**The Collected Scientific Papers of
Paul A. Samuelson**

VOLUME 7

THE COLLECTED SCIENTIFIC PAPERS OF PAUL A. SAMUELSON

Edited by Janice Murray

THE MIT PRESS
Cambridge, Massachusetts, and London, England

© 2011 Massachusetts Institute of Technology

All rights reserved. No part of this book may be reproduced in any form by any electronic or mechanical means (including photocopying, recording, or information storage and retrieval) without permission in writing from the publisher.

For information about special quantity discounts, please email special_sales@mitpress.mit.edu

This book was set in Times New Roman by Graphic Composition, Inc. Printed and bound in the United States of America.

Library of Congress Cataloging-in-Publication Data

Samuelson, Paul Anthony, 1915–2009
   The collected scientific papers of Paul A. Samuelson
   Includes bibliographies.
I. Economics—Collected works.
HB33.S2   330.08   65-28408
ISBN 978-0-262-01574-5

10 9 8 7 6 5 4 3 2 1

For his family, and for his friends and colleagues everywhere.

CONTENTS

Volume VII

Editor's Preface

Part VI. Stochastic Theory

460. Long-Run Risk Tolerance When Equity Returns are Mean Progressing: Pseudoparadoxes and Vindication of 'Businessman's Risk'
    Money, Macroeconomics, and Economic Policy, W.C. Brainard, W.D. Nordhaus and H.W. Watts, (eds.). Cambridge, Mass.: The MIT Press, 181–204, 1991. 3
461. Paradise Lost and Refound: The Harvard ABC Barometers
    The Journal of Portfolio Management, 13(3), 4–9, 1987. 23
462. The √N Law and Repeated Risktaking
    Probability, Statistics and Mathematics, Papers in Honor of Samuel Karlin, T.W. Anderson, K.B. Athreya and D.L. Iglehart (eds). San Diego, California and Orlando, Florida: The Academic Press, Inc., 291–306, 1989. 29
463. Asset Allocation Could Be Dangerous to Your Health
    The Journal of Portfolio Management, 16(3), 5–8, 1990. 45
464. The Long-Term Case For Equities and How It Can Be Oversold
    The Journal of Portfolio Management, 21(1), 15–24, 1994. 49
465. The Irreducible Role of Derived Marginal Utility in Dynamic Stochastic Programming
    Pacific Economic Review, 1(1), 3–11, 1996. 59
466. Proof by Certainty Equivalents that Diversification-Across-Time Does Worse, Risk Corrected, than Diversification-Throughout-Time
    Journal of Risk and Uncertainty, 14(2), 129–142, 1997. 68

Contents

467. Dogma of the Decade: Sure-Thing Risk Erosion for Long-Horizon Investors (uncut version of edited article, published as "Dogma of the Day")
Bloomberg Personal, 33–34, January-February, 1997. — 82

468. The Judgment of Economic Science on Rational Portfolio Management: Indexing, Timing, and Long-Horizon Effects
The Journal of Portfolio Management, 4–12, Fall, 1989. — 86

469. At Last, a Rational Case for Long-Horizon Risk Tolerance and for Asset-Allocation Timing?
Active Asset Allocation, State of the Art Portfolio Policies, Strategies and Tactics, R. Arnold and F. Fabozzi (eds.). Chicago: Probus Publishing Co., 411–416, 1992. — 95

470. A Case at Last for Age-Phased Reduction in Equity
Proceedings of the National Academy of Sciences, USA, 86, 9048–9051, 1989. — 101

471. Risk Tolerances, Distributive Inequity, and Track Betters' Equilibrium
Economic Analysis of Markets and Games, Essays in Honor of Frank Hahn, P. Dasgupta, D. Gale, O. Hart and E. Maskin (eds.). Cambridge, Mass.: The MIT Press, 602–620, 1992. — 105

472. Grappling with the Rational Case for Long-Horizon Risky-Equities Tolerance
Speech, University of Rome, Rome, Italy, 5 April 1995. — 124

473. How Best to Flip-Flop if You Must: Integer Dynamic Stochastic Programming for Either-Or
Journal of Risk and Uncertainty, 15(3), 183–190, 1997. — 131

474. Estimating Probabilities Relevant to Calculating Relative Risk-Corrected Returns of Alternative Portfolios
Journal of Risk and Uncertainty, 15(3), 191–200, 1997. — 139

475. Foreword
Continuous-time Finance, R.C. Merton. Cambridge, Mass.: Basil Blackwell, Inc., xi-xii, 1990. — 149

476. Reflections on Investing for Foundations and Colleges
Speech, U.S. Trust/Rutgers University Conference, New York, 17 November 1993. — 151

477. 'Tis Folly to Be Wise
Dow Jones Asset Management, 20–28, March/April 1998. — 158

478. Foreword
Bogle on Mutual Funds, New Perspectives for the Intelligent Investor, J.C. Bogle. New York: Irwin Professional Publishing, iii-iv, 1993. — 162

479. Foreword to "The Theory of Security Pricing and Market Structure," M.E. Blume and J.J. Siegel
Journal of Financial Markets, Institutions and Instruments, 1(3), 1–2, 1992. — 164

480. Comment: Clarifying Getting Older and Getting Richer Effects
Journal of Private Portfolio Management, 2(1), 25–26, 2000. — 166

481. Foreword
Finance, Z. Bodie and R.C. Merton. Upper Saddle River, New Jersey: Prentice-Hall, v, 2000. — 168

482. The Classical Theory of Commodity Money Under a Microscope
From Classical Economics to the Theory of the Firm, Essays in Honour of D.P. O'Brien, R. Backhouse and J. Creedy (eds.). Cheltenham, UK: Edward Elgar, 47–64, 1999. — 169

Contents

483.	Modern Finance Theory Within One Lifetime *Mathematical Finance-Bachelier Congress 2000*. H. Geman, D. Madan, S.R. Pliska and T. Vorst (eds.). Berlin, Heidelberg and New York: Springer Verlag, 41–45, 2001.	187
484.	One Way to Measure How Much Second Best 'Second Best' Is *Economic Theory, Dynamics and Markets, Essays in Honor of Ryuzo Sato*, T. Negishi, R. Ramachandran and K. Mino (eds.). Norwell, Mass.: Kluwer Academic Publishers, 1–17, 2001.	192
485.	A Small Pearl for Doctor Stiglitz's Sixtieth Birthday: When Risk Averters Positively Relish 'Excess Volatility' *Economics for an Imperfect World, Essays in Honor of Joseph E. Stiglitz*, R. Arnott, B. Greenwald, R. Kanbur and B. Nalebuff (eds.). Cambridge, Mass.: The MIT Press, 11–16, 2003.	209
486.	The Backward Art of Investing Money *The Journal of Portfolio Management*, 30–33, September 2004.	215
487.	Foreword *Louis Bachelier's Theory of Speculation, the Origins of Modern Finance*. Trans. M. Davis and A. Etheridge. Princeton: Princeton University Press, vii–xi, 2006.	218
488.	Is Personal Finance a Science? *The Future of Life-Cycle Saving and Investing*, Z. Bodie, D. McLeavey and L.B. Siegel (eds.). Charlottesville, Virginia: The Research Foundation of CFA Institute, 1–4, 2007.	223
489.	Asymmetric or Symmetric Time Preference and Discounting in Many Facets of Economic Theory: A Miscellany *Journal of Risk and Uncertainty*, 37(2/3), 107–114, 2008.	227
490.	The Economic Brownian Motion Speech, American Philosophical Society, Philadelphia, 11 November 1960.	235
491.	An Enjoyable Life Puzzling over Modern Finance Theory *Annual Review of Financial Economics*, 1, 19–35, 2009.	245
492.	On the Himalayan Shoulders of Harry Markowitz *Handbook of Portfolio Construction: Contemporary Applications of Markowitz Techniques*, J.B. Guerard (ed.). New York: Springer U.S., 125–132, 2010.	262
493.	Book Review of *Beat the Market: A Scientific Stock Market System*, E.O. Thorp and S.T. Kassouf *Journal of the American Statistical Association*, 63, 1049–1051, 1968.	270

Part VII. Current Economics and Policy

494.	The Present State of Economic Science and Its Probable Future Development *Zeugen des Wissens*, H. Maier-Leibnitz (ed.). Mainz: v. Hase & Koehler Verlag, 1986. Reprinted *Journal of Business Administration*, 18(1/2), 21–32, 1988/89.	275
495.	The Science of Economics at Century's End *Mainichi Shimbun*, 65, 17–23, 1988.	287
496.	The Number One Economic Problem is the Structural Budget Deficit *Business, Economics and the Oval Office, Advice to the New President and Other CEOs*, *Harvard Business Review*, 6, 67–69, 1988.	293
497.	A Personal View on Crises and Economic Cycles *The Risk of Economic Crisis*, M. Feldstein (ed.). Chicago: The University of Chicago Press, 167–170, 1991.	296

Contents

498. Has Economic Science Improved the System?
American Society, Public and Private Responsibilities, W. Knowlton and R. Zeckhauser (eds.). New York: Harper Collins Publishers, 299–315, 1986. 300

499. Thoughts on the Stockholm School and on Scandinavian Economics
The Stockholm School of Economics Revisited, L. Jonung (ed.). New York: Cambridge University Press, 391–407, 1991. 317

500. The To-Be-Expected Angst Created for Economists by Mathematics
Eastern Economic Journal, 20(3), 267–273, 1994. 334

501. How Not to Cure the Imbalance of Trade, published as "Where Iacocca and Common Sense Err"
The New York Times, 15 September 1985. 341

502. U.S. Economic Prospects and Policy Options: Impact on Japan-U.S. Relations
Unkept Promises, Unclear Consequences: U.S. Economic Policy and the Japanese Response, J.A. Rizzo and R. Sato (eds.). Cambridge: Cambridge University Press, 109–136, 1988. 345

503. The Past and Future of International Trade Theory
New Directions in Trade Theory, J. Levinsohn, A. Deardorff and R.M. Stern (eds.). Ann Arbor, Michigan: The University of Michigan Press, 17–22, 1995. 373

504. American and European Economic Divergences at Century's End
Lecture, Institut d'Economic Industrielle, University of Toulouse, Toulouse, France, 9 May 1996. 379

505. How Economics Has Changed
Journal of Economic Education, 18(2), 107–110, 1987. 388

506. Leaning Against What Inflationary Wind?
Challenge, 36(5), 20–26, 1993. 392

507. Economic Science Grapples with Dilemmas of International Finance
Lionel Robbins Memorial Lecture, Claremont College, California, 28 January 1991. 399

508. Recurring Quandaries in International Trade
Keynote Address, Conference on International Finance Markets, New York University, New York, 5 May 1988. 408

509. Realities for a Fine June Day
Speech, Harvard Business School Class of 1948 Reunion, Cambridge, Massachusetts, 5 June 1993. 414

510. Informal Thoughts about Macroeconomics
Roundtable Discussion, Banca d'Italia, Rome, Italy, 3 October 1997. 420

511. Two Gods That Fail
Challenge, 42(5), 29–33, 1999. 426

512. Foreword
Passion and Craft, Economists at Work, M. Szenberg (ed.). Ann Arbor, Michigan: The University of Michigan Press, xi-xiv, 1998. 431

513. Book Review of *Globalization and the Theory of Input Trade*, R.W. Jones
Review of International Economics, 9(3), 547–549, 2001. 435

514. Innovational Progress Sans Thrift
Japan and the World Economy, 14(3), 281–284, 2002. 438

515. The State of the World Economy
Monetary Stability and Economic Growth, A Dialog Between Leading Economists, R.A. Mundell and P.J. Zak (eds.). Cheltenham: Edward Elgar Publishing Limited, 24–37, 2002. 442

Contents

516. Pure Theory Aspects of Industrial Organization and Globalization
Japan and the World Economy, 15(1), 89–90, 2003. — 456
517. A Few Theoretical Aspects of Deregulation
Japan and the World Economy, 15(1), 131–133, 2003. — 458
518. The Pros and Cons of Globalization
Japan and the World Economy, 18(4), 593–594, 2006. — 461

Part VIII. Miscellany

519. The Law Beats Maxwell's Demon
Scientific Correspondence, *Nature*, 347(6), 24–25, 1990. — 467
520. Conserved Energy Without Work or Heat
Proceedings of the National Academy of Sciences, USA, 89, 1090–1094, 1992. — 469
521. Economics and Thermodynamics: von Neumann's Problematic Conjecture
Rational Interaction, Essays in Honor of John C. Harsanyi, R. Selten (ed.). New York: Springer-Verlag, 377–389, 1992. — 474
522. Factor-Price Equalization by Trade in Joint and Non-Joint Production
Review of International Economics, 1(1), 1–9, 1992. — 492
523. Altruism as a Problem Involving Group versus Individual Selection in Economics and Biology
American Economic Review, 83(2), 143–148, 1993. — 501
524. Facets of Balassa-Samuelson Thirty Years Later
Review of International Economics, 2(3), 201–226, 1994. — 507
525. Foreword
The Political Economy of the New Left—An Outsider's View, A. Lindbeck. New York: Harper & Row Publishers, ix-xxi, 1971. — 533
526. On Just How Great 'Great Books' Are
European Journal of the History of Economic Thought, 8(3), 301–308, 2001. — 546
527. Reflections on How Biographies of Individual Scholars Can Relate to a Science's Biography
Foreword, *Inside the Economist's Mind, Conversations with Eminent Economists*, P.A. Samuelson and W.A. Barnett (eds.). Oxford: Blackwell Publishing Ltd., viii-x, 2007. — 550
528. An Interview with Paul A. Samuelson, by William Barnett
Inside the Economist's Mind, Conversations with Eminent Economists, P.A. Samuelson and W.A. Barnett (eds.). Oxford: Blackwell Publishing Ltd., 143–164, 2007. — 553
529. Advance of Total Factor Productivity from Entrepreneurial Innovations
Entrepreneurship, Growth, and Public Policy, Z.J. Acs, D.B. Audrestch and R.J. Strom (eds.). Cambridge and New York: Cambridge University Press, 71–78, 2009. — 575

Part IX. Biographical Writings

530. The 1985 Nobel Prize in Economics
Science, 231, 1399–1401, March 1986. — 585
531. Jacob Viner 1892–1970
Remembering the University of Chicago Teachers, Scientists, and Scholars, E. Shils (ed.). Chicago: The University of Chicago Press, 533–547, 1991. — 588
532. Irving Fisher 1867–1947
Irving Fisher's 'The Nature of Capital and Income', M. Tochtermann (ed.) (published in German). Dusseldorf: Verlag Wirtschaft und Finanzen, 47–55, 1991. — 602

Contents

533. An Economist's Economist
     Obituary of Walter Heller, *The New York Times*, 23 June 1987. — 611
534. Robert Solow: An Affectionate Portrait
     Journal of Economic Perspectives, 3(3), 91–97, 1989. — 613
535. Galbraith as Artist and Scientist
     Unconventional Wisdom, Essays in Economics in Honor of John Kenneth Galbraith, S. Bowles, R. Edwards and W.G. Shepherd (eds.). Boston: The Houghton Mifflin Co., 123–128, 1989. — 620
536. Tribute to Nicholas Georgescu-Roegen on His 85th Birthday
     Libertas Mathematica, 10, 1–4, 1990. — 626
537. Schumpeter, Joseph Alois (with "1991 Afterthoughts on Schumpeter," unpublished)
     Dictionary of American Biography, Supplement 4, 1946–1950, J.A. Garry and E.T. James (eds.). New York: Charles Scribner's Son, 720–723, 1974. — 629
538. Gottfried Haberler (1990–1995)
     The Economic Journal, 106(439), 1679–1687, 1996. — 637
539. Gibbs in Economics
     Proceedings of the Gibbs Symposium Yale University May 15–17, 1989, D.G. Caldi and G.D. Mostow (eds.). Providence, Rhode Island: American Mathematical Society, 255–267, 1989. — 646
540. Remembering Joan
     Joan Robinson and Modern Economic Theory, G.R. Feiwel (ed.). New York: The New York University Press, 121–143, 1989. — 659
541. The Fitness Maximized by the Classical Canonical Economy: A Theme from Houthakker and R.A. Fisher
     Aggregation, Consumption and Trade, Essays in Honor of H.S. Houthakker, L. Phlips and L.D. Taylor (eds.). Dordrecht: Kluwer Academic Publishers, 9–19, 1992. — 682
542. Leontief's 'The Economy as a Circular Flow': An Introduction
     Structural Change and Economic Dynamics, 2(1), 177–179, 1991. — 693
543. Homage to Chakravarty: Thoughts on His Lumping Schumpeter with Marx to Define a Paradigm Alternative to Mainstream Growth Theories
     Capital, Investment and Development, Essays in Memory of Sukhamoy Chakravarty, K. Basu, M. Majumdar and T. Mitra (eds.). Oxford: Blackwell Publishers, 244–258, 1993. — 696
544. Tribute to Wolfgang Stolper on the Fiftieth Anniversary of the Stolper-Samuelson Theorem
     The Stolper-Samuelson Theorem, A Golden Jubilee, A.V. Deardorff and R.M. Stern (eds.). Ann Arbor: The University of Michigan Press, 343–349, 1994. — 711
545. Tribute to Jan Tinbergen: One Exact Match for Economics and Physics
     Indian Journal of Applied Economics, 5(3), 1–16, 1996. — 718
546. Gustav Cassel's Scientific Innovations: Claims and Realities
     History of Political Economy, 25(3), 515–527, 1993. — 734
547. Piero Sraffa (1898–1983) (published in Italian as "Un genio con poche opera")
     Corriere della Sera, 6 March 1983. — 747
548. Knut Wicksell (published as "Wicksells Werk und Persönlichkeit - Eine kritische Analyse in moderner Sicht")
     Foreword to Faksimile-Edition of Wicksell's "Finanztheoretische Untersuchungen," *Klassiker der Nationalökonomie* (published in German). Dusseldorf: Verlag Wirtschaft und Finanzen, 25–36, 1988. — 751

549. Some Memories of Norbert Weiner
Proceedings of Symposia in Pure Mathematics, Vol. 60, The Legacy of Norbert Weiner: A Centennial Symposium, D. Jerison, I.M. Singer and D.W. Stroock (eds.). Providence, Rhode Island: American Mathematical Society, 37–42, 1997. 761

550. Gottfried Haberler as Economic Sage and Trade Theory Innovation
Wirtschafts Politische Blätter, 37, 310–317, 1990. 767

551. Wicksell and Neoclassical Economics
The New Palgrave: A Dictionary of Economics, Vol. IV, J. Eatwell, M. Milgate and P. Newman (eds.). London and Basingstoke: The Macmillan Press, 908–910, 1987. 775

552. Harold Freeman (1909–1997)
Memorial Service Tribute, MIT, Cambridge, Massachusetts, 10 March 1998. 778

553. My John Hicks
Indian Journal of Applied Economics, 7(4), 1–4, 1998. Reproduced in *John Hicks, His Contribution to Economic Theory and Application*, K. Puttaswamaiah (ed.). New Brunswick and London: Transaction Publishers, 1–4, 2001. 782

554. Foreword
Trade, Welfare, and Economic Policies, Essays in Honor of Murray C. Kemp, H. Herberg and N. Van Long (eds.). Ann Arbor: The University of Michigan Press, vii-viii, 1993. 786

555. Foreword
Bioeconomics and Sustainability, Essays in Honor of Nicholas Georgescu-Roegen, K. Mayumi and J.M. Gowdy (eds.). Cheltenham, UK and Northampton, Mass.: Edward Elgar Publishing, xiii-xvii, 1999. 788

556. Book Review of *The Economics of Irving Fisher. Reviewing the Scientific Work of a Great Economist*, H-E. Loef and H.G. Monissen (eds.).
European Journal of the History of Economic Thought, 8(2), 263–270, 2001. 793

557. A Personal Tribute to John Harsanyi
Games and Economic Behavior, 36, 28–29, 2001. 801

558. David Ricardo (1772–1823)
International Encyclopedia of the Social and Behavioral Sciences, N.J. Smelser and P.B. Baltes (eds.). Oxford: Pergamon, 13330–13334, 2001. 803

559. My Bertil Ohlin
Bertil Ohlin, A Centennial Celebration (1899–1999), R. Findlay, L. Jonung and M. Lundahl (eds.). Cambridge, Mass.: The MIT Press, 51–61, 2002. 808

560. Edmund Phelps, Insider-Economists' Insider
Knowledge, Information and Expectations in Modern Macroeconomics, in Honor of Edmund S. Phelps, P. Aghion, R. Frydman, J. Stiglitz and M. Woodward (eds.). Princeton: Princeton University Press, 1–2, 2003. 819

561. Reflections on the Schumpeter I Knew Well
Journal of Evolutionary Economics, 13(5), 463–467, 2003. Reproduced in *Entrepreneurship, the New Economy and Public Policy, Schumpeterian Perspectives*, U. Cantner, E. Dinopoulos and R. Lanzillotti (eds.). Berlin, Heidelberg and New York: Springer-Verlag, 2005. 821

562. A Portrait of the Master as a Young Man
Wassily Leontief and Input-Output Economics, E. Dietzenbacher and M.L. Lahr (eds.). Cambridge: Cambridge University Press, 3–8, 2004. 826

563. Abram Bergson, 1914–2003, A Biographical Memoir by Paul A. Samuelson
    Biographical Memoirs, vol. 84. Washington, D.C.: The National Academies Press, 3–14, 2004. 832
564. Samuelson on Harry [Gordon Johnson], the Full Achiever
    The American Journal of Economics and Sociology. 60(3), 601–606, 2001. 841
565. Franco: A Mind Never at Rest
    Banco Nazionale del Lavoro Quarterly Review, 58(233/234), 5–6, 2005. 847
566. Alice Bourneuf
    Notable American Women, A Biographical Dictionary Completing the 20th Century, S. Ware (ed.). Cambridge, Massachusetts and London: The Belknap Press of Harvard University Press, 72–73, 2004. 852
567. Affectionate Reminiscences of Richard Musgrave
    FinanzArchiv, 64(2), 166–168, 2008. 854
568. An Economist Even Greater Than His High Reputation
    Markets, Money and Capital: Hicksian Economics for the Twenty First Century, R. Scazzeri, A. Sen and S. Zamagni (eds.). Cambridge: Cambridge University Press, 49–51, 2009. 857
569. Remembering Milton Friedman
    Milton Friedman, Nobel Monetary Economist, a review of his theories and policies, K. Puttaswamaiah (ed.). Enfield, New Hampshire: Isle Publishing Company, 31–36, 2009. 860
570. A Few Remembrances of Friedrich von Hayek (1899–1992)
    Journal of Economic Behavior and Organization 69, 1–4, 2009. 866
571. Thünen: An Economist Ahead of His Times
    The Isolated State in Relation to Agriculture and Political Economy, Part III: Principles for the Determination of Rent, the Most Advantageous Rotation Period and the Value of Stands of Varying Age in Pinewoods, Johann Heinrich von Thünen, U. van Suntum (ed.). New York: Palgrave Macmillan, St. Martin's Press, xii-xiv, 2009. 870
572. The Schumpeter Circle at Harvard: 1932–1950
    Journal of Evolutionary Economics, Forthcoming in a special issue on Joseph Schumpeter. 873
573. The Richard Goodwin Circle at Harvard (1938–1950)
    Computable, Constructive and Behavioural Economic Dynamics, Essays in Honour of Kumaraswamy (Vela) Velupillai, S. Zambelli (ed.). Abingdon: Routledge, 49–54, 2010. 878

Part X. Autobiographical Writings

574. My Life Philosophy: Policy Credos and Working Ways
    Eminent Economists, Their Life Philosophies, M. Szenberg (ed.). New York: Cambridge University Press, 236–247, 1991. 887
575. Statistical Flowers Caught in Amber
    Statistical Science, 6(4), 330–338, 1991. 899
576. On the Historiography of Economics: A Correspondence (with Mark Blaug and Don Patinkin)
    Journal of the History of Economic Thought, 13(2), 144–158, 1991. 908
577. The Passing of the Guard in Economics
    Eastern Economic Journal, 14(4), 312–329, 1988. 923
578. Economics in Our Time
    Speech on the occasion of the 90th anniversary of the Nobel Prize. Stockholm, Sweden, 6 December 1991. 935

579. Me and Kennedy
Speech, Examiner Club, Boston, Massachusetts, 3 January 1994.   950
580. At Eighty: MIT and I
Speech, Paul A. Samuelson's MIT 80th birthday party, Boston, Massachusetts, 30 April 1995.   964
581. Paul Anthony Samuelson (b. 1915) (interview)
The Coming of Keynesianism to America, Conversations with the Founders of Keynesian Economics, D. Colander and H. Landreth (eds.). Cheltenham, UK: Edward Elgar Publishing Limited, 145–178, 1995.   969
582. Credo of a Lucky Textbook Author
Journal of Economic Perspectives, 11(2), 153–160, 1997.   1003
583. On Collaboration
The American Economist, 40(2), 16–21, 1996.   1011
584. Joint Authorship in Sciences: Serendipity with Wolfgang Stolper
Journal of Institutional and Theoretical Economics, 143(2), 235–243, 1987.   1017
585. The Fallibility of Economic Science
Third Julius Steinberg Memorial Lecture, The Wharton School of the University of Pennsylvania, Philadelphia, 2 October 1985.   1026
586. How *Foundations* Came To Be
Paul A. Samuelson's "Foundations of Economic Analysis," Vademecum zu einem Klassiker der Gegenwart, J. Niehans, P.A. Samuelson and C.C. von Weizsäcker (published in German). Dusseldorf: Verlag Wirtschaft und Finanzen, 27–52, 1997. Published in English (abridged) in *Journal of Economic Literature*, 36(3), 1375–1386, 1998.   1039
587. A Golden Birthday
Economics, 16th edition, P.A. Samuelson and W. D. Nordhaus. New York: Irwin McGraw-Hill, xxiv-xxvii, 1998.   1059
588. Foreword
Economics, An Introductory Analysis, P.A. Samuelson. Reissued first (1948) edition. New York: McGraw-Hill, iii-iv, 1998.   1063
589. Samuelson's *Economics* at Fifty: Remarks on the Occasion of the Anniversary of Publication
Journal of Economic Education, 30(4), 352–355, 1999.   1065
590. Economics and the Kennedy Presidency
Speech, Brookings Institution, Washington, D.C., 12 November 1999.   1069
591. The First Fifteen Nobel Laureates in Economics, and Fifteen More Might-Have-Beens
Speech, Lindau Economics Nobel Laureates Conference, Lindau, Germany, September, 2004.   1072
592. Paul A. Samuelson
The Changing Face of Economics, Conversations with Cutting Edge Economists, D. Colander, R.P.F. Holt and J.B. Rosser, Jr. (eds.). Ann Arbor: The University of Michigan Press, 309–313, 2004.   1078
593. Pastiches From an Earlier Politically Correct Academic Age
Editing Economics: Essays in Honour of Mark Perlman, H. Lim, U.S. Park and G.C. Harcourt (eds.). London and New York: Routledge, 47–55, 2002.   1083
594. Memoirs of an Early Finance Theorist
Modern Risk Management: A History, introduced by P. Field. London: Risk Books, 587–589, 2003.   1092
595. Three Moles
Bulletin, 62(2), 83–84, 2009.   1095

Contents

    596. Paul A. Samuelson (interview)
         Roads to Wisdom, Conversations with Ten Nobel Laureates in Economics, K.I. Horn. Cheltenham: Edward Elgar Publishing Limited, 39–57, 2009.   1097
    597. In Search of George Stigler and the Chicago School—A Conversation with Paul Samuelson
         Southside Blues: Conversations in Search of George Stigler, C. Friedman. Cheltenham: Edward Elgar Publishing, forthcoming.   1116

Contents of Volumes I–VI   1139

Acknowledgments   1171

Index   1193

EDITOR'S PREFACE

Paul Samuelson never used a word processor. Rather, he famously wrote his thoughts and teachings in longhand, with a ballpoint pen, on yellow or white legal pads always within easy reach. That pen was prolific, as we all know. Even so, I always marveled that he could stop mid-sentence and walk away from something he was so engrossed in writing. He said that ability came from having six children to respond to. Now that pen is forever laid down.

Because of family genetics, Paul was astonished to have lived as long as he did. But he never ran out of things to think about, to correct, to interpret, to pronounce upon, or to provoke thought; his prolific pen continued to race across legal pages until just a few months before his death. Scores and scores of unpublished, incomplete manuscripts attest to his contemplating the endless variety of topics that interested him. Even after his pen gave out in his final weeks, Paul's mind continued to dwell on economics: just four weeks before his death he was interviewed on BBC Radio, addressing key issues in the global financial crisis. "My country needs me," he would often tell me.

Since I joined his "workshop" in 1990, Paul and I worked together to decide which articles should be included in these last two volumes. Because it was not his nature, he declined several urgings to write an autobiography. However, these two volumes do end up having more of a biographical and autobiographical character than the first five. There are more tributes to lost friends and colleagues, and more speeches and interviews of both a personal and historical nature.

Editor's Preface

Articles are arranged in ten parts, with the larger sections being on classical and neoclassical economics, stochastic theory, and current policies. Obvious typographical errors have been corrected, but no substantial changes have been made to the original publications, with two exceptions. In an effort to make the piece more understandable—he did not cotton to being called protectionist—he and Erkko Etula revised the two original appendices to his provocative "Where Ricardo and Mill Rebut and Confirm Arguments of Mainstream Economists Supporting Globalization." Those important appendices appeared only on the 2004 website of *The Journal of Economic Perspectives*, which published the article, and were therefore overlooked. He also wished to add an unpublished "Afterthought" to his *Dictionary of American Biography* text on Joseph Schumpeter.

Three early contributions omitted from previous volumes are reproduced here: Economic Brownian Motion (1960), a Foreword to *The Political Economy of the New Left* (1971), and a book review of *Beat the Market* (1998) with an added 2009 Preamble.

Paul believed that leaving in the page numbers of the original articles helped readers, so I have carried on that tradition which first appeared in volumes four and five.

The Acknowledgments section at the back of the volumes lists the strict chronological order of the contents.

I owe thanks and gratitude to a warm and wonderful team (Michael Sims, Jane Macdonald, and Emily Taber) to work with at the MIT Press, to the Sloan Foundation for support, and to Robert Solow for guidance in preparing these volumes. Most of all, I count my nearly twenty years of working with Paul Samuelson as lucky, rich, and unequalled. I feel privileged to have worked alongside this extraordinary economist, the man who guided that prolific and irrepressible pen with a twinkle in his eye.

Janice Murray
Cambridge, Massachusetts
September 2010

PART VI.

Stochastic Theory

460

7   Long-Run Risk Tolerance When Equity Returns Are Mean Regressing: Pseudoparadoxes and Vindication of "Businessman's Risk"

Paul A. Samuelson

The dogma that total returns of common stocks are a random walk through time is being questioned in favor of the hypothesis that, in long periods of investing, epochs of high total returns tend to be followed by epochs of low, and vice versa.[1]

7.1   Plausible Conjectures

To the degree that this is empirically confirmed, the following conjectures might seem plausible at first thought:

1. The "rebound model" ought to provide the long-horizon investor with a probability distribution of total returns that is more bunched around its position of central tendency than is the case for the "random-walk model." (If the autocorrelation of returns were positive instead of negative as in the *rebound* model, the opposite would be expected—namely, a swelling of long-period variance in such a "momentum model" relative to the *random-walk* reference model.)

2. Risk-averse investors, with strictly concave long-term utility functions, if they are constrained to follow a fixed-proportions-through-time portfolio strategy (a "myopic" strategy), other things equal (whatever that reasonably means), will tolerate in the *rebound* case a higher portfolio fraction of risky common stocks and a lower fraction of lower-yielding-but-safe cash instruments than in the random-walk case. (In the *momentum* model of positive autocorrelation, the same conjecture involves a lower optimal-myopic fraction in risky equities).

3. The longer the investor's time horizon—as where she has concern for portfolio returns 30 years ahead rather than 10 years ahead—then the greater will be the quantitative effects described above.

3

4. Finally, a verifiable departure from random-walk intertemporal independence of returns creates a prima facie case for "timing" decisions. A la Tobin, Modigliani, and Shiller, the canny investor faced with the rebound case will lighten up on equities following a period of boom, and will plunge back into equities more intensively after a rash of bear markets.

7.2 The Canonical Test Case

As Tolstoy almost said: "All random walks are pretty much alike, but departures from time independence can take on an infinity of different forms."

In the interests of simplicity, I examine simple 2-by-2 Markov processes: In one 5-year period, the total return can be "high" or can be "low"; call these alternative growth states $(+, -)$. To keep the analysis simple, I will concentrate on choice between *safe cash* and an equity that either triples the principal or loses it all.

In the random walk, regardless of whether last period experienced $+$ or experienced $-$, the probability of this period's $+$ is the same:

$$\text{Prob}\{X_t = + | X_{t-1} = +\} = \text{Prob}\{X_t = + | X_{t-1} = -\} = a. \tag{1}$$

Its relevant Markov matrix has, by definition, identical rows:

$t-1 \diagdown t$	$+$	$-$
$+$	a	$1-a$
$-$	a	$1-a$

$$0 < a < 1. \tag{2}$$

Stocks rise on the average in the long run. Therefore it is realistic to make

$$a > \tfrac{1}{2} > 1 - a. \tag{3}$$

Readers, however, can test a general conjecture by any example, and therefore the simplicity of the ultrasymmetric case, in which $a = \tfrac{1}{2}$, may commend itself to them.

How is the rebound model's Markov matrix to be written? For it

$$b = \text{Prob}\{+|+\} < \text{Prob}\{+|-\} = c. \tag{4}$$

Its Markov matrix becomes

$$\begin{bmatrix} b & 1-b \\ c & 1-c \end{bmatrix}, \quad 0 < b < c < 1. \tag{5}$$

If we are to be realistic in recognizing that +'s occur more often on the average than −'s (i.e., stocks do have an upward trend), then the simple average of b and c will have to exceed $\frac{1}{2}$—as (7c) will reveal.

Not to be comparing cheese and chalk, I will make long-run opportunities for gain the same by stipulating that the parameters in the rebound model are tuned so as to give us the same long-run, *unconditional* probabilities of +'s and of −'s as obtain in the random-walk case.[2] These "ergodic probabilities" are the left-hand row *eigenvectors* of the relevant Markov matrices:

$$[q \quad 1-q] \begin{bmatrix} a & 1-a \\ a & 1-a \end{bmatrix} = [q \quad 1-q] \equiv [a \quad 1-a]. \tag{6}$$

For the tuned rebound model, we have the following relation that is solvable for an infinity of admissible (b, c) pairs:

$$[a \quad 1-a] \begin{bmatrix} b & 1-b \\ c & 1-c \end{bmatrix} = [a \quad 1-a]. \tag{7a}$$

This gives the desired linear constraint that the (b, c) pairs must satisfy

$$ab + (1-a)c = a, \tag{7b}$$

$$0 < a = \frac{c}{1+c-b} < 1. \tag{7c}$$

The dramatic ultrasymmetric case involves

$$\begin{aligned} a &= \tfrac{1}{2} = 1 - a, \\ b &= 1 - c < \tfrac{1}{2}. \end{aligned} \tag{8a}$$

For b set equal to $\tfrac{1}{3}$, we then have

$$\begin{bmatrix} \tfrac{1}{2} & \tfrac{1}{2} \\ \tfrac{1}{2} & \tfrac{1}{2} \end{bmatrix}: \text{ random walk,} \tag{8b}$$

$$\begin{bmatrix} \tfrac{1}{3} & \tfrac{2}{3} \\ \tfrac{2}{3} & \tfrac{1}{3} \end{bmatrix}: \text{ rebound model,} \tag{8c}$$

$$\begin{bmatrix} \tfrac{2}{3} & \tfrac{1}{3} \\ \tfrac{1}{3} & \tfrac{2}{3} \end{bmatrix}: \text{ momentum model.} \tag{8d}$$

All three of these cases have been pre-tuned into comparability: Just as the random-walk process involves as many +'s as −'s in the unconditional long run, so do these other processes—as the reader can verify by calculating their ergodic [$q \quad 1 - q$] probabilities in the (6) and (7) way—to arrive at the [$\frac{1}{2} \quad \frac{1}{2}$] row vector.

7.3 One-Period Time Horizons: Logarithmic Utility

We can now test the plausible conjectures of Section 7.1. If they are to be valid in general, they must be verifiable for any concave $U(W)$ function whose expected value is truly being maximized.

The fashionable case of logarithmic utility (or "Bernoulli" utility à la 1738) is the temptingly simple example to experiment with. (*Warning:* It is a well-known phenomenon that often logarithmic utility with its unitary elasticity of risk tolerance, $-WU''(W)/U'(W)$, is the razor's-edge case betwixt opposite-signed comparative statics. Alas, the stated conjectures failed to consider this possible treachery, and they will be seen to founder precisely on this shoal!) Let us put the plausible conjecture(s) to the test.

Here is the derivation of the simple one-period optimal portfolio allocation between (1) safe cash, with its zero return, and (2) an equity that with even-odds either triples your money or gives you nothing. The one-period Bernoulli maximizer finds that he must keep three-quarters of wealth in safe cash and one-quarter in the lucrative-but-risky equity—$w^* = \frac{1}{4}$:

$$u^*[w^*] = \underset{w}{\text{Max}} \left[\tfrac{1}{2}\log(1 - w + 3w) + \tfrac{1}{2}\log(1 - w + 0w)\right]$$

$$= u^*[\tfrac{1}{4}], \tag{9}$$

where w^* is the unique root of the necessary-and-sufficient first-derivative condition

$$\frac{du^*}{dw} = 0 = \tfrac{1}{2}(2)(1 + 2w)^{-1} - \tfrac{1}{2}(1 - w)^{-1},$$

$$w^* = \tfrac{1}{4}. \tag{10}$$

This w^* is optimal for the random-walk case. For the one-period problem, the optimal fraction for the rebound case works out to be the same as this w^* if the rules of the game require Bernoulli to have selected w with no knowledge of whether the decision comes just following occurrence of + or of −. The rebound case, in other words, is constrained as part of the thought experiment to have the same relative frequencies of +'s as the random-walk case: 50–50 in the very simplest numerical example, and hence it presents in the one-period horizon the same maximum problem as in (9) and (10).

Conditional upon knowing that + has just occurred—a tripling of the equities initial principal—the one-period investor who is permitted to be nonmyopic will optimally hold only cash in the next period. Or, conditional upon knowing that − has just occurred, the equity having just had its principal washed out, the Bernoulli investor will want to plunge by putting half of wealth in the risky security. These *timer's* solutions for w_+^* and w_-^* arise as following:

$$u^*[w_+^*] = \operatorname*{Max}_{w} [\tfrac{1}{3}\log(1 + 2w) + \tfrac{2}{3}\log(1 - w)]$$

$$= u_+^*(0), \tag{11a}$$

where $w_+^* = 0$ is the root of

$$\tfrac{1}{3}(2)(1 + 2w)^{-1} - \tfrac{2}{3}(1 - w)^{-1} = 0. \tag{11b}$$

Similarly, after − has been observed,

$$u^*[w_-] = \operatorname*{Max}_{w} [\tfrac{2}{3}\log(1 + 2w) + \tfrac{1}{3}\log(1 - w)]$$

$$= u_-^*(\tfrac{1}{2}), \tag{12a}$$

where w^* is the root of the (12b) relation that would be attained by interchanging in (11b) the $(\tfrac{1}{3}, \tfrac{2}{3})$ factors.

For the Bernoulli case with general $(p, 1 - p)$ probabilities in the $E\{U(W)\}$ maximand, the optimal w is the root of a linear equation:

$$u^*[w^*] = \operatorname*{Max}_{w} [p\log(1 + 2w) + (1 - p)\log(1 - w)], \tag{13}$$

where w^* is the root of

$$(1 + 2w)(1 - w)u'[w] = 0 = (3p - 1) - 2w, \tag{14a}$$

$$w^* = \frac{3p - 1}{2}. \tag{14b}$$

7.4 One-Period Nonlogarithmic Case

For $U(W) = -1/W$, an empirically more realistic case than Bernoulli's, the expected-utility calculus corresponding to (9) through (14) involves solving quadratic equations (alternatively, in the special two-outcome cases, solving linear equations like those involved in the log-utility case). Now with one-period horizon we have

$$u[\bar{w}] = \underset{w}{\text{Max}}\left[-\tfrac{1}{2}(1+2w)^{-1} - \tfrac{1}{2}(1-w)^{-1}\right]$$

$$= u[0.1213\ldots], \qquad (15)$$

where $\bar{w}$ is the root of

$$u'[w] = 0 = (2)(\tfrac{1}{2})(1+2w)^{-2} - \tfrac{1}{2}(1-w)^{-2},$$

$$0 = 2w^2 + 8w - 1,$$

$$\bar{w} = \frac{-8+\sqrt{72}}{4} = 0.1213\ldots. \qquad (16)$$

For general one-period probabilities, $(p, 1-p)$, the investor with $(-1/W)$ utility will select optimal $\bar{w}$ as the root of a quadratic equation. Here are the derivations corresponding to the Bernoulli cases (13) and (14).

$$u[\bar{w}] = \underset{w}{\text{Max}}\left[-p(1+2w)^{-1} - (1-p)(1-w)^{-1}\right], \qquad 0 < p < 1, \quad (17)$$

where $\bar{w}$ is the root of

$$(1+2w)^2(1-w)^2 u'[w] = 0$$

$$= 2p(1-w)^2 - (1-p)(1+2w)^2$$

$$= (6p-4)w^2 - 4w + (3p-1). \qquad (18)$$

The solution is therefore

$$\bar{w} = \frac{1}{4}, \qquad p = \frac{2}{3}, \qquad (19a)$$

$$\bar{w} = \frac{4+\sqrt{72p(1-p)}}{4(3p-2)}, \qquad 0 < p < \frac{2}{3}, \qquad (19b)$$

$$\bar{w} = \frac{4-\sqrt{72p(1-p)}}{4(3p-2)}, \qquad \frac{2}{3} < p < 1. \qquad (19c)$$

If borrowing is prohibited so that $\bar{w}$ cannot be negative, the solution in (19b) is to be replaced by $\bar{w} = 0$ when $p < \tfrac{1}{3}$.

Now I permit you, like Bernoulli, to be a timer. If last period showed +, you now face $(\tfrac{1}{3}, \tfrac{2}{3})$ probabilities of dollar returns of $(3, 0)$ for each dollar put in the stock now. Being risk averse, like Bernoulli you also shun such a "fair" gamble, setting $\bar{w}_+ = 0$:

$u'[\bar{w}_+] = 2(\frac{1}{3})(1 + 2w)^{-2} - \frac{2}{3}(1 - w)^{-2}.$

$$\bar{w}_+ = 0 \qquad (20)$$

After last period shows $-$, you solve

$u[\bar{w}_-] = \underset{w}{\text{Max}} \; [-\frac{2}{3}(1 + 2w)^{-1} - \frac{1}{3}(1 - w)^{-1}]$

$$= \bar{u}[\tfrac{1}{4}], \qquad (21)$$

where $\bar{w}_-$ is the root of the quadratic equation implied by the vanishing of $u'[w]$. In accordance with (18) and (19b),

$$0 = 0w^2 + 12w - 3, \qquad \bar{w}_- = \tfrac{1}{4}. \qquad (22)$$

Note that the Bernoulli timer oscillates between (w_+^*, w_-^*) of $(0, \frac{1}{2})$, averaging out *exactly* to the w^* of $\frac{1}{4}$ of the myopic investor. This is a singular property of the (log W) case with its (14b) linearity and it holds for any $[b, c]$ in (5).

You as a more realistic risk averter will have an equity exposure as a timer that oscillates between $(\bar{w}_+, \bar{w}_-)$ of $(0, \frac{1}{4})$, which averages out to exceed (slightly) your myopic nontiming $\bar{w}$ of $0.1213\ldots < 0.125$. For Cramer's 1728 case of $(W^{1/2})$ the opposite inequality will obtain.

The final summary will collect these various findings about optimal portfolio allocations in the relations (49)–(52).

7.5 Multiperiod Horizons

An old Chinese proverb says, A journey of a thousand miles begins with *two* steps (two rather than one because the one-period problem is degenerate).

For the two-period horizon, when faced with a random walk, we know that there are three distinct outcomes, so to speak: $++$ and $--$, and $+-$ or $-+$; 2 favorable draws for the equity, 1 such favorable draw, or 0 favorable draws. Their respective probabilities are known from the binomial coefficients of Pascal's triangle to be $(\frac{1}{4}, \frac{1}{2}, \frac{1}{4})$.

Bernoulli can now solve for the myopic optimal two-period w^*, using these random-walk probabilities and the indicated *multiplicative* (!) outcomes:

$u^*[w^*] = \text{Max}\{\tfrac{1}{4}\log(1 + 2w)^2 + \tfrac{1}{2}\log[(1 + 2w)(1 - w)]$

$\qquad\qquad\qquad\qquad\qquad + \tfrac{1}{4}\log(1 - w)^2\}$

$$= \underset{w}{\text{Max}} \, [(2)(\tfrac{1}{4}) + \tfrac{1}{2}] \log(1 + 2w) + [\tfrac{1}{2} + (2)(\tfrac{1}{4})] \log(1 - w)$$

$$= u^*[\tfrac{1}{4}]. \tag{23}$$

By equating du^*/dw to zero for (23), the reader can verify this optimality selection [noting that (23) reduces to (9) multiplied by 2].

Why did this two-period myopic w^* give Bernoulli the same $\tfrac{1}{4}$ as in the one-period random-walk case? Since log W displays constant-*relative*-risk aversion, we have to expect this; even more generally, for other members of this Santa Claus isoelastic family, the random walk is shown in Samuelson (1969) to give us the same myopic w for time horizons of $T = 1, 2, 3, \ldots$. Thus, for 1728 Cramer utility of the form $W^{1/2}$, the random-walk case gives the same myopic w^* independent of time horizon T. Since Gabriel Cramer is less risk averse than Daniel Bernoulli, his invariant w^* exceeds Bernoulli's $\tfrac{1}{4}$. Similarly, in the still more realistic case observed by econometricians, where $U(W) = -1/W$, the random walk calls out an invariant w^* smaller than $\tfrac{1}{4}$, namely, $0.1213\ldots$.

Now turn to the two-period rebound case. The same three possible multiplicative outcomes for wealth can alone occur. But now they occur with probabilities different from the Pascal random-walk point binomial case. Intuitively we expect more frequent reversals, hence greater number of cancellations toward the middle rather than runs of the $++$ or $--$ type. Gabriel (1959) gives the asymptotic and exact distribution for our Markov case. In any case by brute-force enumeration we can verify that this cancellation does take place. Conditional on your not knowing the prior period's outcome, here are the calculated probabilities of the rebound outcomes, with the contrasting random-walk results indicated in parentheses.

The rebound process does indeed bunch closer around the middle than the random walk. But you would be wrong to think that this persuades the risk-adverse Bernoulli to plunge deeper into equities when his time horizon exceeds one period. Correct calculation shows that Bernoulli chooses to invest the same w^* of $\tfrac{1}{4}$ *whatever his time horizon* and whether he faces the rebound, or momentum, or random-walk process. In the rebound case, myopic Bernoulli acts as follows:

$$u^*(w^*) = u^*(\tfrac{1}{4})$$

$$= (\tfrac{1}{6}) \log[(1 + 2w^*)^2] + (\tfrac{4}{6}) \log[(1 + 2w^*)(1 - w^*)]$$

$$+ (\tfrac{1}{6}) \log[(1 - w^*)^2]$$

$$= (\tfrac{6}{6}) \log(1 + 2w^*) + (\tfrac{6}{6}) \log(1 - w^*). \tag{24}$$

Thus (24)'s multiplicand is a constant times that of (23) or (9), entailing unchanged nontimer's w^* for Bernoulli of $\frac{1}{4}$! (Parenthetically, a Latané 1956 investor who purports to maximize his probability of a highest growth rate exhibits Bernoulli's behavior, including his singular invariance with respect to time horizon.)

Clearly the original conjecture is not a generally valid result, paradoxical as this may at first seem to be the case.

One counterexample kills a purported general theorem.

7.6 Booby Traps

Perhaps the head spins. "The random-walk process increases the process's *variance*, does it not?" Yes, it does increase variance. "Risk averters shun enhanced variance, do they not?" Well, that depends. A mean-preserving alteration of a probability distribution that moves probabilities out from that mean does unequivocally worsen your expected $\{U\}$ if you have the concave $U(W)$ of a risk averter.

But this last is not what is involved in our tuned comparison. Table 7.1 enables you to calculate that at the same time that the move to a rebound process lowers your variance of multiperiod return it lowers (!) any specified portfolio's mean. How you react to this compound change must depend on your Arrow-Pratt risk coefficients, $-U''/U'$ or $-WU''/U'$, – – or, in other words, on where you choose to be on the optimal Markowitz (1959) mean-variance frontier. And how the cookie crumbles, for logarithmic utility involves inert decision making. For $U = W^{1/2}$ or $U = -1/W$, it is two different ball games.

So the paradox is only a pseudoparadox once you are alerted to all the subtleties.

It would be uncandid to ignore failures of heuristic reasoning. My personal intuition had suggested that if I were a Bernoulli or any risk averter, as a long-run investor I would prefer the opportunity to face a rebound rather than a random-walk process, even if I opt for the *same* myopic strategy, $w_T^* = w^*$, in both cases and for all time periods. Table 7.1 shows that conjecture to be false. Actually only a Bernoulli myopic investor is indifferent to the strength and sign of the autocorrelation when our pretuning of ergodic probabilities is adhered to. Our required pre-tuning, when applied to the logarithm's special separability property, forces this indifference on him.

The way has been posed to state the following theorem, which holds for any number of periods and for the random-walk and rebound Markov matrixes with any tuned ergodic probabilities:

Table 7.1
Probabilities of outcomes for alternative time horizons

Two-period outcomes	$(1 + 2w)^2$	$(1 + 2w)(1 - w)$	$(1 - w)^2$
Rebound probabilities	1/6	4/6	1/6
Random-walk p's	1/4 > 1/6	1/2 < 4/6	1/4
Rebound p's after +	1/9	6/9	2/9
Rebound p's after −	2/9	6/9	1/9
Three-period outcomes	$(1 + 2w)^3$	$(1 + 2w)^2(1 - w)$	$(1 + 2w)(1 - w)^2$	$(1 - w)^3$
Rebound p's	1/18	8/18	8/18	1/18
Random-walk p's	1/8 > 1/18	3/8 < 8/18	3/8	1/8
Rebound p's after +	1/27	10/27	14/27	2/27
Rebound p's after −	2/27	14/27	10/27	1/27
Four-period outcomes	$(1 + 2w)^4$	$(1 + 2w)^3(1 - w)$	$(1 + 2w)^2(1 - w)^2$	$(1 + 2w)(1 - w)^3$	$(1 - w)^4$
Rebound p's	1/54	12/54	28/54	12/54	1/52
Random-walk p's	1/16 > 1/54	4/16 > 12/54	6/16 < 28/51	4/16	1/16
Rebound p's after +	1/81	14/81	42/81	22/81	2/81
Rebound p's after −	2/81	22/81	42/81	14/81	1/81

Theorem: Maximizing $E\{\log\}W$ over any time horizon, $T = 1, 2, \ldots$, leads to the same myopic strategy, independently of both T and the degree of autocorrelation that departs from the random-walk's intertemporal independence—provided only that the ergodic probabilities are ensured to be the same. This gives no scope for extra young-person's equity tolerance.

For general proof of the special invariances inherent in the case of log W, I need only remark on the factorization property of the logarithm: for it any sum of utility outcomes, such as

$$p_{..}\log[(1 + 2w^1)(1 + 2w^3)\ldots(1 + 2w^k)(1 - w^4)\ldots]$$
$$+ q_{..}\log[(1 + 2w^2)(1 + 2w^4)\ldots(1 - w^1)(1 - w^3)\ldots], \quad (25)$$

factors into *separate linear* terms involving any specified period's w^t strategy. Thus in the above example the maximand for, say, period 3's w^3 becomes free of all other periods' w's:

$$p_{..}\log(1 + 2w^3) + q_{..}\log(1 - w^3) + \text{remainder}, \quad (26)$$

where the remainder that involves the other w's is irrelevant to the maximizing strategy. Only the single-period $p_{..}/(p_{..} + q_{..})$ counts in the decision. Put another way, the expected value of a sum is the sum of the expected value of the separate variates independently of their intercorrelations, and only the log W form factors into a simple sum of terms involving each separate period w^t.

Remark: Even for the log W case, if Bernoulli is constrained to pick an invariant T-period w_T^* while knowing whether $+$ has just occurred, for small T that anterior information will engender a greater timer's deviation from $\frac{1}{4}$ than it will for large T. As one can see from table 7.1, the larger is T the less different will be the rebound p's following $+$ from those following $-$; last period's information fades fast in its useful value in a simple Markov process, but it does have its day of relevance.

The Copernican hypothesis was at first called the rape of the senses. So much for the validity of raw intuition. The case of logarithmic utility, which respects risk aversion, does demonstrate that investing for the long run need not coax out more average exposure to equity risk than investing for a single period, even when stocks do predictably rebound.

When we leave Bernoulli's utility for more realistic utility functions, can something be saved for raw intuition?

7.7 Intuition At Last Vindicated

Numerous estimates have been made of the elasticity of relative risk aversion that will best rationalize the time-series and cross-sectional data of the actual securities market. With remarkable consensus it is agreed that realistic $-WU''(W)/U'(W)$ coefficients are above the unity of the $\log(W)$ case. People seem to act as if they are more risk averse than Daniel Bernoulli would be.

To dramatize this, I will examine in detail the following utility function with constant relative risk aversion:

$$U(W) = -\frac{1}{W} \tag{27}$$

$$-\frac{WU''(W)}{U'(W)} = 2 > 1 \quad \text{of Bernoulli}.$$

We have seen [in the paragraph following (23)] that this one-period investor has an optimum fraction in equities, w^1, that is less than the w^* of Bernoulli:

$$w^1 = 0.1213\ldots < w^* = \tfrac{1}{4}. \tag{28}$$

Although $-1/W$ belongs to the utility family that yields the same myopic $\bar{w}$ independently of the time horizon T *under the random walk*, we cannot take for granted that the rebound process over two periods will evoke this same w^1 of the one-period problem.

We separately solve for optimal w^2 for a two-period-horizon investor who is constrained to adhere in all periods to the same $\bar{w}$ (and who therefore is forbidden to be a "timer"!). From table 7.1,

$$u_2(\bar{w}^2) = u_2(0.1463\ldots)$$
$$= \underset{w}{\text{Max}}\,[-\tfrac{1}{6}(1 + 2w)^{-2} - \tfrac{4}{6}(1 + 2w)^{-1}(1 - w)^{-1} - \tfrac{1}{6}(1 - w)^{-2}], \tag{29}$$

where $\bar{w}^2$ is the root of the following *cubic* equation:

$$6(1 + 2w)^3(1 - w)^3 u_2'(w) = 0$$
$$= 4(1 - w)^3 + 8(1 - w)^2(1 + 2w)$$
$$\quad - 4(1 - w)(1 + 2w)^2 - 2(1 + w)^3. \tag{30}$$

By speedy Newton iteration, we find that

$$w^2 = 0.1463.. > w^1 = 0.1213\ldots. \tag{31}$$

At long last we have found a rational derivation for long-horizon investors being more equity tolerant than short-horizon investors.

By solving a $(T + 1)$-degree polynomial, we can demonstrate that every increase in T does raise the optimal w^T for our $(-1/W)$ investor who faces a rebound process. Facing a momentum process, her T-dependence would go the other way.

Remark: The rebound process is itself kind of an asymptotic log-normal random walk in the sense that it keeps spreading indefinitely in its probabilities. A $\sqrt{T}$ law eventually operates as in the case of the simple random walk, but Gabriel's (1959) asymptotic-variance coefficient of T is a finite fraction of the coefficient characterizing the simple random walk. (The momentum process gives T a coefficient of more than unity—consistent with observed short-term market behavior.)

The present Markov processes, in short, do not fulfill completely the fundamentalist expectations of a Modigliani, Tobin, Shiller, or Samuelson. We expect economic reality to impose reflecting barriers to where the real value of the S&P 500 can eventually go. That entails more than a tendency toward rebounding in stochastic growth rates.

It reflects the presumed fact that when factor shares and capitalization coefficients are bid to levels far from micro and macro roots of Keynes-Walras-Lucas economic relations, the odds veer toward corrective pricing patterns. (*Warning:* This does not imply that canny investors have to be able to earn excess returns from the indicated rebounds!)

As I explained in my contribution to the Leonid Hurwicz *Festschrift*—in Samuelson (1986, vol. 5), the completion of the trilogy of Samuelson (1965, 1973) explaining why and how speculatively anticipated prices vibrate randomly—it is the *cumulative total return* of any portfolio that obeys white-noise-martingale structure: This is quite consistent with the market price of a stochastic rent-bearing acre of land showing *systematic negative autocorrelation*, as anticipated high runs of juicy rents can be expected to be amortized at a rate just big enough to compensate for the high dividend rents themselves. (As we say in the elementary texts, you might reread the previous sentence.)

7.8 How to Time

Investors with Bernoulli's logarithmic utility will follow the same unrestricted timing rules whatever their ultimate time horizon may be. That is a theorem when pre-tuning is respected:

$$w_+^1 = w_+^2 = \cdots = w_+^T \leqslant w_-^T = \cdots = w_-^2 = w_-^1 \quad \text{for Bernoulli.} \tag{32}$$

For the pure random walk the best way to time is not to time at all. Bernoulli then invests one-fourth in equities, always rebalancing the portfolio at each period so that

$$w_+^T = w_-^T = w^* = \tfrac{1}{4}, \quad t = 1, 2, \ldots: \quad \text{random walk.} \tag{33}$$

When this Bernoulli faces the rebound process, as a timer he raises his w_- following upon a weak stock performance in the previous period. Thus

$$w_+^T \equiv 0 < w^* = \tfrac{1}{4} < \tfrac{1}{2} \equiv w_-^T, \quad T = 1, 2, \ldots. \tag{34}$$

Already back in (25) proof was sketched for these special logarithmic invariances. Clearly Bernoulli's case is singular, being so to speak, too clever by 'arf.

7.9 Dynamic Programming Solutions for Multistage Timing

The investor more risk averse than Bernoulli used the myopic solutions of (27) and (28) that were suboptimal in the sense that they did not take into account the useful information available to the investor facing the rebound process. Since the investor knows last period's equity results, she knows how this period's prospective probabilities have changed and knows she should use that knowledge.

Instead of always opting as a one-period investor for myopic w^1, we have already seen that she should seek (w_+^1, w_-^1) depending upon which of $(+, -)$ just previously prevailed. Similarly the two-period investor can do better now than $\bar{w}^2$ or than $[w_+^1, w_-^1]$ by seeking (w_+^2, w_-^2) depending on which of $(+, -)$ previously prevailed. [By recursion, for any T and knowing (w_+^t, w_-^t) for all $t < T$, she will want now to calculate optimal $[w_+^T, w_-^T]$.]

We have already calculated her one-period timing strategies: $(w_+^1, w_-^1) = (0, \tfrac{1}{4})$. Knowing them, the investor can now solve for her two-period-horizon w_+^2 or w_-^2. When + previously prevailed, she picks her $\bar{w}_+^2$ now, using what she knows about how she will act in the final period. Each of the two-period outcomes $(+ +, - +, + -, - -)$ occurs with its calculable probabilities of $(1/9, 4/9, 2/9, 2/9)$. Here then is her maximand and relevant quadratic equation:

$$u_+[w_+^2] = \underset{w}{\text{Max}}\, [-(\tfrac{1}{9})(1 + 2w)^{-1}(1 + 2w_+^1)^{-1} - (\tfrac{4}{9})(1 - w)^{-1}(1 + 2w_-^1)^{-1}$$

$$- (\tfrac{2}{9})(1 + 2w)^{-1}(1 - w_+^1)^{-1} - (\tfrac{2}{9})(1 - w)^{-1}(1 - w_-^1)^{-1}]$$

$$= (\tfrac{1}{9})\, \underset{w}{\text{Max}}\, \{-[1 + 2](1 + 2w)^{-1} - [4(\tfrac{2}{3}) + 2(\tfrac{4}{3})](1 - w)^{-1}\}$$

16

Long-Run Risk Tolerance When Equity Returns Are Mean Regressing

$$= (\tfrac{25}{27}) \underset{w}{\text{Max}} \left[-(\tfrac{9}{25})(1 + 2w)^{-1} - (\tfrac{16}{25})(1 - w)^{-1} \right]$$

$$= \bar{u}_+ [0.0198193\ldots], \tag{35}$$

where w_+^2 is the root of

$$(27)(1 + 2w)^2(1 - w)^2 u'_+[w] = 18(1 - w)^2 - 16(1 + 2w)^2$$

$$= 2[23w^2 + 50w - 1] \tag{36}$$

$$w_+^2 = (\tfrac{1}{46})[-50 + (2{,}500 + 92)^{1/2}] = 0.0198193\ldots > 0 = w_+^1. \tag{37}$$

From (35)'s last line, we see that her dynamic programming problem in two stages reduces down to formal similarity with a one-stage problem, but with the apparent odds shifted from 2 to 1 against a gain to the more favorable 16 to 9 against! Naturally then she raises her w_+^2 to a positive level from her w_+^1 level of zero.

Similarly, when she solves for two-stage w_-^2 following a market decline, her apparent odds have shifted to better than 2 to 1 in favor of a gain in this first period; hence she raises her w_-^2 to above the $\tfrac{1}{4}$ of her w_-^1. After a $-$, her probabilities for the four possible outcomes are calculable as [2/9, 2/9, 4/9, 1/9], which is the mirror image of those used in (35). Therefore

$$u_-[w_-^2] = (\tfrac{26}{27}) \underset{w}{\text{Max}} \left[-(\tfrac{18}{26})(1 + 2w)^{-1} - (\tfrac{8}{26})(1 - w)^{-1} \right]$$

$$= u_-[0.272078\ldots]. \tag{38}$$

$$27(1 + 2w)^2(1 - w)^2 u'_-[w] = 0 = 36(1 - w)^2 - 8(1 + 2w)^2$$

$$+ 4[w^2 - 26w + 7] \tag{39}$$

$$w_-^2 = (\tfrac{1}{2})[26 + (676 - 28)^{1/2}] = 0.272078\ldots > 0.25 = \bar{w}_-^1$$

By now it will be clear how, knowing $[\bar{w}_+^1, \bar{w}_-^1; \bar{w}_+^2, \bar{w}_-^2]$, the investor can solve recursively for $[\bar{w}_+^3, \bar{w}_-^3]$; hence it is clear how she solves recursively for any T's $[\bar{w}_+^T, \bar{w}_-^T]$. I leave to the reader how to deal with the cases of $-1/W^2$ or $-1/W^N$. For N an integer, calculating $(w^1, w^2, \ldots)$ will involve solving polynomials of respective degrees $(N + 1, 2N + 1, 3N + 1, \ldots)$, but solving for $(w_+^1, w_+^2, \ldots; w_-^1, w_-^2, \ldots)$ will never involve polynomials of greater degree than $N + 1$.

Arithmetic examples need to be augmented by formal, general proof. As in Samuelson (1990)'s *fundamentalist* variant of this chapter,[4] consider the general family of *constant relative risk aversion*:

$$U(W) = \frac{W^\gamma}{\gamma}, \quad 0 \neq \gamma < 1. \tag{40}$$

As in effect already done earlier, define for it the one-period maximized $E\{W_1\}$:

$$u_\gamma[p] = u_\gamma[p; w_p] = \underset{x}{\text{Max}}\, u_\gamma[p; w]$$

$$= \frac{\text{Max}_w\,(p[1 + 3w]^\gamma + [1 - p][1 - w]^\gamma)}{\gamma},$$

$$= \frac{p[1 + 3w_p]^\gamma + [1 - p][1 - w_p]^\gamma}{\gamma}. \tag{41}$$

Since greater probability for a gain improves you, and coaxes you to invest more in stocks, the following inequalities hold

$$\frac{du_\gamma[p]}{dp} > 0,$$

$$\frac{dw_p[p]}{dp} > 0. \tag{42}$$

Depending on whether γ is positive or negative, we have the following inequalities: for $p > q$,

$$\frac{u_\gamma[p]}{u_\gamma[q]} > 1, \quad \gamma > 0, \tag{43a}$$

$$\frac{u_\gamma[p]}{u_\gamma[q]} < 1, \quad \gamma < 0. \tag{43b}$$

The last case of negative γ applies for realistic investors with greater risk aversion than Bernoulli's log W, and in particular for our case of $-1/W$.

The latter's two-period maximum problem, after a little manipulation, can be written so that (35) looks like

$$u_+[w_+^2] = \underset{w}{\text{Max}}\,(-[1 + 3w]^{-1}\tfrac{1}{3}u_{-1}[\tfrac{1}{3}] - [1 - w]^{-1}\tfrac{2}{3}u_{-1}[\tfrac{2}{3}])$$

$$= u_{-1}[h](\tfrac{1}{3}u_{-1}[\tfrac{1}{3}] + \tfrac{2}{3}u_{-1}[\tfrac{2}{3}])$$

$$= u_{-1}[h; w_h](\tfrac{1}{3}u_{-1}[\tfrac{1}{3}] + \tfrac{2}{3}u_{-1}[\tfrac{2}{3}]), \tag{44}$$

where h is defined by

$$\frac{h}{(h-1)} = \frac{1}{2}u_{-1}\frac{[1/3]}{u_{-1}}\begin{bmatrix}2\\3\end{bmatrix} > \frac{1}{2}. \tag{45}$$

Long-Run Risk Tolerance When Equity Returns Are Mean Regressing 197

By virtue of inequalities (42) and (43b), we can then derive

$$h > \tfrac{1}{3}, \quad w_h \equiv w_+^2 > w_{1/3} \equiv w_+^1. \tag{46}$$

The reader may in a similar way prove that

$$u_-[w_-^2] = u_{-1}[r, w_r](\tfrac{2}{3}u_{-1}[\tfrac{1}{3}] + \tfrac{1}{3}u_{-1}[\tfrac{2}{3}]), \tag{47}$$

$$r > \tfrac{2}{3}, \quad w_r \equiv w_-^2 > w_{2/3} \equiv w_-^1. \tag{48}$$

For $w^{1/2}$ or any positive γ, obvious reversals in sign of comparative-states effects are similarly proved.

7.10 Summary

We can wrap up the general rules deduced for investors uniformly more risk averse than the Bernoulli utility maximizer.

Theorem The longer the horizon, other things equal, the greater should be the exposure to lucrative but risky investments when the investor faces a rebound process and has constant relative risk tolerance that exceeds that of Bernoulli.

$$0 = w_+^1 < w_+^2 = 0.0198193.. < w_+^3 < \cdots < w_+^\infty \tag{49}$$

$$w_+^T < w_-^T, \quad T = 1, 2, \ldots. \tag{50}$$

I believe that even for $T = \infty$, (50)'s strong inequality holds: Timing pays even for the longest-run investor when the rebound process applies. Also

$$0.25 = w_-^1 < w_-^2 = 0.272078 < w_-^3 < \cdots < w_-^\infty. \tag{51}$$

For myopic investors constrained to keep their $\bar{w}_T$ unchanged once they have embarked on a T-period investment program, we've seen that a longer time horizon also entails more equity tolerance:

$$w^1 = 0.1213.. < w^2 = 0.1463 < w^3 < \cdots < w^\infty < 0.25 \quad \text{of Bernoulli.} \tag{52}$$

Qualification: When w's cannot be negative or in excess of unity, some of the strong inequalities might become weakened to equalities. I suspect that $\bar{w}^\infty$ is strongly bounded by (w_+^∞, w_-^∞).[3]

Naturally all these inequalities go into reverse (1) when we replace $U = -1/W$ by $U = W^{1/2}$ or any other such function that is less risk averse than Bernoulli (but still risk averse), and (2) when we replace a rebound process by a momentum process that is on the other side of a random walk. All the inequalities are replaced by equalities when the utility is Bernoullian and/or the process is white-noise random walk.

Although my examples involve a special equity with even-odds tripling of principal or washing it out and involve simple Markov processes, abstract analysis should confirm the robustness of my qualitative conclusions.

My three-decade search for confirmation of enhanced risk tolerance among long-horizon investors has thus, in a satisfying sense, achieved success. It is hard to believe that somewhere in the literature there is not already explicit anticipation of so important a result.

A final caveat may be in order against overtouting this deductive qualitative result. Since it takes a long time to duplicate statistical samples of long-term epochs, our confidence in the strength of the rebound deviation from the random walk must be guarded. Moreover the size of the alleged effect, particularly after we discount for the possible one-time nature of the 1920–45 swings of the Great Depression and World War II, may not be too great qualitatively. My examples, where $(\frac{2}{3} \quad \frac{1}{3})$ and $(\frac{1}{3} \quad \frac{2}{3})$ were substituted for $(\frac{1}{2} \quad \frac{1}{2})$, might themselves be considered rather exaggerated contrasts.[5] And even they do not generate vast time-horizon effects on portfolio fractions. For all these reasons a certain caution toward the new results would seem prudent.

Notes

I owe thanks to the MIT Center for Real Estate Development for partial support, and to Aase Huggins, Ruth Pelizzon, and Eva Hakala for editorial assistance. A brief literary distillation of the present discussion is in Samuelson (1988). Dr. Andrew Solow of the Woods Hole Oceanographic Institution provided me with the Gabriel reference.

1. See L. H. Summers (1986), J. M. Poterba and L. H. Summers (1987), and E. F. Fama and K. R. French (1988) for evidence that variances of stock-price changes do not grow linearly with time as they would if a true random walk held. Instead in short periods they grow a bit faster than T, showing weak positive autocorrelation. For longer periods of time the autocorrelation becomes significantly negative. Since stocks marched up the hill in the 1920s, down the valley in the early 1930s, and showed influence of a strong business cycle in the 'tween-the-wars years, this phenomenon is stronger for the 1925–45 period than for the 1945–85 period. The Fama-Summers paradigm has some resemblance to the views of Modigliani, Tobin and Brainard, and Shiller, according to which the market is not necessarily *macro* efficient. Instead it undergoes self-fulfilling waves above and below fundamentalist values: Thus Tobin's q (which is the ratio of the securities-market valuation of

America's earning assets to their reproduction cost) undulates below and above unity, with perhaps some tendency to regress back toward its sustainable equilibrium value. See F. Modigliani and R. Cohen (1979), J. Tobin and W. C. Brainard (1977), R. Shiller (1986), and Samuelson (1986). Lawrence Summers properly notes: "Although the relative weakness of the negative autocorrelation in the post-1950 data does militate against the extra risk tolerance for equities adduced here, the reduced volatility of stocks in those years works *ceteris paribus* to justify some enhanced equity tolerance."

2. It can be shown that this is equivalent to tuning the mean log-outcomes to be the same for the rebound as for the random-walk process. A reader may prefer some other "tuning" normalization. In any case this chapter's main point—that x^1 and x^{1+T} may rationally differ—is valid independent of any normalization.

3. In seeking the asymptotic w's appropriate to T, one might at first be tempted by the log-normal approximation. I must warn against any such temptation. It is true that for each positive w, the *normalized* variate $\sum_1^T \log[(1-w) + wX_j] - E\{\log[(1-w) + wX]\} \div \text{Var}\{\log[(1-w) + wX]\}\sqrt{T}$, does have a limiting distribution that approaches the Gaussian. But it is not true that use of that surrogate Gaussian will give one the correct long-term portfolio w's. To see this, contemplate a second equity that differs from our $(0, 3; \frac{1}{2}, \frac{1}{2})$. Let its outcomes be $(A, B; p, 1-p)$. With cunning we can tailor the trio (A, B, p) to have the same optimal Bernoulli w^* of $\frac{1}{4}$ for *all* T. And we can tailor them to have, for $T = 1$, the same $E\{\log W_1\}$. However, almost always the old and new portfolios will *not* display the same $\text{Var}\{\log W_1\}$. Therefore, using log-normal surrogates will result in different w's for the two portfolios at large T, even though exactly the same w^* of $\frac{1}{4}$ is mandated at every T, however large! This demonstrates the treachery of log-normal surrogates.

4. When price changes satisfy a Markov matrix, the real value of any stock relative to a pea or a house spreads probabilistically to infinity—hardly a fundamentalist's paradigm. In Samuelson [1988] I therefore investigated the following fundamentalist's paradigm: the *trend* of a stock price is a deterministic exponential path: when price at t is below trend value, the probabilities of price gains are assumed to be large relative to losses; and when P_t is above trend, probabilities of price drops grow at expense of rises. Such a Markov process entails for (price/trend) in the far future a definite ergodic probability distribution. Fortunately, all the pleasing qualitative results of the present paper can be confirmed to be valid also for the fundamentalist's paradigm!

5. On the other hand, there is some empirical warrant, as in Pindyck (1988), for using $-1/W^2$ rather than my $-1/W$. That would intensify the quantitative importance of my time-horizon effects.

References

Bernoulli, D. 1738. "Specimen theoriae novae de mensura sortis." *Commentarii*. St. Petersburg Academy. Translated in *Econometrica* 22 (1954): 23–36. Reprinted in

Precursors in Mathematical Economics: An Anthology, ed. W. J. Baumol and S. M. Goldfield. Series of Reprints of Scarce Works on Political Economy, No. 19. London: School of Economics and Political Science, 1968, pp. 15–26.

Gabriel, K. R. 1959. "The Distribution of the Number of Successes in a Sequence of Dependent Trials." *Biometrika* 51: 454–460.

Latané, H. A. 1956. "Criteria for Choice among Risky Ventures." *Journal of Political Economy* 67: 144–155.

Modigliani, F., and Cohn, R. A. 1979. "Inflation, Rational Valuation and the Market." In *Financial Analysts Journal*: 24–44. Reprinted in *Saving, Investment, and Capital Markets in an Inflationary Economy*. Cambridge, MA: Ballinger, 1982, pp. 121–165.

Pindyck, Robert S. 1988. "Risk Aversion and Determinants of Stock Market Behavior." *Review of Economics and Statistics* 70, 2: 183–190.

Samuelson, P. A. 1965. "Proof That Properly Anticipated Prices Fluctuate Randomly." *Industrial Management Review* (Spring). Reprinted in *Collected Scientific Papers of Paul A. Samuelson*, vol. 3, ed. R. Merton. Cambridge: MIT Press, 1972, ch. 198, pp. 782–790.

Samuelson, P. A. 1973. "Proof That Properly Discounted Present Values of Assets Vibrate Randomly." *Bell Journal of Economics and Management Science* 4, 2: 369–374. Reprinted in *Collected Scientific Papers of Paul A. Samuelson*, vol. 4, ed. H. Nagatani and K. Crowley. Cambridge: MIT Press, 1977, ch. 241, pp. 465–470.

Samuelson, P. A. 1986. "Stochastic Land Valuation: Total Return as Martingale Implying Price Changes—A Negatively Correlated Walk." In *Preferences, Uncertainty and Optimality, Essays in Honor of Leonid Hurwicz*, eds. J.S. Chipman, D. McFadden, M. Richter. Boulder, CO: Westview Press, 1990.

Samuelson, P. A. 1988. "Long-Run Risk Taking in a Fundamentalist Model of Equities." MIT Working Paper. June.

Samuelson, P. A. 1990. "Asset Allocation Could Be Dangerous to Your Health." *Journal of Portfolio Management* 16, 3: 5–8.

Shiller, R. 1986. "Stock Prices and Social Dynamics." *Brookings Papers on Economic Activity*: 457–498.

Tobin, J., and Brainard, W. L. 1977. "Asset Markets and the Cost of Capital." In *Economic Progress, Private Values and Public Policy: Essays in Honor of William Fellner*, eds. R. Nelson and B. Balassa. Amsterdam: North-Holland, 1977, pp. 235–262. Reprinted in Tobin, J., *Essays in Economics: Theory and Policy*. Cambridge: MIT Press, 1982.

Samuelson, P. A. 1986. "Stochastic Land Valuation: Total Return as Martingale Implying Price Changes—A Negatively Correlated Walk." In *Preferences, Uncertainty and Optimality, Essays in Honor of Leonid Hurwicz*, eds. J.S. Chipman, D. McFadden, M. Richter. Boulder, CO: Westview Press, 1990.

Paradise Lost & Refound: The Harvard ABC Barometers

Plus some insights into Town–and–Gown in the world of finance.

Paul A. Samuelson

These unauthenticated memoirs were evoked by Peter Bernstein's editorial queryings. Rather than check carefully the historic facts described here, I leave to some future researcher the identification of any myths that have crept into the oral traditions of my generation. I only tell it, as it was told to me! I owe thanks to the MIT Center for Real Estate Development for de Medici support of macroeconomic research.

By unhappy chance, Harvard University got into the forecasting business during the 1920s. Many of the great names in its economics department were connected with the Harvard Economic Society, a commercial venture that used some of its revenue to start and continue the *Review of Economic Statistics,* renamed the *Review of Economics and Statistics* in the 1930s when Seymour Harris was its editor.

Warren M. Persons (1878-1937) was a Harvard statistician who, around World War I, was an expert on the theory of index numbers. Apparently, Persons had the notion of starting a forecasting service. It must have prospered early, as the handsome outsize volumes of the *Review of Economic Statistics* were subsidized by the Harvard Economic Society. Besides Persons, other Harvard luminaries must have received some income from this commercial venture: C. W. Bullock, John H. Williams, Edwin Frickey, and perhaps Allyn Young were a few such. The statistician W. L. Crum was presumably brought to Harvard in part because the Harvard Economic Society needed his mathematical skills.

The story is an interesting one, but in the end an unhappy case study of the risks a university runs when it lends its name to for-profit activities.

THE BAROMETERS

The most memorable activity of the Harvard Economic Society, and certainly its most interesting scientific contribution, was its famous A, B, and C barometers of business activity. These were the forerunners of the leading, current, and lagging indicators later developed at the National Bureau of Economic Research by Arthur F. Burns and Wesley Mitchell, by Geoffrey Moore, and later, in connection with the federal government's statistical services, by Julius Shiskin.

Persons, as I recall it, collected numerous time series. Some had downturns and upturns that occurred on the average a bit *earlier* than most of the series: He classified these as A or *leading* series, and the A barometer was a mean of them. Some of the series tended to move down and move up a bit *later* than the mob: These were the *lagging* series classified under C. The rest were B series, which more or less constituted *current indicators.* Although the act of clas-

---

PAUL A. SAMUELSON is Institute Professor Emeritus at MIT in Cambridge (MA 02139). A former student recently described him as "a human main frame, linked with a spreadsheet on a PC."

sification was mechanically empirical, the A series tended to represent Speculation; the B series were to represent Business; the C series, called Money, tended to be such finance items as interest rates and the stock of money.

The hope was to find in the A series a philosopher's stone that would tell customers when to get into the wild and woolly stock market of the 1920s and when to get out. (Even in my time at Harvard, just outside the walls of the Yard was the office of Curtis & Jackson — later merged with Paine Webber. Students and bold assistant professors could chance their arm against Lady Luck at little personal inconvenience.)

Persons used graphical methods, such as transparent charts that could be shifted until the series in question got into phase with the mean of the business cycle. Also, I seem to remember, he used cross-correlations of the form $r[x_t, y_{t+k}]$. If this Personian r reached its maximum for k equal to the positive integer 3, that was interpreted to mean that x tended to move three months earlier than y did. For k negative, y led x.

Students of monetarism will be surprised only momentarily that M tended to be in the C, or lagging, barometer rather than in the A, or leading, barometer. Any early positivistic Friedman could handily resolve this violation of what today might be called "Granger causality" by noting that M's growth rate (or first difference) tended in smooth oscillations to precede in its turning points M's own turning points: If M_t was in C, dM_t/d_t or $M_t - M_{t-1}$ tended to be in A.

SUCCESS!

The mail and the money rolled in — rolled into Holyoke and Little Halls, the holy temples of the old Harvard economics department in pre-Littauer days. President Emeritus A. Laurence Lowell once told me that one of his smarter moves was to divorce Harvard from the Harvard Economic Society: He just felt that this was not the kind of activity a university should be engaged in. (President Eliot apparently had no such compunction when he lent his name to the Five Foot Shelf of *Harvard Classics*, with which our parents used to line their bookshelves, and which we used as trots to help translate the *Aeneid*. There were no biologically instructive items in Eliot's selection: Much of what my generation knew about sex had to come from the famous eleventh edition of the *Encyclopedia Britannica*.)

Lowell's is a good story, which speaks well for his acumen and caution. But perhaps it wells out from imperfect memory, as some of my elders who have heard me tell the tale claim that it was well after October 1929 that the would-be money fructifiers were driven out of the temples of Holyoke and Little Halls. In any case, they moved only a few paces down Massachusetts Avenue, and their advertisements and letterheads still carried Harvard Square as their address.

UNTIL THE CRASH

Legend has it that the Harvard Economic Society let its customers down badly in the 1929 crash. Twice I heard Leonard Crum agree to recount for graduate students the failure of the barometers to predict or even recognize the 1929 financial panic. Really he had little to glean from the experience, coming up only with remarks like the following:

"There was one statistical clerk [maybe Dorothy Wescott?] who said she didn't like the looks of the ABC barometers. But we failed to heed her warning."

"Perhaps if Allyn Young had not died in 1928, the Harvard Economic Service would have done less badly."

Needless to say, empiricists who live by the sword die by the sword. The customers melted away, and the professors had to go back to teaching Radcliffe sections for their pin money. A number of economist stars, young and old, dropped a bundle in the 1929 crash. Some dowagers in Cambridge were still saying in my time: "I shouldn't have listened to Lauchlin Currie's guesses." A Back Bay society dentist, in the late 1930s, when he held me captive in the chair, used to complain endlessly: "John Williams may be vice president of the New York Federal Reserve Bank now, but in 1929 he sure was optimistic."

I have no reason to single out the Persons barometer methodology as particularly misleading in a time when a tulip-mania craze was sweeping both Wall Street and Main Street. Actually, though, it is of scientific interest that the National Bureau upper turning point of the late-1920s business cycle is marked in mid-1929, months prior to Black Friday of October 1929. Only rarely in history does the stock market *follow* the coincidental indicators instead of *leading* them. (When I am dead, I will not so much be remembered for my countless wisdoms as for my flippant remark: "Yes, Wall Street does call the turns of business. The Dow Jones index has predicted *nine* of the last five recessions.")

The fact that stock prices, for whatever reason, are so early an indicator of cyclical downturns suggests that speculators ought not to have hoped for much from subscribing to the ABC barometers. What the speculator wants is the time series that comes *before* the A series: They want Irving Berlin's pup, the "pup who gets the bugler up!" Such pups are hard to locate, and expensive to rent. Thus, it was a legend of the 1930s that Roger Babson, the sage of Wellesley Hills, had predicted the Wall Street collapse of 1929. Indeed he had. But Babson did it first in 1925 — a call that did not do a lot for the net worth of his clients.

In the middle of the 1930s, the *Review of Economic Statistics* was still carrying in an unenthusiastic way the ABC barometers in each quarterly issue. One day these disappeared from the new mailing. Few noticed. The universe and economic science carried on.

THE PHOENIX FLIES AGAIN

The museums of science are replete with fossils of species that could not last the course. The leading-coinciding-lagging indicators might be buried forever in old footnotes. But occasionally Sleeping Beauty is brought back to life by the kiss of a new Prince Charming. It must have been Arthur F. Burns who played the Prince. As the historian of science Robert K. Merton would expect, Darwins and Wallaces come in pairs like Newtons and Leibnizes. So it was with Burns and Persons. Impressed as he was by the regularities of the business cycle that the Mitchell group at the National Bureau had discerned and classified, it was only natural for Burns to look for regularities of phase shifts. And, working with Moore (and, later, with Shiskin), Burns found regularities that we economists still use today.

The ABC barometers live on in the Leading Indicators methodology of government agencies and private forecasters. What I still continue to find astonishing, but which I gratefully accept, is the finding that the mechanical leading indicators — imperfect as they are — still convey useful information. Even more surprising, they still stand up well in comparison with a myriad of close cousins. Like the late Tjalling Koopmans, I prefer paradigms that combine plausible Newtonian theories with observed Baconian facts. But never would I refuse houseroom to a sturdy fact just because it is a bastard without a name and a parental model.

CHARLES RIVER LEGENDS

We can appraise the influence of the Harvard Economic Society better if we know something about how the depression hit a community like Cambridge and a university like Harvard. Stories become taller in their retelling.

More than once I heard the following doubtful tale. One March morning in 1933, a Radcliffe student was supposed to have put to her money and banking professor the following question: "Professor Williams, could all the banks be shut down?" "No, that is quite impossible," he is reported to have replied. "What then does this headline in the *Boston Herald* mean, sir?"

The story is too pat to have a plausible ring. Perhaps it was accorded a false credence because reliable legend tells that the janitor in Holyoke Hall had to lend the department members funds to carry them through the Bank Holiday, because he was the only one in the building to have withdrawn his funds from the Cambridge Trust Company.

Wait, though, before we infer that the amateur is a better forecaster than the expert. It would perhaps not have been considered quite good form for professors to initiate a run on the banks. All my teachers knew well the opprobrium that descended on Professor Arthur Dewing, finance expert at the Harvard Business School, when, against the pleas of distraught bankers, he withdrew a large amount of gold from the Harvard Trust and put it in a bank deposit vault for safekeeping. Rightly or wrongly, this was considered the unsocial act of a survivor at sea who, in bolting out of the lifeboat, rocks it into hazardous instability.

For a score of years, Dewing would justify his behavior even to casual strangers, averring that, as a fiduciary for his public utility companies, it had been his duty to conserve their assets. (We graduate students believed the story that Dean Donham of the Harvard Business School asked for Dewing's formal resignation in order to alleviate public criticism but that, immediately on receiving that document, Donham proceeded to accept it. Do things happen like this outside C. P. Snow novels?)

Although the Harvard Economic Society happened to put some of its reliance on the ABC barometers, the service was essentially one of those many desert blooms called into existence by the sunshine of a long bull market. The cartoon books were full of similar debacles. "Where are the Customers' Yachts?" and "Oh Yeah?" were only two of the many titles of works in this genre.

AN EARLY KEYNESIAN CONTROVERSY

The magnificent collected works of John Maynard Keynes remind me of an old dispute about the 1920s bull market. Keynes and Ralph Hawtrey were on one side of the debate. Among those on the other side were Carl Snyder of the Federal Reserve Bank of New York and that same Bullock whom I have already mentioned in connection with the Harvard Economic Society. The issue deserves some paragraphs.

Bullock was a leading Harvard elder throughout the first third of the century, along with Frank

Taussig (truly a great scholar, and dean of American economists), Thomas Nixon Carver, and the wordless great man in economic history, Edwin F. Gay. These well-paid luminaries did not get along well with one another, as the failure of Taussig's prize pupil in Jacob Viner's oral examination attests.

Bullock's fiefdom was public finance, and he brought to it a knowledge of Greek and Latin and perhaps some smattering of Hebrew and Aramaic. In case you are too dull to guess how that confers deep insight into taxation and fiscal policy, Bullock's writings would have driven home to you that throughout all history unbalanced budgets contrived the downfall of Greece and the decline of Rome. Bullock's disciples, Harold Hitchings Burbank at Harvard and Harley Lutz at Princeton, perpetuated his theses.

Although Ralph Hawtrey and John Maynard Keynes were scholars of deeper analysis and wider reputation, one cannot in retrospect be sure that theirs was a more correct position than Bullock's in the late 1920s. Hawtrey and Keynes discerned no deep danger to the United States and the world macroeconomy from the Wall Street Bubble. Although Bullock could not articulate the precise basis for his apprehension, he had forebodings that the speculative "excesses" in Wall Street would lead to future disasters: As it had been in Sodom and Gomorrah, so might it come to be in New York and Chicago.

Some features of the securities markets in 1986 would no doubt be regarded by a Rip van Bullock as equally ominous. Rather than dismiss as ridiculous any such fears, I would have to take more comfort from the consideration that what was crucial for the Great Depression was not so much the October 29 Crash as the cumulative falling dominoes of bank failures, mortgage foreclosures, and bankruptcies that were subsequently allowed to take place in that era of relative laissez-faire.

UNIVERSITY FINANCES

Harvard and Cambridge were if anything less hard hit by the depression than most places. I remember few Greater Boston banks failing after 1935. When I once told the story that no local bank would take a Harvard student's deposit in those days, it was not to document the rigors of the academic life but, rather, to report on the possible relevance of a contemporary liquidity trap.

President Lowell's successful wooing of Mr. Harkness for the House system meant that Dunster and Lowell Houses were built in the teeth of the Great Depression, costing the economy in the end possibly a negative amount. Professors who kept their jobs in some cases never had it so good as in the slump. Instructors in the Harvard economics department earned as much as $2500 a year, more perhaps than full professors at some land grant institutions and certainly several times what Harvard assistants in philosophy and the humanities were doled out. The best and the brightest in mathematics, physics, and biology — as certified by the National Research Council — were unable to a man to find jobs, much less permanent chairs, in the years just after 1933–1934.

The total returns earned on the Harvard portfolio in the years 1930 to 1939 can hardly explain its having been an oasis of serenity. Like others' organs, the Harvard nose was being ground down by the deflation, but it was a very long nose to begin with. The assets of universities were not to be unitized for another thirty years at least, so no one knew which universities did well as investors and which did badly. One had to settle for impressions. Hopkins, McGill, and Stanford were among those considered not to have been lucky in the depression years. Harvard was supposed to have done better than Yale. Once reputation is formed, however unwarrantedly, it tends to have a life of its own. One suspects that Yale did less badly than the casual world believes — and that Harvard did less well.

TRUE "THAT THOSE WHO TEACH, CAN'T"?

A treasurer of Harvard, William Claflin, once told me at a Society of Fellows dinner: "I have only two rules for investing the Harvard portfolio. Never consult the Economics Department, and never consult the Business School." Would that it were so simple!

Later in the postwar period, there were times when the University of Chicago, Rochester, (Connecticut) Wesleyan, the Alumni Foundation of the University of Wisconsin, and one or another educational institution were rumored to be particularly astute and innovative as investors. Often their short-term reputations were based on no more than the happenstance that the institution in question happened to allocate a high fraction of wealth to common stocks or unconventional equity instruments when markets were strong. By the time their college treasurers levitated up to important positions with a large Wall Street firm, their green thumbs too often reverted to the gray mean.

One needs sophisticated academic theory to understand the Mandelbrot–Pareto–Levy and less leptokurtic probability distributions that conduce to spurious appearances of superlative performing ability. Those who decry broad diversification or "settling for mediocrity" often have no conception of how to discern and test *long-run risk-corrected* investment prowess. Thus, in its fifteen years of existence, the

Common Fund (set up to permit smaller schools and colleges to pool their assets under professional management) has earned a higher "alpha" of total return than has the S&P 500 Index or CREF. Insiders understand that most of this superiority came from one of many money managers — one terminated at this time. Hiring several money managers and firing those with least recent luck has yet to be authenticated as the best strategy or even as a good strategy.

Irving Fisher, now recognized to have been a great scholar, became a laughingstock for his bullish pronouncements. Keynes's scholarly prowess did not inhibit his investment judgment. The typical college at Oxford and Cambridge tended to have on its endowment board one or more economist dons. I doubt that a Richard Kahn, a James Meade, or a Brian Reddaway lowered the batting averages of their ancient colleges. Certainly it was not long after Claflin jested that modern finance theory, from the pens of Harry Markowitz, John Lintner, Irwin Friend, and William Sharpe, demonstrated its usefulness to money managers. CREF, the largest common stock fund in the world, has benefited much from its trustees drawn from the world of professional finance. From my own observations over a long period of years, I would have to conclude that, at the same time, CREF's academic trustees have brought to the common effort much that the Claflins of the world neglect at their peril.

Paul Cabot was certainly one of Harvard's more effective treasurers. In retrospect, was it wise that his antipathy to government and to debt was permitted to delay Harvard's taking advantage of tax-exempt borrowing for the building of dormitories? Did Harvard's descending to the public trough kill off private philanthropy, as State Street pundits had warned would be the case?

When Seymour Harris led a 1951 revolt of the Harvard faculty against investing all of professors' pensions in fixed-principal securities, that move coincided with Vannevar Bush's threat to pull the Carnegie Institution out of TIAA. William C. Greenough's proposal for variable annuities based on the changing market values of a representative portfolio of common stocks therefore got its chance when TIAA established CREF in 1952. Meanwhile, back at the Harvard Yard, Cabot grudgingly awarded the rebelling activists a pension contract yielding as much more than 3-odd percent as the declared yield on the market value of the Harvard portfolio exceeded that percent.

The result was an incipient disaster. Neither Cabot nor the rebel professors realized that the latter were selling out their birthright for a mess of pottage that left all the capital gains of the Harvard portfolio with the university and not with the professors. Had a competent assistant professor of finance been commissioned to study the setup at an early stage, the disaster might have been averted, and a later Harvard administration could have been spared the need to devise Robin Hood compensations for a generation of professors who had opted against CREF–TIAA and for the unfavorable local option.

A modern reader may be tempted to say, "Surely, when observers examined the *total returns* of CREF-TIAA, the Harvard portfolio, and the contractual provisions of the Harvard-controlled defined-benefit pensions, they would have recognized early on the inadequacy of the local alternative to CREF-TIAA."

Such a remark would betray naivete. No university provided data for observers to calculate total returns and other data that would enable an auditor to know whether its endowment was being poorly or cannily invested. I have no way of judging whether Henry Shattuck, or Claflin, or Cabot were astute investors. In the absence of unitization, neither can anyone else. To its credit, Harvard was one of the first finally to unitize its holdings so that a) *total returns* could be estimated, and b) a donor could discover when the university's central headquarters was standing to usurp the future capital gains from his/her gift. (Threat of suits by donors, I seem to remember, helped speed overdue action on this unitization front.) *After* Harvard moved, so did MIT and Yale — as so often is the case. Let us be grateful.

GOING FOR IT

Judging performance of college and foundation trustees inevitably recalls McGeorge Bundy's pressure, from the Ford Foundation and onto non-profit organizations, to pursue a more aggressive strategy for improved expected return. Just when James Tobin's q factor — the ratio of what the economy's assets sell for in Wall Street, relative to what it would cost (net) in goods markets to construct such assets — was warning against possible overvaluation of equities, the Robert Barker report commissioned by Bundy urged colleges to invest more rationally. What Barker *et al.* meant to communicate was, "Be more rational." I fear this was interpreted by readers as, "Be more bold — especially if you hope for Ford Foundation grants."

I do not fault Bundy or Barker. I do reproach the economist members of the Barker committee, good friends of mine (Howard Bowen and James Lorie), for not incurring personal unpopularity by insisting in a minority dissent to the effect that long-run riskiness received inadequate attention in the Barker report. Academic scholars in economics departments and business schools — Eugene Fama, Fischer Black, Robert C. Merton, Myron Scholes, and a myriad of others — do have inputs that college treasurers, pension managers, and mutual fund directors will neglect only at their peril.

THE HOLY SANCTUM

All this, I agree, is a fair distance away from the comedy-tragedy of the Harvard Economic Society. Still, this digression to efficient market theory does bring up a basic question.

Even if the A barometer contains some useful knowledge for predicting share price declines, who is to say that this knowledge is not *already* registered in Wall Street pricings?

What is truly discouraging — or reassuring? — is the considerable evidence that the universe of those who seek to be "timers," and vary the fractional shares of their portfolios committed to common stocks in the hope of enlarging average long-term total return, in fact fail to achieve on the average any plus gain in comparison with simply buying and holding a fixed fraction of common stocks.

First it was my physicist and electrical engineer colleagues who became instant millionaires. Now it is the turn of the molecular biologists. That is their business. But as the comic-sad history of the Harvard Economic Society reminds us, it is the university's main business to mind its soul.

462

The $\sqrt{N}$ Law and Repeated Risktaking

Paul A. Samuelson[*]

Massachusetts Institute of Technology

1. INTRODUCTION AND REVIEW

P.A. Samuelson (1963) pointed out a widespread fallacy concerning how insurance works: it is not by *adding* independent risks that risk exposure is eased, but by *subdividing* through pooling the added risks. Insuring 100 independent ships increases risk 10-fold over insuring 1 ship; by pooling risk coverage of the 100 over 100 insurers, we reduce the risk on each to effectively one-tenth.

This topic evoked considerable discussion: e.g., L.L. Lopes (1981), A. Tversky and M. Bar-Hillel (1983), S.H. Chew and L. Epstein (1988), J.W. Pratt and R.J. Zeckhauser (1987), P.A. Samuelson (1988); but since it appeared in a limited-circulation journal, some recapitulation will be useful.

AMS Subject Classification: Primary 90A09.
Key words and phrases: Proper utility, insurance, risk aversion.

[*] I owe thanks to the MIT Center for Real Estate Development for partial support; to Aase Huggins, Eva Hakala, and Martha Adams for editorial assistance; to Gerard Gennotte for needed mathematical auditing; and to discussions with Joram Mayshar of Jerusalem University, Joseph Stiglitz of Stanford, and to Richard Zeckhauser and John Pratt of Harvard. John Pratt's companion piece provides an interesting alternative proof of my analysis and ingenious findings in its own right.

The exposition began with Stan Ulam's whimsy that, *A coward is one who won't bet either way on a favorable gamble.* Actually, it can be rational for a maximizer of expected utility, of $E\{U(W)\}$ with $U(W)$ strictly concave and in this sense risk averse, to refuse a sizeable bet favorable in money if dollars of gain bring less marginal utility than dollars of loss take away. For $U(W)$ a *smooth* concave function, Ulam would be correct to require that a sufficiently-scaled-down favorable bet be accepted.

I quoted the discussion of Ulam's remark by an unnamed colleague, who asserted he would shun an even-odds bet with $200 gain and $100 loss—but would embrace a set of a large enough number of such independent bets. Since it will be seen that it was gratuitous for me to attribute to my colleague reliance on a fallacious version of the Law of Large Numbers, I can identify him as E. Cary Brown, my long-time MIT boss. The Brownian motive need not have been a belief that, when a favorable gamble is repeated a large enough number of times N, it is virtually certain to leave you ahead.

Stock market letters and baseball announcers do often assert what boils down to the following false version of the Law of Large Numbers: after 1000 or more plays of a gamble, you are virtually certain to be near to 1000 times the expected gain per play; or

> If each play of gamble brings positive expected return, $E\{X_j\} = \mu > 0$, then

(1.1) $$\text{Prob}\{|(X_1 + \ldots + X_N) - N\mu| < \epsilon\} \to 1,$$
$$\text{for } 0 < \epsilon \ll 1, \quad \text{as } N \to \infty.$$

"In the long run, the odds dominate and chance errors cancel out."

Mathematicians know this to be monstrously misleading as stated, since for any $1/\epsilon$ however large, as N gets larger and larger it becomes virtually certain the $\sum_1^N X_j$ will diverge absolutely from $N\mu$ by more than $1/\varepsilon$. Riskiness does not cancel out for the longterm investor in a random-walk course, but rather grows like $\sqrt{N}$. This is so even though it is mathematically valid to assert that, for all positive ϵ,

(1.2) $$\lim_{N \to \infty} \text{Prob}\left\{\left|\frac{\sum_1^N X_j}{N\mu} - 1\right| < \epsilon\right\} = 1$$

30

$$\lim_{N\to\infty}\left\{a<\frac{\sum_1^N X_j-\mu N}{N^{1/2}\sigma}\right\}<b = \int_a^b (2\pi)^{-\frac{1}{2}}e^{-\frac{1}{2}t^2}dt\;,$$

where $\sigma^2 =$ Variance $\{X_j\} < \infty$; and also

$$\lim_{N\to\infty} \text{Prob}\left\{\sum_1^N X_j > 0\right\} = 1\;.$$

These Law-of-Large-Number and Central-Limit-Law truths do not justify belief that, when a favorable bet is repeatable a large enough number of times, it must end you up ahead. Nor should you be misled into following decisions simply because, with limiting probability of unity, they will leave you ahead—as in the dubious longrun investing counsel of Latané, Kelley, Breiman, Markowitz, Hakannson, and others. How much disutility harm you suffer when you are behind must rationally be given its proper weight. (Samuelson (1972, 1977, 1986, Chs. 204, 207, 245, 246, 329) nags away on this.)

Despite (1.2), there are many probability gambles with positive money gain $E\{X_j\}$, such that for admissible strictly-concave $U(W)$ of risk averters, for *all* N it will be the case that

$$(1.3)\qquad E\left\{U\left(W_0 + \sum_1^N X_j\right)\right\} < U(W_0)\;.$$

The possibility of (1.3) could be verified by inductive calculation for the numerical case

$$(1.4)\qquad U(W) = -2^{-W}\;,$$
$$\text{Prob}\{X_j = -1\} = 1/2 = \text{Prob}\{X_j = 1+\epsilon\}\;,\qquad 0 < \epsilon \ll 1.$$

For (1.4) it can be shown that (1.3)'s left-hand side diminishes with each increment of N above $N = 0$.

Constructively, Samuelson (1963) stated the theorem that, a maximizer of $E\{U(W)\}$ who is risk averse enough to refuse a specified favorable bet *at every* W_0 level cannot ever rationally accept a set of $2, 3, \ldots$, or $N, \ldots$ such favorable bets. (Remark: Recently Chew and Epstein (1988) showed that a risk-averse investor, who satisfies the axioms of Mark Machina (1982) that are weaker than those of the Expected $\{U\}$ dogma, is *not* bound by the 1963 theorem.)

2. PRESENT PURPOSES

The following problem naturally suggests itself as one aspect of the property Pratt and Zeckhauser (1987) call "proper" utility: *For what $U(W)$ functions is it the case that, whenever you are indifferent to 1 of a specified favorable gamble, you will also be indifferent to $2, 3, \ldots, N, \ldots$ of such gambles as a set?* And vice versa, in the sense that being indifferent to K such gambles means you will be indifferent to any J such gambles, $J \gtreqless K$? Once we are given a $U(W)$ function that meets this repeated-indifference test, we are assured that it will also reject (or accept) 2 repeated independent gambles whenever it rejects (or accepts) one such gamble.

The resulting restriction on $U(W)$ is the rather natural one adepts at portfolio theory would guess it to be—namely constancy of absolute risk aversion. Of greater interest are the functional equations derived here to tackle the questions. In half a century of theorizing about economics, I have rarely encountered any importance in the third derivative of a function, as with $U^{(3)}(W)$, much less encountered importance in such higher derivatives as the fifth and sixth derivatives of relevant economic functions.

Also, there is independent interest in the alternative approach to the posed problem used by John Pratt (1989) in a companion paper evoked by our private discussions. I have no doubt that still other approaches could be useful.

3. AMBIGUOUS CASES AND REASONS TO SELF-INSURE

Before analyzing the posed problem, I should mention that the cited 1963 theorem is of limited economic application. Thus for investors with constant relative risk aversion, a popular textbook case, at large W_0 values the specified favorable gamble is effectively scaled down enough in size to make it acceptable; therefore, the premise of the 1963 theorem is not met. Indeed, the ruling empirical dogma—as in K.J. Arrow (1964)—hypothesizes that people typically have diminishing absolute risk aversion, so that $-U''(W)/U'(W)$ drops indefinitely with W. Hence, at high enough W, practically everyone will come to accept the original *single* favorable gamble. So my theorem may be in the Pirandello role of a syllogism looking for an application. Who therefore is to say that Brown, contemplating the odds that he will end up at such high W levels after undertaking a *large* number of favorable gambles, is irrational? In the original version of this paper circulated, I worked out such a valid defense for him by using the pioneering E.D. Domar and R.A. Musgrave (1944) $U(W)$, which consists of straight lines meeting at a corner so that each dollar of loss hurts more than each dollar of gain by a constant multiple. (Below, between Equations (5.7) and (5.8), I describe another defense for Brown along lines suggested by John Pratt.)

Although constant-relative-risk-aversion $U(W)$ functions elude the grasp of the 1963 theorem, we must not infer from this that Brown with such a utility may rationally accept a repeated number of a gamble that is singly unacceptable. That is not possible since such utilities are not, in the pejorative terminology of Pratt-Zeckhauser (1984), so "improper."

Thus, suppose I have Bernoulli logarithmic utility, $U = \log W$. Suppose I have W_0 so low that I will reject the favorable gamble

$$(3.1) \quad \text{Prob}\{X_1 = H + h\} = \frac{1}{2} = \text{Prob}\{X_1 = H - h\}, \quad 0 < H < h.$$

Then I can never, at such W_0, accept the package of 2 independent such gambles.

Thus,

$$\frac{1}{2}\log(W_0 + H + h) + \frac{1}{2}\log(W_0 + H - h) < \log(W_0), \quad 0 < H < h,$$

implies

$$\frac{1}{4}\log(W_0 + 2H + 2h) + \frac{1}{2}\log(W_0 + 2H + h - h) + \frac{1}{4}\log(W_0 + 2H - 2h)$$

$$(3.2) \qquad\qquad\qquad < \log(W_0).$$

Similarly, Pratt-Zeckhauser (1987) proved for any function $W^{1-C}/(1-C)$, $0 < C \neq 1$, that refusal of one favorable bet implies refusing any integral number of such independent bets. The whole family is in this Pratt-Zeckhauser sense "proper."

The present problems have practical concern beyond that for gamblers or portfolio investors. Since insurance companies charge a premium that more than covers their loss risk, when I desist from buying insurance on an item, I am embracing a favorable gamble. When I do insure the item, I am refusing a favorable gamble.

Most individuals with 1 or 2 autos prefer to buy insurance. Many corporations with fleets of trucks or taxis are willing to self-insure. Is this rational?

It may be. Thus, the firm with trucks may already have many shareholders. What is called self-insuring may then really be a case of subdividing risk by sharing it among many different risk bearers. In terms of Samuelson (1963), we are then dealing with the $1/\sqrt{N}$ law—not the $\sqrt{N}$ law. "Self" insurance is then only a hidden form of pooling insurance.

Here is a different argument. The accounting reports of a 1-car taxi company will oscillate wildly in the absence of insurance. The decision whether to buy into the company will be contaminated by noise in the data due to stochastic risk. While it is true that the company with 100 taxis will have 10 times the oscillations in accident payments, their *percentage* importance in per share earnings of the large company will be only one-tenth as great. So there is less accounting objection to self insurance that comes with size. So goes this second line of argument. On examination, it also appears to involve the $1/\sqrt{N}$ rather than the $\sqrt{N}$ law. (To be sure, the $1/\sqrt{N}$ law would not be valid in its sphere if it were not the case that the $\sqrt{N}$ law is valid in its: really, they are two aspects of the same truth.)

Here is a third consideration. Suppose 1 person owns the huge company. It is her utility function that is alone relevant. And, almost by definition, the W in her $U(W)$ function is a large one. Insuring a single taxi, looked at from her perspective, has been scaled down to a degree that makes this favorable gamble attractive. And if she is rich enough, the same logic will make it desirable to self-insure for a great number of taxis. (Rather than self-insure on M of N taxis, insuring the other N-M completely, it will no doubt be better to make more complicated reinsurance contracts that involve various deductibility clauses. Details about avoidable transaction and information costs become critical in arriving at the optimal arrangement.)

Clearly, $\sqrt{N}$ laws cannot be alone decisive. If she is rich as Croesus, but has $(-e^{-CW})$ utility, it will be seen that the size of her fleet will not affect her self-insurance decisions.

4. DEFINING $U(W)$ NEUTRAL TOWARD REPETITION OF RISKS

$U(W)$'s come in several general categories: i) Those on the razor's edge where, if you will accept (reject, or be indifferent to) 1 favorable gamble, you will also accept (reject, or be indifferent to) 2, 3, ..., of such independent gambles. ii) Those in which you will take some maximum number M of such gambles, or less, but not more than M, where $M = 1, 2, \ldots$. iii) those in which you will take some minimum number M or more, but *will not take less than M*. iv) Those with more idiosyncratic properties. Depending upon the W level in question, one may of course generally go from one category to another. And of course, gambles of different compositions may affect one differently. However, for gambles sufficiently "compact" or "small," the composition of the gamble will presumably become immaterial.

Category i) is in a sense the razor's-edge border between the next two categories and our problem is to characterize its $U(W)$s.

To explore where i)'s broad border of indifference falls, I first proceed heuristically, asking the following question: For what local properties of the $U(W)$ function will it be the case that, when I am broadly indifferent about taking either one of the two specified (independent, compact, identical) gambles, I am also broadly indifferent to taking both of them together?

Suppose my $U(W)$ is such that at W_0 I opt to just take 1 of a sufficiently-favorable gamble that gives me with even odds a gain of $H+h$ or a loss of $h-H$. With what new utility function (of W near W_0) do I subsequently contemplate whether to take a second such independent gamble? My new ("post-one-gamble") utility function will be $\overline{U}(W)$ defined as follows.

$$(4.1) \quad \overline{U}(W) = \frac{1}{2} U(W + H_1(h; W_0) + h) + \frac{1}{2} U(W + H_1(h; W_0) - h),$$

where

$$(4.2) \quad H_1(h; W_0) = 0h + (-U''(W_0)/U'(W_0))h^2 + \text{higher powers of } h,$$

and $H_1(h; W_0)$ is the unique root of

$$(4.3) \quad \frac{1}{2} U(W_0 + H_1(h; W_0) + h) + \frac{1}{2} U(W_0 + H_1(h; W_0) - h) = U(W_0).$$

Within Category i), one expects the risk coefficient of $\overline{U}(W)$ to equal that of $U(W)$:

$$\text{(4.4)} \quad -\frac{U''(W)}{U'(W)} = -\frac{\overline{U}''(W)}{\overline{U}'(W)}$$
$$= -\frac{U''(W+H_1+h) + U''(W+H_1-h)}{U'(W+H_1+h) + U'(W+H_1-h)}.$$

Now, for h small, and h^3 negligible compared to h^2, we apply Taylor's expansions to the numerator and denominator, to get

$$\text{(4.5)} \quad -\frac{U''(W)}{U'(W)} = -\frac{U''(W) + (-1U^{(3)}U''(-U')^{-1} + U^{(4)})h^2 + \cdots}{U'(W) + (-1U''U''(-U')^{-1} + U^{(3)})h^2 + \cdots},$$

where third, fourth, and higher derivatives of U are written as $U^{(3)}$, $U^{(4)}$, ... For (4.5)'s equivalence to hold approximately near W, we must have to a good approximation,

$$\text{(4.6a)} \quad \frac{U^{(4)}}{U'} = 2\left(\frac{U^{(3)}}{U'}\right)\left(\frac{U''}{U'}\right) - \left(\frac{U''}{U'}\right)^3.$$

In terms of the absolute risk-aversion function, $A = -U''/U'$, this 4th order equation in U becomes the 2nd order differential equation:

$$\text{(4.6b)} \quad A''(W) = A'(W)A(W).$$

This is one necessary condition on admissible $A(W)$. An important subclass of (4.6b)'s solutions is verified to be the well-known case of constant-absolute-risk aversion:

$$\text{(4.7a)} \quad A(W) \equiv a > 0,$$

$$\text{(4.7b)} \quad U(W) = b + d\left(-e^{-aW}\right), \quad (d,a) > 0, \; -\infty < b < +\infty.$$

There is a more general 2-parameter infinity of other solutions to (4.6b), each uniquely defined for

$$\text{(4.8a)} \quad \tilde{a} = A(W_0) > 0, \quad A'(W_0) = \overline{a} \gtreqless 0,$$

(4.8b) $$A(W) = f(W;\tilde{a},\overline{a})\ .$$

With $\tilde{a}$ prescribed positive, $A(W)$ will be positive and risk averse in some interval around specified W_0. For $\overline{a}$ prescribed to vanish, we have (4.7)'s special case; and, as will be seen, this is the only admissible case when necessary conditions additional to (4.6b) are deduced to hold.

If all we require is a rough approximation to indifference, then any member of the $f(W;\tilde{a},\overline{a})$ family will be very nearly indifferent about repeating just-indifferent bets that are small in scale.

As we introduce higher-order terms in $(h^3, h^4, h^5, h^6, \ldots)$ in the Taylor's expansions of (4.4)'s numerators and denominators, and eschew approximations, we deduce further necessary conditions involving $A(W)$'s higher derivatives. We soon discover that having to satisfy additional necessary conditions beyond (4.6b) narrows the admissible $A(W)$ functions to the case of *constant*-absolute-risk aversion (including of course the risk-neutral case where $A(W)$ vanishes and U is linear in W).

5. EXACT DERIVATION

I shall now show that strict constancy of $A(W)$ is a necessary as well as sufficient condition for our defined neutrality toward repetition of just-indifferent gamble.

First, define the respective premium that you must be given as a bribe to induce you to tolerate an even-odds chance of gaining $+h$ or losing it. In (3.1) this was called H_1 or $H_1(h;W)$ when a single-gamble indifference is involved.

To deal with 2 repetitions of a gamble and your indifference, define H_2 or $H_2(h;W)$, the premium you must be bribed to be just willing to chance 2 independent bets that each yield $+h$ and $-h$ with even odds.

Clearly, H_1 and H_2 are defined as roots of the following respective equivalences:

(5.1) $$\frac{1}{2}U(W + H_1 + h) + \frac{1}{2}U(W + H_1 - h) = U(W)\ ,$$

$$0 < H_1 = H_1(h;W) < h\ ,$$

$$(5.2) \quad \frac{1}{4}U(W+H_2+2h)+\frac{1}{2}U(W+H_2+0)+\frac{1}{4}U(W+H_2-2h) = U(W),$$

$$0 < H_2 = H_2(h;W) < 2h.$$

Category i) consists then of the $U(W)$s such that it will be exactly the case that the bribe to just take 2 bets must be exactly twice the bribe to just take 1 bet.

For what $U(W)$s will it be the case that

$$(5.3) \quad H_2(h;W) \equiv 2H_1(h;W)$$

In terms of formal Taylor's expansions

$$(5.4a) \quad H_1 = 0 + 0h + A(W)h^2 + (1/3!)H_1^{(3)}(0;W)h^3 + (1/4!)H_1^{(4)}(O;W)$$

$$+(1/5!)H_1^{(5)}(O;W) + (1/6!)H_1^{(6)}(0;W) + R_7,$$

$$(5.4b) \quad H_2 = 0 + 0h + (2)A(W)h^2 + \sum_{j=3}^{6}(1/j!)H_2^{(j)}(0;W)h^j + \text{Remainder}.$$

The requisite derivatives of H_2 and $2H_1$ in (5.4a) and (5.4b) must be made to match in accordance with (5.3)'s requirement. It can be verified that each jth order derivative of an H depends on all U derivatives up to that same order, and therefore depends on all A derivatives up to order $j-2$.

$$(5.5) \quad 2H_1^{(j)}(0;W) = g^j(A(W), A'(W), \ldots, A^{(j-2)}(W)),$$

$$H_2^{(j)}(0;W) = G^j(A(W), A'(W), \ldots, A^{(j-2)}(W)).$$

Thus, equating coefficients we verify relations binding on admissible $A(W)$'s such as

$$(5.6) \quad \begin{aligned} 0 &= G^4(A, A', A'') - g^4(A, A', A'') \\ &= A''(W) - A'(W)A(W), \end{aligned}$$

as in (4.6b). Because the odd fifth derivatives vanish for all U and A functions, we need only adjoin to (5.6) the matching of sixth derivatives of $2H_1$ and H_2. When Professor Gerard Gennotte of UC (Berkeley) was an MIT graduate student, he kindly slogged through the monstrous calculations to deduce finally that we must in the end adjoin to (5.6) the further necessary condition

(5.7) $$0 = A(W)A'(W)^2 \ .$$

Joseph Stiglitz, doodling during my Stanford lecture on this subject, arrived at this same conclusion.

Together (5.6) and (5.7) do entail the constancy of $A(W)$ and of absolute risk aversion.

This completes the demonstration that the only risk-averse $U(W)$ that leads to indifference toward repetition of indifferent gambles is (4.7)'s $-e^{-aW}$.

What holds for indifference holds also for strong preference. Thus, iff my $A(W)$ is constant, when I accept 1 gamble, I will accept $2, 3, \ldots$ gambles. Likewise for rejection decisions.

Now Pratt's suggested defense for Brown can be sketched. For all W less than a critical W_1, let Brown have constant risk aversion—say at $A(W) \equiv 1$ as for $-e^{-W}$. Let him face the single even-odds bet $(-1+H, 1+H)$ where e^H is epsilon below $\frac{1}{2}(e + e^{-1})$. Then for all W_0 below $W_1 - 1 - H$, Brown will definitely refuse a single bet, albeit just barely refuse it. Above $W = W_1$, let Brown's $A(W)$ fall off smoothly from unity, to level off at $1/2$ for all W above $W_3 > W_1$. Since Brown has been made to be more appreciative of gains to any W above W_1 than he was before, and since he would in any case have almost been willing to have taken a single gamble, we deduce that there is an identifiable initial wealth level, call it W_2, $W_1 - 1 - H < W_2 < W_3$, at which he will just be indifferent to taking a single gamble (and, for initial W_0 above W_2 he will gladly accept a single gamble). Now we realize that for all initial W_0's on the interval $(W_1 - H - 1, W_2)$, Brown will reject the single gamble but definitely want to take 2 gambles—because the attractiveness of winning 2 in a row has been made finitely large, which is enough to outweigh the arbitrarily small unattractiveness contrived for the single gamble. QED, namely such a Brown is proved to be rational to refuse a single gamble while accepting a multiple repetition of it.

Let me record a remark about mathematical heuristics. The present demonstration of constancy of absolute risk aversion involved only special probability gambles—2 outcomes at even-odds. Yet practitioners in this field can have an easy mind that the result extends to *any* (non-degenerate) probability distribution.

Thus, replace the even-odds case by a probability-density gamble:

(5.8) $$\int_{-\infty}^{\infty} p(h)h\,dh = \mu > 0 \ .$$

For it, neutrality toward repetition of a just-acceptable gamble replaces the few-term sums of (5.1) and (5.2) by the following integral equations involving $U(W)$:

If $H_1(W)$ is the unique root of

(5.9) $$\int_{-\infty}^{\infty} dh\ U(W + H_1 + h)p(h) = U(W) \ ,$$

and $H_2(W)$ the root of

(5.10) $$\int_{-\infty}^{\infty} dh\ U(W + H_2 + h) \int_{-\infty}^{\infty} p(h - h')p(h')dh' = U(W) \ ,$$

then only for

(5.11) $$U(W) = b - de^{-aW} \ , \quad d > 0\ , a > 0\ , \quad -\infty < b < +\infty \ ,$$

is

(5.12) $$H_2(W) \equiv 2H_1(W) \ .$$

This remarkable simplicity is encountered again and again in this branch of probability. If at every wealth level I invest the same amount in one specified kind of equity, then for any other specified kind of equity we know my $U(W)$ is such that my absolute investment is independent of initial wealth level.

Thus, define $x = f_j(W)$ as the root of

(5.13) $$0 = \int_{-\infty}^{\infty} dh U'(W - x + xh)(h - 1)p_j(h) \ , \qquad j = 1, 2 \ .$$

Then the $U'(W)$ that assures

(5.14) $$f_1(W) \equiv f_1(1) \ ;$$

namely $U' = be^{-aW}$, also assures

(5.15) $$f_2(W) = f_2(1) ,$$

even though $p_1(h)$ and $p_2(h)$ are very different densities. We should count our blessing that such simplicities do obtain.

Depending on the algebraic sign at any particular W of (4.6b)'s $A''(W) - A'(W)A(W)$, and of $A'(W)$ itself, one expects to be able to state various strong *local* theorems: thus, for the former of a specified sign, if you will reject 1 of a particular sufficiently small gamble, you must reject 2 of it; or, for alternative specified sign, even if you reject 1 sufficiently small gamble, you will want to accept some number of them. Even more intricate local uniformities can be deduced such as, if you just barely reject 1 sufficiently small gamble, and $A'' - a'A$ is of a specified sign, you will accept some multiple of those gambles. John Pratt (1989), in his companion paper, states and proves a number of such delicate relationships.

6. FINAL REFLECTIONS

One can win a logical victory and lose an actual war. Academics have long warned practical money managers against a naive belief that investors for the long run can prudently invest more heavily in risky equities because time diversification will tend toward cancelling out risk when repeated plays are involved. For three decades those same academics have pointed out that rational portfolio managers, confronted by random-walk stock prices and possessing constant relative risk aversion, will select the same equity exposure when old as when young.

In the last few years statisticians have begun to believe that there is negative autocorrelation in price changes over periods measured in years rather than in days or weeks. It would be wrong to think that this new element of enhanced cancellation of risk over time would provide a rational basis for all long-horizon investors to hold relatively more equities than short-horizon investors would hold. No such sweeping result is valid: thus if you act to maximize expected value of log(Terminal Wealth), à la Daniel Bernoulli, you will choose the same equity fraction when old or young; if you act to maximize expected value of $\sqrt{W}$, à la Gabriel Cramer, you will be *more venturesome when old* than when young. But if you are like most investors, and seem to act as if more risk averse than Bernoulli, I was able to announce at the May 1988 Tobin *Fest* at Yale the following confirmation of practical investors' folk wisdom: *Even when long-run riskiness still grows eventually in proportion to $\sqrt{\text{Time Horizon}}$, you as a youngster with many periods ahead of you should hold more of risky equities than your older uncles should.*

There is a second question. Would empirical findings of significant long-period negative autocorrelation in equity price changes, and/or new findings concerning attitudes toward repeated gambles, weaken or strengthen the criticisms of Latané-Kelly-Breiman strategy of maximizing "long-term growth?" I believe that a rational person who is truly more risk averse than a Daniel Bernoulli will remain adamant in eschewing this irrelevant counsel and will perceive that any notion of long-run utility dominance is illusory.

Thirdly, what theory of the distribution of wealth and income can we fabricate from the assumption that all of us are confronted in life with quasi-independent favorable gambles that are repeatable? If very poor and very rich people are hypothesized to have lower risk tolerance than those in between (because the poor are desperate to avoid utter poverty, and the rich are jaded about becoming super-rich), then the middle classes will constantly be relatively more venturesome, and will accordingly be better rewarded (per dollar of wealth). Many of them tend to rise in affluence; some by chance sink into poverty. So long as some of the poor, like some of the rich, will move to the adjacent class, we can indeed deduce an evolution to an ergodic wealth-distribution steady state.

The following Markov transition matrix, M, captures our hypotheses:

(6.1) (Prob {going from class i at time $t-1$ to class j at t}) = (M_{ij})

$$= \begin{pmatrix} 0.5 & 0.5 & 0 \\ 0.2 & 0.5 & 0.3 \\ 0 & 0.5 & 0.5 \end{pmatrix}, \quad \begin{cases} j=1 & \text{means being poor} \\ j=2 & \text{means middle class} \\ j=3 & \text{means being rich} \end{cases}.$$

Half of each class stand to remain in the same class. Half of the rich descend to the middle class. Half of the poor rise to the middle class. Whereas three-tenths rise to affluence from the middle class, only two-tenths of them fall into poverty.

The limiting ergodic state, given by the rows of powers of M, M^t as $t \to \infty$, puts half the people ultimately in the middle class, twenty percent in poverty, and thirty percent in the upper crust.

Schumpeter was right. Capitalism is like a hotel. Its upper rooms are always full, but the occupants are constantly changing according to the fortunes of competition.

REFERENCES

Arrow, K.J. (1964), Aspects of the Theory of Risk-Bearing, *Yrjo Jahnsson Lectures*, Yrjo Jahnsson Foundation, Helsinki.

Bernoulli, D. (1738), Specimen theoriae navae de mensura sortis, *Commentarii*, St. Petersburg Academy. Translated in *Econometrica*, **22** (1954), 23–36; reprinted in *Precursors in Mathematical Economics: An Anthology*, Baumol, W. and Goldfield, S., eds., Series of Reprints of Scarce Works on Political Economy, No. 19, London: School of Economics and Political Science, 1968, 15–26.

Chew, S.H. and Epstein, L. (1988), The law of large numbers and the attractiveness of compound gambles, *Journal of Risk and Uncertainty*, **1**, 125–132.

Domar, E.D. and R.A. Musgrave (1944), Proportional income taxation and risktaking, *Quarterly Journal of Economics*, **58**, 388–422.

Lopes, L.L. (1981), Decision making in the short run, *Journal of Experimental Psychology: Learning, Memory and Cognition*, **7**, 377–385.

Machina, M. (1982), 'Expected utility' analysis without the independence axiom, *Econometrica*, **50**, 277–323.

Markowitz, H.L. (1959), *Portfolio Selection: Efficient Diversification of Investments*, John Wiley and Sons, Inc., New York.

Pratt, J.W. (1989), Some results on repeated risktaking in *Probability, Statistics and Mathematics*, Anderson, T.W., Athreya, K.B., and Iglehart, D.L., eds., London: Academic Press, 211–244.

Pratt, J.W. and R.J. Zeckhauser (1987), Proper risk aversion, *Econometrica*, **55**, No. 1, 143–154.

Samuelson, P.A. (1963), Risk and uncertainty: a fallacy of large numbers, *Scientia*, 6th Series, April-May. Reprinted in *Collected Scientific Papers of Paul A. Samuelson*, Volume 1, 1966, MIT Press, Cambridge.

Samuelson, P.A. (1972, 1977, 1986), *Collected Scientific Papers of Paul A. Samuelson*, MIT Press, Cambridge, Volumes 3, 4, and 5.

Samuelson, P.A. (1988), How a certain 'internal consistency' entails the expected utility dogma, *Journal of Risk and Uncertainty*, **1**, 339–343.

Tversky, A. and M. Bar-Hillel (1983), Risk: the long and the short, *Journal of Experimental Psychology: Learning, Memory and Cognition* **9**, 713–717.

Asset allocation could be dangerous to your health

Pitfalls in across-time diversification.

Paul A. Samuelson

The most recent god that failed has been asset allocation strategy — which claims to be able to detect at any time whether equity investors are to be well rewarded for taking on risks or poorly rewarded. By giving low weight to equities when they are prone to do poorly and high weight when prone to do well, asset allocation techniques are seen to be a variant of timing methods.

Asset allocators' finest hour came just before the October 1987 worldwide crash when they kept their devotees from losing 23% of portfolio value in a brief time period. Recent success in Wall Street breeds customers; and during 1988–1989 many converts of the asset allocators ruefully missed the high total returns garnered by stocks here and abroad. Whether 1990 will compensate cannot now be known.

In a digression in an essay reflecting on the surprising efficiencies of speculative markets and the historical successes of indexers (Samuelson [1989]), I pointed out how costly it can be to act like a market timer when in fact you lack ex ante and ex post ability to discern over- and undervaluation of the market as a whole.

In particular I mentioned the case of an MIT professor who in one year went back and forth sixteen times between all-equities and zero-equities. No load was charged for the switches, and because no academic fool could be so unlucky as to have been wrong every time in his moves, one at first careless thought might suspect that he had done himself little harm.

While his complacent colleagues stayed all year long half-and-half in stocks and fixed-principal assets, this professor would seem to have achieved his half-and-half mix by *across-time diversification* (so to speak, Monday–Wednesday–Friday in stocks and Tuesday–Thursday–Saturday in bonds).

As I argued then, this evaluation would indeed be a careless underestimation of the inefficiency of across-time diversification. My demonstration of this insufficiently noticed point, constrained by space and the limits of mathematical sophistication, followed a four-period scenario in which the modal outcomes of stock and cash were seen to work out better on a risk-corrected-mean basis for those who eschewed across-time diversification.

Because the point occasioned some correspondence with practical investors, and is in any case important in its own right, I present here a terse demonstration of the costliness in a random-walk model of across-time diversification in comparison with optimal at-each-time diversification for rational investors who seek to maximize the expected value of terminal utility of wealth and who have a specified constant relative risk aversion.

I must not pretend to prove too much. If you do have timing ability, flaunt it! But in the absence of Napoleonic pretensions to clairvoyance, your rational flauntings are more likely to involve switches of a few percent in your equity fraction around some optimal intermediate level rather than the swings from 100%

PAUL A. SAMUELSON is Institute Professor of Economics Emeritus at the Massachusetts Institute of Technology in Cambridge (MA 02139). He owes thanks for partial support to the MIT Sloan School of Management; for editorial assistance to Aase Huggins and Eva Hakala; and to Robert C. Merton for insightful discussions.

in stocks to 10% in stocks that characterized many asset allocation systems in the last two years.

ASSUMPTIONS

Suppose safe cash has a constant total return. Let a specified portfolio of equities have a total return that is a random variable whose outcomes can be better or worse than cash in each period: Posit the null hypothesis that each period's distribution of total returns is independent of any other's (a random walk). Begin with my having the logarithmic utility proposed by Daniel Bernoulli in 1738, U(W) = log W, where W is terminal wealth after T periods from now.

It is well-known, as in Merton [1969] or Samuelson [1969], that if I am a rational maximizer of such declared expected utility, I shall do best *if I myopically put the same w_t fraction of my portfolio into equities during every period.* For every w_t,

$$w_T^* = w_{T-1}^* = \ldots = w_1^* \qquad (1)$$

For expositional simplicity, let $w_t^* = \frac{1}{2}$.

The arithmetic mean, or expected value, of the dollar outcomes of the portfolio that is 100% in stocks must be greater than the safe cash outcome of $1 + r_0$ — else I'd hold none of that risky equity portfolio. What interests Bernoulli, however, is its geometric mean. This can be less than or greater than $1 + r_0$. Call it Case 1 when G.M. of stocks alone $= 1 + r_1 > 1 + r_0$, and Case 2 when $1 + r_1 < 1 + r_0$. Write $1 + r_{1/2}$ for the G.M. of the fifty–fifty portfolio.

Consider twins: A always puts fifty–fifty into stocks and cash; B half the time, and with no serendipity with respect to "timing," puts 100% into stocks and the other half puts all into cash.

It is important to realize that the geometric mean of the fifty–fifty portfolio is greater than "the greater of the G.M. of cash or the G.M. of pure stocks." Why? Because that is what is meant when we say that I as a Bernoulli utilitarian will maximize E[log W] by selecting as my fractional equity share, w_t^*,

$$0 < w_t^* = \frac{1}{2} < 1. \qquad (2)$$

Then, recognizing that the log of the G.M. is the E[log W], we write

G.M. of cash < G.M. of 50-50 > G.M. of pure stocks. (3)

This can be rewritten as

$$1 + r_0 < 1 + r_{1/2} > 1 + r_1 \qquad (3a)$$

$$1 + r_{1/2} > 1 + \text{Max}(r_0, r_1) > 1 + \tfrac{1}{2}(r_0 + r_1). \qquad (3b)$$

We can now describe how badly or well people will fare pursuing different strategies, assuming each starts out with the same initial wealth. The certainty equivalent for an investor in cash only will grow like

$$W_0(1 + r_0)^t, \ t = 1, 2, \ldots, T. \qquad (4)$$

Perhaps think of this as 3%, with $1 + r_0 = 1.03$.

The certainty equivalent for a Bernoulli who rashly holds only stocks will grow like

$$W_0(1 + r_1)^t, \ t = 1, 2, \ldots, T. \qquad (5)$$

This certainty equivalent is the amount of safe wealth that gives him as much expected utility as his lucrative-but-risky stocks-only portfolio would give. Perhaps set it at 4%, or 1.04.

The certainty equivalent for the rational non-timer grows better than either of the above, growing like

$$W_0(1 + r_{1/2})^t > W_0 \text{Max}[1 + r_0, 1 + r_1]^t \qquad (6)$$

The left side of (6) is the growing amount of safe wealth that just matches the expected utility from holding the optimal proportion of stocks. For a numerical example, suppose it to be 6%, with $1 + r_{1/2} = 1.06$.

The delusioned timer who embraces across-time diversification on a fifty–fifty basis has a certainty equivalent that grows like

$$W_0[(1 + r_0)(1 + r_1)]^{t/2} < W_0(1 + r_{1/2})^t. \qquad (7)$$

As the G.M. of 1.03 and 1.04 is 1.035, the left-hand side grows only like $(1.035)^t$: Its shortfall from $(1.06)^t$ is the penalty inherent in across-time diversification.

You may wonder whether I have stacked the deck against across-time diversification. After all, my w_t^* of $\frac{1}{2}$ picked $\frac{1}{2}$ because it was truly the best fraction to pick. Why stick the across-time diversifier with this *same* fifty–fifty fraction? Surely, let him pick the *best fraction of the time* to be solely in stocks. Call it v^*, with $1 - v^*$ being the fraction of time to be solely in cash:

$$v^* \gtreqless w_t^* = 1/2.$$

When Robert Merton and I each analyzed how to select optimal v^*, we both were surprised to discover the solution is a bang-bang one. Either v^* is 0 or 1 depending upon whether $1 + r_0 > 1 + r_1$ or $1 + r_1 > 1 + r_0$! (In our numerical example, 1.04 > 1.03 and $v^* = 1$.)

It is never mandatory to diversify *across* time. Your best *across-time* diversification is to stay always in the pure strategy that is maximal in *its* E[log W]! If that seems like folly, so much the worse for trying to time in a random-walk model.

Now it can be verified that you stand to average out worse even with your best v^*, as (6) showed that your certainty equivalent now grows like

$W_0\{\text{Max}[1 + r_0, 1 + r_1]\}^t < W_0(1 + r_{1/2})^t.$ QED   (8)

In our example, $W_0(1.04)^t < W_0(1.06)^t$. Thus, even in the best bang-bang solution you are losing one-third of your obtainable 6% certainty equivalent!

GENERALIZATIONS

Everything said here about Bernoulli logarithmic utility holds qualitatively when we replace log W by $W^{1/2}$ or by $-W^{-1}$, or $-W^{-2}$, ..., or W^γ/γ with $0 \neq \gamma < 1$. Thus, for $-W^{-1}$ we speak of the *harmonic mean* instead of the *geometric mean* — and likewise for the properly defined γ *mean*. A brief Mathematical Appendix gives details.

In all cases you will pay dearly in expected utility terms for a fancied ability to time. It is not merely that you fail to garner the better *mean* return, but you pay as well the bitter price of losing risk-reducing diversification. It is a corollary that a system that has modest true ability to time will bring you less final net benefit to the degree that it involves some bad side effects of *across-time* diversification.

CAVEATS

Suppose you correctly recognize that what you face is *not* a white-noise process but rather a red-noise process showing "mean reversion" and detectable negative autocorrelation à la Poterba–Summers [1988] or Fama-French [1988]. Then, as described in the Tobin-*fest* paper of Samuelson [1988a], your w^*_{t+1} will be optimally lower when your w^*_t is optimally higher. For the w^*_ts to oscillate out of the $(0.40, 0.60)$ interval around ½ would presuppose a Markov process that is very red indeed. The danger in the dividend discount models that the asset allocator tends to appeal to is that *their very appearance of scientific objectivity seductively leads to the hubris of believing in the wisdom of vast swings in equity holdings*.

Even a modest ability on the part of a would-be timer to recognize occasions when the mean returns of stocks are high and are low can be rationally indulged *on a small scale* despite this article's strictures concerning induced riskiness costs. Why? Because any w_t near to the optimal w^*_t is almost as good as w^*_t, for the reason that all smooth maximums are virtually horizontal curves with a shortfall from the maximum that has the extreme smallness associated with the square of $(w_t - w^*_t)$. When this evil is small, it is overweighed by any true ability to discern an improvement in the mean of equities, an ability that brings you benefit that varies with the first power of $(w_t - w^*_t)$.

The logic of the paragraph above, alas, cannot justify the broad swings in the equity fraction that so many asset allocation systems recommend. When the asset allocators go back to the drawing boards, they can benefit from the analysis here by putting the strong burden of proof against each further recommended change in $w_t - w^*_t$. (Remark: Sometimes practical men say that they don't know their own U(W) function. I agree that, if you don't know where you want to go, it becomes rather pointless to discuss how best to go there. However, not knowing whether my U(W) is $-1/W$ or $-1/W^2$ cannot justify my acting as if I were indifferent to risk. Wherever you are between the two cases of the previous sentence, my warnings apply.)

After the surgeon general has warned that cigarettes can be dangerous to your health, honesty compels few qualifications, for there are less pyrrhic ways of avoiding overweight. The case against timing is less conclusive in principle because the strong evidence in favor of *micro*efficiency of security markets lacks power as a proof of the *macro*efficiency of general stock levels.

Thus, as mentioned, Samuelson [1988a] deduced a limited efficacy for timers in a Markov process where the probability of a rise in general equity prices in the period ahead is weakly reduced by a rise in last period's prices — the "red noise" departure from white noise probabilities. In a circulated unpublished study, Samuelson [1988b], there was also similarly deduced a role for timing in a fundamentalist's model involving an invariant probability distribution for the S&P around a postulated exogenous geometric trend.

All the more important becomes this article's warning against the pitfalls intrinsic to across-time diversification. The optimal variations in equity fractions that I deduced for the prudent timer were moderate. Why?

Consider the case when I operate without fire insurance on my house. Most times I notice no cause for regret. But actually the clock of risk is always running against me. Always? Yes, even though on rainy days with lightning-free skies, and when the children and help are away on vacation, my amount of fire insurance might rationally be lightened. Once I have the hubris to program for each day a variable coverage of fire insurance, human nature is all too likely to dull my recognition of the ominous clock of risk that is always running against the uninsured in some degree. That week when the timer garners a capital gain by undiversifying his portfolio, does he realize that he should be debiting against his gain in mean the insidious rise in riskiness that was inseparably involved?

The would-be timer needs the message of this paper more than agnostics do. For it will keep to the forefront of his benefit–cost calculus the increasing riskiness inherent in *sizable across-time departures from diversification* — for what I have called euphemistically *across-time diversification* is more accurately to be dubbed across-time deviations from diversification. The easier part of being a timer is judiciously selling before peaks. The hard part is being sure to buy back before the market has already reachieved its earlier peak.

REFERENCES

Fama, E.F., and K.R. French, "Permanent and Temporary Components of Stock Prices," *Journal of Political Economics* 96 (1988), pp. 246-273.

Merton, R.C. "Lifetime Portfolio Selection under Uncertainty: The Continuous-Time Case." *Review of Economic Statistics*, August 1969, pp. 247-257.

Poterba, J.M. and L.H. Summers, "Mean Reversion in Stock Returns: Evidence and Implications," *Journal of Financial Economics* 22 (1988), pp. 27-59.

Samuelson, P.A. "The Judgment of Economic Science on Rational Portfolio Management: Indexing, Timing, and Long-Horizon Effects," *Journal of Portfolio Management*, Fall 1989, pp. 4-12.

———. "Longrun Risk Tolerance When Equity Returns Are Mean Regressing: Pseudoparadoxes and Vindication of 'Business Man's Risk'." In *Macroeconomics, Finance and Economic Policy: Essays in Honor of James Tobin*, W. Brainard, W. Nordhaus, and H. Watts, eds. Cambridge, MA: MIT Press (a 1988 paper forthcoming in 1990 or 1991).

———. Longrun Risk Tolerance in a Fundamentalist Model of Equities." MIT Working Paper, June 1988.

MATHEMATICAL APPENDIX

1. Cash is assumed to have a safe total return of r_0 in each period. Each dollar invested in the common stock has a total return in each period that is the random variable $X_t - 1$, where $(\ldots, X_{t-1}, X_t, X_{t+1}, \ldots)$ are identically and independently distributed:

$$\text{Prob}[X_t \leq x] = P(x); \; P(x) \equiv 0, \; x < 0 \quad (A1)$$

$$E[X_t] > 1 + r_0 = R \quad (A2)$$

$$\text{Var}[X_t] > 0, \; P(R-) > 0 \quad (A3)$$

2. One-period maximization involves

$$\underset{w}{\text{Max}} \; E\{U[W_0(1-w)R + W_0 w X_1]\}$$

$$= E\{U[W_0(1-w^*)R + W_0 w^* X_1]\} \quad (A4)$$
$$= \bar{e}(w^*)$$

where w^* is the unique root for w of

$$0 = E\{U'[W_0(1-w)R + W_0 w X_1] W_0 [X_1 - R]\} \quad (A5)$$

For $1 > \gamma \neq 0$ and $U(W) = W^\gamma/\gamma$, we write w^* as w_γ. For $U(W) = \log W$, we write w^* as w_0 and can verify that $w_\gamma \mapsto w_0$ as $\gamma \mapsto 0$. Note that as γ falls from 1, w_γ declines, reaching 0 as $\gamma \mapsto -\infty$. For $\gamma \leq 0$ and $P(0) > 0$, $w_\gamma < 1$.

For $1 > \gamma \neq 0$, the *certainty equivalent* that is as good as having $\bar{e}(w)$ can be written as

$$W_0(1 + r_w[\gamma]) = \gamma[\bar{e}(w)^{1/\gamma}] \quad (A6)$$

$$W_0(1 + r_0) < W_0\{1 + r_{w_\gamma}[\gamma]\} > W_0(1 + r_1) \quad (A7)$$

3. For time-independent processes,

$$E[Z_1 \ldots Z_T] = E[Z_1] \ldots E[Z_T] \quad (A8)$$

Therefore, for $T \geq 2$ and $\gamma \neq 0$, our multi-period maximization can be shown to reduce to myopic behavior, with

$$(W_0^\gamma/\gamma) \underset{w_1 \ldots w_T}{\text{Max}} E\left\{ \prod_1^T [R + w_t X_t - w_t R]^\gamma \right\}$$

$$= (W_0^\gamma/\gamma)[E\{[R + w_\gamma X - w_\gamma R]^\gamma\}]^T = \bar{e}(w^*)^T \quad (A9)$$

$$> (W_0^\gamma/\gamma)(\text{Max}[R^\gamma, E\{X^\gamma\}])^T \quad (A10)$$

The optimizing *certainty equivalent* will grow like

$$W_0\{1 + r_{w_\gamma}[\gamma]\}^t, \; t = 1, 2, 3, \ldots, T \quad (A11)$$

4. The maximization problem for the *across-time diversifier* becomes bang-bang, taking the following form: For $\gamma \neq 0$ and $0 \leq v \leq 1$,

$$(W_0^\gamma/\gamma) \underset{v}{\text{Max}}[(R^{\gamma T})^{(1-v)}(E\{X^\gamma\}T)^v]$$

$$= (W_0^\gamma/\gamma)[\text{Max}(R^\gamma, E\{X^\gamma\})]^T \quad (A12)$$

From the inequalities of (A7) and (A10), the *across-time diversifier* clearly does worse than the non-timer, with *certainty equivalent* of

$$W_0\{\text{Max}[1 + r_0, 1 + r_1]\}^T < W_0\{1 + r_{w_\gamma}[\gamma]\}^T \quad (A13)$$

For the Bernoulli case, where $\gamma \mapsto 0$, (A9) and (A12) are replaced by

$$\log W_0 + TE\{\log[R + w_0 X - w_0 R]\}$$
$$> \log W_0 + T \text{ Max}[\log R, E\{\log X\}] \quad (A14)$$

5. Asset allocators have the possibility of being helpful when we replace probabilistic *independence* (or the weaker *martingale* process) by red-noise *mean reversion* or *negative* autocorrelation. Now (A1) is replaced by

$$\text{Prob}\{(p_{t+1} - p_t)/p_t \leq x \mid p_t = y\} = P(x \mid y) \quad (A15)$$

$$\partial P(x \mid y)/\partial y > 0, \; (\partial/\partial y) E\{(p_{t+1} - p_t)/p_t \mid p_t = y\} < 0 \quad (A16)$$

Somehow the asset allocators are supposed to have knowledge from dividend discounting models of (A16)'s inequalities that other investors do not have or do not believe in. What evidence would convert us to that view? Finally, even if (A16)'s inequalities have the indicated signs, unless their quantitative magnitudes are believed to be substantial, only modest variations of w_t^* around w_γ would be justifiable.

The Long-Term Case for Equities

And how it can be oversold.

Paul A. Samuelson

In the first issue of the *Journal of Portfolio Management* (Samuelson [1974]), I interpreted the evidence to speak largely in favor of markets being efficient: The ball was said to be in the court of those who allege that activist judgment can improve on broad diversification-cum-lean expense ratios. Microefficiency in the pricing of stocks, bonds, futures, and derivatives, I argued, was not a mysterious dogma — like the manifest impossibility of creating a perpetual motion machine. A few stars with superior information and clever ability to squeeze excess risk-corrected returns from those data could earn high rents; but investors will find it hard to identify the stars from the merely lucky; and after competition makes you pay top dollar for superior advice, most investors can eke out for themselves only skimpy excess returns.

To commemorate this Journal's fifteen years of success (Samuelson [1989]), I reviewed the cogency and accruing empirical verisimilitude of that agnostic questioning of activistic judgmental investing. By and large, the ball that was put in the court of the would-be judgment-mongerers never did get returned with point-winning velocity. The jury of history did not find systematic inefficiency that exercisers of judgment could use to achieve excess risk-corrected returns.

We can expect the debate to go on. And that tells you something about the approximate microefficiency of the organized markets where widely owned securities are traded.

PAUL A. SAMUELSON is professor emeritus of economics at the Massachusetts Institute of Technology in Cambridge (MA 02139).

OUTLINE OF TOPICS

Today, for the Journal's twentieth issue, let me begin with a critical discussion of the new orthodoxy that favors 1) Buy and Hold Diversified Equities If You Are a Long-Horizon Investor, with the Assurance of History and the Law of Large Numbers that 2) Riskiness Is Bound to Cancel Out Over Many Investment Periods so that Equities in the End Will Outperform Low-Yield Safe Securities.

Then I explain why my belief in *micro*efficiency is compatible with skepticism about *macro*efficiency of the general market level. This opens the possibility that asset allocation and "timing" might deliver superior performance. The ex post evidence does not confirm this hope. In any case, I explicate the doctrine of "Sin, But Sin Only A Little," when succumbing to temptations of non-index investing.

A third section, which can be skipped or skimmed, recapitulates major fallacies of belief that continue to infest the sophisticated investment community.

Finally, the question presents itself as to whether the resources devoted to the futile attempt to beat the investing crowd are not socially excessive.

THE NEW MESSIAH: BUY AND HOLD EQUITIES FOR SURE-THING LONG-RUN SUPERIOR PERFORMANCE?

My cold blanket of caution about activist asset allocation timing, which is argued out in the next section, may make readers think I have climbed on today's bandwagon of Become A Long-Term Investor Who Buys and Holds in the Confidence Acquired from History, Which Assures that Stocks Do Better in the Long Pull than Non-Stocks Do.

As will be seen, I give two cheers at most for this new dogma. There have been worse dogmas. And there will be worse ones to come. However, as I shall explicate, once everyone comes to believe in and act on Always Hold Stocks, that tactic will self-destruct in the way that the Tokyo Equity Bubble self-destructed after New Year's Day 1990.

The long-run case for equities is alleged to be ironclad. Once your investment horizon exceeds six to ten years, *throughout all history*, stocks have left you ahead of your timid sister's bonds and overnight cash. QED.

To clinch the conclusive, rely on the good old Law of Large Numbers, which (allegedly) causes variance to go to zero as the investment horizon approaches infinity in the limit. Don't reexamine yearly your total returns, just as you ought not to pull up your flowers to examine their roots. That way you would only sleep badly and whipsaw yourself into regret and inefficiency. Buy Vanguard Indexes on *all* bond and stock securities, domestic and international and long and short, in predetermined proportions depending upon your risk tolerance and age-related investment horizon. Then practice *salutary neglect* (except for occasional rebalancings to keep your ratios approximately constant).

That is not *my* advice. That is the current wisdom among many investors and advisors. Here are some relevant reactions.

1. The Law of Large Numbers does *not* reduce riskiness toward zero as the investing period extends toward infinity. If you are maximizing the expected logarithms or expected square root of your wealth at retirement, you will hold exactly the same portfolio proportions *at every age*. Thus, there cannot be any sure-thing syllogism pushing long-term investors into more equity tolerance than short-term investors. (Yes, when you are young, stocks may have more time to recover from crashes, but they also have more time to encounter crashes!)

2. Sleeping well for irrational reasons, you may say, is as good as sleeping well for rational reasons. I do not pronounce on that. Dollar-averaging gives many folk the comfort to get into stocks. Bully for them. This denies not at all the truth that dollar-averaging cannot improve risk-corrected expected performance. There are dozens of other rules and maxims whose attractions have naught to do with their genuine merits to optimize mean-variance results. For a fiduciary trustee of a large endowment to act on them is a blunder if not a crime; but who am I to advise you on how best to deal with your parent-in-law?

3. We have data for, say, 150 years of bond and stock price quotations. That's about 2,000 monthly observations, 50,000 daily observations, and in some cases up to 400,000 hourly observations. It does not follow that we have 4×10^5 bits of information in favor of the proposition that over invest-

ment periods longer than ten years, the higher your equity exposure, the higher your *cumulative* return.

Impressive, so large a sample? Not really. Overlapping moving averages are not each independent data points or degrees of freedom. Even when we correct for that obvious consideration, keep repeating to yourself firmly:

We have only *one* history of capitalism. Inferences based on a sample of one must never be accorded sure-thing interpretations. When a thirty-five-year-old lost 82% of his pension portfolio between 1929 and 1932, do you think it was fore-ordained in heaven that later it would come back and fructify to +400% by his retirement at sixty-five? How did 1913 Tsarist executives fare in their retirement years on the Left Bank of Paris?

It is a dogma, not a guaranteed fact, that financial data are generated by a *stationary probability* process. You are a fool if you wake up each morning and say the universe was born anew today with new rules. You are also a fool if you think that history can be read to teach necessitous lessons. The art of practical decision-making is to try to glean from experience what aspects of it are likely to have relevance for the future. The Bible tells us, "There is a time to remember, and a time to forget." But the Good Book does not inform us just how to ascertain those times.

My point is not that of sage nihilism. Let my debunking be more specific. Suppose you believe that the past percent daily price moves of the Standard & Poor's and the Bond Index can be put into a huge urn. Suppose you believe that future S&P and bond changes will be *random* draws from that urn. Is it then the case that there is such a preponderance of superior equity moves over bond moves (taking into account, of course, all dividends and interest coupons) that in any long sequence of time (such as ten or twenty or forty years) no non-paranoid, long-term investor could be rationally tempted *not* to invest virtually solely in equities?

I have seen scores of investment discussions that do, in effect, put the matter that way when they make the case for long-term sticking with equities. They think the Law of Large Numbers clinches their case before any rational jury.

They are wrong.[1] To see that there is no such long-term dominance, consider how a rational Bernoulli (desiring to maximize the expected value of his logarithm of wealth outcomes) will act each day, each month, and each year at every age, in his long life. He will *always* desire the same limited exposure to equities. He abjures regret. He ignores whether he beats his twin in duels over long or short contest periods. All he does is act to maximize the geometric mean of his terminal wealth in all its likely possible outcomes, and that leads him myopically to ignore his age. His case is a counterexample to any belief that the Law of Large Numbers serves to wash out short-term riskiness when the investment horizon is long enough. And there is an infinity of other such counterexamples.

Restudy the paradoxical case of myopic age-independent prudence if ever sure-thing dominance tempts you. Suppose you have a utility function and act to maximize its expected value. Suppose you face a probability process that is stationary and with each period's probabilities being independent of any earlier or later period's. Suppose further that your own utility function is risk-averse but displays the property of having constant relative risk aversion.

(This means that with a million dollars of wealth, or two million, or only one hundred thousand, you will rationally select the *same portfolio proportions*. Also, we assume that you can't affect the prices at which you sell or buy, and your transaction and tax costs are negligible.)

Then it is an exact theorem that *The Investment Horizon Can Have No Effect on Your Portfolio Proportions*. See Samuelson [1969].

Now let me recapitulate exceptions to this result.

1. If you are a young professional with future non-securities market earnings, since those human capital prospects cannot be efficiently capitalized or borrowed on, to keep your equities at their proper fraction of *true total wealth*, you should early in life put a larger fraction of your liquid wealth in common stocks. Late in working life, when your human capital has been depleted in total value and your *liquid* wealth has accordingly risen by accumulation, your fractional holding of equities will *seem* to have fallen even when it hasn't, reckoned in terms of the proper total of (human + liquid capital).

    This rational pattern is, however, no genuine exception to the uniform-equity share tactic. (Remark: As Robert Merton has emphasized, when your human earnings correlate positively with equity gains, that should cause you to lean somewhat against equity holding. Similarly, limit your holding of ESOPs (in your employing firm) that will go bad just when you lose your job. Brokers whose wages rise and fall with bull and bear markets should somewhat downplay common stocks in their private portfolios — unless their job gives them a (legal) edge in knowledge about future stock moves.)

2. Bodie, W. Samuelson, and Merton [1992] have cogently deduced an argument for rationally biasing your holdings toward equities when you are young — for the reason that you can then hope to work harder later to compensate for unlucky common stock losses. (Warning: This is not the fallacious point that losses incurred when young can be made up by a longer time remaining in which the market might by chance come back.)

3. In the Tobin *Festschrift,* Samuelson [1991] justifies a life-cycle pattern of diminished equity tolerance with age based upon the hypothesis — of Fama and French [1988] and Poterba and Summers [1988] — that equity prices do not move in a white-noise pattern but rather tend to be mean-reverting in what I call a *red-noise* pattern of *negative* serial *auto*correlation. Thus, if low depression Wall Street prices tend to be followed by extraordinary total returns, and if high bubble prices tend to be followed by extraordinarily low or negative total return, then someone who is very risk-averse in comparison with a Bernoulli should rationally step-up her equity fraction *and should be more risk-tolerant when young than when old.* That was my finding.

(Note too that red-noise processes are more promising for would-be "timers" than are white-noise processes. And one understands that blue-noise processes involving positive serial autocorrelation of price moves lend legitimacy to momentum technicians who pile onto price trends in either direction. Paradoxically, when old, such chartists should be most bold!)

Light is thrown on various fallacies in use of the Law of Large Numbers when you realize that persons more risk-tolerant than Bernoulli are forced by red-noise processes to *increase* their equity exposure as they get closer to their terminal time of pension accumulation. The geriatric plunger becomes demonstrably rational!

It is worse than an anticlimax for me to warn that the case for mean-reverting *red* noise is not very strong. The fact of the Great Depression imparts much of its credibility. In the Age After Keynes, is that a fact that we should remember vividly?

4. Finally I come to what may most convincingly lie at the base of the common predisposition to speak of "a business person's risk," and to contrast it with the widow-and-widower safe choices. People may be less risk-tolerant in absolute terms when they face poverty than when they are affluent. Indeed most economists are more confident than I am that the preponderant pattern is *relative risk tolerance* that declines with wealth while absolute risk tolerance grows with wealth.[2]

However, I did get definite and reasonable results (Samuelson [1989]) when people insist on the paramount importance of a minimum $\overline{W}$ attainment. Thus, let me maximize U = log (W − $\overline{W}$), $\overline{W}$ > 0. In that case, if at age 65 − T, my initial W_0 exceeds $\overline{W}/(1 + r)^T$, where r is the safe rate of interest, I will put into a safe sinking fund $\overline{W}/(1 + r)^T = S_T$. The rest I invest in stocks to a fixed fraction (à la Bernoulli). As the horizon period T gets small, my swollen non-equity total, swollen because of the S_T non-equity add-on — gets more swollen.

Result: For all W_Ts not too small, my f(W, 65 − A) does, ceteris paribus, decline with A — in accordance with the vulgar presumption. (For W_T less than $\overline{W}/(1 + r)^T$, the model breaks down by being ambiguous. There is no way then for you to avoid the infinite misery of ending up with less than your *mandatory* goal.)

However, the above deals only with life-cycle investing for the accumulation time of life while you have no need to draw on assets for current consumption needs.

5. As Robert Merton pointed out to me (see Samuelson [1989]), this 1989 vindication of the popular belief goes into reverse for the pure *rentier's* life-cycle investing. If I insist on a minimum consumption level at every age, as when I maximize the expected value of the integral of $\int \log (C_t - \overline{C})dt$, then the sinking fund I must put into safe non-equities *diminishes* as my age grows and brings me nearer to death (which is Modigliani life-cycle extinction). When less of my wealth is preempted for mandatory sinking fund, more of it goes into Bernoulli's fixed fraction in equities. That means as

rentier, other things being equal, I go deeper into equities as I age! Will they believe that in the cocktail lounges near Wall Street?

6. Heretically, I suggest as a good example to test economists' approved dogma is where their presumption is reversed — as in the case U(W) = log (W − 1), where my *relative risk tolerance* rises with wealth. My computation demonstrates that my two-period investing is then truly systematically more equity-tolerant than my one-period investing. A two-period horizon investment *biases* my chosen equity fraction upward for this reversal of the economists' favorite presumptions? If so, hadn't economists better start whistling a different tune?

7. Here are some further mathematical misunderstandings. The Law of Large Numbers is a perfectly valid principle in probability. So is the Central Limit Theorem, which states how sums of independent (finite-variance) variates approach more closely in some sense the normal distribution (of Gauss), and which states how *products* of independent variables come to approximate to the lognormal distribution when the number of components becomes large.

But a valid theorem can be misapplied in dozens of ways. One popular fallacy is to advise people to "maximize the growth rate of their portfolio" by adjusting risk so as to maximize in each period its geometric mean (expected logarithmic mean). Latané, Kelley, Breiman, Cover, and a host of rediscoverers of the wrong wheel recommend it. What they can prove is this.

Suppose you act to maximize in each period the expected log of your portfolio. I, your twin, act systematically different from you in some fashion. Then as the number of independent periods becomes large, your probability of "outperforming" me cumulatively rises more and more above 1/2 and nearer and nearer to unity. And so, we are told, *your* strategy is the peachy sure-thing recipe for good behavior.

I understand and am unimpressed. It's kids' stuff to fight duels. I am more risk-averse than Bernoulli, and he for quite a different reason will follow *your* geometric mean strategy. My U (wealth) function forces me, say, to maximize the harmonic mean of my portfolio: That makes me hold more safe stuff and less equity stuff than you.

Am I sure-thing outperformed? Of course not, as I have explained in n + 1 articles, one of them all in words of one syllable. No matter how great is T, sometimes I beat you, my twin. By my lights you often beat me *trivially*. Bully for you. When I apply my proper yardstick to the worth of your victories and net them against the worth of my (fewer) victories, I triumphantly laugh at your irrelevant argument.

The point is that the crowd I criticize gets your consent *only because of your misunderstanding*. They wrongly think that prob → 1 as T → ∞ means that your bold strategy becomes clearly smarter when the investment horizon becomes long enough. Not so. For every T from here to infinity, I verify how stupid I would be to follow my twin's practice. If my twin truly has *my* degree of risk aversion, she is thwarting her own druthers because she has been sold a mess of potage.[3]

SELF-DESTRUCTION OF A DOGMA

Finally, let me explain why this hold-for-the-long-pull tactic will self-destruct if ever it becomes universally believed in. If you adhere to the dogma that stocks must beat bonds in the long-enough run, there is no P/E level that the market averages out to at which you will take in sail. A Ponzi bubble is ever possible, and given past psychologies of boom and bust, ever-higher P/E ratios become a self-fulfilling prophecy.

I cannot prove to you that every bubble must burst. After all, anything can be carried on to twice where it has already reached. But anyone who believes in not-completely-inefficient macro-models will agree that, at high enough P/E ratios, equities will cease to display *in the future* their historical superiority over bonds. QED. The urn from which future draws get taken is altered *endogenously* by one-way movements of market levels.

A concrete example may be more convincing than several fancy syllogisms. Consider Tobin's q (see Brainard and Tobin [1968]). It tries to compare (A) in its numerator, what you have to pay for all society's productive assets if you buy them in the financial marketplace, with (B) in its denominator, what it would cost you to hire carpenters and engineers to produce those assets at current carpenters' and engineers' wages per unit of product.

Can you really believe that, once buy-equity dogma bulls Tobin's q up to 1-1/2, 2, 5, or 10, that the next generation of true believers will succeed in retiring with those hoped-for capital gains to spend? Come on, now.

To protect the innocent, let me omit names but address protests that have been made to me by two readers of these paragraphs. Both come from sophisticated investment counselors; call them A and B.

A protests as follows:

> We know that a bond can give you in the long run only its contractual interest rate. By contrast, a stock can deliver you positive capital gains, and under progressive steady-state capitalism a positive gain surely must beat a zero gain?

I am unshaken. As the decades go by, the cautious investor in bonds can enjoy a rising real income stream if the real rate of interest at which he or she refunds old bonds displays a rising trend. There is no arithmetic-ordained inferiority of bonds compared to stocks.

To this A gives a rebuttal: "Historically, real interest rates have been meandering rather than displaying a rising trend." Agreed. But that is not an arithmetical necessity, but rather a factual happenstance.

I must go deeper in my answer. I suspect A believes that by owning things — shovels and land or share certificates that are evidence of your owning them — you stand to gain the fruits of historical progress. But is *that* true?

If the nation will need more power generators, the rentiers who own today's inventory will find their ownership diluted if they live off the current earnings of their utility stocks. (If the company plows back some earnings rather than paying them all out in dividends, the rentier must sell off some shares in order to spend all after-tax earnings on consumption.) The new savers in a growing population that is getting richer will get the ownership of the more numerous generators.

I must meet the further objection:

> What about Schumpeterian innovations and the extra nuts and fruits that they make possible? Aren't *these* a superior source of returns to stockholders that bondholders don't get?

The answer is:

> Neither equity-holding rentiers nor bondholding rentiers have a lock on Schumpeterian prof-

its. Much of the profits will go as temporary or quasi-permanent rents to the innovators themselves. Many of the innovations will actually decimate the interest yields of old and obsolete capital equipment. Even in those important cases where innovation is complementary to old machines and augments *their* marginal productivities, the Modigliani-Miller theorem demonstrates that the division between debtholders and equityholders cannot be shown to favor one rather than the other.

In the interest of brevity I discuss B's point in an endnote.[4]

A MISCELLANY OF MISCONCEPTIONS AND RECTIFICATIONS

It is useful to review what good sense — common or otherwise — has to suggest about various fundamentals.

1. *What's already discounted.* Folk wisdom (or was it Will Rogers?) says: "Buy land. They ain't making any more of it." What folk wisdom forgets is that, "*Everyone* knows land is limited in supply; and what everyone already knows can't help but get already built into today's competitive bids."

2. *The square-root law of lower variability.* Folk wisdom says: "Don't put all your eggs in one basket." That nominates the canny principle of *diversification*. When instead of putting $40,000 into one stock, you divide it over four *independent* stocks, each equally risky and each with equal mean total returns, you stand to halve your riskiness while leaving your expected mean return unchanged.

    Who says that? Something more powerful than folk wisdom says that. It is the statistical Law of Large Numbers.

3. *Settling for (canny) mediocrity.* Don't rush to sell folk wisdom short. Always it speaks with forked tongue. Folk wisdom (this time I mean Mark Twain) said: "Put all your eggs in one basket — *and watch that basket.*" Old-timers will remember that this was the watchword of Gerald Loeb's bestseller, *The Struggle for Investment Survival*. That guide made fortunes for a few. I suspect it decimated nest eggs for a vast multitude.

    Just what do you watch for? Even the great

John Maynard Keynes, when he first became head of a big insurance company, opined: "At any time buy only one stock: the best one going. When it loses that distinction, replace it by the new best one." That was more worthy of Will Rogers than of Keynes. And, later, Keynes learned better.

4. *Random-dart misunderstanding.* Notice how this emphasis on diversification rebuts the common error of believing that, under random walk conditions, prudent investors will throw a dart at the financial page and invest in the one or few items that get hit. A random walk market more correctly compels you to throw a laundry towel at the whole financial page and invest in pretty much everything there in dollar weights proportional to each stock's relative dollar market capitalization (i.e., more dollars in autos than in bubble gum, and more dollars in General Motors autos than in Ford, Dodge, or Mazda autos).

Because I once testified before a Senate Committee on this subject, Senator Mondale used to compare a random-dart portfolio of half a dozen stocks with the S&P index or with best-buy recommendations of several market pundits. The newspapers periodically carry on this same contest. Replication of a misleading test, alas, does not make it any less misleading.

5. *How negative covariance truly diversifies.* Before leaving the subject of diversification, I should make a qualification: When you split a dollar equally over four independent stocks, you halve the chance of riskiness. But most stocks tend to be positively correlated, which means in pragmatic reality you actually less than halve your risk. And, extreme diversifying does run into diminishing returns. A judicious sample of 300 stocks could give you most of the efficiency that the S&P 500 could give you — as far as the Law of Large Numbers is concerned.

However, most such short cuts are *not* judicious — in the sense that most (of the many possible) selections of 300 out of 500 will tend to have biased means as compared to the whole market. By inadvertence you will be sticking yourself with too many or too few utilities (or "cyclicals" or low P/E stocks or...) — any of which pathologies will be penalized in a nearly efficient market universe on a risk-corrected basis.

If (!) gold stocks were truly reverse-correlated with the bulk of your equities, you could afford to buy those lemons in limited degree because their reducing your overall risk compensates for their great volatility and subpar mean return. Our grandparents told us that bonds were a good hedge for stocks, and vice versa. These days we have to warn our daughters that equities and bonds display astonishing *positive* correlation. Times change. And will change again.

6. *The hidden cost of even good ideas.* Suppose you are in a high tax bracket. You discover that, even when Stock A has the same total return as Stock B (think of Berkshire-Hathaway), which *never* pays a dividend, B leaves you with less tax to pay. What follows from your clever perception?

Well, you might hang up on the broker who tells you to put long growing B-H in your self-directed IRA tax shelter. Instead you can make sure it is the high-dividend utility that goes into your IRA, while your B-H is held at home until after the Grim Reaper absolves your heirs from all accrued capital gains tax liability. Your overall portfolio is kept in overall market diversification. That's one way to cash in on your perception.

A second way is to lean toward stocks whose total return *comes least from dividends.* However young you are, you can delay "realizing" your capital gains tax liability by holding such stocks longer. Since time is money when the interest rate is positive, you are in effect getting an interest-free loan from the government; and that should put you ahead of your unimaginative twin.

But beware of dangers. When your computer screen selects for you a portfolio of low-dividend beauties, it's dollars to doughnuts that such a portfolio is thrown out of balanced diversification over the whole market. Your public utility representation is skimpy. Your growth companies are bloated in fractional representation. You have made an expensive bargain with the devil.

In return for hope of a somewhat higher after-tax mean total return, you are risking the excess volatility and risk that inhere in departures from what the Law of Larger Numbers could impart to you. Maybe you'd be better off to buy the whole market on borrowed leverage, with your interest payments deductible from your tax bill? But again beware of danger. That way you might be buying a better *mean* after-tax return but in a *trade-off with higher volatility and risk*; and note that you have made yourself be underrepresented net in fixed-interest assets and overrepresented net in equities.

What is the moral? Never do anything that departs from the overall index of equities (big and small, foreign and domestic, ... and...) cum index of the whole bond market? That is too chaste. Wherever you discern a tempting "edge," yield to it *but yield only a little*.

"Sin" — but only a little. Can that be theologically or *rationally* sound doctrine? Yes, for a mathematical reason. Departing from a *maximal* position *at first* costs you negligibly little: Your loss begins like a negligible squared fraction; $(1/10)^2$ is only 1/100! By contrast, your gain in the mean from exploiting a tax loophole begins like a first power: $(1/10)^1$ is all of 0.1 >> 0.01!

7. *Too clever by 'arf in "timing."* This sin-but-little is a *general* principle that applies everywhere and not just in the domain of taxmanship. A notorious temptation is to try to *"time* the general market."

In fancy nomenclature, this is the fine art of asset allocation. Sell just before or just after the whole market peaks. Park your profits in money market funds. Then, just before or just after the whole market bottoms out, buy back into it. Your profits in comparison with buy-and-hold will be enormous. *If* you can do it. If. Experience shows that out of a thousand money managers and private investors only a small fraction in fact succeed in buying back in at a lower average price than they have sold out at.

That's the mediocre crowd. You are wonderful you. But, as Thomas Cromwell said: "I beseech you in the bowels of Christ to consider that (wonderful) you may be wrong." Or may be sometimes wrong. Among the asset allocators there are *confident* ones; they move from ninety-ten in stocks-bonds to five-ninety-five in stocks-bonds. That implies a degree of self-confidence bordering on *hubris* and self-deception. Over the decades, when both groups of asset allocators have equal *limited* (!) ability to "time," the *cautious* chaps who alternate between sixty-five-thirty-five in stocks-bonds and sixty-forty are likely to end up with a superior risk-corrected total return score.

As revealed in this Journal (Samuelson [1990]), it is a fatal mathematical fallacy to think that *diversifying across time* — as, for example, when you hold zero-one hundred stocks-bonds a third of the time and one hundred-zero two-thirds of the time — is just as variance-reducing as to hold sixty-six and two-thirds-thirty-three and one-third *all* the time. You pay through the nose in excess volatility from diversifying primarily across time rather than at every period of time. Only geniuses at timing or lucky sailors and drunks can be ahead when paying such a secret toll.

Every departure from indexing that you hope will put you ahead — as when you give eight money managers with different styles one-eighth each of your portfolio to manage — when the resultant ends far from diversification agreement with the overall index, your risk-corrected long-run performance is in jeopardy to a degree that you are not able even to estimate. (On the other hand, having eight people in such disagreement that they fortuitously cancel out to produce for you the whole market itself — well, that is an expensively inefficient way of becoming a closet indexer!)

8. *False insurances.* The Surgeon General must warn you against arbitrary avoiding of "regret" and of "probability of specifiable loss." Space does not permit more than bare mention of similar mathematical calculations that *seem* to be persuasive. But when you truly understand them, they lose that persuasiveness.

Investors in volatile futures funds are provided with "guarantees" that after five years they will at least get their principal back. Big deal. It's *their* money that is, in part, set aside and put into zero-coupon safe bonds. They stand to lose their "opportunity gains" and think they stand not to lose anything. No one sent them the bill for those zero-coupon bonds. They pay it by giving up the opportunity to make the gains that are hoped for from those astute futures investments.

9. *Debunking portfolio insurance, stop losses, and other misconceptions.* Today any person of IQ 100 can buy from a 140-IQ mathematician various "derivatives" that will sacrifice their assets' *extreme gains* in return for giving them *lower probabilities* of various *losses.* Is that better than buying less of volatile stocks? The normal-IQ chaps haven't a clue. The Ph.D. whiz kid, for a fee, can give them a clue.

You can be sure that when a Cincinnati soap company and a German metals company each lose hundreds of millions of dollars in a New York bank's "safe deal," it was all in the misapprehension that "extra yield without extra risk" was being bought. When you get a perfect hedge, you get essentially the safe interest rate (minus some transaction costs) — because all the Black-Scholes formulas are based on that safe rate of interest! Furthermore, exact Black-Scholes pricing never provides true safe hedges. No one can know with precision or certainty that the standard deviation parameter of volatility in the quoted Black-Scholes formula will be near next period's ex post volatility.

Derivatives can be useful when A with one tolerance for probability distribution of gain and loss meets B with a different tolerance. Jack Sprat and Mrs. Sprat, as consenting adults in a broad market, swap fat for lean, and both are better off. So it could be with derivatives bought and sold by equally informed adults with different risk tolerances and endowments.

10. *Reconsidering the wisdom of switching from past losers to present winners.* In the real world, success begets, if not success, new customers. Pension funds and endowments switch to last year's performers. If Magellan Fund was hot in 1990 or 1992, in 1993 it grows mightily.

There is some evidence that last year's winners tend to repeat next year. But it is very slight. Mostly the effect comes from the fact that really bad funds stay bad. Their expenses are high, and their choices stay haphazard. (No one can turn a profit selling them short, so the lemons stay being lemons!) When you pare them away and concentrate on the serious contenders, the five-year serial autocorrelations become tenuous, and very few systematically display excess risk-corrected (after-tax) returns.

There must be some (debunking) moral in this as to what the social marginal productivity is of the vast resources devoted to the universe of finance.[5]

MACRO-INEFFICIENCY?

I have considerable belief in *micro*efficiency of liquid organized markets. I am doubtful about any great *macro*efficiency. General Motors' common stock gets priced before and after dividend payments to preclude easy pickings. GM convertibles sell about right in ratio to GM common and GM preferred. (For a small firm, followed by few investors, I'd have to modify this plug for *micro*efficiency.)

Why then shouldn't I believe that the level of the whole equity index gets prices right in good times and bad? The difference is that when Franco Modigliani sees a mispricing of GM common and preferred, he and others can make profits doing what corrects that discrepancy. And that's why the microefficiency gets wiped out as soon as it becomes significant enough to be recognizable.

How does the story run when, in the late 1970s Professor Modigliani opined that the Dow was below 1,000 "irrationally," in the sense that he believed it would be at least 1,400 if investors and speculators understood how not to double-count the bad effects on corporations of then-current inflation? All he could do was write about it. Arguing with the tape by selling the general index short could be costly, and in any case ineffective, while animal spirits were what they were and analysts' shortcomings were what they were.

That is why I stand with Shiller [1986] as a doubter of market macroefficiency.

Caveat: I suspect that gross *macro*-mispricings will, as in Japan during the period 1987-1992, create some tension toward correction. Therefore, I would expect a kind of bounded degree of macro-inefficiency to prevail most of the time in the long run. Although I personally am cautious in trying to "time," when Tobin's q wanders too far from its historic haunts, I find myself making modest changes in degree of equity exposure. Who's being human now?

ARE RESOURCES GROSSLY OVERAPPLIED TO FINANCIAL MARKETS?

To the degree that markets are approximately microefficient, and practitioners are not very successful at timing, why should so many people be necessary to deal in securities? Why can't we all leave most of the job to, say, Vanguard, and save investors most of the loads and expenses that they are charged?

There is a lot to that view. And a society like Japan gives investors a much more expensive deal than our investors can get. Perhaps there is some comfort in the fact that, like supermarkets and chain stores, Wall Street and Chicago are slowly becoming leaner in their usurping of scarce resources.

Information is not a free good. Just as you must kiss many frogs to catch a prince, maybe a lot of meaningless noise trading is needed to keep markets liquid and efficient. Maybe.

ENDNOTES

[1] See the excellent discussion of Kritzman [1994], which reinforces the points made in Samuelson [1969, 1974, 1989a, 1989b, 1990, 1991] and Bodie, Merton, and W. Samuelson [1992].

[2] In technical notation $-WU''(W)/U'(W)$ allegedly grows with W, while $-U''(W)/U'(W)$ declines with W. This popular dogma may trace among economists to Kenneth Arrow's classic 1965 Finnish lectures on risk-bearing (where he is preoccupied with difficulties concerning completeness of decision-making that could arise from unboundedness of the U(W) function) (see Arrow [1971]). On reflection, I find it more plausible that relative risk aversion diminish with wealth. Using this axiom, I have work in process that *deduces* the conventional dogma of greater risk tolerance for long-term investors. The deduction hinges on the fact that real rates of interest and mean real rates of total return for stocks tend both to be positive. Therefore, with the same W now, the long-period investor can expect to have greater W_0 at retirement than the short-period investor can at retirement. That excess of future wealth is what justifies greater risk tolerance now. Let X_T^* be the function $f(W_T, 65 - Age) = f(W_T, T)$: The deduction establishes that f is monotone increasing in both its arguments.

[3] Table 1 in Kritzman [1994] depicts confidence intervals to compare performance of bold and of cautious strategies for T = 1, 2, ..., 20, ..., investment periods. Such tables can be made to show always: For T large enough, the tactic with the higher geometric mean will beat the other at the specified confidence level of 95%, or 99%, or 99.9999%. Is this proof of relevant stochastic dominance? Of course not. As Kritzman suggests, it is déjà vu: Latané, Kelley, Breiman all over again. The syllogism boomerangs.

[4] B avers: "It is irrational for most long-run investors to be very risk-averse. Where is the *long-run* risk? People are myopic and therefore paranoid. That's great for rational me. Their fears provide me with my bargains."

In a nutshell, B begs the issue. No one can prove to *me* that *I am too risk-averse*. Long-run risk is not ignorable.

[5] If ever people stop gathering costly information that is socially valuable because they all come to believe in microefficient markets, will that theory of microefficiency self-destruct? No. The paradox is avoided because, when it begins to have bite, the rewards to information gathering rise enough to monitor away excess market inefficiencies. There is, though, one reason why *laissez-faire* can fail in optimality. The info you gather at a cost to you can leak to benefit others. That creates a familiar "externality" that impairs Pareto optimality and justifies *social* subsidy to information gathering and dissemination.

REFERENCES

Arrow, K.J. "Aspects of the Theory of Risk-Bearing." Reproduced as Chapters 2 and 3 in *Essays in the Theory of Risk-Bearing*. Chicago: Markham, 1971.

Bodie, Zvi, Robert Merton, and William Samuelson. "Labor Supply Flexibility and Portfolio Choice in a Lifecycle Model." *Journal of Economic Dynamics and Control*, Vol. 16, No. 3 (July/October 1992), pp. 427-450.

Brainard, William C., and James Tobin. "Pitfalls in Financial Model Building." *American Economic Review (Papers and Proceedings)*, May 1968, pp. 99-122.

Fama, E.F., and K.R. French. "Permanent and Temporary Components of Stock Prices." *Journal of Political Economics*, Vol. 96, No. 2 (1988), pp. 264-273.

Kritzman, Mark. "What Practitioners Need to Know...About Time Diversification." *Financial Analysts Journal*, January-February 1994, pp. 14-18.

Poterba, James, and Lawrence Summers. "Mean Reversion in Stock Returns: Evidence and Implications." *Journal of Financial Economics*, 22 (1988), pp. 27-59.

Samuelson, Paul A. "Asset Allocation Could Be Dangerous to Your Health." *Journal of Portfolio Management*, Spring 1990, pp. 5-8.

——. "A Case at Last for Age-Phased Reduction in Equity." *Proceedings of the National Academy of Science*, November 1989a, pp. 9048-9051.

——. "Challenge to Judgment." *Journal of Portfolio Management*, Fall 1974, pp. 17-19.

——. "The Judgment of Economic Science on Rational Portfolio Management: Indexing, Timing, and Long-Horizon Effects." *Journal of Portfolio Management*, Fall 1989b, pp. 4-12.

——. "Lifetime Portfolio Selection by Dynamic Stochastic Programming." *Review of Economic Statistics*, August 1969, pp. 239-246.

——. "Long-Run Risk Tolerance When Equity Returns Are Mean Regressing: Pseudoparadoxes and Vindication of 'Businessmen's Risk'." In W.C. Brainard, W.D. Nordhaus, and H.W. Watts, eds., *Money, Macroeconomics, and Economic Policy*. Cambridge, MA: The MIT Press, 1991, pp. 181-200.

Shiller, Robert. "Stock Prices and Social Dynamics." *Brookings Papers on Economic Activity*, 1986, pp. 457-498.

THE IRREDUCIBLE ROLE OF DERIVED MARGINAL UTILITY IN DYNAMIC STOCHASTIC PROGRAMMING

PAUL A. SAMUELSON[1] *Massachusetts Institute of Technology*

Abstract. Using the important case of multi-period investing between a safe asset with a low mean return and an equity basket with a higher total return but a riskier one, this analysis demonstrates that the relevant stochastic programming involves irreducibly recursive variational relations. The "direct" Lagrange–Chow procedure is related to the derivatives of the Bellman "indirect" algorithms and shown to require essentially the same computations save only for standard integrations or taking of first derivatives. To demonstrate that the comparison is unchanged when a vector of control variables must be optimized in a many-period stochastic scenario, the problem is solved for a rentier to both decide how much to save in each period and how much to put of each period's investment into risky securities.

1. INTRODUCTION

Professor Gregory Chow (1992, 1993) has contrasted two alternative methods for solving optimal dynamic programming algorithms: the Bellman-like "indirect" approach which works backward from the terminal future period by period to the present, and which calculates at each stage a derived utility that determines how at that stage the optimal value of a decision-control variable is to be solved for; and Chow's preferred Lagrangian-multiplier "direct" method that eschews explicit recognition of any derived utility functions as such. If I understand his summing up, Dr Chow points out that the too-little-known direct Lagrangian procedure delivers all the optimal solutions that the popular indirect-utilities method can deliver, and does so more economically in the sense that redundant laborious calculations of any indirect utilities can be avoided.

One must agree that both methods produce the same usable result, and agree that it is regrettable if the popular indirect method has eclipsed attention by scholars from the efficient and effective direct Lagrangian approach. We are all in Gregory Chow's debt for a cogent and needed important reminder.

Having said that, in this paper I explicate how both methods are *identical* (a) in their logic and irreducible numerical calculations; and (b) in their common need to calculate recursively *all* the derived MARGINAL utility functions

---

[1] I owe thanks to Professor Gregory Chow of Princeton University for valuable correspondence; to Janice M. Murray of MIT for editorial assistance; and, for partial support, to the Japan–US Center of the New York University Stern School of Management where I am the Long-Term Credit Bank of Japan Visiting Professor of Political Economy.

Address for correspondence: Paul A. Samuelson, Massachusetts Institute of Technology, Boston, MA 02139, USA.

© Blackwell Publishers Ltd 1996. 108 Cowley Road, Oxford OX4 1JF, UK and 238 Main Street, Cambridge, MA 02142, USA.

(except the final one). I have capitalized the word "marginal" to bring out the crucial role in the problem for the sequence $[dU_0(W_0)/dW_0, dU_1(W_1)/dW_1, \ldots, dU_{T-1}(W_{T-1})/dW_{T-1}]$, the indirect *marginal* utilities that are first derivatives of the Bellman-like direct utilities $[U_0(W_0), U_1(W_1), \ldots, U_T(W_T)]$. By simple integration – "mere quadrature" – we can go from the $[U'_t(W_t)]$ sequence to the Bellman $[U_t(W_t)]$ sequence; and, in reverse, the $[U'_t(W_t)]$ sequence follows from $[U_t(W_t)]$ by simple differentiation.

Doctor Chow recognizes that, in calculating the Lagrangian multipliers in the "direct" algorithm, a set of them is exactly the derived marginal utility sequence. Rightly, this fact disarms any criticism of the direct algorithm on the ground that it *fails* to provide the useful information desired by those who value the indirect utilities for their own sake. So to speak, by a mere quadrature, the direct method gives all that the well-known indirect method can yield.

Agreed. But, as will be seen, this knife cuts both ways. It would be a misunderstanding of the valuable Chow message to be left with the impression that the users of the Bellman indirect method are *wasting much scarce computational time and energy* that could be saved by scrupulous adherence to direct Lagrangian multipliers alone. In the total metric of computational time and energy, this note will show that the Bellman add-on is rather minuscule – and in return you do get what many of us find to be often valuable for their own sakes, namely explicit knowledge of the many along-the-way period-ahead indirect utilities. (Note: I use the word utility for *any* pay-off function; dollars or ergs or anything else could be a "utility.")

2. A BASIC EXAMPLE: PORTFOLIO INVESTING FOR DIFFERENT TIME HORIZONS

You can invest dollars today in a *safe* security that will deliver tomorrow (the next period) A dollars, where $A = 1 + r \geq 1$. Alternatively, you can invest your present wealth of W_1 partly in a chancy stock whose "total return-plus-principal (per dollar)" is the random variable Z, where

$$\text{Prob}\{Z \leq z\} = P(z), \quad P(z) \equiv 0 \text{ for } z < 0 \tag{1}$$

$$E\{Z\} > A, P(A) > 0; E\{Z\} = E_1\{Z_1\} = \cdots = E_T\{Z_T\} \tag{2}$$

so that risk-averse folk will put some finite positive fraction, x_t^*, in stocks.

As a two-period investor you begin with W_2 and optimally invest the fraction x_2^* in stocks; and then later, after chance reveals how that period's stock initially did, you will optimally invest the fraction x_1^* of your resulting W_1 in stocks for the one period left to go. For simplicity, I assume that you act to maximize the expected value of your well-defined utility function of terminal (e.g. "retirement") wealth, W_0:

$$\text{Max } E\{U(W_0)\} \quad U'(W_0) > 0 > U''(W_0) \text{ for } W_0 > 0. \tag{3}$$

A simplifying assumption is that in every period, the process is *stationary* and *independent*, involving the *same* $P(z)$ probability function:

$$\text{Prob}\{Z_1 \leq z_1 \text{ and } Z_2 \leq z_2 \text{ and } \ldots Z_T \leq z_T\} = P(z_1)P(z_2)\ldots P(z_T). \tag{4}$$

© Blackwell Publishers Ltd 1996

This is a standard "dynamic stochastic programming problem" and an important one in the literature of modern finance. Among practical investors it is a dogma that the long-horizon investor will harbor greater risk tolerance for chancy-but-high-mean-return stocks than the short-period investor. Thus, when $(W_T, W_{T-1}, ..., W_2, W_1)$ is the actual wealth sequence faced by you at each stage, and when $(X_T[W_T], X_{T-1}[W_{T-1}], ..., X_2[W_2], X_1[W_1])$ is the sequence of optimal equity fractions in the portfolio, the popular dogma asserts that

$$X_1[W] < X_2[W] < \cdots < X_{T-1}[W] < X_T[W]. \tag{5}$$

T stands for T periods ahead before the terminal date; 1 stands for one period ahead before that terminous; and so forth in between.

For some specified A and $[U(W_0) \, P(z)]$ functions, the popular dogma will be confirmed – as for $A > 1$ and $U(W_0) = \ln(W_0 - 1)$. But for others, it will be denied – as in the well-known "myopic" cases of $X_t[W] \equiv X_1[W]$ when $U(W_0) = \log W_0$; or $W_0^{1/2}$; or $-W_0^{-2}$; or W_0^γ/γ, $1 > \gamma \neq 0$, which has constant relative-risk-aversion.

Bellman-like indirect utilities or Chow-recommended direct Lagrangian procedures can solve any such problem. What I will show here is that no valid solution can avoid calculating recursively the sequence of derived *marginal* utility functions; and that when this is done, whether you dub the algorithm "direct" or "indirect," Chow–Lagrangian or Bellman-indirect, the *irreducible* calculations are *exactly the same* (and, from them, by quadrature alone you will have calculated complete knowledge of the derived utility functions $[U(W_0) \equiv U_0(W_0), U_1(W_1), ..., U_T(W_T)]$). Notice that no Chow assertion has been denied; but note too that the computational disadvantages of either method are demonstrated to be minor.

3. ONE-PERIOD SOLUTION

This case is so simple that it is virtually outside the realm of *dynamic programming*. But all journeys do end with their last step. Succinctly, you penultimately begin with W_1 and decide how to allocate it optimally between safe cash of $(1 - x_1^*)W_1$ and chancy stock of $x_1^* W_1$, to end with the random variable of W_0 that stands to have best Expected $U(W_0)$ or Expected $U_0(W_0)$. Here are the specific calculations:

$$u^1(W_1; x_1) \equiv E\{U_0(W_0)\} \equiv E_1\{U_0(W_1 A + W_1 Z_1 x_1 - W_1 A x_1)\}$$
$$= \int_0^\infty U_0(W_1 A + W_1 z_1 x_1 - W_1 A x_1) dP(z_1) \tag{6}$$

where the Stieltjes-integral formulation covers both discrete probabilities and probability densities.

By definition,

$$\underset{x_1}{\mathrm{Max}}\, u^1(W_1; x_1) = u^1(W_1; x_1^*) \equiv u^1(W_1; X_1[W_1]) \equiv U_1(W_1) \tag{7}$$

where
$$x_1^* = X_1[W_1] \tag{8}$$
is by definition the unique positive root for x_1 of
$$0 = \partial u^1/\partial x_1 \equiv u_x^1(W_1; x_1) \equiv E_1\{U_0'(W_1A + W_1Z_1x_1 - W_1Ax_1)W_1(Z_1 - A)\}. \tag{9}$$

Remark: The maximum is an interior one here, with no need for the inequalities of Kuhn–Tucker concave programming.

Should one have some interest in (7)'s defined *indirect* utility function $U_1(W_1)$, either for its own sake or for its possible usefulness in calculating next section's optimal two-period equity fraction, $x_2^* = X_2[W_2]$, it is defined as

$$u^1(W_1; X_1[W_1]) \equiv U_1(W_1) \equiv E_1\{U_0(W_1A + W_1Z_1X_1[W_1] - W_1AX_1[W_1])\}$$
$$= \int_0^\infty U_0(W_1A + W_1z_1X_1[W_1] - W_1AX_1[W_1])\,dP(z_1). \tag{10}$$

Then $U_1'(W_1)$ can be defined by *either* of the two following equivalents:

$$u_W^1(W_1; X_1[W_1]) + u_x^1(W_1; X_1[W_1])X_1'[W_1] = u_w^1(W_1; X_1[W_1]) + 0 \tag{11a}$$
$$= (d/dW_1)U_1(W_1), \text{ where } U(W_1) \text{ was defined in (10)} \tag{11b}$$

or

$$= E_1\{U_0'(W_1A + W_1Z_1X_1[W_1] - W_1AX_1[W_1])(A + [Z_1 - A]X_1[W_1]$$
$$+ W_1[Z_1 - A]X_1'[W_1])\}$$
$$= AE_1\{U_0'(W_1A + W_1Z_1X_1[W_1] - W_1AX_1[W])\} + 0 + 0. \tag{11c}$$

Note that (11c)'s way of defining $U_1'(W_1)$ requires *no* knowledge of $U_1(W_1)$ itself and even no knowledge of $U_0(W_0)$ as against $U_0'(W_0)$!

Three remarks are in order. First, if a solution is needed for only one period and for a single specified W_1, the labor of computing the quadrature(s) that gives $U_1(W_1)$ or gives $U_1'(W_1)$ over a range of W_1's can be spared. Richard Bellman would not have disagreed with this.

Secondly, even if one will be confronted with only one $W_1 = \overline{W}_1$, or with W_1's in some narrow range around $\overline{W}_1$, the stochastic possibilities of experiencing $U_0(W_0)$ values outside the narrow range near $U_0(AW_1)$ are compelling; and therefore you need to calculate the raw materials that $U_0(W_0)$ depends on over a range of W_0 that could even be anywhere on $[0, \infty]$. Thus, if $P(z)$ is log–normal all of $U_0'(W_0)$ becomes relevant.

Thirdly, for the degenerate one-period case, Bellman and Chow minimal calculations are identical.

4. TWO-PERIOD HORIZONS

As a two-period investor, you start with W_2 and your immediate decision will be how to calculate $x_2^* = X_2[W_2]$. But to do this, you will have to utilize the results from the above one-period problem, needing to know for all W_1's that could emerge from your $x_2^*W_2$ choice how their outcomes are to be weighed by you now.

© Blackwell Publishers Ltd 1996

Here are the Bellman-like calculations. Define as before

$$U_1(W_1) \equiv u^1(W_1; X_1[W_1]) \equiv E_1\{U_0(W_1A + W_1Z_1X_1[W_1] - W_1AX_1[W_1])\}. \quad (12)$$

It follows that

$$U_1'(W_1) \equiv (d/dW_1)U_1(W_1), \text{ or equivalently (!)} \quad (13a)$$

$$\equiv E_1\{U'(W_1A + W_1Z_1X_1[W_1] - W_1AX_1[W_1])(A + 0 + 0)\} \quad (13b)$$

$$u^2(W_2; x_2) \equiv E\{U_1(W_1)\} \equiv E_2\{U_1(W_2A + W_2Z_2x_2 - W_2Ax_2)\}. \quad (14)$$

Also

$$0 = u_x^2(W_2; x_2^*) = E_2\{U_1'(W_2A + W_2Z_2x_2^* - W_2Ax_2^*)(Z_2 - A)W_2\}$$
$$= u_x^2(W_2; X_2[W_2]) \quad (15)$$

where

$$x_2^* = X_2[W_2] \text{ is the unique positive root for } x_2 \text{ in (15)}. \quad (16)$$

It can be proved that strong concavity restrictions on $U_0(W)$ entail that $U_1(W)$ is also qualitatively concave:

$$U_1'(W_1) > 0 > U_1''(W_1). \quad (17)$$

We see that, with no explicit reliance on $U_0(W)$, $X_1[W_1]$ and $U_1'(W_1)$ can be calculated from $U_0'(W)$. This is what Chow's point does establish and similar validity holds for all t.

5. THE MANY-PERIOD PROBLEM

This section's analysis of the general multiperiod calculations will confirm that the following sequence of pairs self-generate themselves:

$$\{U_0[W]\} \to \{U_0'(W)\} \to \{X_1[W]U_1'(W)\} \to \{X_2[W]U_2'(W)\} \to$$
$$\cdots \to \{X_{T-1}[W]U_{T-1}'(W)\} \to \{X_T[W]\}. \quad (18)$$

Note that the sequence $\{U_1(W)U_2(W) \ldots U_{T-1}(W)U_T(W)\}$ is *not* needed in this mode of calculations, but note too that the simple integration of (20) below will yield $U_t(W)$ from (18).

However, it is true that the *desideratum* of the $\{X_1[W] \ X_2[W] \ldots X_{T-1}[W] \ X_T[W]\}$ sequence is also calculable from the alternative self-generating "Bellman" sequence

$$\{U_0(W)\} \to \{U_0'(W)\} \to \{X_1[W] \ U_1(W) \ U_1'(W)\} \to$$
$$\{X_2[W] \ U_2(W) \ U_2'(W)\} \to \cdots \to \{X_T[W] \ U_T(W)U_T'(W)\}. \quad (19)$$

And, as already discussed, always

$$U_t(W) \equiv U_t(\overline{W}) + \int_{\overline{W}}^{W} U_t'(v)dv, \quad U_t'(W) = (d/dW)U_t(W), \quad t = 0, 1, \ldots \quad (20)$$

The heavy burden of concave-programming calculation is not in performing simple integrations and differentiations of known functions, and Dr Chow's readers will want to remind themselves of this important truth.

Here are the equations that generate (18)'s direct ("Lagrangian") sequence functions. For $U'_0(W_0)$ given, and for $t = 1, 2, \ldots, T$:

$$0 = E_t\{U'_{t-1}(W_tA + W_tZ_tx_t^* - W_tAx_t^*)[Z_t - A]\} \tag{21a}$$

$$x_t^* = X_t[W_t] > 0, \tag{21b}$$

$$U'_t(W_t) \equiv AE\{U'_{t-1}(W_tA + W_tZ_tX_t[W_t] - W_tAX_t[W_t])\}. \tag{21c}$$

For $t = 1$ we have the first triplet of (18); for $t = 2$, the second triplet; ...; and for $t = T$, the last triplet's $U'_t(W_t)$ of (21c) does not have to be calculated.

If desired, Bellman's indirect utilities can be derived from

$$U_t(W) - U_t(\overline{W}) = \int_{\overline{W}}^{W_t} U'_t(v)\,dv. \tag{21d}$$

6. GENERALIZATIONS

Much of the traditional literature on the calculus of variations and on dynamic programming deals with the special case of *additive-independence* when today's payoff is added to payoffs of tomorrow and yesterday. In concluding, it will be instructive (a) to be more general, while (b) showing that in each period you still have to decide *its* control variable(s) using results of *past* stochastic draws but being necessarily ignorant of *future* random draws.

It suffices to consider first a rentier–saver who consumes in three consecutive periods (c_2, c_1, c_0). Her utility of that vector of consumption is concave $U(c_0, c_1, c_2)$, both *ex ante* and *ex post*. Wealth of W_2 gets invested and results in W_1 *after* optimal stock fraction of x_2 and optimal c_2 were determined and (of course) depending upon what the luck of the draw was for Z_2. W_1 needs in turn to get optimally divided between c_1 and reinvestment. Simultaneously with x_1, c_1's best magnitude must get selected – in this and all matters so as to maximize $E\{U(c_0, c_1, c_2)\}$ subject to the constraints and knowledge of the situation at each stage.

The financial constraints involving (W_t, x_t) are as before, but added to the problem are the new endogenous control variables for c_t. Now, with $c_0 = 0$:

$$W_{t-1} + c_{t-1} = W_t(A + Z_tx_t - Ax_t), \qquad t = 1, 2, \ldots, T > 1. \tag{22}$$

For notational usefulness, define

$$U^0(W_0, c_1 \mid c_2, \ldots, c_T) \equiv U(W_0, c_1, c_2, \ldots, c_T). \tag{23}$$

This prepares the way to identify Bellman indirect functions for each $1 \leq t \leq T$: $U^t(W_t, c_{t+1} \mid c_{t+2}, \ldots, c_T)$. It will also be notationally convenient to designate

© Blackwell Publishers Ltd 1996

the following partial derivatives for $t = 1, 2, \ldots, T$:

$$\partial U^{t-1}(W_{t-1}, c_t | c_{t+1}, \ldots)/\partial W_{t-1} \equiv U_W^{t-1}(W_{t-1}, c_t | c_{t+1}, \ldots)$$
$$\partial U^{t-1}(W_{t-1}, c_t | c_{t+1}, \ldots)/\partial c_t \equiv U_c^{t-1}(W_{t-1}, c_t | c_{t+1}, \ldots). \tag{24}$$

Contemplate the last step first, when $t = 1$. We know W_1 and pick best stock fraction and best present consumption, (x_1^*, c_1^*), while then knowing what past $(c_2, \ldots, c_T)$ were and what random stock outcomes $(Z_2, \ldots, Z_T)$ were. Then

$$\underset{x_1, c_1}{\text{Max}}\ E_1\{U^0([W_1 - c_1][A + Z_1 x_1 - A x_1], c_1 | c_2, \ldots, c_T)\}$$

$$\equiv U^1(W_1, c_2 | c_3, \ldots, c_T), \text{ def of } U^1 \text{ function} \tag{25a}$$

$$\equiv E_1\{U^0([W_1 - c_1^*][A + \{Z_1 - A\}x_1^*], c_1^* | c_2, \ldots, c_T)\} \tag{25b}$$

$$\equiv E_1\{U^0([W_1 - C^1\{W_1 | c_2, \ldots, c_T\}][A + \{Z_1 - A\}X^1\{W_1 | c_2, \ldots, c_T\}],$$
$$C^1\{W_1 | c_2, \ldots, c_T\} | c_2, \ldots, c_T)\} \tag{25c}$$

where

$$(x_1^*\ c_1^*) = (X^1\{W_1 | c_2, \ldots, c_T\}\ C^1\{W_1 | c_2, \ldots, c_T\}) \tag{26a}$$

is the unique vectoral root of the following first-derivative maximal conditions:

$$0 = \partial E_1\{U^0(\ )\}/\partial x_1 \equiv [W_1 - c_1] E_1\{U_W^0([W_1 - c_1]$$
$$[A + \{Z_1 - A\}x_1], c_1 | c_2, \ldots)(Z_1 - A)\};$$
$$\equiv E_1\{U_W^0([W_1 - c_1][A + \{Z_1 - A\}x_1], c_1 | c_2, \ldots)[Z_1 - A]\},$$
$$\text{for } W_1 - c_1 > 0; \tag{26b}$$

$$0 = \partial E_1\{U^0(\ )\}/\partial c_1 \equiv E_1\{U_c^0([W_1 - c_1][A + \{Z_1 - A\}x_1], c_1 | c_2, \ldots)\}$$
$$- A E_1\{U_W^0([W_1 - c_1][A + \{Z_1 - A\}x_1], c_1 | c_2, \ldots)\}. \tag{26c}$$

What has been done for $t = 1$, given $U^0(\ )$, can evidently be done in the same pattern for any t – to give recursively decision functions $(X^t\{W_t | c_{t+1}, \ldots\}$ $C^t\{W_t | c_{t+1}, \ldots\})$, and to define $U^t(W_t, c_{t+1} | c_{t+2}, \ldots, c_T)$ recursively in terms of $U^{t-1}(W_{t-1}, c_t | c_{t+1}, \ldots, c_T)$, all this in the spirit of Bellman's indirect methods.

Here is how it goes:

$$\underset{x_t, c_t}{\text{Max}}\ E_t\{U^{t-1}([W_t - c_t][A + \{Z_t - A\}x_t], c_t | c_{t+1}, \ldots, c_T)\}$$

$$= E_t\{U^{t-1}([W_t - c_t^*][A + \{Z_t - A\}x_t^*], c_t^* | c_{t+1}, \ldots, c_T)\} \tag{27a}$$

$$\equiv U^t(W_t, c_{t+1} | c_{t+2}, \ldots, c_T), \text{ def. of } U^t \text{ function} \tag{27b}$$

$$\equiv E\{U^{t-1}([W_t - C^t\{W_t | c_{t+1}, \ldots, c_T\}][A + \{Z_t - A\}X^t\{W_t | c_{t+1}, \ldots, c_T\}],$$
$$C^t\{W_t | c_{t+1}, \ldots, c_T\} | c_{t+2}, \ldots, c_T)\}. \tag{27c}$$

© Blackwell Publishers Ltd 1996

Then, just as in (26) when t had equalled 1, $(x_t^*\ c_t^*) = (X^t\{W_t|c_{t+1}, ..., c_T\}\ C^t\{W_t|c_{t+1}, ..., c_T\})$ is by definition the unique vector root of

$$0 = \partial E_t\{U^{t-1}(\ )\}/\partial x_t$$
$$\equiv E_t\{U_W^{t-1}([W_t - c_t][A + \{Z_t - A\}x_t], c_t|c_{t+1}, ...)[Z_t - A]\}[W_t - c_t] \quad (28a)$$
$$0 = \partial E_t\{U^{t-1}(\ )\}/\partial c_t$$
$$\equiv E_t\{U_c^{t-1}([W_t - c_t][A + \{Z_t - A\}x_t], c_t|c_{t+1}, ...)\}$$
$$- AE_t\{U_W^{t-1}([W_t - c_t][A + \{Z_t - A\}x_t], c_t|c_{t+1}, ...)\} - 0x_t. \quad (28b)$$

The last term vanishes in (28b) as an implication of (28a). And in (28a), the positive $[W_t - c_t]$ factor can be cancelled out.

Recall that the Lagrange–Chow "direct" procedure, in the search for the best single control variable x_t^*, could dispense with the $[U_t(W_t)]$ sequence and utilize only recursive definition of that sequence's respective derivatives $[dU_t(W_t)/dW_t]$. The same holds here and the rigorous proof is completely analogous. If you wish, you can plan not to calculate the U^t functions. Merely adjoin to the variational relations (28) the recursive identifications implied by what you have ignored. For $t = 1, ..., T$:

$$U_W^t(W_t, c_t|c_{t+1}, ...) \equiv AE_t\{U_W^{t-1}(W_{t-1}, C^t\{W_t|c_{t+1}, ...\}|c_{t+1}, ..., c_T)\} \quad (29a)$$
$$U_c^t(W_t, c_t|c_{t+1}, ...) \equiv E_t\{U_c^{t-1}(W_{t-1}, C^t\{W_t|c_{t+1}, ...\}|c_{t+1}, ..., c_T)\}. \quad (29b)$$

Remember that W_{t-1}, with (W_t, x_t^*, c_t^*) fixed at inherited and calculated levels, is itself a random variable over which the $E_t\{\ \}$ expected value can be taken. In the last two relations, instead of writing the short W_{t-1} symbol, the reader is free to write out the $[W_t - c_t^*][A + \{Z_t - A\}x_t^*]$ symbols.

6.1. *Discussion*

When the problem involves optimal decision-making about a vector of control variables, Lagrange–Chow or anyone must recursively calculate and record a vector of new functions. By contrast, the zealous followers of Bellman need calculate only one scalar function at each t, provided only that they do not mind the rather easy operation of calculating its $\partial U^{t-1}/\partial W_t$ and $\partial U^{t-1}/\partial c_t$ partial derivatives.

This re-emphasizes that there is no true sizeable discrepancy in work involved in the alternative direct or indirect solution algorithms.

6.2. *Remark*

For the pragmatist interested only in the needed decision rules, it can be shown that for the conventional case of additively independent intertemporal payoffs $U = \sum_0^T V_t(c_t)$, all *past* consumption magnitudes $(...|c_{t+1}, c_{t+2}...)$ alter not at all the $[X^t\{\ \}\ C^t\{\ \}]$ decision functions. Now they can be written simply as $[X^t\{W_t\}\ C^t\{W_t\}]$, just as in the scalar problem where only retirement-day wealth was in the maximand.

© Blackwell Publishers Ltd 1996

BIBLIOGRAPHY

Bellman, R. (1957) *Dynamic Programming*, Princeton, NJ: Princeton University Press.
Chow, G. (1992) "Dynamic Optimization without Dynamic Programming," *Economic Modelling* 9, January, 3–9.
—— (1993) "Optimal Control without Solving the Bellman Equation," *Journal of Economic Dynamics and Control* 17, 621–30.
Phelps, E. (1962) "The Accumulation of Risky Capital: A Sequential Utility Analysis," *Econometrica* 30, 729–43.
Samuelson, P. A. (1969) "Lifetime Portfolio Selection by Dynamic Stochastic Programming," *Review of Economics and Statistics* 51, 239–46. Reproduced as Chapter 204 in *The Collected Scientific Papers of Paul A. Samuelson*, Vol. 3, Cambridge, MA: MIT Press, 1972.

© Blackwell Publishers Ltd 1996

Journal of Risk and Uncertainty, 14:129–142 (1997)
© 1997 Kluwer Academic Publishers

Proof by Certainty Equivalents That Diversification-Across-Time Does Worse, Risk Corrected, Than Diversification-Throughout-Time

PAUL A. SAMUELSON
Department of Economics, E52-383C, Massachusetts Institute of Technology, Cambridge, MA 02139-4307

Abstract

For those with *constant* relative-risk-aversion, one can calculate an easy and exact measurement of their *risk-corrected total return* per period by use of an appropriate "*power* mean": the Geometric Mean when $U = \log$ Wealth; the Harmonic Mean when $U = -W^{-1}$; and the general $(\Sigma p_j W_j^\gamma)^{1/\gamma}$ mean when $U = W^\gamma/\gamma$, $1 > \gamma \neq 0$. This subjective risk-corrected return compounds over multiple periods formally the way money returns compound: $1 + r_1$, $(1 + r_1)(1 + r_2)$, ..., $\Pi_1^T(1 + r_t)$. For them, this approach can dramatize the inefficiency of being (say) half the time in each of two *independent* and *identically distributed* securities; 100% is then lost of the benefit from being all the time 50-50 in each; actually, being half the time in each is as bad as being all the time in either one, which is equivalent to being completely undiversified. More generally, there is proved here that, for *any* risk-averse $U(W)$ and time-independent probabilities, optimal diversification *within* each time period outperforms generically any and all patterns of *across-time* diversification. The variety of proposed risk-corrected returns can give useful approximations for different classes of investors—widows and orphans, pension fiduciaries, high-flying plungers, and so forth—to replace or extend Markowitz, Sharpe, Treynor, or Modigliani-Modigliani measures of corrected performance.

Key words: certainty equivalents, risk-corrected diversifications

JEL Classification: D80, G00

An Ivy League college professor, under the illusion that he possessed acumen to "time" the market, used his privilege in a self-managed tax-sheltered account to switch costlessly 16 times in one year from 100% in cash to 100% in a stock index. As it turned out, neither he nor one who were to zig when he zagged gained from the activism (and, of course, some transaction costs were generated that fell on others). It was an inexpensive lesson, he thought: "Whereas passive colleagues were 50% in stocks and in a safe security all the year, I averaged 50% in each over the year as a whole—a wash."

That is a fallacy. Diversification *across time* fails to deliver the *risk-corrected* return that diversification *throughout time* can do. See Samuelson (1989, 1990) for a demonstration of this important distinction, which has a special significance in tempering optimal "asset allocation" programs: You must have great timing prescience *gross* to overcome the *deadweight loss* inherent in shifting strongly between stocks and nonstocks in the hope of delivering superior *net* risk-corrected returns over the years.

What is needed is rigorous mathematical-statistical proof. Here I first present it succinctly for that important class of cases where "risk-corrected return" can be given an exact operational definition free from all mean-variance approximations. For such cases, pertaining to those with *constant relative risk aversion*, it is shown how useful is the expository device of "certainty-equivalent" wealth levels, $\hat{W}$, which serve as effective surrogates for actual random-varying W levels.

Final discussion appraises the robustness of the presented ideal models and suggests qualifications needed for the most general cases. Then, in response to a referee who I hope will publish his proof that the result here generalizes to any concave $U(W)$ function, I present my own general theorem with its intuitive proof.

1. Review of assumptions

An investor, you, chooses how to allocate initial wealth in a portfolio between (a) safe cash with a sure money return rate per period of $1 + r = R \geq 1$, and (b) a risky stock with assumed probability distribution, $P(z)$, for its random-variable outcome rate Z for each dollar put into the stock.

$$\text{Prob}\{Z \leq z\} = P(z). \tag{1a}$$

To assure limited liability

$$P(z) \equiv 0 \text{ for } z < 0. \tag{1b}$$

To rule out infinite arbitrage

$$1 > P(1 + r) > 0. \tag{1c}$$

If risk-averse investors are to buy the stock

$$E\{Z\} = \int_0^\infty z dP(z) \equiv \int_0^\infty zP(dz) > 1 + r. \tag{1d}$$

The Stieltjes' integral in (1d) handles both discrete probabilities—$p_1 + \ldots + p_n = 1$—and probability densities, where $dP(z) \equiv P(dz) \equiv P'(z)dz$.

In our dynamic stochastic processes, $1 + r$ holds in every period t; and the stock's successive Z's obey the same $P(\ )$ and are independent period by period. Thus,

$$\text{Prob}\{Z_1 \leq z_1, \ldots, Z_T \leq z_T\} = P(z_1) \ldots P(z_T) \tag{2a}$$

$$\text{Prob}\{Z_{t+1} \leq z_{t+1} | Z_t = z_t\} = P(z_{t+1}), \partial P/\partial z_t \equiv 0. \tag{2b}$$

These "white-noise" assumptions would become "red-noise" when mean *reversion* and *negative* autocorrelations obtain; and would become "blue-noise" when momentum processes involve *positive* autocorrelations. I do not address such generalizations here. Readers, however, can straightforwardly replace my single stochastic stock with a portfolio selected from a bevy of such; and can replace $E\{U\}$ as a maximand by any smooth risk-averse, Machina-like functional.

2. One-period portfolio choice

You begin with initial wealth, $W_1 = \bar{W}$. You must decide what fraction x_1 to put initially into the stock and what fraction $1 - x_1$ to put into safe cash.

Your terminal wealth W_0 becomes the random variable

$$W_0 = \bar{W}(1 + r)(1 - x_1) + \bar{W}Z_1 x_1. \tag{3}$$

If risk-neutral, you would select x_1 to maximize Expected $\{$money $W_0\}$. Because (1d) asserts that the stock constitutes a "better than *fair* game," a risk-neutral person would want to make x_1^* infinitely large, borrowing at $1 + r$ to leverage to whatever degree were feasible.

But you are risk averse with a strongly *concave* utility function

$$U = U(W), \; U'(W) > 0 > U''(W) \tag{4}$$

almost everywhere.

Your optimality problem is the following

$$\underset{x_1}{\text{Max}}\, E\{U(W_0)\} \equiv \underset{x_1}{\text{Max}}\, E\{U(\bar{W}[1 + r][1 - x_1] + \bar{W}Z_1 x_1)\} \tag{5a}$$

$$= \underset{x_1}{\text{Max}} \int_0^\infty U(\bar{W}[1 + r][1 - x] + \bar{W}z_1 x_1)\, dP(z_1) \tag{5b}$$

$$= \underset{x_1}{\text{Max}}\, u^1(x_1; \bar{W}) = u^1(x_1^*; \bar{W}), \text{def of } u^1(\,), x_1^* \tag{5c}$$

$$\equiv u^1(X_1[\bar{W}], \bar{W}) \equiv U_1(\bar{W}), \text{def of } U_1(\bar{W}), X_1[\bar{W}] \tag{5d}$$

where $x_1^* = X_1[\bar{W}]$ is the unique positive root for x_1 of

$$\partial E\{U(W_0)\}/\partial x_1 = 0 = \int_0^\infty U'(\bar{W}[1 + r][1 - x] + \bar{W}z_1 x_1)(z_1 - R)\, dP(z_1). \tag{5e}$$

3. "Certainty equivalents"

Equivalent to maximizing through choice $E\{U(W_0)\}$, it will now be explained, is to maximize the following defined Certainty Equivalent Wealth of Actual Stochastic Wealth.
Consider

$$u = U(W), \ U'(W) > 0 \tag{6a}$$

and its inverse function

$$U = U^{-1}[u] \equiv \phi[u], \ \phi' = 1/U' > 0 \tag{6b}$$

$$W \equiv U^{-1}[U(W)]. \tag{6c}$$

Now solve for $\hat{W}$ the following implicit relation

$$U(\hat{W}) = E\{U(W_0)\} = E\{U(\bar{W}[1 + r][1 - x_1] + \bar{W}Z_1 x_1)\} \tag{7a}$$

$$\hat{W} = U^{-1}[E\{U(\bar{W}[1 + r][1 - x_1] + \bar{W}Z_1 x_1)\}] \tag{7b}$$

$$= U^{-1}[u^1(x; \bar{W})] = \omega(x; \bar{W}). \tag{7c}$$

$\hat{W}$ is thus the well-defined certainty-wealth equivalent to the initial $\bar{W}$ that is invested into a portfolio consisting of the fraction x_1 in stock and $(1 - x_1)$ in the safe security; and where $E\{U(W_0)\}$ is your *ex ante subjective* evaluation of the worth of the portfolio to you corrected *fully* for riskiness. Note that $\hat{W}$ is two-ways subjective: It depends on your *psychological* evaluation of gains relative to losses; and, also, it depends on your *personal* probability beliefs about how the risky stock(s) behaves as a random variable. In math speech, $\hat{W}$ is a *function* of $\bar{W}$ and at the same time is the (7b) *functional* of the $U(W)$ and the $P(z)$ functions.

4. Constant relative-risk-aversion

There is a special class of $U(W)$ functions for which $\bar{W}$ matters not at all in determining best portfolio *proportions* and the ratio $\hat{W}/\bar{W}$; and in which the time-horizon, *myopically*, does not matter at all. This class consists of the functions with *constant relative risk aversion* in the sense of Arrow–Pratt's $-WU''(W)/U'(W) = A(W)$ defined measure. For this class, with $A(W) \equiv \bar{A}$, which includes Bernoulli's $U = \log W$ and includes $U = W^\gamma/\gamma$ with $1 > \gamma \neq 0$, $\hat{W}/\bar{W}$ depends *only* on x_1 independently of $\bar{W}$ scale. For this CRRA class, it is easy to deduce that

$$\hat{W} = \bar{W}\omega_\gamma(x), \ \partial \omega_\gamma(x)/\partial \gamma < 0. \tag{8}$$

IN- VS. -ACROSS TIME DIVERSIFICATION

Generally, as γ moves downward from being close to unity (where you would be risk neutral), your equity tolerance declines. When γ falls close to zero (where, so to speak, you would have the middling risk aversion of a Daniel Bernoulli), you are more risk averse than when $\gamma = 1/2$. As γ falls farther and farther below zero, your risk aversion uniformly rises—until, as $\gamma \to -\infty$, you approach the minmax paranoia of one who is obsessed by the worst that can happen, however low its positive probability may be.

Three numerical cases can serve the present purpose:

1. In the middle is Bernoulli's ln W, where *marginal* utility of a loss doubles as your wealth halves. A Bernoulli can be shown to choose in portfolio and other stochastic decision making so as to want to pick the biggest feasible *Geometric Mean of Money* outcomes: The *G.M.* is his *certainty equivalent* $\hat{W}$. By contrast a risk-neutral person would act to maximize money's *Arithmetic Mean*.
2. More risk averse than Bernoulli are those who act to maximize $E\{U(W_0)\} = E\{-W_0^{-1}\}$, $\gamma = -1$. It is as if they choose to pick that which gives the highest *Harmonic Mean of Money* outcomes, and for them the portfolio's Certainty Equivalent is $\hat{W} = H.M. < G.M. < A.M.$ Historical and cross-sectional statistical studies of what best accords with observed equity premia suggest that $H.M$ is more realistic than log W_0.
3. Least realistic perhaps is $W^{1/2}/(1/2)$, which was the $U(W)$ proposed by Crämer in 1728. Its Certainty Equivalent is a weighted-mean, the "square of the mean square root" (not to be confused with the standard deviation, which is "the root of the mean square"). This falls between the Geometric and Arithmetic means.

Here is derived the exact Certainty-Equivalent formula for log W.

$$u = \ln W \leftrightarrow W = U^{-1}[u] \equiv e^u = \exp[u] \tag{9a}$$

For $\bar{W}$ 100% in safe cash with sure $(1 + r)$ outcome, trivially

$$U(\hat{W}) = \ln \hat{W} = U(\bar{W}[1 + r]) = \ln(\bar{W}[1 + r]) \tag{9b}$$

$$\hat{W} = \exp[\ln \bar{W}(1 + r)] = \bar{W}(1 + r) = \bar{W}\omega_0(0). \tag{9c}$$

When all your wealth goes 100% into the stock, $\hat{W}$ becomes the weighted *G.M.* of Z:

$$\hat{W} = \exp\left[\int_0^\infty \ln(\bar{W}z)\, dP(z)\right] = \bar{W}\omega_0(1). \tag{10}$$

For fractions $[x\,; 1-x]$ respectively in stock and safe cash,

$$\hat{W} = \exp\left[\int_0^\infty \ln(\bar{W}[1+r][1-x] + \bar{W}zx)\, dP(z)\right] \tag{11a}$$

$$= \bar{W} \int_0^\infty [\ln ([1 + r][1 - x] + zx) \, dP(z) = \bar{W}\omega_0(x)] \tag{11b}$$

$$\equiv G.M. \text{ of } W_0. \tag{11c}$$

Now, consider the general case where $1 > \gamma \neq 0$,

$$u = U(W) = W^\gamma/\gamma, \gamma \neq 0 \tag{12a}$$

$$W = U^{-1}[u] = [\gamma u]^{1/\gamma} = (\gamma^{1/\gamma})u^{1/\gamma}. \tag{12b}$$

For 100% in safe cash, at sure rate $(1 + r)$, trivially

$$U(\hat{W}) = \bar{W}^\gamma/\gamma = U(\bar{W}[1 + r]) = (\bar{W}[1 + r])^\gamma/\gamma \tag{13a}$$

$$\hat{W} = \bar{W}(1 + r) = \bar{W}\omega_\gamma(0). \tag{13b}$$

For 100% in the stochastic stock

$$\hat{W} = \bar{W}[\int_0^\infty z^\gamma dP(z)]^{1/\gamma}/\gamma \equiv \bar{W}\omega_\gamma(1). \tag{13c}$$

For $[x; 1-x]$ in the stock and in cash respectively,

$$\hat{W} = \bar{W}[\int_0^\infty ([1 + r][1 - x] + zx)^\gamma dP(z)]^{1/\gamma}/\gamma$$

$$\equiv \bar{W}\omega_\gamma(x), \text{ a generalized weighted mean.} \tag{13d}$$

5. Illustrative numerical scenarios

Suppose for concreteness that $1 + r = 1.05$, as when a money market fund stays always at $1 per share and pays 5% interest with assured certainty. Let your stock alternative give at *even odds twice* 1.05 or *half* 1.05. That makes the stock better than a fair gamble, because its mean or Expected money outcome is

$$E\{Z\} = 1.05 \left[\frac{1}{2}(2) + \frac{1}{2}(1/2)\right] = (1.05)(1.25) = 1.3125. \tag{14}$$

This is a 31+% money return.

How much does the stock's better money return need to be discounted for its riskiness—its volatility? Our $\hat{W}$ measure or certainty equivalent to 100% in stock gives an exact answer for *Bernoulli*—as follows:

$$\hat{W} = G.M. = \hat{W}(1.05)\sqrt{(2)(1/2)} = \hat{W}(1.05). \tag{15}$$

In this numerical example, the 1.3125 of *A.M.* gets knocked down for risk to 1.05: no better and no worse than cash itself!

For the even more risk-averse Harmonic Mean maximizer, who possesses $\gamma = -1$,

$$\hat{W} = H.M. = \hat{W}(1.05)\frac{1}{\frac{1}{2}(2) + \frac{1}{2}(1/2)} = \hat{W}(1.05)\frac{2(1)(1/2)}{2 + (1/2)}$$

$$= \hat{W}(1.05)(1 - .20) = \hat{W}(1 - .16) < \hat{W}(1.05). \tag{16}$$

For her, the risk-corrected return of the stock is *minus* 16%! Better to be in 5% cash.

What about the Crâmer type with $\gamma = 1/2$? This macho person calculates for 100% in the stock

$$\hat{W} = \bar{W}(1.05)\left(\frac{1}{2}[2]^{1/2} + \frac{1}{2}[1/2]^{1/2}\right)^2$$

$$= \hat{W}(1.05)(3/4)\sqrt{2} = \hat{W}(1.05)(1.0606601..)$$

$$= \hat{W}(1.113691..) > \hat{W}(1.05). \tag{17}$$

Even for this macho risk bearer, the gross money return needs discounting for proper risk correction. But still, he'd rather be 100% in the stock with its risk-corrected 11% total return than 100% in the safe stuff with its 5%.

But now our mathematics teaches us that water can indeed rise above its own source. Yes, Virginia, within–time diversification does provide a free lunch. For Bernoulli, by mixing half and half the cash and stock items, with their similar 5% risk-corrected returns, by magic he ends up with the following risk-corrected return raised to 11+%!

$$\hat{W} = \bar{W}(1.05)\left[\frac{1}{2} + \frac{1}{2}(2)\right]^{1/2}\left[\frac{1}{2} + \frac{1}{2}(1/2)\right]^{1/2}$$

$$= \hat{W}(1.05)[(3/4)\sqrt{2}] = \hat{W}(1.05)(1.0606601..)$$

$$= \hat{W}(1.113691). \tag{18}$$

By numerical coincidence (18)'s answer happens to give the same number as (17)'s. However, the reader will be able to calculate—using Equation (21e) below—that a diversified mixture of stock and cash can also raise for a macho Crâmer his risk-corrected return to well above 11%—actually to 21 + %, which is a discount-for-risk of only one-third off the money return itself.

Proper optimal diversification is thus seen to more than double risk-corrected returns of pure cash or pure equity in many of these examples. What about the peripatetic gunslinger professor? In those cases where 100% in either security brings only 5% of risk-corrected return, all of the attainable excess return over 5% is being lost. To put it in numerical perspective, suppose the professor has both $\ln(W)$ and a $500,000 nest egg. By diversifying across time, and subjectively earning 5% instead of 11%, doing the wrong thing, he is in effect throwing away $28,595 of his $500,000 $\bar{W}$ in each and every period!

A second computation will drive home the essential point. Going from logarithmic utility to the more realistic case of the Harmonic Mean, I enhance the stock's returns to ensure that its risk-corrected return does not fall short of cash's: With even odds, let its gain now be 1.05(2) (5/4) and let its loss be 1.05(1/2) (5/4). Computation of $H.M.$ then shows that being 100% in the stock now produces only the same risk-corrected 1.05 as safe cash does.

Being 50–50 in cash and in stock will do still better. (Indeed $x_1^* = 4/9$ can be shown to be best of all, but $x_1 = 1/2$ is a good approximation to that.) Here again the peripatetic professor is dead wrong to think that being one period in each averages out to the same happy diversification that comes from being *always* near to 50–50 in both. Actually, in this as in the earlier contrived example, diversification across time accomplishes *zero* true diversification! By contrast, true optimal diversification will be shown to here increase your risk-corrected return by from 1.05 to 1.16 2 / 3 %! Doing it right gains most for those who are most risk averse.

6. When your optimal equity ratio rule is linear

Equation (5e), the general equation to determine the numerical equity ratio x_1^*, assumes the remarkably simple *linear* form when (a) $U = \ln W$ or $U = W^\gamma/\gamma$, and (b) when the risky security has only *two* outcomes—a gain relative to cash's and a loss relative to cash's. Thus, let $P(z)$ in (1) have the following property:

$$\text{Prob}\{Z_1 = \bar{W}[1 + r][1 + g_j]\} = p_j;\ j = 1,2 \tag{19a}$$

$$p_j > 0,\ \sum_1^2 p_j = 1,\ \sum_1^2 p_j g_j > 0,\ g_2 < 0 \tag{19b}$$

In that case, for $U = \ln W$ à la Bernoulli

$$u^1(x_1; \bar{W}) = \sum_1^2 p_j \ln(\bar{W}[1 + r][1 + g_j x_1])$$

$$= \sum_1^2 p_j \ln(1 + g_j x_1) + \ln(\bar{W}[1 + r]) \tag{20a}$$

$$\partial u^1/\partial x_1 = 0 = \sum_1^2 p_j g_j [1 + g_j x_1]^{-1}$$

$$= [1 + g_1 x_1]^{-1}[1 + g_2 x_1]^{-1}[\sum_1^2 p_j g_j + g_1 g_2 x_1] \tag{20b}$$

$$\therefore x_1^* = \sum_1^2 p_j g_j / g_1 (-g_2) > 0. \tag{20c}$$

Thus, when as in (18) above the stock produces with even odds *twice* the $[1 + r]$ cash outcome or half that, Bernoulli's best x_1^* is verified to equal 1/2. This reconfirms that diversifying 50–50 into the stock and into the safe stuff more than doubles your risk-corrected certainty equivalent return, from 1.05 to (1.1136931).

What was just done, solving for x_1^* in the log W case, can now be generalized for W^γ/γ with $1 > \gamma \neq 0$. Equation (20) becomes

$$u^1(x_1; \bar{W}) = (\bar{W}[1 + r])^\gamma (\gamma)^{-1} \sum_1^2 p_j (1 + g_j x_1)^\gamma \tag{21a}$$

$$\partial u_1/\partial x_1 = 0 = (\bar{W}[1 + r])^\gamma [\sum_1^2 p_j g_j [1 + g_j x_1]^{\gamma - 1}]. \tag{21b}$$

Canceling out $(1 + g_1 x_1)^{\gamma - 1} (1 + g_2 x_1)^{\gamma - 1}$ and rearranging terms then gives

$$(p_1 g_1)(1 + g_2 x_1)^{\gamma - 1} = (-p_2 g_2)(1 + g_1 x_1)^{\gamma - 1} \tag{21c}$$

$$(p_1 g_1)^{1/(1-\gamma)}(1 + g_1 x_1) = (-p_2 g_2)^{1/(1-\gamma)}(1 + g_2 x_2) \tag{21d}$$

Writing $1/(1 - \gamma)$ as α, we find that (21c) implies

$$x_1^* = [(p_1 g_1)^\alpha - (-p_2 g_2)^\alpha]/[(p_1 g_1)^\alpha g_1 - (-p_2 g_2)^\alpha g_2] \tag{21e}$$

For $\gamma = -1$, the H.M. case, the reader can verify that $(p_1, p_2, g_1, g_2, \alpha) = (1/2, 1/2, (2)(5/4) - 1, (1/2)(5/4) - 1, 1/2)$, and we can calculate $x_1^* = 4/9$. Here, with optimal diversification in two periods, your certainty-equivalent H.M. works out to

$$\hat{W}^* = \bar{W}[1.05]^2[1.111...]^2 = \bar{W}[1.36111...] \tag{22a}$$

as against

$$\hat{W} = \bar{W}[1.05][1.05] = \bar{W}[1.1025] \tag{22b}$$

for the misguided professor who in one period is 100% in cash and in the other period is 100% in the stock. From any original $500,000, this savant would be subjectively throwing down the drain almost $70,000 in each investment period!

7. The exact theorem stated

Theorem. For those with *constant relative risk aversion*, always being optimally $(x_1^*; 1-x_1^*)$ in stocks and cash beats out in *Certainty Equivalent* $\hat{W}^*$ the alternative tactic of being x_1^* fraction of the subperiods 100% in the stock and the rest of the times being the $1 - x_1^*$ fraction of them 100% in cash.

It will suffice to consider the special case where x_1^* happens to be 1/2. In that case, after two periods

$$\text{Max}_x \hat{W} = \bar{W}[1 + r]^2[\omega_\gamma(1/2)]^2 > \bar{W}[1 + r]^2 [\omega_\gamma(0)\omega_\gamma(1)] \tag{23a}$$

inasmuch as, by definition,

$$\omega_\gamma(x_1^*) > \omega_\gamma(0), \omega_\gamma(x_1^*) > \omega_\gamma(1). \quad \text{QED.} \tag{23b}$$

8. Many-period diversification

Investing is rarely a one-period affair. Fortunately, the present proof of the superiority (under constant relative risk aversion) of diversifying *throughout* time over *across* time holds nicely for any number of time periods. The explicated Certainty Equivalent risk-corrected return can now be shown to compound over two or more periods exactly the way safe interest compounds: A sure $1 + r_1$ in one period becomes $(1 + r_1)(1 + r_2)$ in two periods; and in T periods we have $(1 + r_1)(1 + r_2) \ldots (1 + r_T)$, which does equal $(1 + r)^T$ if all the cash r's are the same. Similarly, let $1 + \rho_t$ be the risk-corrected (subjective!) return for the tth period as reckoned by my proposed Certainty Equivalent methodology (for a person with constant relative risk aversion $1 - \gamma$, and faced by a specified $P(z)$ stock-outcome probability function). Then it can now be shown that the compoundings $(1 + \rho_1)$, $(1 + \rho_1)(1 + \rho_2)$, ..., $(1 + \rho_1) \ldots (1 + \rho_T)$ do apply.

Recall that

$$\hat{W}_1^* = \bar{W}[1 + r] \omega_\gamma(x_1^*) \tag{24a}$$

$$\equiv \bar{W}[1 + r][1 + \rho_1^*], \text{ def. of } \rho_1^* \tag{24b}$$

Remember that x_1^* is the optimal equity fraction that maximizes your $E\{U(\ )\}$. Under white-noise market-efficiency stationarity, for your fixed γ, myopically

$$x_1^* = x_2^* = \ldots = x_T^* = x^* \tag{25a}$$

$$\rho_1^* = \rho_2^* = \ldots = \rho_T^* = \rho^* \tag{25b}$$

$$\hat{W}_T^* = \bar{W}[1 + r]^T[1 + \rho^*]^T \tag{25c}$$

By extension the proved superiority theorem cogently implies that

$$\hat{W}_T^* > \bar{W}[1 + r]^T \omega_\gamma(x_1) \omega_\gamma(x_2) \ldots \omega_\gamma(x_T) \tag{26a}$$

for *any* choice of $(x_1 \ x_2 \ \ldots \ x_T) \neq (x^* \ x^* \ \ldots \ x^*)$. This follows from the strong maximal condition

$$\omega_\gamma(x^*) > \omega_\gamma(x) \text{ for any } x \neq x^* \tag{26b}$$

The reader will realize how known changes in the $P(z)$ function as time passes will have to lead to calculable alterations in best x_t^*.

9. Discussion

The tenor of the present analysis puts the burden of proof on those who are tempted to be timers. Yes, do time if you do have genuine timing ability—but do so in prudent damped-down degree because of the demonstrated deadweight loss entailed by faulty diversification.

Here is a brief hint as to how to moderately use such genuine "timing ability" as you do have. The Bernoulli case is broadly indicative of what holds for all γ.

Instead of specifying even odds that the stock entails either (2) [1.05] or (1/2) [1.05], let the odds be even for the outcomes $2y(1.05)$ and $(1/2)y(1.05)$, where y is some random-variable *scale* parameter. Let's stipulate that, at time $t - 1$, you know the value of a variate v_{t-1} that is *correlated* with the random draw of y_t. For example

$$y_t = \bar{v}_{t-1} + \{\varepsilon_t\} \tag{27}$$

where $\bar{v}_{t-1}$ is known to equal alternately either 1/2 or 1 1/2, and where ε_t with even odds equals $+1/8$ or $-1/8$.

Surely, whenever you know that $\bar{v}_{t-1}$ has been high and that *a fortiori* y_t is likely to be high, then you ought to *raise* your x_1^* decision variable. In a straightforward way you now solve an augmented $E\{U(W_0)\}$ problem—augmented by pooling knowledge of the $\{\varepsilon_t\}$ probability information with your $P(z)$ belief. Rash folk may be led by overconfidence to change x_1^* violently, just as if they had exact knowledge of the as yet unknown ε_t variate. You should optimally eschew such violence.

The present article warns against much more than rash timing decisions. It warns also against hyper-activisms that are tempted out by hope of making rewarding sectoral bets that pull the composition of your equity portfolio away from the broad diversification that normally leads to maximal risk-corrected return. Yes, do overweight in health care or finance stocks when your evidence is strong that they will outperform the market. The harm you do yourself in unbalancing diversification begins small near the normal optimum: The square of a fraction begins tiny. But as you press your wish for *excess mean*, your self-imposed harm from augmented riskiness shoots up. Good theology says: If you must sin, sin little. Sin is sin because it promises more than it can deliver.

The Harmonic, Geometric, and various other power means used here will be recognized to resemble closely the Constant-Elasticity-of-Substitution (CES) production functions widely used in modern microeconomics. See Arrow et al. (1961). Examples are $((\Sigma_1^n c_j V_j^{-1})^{-1}$, $(\Sigma_1^n c_j V_j^{1/2})^2$, $(\Sigma c_j V_j^\alpha)^{1/\alpha}$, and of course Cobb–Douglas's $\Pi_1^n c_j V_j^{k_j}$, $\Sigma_1^n k_j - 1 = 0 < k_j$. In the probability context, $\Sigma_1^n c_j = 1$.

As soon as we leave models with constancy of relative-risk-aversion, ambiguities arise concerning how to calculate crisp risk-corrected returns. For one period, as in Equation (7) above, we can define certainty equivalents as

$$U(\hat{W}_1) = E\{U(\bar{W}[1+r][1-x_1] + \bar{W}[1+r]Z_1 x_1)\} \tag{28a}$$

$$U(\hat{W}_1^*) = \underset{x_1}{\text{Max}}\ U(\hat{W}_1) \tag{28b}$$

$$\hat{W}_1^* = \underset{x_1}{\text{Max}}\ U^{-1}[E\{U(\bar{W}[1+r][1+\{Z_1-1\}x_1^*])\}] \tag{28c}$$

$$= \omega_1(X_1[\bar{W}_1], \bar{W}_1) \tag{28d}$$

$\hat{W}_1^*/\bar{W}$ not independent of $\bar{W}$ in the general case. \hfill (28e)

What about two or more periods? It is not the *optimum optimorum* to decide in advance to limit yourself to $x_1 \equiv x_2$. Now, as discussed in Chow (1993) and Samuelson (1996), you must use Bellman–Lagrange dynamic stochastic programming procedures.

No longer can we deduce that, for some definable ω of (x) function,

$$\hat{W}_2 = \hat{W}_1 \omega(x^*) = \bar{W}\omega(x^*)^2 \text{ or } \hat{W}_T = \bar{W}\omega(x^*)^T \equiv \hat{W}_{T-k}\omega(x^*)^k. \tag{29}$$

The difficulty is intrinsic. (Of course, if over all the ranges of W_t that will occur and that are near enough to $\bar{W}$, the Arrow–Pratt $A(W)$ *approximates* to constancy, then the simple compounding deduced thus far in this article will be very nearly valid.) The final section deals with nonconstant relative risk aversion, the general case.

10. The completely general theorem

Dropping completely any constancy of relative risk aversion, I conclude with proof that for all concave or risk-averse $U(W)$ functions, across-time diversifications must be inferior to within-time diversification for all portfolios choosing between safe cash and stochastic stocks that enjoy a higher expected money return.

Consider multiple time periods: $t = 1, 2, ..., T > 1$. You begin with $\bar{W}_T$ and wish to end up with the best $E\{U(W_0)\}$, where

$$W_{t-1} = W_t[R(1 - x_t) + RZ_t x_t], t = T, T - 1, ..., 2, 1 \tag{30a}$$

$$E\{Z_t\} = \int_0^\infty zP(dz) > R \geq 1 \tag{30b}$$

and you wish to select $(x_T^*, ..., x_2^*, x_1^*)$ so as to achieve $\text{Max} E\{U(W_0)\}$.

The Bellman–Lagrange dynamic stochastic programming algorithm for this involves recursively resolving for the sequence $(U(W) \equiv W_0(W), U_1(W), ..., U_{T-1}(W); X_1[W], X_2[W], ..., X_T[W])$ by means of the recursion relations

$$0 = W_t \int_0^\infty U'_{t-1}(W_t R + R[z_t - 1]x_t^*) R(z_t - 1) dP(z_t), x_t^* \equiv x_t[W] \tag{31a}$$

$$U_t(W_t) \equiv \int_0^\infty U_{t-1}(W_t R + W_t R[z_t - 1]X_t[W_t]) dP(z_t), t = 1, ..., T. \tag{31b}$$

It is well known that when $U(W)$ is strictly concave, so will be all Bellman derived utility functions $U_t(W)$. In that case, when at each time t you solve (31a)'s one-period problem, your optimal x_t^* *must* be positive by virtue of (30b)'s assurance that the equity investment is a better-than-fair option in comparison with safe cash's total money return of R. Because the flip-flop between all cash and all stocks involves some x_t^*'s being zero, that kind of diversification against time has thus been effectively ruled out as a solution to (31a). QED.

Remarks: A similar proof will rule out flip-flopping a little bit above and below the actual best $\{x_t^*\}$ numbers. Such timing ploys are warranted only when the postulate of white noise is replaced by one in which you have a private Maxwell Demon (or other model) that does accurately vouchsafe to you valid timing prescience. Also, this proof will apply to stochastic choice criteria that depart in the Machina (1982) manner from the dogma of Expected {Utility} maximization: Any cardinal *functional* of the Probability distribution of W outcomes will be covered provided only that it is uniformly "risk-averse" and suitably smooth.

The reader should appreciate that the Markowitz–Tobin efficiency frontier in the (mean, variance) space has been left behind in the present discussion. Instead of Sharpe (1966) ratio, or Jensen (1968) or Treynor (1965) or Modigliani-Modigliani (1996) measures, I am proposing that we appraise past performance of a specified fund in terms of the S&P or other market measure by calculating for each their past Harmonic Mean, or Geometric Mean, or whatever Mean your relevant best approximation γ calls for. That way you can debunk performance in a bull market that comes merely from explicit or implicit *leverage* rather than from ability to pick winners.

Acknowledgments

I owe thanks to the Center for Japan–U.S. Business and Economic Studies at the NYU Stern School of Business, where I am the Long-Term Credit Bank of Japan Visiting Professor of Political Economy. I am again in debt for editorial assistance to Janice M. Murray, my coworker at MIT. The late Stan Ulam, who 60 years ago challenged me to assert a proposition in economics that was both nonobvious and true, motivated from the grave writing up this research.

References

Arrow, Kenneth J., Hollis A. Chenery, Bagicha S. Minha, and Robert M. Solow. (1961). "Capital-Labor Substitution and Economic Efficiency," *Review of Economics and Statistics* August, 225–250.

Chow, Gregory. (1993). "Optimal Control Without Solving the Bellman Equation," *Journal of Economic Dynamics and Control* 17, 621–630.

Jensen, Michael E. (1968). "The Performance of Mutual Funds in the Period 1945–1964," *Journal of Finance* May, 389–415.

Machina, Mark. (1982). "'Expected Utility' Analysis Without the Independence Axiom," *Econometrica* 50, 277–323.

Modigliani, Franco, and Leah Modigliani. (1996). "The Modigliani-Modigliani Measure of Risk Adjusted Performance (MAP)." Paper presented at the Financial Economists Roundtable, Newport, RI, July 8, 1996.

Samuelson, Paul A. (1989). "The Judgment of Economic Science on Rational Portfolio Management: Indexing, Timing, and Long-Horizon Effect," *Journal of Portfolio Management* Fall, 4–12.

Samuelson, Paul A. (1990). "Asset Allocation Could Be Dangerous to Your Health: Pitfalls in Across-Time Diversification," *Journal of Portfolio Management* Spring, 5–8.

Samuelson, Paul A. (1996). "The Irreducible Role of Derived Marginal Utility in Dynamic Stochastic Programming," *Pacific Economic Review* 1, 3–11.

Sharpe, William F. (1966). "Mutual Fund Performance," *Journal of Business, Supplement on Security Prices* 39, 119–138.

Treynor, Jack L. (1965). "How to Rate Management Investment Funds," *Harvard Business Review* January–February, 43, 63–75.

467

DOGMA OF THE DECADE: SURE-THING RISK EROSION
FOR LONG-HORIZON INVESTORS
Paul A. Samuelson, January, 1997

    America is living in the biggest stock market boom in our history. Wall Street beats out in total return London, Paris, Frankfurt, Hong Kong and Singapore; but markets, almost everywhere, are in a one-way rise. The Roaring Twenties has by now been well-surpassed both in duration and broadness of public participation. And the long bull rise from 1942 to 1962 cannot compare with today's ongoing explosion in equity values.

    Many well informed observers find this puzzling. The Main Street U.S. economy is to be sure doing well: the incumbent President Clinton benefitted when our real GDP growth rate in the 1990s puts to shame European and Japanese performances; the same holds when America's net job creation on a population-corrected basis beats that of leaders abroad. Moreover, inflation of the price level has been reassuringly contained up until now.

    However, it is an open secret that we also live now in the new Ruthless Economy, where downscaling and disappointing productivity growth makes the middle- and lower-income classes newly apprehensive and stagnating in their earnable living levels.

    I cannot predict future moves in the Dow-Jones Index, but I do not find the contemporary bull market puzzling. One dogma now pervades investors in Wall Street, LaSalle Street and Main Street and it suffices to explain the story. Here is that dogma in a nutshell.

> Be a long-term investor. Buy and hold a diversified portfolio of common stocks. One hundred and fifty years of experience -- a sample of 12 x 150 = 1,860 monthly data of experience -- demonstrate that *always* those who invest for at least a fifteen-year horizon do come out ahead of their timid brethren by investing in equities rather than bank accounts, money-market funds or diversified indexes of bonds. This is a two-way truth. What the *facts* of economic history prove is allegedly further proved by the *mathematical laws* of probability: the Law of Large Numbers, which insures our ships at sea and life expectancies at home, supposedly guarantees that when the number of uncertain coin tosses, N, becomes large, the probability of equality between numbers of heads and tails mathematically converges to 1 as N goes to infinity. So, allegedly, with the superiority of stocks for large-N investor horizons.

2

    If true, this is a compelling dogma. It makes for good sleep at night and comfortable retirement living. (Only brokers who live on churning accounts, or IRS tax collectors who levy on capital gains actually realized when portfolios turn over, would care to keep this good-news formula quiet.)

    Is the dogma true as told? Alas, No. Nevertheless, those who believed in it before and after the great October 19, 1987 worldwide Stock Crash are smiling all the way to the bank (or, better, to the mutual fund). And Asset-Allocating Timers, like Mr. Vinik who used to run the biggest Magellan Fund for Fidelity, regret they had not drunk deeper of the good whisky that delivers the joy and peace being now exported to Main Street from Wall Street.

    Here is how to test the *correct* statistical influence of time horizon N on rational equity tolerance. Since we have only one history of markets, we need to go beyond that sample of 1 (which constitutes a lot less than a sample of 1,850 independent items).

    First, write down all those 1,850 percentage changes in stock prices on as many slips of paper. Put them in a big hat. Shake vigorously. Then draw at random a new couple of thousand of tickets, each time replacing the last draw and shaking vigorously. That way we can generate as many *new* representative possible histories of *future* equity markets.

    Second, is it true that in *all* these histories you *always* come out ahead in stocks rather than safe-but-less-volatile securities? Definitely not. Most of the time the buy-and-hold common stock investors *do* beat their more cautious neighbors; and, as the time horizon N becomes larger, the odds do grow that the plungers will win the duel. But it is also true that large N *brings bigger losses* in those inevitable times when you do lose. Canny risk averters should always keep in mind, in a rational non-paranoid way, the pains they will feel in those probability-calculated *bad outcome* scenarios. (Ask yourself: Will stepping down toward a poverty level, when that rarely but inevitably does happen, outweigh for me the pleasures that occur in those likely outcomes when my equity nest egg does increase?) When each of us tries to do that, those of us who are more truly risk averse will rationally hedge our bets by holding down our portfolio's fraction exposed to volatile equities.

    Yes, in those new histories that the future will bring -- even when past probabilities still do operate intact -- you definitely could lose and lose big no matter whether you have 10 or 20 or 80 years to go before retirement. (And for calculating folks of the kind who would pick the same stock/cash fraction at a million dollars of wealth as at a hundred thousand dollars, it is a mathematical theorem: Select for time horizon N = 20 *exactly* the same equity fraction as for N = 10 or 1 or 80!)

83

The current dogma proves too much. If 60 percent in stocks beats 50 percent sure thing, then 100 percent beats 60 percent: and leveraging to put 110 or 200 percent in stocks beats 100 percent! Stop-loss orders and rebalancings, hedge fund plungers have learned the hard way, cannot rebut the stern theorem: If you always hold more than 101 percent in stocks, in long enough time the Law of Large Numbers implies that the probability goes to one you will go bankrupt.

Are you still doubtful? Unconvinced? Let's go from academic mathematics to practical insurance. Dr. Zvi Bodie of the Boston University School of Management, acclaimed Mr. Pension Expert, will be our guide in buying portfolio insurance covering any shortfalls of outcome below the 3-5 percent *safe* rate of total return available from past money market funds. What insurance premium must the one-year investor pay to be guaranteed *against* ending up with *less* than the safe five percent of a Money Market Fund? And what $Premium_N$ must one pay for time horizons $N = 2, 4, 10, 40, \ldots$ so as assuredly not to go below safe rates of total return? The Black-Scholes options formula, Dr. Bodie points out, must be used by any insurance firm that you can count on to stay solvent. (The Ponzi shop down the street will quote better terms but don't shoot your own knee!) Does $Premium_N$ go *down* as N grows -- as would be the case if the current dogma with its misunderstanding of the Law of Large Numbers implies?

No. And No. The bad news is that the $Premium_N$ *grows* with N, and when N gets to infinity the Premium eats up *all* your excess return! Some bargain. Total risk *grows* rather than diminishes with the time horizon. Overhead loads and insurance company profits aside, *whenever you pay the needed premium to cover any losses that go below the modest safe rate, you are left only with that safe rate*! The First Two Laws of Thermodynamics dictate: No Perpetual Motion Machine is possible. The same goes for the Black-Scholes-Bodie Thirteenth Law of (Probability) Economics: No extra gain without the pain of risk exposure.

I warn again being misunderstood. Professor Samuelson does not advise against 100% in equities; or 110%; or 80%; or 10%. I can demonstrate reasons why folks who do understand *their* own degree of risk tolerance will want to just buy and hold diversified common stocks. And can demonstrate why more risk averse folks should eschew current fashions. My point is this: Don't do what you do for the mistaken reasons given by the current dogma.

One last warning. During the last 150 years stocks did as well as they did because most folks did *not* act on the dogma.

If ever in the future belief in this dogma becomes virtually unanimous, it must self-destruct. We will then be in a Japan-like stock and land bubble -- with no anchor for prudent value. No cap can then be found for Price/Earnings ratios. When 15 becomes 20 and 20 becomes 80, and 80 becomes the over-200 P/E of the 1987 Nippon Phone company, only those innocents who believe in the Tooth Fairy will believe that new buyers of the Dow must in the mass end up with yachts that their cautious neighbor can't afford.

Caveat Emptor. Let the buyer beware -- an old dogma not yet repealed by science.

The judgment of economic science on rational portfolio management: Indexing, timing, and long-horizon effects

"Forsake search for needles that are so very small in haystacks that are so very large."

Paul A. Samuelson

Think Tank: One out of twenty alcoholics can learn to become a moderate social drinker.

Experienced Clinician: Even if true, act as if it were false, for you will never identify that one in twenty, and in the attempt five in twenty will be ruined.

Under the title "Challenge to Judgment," I wrote in the first issue of this Journal that the ball was in the court of the conventional believers in discretionary portfolio selection. The vast preponderance of pre-1974 statistical evidence suggested the following:

1. The security analyst industry does *not* on the average perform quite as well over time as an indexed portfolio that passively holds stocks in proportions approximating their respective market capitalizations.
2. Those lucky money managers who happen in any period to beat the comprehensive averages in total return seem primarily to have been merely lucky. Being on the honor roll in 1974 does not make you appreciably more likely to be on the 1975 honor roll. Indeed, one can add that a year's winners as a group are prone to larger-than-average variability of performance and no better long-run mean performance: for the reason that you have a better chance to look like a great performer if you manage less money, if you diversify less, if you favor high-beta and high-variance stocks, and this would remain true even if large endowments stood to do just as well as small, and if volatile individual stocks promised no better means than less volatile stocks.
3. If money managers do not on the average deliver superior performance, and if high turnover of selections merely generates high transaction costs (explicit brokerage commissions plus hard-to-calculate other costs), then a buy-and-hold program of broad diversification is the canny way to go. (Diversification means international as well as domestic, fixed-principal securities as well as equities, real estate as well as market securities, possibly even a modicum of commodity and fi-

PAUL A. SAMUELSON is Institute Professor of Economics Emeritus at the Massachusetts Institute of Technology in Cambridge (MA 02139). He owes thanks for partial support to his Long Term Credit Bank of Japan Visiting Professorship at the Japan-U.S. Center for Economics and Business at New York University's Stern Graduate School of Management Science. He also owes thanks to Aase Huggins and Eva Hakala for appreciated editorial assistance; and thanks again to Robert C. Merton for valuable conversations.

nancial futures. It entails what critics of TIAA–CREF like to call "settling for *mediocrity*," an odd phrase to use if the superstar returns are not attainable on a risk-corrected basis.)

4. In 1974 the findings of economic science did not, in my interpretation, provide either deductive proof or cogent empirical evidence that security markets were so "strongly efficient" as to make it implausible that *any* persons or methods could beat the odds on a risk-corrected basis. People differ. Some lose their money fast, some slow. Some may react quickly to new relevant information; some may have better access to such information, perhaps because they have invested resources in acquiring that access. Some people discern and calculate the relevant odds better than others. Such folk can make fortunes from their talents. They are worth hiring by those with plentiful capital and the acumen to recognize a genuine talent for long-run performing.

My point was that the competitive market would be expected to bid up the rents of such extraordinary investors, so that much of the excess total return they could garner for you would be theirs and not yours. (As hundreds of the largest portfolios of pension funds, universities, mutual funds, insurance companies, and foundations, which could best afford to hire this best talent, do not in recorded fact do better than indexed portfolios, there cannot exist very many superstars, and those who exist must be very hard indeed to recognize.)

HOW NOW? SAME STORY

Fifteen years have passed since my "challenge to judgment." What has been the further testimony of the 1970s and 1980s? What, in sum, is the judgment of 1989 economic science on the challenge to judgment?

Broadly speaking, the case for efficient markets is a bit stronger in 1989 than it was in 1974, or in 1953 when Holbrook Working and Maurice Kendall were hypothesizing that stock and commodity price changes are pretty much a random walk (or a white-noise martingale). Out of the thousands of published and unpublished statistical testings of various forms of the hypothesis, a few dozen representing a minuscule percentage have isolated profitable exceptions to the theory.

The story is not quite so bad as the story of ESP or other parapsychological phenomena. Weak trace elements of clairvoyance are occasionally reported, but on examination they accumulate into nothing interesting. As my children used to say: BORING. BORING.

So it is with the few not-very-significant apparent exceptions to weak efficiency of markets. Here are examples of minor exceptions to micro-efficient markets.

1. Maybe closed-end funds that sell at a discount to asset value give the calculating investor a slim edge. (Warning: unrealized capital gains and/or high management expenses may justify a generous discount.) A stock exchange member, who is best positioned to engage in short-selling, might garner small pickings from selling short the newly offered closed-end funds that persuasive salespeople sell to unsophisticated buyers even though their price is likely to soon go to a discount below initial asset value. There is probably a better way to make a small living.

2. Small stocks have risen relative to large capitalization in January for several years. Mondays fare differently from Fridays. Opening and morning price movements have been observed to differ from late-day movements. Perhaps as fast as people recognize these oddities and begin to act on them, they will disappear as systematic effects?

3. Occasionally, and particularly in emergency times, arbitragable price discrepancies appear on the screen. Quick small killings may then be possible. It is a living but it does not come without some work and intelligence. For program arbitrageurs, particularly those with plentiful capital and facing insiders' commission and short-selling rules, persistent profits may be attainable. Pension funds and foundations, as well as ordinary private investors, might better ignore these exotics.

4. A few hundred trend-following traders may display a genuine knack for earning supernormal profits. Some scores of thousands of others, who to themselves look like such virtuosi and appear to you and me indistinguishable from them, constantly erode their principal trying to do the same things. If you doubt my cynicism, contemplate how bad the mob does in public trading contests. If you doubt my limited gullibility as to the existence of successful traders, study intensively the fortunes of the existent set of successful futures traders with excellent batting averages over the decades. They become very rich, and many stay rich. Some of those who end being shot down in flames do so because their risk tolerance causes them to pyramid: Then they must be right not most of the time but all of the time — a manifest impossibility.

A CASE STUDY

What I believe can be dramatized by a true case. A new foundation deliberated on how it should invest a portfolio that was somewhere between $100 million and $1 billion. It consulted some consultants (and some academics like me). After dithering in cash throughout much of the 1982–1985 bull market, it decided to hire eight money managers — a perfect copout. It drops the worst periodically and adds new hopefuls. Its results are way short of mediocre: Its deadweight costs could support a well-run portfolio of $10 billion. The donor does not even acquire peace of mind from this absolutely standard mode of operation. (The eight managers all have good reputations; the consultants who help pick the managers all have good reputations. Should one weep or giggle?)

A SECOND CASE STUDY

During the same period a donor left an Ivy League university a few million dollars, specifying that the gift had to be separately identified in the portfolio and separately invested. The busy treasurer asked a faculty committee to spend an hour deciding how these funds should be invested for the next five years.

With no deep thought they recommended:
1. Put 60% in stocks, 25% in money market funds, and 15% in junk bonds.
2. Specifically, put half the stocks in the Vanguard Index Trust (S&P 500); one-third in the Windsor Fund; one-sixth in the Explorer Fund, concentrating on emerging venture enterprises. Because of low expense ratios, Vanguard money market and bond funds were selected.

Like Rip Van Winkle, everyone went to sleep. After some years the portfolio had grown enormously. The Explorer Fund did most poorly, the Windsor Fund best; the Index Fund caught the 1984–1987 rise, the post-Crash fall, and the post-post-Crash rise. So passive was the monitoring that there was no rebalancing of equities when they came to exceed 80% of the portfolio.

The total cost of administering the several-million dollar portfolio was below one-half of 1% of asset value. MBA candidates around the country would nevertheless award this caper an A+ — not because it happened to be so lucky but because it adhered so well to Markowitz–Sharpe precautionary wisdoms. (The fact that one-third of the equities were given to John Neff at Windsor rather than to the Index Trust revealed that the advisors were not fully subscribers to the dogma of efficient markets!)

EXCEPTIONAL TALENTS

To dramatize that I have no methodological reluctance to believe that some persons can systematically garner superior risk-corrected returns, I have a little list. It is the meagre fruits of a lifetime of observation and research, and it makes no pretence to being complete or even optimal.

Warren Buffett. He is on everyone's list. Although a professed disciple of Benjamin Graham's fundamentalism, Buffett's edge comes from his genius, not his precepts. When Buffett says, shucks, it's easy; all you have to do is look for a business that has a franchise — don't you believe it. The franchise International Harvester once had is long gone. When Berkshire Hathaway, Buffett's fund, bought into the *Washington Post*, it was anything but clear that this would turn out marvelously well. (I was at that time a Buffett groupie, and I was a *Newsweek* columnist in the *Post* stable; nevertheless I lacked a rational conviction for adding to my portfolio more of *Washington Post* stock, just as at the present time I am in doubt about Buffett's Salomon acquisition.) Will Rogers says to buy stocks that are going to go up. Graham and Buffett say to buy stocks that are bargains. No cinch to do! (The treasurer of the National Academy of Sciences sent members of the finance committee copies of a *Forbes* item describing how Grinnell College took millions of capital gains on a TV station purchase suggested by Buffett. To the treasurer's query, "Why doesn't the Academy do this sort of thing?" I replied, "Good idea. How do we start?")

Knowledge of Buffett's skills may be already fully discounted in the marketplace. Now that B–H has gone up more than a hundredfold, it is at a premium to book value. Buffett himself reports doubts that he can find for the growing total that he must invest opportunities comparable to those in the past.

In short, the market shows some efficiency in recognizing the occasional genius. (Remark: One trait Buffett does have that is attractive to me is this: There is ample evidence from Buffett's past behaviors that he acts exactly as much for me as a minority stockholder as for himself. That is rare, not common, and by itself warrants some premium.)

John Templeton. His record in picking international stocks is superlative over a long period of time. Although it went against the aesthetic grain, I once paid a minuscule load to invest in one of the Templeton funds. I had no reason for regret, even though the results would have been even more impressive if Templeton had not shared my own fears that the Japanese stock market was in a bubble.

Mr. Templeton, however, is past three score and ten. "What will you do for me next?" is the question asked in the hard-boiled marketplace. (Remark: A Templeton generally performs better than his stated analyses would cause you to expect. It is not that his public remarks are silly or naive; it is that most speakers with those views could not win a high school stock-picking contest.)

John Neff. The Windsor Fund has been a success story for so long that ordinary statistical significance tests do not deny its positive risk-corrected expected "alpha." Its staff is small; its rationalizations are reasonable.

Most of the time the Vanguard Group closes Neff's funds to new money now that their total size handicaps potential returns per dollars. That undermines them as a useful exception to the efficient market dogma.

Kurt Lindner, Michael Price, Peter Lynch. Again, here are names of long-term performers. Again, the world has already beaten paths to the Lindner funds, the Mutual Shares fund, and the (Fidelity) Magellan fund, bringing on the law of diminishing returns associated with size of principal. Again, intermittent or permanent closing of the funds to new money has taken place. Again, our stories about exceptions to efficient markets are partially undermined so far as practical investing opportunities are concerned.

Paul Tudor Jones. Operating as short-term traders in various futures markets (financial instruments, foreign exchange, grains, metals, meats, bonds, options, stock indexes, and particular equities), the Tudor Funds and related funds directed by Jones have generated a record in recent years that would be hard to happen in a random-walk model. Nineteen eighty-seven, the year of the Market Crash, is said to have brought to Jones many tens of millions of dollars, with Black Monday itself bringing record trading gains.

A clipping service that brought you all public utterances by Jones would not inspire confidence in a hard-boiled econometrician: Elliot Waves, Fibonacci numbers, and various Prechter paradigms sound to many like science fiction. Yet the knack for positive gains must puzzle the unbiased observer who believes in strong versions of efficient markets. (Amos Hostetter, Sr., whose picture is on the wall of the Commodities Corporation in Princeton, quietly garnered positive returns in commodity trading over virtually every year in the half century before his death. CC assigned an apprentice to learn his methods, and a small privately printed book summarizes the findings. Armed with this volume, I doubt that I could perform well — illustrating again that the art of the proficient trader is indeed an art and not a reproducible scientific method; if this description of mine is near the mark, that does not necessarily imply any mysticism or "luck" involved in Jones–Hostetter processes nor does it deny the extreme rarity of the skill in question and the extreme difficulty of identifying where it exists. Remember again how *badly* the rank and file do in audited trading contests, and these are largely professionals who have devoted years and fortunes to developing trading skills!)

Whenever a Paul Tudor Jones makes millions for a few people, the attempt of thousands of people to identify or be a similar success entails losses of hundreds of millions to a thousand others. Such attempts of course contribute to "market liquidity" and to the overhead of a vast brokerage industry.

Is that the end of my list? No, a few more names could be ventured. (Also, some superstars of former years may have lost their superlative batting averages. Remember Tsai and Alger? This reminds us that life may not be a *stationary* time series, and all tests of significance do need to be taken with a grain of salt.)

If each analyst in the Long-term Top Dozen is so very good, why is it still prudent to diversify among them? That is because the market is a fickle mechanism. Methods that work well today — low P/Es, franchise companies, glamorous growers, low-capitalization companies — can become overpopular and thereby self-destruct. There is a time to remember and a time to forget.

I conclude this *ad hominem* section with its indicated finding: A thousand to ten thousand money managers all look about equally good or bad. Each expects to do 3% better than the mob. Each has put together a convincing story. After the fact, hardly ten out of ten thousand perform in a way that convinces an experienced student of inductive evidence that a long-term edge over indexing is likely. As with the alcoholics in my article's initial quotation, it may be the better part of wisdom to forsake search for needles that are so very small in haystacks that are so very large.

RX FOR CANNY INVESTING

The same wisdom is suggested for the largest common stock fund in the world (College Retirement Equities Fund with more than $40 billion of assets) or for the middling investor with assets from $40 thousand to $40 million.

1. Decide what proportions of wealth in common stocks, money market funds, and longer-term bonds your own risk tolerance leaves you comfortable with (e.g., 60% in stocks, 25% in money market funds, 15% in bonds). There is no scientific way to determine what is optimal for these fractions.
2. Put 80% to 100% of your targeted equity portfolio in a no-load version of an index fund (e.g., Vanguard's Index Trust for the S&P 500 and possibly its smaller-stock tier; or Wells Fargo's similar vehicles; 10% to 25% in similar foreign market vehicles also makes sense.). The *full* management and other inclusive fees ought to be as low as three-tenths of 1% of principal per year — in contrast to

the usual 1% to 2% in the mutual fund, pension, and trust worlds.
3. Lean-cost bond and money funds are similarly indicated.

The investor who runs a portfolio of five to fifty asset items is (usually) being self-indulgent. The hobby can be an expensive one over forty years of the individual's life cycle. Blowing a thousand dollars a year at the gaming tables of Las Vegas might be a comparative bargain, but of course the gratifications to the ego may be less for many temperaments that are not so much desirous of taking risks as of proving an ability to beat life's odds by personal cleverness.

As funds accumulate in active life, purchases can be made in the indicated proportions (or, more accurately, can be made so as to keep the totals *rebalanced* to those proportions). Sales (in retirement, for educational expenses, for extraordinary consumption purposes) can be guided by the same balancing considerations.

TO TIME OR NOT TO TIME?

No-load mutual fund vehicles offer an efficient mode for the would-be "market timer," who desires to sell stocks dear, putting the proceeds into bonds that are about to rise, . . . , and so forth in a cycle of extra total returns.

There is a trap here. As will be discussed, many call themselves cyclical timers; but God chooses few to be net winners over each cycle. "Be good, Sweet Maid, and let them that will be clever." This can be good advice for prudent investors too — as the dismal timing record of college endowments has suggested.

My university, MIT, arranged for professors to be able to invest special tax-deferred funds in an insurance company's program that permitted by a phone call switches from an equity fund to a bond fund or vice versa. One MIT professor — I hope it was a chemical engineer and not an economist — the first year switched sixteen times back and forth between stocks and bonds!

At first uncritical thought, I decided that no one could be so clever or unlucky as to hurt one's self much during so many quasi-random switches. So to speak, this timer at first appeared to me to be equivalent to a sedate colleague who all twelve months of the year kept 50% in stocks and 50% in bonds.

I was wrong to think this. Diversification across time is *not* the same as diversification during each time period. Instead it involves a *lowered* risk-corrected mean return.

Here is a crude hint as to why random diversification across time is an inefficient way to diversify. Suppose Professor A can invest in safe cash and be sure of getting back each dollar of principal, or can buy a stock that doubles each dollar when a coin shows heads and halves it when tails comes up. All tosses are randomly fair and independent. Dr. A (foolishly) half the time puts 100% in stocks, half the time 100% in cash. An orthodox colleague, Professor B, at *all* times puts half in cash and half in stocks.

Consider four time periods when H and T each come up twice (but in an unpredictable order). See how A's initial $10,000 ends up growing more slowly in the four periods than does B's:

A's Terminal Wealth = $10,000 $(2)(1)\left(\frac{1}{2}\right)(1)$

= $10,000

B's Terminal Wealth = $10,000 $\left[\frac{1}{2} + \frac{1}{2}(2)\right]^2 \left[\frac{1}{2} + \frac{1}{2}\left(\frac{1}{2}\right)\right]^2$

= $10,000 $[3/2]^2[3/4]^2$

= $12,656.25 > $10,000   QED

More rigorous proof of the inefficiency of time diversification as against genuine diversification might go as follows. Suppose both A and B are risk-averse, as for example being maximizers of the Expected Utility of their wealth outcomes in the Bernoulli fashion, MaxE[logW]. When all equally likely four-toss coin outcomes are enumerated, [HHHH, THHH, . . ., TTTT], calculation will show it to be the case that it is exactly as if A threw away one-ninth of the initial $10,000 to indulge the whim of possessing timing ability. Dull B can, so to speak, laugh all the way to the bank with an extra $1,111.11 of equivalent well-being. (Of course, if A really had a Maxwell Demon that gave omniscience, A's terminal wealth in the HTHT case would have been a whopping $40,000 [= $10,000(2)(1)(2)(1)]; in the HHHH case, it would be $160,000! Yes, and if my Aunt Sally had wheels, she'd be a stagecoach.)

MACRO VERSUS MICRO EFFICIENCY

I believe the evidence is strong in favor of considerable market efficiency at the *micro* level. Thus, if GM stock did not generally decline between a before-dividend and after-dividend date, you and I could buy it and profit overnight from receiving its dividend, while selling it the next day. In doing so we would correct the inefficiency and make money in the process. Thus, a security's price is always bid to a level from which we must expect it could subsequently either rise or fall. That is the "martingale" property of an efficient market as against a "sure-to-rise" property. For early deductive enunciation of this theorem on prior discounting, see P. Samuelson [1965].[1]

Suppose, however, a Professor Modigliani

thinks in 1975 that the level of the Dow Jones or S&P index is too low — perhaps because Tobin's Q ratio is way below unity[2] or because investors don't properly know how to allow for inflation. What can he do about it? Modigliani cannot make money arbitraging out any discordant relationship. Indeed, even if he is right, Modigliani could lose his shirt arguing with the tape that can continue to make the same mistake that it has long been making.

We see why there are two camps among the economic scientists. Fischer Black's mantra is that the market is always in equilibrium: during Black Monday, on the previous Friday or Monday, and on the day after Monday. Robert Shiller of Yale believes the market is capable of generating self-fulfilling oscillations above and below any fundamentalist's discounted dividend parity.

On the whole, I side with Shiller and Modigliani and am prepared to doubt *macro* market efficiency.

This gives one hope for a rational approach toward "timing." However, hope is no guarantee that net success will reward the attempt to time.

Wall Street is always winning yesterday's war. The few asset allocation programs that lightened up on equities before October 1987 got great publicity. Naturally therefore 1988 and 1989 witnessed many popular asset allocation strategies. Alas, in view of the recovery of equities from November 1987 to mid-1989, the short-term results have been rather dismal for those portfolios light on equities during the 1989 bull market.

Remark: Roger Babson was famous for correctly calling the 1929 Crash. Not many remember that Babson turned bearish as early as 1925, so that few of his faithful clients benefited net from this early asset allocation service. Similarly, the astute investor Laurence Tisch was bearish long before the eventual 1987 Crash. NYU and the Twentieth Century Fund must rue the advice that made them miss the 1982-1987 bull market. The critical test of a timing attempt is not whether it led to selling before the peak; did it lead you to buy back in while prices still were lower than when you sold? That is the crucial question.

RED RATHER THAN WHITE NOISE?

Modern experts in finance — examples are Fama and French [1988] and Poterba and Summers [1987] — begin to put some credence in deviations from the strict random walk dogma. Over time horizons as long as a few years, they think to be able to discern some mean-reversion patterns of negative serial autocorrelation. Instead of "white noise" this is "red noise."

If truly significant, mean reversion entails modification in certain dogmas of rational behavior.[3] As I shall show, the scientific case for *long-run* equity investing is provided with some rescue.

RATIONAL AGE EFFECTS ON RISK-TAKING?

1. As you grow older and the time horizon of your investing shortens, should you rationally cut down on your exposure to lucrative but risky equities?

2. And, when you are young with many chances ahead to recoup any transient losses, can you afford to take a "businessman's risk?"

3. Can college endowments and portfolios of permanent foundations, expecting to be operating and growing virtually forever, by the same logic largely ignore short-run riskiness and invest heavily in common stocks with high average mean returns, relying on "diversification over time and the cancellations of repeated chances in the Law of Large Numbers"?

These are old and basic questions. The conventional wisdom gives them an affirmative answer:

1. Long-horizon investors allegedly can, *ceteris paribus*, tolerate more risk and thereby garner higher mean returns.

2. The rational age-specific pattern of asset allocation allegedly involves some tapering down with maturity of equities relative to lower-variance assets.

3. Thus, although CREF is careful not to express judgments about optimal strategies for its professional participants to follow, readers of TIAA–CREF's many publications could be forgiven for tacitly presuming that it is more normal at advanced ages to shift from the equities of CREF to the bonds and nominal-principal investments of TIAA than vice versa.

Like so much that belongs to the conventional wisdom, this described dogma has not as yet earned the *imprimatur* of science. Thus, when Samuelson [1969] was motivated to investigate rational life-cycle investing for those who maximize expected utility and who possess constant-relative-risk aversion, there emerged the surprising theorem that your uncle with few years to go should hold exactly the same fraction of wealth in risky *(random-walk)* stocks as he did when young and as you do now. This mandate that rational investors should be *myopic*, ignoring the length of their time horizon, is a specific denial of the conventional wisdom.

HOW TIME ADDS TO RISK

How is such a nihilistic result possible? Here are relevant considerations.

Repeated investing over many periods does not cause risk to wash out in the long run. Insurance companies do not eliminate total risk by insuring more and more ships. As shown in the discussion of fallacies of interpreting the Law of Large Numbers in Samuelson [1963], each new independent risk adds to the *absolute total* of risk. But *total absolute* risk grows as the *square root* of the number of *independent* ships insured and not in proportion to their numbers. It is the *subdividing* of risk by bringing in new members to the insuring syndicate that, together with bringing in new independent ships, does reduce the *relative* riskiness per dollar. ($\sqrt{N}$ does grow with N; but making the denominator in Total Riskiness/Total Number of Insurers be proportional to N does produce $\sqrt{N}/N$, which does decline like $1/\sqrt{N}$ toward zero.)

The diversification over time that a pension fund or young person achieves when investing over many periods thus cannot cancel out or effectively reduce the dispersion of wealth outcomes that occurs at distant dates in the future.[4]

A LOOPHOLE?

All the above applies to equity markets that are truly *random walks*. Now that Poterba and Summers [1987], Fama and French [1988], Modigliani and Cohen [1979], Tobin and Brainard [1977], and other observers are providing evidence that — *over long periods of time, epochs of strong equity returns tend to be followed by epochs of weak, and vice versa* — at long last I am able to deduce some *rational* basis for the conventional wisdom according to which long investing horizons do call for more equity exposure than short horizons do.

I spelled out the mathematical derivation at the May 1988 Tobin Colloquium at Yale. See Samuelson [1988] in the *Festschrift* for James Tobin for details. Here I shall merely sketch the nature of the argument.

When equity return rates of one five-year period are *negatively correlated* with those of the last such period, Samuelson [1988] demonstrates that extreme runs tend to be self-cancelling, making the wealth outcomes at the end of a long horizon bunch up around their middle in comparison with the log normal outcomes of the *random walk*. Paradoxically, such a bunching around the middle does not compel all risk averters to plunge more heavily into equities. For risk-averse investors who maximize Expected Value of their utility, which happens to be the logarithm of wealth (à la 1738 Daniel Bernoulli), *the time horizon turns out not to matter at all* — both in the Poterba-Summers *rebound* model and the *random-walk* model.

However, the bulk of the empirical evidence, cross-sectional and from time series, is that real-life investors are *more risk-averse* than Bernoulli. Instead of having a utility function like log(Wealth), their behavior is better rationalized if we hypothesize for them something like

$$U(W) = -1/W \text{ or } -1/W^2$$

When I calculate for $(-1/W)$ the one-period and two-period optimal equity shares in the *rebound* case, I deduce that the longer time horizon does mandate some greater tolerance for lucrative but risky stocks. QED. (The intuitive reason for the result is that a bad outcome for my equities in a pre-ultimate period just ahead is not so bad because it shifts the odds toward a remunerative rebound, a consideration that relieves equity exposure of some of its abhorrent short-run riskiness.)

A twenty-year quest to justify long time-horizon risk-taking has thus finally been successfully rewarded.

Good things come in threes. In the next section I present a second rational basis for being more risk-tolerant when young than when old. This second basis holds even in a random-walk world. Simultaneously and both independently of me and unknown to me, Professors Zvi Bodie and William F. Samuelson have developed a quite different third basis for greater risk tolerance on the part of a worker when young than when old: The Bodie-Samuelson theorem holds even in a random-walk world and rests on the greater opportunities of the young to compensate for risky outcomes by working harder or less hard.[5]

William C. Greenough, longtime chairman of TIAA-CREF and creator of the CREF variable-annuity pension vehicle, and I as CREF trustee engaged in amiable debate for many years on the following issue. Greenough expressed the hope that the fact that CREF can be fairly sure of net growth and of little need for liquidity to redeem participants' holdings ought to be to our advantage as investors. So to speak, as very long-horizon investors, we ought to be able to tolerate more riskiness, in the sense that many short-run ups and downs can be expected actuarially to cancel out. Putting Greenough's argument in my parlance, cannot we at CREF aim at every point in the short run to be on the Markowitz *efficiency mean-sigma frontier* at a higher-mean and higher-variance location, counting actuarially on our *long-run* forty-year participants ending on a high-mean–low-variance point that is non-attainable by short-run investors subject to irreducible liquidity concerns? A similar supposition (or fallacy?) seemed to underlie the famous 1969 Barker-Bundy Report of the Ford Foundation, which was interpreted to be telling colleges to be bold in equity investing just as the 1942–1966 bull market was ending.[6]

To this I replied with theoretical doubts. Under time-independent probabilities, variance does not cancel out in even the longest runs (instead growing proportional to time). A foundation investing for a five-year horizon, I argued, could do just as well investing in the few-thousand corporation universe that CREF invests in as CREF can hope to do. Whatever edge TIAA might have because of its assured growth pattern, CREF could have no similar positive edge in the competitive equity market. So I argued. The Samuelson [1969] finding was put forward, according to which any investor with constant-relative-risk aversion and facing a random-walk world is deduced to choose rationally the same equity fraction in her portfolio when aged thirty as when aged sixty-five and almost ready to retire.

Suppose, however, that my utility of terminal wealth at age seventy is all that I really care for. I am concerned to get the probability distribution of such terminal wealths that is most desirable: high mean, low dispersion about the mean, and so forth.

Now at last I find a new argument that weighs in on Greenough's side. Agreed that if my U(terminal W) is like log W, the Samuelson result of zero age effects on equity fraction is vindicated. Suppose, though, human nature is such that we are each most anxious *not to fall below a "subsistence" level of terminal wealth* — so that log(W - S) and not log W is the utility whose Expected Value we seek to maximize.

In that case Greenough's contention is correct that older people will put less into risky stocks when they have fewer years to go before the terminal date of retiring or bequeathing. Samuelson [1988] explains this truth by pointing out that the present discounted value of the terminal subsistence wealth, which is $S/(1 + i)^T$, must in effect be put into escrow in the form of safe cash or money market funds. As T, the time left in the horizon, shrinks, $S/(1 + i)^T$ will rise, thereby displacing from one's equity portfolio a larger and larger fractional share. QED for the contention that oldsters should more likely transfer from CREF to TIAA than vice versa (if such reverse transfers were permissible).

THE BODIE-OTHER SAMUELSON EFFECT

Suppose I can work harder or less hard. (I can moonlight and give up leisure; can consult; teach summer school; retire later; and so forth.) Most dramatic would be that case of Alfred Marshall where my marginal utility of leisure happens to be constant: Always I work up to the point where I consume the same market baskets of consumption goods, that precise amount that brings my marginal utility of consumption to equality with my unchanged marginal disutility of work.

In this dramatic case, any extra dollar of rentier wealth entails no extra consumption of goods, instead causing only leisure to rise.

When I am young, I can dare to plunge heavily in high-mean, high-variance equities. Why? Because if luck turns out bad and I lose principal, I can and will always choose to work enough more to keep my consumption up. (Of course, I cannot subtract further from leisure when all my leisure has been usurped by work; beyond that point we have lost Marshall's dramatic case of relative marginal disutility that is constant.)

The reader may contemplate two cases. In case 1, my final year's supply of labor has already been determined by me. As a very short-period investor, I must be chary of putting too much in equities lest by bad luck I am unable to afford my minimum of subsistence.

My younger brother has two years to go in making his penultimate decision on the fraction to put into stocks. He realizes that if bad luck leaves him with low principal as he comes to his final year, he can plan to compensate by supplying more labor. The consequences to him of a loss from a lucrative gamble are seen to be less. Rationally the younger brother puts a larger fraction into attractive-but-risky equities than does the older brother. QED.

The reader is referred to the original and cogent exposition of Bodie and William Samuelson. Again Greenough is vindicated!

FINALE

This article has been written to be provocative. I hope it will demonstrate that the modern theory of finance has much to offer the experienced practitioners in the securities industry.

Also I hope that the new findings reported on here will demonstrate that the theory of finance is not a perfect and completed paradigm. There is much still to be learned.

---

[1] Benoit Mandelbrot and Eugene Fama each did independent formulations of discounting and efficiency.

[2] Q is defined as Numerator/Denominator = N/D, where D is the calculated total cost of *producing* in commodity markets America's earning assets; and N is the calculated total value for which those assets sell in our securities markets. (Of course difficult measurements of depreciation and of debt financings are involved in estimating Q numerically.) When I was a new textbook author in the late 1940s, I judged Q to be an attractive fraction, but by 1965 the long bull market had raised Q far above unity. Although N in 1989 is now about where it was just prior to Black October of 1987, D is presumably 10% to 15% higher.

[3] Consider simple so-called Markov processes in which successive five-year periods register a "+" or a "−" (presumably with a greater probability of + than − in a growing, inflation-prone system). Under a *random walk* model, the probability of + following an observed −, call it $P_{+,-}$, will be the same as $P_{+,-}$, the probability of + after − has been observed. In a mean-reverting, red-noise, or "rebound"

process, we instead have P_{+-} greater than P_{++}. A "momentum" or "blue-noise" process involves *positive* autocorrelation and P_{++} greater than P_{+-}. (Warning: If giant swings like that of the post-1929 Depression are expected to be obsolete, the Poterba–Summers and Fama–French evidence for mean reversion is weakened.)

[4] There is a misleading spurious parallel between the decline of $\sqrt{N}/N$ with time horizon and the decline with $\sqrt{N}$ of the variance of a portfolio's *mean* annual return with N. For independent probabilities, Variance [log(mean annual return)] $\to 0$ as $1/\sqrt{N} \to 0$. However, the dispersion of my terminal year's log Wealth, $Var[logW_N]$, does rise with N in proportion to N and, *ceteris paribus*, that does lower my $Exp[U_N(W_N)]$.

[5] See P.A. Samuelson [1989]; also, Bodie and Samuelson [1989].

[6] See Barker [1969].

REFERENCES

Barker, R. *Managing Educational Endowments*. Report to the Ford Foundation from the Advisory Committee on Endowment Management, Robert Barker, Chairman, 1969.

Bodie, Z., and W.F. Samuelson. "Labor Supply Flexibility and Portfolio Choice." National Bureau of Economic Research Working Paper, 1989.

Fama, E.F., and K.P. French, "Permanent and Temporary Components of Stock Prices." *Journal of Political Economy*, Vol. 96, No. 2, 1988, pp. 264-273.

Modigliani, F., and R.A. Cohn. "Inflation, Rational Valuation and the Market." *Financial Analysts Journal*, March/April, 1979, pp. 24-44.

Poterba, J.M., and L. Summers. "Means Reversion in Stock Returns: Evidence and Implications." Cambridge, MA: National Bureau of Economic Research, March 1987.

Samuelson, P.A. "A Case at Last for Age-Phased Reduction in Equity." *Proceedings of the National Academy of Science*, forthcoming 1989.

———. "Challenge to Judgment." *Journal of Portfolio Management*, Vol. 1, No. 1, Fall 1974, pp. 17-19. Reprinted in *Collected Scientific Papers of Paul A. Samuelson*, Vol. IV, H. Nagatani and K. Crowley, eds., Chapter 243, pp. 479-485.

———. "Lifetime Portfolio Selection by Dynamic Stochastic Programming." *Review of Economics and Statistics*, Vol. 51(3), August 1969, pp. 239-246. Reprinted in *Collected Scientific Papers of Paul A. Samuelson*, Vol. III, R. Merton, ed., Chapter 204, pp. 883-890.

———. "Longrun Risk Tolerance When Equity Returns Are Mean Regressing: Pseudoparadoxes and Vindication of 'Business Man's Risk'." Lecture at the May 7-8, 1988, Yale Symposium in honor of James Tobin's seventieth birthday.

———. "Proof that Properly Anticipated Prices Fluctuate Randomly." *Industrial Management Review*, Spring 1965. Reprinted in *Collected Scientific Papers of Paul A. Samuelson*, Vol. III, R. Merton, ed., Chapter 198, pp. 782-790.

———. "Risk and Uncertainty: A Fallacy of Large Numbers." *Scientia*, 6th series, 57th year April-May 1963, pp. 1-6. Reprinted in *Collected Scientific Papers of Paul A. Samuelson*, Vol. I, J.E. Stiglitz, ed., Chapter 16, pp. 153-158.

Shiller, R. "Stock Prices and Social Dynamics." *Brookings Papers on Economic Activity*, 1986, pp. 457-498.

Summers, L.H. "Does the Stock Market Rationally Reflect Fundamental Values?" *Journal of Finance*, Vol. 41, 1986, pp. 591-601.

Tobin, J., and W.L. Brainard. "Asset Markets and the Cost of Capital." In *Economic Progress, Private Values and Public Policy: Essays in Honor of William Fellner*, R. Nelson and B. Balassa, eds. Amsterdam: North-Holland, 1977, pp. 235-262. Reprinted in J. Tobin, *Essays in Economics: Theory and Policy*, Cambridge, Mass., MIT Press, 1982.

CHAPTER 19

At Last, A Rational Case for Long-Horizon Risk Tolerance and for Asset-Allocation Timing?

PAUL A. SAMUELSON
INSTITUTE PROFESSOR EMERITUS
MASSACHUSETTS INSTITUTE OF TECHNOLOGY

1. As you grow older and the time horizon of your investing shortens, should you rationally cut down on your exposure to lucrative but risky equities?
2. And, when you are young with many chances ahead to recoup any transient losses, can you afford to take a "business man's risk?"
3. College endowments and portfolios of permanent foundations, expecting to be operating and growing virtually forever, can they, by the same logic, largely ignore short-run riskiness and invest heavily in common stocks with high average mean returns, relying on "diversification over time and the cancellations of repeated chances in the Law of Large Numbers?"
4. After stocks have extraordinarily risen in value, should you rationally lighten up on them? After they have been languishing unusually long in price level, should you time your portfolio choices by

leaning against the wind in the general direction of taking on an extra fractional share of equities?

These are old and basic questions. The conventional wisdom gives them an affirmative answer:

> Long-horizon investors allegedly can, *ceteris paribus*, tolerate more risk and thereby garner higher mean returns.
>
> The rational age-specific pattern of asset allocation allegedly involves, as you age, some tapering down of equities relative to lower-variance assets.
>
> Thus, although CREF is careful not to express judgments about optimal strategies for its professorial participants to follow, readers of TIAA-CREF's many publications could be forgiven for tacitly presuming that it is more normal at advanced ages to shift from the equities of CREF to the bonds and nominal-principal investments of TIAA and CREF than vice versa.
>
> Contending that markets do not go one way indefinitely, contrarians counsel that investors downplay equities when their price/earnings ratios have become high and their Tobin-q-ratio has run way past unity. Practical investing counselors endorse "timing" in principle while admitting that experience turns up little documentation that would-be timers have fared well.

Like so much that belongs to the conventional wisdom, this described dogma has not as yet earned the imprimatur of science. Thus, when Samuelson (1969) was motivated to investigate rational life-cycle investing for those who maximize expected utility and who possess constant-relative-risk aversion, there emerged the surprising theorem that your uncle with few years to go should hold exactly the same fraction of wealth in risky (*random-walk*) stocks as he did when young and as you do now. This mandate that rational investors should be *myopic*, ignoring the length of their time horizon, is a specific denial of the conventional wisdom.

HOW TIME ADDS TO RISK

How is such a nihilistic result possible? Here are relevant considerations.

Repeated investing over many periods does not cause risk to wash out in the long run. Insurance companies do not eliminate total risk by insuring more and more ships. As shown in my discussion of fallacies of interpreting the Law of Large Numbers (Samuelson 1963), each new independent risk adds to the *absolute total* of risk. But *total absolute* risk grows as the *square root* of the number of *independent* ships insured and not in proportion to their numbers. It is the *subdividing* of risk by bringing in new members to the insuring syndicate that, together with bringing in of new independent ships, does reduce the *relative* riskiness per dollar. ($\sqrt{N}$ does grow with N; but making the denominator in Total Riskiness/Total Number of Insurers be proportional to N, does produce $\sqrt{N}/N$ which does decline like $1/\sqrt{N}$ toward zero.)

The diversification over time which a pension fund or young person achieves when investing over many periods thus cannot cancel out or effectively reduce the dispersion of wealth outcomes that occurs at distant dates in the future.[1]

In Chapter 18, it is demonstrated that, if the probabilities that stocks and bonds are subject to in successive periods are broadly independent, the twin who is half the time in stocks and half the time in bonds will experience over a lifetime a demonstrably worse risk-adjusted return than the twin who is always 50% in each. (Of course, if you have a magic demon that tells you when bonds will soar and when stocks will zoom, then you and the Tooth Fairy should follow Will Rogers' formula for being a perfect timer by only buying securities that are going to appreciate.)

A LOOPHOLE UNDER MEAN-REGRESSION?

All the above applies to equity markets that are truly *random walks*. Now that Poterba and Summers (1987), Fama and French (1988), Modigliani and Cohen (1961), Tobin and Brainard (1977), and other observers are providing

---

[1] There is a misleading spurious parallel between the decline of N/N with time horizon and the decline with $\sqrt{N}$ of the variance of a portfolio's *mean* annual return with N. For independent probabilities, Variance {log (mean annual return)} → 0 as $1/\sqrt{N}$ → 0. However, the dispersion of my terminal year's log Wealth, Var{logW_N}, does rise with N in proportion to N and *ceteris paribus* that does lower my Exp $\{U_N(W_N)\}$.

evidence that — *over long periods of time, epochs of strong equity returns tend to be followed by epochs of weak, and vice versa* — at long last I am able to deduce some *rational* basis for the conventional wisdom according to which long investing horizons do call for more equity exposure than short horizons do.

> Theorem: For a *white-noise* process of a random walk, where percentage price changes of stocks tomorrow are truly independent of yesterday's changes, would-be timers are shooting themselves in the leg. So to speak they lose two ways: in geometric mean return and in volatility of return.
>
> By contrast, when white noise is replaced by *red noise* so that the next several-years' return is negatively auto-correlated with the last several-years' return, then lower fractional shares in equities should follow upon higher fractional shares. Indeed, when the process involves *violet noise*, meaning that next week's expected change in price is positively correlated with last week's change, you should be a timer in the style of a momentum trader — piling on to any price trends (and helping to make them worse?).

Samuelson (1991) confirmed that the spirit of the above theorem holds for a fundamentalist's model that goes beyond a red-noise process involving a Markov matrix that makes serial correlations of price changes be negatively autocorrelated. Such Markov processes still have the dubious implication that, if we wait long enough, *real* stock prices can wander anywhere with one GM share being worth less than a peanut or more than the annual GNP.

Also, suppose you have rational reason to believe that real stock prices tend to be in an invariant percentage probability spread around some exponential real time trend. Such a fundamentalist model entails optimal portfolio choice by cautious people that is more risk tolerant for the long horizon than for the short. And it does imply that the canny timer should lighten up on stocks when they have risen above trend and load up when they have fallen behind trend. Clearly as such a fundamentalist contrarian timer, you must belong to an elite minority — for if everyone shared your Bayesians, the S&P-500 would not be going through its Shiller-Keynes gyrations.

I have spelled out the mathematical derivation at the May 1988 Tobin Colloquium at Yale, held to honor James Tobin on the occasion of his

Seventieth Anniversary. See Samuelson (1991) for details. Here I shall merely sketch the nature of the argument.

When equity return rates of one 5-year period are *negatively correlated* with those of the last such period, my Tobin-fest essay demonstrated that extreme runs tend to be self-cancelling, making the wealth outcomes at the end of a long horizon bunch up around their middle in comparison with the log-normal outcomes of the *random walk*. Paradoxically, such a bunching around the middle does not compel all risk averters to plunge more heavily into equities. For risk-averse investors who maximize Expected value of their utility, which happens to be the logarithm of wealth (à la 1738 Daniel Bernoulli), *the time horizon turns out not to matter at all* — both in the Poterba-Summers *rebound* model and the *random-walk model*.

However, the bulk of the empirical evidence, cross-sectional and from time series, is that real-life investors are *more risk averse* than Bernoulli. Instead of having a utility function like log(Wealth), their behavior is better rationalized if we hypothesize for them something like

$U(W) = -1/W$ or $-1/W^2$

When I calculate for $(-1/W)$ the 1-period and 2-period optimal equity shares in the *rebound* case, I deduce that the longer time horizon does mandate some greater tolerance for lucrative but risky stocks. QED. The intuitive reason for the result is that a bad outcome for my equities in a pre-ultimate period just ahead is not so bad since it shifts the odds towards a remunerative rebound, a consideration that relieves equity exposure of some of its abhorrent riskiness.

There is also deduced to be a case for being a *market timer*, reducing equity share after a boom epoch and raising it after bear markets. However, following a crash year like 1987, there is probably already an excessive fad for "asset allocation" models that try to "time." In the present age of capital-gains taxation at full marginal rates, the burden of proof has shifted against turnover. One should also ponder over the final caution in my Tobin paper:

> A final caveat may be in order warning against overtouting this deductive qualitative result. Since it takes a long time to duplicate statistical samples of long-term epochs, our confidence in the strength of the *rebound* [red-noise] deviation from the *random walk* must be guarded. Moreover, the size

99

of the alleged effect, particularly after we discount for the possible one-time nature of the 1920–1945 swings of the Great Depression and World War II, may not be too great quantitatively. For these reasons, a certain caution toward the new results would seem prudent.

REFERENCES

Fama, E.F. and French, K.P., "Permanent and Temporary Components of Stock Prices," *Journal of Political Economy* 96, No. 2, 1988, pp. 246–273.

Poterba, J.M. and Summers, L., "Means Reversion in Stock Returns: Evidence and Implications," Cambridge, MA: NBER, March 1987.

Samuelson, P.A., "Lifetime Portfolio Selection by Dynamic Stochastic Programming," *Review of Economics and Statistics* 51(3), August 1969, pp. 239–46; Reprinted in *Collected Scientific Papers of Paul A. Samuelson* Vol. III, R. Merton (ed.), Chapter 204, pp. 883–90.

_____, "Risk and Uncertainty: A Fallacy of Large Numbers," *Scientia*, 6th series, 57th year, April/May 1963, pp. 1–6; Reprinted in *Collected Scientific Papers of Paul A. Samuelson*, Vol. I, J.E. Stiglitz (ed.), Chapter 16, pp. 153–158.

_____, "Longrun Risk Tolerance When Equity Returns are Mean Regressing: Pseudoparadoxes and Vindication of 'Businessman's Risk'," in Brainard, W., Nordhaus, W., and Watts, H. (eds.), *Macroeconomics, Finance and Economic Policy: Essays in Honor of James Tobin.* Cambridge, Mass.: MIT Press, 1991.

_____, "Asset Allocation Can Be Dangerous To Your Health: Pitfalls in Across-time Diversification," *Journal of Portfolio Management*, 16, 1990, pp. 5–8.

Shiller, R., "Stock Prices and Social Dynamics," *Brookings Papers on Economic Activity*, 1986, pp. 457–498.

Tobin, J. and Brainard, W. L., "Asset Markets and the Cost of Capital," in *Economic Progress, Private Values and Public Policy: Essays in Honor of William Fellner,* eds. R. Nelson and B. Balassa, 1977; Amsterdam, North-Holland, pp. 235–262. Reprinted in Tobin, J., *Essays in Economics: Theory and Policy,* Cambridge, Mass., The MIT Press, 1982.

A case at last for age-phased reduction in equity

(random walk/expected utility/subsistence consumption-wealth)

PAUL A. SAMUELSON

Department of Economics, Massachusetts Institute of Technology, Cambridge, MA 02139

Contributed by Paul A. Samuelson, June 7, 1989

ABSTRACT Maximizing expected utility over a lifetime leads one who has constant relative risk aversion and faces random-walk securities returns to be "myopic" and hold the same fraction of portfolio in equities early and late in life—a defiance of folk wisdom and casual introspection. By assuming one needs to assure at retirement a minimum ("subsistence") level of wealth, the present analysis deduces a pattern of greater risk-taking when young than when old. When a subsistence minimum is needed at every period of life, the *rentier* paradoxically is least risk tolerant in youth—the Robert C. Merton paradox that traces to the decline with age of the present discounted value of the subsistence-consumption requirements. Conversely, the decline with age of capitalized human capital reverses the Merton effect.

DEBATED AGE EFFECTS

Folk wisdom recommends that we should be more risk tolerant when young, reducing as we approach retirement the fraction of wealth put into risky equities and increasing our safe-cash exposure. However, Samuelson (1) found that a rational maximizer of expected utility, even though subject to constant relative risk aversion and facing random-walk securities returns, would rationally invest the same fraction in equities at all ages. This result held despite the young person's "having more opportunities and time to recoup from initial bad luck;" and despite the law of large numbers guaranteeing a tendency for securities to live up over many repeated independent periods to their intrinsic superior profitability over safe-cash assets. Leland (2), Mossin (3), Merton (4), and Hakannson (5) arrived at this same null result.

By dropping the assumption of white-noise martingales in favor of mean-reverting negative serial correlation, Samuelson (6, †) was able to confirm, however, the qualitative wisdom of folklore for investors with constant relative risk aversion extended that of Bernoulli's logarithmic utility. (For $U = -1/W^{|\gamma|}$, Merton obtains that under mean reversion, many-period investors will be more risk-taking than few-period investors.)

Also, Samuelson (ref. 1, p. 245) had noted the uncontroversial result concerning "businessman's risk." Suppose I face annual earnings from work, known to be constant over preretirement years. The capitalized (present discounted) value of this *human capital* declines as I age and as my time to retirement shrinks. Therefore, if I hold equities in constant fraction to my total wealth—defined as portfolio wealth plus human capital—my observed portfolio fraction in equities will be seen to decline rationally with age. (With negative human capital, as when I owe a specified number of periodic cash installments, the reverse of the folk-wisdom pattern is of course entailed.)

The present analysis deduces a third, new, case for age-phased riskiness reduction. It retains the random-walk assumption of uniform and independent probability distributions, and it continues to ignore human-capital complications. Its new element is recognition of the realistic fact that many people save toward assuring for themselves or their heirs a certain minimum ("subsistence") level of wealth. It is proved here that, when we replace $U = \log W$ or $U = W^\gamma/\gamma$ by

$$U = \log[W - S] \text{ or } (W - S)^\gamma/\gamma, \quad 0 \neq \gamma < 1, S > 0, \quad [1]$$

where U = utility, W = terminal wealth, S = minimum terminal wealth insisted on, and γ = parameter of relative risk tolerance, then the fraction rationally allocated to equities decreases with age toward retirement, confirming folk wisdom.

Zvi Bodie and William Samuelson have deduced (7) an independent new reason for greater risk tolerance when young. It stems from the fact that I can plan to work harder if my risks early turn out adversely.

It will suffice for the present demonstration to consider the simplest case of a single risky stock and safe cash. However, the result and its proof are general, and I provide for the reader the illustrative exact formulas that hold for the lognormal Brownian motions of Merton (4, 8, 9).

I owe to Robert Merton also a seemingly paradoxical reversal of folk wisdom on age and risk-taking. This specifies a realistic case where I must rationally be less risk-taking when young (or when I am early in retirement)! It occurs when I act to maximize the expected (Exp) value of summed consumption utilities, $U[C_t]$, over each of the time periods until retirement, of future periods (t) under the realistic proviso that I am wary of ever falling in consumption below each period's minimum-subsistence consumption of positive Q. Instead of maximizing

$$\text{Exp } \Sigma_t U[C_t] = \text{Exp } \Sigma_t C_t^\gamma/\gamma,$$

I maximize

$$\text{Exp } \Sigma_t (C_t - Q)^\gamma/\gamma, \quad 0 < \gamma < 1, Q > 0. \quad [2]$$

When young, I here face for many periods the necessity of assuring the Q subsistence consumptions; therefore, I must lock into safe-cash much of my portfolio when I am young. As I age and the periods left of life shrink, I need lock less of wealth in safe cash and therefore will display more tolerance for risky equities as I mature! (The earlier example of negative human capital explicates and dispels the Merton paradox, just as the case of positive human capital explicates this paper's new validation of folk wisdom's contention that a bequeather plays safe increasingly when being older.)

In real life the quantitative importance of the desire to provide a minimum of bequest must vie with the quantitative importance of Merton's subsistence-consumption level. Therefore, simple folk wisdom is seen to be too simple, a general finding itself glimpsed by folk wisdom.

The publication costs of this article were defrayed in part by page charge payment. This article must therefore be hereby marked "*advertisement*" in accordance with 18 U.S.C. §1734 solely to indicate this fact.

†Samuelson, P. A. (1988) *Longrun Risk Tolerance in a Fundamentalist Model of Equities*, Working Paper.

REVIEW OF STANDARD MODEL

In each period a dollar of safe cash is sure to have a total return of r, the safe rate of interest: $r \geq 0$. Each dollar in the risky security has a total return that is in each period t an independent random variable, $X - 1$, where

$$\text{Prob}\{X \leq x\} = P(x), \text{ where } x \text{ is outcome per \$,} \quad [3]$$

$$P(1+r) > 0, P(x) = 0 \text{ for } x < 0 \quad [4]$$

$$\text{Prob}\{..X_t \leq x_0, X_{t+1} \leq x_1, ..\} = ..P(x_0)P(x_1).. \quad [5]$$

$$\text{Exp}\{X\} = \int_{-\infty}^{\infty} x \, dP(x) = \mu > 1 + r \quad [6]$$

$$\text{Var}\{X\} = \int_{-\infty}^{\infty} (x - \mu)^2 \, dP(x) = \sigma^2 > 0. \quad [7]$$

Under our random-walk assumptions of Eqs. **3–7**, you are assumed to act like an expected {utility} maximizer who is risk-averse—as in Eq. **1** above.

Subject to the stipulations of Eqs. **1** and **3–7**, you will assuredly always invest something in safe cash and something in the risky stock. Thus, when you have only one period to go, you will determine to pick your optimal fraction of portfolio in equities by the following procedure: writing W_1, r, w_1, and $X_1 - 1$ as your initial wealth, the interest rate, your fraction in equities, and the random-variable total returns from \$1 in risky stock, respectively, you seek

$$\underset{w_1}{\text{Max Exp}}\{U[W_1(1 + r)(1 - w_1) + W_1 w_1 X_1]\}$$

$$= \text{Exp}\{U[W_1(1 + r)(1 - w_1^*) + W_1 w_1^* X_1]\}$$

$$= \int_{-\infty}^{\infty} U[W_1(1 + r)(1 - w_1^*) + W_1 w_1^* x_1] \, dP(x_1)$$

$$= U_1^*[W_1], \quad [8]$$

where the optimal fraction in equities,

$$w_1^* = f_1(W_1) \quad [9]$$

is the unique fractional root for w of

$$0 = \int_{-\infty}^{\infty} U'[W_1(1 + r)(1 - w) + W_1 w x]$$

$$\times (x_1 - 1 - r) \, dP(x). \quad [10]$$

As is typical in dynamic programming, knowing W_T when there are T periods to go and having already solved recursively relations just like Eqs. **8–10** for $U_1^*(W), U_2^*(W), \ldots$, $U_{T-1}^*(W)$, we can solve for our best w_T^* fraction as follows:

$$\underset{w_T}{\text{Max Exp}}\{U_{T-1}^*[W_T(1 + r)(1 - w_T) + W_T w_T X_T]\}$$

$$= \int_{-\infty}^{\infty} U_{T-1}^*[W_T(1 + r)(1 - w_T^*)$$

$$+ W_T w_T^*(x_T - 1 - r)]dP(x_T)$$

$$= U_T^*[W_T], \quad [11]$$

where

$$w_T^* = f_T(W_T) \quad [12]$$

is the unique fractional root for w of

$$0 = \int_{-\infty}^{\infty} U_{T-1}^{*'}[W_T(1 + r)(1 - w) + W_T w(x - 1 - r)]$$

$$\times (x - 1 - r) \, dP(x). \quad [13]$$

Folk wisdom translates into the unqualified claim that

$$f_T(W) > f_{T-1}(W) > \ldots > f_2(W) > f_1(W). \quad [14]$$

Around 1969 many investigators deduced that this cannot be in general true:

$$\text{for } U = \log W \text{ or } W^\gamma/\gamma, \quad [15]$$

all risk-averse persons follow decision rules that are "myopic"; namely, they set

$$f_T(W) \equiv f_{T-1}(W) \equiv \ldots \equiv f_1(W) = w_\gamma^*, \quad [16]$$

where w_γ^* is the w root of

$$0 = W^\gamma \int_{-\infty}^{\infty} [(1 + r)(1 - w) + w(x - 1 - r)]^{\gamma-1}$$

$$\times (x - 1 - r) \, dP(x) \quad [17]$$

and is thus independent of W at every stage. [Remark: As $\gamma \to 0$, $w_\gamma^* \to w_0^*$, the optimal equity fraction for the log W case. Using $(W - 1)^\gamma/\gamma$ rather than W^γ/γ for U makes no difference and does let us cover the log W case by the limiting form of $(W^\gamma - 1)/\gamma$ as $\gamma \to 0$.]

HANDLING SUBSISTENCE BY ESCROWED CASH

Our myopic solution for w_γ^* in Eq. **17** enables us to handle the subsistence S in the U of Eq. **1**. Whenever there are T periods to go, our problem is feasible only if

$$W_T > S/(1 + r)^T. \quad [18]$$

Only if we can set aside in safe cash $S(1 + r)^{-T}$ can we ensure against the worst-case scenario where, in every period remaining, our equity's worst-luck outcome leaves us unable to avert the infinite catastrophe of not being able to bequeath at least S.

Therefore, in effect we must lock in $S/(1 + r)^T$ into a safe-cash escrow, knowing it will grow through the stages $[S/(1 + r)^{T-1}, \ldots, S/(1 + r), S]$. The remaining investable portfolio goes through the stages $[\tilde{W}_T, \tilde{W}_{T-1}, \ldots, \tilde{W}_1, \tilde{W}_0]$, where these wealths are constrained to grow exactly as indicated by the relations

$$\tilde{W}_{t-1} = \tilde{W}_t[(1 + r)(1 - \tilde{w}_t) + \tilde{w}_t X_t]$$

$$= W_{t-1} - S(1 + r)^{1-t}, \quad t = T, T - 1, \ldots, 1. \quad [19]$$

In Eq. **19**, $\tilde{w}_t$ is the fraction of the freed-up portfolio invested in the common stock, when there are still t periods to go, and $X_t - 1$ is that risky security's rate of total return. Since our escrowed lock-in takes care of the S in our maximand's $U(W_0 - S)$, if we use the $\tilde{W}_1$ freed-up variable, our maximand is precisely in the 1969 Santa Claus form of Eqs. **8–13**, with the myopic solution of Eqs. **16** and **17**:

$$\tilde{w}_t^* = w_\gamma^* > 0, \quad t = T, T - 1, \ldots, 2, 1. \quad [20]$$

The actual portfolio, inclusive of its cash-escrowed component, displays the lower w_t^* proportion given by

$$w_t^* = \tilde{w}_t^*(\tilde{W}_t/W_t) = \tilde{w}_t^*(W_t - S[1 + r]^{-t})/W_t$$

$$= \tilde{f}_t(W_t) = w_\gamma^* - w_\gamma^*(S)/(1 + r)^t W_t. \quad [21]$$

Therefore, in agreement with folk wisdom, for $r > 0$ Eq. **21** does translate into

$$\tilde{f}_T(W) > \tilde{f}_{T-1}(W) > \ldots > \tilde{f}_2(W) > \tilde{f}_1(W) \quad [22]$$

because of the inequality

$$S/(1 + r)^T < S/(1 + r)^{T-1} < \ldots < S/(1 + r). \quad [23]$$

Q.E.D.

THE MERTON PARADOX

Unlike the previous bequest scenario of Eq. 1, here Eq. 2's many-period consumption scenario needs the following amount in safe-cash escrow to assure the subsistence-consumption Q of each period left to go:

$$G_T = Q(1 + r)^{-1} + Q(1 + r)^{-2} + \ldots + Q(1 + r)^{-T}$$

$$= Q[1 - (1 + r)^{-T}]/r, \quad 1 + r > 0 \quad [24]$$

$$> G_{T-1} > G_{T-2} > \ldots > G_2 > G_1. \quad [25]$$

Define the freely investable portfolio when there are t periods to go by

$$\tilde{W}_t = W_t - G_t, \quad (t = T, \ldots, 2, 1). \quad [26]$$

Its $\hat{w}_t^*$ proportions held in equity are for all t the constant w_γ^*, because using the $\tilde{W}$s in our maximization permits us to ignore the Q terms in the maximand, which already were taken care of by our declining sinking fund.

In short, the whole portfolio's true equity fractions end up given by

$$w_t^* = w_\gamma^*(W_t - E_t)/W_t$$
$$= w_\gamma^* - w_\gamma^*(E_t/W_t) = \hat{f}_t(W_t). \quad [27]$$

In view of the inequalities of Eq. 25, we verify Merton's paradoxical increase in equity tolerance with age:

$$\hat{f}_T(W) < \hat{f}_{T-1}(W) < \ldots < \hat{f}_2(W) < \hat{f}_1(W). \quad [28]$$

Q.E.D.

DISCUSSION

The present analysis dealt either with constant relative risk aversion or with subsistence-level parameters that make relative risk aversion decline from its infinite magnitude at the subsistence level to its constant level at large values of the utility function argument. (Absolute risk aversion in the Pratt–Arrow sense declines with well-being in all of our cases examined.)

Folk wisdom is shaky on just how risk aversion does change with affluence. Academic sages usually opine that (*i*) absolute risk tolerance rises with affluence, while (*ii*) relative risk tolerance may fall. The present subsistence terms, S and Q, do not accord with the second of these speculations.

This suggests we ought to be prepared for complicated age effects, where almost anything can happen and

$$f_T(W) > f_{T-1}(W) \text{ for some } W \text{ and } T \text{ intervals}$$
$$< f_{T-1}(W) \text{ for other } W\text{s and } T\text{s.} \quad [29]$$

More general than either Eq. 1 or 2 is the maximand

$$\text{Exp}\{\Sigma(W_t - S_t)^\gamma/\gamma\}, \quad [30]$$

where the sequence $(S_T, \ldots, S_1)$ can be arbitrarily specified positive numbers. At any time with t periods left in the planning horizon, our locked-in cash escrow has the present discounted value of

$$V_t = S_t(1 + r)^{-1} + S_{t-1}(1 + r)^{-2}$$
$$+ \ldots + S_1(1 + r)^{-t}. \quad [31]$$

By reasoning already established, we derive the most general result:

$$w_t^* > w_{t+1}^* \text{ iff } V_t > V_{t+1}$$
$$< w_{t+1}^* \text{ iff } V_t < V_{t+1}$$
$$= w_{t+1}^* \text{ iff } V_t = V_{t+1}. \quad [32]$$

Finally, consider the following Merton model of instantaneous probabilities in continuous time. Denoting the passage of time by positive growth in y, $y = T - t$, safe cash grows like e^{Ry}, where $e^R = 1 + r \geq 1$. The optimized portfolio of securities obeys the following Ito–Wiener process

$$dW = [R + w(\alpha - R)]W \, dy + wW\sigma dZ,$$
$$\alpha > R \geq 0, \sigma > 0. \quad [33]$$

Suppose I select w_t over $T < t < 0$ to achieve the following maximized expected {utility}:

$$[W(0) - S]^\gamma/\gamma, \quad 0 \neq \gamma < 1. \quad [34]$$

It is well known from Merton (4, 8, 9) that when $S = 0$, we are in the myopic case

$$w_t^* \equiv (\alpha - R)/\sigma^2(1 - \gamma) = w_\gamma^*, \quad -\infty \leq \gamma < 1. \quad [35]$$

As before we will want to set up an escrow fund F_t to assure the positive S subsistence need, leading to

$$\tilde{W}_t = W_t - F_t = W_t - Se^{-Rt}, \quad dF_t/dt > 0.$$
$$F_t = Se^{-Rt}, \text{ rising as } t \to 0. \quad [36]$$

Then by earlier arguments, we can write for positive S and R

$$w_t^* = w_\gamma^*[\tilde{W}_t/W_t] = w_\gamma^*[1 - S/e^{Rt}W_t] = \tilde{f}(W_t) \quad [37]$$

with Eq. 36 implying that

$$\tilde{f}_T(W) > \tilde{f}_t(W) \text{ for } T > t > 0. \quad [38]$$

The Merton paradox applies to the case where, instead of maximizing the terminal-bequest utility of Eq. 1, I am given initial W_T and select (C_t, w_t) to achieve the maximand of Eq. 2:

$$\text{Max}\left[\text{Exp}\left\{\gamma^{-1}\int_0^T (C_t - Q)^\gamma dy\right\}\right]. \quad [39]$$

Now add to the coefficient of dy in Eq. 33 an appendage of $-C$, with the understanding that C cannot be negative. Now

$$\hat{W}_t = W_t - E_t = W_t - Q[1 - e^{-RE}], dE_t/dt > 0, \quad [40]$$

$$w_t^* = \hat{w}_t^*(\hat{W}_t/W_t) = w_\gamma^*(1 - E_t/W_t) = \hat{f}(W_t), \quad [41]$$

$$\hat{f}_T(W) > \hat{f}_t(W) \text{ if } T > t > 0. \quad [42]$$

If we consider a third problem where we maximize a positive weighted average of the maximands of Eqs. 34 and 39, the quantitative strength of the weights has no effect on the optimal

$$w_t^* = \bar{f}_t(W_t) = w_\gamma^*[1 - (F_t + E_t)/W_t]$$
$$= w_\gamma^* - w_\gamma^*[(Q - RS)(e^{-Rt}/R) - (Q/R)]W_t. \quad [43]$$

As S/Q rises from zero to a large enough magnitude, $\bar{f}_t'(W)$ changes sign.

The presence of nonrisky human capital also raises young people's equity tolerance. {However, if their wage earnings are positively correlated with stocks' performance, this conclusion needs modifying. If wage prospects are risky but are independent of equities' risks, Pratt (10) would point out that having certain $U[W]$s would entail my having less tolerance for one class of independent risks when another class's riskiness rises. Folk wisdom, I fear, is not up to these subtleties: when in doubt, it perhaps simplistically expects increasing independent risks to be increasingly marginally painful?}

I owe thanks to the Massachusetts Institute of Technology Center for Real Estate Development for partial postdoctoral fellowship aid; to Aase Huggins and Eva Hakala for appreciated editorial assistance; and to Robert C. Merton for stimulating discussions.

1. Samuelson, P. A. (1969) *Rev. Econ. Stat.* **51,** 239–246; reprinted (1972) in *Collected Scientific Papers of Paul A. Samuelson,* ed. Merton, R. C. (MIT Press, Cambridge, MA), Vol. 3, pp. 883–890.
2. Leland, H. E. (1968) Dissertation (Harvard Univ., Cambridge, MA).
3. Mossin, J. (1968) *J. Business* **41,** 215–229.
4. Merton, R. C. (1969) *Rev. Econ. Stat.* **51,** 247–257.
5. Hakansson, N. H. (1970) *Econometrica* **38,** 587–607.
6. Samuelson, P. A. (1990) in *Macroeconomics, Finance and Economic Policy: Essays in Honor of James Tobin,* eds. Brainard, W., Nordhaus, W. & Watts, H. (Massachusetts Institute of Technology Press, Cambridge, MA), in press.
7. Bodie, Z. & Samuelson, W. F. (1989) *Labor Supply Flexibility and Portfolio Choice,* Working Paper (National Bureau of Economic Research, Cambridge, MA).
8. Merton, R. C. (1971) *J. Econ. Theory* **3,** 373–413.
9. Merton, R. C. (1990) *Continuous Time Finance* (Blackwell, Oxford), in press.
10. Pratt, J. W. (1988) *J. Risk Uncertainty* **1,** 395–413.

471

Risk Tolerances, Distributive Inequality, and Track Bettors' Equilibrium

Paul A. Samuelson

At the 1950 World Mathematical Congress, Robert Bishop weighed the empirical and theoretical evidence bearing on the Friedman-Savage (1948, 1952) hypothesis that people act to maximize the expected value, $E\{U(W)\}$, of a utility that is a function of wealth with double inflection points at some intermediate level of W. Bishop raised doubts, not since dispelled, that researchers had ever been able to identify the critical W range that the Friedman-Savage theory calls for.

What struck me most was Bishop's demonstration that such an interval of increasing marginal utility, if it were to exist, would self-destruct in the sense that its inhabitants would be inveterate gamblers who would cause themselves to be propelled out of it and into the absorbing wealth levels below and above it, where the von Neumann $E\{U(W)\}$ criterion would forbid any gambling at fair odds.

One sage's *reductio ad absurdum* is another conquistador's *tour de force*. By the time of the famous 1962 Paris conference on risk—famous because Kenneth Arrow announced there his fundamental breakthrough concerning contingent markets for different outcomes of the state of nature—Milton Friedman had traced much of observed income and wealth inequality to the life-cycle choices of risk that we each have embraced. As I explained to John Hicks at Oxford on my way home from Paris, when he asked me what had gone on there: "Those unequal beds we all lie in are supposed to be beds we made for ourselves, as Rockefeller was lucky in his long-shot bets and Micawber was unlucky in his."[1]

Because the Bishop effect planted a seed in my mind that germinated only four decades later in a model of an ergodic wealth distribution, let me explicate this effect. Divide reality into three ranges, with the poor and the rich, who are risk averse, surrounding a middle range of risk relishers. Fair gambles can be contrived virtually costlessly. Neither the rich nor the poor are willing to engage in such zero-sum activities. But the risk relishers go at it with vigor. If all of them began deep in the middle, after a few turns of the roulette wheel the winners and losers will have moved toward the two extremes. It is a standard theorem in sequential analysis and gambler's ruin that, in enough time, with probability approaching 1, all the risk relishers will have disappeared into the absorbing barriers of the rich or the poor, where their itch will have been eliminated. (You may quibble that one orphan could be left stably in the middle range. However, by sweetening the odds a bit above fair odds, the orphan could coax from the risk averters above or below enough action that he will end up out of the middle. Alternatively, we can posit that Mother Nature throws up for him and anyone fair bets that by chance will either use up his principal or garner him a compensating profit. In either case the asymptotic state is an empty Friedman-Savage domain.)

The weight of the evidence suggests that in most societies, in *every* income range, some individuals will engage in recreational gambling: at the track, with the bookies, in periodic purchases of lottery tickets, over the bridge or poker table, down at Merrill Lynch, or hanging on the street corner waiting for a frog to lunge to the right or the left. Some people eschew (or minimize) such activities at every income level. Markowitz (1952b) sensibly suggested that hysteresis obtains, so that the Friedman-Savage inflection points recreate themselves for both winners and losers somewhere above *wherever* they subsequently land. (Again, at *any W*, they both buy insurance and back long shots.) The late Jimmie Savage, not one to take any old Yes for an answer, repudiated the Markowitz rescue line, saying that he would disown such a version of his own theory as uninteresting. My advice to Savage was to cut his losses and accept whatever scientific truth Nature doles out. We do want a handle on recreational gambling, and the Markowitz-Bishop twist of the Friedman-Savage effect can provide us with one—as I shall show in my later modeling of racetrack equilibrium. (Standing friction acts in real life just like the Markowitz construct: a rough block stays anywhere you place it on a rough inclined plane; its potential energy function has a V-bottom that follows it wherever it goes. Not elegant? Not economical in the sense of Mach? Too bad, Dr. Savage and Dr. Samuelson. Like Margaret Fuller, we must "accept the universe" and whatever ways the cookie crumbles.)

Risk Tolerance That Falls, Rises, and Falls

A major use of wavy total utility functions is to give us some handle on modeling recreational gambling. Many of my subsequent pages will be devoted to illustrating the general equilibrium for bettors in a parimutuel system. Before doing this, let me mention briefly how this generalized Friedman-Savage world is particularly lethal with respect to (mean, variance) approximations (discussed by Hicks (1935), Marschak and Makower (1938), Tobin (1958), Markowitz (1959), Latané (1959), Sharpe

(1964), Samuelson (1967, 1970, 1983, 1989) and many others) and how waviness in risk tolerances can generate models of ergodic income distribution that differ materially from those of the Pareto-Champernowne type. (See Champernowne 1953.)

The two parameters of mean money return and variance are known to be sufficient for decision making under the unrealistic and singular case where the utility function of wealth, $U(W)$, is quadratic; and/or under the case that violates limited liability, where securities have returns that obey a multi-variate Gaussian probability distribution. Except as a qualitative surrogate to describe general behavior of risk bearers, mean-variance analysis is understood to be primarily approximative. Samuelson (1970), in the context of the debates among Borch (1969), Feldstein (1969), and Tobin (1969) about mean-variance, defended these tools as giving limiting approximations when outcomes become more and more bunched by "compact probabilities." Fortunately, the Merton (1969, 1990) world of instantaneous Wiener-Ito probabilities offers a valuable paradigm in which the mean and the variance become exactly sufficient parameters for choice.

Generally, one does not sensibly cavil at a two-term Taylor expansion that provides approximating insight. But—as is developed below, and explicated in Samuelson (1990a,b)—the recreational gamblers in a Friedman-Savage universe traverse small finite domains where things can get worse before they get better. There is an irreducible threeness (rather than twoness) involved in their decision making. "Why the heavy weather?" you will ask. "Use a three-term Taylor expansion, adjoining to the two moments of (mean, variance) a third moment of skewness." Alas, the derivatives at initial wealth, $[U'(W), U''(W), U'''(W)]$, cannot quite capture the requisite intricacies of the problem. That this is not a capricious consideration is exemplified by the laudable attempt of Quandt (1986) to *deduce* the observed relative unprofitability of bets on long shots by heuristic reasoning that reverses the role of variance from that of a "bad" for risk averters to that of a "good" for risk-relishers at the track.

As was mentioned above, Bishop (1950) and Friedman (1953) would have expected the wealth range around the double inflection points to empty themselves out as their inhabitants gambled out of them. More pedantically, one envisages an ergodic probability distribution with low but positive numbers in that wealth interval—this under the realistic proviso that Nature is constantly throwing up to everyone investment

107

gambles that are favorable in money terms. Although the Friedman-Savage interval tends always to empty itself, it is always gaining some new entrants from those people above and below it who have been enticed into favorable investment bets that land them there.

Economists like Markowitz, Bishop, and me, who doubt that there exist identifiable wealth intervals where the average person loses risk aversion, are led to a different ergodic theory of income distribution by the considerations of the last paragraph.[2] In Samuelson (1989), I assume positive relative-risk aversion of the Arrow-Pratt type:

$$-WU''(W)/U'(W) = A(W) = A(W) > 0 \text{ for all } W.$$

If the very rich and the very poor have a high $A(W)$ while the intermediate class has a lower $A(W)$, then those in the middle will be more venturesome and will tend by chance to rise or fall out of their initial class. Realistic considerations of tax transfers, bequests, wage earnings, and consumption needs will complete the model and provide the reflecting barriers that keep the system's asymptotic ergodic probabilities positive in all ranges of W.

The Pareto-Champernowne distribution, by contrast, requires that *all* within the Pareto range face the *same* relative decision processes as those above them in the wealth scale. See, for example, Van der Wijk's well-known law of the exact Pareto distribution—which Chipman (1976) has traced to Bowley early in the century and to a long line of writers who preceded Van der Wijk (1939).

Sport of Kings: Recreational Gambling

Can models of wavy $U(W)$ that can rationalize recreational gambling generate exact models of bettors' equilibrium?

The crowd has a wisdom few members possess. The collective of consensus business-cycle forecasters usually outperforms in the end any one of the group—certainly any random member of it. Picking the winner at a horse race by tossing a fair coin in your own private cave is hardly optimal. Nor is going by euphony of name, in disregard of the horse's attributes, lineage, and past performances. Alas, when everyone is as free to study horses' haunches, pedigrees, and running records as you are, the profitability of such efforts can self-destruct.

At the parimutuel tracks, horse A will be regarded as more likely to win than horse B. When more bets are laid on A than on B in a two-horse race,

A becomes the favorite and B becomes the long shot. Statistics show that in real life favorites do win more often than long shots. That is the bottom line. (This doctrine of a Smithian invisible hand that leads the mob to wise forecasting will be developed below as law I, and will be modified in law II to a closer approximation.)

All this is to say that the "objective probabilities" in an H-horse race for each horse to win, $(p_1, \ldots, p_h, \ldots, p_H)$, tend to be correctly estimated by the observed fractions bet at the totalizer on the respective horses, $(y_1, \ldots, y_h, \ldots, y_H)$, where

$$y_h = b_h n_h \bigg/ \sum_1^n b_j n_j, \tag{1}$$

n_h = fraction of all betters who bet on horse h, (2)

b_h = average dollar bet on h, (3)

$$1 = \sum_1^H y_j = \sum_1^H n_j = \sum_1^H p_j, \tag{4}$$

Rankings of $(p_1, \ldots, p_H)$ and $(y_1, \ldots, y_H)$ "tend to agree." (5)

Suppose races were handicapped so as to try to equalize the probability of winning for every horse, say—by having experts estimate how much extra weight the superior horse must carry. Under perfectionist handicapping, by definition, when there are H horses in the race each has a $1/H$ chance of coming in first. If people correctly believed in perfect handicapping, bets should tend to be made equally on all horses at the totalizer, so there would be no long shots and no favorites. In a two-horse race, A and B would promise the same odds; if that tended momentarily not to be so, independent of risk aversion and tolerance, rational hedonists would prefer to bet on the (spurious) long shot. Over many races, horses that were slight favorites by virtue of Brownian wobble alone would not show any tendency to win more often than the (spurious) long shots; and (5) would need modifying. A world with perfect handicappers might be a dull one for spectators.

Race betting under a totalizer system lets the bettors, all together, set the odds that each faces. Those of us who wisely bet on the horse that does win will receive all the money that is bet on all the horses—but subject to the fractional take by the track and the tax collector. Call this take factor t.

109

Ordinarily it is a fraction around $\frac{1}{5}$ or $\frac{1}{6}$. A negative t is rarely seen in real life, since it would involve an outright subsidy from some outsider. Even $t = 0$ would require someone to be an altruist.

The Complete Model of Bettor's Equilibrium: Premises

Suppose that H horses run a race, and a large number of spectators can bet on any one of them to win. Take as known the objective probability that horse h will win:

$$0 < (p_1, \ldots, p_h, \ldots, p_H), \text{ a specified vector.} \tag{6}$$

All bettors believe in these probabilities.

For simplicity, all bettors are to have the same tolerance for risk, each acting to maximize the expected value of his utility-of-wealth function, $U(W)$, which is the same function for all. Economists most often deal with risk-averse individuals, who display

$$U'(W) > 0 > U''(W), \quad W > 0 \tag{7}$$

and

$$U'(W) \to \infty \text{ as } W \to 0, \quad U'(W) \to 0 \text{ as } W \to \infty. \tag{8}$$

Recreational betting would stop in its tracks for such people until a research subsidy from the National Science Foundation made possible the negative t that would coax them into action.

To motivate bets of finite amount in the negative-sum game being run at the tracks, it suffices to posit a Friedman-Savage interval where $U'(W)$ rises for a range. Realism suggests that the Markowitz-Bishop version be assumed: Whatever the bettor's wealth just before his arrival at the track (call it $\overline{W}$), the same reversal of sign of $U''(W - \overline{W})$ recreates itself in $\overline{W}$'s neighborhood. It costs nothing to regard all spectators as starting with the same $\overline{W}$.

An elegant device to motivate a bettor's model, I have found, is to assume a *cusp* in the utility function at $\overline{W}$ itself: Below $\overline{W}$, U follows a strictly concave branch, $f(W)$; above $\overline{W}$, U follows a similar branch, $g(W)$; but $f'(\overline{W}-)$ is assumed to be below $g'(\overline{W}+)$, so that the essence of the Friedman-Savage and Markowitz-Bishop qualitative phenomena is contrived to be localized into a marginal-utility quantum up-jump at the point of initial wealth itself. Mathematically, cusped utility can be described as follows:

$$U(W - \overline{W}) = f(W - \overline{W}), \quad W \leq \overline{W} \tag{9a}$$

$$= g(W - \overline{W}), \quad W \geq \overline{W}; \quad f(\overline{W}) = g(\overline{W}) \tag{9b}$$

$$f'(W) > 0 > f''(W), \qquad g'(W) > 0 > g''(W). \tag{9c}$$

By dimension convention, we can stipulate a marginal utility of unity where W approaches $\overline{W}$ from below:

$$f'(\overline{W}-) = L = 1, \quad g'(\overline{W}+) = 1 + \Delta = R > 1, \tag{9d}$$

$$[-f''(\overline{W}-), -g''(\overline{W}+)] > 0 \text{ but otherwise arbitrary.} \tag{9e}$$

At the extremities of positive W, $f(W)$ and $g(W)$ obey (8). For total and marginal utility the pictures are ζ and $\backslash\!\backslash$.

For horses not too badly matched and the house's take factor large enough, all bets can be kept small enough so that the three parameters $[\Delta, -f''(\overline{W}-), -g''(\overline{W}+)]$ will essentially dominate the equilibrium solution's form—sophisticated "compact probabilities" for which m and σ^2 are *not* sufficient parameters!

All betting must be through the totalizer. I assume that one person bets on only one horse to win. For brevity I forbid bets on a horse to "place" or "show" (i.e., to come in at least second or third); I also forbid or ignore betting on more than one race per afternoon at the track, eliminating bets that require picking the winner in several races (e.g., daily doubles).

Recall that the totalizer gives the winners on horse h all that anyone has bet on any horse minus the track's fractional take of t times the total amount bet.

Mark Twain said that it is differences of opinion that make horse races. This is a one-third truth. Differences of risk tolerance can also motivate positive bets among persons with the same views about the probabilities. The present model abstracts from both of the above truths. (More exactly, I conceive of them as providing clustering approximations that wobble around the equilibrium points defined by this model.) What was understood by Twain, but not pithily enunciated, was that positive relish for risk taking can generate bets among people alike with respect to probability expectations and tolerances for risk. Cusped utility, or some other Markowitz-Bishop construct, formalizes the entailed equilibrium.

Preview of General Equilibrium's Properties

For broad domains of the specified parameters $(p_1,\ldots,p_H;t)$, it can be shown that a unique equilibrium will define itself, determining positive values for the $2H - 1$ independent unknowns comprising the $(\bar{b}_1\ldots\bar{b}_H)$ positive bets and the $(y_1\ldots y_H)$ fractions of total bets wagered on each horse. Of course, these solution values will be a functional of the $U(W - \overline{W})$ function specified; and they will be a function of the parameters $(p_1,\ldots,p_H;t)$:

$$0 < \bar{b}_h = B_h\{p_1,\ldots,p_H;t\}, \quad h = 1,\ldots,H \tag{10a}$$

$$0 < y_h = Y_h\{p_1,\ldots,p_H;t\}, \quad \sum_1^H Y_j\{p_1,\ldots,p_H;t\} \equiv 1. \tag{10b}$$

(Although it will be shown that each expression in (10a) can be written as $B\{p_h;t\}$ independent of h, where p_h is a scalar rather than a vector, a similar invariance will not hold for each $Y_h\{p_1,\ldots,p_H,t\}$ function.)

If t were made so large as to seem confiscatory, there might be no bets made at all and an indeterminate Y vector would result. Also, were we to let $U(W)$ have multiple inflection points, there could well be a multiplicity of solutions. For $U''(\overline{W})$ positive and t not too large, all will be risk relishers motivated to bet. And if $U''(W)$ were assumed to be positive for W everywhere on $(-\infty,\infty)$—the case too many writers seem tacitly to accept—motivated bets would be *unbounded* in size and no proper equilibrium would seem definable.

The advantage of my proposed exact model is that it permits us to test conventional wisdoms:

Betting Law I The relative odds at the track tend to approximate the *ex post* probabilities of winning. If the vector of relative shares bet on the horses, $[y_1\ldots y_H]$, agreed with *ex ante* and *ex post* probabilities, $[p_1\ldots p_H]$, law I would be exact, a stronger version of equation (5):

$$P = (p_1,\ldots,p_H) = (y_1,\ldots,y_H) = Y. \tag{11}$$

Betting Law II Because of the house's take, bets on every horse tend to be unfavorable gambles. However, "long shots" with lowest p_h tend, statistics reveal, to have the worst relative odds; "favorites" with highest p_h tend to have the least unfavorable odds, and indeed runaway favorites can be worth betting on even to a canny risk averter. One weaker way to express law II would be this:

If $p_1 \leq p_2 \leq \cdots \leq H^{-1} \leq \cdots \leq p_H$,

$$y_1/p_1 \geq y_2/p_2 \geq \cdots \geq y_H/p_H. \tag{12}$$

Poincaré paraphrased a witty friend: "Everyone believes in the normal (Gaussian) law: theorists because they think it is a fact of experience; empiricists because they think it a valid deduction of mathematical theory." Today every schoolchild knows that many data depart from normality, and that well-founded axioms can entail systematic departures from normality. I must agree that most data do bear out law II's modification of law I; but I hope to show that Quandt (1986) cannot validly *deduce* that law II has to hold for risk relishers motivated to bet at the tracks.

Laws I and II: Bottom of the Bottom Line

To speak of the "true objective probabilities" for horses 1 and 2 to respectively win in a two-horse race smacks of metaphysics. Frank Ramsey, a logician and philosopher in the class of Frege and Russell, purported to define meaningful personal or subjective probabilities in terms of betabilities and not vice versa (see Ramsey 1930). Let me therefore try my hand at a revealed preference approach.

We can imagine the universe of all two-horse races. We have historical samples from it, with statistical records of the odds that obtained for each past race and data on what the odds were on the horse that won. For any past race, know $(y_1, y_2 = 1 - y_1)$. For each, $\text{Max}(y_1, 1 - y_1)$ provides the fractional bet on the favorite, y_f; $1 - y_f$ is the bet on the long shot. From past data on how often the favorite won, for each and every numerical value of y_f on the interval $(\frac{1}{2}, 1)$ we can compile the revealed frequency of victory; this gives the conditional probability distribution

$$\text{Prob}\{\text{favorite won} \mid y_f = x\} = \phi(x), \quad \tfrac{1}{2} \leq x \leq 1. \tag{13}$$

Mob wisdom would mean that $\phi(x)$ rises with x.

Law I can be phrased to express the strict hypothesis

$$\phi(x) \equiv x, \quad \tfrac{1}{2} \leq x \leq 1. \tag{14}$$

This would be Adam Smith's invisible hand of mob omniscience about chances.

Law II can be phrased to say

$$\phi(x) > x, \quad \tfrac{1}{2} < x < 1; \quad \phi(\tfrac{1}{2}) = \tfrac{1}{2}. \tag{15}$$

If you have no outside knowledge about the relative merits of the two horses, but know that the mob has picked a favorite and determined its y_f, then your knowledge of this $\phi(x)$ function and your belief that it applies will be valuable to you. As the putative "true p_f" for you to put in your $E\{U(W)\}$ maximand from which to calculate your best $\bar{b}_f$ bet, you will want to put in law II's $\phi(y_f)$ and not law I's y_f or the agnostic's $\tfrac{1}{2}$.

A Russell-Whitehead theory of types seems almost needed to resolve the circular iteration that this suggests. When bettors start out naive and generate an observable $\phi(x)$, some may become sophisticated; and in using the old $\phi(x)$ in the described fashion, they will alter their behavior and the frequency of different y_f values that clear the market. Law II will then partially self-destruct as more people see merit in betting on the favorite, thereby undermining its relatively favorable odds. The new $\phi(x)$ will be nearer to law I's x than the old one was. The iteration might well converge to a $\phi(x)^*$ function that is self-warranting and which leaves law I only an approximation to law II. Its shape must depend on what the sources are for relevant outside information. Because of the deadweight cost of arbitrage transactions, inherent when t is appreciable, the minority with better knowledge and better deductive capacity cannot generate the dominance relevant to the totals that we are led to expect will obtain in efficient security markets—as those who are most perspicacious accumulate ever more dollars and weighting votes.

Formal Conditions of Bettor Equilibrium: Bet Sizes

Begin with me, a typical individual deciding how much to bet on horse h, or indeed whether to bet anything on h. I feel too small to affect the posted $(y_1, \ldots, y_H)$ odds that I face.

If h loses, as will happen with probability $1 - p_h$, I will end with $\overline{W} - b_h$ when I bet b_h on h. With probability p_h I shall win, and then I receive my prorated share of all the dollars bet on any horse, minus the house's take of t times that total. As a winner who has bet b_h on h, I calculate to end up with

$$\overline{W} + b_h[(1-t) - y_h]/y_h.$$

Therefore, my expected utility of $E\{U(W)\}$ has to be written as

$$e(b_h|y_h;p_h,t) = (1-p_h)U(\overline{W}-b_h) + p_h U(\overline{W}+b_h[1-t-y_h]/y_h). \quad (16)$$

Note that $e(|)$ has no need for an h subscript: its expression is the same function for all horses—it being understood that the relevant p_h and y_h do carry their appropriate h subscript. (A subscript will be used in $e(b,y;p,t)$, as in $e_b(b|y;p,t)$, to denote $\partial e/\partial b$; likewise for $e_y(\ )$, $e_p(\ )$ and $e_{by}(\ )$, and so on.

The optimal bet of $\bar{b}_h$ that I will make on horse h is generated as the solution to the Kuhn-Tucker programming problem

$$\bar{e}(y_h;p_h,t) = \underset{b_h}{\operatorname{Max}}\ e(b_h|y_h;p_h,t) \quad \text{s.t.}\ b_h \geq 0$$

$$= e(\bar{b}_h|y_h;p_h,t), \quad (17)$$

where $\bar{b}_h$ is a root for b_h of the Kuhn-Tucker relations

$$e_b(b_h|y_h;p_h,t) \leq 0, \quad (18a)$$

$$b_h e_b(b_h|y_h;p_h,t) = 0. \quad (18b)$$

Remark Negative bets are excluded because the totalizer will not permit them, being in the business of making commissions rather than giving them away.

If I am risk averse with a $U(W)$ that is everywhere strongly concave, (18) represents conditions both necessary and sufficient. The general Friedman-Savage $U(W)$ can, however, entail a b root for (18) that corresponds to a local minimum for $e(b|\ )$; and then, when $\partial e/\partial b$ is not a strictly concave function of b, we must choose, from (18)'s other pair of b roots, the $\bar{b}$ that corresponds to a *global* maximum.

If $U(W-\overline{W})$ is cusped as in (9), then (18) is also necessary and sufficient: e being a strictly concave function of b_h, $\bar{B}_h$ in (10a) will be a continuous function of its arguments both for concave and for cusped utility. If $U''(W)$ were positive for all W on $(-\infty,\infty)$, such a risk lover could find no finite $\bar{b}_h$ bet that would be optimal. If $U(W-\overline{W})$ has the Friedman-Savage property of possessing double inflection points for W above $\overline{W}$ and otherwise obeys the terminal properties of (8b), then (18) will almost always also define a unique and finite $\bar{b}_h$ even though the $B_h(\ )$ function can have jumps. As mentioned, when $U''(W)$ changes sign on many intervals, the conditions of (18) are necessary conditions for each local maximum but by themselves do not suffice to determine the $\bar{b}_h$ that is (or are) maximum-maximorum.

Where (18) suffices to define a unique $\bar{b}_h$, write it as

$$\bar{b}_h = B\{y_h; p_h, t\}. \tag{19}$$

(Again, recall that B does not itself require an h subscript.)

Here are a few helpful examples. For risk averters facing $t = 0$ and $y_h = p_h$, the gamble is fair and zero is the optimal bet. *A fortiori*, for $0 < t < 1$, a risk averter calculates

$$e_b(0, p_h; p_h, t) = -t\, U'(\overline{W}) < 0, \quad \bar{b}_h = 0. \tag{20}$$

A risk relisher, with $U''(W)$ locally positive near $\overline{W}$, will eschew small unfavorable bets but still may select a finite positive $\bar{b}_h$ à la Friedman and Savage.

The equality variant of (18a) becomes necessary and sufficient when people are risk averse, t is slightly negative, and y_h is sufficiently near p_h. Then (18a)'s equality gives the condition

$$\frac{U'(\overline{W} + b_h[1 - t - y_h]/y_h)}{U'(\overline{W} - b_h)} = \frac{(1 - p_h)/(1 - y_h - t)}{p_h/y_h}. \tag{21}$$

For cusped utility (where the two Friedman-Savage inflection points are concentrated in a quantum up-jump of marginal utility at $\overline{W}$ itself), (18)'s first equality will similarly apply provided t is not too large a proper fraction and y_h is not too far from p_h. Then (21) becomes

$$\frac{g'(\overline{W} + b_h[1 - t - y_h]/y_h)}{f'(\overline{W} - b_h)} = \frac{(1 - p_h)/(1 - y_h - t)}{p_h/y_h}. \tag{22}$$

The comparative statics of the maximizing equilibrium are clear cut:

- $\bar{e}$ is if anything, raised by an increase in p_h, and hurt by an increase in t or y_h.
- A rise in p_h, if anything, induces a larger $\bar{b}_h$ bet.
- A fall in y_h or t, which sweetens the payoff odds on horse h, need not always raise $\bar{b}_h$ since there are opposing reactions (a bit like income and substitution effects). However, for t near enough to zero and y_h near enough to p_h, the $\bar{b}_h$ bet will be small and will be reduced in the naively intuitive way by rises in either t or y_h.

Final Market-Clearing Conditions

It is not enough that a bettor on h is required to make the $\bar{b}_h$ decided on be of optimal quantitative size. Since all are restricted to betting on but one horse to win, every horse will coax out some positive bets only if all the optimal bets $(\bar{b}_1,\ldots,\bar{b}_h,\ldots,\bar{b}_H)$ stand to yield equivalent $E\{U(W)\}$ increments.

Therefore, to the optimum-size-bets conditions of (18) or (21) or (22), H in number, we must adjoin the following $H - 1$ conditions ensuring *equality of ex ante utility of bets on all horses*: In terms of the $\bar{e}$'s of (17), we have

$$\bar{e}(y_1;p_1,t) = \cdots = \bar{e}(y_H;p_H,t). \tag{23}$$

This renders complete our formal model of general equilibrium for parimutuel bettors. Our $2H - 1$ unknowns, $(\bar{b}_1,\ldots,\bar{b}_H;y_1,\ldots,y_H)$, are determined by the $2H - 1$ relations of (18) and (23). Alternatively exposited, if the H $\bar{e}(y_n;p_n,t)$ functions are taken as known entailments of the H relations of (18), then they by themselves provide us in (23) the $H - 1$ relations needed to determine the final $H - 1$ independent unknowns:

$$y_h = Y_h\{p_1,\ldots,p_H;t\}, \quad h = 1,\ldots,H \tag{24}$$

$$\sum_1^H Y_h\{p_1,\ldots,p_H;t\} \equiv 1.$$

Notice that no vanishing of $\partial y_1/\partial p_H$ cross-terms can be expected in (23)–(24).

Mere counting of independent equations to ensure equality of their number with the number of endogenous unknowns was not really good enough for your dad—except of course in the exceptional case of linear relations. We must separately analyze the quality of the equations to decide whether there *exists at least one* positive and finite solution for $(\bar{b}_1,\ldots,\bar{b}_H;y_1,\ldots,y_H)$ and whether an existent solution is *unique*. Experience suggests that proof of uniqueness usually requires stronger hypotheses and more intricate argumentation, but I conjecture that existence proofs can be straightforwardly found.

For the special case of symmetric odds, t a negative number, and the customers all risk averse as in (8),

$$H^{-1} = p_1 = \cdots = p_H, \quad t < 0 \tag{25}$$

it is not hard to demonstrate that a solution exists in the symmetric form

$$H^{-1} = y_1 = \cdots = y_H. \tag{26}$$

This is a singular instance of law I (and of law II!).

For the odds still symmetric, where t is a small enough positive number and where the customers all have (9)'s cusped utility, the same symmetric Y vector is a solution.

By continuity arguments, we can let P be anywhere in a near neighborhood around (25)'s symmetry point and know that a solution for Y near (26)'s symmetry point will be ensured. Likewise for the cusped-utility case: when P is near the symmetry point, an almost-symmetric Y solution is ensured.

The reader can experiment with the tractable case of two-horse races, where (23) reduces to

$$\bar{e}(y_1; p_1, t) = \bar{e}(1 - y_1; 1 - p_1, t) \tag{27}$$

and a graphical examination of existence and uniqueness of equilibrium can be managed for the cusped-utility case.

Pitfalls in the Literature

The noted fact that these final functions in (24), or (10b), cannot be functions of the single scalar p_h, but must be functions of the whole vector, $P = (p_1, \ldots, p_H)$, has grave consequences for the existing horse-race literature. As seen, for $H > 2$ it is quite untrue that cross-terms such as $\partial y_i / \partial p_j$ will all vanish. At once we are alerted to blemishes in the published literature, where virtually all the authorities follow the pioneering lead of Weitzman (1965) and try to deduce a single relation between the probability of any horse winning (calculated *ex post* and now written as π) conditional on its observed payoff y, essentially a variant of (13) above:

$$\pi = \psi(y), \quad y = \psi^{-1}(\pi). \tag{28}$$

For $H > 2$, and even if all races were for the same number of horses, say $H = 8$, there simply is not such an invariant function. (Example: Let $H = 3$ and let p be the probability of some specified horse winning. The remaining probability, $1 - p$, might be divided up evenly between the two other horses if they happen to be well matched. Or one of them could be much more likely than the other to win. The same $\psi^{-1}\{p\}$ function could not be expected to apply to two such different cases—except, possibly, as some vague approximation. In real life, at best there could be in three-horse races a frequency distribution for the various *ex ante* probabilities (p_1,p_2,p_3). After (18) and (23) have converted each vector P into its entailed equilibrium Y, the record book would give us the empirical frequency of horse 1 winning conditional on each observed vector (y_1,y_2,y_3). Using π's to distinguish *ex post* winning frequencies from objective *ex ante* p's, a Weitzman would not be able to observe (28)'s expression for a $\psi(y_1) = \pi_1$; at best he would be able to observe expressions such as

$$\pi_1 = \psi(y;y_2,y_3) = \psi(y_1;y_3,y_2),$$
$$\pi_2 = \psi(y_2;y_1,y_3), \hspace{3cm} (29)$$
$$\pi_3 = \psi(y_3;y_1,y_2).$$

I must leave to a more leisurely occasion further elucidation of where the existing racetrack literature in the economic journals has taken shaky short cuts. See, for example, Ali (1977), Asch et al. (1984), and Ziemba and Hausch (1987).

Law I: Not a Correct Test of Prescience

Actually, even if it were miraculously to be the case that somehow the mob is omniscient in knowing the "true" $(p_1,\ldots,p_H)$, once their risk tolerances entered into the general-equilibrium solution of (24) we should *not* expect (28) or any one-variable correspondence to hold.

The realization of law I is not evidence for exact estimation by the mob.

The reader who has understood how peculiarities of risk tolerance in $U(W)$ result in a known P vector creating an observed equilibrium Y vector *different* from itself will realize that (generally) only when everyone incorrectly estimated the true P could the observed Y happen to equal that true P! (This is true even when all bets are "small" and the probabilities can be regarded as "compact.")

Law II: An Observed Regularity Not a Deducible Result

In Samuelson (1990b) the Friedman-Savage geometry is used to generate an easy counterexample to the contention that risk relishers will, *as a matter of pure logic*, be prone to like betting on long shots so much as to penalize the relative odds offered by such bets. (They have to pay through the nose, so to speak for their kicks.) So goes the allegation. But when people start preponderantly above the Friedman-Savage top inflection point, they can be shown to reverse Quandt's rule.

Here I invite readers to create their own counterexamples, using cusped utility and assuming both t and Δ in (9) to be so small as to keep all $\bar{b}_h$'s small enough to permit us to regard $f(W - \overline{W})$ and $g(W - \overline{W})$ as simple quadratics. By specifying $-f''(\overline{W}-)$ in (9e) to be small relative to $-g''(\overline{W}+)$, the reader will verify that the reverse of Quandt's (1986) usual relation holds. That is, this case gives for $H = 2$,

When $p_1 > \frac{1}{2} > p_2, y_1/p_1 > y_2/p_2$. (30)

As a by-product of this way of creating a counterexample, the reader will realize that even compact probabilities cannot justify (mean, variance) analysis, since at the very least the three parameters $[\Delta, -f''(0-), -g''(0+)]$ are involved in the quadratic approximation to $E\{U(W)\}$. In their neglected early classic on risk, Domar and Musgrave (1944) used cornered utility—where each dollar of loss is treated as more than each dollar of gain—to hint at the same point about the inadequacy of (mean, variance) analysis even locally. The present paper's corner is in $U'(W)$ whereas theirs was in $U(W)$.

Conclusion

Economic theory is a serious business, not a game. The name of the game is understanding and testing observable reality. My first paper (Samuelson 1937) arose from a consideration that I considered too obvious even to mention:

By observing how much more than my loss you must promise me as a gain in a 50-50 coin toss at each wealth level, your recorded

Gain = f(Loss; Wealth)

function can tell you: one, whether I am maximizing the expected value of *any* existent utility-of-wealth function; and two, how fast quantitatively its marginal utility declines with higher wealth levels.

The idea had come to me in my teens while listening to Professor Paul Douglas (later a Marine hero and a Senator) exposit at the University of

Chicago Böhm-Bawerkian notions of additive temporal utilities and alleged time-preference discounting, and my first paper later spelled it all out for testable life-cycle saving behavior.

In a sense I've not advanced far in 56 years from the ruts of revealed preference—or should I say "from the golden highways of empirical science."

Frank Hahn, for whom this paper is a token of homage, is one of those rare minds of whom one can truly say, age does not stale his enthusiasm to insist upon adequate foundations for a proposed theory. Other scholars stay productive into their seventh, eighth, and ninth decades, but that is not quite the same thing. A Hicks stays true to his own star of originality; a Tinbergen stays faithful to his goal for human welfare. To me Hahn has seemed most like the late Jacob Marschak, whose love affair was with the science of economics itself. God bless!

Notes

1. When Hicks remarked "You don't suppose there is anything in that?" my reply was more frivolous than deep. Instead of saying "Actually, as I grow older and more successful, I find more and more merit in the notion," I should have said "Yes, some inequality is generated by differential tolerances for risk; and even more accumulates from differential ability to estimate real-world riskiness." See Friedman (1953) for a discussion of this matter. In particular, there used to be occasional references in the literature to an intermediate income range where fits of the Pareto distribution allegedly encountered a dearth of observations. Friedman adduced this as somewhat confirmatory of the Friedman-Savage phenomenon, employing precisely the Bishop line of reasoning. Before and since 1952, identifications of hollows in the income distribution have proved to be as elusive as the Scarlet Pimpernel. (One nice story involves Lord (Josiah) Stamp. When a tabulation of tax returns turned up a suspicious dearth in one interval, he asked his subordinates at the Inland Revenue Service to look into it. A misplaced packet of returns was conveniently found in a remote closet, clearing up the mystery. One wonders whether under different stopping rules other closets might be discovered, some adding to and others subtracting from Vilfredo Pareto's posthumous fame.)

2. See Keynes (1921) for the following misunderstanding of the mathematics of gambler's ruin:

The true moral is this, that poor men should not gamble and that millionaires should do nothing else. But millionaires gain nothing by gambling with one another, and until the poor man departs from the path of prudence the millionaire does not find his opportunity. If it be replied that in fact most millionaires are men originally poor who departed from the path of prudence [shades of 1952 Friedman], it must be admitted that the poor man is not doomed with certainty. Thus the philosopher must draw what comfort he can from the conclusion with which his theory furnishes him, that millionaires are often fortunate fools who have thriven on unfortunate ones.[1]

> [1] From the social point of view, however, this moral against gambling may be drawn—that those who start with the largest initial fortunes are most likely to win, and that a given increment to the wealth of these benefits them, on the assumption of a diminishing marginal utility of money, less than it injures those from whom it is taken.

(Keynes 1921, p. 320 and n. 1)

Any innuendo of the rich getting richer at the expense of the poor is ill-founded. To act so as to maximize your probability of winning—à la either Keynes or Latané, Kelly, and Breiman—can be a treacherous strategy. Actually, A and B with respective wealths of W_A and W_B, if risk averse, will never gamble with each other. Even when $W_A \gg W_B$, A will refuse to gamble, since for $U_A''(W) < 0$

$$\frac{W_B}{W_A + W_B} U_A(0) + \frac{W_A}{W_A + W_B} U_A(W_A + W_B) < U(W_A).$$

References

Ali, Mukhtar M. 1977. "Probability and utility estimates for racetrack bettors." *Journal of Political Economy* 85 (4): 803–815.

Asch, Peter, Burton G. Malkiel, and Richard E. Quandt. 1984. "Market efficiency in racetrack betting." *Journal of Business* 57 (2): 165–175.

Bishop, Robert L. 1950. Lecture on Expected Utility. World Mathematical Congress, Cambridge, Massachusetts.

Borch, Karl. 1969. "A note on uncertainty and indifference curves," *Review of Economic Studies* 36 (105): 1–4.

Champernowne, David. 1953. "A model of income distribution." *Economic Journal* 63: 318–351

Chipman, John S. 1976. "The Paretian heritage." *Revue Européene de Science Sociale and Cahiér of Vilfredo Pareto* 14 (37).

Domar, Evsey D., and R. A. Musgrave. 1944. "Proportional income taxation and risk-taking," *Quarterly Journal of Economics* 58: 388–422.

Feldstein, Martin. 1969. "Mean-variance analysis in the theory of liquidity preference and portfolio selection." *Review of Economic Studies* 36 (105): 5–12.

Friedman, Milton. 1953 "Choice, chance, and the personal distribution of income." *Journal of Political Economy* 61: 277–90.

Friedman, Milton, and L. J. Savage. 1948. "The utility analysis of choices involving risk." *Journal of Political Economy* 56: 279–304.

Friedman, Milton, and L. J. Savage. 1952. "The expected-utility hypothesis and the measurability of utility." *Journal of Political Economy* 60: 463–474.

Hicks, John. 1935. "A suggestion for simplifying the theory of money." *Economica* N.S. 2: 1–19.

Keynes, John Maynard. 1921. *A Treatise on Probability*. Macmillan.

Latané, Henry A. 1959. "Criteria for choice among risky ventures." *Journal of Political Economy* 67: 144–55.

Markowitz, Harry M. 1952a. "Portfolio selection." *Journal of Finance* 7: 77–91.

Markowitz, Harry M. 1952b. "The utility of wealth." *Journal of Political Economy* 60: 151–158.

Markowitz, Harry M. 1959. *Portfolio Selection*. Yale University Press.

Marschak, Jacob, and Helen Makower. 1938. "Assets, prices and monetary theory." *Economica* N.S. 5: 261–88.

Merton, Robert C. 1969. "Lifetime portfolio selection under uncertainty: The continuous-time case." *Review of Economics and Statistics* 51: 247–257.

Merton, Robert C. 1990. *Continuous-Time Finance*. Blackwell.

Quandt, R. E. 1986. "Betting and equilibrium," *Quarterly Journal of Economics* 101: 201–207

Ramsey, Frank P. 1930. *The Foundations of Mathematics*. Routledge.

Rosett, Richard N. 1965. "Gambling and rationality." *Journal of Political Economy* 73: 595–607.

Samuelson, Paul A. 1937. "A note on measurement of utility." *Review of Economic Studies* 4: 155–61.

Samuelson, Paul A. 1967. "General proof that diversification pays," *Journal of Finance and Quantitative Analysis* 2: 1–13. Reprinted in *Collected Scientific Papers of Paul A. Samuelson*, Volume 3, ed. R. C. Merton. MIT Press, 1972.

Samuelson, Paul A. 1970. "The fundamental approximation theorem of portfolio analysis in terms of means, variances, and higher moments." *Review of Economic Studies* 37 (4): 537–542. Reprinted in *Collected Scientific Papers of Paul A. Samuelson*, Volume 3, ed. R. C. Merton. MIT Press.

Samuelson, Paul A. 1983. *Foundations of Economic Analysis*, enlarged edition. Harvard University Press.

Samuelson, Paul A. 1989. "The $\sqrt{N}$ law and repeated risktaking." In *Probability, Statistics, and Mathematics: Papers in Honor of Samuel Karlin*, ed. T. W. Anderson et al. Academic Press.

Samuelson, Paul A. 1990a. General Equilibrium Model for Parimutuel Track Odds. Working paper, MIT.

Samuelson, Paul A. 1990b. The Geometry of Friedman-Savage and Revealed Preference for Risk Taking. Working paper, MIT.

Sharpe, William F. 1964. "Capital asset prices: A theory of market equilibrium under conditions of risk." *Journal of Finance* 19: 425–442.

Tobin, James. 1958. "Liquidity preference as behavior towards risk." *Review of Economic Studies* 25: 65–86.

Tobin, James. 1969. "Comment on Borch and Feldstein." *Review of Economic Studies* 36 (105): 13–14.

Van der Wijk, J. 1939. *Inkomens- en vermogensverdeling*. De Erven F. Bohn N.V.

Weitzman, Martin. 1965. "Utility Analysis and Group Behavior: An Empirical Study." *Journal of Political Economy* 73: 18–26.

Ziemba, W. T., and D. B. Hausch. 1987. *Beat the Racetrack*. Wm. Morrow.

472

GRAPPLING WITH THE RATIONAL CASE FOR LONG-HORIZON RISKY-EQUITIES TOLERANCE

University of Rome, Rome, 5 April 1995

When I was first invited to speak at the University of Rome, there was a temptation not to accept. After all it was a vacation time. And there was a second consideration. If you have been a writer of textbooks, and adviser to Presidents, people want you to speculate on the future of Capitalism and the Mixed Economy; or to forecast on the next collapse of the dollar; or, in Italy perhaps, to render judgments on Sraffian economics.

In the end I agreed to meet with a small group of graduate students and staff. And to talk about a particular topic in economic theory that would well illustrate what my kind of economic theorist does in any month of a 50-year career.

My chosen topic is from the modern theory of finance. This is a brand new branch of our subject, one which didn't exist before World War II. From the beginning I was in on its development. To drop names, think of Black-Scholes. Robert Merton. Bill Sharpe. Gene Fama. Modigliani-Miller, Harry Markowitz, Kenneth Arrow, and many others. Also, going back into the prehistoric past will be found such now-realized-to-be-relevant names as Bachelier, (even) Einstein, Norbert Wiener, Ito, Bernoulli, Laplace, and von Neumann.

The resulting theory is both beautiful and empirically verifiable. It also is crucial for policy purposes. Do "derivatives" improve the efficiency of The Efficiency Market? Do they add to destabilizing market volatility, thereby increasing the system's vulnerability to 1929 and 1987 crashes and panics?

Problem for Today

Here it is: should long-horizon investors be *rationally* more tolerant of risky equities than short-horizon investors? The emphasis is on the word "rationally." Fads come and go.

Right now the current fashion definitely favors: Be a long-run investor. Just buy and hold. Ignore temporary ups and downs in the New York and Milan stock prices, because over one, two or three decades they will be seen to be truly temporary. *Always* equities deliver a higher *total return* than do alternative assets in every *long* run. Eschew regrets. And accept it that the odds are greatly against those who believe they can "time" their decisions to profitably sell out when the indexes are "high" and buy back in after they have become "low."

In sum, *diversification over time* solves all the risk problems that can be solved for the life-cycle investor.

The same advice is given to the Treasurer of Harvard University, the Ford Foundation, or to the sophisticated manager of any pension fund. Harvard is forever. Act like a long-horizon investor and tilt toward high-means equities despite their riskiness.

Ruling Rationalizations
I have said that it is today's fashion to advise the young to hold a higher fraction of risky equities than the old should do. Actually that has always been the standard doctrine preached by financial advisers.

I was for many years Trustee for TIAA-CREF, the pension fund for colleges and the world's largest private pension fund. Although it pretended not to give any financial or legal advice, its participants could be forgiven for reading into its literature: Begin your career with as high a fraction of your pension portfolio in equities as your risk tolerance can stand; then, before or during retirement be more heavily invested in safe bond and cash items.

Now Wall Street even offers mutual funds tailored for folks born in the 1920s, or 1930s, or in later decades. These are pledged to follow the strategy: Risky stocks when the investment horizon is long (as for example $T = 30$ years); cautious concentration on short-term bonds when T_2 shrinks to 10 or 5.

What then is new? New are the dozens of articles by professors of finance who purport to prove that the Law of Large Numbers is the long investor's friend and savior. Here are typical rationalizations.

1. Calculate how stocks have always beat bonds in economic history when you deal with comparative portfolio performances over every decade since, say, 1850. "Always" means that history confirms a sure thing.

2. Insurance companies can close when they cover one ship. For them two ships are less risky. Better still 100 ships: "Diversification diminishes risk." Diversification across time, holding stocks for 40 years (which is 480 months, 3360 weeks)--makes stocks' excess *total return* a sure thing.

σ_{100} of 100, if not less than σ_1 of 1, is only 10 (and now 100) times σ_1.

$$\sigma_T = \sqrt{T}\ \sigma_1.$$

3. People are too cautious. That makes bargains for rational risk-takers like the Harvard professor who told me that irrational risk aversion by the crowd made bargains for the select few like himself who understand the Law of Large Numbers.

4. How much long-run risk tolerance is good? If 55% in stocks is a bargain, 65% is better. As a member of the Finance Committee of the National Academy of Sciences, USA, that is what I am told. And some of the most sophisticated scientists now write articles with the title, "The Case for 100% Stock Portfolio for

Universities, Foundations and (even) Pension Funds."

5. Buy stocks and forget them. Don't read the financial page. Don't calculate your weekly, monthly, or even yearly ups and downs. Regret is vain regret. It is your psychological enemy. The gardener who uproots his flowers to check on how they are doing ruins the crop.

Where I Stand

By now I have written more than half-a-dozen highly mathematical articles debunking these misunderstandings of how the Law of Large Numbers really works. Alas, as yet, my syllogisms fall mostly on deaf ears.

One young scholar, beginning what will be a promising career, wrote me recently:

> Professor Samuelson, what right do you have to tell people not to be bold in their long-horizon investing? It's a free country, and your vote is no bigger than all those out there. And when it comes to my own pension portfolio, your vote counts for zero and *my* vote counts for 100%.

Of course I am not Mussolini to give orders that all investors must obey, lest they be given castor oil until they agree with my dicta. People's own risk-aversion and risk-tolerance should control their own portfolio decisions. All that I do, or have ever done, is point out carefully when a way of reasoning does not cogently justify the actions that investors think they do.

1. Thus, time does not gradually erode short-term riskiness into negligible long-term riskiness.

2. Thus, the story of how an Italian or American would have fared in the whole of the 1850-1995 economic history is *not* a large-sample sure thing. Looked at one way, an actual history (Adam, Caesar, Napoleon, Lenin, Keynes) is *a sample of one*. Surety does not come from the likes of it.

3. Thus, record from U.S. history every week's percentage changes in the Dow-Jones or Standard & Poor's and write them on a slip of paper. Put all the 1850-1995 several thousand slips of paper into a huge hat and shake them up randomly.

Now let's draw at random new histories, each being a sample of several thousand. Calculate how two siblings compare: A who sticks to allegedly safe fixed-principal bonds; and B who puts 100% into stocks.

Is it a sure thing that B always beats A?

No. Most of the samples drawn do show B better than A in a 40-year pension program. (If T were 50 instead of 40, A's probability of beating B would be lower still.)

That part of the probability statistics is trivially true. But what matters to the rational risk-taker is to tally up *all* the probabilities when A does beat B, and carefully calculate how bad the beatings are (how bad not merely in retirement dollars or retirement lira, but in utility terms of the rational decision-maker). Thus specify your own $U(W_0)$ function where W_0 is the (real) retirement wealth dealt out to you by chance on the day you retire.

If the Law of Large Numbers eroded riskiness to virtually zero, the $E\{U(W_0)\}$ test should confirm today's fad always. Does it? No. And not at all for chaps like me and you if our $U(W_0)$ is like Bernoulli's $\log W_0$; or like Cramer's $W_0^{1/2}$; or like what many econometricians estimate will give good market fit for time series and cross-sectional data, say $U(W_0) = -W_0^{-2}$. For the genus of which these three U's are species, working the problem right for ourselves gives: *Invest the same fraction for a one-year or a 100-year horizon.* (See Samuelson, *Review of Economics and Statistics*, 1959.)

Probability Model

A. $1 in *safe* asset → $(1+$\bar{r}$) one period later: $\bar{r} \geq 0$, $R = 1+\bar{r} \geq 1$

$1 in risky stock(s) → $Z, a random variable with probability density $p(z)dz$

B.   Random Walk: Each successive period has *independent* and *same* random variable

$(Z_1\ Z_2\ ...\ Z_T)$: probability density $p(z_1)p(z_2)...dz_1 dz_2...dz_T$
$\text{Exp } Z = E\{Z\} = \int_0^\infty z p(z) dz = \mu > R = 1+\bar{r}.$

(or else risk-averters won't buy *any* stock)
$0 < \text{Var } Z = \int_0^\infty (z-\mu)^2 p(z) dz = \sigma_1^2.$

C.   One-period-horizon Investor begins with Wealth = W_1. She puts x_1, fraction of

W_1 in stock and $(1-x_1)$ in safe cash. Her final ("retirement") wealth is

$W_0 = W_1(1+\bar{r})(1-x_1) + W_1 Z_1 x_1 = W_1 R + W_1(Z_1-R)x_1$
$= W_1(R+[z_1-R]x_1).$

127

D. Two-period horizon Investor begins with W_2 and puts x_2 fraction into stock.
At the end of that period she has

$W_1 = W_2R + W_2(Z_2-R)x_2 = W_2[R+(Z_2-R)x_2]$.
Later
$W_0 = W_1R + W_1(Z_1-R)x_1 = W_2[R+(Z_2-R)x_2][R+(Z_1-R)x_1]$.

E. For T-period-horizon Investor, we have

$W_{T-1} = W_T[R+(Z_T-R)x_T]$
.....
$W_1 = W_2[R+(Z_2-R)x_2]$
$W_0 = W_T[R+(Z_T-R)x_T] .. [R+(Z_1-R)x_1]$
etc.

Expected Utility Model (Daniel Bernoulli-Laplace-von Neumann)
You act from T-to-0 years from retirement to *maximize* your $E\{U[W_0]\}$, where

$$U'[W_0] > 0 > U''[W_0], \; U[W] \text{ is } concave.$$

(A dollar of loss hurts more than a dollar of gain pleases, diminishing [cardinal] marginal utility of a risk averter.)

One-Period Decision Problem
Seek

$$\text{Max}_{x_1} E\{U[W_0]\} = \text{Max}_{x_1} E\{U[W_1(R+(Z_1-R)X_1)]\}$$

$$= \text{Max}_{x_1} \int_0^\infty U[W_1(R+(Z_1-R)x_1)]p(z_1)dz_1$$

$$= \int_0^\infty U[W_1(R+(z_1-R)x_1^*)]p(z_1)dZ_1$$

$$= \int_0^\infty U[W_1(R+(z_1-R)f_1[W])] \equiv U_2(W_1) \text{ below}$$

where $x_1^* = f_1\{W_1\}$ is unique root for x_1 of

$$0 = W_1 \int_0^\infty [z_1-R]U'(W_1[R+(z_1-R)])p(z_1)dz_1.$$

Example. The family of $U(W_0) = \log W_0$, $W_0^{1/2}$, $-W_0^{-2}$, or $W^\gamma/\gamma, 0 \neq \gamma < 1$, all enjoy "*constant* relative risk aversion," or

$$R_1(W_0) = -W_0 U''(W_0)/U'(W_0) \equiv -(\gamma-1) = 1-\gamma > 0$$

128

$R_1'(W_0) \equiv 0$.

Theorem: $f_1\{W\} \equiv x_1^* \equiv c_\gamma$ for them (proportionality of stocks to wealth)

c_γ grows with γ

Theorem: If $R_1'(W_0) < 0$ (diminishing relative risk aversion), $f_1'\{W_1\} > 0$. The rich feel they can risk *more*.

Two-Period-Horizon Case
This is *exactly* like one-period provided we begin with W_2 and pick $x_2^* = f_1\{W_2\}$ so as to maximize Exp Val of a *new* $U_2(W_1)$ rather than the old $U(W_0) \equiv U_1(W_0)$. Again, we have a new $x_2^* = f_2\{W_2\}$ which is optimal for the two-period horizon *in its first year ahead*.

Skipping details of dynamic programming, here are the procedures and results for the two-period case.

$$\operatorname*{Max}_{x_2} E\{U_2[W_1]\} = \operatorname*{Max}_{x_2} E\{U_2[W_2(R+(Z_2-R)x_2)]\}$$

$$= E\{U_2[W_2(R+(Z_2-R)x_2^*)]\}$$
$$= E\{U_2[W_2(R-(Z_2-R)f_2\{W_2\})]\}$$

where $x_2^* = f_2(W_2)$ is the unique root for x_2 of

$$0 = (\partial/\partial x_2) E\{U_2[W_2(R+(Z_2-R)x_2)]\}$$
$$= \int_0^\infty (Z_2-R) U_2'(R+(Z_2-R)x_2) p(z_2) dz_2.$$

Today's problem is this: What are *sufficient* conditions on $U(W_0)$ or $U_1(W_0)$ so that

$$x_2^* = f_2(W) > x_1^* = f_1(W)$$

for relevant W ranges?

If we can prove it to T = 2, and T = 1, we can prove it for
$$0 < f_1(W) < f_2(W) < f_3(W) < ... < f_{T-1}(W) < f_T(W).$$

Examples of Some *Rational* Reasons for Going Along with the Current Fad
Case 1. Samuelson (1992, *Proceedings of the National Academy of Sciences*)
$U(W) = \log(W-1)$, R = say $1 + .10$.

Here retirement is *infinitely* miserable unless you end with $W_0 > 1$.

Theorem:
$$\frac{f_2(W)}{f_1(W)} = \frac{W-(1.1)^{-2}}{W-(1.1)^{-1}} = \frac{W(1.1)^2-1}{W(1.1)^2-1.1} > 1. \text{ QED.}$$

$$\frac{f_T(W)}{f_1(W)} = \frac{W-(1.1)^T}{W-(1.1)^{-1}} = \frac{W(1.1)^{T-1}}{W(1.1)^T-(1.1)^{T-1}} > 1$$

$$> \frac{f_{T-1}(W)}{f_1(W)} > \ldots > \frac{f_3(W)}{f_1(W)} > \frac{f_2(W)}{f_1(W)} > 1. \text{ QED.}$$

Case 2. $R_0'(W) < 0$ for $U_0(W) \equiv U(W)$
If   Var. of stocks sufficiently small
$0 < \mu - R << 1$,
then
$f_T(W) > f_{T-1}(W)$, $T = 2,3,\ldots$

References

Samuelson, P.A. 1959. "Alvin Hansen and the Interactions between the Multiplier Analysis and the Principle of Acceleration," *Review of Economics and Statistics* 41.2, Part I(May): 183-84.

Samuelson, P.A. 1992. "Conserved energy without work or heat," *Proceedings of the National Academy of Sciences*, 89(February):1090-94.

How Best to Flip-Flop if You Must: Integer Dynamic Stochastic Programming for Either-Or

PAUL A. SAMUELSON
Department of Economics, Massachusetts Institute of Technology, Cambridge, MA 02139-4307

Abstract

Standard portfolio analysis presumes one can blend different securities continuously. When one must choose all of one portfolio or all of another, we are in stochastic digital programming: either-or, zero-or-one choice. The algorithm for doing this optimally is shown to be simpler than in real variable maximizing, a switch from the usual extra complexities of digital programming. The Bellman multi-period dynamic programming is shown, paradoxically, to make it possible for a risk-averse investor to want sometimes to embrace an unfair gamble. The superiority of within-time diversification over across-time diversification carries over to this flip-flop case.

Key words: 0-1 Choice, worthwhile, unfair bets

JEL Classification: D-80, G-00

It is better to diversity a portfolio among securities *within* time than to flip-flop *across* time. But sometimes "either-or" is an intrinsic necessity and then an algorithm is needed to do it optimally. Thus the present paper, which is a sequel to Samuelson (1997), is in the spirit of the Dubins-Savage classic, *How to Gamble if You Must* (1965).

The contemplated analysis deals with a manageable scenario. In contrast to the usual extra complexities induced by integer-programming constraints, this exercise has a solution that involves no dependence on the *marginal* utility function $U'(W)$, and is paradoxically easier to solve than the real-variable programming case. Beyond its own interest, the case throws light on the dialogue between partisans for Bellman derived-indirect utilities (maximands) and classic Lagrange-Chow alternatives. Also, just as quantum restrictions in physics led to new and interesting results, so in this case where control variables are restricted to zero or one, a risk-averse person can be motivated to accept certain unfavorable gambles.

Consider a standard optimal-portfolio problem. You begin with initial wealth of $\bar{W}$. You can allocate it in non-negative fractions $(x_1\ x_2\ \ldots\ x_N)$ among N different securities, which are each and all subject to a joint probability distribution of outcomes per dollar put into them, $(Y_1\ Y_2\ \ldots\ Y_N)$.

$$\text{Prob}\{Y_1 \leq y_1, \ldots Y_N \leq y_n\} = P(y_1, \ldots y_n). \tag{1}$$

There is no presumption that the different alternatives are probabilistically *independent;* $P(\ )$ is presumptively not $P_1(y_1)P_2(y_2) \ldots P_N(y_n)$. However, in so-called "efficient markets" where knowable odds tend to be discounted in advance by numerous avid competitors, between any two time periods t and $t + k$, *intertemporal independence* is often postulated. A further assumption is that of *stationariness*, in which $({}^{t}Y_1 \ldots {}^{t}Y_N), \ldots, ({}^{t+k}Y_1 \ldots {}^{t+k}Y_N)$ all have the same $P(y_1, \ldots, y_N)$ probability distributions.

Let t be the integer denoting time periods ahead until a terminal date of retirement. At any time t, your initial W_t results in the following W_{t-1} after you have somehow selected your best portfolio fractions of $({}^{t}x_1^* \ldots {}^{t}x_N^*)$:

$$W_{t-1} = W_t[{}^{t}Y_1 {}^{t}x_1^* + \ldots + {}^{t}Y_N {}^{t}x_N^*], \quad t = T, T-1, \ldots, 2, 1. \tag{2}$$

In the accumulation of lifecycle savings toward retirement, your final W_0 wealth will then be a random variable dependent upon luck of the draw—i.e., on the $P(y_1, \ldots, y_n)$ function—and on your way of choosing the $({}^{T}x_1^* \ldots {}^{T}x_N^*), \ldots, ({}^{1}x_1^* \ldots {}^{1}x_N^*)$ sequence along the way.

Here it is assumed those choices are made optimally to maximize Expected{Risk-averse Utility of final W_0 wealth}:

$$\text{Max } E\{U(W_0)\}; \quad U'(W_0) > 0 > U''(W_0). \tag{3}$$

In the classic problem where diversification *within* each time period t is feasible, the optimal elements of the $({}^{t}x_j^*)$ vector are generically real non-negative fractions. But in the present "either-or" or "flip-flop" scenario, each and every ${}^{t}x_j^*$ is constrained to be 0 or 1; and at any t only one ${}^{t}x_j$ can be one, so that always ${}^{t}x_1^* + \ldots + {}^{t}x_N^* = 1$. (Heavy transaction costs, market imperfections, or institutional rigidities might mandate 0–1 lumpiness. Or this might arise from mistaken beliefs about *across-time* diversification. See P.A. Samuelson, 1997.)

1. The one-period problem

When $T = 1$, our problem becomes

$$\text{Max } E\{U(W_0)\} \equiv \underset{x_j}{\text{Max }} E\{U(\bar{W}_1 \sum_1^N x_j Y_j)\}$$

$$= E\{U(\bar{W} \sum_1^N x_j^* Y_j)\} \tag{4}$$

where any admissible optimizing (x_j^*) vector will depend on $\bar{W}$.

Since this scenario requires choice of but one out of the N alternative mutually-exclusive different investments, the N marginal probability distributions for the respective

HOW BEST TO FLIP-FLOP IF YOU MUST

[$'Y_j$] variables are critical. These are defined from Equation (4)'s $P(\ )$ function by the following:

$$\text{Prob}\{Y_1 \leq y_1\} = P(y_1, \infty, \ldots, \infty) = P_1(y_1)$$

$$\text{Prob}\{Y_2 \leq y_2\} = P(\infty, y_2, \infty, \ldots, \infty) = P_2(y_2)$$

$$\ldots$$

$$\text{Prob}\{Y_N \leq y_N\} = P(\infty, \infty, \ldots, \infty, y_N) = P_N(y_N). \tag{5}$$

Since $P_1(y_1)$ might refer to safe cash, while $P_2(y_2)$ refers to the S&P 500 Index and $P_N(y_N)$ to General Motors stock or an international security, the $P_j(\ )$ and $P_k(\ )$ distributions can well differ materially in *mean* values and in spread *volatilities*.

Highly relevant for our problem are the N different expected utilities from 100% investments in each of the alternative securities, defined as

$$^1u_j(W_1) \equiv E\{U(W_1 Y_j)\}, \quad j = 1, 2, \ldots, N \tag{6a}$$

$$\equiv \int_0^\infty U(W_1 y_j) dP_j(y_j). \quad j \tag{6b}$$

These Stieltjes integrals handle both probability densities and discrete probabilities. For a density, $dP(y_j)$ is merely a notation for $P'(y_j)dy_j$. For discrete probabilities, the above integral becomes a sum: $p'_j y'_j + p''_j y''_j + \ldots$, $p'_j + p''_j + \ldots = 1$ and $(y'_j y''_j \ldots)$ the various possible outcomes from the dollar put into the jth security. (Remark: any dividends are understood to be combined with capital-gains changes in principal. Taxes and transaction costs are either ignored or have already been properly allowed for.)

We can now rewrite our maximal expected utility from (4), as follows

$$\underset{x_j}{\text{Max}} \ E\{U(\bar{W}_1 \sum_1^N x_j Y_j)\} \tag{7a}$$

$$= \text{Max}[E\{U(\bar{W}_1 Y_1)\}, E\{U(\bar{W}_1 Y_2)\}, \ldots, E\{U(\bar{W}_1 Y_N)\}] \tag{7b}$$

$$= \text{Max}[^1u_1(\bar{W}_1), \ldots, {}^1u_N(\bar{W}_1)] \tag{7c}$$

$$= U_1(W_1), \text{ def. of Bellman derived, indirect } U_1(W) \text{ function.} \tag{7d}$$

Note that two or more of the N investments might, at some $\bar{W}_1$ level, happen to be tied in expected utility. Therefore, the optimal vector (x_j^*) (which of course consists of $N-1$ zeros and a single one) might *not* be a *single*-valued function of $\bar{W}_1$; rather it will then be a *correspondence* between (x_j^*) and $\bar{W}_1$. As far as optimality is concerned the indeterminacy is inessential: you are then quite indifferent as to which of the tied x_j^* optimal vectors are selected. The subsequent probability distribution for W_0 is different depending upon which of the tied winners you happen to select; but their $E\{U(W_0)\}$ or $U_1(\bar{W}_1)$ is exactly the same for them, and that is all that counts for you the decision-maker.

Employ the convention that your original $U(W)$ function can be written as $U_0(W_0)$, the utility to you of each final W_0 wealth. Equations (7) show how from any risk-averse $U_0(W)$ function, we can derive Bellman's indirect utility function $U_1(W)$ measuring how much each W wealth level for you one period earlier is deemed then to be worth to you in the end. The next section goes from $T = 1$ to multiple-period dynamic stochastic horizons where $T \geq 2$. It shows how, at any intermediate t stage, you will want to invest your W_t in a best allocation vector $({}^t x_j^*)$ so as to maximize your calculated Bellman *indirect* utility function $U_{t-1}(W_t)$.

2. The two-period problem

Here you begin with $\bar{W}_2$. Everything relevant about your ultimate $U(W)$—or $U_0(W)$—evaluation of risks and gains is at this stage of the game encapsulated in (7)'s $U_1(W_1)$ function. Concretely, you solve

$$\text{Max } E\{U_1(W_1)\} \equiv \text{Max } E\{U_1(\bar{W}_2 \sum_1^N {}^2 x_y Y_j)\} \tag{8a}$$

$$= E\{U_1(\bar{W}_2 \sum_1^N {}^2 x_j^* Y_j)\}, \text{ def. of optimizing } (x_j) \tag{8b}$$

$$= \text{Max}_j [E\{U_1(\bar{W}_2 Y_1)\}, \ldots, E\{U_1(\bar{W}_2 Y_N)\}] \tag{8c}$$

$$\equiv U_2(\bar{W}_2), \text{ def of } U_2(W) \text{ function.} \tag{8d}$$

Armed with (8d)'s knowledge of the $U_2(W)$ function, by straightforward mathematical induction we know how to solve Bellman's dynamic stochastic programming problem one stage still earlier when then we know only our $\bar{W}_3$ wealth. And so forth, back to $t = T$, the initial $\bar{W}_T$ endowment.

3. The general t-period problem

For each t in the sequence $T, T - 1, \ldots, t, t - 1, \ldots, 2, 1$, and with $\bar{W}_T$ and $U_0(W)$ specified, the following recursion relations constitute our algorithm

$$U_t(W) = \underset{x_j}{\text{Max}}\, E\{U_{t-1}(W\sum_1^N {}^tx_jY_j)\}, \text{def. of } U_t(\ ) \text{ function} \tag{9a}$$

$$= E\{U_{t-1}({}^tx_k^*Y_jW)\}, \text{def. of } k^* \tag{9b}$$

where $({}^tx_k^*)$ is any unity vector element such that it satisfies

$$\text{Every } {}^tx_k^* \text{ is } 0 \text{ or } 1, \sum_1^N {}^tx_j^* = 1 \tag{9c}$$

$$x_k^*\{\underset{j}{\text{Max}}[E\{U(WY_j)\}] - E\{U(WY_k)\}\} = 0. \tag{9d}$$

The calculations are performed so that successively, from left to right, one evaluates

$$U_0(W): ({}^1x_j^*[W]), U_1(W); ({}^2x_j^*[W]), U_2(W); \ldots$$
$$\ldots, U_{T-1}(W); ({}^Tx_j^*[W]), U_T(W). \tag{10}$$

The last $U_T(W)$ function need not be explicitly evaluated.

When the control variables are real variables, it is a theorem that a risk-averse $U_0(W)$ generates all $U_t(W)$'s that are also risk-averse. But when integer programming constrains every x_j to be zero or one, in that quantum world a concave $U_0(W)$ can generate a non-concave $U_1(W)$ or $U_t(W)$—as will be seen (in Figure 1b to come in §5) when risk averters can then embrace unfavorable gambles. It is a theorem that for $U(W)$ with the "myopic" property of constant-relative-risk aversion, $-WU''(W)/U'(W) = A(W) = $ a strict constant, then in the integer as well as real-variable case *all* subsequent derived utilities $U_t(W)$ also possess that property. (Easy proof: In (9) posit that $U_t(W) = c_t W^\gamma/\gamma$. Then $U_{t+1}(W) = (W^\gamma/\gamma)\text{Max}(E\{Y_j^\gamma\}) = (W^\gamma/\gamma)c_{t+1}$. It follows by induction that when $U_0(W) = c_0 W^\gamma/\gamma$, every $U_t(W) = c_t W^\gamma/\gamma$.

Morever, when $A(W)$ has the special property that makes safe cash less attractive to the higher $\bar{W}$ long-horizon investor, that same propensity will hold for the optimizing flip-flop investor as well as for the standard case where the (x_j) controls are real variables.

4. Resolving a pseudo-paradox where risk-averter is led in quantum economics to embrace unfair gambles

When $(x_1, 1 - x_1)$ are non-negative, real-variable control variables that sum to one, always $U_1''(W)$ and $U_t''(W)$ are negative when $U_0''(W)$ is negative. Figure 1(a) tells that story. The concave curve AA depicts $U_1(W)$ when $(x_1, 1 - x_1)$ are frozen at $\bar{W}_A$'s optimal level. Concave BB gives $U_1(W)$ when $(x_1, 1 - x_1)$ are frozen at $\bar{W}_B$'s different optimal levels.

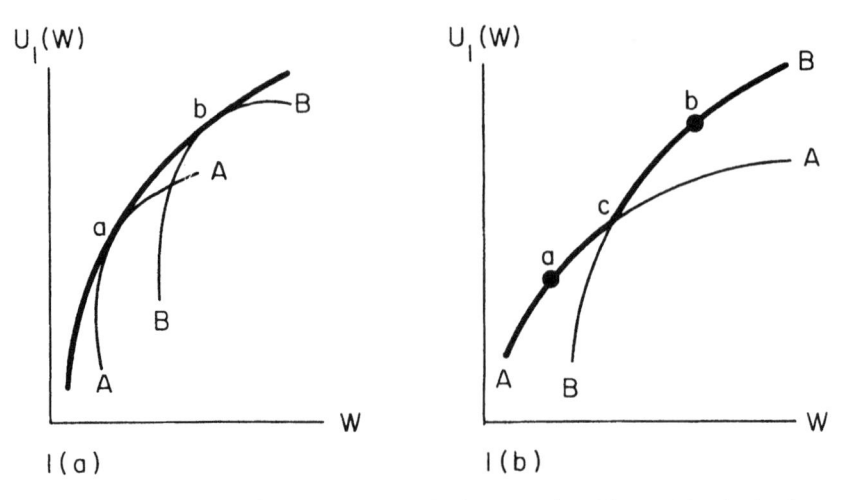

Figure 1. (a) When portfolio choice can be any real fraction, concavity of the U(W) function implies concavity of the indirect Bellman $U_1(W)$ function, as also with $U_2(W),...,U_t(W),...$, (b) Under 0-or-1 bing-bang choice, strict risk aversion of the U(W) can, paradoxically, entail non-concavities of indirect utilities — like Aa..bB — which admit of acceptance of *unfavorable* money gambles at transitional stages!

In standard non-quantum portfolio choice, the osculating *envelope* curve tangential to all the different (..., AA, BB, ...) curves is the defined correct $U_1(W)$ Bellman function. That envelope curve, ..ab.., will then also have to be concave.

The following gives analytical proof of this when x is the real-variable fraction of wealth put into a stock with favorable mean but unfavorable positive volatility; $1 - x$ goes into safe cash with an inferior mean of $1 + r = R \geq 0$.

Define

$$u(W;x) = \int_0^\infty U_0(WR[1-x] + Wyx)dP(y) \tag{11}$$

where a dollar put into the stock has one period later the random-variable outcome Y, with $\text{Prob}\{Y \leq y\} = P(y)$. Define

$$u(W;x^*) = \underset{x}{\text{Max }} u(W;x) = u(W;X[W]) = U_1(W) \tag{12}$$

where $x^* = X[W]$ is the unique root of

$$\partial u/\partial x = u_x(W;x^*) = 0 \equiv u_x(W;X[W]), \ U_1'(W) \equiv u_W(W;X[W]) + 0. \tag{13}$$

From (11) we can verify that $u(W;x)$ is concave in its two arguments, so that almost everywhere

HOW BEST TO FLIP-FLOP IF YOU MUST

$$u_{ww} < 0, u_{xx} < 0, \Delta = u_{ww}u_{xx} - u_{xy}^2 > 0. \tag{14}$$

Now, using (14), calculate

$$U_1''(W) = dU'(W)/dW = d\{u_W(W;X[W])\}/dW$$

$$= u_{ww} + u_{wx}X' = u_{ww} - u_{wx}u_{xw}/u_{xx}$$

$$= (u_{ww}u_{xx} - u_{xw}^2)/u_{xx} = \Delta/u_{xx} < 0. \quad \text{QED.} \tag{15}$$

Figure 1(b) tells the different flip-flop story. Here $U_1(W)$ will generically cease to be concave near to where it is canny to flip-flop to 100% cash on a certain $\bar{W}$ interval, but to flip-flop to 100% in stock at an adjacent $\bar{W}$ interval. The dark "envelope" is now $AacbB$; and at the generic cusp point c, the $U_1(W)$ contour loses its concavity! Note that, in the 1948 Friedman-Savage fashion, near c you will both eschew (large-enough) fair gambles while embracing small unfavorable gambles! Concretely, suppose you can in an initial period choose to accept a small unfavorable gamble, while in your final preretirement period you can invest in one (and only one) of safe cash or in a high-mean volatile stock.

If later you can, as in Figure 1a, optimally *blend* cash and stock, a risk-averse you will never embrace *any* unfair gamble. But in the quantum world of flip-flop, if your initial $\bar{W} = \bar{W}_2$ is near c in Figure 1b, you will welcome a take-it-or-leave-it small unfavorable bet. Why? Because it gives you $\bar{W}_1$ options that average out to better terminal utilities. Counter-intuitive? Perhaps. But, on reflection, still this is the better thing to do in terms of final Expected{(concave!)Utility}.

5. Bellman versus Lagrange

Gregory Chow (1993) and Paul A. Samuelson (1996) have engaged in friendly dialogue about the relative merits and demerits of (a) the Bellman type algorithm that relies on calculation of indirect utility functions like the $U_t(W)$ sequence here, and (b) the classic Lagrange multiplier technique as applied to dynamic stochastic variables. It is agreed that both approaches involve about the same category of calculations in *continuum* retirement-saving problems: while Bellman must calculate the $\{U_t(W)\}$ sequence, Lagrange-Chow must calculate the $\{U_t'(W)\}$ sequence.

The competition with Bellman needs to be re-examined when, as in this non-continuum flip-flop case, there can be no Newtonian derivatives to put in Equation (9)'s maximizing conditions. With 0-or-1 control variables, or with more general *integer* programming scenarios, the Bellman logic still applies fully. Attempting to apply a Lagrange-Chow alternative, leads when the control is integral to *no* algorithm *alternative* to Bellman's!

I also suggest that a reader who wants to get a feel for the either-or scenario should work out an easy numerical $N = 2$ example, where Alternative 1 is safe cash with zero total return whereas Alternative 2 is a chancy stock that either doubles or halves your principal with even odds. For general $U(W)$ and one given $\bar{W}_2$, U needs to be evaluated for at most four different W values. For $U = \log W$, singularly you will always be indifferent between cash and this stock no matter what integer T is. By contrast, for $U = W^\gamma/\gamma$, $0 < \gamma < 1$, always you will buy stock; for $0 > \gamma$, always you will stand pat with cash. For more realistic $U(W)$, such that your relative risk aversion is falling with W while your absolute risk aversion rises with W—as when $-U'(W)/U''(W)$ is a *convex* function in the Christian Gollier (1995) sense—I would conjecture that cash will be held until one's wealth has reached a critical $\hat{W}_t$ level, and conjecture that $\hat{W}_t$ is lower when t is larger. (I hope a referee will publish his proof of this and related conjectures.)

Acknowledgements

For partial support I owe thanks to the NYU Stern School of Business, the MIT Sloan School of Management, and the Alfred P. Sloan Foundation. For editorial assistance I owe thanks to my MIT co-worker Janice M. Murray. I have benefitted also from conversations with Herbert Scarf of Yale.

References

Chow, Gregory. (1993). "Optimal Control without Solving the Bellman Equation," *Journal of Economic Dynamics and Control* 17, 621–30.

Dubbins, Lester E. and Leonard J. Savage. (1965). *How to Gamble if You Must; Inequalities for Stochastic Processes.* New York: McGraw-Hill.

Gollier, Christian. (1995). "Should Young People be Less Risk-Averse?" Paper in process, University of Toulouse, Toulouse, France.

Samuelson, Paul A. (1996). "The Irreducible Role of Derived Marginal Utility in Dynamic Stochastic Programming," *Pacific Economic Review* 1:1, 3–11.

Samuelson, Paul A. (1997). "Proof by Certainty Equivalents That Diversification-Across-Time Does Worse, Risk Corrected, Than Diversification-Throughout-Time," *Journal of Risk and Uncertainty*, 14:163–76.

474

Journal of Risk and Uncertainty, 15:191–200 (1997)
© 1997 Kluwer Academic Publishers

Estimating Probabilities Relevant to Calculating Relative Risk-Corrected Returns of Alternative Portfolios

PAUL A. SAMUELSON
Dept. of Economics, Massachusetts Institute of Technology, Cambridge, MA 02139-4307

Abstract

In making all-or-none choices between alternative securities, Samuelson (1997b) suggested that investors of different risk-aversion should calculate from past samples of those securities their relevant Harmonic Means, or Geometric Means, or other associative means representative of their respective degrees of relative-risk-aversion. Here it is shown how this learning procedure can be improved upon when you have prior knowledge that the securities have log-Normal distributions. Classical estimation theory, concerning *consistent, efficient*, and *sufficient* statistics, is shown to have a cash value by means of the calculable measure of (*ex ante*) "risk-corrected certainty equivalents." Needed qualifications and testings are also presented.

Key words: Certainty equivalents, learning algorithms

JEL Classification: D-80, G'00

Samuelson (1997b) nominated a procedure for measuring comparative risk-corrected total returns for alternative investment options, which purports to be superior to conventional Sharpe, Treynor, Modigliani-Modigliani procedures that are based on mean-variance approximations—superior, that is, for investors who approximate to constant-relative-risk-aversion: $-WU''(W)/U'(W) = \text{constant} > 0$. As a quasi-realistic example—applicable to investors whose $-WU''(W)/U(W) \equiv +2$—some years of data on A and B, respectively (a) the *indexed* component of a large pension organization and (b) its *actively-managed* component, had their respective Harmonic Means calculated: if forced to choose solely A or solely B, that chosen is to be the one with the larger H.M. in the historical sample period.

Friendly questions have been put to me by Duke's Edwin Burmeister and by MIT's Robert Solow. Burmeister asked: "If Canadian penny mining stocks had the same H.M. as the S&P 500 Index, would you really be indifferent between them?" In a related vein, Solow asked: "If option B's total return has an H.M. of 1.05 that involves no variability at all within the sample period, while A has an H.M. of 1.05 that involves much variability within the sample, mightn't you as a risk-averter find yourself drawn toward favoring B?"

Burmeister of course is hinting at doubts about the *stationarity* of the probability process generating penny stock price movements. Solow is wondering whether the Harmonic Mean by itself can encompass all that one feels about one's personal risk tolerance.

139

(The same query could arise for a Bernoulli with logarithmic utility of wealth: is the Geometric Mean then enough?)

One immediate reaction to Solow runs as follows: (a) After I commit myself to

Maximization of Expected Utility ≡
$$E\{U(W \text{ outcomes})\} \equiv E\{-1/W\}, \tag{1}$$

I will be second guessing my own true reaction to riskiness if I go beyond measuring putative Harmonic Means. (b) In the rare cases of exact ties between $H.M._A$ and $H.M._B$, it will be harmless to embrace a lexicographic ordering that breaks ties by selecting the option with clearly "less volatility" (somehow objectively measurable). (c) But when $H.M._A$ is even a trifle bigger than $H.M._B$, my Max $E\{-1/W\}$ will not let me second guess that fact, thus implying that realistically I would *not* be willing to pay anything appreciable for the fetish of breaking ties by using a supplementary criterion of "*ceteris paribus*, eschew gratuitous volatility."

Do these banalities dispose of the debate, dispose of certain tentative heuristic doubts? On reflection, one wants to go deeper into the problem of how a thoughtful investor forms judgements—not on his/her *utility* reaction to outcomes—but on his/her judgments about relevant probabilities. This takes one back to old issues of statistical estimation, and maybe to more modern issues of Bayesian prior and posterior personal probabilities of belief.

1. Specifying a possible scenario

In a textbook example, one can first artificially stipulate that A and B are "known" to have respectively specified universe probability distributions, $[\text{Prob}\{Z_A \leq z\}, \text{Prob}\{Z_B \leq z\}] \equiv [P_A(z), P_B(z)]$, where each Z is the random variable of that security's 1 + total return. Then, if you have thought through and committed yourself to some plausible "sure-thing" Axioms of Ramsey-von Neumann-Marschak-Savage type, you will have already ruled out of court as irrelevant the Burmeister-Solow queries; and you will indeed use the Harmonic Mean when $U(W) = -1/W$, or the Geometric Mean when $U(W) = \log W$, or the Arithmetic Mean when you have *linear* risk-neutral utility. There is here no need to have to calculate these means from finite past samples of A and B data, since by hypotheses you do "know" the $P_A(\ )$ and $P_B(\ )$ probability distributions and can use *them* to calculate exact *universe* integrals:

$$H.M._A = [\int_0^\infty z^{-1} dP_A(z)]^{-1}, \text{ etc.} \tag{2}$$

It is perhaps more realistic, in actual practice, to have to rely only on past data for A and B total returns per period in order to "learn" A's and B's $P(z)$ probability distributions. By heroic idealization, suppose we have finite samples $(Z_A^1...Z_A^N; Z_B^1...Z_B^N)$, $N \geq 1$.

Posit (i) that each and every Z_A^t has the identical distribution for all t, and (ii) that there is "exact independence" between $(Z_A^t, Z_A^{t \pm k})$, and likewise for (i) and (ii) applied to $(Z_B^t, Z_B^{t \pm k})$. This white-noise (or quasi-martingale) property is a stretch, but in markets with many buyers and sellers it could be the case that what is knowable about relevant information tends to get already discounted efficiently into the prices we all face.

Bayesians will say: "If you have *prior* probability beliefs, build them into your estimator for the H.M.$_A$ and H.M.$_B$ parameters." You may reply: "Not being aware of such prior knowledge, I hesitate to pretend to have what I am doubtful about having."

The procedure described in Samuelson (1997b), under this postulated ignorance, nonetheless, seems defensible. *Calculate the sample's H.M. for each of A and B.* Remembering the SEC warning that past performance does not guarantee future results, still you can know that the H.M. of repeated samples is a *consistent* estimator of the universe's true H.M. (With $N = $ only 1, there is no great comfort in that. With N very large, there would be much comfort if the assumption of stationariness could be taken at face value.)

Suppose N is at least 2. Solow's gut feeling is presumably that there must be some useful information in what history is telling us about the relative variabilities of Z_A and Z_B, and the resulting variabilities of N-sample H.M.'s from their universes. In Solow's proposed case, where $Z_B = 1.05$ with certainty, the god who knows what $P_A(z)$ "really" is, can calculate precisely how often an A with a "true" H.M.$_A$ of $1.05 + \Delta$, $\Delta > 0$, will by bad chance in the card deal of history, *sometimes* be passed over by you in favor of B, thereby causing you to suffer a calculable opportunity loss. The 1997 nominated choice criterion will thus give you with calculable probabilities (π, $1 - \pi$), not 1.05 of *ex ante H.M.*$_B$, and not $(1.05 + \Delta)$ of H.M.$_A$, but only the intermediate $\pi(1.05 + \Delta) + (1 - \pi)1.05 = 1.05 + \pi\Delta$. (Neyman-Pearson might speak of Type I and Type II errors: sometimes you pick inferior B, when A would in fact *ex ante* always be better.)

Unless we can posit more prior knowledge, I cannot see how the imperfect 1997 procedure can be improved on. (For N large and probabilities as posited, the procedure will not be very imperfect!)

2. Log normality to the rescue

The assumption of probabilistic *independence* of successive variations in speculative prices is a powerful one. The usual Black-Scholes formula for option pricing is dependent on its implication of log-Normality holding approximately for successive $\{p_{t+1}/p_t\}$ price *ratios* (more exactly, for "total returns"). This is what, years ago, I dubbed the *Geometric* Brownian Motion (contrasting it with Bachelier's 1900 *Arithmetic* Brownian Motion governing independent successive price *differences*, $p_{t+1} - p_t$).

For infinitely-divisible Wiener probabilities defined continuously over instants, an Itô-Merton stochastic differential equation obtains for A and B of the form

$dx = \mu x dt + \sigma x dz$, where dz is a standard Gauss-Wiener process. (3)

This does imply log-Normality for $P_A(z)$ and $P_B(z)$. Thus, for A, after appropriate choice of units for $(\mu, \sigma; \alpha, \beta)$,

$$\text{Prob}\{\log [W(t + 1)/W(t)] \leq x | \alpha_A, \beta_A\} = N([x - \alpha]/\beta)$$

$$\equiv \int_{-\infty}^{x} \exp\left(-\frac{1}{2}[x - \alpha_A]^2/\beta_A^2\right) dx/\beta_A\sqrt{2\pi}. \quad (4a)$$

$$N'(u) = (2\pi)^{-1/2} e^{-1/2 u^2}, \text{ Gaussian density.} \quad (4b)$$

Etc. for B.

Solow's strong example where B's variance is zero and ($Z_B \equiv 1.05$, $X_B \equiv \log 1.05$) will expedite the exposition without compromising its general point. For it,

$$\text{H.M.}_B = 1.05 \quad (5a)$$

$$\text{H.M.}_A = \int_0^\infty e^{-x} N'([x - \alpha_A]/\beta_A) dx/\beta_A \quad (5b)$$

$$= E\{e^{-x_A}\} \equiv \Phi_{-1}(\alpha_A, \beta_A), \text{ def of } \Phi_{-1} \text{ function.} \quad (5c)$$

Provided we know α_A and β_A, we would know *ex ante* H.M.$_A$ and could apply our agreed-to decision rule

Pick A over B if $\Phi_{-1}(\alpha_A, \beta_A) > 1.05$, or (6)

Pick B over A if $\Phi_{-1}(\alpha_A, \beta_A) < 1.05$, or

Be indifferent between A and B if $\Phi_{-1}(\alpha_A, \beta_A) = 1.05$.

Now we can depart from using solely the 1997 *consistent estimator* for H.M.$_A$, namely can depart from solely using sample

$$\text{H.M.}_A = [(1/Z_A^1) + \ldots + (1/Z_A^N)]^{-1} N \gtreqless \text{H.M.}_B = 1.05. \quad (7)$$

That methodology never bothered to utilize *the sample's* calculable

$$\hat{\alpha}_A = (\log Z_A^1 + \ldots + \log Z_A^N)/N \quad (8a)$$

$$(\hat{\beta}_A)^2 = N^{-1} \sum_1^N (\log Z_A^j)^2 - (\hat{\alpha}_A)^2. \quad (8b)$$

CALCULATING RELATIVE RISK-CORRECTED RETURNS

Since we presumably know that $\log Z = x$ has a Gaussian distribution, and definitely know that Maximum Likelihood gives $(\hat{\alpha}_A, \hat{\beta}_A)$ estimators that are *sufficient* (and *efficient*) statistical estimators for $N([x - \alpha_A]/\beta_A)$, I must nominate that we do calculate these last estimators from our past sample and *from them* calculate Equation (5c)'s

$$\Phi_{-1}(\hat{\alpha}_A, \hat{\beta}_A) \gtreqless 1.05. \tag{9}$$

That way we will have minimized the 1997 methodology's proneness to error resulting from inevitable chance variability in the draws of the historical N-sized sample of A's past performance. This can be confirmed by calculation.

Suppose, by singular coincidence, true H.M.$_A$ does equal 1.05. Then indifference truly should prevail (if we knew it) and there is zero error from *any* method used to arrive at H.M.$_A$ (astrology or otherwise!).

Suppose H.M.$_A$ truly does exceed 1.05. Then we ought (if only we knew it) always pick A over B. The 1997 algorithm has a calculable probability of picking B mistakenly: call that $E_N(\alpha, \beta)$. The Maximum Likelihood algorithm now proposed here has its calculable probability of picking B mistakenly: call that $e_N(\alpha, \beta)$.

Theorem 1. Under the log-Normal hypothesis,

$$\text{Always } e_N(\alpha, \beta) \leq E_N(\alpha, \beta), N > 1. \tag{10a}$$

$$\text{For } \Phi_{-1}(\alpha, \beta) \neq 1.05, e_N(\alpha, \beta) < E_N(\alpha, \beta). \tag{10b}$$

$$\lim_{N \to \infty} [e_N(\alpha, \beta)\, E_N(\alpha, \beta)] = [0\ 0]. \tag{10c}$$

No better $e_N(\alpha, \beta)$ function can be found, based on the specified sample data and probability assumptions made.

3. A more risk-tolerant case: Bernoulli's logarithmic utility

Now replace $U(W) = -1/W$ by $U(W) = \log W$. Under the same assumptions of probability stationariness, serial non-correlation, and log-Normality, the same sufficient estimators still apply:

$$\hat{\alpha}_A = \sum_1^N \log Z_A^k/N = \sum_1^N X_A^k/N \tag{11a}$$

$$(\hat{\beta}_A)^2 = \sum_1^N (X_A^k)^2/N - (\hat{\alpha}_A)^2. \tag{11b}$$

143

But now, instead of the Harmonic Mean as what is to be maximal, we have Max($G.M._A$, $G.M._B$):

Pick A if $\hat{\alpha}_A > \log 1.05$, or

Pick B if $\hat{\alpha}_A < \log 1.05$, or

Be indifferent if $\hat{\alpha}_A = \log 1.05$. (12a)

Note that the antipathy toward volatility as such, as when $\beta_A > \beta_B = 0$, which I have gratuitously attributed to Solow's gut feeling, now simply does not rationally have a role. Knowledge of (11b)'s β_A is quite irrelevant: only (11a)'s $\hat{\alpha}_A \gtreqless \hat{\alpha}_B$ criterion matters when

$$G.M._A = e^{\hat{\alpha}_A}, \text{ independently of } \hat{\beta}_A. \tag{12b}$$

4. Risk tolerance exceeding Bernoulli's

Suppose your utility is $U = W^{1/2}$; or is linearly *risk neutral*, $U = W$; or is $U = W^\gamma/\gamma$, $0 < \gamma < 1$. Now, in a sense explicated in (14) to come, you will savor a high $\hat{\beta}$ when that is compensated by a low $\hat{\alpha}$. Now your criterion for maximal choice is a new "γ Mean", $\Phi_\gamma(\hat{\alpha}, \hat{\beta})$:

$$(1.05)^\gamma \gtreqless E\{U(W_A)\} \equiv \int_{-\gamma_0}^{\infty} [\beta_A \sqrt{2\pi}]^{-1} e^{\gamma x} \exp\left(-\frac{1}{2}[x - \hat{\alpha}_A]^2\right)/\hat{\beta}_A^2 \, dx$$

$$\equiv \Phi_\gamma(\hat{\alpha}_A, \hat{\beta}_A), \text{ def of } \Phi_\gamma \text{ function.} \tag{13}$$

Thus γ can be $+1/2$; or for the $A.M._A$ case be $+1$; or for the $G.M.$ case, $\gamma = 0$; and for the $H.M.$ case, $\gamma = -1$. As is so often the case, one's comparative statics (so to speak) changes sign as you pass from one side of log W risk tolerance to the other side: i.e.,

$$\partial\Phi_\gamma(\hat{\alpha}_A, \hat{\beta}_A)/\partial\hat{\beta}_A \text{ has the sign of } \gamma. \tag{14}$$

Our previous Theorem 1, stated for $\gamma = -1$, generalizes as follows: for *all* $\gamma \leq 1$,

$$\text{As } N \to \infty, \partial\Phi_\gamma(\hat{\alpha}_A, \hat{\beta}_B)/\partial\beta_A = 0, \tag{15}$$

so that asymptotically my 1997 *consistent* estimator will be of tolerable accuracy.

In concluding, one must state the suspicion that the literature on stochastic portfolio decision making, along with its useful preoccupation with proper *utility* analysis of gains and losses, can benefit from more study of how we can understand and improve on our beliefs about probabilities.

5. Discussion and qualifications

How much difference does best-efficient estimation make? Here I present a way of giving a cash value to the answer, applicable when the posited probability and utility hypotheses are exactly satisfied.

Illustrate first with the special Bernoulli case where $U = \log W$. Here the *consistent* estimator procedure of Samuelson (1997b) differs not at all from this paper's suggested better procedure of using *sufficient*-statistic estimators, $(\hat{\alpha}, \hat{\beta})$ for the log-Normal sample. However, suppose that, instead of using the sample's *mean* $\log Z_A$, you had used its *median* $\log Z_A$. We know from estimation theory that, in small or large Gaussian samples, the median has only 63.7% the "efficiency" of the mean. This implies that by chance alone, even when A's true $E\{\log W\}$ does exceed $\log 1.05$ by positive Δ, one will with positive probability $(1 - \pi)$ wrongly select B rather than A. As earlier mentioned, your actual longrun achieved $E\{U(W)\}$ will be only $\log 1.05 + \pi\Delta$, where $0 < \pi < 1$.

What needs to be understood is that even though the median is also a *consistent* estimator of $\log Z_a$'s central tendency, using it will give you a lower π and thereby a lower *ex ante* Expected $\{U(W)\}$!

Average log of $(1 + \text{total return})$ or of Z is not a numerically intuitive magnitude. Samuelson (1997a) suggests one calculate for any two alternative algorithms—such as the use of median or of mean—their respective *"certainty equivalents."* Imagine two independent twins, sister and brother, facing the same log-Normal probabilities and possessing identical Bernoulli $U(W)$'s. Each begins with, say, $1 million of wealth. Girl uses the *mean* estimator; Boy uses the *median* estimator. As referee for them I can work out how much more often the boy twin wrongly chooses B over the truly-better A as compared to the savvy girl twin: her π^g exceeds his π^b. That implies he stands to get a probability distribution of *ex post* terminal wealth that is strictly worse than what she stands to get. Both must agree that hers is the better probability spread to be facing. And a referee can calculate for each of these specified probability distributions their determinable *ex ante* "certainty equivalent" dollar measure. This must convince both of them that the *mean* is the better procedure than the *median*.

This concept of "certainty equivalents" was suggested in Samuelson (1997a). Here is its procedure. Contemplate every-way identical twins, Girl and Boy. Girl uses the *sufficient*-statistic *mean* estimator and Boy uses the *consistent* (but inefficient) *median* estimator. As referee let's assume you "know" that A security definitely has a true G.M.$_A$ of say, 1.15, which exceeds G.M.$_B$ of 1.05. That being so, each twin would be best served by always picking A. They, however, must learn from the past sample's random outcome what to do.

Suppose true G.M.$_A$ = 1.15 as against G.M.$_B$ = 1.05. Suppose your size sample has for A a volatility-spread standard deviation that is about equal to $1.15 - 1.05 = 0.10$. Classical estimation theory tells that *means* of samples have a standard deviation that is $(2/\pi)^{1/2} = (.8)$ times *medians'* standard deviation. Gaussian tables tell that Girl's prob-

145

ability of correctly picking A is therefore $\pi^g = .84$ versus Boy's probability of $\pi^b = .79$. Samuelson (1997a) shows how to calculate per dollar of initial wealth a twin's certainty equivalent: $\hat{w} = \hat{W}/\bar{W}$. For Bernoulli's logarithmic utility this becomes, for Girl and Boy respectively,

$$\hat{w}^g = (1.05)^{1-\pi^g}(1.15)^{\pi^g} = (1.05)^{.16}(1.15)^{.84}, \tag{16a}$$

$$\hat{w}^b = (1.05)^{.21}(1.15)^{.74}$$

$$1 > \hat{w}^b/\hat{w}^g = (1.05/1.15)^{\pi^g - \pi^b} \tag{16b}$$

$$= (.913)^{.05} = 0.995459.$$

To sum up: it is just as if Boy, by using the inefficient median rather than the mean, throws away from his initial $1 million the amount $4,500, while Girl smiles all the way to and from the bank.

Of course when G.M.$_A$ and G.M.$_B$ differ but little, the benefit from good estimation procedure largely evaporates. Also, when A is almost as perfectly safe as B, anyone's $1 - \pi$ becomes trivially small; and, at the opposite extreme, where A is so volatile that its sampling variation enormously exceeds $|G.M._A - G.M._B|$, π will end up near $1/2$ whatever the estimation procedure used.

There is a further point concerning possible mis-specification of the log-Normal model. Suppose $\log Z_A$ is actually fat-tailed, near to the Cauchy distribution for example. Boy is not then stupid to prefer the median to the mean. The median is at the least a *consistent* estimator of the Cauchy's central tendency. A careful researcher might well become cautious when his calculated sample means and medians are strongly disparate and give conflicting signals for buying A. The log-Normality hypothesis itself ought to be tested using sample data, and similarly with respect to alternative fat-tailed specifications.

Suppose the twins had each possessed $U(W) = W^\gamma/\gamma$ for $1 > \gamma \neq 0$. The Harmonic Mean maximizer's $U(W) = -1/W$ is such a possible case. Then the *sufficient*-statistic pair, $(\hat{\alpha}_A, \hat{\beta}^2) = (E\{\log Z_A\} \text{Var}\{\log Z_A\})$, could lead one seriously astray if log-Normality is a misspecification for $\log Z$. Then Equation (9)'s suggested comparison of $\Phi_{-1}(\hat{\alpha}, \hat{\beta}) \gtreqless 1.05$ might be using a *non-consistent* estimator for true $H.M._A$! The (Samuelson, 1997b) suggested *sample* $H.M._A$ might possibly then be safer. Another same warning applies for the $W^{1/2}$ and W utility risk-averters.

For a Harmonic Mean Maximizer, or any other member of the constant-relative-risk-aversion family, the certainty equivalence formulas of (16) involve π-weighted Harmonic Means of the ($H.M._A$ and $H.M._B$), namely:

$$H.M. = [\pi(H.M._A)^{-1} + (1 - \pi)(H.M._B)^{-1}]^{-1}. \tag{16c}$$

And similarly, for risk-neutral folk,

$$A.M. = \pi A.M._A + (1 - \pi)A.M._B. \tag{16d}$$

As exposited in Samuelson (1997a), when relative-risk-aversion varies with W, *certainly equivalents* become functionals of $U(W)$ and $\hat{W}/\bar{W}$ will be a function of W.

As in Samuelson (1997b), optimal blending of alternative A's and B's has not been dealt with here. But the same merits and demerits ought to pertain for Maximum-Likelihood estimators, $(\hat{\alpha}, \hat{\beta})$.

I have left to interested readers the straightforward use of the present analysis when B as well as A has positive stochastic volatility. Concentrating on Solow's case where B is a safe security was only to simplify the basic exposition.

All the implicit theorems of the present paper need qualifications when the premised exact axioms become only approximations or when they are definitely rebuttable. Thus, trying to reduce $(1 - \pi)$ to zero by going back in history indefinitely far or by using price changes over time intervals that become indefinitely short—these could be illusory ways to gain precision. The stationariness of probabilities appropriate for 1947–1997 could be inappropriate for the 1807–1997 historical period; and price changes per second need not behave like price changes per day, per month, per quarter, and per year.

As always, *Researcher beware*!

Acknowledgements

My debts to Edwin Burmeister and Robert Solow are evident. I thank a perceptive referee for encouragement to add the final section; and thank Jerry Hausman of MIT for helpful encouragement. I owe thanks to Janice M. Murray for editorial assistance; and, for partial support, to NYU's Stern School of Business, MIT's Sloan School of Management, and to the Sloan Foundation.

References

Bachelier, L. (1900). "Théorie de la spéculation," *Annales de l'Ecole normale supérieure*, 3rd series, 17, 21–86. English translation in *The Random Character of Stock Market Prices*, ed. P.H. Cootner. Cambridge, Mass.: The MIT Press, 1967.

Bernoulli, D. (1738). "Specimen theoriae novae de mensura sortis." English translation in *Econometrica*, 22, 23–36, 1954. Reprinted in *Precursors in Mathematical Economics: An Anthology*, eds. W.J. Baumol and S.M. Goldfeld, Series of Reprints of Scarce Works on Political Economy, No. 19. London: London School of Economics and Political Science, 1968, pp. 15–26.

Modigliani, F. and Modigliani, L. (1997). "Risk Adjusted Performance, How to measure it and why," *Journal of Portfolio Management*, Winter, 23, 45–54.

Samuelson, P.A. (1997a). "Proof by Certainty Equivalents that Diversification-Across-Time Does Worse, Risk Corrected, than Diversification-Throughout-Time," *Journal of Risk and Uncertainty*, 14, 129–42.

Samuelson, P.A. (1997b). "How Best to Flip-Flop If You Must: Integer Dynamic Stochastic Programming for Either-Or," *Journal of Risk and Uncertainty*, 15, 183–190.

Sharpe, W.F. 1966. "Mutual Fund Performance," *Journal of Business, Supplement on Security Prices*, 39, 119–38.

Treynor, J.L. 1965. "How to Rate Management Investment Funds," *Harvard Business Review*, January–February, 43, 63–75.

475

Foreword

A great economist of an earlier generation said that, useful though economic theory is for understanding the world, no one would go to an economic theorist for advice on how to run a brewery or produce a mousetrap. Today that sage would have to change his tune: economic principles really do apply and woe to the accountant or marketer who runs counter to economic law. Paradoxically, one of our most elegant and complex sectors of economic analysis – the modern theory of finance – is confirmed daily by millions of statistical observations. When today's associate professor of security analysis is asked, "Young man, if you're so smart, why ain't you rich?", he replies by laughing all the way to the bank or to his appointment as a high-paid consultant to Wall Street.

Among connoisseurs, Robert C. Merton is known as an expert among experts, a giant who stands on the shoulders of such giants as Louis Bachelier, John Burr Williams, George Terborgh, Keynes, James Tobin and Harry Markowitz, Kenneth Arrow and Gerard Debreu, John Lintner and William Sharpe, Eugene Fama, Benoit Mandelbrot, and the ubiquitous Black–Scholes. (Benjamin Graham occupies another part of the forest.) The pole that propelled Merton to Byronic eminence was the mathematical tool of continuous probability à la Norbert Wiener and Kiyoshi Itô. Suddenly what had been complex approximation became beautifully simple truth.

The present book patiently explicates for readers with imperfect mathematical background the essentials of efficient-market asset pricing. Many of its chapters reproduce articles that have become classics in the literature. Several chapters are new to this book and break novel ground.

I am proud to have figured in the Mertonian march to fame. When a youngster, with an electrical engineering bachelor degree and beginning Cal Tech graduate work in applied mathematics, he decided to be an economist and applied to several graduate schools for admission in economics. All but one, he says, turned him down: MIT, *mirabile dictu*, offered him a fellowship! He worked with me and was a joy to work with. One of the great pleasures in academic life is to see a younger savant develop, evolve into a colleague and co-author – and then, best of all, is the rare sight of the companion at arms who forges ahead of you, as you were able to do at the inflection point of your own career. Robert K.

Merton, anthropological observer of the zoo of scientists (and fond mentor of Robert C.), will want to add this saga to his case studies of how science actually evolves.

To the reader I repeat:
Bon Appetit!

Paul A. Samuelson
MIT

476

REFLECTIONS ON INVESTING FOR FOUNDATIONS
AND COLLEGES
Rutgers Conference, New York, 17 November 1993

I have to begin with a story that I have often told, a true story. One of the Harvard Treasurers I have known, he may have been the stupidest one, told me years ago that he had only two rules for investing the Harvard portfolio. Being young at the time I was eager to learn.

"Rule #1," he said, was "Never consult the economics department."

"And Rule #2 is, Never consult the business school."

In the words of Perot's vice presidential candidate, retired Admiral Stockdale, Why am I here? What are my credentials to pontificate at you practical folk on how you should run your businesses?

Actually I am here because Jim Bicksler is the world's greatest salesman. He wears you down with sweet talk and guile. "You're going to be at NYU anyway, so share your wisdom." I don't fall for such malarkey but even stone, in the end, is worn down by drop after drop of water. And the same holds for bone in the head.

What I told Roger Murray and Jim Bicksler I would do is ramble in a low-keyed way about some of the patterns and changes I've witnessed in fifty years of kibitzing in circles of pension investing, non-profit institutions fighting for survival and growth, mutual fund fads and fashions, and the poor individual investor whom the Bible says we have always with us. Like the roster of customers in each broker's harem, the composition of names changes for Darwinian reasons, but for reasons P.T. Barnum has made clear, the roster neither diminishes nor grows. I may add, that the roster of brokers itself turns over in accordance with Gresham's Law that bad money drives out good, but as fast as Darwin chops off one dragon head, two others spring up to fill Nature's abhorred vacuum.

My biblical text today addresses foundations and colleges. But in all scientific candor, the boiler plate of this sermon could be largely recycled for an audience of pension investors, or of mutual fund managers. How can that be? Harvard and MIT will live forever. That's what our alma mater songs proclaim. So we and the Rockefeller Foundation allegedly can take the long view, ignoring transitory ups and downs in Wall Street quotations. Since it is said to be a fact that equities do better than cash, bonds, or lotteries, the canny university will do better with 50% in stocks than the timid college with 70% in bonds. If an equity fraction of 50% is better than one of 30%, 80% must be better than 50%. You can see where I am going. 100% must be best of all. But why stop there with an ironclad syllogism? Leveraging with debt, our 150% in equities will in the long run history of the Crimson paradise win hands down over Boola Boola's pusillanimous 50% strategy.

What guarantees this? Allegedly the good old Law of Large Numbers -- which keeps our insurance companies solvent and the Brooklyn Bridge standing.

Every baseball announcer knows these things. "Babe Ruth," they aver, "is due to hit because the last three times at bat he struck out."

In the next breath, Red Barber would tell us with equal certitude: "Lou Gehrig is hot. Having hit two home runs in a row, his odds to hit another have now gone up because he is on a roll." Again, that good old Law of Large Numbers, which is so remarkably flexible and so conveniently accurate.

I am not just jiving and having cheap fun. Today's nascent fashion--I will not say fad--is to be a *long run investor*, eschewing futile attempts to out-time the market by asset allocation which sells before the crashes and buys back before the bubbles. The devil can quote scriptures for his/her purposes. And so can the angels. We are told about timers who did sell before Black Monday, October 1987, and did in a timely way buy back for less. Yet when the Common Fund studied the record of a thousand timers, the verdict was a dismal one. A few timers beat buy and hold. A few lost their shirts and undergarments as well. On the average, this time the Law of Large Numbers reported that most bought back too late and at higher than they had sold. For taxpaying investors, capital gains realizations made the picture worse. The new customers for allocation services after 1987 are generally not yet ahead. They hope their better sleep and lower variances compensate for their lower mean.

The trend toward ignoring the short run is not as bad as many earlier trends. However, if you ask me during the question period, I'll explain why it will self-destruct once everyone acts on it. And if time permits, I may be able to explain why the Law of Large Numbers is being abused by its advocates. However, the weaknesses in the stay-invested logic is not in itself a strong argument for asset allocation tactics.

For every time there is a season. A time to buy and a time to sell. Like John Templeton I can quote the Bible. Will Rogers said it all: "Buy stocks that are going to go up. Sell them when they do. If they're not going to go up, don't have bought them."

Good advice. But before making the stew, you must first catch your rabbit. Thus, I am an old-timer on the Finance Committee of the National Academy of Sciences. I have been worth every penny they pay me. One former Academy Treasurer noticed in *Forbes* or *Barron's* a little story about Grinnell College and Warren Buffett. He sent each of us on the committee a photocopy of it. A Grinnell regent knew the Sage of Omaha and asked his help. Iowa is next to Nebraska and blood is thicker than water. So Buffett is supposed to have said something like the following:

> A certain TV station can be bought for X millions. The *Washington Post*, on whose Board I sit, cannot at this time acquire such a station. It might be a good deal for Grinnell.

It was. The photocopy related that after no great delay, what cost $X million was sold for $2X or $3X million. "Why don't we on the Finance Committee do this sort of thing?" our biochemist Treasurer pencilled in on the copy's margin.

I am no dummy and I have a ball pen too. I whipped back to him by 29¢ mail: "I'm all for it. How do we start?"

If Ted Williams granted interviews, he could tell you how to hit home runs. Buffett, whom I have thousands of reasons to admire, is less shy than Williams. He has said in lectures something like the following:

> Shucks, just buy a good business franchise at a favorable price. Stay married to her as long as she stays true to her promise. Forget the efficient-market stuff. Any clear thinker could see the *Washington Post* was undervalued at the price we bought it. And so forth.

Well, I was a columnist for *Newsweek* at that time. Perhaps any fool could see that the parent company was a steal in Wall Street, but I was not that kind of a fool. Also, by the way, I can't hit home runs like Ted, even when I try hard.

Alas, those with a fine touch for beating the market odds don't write as sensibly as they act. Peter Lynch did a great job at the Magellan Fund. I'd never guess it from his books and television interviews. Telling amateurs to invest in a local company that they know makes good chocolate bars seems to me like a joke. That's not what made Ned Johnson's Fidelity organization successful, or helped John Neff turn around the University of Pennsylvania's fortunes.

To woo me, Bicksler faxed me reams of words of wisdom by affluent pundits. T. Rowe Price. My old roommate Bill Greenough of TIAA and CREF. Barney Baruch. Maynard Keynes. John Templeton. There were even some of the indiscretions of P.A. Samuelson.

What did it all add up to? A bit fat zero? Maybe when you subtracted the bad advice from the good, the shortfall from zero was substantial. Somebody should snitch to the Surgeon General about the imperiling of the public's health.

Let me digress briefly on Keynes. He was top economist in this century, to be ranked with Adam Smith and one other in the First Three Economists of all time. Bertrand Russell, himself peerless logician of the century, said that Maynard Keynes was the most brilliant mind he had ever met.

What is more to the point. Keynes made a fortune for King's College, Cambridge. He made and left his own fortune. He headed a large insurance company. Also several investment trusts. And as almost a kid, he ran the British Treasury in World War I.

But here is what our hero said when elevated to head the insurance company. I paraphrase.

> Optimally, you should buy one stock. The best one going. After it has gone up, replace it by the new best-est of the best.

Should we laugh or cry at this hubris, which misses the point about diversification to improve risk-corrected mean return?

Still earlier the boy genius used his economic theory of purchasing power parity to predict that excess German inflation would depreciate the mark. So Keynes sold the mark short. A great call, with much initial success. But later, for a time, the market reversed itself and our pyramiding boy was bankrupt and owed his Father and Bloomsbury friends. Again I must here bring in the Will Rogers who said, "Buy land, they ain't making any more of it." We expect a great economist to ask the question that never occurred to the rope-twirling cowboy: Is the future fall in the mark already allowed for in today's mark-future's quotation? Are the *Washington Post*'s future prospects not already reflected in the price Berkshire-Hathaway must pay for it? Don't the buyers and sellers in the auctions for land all know that acres can't be reproduced like rabbits or mousetraps?

Barney Baruch, one gleans from the history books, made the money he made mostly on insider information and pools that contrived price changes in the short run. In a clearer age there seems nought to learn there.

A card-carrying atheist I know claimed he heard John Templeton explain that, in managing their foundation's foreign investments, he benefitted from help from the Lord. I pointed out to my shaken friend: Morale does matter. A trader going through a divorce or having a bout with John Barleycorn is a poor trader. Don't knock whatever contributes to serenity. But do calibrate results and evaluate promised methods.

I heard at Harvard's Kennedy School on October 14, 1987 what I called George Soros's $10 million lecture. Soros has an attested excellent batting average. And if you own one-third of a successful offshore fund worth billions, you too can give a lecture at Harvard, and on any subject you wish. I went to it, hoping to learn how to get rich quick. What I got was a learned discussion of Karl Popper's methodology of science, improved by Soros's concept that he called reflexivity and his discussion of the decision diary he kept during the previous two years' bull market. (By the way I never did grasp just what reflexivity was. But I did read him to be one just then engaged in getting out of bull positions. By my reckoning, you are out $10 million if you are slowed down from liquidating $1 billion because of a Harvard teaching assignment.)

Well, I seem to have read Soros wrong. Instead of selling stocks generally prior to Black Monday, October 19, 1987, when every world market dropped about 22% in one day, *The New York Times* told us Soros was selling the Japanese market short and hedging his shorts with New York long positions. Soros was right that Tokyo stocks were most overvalued. But the brute fact was that in the 1987 Crash, Japanese stocks fell least. Don't grieve for George Soros. Later he more than recouped; and by early 1990, the Tokyo bubble burst hard. My point is that a George Soros cannot transfer to you or me his ability to anticipate the unknown future.

If time were not so scarce, I would do for *systems* what I have done for *people*. The Vassar system had a vogue in the late 1930s: sell what has gone up most; buy what has gone down. Rebalancing your portfolio, it was claimed, was bound to make superlative returns if quotations continued to oscillate between historical channels. Alas, following that tactic literally gets you out of equities early in new great inflations.

Dollar averaging is another arithmetical panacea sure to make you money. In a random walk world, the axioms it implicitly relies on are simply not true.

Chartists and technicians, like the poor, we have always with us. Like psychoanalysis, there is no way to test the truth of technicians' rules. When I asked Holbrook Working, the great unsung hero who best analyzed speculative prices, about them, he said:

> I've found over 50 years that the chartists generally have holes in their shoes. They explain why they were wrong in the past, and why finally today they've got it right.

Working is worth listening to. But scientific integrity requires me to say that there are a few, rare traders who do laugh all the way to the bank and over a long number of years. But they are hard to find. And they are avaricious chaps who know their own value and know how to exact it.

In a moment I'll sum up briefly on a few do's and don't's for wise investing. But not before I mention a problem that universities and foundations peculiarly face. Every college has a president. N deans. And heads of departments. Foundations have their operating chieftains too. A live-wire president wants to make a perceptible splash. So do the sub-chieftains. Always they are short of spendable income. To them the future is now.

This used to put pressure on endowment committees to tilt toward high-coupon bonds and away from low-dividend stocks. Even at MIT, some of us economists are able to help a besieged treasurer fend off the blandishments of a really able president anxious to push bonds that betoken ready spendable cash. It is irrational for an institution that will presumably live forever to let its decisions about current and future spendings get loused up by what is called a bond's coupon and a stock's dividend.

Total return is what portfolio decisions should alone think about. What can be safely spent in each present epoch should have nought to do with how much of the total return is in the form of bond yield or stock yield. The inflation-corrected rate of total return that can be prudently extrapolated to the future from recent smoothed experience, that is what the institution can prudently now spend. Example: if inflation is at 2½-5%, and total return is around 8-12%, something above 5% of endowment is a conservative estimate of what ought to be available for each year's expenditure.

Having to be liquid should not have to be an important problem for a well-run college or foundation.

Rule 1. *Diversification* is the key to optimizing risk-corrected total return in every run of time. Generally that means holding something of everything out there in about the proportions of their respective aggregate values.

You need not exactly index. You need not index at all. But the burden of proof should be initially against large departures from broad diversification. Small departures, even when wrong, hurt you little. Keep them small or have a good alibi.

Rule 2. Diversifying by hiring many money managers or by throwing a dart at a list of mutual funds is not achieving diversification. Tweedledum and Tweedledee differ from the whole universe of investments, but in unknown ways and you will find it hard to reckon where your resulting portfolio truly stands.

Other things equal, you should have international as well as domestic stocks. Leaving out an industry can easily happen and in the long run it can be costly.

Rule 3. Unless you are of a goodly size, and with some special access to knowledgeable talent, a college or foundation should ask itself: Why do we invest in-house? Why not leave the driving to Greyhound? I mean to Vanguard or Fidelity or some other no-load lean-expense vehicle.

Any organization paying as much as 1% of assets net for all management and trading expense should ask itself whether there is not a better out-of-house way.

Rule 4. There are departures from blind diversification that do pay off. For every one with a plus return, there are two with a minus return. The top dogs of one quarter or year are rarely the top dog of last year or next year. Chasing the latest success is a recipe for turnover, expense, and sub-par performance.

Here is a final story to illustrate. Researchers on alcoholism reported a few years ago: It's not true that alcoholics can never safely become moderate social drinkers. Experience shows that five percent can reform themselves in this way.

I asked an expert in the field: "What about this?" She replied: "Even if true, treat it as if it were false. You will never successfully identify the right five percent. Acting as if you might will end up with 30 percent getting hurt."

What is the moral? If you listen to many presentations, you will be many times tempted. Few put their worst feet forward. For every winner you spot gross, you may encounter more than one after-the-fact loser. Net you are behind.

Within my professional lifetime, finance has been revolutionized by new ways of knowing and evaluating performance. This is a blessing and a curse.

It is a blessing to know how to measure past and present total returns. Harvard superiority over Yale is cut down to genuine size.

It is a curse because there is pressure to perform five percent better than one's peers and three percent better than the broad indexes. The eye on the long horizon is shifted down to: "Who's on first this quarter? This month? This week?"

Digging up the tulip bulbs to see how they're doing makes Mary's garden grow worse. Psychologists have shown that reviewing and appraising performance often makes for inefficient short-horizon investing rather than the reverse.

I believe that sensible low P/E strategy is likely over time to beat glamour-growth investing. When Tobin's q tells me (as it does now) that American assets sell for more in Wall Street than it costs to reproduce them, I am concerned for the longevity of the bull market. But experience warns that these are dangerous thoughts.

At best tilt a few percent toward lower P/E's. And maybe lighten up from 60% equities to 55%. But much greater activism than this is hubris -- or chutzpah. And in the long run the devil drives a hard bargain.

Paul A. Samuelson has described himself as the last "generalist" in economics. In fact, he is one of its leading generals. Now 82, he is perhaps best known as the author of the college textbook *Economics: An Introductory Analysis*. First published in 1948 and currently in its 16th edition, it is the most successful economics textbook ever. Besides his celebrity as a best-selling author and former *Newsweek* columnist, Samuelson was an economic advisor to Senator and then President-elect John F. Kennedy, and from 1977 to 1985 a trustee of the College Retirement Equities Fund, the college teachers' fund known as CREF. He currently serves as a consultant to the Federal Reserve Bank. His many contributions to the field brought him the 1970 Nobel Prize in Economic Sciences.

By his own admission, Samuelson, professor emeritus of economics at the Massachusetts Institute of Technology, is primarily a theorist, combing the academic shadows for stray bands of light. For several decades he has focused considerable attention on finance—what he modestly once called his "Sunday painting"—specifically, the behavior of stock market prices and the effect time has on market risk—two crucial issues that ultimately led to University of Chicago professor Eugene Fama's random walk concept and the efficient market hypothesis.

Many people now believe that if they simply hold stocks long enough—10, 20, 50 years—they will not, cannot, lose money, for statistics show that since 1926 the U.S. equity market has not suffered a loss in any given 15-year period. Therefore, an investor who stays in the market long enough will face less market risk and be assured of making the long-term historical average annual return from stocks.

This new dogma is a fallacy, Samuelson says bluntly. He concedes while it's likely over the long term that stocks will fare better than other assets, to invest on that assumption is dangerous. Risk does not go to zero over long periods, he explains. To think otherwise creates a false sense of security and leads to complacency. The problem is that when stock prices do turn down (as inevitably happens even in the strongest of bull markets) your optimistic equity exposure can overwhelm your gut-level risk tolerance, leading to poor short-term judgments and even outright panic. If you want to put 110% of your net worth into stocks, fine, he says, just don't follow the herd; understand your tolerance for the uncertainties ahead and how it could impact your decision.

How to invest money is a second key aspect of Samuelson's research and a motive for his exploration into the predictability of stock prices. His conclusion: There is none. What will happen tomorrow cannot be known, he contends. "When your broker says, 'Hurry, hurry, you have just enough time to buy,' you know that's almost certainly wrong," Samuelson says. The efficient minds of the market will have long erased any price discrepancy in a given stock. Accordingly, without much hope that Wall Street is paved with overlooked gold nuggets for eagle-eyed portfolio managers to scoop up, Samuelson says most investors, unless they possess intimate knowledge of a company's prospects, are better off placing their bets with a market index. At the same time, he adds, markets themselves are not always so efficient. Instead they are frequently objects of wild swings and speculative euphoria that defy rationality. Samuelson's pragmatic advice in such instances: Don't fight the tape. He says, "When everyone is insane, 'tis folly to be wise." An economist quoting Shakespeare? That's hardly the first time in a long, distinguished career that Samuelson has surprised.

Nowadays, the prevailing attitude holds that owning stocks for the long run reduces market risk. You disagree. Why?

People believe that history shows conclusively that in dozens of 15-year periods, there's never been a time when you didn't do better in equities. That makes it almost a sure thing. And if you're investing for 500 years, it would be a sure thing. If you just don't pull up the tulips by their roots but hold onto them, the long pull is your friend and your risk erodes with the time of your investment horizon.

> "When people believe you can't lose money in equities, everybody's making that true in the short run."

That is not a correct understanding. The history we have is really a sample of one. You bet on Czarist Russian bonds and you lost. If you had bought second-class bonds during the Great Depression in America, you'd have done better than your control who bought high-quality bonds. That's the way the hand of history turned out. If you want to be more statistical, take all the hourly market price changes over the last 150 years, write them down on separate tickets, put them in a big hat, shake thoroughly, and then draw out a new 150 years of history. It is not true that because it's 150 years, it will show stocks doing better.

If history is no proper guide, and assuming no one wants to take undue risk, what explains our love affair with stocks?

If I have to explain why we've had these bull markets year after year exceeding the 1920s—which I can still remember as a high school student—it's that more and more people are being converted to the doctrine that it's prudent to hold equities if you are a long-term, patient holder. As that doctrine spreads, that's going to raise the price-to-earnings ratio of the market. If it became universal, it would actually create no anchor. What P/E ratio is wrong? You then have something like the Japanese market—call it an irrational bubble.

Are you suggesting that we're setting ourselves up for a speculative bubble in U.S. markets?

When people believe you can't lose money in equities, everybody's making that true in the short run. But it will self-destruct if the P/E gets high enough, particularly if you look ahead to 2010 when the baby boomers are ready to retire. People are going to be on the selling end. Your equity premium will disappoint. It could self-destruct in a move to its own new equilibrium. After a time people would say, 'We don't do better over a 15-year period in equities than in bonds,' and so the new dogma might be that it's a matter of indifference.

Surely people aren't indifferent to risk. Doesn't aversion to loss ultimately govern an investor's exposure to equities?

Your risk tolerance is a feature of you, like your nose. Suppose you're the sort of person who really hates coming down in the world. There's a certain minimum retirement nest egg that you would hate like hell to go below. Sure, you'd like to go above it, but the degree of kick you get from going above it, if you weigh the odds, makes it an easy decision. You can then say, 'I'm really risk averse to that degree.' So you set aside an amount of money in safe compound interest to guarantee you meet that minimum, and you play with the rest in equities.

When you're young, because there's so much compound interest to build up, you can afford to be more risk tolerant. This means you will have a higher equity position. The trouble with the current dogma is that if it's true as stated, then being 60% in equities is better than 50%. Being 70% is better than 60%. Being 100% in equities isn't best of all, because 110% is really better. This is not an absurdity. But pushing that dogma will show that it's not intrinsically correct, because the moment you're over 100% not only can your principal be wiped out, but you actually can go into debt.

You've focused extensively on questions of risk tolerance and aging. Should we trim equity holdings as our investment horizon shortens?

It is not automatic that when you turn emeritus you should say, 'I don't have so many years to go and so I can squeeze way down on my equity fraction.' First, you may not understand the number of years you actually have. If you retire at 65, you still have 20-odd years, and to be in those 20 years without equity holdings may be a misunderstanding of your own risk tolerance. The case for changes in equity tolerance through investment horizon is a much gentler case at best, and no sure thing at all.

You mentioned the year 2010 as a source of concern about stock market valuation. What troubles you about this not-so-distant future?

The people who then are going to be consuming their nest eggs are going to put a slight bearish element on the market. That's independent of whether people are turning less equity tolerant. There will be bearish effects on the bond markets as well, though not necessarily to the same degree. If people are generally cashing in their bonds, that's going to raise yields. Two things are going to be involved. One is how you hold your principal, whatever it remains in each year. I'm saying you're actually going to be reducing how your principal grows when you're in your retirement years. You'll be liquidating assets. That's going to act as a depressant on the market's P/E ratio. Capital for new capital formation is going to get scarcer when you've got "dissavers."

"Your risk tolerance is a feature of you, like your nose."

Yet the rush to equities is so unprecedented, perhaps the rules of the game are being rewritten. Why wouldn't investors keep playing until the end?

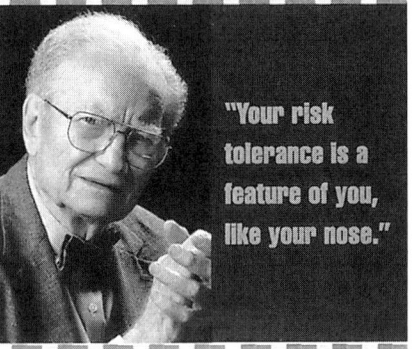

So many people believe the dogma about equities that they'll still say in their old age, 'I'm a patient buy and hold investor, and I'm going to enjoy the higher means.' But they won't have the crutch reassurance that they're still long-term investors and that the risk has eroded. Once you've been successful in equities and until you cease to be successful, you begin to believe there isn't any risk in them. This could become one of the macro factors in anybody's forecast of what's going to happen to equity markets in the first decade of the next century.

An influential aspect of your work involves so-called Time Diversification Theory, which looks at market risk across one's lifetime. If, as you contend, time does not mitigate risk, does time then increase risk?

The relevant risk is how your utility function is affected by what you do now. When are you going to use that money? When are you going to retire? There's too much preoccupation with the mean and not with the variability of the mean. If you generate new histories of how the future can look using the same probabilities as applied in the past, it is not the case that serious losses are squeezed away. Serious losses as your utility may reckon them, may stay the same, get worse, or get lessened in your first year of investing in a long-time horizon.

And, every year that comes up is the first year of what's left.

Time Diversification Theory incorporates two key elements: diversification within time and diversification across time. What is the difference?

Diversification within time is in every instance of time having a spread across various securities. Diversification across time is at different instances being heavily concentrated in one kind of investment as against the other. Monday, Wednesday, and Friday I'm in equities. Tuesdays and Thursdays I'm in bonds. That's not the same as being always 60% in equities and 40% in bonds.

So "within time" offers pragmatic portfolio diversity, while "across time" is nothing more than market timing disguised as tactical asset allocation. What first led you on this course?

What alerted me to this problem was that at MIT, where I teach, professors could put money in a plan consisting of a 100% fixed principal offering, or 100% in an equity fund, or any mixture. With a telephone call you could change the allocation. I learned— to my amusement—that one professor had changed 16 times in the first year. I thought, he can't do any harm to himself because nobody's so stupid as to guess wrong all the time. So he could say at the end of the year, you were 50% all the time in equities, I was 50% too, but I got there by 100/zero and zero/100 in a random movement. That's wrong. He was accomplishing no market timing; he was just taking on extra variability because you don't get the same reduction of risk.

Obviously you wouldn't encourage people to shift equity exposure based solely on how they feel about the market.

The practical moral is: If you must be a timer, be a very modest timer. Don't exaggerate your ability to correctly zig when the market zigs and before the market zags. You've got to have an awful lot of skill in that direction. The harm you do to yourself is pretty small when you go from 55% to 51% and 45% to 49%. Of course, that makes the whole act unexciting.

I tell people, 'You want to leave excitement outside the door when you go into investing. If you want excitement, take $500 and go to Las Vegas. Get it out of your system.' Don't play Russian roulette with your life-cycle savings, which is what most savings are. That's of course why people, who do their own investing and collect stocks like postage stamps, always have a favorite eight names. That's exciting. But decide whether you're in it for thrills or for what your 1040 is going to show at the end of your life.

Your research into the unpredictability of future prices broke new ground more than 30 years ago. Future events cast their shadows before them, you wrote, and prices quickly reflect an asset's intrinsic value. Has your view changed at all?

I believe, from my studies and all the studies I've read of Eugene Fama, Ken French, Harry Markowitz, and Bill Sharpe, that markets are nearly microefficient. By that I mean that the adjustments between the preferred stock of General Motors and its common stock are nicely approximately made. The reason is there are sharp-eyed people, each with slightly different sets of information. When they see the daylight edge of a quasi-arbitrage situation, they act on it and make a lot of money for themselves. But in doing so they wipe out that edge.

In the stock market, what's going to happen the next day cannot be known. When your broker says, 'Hurry, hurry, you have just enough time to buy,' you know that's almost certainly wrong. The price is already in the market, unless he has inside information.

"Once you've been successful in equities and until you cease to be successful, you begin to believe there isn't any risk in them."

You also claim the efficiencies that bring the price of an individual stock into balance do not apply to an overall market. How can that be?

There is no similar macroefficiency. The rational expectation that makes the Dow Jones index right has no foundation. At the end of 1996, Thailand had high credit ratings; everybody was making money. In the middle of 1997, it went the other way. These big swings around any kind of putative fundamental value are the nature of organized markets. You can't make money fighting a Japanese bubble. When everybody is insane, 'tis folly to be wise.

What's your assessment of the U.S. stock market? Do wise heads still prevail?

I never give stock market advice, but I can't help being asked. The most difficult question I've been asked is 'Should I sell?' I was at the 1991 Nobel reunion, the 90th anniversary of the prize, and Markowitz was there, Merton Miller, Sharpe, Milton Friedman, all the usual suspects. Sharpe, who for my money is one of the brightest guys out there, was taking a poll among these really smart guys—us. The majority knew the market was too high. I guess it was about a third of what it is now. So do you sell or buy and hold? It isn't a question of whether you sell out before the peak, but did you buy back at a lower price than the price at which you sold?

You've given much thought to whether an investor, whose stocks have risen in value, should lighten up on them. What's your conclusion?

If you've made a fairly sophisticated calculation of where your balance is, and one part of your portfolio goes way out because of the luck of the deal, you should be rebalancing. That's a great way of controlling risk as against what is in effect pyramiding, or letting your gains run.

Buy and hold doesn't mean letting your winners ride?

I'm talking about this in a white noise market. If you're onto a good thing by insider knowledge, then it could be that success will breed success. It's always tricky. If you've ever listened to baseball announcers, they say, 'Ted Williams is hot, so he's going to hit today.' Or they say, 'Ted Williams hasn't been hitting up to his average, so he's really due.' Each of those assumes a systematic deviation from randomness. White noise would say, 'It's going to be the same each time.' But blue noise, a positive serial correlation, says, 'Things go in runs.' When you've been successful, then tomorrow you're going to be successful.

A big open question is how much mean reversion there is in stocks. I think of it as fairly random, but I honestly can't think that after a decade of sharp gains, the next decade will build up with equally sharp gains. There is a weak regression to the mean. But if you leave out the Great Depression, most of what you get from statistical studies disappears. The white noise, quasi-random walk is the better crude approximation.

Speaking of regression to the mean, how do you regard most portfolio managers today?

There are very few people or organizations who have any presumptive edge over a low-cost, no-load set of indices, particularly on a risk-corrected basis. People used to say that you're settling for mediocrity. Isn't it interesting that the best brains on Wall Street can't achieve mediocrity? This is old hat at the moment because the index of big capitalization stocks is outperforming its usual outperformance. I don't think that's a steady state necessarily.

However, this message can never be sold on Wall Street because it's in effect telling most people to drop dead. But you know the simple story. You're a corporation, and a pretty good pension company comes along and says we'll add a couple of percentage points for you. But it doesn't. On a risk-corrected basis, it doesn't on average equal the index. People say look at the 10% that beat the index. What they don't realize is that generally those are not the same 10%. The hotel rooms of capitalism are always full, said the economist Joseph Schumpeter, but they're full with different people.

> "If you must be a timer, be a very modest timer."

Your advice to individual investors then would be to index a portfolio?

For the ordinary person who isn't looking for thrills, it's not hard to give prudent advice, but it's very dull advice. With indexing, you're diversified in time. And you can sleep well knowing not that your stocks will be stationary in value, but that you've done all that a sensible human being can do for the good cause. Your equity tolerance should be down to your sleeping point.

What are your thoughts on the direction of corporate America today with regard to the future challenges facing U.S. companies and their share prices?

We are in a more ruthless economy. The Fortune 500 once had a significant leisure of oligopoly power, the imperfection of competition. They could be made to share that with labor, and were. That's all gone now. Things are no longer on a lifetime basis, where you got too little when you were young and too much when you were old. Everything is what have you done for me lately? What can you do for me soon? It's a much more intense competition, part of which comes from abroad, but a lot of which is internal.

A lot of it is because of the change in governance on Wall Street. In the old model, nobody had any significant proportion of the shares, surely not management. Management was bureaucratic and lasted forever. That has given way to mergers, acquisitions, conglomerates. A lot of that is to run away from obligations that would have been implicit in the past. So there's a visceral recognition in the labor force that you don't have this lifetime security. Union bargaining power has atrophied tremendously. Government is not in its corner the way that it used to be. As a result—and this is a surprise—the American labor force has shown tremendous flexibility in accepting mediocre jobs, which has not yet been matched in Europe. But I think that's the wave of the future, with all that means for greater inequality and personal instability.

Competition can make a company or a society stronger, but always having to look over your shoulder can be unnerving. Unfortunately, some people won't adapt well.

It is a paradox that just when we need the welfare state more because of the increased inequality that is being thrown up by the new effects of competition, we see almost everywhere an erosion of altruism on the part of the electorate. I write today not of a mixed economy, not of the welfare state, but of the limited mixed economy, the limited welfare state. This isn't because my arteries are harder and I've grown more conservative. I've grown to recognize the new realism that there's a scarce supply of altruism. It needs to be husbanded and used as wisely as we can.

Foreword

The same surgeon general who required cigarette packages to say: "Warning, this product may be dangerous to your health" ought to require that 99 out of 100 books written on personal finance carry that same label. The exceptions are rare. Benjamin Graham's *The Intelligent Investor* is one. Now it is high praise when I endorse *Bogle on Mutual Funds* as another.

I do not speak for myself. What is one person's opinion worth? It is the statistical evidences of economic history that I speak for. Over half a century, professors of finance have studied various strategies for prudent investing. A jury of economists is never unanimous—how could it be in such an inexact science?—but on these lessons of experience there is a remarkable degree of agreement.

1. *Diversification* does reduce, but not eliminate, risk. Buying many stocks, critics say, is "settling for mediocrity." When I was a trustee on the finance committee of the largest private pension equity fund in the world—which handled the old-age savings of the whole university community—we had 30 billion reasons to look into this critique alleging mediocrity. We discovered that the hundreds of money managers who believe in putting only a few eggs in one basket and then "watching fiercely those eggs," alas, produce long-term investment returns that are significantly below those of diversified portfolios. No exceptions? Yes, a few; but a changing group, hard to identify in advance, and prone to regress toward the mean even before you can spot them.

2. For those not in the millionaire class, the need to diversify implies that the sensible and cost-efficient strategy is *not to handle personally* investments needed for those future days of retirement, of home purchases, and of sending offspring to college. "Leave the driving to Greyhound" is not counsel of cowardice and modesty. It's just plain good sense when you reckon the facts about brokerage commissions and the need to keep tax records. All this applies even if you will not go all the way toward "index investing," my next topic.

3. The most efficient way to diversify a stock portfolio is with a low-fee

iii

index fund. Statistically, a broadly based stock index fund will outperform most actively managed equity portfolios. A thousand money managers all look about equally good or bad. Each expects to do 3% better than the mob. Each puts together a convincing story after the fact. Hardly ten of one thousand perform in a way that convinces a jury of experts that a long-term edge over indexing is likely. (For bond and money market portfolios, the canny investor will select among funds with high quality and lean costs.)

4. Enough said about the testimony of economic science. Where John Bogle has added a new note is in connection with his emphasis upon low-cost, no-load investing. I have no association with The Vanguard Group of funds other than as a charter member investor, along with numerous children and innumerable grandchildren. So, as a disinterested witness in the court of opinion, perhaps my seconding his suggestions will carry some weight. John Bogle has changed a basic industry in the optimal direction. Of very few can this be said.

May I add a personal finding? Investing sensibly, besides being remunerative, can still be fun.

Paul A. Samuelson
Institute Professor Emeritus
Cambridge, Massachusetts

June 1993

479

FOREWORD

PAUL A. SAMUELSON, MIT, FEBRUARY 1992

The economic theory of finance is one of the great success stories of our time. Now even Nobel Prizes are given to its innovators—a sign that economic theorists recognize the scientific worthiness of the finance models.

Flowers and medals are all very well but money talks loudest of all. Wall Street has beat a track to the door of those mathematically adept in the arcane arts of finance. Thus, a bright MIT student whose undergraduate thesis I supervised a decade ago recently made the headlines with his over-20-million-dollars earned annual bonus. (His thesis found a random-walk treasury bond market so efficient that no one could garner surplus capital gains, but apparently, subsequent to graduation, he learned how to refute his own findings.)

When a new scientific theory triumphs, is that the end of the story as we allegedly live happily ever afterward? No. Economic statisticians and historians must monitor the speculative markets that are pronounced to be "efficient"—to test whether they stay that way. Marshall Blume and Jeremy Siegel, after reviewing old findings, present for us new evolutionary evidence. If stock prices move in an unfathomable random walk, how can it be that investors in small stocks do better than their conservative cousins? Can we really count on end-of-the-year killings in those small stocks? Once the secret is out, year after year? Rather than report on the off-the-cuff opinions of John Kenneth Galbraith, Milton Friedman, or Paul Samuelson, Blume and Siegel dig out the evolving facts on low capitalization markets. It is a never-ending project.

Market structures do differ. A hundred analysts study changes in IBM earnings and prospects. Few investors have even heard the name of a new over-the-counter company. Is it plausible that two such stocks will display the same statistical structure? Or compare the Tokyo market of the 1990s with that of earlier times when chewing gum and tacit pools held together Japanese stock prices. We need to know the latest wrinkles of evolving market structure. Better still we seek a good theory that will help us, before markets know how they are going to be reformed, guess where they will be evolving toward. I found valuable the authors' account of how market structure affects market inefficiencies.

Modern finance theory is fascinating precisely because it is still open-ended. The rigor of Euclid's geometry, which is the rigor of *rigor mortis*, is quite another thing. Thus, I continue to debunk chartism and technical trading methods. But experience makes me think that a few folk do have an intuitive flair for making money by sensing patterns of momentum. You can't learn to do it from a book, and they can't explain to their daughters how to do it. Neither to you nor to David Rockefeller will these Babe Ruths transfer cheaply the rents of their rare ability. So, for economic science, it is valid to regard speculative prices as effectively white noise. In the same way, experience has persuaded me that there are a few Warren Buffetts out there with high rent-earning ability because they are good at figuring out which fundamentals are fundamental and which new data are worth paying high costs to get. Such super-stars don't come cheap: by the time you spot them their fee has been bid sky high! Their possible existence does not refute the version of market efficiency that I deem scientifically realistic and useful. In my envisaged efficiency equilibrium, rents to ability to grapple with uncertainty are not zero but for the bulk of investors they do average out to be minuscule. Costs incurred to dig out relevant data are positive but competitors grind down the intra-marginal returns sought. The *ex post* stochastic variation of prices diverges from any person's *ex ante* expectations, and it is the heterogeneity of *ex ante* expectations that primarily generates the extensive real world transactions between buyers and sellers.

I state these heresies diffidently and in a low key—for the reason that any and all of my super stars could be merely lucky. There is no escaping chance in the science of finance. Even the beautiful Black-Scholes option formula depends on an *ex ante* parameter of variability whose value we can *never* "know" with precision. Just as a researcher in medicine pools the results of many studies of cholesterol and mortality in a final *meta*-analysis, so are my judgments the upshot of my *meta*-analysis of a lifetime of divergent experiences. Who is to say your different life path is not better than mine?

Reading the present work brings to my consciousness another secret conviction. I do believe in *micro*-efficiency of organized markets. Diversification does raise risk-corrected returns. Holding the broadest index of stocks in your portfolio does enable you to outperform on a risk-corrected basis most money managers. That is the *micro*-efficiency that myriad empirical observations do bear out. But is it the case that modern markets are *macro*-efficient in the sense that the average level of the Standard & Poor's Index or of more comprehensive aggregates is a "correct" appraisal of fundamental wealth and production prospects?

On that question I am agnostic. Markets can produce for themselves self-fulfilling syndromes of optimism and pessimism. If I believed in 1928 that Price/Earnings ratios were too high in Wall Street, I could lose my shirt arguing with the tape. (By contrast, if I perceive a *micro*-divergence between GM's pre-dividend and post-dividend price, it's a favorable calculated risk to bet against it. As I and other experienced cookies do this, we make excess profits from our acts and at the same time our acts work to iron out the aberration.) It is hard enough to define rationally what *macro*-efficiency of the aggregate level of stock prices means, much less believe in it!

Comment: Clarifying Getting Older and Getting Richer Effects

PAUL A. SAMUELSON

PAUL A. SAMUELSON
is a professor at the Massachusetts Institute of Technology in Cambridge.

Since 1969, it has been well-known among finance experts that investors with constant relative risk aversion utility functions, U(W), facing time-independent stationary probabilities, will pick the same equity ratio 1) when young or old, 2) when having high or low wealth to invest, or 3) when facing a one-period investment horizon or a thirty-period investment horizon to (say) retirement. For them, it is false that long-horizon investment is less risky than short — despite gabble about Law of Large Numbers or $\sqrt{N}$ laws of insurance standard deviations.

In Samuelson [1989], I provided a plausible alternative to constant relative risk aversion (CRRA) U(W): One might replace CRRA by "displaced CRRA," or D-CRRA; for this case, people hate mightily being poor in the sense of being stuck with less than minimum tolerable wealth levels. For example, one might name S = $100,000 as the mandatory needed minimum amount at age of retirement 65. Therefore, one might replace a CRRA function like

$$U(W) = \log W \quad (1A)$$

with

$$U(W) = \log(W - S), \; W > S > 0 \quad (1B)$$

If you are like that, at low Ws not far above S you will be rationally averse to any sizable portfolio fraction, x*, in risky equities. As W grows more and more above S, your risk tolerance and x* rise — which does seem realistic. Your richer identical twin will have a higher x* than poor you.

My 1989 mathematics showed something less obvious: At each wealth level, W, you will pick at the beginning of this first contemplated period a lower x* fraction when your $1 million nest egg is directed toward a one-period investment horizon than when it is directed toward a two-period or an N-period horizon. Call the length of your investment horizon N, and contemplate the two-variable function for x* as it depends on present disposable wealth and on the integer N. Then

$$x^* = f(W, N) \quad (2A)$$

For CRRA:

$$f(W, N) \equiv \text{constant},$$
$$f(W, N - 1) = f(W, N) = f(W, N + 1) \quad (2B)$$

However, for displaced CRRA (as, e.g., log (W − S) or $\sqrt{W - S}$), I proved what vindicates the vulgar credo of our day:

$$f(W, N) > f(W, N - 1) > \ldots >$$
$$f(W, 2) > f(W, 1) \quad (2C)$$

I wrote up this analysis and put its results in a non-mathematical subsection of my 1994 article for the *Journal of Portfolio Management*. McNaughton, Piggott, and Purcal [2000] have now pointed out — correctly — that this Samuelson result does not illustrate whether the biographer of typical D-CRRA investors will be able to say: "As they aged, their x* was seen to decline!" Why not? Because life-cycle savers do tend to become wealthier as they age: this trend pushes up W in the f(W, N) function just as the passage of years pushes N down. Therefore, it is ambiguous as to which of the opposing effects will win out on average.

When real interest rates are high and when the "equity premium" is also high, the wealth effect is likely to outweigh the loss-in-time before retirement effect. Then, biographers will generally report growing x* with growing preretirement age.

A useful tip for young savers is this: If you can count on being a steady saver and accumulator, even when young you can bet on having considerably higher wealth in your later years of working life. That justifies, at your present actual modest W nest egg, investing militantly as if you are pretty sure to end up with considerably higher Ws. (It is a heuristic that approximates to the exact Bellman *dynamic* stochastic programming.)

SUMMARY

McNaughton, Piggott, and Purcal [2000] have demonstrated that apples are green. That truth does not negate Samuelson's [1994] deduction that oranges are orange, but it does put readers and me in their debt. Sufficiency conditions like my present log (W − S) can of course be generalized to vindicate your becoming more (or less!) equity tolerant as your investment horizon lengthens.[*]

ENDNOTE

[*]When log (W − S) is replaced by log (W + S), instead of vindicating today's popular view, we contradict it. Now f(W, N) < f(W, N − 1), and ceteris paribus your x* is less when youthfully facing a longer investment horizon. Then, as your wealth and age tend to grow together, your x* will tend definitely to grow with them — the opposite of many vulgar claims.

REFERENCES

McNaughton, Tracey, John Piggott, and Sachi Purcal. "Growing Old Gracefully: Age-Phasing, Targets, and Savings Rules." *Journal of Private Portfolio Management*, Spring 2000.

Samuelson, Paul A. "The Long-Term Case for Equities." *Journal of Portfolio Management*, Vol. 21, No. 1 (Fall 1994), pp. 15-24.

——. "The $\sqrt{N}$ Law and Repeated Risk-Taking." In T.W. Anderson, ed., *Probabilities, Statistics and Mathematics: Papers in Honor of Samuel Karlin*. San Diego: Academic Press, 1989, pp. 291-306.

Foreword

Every year dozens of new textbooks are published. No wonder. As Willie Sutton told the judge about why he robbed banks: "That's where the money is." But only every other decade does there arrive an innovative new work that sets a new pattern of excellence and pedagogy. This Bodie-Merton *Finance* has long been expected. And it proves to be well worth the wait. Good teachability, like good wine, requires much deliberate time.

In the meanwhile, Robert Merton shared the 1997 Nobel Prize in Economics. His was never a case of "if" but only a case of "when," for it has been well said that Merton is the Isaac Newton of modern finance theory. And ever since their graduate student days at MIT, Bodie and Merton have made a productive team. Speaking as one of their teachers, I hail their demonstrating that water can indeed rise above its source. The kind of finance that matters for modern experts goes beyond the tools that have been revolutionizing Wall Street: the pricing of options and other contingent derivatives. Yes, all that is important practically and theoretically. But as this book's coverage shows, it is the Main Street economy of production, capital budgeting, personal finance, and rational accounting that is best illuminated by this overdue breakthrough in teaching.

I moan to myself, "Where were these authors back when I was a student?" Well, the future is longer than the past, and future students will reap the harvest that these innovative teachers have sown.

Enjoy!

Paul A Samuelson

Paul A. Samuelson
Massachusetts Institute of Technology

3. The classical theory of commodity money under a microscope

Paul A. Samuelson

3.1 INTRODUCTION

Prior to the twentieth century the classical economists concentrated on cost of production to determine the supply of their commodity money. Mined gold would be indicative. A measure of agreement prevailed on what was thereby implied. In every short run an early Quantity Theory determined the price level appropriate to a specified stock of M; in the long run, the equilibrium stationary-state supply of M was determined by the technological cost of maintaining the stock of money. Marshall (around 1871), in private notes mathematised J.S. Mill's (1848) treatments of money, providing the major needed synthesis. See the excellent survey in Laidler (1991), and the early Marshallian texts unearthed in Whitaker (1975).

Here I propose to elaborate on the essential ingredients of the full analysis. Imagine a modern quantitative economics graduate school where a term paper is assigned along the following lines:

> Specify a *complete* classical macro model with impeccable (if simplified) classical micro foundations. Summarize its chief behavioural properties and test the degree to which *in it* there prevails strict *real*-neutrality of money. On the basis of your analysis, discuss critically a nominated view[1] that the great 1920–23 German hyperinflation and over-issue of paper German marks occurred in part because the Reichsbank's head, Rudolph Haverstein, and the wartime German Minister of Finance and preeminent textbook author, Karl Helfferich, had been brainwashed in their formative years by the Wilhelm Roscher (1954) textbook's exposition of the faulty classical *cost* theory of money.

---

[1] See Barkai (1989), to which I am obviously much indebted.

Part One here will begin with the extreme classical scenario in which the Labour Theory of Value obtains in a pure form (*sans* scarce land; *sans* produced capital inputs; *sans* essential time-phasing). Part Two, by introducing specialised mining resources and diminishing returns to labour in M production, resolves a basic paradoxical indeterminancy. Part Three introduces various generalisations and qualifications.

3.2 PART ONE: THE EXTREME LABOUR-THEORY-OF-VALUE SCENARIO

How does commodity money fit in with the simplest of all classical microeconomics? In that overly-simple scenario, all goods are timelessly producible out of homogeneous labour at fixed productivities. It is a world of 'natural' prices, set by required or embodied per-unit 'labour' inputs. Smith gives it only a few pages, dealing with deer and beaver.

In addition to n goods useful in themselves – tea, cloth, ... – let me add a metal (gold), which is used solely as a medium for transactions and is valued *only* for the purchases it can facilitate. (Remember the fable of King Midas.) Ditch diggers and opera divas sell their services for this M; craftsmen sell their products for it; all use it to buy the products they opt to consume. Let new production of M be q_0; let $(q_1,...,q_n)$ designate the various useful goods' productions. The unit labour requirements for the $n+1$ goods are respectively the positive technical constants $(a_0; a_1, a_2,...,a_n)$. Let W be the wage or price of labour, in terms of ounces of gold; then real prices – 'natural prices' – are

$$(P_0/W; P_1/W,...,P_n/W) = (a_0; a_1,...,a_n) \qquad (3.1)$$

when all q's are positive. These P_j's are in terms of units of labour. Nominal prices, in terms of ounces of gold, when all q's are positive are

$$(P_0; P_1,...,P_n) = (1; P_1/P_0,...,P_n/P_0)$$

$$= (1; a_1/a_0,...,a_n/a_0) \qquad (3.2a)$$

$$P_0 = 1, W \text{ in ounces} = 1/a_0. \qquad (3.2b)$$

The classical theory of commodity money

Close scrutiny of Equation (3.2) reveals the seeming paradox that no inflation of the nominal (!) price level is ever possible in this extreme model where the durability of M has not yet been formally recognised.

It could be the case that there is more than one metal used as money: say (gold, silver) or (q_0, q_{-1}); and with real labour costs then being $(a_{-1}, a_0; a_1,...,a_n)$. By the same established social convention that could justify gold's serving as money, it could be the case that one ounce of gold *or x* ounces of silver are treated indifferently as always acceptable in any and all transactions. That is asking a lot for the strict constancy of the a_{-1}/a_0 ratio, since any random or systematic change in it (away from x) would by Gresham's arbitrage law entail that only one of the two metals would continue to be produced at all: the cheaper metal would dominate over the now more costly-to-produce one.

Already we notice the inadequacy of this simple labour theory of value to encapsulate a viable classical theory of money. Smith's deer and beaver, once produced, are consumed and need to be produced again and again in the subsequent periods. Pure ingots of gold would be chosen by society to be adopted as its 'money' precisely because of gold's manifest *durability*. q_0 is thus a different kind of thing from this scenario's q_1 or q_n. The stock of M that we add to and subtract from when we make transactions is the cumulation of *all past* $q_0(t)$ productions (minus of course any wearing away or losings, if there are any such).

We can begin with a flow model of productions and consumptions of goods useful in themselves: $[q_1(t),...,q_n(t)]$. Contemplate a flow of $\bar{L}$ total labour that can be allocated as $[L_0(t); L_1(t),...,L_n(t)]$. Here are the production functions that have been implicitly posited up until now:

$$q_j(t) = L_j(t)/a_j > 0, j = 0; 1, 2,...,n. \qquad (3.3)$$

Competitive minimal real prices are thereby defined by

$$P_j = Wa_j \text{ when } q_j > 0, j = 0, 1,...,n \qquad (3.4a)$$

$$P_j \leq Wa_j \text{ when } q_j = 0 \qquad (3.4b)$$

$$W \geq 1/a_0 \text{ when } q_0 = 0 = L_0. \qquad (3.4c)$$

For brevity I shall assume all labourers have the same tastes for consuming $q_j(t)$ and for holding $M(t)$. Then, for total labour supply at constant $\bar{L}$, how shall we write down a 1750 consumer budget constraint in each time period?

Gold being the only durable good, and at first posited to be infinitely durable, we must recognise that today's M stock is the integral of all past $q_0(t)$s:

$$dM(t)/dt = q_0(t) = L_0(t)/a_0. \tag{3.5}$$

How would the competitive market determine the stationary-state allocation of labour: $[L_0; L_1,...,L_n] \equiv [\bar{L} - \Sigma_1^n L_j; L_1,..., L_n]$? In this *timeless* (!) idealisation, if there is not a paradox there is certainly a problem when gold is completely durable. When Smith's (1776) Invisible Hand makes a *teleological* study of what *ought* to happen, gold production should vanish completely! Whatever M somehow earlier came into existence, it will suffice optimally forever. $L_0(t)$ should stay at zero. The representative worker would then spend all his or her WL income on demanding the $[q_1,...,q_n]$ that use up all of $\bar{L}$ among the various positive $[L_1,...,L_n]$. The price of existent M, P_M, would then be divorced from the price of new-mined money.

Bewitched by cost-of-production simplicities for goods readily reproducible, the main classical economists devoted few pages to spelling out a formal theory of consumption demand. As I read them, they took for granted a customary set of tastes and spending proclivities. (J.S. Mill, needing something more definite for his 1829–44 foreign trade model, assumed constant fractions of total income are spent on each of the n goods; a 1990s student might recognize in this Cobb–Douglas or Bernoulli-logarithmic utilities; but Mill's was a purely positivistic approach.)

If there were a teleological Invisible Hand, it would spend all of *society's* $W\bar{L}$ income solely on the $\Sigma_1^n p_j q_j$ goods. When L_0 is thereby fixed at *zero*, it will *not* be the case that goods' gold prices, measured in ounces, will have to be equal to Equation (3.5)'s implied costs of production.

$$(a_1/a_0, a_2/a_0,..., a_n/a_0) = (P_1/P_0, P_2/P_0,..., P_n/P_0). \tag{3.6}$$

Instead Equation (3.6)'s right-hand vector could be *any proportional* mark-up of its left-hand vector.

Paradox: in the purest of pure classical macro models there is lacking in validity the much-quoted dictum: whether or not the quantity theory determines the macro price level in the short run, it is mining cost of production that determines the price level in the long run. For *in it*, we see that a long-run change in a_0 might well have *no* effect on (P_j/P_0) or on W/P_0 or W/P_M.

The classical theory of commodity money 51

What in this purest case does determine the short-run macro price level? I shall address this question in each of two cases: (1) when the money metal is *infinitely* durable; (2) when, as seems more realistic, some minimal fraction of the stock of money does (by the Second Law of Thermodynamics) constantly decay away through wear or loss.

In this latter case, Equation (3.5) for the stock of M must be modified to read:

$$dM(t)/dt = q_0(t) - \delta M(t), \delta > 0. \tag{3.7}$$

This implies that, in the stationary state,

$$M^* = q_0^*/\delta = L_0^*/\delta \, a_0 > 0. \tag{3.8}$$

But *what* long-run M level will prevail in the classical system's steady state? Free workers can go in whatever numbers *they* wish, to work as L_0 rather than as L_1 or L_2 or L_n. In this world, Say's Law applies with a vengeance. There is *always* a job open for *any* worker: any number can go out and pan gold from the posited endless ore-endowed streams. (The labour theory of value does not let us admit that gold-mining jobs might involve more or less utility than cloth producing jobs. As soon as we recognise and admit the differential disutilities of different industries, the Ricardo–Marx–Menger system of natural prices goes quite out the window – as Edgeworth insisted on in his 1890's polemics with the Austrians.)

Up until now I have taken no explicit notice of how, in the short run of the classical commodity scenario, the Quantity Theory was supposed to be operating. Long before there had been written down, $MV = PQ$ relationships, or $M = kPQ$ formal relationships, Copernicus, Locke (1696), Hume (1955) and Ricardo (1817) recognized that *any* level of M stock is as useful as any other to support and sustain a price level of properly-costed-out goods. This is the core notion of *real neutrality*-of-nominal-M; and its truth is what underlies the dogma that *ceteris paribus* the price level is directly *proportional* to the quantity of M.

The reader should realise that I have uncovered a basic problematic indeterminacy of the price level in the purest classical case, based on the indeterminacy of how much labour goes into M mining in excess of or in deficiency of what is needed to just replace and maintain whatever M stock has been in existence.

Alongside the paradox of short-term indeterminancy of the quantity of gold production, there resides the paradox that the long-term nominal wage

173

level, W^*, and the stationary-state stock of M^*, *are* determinate within the commodity theory of money. We must go beyond (3.1)'s discussion of cost and q_0 supply to take account of the public's *demand* for the durable M.

Part Two will analyse in greater detail the pre-1870 Quantity Theory, which already was far advanced. To complete Part One's extreme labour-only scenario, it will suffice to write down (in neoclassical symbolism) the relevant Quantity Equation identity: the demand for money becomes

$$M = (1/V)PQ = k\sum_0^n P_j q_j \qquad (3.9a)$$

$$= kW\overline{L}, \text{ labour theory of value} \qquad (3.9b)$$

$$= kW(L_1 + ... + L_n) + kW(L_0). \qquad (3.9c)$$

In (3.9), M is in ounces of gold; so too are the P's and W; and also q_0 when that is positive. V^{-1} or k is a quasi-constant depending upon institutions and customs. More realistically k should be an endogenous function of various endogenous variables – such as the algebraic rate of growth of W and P; and, as Marshall in an 1871 anticipation of Keynes' liquidity preference wrote down, k is a declining function of the nominal interest rate(s) on people's earning assets. (Eclectic Alfred would have been no 1968 monetarist Milton, who read from history mainly *weak* $\partial V/\partial$ (interest) effects.)

Now my microscope must focus on (3.9)'s supply *ss* relation and at the same time (3.9)'s demand *dd* relation. The basic price level, or its perfect correlative W, cannot generically serve both God and Mammon. Which will prevail at any time t,

$$W(t) = 1/\overline{a}_0 \text{ or } W(t) = [\overline{V}M(t)/\overline{L}]? \qquad (3.10)$$

The answer to the puzzle is to rewrite the question as

$$W(t) \geq 1/\overline{a}_0 \text{ or } W(t) = M(t)\overline{V}/\overline{L}? \qquad (3.11)$$

Then, by logic alone, on the following razor's edge, long-run stationary state equilibrium can alone be defined – namely as

$$W^* = 1/\overline{a}_0 = M^*(\overline{V}/\overline{L}). \qquad (3.12)$$

The classical theory of commodity money

The long-run equilibrium stock occurs only when the two unknowns, M^* and W^*, each satisfy the two independent and compatible equations

$$W^* = 1/\bar{a}_0, \quad M^* = \bar{L}/(\bar{V}\bar{a}_0). \tag{3.13}$$

Note that (3.13) unequivocally implies *real* neutrality of W^*/M^* and every P_j^*/M^*.

Is this a *stable* long-run equilibrium? Where in the short run can the system be found? When $M(t_0)$ starts out *absolutely* (!) too high, what brings it down to M^*?

That is a question easily answered, and confirmatory to stable equilibrium. When $M(t_0) > M^*$, $W(t) > 1/\bar{a}_0$, the wage in gold ounces earnable in the mines. That turns off *all* q_0 production. Thereafter, at the exponential rate of gold decay $\bar{\delta}$, $M(t)$ drops exponentially

$$0 < M(t) = M(t_0)e^{-\delta t}, \quad t_0 \leq t \leq \bar{t} = \ln[M(t_a)/M^*]/\delta \tag{3.14}$$

$$\lim_{t \to t_0} M(t) = M^* = \bar{L}/(\bar{V}\bar{a}_0). \tag{3.15}$$

After a New World strike, the transition back to equilibrium can be a very long-time one.

More perplexing is what must happen when $M(t_0)$ somehow starts below M^*. (An earthquake reduces everyone's cash holdings by 50 per cent.) Then God and Mammon are in logical contradiction. Every worker would rush to the mines if the $1/a_0$ wage they can earn there exceeds the market wage. The people will starve for corn. But will they then stick to their customary, their 'permanent' quantity-equation M/income relation? That would seem absurd, and would lead to the same econometric difficulties that Friedman epigoni fell into in the 1970s when supposing that interest rates would adjust violently to bring people soon back on their *permanent* demand for money. When I am hungry, I will speed up my V rather than go hungrier and, perforce will settle for a lower M/W relationship.

The rush to the mines would produce something like the 'forced saving' of Schumpeter and Hayek – or better, the 'forced *lacking*' of Robertson's *Banking Policy and the Price Level* (1926) induced this time by withdrawal of L_0 from useful-goods production.

Digression: Economic history cannot teach decisive lessons. But, combined with history of economic doctrines, it can nominate useful warnings. Economists love gimmicks to stabilise. Examples are Fisher's compensated-gold content of the dollar and Wicksell's (1898) variant. Benjamin Graham, Frank Graham, Keynes, Hayek, Kaldor, Stanford's Robert Hall and others have sought to stabilise price *levels* by having government purchase at *fixed* nominal prices a market basket of durable and storable goods. All such open tenders, which divorce market demand from actual human needs, desires and personal purchasing power, are prone Gresham-like to set off golden avalanches of sterile accumulation in governmental warehouses. This is particularly likely when lobbyists for sectoral interests operate in a populist democracy. In Hayek's *Prices and Production* (1931) much was made of a scenario in which too many resources go to starting unwise things which will end up getting abandoned after which the people are supposed to starve from shortage of production. That never lasted as a plausible autopsy on the 1929–33 Great Depression. But in the present model, with its extreme constant cost idealisations, the spectre of *everyone* off to the gold mines would be a chilling one.

To abbreviate Part One's exposition, I merely state dogmatically that in no version of monetary theory is it realistic to posit a truly stable demand for money, of MV or $M_1V_1 + MV$ type or of any other type. God is in the details, and so is the Devil there. My remark is quite different from Kahn's Radcliffe testimony declaring V-velocity and the Quantity Theory to be 'bogus' concepts: Kahn had forgotten Keynes' liquidity-preference equation – which Pigou chose to write as $M = PQ/V(r)$, $V(r)$ being a rising function of the interest rate.

3.3 PART TWO: GOLD MINED AT RISING SUPPLY COST

The paradoxical indeterminacy of Part One can be disposed of as soon as we catch up with the classical writers, who generally recognised from the beginning that only certain 'lands' are best suited for gold producing. Labour inputs must realistically be accompanied by natural-resource requirements. Since these scarce specialised mining resources will command competitive rents, any system with 'natural' nominal prices goes out of the window. At best we have what a modern reader would call Marshallian 'normal' prices.

In the simplest model, I may keep all non-M items producible by labour alone, while requiring that q_0 gets produced by L_0 working on fixed and specialised 'land': in modern parlance, by the law of diminishing returns, labour's marginal productivity in gold production falls when L_0 rises; the

The classical theory of commodity money

other side of that same coin reads that q_0 is produced at *rising* supply cost in terms of needed labour. In place of (3.3)'s $q_0 = L_0/a_0$, a modern economist must write a quite different production function for q_0: new gold (in ounces) obeys the concave production function

$q_0 = f(\text{labour}, \textit{fixed} \text{ mine-lands})$

$= f(L_0)$ for short (3.16a)

$f'(L_0) > 0 > f''(L_0)$; diminishing returns. (3.16b)

So long as L_0 is positive, it will be hired up to the point where (in modern parlance) its marginal physical product has become equal to the market wage rate W (in ounces):

$W/P_0 \equiv W = f'(L_0)$ (3.16c)

$\Delta L_0 / \Delta W < 0$. (3.16d)

Total rent of mines, denominated in ounces of gold, in classical parlance is the *residual* of what is left after employer-owners have subtracted from total output the total wages of labour:

$\text{Rent}_0 = R_0 = f(L_0) - WL_0$

$= f(L_0) - L_0 f'(L_0) = R_0(L_0)$ (3.16e)

$\Delta \text{Rent}_0 / \Delta L_0 > 0$. (3.16f)

For pedagogical purposes the reader may contemplate the simplest Cobb–Douglas formula

$f(L_0) = 2\sqrt{L_0}$ (3.17a)

$W/P_0 = W = f'(L_0) = 1/\sqrt{L_0}$ (3.17b)

$R_0(L_0) = \sqrt{L_0} = \frac{1}{2} q_0$. (3.17c)

177

Here rent and wages happen to get 50–50 competitive shares in mining: $WL_0 = R_0$.

Even though all the n useful goods still are priced competitively at $P_j = Wa_j$, nominal prices now depart from labour values in every run when gold is being produced. Now

$$P_j/P_0 \equiv P_j = \text{marginal cost}_j/\text{marginal cost}_0 \qquad (3.18a)$$

$$= [W\,a_j]/[W/f'(L_0)] \qquad (3.18b)$$

$$= f'(L_0)a_j, \quad j = 1,2,...,n. \qquad (3.18c)$$

In modern parlance, equation (3.18) says that all goods' nominal relative prices competitively equal ratios of their *marginal* costs to gold's marginal cost. And *contra* to the labour theory of value, no longer is such a nominal price a technical constant. The scandal which haunts modern discussants of Ricardian systems is that such great authorities as Stigler, Sraffa, Blaug, Hollander, ... while they agree with Ricardo in recognising and admitting that differences in 'time intensities' (which are *absent* in *this* exposition) do vitiate the labour theory of value, they fail to emphasise that so also do non-labour *primary* factors vitiate that singular theory. (Honourable exceptions are Cannan, Wicksell, Viner, Robbins and Barkai, who recognise how positive land rents cannot be 'got rid of as a complication' by recourse to production on external-margin zero-rent lands. Where that external margin, and where *internal* margins, fall are definitely *endogenous* unknowns, materially affected by any change of production mix between mining and cheese or chalk! Numerical experimentation will rebut Ricardo–Stigler presumptions that these distortions are only of small percentage amounts; particularly when produced inputs are needed for production and lands are diverse, they can easily be of 99 per cent importance.)

For macroeconomics of price level the (3.18) relations are relevant. Out of the window goes the dictum that cost of M production impacts price levels *only* in the longest-run equilibrium. Formally *both* blades of Marshall's *SS–DD* scissors operate here in short runs as well as long runs. As will be shown, systematic changes in the right-hand side of $MV = PQ = \sum_0^n P_j q_j$ identities occur even in the shortest run: therefore *M/W invariance* needed for *strict* quantity-theory *real* neutrality does not quite obtain in the classical commodity theory of money. (However, when mining rent, R_0, is only a small fraction of net national product, classical microeconomics will entail a good approximation to real neutrality of W/M and P_j/M ratios, as

The classical theory of commodity money

subsequent analysis will explicate. Much that one sees under a microscope may not be vital for economic history and policy optimisation.)

For a complete classical macro system, we must supplement the (3.16–3.18) micro relations by pre-1870 $MV = PQ$ demand relations – literary of course – bearing on society's *demand* for durable money stock. Forks were made before fingers; before Simon Newcomb, Alfred Marshall, Irving Fisher and Edwin Kemmerer wrote down $MV = PQ$ formalisms, post-Locke writers explicitly described how people's average money holdings would bear positive relation to how much real q's they will be faced with. Even Roscher describes how the same coin may be used several times in a year, possessing so to speak a customary or characteristic velocity of circulation. Present-day textbook expositions about the *definitional* identity of the two sides of the $MV = PQ$ formalism are already in the classicals' pre-mathematical literature. It even gives various reasons why V, or its mirror-twin $1/V = k$, instead of being a strict constant, might realistically be a variable parameter that is a function of various endogenous and exogenous factors.

Now $Rent_0$ must be included in the national income, along with $W\bar{L}$: from the demand side we stipulate that

$$M = (1/\bar{V})\sum_0^n P_j q_j = (1/\bar{V})PQ \qquad (3.19a)$$

$$= (1/\bar{V})[W\bar{L} + R_0(L_0)]. \qquad (3.19b)$$

No longer will W/M and P_j/M variables be strictly constant independently of M – or for that matter independently with respect to dM/dt, which is positively correlated with the magnitude of L_0. Even a steady-state innovation in gold-mining technique, as it changes (W^*, M^*, L_0^*), can strictly speaking perturb W^*/M^* and P_j^*/M^* ratios in a different way than other innovations will do.

I can now combine our complete supply and demand relations with the (3.7) flow-accounting relation

$$\dot{M}(t) = q_0(t) - \delta M(t) \qquad (3.7)'$$

to get a complete dynamic version of the classical commodity theory of money applicable in both short and long runs.

$$\dot{M} = f(L_0) - \delta M \qquad (3.20a)$$

58   *From classical economics to the theory of the firm*

$$M = (1/\bar{V})[f'(L_0)\bar{L} + R_0(L_0)]. \tag{3.20b}$$

In the stationary state, when $\dot{M} = 0$ along with $\dot{L}_0 = 0$, (3.20) becomes two independent relations in the two unknowns: L_0 and M.

$$f(L_0) - \bar{\delta}M = 0 \tag{3.21a}$$

$$M = (1/\bar{V})[f'(L_0)\bar{L} + f(L_0) - f'(L_0)]. \tag{3.21b}$$

When (3.21b) is two-way invertible, it becomes

$$L_0 = \lambda[M; \bar{V}, \bar{L}]. \tag{3.21c}$$

If one uses (3.21b) to eliminate M explicitly from (3.21a), we get the following single equation to determine L_0^*, namely

$$\bar{V}f'(L_0)[1-\delta] + f'(L_0)[\bar{L} - L_0] = 0. \tag{3.21d}$$

If (3.21d) has a single unique L_0^* root, substituting that L_0^* back into (3.21b) will complete our search for the *absolute* (!) M^* long-run equilibrium. Similarly, V^* can be computed from the $W^* = f'(L_0^*)$ relation.

Also, (3.20a) and (3.21d) can be combined to give the following autonomous *dynamic* relation for M:

$$\dot{M} = f(\lambda[M; \bar{L}, \bar{V}]) - \delta M. \text{ QED.} \tag{3.21e}$$

Modern sophisticates know that merely matching the number of unknowns with the number of equations is not good enough. The *quality* of the nonlinear equations matters, particularly when uniqueness of equilibrium is in question. To sidestep tedious (but not trivial) mathematics, I can simplify by supposing $R_0(L_0)$ rent to be small relative to $W\bar{L}$.

Alternatively, I can dispose of rent completely if we suppose that mining is like a public fishery or public common: free entry of workers push and shove their way on scarce resources until each gets the same productivity wage – with no landlord to have to pay off. Under artificial symmetry conditions of mining geography, that could even be a Pareto-*efficient* scenario. In that case equation (3.21b) is replaced by the following, *which sets R_0 to zero and replaces marginal* product $f'(L_0)$ by average product, $A(L_0)$ – also a declining function:

180

$$A(L_0) = f(L_0)/L_0\,;\, A'(L_0) > 0 > A''(L_0).\tag{3.22}$$

In the Cobb-Douglas example of (3.17), much becomes simplified: now

$$\dot{M} = 2\sqrt{L_0} - \delta m \tag{3.21a}'$$

$$M\overline{V} = \tfrac{1}{2}\overline{L}/\sqrt{L_0} \equiv W\overline{L}. \tag{3.21b}'$$

Substituting from (3.21b)' into (3.21a)', gives an autonomous differential equation in M alone that is globally and locally stable

$$\mathrm{d}M/\mathrm{d}t = 2(\overline{L}/\overline{V})M^{-1} - \delta M \tag{3.23a}$$

$$M^* = \sqrt{2(\overline{L}/\overline{V}\delta)} > 0 \tag{3.23b}$$

$$\lim_{t\to\infty} M(t) = M^* \text{ from any positive initial } M(t_0). \text{ QED} \tag{3.23c}$$

This completes Part Two and my detailed analysis of the simplest commodity-money model. Its verdict is complimentary to the acumen of the best classical writers.

3.4 PART THREE: GENERALISATIONS AND QUALIFICATIONS

The existence of a stationary-state M^* can be inferred along familiar classical lines by logical reasoning *sans* mathematics. Very high M means very high W in ounces. That chokes off most potential gold production; and it does so in the face of high δM depreciation. Hence, high M means strongly declining $\mathrm{d}M/\mathrm{d}t$. Similarly, when M starts out low, that entails low gold wage and draws workers into mining even the leanest ore deposits. The outpouring of new gold causes $\mathrm{d}M/\mathrm{d}t$ to be strongly positive. At some inbetween M^* level, we lie in the Goldilocks state which is not too high and not too low. Ah, bliss. (But bliss with labour wasted on producing what adds nought to people's ultimate well-being. Yes, M is *qualitatively* useful. No, more *quantity* of steady-state M enhances no one's pleasure or well-being. This is the basic paradox of every real-neutral monetary theory.)

If we now drop the extreme simplifying assumptions of the previous parts, the modifications and qualifications are fairly obvious. Thus, (1) Marshall (1923) properly notes that when gold or any money unit has decorative use in jewellery, in technical use or electronics, that will introduce a degree of non-neutrality into the theory of money.

Similarly, (2) when money's sole function is no longer as a medium of exchange – as when it is held for a portfolio item in one's nestegg of wealth – then the quasi-constancy of $1/V$ or k is severely compromised. Faced with positive interest rates to be earned on non-M wealth items, folks will dispense with some of that excess cash which would have added to their convenience. Real-neutrality may still be preserved. (See Samuelson (1968) for argumentation on the non-Pareto-optimality of people's thus squeezing down on their cash balances; each is motivated to do so but when *all* do it there is no equivalent convenience-of-transaction gain to anyone. The exact analysis is thorny: suppose we were all to form a social compact to keep more M at hand; and suppose that this gives us the pleasure of being able to be more capricious in random impulse buying; then that will force retailers to keep larger inventories lest items are found to be out of stock; however, there are real social costs to the keeping of larger inventories, so that any gain in consumers' surplus needs to have subtracted from it any loss in producers' surplus.)

(3) Even when M is the only money, non-metal items will spontaneously emerge as partial substitutes for M: paper bank notes, checkable deposits, plastic credit (or debit) cards. As a result the V in $MV = PQ$ becomes systematically and stochastically variable. (My Chicago teachers, Frank Knight, Henry Simons and Lloyd Mints, became enamoured with 100 per cent reserve requirements for checkable bank deposits. Only Jacob Viner realised that, under *laissez-faire, substitutes* for banks were bound to result.)

Before Fisher (1911) introduced $M_1V_1 + M_2V_2 = PQ$, defenders and opponents of the quantity theory recognised that non-metal items in the credit system effectively acted *as if* these were more M. Edwin Cannan insisted that M_2 was not money; it was only something that pepped up V – an empty victory for an old tradition.

The Friedman–Schwartz *A Monetary History of the United States 1867– 1960* (1963) was completed just at the time when checkable bank deposits became widely available to provide an *interest-bearing money*! Whatever historical quasi-constancies had held for demand-for-money functions, one became forced to expect henceforth systemic variability in them. (This was brought home to me in the 1970s when I held six-year (!) stocks of money, bearing 18 per cent safe interest rate. *That M* burned no hole in my pocket tempting me to spend: my C/income and C/wealth ratio bore no relation to

182

my $\Sigma p_j q_j / M$ ratio. And in the future, when *all* of one's equity and bond assets can, by a phone call, be useable to buy gum or TVs, more sophisticated demand-for-money functions will be required.) The reason empirical regressions have not behaved more erratically is that authors mine the data on M_0, M_1, M_2, ..., M_{17}, ..., to chase after the definition which gives the best in-sample fit; rationally to be feared is that out-of-sample projections will lack robustness. Moral: If you must specify Rules for central bankers, specify them *often*.

(4) When *all* the aspects of *time* are restored to the scenario, no essential modifications are required for my earlier micro foundations for classical commodity-money theory. Tea and cloth can like gold also require natural resources. Let all the q's be producible in a time-phased way, with or without produced ('capital') inputs. The same $\sum_{1}^{n} P_j q_j + (WL_0 + \text{Rents} + \text{Interest-costs}_0)$ will enter into the M^* long-run equilibrium and into the converging dM/dt movements toward M^*.

(5) One classical element in Mill was overlooked by Marshall in 1871. Mining is par excellence *not* a sustainable cost function. Along with the positive L_0 input, the q_0 production function will have in it as a depressing argument the cumulative amount of all *past* $q[t]$ mined. Call this $Q_0[t]$. At the least we should replace $f(L_0)$ by

$$q_0 = f(L_0, Q_0); \quad \partial q_0 / \partial L_0 > 0 > \partial f / \partial Q_0, \tag{3.24a}$$

where

$$\int_{-\infty}^{t} q_0 [\int_{-\infty}^{t}] d\theta = Q_0(t). \tag{3.24b}$$

Now we are in the realm of entropy economics à la Georgescu-Roegen (1971). For our logo we need a running-down *hourglass* rather than a periodic *pendulum*. At best our long-run M^* equilibrium and price level P^* will be gently decaying in time if we stick with our metal M. In the classicist's Say's Law world, where all markets clear frictionlessly, this deflation would cause no serious unemployment problems.

Sobering up to face the real world of history and the future, we realise that for a mined gold there is no solid cost-of-production function to build on. Prior to Columbus, gold scarcity was different from what it became in the epoch of Spanish New World Treasure and the secular inflation which it brought. By Georgescu's Second Law of dissipation of concentrated *pure* resource stocks, the system was prone to mark time until new Californian and Australian strikes happened to occur (and which Roscher took notice of). The Klondike and Alaskan strikes occurred late in the nineteenth century – along with the new cyanide process for enhancing recoverable gold from ore – as Haverstein and Helfferich (1903) would have known. After 1929 a popular theory among older economists was that the Great Depression had important roots in the falling of the (gold stocks)/National Income ratios. This was not absurd but it failed to appreciate the degree to which any M_1 was supplementable by M_2 increments; teleologically, the breakdowns in the gold standard speeded up this possibility.

For brevity, I turn to the question of Roscher's possible guilt in brainwashing Reichsbank governors and German Finance Ministers.

Let me depose at the beginning that the Continental authorities lacked sophomoric understanding of early twentieth-century macroeconomics. Even in the face of postwar German politics and resentments over imposed reparations payments, there was no intrinsic necessity to tolerate hyperinflation. Ironically, most of the relations in my version of commodity money are to be found in Barkai's description of Roscher's text – particularly in its post-1878 editions and the American translation. There is in that text the equivalent to $M = \Sigma P_j q_j / V$; and even the equivalent to $M = (\Sigma P_j q_j - M_2 V_2)/V$. As far back as 1810 and the English Bullion Report, Ricardo and contemporaries realised that a paper M could replace gold M. (Presumably they did not know of Franklin's eighteenth-century Pennsylvania episode, in which a *controlled total* of fiat paper M sustained well-behaved price levels and prospering business conditions. If only Haverstein and Helfferich had thought to regard what they were witnessing as precisely what would happen if a governmental alchemist were able to create gold at a near-zero cost and proceeded to spend and lend that stuff in billion-fold extra amount.)

I am not saying that Roscher or his readers understood in a coherent *Gestalt* the elements that were present in his textbook. The magician at a carnival deflects the audience's attention away to irrelevant things so that they will not 'see' what is actually going on in front of them.

President Haverstein even boasted of his virtue in keeping the Reichsbank's lending interest rate in single digits while the inflation rate was in a score of digits. This puts all talk of *Asian* crony capitalism into the shade: the bankers and politicians who had access to any of such cheap money (effectively at explosively-high *negative real* rates of interest) must have made fortunes. (One wonders how the 39-year-old Joseph Schumpeter, who became president of a private bank so-to-speak as a going-away present after he was fired as Austria's Finance Minister, managed to go broke instead of squirrelling away a real fortune. Someone else must have been minding the shop?)

Neither in my version of *classical* monetary theory, nor in its neoclassical successor, could it suffice as good private-banking or central-banking procedure to make *any* and *all* loans that could during inflation times assuredly be able to get paid back. Inflation bubbles, in the times *before* they burst, rescue the worst fools and charlatans. So much for the sanctity of any 'real bills doctrine'.

Just as sixteenth-century price rises were precious-metal based, 1920–3 hyperinflation can be adequately understood as a paper-notes inflation even by lay people unable to understand the intricacies of contemporaneous developments in the credit sphere.

This is to say that I could write a contra-factual history in which a system *without* credit institutions or a metal base could go through the same explosion of bank notes and price levels. In it, once we recognised how V will systemically speed up when $[dP(t)/dt]/P(t)$ becomes astronomical, there would emerge the following same polemical dialogue.

Public to Central Banker: 'Give us more M. We cannot keep up with prices'.
Central Banker: 'We are running the currency presses at top speed and adding zeros to their face value, doing our best to keep up. We are blameless for the inflation; we are just trying to keep up with it'. (Notice there is no confusion here about what is M, or about what are appropriate real and nominal interest rates during more-than-exponential explosions of M and P in a chicken–egg–chicken ... sequence.)

There would also be truth in the following dialogue.

Public: 'Give us more M or there will be depression, unemployment and production shortages'.
Central Banker: 'Unless the political system will tolerate a (transitional?) depression, we dare not cap the M supply'.

In final summary, metallic monetary systems are dominated in logic by controlled fiat-money systems. Only when democratic societies cannot trust themselves to do the pragmatic sensible things might use of shibboleths have merit as second-best feasible devices.

REFERENCES

Barkai, Haim (1989) 'The Old Historical School: Roscher on Money and Monetary Issues,' *History of Political Economy* 21(2), pp. 179–200.
Fisher, Irving (1911) *The Purchasing Power of Money*. New York: The Macmillan Co.

Friedman, Milton (1968) 'Money: Quantity Theory,' *International Encyclopedia of the Social Sciences*, D. Sills (ed.), Vol. 10. New York: The Macmillan Company and the Free Press, pp. 432–47.

Friedman, Milton and Schwartz, Anna Jacobson (1963) *A Monetary History of the United States 1867–1960*. Princeton: Princeton University Press.

Georgescu-Roegen, Nicholas (1971) *The Entropy Law and the Economic Process*. Cambridge, MA: Harvard University Press.

Hayek, Friedrich (1931) *Prices and Production*. New York: Augustus M. Kelley, 1967.

Helfferich, Karl (1903) *Das Geld*. Leipzig. Translated into English as *Money*, I. Infield (trans.). New York: Adelphi, 1927.

Hume, David (1955) *Writings on Economics*, E. Rotwein (ed.). Edinburgh, London, Melbourne: Thomas Nelson and Sons, Ltd.

Laidler, David (1991) *The Golden Age of the Quantity Theory*. Princeton: Princeton University Press.

Locke, John (1696) *Several Papers Relating to Money, Interest and Trade, etcetera*. New York: Augustus M. Kelley, 1968.

Marshall, Alfred (1923) *Money Credit and Commerce*. London: Macmillan & Co.

Mill, John Stuart (1844) *Essays on Some Unsettled Questions in Political Economy*. London: Parker.

Mill, John Stuart (1848) *Principles of Political Economy, with some of their Applications to Social Philosophy*. Published in US, 1880, New York: D. Appleton & Co.

Ricardo, David (1817) *Principles of Political Economy and Taxation*. London: John Murray.

Robertson, Dennis (1926) *Banking Policy and the Price Level*. New York: Augustus M. Kelley, 1949.

Roscher, Wilhelm (1954) *Die Grundlagen der Nationalökonomie*. Stuttgart: Cotta, 1878. Translated into English as *Principles of Political Economy*, J.J. Lalor (trans.). New York.

Samuelson, Paul A. (1968) 'What Classical and Neoclassical Monetary Theory Really Was,' *Canadian Journal of Economics* 1, pp. 1–15.

Smith, Adam (1776) *An Inquiry into the Nature and Causes of the Wealth of Nations*. E. Cannan (ed.). New York: the Modern Library, 1937.

Whitaker, J.S. (ed.) (1975) *The Early Economic Writings of Alfred Marshall, 1867–1890* Volumes 1 and 2. New York: The Free Press. (See particularly Vol. 1, pp. 164–77; Vol. 2 pp. 277–8.)

Wicksell, Knut (1898) *Geldzins und Güterpreise bestimmenden Ursachen*. Jena: G. Fischer. Translated into English as *Interest and Prices: A Study of the Causes Regulating the Value of Money*, R.F. Kahn (trans.). London: Macmillan, 1936.

483

Modern Finance Theory Within One Lifetime

Paul Samuelson

MIT, E52-383
Department of Economics
50 Memorial Drive
Cambridge, MA 02142, USA

Abstract. We meet to celebrate the century birthday of Louis Bachelier's Paris Ph.D. thesis, *Théorie de la Spéculation*. One hundred is a good round number. However, the text of my sermon today is about the genesis of the present modern theory of finance in one academic lifetime – a rare phenomenon in the annals of any science. Although Bachelier's basic breakthrough came in 1900, its scientific beginning must be placed at about 1950. Science is public knowledge. The treasures that were in Gauss's private notebooks were as if they never existed – until he released them in lecture or publication, or until they were later quasi-independently discovered by scholars other than Gauss. When a tree falls in a forest empty of observers or listeners, it is much as if no tree ever fell there at all.

Discovering Bachelier

Discovery of Bachelier's work is a well-known, rather romantic story. It is worth repeating. It begins with blue ditto hectographed post cards sent out by the late Jimmie Savage to several 1950 theorists asking: Any of you know of a French guy named Bachelier who seems to have written a little 1914 book on speculation? I for one had known the name Bachelier. Back in the late 1930's when I and the brilliant Polish-American topological mathematician Stan Ulam were buddies in Harvard's crack Society of Fellows, Stan had mentioned that name. Occasionally Ulam was asked to fill in at Harvard in giving one of its few courses on probability. Later Ulam gained fame at the war-time atomic bomb program in the Los Alamos Laboratory. It was Ulam who repopularized the Monte Carlo method to solve intractable mathematical problems; and still later it was he who got the bright idea that made Teller's hydrogen fusion bomb workable. Besides, I had vague remembrance of a footnote reference to Bachelier in Feller's 1950 classic on *Probability Theory and its Applications, Volume I*. Here are Feller's somewhat patronizing words:

> Credit for discovering the connections between random walks and diffusion is due principally to L. Bachelier (1870–1946). His work is frequently of a heuristic nature, but he derived many new results. Kolmogorov's theory of stochastic processes [first named such, I believe by Bachelier] of the Markov type is based largely on Bachelier's ideas. See in particular L. Bachelier, *Calcul des probabilités*, Paris, 1912.

I may add that it is primarily in Feller's less elementary Volume II, not issued until after the early 1950s, that the Îto-like mathematics gets discussed.

As I expected, the 1914 popular Bachelier exposition was not in the limited MIT library. But a greater treasure was there: the 1900 Paris thesis and the 1912 item. In the superb Harvard Widener Library, I later did find Savage's 1914 reference, along with a post-World War I additional book. After turning the pages of the 1900 masterpiece, I recognized its brilliance: all that was later in Einstein's 1905 brownian motion breakthrough was already in Bachelier and more. When my one-time pupil and colleague Paul Cootner planned to bring out a 1960s anthology of finance memoirs, I urged him to commission an English translation of Bachelier: nuances of original work can get lost on its foreign language readers.

To finish off the Bachelier discovery, his use of the Absolute Gaussian distribution irreducibly resulted in both positive and negative wealth outcomes, something not compatible with the limited-liability feature of common stocks. For that reason I pragmatically replaced his Absolute Gaussians by Log-Normal probabilities: a stock might double or halve at commensurable odds; such a law of proportionate effect, familiar in the theory of skew curves (Gibrat and otherwise), for various additional reasons became the work-horse for Black-Scholes and other option formulas. The astronomer M.F.M. Osborne independently resorted to the same "Geometric Brownian Motion," basing his argument on his own doubtfully persuasive variant of the psychological Weber-Fechner law.

In On the Creation

When I entered the study of economics in 1932 at Chicago, finance theory was not then in the economics curriculum; nor was it in the business school syllabus. Unknown to most of us, Holbrook Working was spending three decades at the Stanford Food Institute working through the statistics of spot commodity prices and futures prices on organized speculative exchanges. I salute him as one of the early heroes of the random-walk story. My task today is to recall and honor these great pioneers of finance, giants who walked the earth in the Neanderthal forests.

To do this I am proposing to fabricate counter-factual science history. If Alfred Nobel can create Nobel Prizes, I can conjure up fictional Samuelson-Nobel Prizes for Finance. Holbrook Working, around 1950, is an early recipient of my Samuelson-Nobel Prize. He also elaborated the theory of hedging and of rational intertemporal storage. From tables of random numbers he constructed diagrams of putative price changes $P_{t+1} - P_t$. When he slyly interspersed their diagrams within undated diagrams of real-market price changes, floor traders could hardly tell the difference. It was like experiments in which laypeople are presented with paintings by (a) modern artists, (b) kindergarten children and (c) inhabitants of mental institutions. In these experiments art critics scored higher in telling them apart than Board of Trader locals did in separating Working's artifacts and the real things.

Let me move past Holbrook Working. Alfred Cowles, III, an heir to a mining and aluminum fortune, contracted tuberculosis and that kept him tied to the salubrious mountain climate of Colorado Springs, Colorado. To satisfy his curiosity and hopefully improve his portfolio performance, Cowles founded the non-profit Cowles Commission to study econometrics. Cowles made some of the first probability studies of forecasting methods, showing that none did better than the best of several ought to do by chance alone. His theoretical tests on runs hinted at random-walk structure for stock prices.

Equally important, Cowles compiled a precursor index to the S&P 500. Every day we see these indexes being used in current appraisals of whether our bull market is or is not grossly overvalued. Cowles therefore also gets early elected to the Samuelson-Nobel Prize.

Prizes must go also to Frank Ramsey, Bruno de Finetti, L.J. Savage, John von Neumann and Jacob Marschak for re-establishing (after Daniel Bernoulli and Laplace) maximizing $\text{Exp}\{U(W)\}$ as a decision criterion.

Nay-sayers can be as important in progress of science as aye-sayers. Awards of my Samuelson-Nobel Prizes should therefore go also to Maurice Allais, whose artful tests have demonstrated that many real-world people will want to violate the Axioms of maximized Expected Utility. Similarly the theoretical generalizations of Mark Machina's non-linear functionals plus the behavioristic experiments rationalized by Amos Tversky and Daniel Kahneman (1974) certainly deserve sharing a top prize in finance. Kenneth Arrow and Gerald Debreu each contributed to Arrow's important concept of complete markets.

Tom Kuhn's 1962 theory of scientific revolutions stressed the key role of new data that refute old notions and launch new ones. The LSE statistician Maurice Kendall, who prided himself on his ignorance of economics, by brute empiricism gave the Royal Statistical Society a 1953 round-up of the serial auto-correlation structure of price-changes in spot commodity markets, futures prices, individual common stock price changes, as well as indexed portfolios of stock price changes. To his surprise and delight, virtually all $r_{\Delta p_t, \Delta p_{t+k}}$ coefficients meandered in the neighborhood of zero, as if by chance alone. He proclaimed this to demonstrate an *absence* of economic law: *white* noise, a tale told by an idiot or by the devil who draws samples of price changes randomly after mixing thoroughly the tickets in a giant urn or hat. (Positive serial correlations that favor runs I later called *blue* noise. Negative serial correlations depicting regression toward the mean, I called *red* noise.)

By report the economist subset in the Royal Statistical Society London audience did not take well this raid from a disciplinary outsider. But with economists' characteristic flexibility and shiftiness, I told them to rally and work the other side of the street: perfect speculation by numerous independent interpreters of arriving new news would be, we came to realize, a sign of higher economic law; as I put it in 1965, an indication of the martingale market theory. "No easy pickings" was the logo on the T-shirt of the prizewinning Kendall and his efficient-market followers.

Mean and variance analysis had informally entered pre-1945 finance theory, as in the heuristic works of Helen Makower & Jacob Marschak and Evsey Domar & Richard Musgrave. But it was Harry Markowitz (1953–59), James Tobin (1958) and William Sharpe (1964), who perfected the important theory of optimal portfolio efficiency by means of quadratic programming. Understandably this (mean, variance) analysis has permeated actual investor practice and richly merits Samuelson-Nobel Prizes, as do also the writings of Modigliani-Miller and Mandelbrot-Fama.

Prizes should not go only to individuals – to Titian and Rembrandt. They should go also to places and institutions: to the Wharton School finance workshops pioneered by Irwin Friend and Stephen Ross; the Berkeley, Stanford and UCLA workshops of Barr Rosenberg, Nils Hakansson and Hayne Leland; the innumerable Chicago experts in finance; the busy Cambridge, Massachusetts workshops of John Lintner, Robert Schlaifer, John Pratt, Richard Zeckhauser, Howard Raiffa, Stewart Myers, John C. Cox, Jonathan Ingersoll, Richard Kruizenga, Paul Cootner and Andrew Lo, to mention only a few. To reward fundamental breakthroughs half a hundred prizes in the 1950–2000 period would not really be enough, particularly in the recent times of Robert Shiller, John Campbell and Jeremy Siegel.

The Holy Grail

I have saved for my all too brief ending the story of the competition to reach the North Pole first. I mean the Black-Scholes-Merton formula for equilibrium option pricing. As the physicist Freeman Dyson documented, Kuhn erred in omitting, as a major cause of scientific revolution breakthroughs, new toolmaking. Behind Galileo and Newton lay the invention of the telescope. Behind Darwin and Crick-Watson lay the invention of the microscope. Behind Black-Scholes-Merton lay Norbert Wiener, A.N. Kolmogorov and Kyosi Îto. I cannot explicate the point better than by quoting the works of the infallible poet:

> Nature and Nature's law lay hid in night;
> God said, Let Îto be! and all was light.

The stochastic calculus, by being able to model instantaneously rebalancing price changes, put rigor into the brilliant conjecture of Fischer Black and Myron Scholes of an instantaneous variance-free hedge. Suddenly the imperfection of mean-variance analysis evaporated away; suddenly the evaluation of a stock's derivative securities, so that neither buyer nor seller stands to gain, becomes clear. The mathematical seed that Bachelier planted, which Wiener blessed, became through the harvestings of Îto, by Fischer Black, Myron Scholes and Robert Merton the Dyson tool-breakthrough which sparked a revolutionary change in finance science.

Each month in journals all over the world, each day and hour in new markets everywhere, we see at work this skeleton key to the miracles of scientific advance. The saga is only bettered by the opposition to the new paradigm along the way. When an older Milton Friedman pooh-poohed it all as "not even economics at all," this only documented Max Planck's dictum that Science Progresses Funeral by Funeral.

And all this in *one* academic lifetime. My academic lifetime. A wise King Alphonse once said: "If I'd been in on the Creation, I could have done a better job of it." Well, I was in on the creation of finance theory. But I could not have done that better job; if I could have, I would have. And I didn't. Science is public knowledge eked out by all our heroes, two steps forward and one step back. A non-random walk, you will agree.

484

1. ONE WAY TO MEASURE HOW MUCH SECOND BEST "SECOND BEST" IS

PAUL A. SAMUELSON

A democracy chooses to spend a fraction of its real GDP on some public good(s). It can finance that expenditure by excise taxes. When I buy a book in the store, I pay a positive excise tax; if I buy it on the web from Amazon.com, that involves no tax. Such an unbalanced pattern of taxing can add avoidable *deadweight loss* to the irreducible real cost of the public good. How can we get a measure of the deadweight loss involved in a specified "second-best" scenario?

Here I sketch a heuristic procedure to do that. To keep the exposition brief and filter out complications that arise from differential incidences of burden on different people, different income groups and different consumer tastes, I focus here on a scenario where all are affected in the same degree.

In Section 1, I describe the economy's technology, its tastes and its public-goods need. Then analysis defines what is the first-best solution to the problem. By contrast, there is worked out the second-best solution(s) when one good is exempted from tax. Section 2 uses *homothetic money-metric utility* to provide a numerical measure of first-best real per capita income; its excess over second-best real income is a *numerical* measure of *avoidable deadweight loss* occasioned by each and any second-best solution. This approach makes no explicit mention of Dupuit-Jenkin-Marshall triangles of "consumers surplus." Section 3 sketches the diagrammatic indifference curves' general solution in the two-dimensional case. In Section 4, scenarios of greater or lesser *elasticities of substitution* are worked out to indicate the Ramsey (1927) and Joseph (1939) findings that a tax which can be avoided by virtue of demand elasticity is *ceteris paribus* a bad tax (i.e., an inefficient tax, productive of deadweight loss). Section 5, qualifications and

1 FIRST-BEST FISCAL SOLUTION VS. SECOND-BEST

Contemplate first two private goods, competitively bought and sold in the non-public sector. Let them each be producible by labor alone: 1 of labor produces 1 of C_1 or 1 of C_2; society's total of labor is specified to be fixed in total supply, $L_1 + L_2 + L_g = 1$ where L_g is the amount of labor needed to produce the public good C_g opted for by democracy's voters. Contemplate the singular case where every consumer chooses to spend *half of disposable income on each of the private goods*. (Later I tackle a case more general than this (1848) Millian case of *constant* fractional expenditures on the private goods; more generally all consumers will then still have common *homothetic* tastes which are symmetric in the $[C_1\ C_2]$ goods.)

Sans public expenditure, define optimal real GDP as unity. With public expenditure of g a fraction of the inelastic total supply of labor, what is the *first-best* solution to the tax problem? As is well-known under Henry George inelastic supply, a fractional income tax on labor at the rate g will leave private real GDP to voters totaling to $1 - g$. When consumers opt to spend $\frac{1}{2}(1 - g)$ equally on C_1 and on C_2, they contrive for themselves total ("money-metric") real private GDP of $1 - g$—which leaves over for government's public good(s) exactly g. Thus, there is *no* deadweight loss superimposed on the irreducible cost of the public good(s) in this scenario's *first-best* configuration!

As a bonus, here in my Santa Claus specification, the *same* first-best configuration can be achieved by optimal 1927 Frank Ramsey excise taxes. This is here achieved by *balanced uniform ad valorem* tax rates on C_1 and C_2:

$$t_1 = t_2;\ \text{prices to consumers}\ 1 + t_1 = 1 + t_2 = 1 + t, \tag{1a}$$

$$\text{price of}\ C_3 = 1 + 0 \tag{1b}$$

Competition's invisible hand leads to each consumer's optimizing (Millian) demand functions

$$C_1 = \frac{1}{2}[1]/[1+t_1],\ C_2 = \frac{1}{2}[1]/[1+t_2] \tag{2}$$

The common tax rate, $t = t_1 = t_2$, has to be that which collects for the government exactly enough revenue for it to buy the labor needed to produce C_g, namely

$$t_1 C_1 + t_2 C_2 = t(C_1 + C_2) = g = t(1-g) < 1,\ t^* = g/(1-g) \tag{3}$$

where for convenience the wage rate of labor is set to be unity as numeraire.

ONE WAY TO MEASURE HOW MUCH SECOND BEST "SECOND BEST" IS

$$C_1^* = \frac{1}{2}(1-g), \; C_2^* = \frac{1}{2}(1-g) \tag{5}$$

Remark: Given symmetry of C_1 and C_2 tastes and demands, one's hunch might be that it would be "unfair" to treat C_1 and C_2 unequally. My analysis depends on no *a priori* hunches. "Fairness" is not a relevant factor. What matters is that unequal tax rates will turn out to be *inefficient for everybody*, being at best a *second-best* solution to society's organization of economics.

Suppose populist democracy for whatever reason decides to exempt C_1 from *any* excise taxation. In the resulting second-best,

$$t_1^{**} = 0 < t_2^{**} \text{ and } C_1^{**} > C_2^{**} \tag{6}$$

Now

$$t_1 = 0, \; t_2 C_2 = g \tag{7}$$

$$C_1^{**} = \frac{1}{2}\frac{[1]}{1+0}, \tag{8}$$

$$C_2^{**} = \frac{1}{2}\frac{[1]}{1+t_2} = \frac{1}{2}\frac{1}{1+gC_2^{-1}}$$

$$= 1 - g - C_1^{**} = 1 - g - \frac{1}{2} = \frac{1}{2} - g \tag{9}$$

$$t_2^{**} = g\bigg/\left(\frac{1}{2} - g\right) = 2g/(1-2g) \tag{10}$$

A concrete numerical example will be helpful. Let one-sixth of GDP, 16 2/3%, be voted for public good(s): then putting $\frac{1}{6}$ for g in Equations (1)–(10) entails

$$t_1^* = t_2^* = \frac{1}{6}; \; C_1^* = C_2^* = \frac{1}{2}\left(\frac{5}{6}\right) = \frac{5}{12} \tag{11}$$

By contrast, for second-best,

$$t_1^{**} = 0, \; t_2^{**} = \frac{1}{2}; \; C_1^{**} = \frac{6}{12}, \; C_2^{**} = \frac{4}{12} \tag{12}$$

2 HOMOTHETIC MONEY-METRIC UTILITY TO MEASURE QUANTITATIVE INEFFICIENCY

In the first-best solution, all individuals end consuming equal per labor amounts of $(C_1^* \; C_2^*)$, namely $(\frac{5}{12} \; \frac{5}{12})$ when $g = \frac{1}{6}$. In the second-best case, where $t_1^{**} = 0$ and $t_2^{**} = \frac{1}{2}$, each ends up with less of C_2 and more of C_1, namely with $(\frac{6}{12} \; \frac{4}{12})$. Who is to say that one solution is better than the other? The citizens themselves each render this judgment. Their 50-50 expenditure on each good reveals that each of them acts as if to maximize the *geometric mean* of $(C_1 \; C_2)$; thus

ECONOMIC THEORY, DYNAMICS AND MARKETS

$$GM^{**}/GM^* = \sqrt{(6)(4)/(5)(5)} = \sqrt{0.96} = 0.9798 = 1 - 0.0202 \qquad (13)$$

It is just as if all people each gratuitously give up 2.02% of their disposable money (and real) incomes. To whom do they give this up? To the State? No. To their neighbor? No. No one gains what all lose. The second-best pattern of non-optimal excise taxing creates precisely that much extra deadweight loss—subtracted from what is unavoidably lost when voters willingly opted to exchange 16 2/3% of before-tax income for the public goods that they wanted.

When the g fractional governmental load is small, the deadweight loss is much smaller: it begins growing like g^2, the small square of g, proportional to $0.01 \times 0.01 = 1/10,000$ when g is only 0.01. When g becomes larger—e.g., approaches 0.5, the maximum that unbalanced $(t_1\ t_2)$ can (in this Millian case) feasibly finance for it—the deadweight loss computable by *money*-metric homothetic utility outweighs g by far: the deadweight loss approaches 100% of attainable private real income! Thus raise g from $\frac{1}{6} = \frac{4}{24}$ to $\frac{11}{24}$. Then the new calculated deadweight loss in GDP (measured from first-best) rises to 73.35%!

Alert readers will already have guessed that deadweight loss is less when fewer goods are exempted from excise taxation. What is much the same thing, when C_1's expenditure is high relative to C_2's expenditure, then exempting C_1 from excise taxation creates a measurably greater deadweight loss.

For proof, keep g at 1/6 but contemplate consumers' tastes that raise C_1's expenditure ratio to 3/4 while lowering C_2's expenditure to 1/4. Then exempting C_1 from any tax (t_1^{**} being set at zero) means that *all* of the labor needed by government will have to be subtracted from the L_2 used for C_2. This leaves each of us ending up consuming in the first-best solution

$$(C_1^*\ \ C_2^*) = \left(\frac{5}{6}\left[\frac{3}{4}\right]\ \ \frac{5}{6}\left[\frac{1}{4}\right]\right) = \left(\frac{15}{24}\ \ \frac{5}{24}\right) \qquad (14)$$

By contrast, in the second-best solution

$$(C_1^{**}\ \ C_2^{**}) = \left(\frac{18}{24}\ \ \frac{20}{24} - \frac{18}{24} = \frac{2}{24}\right) \qquad (15)$$

Now the relevant geometric means involve the weights ($\frac{3}{4}$ and $\frac{1}{4}$). Then the relevant ratio becomes the Cobb-Douglas formula

$$GM^{**}/GM^* = (C_1^{**})^{3/4}(C_2^{**})^{1/4}/(C_1^*)^{3/4}(C_2^*)^{1/4}$$
$$= (15/18)^{3/4}(2/5)^{1/4} = 1 - 0.3064 \qquad (16)$$

Thus the 2.02% deadweight loss, incurred when a 1/6 public load gets no help from excise taxing of C_1's half of private expenditure, explodes to a 30.64% deadweight loss when C_1's three-fourths of private expenditure gets exemption from excise taxation. This gratuitous loss from first-best exceeds the numerically unavoidable loss of 16 2/3% from *laissez-faire*.

3 DIAGRAMMATIC GENERAL SOLUTION

This two-good case lends itself to graphical exposition. In Figure 1 all persons have the same symmetric homothetic indifference contours. The *TT'* frontier shows the technological tradeoff between the goods when total labor is fixed and only the two private goods are to be produced. Inside *TT'* and parallel to it is *AA'*, the feasible tradeoff between *private* C_1 and C_2 when the fraction g of total labor is used up in producing the public good(s) democratically decided on. Homothetic demand, which means *unitary income elasticities* of all private goods, implies that every indifference contour is a radial blow-up of the contour that goes through the first-best equilibrium point F^*, and which is labelled U^*U^*. (Readers need not force U^*U^* to be symmetric rectangular hyperbolae around the 45°-diagonal just because my exposition concentrated on that case.) Only when goods are taxed at equal percentage rate, $t_1 = t_2 = t^*$, will demand be shifted in equal degree from zero-public-good point T^* down to first-best F^*.

By contrast, when C_1 bears no tax, consumers each face the new budget line $TS^{**}Z$, and each achieves the feasible second-best maximum at the S^{**} point where the budget line is *tangential* to the achievable $U^{**}U^{**}$ contour. Money-metric utility for first-best F^* is measured by the length OF^*. Money-metric utility for second-best S^{**} is measured by OM^{**} on the main diagonal (M^{**} is where $U^{**}U^{**}$ intersects that diagonal). In summary, the ratio

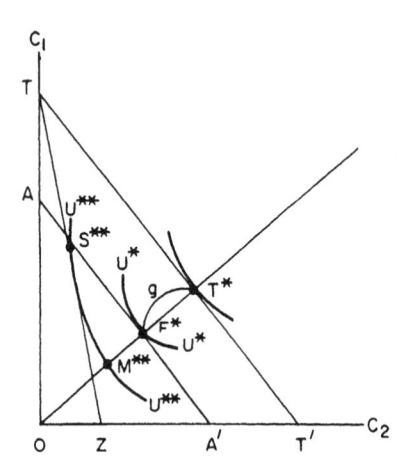

Figure 1. The first-best is at F^*, due southwest of the T^* *laissez-faire* point of zero government. The second-best is at the S^{**} tangency point on the U^{**} contour below the first-best U^* contour, where a TZ pivot through T intersects the AA' frontier and is tangential to the specified indifference curves. Money-metric utilities are measured by the diagonal's OF^* and OM^{**} lengths. $M^{**}F^*/OM^{**}$ measures deadweight-loss ratio. (Plot is qualitative, not exact.)

of ($M^{**}F^*$ length)/(OF^* length) is the *percentage* of avoidable deadweight loss (down to below first-best) due to second-best.

The astute reader will perceive that when the U^*U^* contour is nearly an "L" through F^*, which is when elasticity of substitution σ virtually equals zero, then M^{**} and F^* will almost coincide and deadweight loss is virtually zero—à la 1939 M.W.F. Joseph. (That same reader can dispense with homotheticity in the singular case when *all* individuals have the same indifference tastes and start out from the same TT' endowments. More in Section 5 on this.)

4 HOW SUBSTITUTION ELASTICITY BOOSTS DEADWEIGHT LOSS

Has this 50-50 expenditure scenario *over*-dramatized realistic deadweight loss? Or *under*-dramatized it? To show that neither answer should be Yes, replace homothetic Mill-Cobb-Douglas $2C_1^{1/2}C_2^{1/2}$ by the general symmetric constant-elasticity-of-substitution family, CES

$$U = \left(\frac{1}{2}C_1^\alpha + \frac{1}{2}C_2^\alpha\right)^{1/\alpha}, 1 > \alpha \neq 0$$
$$= M_\alpha(C_1, C_2), \text{general concave } power \text{ mean} \qquad (17)$$

My useful examples will be

$$U = M_{-1}(C_1, C_2) = \left(\frac{1}{2}C_1^{-1} + \frac{1}{2}C_2^{-1}\right)^{-1}, \text{Harmonic Mean} \qquad (18)$$

This has σ less than the unity of Cobb-Douglas-Mill.

For $\sigma > 1$, I use the (1728) Gabriel Cramér square-root Mean, which he nominated to defang the stochastic St. Petersburg Paradox's infinity. Its formula is

$$U = M_{1/2}(C_1, C_2) = \left(\frac{1}{2}C_1^{1/2} + \frac{1}{2}C_2^{1/2}\right)^2 \qquad (19)$$

Pushing Equations (18) and (19) each to their extremes, so that $\sigma \to 0$, or $\sigma \to \infty$, gives us the polar archetypes

$$U = M_{-\infty}(C_1, C_2) = \lim_{\alpha \to -\infty}\left(\frac{1}{2}C_1^\alpha + \frac{1}{2}C_2^\alpha\right)^{1/\alpha}$$
$$= \text{Min}(C_1, C_2) \qquad (18')$$

$$U = M_1(C_1, C_2) = \frac{1}{2}C_1 + \frac{1}{2}C_2, \text{linear mean} \qquad (19')$$

Intuitively readers will perceive that (18') is the case of L-shaped contours cornered on Figures 1's 45° diagonal; and that (19') involves *parallel* indifference *lines* to those going through F^* and T'. When there is no substitution at all, S^{**} and F^* will be seen to coincide and excess deadweight loss evaporates completely.

197

By contrast, (19′)'s case of *infinite* substitutability means that unbalanced excise taxing will cause *all* expenditures on tax-exempted good(s) to evaporate completely. *No* positive-*g* expenditure program can then ever be financed by *any* excise-tax pattern that is at all unbalanced! This extreme is the worst possible for deadweight loss.

Our numerical examples (17) and (18), which bracket the unitary-σ numerical examples of Sections 1 and 2, will confirm the degree to which demand-elasticity does magnify deadweight loss.

Here is brief mathematical explanation. For all α in (17), formulas for first-best and second-best solutions are, respectively

$$C_1^* = C_2^* = \frac{1}{2}(1-g), \text{ first best} \tag{20}$$

For second-best, the solution is the root of the following relations

$$C_1^{**} = 1 - g - C_2^{**} \tag{21a}$$

$$1 + t_2^{**} = \left(\frac{1-g-C_2^{**}}{C_2^{**}}\right)^{1-\alpha}, 1-\alpha > 0 \tag{21b}$$

or

$$1 + (g/C_2^{**}) = \left(\frac{1-g-C_2^{**}}{C_2^{**}}\right)^{1-\alpha} \tag{21c}$$

To focus on the effects of varying substitution elasticities, I keep the *g* share constant at $g = \frac{1}{6}$, for $1-\alpha = 1$, $1-\alpha = 2$ and $1-\alpha = \frac{1}{2}$. Then denoting $6C_2$ by x, here are the three first-best vs. second-best stories.

$1-\alpha = 1$, $\sigma = 1$, Cobb-Douglas Case:

$$C_1^* = \frac{1}{2}\left[\frac{5}{6}\right] = \frac{5}{12}, C_2^* = \frac{1}{2}\left[\frac{5}{6}\right] = \frac{5}{12}: \text{ first best} \tag{22a}$$

$$1 + \frac{1}{x} = \frac{5-x}{x}, x^{**} = 6C_2^{**} = 2, C_2^{**} = \frac{2}{6} = \frac{1}{3} \tag{22b}$$

$$C_1^{**} = \frac{1}{2}, C_2^{**} = \frac{5}{12}: \text{ second best} \tag{22c}$$

This confirms my Sections 1 and 2 findings. Thus

$$M_0(C_1^{**}, C_2^{**})/M_0(C_1^{**}, C_2^{**}) = GM^{**}/GM^* = 1 - 0.0202 \tag{22d}$$

Deadweight loss or $DL_0 = 2.02\%$ as before. (22e)

$1-\alpha = 2$, $\sigma = \frac{1}{2}$ Harmonic Mean Case:

$$C_1^* = \frac{5}{12}, C_2^* = \frac{5}{12}: \text{ first-best} \tag{23a}$$

$$\frac{x+1}{x} = \left(\frac{5-x}{x}\right)^2, x^{**} = 6C_2^{**} = \frac{25}{11}, C_2^{**} = \frac{25}{66} \tag{23b}$$

198

8   ECONOMIC THEORY, DYNAMICS AND MARKETS

$$C_1^{**} = \frac{5}{11}, C_2^{**} = \frac{25}{66}: \text{second best} \tag{23c}$$

$$M_{-1}(C_1^{**}, C_2^{**})/M_{-1}(C_1^*, C_2^*) \tag{23d}$$

$$= \frac{H.M.(C_1^{**}, C_2^{**})}{H.M.(C_1^*, C_2^*)} = 0.9917 = 1 - 0.0083 \tag{23e}$$

$$DL_{-1} = \frac{83}{100} \text{ of } 1\% < DL_0 = 2.02\% \tag{23f}$$

$1 - \alpha = \tfrac{1}{2}$, $\sigma = 2$ (1728) Cramér Case:

$$C_1^* = \frac{5}{12}, C_2^* = \frac{5}{12}: \text{first best} \tag{24a}$$

$$\frac{x+1}{x} = \left(\frac{5-x}{x}\right)^{1/2}, 2x^2 - 3x + 1 = (x-1)\left(x - \frac{1}{2}\right) \tag{24b}$$

Footnote 1 interprets this double root.[1]

$$C_2^* = \frac{1}{6}, C_1^* = \frac{5}{6} - \frac{1}{6} = \frac{4}{6}: \text{second best} \tag{24c}$$

$$M_{1/2}(C_1^*, C_2^*)/M_{1/2}(C_1^{**}, C_2^{**}) = \left(\frac{1}{2}\left[\frac{1}{6}\right]^{1/2} + \frac{1}{2}\left[\frac{4}{6}\right]^{1/2}\right)^2 \Big/ (5/12)$$

$$= (9/24)/(10/24) = 1 - \frac{1}{10} \tag{24d}$$

$$\text{Deadweight Loss}_{1/2} = 10\% > 2.02\% > 0.83 \text{ of } 1\%. \tag{24e}$$

Table 1 sums up this story on how higher-elasticity σ results in more second-best deadweight loss when g is set at $\tfrac{1}{6}$.

Table 1.

Elasticity of substitution σ	0	$\tfrac{1}{2}$	1	2	∞
(Deadweight Loss) (% of private GDP)	0%	0.83% of 1%	2.02%	10%	maximal

---

[1] Note as a digression that the double root of Equation (24b)'s quadratic equations reveals qualitatively the presence of two ("Art Laffer") branches of the tax-burden curve. This means there are two different tax rates on C_2 that can finance the government's g. I shall pick the lower t_2^{**}, equal to $1/x^{**} = 1$ rather than $t^{**} = 1/x^{**} = 2$, so as to concentrate on *minimum* second-best excess deadweight loss. (Remark: the voodoo economics of Reagan 1981 supply-side economics was not vitiated by Laffer's innocuous *logic*; its Achilles Heel was the Laffer-Kemp-Stockman gratuitous assertion that the 1980 U.S. tax system was *already* deep down the declining branch; mainstream economists of both parties testified that economic history did not substantiate this Laffer thesis, but to no avail; subsequent 1981-90 history confirmed their contentions.) Although two out of three of my

199

When we replace CES functions by any concave homogeneous-first-degree money-metric utility functions, the same presumption as in Table 1 holds.

5 QUALIFICATIONS AND GENERALIZATIONS

Now I sketch what happens when I drop some of my simplifications that made for easier and briefer expositions. First, so as not to ignore complications to consumers surplus connected with producers surplus, I shall add to a labor-only technology other needed input such as homogeneous land. Little of earlier *fundamentals* turns out to need qualifying on this account.

Suppose first that all the private and public goods were to use labor and land in the *same* proportions no matter what are the prevailing rent/wage ratios. Then *nothing* really changes in Sections 1 to 4 (so long as both these primary inputs are supplied perfectly inelastically). Then the $(C_1\ C_2)$ trade-off locus is still linear, again displaying constant costs. The first-best equilibrium of $(C_1^*\ C_2^*)$ is still 5/6 of zero-public-goods *laissez-faire* equilibrium when 1/6 of both labor and land resources are withdrawn for public use. Then, too, the deadweight burden added to the intrinsic burden will, when C_2 is alone given a positive sales tax t_2^{**}, entail a similar quantitative percentage loss in money-metric homothetic utility.

Less dull is the analysis when C_2 alone needs land along with labor, while both C_1 and C_g still need labor input only. Here are that model's technologies and tastes:

$$\text{Production functions: } C_1 = L_1; C_g = L_g; C_2 = L_2^{1/2}(\text{Land}_2)^{1/2}$$

$$= L_2^{1/2} \text{ when Land} = 1 \quad (25\text{a})$$

$$L_1 + L_2 + L_g = 1; W = 1 \text{ as numeraire convention} \quad (25\text{b})$$

$$\text{Tastes: } C_1 = \frac{1}{2}(\text{Income}/P_1), \ C_2 = \frac{1}{2}(\text{Income}/P_2) \quad (25\text{c})$$

Under *laissez-faire*, sans any government, the first-best solution would no longer involve equal C^*'s. Instead, because C_1 incurs no land expense, C_1^* will exceed C_2^*. To work out the first-best solution when one-sixth of labor is voted to be needed for public good C_g, the reader can construct a Figure 2 generalization of my Figure 1. Again it is a provable theorem that $t_1^* = t_2^*$ for first-best when factors are all inelastic in supply. Now the TT' production-possibility frontier will be concave and *not* symmetric around the 45° diagonal. A one-sixth withdrawal of total $L_1 + L_2$ will make the private-goods AA' frontier be below TT' by one-sixth of its vertical distance. The new, curved AA' frontier will be tangential to the U^*U^* rectangular hyperbola of indifference at the new first-best F^* point (which will no longer be on the 45° diagonal ray). Where U^*U^* intersects the diagonal-ray (call it M^*) can still be used to give Length OM^* as our measure of first-best money-metric utility.

---

numerical cases involved no double branches, generically multiple branches can occur in any multiplicity.

10   ECONOMIC THEORY, DYNAMICS AND MARKETS

The diagram can handle, but with somewhat more complexity, the second-best case—more complex because now the $TS^{**}Z$ budget line cannot be tangential to $U^{**}U^{**}$ because of the $1 + t_2$ wedge separating marginal-utility ratios and marginal-cost ratios. Still there is defined for us a unique S^{**} point and an intersection point M^{**} where the U^{**} contour intersects the diagonal ray. As before the ratio Length $M^{**}M^*$/Length OM^* depicts money-metric excess deadweight loss. QED.

To calculate and present a first-best solution, I always have two choices. I could, as in Equations (26) below, define a simple calculus problem to maximize money-metric utility. Or, as in Equations (27) below, I could write out *all* the prosaic arbitrage conditions of competitive supply and demand, knowing that Adam Smith's VISIBLE HAND will (under the posited convexities of tastes and technology) achieve the maximum.

Each second-best solution must necessarily be the outcome of the positivistic competition defined by each specified pattern of *unbalanced* excise taxes. When $t_1 \neq t_2$, a $(1 + t_2)/(1 + t_1)$ wedge is inserted between *relative marginal utilities* and *relative marginal costs*. Smith's visible hand is deflected from the bull's eye by the governmental intruder into the machine. (An erudite antiquarian authority castigated me recently for trying to interpret 1776 Smith in these terms. If this be Whig History, *mea culpa*.)

Here is a terse work-out of the arithmetic from the Equation (25) data when $g = \frac{1}{6}$. First-best solution is given by

$$L_1 + L_2 = C_1 + (C_2)^2 = \frac{5}{6} \tag{26a}$$

$$\operatorname*{Max}_{C_1, C_2} \sqrt{C_1 C_2} = \operatorname*{Max}_{C_2} \sqrt{\left[\frac{5}{6} - C_2^2\right] C_2} = \sqrt{\frac{10}{18} \sqrt{5/8}} \tag{26b}$$

$$= \sqrt{C_1^* C_2^*} = \sqrt{(0.555)(0.527)} = 0.541 \tag{26c}$$

For second-beset, competition augments Equation (26a) above by the relations

$$P_2/P_1 = \frac{MU_2}{MU_1} = \frac{1 + t_2}{1 + 0} \frac{MC_2}{MC_1} \tag{27a}$$

$$= \frac{C_1}{C_2} = \left(1 + [6C_2]^{-1}\right)(2C_2/1) \tag{27b}$$

$$= \left(\frac{5}{6} - C_2^2\right) C_2^{-1} = 2C_2 + \frac{1}{3} \text{ or} \tag{27c}$$

$$3C_2^2 + \frac{1}{3} C_2 - \frac{5}{6} = 0, \quad C_2^{**} = -\frac{1}{18} + \frac{\sqrt{\frac{1}{9} + 10}}{6} = 0.474 \tag{27d}$$

$$C_1^{**} = \frac{5}{6} - 0.225 = 0.608 \tag{27e}$$

201

$$\frac{GM^{**}}{GM^*} = \frac{0.537}{0.541} = 1 - 0.0077,$$

$$\text{deadweight loss \%} = \frac{77}{100} \text{ of } 1\% \tag{27f}$$

I am puzzled that deadweight loss has been made so small by the unbalanced presence of land along with labor. (Perhaps a calculator error?)

An assiduous reader can supplement this GM^{**}/GM^* analysis by Harmonic Mean**/Harmonic Mean* or the other risk-aversion(s) in Section 4 also. That should attest to the robustness of the earlier algorithms.

A more serious limitation on the present paradigms comes when we encounter endogenous elasticity of the labor supply. Then $L_1 + L_2 + L_g$ will not remain constant when the burden of total taxes is elevated. Indeed what I have denoted by g should be chosen endogenously by a rational democracy in dependence on how feasible it will be to approximate to first-best tax legislation. However, that additional complexity to tax-incidence analysis from elastic labor supply will not faze the expert mathematical economist. What is important to recognize is that no longer will money-metric homothetic utility of private goods be a defensible magnitude to maximize once ordinal disutilities of labor are part of the "tastes and preferences" story.

Here is a simple example to explore. Suppose that, in the fashion of 1871 Jevons, we each act to maximize the difference between a "utility of goods" and a "disutility of labor or effort." For example,

$$\underset{C_1, C_2, L}{\text{Max}} \log\{\text{Money-metric U}\} - \text{Disutility of [Total] Labor}$$

$$= \frac{1}{2}\log C_1 + \frac{1}{2}\log C_2 - (L_1 + L_2 + L_g)^2, \text{ or alternatively} \tag{28a}$$

$$= \frac{1}{2}\log C_1 + \frac{1}{2}\log C_2 - \delta(L_1 + L_2 + L_g) \tag{28b}$$

where δ is the *constant* [!] marginal disutility of labor. This last constancy is old-fashioned cardinalism with a vengeance, a special case or crutch for 1890 Marshall or 1889 Auspitz-Lieben. I can still give the first-best and any second-best solutions (with $L_g/[L_1 + L_2]$ preassigned or being an endogenous unknown), solvable once we adjoin to private-goods' money-metric utility an explicit role for C_g, as in the homothetic money-metric expression $C_1^{1/3} C_2^{1/3} C_g^{1/3}$. Now, however, GM^{**}/GM^* as a money measure of [ordinal!] utility fails to do justice to the *disutility* which larger or lesser totals for L must entail. I am happy to emphasize this vital qualification lest any reader think that in my dotage I would ever replace ordinalism by a dogma of new money-metric cardinalism. Also, with total L endogenous, neither an income tax nor balanced excise taxes can generically replace lump-sum taxes to ensure first-best!

The advantage of homothetic money-metric utility, when in singular empirical scenarios it can be defined, is that to most of us in a commercial society it seems meaningful to say to ourselves: Batch A of goods is what

$5,000 a month would buy me; if I picked Batch B above Batch A, it is just as if I threw away $1,000 because B is only what I could (and would) buy if monthly income was only $4,000. (This same money-metric measure Samuelson (1997) used to provide rational risk-corrections for diversified portfolios A and B, each subject to stochastic uncertainty. If A's Expected [stochastic] Utility is to me $5,000, and B's to me is $4,000, then investing my initial wealth [of say $3,000] in B rather than A is just like throwing away a big chunk of my initial wealth.)

Fine, then, but only when goods' money-meteric utilities are not contaminated by differences in labor disutility—as in the case here. We must aim at the proper relevant bull's eye and not at some easy non-bull's eye. (J.J. Thompson, the Nobel Laureate who discovered the electron, was told in Cambridge: "Any broker in the city makes twice your salary." Unfazed, J.J. replied: "Yes, but look at the work they must do"—a two-edged rebuke.)

Finally, out of a long list of needed qualifications I mention that for two hundred years economists have known well that demand is NOT homothetic. Engels' Laws document that the ratio of food expenditure to total expenditure falls systematically with income; etc., etc. Even if all people had identical tastes, at different income levels, second-best and first-best would give them different money-metric utilities—and, hence, different measures of avoidable deadweight loss.

Something could be saved from the ruins in an egalitarian society where people's incomes as well as tastes are identical—even if the tastes are *not* homothetic. For the representative man, Batch A and Batch B can be given a commensurable money-metric utility once we agree on a specified vector of prices. Thus, for inelastic supplies of both labor and land, one could replace the $\sqrt{C_1 C_2}$ tastes used in Equations (26) and (27). Replace by what? Replace by any non-homothetic *ordinal* quasi-concave $u(C_1, C_2)$ of "the representative person." At any chosen reference vector of prices, $(\overline{P}_1/W\ \overline{P}_2/W)$, and for labor supply of unity, $L = 1$, solve the following McKenzie (1957) inverse problem of consumer's choice

$$\operatorname*{Min}_{z_1, z_2} \sum_{1}^{2} (\overline{P}_j/W) Z_j \quad \text{s.t.} \quad u(Z_1, Z_2) \geq u(C_1, C_2)$$

$$= E(C_1, C_2; \overline{P}_1/W, \overline{P}_2/W) = E(C_1, C_2) \text{ for short} \qquad (29)$$

The minimized expenditure function $E(C_1, C_2)$ can serve as a money-metric utility. The ratio

$$E(C_1^{**}, C_2^{**})/E(C_1^{*}, C_2^{*}) = 1 - \text{Deadweight Loss} \qquad (30)$$

should work much the way GM^{**}/GM^{*} does in the Mill-Douglas-Wicksell homothetic case.

However, I have to be reserved about pretensions for this dodge. What reference prices would be especially useful? Only in the homothetic case will choosing different reference prices alter not at all the final results. First-best price ratios might possibly nominate themselves in our non-homothetic excise tax case? But remember that we voters cannot be expected to know what would be first-best in a world where we are lucky not to be far far away from it.

My purpose here is not to unveil a new Napoleonic metric calculus of welfare. Rather it is to push advanced economists' thinking toward general equilibrium *Gestalts* and away from the Marshallian partial equilibria which dominated when first I studied economics 70 years ago.

Nor are these approaches confined to second-best taxes. They apply, with all their limitations, to the old problem of estimating how much a modern economy loses on account of monopolistic deviations from competitive marginal-cost pricing. Bergson (1973) commented dubiously on the familiar 1954 Harberger estimate that welfare losses due to monopolistic pricing were back in the first half of the twentieth century but "...a tenth of a percent of national income (p. 87)." This mode of expression is, in its way, a version of money-metric utility. Certainly the methods of my previous sections could have applied as well to stipulated situations in which sectorally prices paid were in excess of appropriately measured marginal costs. Easily fabricated numerical examples, applied to CES functions spread over the spectrum of σ elasticities, can well yield estimates that are considerable multiples of Harberger-Schwartzman-Leibenstein's. Did we really have in 1954 or 1994 reliable estimates of the many supply-demand elasticities to inspire confidence in these matters? I do not know. However, if my hunch is correct that in today's global economy the oligopoly powers of the Fortune-500 companies have been vastly reduced by domestic and international free entries which widen the market and by changes in corporate governance away from the Berle-Means pattern described in my first-edition 1948 *ECONOMICS*, then that has to be quite incompatible with the above Harberger findings.

6 LITERATURE ACKNOWLEDGMENTS

Frank Ramsey's 1927 classic on optimal excise taxing, which was set to him as a problem by A.C. Pigou, is obviously an important source. His results were, at least partially, rediscovered and generalized by J.R. Hicks, H. Hotelling, M. Boiteux, P.A. Samuelson, U. Hicks, Baumol-Bradford, A. Walters, J. Drèze, Diamond-Mirrlees, and others cited in Samuelson (1974). A. Bergson (1936) was an early user of the CES formula employed here, and an omniscient reader will recognize how much I again owe to Bergson (1936, 1938, 1973, 1979, 1980). Peggy (M.W.F.) Joseph (1939) was also an original analyst. Although little referred to here explicitly, the vast consumers surplus literature of Marshall-Dupuit-Jenkin-Hotelling-Allais-Divisia-Robert Bishop-James Morgan-Sono-Harberger overlaps with my problem. More directly I have relied on Roy-Shephard-Houthakker-Samuelson-McKenzie duality theory and my homothetic money-metric utility is one form of *exact* index number theory à la Diewert.

Science is seen here to be a vast evolutionary cooperative process. All this 2000 material could essentially have been written down by Ragnar Frisch and his contemporaries half a century ago.

I recommend that serious readers refer to the vast literature on appraising how differing degrees of prices distortion from *laissez-faire* arbitrage will compromise welfare optimality. See for example the valuable analysis and review in Kunio Kawamata (1974). With Machiavellian subtlety my singular Santa Claus scenarios have been specified so as to rule out the genuine subtleties of the general cases broached by Debreu (1951) and others.

ACKNOWLEDGEMENTS

I acknowledge editorial and referencing aid from Janice M. Murray and partial support aid from MIT and the Sloan Foundation.

References

Auspitz, Rudolf and Richard Lieben. 1889. *Untersuchungen über die Theorie des Preises*. Leipzig: Duncker & Humblot.

Bergson, Abram. 1936. "Real Income, Expenditure Proportionality and Frisch's 'New Methods of Measuring Marginal Utility'," *Review of Economic Studies*, 4:33–52.

—— 1938. "A Reformation of Certain Aspects of Welfare Economics," *The Quarterly Journal of Economics*, 52:310–334.

—— 1973. "On Monopoly Welfare Losses," *American Economic Review*, 63:853–870.

—— 1979. "Consumer's and Producer's Surplus and General Equilibrium," in H. Greenfield, et al., eds., *Theory for Economic Efficiency: Essays in Honor of Abba P. Lerner*. Cambridge, Mass.: MIT Press.

—— 1980. "Consumer's Surplus and Income Redistribution," *Journal of Public Economics*, 14:31–47.

Cramér, Gabriel. 1728. As discussed in I. Todhunter, *History of the Mathematical Theory of Probability*, 1949. New York: Chelsea. Page 220 gives a good account.

Debreu, Gerard. 1951. "The coefficient of resource utilization," *Econometrica* 19:273–292.

Diewert, Erwin. 1976. "Exact and Superlative Index Numbers," *Journal of Econometrics*, 4:115–145.

Harberger, A.C. 1954. "Monopoly and Resource Allocation," *American Economic Review*, 44:77–87.

Hicks, John R. 1956. *A Revision of Demand Theory*, Oxford: Oxford University Press.

Hotelling, Harold. 1938. "The General Welfare in Relation to Problems of Taxation and of Railway and Utility Rates," *Econometrica*, 6:242–269.

Jevons, William Stanley. 1871. *The Theory of Political Economy.* Pelican Classics edn., ed. R.D. Collison Black Harmondsworth: Penguin Books, 1970.

Joseph, Margaret F.W. 1939. "The excess burden of indirect taxation," *Review of Economic Studies,* 6:226–231.

Kawamata, Kunio. 1974. "Price Distortion and Potential Welfare," *Econometrica,* 42:435–460.

Leibenstein, Harvey. 1966. "Allocative Efficiency vs. 'X-Efficiency'," *American Economic Review,* 56:392–415.

Marshall, Alfred. 1890. *Principles of Economics.* London: Macmillan.

McKenzie, Lionel. 1957. "Demand Theory Without a Utility Index," *Review of Economic Studies,* 24:185–189.

Mill, John S., 1848. *Principles of Political Economy, with some of their applications to Social Philosophy.* Two volumes. London: John W. Parker.

Pigou, Arthur C. 1928. *A Study in Public Finance.* London: Macmillan, 3rd edition, 1947.

Ramsey, Frank. 1927. "A contribution to the theory of taxation," *Economic Journal,* 37:47–61.

Samuelson, Paul A. 1947, 1983. *Foundations of Economic Analysis,* Cambridge, Mass.: Harvard University Press.

—— 1948. *ECONOMICS.* New York: McGraw-Hill.

—— 1972. "Unification Theorem for the Two Basic Dualities of Homothetic Demand Theory," *Proceedings of the National Academy of Sciences, U.S.A.,* 69:2673–2674. Reproduced as Chapter 212 in *The Collected Scientific Papers of Paul A. Samuelson,* Vol. 4. Cambridge, Mass.: The MIT Press, 1977.

—— and Swamy, S. 1973. "Invariant Economic Index Numbers and Canonical Duality: Survey and Synthesis," *American Economic Review,* 64:566–593. Reproduced as Chapter 209 in *The Collected Scientific Papers of Paul A. Samuelson,* Vol. 4. Cambridge, Mass.: The MIT Press, 1977.

—— 1974. "Complementarity: An Essay on the 40th Anniversary of the Hicks-Allen Revolution in Demand Theory," *Journal of Economic Literature,* 12:1255–1289. Reproduced as Chapter 208 in *The Collected Scientific Papers of Paul A. Samuelson,* Vol. 4. Cambridge, Mass.: The MIT Press, 1977.

—— 1982. "A Chapter in the History of Ramsey's Optimal Feasible Taxation and Optimal Public Utility Prices," in S. Andersen, et al., eds., *Economic Essays in Honour of Jørgen H. Gelting.* Copenhagen: The Danish Economic

Association. Reproduced as Chapter 296 in *The Collected Scientific Papers of Paul A. Samuelson*, Vol. 5. Cambridge, Mass.: The MIT Press, 1986.

—— 1997. "Proof by Certainty Equivalents that Diversification-Across-Time Does Worse, Risk Corrected, than Diversification-Throughout-Time," *Journal of Risk and Uncertainty*, 14:129–142.

Schwartzman, David. 1960. "The Burden of Monopoly," *Journal of Political Economy*, 68:627–630.

Shephard, Ronald. 1953. *Cost and Production Functions*. Princeton: Princeton University Press.

485

2 A Small Pearl for Doctor Stiglitz's Sixtieth Birthday: When Risk Averters Positively Relish "Excess Volatility"

Paul A. Samuelson

Sometimes, even within the pure realm of deductive mathematics, experimental exploration may generate a conjecture or even a valid theorem. What fruit flies, maize, and phage do for the genetical biologist—serve as convenient special testing grounds for general microbiological truths—simple cases of two-outcome ("binary") investment probabilities can sometimes provide speedy ways of testing modern finance principles. (By modern finance I mean the Bachelier to Black-Scholes-Merton theories and beyond, most of which go back only to about the mid-twentieth century.)

One day I fooled around idly with some finger exercises in portfolio theory and was given a shock of surprise by the mathematics. Which would be better for an investor faced with an all-or-nothing choice between stock A that with even-odds turns every $1.00 of ante into $2.00 or into $0.50, or stock B that turns $1.00 into $4.00 or into $0.25?

Of course the investor's degree of risk tolerance must influence which one is chosen. A risk-neutral investor will certainly go for higher mean-money B rather than A. A near-paranoid investor with scant tolerance for loss will instead pick the less-volatile A even though its mean-money return is only ten-seventeenths that of B.

My custom is to start off with a 1738 Bernoullian who acts to maximize the expected value of log (wealth outcomes). He will be precisely indifferent between A and B. (Some will say, but not I, since A and B are equal and since he is a risk averter who shuns unnecessary volatility, he'll opt for less-volatile A.) Readers will realize that those less risk averse than Bernoulli, such as 1728 Cramer, who maximize $E\{\sqrt{\text{wealth outcomes}}\}$, will opt for B. Contrariwise, a more risk-averse investor than Bernoulli who maximizes $E\{(-1/\text{Wealth})\}$, would pick "safer" A over B.

209

These choosings between *all*-in-stock A or *all*-in-stock B are a bit remote from conventional portfolio problems. In them, an investor can avoid all-or-none choices. Instead she usually will face absolutely safe cash that promises an interest rate worse than A's or B's best outcome but better than either of their worst outcomes. Cash's safe return could be zero, or it could be say 5 percent. For brevity, I'll set it at 0 percent. Whatever the investor's degree of smooth risk aversion, she can always beat A by mixing it with some positive cash ratio.

The same goes for her definite gain from mixing B with some positive cash. MBA quizzes ask students what fraction of the portfolio should optimally be in cash and what remaining fraction in A? Or the B-cum-optimal cash might be the quiz question. For Bernoulli, uncomplicated linear algebra says: $x^* = 0.5$ in cash and $1 - x^* = 0.5$ in A is optimal. By sheer coincidence (of my contrived example), Bernoulli calculates 0.5 cash in B, too!

To be honest, originally I stupidly expected that if one were made to choose between A-cum best cash and B-cum cash, since all A and all B were "equivalent," then the rational investor would do better to break the previous tie by avoiding more-volatile B. I'd have felt less ashamed if I had originally (fallaciously) argued: A-cum cash and B-cum cash will still be equally preferable, when for each the cool cash has optimally quenched their respective volatilities.

One's mathematics shouts out any intuitive errors. Complete optimality calculations of expected log utility of A&Cash and B&Cash show the latter to be definitely the better choice. To ensure that this oddity was not peculiar to the special Bernoulli case, I worked out the $U = \sqrt{W}$ and the $U = -W^{-1}$ cases, only to get the same "counter-intuitive" result.

Capitulating to the $2 + 2 = 4$ arithmetic, I leaped to the general conjecture:

THEOREM Whenever $E\{U(W_A)\} = E\{U(W_B)\} = U(W_{AB})$, and the probability distribution around (W_{AB}) is for B uniformly more dispersed around (W_{AB}) than it is for A, then best $W^*_{B\&C} >$ best $W^*_{A\&C}$:

$$E\{U(W_A)\} < E\{U(W^*_{A\&Cash})\} < E\{U(W^*_{B\&Cash})\} > E\{U(W_B)\}.$$

Admittedly, this was a stretch. Why believe that what holds for *binary* wealth outcomes would hold for *general* multidiscrete-outcome cases and for probability-density cases?

A Small Pearl for Doctor Stiglitz's Sixtieth Birthday

Experience planted that belief stretch. Consider the similar but different case where stocks α and β have the same mean-money outcomes: α converts initial \$1 into $1/2$ or 2 with even odds; β turns \$1 into 0 or $2\,1/2$ with even odds. Then for risk averters who abhor money volatility around the money mean, when

$$E\{W_\alpha\} = E\{W_\beta\} = \overline{W} = 1\tfrac{1}{4} \tag{1a}$$

and

$$\mathrm{Min}\{W_\beta\} < \mathrm{Min}\{W_\alpha\} < \overline{W} < \mathrm{Max}\{W_\alpha\} < \mathrm{Max}\{W_\beta\}$$
$$0 < \tfrac{1}{2} < 1\tfrac{1}{4} < 2 < 2\tfrac{1}{2} \tag{1b}$$

and

$$U'(W) > 0 > U''(W), \tag{1c}$$

then $E\{U(W_\beta)\} < E\{U(W_\alpha)\}$. $\tag{1d}$

Numerous papers on "stochastic dominance" justify the stretch from even-odds binary outcome where

$$\mathrm{prob}\{\mathrm{Max}\,W\} = 1 - \mathrm{prob}\{\mathrm{Min}\,W\} \tag{2a}$$

to the most general probability cases where W can have multiple discrete values.

$$\mathrm{prob}\{W_1 = a_1\} = p_1, \ldots, \mathrm{prob}\{W_n = a_n\} = p_n \tag{2b}$$

$$\sum_1^n p_j = 1;\, p_j > 0 \text{ for } j = 1, 2, \ldots, n. \tag{2c}$$

And the same result applies when W's probability density is $p(W)\,dW = P'(W)\,dW$; and applies as well for the general Stieltjes integral case where

$$\mathrm{Prob}\{W \leq w\} = P(w); \int_0^\infty dP(w) = 1 \tag{2d}$$

$P(w + |h|) \geq P(w); P(0-) = 0,$ limited Liability

$$P(0) \geq 0;\, \lim_{w \to \infty} P(w) = 1. \tag{2e}$$

Having learned something, I was inclined to publish a short note. But then somebody suggested to me that this result was already in Diamond-Stiglitz (1974). I looked there and realized that indeed

211

my brainchild was already floating somewhere there, but exactly where I was not sure. And the same vague uncertainty pertained to Rothschild-Stiglitz (1971).

For a Joe Stiglitz, who exudes theorems hourly from every pore, the best of all presents may be one that leaves to him some task of putting it together correctly. Maybe he will find that my little pearl is after all only a grain of sand?

Rationalizations

I conclude with some informal brainstorming. How intuitively can we understand the pseudoparadox that risk averters who shun money volatility as such, seemingly embrace volatility when choosing between pairs of securities that are on an all-or-none basis exactly indifferent?

Here is one literary consideration. Suppose as an extreme case that A had already been safe cash itself. Then the option to add cash as a diversifier to what is already cash can accomplish nothing for it. Thus

$$A \approx A\&C \approx B \leq B\&Cash.^* \quad QED. \tag{3}$$

Using a reliable intuitive stretch, one realizes that cash usefully improves on volatile B more than it can for an admissible less-volatile A.

A somewhat similar comfort can come from recalling a historical Waugh-Samuelson dialogue. During World War II, Frederick Waugh published "Does the Consumer Benefit from Price Instability?" in the *1944 Quarterly Journal of Economics*. What he proved was that with no time preference and symmetric intertemporal tastes, then over two periods one will be better off buying at $(p + h, p - h)$ prices than at $(p\ p)$ prices. Moonlighting from the wartime MIT Radiation Laboratory, I submitted to *Econometrica* a paper entitled "The Consumer Does Benefit from **Feasible** Price **Stability**" (2002, emphasis added). The meticulous assistant editor lost that accepted paper, and in my zeal to defeat Adolf Hitler I let the matter drop until decades later when the Waugh effect got rediscovered.

My point was not that Waugh's "hypothesis I implies conclusions II" was incorrect. But rather that, if its innuendo persuaded Congress to pass (in the interest of price instability) a law requiring equal

A Small Pearl for Doctor Stiglitz's Sixtieth Birthday

harvests (q q) to be replaced by carryover and storage creating unequal (q + Δ q − Δ), consumer's utility would be *reduced* and not enhanced. Why? Because the entailed unequal (p_1 p_2) auction prices must then definitely violate Waugh's hypothesized ability to purchase at prices that averaged in the mean the same as the equalized equilibrium prices.

What is afoot in the debate is that, by the weak axiom of revealed preference, the direct utility function, $U(q_1, q_2) \equiv U(q_2, q_1) = U(q_1) + U(q_2)$, is quasi-concave in its arguments whereas its *dual* utility function in the normalized price space

$$^*U(p_1, p_2) = \underset{q_1, q_2}{\text{Max}}\ U(q_1, q_2) \text{ s.t.} \tag{4a}$$

$$p_1 q_2 + p_2 q_2 = 1 \tag{4b}$$

must be quasi-convex in its arguments. Something like the flip-flop from concavity to convexity is involved in the Diamond-Stiglitz (or Rothschild-Stiglitz) innovative papers. An easy Mill-Cobb-Douglas case is illustrative. Here

$$U(q_1, q_2) = U(q_1) + U(q_2) = \log q_1 + \log q_2 \tag{5a}$$

$$U(p_1, p_2) = {^*U(p_1)} + {^*U(p_2)} = \log(1/2p_1) + \log(1/2p_2) \tag{5b}$$

$$U'(q) > 0 > U''(q) \text{ and } {^*U'(p)} < 0 <^* U''(p). \tag{5c}$$

Note the crucial reversal of signs in equation (5c).

Similar perhaps to the Waugh effect is the familiar 1817 Ricardian pitch for specialization and trade between Portugal and England. You and your neighbor are each benefitted when, so to speak, you can buy at both your own and your neighbor's scarcity prices.

Acknowledgments

I owe thanks to Janice Murray for editorial assistance; to the MIT Sloan School and the Alfred P. Sloan Foundation for partial support; and, as usual, to Bob Solow for safety-netting.

References

Diamond, Peter, and Joseph Stiglitz. 1974. "Increases in Risk and in Risk Aversion." *Journal of Economic Theory* 8:337–360.

Rothschild, Michael, and Joseph Stiglitz. 1971. "Increasing Risk II: Its Economic Consequences." *Journal of Economic Theory* 3:66–84.

Samuelson, Paul A. 1972. "The Consumer Does Benefit from Feasible Price Stability." *Quarterly Journal of Economics* 86:476–493. Reproduced as chapter 261 in *The Collected Scientific Papers of Paul A. Samuelson*, vol. 4. Cambridge, Mass.: The MIT Press, 1977.

Waugh, Frederick V. 1944. "Does the Consumer Benefit from Price Instability?" *Quarterly Journal of Economics* 58:602–614.

The Backward Art of Investing Money

A take on current finance debates.

Paul A. Samuelson

PAUL A. SAMUELSON is Institute Professor Emeritus at the Massachusetts Institute of Technology.

My title is lifted, I believe, from an essay by Wesley Mitchell entitled, "The Backward Art of Spending Money." Beginning this way will I hope make clear that being a high priest of highfalutin finance theory does not imply that I think rationality in investing behavior is either universal or even widespread.

A sizable fraction of the nation's resources are committed to mutual fund, pension fund, and brokerage organizations. Old and new historical records suggest that their clients could be better served by plain vanilla Vanguards or TIAA-CREFs, and that this would release perhaps 90% of the finance industry's resources to produce other comforts and necessities of life.

Would the efficiency and growth of our mixed economic market be reduced by such a switch to lean and canny diversification? Or would the economy's efficiency and growth be elevated by such a change?

There is no preponderant evidence in favor of the affirmative or the negative on this. In particular, it is probably a romantic myth that departing systematically from a broadest diversification will generate random subsidies to venturesome projects that average out to be socially superproductive. In these days when we hear so much about Schumpeter's *"creative capitalistic destruction,"* we should not ignore *"malignant* capitalistic destruction." The adage, "It is better to have loved and lost than never to have loved at all," is neither a tautology nor a tested empirical truth.

When *The Journal of Portfolio Management* reaches new birthdays, I become motivated by the editors' invitation to record my take on various current finance debates. Here I address some of the more interesting questions.

FINANCE DEBATES

How should the length of the investment horizon affect risk tolerance? This is a complicated question, much misunderstood. I'll discuss it last.

Some mathematicians and engineers used to advocate that we seek portfolio combinations that maximize the portfolio's long-run growth rate. Should one really invest so as to maximize the geometric mean of total returns, as that desideratum mandates? The answer is simple: Only those Laplacians with singular Bernoulli utility, utility of wealth = log(wealth), should seek to maximize geometric mean. It is a stupid desideratum to seek the greatest probability of winning the biggest random lottery.

Markowitz-Sharpe-Tobin quadratic programming in terms of portfolio means and variance is a powerful approximation that has captured real-world converts in the way that smallpox used to infect once-isolated aborigines. Is that truly optimal for investors with widely different Laplacian risk tolerances? Should Laplacians with widely divergent risk tolerances really want the same singular proportionate mixture of risky stocks A and B when combining them with a safe security C? If you understand that the true answer is no, do you understand that a rational investor provided with only knowledge of means and covariances should not waste that limited knowledge on standard quadratic programming? This standard mean-variance quadratic programming is guaranteed to work well only for lowest-risk bettings.

Contemplate a universe with 0% Thaler-Tversky-Kahneman "irrational behaviorists," and contemplate universes with 80% of them, or with a universal 100%. Is it not possibly the case that both the 80% and 0% alternatives could sustain much the same Fama-Samuelson micro-efficient market pricing?

For myself, I believe the evidence is strong that modern Wall Streets are approximately micro-efficient; that is, there are no easy pickings left on the table. Like Robert Shiller and unlike Fischer Black, however, I find this micro-efficiency consistent with macro-inefficiency—in the sense that the overall asset indexes can and do undergo long-term overvaluation and undervaluation oscillations about some smoother trend.

Yes, Virginia, some few traders do beat the so-called random walk market over the long run. But they are hard to identify, and you cannot buy their services cheap—for the reason that others richer than you and more alert than you have already bid up the rents on their talents to the point where they are no longer wonderful bargains. Both in a stationary stochastic scenario and a non-stationary stochastic scenario, many would-be Babe Ruths will for a time enjoy stellar batting averages. Fidelity's Magellan or Vanguard's Windsor funds illustrate my point: Mixing either with the S&P index in every decade does little to augment your risk-corrected return.

Most traders who do well in any year are momentum traders. Unlike the numerous traders with so-so performance, the successful stars do not give back to the changing market all or most of their previous winnings. They do this by a flair for risk avoidance that seemingly cannot be programmed into their systems' formulas. All the veteran stars have a healthy concern about risk, but seemingly they cannot codify their concern.

I illustrate by a little story. Z garnered profits in futures market trading 49 out of 49 years. He became patron saint to a new trading group. They apprenticed to him for a whole year Y, a young trader, who wrote up a privately printed book summarizing Z's various wisdoms. Alas, Y as a trader was himself never able to break even in any subsequent year. (An Ivy League physicist analyzed the acoustics of fine violins. From his laboratory measures he concluded: "The only difference between a Stradivarius and an expensive 1990s manufacture is somewhere in the overtones." Thanks a lot.)

Mathematicians know that stock price changes have short-run serial correlation coefficients that are positive, while longer-run serial correlations are negative. (Blue noise evolves into red noise.) Alas, knowing this doesn't seem to enable one to garner lush trading returns. The Good Book says, "There is a time to remember and a time to forget." Alas, we need a better book to inform us on how and when we should shift our gears.

Self-serving bar associations benefit from the dictum: "He who is his own lawyer has a fool for a client." God must have loved the lone-wolf investor because he made so many of them. More likely it was the Devil, because an accurate tally of how they do as a group over their lifetimes would tell a sorry story. Just as alcoholics bamboozle themselves at the same time that they bamboozle their handlers, lone-wolf investors talk in the locker rooms about their winners, not their losers. Only their spouses and the IRS are aware of their true net losses in what is a negative-sum game.

Most investments are sold, not bought. Reading *Forbes* and *Barron's*, the surgeon general warns, can be injurious to your long-term financial health. There is nothing so dangerous as a good new story. Exciting investing just beggars you faster than the dull kind. That's why Darwinian evolution has made paranoid wives less vulnerable than high-T husbands (T = Testosterone).

Can the heirs to high or moderate wealth buy the brains they did not inherit? We do not have solid and unbiased samples of performance records at the big private banks, big investment brokers, and the big brokerage franchises. That fact by itself is circumstantial evidence that mediocrity reigns there as elsewhere.

Since the early-2000 bursting of the high-tech bubble, the ribbon clerks at Vanguard, CREF, and such have incurred the same percentage losses as the broad equity indexes. How could that not be the case, when their mantra is to end up with a beta of exactly 1.000?

This has bred the quixotic notion that the time is ripe to drop off the wagon and revert to *self*-decision-making. Reinforcing this non-sequitur is that the 2002-2003 upswing in Wall Street has been strongest in the dogs that suffered most in 2000-2001.

Is this case for self-choice cogent? Not really. About half of undiversified portfolios will by definition have better and worse movements around the diversified average. Schumpeter used to say that the top dollar rooms in capitalism's grand hotel are always occupied, but not by the same occupants. Next time instead of oil magnates it will be mall developers or software nerds or investment bankers. Look under the Ivy League's building ivy, and the names you read on the friezes will document Schumpeter's story.

To truncate what could be a long list, following every quasi-crash, people realize how much better they could have done if only they had timed their investments—that is, timed them in accordance with hindsight. Will Rogers put it well: Buy stocks before they go up, and sell them after they stop going up.

Studies of a thousand actual timers tell a dismal story. It's easier to sell when P/Es have soared, but it is hard to get back in before the new balloon goes up fast. And it is a mathematical error to think that a husband who is half the time long and half the time short is only duplicating across time his wife who is always half-and-half in risky stocks and "safe" bonds. If both lack skills to be the first in the mob trying to anticipate cyclical and stock price turning points, and to act ahead of full-time macro experts, it is the husband who suffers the most because he adds to his bad judgments about GDPs his losses from having abandoned optimal security diversification.

As promised, I conclude with some of the complications involved in the length of time horizon debates. In a truly random white noise market, the law of large numbers that reduces the variance of random errors about an unchanging mean by $\sqrt{N}$, does *not* apply. Repeat, does *not* apply.

If my more risk-averse wife maximizes the harmonic mean of cumulative portfolio return, while optimistic I maximize (à la Bernoulli) the geometric mean, each of us as young and old rentiers should freeze our equity ratios at our particular preferred different levels. We differ at age 30. And differ the same way at age 60. The investment crowd finds this hard to understand and believe.

It is another matter if most families have risk tolerance that *increases* with wealth. If 50/50 in stocks and bonds is right for us when our wealth is $500,000 and 75/25 is right at wealth of $5 million, then at 35 we ought to realize that the nest egg in hand is most likely to grow a lot in the next 30 years. Planning for retirement, even at 35 we should set our risk tolerance the way we would if we already had much of the wealth we're likely to have at 55. Ponder the points.

- It's not because actual riskiness erodes over the long horizon that the young with good future wage prospects should raise their equity ratio. It's because of those good prospects, taken into some account *now*.

- Those who know the literature understand other complications: A young professional cannot make liquid the present discounted value of her human capital. That factor can by itself justify that she be more risk-tolerant in the handling of her non-human capital.
- Also, as pointed out by Bodie, Merton, and Samuelson [1992], if a professional can count on working harder to offset any extra losses coming from heavier equity fractions, that can be a valid reason for raising 50%-50% to, say, 75%-25% now.

If in life we will not face the *white* noise of truly random walk but instead will face the *red* noise of mean-reversal, then those of us who are more risk-averse than Bernoulli (more cautious than the geometric mean maximizer) should thereby rationally raise 50%-50% to, say, 75%-25%. (Paradoxically, for those more risk-tolerant than Bernoulli, presence of future mean-reversal red noise will mandate that they drop from 50%-50% to 25%-75%!) Gollier [2001] is the best book on the nuances of this old familiar debate.

SUMMING UP

Post-Bush ideology will in all likelihood permit future workers to withdraw part of their Social Security credits into private self-managed accounts. Why? Because that will work out well for the greatest number? No. It is virtually guaranteed to work out expensively for most people. But the finance industries will make out well, doing their usual mediocre job for their clients who have Social Security funds to invest. Lobbyists will grease the skids to favor a system with gratuitous deadweight losses and inefficiencies.

That's how plutocratic democracy works itself out. Optimists think that people get the democracy they deserve. Pessimists like me fear the optimists are right.

REFERENCES

Bodie, Zvi, R.C. Merton, and W.F. Samuelson. "Labor Supply Flexibility and Portfolio Choice in a Life-Cycle Model." *Journal of Economic Dynamics and Control*, Vol. 15 (1992).

Gollier, Christian. *The Economics of Risk and Time*. Cambridge: The MIT Press, 2001.

To order reprints of this article, please contact Ajani Malik at amalik@iijournals.com or 212-224-3205

Foreword

Mathematical and other scientific research can sometimes have a beauty akin to artistic masterworks. And, rarely, romance can even arise in how science progresses. One notable example of this is the 1914 discovery by the eminent British mathematician, G. H. Hardy, of the unknown mathematical genius Ramanujan—what Hardy called the greatest romance in his professional life.

That story began when the morning post brought to Trinity College, Cambridge, a letter from an unknown impoverished Madras clerk. Instead of giving it a cursory glance, Hardy examined with amazement the several enclosed infinite series. In a flash, he realized they were the work of a genius: a few Hardy already knew; maybe at least one was imperfect; but several were so novel that no mere talent could have discovered them. No need here to rehash the story of the Ramanujan–Hardy collaboration and the tragic early death from tuberculosis of Ramanujan.

As told in the preface below, discovery or rediscovery of Louis Bachelier's 1900 Sorbonne thesis, 'Théorie de la spéculation', began only in the middle of the twentieth century, and initially involved a dozen or so postcards sent out from Yale by the late Jimmie Savage, a pioneer in bringing back into fashion statistical use of Bayesian probabilities. In paraphrase, the postcard's message said, approximately, 'Do any of you economist guys know about a 1914 French book on the theory of speculation by some French professor named Bachelier?'

Apparently I was the only fish to respond to Savage's cast. The good MIT mathematical library did not possess Savage's 1914 reference. But it did have something better, namely Bachelier's original thesis itself.

I rapidly spread the news of the Bachelier gem among early finance theorists. And when our MIT PhD Paul Cootner edited his collection of worthy finance papers, on my suggestion he included an English version of Bachelier's 1900 French text. I salute Davis and Etheridge for their present definitive translation, augmented by their splendid commentaries.

FOREWORD

What adds to Bachelier's fame as a theorist is that he wrote long before Norbert Wiener provided a coherent basis for differential probability space. And even longer before the Itô stochastic calculus became available to Robert Merton or Fischer Black.

Even more impressive to lay students of how modern science evolved is that Bachelier beat Albert Einstein to the punch in analyzing what is essentially Brownian motion. Einstein's 1905 physics was impeccable. But as pure mathematics, Bachelier had already overlapped Einstein's findings and beyond that explicated how Fourier's derivation of the partial differential equation of heat applied isomorphically to the diffusions of probabilities. The famous Fokker–Planck and Chapman–Kolmogorov equations could, therefore, also carry the name of Bachelier first.

Notions today of 'Wall Street as a random walk' did get an important boost from Bachelier. But earlier, as far back as 1930, Holbrook Working's prolific Stanford research on future prices had documented the similarities between random-number sequences and time profiles of actual wheat and stock prices. One must still acknowledge that doctrines of 'efficient markets' did have anticipations in Bachelier.

Early on, discoverers of Bachelier realized that Bachelier's strict text involved price changes subject to absolute Gaussian distribution. By contrast, limited-liability common stocks can both rise and fall, but none of their prices can, by definition, go negative. Therefore, opportunistically I suggested replacing Bachelier's absolute Gaussian distribution by 'geometric' Brownian motion based on log-Gaussian distributions. Independently, the astronomer M. F. M. Osborne made the same suggestion, based on some analogy with Weber–Fechner laws in historic psychology.

Novel notions in science naturally invoke opposition from the ruling savants of normal science. That is why Bachelier's mathematics and efficient-market claims met with resistance—resistance from diverse sources.

(1) If Wall Street was only a casino, then must not 'economic law' be denied? That was the accusation of the economists assigned to frame a vote of thanks for (Sir) Maurice Kendall's 1953 Royal Statistical Society lecture that reported quasi-zero serial (Pearsonian) correlations of price changes for future contracts on commodities, for common stocks, and for indexed portfolios of the above. In post-mortem chatter with my friends who had attended that lecture, I mischievously suggested:

> Work the other side of the street. Economic law in its purest form would expect rationally anticipated prices to bounce quasi-randomly to incoming shocks from unanticipated future events.

viii

(Most of my own half-dozen expositions of market efficiency, based on martingales rather than white noise, definitely do accord with economic fundamentalism. Working, who was a pioneer in recognizing random components, nevertheless compared carry-overs and seasonal pricings for onions (a) when speculative markets were banned as illegal, and (b) when they were legalized. Under (b), runs of good and bad harvests resulted, respectively, in storage and carry-over patterns that matched closely the linear-programming paths generated by an omniscient Robinson Crusoe; without legal bourses, what later became known as 'intertemporal Pareto non-optimality' was the rule in the Hobbesian jungle.)

(2) Old-guard resistance to post-Bachelier finance is well exemplified by the distinguished Nobelist and libertarian Milton Friedman. Early in the 1950s he had reacted adversely to Harry Markowitz's paradigm of portfolio optimization by mean-variance quadratic programming. It was not economics; nor was it at all interesting mathematics. Nor was this a hasty, tentative diagnosis. Forty years later in interviews with Reuters and the Associated Press, this truly great economist opined that the names of Markowitz, Sharpè, and Merton Miller would not be on connoisseurs' lists of 100 likely Nobel candidates. In some university junior common rooms, this incident brought into remembrance Max Planck's methodological dictum: science progresses funeral by funeral.

(3) Decades ago it was still not uncommon for most economists to doubt the usefulness of highfalutin mathematics for a social science like economics. When they overheard palaver about, say, Merton–Itô stochastic calculus, they were 'agin' it'. A different reaction comes from the lively twenty-first century school of 'behavioral economists'. These are well aware that few Wall Street locals can compute whether independent tosses of two fair coins will be more likely to result in both heads and tails rather than in two heads or two tails. So, how can their markets become and stay 'efficient'?

Within the sect of behaviorists, there are sophisticates who develop models in which most persons do diverge from Bachelier-type behavior, and thereby they do open up for more subtle traders temporary profits garnered from correctly correcting aberrant pricing patterns.

(4) Of course the harshest critics of efficient markets are all the brokers and investment bankers whose livelihoods would disappear in a

world of precisely efficient markets. Outnumbering these professionals as critics of market efficiency are the thousands of nongifted individuals who like a gamble but lack any flair at all for successful long-term risk-correct trading. They pursue and do not catch the fool's gold they seek.

Some very rare minds do have the special talent and flair needed for a good long-term batting average. More significant are the large universities, foundations, and millionaire family fortunes. Why do they outperform the noise traders and the small-college treasurers? I believe, but cannot prove, that it is largely because big money can (legally!) learn early more future-relevant information. Of course, those with earlier correct, not-yet-discounted, information do possess a Maxwell Demon that (joke) can defy the second law of thermodynamics.

(5) Perhaps methodologically most interesting—and certainly just that to the great Henri Poincaré, one of Bachelier's mentors—is the basic puzzle of how deductive mathematics usefully illuminates empirical behavior. The Bachelier tribe filters past oscillatory data, to nominate plausible profitable risk-corrected bets and hedges. These are guaranteed to perform well when applied to ideal *stationary* time series.

Real life, in Wall Street or Lasalle Street, or the City of London, never accords perfectly to a stationary time series. Yet, should traders deny *any* stationarity to the economic history record—past, present, or future? A true incident will explicate these points.

Some years ago there was a call option on a certain stock; I will call it Federal Finance. Traders applied to it standard Black–Scholes procedures, utilizing its past (and presumably extrapolatable) 'volatility' parameter. Ribbon clerks and assistant professors at MIT then noticed that, taking account of this call's exercise price, it was being grossly underpriced. So they bought some calls. Instead of their acumen being rewarded, the call went further down in market price. How could that be? A Black–Scholes hedge is a perfect hedge?

Well, there is no perfect hedge. Every Black–Scholes formula needs to have the right numerical volatility factor put in it. Who can ever know such perfection with certainty? The true tale tells its own lesson. Legally, but secretly, Federal Finance had contracted to be taken over at an already determined price. That meant its true volatility parameter became zero, far below past recorded volatilities. All money anted up was lost. (Moral: the crucial moment for intuitive traders is the one in which they compel themselves to disbelieve their own clever model. Time to go fishing, rather than risk more good money going bad. Long Term Capital Management seemingly never reached that crucial moment?)

We all owe gratitude to Professors Davis and Etheridge, whose labors and erudition have provided illuminating homage to a long underrated science hero. *Bon appetit!*

Paul A. Samuelson
June 2006

Keynote Addresses

Is Personal Finance a Science?

Paul A. Samuelson
Institute Professor and Professor of Economics, Emeritus
Massachusetts Institute of Technology
Cambridge, Massachusetts

My assigned presentation title is ill expressed. Its wording might seem to be asking, "Is personal finance an *exact* science?" And, of course, the answer to that is a flat no. If this disappoints anyone in the audience, now is a good moment to rectify your miscalculation by leaving.

What I do hope to address is what kind of inexact science personal finance is. Actually, the earliest political economy—in Aristotle or even the Holy Scriptures—began as the management of the household. You cannot be more low-down personal than that.

My Harvard mentor Joseph Schumpeter, in a crescendo of brainstorming, went so far as to claim that solving the numerical problems of economics—one pig for three hens rather than two or four—was the effective Darwinian evolutionary selection force that made humans become human. Descartes opined, "I think; therefore, I am." Schumpeter out-opined Descartes by asserting, "Because we humanoid primates had to struggle with personal finance, we became human."

In our introductory economics textbooks, Robinson Crusoe always played a starring role—and rightly so. Some 10,000 years ago, agriculture broadly defined was the only existent industry. Each farm and hunting family had little reason to trade with their 20–50 known neighbors—neighbors who were virtual clones of themselves.

I do not jest. As recently as around 1970, one of my innumerable sons spent his summer away from Milton Academy with his "new" temporary mother on a farm in lower Austria. That is a region where no marriage took place before the female candidate proved her fertility by becoming pregnant. Virtually all that the family consumed was grown on their peasant farm. Slaughtering the hog was the big event of the summer—pure personal finance once again.

But alas, devil nicotine ended that bucolic scenario of self-sufficiency. My son's "new" brother became hooked on cigarette smoking. This requires cash. And to get cash, you must shift to some cash crop for the first time. That is how and why personal finance became perforce *market oriented* as it is today almost everywhere.

©2007, The Research Foundation of CFA Institute

I spoke of elementary textbooks. My McGraw-Hill bestseller, *Economics: An Introductory Analysis*, came out back in 1948.[1] For the 50-year celebration of it, I had to reread this brainchild. What I discovered was that, apparently, mine was the first primer ever to devote a full chapter to personal finance—including Series E savings bonds, diversified mutual funds, and how much more income sons-in-law earned who were doctors and lawyers as compared with clergymen, dishwashers, cabdrivers, or stenographers. Fifty years later, I was pleasantly surprised to reread much in the new facsimile edition of that 1948 original, like the following words:

> Of course America's post-1935 social security system, which was formulated in depression times to intentionally discourage saving and to coax into retirement job-hoggers, will have to be abandoned in the future as a pay-as-you-go non-actuarial financial system. Such systems begin with seductively favorable pension rates that are transitional only, and must mandate stiffer contributions in future stationary or declining demographic states.

This was apparently one of my first initiations into overlapping-generation economics. You might say that in my small way, I was then being John the Baptist to latter-day Larry Kotlikoff, who is known deservedly around Central Square as "Mr. Generational Accounting."

Life-cycle finance à la Franco Modigliani recognizes that as mammals, we all do begin with a free lunch. As mortals, we are all going to die. But prior to that event, with few exceptions, we will need to be supported in retirement years by personal finance. And as we used to think before Reagan and the two Bushes, old-age pensions might come partly out of Social Security *public* finance.

My brief words here will focus on personal life-cycle finance. That is a domain full of, shucks, ordinary common sense. Alas, *common* sense is not the same thing as *good* sense. Good sense in these esoteric puzzles is hard to come by.

Here is a recent example. Life-cycle retirement mutual funds are a current rage. Fund A is for the youngster in this audience who will be retiring in 2042; Fund B is for 2015 retirees. Funds A and B both might begin with, say, 65 percent in risky stocks and 35 percent in allegedly safer bonds. But even without anyone having to make a phone call, Fund B will move earlier than Fund A to pare down on risky stocks and goose up exposure to safe bonds.

The logic for this is simple—as simple as that 2 + 2 = 4 and that the next 9 years is a shorter horizon period than the next 36 years. The law of averages, proven over and over in Las Vegas or even at the ballpark, allegedly tells us that riskiness for a pooled sample of, say, 36 items is only half what it is for a pooled sample of only 9 horizon items—the well-known $\sqrt{n}$ *verity*, or maybe *fallacy*.

---

[1] Paul A. Samuelson, *Economics: An Introductory Analysis* (New York: McGraw-Hill Book Company, 1948).

Milton Friedman is assuredly no dummy. Just ask him. Maybe he would recall from his course in statistics that the ratio of $\sqrt{9}$ (i.e., 3) to $\sqrt{36}$ (i.e., 6) measures how less risky stocks are, in the sense that the long-horizon portfolio endures only half the stock riskiness of the short-horizon portfolio. Do not copy down my fuzzy arithmetic. It is only blue smoke, sound, and fury signifying nothing.

I have triplet sons. I will call them Tom, Dick, and Harry to protect their privacy. All three are risk-averse chips off the old block: Unless the mean gains of a portfolio exceed its mean losses, they will avoid such an investment. However, Tom is less paranoid than Dick, whereas Harry is even more risk averse than Dick. Nevertheless, all three will shun life-cycle funds. For each of their 25 years until retirement, each will hold constant the fractional weight of risky equities. Tom's constant is 3/4; Dick's is 1/2; suspicious Harry stands at only 1/4.

How do I know that? Because in my family we eat our own cooking. I have written numerous learned papers denying that the correct law of large numbers vindicates the commonsense erroneous notions about risk erosion when investment horizons grow from 1 to 10 or from 100 to 10,000.

Mine has been the Lord's work. But it has brought me no second Nobel Prize—not even when I go on to write articles using only one-syllable words to rebut the many pure mathematicians who believe that all of us should seek only to maximize our portfolio's long-term growth rates.[2] Georges Clemenceau said that wars are too important to leave to generals. I say, applied math is too important to be left to pure math types!

I do not seem to have made many converts saved from error, however. I console myself by repeating over and over Mark Twain's wisdom: "You will never correct by *logic* a man's error if that error did not get into his mind by logic."

With Zvi Bodie on this program, I can hurry on to new personal finance topics. Housing will be one. Why housing in a personal finance seminar? I will leave it to Yale University's Bob Shiller or Wellesley College's Karl (Chip) Case, but not before articulating my 1958 point that, money aside, people's homes are an ideal contrivance for converting working-age savings into retirement-day dissaving.

President George W. Bush has advocated—so far unsuccessfully—that those of us covered by Social Security should be allowed to transfer into our own accounts our fair share of what has been paid into the public fund on our account. That way, the long-term sure-thing surplus yield of common stocks over bonds can be a wind at our back augmenting our golden years of retirement. Besides, as Libertarians say, "It's our money, not the government's."

---

[2]Paul A. Samuelson, "Why We Should Not Make Mean Log of Wealth Big Though Years to Act Are Long," *Journal of Banking & Finance*, vol. 3, no. 4 (December 1979):305–307.

Do not shoot the piano player—I am only quoting from White House handouts.

I am not a prophet. I cannot guarantee that, risk corrected, stocks will outperform bonds from 2006 to 2050. However, if the U.S. electorate wants to drink from that whiskey bottle and bet on that view, private accounts are not the efficient way to implement such a plan. Ask Massachusetts Institute of Technology's Peter Diamond for sermons on this topic.

A century of economic history about private and public financial markets strongly nominates that one huge public diversified indexed Social Security fund, using both stocks and bonds and both domestic and foreign holdings, will produce for the next generations better retirement pensions along with better sleep at night. One of its unique virtues is beneficial mutual insurance–reinsurance among adjacent generations.

Of course, this sensible—"good sense" sensible—proposal is too efficient ever to be adopted. To adopt it would free some millions of financial employees to transfer into useful plumbing, beer brewing, and barbering jobs.

Never forget the old saw, "Insurance is sold, not bought." The same goes for stocks, bonds, and lottery coupons. Borrowing from Abraham Lincoln, I can say that God must love those common folk that behavior scientist economists write about because She made so many of them.

Fortunately, there have been some good social inventions. If the poet Browning were to ask me, "Did you once see Shelley plain?" I would have to answer no. But I did see up close my Harvard graduate school buddy Bill Greenough. It was his Harvard PhD thesis that invented for TIAA-CREF the *variable lifetime annuity* invested efficiently in common stocks. And early on, I did write blurbs for Jack Bogle's successful launching of Vanguard's no-load rock-bottom fee S&P 500 Index stock mutual funds.

Along with the hero who invented the wheel and the heroes who discovered how to make cheese cheese and how to make cider hard cider, in my Valhalla of famous heroes, you will find the names of Greenough and Bogle.

My final words are cut short by this audience's well-fed drowsiness. I will leave as a question for later discussion: Will hedge funds make our golden years more golden, or will the new concoctions of option engineers, instead of reducing risks by spreading them optimally (in fact, by making possible about 100 to 1 over leveraging), result in microeconomic losses for pension funds and, maybe someday, even threaten the macro system with lethal financial implosions?

Good teachers always end their lectures with a question.

Asymmetric or symmetric time preference and discounting in many facets of economic theory: A miscellany

Paul A. Samuelson

Published online: 7 August 2008
© Springer Science + Business Media, LLC 2008

Abstract Factual accounts of how different people actually do discount future events and do over-estimate and under estimate the likelihood of future gains and losses are seen to vary with time and place. Lifetime distributions of wealth and income correlate with choices by those who live mostly for the present and against those who think now about differential future outputs. Rates of time discount and degree of optimism (rational vs. irrational) are seen to overlap ambiguously. Each "behaviorist" pattern can be matched by its reversed pattern.

Keywords Present-moment bias · Stochastic optimizing of expected utility outcomes · Associative means for post-1738 Laplacians

JEL Classification D90 · B21 · D80

The task of anthropologists, and of economists also, is to collect anecdotes that may or may not lend themselves to testable conjecturing. In actual economic life, and in the writings of economists, the phenomena of how people treat the present and the future (and the past, too) offer a rich treasure trove of varied behaviors. Before treating time discounting, a basic caveat should be articulated.

Naturalists in biology, and in economics too, deal in a special calculus. Almost any "truth" that they nominate can be matched by "a negation of that truth" which is also a "truth."

This could drive a pedantic logician wild because in a consistent logical system, stipulating that both A and not A are "true" enables you to prove that *any*thing and *every*thing (and *nothing*) is true.

Folk lore, after all, is a collection of old anecdotes. "Absence makes the heart grow fonder." But that does not deny the grain of wisdom in the saying, "Out of sight, out of mind." Pascal wrote that the heart has reasons that reason will never

P. A. Samuelson (✉)
Institute Professor Emeritus, Department of Economics, MIT, E52-383C, 50 Memorial Drive, Cambridge, MA 02142, USA

know. I say that behavioral economics scores when it fruitfully nominates contradictory evidence and studies its relative empirical frequencies.

Time discounting

The busy bees work hard all summer long to fill their winter honeycombs. Grasshoppers, however, consume all they can consume. (Maybe not so dumb if grasshoppers are scheduled to die before autumn is over.) I once asked my mother-in-law, who was omniscient about her Wisconsin hometown neighbors, whether a certain local was a tightwad. She replied, "Yes, indeed. He saves every year even if in a lean year he has to borrow to save."

By contrast there once was a legendary New England village pariah who had done the most awful thing—namely, he had trenched on family capital.

The early utilitarian Jeremy Bentham contrasted "impure pleasures" and "pure pleasures." Among the latter he was not judgmental, agreeing that doggerel and epic poetry were equally valuable if you thought them to be. An impure pleasure he defined as one that pleased you in the beginning but during subsequent times brought you even weightier *dis*-utilities.

One source of interest: lending to the thriftless

Since the beginning of recorded history, in every country there appeared specimens of the third oldest profession: money lenders who advance work buddies $4 on Friday in expectation of getting paid $5 on Saturday. That's compound interest with a vengeance.

My next anecdote involves no money, but does relate to discounting the likely future. A friend who was a worthy economics professor sailed with his World War II regiment to Alexandria, Egypt, on their way to the Asia Minor oil lands of the U.S.S.R. Upon their arrival in Alexandria, the medical officer harangued the troops: "Alexandria is at this time the cesspool of the world. The syphilis bug here makes your nose fall off in only 3 weeks. Hang easy until we go through the Suez Canal to arrive in Port Said and paradise."

The audience divided up 10 to 90. My friend and the other middle class officers cowered in their bunks aboard ship. The enlisted men all jumped ship, muttering to themselves, "It's no worse than a bad cold." Simultaneously they were heavily discounting the future, and grossly misjudging the probability of bad outcomes.

I dare to think that here we have a parable explaining one main difference between society's rich and society's poor. The latter tend to live (exogenously and endogenously) *in the present*. By contrast, the self-made rich keep their eye on subsequent moves in the chess game of life. And one reason they do end up rich is that from early on they have cultivated a wholesome respect for the possibility of losses.

Behavioral economics uses the awkward name "hyperbolic" time preference, for extreme over-emphasis on the present moment.

Lest you think it is only males who display hyper-myopia, I call attention to an item in the prestigious *New England Journal of Medicine*. Ten years after AIDS jumped from beasts to humans, an Ivy League college medical department interrogated its volunteering female students about their safe-sex precautions. These had reportedly changed little in that decade, the poll reported. Hard to believe, yes. But significant even if only half correct. In this example the factor of *time* discounting interacts with misguided optimism about the probability of bad outcomes.

Sex is only one of the powerful factors in human behavior. Neurologists report that along with the brain in the head, the alimentary canal can be regarded as a competing and cooperating second brain. This helps explain why fighting against becoming unhealthily fat is such a perpetual battle, and so often a losing one. Paradoxically, success of modern medical research in combatting cardiovascular disease gets offset by age-related diabetes induced by overeating.

As Mark Twain said, "Shucks, quitting smoking is easy. I've done it hundreds of times."

Chicago economics has a tautology to explain any behavior or its opposite. People who smoke do so because they get greater utility doing whatever they do. While Gary Becker was still in diapers, Chicago professor Paul Douglas (later marine and then Senator Douglas) was my 250-pound lecturer on Marshallian economics. I, fresh out of high school, was shocked when he lit up a cigarette in class. Later I was shocked again when he chastised a fellow student who had followed suit with the command: Douse that fag.

Douglas explained his smoking in a non-Beckerian way. He said, "I don't smoke because it gives me pleasure. It is a filthy habit which will shorten my life expectancy. I light up this new cigarette only because it reduces my discomfort from not getting my needed dollop of nicotine." Somehow I deemed that a better description of addiction than a sentence which reads: By definition, I smoke because I smoke.[1]

Closely related to the above is whether purist economists should admit into their axioms of stochastic choice *a separate love of gambling*. Milton Friedman said No, and drafted his Chicago neighbor Jimmie Savage to help formulate enough epicycles in one's Laplacian utility functions to rationalize behavior by people not too rich and not too poor who happen to be "risk averse for small bets" and simultaneously "risk relishers" for long shots at unfavorable odds.

Since "potters fields" are full of the corpses of people who died broke after being born with silver spoons in their mouths, why bother with casuistic denials about love of gambling and love of risk-taking? If there was no "love of danger"—no thrilling rush of adrenaline—why would people pay $75,000 and risk longevity to try to climb Mt. Everest? The 60-year-old widow who usually loses $20 every Thursday

---

[1] Gary Becker (1976) sometimes does cogently describe the pleasures some smokers want and do receive. Many testify that the day's first cigarette with morning coffee is the high point of their day. Mathematicians often do use coffee to sharpen their minds. And some report that after giving up smoking, they enter a period of reduced acuity and originality. Common mythology claims that a cigarette smoker on the building crew is worth double the pipe smoker. This leaves us uninformed on the relative efficiency of those who never smoke. Some surveys report that these days young girls are more prone than young boys to smoke. One explanation is that to quit smoking is to risk gaining the extra weight that will make you less attractive and less popular. Studies of metabolism apparently confirm that in the immediate aftermath of giving up cigarettes, on average weights do rise.

playing bingo at the local church knows she is buying friendly conversations that are worth to her more than $20 can buy her at Wal-Mart. She does not fool herself that she is making a canny investment. And neither do weekenders in Las Vegas believe that their few hundred dollars (dedicated to be lost) will escape the casino owners.

More difficult to classify are the millions of activistic traders in the stock market. Most of them like to believe that they are among the singular few who can "time" profitably the ups and downs of the ticker tape. They seek to prove to themselves and others that they are ultra-smart.

Understanding of intertemporal discounting becomes more complex when stochastic uncertainty enters the picture. Today aging patients often have to choose whether to have surgery or stay with a medicinal treatment for congestive heart failure: make your choice, say, between a one-third probability of immediate death on an operating table against a two-thirds probability of a lingering good-quality life.

However, nought is entirely new under the sun. Diderot and other eighteenth century probabilists analyzed similar choices between exposing oneself to cowpox or to a seemingly less virulent variety of smallpox as a form of insurance against later death from plain-vanilla smallpox. The cost of the insurance could not be measured in gold coins. Its cost was experiencing, at estimable odds, a shift from good health now to possible premature death just around the corner.

It has been well said that intertemporal capital theory is the Mount Everest in theoretical political economy. Even the cuneiform tablets of the Babylonians contained primitive formulas for compound interest.

For deep mathematical reasons "simple interest" is less simple than "compound interest." As tots we learn facts about spacial perspective, so we stop being astonished that the same tree looks bigger up close than it does far away. Time, too, has its perspective.

People continue to be amazed by how gigantic exponential growth can become. Thus, readers of my introductory *Economics* (Samuelson 1948, 1980) would remember at exam time that the $24 paid to Native American Indians for the island of Manhattan did, a few hundred years later, accumulate at six percent compound interest to match the hundreds of billions of 1960 dollars that New York real estate then sold for. A bright student from Ohio wrote a dissenting letter: "Dear Author, you say today's total value of NYC is $X. Surely you err. A better guess would be $Y>$X."

I assigned my young research assistant to carefully work out the puzzle. In an hour she came back with the laconic remark: "Boss, write to her that if the six percent interest rate falls short, tell her to try 6.3%."

Homer's *Odyssey* recognized the problem of plan consistency and plan inconsistency long before economist Robert Strotz (1956) grappled with it. Ulysses knew that visiting the island of the Sirens meant certain death. He knew also that the songs they sing are irresistibly sweet. So he sealed the ears of his ship's crew with wax and commanded them to ignore any command from him to be released from being tied to the mast of the ship. Under these precautions he dolefully survived the poisonous sweet temptations to frolic with the Sirens.

Many ordinary folk, like Johnson's Boswell, go out each night knowing that they will hate themselves the next morning for doing what they are about to do. As Pascal ought to have said, the Heart has un-reasons that Reason will never know.

Mainstream insights into equilibrium discount rates

Adam Smith (1776) and his contemporaries sensed correctly that the real productivity of human labor and nature's resources could be augmented by the help of produced capital inputs. This even in the absence of any Schumpeterian technological or entrepreneurial innovations.

Presumptively the Laws of Diminishing Returns would come into play when each of the capitals came to have less and less of labor and land to work with. Names of important scholars would be Nassau Senior (1836), Eugen von Böhm-Bawerk (1884, 1889), Irving Fisher (1907), Joseph Schumpeter (1912), Frank Ramsey (1928) and Robert Solow (1955, 1956).

Successful accumulation of incremental capital could be attained only by someone's thriftily abstaining from available current consumption. When this process did raise the productivity of labor and land inputs, it mandated that the new uniform safe interest (or profit) rate would fall. Indeed (*pace* Frank Knight) it could fall to zero—the Golden Age State of Euthanasia of the Rentier where all of the maximized Golden Rule Social harvest would accrue to workers' wages and landowners' real rents.

Opposition to interest as excessive usury

Karl Marx (1867) espoused the "heretical" position that machinery and factories were merely "dead (past) labor" which was undeserving of a net permanent share of the social harvest. He must have surmised this on a bad-hair day, but never did he escape from his own brainchild.

Apart from Marx both the Old Testament and Aristotle declaimed against "interest as *usury*." The Catholic Schoolmen in Renaissance times—like St. Thomas Aquinas—deplored on ideological grounds the existence of a positive interest rate on loans. Rabbits and corn seed were "fertile," according to Aristotle. By contrast money and gold were "sterile" and therefore undeserving of earning positive interest geared to the length of time for the loan. (All such heretical writers held in their mind's eye the spectacle of a rich, fat lender with superfluous luxuries lending monopolistically to poverty-stricken borrowers at levels of interest that only the desperate would agree to.) Catholic Schoolman Aquinas deemed it a violation of "distributive justice between rich and poor" to countenance positive interest on interpersonal loans.

Mainstream economic historians believe that the Calvinist-Lutheran revolt against Catholicism sparked the post-Renaissance Industrial Revolution in Britain and Holland. By contrast Spain and Latin America stagnated under the Catholic church's condemnation of interest.

Parallel to Biblical-Aristotelian-Catholic Schoolmen's condemnation of the charging of interest on interpersonal loans came the independent Islamic stricture against the legitimacy of interest as a cost for loans, or as a source of permanent consumable income. (Pakistan's founding constitution makes plain its Islamic opposition to interest.)

Whenever kings or parliaments or religious heads impose restraints on market transactions between consenting adults, black markets or gray markets tend to develop spontaneously.

Prior to and during the Counter-Reformation, within the Catholic church personal loans at hidden interest rates continued to be made. One dodge was as follows: Zero interest is ordained; but if I am late in paying you, it is legitimate for me to have to pay you a penalty charge. Soon custom develops that you'll lend me at zero interest in the expectation that I will purposely miss the contractual date. That penalty charge will typically be higher on a loan with a 2-year duration than for a loan with a 1-year duration. Covertly interest is thus being paid and interest is being received. If I surprise you by not paying off the loan "late," next time you will not lend to me.

Or consider the following example of what modern economists call "opportunity cost." Turgot (1766), the great French contemporary of Smith, argued: "Yes, money and gold coins are sterile when held in pockets or vaults. But money today can buy fertile land whose annual rents will accrue to you as investor. Fair then it must be to charge without using the word 'interest' the same percentage rate earnable per invested dollar in land." (Land sells, say, at so-called 20-years-purchase. When you have collected 20 years of land rents in harvest corn, and then sold back the land in order to repay the loan, you were in reality earning exactly five percent interest per year on your maintained permanent principal.) QED.

Mideast oil tycoons, by buying General Motors common stock that pays say dividends of $5 per year, when GM stock always sells for $100 per share, will in actuality be earning five percent interest per year. This example shows how orthodox believers in Islam can and *do* avoid sin in the modern world of organized finance.

One esoteric puzzle emerges. Except in permanent stationary or dynamic evolving steady states, price ratios of different goods will fluctuate: How then could society have *one* single safe rate of interest? When corn's price relative to wheat's price is falling—even in a predictable fashion—then in Arrow and Debreu (1954) complete-markets equilibrium when a loan today of 100 grains of corn brings me 105 corn grains tomorrow, it would have to be the case that a loan of 100 grains of wheat will bring *less than* 105 grains of then-more-dear wheat grains!

In sum, *own* interest rates in wheat differ from *own* interest rates in corn except in singular scenarios. This brainchild discovered by Piero Sraffa (1932) was (incoherently) picked up in John Maynard Keynes's *General Theory* (1936). Pity the "green" policy committee devoted to conservation of ecological resources when they may have to cope with hundreds of different own rates of discount!

Suffice it to mention here that we cannot optimally plan for and price out good "green" policies without facing up to such queries as these: Will our grandchildren be better off than us? If so, why should we stick to current market rates of interest as discount parameters in our maximands?

Does it make a difference? Yes. Purifying tomorrow's water supplies is worth doing more intensively now if the future utilities of those waters should be evaluated now with *zero* discounting, even though Wall Street generally charges today closer to 6% interest.

Fallacies and paradoxes?

Frequent actors on stage in economic seminars are Robinson Crusoe and *Homo economicus*. One hesitates to throw a stone at Crusoe who, after all, was only a bourgeois, muddling-through Englishman. *Homo economicus* we try to hold to a higher standard.

One classical problem concerns lifetime, life-cycle portfolio investing for late-in-life retirement spending. Popular innuendo hints that it is irrational not to become more risk averse when investing at an old age with fewer future-horizon periods ahead to invest in.

Lay people and Wall Street pundits have this puzzle all wrong. Strangely, too, some mathematical sophisticates also give other irrational advice. The mob believes erroneously that "riskiness" diminishes when you will be averaging gains and losses over N periods rather than over only one or two periods. Why that belief? Advanced statistics does teach that means of a random sample size of four will have a standard deviation that is half that for a sample with $N=1$. *Ergo*, (by an erroneous reference to some not incorrect "Law of Large Numbers") optimal investing over a time of N periods can (*allegedly!*) better afford risky stocks and fewer "safe" bonds.

When I became a TIAA-CREF trustee and served on the CREF equities finance committee, it was my duty to correct all such heresies about *always* shifting in old age to safer portfolios—as earlier Trustee Milton Friedman had prescribed.

Similarly, I had to shoot down the contention of mathematicians Kelley, Breiman and Latané that both risk-tolerant Jack Sprat and his risk-abhorring wife should always be *geometric-mean* maximizers for all N horizons, however large or small. That does defy good sense (even though it will serve one *well* in a *foolish duel* to beat the portfolio performance of one's brother-in-law). Being first best may cater to your vanity, but it does not butter the parsnips of *your* optimal lifetime Expected Utility.

Moral: If you are going to be *Homo economicus*, do mind your syllogisms and lemmas. For brevity, I'll cite for correct life-cycle portfolio strategy, Christian Gollier (2001).

The excessive equity premium puzzle

I'll conclude with the alleged "*Excessive* Equity Premium" (calculated in the long run to "irrationally" exceed the lower average returns from bonds). In a nutshell, it is a confirmable fact that, almost always, for 100 years the total returns on stocks over any 20 years did exceed the total return on bonds. Why then shouldn't a perfect market erode away this discrepancy?

Personally, I perceive no paradox. The spread that can and will occur for a stock portfolio to drop below that for a bond portfolio can and often will be great. That means that there will be times when your stocks will fall much in value. Hating to incur losses is in no way irrational. The pains we get from coming down in the world will be graver than most people believe *ex ante*. That can justify a need for higher average returns on stocks than on bonds. Paradox resolved.

Final reminder

Economic history and probability theory can be useful. But never forget that economics can at no time become an exact science for the reason that actual economic history is not ever what mathematicians call a *"stationary* probability distribution." There are thus no exact simple rules to learn how to benefit from knowledge of the past. None at all.

References

Arrow, K., & Debreu, G. (1954). Existence of an Equilibrium for a Competitive Economy. *Econometrica, 22,* 265–90.
Becker, G. (1976). *The Economic Approach to Human Behavior.* Chicago: University of Chicago Press.
Böhm-Bawerk, E. (1884). *Kapital und Kapitalzins. Erste Abteilung: Geschichte undKritik der Kapitalzins-Theorien.* Translated as *Capital and Interest.* London: Macmillan, 1890. South Holland, Ill.: Libertarian Press, 1959.
Böhm-Bawerk, E. (1889). *Kapital und Kapitalzins. Zweite Abteilung: Positive Theorie des Kapitales.* Translated as *The Positive Theory of Capital.* London: Macmillan, 1892. South Holland, Ill.: Libertarian Press, 1959.
Fisher, I. (1907). *The Rate of Interest.* New York: Macmillan.
Gollier, C. (2001). *The Economics of Risk and Time.* Cambridge, MA: The MIT Press.
Keynes, J. M. (1936). *The General Theory of Employment, Interest and Money.* As reprinted in *The Collected Writings of John Maynard Keynes,* Vol. VII. London: Macmillan, for the Royal Economic Society.
Marx, K. (1867). *Das Kapital.* Translated as *Capital,* Vol. 1. Hammondsworth: Penguin Books, 1976.
Ramsey, F. (1928). A Mathematical Theory of Saving. *Economic Journal, 38,* 543–49.
Samuelson, P. A. (1948, 1980). *Economics.* New York: McGraw-Hill.
Schumpeter, J. (1912). *The Theory of Economic Development.* Leipzig: Duncker & Humboldt. Translated by R. Opie. Cambridge, MA: Harvard University Press, 1934.
Senior, N. (1836). *An Outline of the Science of Political Economy.* New York: Kelley Reprint, 1965.
Smith, A. (1776). *An Inquiry into the Nature and Causes of the Wealth of Nations.* E. Cannan, ed. New York: The Modern Library, 1937.
Solow, R. (1955). The Production Function and the Theory of Capital. *Review of Economic Studies, 23*(2), 101–108.
Solow, R. (1956). A Contribution to the Theory of Economic Growth. *Quarterly Journal of Economics, 70* (1), 65–94.
Sraffa, P. (1932). Dr. Hayek on Money and Capital. *Economic Journal, 42,* 42–53.
Strotz, R. (1956). Myopia and Inconsistency in Dynamic Utility Maximization. *Review of Economic Studies, 23,* 165–80.
Turgot, A. R. J. (1766). *Reflections on the Production and Distribution of Wealth.* Translated in P.D. Groenewegen, *The Economics of A.R.J. Turgot.* The Hague: Martinus Nijhoff, 1977.

490

THE ECONOMIC BROWNIAN MOTION
American Philosophical Society, Philadelphia
11 November 1960

I.

It is not easy for a Smith or a Brown to win fame, but Adam Smith made the grade. And so did an Englishman, Robert Brown, when in 1827 he noted in the microscope the perpetual dance of life and had the wit to comment on it. The rest of the story is now classic; how in the years after 1905 Einstein, Schmolukowski and a long chain of distinguished physicists worked out the theory of the random process in which a visible colloidal particle is bombarded by the random collisions of invisible molecules, and from whose resulting drunken-sailor walk the existence and number of molecules can be cleverly inferred. Equally classic is the development of the mathematical theory of the Brownian motion by Wiener, Levy, Komologorov, Cramer, Doob and a long chain of distinguished writers in the mathematical theory of probability and stochastic processes.

What is known but to a few in the history of thought is the fact that the first path-breaking work on these stochastic processes arose out of the study of economics--or more particularly the stock market. In 1900, five years before Einstein's classic paper, a mathematical student of Henri Poincare, Louis Bachelier, published his doctoral thesis, "*Théorie de la speculation.*" It is not recorded that this made the fortune of its author or anyone else, but Bachelier's monograph is a fertile precursor of what would today be called the theories of stochastic processes. Thus, the so-called Fokker-Planck partial differential equation of probability is already in Bachelier and his demonstrations are much more interesting and general than those of Einstein.

Bachelier, apparently, has never been very well known. Those few writers who know his name think of him primarily as the imaginative but non-rigorous person whose writings inspired Komologorov to do great things with stochastic processes. This does him much less than justice, for while in truth his standards of rigor were not those of the post-war mathematical classroom, his concepts were novel and powerful and he was not more heuristic than the bulk of the great writings of the past.

I may add that my own acquaintanceship with the works of Bachelier date back only half a dozen years. Dr. Richard J. Kruizenga, now of the Standard Oil of New Jersey economics department, was writing an excellent thesis on so-called "puts and calls" under my direction. After much clever and original work he was about to hand in his thesis when Professor L.J. Savage, then at the University of Chicago, sent a round-robin letter to a number of mathematical economists asking whether any of them had ever heard of a Bachelier who had published in 1914 a popular exposition called

La jeu, la chance et le hasard, and which purported to present a theory of speculation along with innumerable empirical proofs of its validity. No copy of this work is apparently to be had anywhere in the Cambridge vicinity, but I was led to consult Bachelier's 1900 and later mathematical works. Chance can deal hard blows to young scholars for, lo and behold, much of Kruizenga's original work was nicely duplicated there--if duplicated is the right word. Fortunately, the two contributions did not completely overlap.

My own personal interest was involved, for one of the phenomena that had bothered me in the Kruizenga research continued to bother me after I had read Bachelier. According to the Bachelier-Kruizenga theory of price formation according to the random-walk, white-noise hypothesis, the market price of a call or put option should increase about with the square root of its time duration (for reasons that will be explained). This implies that an option with a long enough time duration should ultimately become worth more than any preassigned number--the total supply of money in the world, the price that most Pauls will pay to play the game in Bernoulli's St. Petersburg paradox, or anything else. While long ago, like the other irresponsible economists of my generation, I overcame my fear of large numbers, my reason could not convince me that one would ever pay more for the extended privilege of buying a share of General Motors stock more than the present market price at which one has in effect a perpetual call on the stock. What is the same thing--so long as limited liability attaches to stock ownership--why would anyone ever pay as insurance against loss the cost of a put that exceeded that value? Yes, by the Bachelier-Kruizenga square-root law for the absolute Brownian motion, the cost of such a put could become indefinitely large.

To overcome this basic and paradoxical contradiction, I reformulated the hypothesis of a sort of "relative rather than absolute random walk." And it is this "economic Brownian motion" that my title refers to. The new hypothesis does not get rid of the paradox and seems to come closer into agreement with economic observations, but there will be no time today to discuss the problem of empirical verification.

II.

Surely some must wonder whether I am pulling hats out of rabbits or pulling legs in suggesting that the refined and idealized concepts of mathematical probability have anything to do with something so complicated as the competitive market in which September Chicago wheat gets priced from moment to moment. How can that casino we call the stock market, dependent as it is on psychology and a thousand events, be remotely likened to a stochastic process?

3

Let me hasten to make what the SEC calls full disclosure. I make no pretense of developing formulas for out-guessing the stock market and seats near to a broker's telephone will not give my listeners any advantage. But I am quite in earnest in pointing out that there are countless optimists who proceed on the assumption that price changes are *not* like the Brownian motion, that simple little rules can be found by empirical investigation of past structure of price changes that will enable the speculator or investor to predict with some success future movements of prices from knowledge of past prices alone. Everyone you meet in Wall Street denies that he is a chartist; but when pressed, most will admit that some of their best friends are, and that they spend much of their time looking for resistance trends, heads-and-shoulders formations, and other configurations that only an organic chemist could understand.

The best, but perhaps not the most scientific, evidence for the worthwhileness of a random-walk assumption about price changes comes from an *ad hominem* remark of Holbrook Working. After decades of study of commodity prices at Stanford's Food Research Institute, Working once observed that most men who are ardent chartists appear on closer observation to have holes in their shoes (not as I almost Freudianly said, in their heads). To be sure the test implied by the ancient jibe, "If you're so smart, why ain't you rich" cannot be regarded as an optimal one.

Actually, there is a good deal of evidence, some of it unpublished, suggesting that price changes in competitive markets are fully independent in the following sense: Merely from knowing past price changes you are not able much to improve your predictions of the direction or degree of future price changes.

Working himself has made certain tests relevant to the existence of systematic auto-correlation of price changes in commodity futures--including preparing artificial times series from first differences that are taken from tables of random numbers--to see whether readers can guess their origin. Maurice Kendall in 1953 published tests of serial correlation on a variety of price changes in organized markets and seemed to find remarkably little deviation from pure randomness or "white noise." Years ago I experimented with various crude length of runs of plus or minus price changes, and discovered to my surprise how little were the deviations from what could be theoretically expected from various chance hypotheses. I am sure that other systematic and unsystematic tests have been made by various statisticians *and* scholars.

The upshot of all these is not that the Brownian movement hypothesis has been firmly grounded in experience. But, with some exceptions to be mentioned, most studies show that there is much less of predictive structure in these time series than might at first have been expected.

A few exceptions have been noted. Thus, Sidney Alexander of MIT's School of Industrial Management tested wheat price changes for randomness of runs, with good verification over long periods of time. Yet in connection with weekly American stock prices, he sometimes found that slightly more elaborate Markoff transitional matrixes would fit the data better. Thus, he formulated the rule: If a minus price change has just been observed, the odds are even that the next change will be plus or minus; but if a plus has just been observed, then the probability that the next item will be plus is .6, not .5. This, reflecting as it does the known trend in stock prices, is the best confirmation known to me of J.P. Morgan's dictum: Never sell America short. But I must add with Alfred Marshall: All short statements in economics are untrue, with the possible exception of the one I am now making.

There is perhaps one further bit of negative evidence. The Russian statistician Eugen Slutsky some forty years ago showed that it was easy to produce by various moving averages and differencing of purely random numbers, stretches of time series that looked very much like those of English business cycles back in good Queen Victoria's days; and Frisch, Tinbergen, Walker, Yule, Wold, the Adelmans and others have developed the theory of stochastic auto-regressive processes that can yield irregular fluctuations quite like those we observe in modern business cycles. Yet I have heard it to be true that when Working showed some of his simple artificial series built from random-walk differences to professional commodity specialists, they reported their feeling that in some subtle way the series did not look quite like the real thing--reminding me of a friend who claimed the only difference between his violin and a Stradivarius was in the "overtones."

III.

I must be brief on the basic question as to "why" price changes might be thought to be like some simple probability process. Bachelier himself, in good Laplacian tradition, glorified the very complexity and numerosity of the background forces that presumably combined to produce observed movements. He asserted it was hopeless ever to look for causes, and took refuge in the general notion of the central limit theorems of probability--namely that the superposition of many independent small forces, themselves not necessarily "normally" distributed, would produce in the limit a normal or Gaussian distribution.

This, I believe, overdoes things. Certainly the search for causes in any complex field will be a hard one; and certainly the methods of statistics and probability will have their place in any description. But it does not follow that out of sheer ignorance comes beautiful knowledge about probabilities: a special kind of "balanced ignorance" would be needed to ensure that the hypothesis of a central limit theorem or of a Wiener process are adequately met. There is no grand uncertainty principle in economics of the Heisenberg type, and unlike the quantum physicist we cannot work the other side of the street and draw comfort from ignorance.

There is, though, a much more peculiarly economic reason for expecting that price changes will be like that of an unbiased random walk. Bachelier and very many economists have pointed out that price in the wheat or stock market is the resultant of the opposing forces of numerous sellers and buyers. There is a sense then in which it would be self-contradictory to speak of a "general, and correct expectation that price will rise." For if people generally knew that the future price would be up, they would already have bid it up.

It is this second factor-that the market has already discounted any known biases thereby removing them--which is the most powerful argument for the usefulness of the present stochastic approach.[1]

For the remainder of this paper I shall accept the general notion that price changes constitute a "fair game" (or what is technically called by probabilists a "martingale"). This is to be regarded only as a first approximation model, around which various adjustments are to be made. Naturally certain qualifications having to do with the treatment of dividends on stocks will have to be made, since economists will realize that the opportunity cost of earning pure interest on safe securities will be relevant to share pricing. Indeed the very presence of stochastic dispersion in share prices probably implies that they will have to offer a sweeter mean yield than riskless securities; and anyone troubled by the present assumption of unbiased first moments is free to think that this is true only after certain yield adjustments have been made. (For example, the dividend may already take account of riskiness; or all of the prices that I talk about could be regarded not as actual quoted prices but as some kind of "present discounted value of prices," it being understood that the proper discount factor appropriate to securities of this degree of stochastic dispersion and riskiness has been already applied.)

IV.

With cruel brevity, I can describe the present model. Let x_t be the price of a given stock or futures contract as quoted time t. Then x_0 is the present quoted price and it is known with certainty to be itself. An instant later it will be different. But the present price has been adjusted by supply and demand so that the mean, or expected change between now and any future time, is exactly zero. This can be summarized by the following probability distributions:

$$\text{prob}\{x_t \leq x\} = F(x,t).$$

Because the present x_0 is known with certainty
$$F(x,0) = 0, x < x_0 = 1 \; x \geq x_0,$$
and because of our fair-game assumption
$$E(x_t|x_0) = \int_{-\infty}^{\infty} x_t dF(x,t) \equiv x_0 \text{ for all t,}$$
with the passage of time and occurrence of unknown events, the dispersion of x_t can be expected to increase. In fact, if we make Bachelier's absolute Brownian motion assumption, successive changes in prices are independently distributed. His full assumption can be summarized in the basic axiom of independence and uniformity

(1) $$F(x,t_1+t_2) \equiv \int_{-\infty}^{\infty} F(x-X,t_1)F(X,t_2)$$
$$\equiv F(x,t_1)*F(x,t_2).$$

He goes further and assumes that this holds for all real t, not merely for integral values of t. Thus, an event an instant away from now is itself the result of an indefinitely large number of intervening instants.

By four different arguments, Bachelier goes from Equation (1) to the normal or Gauss-Wiener form for the probabilities:

(2) $$F(x,t) = \int_{-\infty}^{x} \frac{1}{\sqrt{2\Pi}} \exp\left[-\frac{1}{2}\left(\frac{X-x_0}{\sqrt{t}\sigma}\right)^2\right] \frac{d(X-x_0)}{\sqrt{t}\sigma}$$

where σ^2 is the variance of x_1. Thus, the absolute Brownian motion means that $F(x,t)$ is a normal distribution with unchanging mean x_0, but with dispersion that grows with the square root of t.

Market data on puts and calls give a measure of confirmation of all this. Thus, the ideal mathematical value of a call option giving one the right to periods from now to buy the stock at present market price x_0 can easily be shown to be

$$C = \int_{x_0}^{\infty} (x-x_0)dF(x,t),$$

which is the only value it can have if the fair-game rule holds for all transactions. The corresponding value for a put (which gives one the right to sell the stock after t periods at x_0) is

$$\underline{P} = \int_{-\infty}^{x_0} |x-x_0| dF(x,t)$$
$$= C \text{ because } \int_{-\infty}^{\infty} (x-x_0)dF(x,t) = 0.$$

Thus, Bachelier can write
$$C(t) = k\sigma\sqrt{t} = \underline{P}(t),$$
where k is a determinate decimal.

In fact, six-month calls do sell for about 40 per cent more than

240

do three- month calls, in accordance with the absolute Brownian motion (i.e., $\sqrt{2}$ = 1.4 approximately). (Another demonstration that probability motions *are* applicable comes from the following empirical phenomenon: if the exercise price of a call is say $1 away from x_0, its value is not changed by $1 but by about one-half a dollar--just what would be predicted by a theory involving quasi-symmetric probability distributions. The fact that calls sell for more than puts, even after one has corrected for dividend treatment, is in disagreement with this first-approximation theory and itself only possible because of brokerage charges, interest, and other market frictions.)

In physics the Brownian motion is known to be invalid for t very small. In economics it must merely be invalid for very large t. Thus, one might pay 20 per cent of U.S. Steel's market price ($75 per share, 11/10/60) for a six-month call at market. If we quadruple six months and go to a two-year call, one might pay 40 per cent in accordance with the absolute Brownian hypothesis. But who can believe that for an eight-year call--equals 2×2×2--any sane person would pay 160 per cent when for 100 per cent he can get a *perpetual* call by buying the stock outright.

Evidently the absolute Brownian motion of the Bachelier-Einstein type cannot be economically admissible, even though it provides good approximations for a limited time period. The root difficulty with an absolute Brownian motion comes from the fact that its probabilities radiate from positive prices to the absurd region of negative prices--wherever, because of limited liability on shares, they can become worthless but never negative in value.

V.

Once alerted to the Brownian drawbacks, we see other deficiencies. Why as a stock changes in price should its percentage variability change? Shares can always be split or set at any denomination, and if there is any advantage in doing so we should assume that all such splits have been made. (The alleged great advantage of splits is not borne out by theory or experience.)

At the present level of approximation, we surely ought to invoke the Gertrude Stein lemma: "A dollar is a dollar is a dollar." The absolute level of price should never matter. So years ago I proposed as the economic Brownian motion a simple theory based on *relative* changes. The basic assumption of the relative Brownian motion is that each dollar's worth of stock or commodity is subject to a uniform and independent distribution of relative increments. The following axioms replace Bachelier's:

$$E(x_t|x_0) \equiv \frac{t}{t}x_0 \text{ as with Bachelier;}$$

but instead of his Equation (1) we have

(3) $$F(x,t_1+t_2) \equiv \int_0^\infty F\left(\frac{x}{x'},t_1\right)dF(x,t_2)$$
$$\equiv (F(x,t_1)\#(F(x,t_2)),$$

where I have coined a symbol # for the above special kind of percentage convolution or *faltung*. (The symmetry of t_1 and t_2 in Equations (1) and (3) is obvious.)

If Equation (3) is to hold, and if we add some regularity assumptions so that of all the class of infinitely-divisible functions of the Levy-Khintchine type only the Gaussian is admissible, then the economic Brownian motion is describable by the well-known log normal distribution

(4) $$F(x,t) = \int_0^{\log x} \frac{1}{\sqrt{2\Pi}} \exp\left[\frac{1}{2}\left(\frac{\log x - \mu_1 t}{\sqrt{t\mu_2}}\right)^2\right]\frac{d \log x}{\sqrt{t\mu_2}}$$

where $\mu_1 = E(\log x_1|x_0) < 0$
$\mu_2 = \text{Var}[\log x_1] > 0.$

The fair-game assumption makes μ_1 and μ_2 simply related.

I shall not repeat here the calculation of the value of a call for all t, but shall merely say that the resulting function does have the desired properties

$C(t) \sqrt{t}$ for small t
$C'(t) > 0$ for all t
$\lim_{t\to\infty} C(t) = x_0.$

I may also add a paradox of my own. If the log normal form is regarded as only asymptotically attained instead of instantaneously so as a result of the Bachelier insistence that t can be any real fraction, however small, it need *not* be true that

$$\int_0^\infty (x-x_0)\lim_{t\to\infty} dF(x,t) = \lim_{t\to\infty}\int_0^\infty (x-x_0)dF(x,t) \equiv 0.$$

This is really a cheap paradox that will not surprise any mathematician who is properly wary of limits.[2]

VI.

In conclusion, I ought to point out some very paradoxical implications of relative Brownian motion.

1. It implies that it is practically certain that everyone buying

stocks will be practically ruined. More precisely,
$$\lim_{t \to \infty} F(x,t) = 0, x > 0 \text{ for the log normal distribution.}$$

2. Yet all along we have a "fair game" with
$$E(x_t | x_0) \equiv x_0,$$
the few winners winning so much as to balance with limited losses of the vast majority of the stocks.

Any experienced investor will realize the germ of truth in this, knowing that the large gains he makes on a few stocks are compensation for many small losses. Middle observers, who abjure the arithmetic-mean index numbers, lose sight of this fact in employing geometric-mean index numbers that *are* biased downward. (In the U.S. few beat the Dow Jones Industrial index; in the U.K., most people beat the Financial Times Index, not realizing that it is a geometric mean and that any fool can beat it by putting its stocks in his portfolio!)

Whether one should drop the fair-game hypothesis, or introduce a source of new stocks, time will not permit me to discuss on the present occasion.

Footnotes

1. In connection with spot prices for a good like wheat, there are strong reasons to expect systematic seasonal and other biases in the data. Hence, I long felt uneasy over the evidence that such changes in such spot prices did agree so well with the Brownian motions. Granted that many stochastic factors such as weather are operative, we still have no reason to expect a factor like weather to show serially unauto-correlated behavior since meteorological persistence is a fact of nature. Fortunately for my peace of mind, I have been able to work out the following very general theorem: No matter what is the stochastic structure of spot prices, if the prices of futures are always equated to the expected value of spot prices, then the resulting series of future prices *will* necessarily have unbiased increments. This is a deductive theorem and not a uniformity of nature; but to the degree that the hypothesis about expected values is valid, it will be of empirical relevance.

2. Corresponding to his Equations (1) and (2), Bachelier years before Einstein derived the basic partial differential equation for diffusion of probabilities (of which the so-called Fokker-Planck equation is a transparent generalization)

$$C^2 \frac{\partial F(x,t)}{\partial t} \frac{\partial^2 F(x,t)}{\partial x^2} + bx \frac{\partial F(x,t)}{\partial x}.$$

Corresponding to my Equations (3) and (4) is the basic partial differential equation of the relative Brownian motion

$$\frac{\partial F(x,t)}{\partial t} \equiv \frac{\mu_2}{2} x^2 \frac{\partial^2 F(x,t)}{\partial x^2};$$

or if we relax the dependence of μ_2 and μ_1, we get the slightly more general form

$$\frac{\partial F(x,t)}{\partial t} + ax^2 \frac{\partial^2 F(x,t)}{\partial x^2}$$

where the parameters a and b are simple functions of μ_1 and μ_2.

References

Bachelier, L. 1900. Théorie de la speculation, *Annales de l'Ecole normal supérieur*, 3rd series, 17:21-86. Trans. by A.J. Boness in P.H. Cootner, ed., *The Random Characters of Stock Market Prices*, Cambridge, Mass., The MIT Press, 1967.

Bachelier, L. 1914. *La jeu, la chance et le hasard*. Paris, E. Flammarion.

Einstein, A. 1905. On the Motion--Required by the Molecular Kinetic Theory of Heat--of Small Particles Suspended in a Stationary Liquid, *Annalen der Physik*, 17:549-60.

Kendall, M. 1953. The Analysis of Economic Time-series, Pt. 1: Prices, *Royal Statistical Society Journal*, Ser. A, 116: 11-25.

Kruizenga, R. 1956. Put and Call Options: A Theoretical and Market Analysis. Ph.D. thesis, Massachusetts Institute of Technology, Department of Economics, Cambridge, Massachusetts.

491

An Enjoyable Life Puzzling Over Modern Finance Theory

Paul A. Samuelson

Department of Economics, Massachusetts Institute of Technology, Cambridge, Massachusetts 02139

> **Abstract**
>
> This is a terse account of group creation of modern finance theory; and a sampling of my prosaic autobiographical investing and consulting for nonprofit academies. Eschewing 1900 Bachelier and 1905 Einstein white noise randomness, my martingale version of market *micro* efficiency invoked no violation of economic law. My attempts to establish pricing theory for options fell a bit short of the Black-Scholes-Merton Holy Grail. For life cycle investing, mathematicians' maximum growth Kelly criterion was debunked, as were vulgar notions that necessarily riskiness is averaged downward for long-term investors. Popular Markowitz-Tobin quadratic programming was shown to hold generically only for smallest price variations or for unrealistic risk-aversion functions. Because economic history at best obeys only quasi-stationary probabilities, no sure-thing formulas will ever be definable. Excess returns—excess "alphas"—can result only from early new "insider" knowledge, however acquired—legally or illegally. Boo hoo.

> An irrational passion for dispassionate rationality can take the pleasure out of life.
>
> John Maurice Clark, c. 1920
>
> Not for people like me.
>
> Paul A. Samuelson

INTRODUCTION

In a too-kind summing up on my contributions to finance theory, Robert C. Merton counts that most of my best papers in that field were done after I'd reached the age of 50. Since he counts cards well, he must be right. My ego does not object to being linked with such Methuselah masters as Verdi.

But actually my maiden 1937 publication, "Some Aspects of the Pure Theory of Capital" (Samuelson 1937), written just when becoming eligible to vote, was on present-discounted value of future cash receipts. At that time intertemporal capital theory, still the Mount Everest of economic science, was already one of my principal preoccupations.

In more than one keynote lecture I have remarked that modern frontier finance theory dates back to one lifetime. My innuendo was not that merely by my being alive at the creation I was that theory's progenitor. A true history of this subject nicely confirms *père* Robert K. Merton's thesis that scientific advances are almost always a *group* creation. This documents that Newton-Leibniz, Darwin-Wallace, and Joule-Mayer-Helmholz-Kelvin-Clausius-Gibbs *group* discoveries are the rule and that Carlylean unique geniuses are the exception to the rule.

When I once called myself a "Sunday painter" dabbling in stochastic finance, that was not meant to belittle finance theory as a branch of serious economic theory. Such a peculiar view was expressed again and again by the late Milton Friedman, a dizzy view that I still find incomprehensible.

In this meandering account of my travels in the land of finance, I would like to be mostly camera. I was at the right places at the right times and had a front-row spectator seat. However, as happened so often in the seminar or lecture hall, I couldn't stay out of the act. (At Quaker meetings, one talks only when God tells us to.) No Quaker I, but something often provoked me into interruption.

Nabokov-like, I here say to myself: Speak memory. Eschew terse elegance and proof and false bravado. So, readers beware.

THE BEFOREMATH

I was reborn, born as an economist, at 8:00 a.m. on January 2, 1932, in the University of Chicago classroom. But you might say that unusually interesting economic history had earlier already impinged on me prenatally.

During my first few years of life, the heavy spending by the World War I belligerent nations brought 12-h, seven-days-a-week shifts at U.S. Steel's massive new Gary, Indiana plant. Middle European Slavs, riding their bikes to work, are still part of my Freudian memories. Etched there, too, is the memory of the postwar 1919–1921 recession. And I can dimly recall imported Mexican workers emerging from Gary's many rail stations to do their strike-breaking duties.

Of course, I took for granted my family's relative affluence from the World War I spendings, which after Keynes's (1936) classic *General Theory*, we came to call "multiplier spending and respending." Then at age 10 I learned the downside of boom and bust. My family achieved a small fortune in Florida real estate the hard way: they started out with the proverbial larger fortune. Before reaching my teens, I played cops and robbers on the Coral Gables acres populated by half-built homes destined never to be completed. In the 1929–1939 period, both at Chicago and Harvard, we called such abortions "Hayeks," after Austrian Friedrich von Hayek (1931) who wrote about such stuff.

To hurry on, I skip to early 1929. My young freshman algebra teacher perused the financial pages after class. Too often a teacher's pet, I lingered on with her. Together we selected as winner stocks Atwater Kent radios and Auburn Motors. I shared the choosings; she bore the losses after the October Wall Street Crash.

In the early 1930s, while attending at Chicago the world's most revered conservative economics classes, I could not reconcile what I was being taught with what I observed in the world outside of academia. Four summers, up to my 1935 B.A. graduation, I spent on Lake Michigan's sandy beach. That was not because I was lazy. (I *am* lazy when it comes to doing things I find boring.) Nor was it because my family was filthy rich. A job, any job, would have been most welcome then.

But I learned from observing the experiences of my Chicago classmates. Some of them would apply to more than a hundred places for any kind of a summer job. Zero acceptance was their report to me. So I never felt a twinge of guilt. However, if I had a Boswell, he might conjecture that I would probably become a likely convert to a John Maynard Keynes when and if he pioneered a new disequilibrium economics. Actually, I became a cafeteria Keynesian in the years before Keynes's 1936 *General Theory*.

In summing up, it can be said that I became infatuated and obsessed with economics as a lifetime study in good part because in my first two decades of life macroeconomic factual history was so turbulent and nonoptimal. I presume that many a doctor felt similarly called to medicine because of contemporary plagues that robbed so many folk of their three-score-and-ten longevity.

SOME EARLIEST PERSONAL FINANCIAL EXPLORATIONS (1935–1955)

Curiosity—scientific curiosity—motivated my varied early personal investing. I was not averse to earning a good net risk-corrected total return. But I, and after 1938 wife Marion Crawford and I, were comfortably off on our joint earnings. Thus, essentially the sole reason I started my research into the pricing of put and call options came from my (mistaken!) conjecture that the difference between the market prices of puts and calls would give the macro researcher some exact objective measure of whether investors were becoming expectationally more bullish or more bearish. (Later I developed with a thesis advisee a two-component vector calculus which proved that arbitragers would, under ideal conditions, keep like puts and like calls *approximately equal* (!) in price.)

(Approximate equality of put and call prices for puts and calls needn't rob options of any useful prediction hypotheses. Thus, back in October 1987, when the Dow index fell the fastest ever in one day—22%!—the Vix index of implied volatility earlier soared. That led one economic historian to declare that such a rise is a good forecaster of declining stock prices. In the 1987 case, the spread of the new device of "portfolio insurance" did contribute much to the decline. However, that same economic historian doing due diligence could have found in the statistical record cases where exogenous increases in *bullishness* [rather than bearishness] could be the true cause of a spike up in the volatility index.)

In 1968 I wrote a critical review of the Thorp-Kassouf (1967) book *Beat the Market* (Samuelson 1968). My main dissent was against their suggestion of easy money from merger arbitrage. Though I had done well with the Packard-Studebaker merger, it had been a harrowing—not an easy—experience. Shorts were hard to execute; short squeezes were a chronic danger. When an acquaintance tried to sell me puts I warned him not to do so, thereby risking a "short squeeze." He regretted not believing me. I do recall a similar story from an earlier time involving Molybdenum Corporation warrants that were destined to expire worthless. But it sure was hard to keep them short, and there were short squeezes and short scares that the intrinsically worthless warrants might have to be purchased for delivery with more shorts outstanding than warrants available to deliver. This fits the Thorp-Kassouf domain. I recall buying puts on the warrants, thereby giving up much of the potential profit, but realizing some of it.

That 1968 item somehow never got included in my *Collected Scientific Papers* (Samuelson 1966a, 1966b, 1972, 1977, 1986). Maybe that was because I regretted my harsh tone. But in retrospect I relish my nihilism that *no perfect hedge is ever possible*. You will ask, what about the Black-Scholes-Merton hedge for log-normal probability distributions? Even that always does depend on an *unknowable* correct volatility parameter. (My 1966 nihilism prepared me for the 1998 Long-Term Capital Management debacle *after* it happened, but not before. Hyper-leveraging, plus off-the-chart exogenous shocks, trumped normal expectations, I think. But we may never know.)

During my 1935–1940 Harvard years I enjoyed a lot of leisure time. That was because, as I learned to my surprise, I was better prepared than the 50-odd other Harvard graduate students for the reason that at Chicago I had taken far more economics courses than my fellow students had.

Then, at the economics headquarters, where Harvard's house journal—the *Quarterly Journal of Economics*—had its office, there was spread out on a big table current exchange magazines from *The Economic Journal*, the *Journal of Political Economy*, *Economica*, *Econometrica*, the *Review of Economic Studies*, etc. Foolishly, I devoured each and all of them. So that gave me a jump start in understanding the early finance publications by Alfred Cowles, III, Holbrook Working, and other statisticians.

Many traders I have known started out in their idle moments doing thought experiments with successive days' financial pages. When these seemed to work out in their favor, they began to frequent brokerage houses and various exchanges. Of course, often they learned that what seemed to work out on paper, with "virtual" rather than "real" money, could be a bit misleading. When you want to sell short, you have to wait for an uptick in the stock's price. Sometimes you are at the end of a long queue, and either you never can make the trade or you can make it only *after* your discerned profit opportunity had already disappeared.

Early in my marriage to Marion Crawford Samuelson, she came into a moderate legacy. That needed to be cannily invested. 1938 was a pretty good time to begin. We were young. Our elders were burned so badly in the 1929–1932 years as to leave for us some good opportunities: corporate shares were available with seven-to-one price/earnings ratios, along sometimes with an additional 5% or 6% dividend yield.

My knowledge of orthodox and Keynesian macro theory perhaps provided a further small edge (not to be exaggerated). Example: Hotels built in the 1920s could be bought in the mid-1930s at a price far below their reproduction cost. Two MIT grads, Ernest Henderson and Robert Moore, bought the Commander Hotel opposite the Cambridge Common for $5,000 and an assumed mortgage. That's how the Sheraton chain got started. Same with the Hilton hotels. Applying some scientific management and some refurbishing created good profit opportunities. Later, when hotels had to be built new, Marion and I moved on to other investments.

Here is a second example, happy enough in terms of profitability but disillusioning for me as an idealistic do-gooder. My first MIT secretary revealed that she had invested in a saving plan which paid a 2%–3% interest yield, but only if she *never* missed an installment payment. Since new U.S. Series E savings bonds matched and beat that deal, I realized that investing in the management of her kind of company was the way to go.

It would be a better world if the most ethical sectors had the best returns. Instead, when thoughtful people won't deign to invest in cigarette companies, irresponsible investors may be able to do well by being irresponsible.

Warren Buffett, in his later Buffett-Munger phase, has favored "franchise" companies. These, most often, are what economics lecturers call "oligopolies" rather than hard-sod competitors. Alas, monopolies, duopolies and oligopolies are not the ethical utopias that Adam Smith's Invisible Hand would create under most active competition.

If ever I hoped that my Wall Street winners would do best for the good of society, experience dashed such naive hope. A company that sold automatic cancer insurance to Japanese employees, but whose fine print precluded their paying out very many claims, was a profitable investment hard to beat.

EFFICIENT MARKET HYPOTHESES

From writings by Holbrook Working at Stanford and by statistician Maurice Kendall at the LSE, I understood that price changes of corn or pork bellies—spot prices or futures prices—when plotted as time series did look much like a truly random walk. (All this was before a postcard was sent by Jimmie Savage from Yale to a number of us economists asking if any of us knew a small 1914 book by a French mathematician Louis Bachelier, whose title had to do with a theory of speculation. I turned out to be his only respondent.) After I found in MIT's math library Bachelier's (1900) Paris Ph.D. thesis (supervised by no less than Henri Poincaré), I persuaded Paul Cootner (1974) to publish an English translation of this seminal work; Bachelier's work actually dominated Einstein's (1905) analysis of Brownian motion.

Working had reported that when he fabricated random walk data and plotted them along with actual historical Board of Trade price data, the locals at the Chicago Board of Trade he showed them to could not accurately guess which was which. (Art critics, when made to choose between kindergarten daubs, insane asylum artists, and *avant garde* art, did much better than those Chicago locals!)

My admired young friend, the late Dutch-American Hendrik Houthakker, was one listener at Kendall's Royal Statistical Society lecture. He and other economists there took offense to Kendall's innuendo that real-life price movements were chance data *not at all subject to any fundamental economic laws.*

My reaction differed: Work the other side of the street and argue instead that when many buyers and sellers, each with different information, come together in a competitive auction market, then absence of *ex ante* discernable predictive trends was a sign of economic law working at its best. Anything that was almost sure to happen would already have been made to happen. (That bred four of my needed follow-up articles about "efficient markets.") Again, as with Newton and Leibniz or Darwin and Wallace, multiple economists were arriving at similar new insights, independently and cooperatively.

One admired youngster was Eugene Fama at the University of Chicago. At Tufts University near Boston he had been a football player from nearby, concentrating with honors on Romance languages. Only a few years later Fama had become a Chicago full professor and a much-cited world authority. Independent of my writings on the efficient market hypothesis, Fama had provided his own conjectured hypotheses. (In my considered judgment, the Stockholm savants ought to have honored Fama to share with other worthies in the Nobel Prize in economics. The $300 million Booth gift to Chicago's graduate business school owed much to the Fama workshop, which in terms of some metric beats a Stockholm gold medal by more than a hundred to one!)

From the beginning I could not believe that the "efficient market" hypothesis was dependent on a pure Brownian motion white noise or any truly random random walk. Place a minuscule colloidal molecule on a horizontal table that covers unlimited acres. Bombard it from every direction with thousands of minute atoms; and then if you wait long enough that original molecule can have traveled a billion miles in one direction. That's truly a random Bachelier-Einstein walk, but not my notion of economic fluctuations.

Taken literally, a random walk dictates with certainty that in time the price of a luxury Rolls Royce relative to the price of one green pea can reach equality or any ratio you can name. I didn't even then know the name of a statistical martingale. But this was the kind of chance variation which would emerge when many different traders, possessed of different information (true or false), bought and sold stocks or bonds. Bachelier's math of 1900 and Einstein's math of Brownian motion might be hard to tell apart from martingales in short runs, but they were a different species in the finance zoo.

PEOPLE MAGAZINE SNAPSHOTS OF INVESTORS WITH LONG-RUN POSITIVE ALPHAS

Will Rogers once wrote (in my paraphrase), "Buy stocks that are going to go up. When they're going to go down, sell them!" Good work if you can get it. Only a few can.

Among economists John Maynard Keynes (1883–1946) did well over a lifetime. He had a high I.Q. and must have been a better-than-average bridge player. Apparently some of his triumphs in currency trading stemmed from his micro- and macroeconomic hunches. However, after scoring well on bets that Germany's postwar inflation would cause the mark to depreciate, he did go virtually bankrupt when for a few months the mark reversed from its down trend. A kindly City friend enabled him to avoid bankruptcy, a fate worse than death in the post-Edwardian Age. (Again in 1929 a number of people incurred losses when a Keynes-Robertson speculative fund did badly. I learned this from Lionel Robbins. However, in autumn 1932, German Professor Hans Neisser heard Keynes give a lecture at Cambridge, in which he said, "Right now is your lifetime opportunity. Borrow and beg to invest in diversified common stocks that are going to recover now that the pound has ceased to be over-valued." Not a shabby call.)

However, with my degree of risk intolerance, I would hesitate to put my entire nest egg in Keynes's hands only. Successes tempted him to leverage up. That means you have to be rarely wrong, a higher hurdle than to be mostly right.

I skip rapidly to Yale's Irving Fisher. This truly great American scholar, who married into a fortune, was the son of a poor Protestant minister. Around 1919 he earned for himself a bundle by inventing a visible Rolodex-like filing system. Then, as a 1920s Wall Street investor, he scored well until the October Crash brought margin calls to him that he could not meet. He became a virtual bankrupt.

Around 1931, Fisher's statistical measures convinced him that the Dow Jones Index had hit its bottom. He then advised the public to newly invest at what he believed had become bargain prices. Alas, that was a second bad guess. His wife's nest egg and his own were lost. His sister-in-law, who was president of Wellesley College, as an amateur Bayesian avoided letting Irving lose her fortune too.

Traders successful over a long time period, in my experience, generally do have a wholesome respect for risk. When things first go against them, their chosen model would say: "Expected profits will be higher still." However, for canny traders *the moment comes when they have to doubt their own model*. At that point they close positions and go fishing. (In 1998, the Long-Term Capital Management group apparently never did try to go fishing.)

I intrude into this section a brief account of David Ricardo's legendary advice to his friend Robert Malthus just before the 1815 Battle of Waterloo: "Invest now in British bonds, which will go up when Napoleon meets defeat at Waterloo." Though tempted, Malthus didn't care to do so risky a thing. (See Sraffa, 1951, volume 7.) Too bad for him. But why was Ricardo so confident? After the event, Britain's commander, the Duke of Wellington, said: The Waterloo victory was a close-run thing. Had the Prussian allies of Britain not arrived at the battlefield late in the day, things might have turned out differently.

Facts gathered by Piero Sraffa, Ricardo's biographer, seemed to be these. Ricardo did have an observer near the battlefield. He by fast horse brought the news to the nearest harbor where a packet ship was on the wait. So very early Ricardo in London did know the outcome, and did personally convey the news to the English government.

It is interesting how Ricardo reacted to the news. On his customary chair at the Exchange, he *sold* (!) British Treasury stuff again and again. The other traders saw this, and suspecting that he would know the true story, they joined in the selling. Then, suddenly, Ricardo reversed course and bought and bought. It was his biggest coup ever, and enabled him to retire from active trading and become a passive rentier investor for the rest of his life.

I have two reactions. If not illegal, an ethical purist would have to fault Ricardo for in effect profiting from his own spreading of false rumors. In this millennium that might be something to criticize or even to litigate about. Second, it could be the case that Ricardo was not depending solely on a Napoleon defeat. Instead, he could have made a shrewd bet that *volatility* would in any case spike up. And then he, on the exchange floor, could hope to nimbly benefit his own purse and Malthus's too.

Note that I have written naught about the legendary Rothschilds' role in pre- and post-Waterloo speculations. Actually, Ricardo put them in the shade. And truth to tell, as money lenders to the crowns of Europe, the Rothschilds might have privately prayed for a continuation of French and English wars.

EXISTENCE OF A FEW HARD-TO-FIND, EXPENSIVE-TO-HIRE MAGICIANS

Investors such as Warren Buffett are strong and rare exceptions to the efficient market dogma. My take on that topic boils down to something like the following.

There are no easy pickings in Wall Street. Still, some tenors are better than other tenors; some billiard sharks will win most of the time. Why not then expect that a scarce subset of speculators can enjoy a "positive alpha" during most of their active lives, meaning by those words risk-corrected extra returns as compared to 99% of the trading mob. Such talents are hard to find. And they don't provide their services on the cheap. Lastly, even those guys' "hot" hands often do turn cold.

I never considered myself to be an A+ trader. What I did become was a useful monitor of traders. I skip here my long years as activist charter investor and Board of Directors member for the Commodities Corporation in Princeton. Space does not allow me to go into that intricate story. I learned to carefully abstain from influencing successful traders by offering them my macroeconomic views. Most of such views were registered already in yesterday's and today's markets. Star traders—such as Bruce Kovner's Caxton and Paul Tudor Jones—somehow had the knack to go beyond what was already in today's financial pages. To maintain their positive alphas required a concentration that for me had to be devoted to *avant garde* scientific economic discoveries.

MICRO EFFICIENT MARKETS THAT ARE MACRO INEFFICIENT

Experience quickly teaches that, if it is common knowledge that General Motors will pay a $100 dividend per share to GM shareholders on August 15, the following caper will not work: 1. Shortly before August 15 buy GM shares; 2. collect their dividends on August 15; then 3. on August 16 sell those shares you recently bought; finally 4. presto you are a sure-thing winner. Of course not. Instead, in reality, past the date of receiving the dividend, each GM share will drop in price by the amount of that dividend. In words, markets do tend to be *micro* efficient. *Only when you know new correct news that others don't yet know can you capture easy returns in micro-efficient markets.*

Does that mean that every rise and fall in the indexes of most stock prices are rational reactions to knowable correct news? Not at all. The big cumulative swings in mean prices that economic historians document—as in 1929–1934 or 2007–2008—are well-known features of historic business cycles. Only those who are naive think it easy to be a successful "timer"—defined as one who sells out stocks just before the S&P 500 index will turn down; then buys back in only when stocks are at their nadir.

Study after study reports how dismal are the records of a thousand would-be timers. Maybe it is easier to sell near the top than to know when the bottom is near. When nonfalse recoveries occur, they tend to advance fast. Again, what makes *macro* efficiency impossible is the hard fact that economic history is at best *quasi-stationary* time series. That quasi kills all certainties.

DECISION-MAKING UNDER UNCERTAINTIES

Economics appealed to me because I enjoyed looking for theoretical understandings of empirical reality. The longer I studied and taught economics, the more dissatisfied I became with mere theoretical cleverness or high IQ's.

Even when I began to write more popular journalism, I tried never to leave my mathematical insights back at home. The good journalist, by definition of the word "good," has to be a good *contemporary* economic historian. He has to mobilize what is knowable about already past history into conjectures about what *future* economic history is likely to be.

Bob Solow has for more than half a century occupied an office adjacent to mine. When young he would say, if you don't regard probability theory as the most interesting subject in the world, then I feel sorry for you. I always agreed with that. However, probability with zero applications to the real world I found to be dull measure theory.

Much of the satisfaction felt by the researcher comes from making probability math the servant of policy choice. *Evidence-based* medicine is the jargon for what I am talking about. Early on I would confer with my internist, using words like the following. Deciding to take a cholesterol-reducing statin pill should be done by me in much the same way that I come to decide to buy General Motors stock and sell General Electric stock. (After my eightieth birthday, when we got what was my first dog, I used the same methodology when consulting his vet.)

One could ask, Why for the last several decades have you subscribed for and read the prestigious weekly *New England Journal of Medicine*? Did you regret not becoming an M.D.? There is no iota of such a regret. It is because modern medicine tries to examine— "with dispassionate rationality"—what alternative treatments may minimize risk and maximize cure that I selfishly indulge in such extracurricular reading. Many professors relax by playing chess or bridge. That stuff is too much like my own economic research to tempt me.

Honesty compels me to admit that "curiosity" often trumps utilitarian motivation. Thus, I've written quite a lot on basic similarities between the paradigms of competitive microeconomics and the paradigms of classical thermodynamics. These papers appeal to a small jury of curious scholars. And again, after my 1970 sojourn to Stockholm somewhat liberated me from the grindstone of economics, I wrote half a dozen biological papers on Mendelian dynamics. Always unsolved problems motivate trying to solve them. The reward is not dollar royalties; nor even oodles of citations. My thousandfold newspaper columns have nuances unappreciated by most of their million readers.

MODUS OPERANDI

I caution myself from enjoying any rush from trading triumphantly. When my math recommended wide diversification with low, low turnover, I ate my own cooking. Especially after John Bogle created the customer-oriented Vanguard Group, with its lean, lean management costs and low turnover, my time and energies got freed up to concentrate on week days on revealed preference and comparative advantage foreign trade theory.

You can't make bricks without sand and straw. *Value Line* was what I used as a convenient data source. Its evaluations of bargains and duds I deemed to be less useful than its database.

Also, despite my chronic risk aversion, my self-confidence (or over-self-confidence) led me, while eschewing margin loans, to lean toward the deliberate high volatility of leveraged firms. In effect, decades before the legendary Modigliani-Miller (1961) theorem was published, I was disbelieving in it because I knew that I could not borrow personally at interest rates available to successful corporations.

253

DIGRESSION ON THE MODIGLIANI-MILLER MISUNDERSTOOD THEOREM

Top MIT graduate students would too often write exam passages like the following: Modigliani-Miller have proved that any and every corporation can *indifferently* employ much or little positive leverage and much or little negative leverage. *Ergo*, societies of rabid risk-relishers will end up with the same degree of risk taking as societies of paranoid risk averters.

This is quite wrong. What Modigliani-Miller asserted boils down to is only a weak tautology: Under idealized conditions where everyone can borrow or lend at the same interest rate, whenever I am interested in a particular corporate activity, no matter what degree of (algebraic) leveraging it has chosen, I can, by my own borrowing or lending, *offset exactly* whatever I don't like about *its* choices.

Here is briefest proof of my take on what will be a society's optimal degree of risk taking. Crusoes on two different islands can harvest the corn they live on by each choosing between two different known technologies. Technology A grows *with certainty*, rain or shine, 1^A bushels of corn per unit of land; Technology B harvests 4^B or $\frac{1^B}{4}$ of corn, at even 50-50 odds depending on whether the season is rainy or dry, respectively.

"Dan" Crusoe on his island will (rightly) choose to put half his land acres into B and half into A because Dan agrees with Daniel Bernoulli (1738), whose Laplacian utility function was *logarithmic*: $U(\text{Corn Crop})^{\text{Dan}} = \log(\text{Corn Crop})$. However, "Gabriel" (Kramer) Crusoe on his island is *less* risk averse. His Laplacian utility function is $U(\text{Corn Crop})^{\text{Gabe}} = \sqrt{\text{corn crop}}$. Baby calculus shows that Gabe Crusoe will put *all* his land into the riskier B technology. (Readers can confirm by use of freshman calculus those two clashing degrees of diversification.)

Only by misunderstanding what Modigliani-Miller concocted could readers doubt that it matters much to Dan on his island, and much to Gabe on his, for each to get only *his* desired best degree of optimal diversification. The same holds for divergent societies made up of many Dans only or of many Gabes only (QED).

In an article dedicated to the great Harry Markowitz on an occasion for his eightieth birthday (Samuelson 2009), I show that 500 Dans will end up with equilibrium contracts with 500 Gabes in Arrow-Debreu complete markets. Gabes will give Dans specified amounts of corn in the bad dry seasons in return for receiving from Dans specified amounts of corn in good wet seasons.

BACK TO EARLY PAS INVESTING

Value Line did not purport to help me separate winners from losers in the put-and-call option markets. There, for data, I relied on a Fried letter that cost a couple of hundred dollars per year. It would say things like: Buying the calls on the RKO Corporation warrant will yield a 1000% profit, etc. Looking into the future, Fried might tell me: If stock A rises by 10%, a call on A will rise by 22%; but if A drops by 20%, the call will drop by only 10%. If you can believe that sort of thing, I have a good bridge to sell you at a bargain price.

One of my MIT students would borrow my Fried letter periodically. Once he said to me, "Why do you waste your money? That dope sheet is rarely right." Unfazed, I replied,

"Actually, if I get one or two good ideas, they're worth more than a few hundred bucks." Later I regretted my overly quick response. The next day I corrected the previous day's reply: "If I get one or two good ideas *net*, that's money in the bank."

Most hot tips in *Barron's*, *The Wall Street Journal*, or *Forbes* lead to fool's gold, not the real stuff. Bombarding yourself with lots of plausible stories is guaranteed to accelerate the turnover of your portfolio and help pay for your broker's yacht. As true today, in the twenty-first century, as it was in the mid-twentieth century.

NO SURE THINGS?

From 1938 to 1941 Pearl Harbor, one could smell an upcoming World War II. Surely Boeing Aircraft stocks would be both safe and extra profitable? But no. For whatever reason, in that period of run up to U.S. participation in World War II, one could, and did, register losses from Boeing stocks. Go figure.

This brings back to mind the crucial already mentioned truth that "economic history obeys no *stationary* probabilities." *No* means none at all. At best, the keenest trader is faced only with quasi-stationary approximations.

The good traders I've known were not necessarily adept at advanced mathematical probability. But still they did have a wariness against risk. A trader could have a hot hand for a lengthy period of time. However, when changing reality deviated from the hunches that had been utilizing so well, the hot hand could turn cold—sometimes permanently cold.

Experience confirms that successful traders cannot explain in Wharton School seminars how you or I can be good traders. Example: Amos Hostetter, Sr., commodity broker and trader, could score positively in say all of 40 years. This encouraged Princeton's Commodity Corporation to assign to him a Boswell, who would write out the Hostetter wisdoms in a privately printed book. Alas, that Boswell remained the mediocre trader he had previously been.

I suggest a second example. Warren Buffett has been no slouch as an investor. His explanations are simple. You look for and find a good company—say *The Washington Post*. If your chemistry and theirs are compatible, you quickly shake hands. And, as it says in *Brothers Grimm* or *Mother Goose*, all of you then live happily and profitably forever after.

When I hear this, I pinch myself and remind myself that Joseph Schumpeter at Harvard brainwashed me into believing that there are no permanently "good franchise" companies. (In fairness to Buffett, he translates "permanently hold" into "hold for a long time.")

STINT AS BOARD DIRECTOR AT ADDISON-WESLEY PUBLISHERS

MIT before World War II was the biggest technology university, and arguably MIT and Cal Tech were world leaders in engineering and sciences. However, after and during World War II, MIT got co-opted into a physical and biological sciences powerhouse.

That's why it was natural for me to buy some shares in the new Addison-Wesley publishers, which started in Kendall Square, Cambridge, a stone's throw from my office. It prospered from its best seller, George Thomas's *Calculus* textbook. Same story for Sears' physics texts. Because Addison-Wesley employed a German typesetting expert on math printing, it was a canny bet that the new small firm would grow.

On account of what financial engineers call access to public idiosyncratic knowledge, I bought 50 shares again and again. I had previously always steadfastly refused to serve on corporation boards as a director. I reluctantly agreed to serve temporarily on the Addison-Wesley board to represent its Class B nonvoting shareholders. At first this meant only an occasional quarter-mile walk from my MIT office. A minor secondary motive was curiosity: How will a mathematical economist judge from the inside the rationality and irrationality of small business sociology and anthropology?

Both purposes were served well. What I observed seemed to me to disagree with much of the current reports by Oxford and Harvard Business School interviewers who pooh-poohed the importance of interest rates to real-life firms. Only when credit became more plentifully available did Addison-Wesley move to impressive new headquarters on the legendary Massachusetts Route 128. That sweetened life for Addison-Wesley's earliest staff and possibly helped enlist new textbook writers. But maybe moderate expansion of the Kendall Square spartan space could have been a better deal for both Class A and Class B share owners.

Once a year, Addison-Wesley did have to be free of debt to its lead banker, the First National Bank of Boston. A promising plan to start early a West Coast branch near to Silicon Valley was definitely delayed by liquidity restraints.

Also, one could observe that early employees of successful firms received compensation benefits beyond what was being paid for janitors, secretaries and salespersons in adjacent neighborhood firms. All know that in Seattle a thousand millionaires were spawned by Microsoft. That same qualitative effect will be found in small businesses, too.

This is how and why I bowed out from board directorships. The original Addison-Wesley owner was the print salesman who served a number of MIT departments. He thereby owned in perpetuity more than 50% of Addison-Wesley's voting shares. His right-hand go-getter—I'll call him "Bailey"—was energetic and experienced. Mostly, it was he who most authors, and would-be authors, dealt with when Addison-Wesley shifted to book publishing.

One day the activist go-getter came to me to say that he was losing sleep at night realizing that he could never achieve 50%+ ownership of the voting power. I had never signed up to be an ombudsman; I certainly didn't want to know which insider subgroups were against other subgroups. Therefore, I advised Bailey to go to wherever he could get some sleep. (He did. And for a while prospered.)

I resigned quietly as a director, pleading that my economics research mandated that. One problem remained. I wanted to sell all of my shares, even at the beaten-down price that they would bring if dumped suddenly on the market. So cannily, I began to feed gradually to the pink-sheet brokerage marketplace a few hundred shares at a time. My good sleep would trump a few thousand dollars of lost capital gains. Why *lost* capital gains? Because every one of the thousands of readers of Samuelson's *ECONOMICS* (Samuelson 1948, 1980; Samuelson & Nordhaus 1985, 2010) knew that "increase in supply will *lower* price."

Instead, in this instance the more shares I fed the pink-sheet market, the higher went Addison-Wesley's share price! I came to realize why. When few shares were being bought and sold, few brokers knew or cared about Addison-Wesley. Added shares announced for sale motivated brokers and investors to study Addison-Wesley's salubrious profitability.

Moral: To understand economics you need to know not only fundamentals but also its *nuances*. Darwin is in the nuances. When someone preaches "Economics in one lesson," I advise: Go back for the second lesson.

USEFUL PERSONAL CODE

Early on I chose not to serve as a paid economic expert in court litigation cases. I could afford to do that. I did not criticize those who did. Our whole system of jurisprudence is based squarely on adversary procedures. When you accept to testify for one interested party in a litigation, you have given up your freedom to bring to court any truth prejudicial to your client. Once you accept the Queen's shilling, you have lost the freedom to seek out truth.

A different set of considerations applied when Chairman John Bogle sounded me out for board membership of the Vanguard Group. I refused in accordance with my usual resolve. But, as I explained, that was not at all because I disagreed or disapproved of Vanguard's functioning. Mentally, I awarded A++ grades to Vanguard and Bogle, as almost the only mutual fund group dedicated solely to its client's interests. My reason for refusal, I explained, was this: In my many finance writings, I remain *freer to enthuse* about Vanguard than I would have been as a board director.

TIAA-CREF TRUSTEE: 1974–1985

Bill C. Greenough was a roommate of mine in the Harvard Graduate School. His Ph.D. thesis on "variable annuities" first persuaded TIAA (and later others) to set up retirement funds partly invested in equities. So shortly after age 35 he was President of the TIAA and later Chairman of TIAA-CREF. He long wanted me to become a trustee. However, for whatever reasons MIT did not use TIAA-CREF for its retirement funds, thereby thwarting Greenough's wish. When in 1973 MIT did adopt certain catch-up supplementary retirement options, I could and did put some of my money into TIAA-CREF venues. That empowered Greenough to get me elected as a trustee.

I took $20–$80 billion seriously. Appointed to the Finance Committee of (equity) CREF, I pursued my usual activist ways. (I am a resolute polite troublemaker who asks questions about any and all current procedures.) I strongly urged for more foreign stocks in the CREF funds. You didn't have to be a genius to advocate that.

Always CREF finance committees consisted of both academics and Wall Street money managers. Before and after my time, most academics favored broadly diversified "indexing" for so large a fund as ours. Opposed to this were many of the nonacademics who believed in opportunistic picking out of best stocks. Peace prevailed when a compromise was agreed upon that put most of the portfolios in low-turnover, no-load, broad indexes ("Vanguard" type tactics), and the lesser residual in judgmental stock portfolios. This latter group did not do badly in my time (although earlier it had done less well).

However, a couple of the other academics and I debated against certain legacy views. First, since TIAA-CREF had a captive *growing* clientele, it allegedly did not have to worry about enjoying liquidity at all times. That, I argued, did not provide us with a positive alpha edge. Second, prevailing dogma, inside TIAA-CREF and outside it, *opined that investing for the long run over a time horizon of many years causes riskiness to erode downward*. Several of my published works raised doubts about that.

Reported to me was that Milton Friedman, a trustee before my time, had disagreed with my later heresies. At Columbia, Friedman had learned some Laws of Large Numbers that allegedly negated my views. I said stubbornly: Who's afraid of Virginia Woolf? Who's afraid of Milton Friedman and *his* odd version of the Law of Large Numbers?

NON-PROFIT FINANCE COMMITTEES

I will not dwell upon the few occasions when the MIT endowment and treasury offices benefitted from consultations with Professors Solow, Modigliani, Merton, Fischer Black, and me. (In the 1970s stagflation, bond yields soared high above equity dividend yields. Most of the deans and at least one of the MIT presidents wanted to bail out of stocks so as to be able to have "more income to spend out of." We professional nerds did MIT's future a good turn by lending support to the treasurer's office specialist demurrals.)

I've known personally almost a dozen Harvard treasurers. One of them, perhaps not one with the highest I.Q., told me his "two rules" in running the Harvard endowment: 1. Never consult the economics department. 2. Never consult the business school.

The story about the Harvard treasurer who was skeptical over new-fangled finance theory reminds me to comment on the stunning successes in the 1985–2005 period of a new type of investor for top universities and foundations—Yale, Harvard, Princeton, and Stanford, for example. Wanting to be scrupulously honest about the reality of our markets being a microefficient pricing regimen, when I started to write up this topic I did have to ask myself: Aren't Treasurer David Swenson at Yale and his like elsewhere in the Ivy League clear refutations of the claim that nobody and no system scores long-run positive risk-corrected alphas?

However, I must revise my admission that the Yale-Harvard kind of trading does rebut the efficient market hypothesis. I was wrong to declare that these biggest universities and foundations had learned how to squeeze extraordinary risk-corrected long-run total returns on their portfolios. Yale-Harvard type *alternative* investing collapsed in 2007–2008. Instead of there being "much gain with no pain," the post-2007 meltdown of new financial engineering instruments did dry up the private financing that Yale-Harvard type investing crucially depended upon.

So, as yet, there is no magic formula for sure-thing "alpha" gains (in the long run on a risk-corrected basis)! So far only those with earlier knowledge of *changed* news—illegally or legally arrived at—can be top winners in today's financial markets.

I would be remiss if I did not mention that outfits like the Medallion Fund from the stables of the Renaissance Group on Long Island and under the direction of James Simon (math star formerly Chairman of the Stonybrook Math Department) rely on super high-speed computer buy-and-sell orders. They, along with a Goldman Sachs high-speed computer group, seem almost to coin gains endlessly. They beat other traders to the new punches. Then, later, they earn a premium when they sell or buy with ordinary traders and with the last-in-line smaller traders. Medallion insiders must laugh at the notion of an efficient market dogma! Whether future regulation can plug this loophole, I don't know.

THE GLOBAL MELTDOWN EXPORTED FROM U.S. WALL STREET

While writing the rest of this memoir, I had not planned to add this last section on how a down bubble in real estate following an up bubble in real estate *recreated* global panics, bankruptcies and economic chaos reminiscent of the 1929–1939 Great Depression. To tell the candid truth, I had never expected in my long lifetime to experience once again so much of what I have vividly remembered from the early 1930s when my serious study of political economy had begun in January 1932. This has been *déjà vu* with a vengeance.

To my surprise, the best and the brightest—at MIT, Harvard, or Stanford—when they wrote about the Great Depression in the 1970s and 1980s were almost as much off base about that 1930–1939 disequilibrium economy as Milton Friedman & Anna Schwartz (1963) had been in their book on money, spelled with a capital M. Their cardinal error was to overplay the role of central banks like the Federal Reserve and the Bank of England, and to underplay the role of sustained large deficit budgetary spending in bringing U.S. and German employment virtually back to full employment levels by 1939.

Put another way, oddly around 1950, Milton Friedman reverted back to the MV = PQ tautology of Irving Fisher (1911) and Alfred Marshall (1923). (What is so odd in this is that for the period 1950–2008, innovation of computers balkanized M beyond M_0 and M_2 into M_0 to $M_{seventy-eleven}$.) Even with only M_2 in the relevant picture, Friedman's conjectured constancy for its Velocity (short term, long term, during up booms and down booms) was whimsically off the chart. (Canada, with few banks to fail, maintained its M's in the Depression in contrast to the U.S.; yet both places had similar collapses in real output, employment, and price levels.)

Irving Fisher in America and Knut Wicksell in Sweden, both early believers in such a 1911 Quantity Theory of Money, came to know better after World War I. And thereby they died better macroeconomists than they had been. Dr. Friedman lacked ability to feel regret or to change. He continued to misconstrue equivalence between "Money matters" and "*only* Money matters."

All scholars are toast after a few decades in a dynamic science. However, my sole reason for mentioning what a poor macro paradigm monetarism proved itself to be in the last third of the twentieth century, is that those 1980s Ph.D. thesis writers on the Great Depression were led down the garden path to a powerful influence of unorthodox fiscal policy in the 1933–1939 recovery period. Macro experts trained in the 1970s and 1980s were ill-prepared for the post-2007 meltdown.

I suspect that future rocky post-2008 behavior on Main Street—globally and in the United States—will need to be stabilized by some heavy deficit spending. On the Chicago Midway that I knew as an undergraduate, Henry Simons, Jacob Viner, and Charles Hardy created a cogent oral tradition that justified large budgetary deficits and utilization of new agencies like the Reconstruction Finance Corporation that would knowingly make some investments that would not pay off. In those days there were *liquidity traps* and *paradoxes of thrift*, whereby extra savings served only to *reduce* (!) investment. In such time what would be imprudent in "normal" times, became both prudent and necessary. Evidence: After the 1931 devaluation of the U.K. pound, the places loathe to devalue and deficit spend (like France) suffered badly in comparison with the places (like Belgium) that devalued its franc.

Alas, Alan Greenspan at the pre-2006 U.S. Federal Reserve, Governor Mervyn King at the Bank of England, and Greenspan's successor Governor Ben Bernanke were slow off the mark to move away from mere inflation targeting. Bad economic news should have taught them that the time to preach about moral hazard should have been *before* Rome is burning and not while it is burning.

I lack space to indict the many whose deregulations and conflicts of interest created the tinder for the recent burning of Rome. Suffice it to mention that this may have been the first time in history that what used to be a plain-vanilla down bubble in real estate impinged on the new fiendish, frenzied Frankenstein creations in financial engineering. These brainchildren of MIT, Chicago, and Wharton could have rationalized investing and sharing of risks—and thereby reduced unnecessary riskiness. But this time actually they blinded transparency and caused CEOs to hyper-leverage without knowing that they were doing so. Securitization of mortgage was only one part of the new terrible iceberg. In fairness, as pointed out to me by MIT Professor Andrew Lo, as early as 1970 the federal government and private Wall Street promoted securitizing mortgages. Maybe what has been needed is not fewer financial engineers, but rather more and better financial engineers enforcing prudent social versions of corporate governance and regulation.

Moral: free markets do not stabilize themselves. Zero regulating is vastly suboptimal to rational regulating. Libertarianism is its own worst enemy!

WINDUP

Markets are not perfect, which is true even for rationally regulated markets. Nevertheless, over the last thousand years every attempt to organize sizeable societies without important dependence on markets has generated its own failures, à la Marx, Lenin, Stalin, Castro, Mao, and many more.

Limited *centrist* societies with regulated markets and a rule of law are those "serfdoms" that von Hayek (1944) [and Friedman (1962) too] used to warn us about. That tells us something about them rather than something about Genghis Khan or Franklin Roosevelt. It is paranoid to warn against inevitable slippery slopes downward to hell once individual *commercial freedoms* are in anyway infringed upon. Paranoidal guesses are as prone to misfire as are utopian delusions about the self-correcting mechanisms of a pure *laissez-faire* market economy, or an ideal *centrist* economy. Willy nilly I am compelled to be a dull *centrist*. I applaud the Ben Bernanke who flexibly moved beyond orthodox inflation targeting by the Fed.

DISCLOSURE STATEMENT

The author is not aware of any affiliations, memberships, funding, or financial holdings that might be perceived as affecting the objectivity of this review.

LITERATURE CITED

Bachelier L. 1900. Théorie de la spéculation, *Ann. École Normale Supér.* 3rd Ser. 17:21–86. Transl. AJ Boness, 1974, in *The Random Character of Stock Market Prices*, ed. PH Cootner pp.17–78. Cambridge, MA: The MIT Press (From French)

Bachelier L. 1914. *Le Jeu, la Chance Hasard. Bibliothéque de Philosophie Scientifique.* Paris: E Flammarion. 320 pp.

Bernoulli D. 1738. Exposition of a new theory on the measurement of risk. Transl. L Sommer, 1954, *Econometrica* 22:23–36 (From Latin)

Cootner P, ed. 1974. *The Random Character of Stock Market Prices*, pp. 17–178. Cambridge, MA: MIT Press

Einstein A. 1905. On the motion—required by the molecular kinetic theory of heat—of small particles suspended in a stationary liquid. *Ann. Phys.* 17:549–60

Fisher I. 1911. *The Purchasing Power of Money.* New York: Macmillan

Friedman M. 1962. *Capitalism and Freedom.* Chicago: Univ. Chicago Press. 202 pp.

Friedman M, Schwartz A. 1963. *A Monetary History of the United States 1867–1960.* Princeton, NJ: Princeton Univ. Press. 888 pp.

Keynes JM. 1936. *The General Theory of Employment, Interest and Money.* Reproduced in *The Collected Writings of John Maynard Keynes*, Vol. 7. 1973. London: Macmillan for the R. Econ. Soc.

Marshall A. 1923. *Money, Credit and Commerce.* London: Macmillan

Modigliani F, Miller MH. 1961. Dividend policy, growth and the valuation of shares. *J. Bus.* 34:411–33

Samuelson PA. 1937. Some aspects of the pure theory of capital. *Q. J. Econ.* 51:469–96

Samuelson PA. 1968. Review of Kassouf, T and E Thorp, Beat the Market: A Scientific Stock Market System (1967). *J. Am. Stat. Assoc.* 63:1049–51

Samuelson PA. 1966a, 1966b, 1972, 1977, 1986. *The Collected Scientific Papers of Paul A. Samuelson.* Vols. 1–5. Cambridge, MA: MIT Press

Samuelson PA. 2009. On the Himalayan shoulders of Harry Markowitz. In *Handbook of Portfolio Construction: Contemporary Applications of Markowitz Techniques*, ed. J Guerard Jr. New York: Springer. In press

Samuelson PA, Nordhaus W. 1985, 2010. *Economics.* New York: McGraw-Hill.

Sraffa P, ed. 1951–1973. *The Works and Correspondence of David Ricardo*, with MH Dodd, Vol. 7. Cambridge: Cambridge Univ. Press R. Econ. Soc.

Thorp EO, Kassouf S. 1967. *Beat the Market, a Scientific Market System.* New York: Random House. 221 pp. See especially the fiftieth anniversary edition with introduction by Milton Friedman. Chicago: The University of Chicago Press

von Hayek F. 1931. *Prices and Production.* London/New York: G. Routledge/August M. Kelley 176 pp. 2nd rev. ed.

von Hayek F. 1944. *The Road to Serfdom.* Chicago, IL: Univ. Chicago Press 1944

Chapter 5
On the Himalayan Shoulders of Harry Markowitz

Paul A. Samuelson

Few scientific scholars live to see their brain children come into almost universal usage. Harry Markowitz (1952, 1959, 2008) has been such an exceptional innovator. His quadratic programming Mean-Variance algorithms are used daily by thousands of money managers everywhere.

When a quantum upward jump occurs, Robert K. Merton and other historians of science tell us that usually more than one scholar contributes to the advance – as with Newton and Leibniz or Darwin and Wallace. When we cite Markowitz–Tobin–Lintner–Mossin–Sharpe methodologies, we pay tribute to the creative interactions among and between the innovators.[1]

Genuine scientific advances all too often do meet with resistance from historical orthodoxies. Max Planck (1900, 1901) gained eternal fame for himself when ("as an act of desperation") he introduced *quantum* notions into classical physics. Was he instantly and universally applauded? Not quite so. Autobiographically, he had to declare that old guards are slow to accept new-fangled theories. As they are so often resistant to new methodologies, the new orthodoxy gets born only after they die one by one. Planck sums it up: *Science progresses funeral by funeral*!

Harry Markowitz encountered the Planckian syndrome early on. At Markowitz's Chicago 1952 oral Ph.D. exam, Professor Milton Friedman made waves against quadratic programming, declaring that it was not even economics, and neither was it interesting mathematics.

Any savant can have a bad hair day. But again, almost half a century later, when Markowitz shared with Merton Miller and Bill Sharpe the 1990 Nobel Prize, Dr. Friedman told the Associated Press that those awardees would not be on anyone's long list of 100 deserving names. Was this Chicago jingoism? Hardly. Markowitz and Miller were both Chicago guys. (However, maybe Markowitz owed more to his Rand think-tank sojourn than to his years on the Midway? Bill Sharpe, a West Coast UCLA product, did learn much around Rand from Chicagoan Markowitz.)

P.A. Samuelson (✉)
Massachusetts Institute of Technology, Department of Economics, E52-38C Cambridge, MA 02139

[1] Tom Kuhn had documented in MIT lectures that the basic thermodynamic Law of Conservation of Energy owed much to at least a dozen quasi-independent researchers. And no two of them gave identical interpretations and nuances!

J.B. Guerard (ed.), *Handbook of Portfolio Construction: Contemporary Applications of Markowitz Techniques*, DOI 10.1007/978-0-387-77439-8_5,
© Springer Science+Business Media, LLC 2010

One's ignorance can be self-costly. The oral records in the TIAA-CREF files reveal that Trustee Dr. Friedman believed the heresy that investing for four independent periods necessarily mandated being more heavily in risky stocks than would be the case for two or one period investment. Elementary, my dear Dr. Watson. Elementary, yes. But quite wrong, Dr. Friedman. Samuelson (1969) is one of dozens of references that explicate the very common Friedman fallacy.

It was no accident that Harry's 1959 classic book was published at Yale and not at Chicago. In the mid-fifties, Chicago had spewed out its Cowles team of Koopmans, Marschack, and the other Nobel stars. Strangely, it made no Herculean efforts to keep Kenneth Arrow from going to Stanford.

In sports, records are made to be broken. In cumulative science, each new breakthrough will in time be challenged by new generations. Even peerless Albert Einstein, after repeated triumphs during the first two-thirds of his scientific life, spent the last third on lost causes.

"What have you done for me lately?" is science's ungrateful dictum.

Having been stimulated by Markowitz early and late, I compose this present brief note in homage to Harry. It does stray a bit beyond quadratic programming to general Laplacians' Kuhn-Tucker concave programming. Explained here is the tool of an investment gamble's "Certainty Equivalent," which for Laplacians will be (*necessarily*) an "Associative Mean" of feasible wealth outcomes. This procedure costlessly bypasses people's *subjective* utility function for risk. An *external* jury of observers can hone in exactly on any guinea pig's certainty-equivalent risk functions from that person's decisions among alternative risk options.

I also discuss whether the Modigliani-Miller theorem could validly tell Robinson Crusoe (or any society) that the *degree of leveraging and diversifying can be a matter of indifference*; also I discuss possible exceptions to the Tobin (1980) (one-shoe-fits-all) theorem, which defines *unique* proportions of risky stocks allegedly invariant with respect to even huge differences among different people's degree of risk aversion. Also, the Sharpe (1970) ratio can be shown to become problematic as a normative guide. Finally, the present model is a good one to test what it means to define when a risk-taker is or is not being adequately (optimally) rewarded for bearing risk.

5.1 Crusoe Saga to Test for a Society's Optimal Diversification and Leveraging

Yale's great physicist, Willard Gibbs, once wisely said, "Mathematics is a language." Here for brevity and clarity, I shall mostly use math-speak in place of words.

I posit a single Robinson Crusoe on his isolated island. He lives on corn harvest produced by his unit labor: $L = 1$. (Ignorable land is superabundant and therefore free.) He knows only two alternative technologies, A and B.

A: 1^A of $L^A \to 1^A$ of corn, with certainty in both wet and dry seasons
B: 1^B of $L^B \to \frac{1}{4}B$ of corn when wet season prevails, or 4^B of corn when dry season prevails.

263

5 On the Himalayan Shoulders of Harry Markowitz

Crusoe knows that wet or dry seasons are random variables with 50–50 probabilities:

$$p_{\text{wet}} = p_{\text{dry}} = \frac{1}{2} = p_j, j = 0, 1. \tag{5.1}$$

I add that Crusoe is a "Laplacian" à la Daniel Bernoulli (1738), whose stochastic choices target *maximal* Expected Utility of Outcomes:

$$\text{Max} \, \Sigma_0^1 p_j U(W_j) \equiv \text{Max} \left\{ \frac{1}{2} U(W_0) + \frac{1}{2} U(W_1) \right\} \tag{5.2}$$

where (W_0, W_1) are *dry* corn harvests and *wet* corn harvests, respectively.

The new-ish tool I utilize primarily here is the concept of a gambler's or an investor's stochastic "Certainty Equivalent." For Laplacians, it defines itself as $W_{1/2}$ in the following way:

$$\frac{1}{2} U(W_0) + \frac{1}{2} U(W_1) = U\left(W_{1/2}\right) \tag{5.3}$$

$$W_{1/2} = M[W_0, W_1] = \text{Certainty Equivalent function} \tag{5.4}$$

$$\equiv U^{-1} \left\{ \frac{1}{2} U(W_0) + \frac{1}{2} U(W_1) \right\} \tag{5.5}$$

where the inverse function

$$U^{-1}\{y\} = x \longleftrightarrow y = U(x) \text{ notationally.} \tag{5.6}$$

The $M[W_0, W_1]$ function is a *general* mean of corn outcomes. But also *singularly*, it is what mathematicians call an Associative Mean (or quasi-linear mean) à la Hardy–Littlewood–Pólya (1952). Equations (5.7) and (5.8) describe M's full content:

$$\text{Min}\{W_0, W_1\} \leq M[W_0 W_1] \leq \text{Max}[W_0, W_1] \tag{5.7}$$

$$M[W, W] \equiv W. \tag{5.8}$$

Without proof, I give one of many Abel-like functional equations that our Laplacian Associative Mean must obey, by definition:

$$M[W_0, W_1] \equiv W_{1/2}; M\left[W_0, W_{1/2}\right] \equiv W_{1/4}, M\left[W_{1/2}, W_1\right] \equiv W_{3/4}. \tag{5.9}$$

Then

$$M\left[W_{1/4}, W_{3/4}\right] \text{ must exactly equal } M[W_0, W_1]! \tag{5.10}$$

In short,

$$M[W_0, W_1] \equiv M(M\{W_0, M[W_0, W_1]\}, M\{W_1, M[W_0, W_1]\}). \quad (5.11)$$

This math-speak esoteric stems only from the following trivial arithmetic tautology:

$$U(W_{1/2}) = \frac{1}{2}U(W_0) + \frac{1}{2}U(W_1) \quad (5.12)$$

$$\begin{aligned} U(W_{1/4}) &= \tfrac{1}{2}U(W_0) + \tfrac{1}{2}\{\tfrac{1}{2}U(W_0) + \tfrac{1}{2}U(W_1)\} \\ &= \left(\tfrac{3}{4}\right)U(W_0) + \tfrac{1}{4}U(W_1) \end{aligned} \quad (5.13)$$

$$\begin{aligned} U(W_{3/4}) &= \tfrac{1}{2}U(W_1) + \tfrac{1}{2}\{\tfrac{1}{2}U(W_0) + \tfrac{1}{2}U(W_1)\} \\ &= \tfrac{3}{4}U(W_1) + \tfrac{1}{4}U(W_0) \end{aligned} \quad (5.14)$$

$$\therefore \frac{1}{2}U(W_{1/4}) + \frac{1}{2}U(W_{3/4}) = \left(\frac{3}{8} + \frac{1}{8}\right)U(W_0) + \left(\frac{1}{8} + \frac{3}{8}\right)U(W_1) \quad (5.15)$$

$$= \frac{1}{2}U(W_0) + \frac{1}{2}U(W_1). \text{ QED} \quad (5.16)$$

5.2 Modigliani-Miller Misunderstood

Exam takers too often write: It is a matter of indifference whether General Motors or General Electric increases each shareholder's leverage by floating debt a little or a lot. Whatever the firm spikes up (or down) can be offset by each shareholder's counter algebraic leveraging. What holds for any one corporation allegedly holds (sic) for society. A specified society can allegedly and indifferently leverage (and diversify) little or much.

Let us test this misunderstanding using these above equations from (5.1) to (5.16) for a special Crusoe, who happens to ape the medium risk tolerance of 1738 Daniel Bernoulli. Bernoulli happened to believe that when wealth doubles its *marginal* utility – $dU(W)/dW$ – halves. Such a $U(W)$ must be

$$U(W) = \log W; \frac{1}{2}U(W_0) + \frac{1}{2}U(W_1) \equiv \frac{1}{2}\log W_0 + \frac{1}{2}\log W_1. \quad (5.17)$$

Skipping mathematical proof, I will assert that this Crusoe – call him Dan Crusoe – will necessarily be a "Geometric Mean maximizer," i.e., for him

$$M[W_0, W_1] \equiv \text{GM} \equiv \sqrt{W_0 \cdot W_1}. \quad (5.18)$$

What will then have to be his stochastic choice between applying his $L = 1$ to A only, to B only, or to some combination of positive fractional L^A and L^B? Applied to Equation (5.18) the A and B parameters, we calculate:

$$\sqrt{\frac{1}{4}^B \cdot 4^B} = 1^B = \sqrt{1^A \cdot 1^A} = 1^A. \tag{5.19}$$

This demonstrates that A only and B only are indifferently choosable. His GM function can also tell the story that, as if by magic, diversification between both A and B guarantees a Certainty Equivalent corn harvest *above* (!) 1^A or 1^B.

By repeated trial and error, or by use of baby Newtonian calculus, Dan can discover that his *maximal* Certainty Equivalent will be 25% above 1, achievable only when he divides his labor (singularly!) 50–50.

For $L^A = \frac{1}{2} = L^B$, the GM becomes

$$\sqrt{\left[\frac{1}{2}(1^A) + \frac{1}{2}\left(\frac{1}{4}^B\right)\right] \times \left[\frac{1}{2}(1^A) + \frac{1}{2}(4^B)\right]} = \sqrt{\frac{5}{8} \cdot \frac{5}{2}} \tag{5.20}$$

$$= \left(\frac{5^{A\&B}}{4}\right)^* > (1^A)^* = (1^B)^*. \tag{5.21}$$

The exact calculus algorithm to find Crusoe's optimal fractional value for L^B—call it x^*—is as follows:

$\text{Max}_x (\text{GM})^2 = \text{Max } f(x)$, where

$$U(x) = \left(1 - \frac{3}{4}x\right)(1 + 3x) \tag{5.22}$$

$$U'(x) = \left(2\frac{1}{4}\right) - 2\left(2\frac{1}{4}\right)x \tag{5.23}$$

$$U'(x^*) = \left(2\frac{1}{4}\right) - 2\left(2\frac{1}{4}\right)x^* = 0 \tag{5.24}$$

$$\therefore x^* = \frac{1}{2}^* \text{ QED.} \tag{5.25}$$

For $\left(\frac{1}{16}, 16\right)$ or (N^{-1}, N), the same singular $\frac{1}{2}^*$ must occur for Crusoe with log utility.

Equations (5.17)–(5.25) justify the paradox that embracing extra volatility *cum* a cash quencher can jack up a risk-taker's Certainty Equivalent through the magic of one's optimal diversifying. Technology B, when half its volatility is quenched by safe A, increases Crusoe's Certainty Equivalent by 25%, because $1 + \frac{1}{4}$ is 25% greater than $1 + 0$. Equations (5.17)–(5.25) spelled out that story.

Energetic readers can test their comprehension by replacing the A and B story by an A and C story, where C has replaced $\left(\frac{1}{4}^B, 4^B\right)$ by $\left(\frac{1}{16}^C, 16^C\right)$. C's extreme volatility *cum* $L^A = \frac{1}{2} = L^C$, achieves a certainty equivalent far better than 25%, as readers can verify.

5.3 Summary

Societies that differ in individuals' risk tolerance will, and should, end up differing much in their equilibrium degree of diversification. A thousand Crusoes just like Dan, on similar islands and with similar known technologies and similar endowments of productive inputs, will all cleave to the same well-defined, one-and-only optimal degree of diversification.

5.4 Mutual Reinsurances' Twixt Different-Type Persons

By contrast, if say 500 islands are populated by Harriet Crusoe Harmonic Mean maximizers and say 500 are populated by Dan Crusoe Geometric Mean maximizers, then much as in the 1817–1848 Ricardo-J.S. Mill theory of trade according to comparative advantage, both groups can be made better off by the existence of folks *unlike* themselves. On another occasion, I hope to show how the Dan Crusoes will trade (in complete Arrow-Debreu markets) with the more risk-averse Harriet Crusoes. Guess whether the Harriets will import or export corn in dry seasons with the Dan's and whether in wet seasons the direction of trade gets qualitatively reversed.

People who differ can thus mutually benefit from insurance contracts with each other. However, I warn that such Pareto-optimal equilibria need not be at all "fair." Notice that for ethicists who value equally Harriet and Dan types, an exogenous increase in relative number of Harriets "unfairly" impoverishes Harriets and fructifies Dans. (When Genghis Khan gives himself *all* which is produced, that is a Pareto Optimal state in the sense that every departure from it hurts someone. However, what is just or fair or ethical when that happens?)

5.5 A Few Final Words on Quadratic Utility

A risk-averse Crusoe could have had, for certain ranges of corn outcomes, a quadratic utility of the form:

$$U(W) = W - \frac{1}{2}bW^2; \, b > 0, W < b^{-1}, \tag{5.26}$$

5 On the Himalayan Shoulders of Harry Markowitz

where large positive b parameter implies greater risk aversion. Thus a Laplacian Dan Crusoe and a Laplacian Harriet Crusoe could differ in that Dan's b would be less than Harriet's b. Both of them would be queer birds, who become more risk averse at large wealth than at small wealth.

Markowitz–Tobin–Sharpe quadratic programming could handle such birds. And for them the Sharpe ratios and Tobin one-shoe-fits-all riskiness might well apply.

Moreover, my special wet vs. dry universal effects that are common to everybody has permitted Harvard Ph.D. Erkko Etula to write out for publication the Markowitz quadratic programming story in terms of means and variances (μ, σ^2) that I have largely ignored. However, that precise story would be a sub-optimal usage for (μ, σ^2) in the case of the Laplacians and I have described who are Geometric Mean and Harmonic Mean maximizers.

Mr. Etula has shown how and when the Tobin theorem does or does not apply. And Etula's equations for Certainty Equivalents, expressed in terms of μ and σ, can replace the equation(s) for quadratic utility. By contrast, for log W utility, $\sqrt{W}$ utility and $-1/W$ utility respectively:

$$\text{For GM, } M[W_0, W_1] \equiv M[\mu - \sigma, \mu + \sigma] \equiv \sqrt{(\mu - \sigma)(\mu + \sigma)} \equiv \sqrt{\mu - \sigma^2} \tag{5.27}$$

$$\text{For HM, } M[W_0, W_1] \equiv [(\mu - \sigma)(\mu + \sigma)]/\mu = \mu - \sigma^2 \mu^{-1} \tag{5.28}$$

$$\text{For } M[W_0, W_1] = \left[\frac{1}{2}\sqrt{W_0} + \frac{1}{2}\sqrt{W_1}\right]^2$$

$$= M[\mu - \sigma, \mu + \sigma] = \left[\frac{1}{2}\sqrt{\mu - \sigma} + \frac{1}{2}\sqrt{\mu + \sigma}\right]^2 \tag{5.29}$$

$$\text{For } U(W) = W - \frac{1}{2}bW^2, W < b^{-1},$$

$$M[W_0, W_1] = \mu - \frac{1}{2}b(\mu^2 + \sigma^2), \mu + \sigma < b^{-1} \tag{5.30}$$

Notice that in every one of these Laplacian risk-averse cases, higher μ is good and *ceteris paribus* higher σ^2 is bad. Sharpe could find four different "Sharpe ratios" to recommend.

As Etula has confirmed, when wet-dry dichotomy is replaced by [very wet, little wet, no wet at all,...], μ and σ's first two moments cannot tell the whole important skewness, kurtosis, and other vital parts of the story. This has been insufficiently recognized for decades. Only for Itô-Merton–Bachelier *instantaneous* probabilities is quadratic programming precisely accurate. (See Samuelson, 1970.)

5.6 Settling What Must be the Optimal Return for the Risks One Takes

The simple, clean Crusoe case can explicate just what has to be the reward a Laplacian needs to get to compensate for the riskiness chosen to be borne.

By the Newtonian choosing of Dan Crusoe's best Geometric Mean, he has stopped taking on extra riskiness just where his Certainty Equivalent drops off net from its maximum. Recall Equations from (5.20) to (5.25).

Therefore, Dan Crusoe and Harriet Crusoe, or Markowitz–Tobin–Sharpe quadratic programmers, do end up with optimized Equation (5.30)'s $\mu - b(\mu^2 + \sigma^2)$ at the point where marginal riskiness is in definitive balance with marginal reward.

No rational Laplacian fails to be rewarded for the riskiness they choose to bear in the singular $U = W_{-1/b}W^2$ case QED.

Acknowledgments I acknowledge the help from Erkko Etula, patient editorial help from Janice Murray, and from the Alfred P. Sloan Foundation for my MIT post-doctoral fellowship.

References

Bernoulli, D. 1738. Exposition of a new theory on the measurement of risk, *Econometrica* 22 (January 1954): 23–36, a translation from the Latin.

Hardy, G.H., Littlewood J.E., and Pólya G. 1952. *Inequalities*. Cambridge, UK and New York, Cambridge University Press.

Markowitz, H. 1952. Portfolio selection, *J Finance* 7. 1:77–91.

Markowitz, H. 1959. Portfolio Selection, Efficient Diversification of Investment. Monograph 16. Cowles Foundation for Research in Economics at Yale University, New Haven, Connecticut.

Markowitz, H. 2008. CAPM investors do not get paid for bearing risk: A linear relation does not imply payment for risk, *J Portfolio Manag* 34 2:91–94.

Planck, M. 1900, 1901. On the law of distribution in energy in the normal spectrum, *Ann Phys* 4:553ff.

Samuelson, P.A. 1969. Lifetime Portfolio Selection by Dynamic Stochastic Programming, *Rev Econ Statistics* 51. 3:239–246.

Samuelson, P.A. 1970. The fundamental approximation theorem of portfolio analysis in terms of means, variances, and higher moments, *Rev Econ Statistics* 37. 4:537–542.

Sharpe, W. 1970. *Portfolio theory and capital markets*. New York, NY, McGraw-Hill Book Company.

Tobin, J. 1980. *Asset accumulation and economic activity*. Oxford, Basil Blackwell.

In 1968 I wrote a critical review of the Thorp-Kassouf (1967) book *Beat the Market* [Samuelson, P.A., *Journal of the American Statistical Association*, Vol. 63, September, pgs. 1049-1051]. My main dissent was against their suggestion of easy money from merger arbitrage. Though I had done well with the Packard-Studebaker merger, it had been a harrowing--not an easy--experience. Shorts were hard to execute; short squeezes were a chronic danger. When an acquaintance tried to sell me puts I warned him not to do so, thereby risking a "short squeeze." He regretted not believing me. I do recall a similar story from an earlier time involving Molybdenum Corporation warrants that were destined to expire worthless. But it sure was hard to keep them short, and there were short squeezes and short scares that the intrinsically worthless warrants might have to be purchased for delivery with more shorts outstanding than warrants available to deliver. This fits the Thorp-Kassouf domain. I recall buying puts on the warrants, thereby giving up much of the potential profit, realizing some of it. That 1968 item somehow never got included in my *Collected Scientific Papers*... Maybe that was because I regretted my harsh tone. But in retrospect I relish my nihilism that no perfect hedge is ever possible. You will ask, what about the Black-Scholes-Merton hedge for log-normal probability distributions? Even that always does depend on an unknowable correct volatility parameter. (My 1968 nihilism prepared me for the 1998 Long-Term Capital Management debacle after it happened, but not before. Hyper-leveraging, plus off-the-cart exogenous shocks, trumped normal expectations, I think. But we may never know.)

Paul A. Samuelson, "An Enjoyable Life Puzzling Over Modern Finance Theory," *Annual Review of Financial Economics*, Vol. 1, December, 2009, pg. 22.

Beat the Market: A Scientific Stock Market System. Edward O. Thorp and Sheen T. Kassouf (Random House, New York, 1967), 221 pages, $7.95.

PAUL SAMUELSON, *Massachusetts Institute of Technology*

JUST as astronomers loathe astrology, scientists rightly resent vulgarization of their craft and false claims on its behalf. Although this book sins less than many, a reviewer for this journal must debunk its claims even though, paradoxically, only the readers of a journal like this are capable of making any money by the methods it recommends. Most of its buyers will not understand it or read it through. A few will enjoy reading it. A smaller few will lose a little money as a result of it. Still fewer might make a bit from it, and enjoy experimenting with its methods. (With the same effort, they might do as well by other methods.) As is candidly said, the book will make more money for its authors than any other use of its system could. Because Thorp wrote *Beat the Dealer*, a fairly well-known book telling how to take advantage of the slightly favorable odds in blackjack that gambling houses often offer, his name will help sell the book. Actually, there is only one page of discussion (at p. 200) that requires the skill of a statistician like him; the rest could have been written by the economist Kassouf, whose work in evaluating warrants has received some deserved attention—for identifying, by multiple correlation, factors upon which predictions of price changes can be based. In the present book this is barely mentioned, the emphasis being upon the misleading impression created that there is something in the mathematics of hedging that makes it possible to beat the market. The Pure Food and Drugs Administration should enjoin the authors from making such misleading claims, or at least require them to take out of the fine print, so to speak, the warnings showing they know better.

In a nutshell, warrants (which give you the right to buy the common stock of a particular company at a stated exercise price at any time during a stated period) are sometimes overpriced relative to the common stock price as they near their termination date—overpriced in the sense that investing in a hedge (in which you buy the common stock and sell the warrants short) is likely to offer you a nicely positive mathematical expectation. Because there is a strong positive correlation between the movements of the common and the warrant, the hedge's positive mean is likely to be accompanied by a low dispersion.

There is nothing new in this. There is nothing certain about it. What gives the book its appeal is the fact that their recommended type of hedge would, over the historical decades since 1930, have earned percentage returns stated to be about 25 per cent per year. That the authors have themselves made some money using the system is supposed to be especially impressive. Those of us who know lots of rich men are less impressed. Whether future warrant price relationships will form a stationary time series with similar properties to those of the past is, of course, not certain. As the authors state, their book may reduce the opportunities for profit. (They ingenuously add that if there is then a recognizable overshoot, by *reversing* their strategy the gentle reader can make money). My guess is that the book will in the short run have an effect toward minimizing its own worth; but after it has been remaindered at the local drug store, life will go on much as in the past.

Most of the book deals with the arithmetic of the problem, which is complicated enough. Little, too little, grapples with the probability aspects. The cornerstone of the analysis is the fact that when a warrant is at its expiration date, arbitrage sets almost-exact limits on its value relative to the common stock. If one warrant permits me to buy the common at an exercise price of E, and if the common has a price of P, then *at expiration* the price of the warrant p must be the following non-analytic function, $p = \text{Max}(0, P-E)$. If you can't verify this, give up. (Once when I was studying the Put-and-Call market, the late Herbert Filer said to me: "You'll never understand this business; it takes a European kind of mind to do so.")

Suppose we have an opinion of the probability distribution that this terminal P will have, given our knowledge of current P^* and p^*; then the probability distribution of p can be derived from it—and hence the probability distribution of gains or losses from selling or buying both the warrants and common. A hedge is merely a linear combination of these prices, and the probability distribution of it can be appraised. Hence, all I must do is compute the expected value of the utility to me of different outcomes that will emerge for each (algebraic) portfolio choice.

To make stew, first catch your rabbit. The book should have spent most of its time telling us how to decide when a rabbit is fit for stewing. Instead it prattles on mostly about the scientific certainty of its message.

It does have one interesting, but possibly misleading, theorem or hint of one. (What do you expect these days for eight dollars?) On p. 201, it is shown that if the probability distribution of terminal P is skewed to the right relative to present P^* (more precisely that Prob $(P \geq p^*+t) \geq$ Prob $(P \leq p^*-t)$, and if $P^* = .5E$, then buying the Warrant at $.3E$ is sure to give you an *expected* gain less than what the stock will give you. Hence, an even hedge must have a positive expectation. No proof is given other than the laconic, "The argument is standard measure-theoretic," but one can see how the argument goes. According to my back-to-the-envelope calculation, this same innocent "skewness" argument leads to the result that when a stock is below half its exercise price, its warrant at *any* price above zero is overpriced in the sense that it has an inferior first moment to the stock. I think this is pretty, and I got my money's worth because I can use the hint to develop some limits on the functions in the theory of rational warrant pricing.* But it confirmed my immediate reaction that the book errs in claiming that the skewness assumption is a "weak" one. The fact that there is some evidence for log-normality of price changes does not necessarily imply

271

such skewness: indeed if prices are a weak-trend random walk, log-normality implies a different kind of skewness. Moreover, suppose the theorem true. It does not tell us that we would not be better off buying the common stock: the answer to that must depend upon our own tradeoff between mean and variance, on margin costs, etc. Obviously both authors have much to contribute that does not appear in this book.

Enough has been said except for a few specific warnings. Fig. 4.1 on p. 45 shows, but does not sufficiently stress, that losses are possible from *any* hedge. The even-hedge has its loss shown in the negative quadrant. The other hedges should also have been extended into the negative quadrant. Of course, the authors deem such losses unlikely. Let *us* form that judgment. The authors mislead themselves in thinking that losses can be avoided by changing one's mind *before* (!) entering the negative quadrant. This is a species of the genus of fallacies based upon a belief that stop-loss orders can change the odds. If we drop the strategy of inevitably holding the hedge until termination date, none of the functions shown apply! (Example: in one minute my warrant may go up relative to the common, and a transaction completed *then* will show a loss of the type that cannot be represented in their charts.) In dynamic programming, we can always vary our strategy—but this book's analysis tells me nothing about how to play such a strategy. For that they need a probability theory of warrant pricing. Their book, with justice, might have been called *End Game*. Or, it seemed to this reviewer, one might steal the title of the classic Brazilian novel by Machado de Assis, *Epitaph For a Small Winner*.

One final warning. It is not the case that one can follow a system like this with little effort. Much of one's profits will be implicit wages, perhaps less than one can garner in other pursuits. For one cannot always execute transactions at the prices that later appear in the records. In making his profits, Kassouf by his own account had to work like a Trojan. Example: the 1962 expiration of Molybdenum warrants was this system's finest hour. I know intimately the man who had the largest short position in that stock: he made money; most of his friends who imitated him lost money; those who sold him puts on the warrants lost a lot of money because they could not keep the warrants borrowed to maintain their short sales—an outcome which Kassouf now says they could have avoided if they had shown sufficient ingenuity and effort. Maybe someone should write a book on how, by use of ingenuity and effort, one can make a dollar. But that would never sell.

* The second edition of P. Cootner, ed., *The Random Character of Stock Market Prices* (MIT Press, 1967), reproduced from the *Industrial Management Review*, 1965 articles by H. P. McKean, Jr. and me on rational warrant pricing.

PART VII.

Current Economics and Policy

2

The Present State of Economic Science and Its Probable Future Development *

Paul A. Samuelson
Massachusetts Institute of Technology

Economic activity is the oldest of the arts and economics is the newest of the sciences. The science of political economy is in a state of vigorous growth all over the globe. The sheer bulk of available factual knowledge is vastly greater than ever before, and the degree of sophistication involved in economic theorizing and measurement would not only astonish Adam Smith and other classical scholars but would also amaze Joseph Schumpeter and my other great teachers of fifty years ago. More economists are now alive than have ever lived since the beginning of time; more additions are made each decade to the literature of political economy than used to occur in a century.

Surely such a field defies brief description? And when it is realized that there is not universal agreement on one single correct school of economics, you may well wonder whether anything less than a treatise or bookshelf can do justice to my ambitious title. Nevertheless I believe that certain broad trends can be usefully identified. The whole can be made to be simpler than the sum of its parts.

I can paint with a broad brush a tolerably accurate picture of the present state of economics. Pinpointing where this science will be in 1990 or 2000 is of course another matter. Let me illustrate by an example. Lionel Robbins, who recently died, was a great economist at Oxford and the London School of Economics in the years 1920 to 1980. Active in helping run the U.K. World War II economic mobilization, Robbins (Lord Robbins, as he was to become) knew everybody; everybody knew him. Yet, some forty years ago in a scholarly presidential address, this great scholar made the confident prediction that the use of mathematics in economics and econometrics was a temporary vogue, a fad that would soon pass away. You have only to look into any learned journal in the economics library to realize how wrong Robbins was both quantitatively and qualitatively.

This raises the question, you may ask, whether economics indeed deserves the title of being a science? My point is not to sow such doubts. For consider a case from the hard sciences, the case of Lord Rutherford, the greatest experimental physicist of the first third of the twentieth century. After the neutron was discovered in his Cambridge laboratory, he was asked to speculate whether splitting the atom might some day become a source of useful power. Although then at the height of his wisdom, Ernest Rutherford made the wrong guess that there was some not-yet-understood law of nature that prevents us from getting out of a physics operation more of energy than we have put into it.

The essence of every science is to develop in ways not predictable in advance. So to speak, if we knew just where we were going to go in science, we'd already have marched there.

So, here I shall not presume to do the impossible. What I can usefully do is what all my life as a productive scholar I have had to try to do -- to weigh the evidence and appraise the logical plausibility of each developing trend, endeavoring to pay most attention to those developments for which the odds seem favorable. This involves of course constant refocussing as one learns from new surprises. As we say in practical forecasting, "If you must forecast, forecast often."

Geographic Convergence

Mainstream economics is recognizably similar over most of the globe. What, in Moscow too? It is true that the elementary textbooks employed to inculcate "sound economics" into college freshmen read very differently in the socialist states of Eastern Europe than they do in free-enterprise Texas. But if you examine the technical economics of the Soviet Academies' memoranda and reports, and cut through the verbiage and vocabulary to reach actual content, you will discover that certain principles and relations occur in common.

Two centuries ago this mainstream economics was primarily British economics: Adam Smith, David Ricardo, and John Stuart Mill were the classical writers who tried to forge political economy as a largely *deductive* science. Looking back, we realize that they overglorified the power of *a priori* reasoning in one's isolated library and exaggerated the exactitude of alleged economic laws.

Classical economics was a successful export abroad. Educated people, in Moscow or Philadelphia or Berlin, knew of the serendipitous "invisible hand" of

Adam Smith that channeled each person's selfish action to achieve the social good. Still, in the rapidly developing New World of America, the dismal science of diminishing returns and Malthusian overpopulation met with resistance. And on the continent where the industrial revolution came late, a romantic and nationalistic school of German economists suspected that Smithian laissez faire was an unconscious rationalization of the interests of the rising bourgeois class; and that Ricardian free trade was an apologetic for a regime favorable to quick-off-the-mark Britain as against economies that were delayed in their domestic industrialization.

Friedrich List provided a century and a half ago a good example of a backlash to classical economics. Migrating from Germany for a sojourn in the United States, List perceived a need to protect infant industries by temporary tariffs. On his return to Germany he wrote up his heretical view that the state should interfere with laissez faire in order to promote industrialization of a young economy. The reception of a scientific theory, along with depending upon its empirical accuracy and elegance of analytical description, can also depend upon whether a society is ripe to approve of its message. List's heresy was well received in nineteenth century Germany and North America, and throughout the preindustrial nations there is still within our own times strong sentiment toward import quotas and protective tariffs for developmental stimulus.

Despite the above offshoot, there is a clearcut main avenue of descent from classical economics to the international mainstream economics of the 1980s. Just when John Stuart Mill's *Principles of Political Economy* (1848) perfected and embalmed classical economics in two volumes, decadence began to set in.

Fortunately, by the last quarter of the nineteenth century, rejuvenation of classical economics occurred. Now it was no longer an English affair: joining with Jevons of Manchester to formulate the neoclassical economics that was heir to classical economics were Walras and Pareto of Lausanne, Menger and Böhm-Bawerk of Vienna, Wicksell and Cassel of Scandinavia, John Bates Clark in America, and many other writers of the period 1870 to 1930. Neoclassical economics was less *a priori* than classical economics; less preoccupied with Malthusian diminishing returns, more optimistic about technical progress; more proficient in the analysis of supply and demand, digging deeper into the structure of utility preferences and consumer choice.

277

Crosscurrents

Traffic on the main highway of history never tells the full story. The continental environment that was resentful of orthodox economics and receptive to List's heresies nurtured an anti-classical movement called the German Historical School, associated at first with Roscher and later with Schmoller. The emphasis was away from deductive theory and toward empirical fact; on dynamic stages of economic development -- primitive culture of hunters and croptenders, feudalism, post-reformation capitalism, and then presumed evolution past capitalism into socialism and communism.

A century ago American economists, finding no graduate schools at Oxford and Cambridge, migrated from one German university to another, attending lectures of Sombart, Wagner, and various so-called "socialists of the chair," and writing detailed historical Ph.D. dissertations on the minutiae of economic history. They brought back to America a movement called Institutionalist Economics which flourished fitfully from 1890 to 1930, and enrolled such eminent names as Thorstein Veblen, Wesley Mitchell, J.R. Commons, and Richard T. Ely. A politically more conservative version of this anti-theory school flourished during the 1920s in the American business schools, where future executives of Fortune-500 multinational corporations received their training by means of the case-study approach.

Today in the 1980s virtually no trace of the Institutional or Historical School can be found in university life or research institutes. As neoclassical economics veered in the direction of statistical measurement or "econometrics," institutionalist empiricism was absorbed into the central channels of mainstream economics.

Marxian Challenges

A more lasting challenge to mainstream economics is provided by Marxism. It has been often said that the doctrines of Karl Marx rose out of German philosophy, French socialism, and British classical economics. The geneaological chart of classical economics divides after Ricardo: paralleling the mainstream channel of neoclassical economics has been the critical branch of Marx and Engels, of Lenin, Stalin, and Mao. It is idle to speculate what would today be the scientific status of Marxian economics had there never been Lenin's successful revolution of 1917. A bald fact of history is that a billion people live today in societies that formally at least profess allegiance to the economics of Karl Marx. Islamic economics may not receive many hours of discussion in the seminar rooms of MIT, but still an analyst of Iran would be ill-advised to give that subject short shrift.

New Left activism among university students in the late 1960s renewed some interest in Marxian political economy. But most of the response was among sociologists and philosophy students rather than in schools of economics and business. Even in Japan, where only a generation ago more than half of economics professors considered themselves to be Marxians, there is relatively little input into the literature of economic science originating from this wing of the profession. China today is reeling uncertainly away from Mao's centralism and is flirting skittishly with price mechanisms and incentives of the market.

Synthesis and Dissolution

By 1930 neoclassical economics was riding high. Economics professors advised banks and wrote newspaper columns in praise of the boom in stock prices going on in Wall Street and other world bourses. The great depression of the 1930s came as a surprise to all the experts: John Maynard Keynes had just published a two-volume *Treatise on Money* that downplayed the business cycle; President Herbert Hoover, an activist engineer, commissioned a study on *Recent Social Trends*, which at the very brink of the great economic crash opined that all was well with the world economy.

For several years bankruptcies and bank failures proliferated. Unemployment swelled, reaching in both Germany and the United States a rate of 25 percent of the working force. By 1931 the gold standard collapsed like a house of cards: exchange rates floated with the winds of supply and demand; exchange and capital controls, import quotas and tariffs, and bilateral trade agreements balkanized the international division of labor built up over a century and restored after the Versailles Peace Treaty.

The tragic slump was bad for starving workers and farmers, who were understandably polarized to vote for the extreme right and the extreme left. Profits were decimated and lifetime savings wiped away. Global production fell for a decade and the capital formation and technical innovations upon which longrun progress depend were aborted by the slump.

Keynesian Revolution

Bad as the depression was for the real world, it served as a powerful stimulant to economic science -- in the same way that horrible plague provides grist for the bacteriologist's mill. Neoclassical economists had gone far in studying historic business cycles: ordinary few-year oscillations in trade; major cycles almost a decade in length; and suspected waves of longer duration. But neoclassical equilibrium theory had no paradigms to explain mass unemployment -- poverty midst plenty.

Thus, at the depths of the slump a libertarian like Friedrich Hayek could warn against providing any purchasing power to the needy poor, lest this thereby distort the balance between consumption and investment spending. Keynes' 1936 classic, the *General Theory of Employment, Interest and Money,* provided economists with a new paradigm to handle macroeconomic policy. (The word "macroeconomics" still needed to be invented then.) Foreshadowers of Keynes -- Ohlin, Myrdal, and Frisch in Scandinavia, and John Maurice Clark in the United States -- were given a respectable scientific model to study and operate.

By the eve of World War II, an amalgam of neoclassical and Keynesian economics had swept the field. Historical studies show that the Allied war mobilization was the most thorough and effective ever achieved. It was a triumph of democratic dedication, but also a triumph for economic science in application.

The Miracle Third Quarter of the Century

The scholarly discipline of economics that came out of the war was much improved in knowledge and in confidence. The successful Marshall Plan and MacArthur Occupation of Japan added to economists' hubris. Despite the doubts about the vigor of "capitalism in an oxygen tent" that had been expressed by Schumpeter and pre-Keynesians, the mixed economies soared in the post-Keynes epoch.

What Europe had not been able to accomplish after World War I, succeeded admirably after the German Currency Reform and throughout the formative decades of the Common Market. Europe narrowed the gap between it and the United States. Japan leaped from being a poor and defeated Asian country to rapid industrialization and onward to become the third largest economy in the world -- subordinate only to the more populous United States and Soviet Union. (Of course in terms of per capita real income Japan exceeds the Soviet Union by almost 50 percent; and by the end of the century Japan's per capita real income looks likely to exceed that of Western Europe and then go on to overtake the U.S. standard of life. Already her actuarial life expectancies at birth are second to none.)

Graduate training in economics expanded greatly from 1950 to 1985. MIT, Stanford, Harvard, Chicago, Cambridge, Oxford, Stockholm, Bonn, Rotterdam, Louvain, and other hotbeds of mathematical rigor attracted the best students from all over the world. Millionaire professors were created overnight as the giant computers of Otto Eckstein's DRI and Lawrence Klein's Wharton-Penn Model were hired to provide forecasts for the multi-national corporations of the postwar period.

The complacency index of modern economics, future history books will record, peaked out around 1965 when the Kennedy-Johnson golden age of Camelot was at its zenith -- before the miasma of the Vietnamese war took over, and prior to onset of the stagflation that pricked the bubble of the infallible mixed economy and welfare state.

Erosion of Consensus

In science it is always the case: The king is dead; long live the new king! The Neanderthal Keynesianism of the 1930s could emphasize fiscal policy and underplay central-bank monetary policy during depression eras when short-term interest rates were virtually zero. By 1955 it was obvious that variations in the supply of money would have substantial effects upon interest rates, levels of nominal wealth, and upon the total of spending and production.

The recognition that "Money does matter" led to an overreaction by a new school who called themselves "monetarists". In their unguarded formulations, zealous followers of Chicago's Professor Milton Friedman sometimes fell into the fallacious syllogism, "Hence, money *alone* matters." Monetarists advocated a steady rate of growth of the money supply, with no yielding by the Federal Reserve, the Bank of England, or the *Bundesbank* to the temptation of trying to lean against the winds of forthcoming recession or inflation. Adherence to such a credible growth rule, monetarists admitted, would not create a new perfect Eden; but, given the perversity of politics and the complexities of long and variable dynamic lags, monetarists believed that stabilizing the trend of the money supply would produce the best feasible macroeconomic policy.

Able monetarists, such as Karl Brunner of Bern and Rochester, enjoyed much success in persuading European governments to eschew fine tuning and activist stabilization policies. At the same time American Keynesians, such as Franco Modigliani, James Tobin, and Robert Solow, were evolving into an eclectic post-Keynesianism that played up the role of asset stocks and liquidity

281

in affecting flows and that tried to synthesize the policy weapons of fiscal and monetary policy.

A more fundamental challenge to the post-Keynesian eclectic mainstream than from the monetarists came from a new camp called "Rational Expectationists" or the school of "New Classical Economists." Led by Robert Lucas and Thomas Sargent, rational expectationists appealed to countless modern statistical studies demonstrating market efficiency in stock and bond pricing. Share prices in New York and London, staple prices in Chicago or Liverpool, fluctuate with each new arrival of news but do so in such a way as to leave their next-period movement subject only to random chance. "If the Wall Street auction market for IBM common stocks yields market prices characteristic of what can be 'rationally expected'," the New Classical writers argued, "then we should base our expectations of what is going to happen to the country's *gross national product* on a model that assumes wisdom among all actors in the economic drama to anticipate what will happen in a *market-clearing* equilibrium."

These new conclusions are quite revolutionary. If true, they imply that the government cannot stimulate unemployment in an economy -- except in the shortest run. If the Federal Reserve is creating new money, and people will have learned about the process, the only effects will be to raise the price level and to leave unemployment and excess capacity just where they were.

It is not facts that kill an old theory. As Schumpeter used to say even before Thomas Kuhn's *The Structure of Scientific Revolutions* was conceived, "It takes a theory to kill a theory." As mainstream macroeconomics and monetarism failed to solve the problems of *stagflation* -- a new disease in which, at the same time that unemployment is high and growing, price and wage levels experience accelerating inflation -- the cream of younger economists found rational expectationism an exciting hypothesis.

Alas, in the Reagan and Thatcher crusades to bring down inflation, the history of the 1980s belied the hopes of those who believed that a credible monetary policy to reduce inflation would succeed with relatively little cost in terms of induced stagnation. Dozens of studies at the National Bureau of Economic Research, hoping to vindicate the hypotheses of rational expectations and using the most powerful methods of modern econometrics, have commonly found that modern reality deviates from that paradigm in a statistically significant way.

Where We Stand: Bird's-eye View

Modern economics is in a lively stage. On the left it is challenged by disciples of John Kenneth Galbraith and by Italian and Indian neo-Keynesians of the Sraffa-Kaldor-Robinson school. On the right there is the Chicago-School insistence on the optimality of market mechanisms. Macroeconomic policy is subject to lively debate by eclectic mainstream post-Keynesians, monetarists, and rational expectationists.

Business cycle prediction utilizes the largest and fastest of modern computers. Modified Keynesian macromodels predominate at OECD and among the large consulting firms and banks. Errors of forecasts are much fewer than before the war. But several years ago it became apparent that accuracy was not converging toward precision: it is as if there is a Heisenberg-like *indeterminacy principle*, specifying that we may go just so far and no further in reducing down the variance of our estimates.

Outsiders complain that the trouble with economists is on how much they disagree. From six economists six different opinions, the canard claims. I have to disagree. Economists if anything tend to agree too much among themselves. And what they agree on is that last year's wisdom was wrong and needs to be replaced by this year's.

Here are some crucial questions that I think command among economists a remarkable consensus, and often their answers are at variance with those from non-economist groups.

1. *Flexible exchange rates, imperfect as they are, must be preferred to pegged exchange rates*. Restoring the gold standard cannot succeed inasmuch as modern electorates will not adhere to the rules of the gold standard that can alone keep it viable. (Do all economists agree on this? Of course not. Relatively more in France would disagree, and relatively more among the older generation. But at any World Economic Congress with a thousand attendants, 900 I believe would agree.)

2. *Most of a nation's resource allocation is best left to the market mechanism*. Even in Eastern Europe or in a Scandinavian welfare state, centralized fiats cannot deliver the goods of a growing, efficient, and equitable society. Government, as so to speak a mutual-reinsurance agency, can of course use its transfer powers to rectify partially the most severe of the inequalities and inequities dealt out by the pricing system.

3. *Irreplaceable natural resources and environmental interdependencies do constitute future problems of importance, but Club of Rome pronouncements of Doomsday downplay the contribution that rationing of scarcity by market pricing can contrive and overlook the age-old struggle against the law of diminishing returns that is provided by scientific discovery and technological innovation.*

When economists from New Delhi, Budapest, and either Cambridge meet, it is a testament to the scientific content of economics that there is so much for them to discuss and to agree upon. This does not deny that scientists who begin with different value premises will end up with differences in policy recommendations. *Those* differences of opinion are quite compatible with agreement on questions of scientific fact: thus, I may favor redistributive income taxes and my old friend Milton Friedman may oppose them; that doesn't mean I deny that those taxes and transfers can do damage to efficiency and growth, but may merely reflect the fact that my value judgments deem those costs are more than offset by gains in human ethics and dignity.

Through a Class Darkly

Where is economic science going? One good way to present guesses on this important matter is by means of a number of short questions and answers.

Question. Is political economy on the verge of a great breakthrough -- like the Crick-Watson discovery of double-helix DNA in molecular biology?

Answer. There is no evidence for this. Nor is there evidence of a fallow period in economic science, as a multitude of researchers move down trails of diminishing returns. Complacency among macroeconomists has oozed away since 1965, and deservedly so. Within the field of microeconomics -- the study of pricing and production within particular sectors of the economy -- rapid progress continues to take place. Economists, like invading barbarians, are spreading imperialistically into law, population studies, and sociobiology.

Question. Is it correct that the economics profession is growing more "conservative?"

Answer. Yes. The failures of socialism to deliver enviable economic performance in Eastern Europe and Mainland China are instilling new respect for market pricing among students of economics. (It is another thing among the populaces in poor African, Asian, and Latin American countries newly released from colonial domination.) My own concern is that we never forget to ask,

"Efficiency for what?" I favor economics with a heart, and my scientific studies are reassuring that this does not require economists with wooly heads. If setting minimum wages too high will create youth unemployment, and rent ceilings will encourage arson in the slums, let people of goodwill recognize these cool truths in legislating optimally.

Question. Has the epidemic of mathematics in economics and econometrics run its course?

Answer. Definitely no. The leaders in our profession take these tools for granted. Excesses of formalism and sterility, experience suggests, will primarily be corrected *from within* the ruling circles of a science and not by outside sages or prophets. A Maxwell or an Einstein, rather than a Goethe, improves upon a Newton.

Question. What big problems loom ahead for economic science? Was Thomas Carlyle right when in the last century he called economics "the dismal science?"

Answer. The business cycle is not, like smallpox, now extinct. Nor is the evil of inflation a past problem to be read about in the history books. The science of economics is nourished by the fresh questions arising in the course of economic history, and each new decade brings its copious supply of new problems and issues.

Since the Nobel Prize in Economics was instituted in 1969, twenty-two Laureates have been honored for scholarly achievements in such diverse areas as international finance, GNP forecasting, economic history and development of backward regions, risk, general equilibrium, economic philosophy and methodology and much more. Before the twentieth century comes to an end, this list will be more than doubled in length as younger scholars create new economic theories and test quantitatively existing paradigms and hypotheses.

Where economic science is concerned, as in other domains of basic knowledge, it remains true that the future is longer than the present.

* ACKNOWLEDGEMENT

These remarks were originally stimulated by a request from the Daimler-Benz Company, on the occasion of the 100th anniversary of the automobile -- 1886-1986 -- to summarize the status of economic science. I make reference to the volume *Zeugen des Wissens* edited by Heinz Maier-Leibnitz and published by Hase & Koehler, Mainz, 1986. Reprinted with permission of v. Hase & Koehler Verlag.

495

The Science of Economics at Century's End
Paul A. Samuelson, 7 November 1988

Political economy has come a long way in the twentieth century. The number of professional economists has grown enormously in the last few decades; that number continues to grow.

When I began the study of economics at the University of Chicago more than half a century ago, Britain was still the homeland of advanced economics. As measured by sale of economic textbooks, American economists already vastly outnumbered British and British-Empire economists *quantitatively*. But *qualitatively* we spent our time reading and discussing the works of Alfred Marshall (dead almost a decade) and the live A.C. Pigou, J.M. Keynes, D.H. Robertson, and Lionel Robbins. German economics had long since lost its appeal as too little theoretical: on the continent we recognized writers of The Austrian School (Schumpeter, Hayek, and the earlier generation of Carl Menger and Böhm-Bawerk), and such Northern European scholars as Cassel, Wicksell, Heckscher, Frisch, and Tinbergen. No pre- or post-Revolution Russians were deemed worth reading. Needless to say we could not read Japanese, and if there were any pre-1930 Japanese economists worth attending to, we were quite unaware of them.

Actually, the American economics of Irving Fisher, J.B. and J.M. Clark, Wesley Mitchell, Frank Taussig, Allyn Young and Frank Knight, Jacob Viner and Harold Hotelling was better than it was then reputed to be. In accord with what the sociologist of science Robert K. Merton calls the Matthew Effect ("To him who hath shall be given"), the leaders at Cambridge, Oxford, and the LSE received more than their just due--just as the Impressionist painters of France stole the limelight from meritorious pioneers elsewhere.

These banal facts of history are worth noting because, when Japanese scholars began to go abroad in the 1920s and to be influenced by foreign writers, it is my impression that they paid a disproportionate amount of attention to the various German schools. One wonders why. Surely the difficulty of German as a language cannot have been materially less than that of English? Perhaps the attractiveness for *technical* and *scientific* imitators of the pre-World War I German universities spread over to the social sciences? Or, could the abstractness of German philosophical thought in the social sciences have had some resonance with the Japanese mind-set of the Meiji period of restoration?

In any case it was a fateful choice, since only in Germany did a tradition of Marxian economics live on. My teachers did not suppress the impulse to teach me Marxian economics. Rather it never occurred to them to be tempted, as they would have put it, to waste my time and theirs with such irrelevances.

In any case, twenty years after the 1932 date when I began

economic study, America had become the dominant force in modern economics. Maurice Allais complained bitterly of the American Juggernaut at the 1952 Paris Conference on Risk. My great English uncles and aunt still carried on magnificently--Harrod, Lerner, Joan Robinson, Kaldor, Hicks, Meade--but they were not reproducing themselves among gifted students. Hitler had made America a free gift of continental scholars--Schumpeter, Leontief, Haberler, Lange, Marschak, von Neumann, Koopmans, and innumerable others. Even the Keynesian torch was carried farthest and fastest in the New World.

A Morishima might still study in Oxford, but most Japanese graduate students who went abroad after 1950 came to America: to Harvard, Hopkins, MIT, Chicago, Rochester, and Stanford. Those appointed to non-Marxist chairs at Tokyo, Osaka, Keio, Kyoto, Hitotsubashi, and elsewhere increasingly had spent a tour of duty doing graduate study in America. The traditional inbreeding, in which great Japanese universities tended to recruit their faculties from among their own students, was perhaps favorably weakened by the random pattern of choosing American universities. (Remark: An economist at *L'Ecole Polytechnique* in Paris is hardly acquainted with an economist at the Sorbonne's Faculty of Law. By contrast, I and my early MIT colleagues all had Ph.D.'s from Harvard, or Chicago, or ...).

Major Twentieth Century Trends
The first third of this century was rather a fallow period for economic science. Marshall rested on his neoclassical oars. Wicksell and Pareto had already done their great work at the century's beginning. After the death of Engels, Marxism grew as a political movement on the Continent but languished as a developing science.

Then, after 1930 at least three revolutions broke out. There was the Chamberlin-Robinson revolution involving *imperfect competition*. There was the *Keynesian* revolution in macroeconomics. There was the *econometric* revolution involving the increased use of mathematics in economic theory and in economic statistics.

The world has never been the same. Suddenly the elder-statesmen Lionel Robbins and Edwin Cannan had lost their audiences. Now it was the turn of Frisch, Hotelling, Leontief, Hicks, Samuelson, Haavelmo, Arrow, Debreu, Friedman, Tobin, Modigliani, Morishima, and a flood of others.

Even dormant Marxism came to life in the tumultuous sixties. Paul Sweezy had written the subject's primer for mainstream-trained economists as far back as 1942. The age of Sraffa created a whole cottage industry of *matrix* Marxism. When my own publications in this area began more than thirty years ago, my old buddy Shigeto

3

Tsuru informed me that much of its content was already in the Japanese vernacular. I believed him, recalling Kei Shibata's pre-war writings and, later, being able to read the translations of Professor Okishio and other post-war scholars.

There is the old philosophical puzzle of how to characterize a tree that falls in a forest where none can hear it. A scholar of good will must feel some of the same puzzle in trying to appraise a vast layer of Japanese economic scholarship in the Marxian tradition. We learn with incredulity that half of Tokyo or Kyoto University consists of Marxist scholars whom we have never met, whose names we do not know, and whose research never sees the light that reflects into western eyes. It is like a physics world of coexisting but never interacting matter and anti-matter. Several years ago the editor of a learned journal of maximal circulation asked me whether they should publish a proposed translation of a great Japanese Marxist. I counseled: "Yes, once you verify that it is not a hoax or parody." They did publish. But, as far as can be apprehended, it was like a stone cast into a pool that leaves nary a ripple. Even our local village Marxists seemed to display little interest, perhaps to their own loss.

It says something about the bureaucratic structure of academic life that so much of the Marxist school remains entrenched in Japanese economic chairs. Thirty years ago I was told that the mainstream wing was beginning to be dominant. Twenty years ago I heard the same story. It makes one wonder whether Max Planck's bittersweet appraisal applies in Japan: "Funeral by funeral science makes progress."

Where half of the academy answers to a different drum beat and is gauged by a different set of standards, both halves are undermined. How often I have witnessed enthusiastic and able students, who have returned to Japan on fire to do important research, only to have them be placed on the lowest step of the escalator and over the years lose their enthusiasm and knowledge of the research frontier. Even the calling of being a great teacher has lost out to bureaucratic inertia. And this in a society demonstrated to possess a hundred million over-achievers!

High Tide of Camelot
The middle third of the twentieth century was the period of greatest global economic progress. Joseph Schumpeter's "capitalism in an oxygen tent" failed to describe the mixed economy's sprint in the Age After Keynes. What did not happen after World War I--namely a rapid catch-up to America by the industrialized regions of Europe and the Pacific Basin--did occur after World War II. (Only compare the weak 1925 Austria of Mises, Hayek, and Machlup with the dynamic Austria of 1955-1980.)

Success in the real economic world seemed at first to be paralleled by triumphs in economic science. John F. Kennedy's Camelot of 1961-65 seemed kind of proof that the economic science of linear programming, game theory and input-output, of Keynes-Tinbergen model building and Klein-Eckstein forecasting was converging toward the maturity of an accurate science. Hubris and over-confidence were understandable temptations.

The stagflation of the Vietnam War epoch was exacerbated by the supply shocks of OPEC and the premonitions of environmental decay and Club-of-Rome resource scarcities. Confidence in Keynesian fine tuning evaporated when whatever policy advisers prescribed to help the stagnation part of stagflation only worsened the inflation aspect, and what helped the inflation evil aggravated the unemployment evil.

In science as elsewhere revolution breeds counter-revolution. As multi-national corporations competed with each other globally, widening the extent of the market and weakening the market power of each giant, interest ebbed away gradually in Chamberlinian imperfections. A Chicago doctrine of near-enough-to-competition gradually evolved. My suspicion is that the Chamberlin-Robinson revolution deserves some comeback on the bourse of economists' preferences.

Model T Keynesians, which had stressed income flows rather than financial stocks, required scientific evolution and adaptation. Professor Milton Friedman's monistic monetarism represented the over-reaction so often encountered in the history of science. The persuasive skills of one articulate polemicist at first served the good cause of accelerating the evolution beyond 1939 Keynesianism. Friedman, Tobin, Modigliani, and others elaborated needed Keynesian wealth effects. Once Friedman was prepared to admit that neoclassical economics called for a systematic positive relationship between the *velocity* of money and the level of interest rates sacrificed by money holders, a better macroeconomic synthesis was achieved. Alas, in Britain the evolution away from Model T Keynesianism was fatally slowed down by ancient ideologies and allegiances.

A more serious challenge than monetarism to post-Keynesian mainstream eclecticism is "the new classical economics of the rational expectationist school." This school is associated with such names as Robert Lucas, Thomas Sargent, Robert Barro, and many younger macroeconomists. By contrast monetarism is a one man's show--a sideshow. If the claims of the New Classicists were verifiable--that money is "neutral" even in the quite short run, that policy interventions cannot have *real* effects save when first sprung as a surprise--this would be a true counter revolution. If...

Actually, the Lucas-Sargent thesis is neither plausible in its strong form nor, even in its weak form, borne out under specific econometric testing. Its explicit forecasts have proved in the 1980s to be mostly misleading if not perverse. (An example is the silly Barro forecast that, when the Reagan government contrived a huge structural fiscal deficit, we citizens would Ricardo-like now increase our personal saving rate enough to pay our future taxes. An example is Sargent's expectation that the taming of inflation in the early 1980s would be nearly as costless as the 1923 German inflation reform.)

Eclecticism wins hands down in economics. In a weak-weak form, Lucas economics will help keep modern Keynesianism realistic. Actually, much modern anti-Keynesianism is only verbal. My Harvard neighbor, Martin Feldstein, dubs himself anti-Keynesian. I discern in his writings A Modern Keynesian Who Chooses to Call Himself Anti-Keynesian. Even Friedman and Brunner-Meltzer, when they wrote out their explicit monetarist equations, turned out to be Tobins in their comparative statics and logical structure.

A successful counter-revolution against mathematics in economics and statistics never could develop. The cure for disillusionment with the potency and magic of mathematics turned out to be, alas and prosaically, even further use of technical mathematics. What did have to be given up was unwarranted self-confidence in the perfection of economic science.

The upshot of the Marxian upsurge of the 1960s was the realization that the novel paradigm of surplus value was, as Böhm has predicted, a sterile detour. *Normatively* equal-profit-rate prices of production won hands down against equal-markups on direct wage costs alone. *Positivistically* there had never been merit in *Capital's Mehrwert* innovations. Karl Marx did make one important analytical contribution: his tableaus of reproduction and balanced growth are a stepping stone from Quesnay to von Neumann, Leontief, Tsuru, and Sraffa; but this innovation is within the economic mainstream and not a point in favor of *Capital's* alternative paradigm. To describe and understand the laws of motion of 1940-1990 political economies, the $\Sigma s_j / \Sigma v_j$ paradigm was a sterile regression and digression. To understand the 1930-1985 events of my time I would gladly have accepted help from Marx or the devil. Alas, in the paragraphs of Dobb, Sweezy, Baran, Mandel, Sraffa, and Garegnani there were to be found no insights into the modern economic history of Europe or America, Asia or Africa, or even the USSR itself.

The stagnating efficiency of East European socialisms and mainland China did much to swing the jury away from the Lerner-Lange debaters and toward the Hayek-Mises camp. When Scandinavia and the Low Countries began to encounter more than half of the GNP going through the channels of government, the usefulness of the market mechanisms received a new dramatization.

The ideology of the economist clerks has turned increasingly conservative in my lifetime. Some of this I find aesthetically and ethically distasteful. Some I must admit results from empirical observation of the pragmatic limitations of egalitarian programs. Back in the 1960s excited students asked me to debate my great linguist colleague Noam Chomsky. It was on my home departmental grounds and he of course was not a trained economist. Still against so eloquent a philosopher and formidable a polemicist, I would gladly have settled for a tie. Except for duty I could have spared the pleasure of it.

In tranquility, as I went over the discussions in memory, I realized that it was Professor Chomsky's vision that the business of economics in the real world might best be carried on by the cooperative principles that are supposed to rule in a kibbutz. And I also realized how odd such a belief would be regarded by 99.44% of the economists in the West, the Third World, and the then socialist Second World.

"It does move," Galileo whispered under his breath about the globe at his inquisitorial trial for heresy. "But there is a hard core of economic science, rooted in historical experience and plausible deductive entailment. This century can be proud of the depth of understanding it has been able to add to the legacy of earlier centuries." That is what I have to say out loud in my serious moments.

The number one economic problem is the structural budget deficit.

Paul A. Samuelson

There is no evidence that a president has any way of substantially raising the low propensity to save among American families – the central challenge facing the U.S. economy. What a president can do, and has a duty to do, is to reduce the major disincentives to thriftiness associated with current government policies.

Prescription must wait upon diagnosis. The 1981 Reaganomics program of budget director David Stockman, Representative Jack Kemp, and academic publicist Arthur Laffer foundered on its faulty diagnosis that the administration had inherited a disastrous economic Dunkirk. The neo-right supply-siders reasoned that, by removing the deathbed tax chains that were holding down the system, they would unleash a new spirit of productivity improvement and splash the Treasury with budget surpluses. Less of tax rates, proclaimed the Laffer curve, meant more of tax revenues.

Politics aside, there was no warrant in economic history or macroeconomic analysis for this rash program of multiyear, across-the-board tax cuts. Democratic party experts such as the late Walter Heller and President Carter's economic adviser, Charles Schultze, testified before Congress in 1981 that what has happened would happen. To show that economics, poised between an art and a science, is more than a cacophony of ideologues and hired guns serving the business trade associations and labor unions, these Democratic warnings were backed up by mainline Republican economists: Alan Greenspan, subsequently named Paul Volcker's successor as chairman of the Federal Reserve Board; Martin Feldstein, subsequently named President Reagan's second chairman of the Council of Economic Advisers (CEA); Herbert Stein and Paul MacCracken, CEA chairmen for presidents Nixon and Ford.

Controlled experiments are impossible in economics. What the supply-siders practiced, we have to live with. So at century's end, when the new economic history textbooks are written, they will look back on the Reagan legacy in more or less the following terms:

☐ The 1980s have witnessed a basic structural budget deficit of unprecedented magnitude and persistence, averaging a colossal 3% + of the nation's

> **The structural deficit is the devil's recipe for a low-saving American economy.**

gross national product. A "basic" deficit is different from a Keynesian-type "cyclical" deficit in that after the nation returns to full employment, the basic deficit persists at a level that makes the public debt rise as a percentage of GNP – something not seen in the times of Truman, Kennedy, Johnson, Nixon, Ford, or Carter.

☐ Real interest rates – actual money interest rates with the annual inflation rate subtracted out of them – have been higher during the Reagan epoch

Paul A. Samuelson is Institute Professor Emeritus at MIT, a Nobel laureate, and the author of a textbook that has been used to teach economics to college students for the last 40 years.

than at any time since Coolidge and Hoover. Real interest rates were zero or negative in the days of Nixon and Carter. Today, hot and cool money in Japan and Germany lusts for the returns on our Treasury and corporate bonds, and only the risk of dollar depreciation limits the avalanche of their capital exports to us.

Tame the deficit with expenditure cuts and tax increases.

☐ America's balance-of-payment deficit is a new and chronic phenomenon, persisting each year in excess of $100 billion. In 1980, the United States was the world's largest creditor nation, having built up since 1914 a vast cumulative total of net foreign investments. By 1985, we had eaten up all of our patrimony. Three years later, we are the world's largest debtor nation. We have been selling the farm and the shop to foreigners, selling U.S. public debt, office buildings and hotels, big-company common stocks and bonds, branch-plant installations. The most optimistic analysts expect our net foreign indebtedness to be growing into the early 1990s. The pessimists warn against the buildup of interest on interest.

These three cold economic realities are closely related. The proximate cause of chronic balance-of-payments deficits and high real interest rates is the new evil in American life—the basic structural fiscal deficit.

This is not an evil in the sense that it will trigger a recession, in 1989 or at some subsequent date, or that it threatens us with inflation accelerating from trot to canter to double-digit gallop and finally racing to banana-republic hyperinflation.

The evil is more insidious than that. It is a long-term evil. And precisely because it is a long-term evil, the political resolve to cope with it is difficult to forge.

The evil of a basic structural deficit is that it is the devil's recipe for a low-saving American economy, for a low domestic-owned capital formation program. Since the level and growth rate of U.S. standards of living and productivity depend, genuine supply-side economics tells us, on the twin elements of capital formation and new technical knowledge, the long-run evil will outweigh the feared short-run evils of recession and inflation.

Of course, not all the news is alarming. Before completing the current diagnosis out of which new economic prescriptions must stem, let me record the elements of strength in the American economy that President Reagan will bequeath to his successor.

☐ The United States still earns and enjoys the world's highest real income per capita. If we call the U.S. level 100 and do the computations correctly, Canada is next to us in the high 90s. Norway, West Germany, Sweden, and Switzerland are all below 90. Japan is scarcely yet at 80, but slowly catching up with Europe. The Soviet Union is below 50.

☐ Since the OPEC crisis of 1973, the United States has created 33 million new jobs. Jobs for women, jobs for immigrants, jobs for infants of the baby boom now grown up. By comparison, the entire Common Market has created barely 5 million new jobs over the same period. America must be doing something right! True, most of the jobs are in the services sector, and many are modestly paid. But it would be costly hubris to prefer no new jobs rather than to accept wage levels below those of the male union elite in manufacturing and the government sector.

☐ The double-digit annual rates of accelerating inflation that began the 1980s were tamed by Paul Volcker's Federal Reserve tightness—down to current inflation rates averaging around 4%. The cost in terms of two recessions was indeed bloody, but luck has been with us in the continuing moderation of wage settlements since 1984.

☐ The drastic therapy of three years of dollar depreciation (halving the dollar vis-à-vis the Japanese yen and the German mark) has finally made our producers competitive with foreign exporters. Factories turning out Caterpillar tractors in Illinois, Cummins engines in Indiana, and Scott paper in Maine are on round-the-clock shifts. U.S. industry operates at an impressive 83% of capacity, while steel and chemicals are at 97%. Overall U.S. productivity growth has

> Dollar depreciation provides the kind of evenhanded protection that political economy commends.

been disappointing in the years of Reagan supply-side economics, but the Toynbeean challenge of imports has spurred a commendable rate of productivity growth in our manufacturing sector. Dollar depreciation has provided the kind of evenhanded protection that political economy commends. To a degree, it has taken the wind out of the sails of the lobbyists for quotas and tariffs.

☐ Some reduction in cold-war tension moderates the buildup in real defense expenditures that burdens the American productive system. After a steady rise from 1981 at a 6% annual rate, real defense expenditures have already peaked out. The outlook is for no new increases into the next decade, which lightens their ratio to the GNP.

☐ After one soberly discounts the Club of Rome hysteria over imminent limits on growth, rational concern for conservation of the environment can be consistent with continued moderate growth of North American and European living standards well into the next century – at the same time that developing regions of Asia, Africa, and Latin America are improving their life expectancies and amenities of consumption.

The art of policy judgment is putting first things first. The new president's first year in office should concentrate on gradual reduction of the basic structural budget deficit from some 3% of our $4 trillion GNP toward 2%, then 1%, and by 1992 elimination of all of the deficit that is basic and not cyclical.

When Senator George Aiken was asked how America might get out of Vietnam, he replied: "In ships." When asked how to tame a basic deficit, one must answer prosaically: "By expenditure cuts and tax increases."

Our present policy dilemma is not merely, or primarily, a Washington impasse between one political party and the other, between Congress and the White House, between left-of-center and right-of-center politicians frolicking along the Potomac. No, ours is a Main Street dilemma.

We all love low tax rates. We prefer ceilings of 28% to ceilings of 50%, 70%, 77%, or 91%. We all want safe borders and skies secure against nuclear attack. We all want a better and more benign environment. Most of us want to honor promises to future Social Security participants. Many wish to strengthen minimal networks of support against catastrophes of sickness and destitution.

In short, what we want is a configuration of inconsistencies. These inconsistencies must be resolved. Economics does not proclaim that all the correction must be by way of tax increases. Or by way of expenditure elimination. Or by some magic 50-50 combination of each. What is clear to observers of realistic politics is that the impasse will continue – as it did in 1985, 1986, and 1987 – if one bloc insists that all the deficit improvements must come via the route of expenditure controls, while another bloc is just as stubborn in requiring the correction to proceed by way of new taxes.

To a first approximation, it is not crucial economically whether new tax revenues come from a value-added tax, consumption taxes, the closing of loopholes, or increments in top marginal rates from the income tax system. With regard to spending, political compromises may have to give on many fronts. Defense initiatives are not sacrosanct. Farm and entitlement programs are unlikely to remain intact in any successful effort.

The new president, backed by the electoral majority that put him in office, should address the number

> The electorate frightened the candidates away from even discussing vital economic issues.

one economic problem of the basic structural deficit, eschewing the pattern of President Reagan and Speaker O'Neill in the wake of the 1984 election. It would be amusing, if it were not so scandalous, that the electorate has frightened away all candidates from even discussing vital economic issues.

Fortunately, once elected, the new president will not be boxed in by campaign promises and omissions. FDR ran in 1932 on a balanced-budget platform. John F. Kennedy promised the leaders of both houses of Congress that he would try to balance the budget. Franklin Roosevelt was applauded by his depression constituency for changing his programs, and JFK got the country moving again by a judicious dosage of cyclical deficit and tax reduction.

The next president will face the opportunity for leadership when 1989 rolls around.

HARVARD BUSINESS REVIEW November-December 1988

3. Paul A. Samuelson
A Personal View on Crises and Economic Cycles

Economic science is prone to cycles of theoretical fads. Before 1929, pundits believed that prosperity in agriculture was necessary if the economy was to be prosperous. "Food will win the War and write the Peace." That was First World War boilerplate, still being muttered by Jeremiahs of the mid-1920s who warned that hard times on the farms would bring on a world debacle.

After 1929 the saying that Wall Street crashes cause Main Street slumps became dogma. As recently as 1962, when President Kennedy lost his patience with Roger Blough of U.S. Steel, the resulting crack in the Dow Jones indexes was feared to entail a National Bureau recession for the American economy. At least that is what you would have learned if, trapped in any Sheraton Hotel and having exhausted the Moody Bible, you read the autobiography planted there by Ernest Henderson, the founder of the Sheraton hostelry chain and a self-taught expert in macroeconomics. Henderson, exaggerating my Rasputin powers over J. F. Kennedy, called me in to say: "Tell your man that in six months time we'll be in a real bad recession unless he backs down from his business bashing." I solemnly recorded in my little black Coop book that a recession would arrive by November 1962. But such are my powers over the head of state that by that date the GNP was in a nice recovery from its mini-growth-recession of earlier 1962. The post-Blough hiccough in the production index, by the way, was about what Franco Modigliani's MIT-Penn-Fed model predicted ought to result from the realized loss in consumer wealth and from the increase in the cost in investment funds implied by the drop in price/earnings ratios of common stocks.

Flushed with this imposing sample of victory, I had to wonder when Stan Fischer and Bob Merton scolded us economists for not taking the stock market more seriously as a macroeconomic phenomenon. Lay people take it too seriously. But economists, Fischer and Merton complained, do not take it seriously enough. Nonetheless, Modigliani and I discounted after 19 October 1987 the dire predictions that a worldwide recession was in the cards. (So did *all* of the 50 consensus forecasters followed by Blue Chip Indicators.) True, the drop in share wealth in October 1987 was fully the equal of the drop in share wealth in October 1929; and, internationally, the crisis and price attrition was in 1987 even more uniform than in 1929. True also, after 1929 came the worldwide depression that was not to be exorcised completely until World War II itself. However, although Franco and Jim Tobin and Bob Solow and I knew that Model-T Keynesianism had to add wealth magnitudes to its flow determinants, we also knew that it was only vulgar journalists who believed that the 25 percent rates of unemployment in 1933 United States and Germany were Granger-caused by the exits of capitalists from the unleaning towers of Wall Street.

As hundreds of banks failed, runs on 15,000 banks caused many thousands more of them to fail. The velocity of high-powered money rationally nose-dived as people chose to hold more currency and less deposits; the result was that, despite the contrived increase in the total of high-powered money throughout the early 1930s, the total nominal GNP shrank by half from 1929 to 1933. Monetarists, wise in their later time, indicted the Fed authorities for not creating whatever high-powered money it would have taken to keep money × velocity ahead of the eroding price level. Although no one could have beaten such a tautological rap, I concur in the view that departing militantly from orthodox finance in 1931 could have reduced greatly the historical decline in high-powered velocity and thereby saved much human suffering and economic waste.

Then, If Not Now?

Was there ever a cogent case for the thesis that panics and crises play a key role in economic slumps of real output and employment?

If you read the early literature on good times and bad times, you will get the impression that panics and crises were more important in the mechanism of business cycles back in the nineteenth century than they are now or have been since, say, 1913. I doubt that this is a safe guide to reality. Much of the alleged change in the role of panics must surely be an artifact of economists' previous lack of statistical knowledge about true economic history.

John Hicks in his last book exemplifies the fallacy. In *A Market Theory of Money* (Oxford University Press, 1989), Hicks writes: "Nineteenth-century cycles (were) not statistical cycles but a succession of crises" (vii). "I want to insist that this [concept of a statistical cycle] is not what Jevons and his contemporaries can have had in mind. . . . They were thinking of the sequence of trade crises which had marked the preceding half-century, occurring in 1825, 1837 (especially in America), 1847, 1857, and 1867" (94).

The weight of the evidence to me points otherwise. If a Christina Romer were able to go back and construct a representative index for the nineteenth century of real production, employment, price levels, investment, and profits, Lombard Street would perhaps be no more important in understanding Mitchell-type business cycles than Wall Street was in the 1920s or in the 1945–89 period.

Schumpeter hailed Clement Juglar as a great business-cycle pioneer—and named the intermediate business cycle after him—because he was allegedly the first to move from the crisis paradigm to the Mitchell-Hansen paradigm.

Adam Smith prattled about the division of labor in *The Wealth of Nations* without showing in his text any appreciation that the Industrial Revolution was bursting out around him. Nor could he have learned better from his excellent library.

So it was with Henry Thornton and John Stuart Mill. Their chronicles lack power as evidence for my present query: If Wall Street crashes have limited effects on Main Street in the last few decades of the twentieth century, was it truly different in 1929 and 1889 and 1839 and 1789?

I must be careful not to overstate my doubts. It may well have been the case that in earlier times the ratio of the value of stocks and bonds listed on bourses was *less* in relation to national wealth and GNP than in the post–World War II epoch. The Modigliani-Tobin partial derivatives, partial (consumption)/partial (wealth), may also have been smaller then rather than larger. And the effects of Lombard Street on the changes in the cost and availability of funds to finance investment may also have been limited the more we go back in history.

Nonetheless, I do not wish to deny—nay I want positively to emphasize—the fact that before 1930 we were in pure capitalism, whereas in 1987 we are a case of the mixed economy. The ability of a crisis/panic in Wall Street or Lombard Street to tip off a cascade of failures of unregulated banks was assuredly greater in history than it is or has been since 1933. The money supply itself in the old days tended to be a casualty of the crisis in a way that is no longer true. This is major.

Another way of putting things is this. In Gladstone's time, as in the time of Herbert Hoover, there was an effective political presumption toward long-run stability of the price level. Although Britain since 1688 never lived up to its presumption of balanced fiscal budgets, never was there acceptance by the official elite that the gold standard could be ignored as a constraint and that deliberate deficit spending was an admissible and admirable tool of policy.

Why was the prophet Hyman Minsky for so many decades a voice crying out in the wilderness? "A qualitative credit crisis is in the intermediate-term cards. Wolf! Wolf!"

The answer for his long wait has to be found in the laws of behavior of populist democracy in the "Age after Keynes." Every three years when I came to revise my textbook, two main charts would jump off the page to command my attention. One was the trendless behavior of real wages from about 1250 to 1750, followed by a sea change to a rising trend of the real wage rate in the "Age after Newton." The other was the trendless behavior of staple prices in Europe and North America, as postwar deflations undid the peaks of wartime inflation—followed, since 1932 and the "new deals" in America and Europe, by a remorseless upward trend in the cost-of-living index.

On every proper Richter scale, the 1987 crash rivaled that of the 1929 crash. By contrast with journalists, mainstream economists correctly computed that the late-1987 25 percent erosion of worldwide asset values was prone to reduce by about 1 percent per annum the likely 1987–89 growth in global output. Had you told those economists to factor into their IS-LM diagrams the worldwide acceleration of the money supply induced by the October 1987 crash, their regressions would have projected the continuance of the 1982 recovery that history has recorded in 1988–89.

I should not need to say it, but I will say it: Reacting and overreacting to each and every market crisis by macro policy can alter the historic pattern of GNP response to panics. But such Pavlovian responses cannot be guaranteed to give us a pattern of economic history that is aptly described by the Good Fairy who says, "And they lived happily ever afterward, with minimal unemployment, price stability, and growth in output characterized by almost-unit roots." There will return times when markets crash against a background of stagflation. Then engineering more money to prevent drops in real output will add to policy dilemmas connected with increases in prices.

CHAPTER 13

Has Economic Science Improved the System?

Paul A. Samuelson

The fifty years of the Kennedy School's existence, which coincide with the interval of time from Harvard's 300th to 350th anniversary, by good chance also coincide with the Age After Keynes. This is therefore a fitting time to take stock, to review how the macroeconomic system has changed during the crucial half century from 1936 to 1986. Also, a birthday party is an occasion to recall briefly what role Harvard University played in this time of Kuhnian revolution in economic science.

TESTIMONIALS

Yes, the world economy is more stable than it was in pre-1929 capitalism. Yes, the birth of macroeconomics did irreversibly advance the science of political economy, and this new knowledge does deserve some of the credit for the better performance of the economic system. No, the advance has not been uniform in all respects: Mindless societies have long been capable of engineering inflations for themselves; but today the prudent odds *against* long-run stability of the price level have certainly risen.

I base these conclusions on the reading of economic history, consciously resisting the temptations to regard the years of our youth as

---

I owe thanks to the MIT Center for Real Estate Development for financial support and to Aase Huggins for editorial assistance.

the years of the universe's glory. By sheer good luck I was born as an economist when pure capitalism was in its heyday. All of neoclassical economics conspired, so to speak, to produce my teachers—and me. It was Sophie Tucker who said, "I've been rich, I've been poor. Believe me, rich is better." My generation enjoys a priceless advantage: We lived through the revolutionary transition. Later scholars can benefit from the cumulative record, which includes among other things the legacies we leave them. History, however, never gets things right. The immediacy of experience while it is happening—the contrast with what went before with what will happen later—is something which if you don't have it there is no way you can get it.

QUALIFICATIONS: THE PERSISTENCE OF BUSINESS CYCLES

Understatement is the optimal form of emphasis. So please be warned: Business cycles still persist. The best forecasters of output, unemployment, profits, security prices, and price indexes are trained economists. Their batting averages in predicting are better than they were one, two, or three generations ago. But these best batting averages are still not very good; and the trend of their mean-precision is not a hopeful one, showing no asymptotic rendezvous with bullseye accuracy.

The Age of Keynes happens to coincide more or less with the post-World-War II epoch. Suppose you make a plot of annual or quarterly percentage changes in real gross national product. The pre-1940 data look to have been drawn by a different hand than that which penned the post-1945 picture—a more exuberant hand. Growth still moves in fits and starts. But now the fits and starts seem tamer.

Crude tests like these, to be sure, do not count for much in a complex subject like economics. Fluctuations in the production index became perceptibly more virulent in the quarter century after the Federal Reserve was founded in 1913. Yet the monetarist economists who concluded from this that the Federal Reserve was a failure were victims of the post hoc ergo propter hoc fallacy. When other things have not been held constant, one must be wary in attributing causation to changes in the thing that happens to have caught one's eye.

The Kaiser had more to do with World War I than Governor Strong of the Federal Reserve.

Here is a first qualification we must apply to the apparently more stable post-1945 macro behavior. Does it appear stable, merely because the between-the-wars period was so singularly unstable? Not a little of the improvement does seem subject to this discount. But not all.

There is a second trap we must beware of. Someone asked William James what he thought of his brother's post-1900 style as a novelist. William laughed off the question, saying: "There is no new style. It's just that Henry has a new secretary and she doesn't cut out all the digressions the old one used to do." The new hand that plots the post-World-War II data may simply differ idiosyncratically in penmanship and measurement from the old one that limned the pre-World-War II data.

Professor Christina Romer of Princeton University has looked into this issue. In her Ph.D. dissertation comparing modern and earlier methods of measuring unemployment and production changes, Romer showed that some of the putative reduction in cyclical instability was spurious, a figment resulting from cruder estimation procedures used in earlier times.[1] If we used those same procedures to describe the 1970s and 1980s, the resulting time series of macro data would more closely resemble the ups and downs of the pre-Keynesian era.

Romer's readers will be struck by two other deflating points. Services have grown in importance relative to manufactured goods. If services are by their nature less prone to cyclical variations than goods, then even if there have been no improvements in the behavior laws and mechanisms of the market economy, the mean amplitudes of cyclical fluctuations could show a declining trend. To the degree that only this is involved, economists would have no warrant for claiming that their science had yielded real-world successes.

The enlarged role of government in the GNP raises a similar question. My Harvard mentor Alvin Hansen, leading fiscal scholar of a generation ago, hypothesized that dollars of public expenditure would be less prone to oscillate cyclically than dollars of private expenditure. So he would have expected the mixed economy to evolve toward greater cyclical stability than undiluted capitalism would. Although Hansen was rightly called the American Keynes and the most prolific architect of policy implications from Keynes's 1936 *General Theory*, he would cheerfully have acknowledged that the new paradigms of macroeconomics deserved only part of the credit for the worldwide growth spurt in the second third of the twentieth century.

Incidentally, historians of thought have failed to note Hansen's claim that the stagnation he feared for a mature *laissez-faire* society had been considerably exorcized by growth of the public sector in the modern mixed economies. To a reader of Romer, Alvin Hansen would say from beyond the grave: "Since one of the scientific reasons for advocating a mixed rather than a *laissez-faire* economy was its discerned greater macro stability, it is not fair to treat the expanded role of government as a mere happenstance like that of the expanded weight of services in the GNP." Fair enough. But the knife cuts two ways. When we come to examine the swollen rates of unemployment in present-day welfare states like Denmark and the Netherlands, we must debit them and certain pathologies of stagflation against the mixed economies that Hansen's generation helped to promote.

The reduced importance of agriculture in the modern economy ought, I think, to increase the cyclical variability of the GNP and magnify the task of macroeconomic stabilizers. I say this because the variability of farm quantities tends to respond to a different drumbeat than the trade cycle—to weather, pestilence and the like. The total *value* of farm production tends toward relative stability; flexibility in the prices that farm goods fetch at auction permits quantities produced to resist the business cycle. By contrast, when natural rubber in Malay gets replaced by synthetic rubber produced by a Fortune 500 company, a drop in demand causes whole plants to be shut down, with the implied swings in production and in employment. All the more credit therefore to macro management if Christina Romer does not observe a rising trend in cyclical amplitude in the post-1929 Galbraithian world of *Fortune's* favorites.

Geoffrey Moore, the chronicler of the business cycle at the National Bureau of Economic Research, observed that recoveries have lasted longer and recessions have ended sooner in the years since World War II. Those same miracle years, however, involved higher *mean* growth rates for Europe, North America, and the Pacific Basin. Moore does not consider a period recessionary unless output declines absolutely. If years of growth recession were tallied, we would find that the economy has been in recession roughly half the time since the war, as it was in the years before, and (almost by definition) half the time in expansion. We moderns should congratulate ourselves only if the lengths of *complete* cycles rise and, more important, the mean shortfall from potential GNP is reduced. By this better measure, some of the postwar improvement in performance must have been lost since 1973 in most of the OECD economies.

To sum up: Even after allowing for the special virulence of the interwar years, my judgment is that the post-1945 economy is performing better macroeconomically than the pre-1920 economy. Depressions, like those of 1893, 1873, and 1836–41, are less likely to reoccur and be allowed to persist. (The macroeconomics of World War II itself was greatly shaped by post-Keynesian knowledge as well, and was distinctly better than macroeconomics of World War I, the Civil War, or the Napoleonic Wars.) On reflection, I believe we owe much to scholars who scientifically elaborated the inadequacies of neutral-money dogmas in less than long-run economic scenarios. My own work has benefited from Keynes's changing the emphasis away from ups-and-downs around some "normal" level and toward attaining the growth in potential GNP achievable through high employment and a fuller realization of that potential. A price has been paid for this benefit: In a system where the good news from stimulus comes before the bad news, the temptation toward overambitious activism bedevils modern democracies.

THE DOG THAT WAGS THE TAIL

An anthropologist visiting from Mars will find our world very different from the world of 1929 or 1932. A toll of bank failures that would have caused chains of bankruptcies in 1931, the observing anthropologist would now find, creates imperceptible waves in Wall Street and not even a ripple in the GNP accounts. Some scholars have grown from youth into maturity warning about the wolf of a credit breakdown. The shocks of OPEC, the chicaneries of the oil patch and real estate manias, and political crises around the globe have provided raw material for a conflagration that could make the crises of 1929–31 look like an innocent flicker in a fireplace. Yet Cassandra's hour has never come.

Is the Age of Keynes so very different from the past? Maynard Keynes blew his own horn and the horns of all of us scholars who itch for the power to affect the world and to improve its well-being by virtue of our scientific breakthroughs. His much-quoted rhetoric caters to our vanity and dreams of glory:

> ... [T]he ideas of economists and political philosophers, both when they are right and when they are wrong, are more powerful than is commonly understood. Indeed the world is ruled by little else. Practical men, who believe themselves to be quite exempt from any intellectual influences, are usually the slave of some defunct economist.... Soon or late, it is ideas, not vested interests, which are dangerous for good or evil.[2]

This is heady stuff, exquisitely brewed. But is it believable? Consider the New Deal of Franklin Delano Roosevelt. It was an example par excellence of deficit spending. Was this, though, because some past ideologue had captured the mind of the new president? Certainly FDR learned nothing in his economic classes under Professor Frank Taussig at Harvard University to push policy in this direction. It was the Great Depression itself that made him renege on his campaign promises to balance the federal budget. To be sure, there is always an academic witch doctor readily at hand to rationalize whatever the prince wants to do. In 1933 it happened to be G. F. Warren, a Cornell farm economist who turned up with confused statistical proof that the price level would inevitably rise if only FDR lifted the buying price the U.S. paid for gold. Only later did Keynes have an interview with Roosevelt, which both dashed Keynes's expectations for the president's economic literacy and left FDR quite unimpressed.

A Roosevelt was no more needed to create a depression deficit than a Newton or a Leibniz was needed to invent calculus, which essentially created itself when the time was ripe. What great hero invented the English language? Surely not Samuel Johnson or Noah Webster, nor even William Shakespeare or the Earl of Oxford.

From earliest times, business recessions unbalanced budgets. Not until 1937 or later did a self-consciously Keynesian clique have any influence in the New Deal regime. In lecturing on various continents, I used to play down the bogeyman of another 1929-32 crash and financial crisis by arguing, "We in populist democracy have eaten fruit of the tree of *knowledge* and there is no going back to Herbert Hoover's undiluted capitalism, etc., etc." Once the electorate got the taste of apple in its mouth, the niceties of science were no longer required. If printing bits of green paper can keep 15,000 banks from going bust, the paper will be printed no matter which political party controls the White House. It is easy for a monetarist historian to look back at the years of the banking crisis and regard as silly the Federal Reserve's concern in 1931 for the adequacy of its gold reserves; easy indeed to imagine might-have-been scenarios in which the Fed created whatever supply of new reserves was needed to offset the decline in our total money supply occasioned by frightened people's converting their bank deposits to currency. But such bold departures from the conventional wisdom were never on the agenda. Academics who insisted on them would have risked losing their relevance and influence as well as being categorized with the easy-money cranks we have always with us.

Keynes was not completely wrong about scientific ideas and public policies. But he exaggerated. The Reagan administration provides a fine example. I can find no relation between the president's State of the Union messages and the prosaic studies of growth by our leading scientific authorities such as Harvard's late Nobelist, Simon Kuznets, or Edward Denison, the author of the definitive study *Trends in American Economic Growth, 1929-1982.*[3]

THAT GOLDEN AGE

Harvard has played an honorable role in the macrorevolution of 1936 to 1986. After Alvin Hansen was called to the first professorship of the Littauer School of Public Administration in 1936—later to become the Kennedy School of Government—Harvard experienced a renaissance in macroeconomics. Reviewing the definitive study commissioned in 1948 by the American Economic Association, *A Survey of Contemporary Economics*, George Stigler ironically complained that the old-school crimson tie was everywhere, in the choice of authors and in the authorities cited.

Before the Littauer School was established, little important work in modern macroeconomics had been done at Harvard. The joint volume on the *Economics of the Recovery Program*, put out by Joseph Schumpeter, Wassily Leontief, Edward Mason, Seymour Harris, Edward Chamberlin, O. H. Taylor, and other younger Harvard faculty, documents the sad irrelevance of neoclassical economics for the Great Depression.[4]

A fiftieth birthday party is a time for nostalgia and celebration. John Williams, the first dean of the Littauer School, formed with

Alvin Hansen a remarkable duo. If to teach is to affirm, then Williams should have become a banker full time. But if to teach is to raise doubt, Williams was a brilliant success. Actually, Williams' cracker-barrel, seemingly relaxed manner made him a splendid teacher. He recruited hundreds of undergraduates to major in economics.

Inevitably Hansen, the pioneer of a new scientific paradigm, stole the show and attracted the bulk of the graduate students destined to become eminent. Robert Roosa, Paul Volcker, and Henry Wallich (who was in both camps) are only a few of the proteges Williams launched at the Federal Reserve Bank of New York, where from the early 1930s to mid-century Williams was vice president and research sage.

If people who need people are the happiest people in the world, then this first Kennedy School dean ought to have been miserable. Actually, he was merely reserved and aloof—almost indolent as a good dean who is determined to maintain his creative scholarship should be. After his retirement, Williams lived for decades as a recluse from colleagues and students.

It does both Hansen and Williams enormous credit that they never undercut each other in the classroom or outside. It was rarely like this in the continental universities and certainly not in the London School of Economics, Cambridge, and Chicago bullpens, where the disciples of the competing stars were pitted against one another not merely on class and ideological issues but also on mundane questions of methodology. Needless to say, the incivility of the 1965 to 1975 era was never dreamed of, even by the warring Oxford dons.

Since Hansen had the disproportionate power for aggression, I suppose he merits the greater praise. Still, it would have been understandable if Williams had nursed resentment that his turf had been taken over. And yet that private individual could say, on the occasion of both men's retirement, that Alvin Hansen had been the best friend he had ever had in academic life. God bless!

Besides Hansen and Williams, Harvard in that golden age had Gottfried Haberler, Joseph Schumpeter, Seymour Harris, and Sumner Slichter as sage macroeconomists. Good students of any bent could find a role model to emulate.

After Edward Mason became Dean of the Littauer School, it finally became more than simply an augmentation of the resources available to the economics and government departments. His leadership, and that of Don Price, takes me beyond my period and beyond macroeconomics as such.

THE MIXED-ECONOMY MIRACLE

By the time Joseph Schumpeter died in 1950, he had become perhaps the world's most cited economist. His 1942 *Capitalism, Socialism and Democracy* made many valuable observations on the passing of *laissez faire* and the march to socialism.[5] Within and between its lines were warnings on problems to come for the welfare state.

Yet Schumpeter failed to realize how dynamic the mixed economies—his "capitalism in an oxygen tent"—would prove to be in the 1945 to 1970 period. Never before or since has global real output grown so rapidly and enduringly.

Like leaders of the school of rational expectationists (the new Classical school), Schumpeter believed that prices and wages adjust to clear markets without inflicting on the economy lasting unemployment or excess capacity. The markets get it right; government can do little good and much harm. (To Schumpeter's credit, he did foresee periods of unemployment longer than those admitted in the models of Robert Lucas, Thomas Sargent, Robert Barro, and other leading rational expectationists.)

How could a Robert Lucas or a Joseph Schumpeter account for miraculous 1945 to 1970 growth? If markets were clearing in 1929 to 1939, how could the kiss of monetary demand achieve postwar miracles? For that matter, how could the rearming of Hitler's Germany wipe out the 25 percent unemployment rate in the depressed economy he took over?

Lucas's followers have to attribute any Federal Reserve success in expanding output to the fact that their monetary expansion catches the market by surprise. Participants in the world economy might be said to be pleasantly surprised by the first mindless pump primings of Hitler and Roosevelt. But what everyone comes to expect year after year can hardly be considered unanticipated or transitory. The crude fact described in econometric terms by Northwestern's Robert J. Gordon—that for more than a century each 1 percent change in nominal GNP decomposes in the short run into 2/3 percent change in real output and 1/3 percent change in price level—accords ill with the Schumpeter-Lucas presumption in favor of Say's law, which denies that any underutilization of resources, much less mass unemployment, can persist. Wesley Mitchell and the empirical business cycle theorists, who along with the Fisher-Wicksell quantity theorists were the only Model T macroeconomists in the neoclassical paddocks, simply ignored Walrasian clearing-of-the-market concepts when they confronted the facts of business cycle history.

Rational expectationists can produce (1) a model in which cyclical variations in output are due solely to subjective desires to substitute at one time more leisure for bread and at another time more bread for leisure. Alternatively, (2) they can produce a model in which a typical intervention, such as a devaluation, expands an economy only because it has not been anticipated and cheats workers of what they had expected. But this does not compel me as an observer of the successful 1936 Belgian devaluation to believe a classicist story that in 1935 Belgian workers wanted leisure whereas in 1937 they wanted to work, nor that Swedish workers were taken by surprise when their real wage fell in consequence of the new Labor Government's contrived 1983 devaluation of the *krona*, a fact about austerity that had been explained to them in advance of the act. However, my refusal to read into the real world the model of the rational-expectationists' seminar room should not blind me to the fact of experience: Competitive advantage from a 1986 devaluation is likely to be less lasting than from a 1936 devaluation of the same magnitude.

The most flagrantly optimistic forecast for the Federal Reserve before the 1974 debacle came from a leading economist using his rational expectation paradigm. When the DRI forecasting service provided its clients with projections based upon rational-expectationist models, the errors of estimate were enormously large. The infamous Laffer-Ransom forecast of the Nixon Treasury was, I believe, the first quantitative rational-expectationist forecast. A post mortem done in 1980 by Thomas Sargent on the 1923 German hyperinflation suggested that a stabilization, if creditable, could be accomplished with minimal unemployment and distress. A reader of this assessment would have been poorly prepared to understand the 1980 to 1983 crusade against inflation by Carter and Reagan. Even less prepared would that reader be for the qualitative and quantitative features of the so far successful Israel program against inflation since mid-1985.

Those who estimate the structural coefficients of the MIT-Penn-FRB model have not seen their coefficients self-destruct, as the Lucas critique ordains they should. The true causal structure of the economy can only be conjectured of course, but the system's recent responses to Federal Reserve actions generally accord better with older textbook macroeconomics than was the case in the early 1970s. I must warn, though, that in the future steady state, fine-tuning by the Fed cannot be counted on to work as exquisitely as it did in mid-1982 to mid-1983. Then Wall Street wanted to believe in the prospect that extra M (money) would largely impinge on Q (quantities) and not on P (prices), and would thus lower rather than raise interest rates and stocks' earnings yields.

I turn now from critiques of stabilization programs by rational expectationists to critiques by monetarists. Experience shows that money does matter. It does not follow, though, that money alone matters. Nor that a rule of constancy in the growth rate of the M-supply is the best we can hope to have. Past great economists, Hawtrey of England and Cassel of Sweden, believed that central bank expansion of M in 1930-31 could have done much to forestall some of the excesses of the Great Depression. But to agree with them on this does not oblige me to believe the monetarist tenet that in a period like 1938-39 monetary policy would have equal potency to raise GNP and that fiscal policy would lack such potency. Let me explain the matter in common-sense terms.

In 1938-39 the Treasury bill rate of interest was often minimal: 3/8 of 3/8 of 1 percent. Suppose the Fed then engaged in an open-market purchase, its principal weapon to expand the money supply. It spits out new M in exchange for taking in Treasury bills. Maybe it pushes the interest rate down to 3/8 of 3/8 of 3/8 of 1 percent. To what good? When monetary policy pushes on a string, the new M it creates induces a drop in the velocity of circulation, V. The product, MV (i.e., the GNP) is only little increased.

Keynes gave economists a good handle on this. But that is not reason for Keynesians to get frozen in such deep-depression mindsets; and the Modiglianis, Tobins, Musgraves, Solows, and other post-Keynesians did react to changes in the feel of the system in the 1940s and 1950s to make their paradigm eclectic. Having an open mind does not, however, mean having an empty one. Recognizing that M changes MV does not require one to swallow the monetarist rejection of neoclassicism in favor of the odd belief that when fiscal policy raises interest rates, this will have negligible effects on V and hence negligible effects on GNP.

Were discretionary judgments made by the Federal Reserve under Eccles, Martin, Burns, and Volcker generally perverse or beneficial in the 1936 to 1986 period? Factoring out democracy's insistence upon aiming for an unemployment level lower than the economy can accommodate without inflation, I feel the report card is a modestly good one. It is politically naive to believe that a steady-money-growth rule was on the feasible menu of choice or that by embracing such a rule we could have achieved price-level stability and a downward trend in the system's natural rate of unemployment.

Monetarism has not been so interesting a scientific development as rational expectationism. One preoccupation of today's young economists is to construct plausible micro foundations for macro paradigms. When the *General Theory* was in its first year, we economists recognized that the emperor had sparse micro clothes. We soon found we could live with that. Better a foundationless macro that allowed us to grasp the macro facts than a paradigm with impeccable foundations that lacked relevance. Sticky wages and imperfect competition, along with plenty of Pareto non-optimality, were prices of admission we were prepared to pay in order to play the best wheel in town.

Much useful work has been done in the last dozen years exploring and devising better micro foundations. (Example: Once you put the wage itself into the production function relating output and labor input, new comparative statistics can arise and some of the observed rigidities become illuminated.) It is not clear, however, that the improvements in foundations have done very much to enable our superstructures to accomplish *their* function more effectively—to provide better hypotheses concerning present and future behavior of the macro system under alternative policy scenarios. I am an optimist. I have faith that hard work by intelligent people, subject to ruthless peer review, will bear fruit as well as light. Experience has convinced me that the sterilities and puerilities of a subject will not be corrected by hostile criticism from sages. Rather, corrections will have to come from within.

SOUR FRUITS OF THE WELFARE STATE

The long duration of the postwar miracle is more surprising than its occurrence. As early as 1945 Alvin Hansen and Lord Beveridge predicted that postwar full-employment economies would encounter rising price levels whenever a free labor market had to cope with full utilization. Before I heard of the famous Phillips Curve relating price-level changes to the rate of unemployment,[6] I doubted the compatibility of really full employment, free markets, and stationary price levels. Indeed Joan Robinson, in her 1937 *Essays on Employment*, had criticized Keynes's optimism that the wage and price level would not rise until some full-employment level had been reached.[7]

By the mid-1960s inflation was accelerating worldwide, presaging the passing away of the postwar miracle. It was the recurrent fact of stagflation, and not newly validated monetarist findings concerning the stability of money's velocity of circulation, that undermined the popularity and self-confidence of post-Keynesians.

A better way of putting the problem is this. The transfer programs of the welfare state were drastically reducing the ability of economic slack to restrain inflation. Unemployment levels that good people considered intolerable were already too low for maintaining price stability. So-called natural rates of unemployment had become ethically unnatural because of the ever-weightier transfer-welfare programs of Scandinavian, Dutch, British, and North American societies.

As an example, consider black male unemployment. During and immediately after World War II, unemployment was lower for black males than for white males. Since 1960 the story is quite the reverse. Short-run stimuli to aggregate demand can reduce the reported unemployment rates among young black males. But to get those rates down to what any humanitarian would consider a decent, tolerable level would require demand-stimulus policies guaranteed to produce accelerating rates of inflation.

The welfare state in this sense self-destructs. People learn how to adjust to the new rules of the game, and these days they learn faster than they used to. Every mainstream economist should recognize that effects on price levels are not as long delayed as they were in the past. But this is not to deny the usefulness of the paradigm suggesting that money does not affect real quantities, at least not in the short run, and that deviations from such neutrality can only be the result of people's being one-time cheatable in their expectations.

The official data on inequality of incomes show great constancy between 1945 and 1985, with a bit more inequality in the last part of the period (albeit less than at the 1929 apotheosis of capitalism). I believe that true inequality, measured over people's entire lifetimes, has significantly decreased in the mixed economy. More people went to bed hungry, more children had rickets because their parents were unlucky or feckless, when I began my economic studies than is the case today in North America and Europe. This is not the outcome of the *laissez-faire* market economy. It is the effect of government's second-guessing the pre-tax imputations of incomes. All such interventions exact their toll in distortions and inefficiencies. A social welfare function that values minimal living standards for all will accept some such inefficiencies: What is worth accomplishing is worth paying for.

Particularly in northern Europe, populist democracy may have pushed the welfare state beyond what the society would prefer if the true tradeoffs were understood. Certainly the post-1973 quickening of inflation around the globe tended to increase the fraction of the GNP passing through the public purse. The shift occurred insidiously, with no town meetings held to deliberate the issues and produce a considered public consensus. Taxpayer revolts and swings to the right may reflect this overshoot. As a professional economist I cannot pontificate on the value judgments here involved.

Students of economic history can address such positivistic questions as whether the welfare states have reached limits of taxation and whether the GNP growth rates that Edward Denison measures are critically reduced by over-high marginal tax rates. When top marginal income-tax rates were 91 percent or 77 percent or 70 percent, the apparent Kuznets-Denison productivity growth rates in the OECD nations were not perceptibly lower than when top rates were 50 percent or less.

The Reagan era has significantly lowered lifecycle tax burdens on the affluent half of the populace, both absolutely and in comparison with the burden on the other half. This charge has not produced a renaissance in entrepreneurship or true supply-side effectiveness, nor does any significant improvement in these trends seem likely by the end of the century. People do react to after-tax incentives, and any good economist can devise a tax system that, other things equal, should somewhat improve America's supply-side performance in the last dozen years of the century. But these are small-scale effects except under utopian assumptions.

My concern about the mixed economy is far broader than the level of marginal income-tax rates or the double taxation of saving in comparison with a single taxing of consumption. When a corporation in Italy or Norway, whether publicly or privately owned, is pressured to continue hiring people to produce goods for which there is no commercial market, the whole purpose of economic life may become insidiously perverted. And this may happen in such a way that no one will be able to tell how far the society has drifted from using its resources to satisfy the desires and needs of its populace.

The reduction in national thrift that results from providing social security to people on a pay-as-you-go basis can be offset, if that be desired, by a budgetary surplus. More worrisome is the question of whether most people really want to be retired by the age of sixty-five or whether this odd fact of life is the artifact of public and private pension arrangements that heedlessly load the dice in favor of self-fulfilling habits and trends favoring very early retirement.

Since 1973 productivity growth has slowed all over the world, Japan being no exception. We Americans naturally look for scapegoats to explain our lagging performance. One view in vogue around 1980 was provided by Harvard Business School professors Robert H. Hayes and William J. Abernathy, under the provocative title "Managing Our Way to Economic Decline."[8] Their culprits are business executives trained at Harvard, Stanford, and Wharton to apply present-discounted-value algorithms in deciding investment programs. Hayes and Abernathy see contemporary managers as today-minded, myopic to all but tomorrow's rise in the Wall Street price of their corporation's stock. How different from the long-sighted Japanese executives, who are quite innocent of mathematical techniques and work while we sleep to rob us of our traditional markets.

I know of no cogent evidence for the Hayes-Abernathy thesis, not even good anecdotes—I mean, case studies. The capital-budgeting techniques based on present-discounted-value computations are devised precisely to render unto the distant future its proper due: If and only if a project meets the common standard set by other projects can it justify its existence. Such modern algorithms correct for the genuine myopia involved in old-fashioned payout-period rules of thumb ("only if *A* pays for itself in 3 years will we invest in it").

Admittedly, much high-paid Wall Street talent spends much time on first organizing conglomerate mergers and then engineering leveraged buyouts that spin off corporate components. Whether that talent could have alternative uses in pushing slide rules or forging better mousetraps we can leave moot. Let me merely suggest that a Boone Pickens finds his easiest pickings when a Roger Blough insists on plowing back into low-profitability steel investment the funds accruing to owners of steel firms. Corporate raiders may sometimes be led by Adam Smith's invisible hand to accomplish Pareto-optimality wonders.

Valid supply-side economics, as against the snakeoil kind, stresses capital formation (which includes more than equipment), natural resources, and knowledge (engineering and managerial knowhow along with basic science). I suspect that the GNP value of higher education has been exaggerated by the writers on human capital who fail to recognize that educational certification is important primarily as a form of signaling. In an affluent society where children spell less well and enjoy more copious civil liberties, why should the use of marijuana stop at the factory gate or the office door? The residual in the production function that can be positive can also be negative. The Uncle Tom, who was an exploited object, was a worker profit-seekers would want to employ. While a sociological revolution is in process, the producer's surplus from inputs rising in the scale of human dignity may sometimes languish.

Instead of creating a paradise, generous income transfers have left Greenland Eskimos prey to the discontents that come with lack of purpose. Nor is this problem limited to esoteric cultures. All human societies evolved under Adam's curse of the need to earn one's bread. As science lightens that burden for people in the advanced nations, and as the collusions we call government take on an ever-larger share of crucial decisionmaking, a people can do to itself what good intentions have done to the aborigines.

In summary, although economics has thus far accomplished much, there is much still to do. Political economy can use scholars with the wisdom of Joseph Schumpeter and the vision of Martin Luther King.

NOTES

1. Christina Romer, "Spurious Volatility in Historical Unemployment Data," *Journal of Political Economy* 94, no. 1 (February 1986): 1-37.
2. John Maynard Keynes, *General Theory of Employment, Interest and Money* (New York: Harcourt, Brace and Co., 1936).
3. Edward F. Denison, *Trends in American Economic Growth, 1929-1982* (Washington, D.C.: The Brookings Institution, 1985).
4. Douglas V. Brown et al., *Economics of the Recovery Program* (New York: McGraw-Hill, 1934).
5. Joseph Schumpeter, *Capitalism, Socialism and Democracy* (New York: Harper and Brothers, 1947).

6. Alban W. Phillips, "The Relation between Unemployment and the Rate of Change of Money Wage Rates in the United Kingdom 1861–1957," *Economica* (November 1958).
7. Joan Robinson, *Essays in the Theory of Employment* (New York: Macmillan, 1937).
8. Robert H. Hayes and William J. Abernathy, "Managing Our Way to Economic Decline," *Harvard Business Review* 58, no. 4 (July–August 1980).

CHAPTER 17

Thoughts on the Stockholm School and on Scandinavian economics

PAUL A. SAMUELSON[1]

We are gathered to celebrate the fiftieth anniversary of something, that something being what Bertil Ohlin defined in 1937 as the Stockholm School. At the same time we could be said to be celebrating the fiftieth birthday of Erik Lundberg's 1937 book, *Studies in the Theory of Economic Expansion.* Or, becoming more personal, we are celebrating also the fiftieth anniversary of Erik Lundberg's thirtieth birthday and thereby acknowledging his three score and twenty milestone.

On this occasion I do not want to focus primarily on the single big question: Did that collective called the Stockholm School independently generate the same paradigm that Keynes published in his 1936 *General Theory of Employment, Money and Interest?* Bertil Ohlin certainly claimed that to be the case in his famous *Economic Journal* articles of 1937. Abba Lerner (1940) and Don Patinkin (1978, 1982) have documented their disagreements with this Ohlin claim, and I must record a measure of agreement with their objective discountings.

I find it useful to broaden my discussion. Stockholm is one city in Sweden, and Sweden is one country in Scandinavia, a region whose scholars understand each others' languages. I believe that Scandinavian economics is a useful category to survey and analyze. At the least, it was that prior to the mid-twentieth century when English became the lingua franca for economic science pretty much everywhere in the world.

Teleologists postulate that if our coat sleeves contain buttons, they must have been put there by the Darwinian gods for a purpose. Separation of the species must, by similar reasoning, perform an ecological function. Differentiation of languages has since the time of the Tower of Babel permitted different places to have somewhat different scientific and scholarly traditions.

This has disadvantages and advantages. During World War II in the U.S. scientific defense establishment, there was sometimes a deliberate design to set independent research parties working on the same task.

They might even be prohibited from communicating with each other, lest the chance originality of a fresh approach be inhibited. Working against this Balkanization was of course any economy of scale in research. Ideally, the best of both worlds might perhaps be attained by use of a referee, who learns all that each source discovers but only selectively communicates to any what is deemed best for them to know. F. Y. Edgeworth at the turn of the century was just such an economist referee.

The separate languages of English, French, German, Dutch, Russian, and Swedish-Danish-Norwegian willy-nilly used to occasion something of such a mixed pattern of decentralization and centralization in economics. Educated scholars knew their own language and one or more universal tongues, such as Latin, French, or English. But knowing a foreign language and being really comfortable in it are different things. Clifford Truesdell, editor of Euler's works and a rational mechanist, has regretted that science abandoned the easy renaissance Latin that was the Esperanto for Newton and Euler.

Spatial localization, even within one language, can produce and sustain some differentiations of emphasis: The Austrian Deductive School begun by Carl Menger, so different from the German Historical Schools, provides a case in point. The universities of northernmost Europe gained in unity of viewpoint from their unity of language. And yet, with the possible unimportant exception of Finland, the German and English tongues were sufficiently similar to those of Scandinavia to keep the various subcultures interconnected.

As far as the world of scholarship is concerned, the fifty years just gone by have tipped the previous pattern of differentiation in the direction of an all-encompassing English. A Maurice Allais who writes only in French may risk his right to a fair hearing, and involved here is the language of Voltaire and Benjamin Franklin. Once upon a time a young scholar published his less-than-best articles in the local-language journal. Or she might have two reputations: the one first earned at home, and the same one earned abroad.

Much that once upon a time was now no longer obtains. We have added some geographically dispersed academic journals in English and lost some native-language journals. The process is a self-perpetuating, self-aggravating one. The less modern students know non-English languages, the less they need to know them. More gets translated into English. More gets originally published in English. If a generation of scholars go off on a tangent, or stagnate, they tend to do so everywhere together. The flame of civilization does not burn on in Timbuktu or Copenhagen when it is flickering away in Cambridge or Rome. When one species dominates all of nature, the risk of extinction when the environment rolls new dice is hardly reduced.

The broad view

For almost a century Swedish economics has been first rate. The quartet of Knut Wicksell, Gustav Cassel, Eli Heckscher, and David Davidson compares well with Britain's Francis Edgeworth, Maynard Keynes, Alfred Marshall, and A. C. Pigou; with America's Irving Fisher, John Bates Clark, Frank Taussig, and Frank Knight; with Austria's Carl Menger, Eugen von Böhm-Bawerk, Josef Schumpeter, and Friedrich von Wieser; with Italy's Vilfredo Pareto, Enrico Barone, and Maffeo Pantaleoni; and with France's Léon Walras, A. A. Cournot, and Jules Dupuit.

The first Swedish giants begot new Scandinavian stars: Bertil Ohlin, Erik Lindahl, Gunnar Myrdal, Ragnar Frisch (of Norway), and Erik Lundberg, to name just a few.

Moreover, Sweden after 1930 was moving into the stage of State Interventionism. The prescriptions of economists were in demand. Nature abhors a vacuum. And if academic economists will not fill that demand, a kind of Gresham's Law will operate to call forth a requisite supply from elsewhere. Swedish academic economists were only too eager in the first half of this century to supply political advice and activism. After Britain was forced to devalue the pound in September of 1931, Scandinavia detached from the old gold parities with her. And this gave Swedish economists the opportunity to prescribe internal macroeconomic stimulation. In the end, as Seymour Harris (1936) was one of the first to discern, the 1931 devaluation was not so much a beggar-my-neighbor tort by Britain and the Sterling Bloc against France, Belgium, and the United States as it was the liberating device that permitted the Sterling Bloc to engineer internally their early autonomous recovery: What importing they ceased to do by virtue of the depreciation-induced dearness of imports was largely offset by the incremental demand for imports occasioned by their incremental level of aggregate income. In Sweden even the conservatives Cassel and Heckscher were money activists in the depression, to the nation's benefit.

The four economists who were commissioned in late 1931 by the Committee on Unemployment – Ohlin, Myrdal, Hammarskjöld, and Johansson – and who published their separate results in the 1933–5 period, were all de facto effective-demand economists. I only wish I knew Swedish so that I could compare their intuitions with those of heterodox contemporaries in Europe and North America. Nor should we make too much of the testimony of Ernst Wigforss, the laborite finance minister after 1932, that he was little affected by Sweden's domestic economists. That is standard drill. Roosevelt's Secretary of the Treasury, Henry Morgenthau, Jr., was if anything anti-Keynesian. And most 1933–6 New Deal policies relied little on respectable macroeconomic analysis. Nonetheless, the influence of Lauchlin Currie, Alvin Hansen, and Keynesianism was important for 1936–80 American fiscal policy. Live, as well as dead, economists have influence that those influenced are not always fully aware of.

A formal theory of output as a whole

Bertil Ohlin was not a shrinking violet when it came to making claims for the originality of either his international trade innovations or his macroeconomic innovations. I judge Bertil to be less diffident in this regard than Knut Wicksell was. Knut valued himself, I am sure, but at this moment the only explicit claim for originality that I can recall his making was in connection with his 1923 assertion concerning the detection of alleged logical error in Ricardo in his third edition's chapter on machinery where David contended that a viable invention could depress a society's real gross equilibrium product. Wicksell (1923 and 1981, p. 201) remarks, "I may be mistaken but as far as I know I am myself the first who has pointed out that Ricardo's conclusion as to a possible diminution of the gross product is *wrong*." [It is ironical that Knut happens to be incorrect on this point, as is argued in Samuelson (1988, 1989)!]

Gustav Cassel by contrast was notorious for his excessive immodesties and his unannounced borrowings from others. Fate has taken a cruel revenge. Both in Scandinavia and abroad Cassel is, I believe, valued below his true worth, which certainly puts him in the first ten of the turn-of-the-century scholars. If we devise a coefficient for blowing one's own horn, and put Gustav at 100 and Knut at 5, I fear Bertil must be placed around 30. That means his contentions do need careful auditings. Prior to refreshing my impressions from Lerner and Patinkin, on rereading Ohlin (1937) I was struck by the following thoughts.

Wicksell's price-level preoccupation

Ohlin exaggerated, I believe, when he wrote (1937, p. 53) that Wicksell's 1898 classic and his later writings contained "the embryo of a 'theory of output as whole.'" If we write nominal output as PQ, my recent rereadings of Wicksell surprised me by his preoccupation with the P factor to the neglect of the Q. Wicksell rashly advocated restoration of exchange parities after World War I, playing down the toll on Q to be expected from an overvalued currency. His polemics with Ricardo espouse curing unemployment by having wage rates float downward to clear markets – in simple Say's Law fashion. Wicksell's business cycle theory was concerned with Spiethoff-like exogenous technical shocks, resonating with the system's endogenous natural periodicities (like a child's rocking horse, as he put it). Wicksell's well-known cumulative processes, which Ohlin and his generation are so concerned with, primarily involve longtime trends in dP/dt that will result from discrepancies between Wicksell's natural interest rate and the market interest rate. Those few passages in Wicksell's writings that go beyond this are to me remarkable for their rarity.

Wicksell was a *quantity theory* economist. He says so and Ohlin's generation would be wrong to deny this. Wicksell does go beyond those who regard M as purely exogenous and V as constant in a $PQ = MV$ tautology. Systematic discrepancies between the natural and market interest rates drive M upward (or downward); and any resulting trend for the right-hand side of the tautology, Wicksell regards as working its effects chiefly on the trend in P and not primarily or systematically on Q.

When Wicksell emphasized alterations in "credit," engineered by the banks even when the total of metal M was little changing, he does seem to have in the back of his mind a theory of augmentable V velocity. In terms of Irving Fisher's 1911 identity

$$PQ = MV + M'V'$$

where these velocities are altered to be "income" rather than "transaction" velocities, and where M' is some kind of *bank* money. Wicksell did seem to believe that the PQ/M ratio was manipulatable by engineering *market* interest rates above or below *real interest rates in natura.* But it is fatal to Ohlin's claims concerning pre–*General Theory* innovations that Wicksell regarded contrived variations in the right-hand side of either tautology as having its effects almost exclusively on the P factor alone. What Wicksell liked about Irving Fisher's macroeconomics was not his suggestive debt-deflation theory of depressions or his money-illusion preoccupation. Rather it was primarily to improve Fisher's gimmicks for stabilizing P that Wicksell concerned himself in writing for the *Quarterly Journal of Economics* an article that F. W. Taussig refused just prior to World War I.

Ohlin tries to make something of the fact that Wicksell, and later his protégé Erik Lindahl, speak of PQ as being determined by a flow of spending out of "income." Arthur Marget, I seem to recall, found similar turns of phrase in Ralph Hawtrey, Josef Schumpeter, and Léon Walras. This is thought to be a move away from having the stock of M or of (M,M'), generating the spending that constituted PQ with the help of some V or (V,V') concept of velocity. Be that as it may, why is such a paradigm a necessary departure from a doctrine of neutrality-of-the-absolute-price level? The left-hand expression PQ can involve primarily trends in P alone even when the right-hand side is varied in its formulation.

The tyranny of a doctrine of neutral money in the short run, which clouded the mind of Lloyd Mints, my first teacher of macroeconomics at Chicago, is coming somewhat back into fashion. The most that I can concede to Ohlin is that scholars with an income-stream approach to PQ are less likely to reify short-run velocity of M if their expositions skirt around the mentioning of V symbols.

Other Swedish macrotheorists

The original title suggested for this piece was something like "Influence Abroad of the Stockholm School." Had I not broken away from that label, this might have been an embarrassingly short lecture. Using myself and my many friends as guinea pigs, I might have summed up tersely as follows:

1. Erik Lundberg's numerical sequences (linear difference equations) were widely read in 1937 and thereafter.

2. Ohlin's 1937 claims for a Stockholm School were widely read. We gave him the benefit of the doubt but had no way to confirm his contentions.

3. Ragnar Frisch's work in Oslo and in the 1933 Cassel *Festschrift* were well known. So was his 1931 work on the acceleration principle, which benefited from his 1931 American sojourn with Alvin Hansen in Minneapolis.

4. Save for John Hicks, few of us knew Lindahl's work – except his thesis carrying forward the public-goods concepts of Wicksell. Late in the 1930s Lindahl's work to clarify time-phased concepts of income *was* well thought of but not carefully studied outside of Hicksian circles.

Lindahl did publish in 1939, and perhaps even as early as 1930 in Swedish, a definitional equation that I can write as

Total spending = consumption spending + investment spending
$$= E = P_c Q_c + P_I Q_I$$

$P_c Q_c / E = 1 - s$, a hypothetical parameter that is constant. But this system leaves us shy of the equations needed to have a determinate theory of (E, Q_c, Q_I, P_c, P_I). Someone should check whether he stipulated something about P_tQ_t as an exogenous creature of animal spirits or otherwise. Unless he did that, Lindahl would seem not to have reached as far as Kahn (1931), and those who know Swedish should tell us just when Lindahl first did what he did do.

5. Having caught echoes of Gunnar Myrdal's *ex ante* and *ex post* terminology, we expected great things from translation of his 1933 *Monetary Equilibrium*. Using myself as typical, we found the book anticlimactic. My first reading of it discerned even less on systematic variation of Q in PQ than even such austere critics as Abba Lerner and Don Patinkin have been able to unearth.

6. After World War II, I heard Bertil Ohlin at Harvard say new and exciting things about the economics of over-full-employment. When I early tried out in Stockholm my notions of a liberal pro-investment policy based on austere fiscal programs fully compensated by easy-money programs, I learned this was old hat there – called by critics of Gunnar Myrdal, "the socialization of thrift."

7. Scandinavia's second golden age in economics – say from 1930 to 1950 – seemed to regress back eventually toward the mean. The diagnosis I heard about most on my visits to Northern Europe was to the effect that temptations of public service and consultancies to banks, corporations, and international agencies caused the wine of talent to be consumed too green. I added on my own, diplomatically only in my own boudoir, that the cynicism toward mathematics in economics and econometrics expressed by most of Sweden's wise academics conduced to her falling behind in the treasure hunt of recent science. (I had to admit that Frisch's capture of Norwegian academic economics, which certainly was not anti-mathematics in ideology, did not forestall that country's retrogression as a place for sabbatical visits by leading young economists. And the Netherlands, after a longer-lasting time in the sun, also seemed to lose ground relative to the colossus of America with its affluent resources for research support.)

Tracing origins

Although I do not focus here on the degree to which a Stockholm School anticipated Keynes's *General Theory,* independently formulated it, or influenced non-Scandinavian economists in developing such macroeconomics, let me say a few words on this subject. Reversing Axel Leijonhufvud's thesis by 180 degrees and disagreeing gently with Robert Clower, I identify what was scientifically important in Keynes as the macroeconomic paradigm that the advanced and elementary texts dub to be Keynesian. (This does not belittle Keynes's personal wisdoms, nor his never fully articulated perceptions and hypotheses. It puts them in their proper place within the history of the living science of economics.)

The single most important core of the Keynesian revolution was its theory of output as a whole as determined by effective demand, which is a sea change from Walrasian market-clearing equilibrium. In baldest form this can be written as

$$\begin{aligned}
&\text{Income} = \text{consumption} + \text{investment} \\
&Y = C + I \quad \text{definition} \\
&C = f(Y), 0 < f'(Y) < 1 \quad \text{propensity to consume} \\
&I = \bar{I} \text{ or } \bar{I}(t) \quad \text{autonomous investment}
\end{aligned} \quad (1)$$

This is the "multiplier" doctrine.[2] Its formulation, in my view, antedates the early 1936 publication of Keynes's book. As an example, there is Richard Kahn's 1931 *Economic Journal* paper. J. M. Clark quasi-independently arrived at similar notions when studying for the Carnegie Foundation the economics of World War I, and how belligerents' demand for U.S. exports induced a positive (but *limited*) rise in our output. J. M. Clark's *Economics of Planning Public Works* was published in 1935, before the *General Theory* but with knowledge by then of Kahn's work and Keynes's 1933 *Means to Prosperity*. I shall show that Clark's dynamic sequences, which resemble some in Erik Lundberg (1937), D. H. Robertson (1939), and Fritz Machlup (1939), are *logically isomorphic* with my equation (1) and thus spell out the essential identity between Kahn of 1931 and Keynes of 1936. I do not expect Don Patinkin will agree with this, but on the present occasion I am under oath to give my opinion.

Many writers other than Clark presented, in the years 1932–5, analyses much like his in their essential content. I pick these dates because my own study of economics begins with the New Year of 1932 and I am staying with my own impressions. Sumner Slichter, I recall, in his published lectures given in Utah, stressed that consumption is passive and driven by active investment. (Slichter regarded himself as anti-Keynesian. When I mentioned to Alvin Hansen years after Slichter's death how implicitly Keynesian Slichter had often been, suggesting he had never realized it, the gentle Hansen said uncharacteristically: "I always thought of Sumner as a closet Keynesian.")

I concede that the historian of thought wishes to distinguish between writers who self-consciously utilize what they perceive to be a new paradigm and those who are driven by the new data to depart, without always realizing it, from accepted paradigms. Don Patinkin thus does have a point. But so do I. And in connection with this conference, I have to judge that the Swedish economists of the 1931–4 period coherently analyzed the increase in real and nominal income that would be generated by unconventional fiscal stimuli. In those years of the Great Depression, those Swedes would have regarded as a crank a John the Baptist (to Robert Lucas) who insisted on Say's Law, market-clearing mechanisms, and neutral-money responses of the price level to continued programs of fiscal and central-bank stimulus. Unlike Patinkin, I would not so curtly dismiss Frisch's models of circulation planning as not being pre-Keynes stepping stones.

In my reading, Maynard Keynes at the 1931 Harris Foundation conference already showed signs of postulating equation (1)'s $f(Y)$ propensity-to-consume function.[3] Although Michal Kalecki almost missed having equation (1)'s system for Y because of his extreme preoccupation with the profit-investment nexus, I believe Patinkin strains at a gnat when he seems to deny as a consumption function Kalecki's 1939 form of $f(Y)$, in which $f'(Y)$ is the constant fraction of income that workers receive in a world where capitalists save *all* of their extra income and workers save *none* of theirs. That constitutes a well-defined propensity-to-consume function. I regard the claims on behalf of Kalecki's originality by Joan Robinson and Lawrence Klein as overblown, and I regard Kalecki's polar case of workers' and capitalists' saving propensities as empirically bizarre. But once Kalecki at whatever date came to stipulate an equation relating the share and magnitude of profits to each level of income, Kalecki's investment-profit multiplier model did become logically isomorphic with my system in equation (1).

The wider Keynesian system involves, along with Y, the variables for interest rates and for endogenous investment – all as being affectable by the exogenous stock of money M. A dozen reviewers of the *General Theory,* most of whom were in constant contact with Keynes, discerned in that book the following amplification of equation (1):

$$Y = C + I \qquad\qquad\qquad\qquad\qquad\qquad (2a)$$
$$= f(Y) + g(r,Y) \qquad g_r < 0, 0 < g_y < 1 - f' < 1$$
$$M = m(Y,r) \qquad m_y > 0, m_r < 0 \qquad\qquad (2b)$$
$$= Y/V(r) \qquad \text{say, } V'(r) > 0$$

Relations between output, Y, and employment, E, were also specified in Keynes (1936).

Once deep-depression conditions were left behind, endogenous changes in the price level, P, became a concern. By 1940 relations like $PY = y$ were studied; M in the equation (2b) $m(Y,r)$ relation was replaced by M/P; and relations determining (P, nominal wage rate) were beginning to be investigated.

Where equation (2) differs from equation (1), I believe the pre-1936 anticipations of Keynes are harder to identify. Thus, the Chicago tradition that I knew so well in 1932-5 involved (a little but) precious little of equation (2). Nor were Irving Fisher's formalisms much better, despite his perceptive fears of debt deflation. What I would have to add to Patinkin's excellent debunking of a mythical subtle oral tradition at Chicago is that Patinkin exaggerates the degree to which the Chicago of 1925-40 differed from the universal $MV = PQ$ orthodoxy. As an example, all ten of the Big Ten universities subscribed to Fisher-Marshall-Pigou-1923 Keynes paradigms.

Let me analyze the 1935 Clark dynamics to show that it and Kahn (1931) are indeed predecessors to the equation (1) 1936 multiplier doctrine, in quite the same sense as historians of science have properly regarded Galileo's falling-body analysis as a predecessor of Newton's gravitational laws and a breakthrough away from Aristotelian physics.

Clark (1935, pp. 91-2) contemplated the difference equation

$$Y_t = C_t + I_t \quad t = \ldots, -1, 0, 1, 2, \ldots \qquad (2)$$
$$= \tfrac{2}{3} Y_{t-1} + I_t \quad I_t \equiv 0, t < 0;\ I_t \equiv \overline{I} > 0, t \geq 0$$

He graphs its solution

$$Y_t = (1 + \tfrac{2}{3} + \ldots + \tfrac{2}{3}^t)\overline{I} \qquad (3)$$
$$= \frac{\overline{I}}{1 - \tfrac{2}{3}}(1 - \tfrac{2}{3}^{t+1})$$

$$\lim_{t \to \infty} Y_t = Y_\infty = \frac{\overline{I}}{1 - \tfrac{2}{3}} \qquad (4)$$

where Y_∞ is seen by any reader to be definable precisely as in my equation (1), namely, by

$$Y_\infty = C_\infty + I_\infty = (MPC)Y + \overline{I} \quad Y = \frac{\overline{I}}{1 - MPC}, \qquad (5)$$
$$0 < MPC < 1$$

Clark's graph of the asymptotic steady states makes clear equation (1)'s paradigm for "output as a whole" as determined by the response to autonomous investment of income so as to achieve the level of induced saving that matches postulated investment. QED.

If we grant the logical isomorphism to Keynes's equation (1) in Clark (1935), can we logically refuse it to Kahn of 1931 and Keynes of 1933? Not by my canons of hair splitting.

History-of-science precedent

A word about Galileo. Using hymn singing as his clock, he could observe that a ball released a short distance above the earth will display short-period downward ("average") velocities proportional to the odd digits: 1, 3, 5, ... Not knowing calculus, Galileo still had the perception of an *instantaneous* velocity – which would be 2 at the time just between the time intervals with adjacent average velocities 1 and 3, and likewise for 4 between 3 and 5, and so forth – a serendipitous simplification provided by the quadratic case. The total distances fallen by the end of the time intervals (1, 2, 3, . . .) were seen by him to be 1, 1 + 3 = 4, 1 + 3 + 5 = 9, . . . ; these were perceived to obey the quadratic formula (1, $2^2, 3^2, 4^2, \ldots, t^2$), or

$$\text{distance} - (\text{velocity})^2 \equiv \text{constant} = 0 \tag{6}$$

The above formula[4] was later generalized by Leibniz and others to the law of conservation of (mechanical) energy.

Now for Newton. He regarded the ball as being attracted (or "accelerated") toward the earth's center by a force proportional to 1/(radius of earth + altitude of ball)$^2 \approx$ 1/(radius of earth)^2, an approximate constant.

Therefore, Newton can write in terms of second and first time derivatives

$$\ddot{x} = -g, \dot{x} = 0 - gt, x = x^0 - \tfrac{1}{2}gt^2 \tag{7}$$
$$\dot{x}^2 + g(x_0 - x) = \text{kinetic energy} + \text{potential energy}$$
$$= \text{constant} = 0$$

I say we are using hindsight, not to *read into* Galileo what was never there but rather to perceive what was genuinely there [even though he did not *always* correctly understand it perfectly – as, for example, when in earlier decades he made $x - x^0$ proportional to velocity rather than (velocity)^2, an error he later came to recognize clearly].

Discussion

Let me sum up. I do agree with Lerner (1940) and Patinkin (1982) that Ohlin exaggerated (1) the sense in which Wicksell ever had a theory of "output as a whole" or a theory of effective demand or a theory of *systematically unneutral* money; (2) the sense in which Myrdal's 1933 *Monetary Equilibrium* had a *formal* model for endogenous *real* GNP; or (3) the sense in which Lindahl and Ohlin ever had such an articulated model. But Ohlin and the other economists commissioned by the government to write about the depression of the early 1930s did not have to have such an explicit model to take for granted that measures which expand the total of $PQ = \Sigma p_j q_j$ can be expected *systematically* to increase Q.

This is not saying a lot. Every village crank, including those who could not reason clearly, believed as much. But in the groves of academe that I first entered, particularly in the solemn hours devoted to theory and methodology, this was never explicitly accepted – even by those who in less solemn hours lapsed into good sense and signed petitions for fiscal deficits and Fed expansionisms. Where was Robert Lucas when the Great Depression raged? He was everywhere, and an agnostic like Harvard's John Williams, who confessed to not knowing how to refute conclusively Foster and Catchings, was an object of some pity and condescension.

I need to make another point. When a Patinkin or a Samuelson takes notice in the 1970s of a passage written in the 1930s that refers explicitly to price level stabilization, or to reflation to restore, say, a 1925 price level, there is a danger that this will be misinterpreted to be evidence for that earlier writer's being preoccupied with P in PQ and *not* at all with Q. Having lived as an economist in those earlier times, I can affirm boldly that this would be a gross mistake. All of us acutely desired a rise in Q, and our espousal of a rise in PQ was in the hope that Q would be raised – especially since, during those years of the Great Depression, we were for once relieved of the usual concern about P rises because defending the slump's trough of the price index was not deemed something worth sacrificing for. (To their shame many Fed officials and some civil servants did worry about the bogey man of inflation even in 1931 and 1932!) Only after 1936 did inflation loom up for sensible humanitarians again as an evil in its own right. When one reads Myrdal, Lindahl, Cassel, and Ohlin, one must keep this in mind, realizing that they did correlate rises in P with desired rises in Q; and the same was then true of Seymour Harris, Henry Simons, and the writer of my various term papers. This imprecision of speaking did little harm until, during World War II, an occasional naive Congressman objected to needing controls and limitations on prices on the ground that "the price level was still not back to 100."

Today we have a new reason to accord more value to pre-Keynes pioneers who thought in terms of effective demand even before their thoughts had firm foundations in explicit economic theory. (Here I make a point like that in Bob Clower's paper.) Our new reason is that modern critics of Keynes have rediscovered what we early converts to Keynes well knew but chose to conveniently forget: The system (1), as well as the system (2a) and (2b), does lack firm "foundations," micro or otherwise. Better no foundations than bad ones! As a reduced form description, (1) served us better than any Lucas-Sargent rationalization could have done. As Oliver Heaviside said in exasperated reply to the critics of his pioneering but intuitive electrical engineering operators, "Shall I refuse my dinner because I do not know the laws of digestion?"

Don Patinkin has raised to new levels the history of science as applied to economics. I applaud his insistence on written documentation to validate remembrances and vague claims by interested witnesses. But sometimes, looking into a microscope, we lose the *gestalt* apparent to the naked eye or perhaps perceivable only in the aperture of a telescope.

When one puts the microscope on Galileo, one fails to find in him so simple a Newton concept as a second-order differential equation

$$d^2/dt^2 = f(x, dx/dt)$$

much less an inverse-square law of acceleration. Although Galileo fails this Patinkin-like test for anticipation of Newton, commentators are right to stress Galileo's recognition that the burden of proof is on the assertion that a velocity will change: A new force is needed to produce an acceleration, not to continue a velocity – which is a tremendous emancipation from Aristotle's basic notion.

Or consider the famous 1744 incident at the Court of Frederic the Great, where Maupertuis enunciated the principle of least action and Euler magnanimously made sense out of the sounds Maupertuis was perpetrating. A Patinkin could rightly demonstrate that Maupertuis never discovered Euler's principle that a cannonball's path in a vacuum provides a minimum of the *difference* between its kinetic and potential energy, as compared to all other paths that conserve the same *total* of those energies. So what credit ought Maupertuis to get for his bombastic claim? I would say he deserves a lot of credit for conjecturing a basic minimum principle in nature (but only if the jury determines that what he intuitively had in mind was not already old hat, was not, for example, already tacitly contained in Hero's ancient writings on light as following a path of least time of arrival or in Fermat's similar speculations about optics).

Patinkin's colleague Yehuda Elkana must surely be right that the different discoveries of the nineteenth-century first law of conservation of energy were not identical in their expositions and findings. That does not mean Tom Kuhn is wrong in enumerating twelve quasi-independent discoverers of that law. When I have made a discovery in economics, my second paper on the subject might well dominate the first paper. Still, it is usually the first one, rough as it is and incomplete as it may be, that most represents the incremental innovation to knowledge. As Littlewood said to Hardy – or was it the other way? – most famous first proofs of important theorems are crude. Later the elegant undertakers and tailors take over. If the proofs could be easy and slick, their dates of discovery would have been earlier ones.

What strikes me as I review Mertonian stories about doubletons and multiple discoveries in science – Darwin and Wallace, Newton and Leibniz, Joule and Mayer, Jevons, Menger, and Walras – is not how genuinely different their versions are, but rather how oddly similar they may be. The laws of probability are defied when it is Malthus's population theory that led Darwin to the notion of natural selection as he climbed a country stile and that also led Wallace in a Malayan fever to the same apprehension. Jevons and Walras even made the same mistake about the necessity for utility to be cardinally measurable! The contemporaneous discoveries of the so-called balanced-budget theorem – earlier by Jörgen Gelting, Keynes, William Salant, Samuelson, Harold Somers, Hansen-Perloff, and Kaldor, and later by Henry Wallich, Richard Goodwin, Trygve Haavelmo, Gottfried Haberler, Everett Hagen, Richard Musgrave, Tom Schelling, and Arthur Smithies – differed in expositions and emphases but agreed in the essentials of the phenomenon.

There were many Molière characters speaking Keynesian prose in the depression years before 1936. What Keynes's *General Theory* gave us, which Ohlin's inspired journalisms could not at all offer, was a new manageable paradigm that we could explicitly express – and test, and criticize, and improve, . . . , and be bewitched by.

Long before Kuhn, Schumpeter used to insist that old theories are not killed by simple facts: It takes a new theory to kill an old one. The mind cannot operate in terms of a melange of sensations. It needs a road map to perceive patterns of regularity and persistence.

So pervasive is the Keynes version that in the same year that a Martin Feldstein or Arthur Burns is castigating the model, his journal papers are utilizing it. To dig the Keynes paradigm's grave, I must use the shovel that it was the first to provide. That, I suppose, after half a century is true fame in science.

If we are candid, we must say that Ohlin's Stockholm School is now part of history – occupying an honorable niche to be sure, but not in 1987 at the cutting edge of economic science.

Notes

1. I owe thanks for partial support to my MIT Sloan School of Management's postdoctoral fellowship and for editorial assistance to Aase Huggins and Ruth Pelizzon.
2. Equation (1) becomes more elaborate once disposable income, which equals $Y -$ Taxes, becomes the argument in $f(\ )$; and when we have to add to $\overline{I}$ a term $\overline{G}$ for governemnt expenditure; and when Taxes is postulated to be a stipulated function $T(Y)$, $0 < T'(Y) < 1$. Similarly, an open economy requires the further variables of the Harrod-Keynes-Metzler type.

    I see from Robert Clower's contribution to this volume that he regards the system (1) here, and my later (2a) and (2b), not as the essential Keynes *General Theory* but rather as a "Samuelson" fabrication. I protest the great honor. Harrod, Hicks, Lange, Reddaway, Meade, J. Robinson, Lerner, and many others wrote down *exactly* this system. I did invent the 45° Keynesian cross as a device for classroom exposition.
3. Patinkin may magnify the probability that Myrdal read the Harris Foundation proceedings and forgot about it. The circulation of that item was minuscule. I never saw it until years after my own Chicago sojourn, and a citation count would show how little was its ripple.
4. To avoid calculus, in equation (6) Galileo can replace (velocity)^2 by (centered-average-velocity)^2.

References

Clark, J. M. (1935), *Economics of Planning Public Works*. Washington, D.C.: U.S. Government Printing Office.

Committee on Unemployment (1931–5), Commissioned reports by Hammarskjöld, Johansson, Myrdal, and Ohlin; and Final Report on *Remedies for Unemployment* (all in Swedish).

Frisch, Ragnar (1933), "Propagation Problems and Impulse Problems in Dynamic Economics," in *Economic Essays in Honour of Gustav Cassel*. London: George Allen and Unwin.

  (1934) "Circulation Planning: Proposal for a National Organization of a Commodity and Service Exchange," Parts I–II, *Econometrica* 2 (July), 258–336; 2 (October), 422–35.

Harris Memorial Foundation (1931), *Unemployment as a World Problem*, Q. Wright, ed., Chicago: University of Chicago Press.

Harris, Seymour (1936), *Exchange Depreciation*. Cambridge, Mass.: Harvard University Press.

Kahn, R. F. (1931), "The Relation of Home Investment to Unemployment," *Economic Journal*, 41 (June), 173–98.

Kalecki, M. (1971), *Selected Essays on the Dynamics of the Capitalist Economy 1933–1970*. Cambridge: Cambridge University Press.

Keynes, J. M. (1923), *A Tract on Monetary Reform.* London: Macmillan.
  (1933), *The Means to Prosperity.* London: Macmillan.
  (1936), *The General Theory of Employment, Interest and Money.* London: Macmillan.
Leijonhufvud, Axel (1968), *On Keynesian Economics and the Economics of Keynes.* New York: Oxford University Press.
Lerner, Abba P. (1940), "Some Swedish Stepping Stones in Economic Theory," *Canadian Journal of Economics and Political Science,* 6 (November), 574–91.
Lindahl, Erik (1939), *Studies in the Theory of Money and Capital.* London: Allan and Unwin.
Lundberg, Erik (1937), *Studies in the Theory of Economic Expansion.* London: P. S. King & Son.
Machlup, Fritz (1939), "Period Analysis and Multiplier Theory," *Quarterly Journal of Economics,* 54 (November), 1–27.
Myrdal, Gunnar (1939), *Monetary Equilibrium.* London: W. Hodge (English translation and revision of 1932 Swedish and 1933 German versions).
Ohlin, Bertil (1937), "Some Notes on the Stockholm Theory of Saving and Investment," *Economic Journal,* 47, 53–69, 221–40.
  (1978), "Keynesian Economics and the Stockholm School, A Comment on Patinkin's Paper," *Scandinavian Journal of Economics,* 80 (No. 2), 144–7.
  (1981), "Stockholm and Cambridge: Four Papers on the Monetary and Employment Theory of the 1930s." Posthumously edited by O. Steiger. *History of Political Economy,* 13 (Summer), 189–255.
Patinkin, Don (1978), "On the Relation between Keynesian Economics and 'The Stockholm School,'" *Scandinavian Journal of Economics,* 80 (No. 2), 135–43. Reprinted in 1982 book below.
  (1981), *Essays on and in the Chicago Tradition.* Durham, N.C.: Duke University Press, Chapters 10–12.
  (1982), *Anticipations of the General Theory? And Other Essays on Keynes.* Chicago: University of Chicago Press.
Robertson, D. H. (1939), "Mr. Clark and the Foreign Trade Multiplier," *Economic Journal,* 49, 354–6.
Samuelson, P. A. (1988), "Mathematical Vindication of Ricardo on Machinery," *Journal of Political Economy,* 96, 274–82.
  (1989), "Ricardo Was Right!" *Scandinavian Journal of Economics,* 91, 47–62.
Slichter, S. H. (1934), *Towards Stability – The Problems of Economic Balance.* New York: Henry Holt and Co.
Wicksell, Knut (1936), *Interest and Prices,* English translation of 1898 German edition. London: Macmillan.
  (1923 and 1981), "Ricardo on Machinery and the Present Unemployment," *Economic Journal,* 91, 200–5, a paper rejected by Keynes in 1923–4 and reproduced with commentary by L. Jonung in *Economic Journal,* pp. 195–

205, under the above title plus the subtitle "An Unpublished Manuscript by Knut Wicksell."

500

THE TO-BE-EXPECTED ANGST CREATED FOR ECONOMISTS BY MATHEMATICS

Paul A. Samuelson
Massachusetts Institute of Technology

Professors Quddus and Rashid [1994] have provided useful samples that confirm what I predicted more than four decades ago — that the virus of mathematics would spread in economics and cause grave psychological discomfort in those scholars who lag behind the external-margin frontier of its extreme cultivation.

The authors present a selection of quotations from writers of eminence who by and large have themselves pioneered in the use of mathematics in economics. Yet *even they* warn against others who carry mathematics *too far*. Admissions against self-interest, jurists know, carry special weight in court.

In response to the editor's request for any reactions by me, I jot down a few thoughts.

BOTTOM LINE

Whatever the *ad hominem* interest of this discussion, it neither adds to nor subtracts from an effort to judge what is the optimal degree of use of mathematics by end-of-century economists.

PREDICTABLE REACTIONS

I do not find the number and eminence of the quoted savants at all surprising. One could double or quadruple these samplings. And oral denunciations of pseudo-mathematicians far exceed in expletives the cautious wordings culled from journals and printed interviews.[1]

EXPLANATORY PARADIGM

I have a fancy [quasi-mathematical] model to rationalize the quotations presented. It employs the *exact* [truncated] *Pareto Distribution*. As is well known the empirical distribution of large incomes obeys pretty well the P.D. property: "However high is your income, there are people richer than you. Calculate the mean income of such people and, no matter what yours is, their mean is always two to three times your income. There is never reason to cease complaining about others' 'excesses.'"

So it is with mathematical pretension as judged by degree of complexity that each scholar averages. Hicks and Allais used much math. (My teachers Jacob Viner, Frank Knight, and Edward Chamberlin would swear to [and at!] that.) But there are others who use more. And this is even more true about each of us as we age. "This far and no further," is our natural motto. (That is tautology, for if we believed in the usefulness of greater complexity, we would engage in it ourselves and recalibrate the frontier from which we complain.)

THE ONCE-AND-FOREVER BATTLE

Historians know that ever there is a *Methodenstreit* between shirt-sleeve hard-fact economists and fancy-dan theoretical economists. Thus, if you want quotes, turn to the 1880s writings of John Kells Ingram, the enemy of theory and "the leading advocate" in Britain of "the historical method." He was no great shakes, but the burden of his complaint against "vicious abstraction" and the deductive methods had to do with his revulsion against the *geometric diagrams* of his age! Who but antiquarians these days reads Cliff Leslie, the best of Jevons' opponents?

MATHEMATICS THE HANDMAIDEN

It was Nicky Kaldor — no mathematician he — who said: "Think of the power of the mathematical method: it enabled a mediocre high-school teacher like Erich Schneider to become a respected scholar." That was malicious and snobbish.

But Charles Darwin said something of the same in a nicer way: "I have always envied those who had the gift of mathematics because it was as if they possessed an extra sense that I lacked." His cousin, Francis Galton, one of the most creative persons who ever published, independently expressed a similar sentiment when he thanked a Cambridge friend who wrote out the Bravais mathematics of bivariate Gaussian distributions that unified and clarified Galton's own ingenious reinvention of the wheel of *correlation* theory.

HOW TO SNOW THE COMPETITION

One could compile a compendium of quotations on how careerists can use the complexity of mathematics to snow their superiors, rivals, and pupils. One way of being vaccinated against being snowable is to acquire some competence in mathematics, but there will have to be better reasons than that to justify diverting energies from the study of rhetoric and the Statistical Abstract.

Science, in my observation, is somewhat self-purifying. The Native American adage tends to apply: "You fool me once, shame on you. You fool me twice, shame on me." I do not wish to over-glorify the self-monitoring process.

On the other hand, the burgeoning movements of anti-science, which quite transcend economics and profess to see in mainstream physics, biology, and medicine only a self-serving coterie of reciprocal back-scratchers, have thus far not been observed to display convergence toward some different version of verifiable and useful science. Dissident movements have special characteristic dynamics, which display weak correlations with any accumulation of reproducible findings.

BITS OF WHAT, FOR WHAT?

The authors correctly say, "To us quotes are what data [are] to a statistical paper" [1994, 253]. As will be developed further, their article illustrates the strengths and weaknesses of quotations as evidential data.

When Jane Doe discovers and justifies a novel fact that is true, in the end this is just as important as when Albert Einstein discovers that fact. When Einstein, or Goethe, says,

> I do not like you, Dr. Fell
> The Reason why I cannot tell.
> But this I know and know full well,
> I do not like you, Dr. Fell.

this testifies something to the great person's mood and digestion of the moment. What else it signifies is problematic.

There can be no unqualified criticism of using quotations as evidence. For the description and documenting of *attitudes* they are indispensable. Still they are truncations of the full texts, and with some authors there can be found quotations that contradict or qualify each other; where this is so there is a duty to present more than one quotation. That is why a perceptive paraphrase can sometimes be more representative than an exact quotation. When confronted with a paraphrase, the reader cannot always tell the difference between a perceptive paraphrase and a misleading summary. By reputation some paraphrasers earn our tentative credence, just as by reputation we learn to distrust some who select for verbatim quotation what rereading the text shows not to be faithfully representative. Although such misleading selection can be artful and deliberate, as often it is semi-unconscious among temperaments who, in Samuel Johnson's phrase, "argue for victory" and who are prone to read into others agreement with and confirmation of their own views.

The study of attitudes is respectable in its own right. But the truth of a proposition cannot be well tested by a count of the number of noses of those who believe in that truth and of those who doubt it. Weighting the number of yea-sayers by their quality cannot do much to redeem the quotation technique as a tester of logical cogency or of empirical relevance.

SAD CALLS RECALLED

Let me adduce two examples of great scholars who prophesized independently while at the top of their powers that mathematical economics was a passing fad that more or less deserved its impending decline. I refer for one to Lionel Robbins at the end of World War II.

Even sadder to me was the essay written by my Chicago teacher Jacob Viner to introduce the 1936 *Festschrift* for his Harvard teacher Frank Taussig, then the dean of American economists. Viner was justly called the most erudite economist of his time: he was then but a year away from publishing his classic doctrinal *Studies in International Economics*. He had in the years just before returned from helping establish in the New Deal Treasury Department a corps of professional economists. In a great Chicago department that was a bit stronger on ideology than on wisdom, Viner stood out as an economist of eclectic judgment and subtle knowledge. And I will remind readers of what they know by hindsight but which Viner could of course not yet know in 1936 — of the impending explosive renaissance in trade and finance to be associated with the names of Lerner, Leontief, Meade, Tinbergen, McKenzie, Stolper, Samuelson, Metzler, Pearce, Kemp, Jones, Johnson, Mundell, and innumerable others, *all of whom by Viner's standards had to be regarded as mathematical economists*.

One doesn't know whether to cry or laugh at Viner's conclusion that math had been carried about as far as it could usefully go in post-Taussig international trade. I will not quote selectively from Viner's text; however, as Casey Stengel used to say, "You could look it up in the book."

QUOTING THE UNIVERSE

My title here refers to the corpus of folklore, fables, aphorisms, and *bons mots* that have survived the Darwinian competition of time. These also our authors could count as units of data. But note the pitfalls in trying to distill from them, say, a guide to ethics or to tactical habit formation.

You know the names that appear most frequently in *Bartlett* or the Oxford Volumes of quotations: Mark Twain, Oscar Wilde, Bernard Shaw (*not* Will Rogers), Ambrose Bierce, La Rochefoucauld, Karl Kraus (less than he should), and all the other usual suspects. Perhaps the greatest name of all is that of Anonymous. Her/his pearls cast before us, by definition, must stand on their own merits without the boost that comes from the name of genius such as Smith or Keynes or Einstein. The same can be said for the Bible, Homer, and Shakespeare (whomever he/she may have been). Moreover, I have noticed that many of the best of the Twain or Wilde sayings are those of doubtful attribution.

To get into the quotation anthologies, don't work to formulate *a new truth*. Repackaging an old untruth will prove as rewarding. Indeed many of our happiest old chestnuts consist of phrasing in an interesting way what catches our attention for its patent falsehood.

As with any industry based on selecting quotations, ransacking folklore to create a code of conduct and belief is peculiarly sterile. Folklore's point is to assert propositions and their exact opposite. Do animal spirits today caution you against explicit risk taking? Then you utter solemnly, "Don't put all your eggs in one basket." Do you wake up hellbent to take a flyer? Then you quote Mark Twain: "Put all your eggs in one basket and—WATCH THAT BASKET!" [as if watching something averts the harm it can do you.] Did Will Rogers really say: "Buy land, they ain't making any more of it"? Efficient-market economists will laugh, not *with* the cowboy, but *at* him. They like better, and like it for its absurdity not truth, his alleged saying: "Only buy stocks that are going to go up. After they have gone up sell them. If they fail to go up, don't have bought them." If Will Rogers "never met a man he didn't like," that ought to disqualify him from any jury. "An open mind is [too often] an empty mind."

In societies professing to believe in astrology, astrology serves a purpose unrelated to its ability (inability?) to predict future events. Like tossable coins, astrology breaks ties. If I like (dislike) a prospective son-in-law, astrology will come to my rescue. Exactly so with folklore.

I am free to choose between: "Out of sight, out of mind" and "Absence makes the heart grow fonder." To choose between: "Never look back, someone may be gaining on you" and "Always learn from your mistakes" Between: "An eye for an eye" and "Turn the other cheek." From "Penny wise and pound foolish" and "Take care of the pence and the dollars will take care of themselves," or "Many a mickle makes a muckle."

From my own writing a sharp-eyed reader can line up clauses pro more math in economics and clauses pro more common sense. (Years ago my colleague Charles Kindleberger was vastly amused when his former student, Jaroslav Vanek called him up to say: "I've changed my mind about flexible exchange rates." "Why did you do that?" Charlie asked. "Because I found a mistake in sign in one of my determinants." CPK thought that deliciously funny. My reaction to him was "How do *I* ascertain where (uncommon!) good sense lies except, so to speak, by the signs in my determinants?" Into which of the two PAS pro-and-con columns would this last sentence go?)

AN EXPLANATORY EPICYCLE

All the esteemed people quoted I happen to know quite well. Earlier I gave a Pareto Distribution paradigm to rationalize the quotations data. Now I venture a factor-analysis addendum *ad hominem*.

People in any group differ in the degree to which they are "Napoleonic." In advance of observing the facts, one hypothesizes that "The more Napoleonic the scholar, the more content that person is with his/her own choice of mathematical complexity; and the more critical such persons will be of the level of mathematics employed by those who use more of it than they and those who use less of it."

By applying this regression-variable to the authors' data, it seemed that as much as one-third of the observed variance could be explained by my calculated $R^2 = .33\ 1/3$. (Correction for degrees-of-freedom have not been made because that would be a just-unnecessary refinement.)

HOW REPRESENTATIVE OF THE UNIVERSE IS A SPECIFIED SAMPLE?

Here is an additional empirical finding that has to do with understanding the pitfalls involved in using quotations as your evidential data. Necessarily quotations are *incomplete* samples. *Context* can be significantly lost.

Thus, consider the Debreu quotation. I do not have his Presidential Address at hand, so I cannot judge exactly how to interpret his words. The authors perhaps expect their readers to interpret Debreu to be complaining about the overuse of mathematics. And indeed he may have meant precisely that. However, as I read the literal words of their selection, I could be forgiven for construing those words to say: "Without prejudice to the actual worthwhileness of mathematics in economics, it is a pity that so much of today's economics cannot be readily understood by so many of today's economists."

I am on safer ground when I refer to the authors' quotations from my 1951 AEA Boston Convention address, Samuelson [1952]. The authors seem to interpret my warning to young economists of the day (that they are likely to be handicapped without mathematics) as implying that "much of the criticism of mathematical applications ... can be explained as an irrational reaction ..." [1994, 252]. I confirmed, when I reread my text, that its actual purpose that day was ".. not to praise mathematics, but slightly to debunk its use in economics" [1952, 56].

"Aha," a reader may be tempted to declare, "this means the authors could have coupled Samuelson's name with those of Allais, Hicks, Georgescu-Roegen, Frisch, and their other nay-sayers."

You will reckon I am a hard person to please when my retort to that would be that this inference would equally damn the use of quotation snippets as evidential data in the search for testable truth of what was said and what was intended to be meant.[2]

A FINAL QUOTATION

As some sage has said,

"Science advances funeral by funeral."

NOTES

1. See the paper by Haim Barkai [1993] entitled, "The *Methodenstreit* and the Emergence of Mathematical Economics" for documentation of the fractal property: the nineteenth century and *every* time period witnesses a similar debate about mathematics. My only difference with Professor Barkai's fine paper is this: a dichotomy between fact gatherers and theory spinners omits a third of the debate; there are mathematics-mongerers like me who are positivistically fact-obsessed and vigorous opponents of *a priori* deductionists. Don't put us in bed with Menger, von Mises, and Robbins.
2. After I delivered my AEA address in Boston, Robert Bishop gave our venerable teacher Edward H. Chamberlin a lift back to Harvard. "How did you like Paul's lecture?" Bob asked. Our mutual teacher replied: "I didn't like it." "What did you find to object to in it?" "Well, it wasn't what Paul said, as what I knew he was thinking." There's context for you! Even republishing the full text of a paper can be problematic for Aesopian writers.

REFERENCES

Barkai, H. The *Methodenstreit* and Emergence of Mathematical Economics. Working Paper #266, Hebrew University, March 1993. Original English version of the German publication, Der Methodenstreit und das Aufkommen der Mathematischen Ökonomie, in *Vademecum zu einem Klassiker der Preistheorie*, edited by B. Schefold. Klassiker der Nationalökonomie Series, Düsseldorf: Die Handelsblatt Bibliothek, 1993, 61-84.

Debreu, G. The Mathematization of Economic Theory. *American Economic Review*, March 1991, 1-7.

Ingram, J. K. in *The New Palgrave Dictionary of Economics*, edited by J. Eatwell, M. Millgate and P. Newman, Vol. 2. London: Macmillan, 1987, 851.

Quddus, M. and Rashid, S. The Overuse of Mathematics in Economics: Nobel Resistance. *Eastern Economic Journal*, Summer 1994, 251-66

Samuelson, P. A. Economic Theory and Mathematics: An Appraisal. *American Economic Review*, 1952, 56-66. Reproduced as Chapter 126 in *Collected Scientific Papers of Paul A. Samuelson*, Vol. 2, Cambridge, MA: The MIT Press, 1966, 1751-61.

Viner, J. Introduction: Professor Taussig's Contribution to the Theory of International Trade. Chapter I in *Explorations in Economics: Notes and Essays Contributed in Honor of F.W. Taussig*. New York: McGraw-Hill Book Company, 1936, 3-12, particularly 11-12.

501

How Not to Cure the Imbalance of Trade
Paul A. Samuelson, MIT, September 1985

There is usually a simple common-sense solution to any economic problem. And usually it is wrong.

America's trade deficit is a perfect example. Here is the common-sense understanding of it--by Lee Iacocca of Chrysler, Lane Kirkland of the AFL-CIO, your brother-in-law at the Kiwanis Club, and your state's Democratic and Republican senators.

The Japanese undersell our manufactures and kill off thousands, even millions, of jobs. Often these are our best industrial jobs, for example the $25,000 slots in the auto or steel industry upon which United States real income supremacy has allegedly always been based.

Diagnosis: Imports from the Pacific Basin are stealing elite jobs from America, dragging down our standard of living to that of the less-affluent nations abroad.

Prescription: If thy eye offend thee, pluck it out. By import quotas or protective tariff surcharges, preserve manufacturing employment in the United States and reduce the over-seven-percent unemployment rate that plagues the Reagan era. That way keep the United States average real income level ten percent higher than the leading nations of Europe, twenty-five percent higher than Japan's per capita income, and more than twice the level of South Korea, Singapore, and the Soviet Union.

Red Herrings

Have I not put the matter too starkly? After all, GM and U.S. Steel spokesmen do not come out and damn free trade unequivocally. What they ask for is "fair trade," a level playing field on which all can compete.

The Japanese and the French, as any trade association lobbyist can document, may talk free trade but their governmental and business bureaucracies in fact practice a thousand subtle forms of discrimination against American imports. So angry businessmen say, don't let the ideology of free trade stand in the way of rectifying the unbalance. If the only language that the Japanese will understand is force, then let's give them an explicit quota to match their implicit trade impediments and thereby wrest concessions from them.

Besides, it is only *temporary* protections our industry needs --just until we "get our house in order" and make the needed adjustments--that is what they say and, the record will show, that is what the steel and textile industries have been saying for lo thirty years now.

I agree the Japanese should shape up and dismantle their obstructions against meat, rice, and citrus imports. In their own self interest they should stop the old-school-tie reciprocity that gangs up

341

spontaneously against any alien competitors. But the detailed evidence is overwhelming in stressing that, were imports into Japan to become perfectly freed from impediments, the dollar change rate would still remain so high as to leave us with a tremendous and a growing bilateral trade deficit with Japan.

Moreover there is nothing temporary about most of this massive shift in dynamic comparative advantage against our older routine manufactures. Buying us more time will not lead to putting our house in order but rather will widen America's productivity-cost disparity. The infant industries of steel, autos, shoes, and textiles that seek protection are creatures late in the cycle of life and not babies that will outgrow their weaknesses.

Hard Issues

So let us look free trade squarely in the eye. Is it bad or good for America?

If the winds of free trade now blow against the formerly high U.S. standard of living, can a bootstrap operation that protects against import competition succeed phoenix-like in restoring and raising the typical American's standard of living? And if the answer is, "Yes, protection can bootstrap us to greater prosperity," then why is protection not also the desired solution for Western Europe's over-ten-percent rates of unemployment?

Most readers, I suspect, will find the above diagnosis and prescription rather plausible. They will be surprised to be told that 95 percent of the economists at any world economic congress deem it to be a tissue of fallacies. (I write "95 percent" because economics is not a hard science like thermodynamics where virtually all of the experts can agree on basic truths. It confirms my point that, recently in *The New York Times* Professor John M. Culbertson of the University of Wisconsin, a member in good standing of the American Economic Association, rejected the simple arithmetic of Ricardian comparative advantage and deduced harm to American well-being from the lowness of Japanese real wages.)

Cold Truths

Here by contrast is what the lessons of economic history and the principles of economic analysis suggest is the better way to understand and cure our present plight.

Diagnosis: 1) Since 1950 the typical American has had a rise in real income of about 93 percent. A respectable fraction of this gain came from technical progress abroad (the cost cutting lobbyists complain about). Our purchases from abroad give us the benefit of the services of foreign workers and resources; at the same time that this is a bargain to us, it raises the real wage rates of workers abroad as a wider circle of consumers bid for their services. Examine a 1950

Sears catalog and the equipment in a 1950 hospital; do the same for 1985, and realize that much of *our* real gains do stem from cheaper imports.

2) Dogmatic free traders insist that *everyone* must be helped by untrammeled trade. They are wrong.

Inventions in Japan that greatly cheapen goods we buy from them can hurt the Japanese standard of living while helping ours. Japanese inventions that enable them to take over goods we formerly exported can hurt the average U.S. income. But is a cold blow from a hurricane helped if we react to it by shooting ourselves in the foot?

Has America the monopoly power to revise the term of trade between the prices we get for exports and what we pay for imports by a policy of self-sufficient autarky? By a policy of *selective* quotas and tariffs? "No", is the clear-cut answer to the question of autarky. "Almost certainly not," is the answer of the hundreds of studies that have appraised quantitatively the policy of optimal monopoly tariffs. Remember, this is a game that two can play, a case of pull-Devil pull-baker, and everyone the loser.

3) A correct diagnosis must recognize that it is the 50-percent overvaluation of the dollar under Reagan policies that has exacerbated our trade deficit. Tourists from abroad can't afford our prices; Caterpillar tractors can't be competitively produced in North America.

Bad luck for our usually lucky president? No, not luck at all. The $200 billion fiscal deficits engendered by Reaganomics, preempting much of private domestic saving, bid up real interest rates here. Chasing these swollen yields, capital funds flow in from abroad and bid up the free-floating dollar exchange rate. Detroit and Pittsburgh cry but continue to vote for plucky Ronnie.

Arithmetic cares nought for politics and heartache. Since January 1981, Reaganomics has entailed our selling the ranch to foreigners--the old capital stock built up from Washington's day, and much of the new capital investment coaxed out by Reaganite tax incentives. When Reagan leaves the White House, America will be a net debtor just as we were in the nineteenth century, owning less abroad than foreigners own here.

Prescription: 1) If thy eye hurts, treat it. Reagan and Congress should of course raise taxes and cut expenditures to augment U.S. thriftiness.

2) The Fed, keeping a wary eye out for undue inflationary pressures when they later become apparent, should lean now against the wind of high real interest rates. If this helps push the dollar down as it has been doing since February, let Volcker and his team rejoice not desist. (The inflation component that arises from the dollar's fall toward equilibrium is a necessary cost of fixing up the economy. Let Wall Street greet it with hosannahs!)

3) If America insists on going its thriftless way in the Reagan fashion, this implies that our real wage rates in manufacturing must be lowered to clear the market and forestall mass unemployment. Workers and union leaders, facing the Hobson choice between permanent close-downs and lower real wages, must eschew the temptation toward suicidal bravado.

The public, given the stark choice between common sense and good sense, faces a challenge few generations have known.

CHAPTER 5

U.S. economic prospects and policy options: impact on Japan–U.S. relations

PAUL A. SAMUELSON

A Japanese renaissance

One of mankind's oldest myths, long antedating Tchaikovsky's ballet or Grimm's fairy tales, is the legend of the sleeping beauty who is awakened back to life by the kiss of a prince charming. What we are not told is whether, after the princess is brought back to life, the couple really did live happily ever afterward.

Were there no quarrels? Did the wife come to outstrip the husband in earning power? What kept their balance of payments in equilibrium? The tale ends just when the real-world problems begin.

If it is not too fanciful, think of 1945 Japan as the helpless and sleeping beauty. Cast the MacArthur occupation authority in the role of the prince charming. In doing so, no prejudgment is being made about how the credit should be divided for bringing about the postwar Japanese miracle. After all, even in the folk story, it is possible that the princess was already awakening of her own accord and that the prince was merely a lucky passerby who happened to appear on the scene at the critical moment.

The takeoff of the Japanese economy after 1945 might even be considered a second rerun of the sleeping beauty legend. The first would have to be the case of Commodore Perry's opening up of Japan just prior to the Meiji Restoration. Admittedly, the 1950–75 takeoff of Japan does have to be re-

---

I owe thanks for professional insights to Dr. Ryuzo Sato, Director of the Center for Japan–U.S. Business and Economic Studies, New York University, and Visiting Professor, Kennedy School of Government, Harvard University; also to the MIT Sloan School of Management for a Gordon Y Billard Fellowship that provided research opportunity; and to Aase Huggins for valuable editorial assistance. More than 50 leading American forecasters provided indispensable inputs relevant to the current econometric scene.

A summary of this project's research findings and relevant viewpoints was presented at the NYU Center for Japan–U.S. Business and Economic Studies on December 4, 1985, under the title "The U.S. and Japanese Economies in the Remaining Reagan Years." This chapter reproduces most of that lecture, with some modifications suggested by the valuable discussions there.

109

110 Paul A. Samuelson

garded as something of a miracle. However, those who know about Japan's progress from, say, 1860 to 1905 ought to have been somewhat prepared for the postwar spurt. A miracle is more surprising the first time it happens than the second time around!

This chapter surveys and analyzes macroeconomic developments affecting Japan–U.S. trade imbalances and trade relationships for the remaining years of the Reagan administration. From these positivistic findings must flow the policy recommendations that are implied.

Such a big topic can never be finally resolved. What I can do, however, is to present some of my tentative findings and hypotheses.

That I shall raise more questions that I can answer requires no apology. For in an inexact science like political economy, posing the right questions to investigate and ponder over is an important part of the battle.

Success story

Americans are alarmed to find that we have a large adverse balance of payments on current account. This is a dramatic reversal from the 1950s, when the rest of the world complained resentfully of a chronic "dollar shortage."

The time interval from dollar shortage to the present is precisely the epoch of the postwar Japanese miracle. In 1950, Japan was a poor oriental country with life expectancies still in the fifties. No wonder the Japanese retirement age became set early.

As best we can estimate, the 1950 per capita real income of Japan, in ratio to that of the United States expressed as 100, was only 17 – or about one-sixth (Table 5.1). Then things changed. And how they did change!

By 1955, Japan was almost at one-fourth of the U.S. living standard. By 1960, it had reached one-third. Some time between 1965 and 1970, Japan went past one-half our level, having already surpassed the Soviet per capita level along the way. After 1970, Japan left Britain behind.

By the time of the 1973 OPEC crisis, Japan had reached two-thirds of the American level of living.

Where does Japan now stand? I suspect that most people have an exaggerated estimate of Japanese productivity. Sometimes Americans think that each Japanese worker is seven feet tall. Moreover, Japanese management is supposed to have secret weapons of compromise and consensus agreement and to possess mysterious procedures that ensure perfect quality control.

At White House meetings, I have heard American businesspeople and trade unionists complain that the Japanese work too hard; in the manner of Benjamin Franklin and Max Weber, they save too much; and to top off the indictment, they are just too damned smart.

The statistical facts do not quite bear this out. As of 1985, Japanese produc-

U.S. economic prospects and policy options 111

Table 5.1. *Per capita real incomes
(expressed as percentage of U.S.)*

	1950	1955	1960	1965	1970	1975	1980
United States	100	100	100	100	100	100	100
Japan	17	23	33	43	64	68	72
USSR	30	33	40	42	47	50	48
West Germany	40	54	71	71	79	81	86
South Korea	11(1953)	12	12	12	17	21	25
United Kingdom	56	59	65	63	64	65	65
India	7	7	8	7	7	7	6
China	$6\frac{1}{2}$	$8\frac{2}{3}$	$9\frac{3}{4}$	$9\frac{1}{3}$	$10\frac{2}{3}$	$12\frac{1}{3}$	14
Taiwan	10	12	13	15	20	24	31

Source: Robert Summers and Alan Heston, "Improved International Comparisons of Product and Its Composition: 1950–1980," *Review of Income and Wealth* (June 1984).[1]

tivity still trails U.S. productivity. Calling U.S. per capita real income 100 in 1986, I estimate Japan's per capita income to be somewhere around 80. This puts Japan perceptibly below Canada, Norway, West Germany, France, Sweden, Switzerland, and Denmark.

True, Japanese life expectancies now average out to the high seventies, making them second to none. True, by the end of the century Japan will move toward or beyond the top of the list in per capita real income, provided only that it continues to enjoy annual growth rates that average out 2 percentage points greater than ours. Since the Soviet population is more than double that of Japan, in terms of *total* rather than *per capita* real GNP, by the year 2000 the ordering will still be the United States first, and the USSR and Japan next, without much difference between the second- and the third-place nations. For all China's population size, even if the post-Mao economic reforms work out well, China will still not come close in total economic weight to the Big Three – or, if we include all of Western Europe in a Common Market bloc, China will still trail the Big Four.

Not a zero-sum game

I do not care for the sporting-page way of looking at economic rivalries. From the time in 1870 when Bismarck unified Germany, England and third-party observers could envisage in Germany a rival who eventually would threaten the hegemony of the British Empire.

The German GNP grew faster than the British. Science in the Wilhelmine universities spawned the successful German chemistry and electricity indus-

347

tries. As far as economics is concerned, this could have been a fruitful competition and rivalry. German progress did not have to be bought at the price of British progress any more than nineteenth-century American progress had to be at the expense of the British Empire's standard of welfare.

Otto von Bismarck has much to answer for at the bar of historical judgment. Provoking two wars, against Austria and France, Bismarck bequeathed to the vain Wilhelm II an unstable legacy. World War I was the bitter fruit of Bismarckian adventurism, and Hitler's World War II was part of the total bill.

None of this served an economic purpose or followed inevitably from economic causation.

This basic truth needs emphasizing in our own time. From 1950 to 1975 the mixed economies of Western Europe and the Far East gained mightily on the United States. In 1945 the 6 percent of world population who were Americans must have enjoyed almost half of global GNP. By 1980 this had dropped to only a quarter of global GNP.

Foreigners' gain was not our loss. Their gain was part of the acceleration of global real output that occurred in the third quarter of the twentieth century and that was widely shared by both developing and industrialized regions. The point is that this step-up in global GNP was also shared by us in North America: In terms of U.S. history over two centuries, the 1946–73 years were marked by generous real growth – even though West Germany, Japan, and the Common Market were gaining on us.

Attention should be directed to the remarkable fact that Japan's post-1950 prosperity has owed nothing to military expenditures. Early in this century, Lenin, Hobson, and Rosa Luxemburg propounded a theory of imperialism that has much appeal in Marxian circles. According to their thesis, advancing economies like those of Germany and Japan must necessarily run out of purchasing power as their masses receive too little effective income to keep employment full. Only by imperialistic adventures in colonies and war can the metropolitan center keep itself going.

So much for science fiction. What are the midcentury facts in this age after Keynes? Japan has about the lowest ratio of military personnel to total population of any nation. Indeed, if we adjust for relative wealth, Japan joins with Switzerland and Canada in having *negative* ratios! Japan at the point five-sixths through the twentieth century displays the precise reverse of the Bismarck pattern of Germany at the two-thirds point of the nineteenth century.

This demonstration is good for the world. It is good for Japan. If and when Japan becomes tempted to bring its military might into relation with its economic might, I hope Tokyo and Washington will be reminded of the salutary truth that economic welfare no longer has to depend on political power.

Table 5.2 gives data on the degree to which different economies are "militarized." If one divides nations according to whether they are non-Marxist or Marxist, it appears that the latter tend to experience a greater degree of militarization.

The present crisis in U.S.–Japan relations

To recapitulate, the sober truth is the reverse of the proposition that Japan's growth robs America's growth. Here is how I put it in a *New York Times* article of September 15, 1985:

Since 1950 the typical American has had a rise in real income of about 93 percent. A respectable fraction of this gain came from technical progress abroad (the cost cutting lobbyists complain about). Our purchases from abroad give us the benefit of the services of foreign workers and resources; at the same time that this is a bargain to us, it raises the real wage rates of workers abroad as a wider circle of consumers bid for their services. Examine a 1950 Sears catalog and the equipment in a 1950 hospital; do the same for 1985, and realize that much of *our* real gains do stem from cheaper imports.

Although Japan's name is not mentioned in the above paragraph, it, more than any other country, deserves credit for the U.S. standard-of-living progress that is associated with cheaper imports. I am not oblivious to the problems faced by manufacturing industries in America that are associated with new foreign competition and shall address this serious matter. What I want to stress is the beneficent face of the coin.

Good policy for both countries will want to preserve the mutual-benefit aspects while trying to minimize or contain the transitional burdens.

Pure theory of trade

I have written several major articles on the basic economics of the Pacific Basin's challenge to Europe and North America. Since I cannot go into all the fine details, let me merely cite these publications: my 1972 Little Nobel lecture entitled "International Trade for a Rich Country"; my German Symposium piece of 1981 "To Protect Manufacturing?"; my detailed analysis in the recent Saburo Okita *Festschrift,* entitled "Analytics of Free-trade or Protectionist Response by America to Japan's Growth Spurt"; and my brief summary in defense of free trade rather than protection that appeared in the *New York Times* of September 15, 1985.

Two truths need underlining.

1. The living standard of American workers and capitalists is on the average increased when Japan or Korea makes technological advances in producing goods that we characteristically import from them.

Table 5.2. *Marxism and militarism: force ratios of Marxist and non-Marxist regimes*

Selected non-Marxist countries	Force ratio	Wealth-adjusted force ratio	Marxist countries	Force ratio	Wealth-adjusted force ratio
Western Hemisphere			Albania	18.9	19.6
United States	9.1	4.6	Angola	6.4	7.1
Canada	3.3	−0.9	Algeria	6.0	5.2
Mexico	2.0	0.4	Benin	0.8	4.1
Guatemala	2.3	2.8	Bulgaria	19.7	17.6
Honduras	3.9	5.7	Burma	4.9	9.3
El Salvador	5.4	6.8	Cape Verde	10.0	12.9
Costa Rica	1.5	2.6	China (Mainland)	4.3	5.9
Colombia	2.6	2.6	Congo	10.0	10.4
Venezuela	3.2	1.1	Cuba	23.5	22.7
Brazil	3.6	2.7	Czechoslovakia	13.8	10.0
Argentina	6.0	3.9	Ethiopia	8.2	12.9
Chile	10.3	9.2	Germany (East)	14.0	10.0
Europe			Guinea	3.2	6.4
United Kingdom	5.8	2.0	Guinea-Bissau	5.0	9.4
France	8.9	4.7	Hungary	10.5	7.5
West Germany	7.8	3.6	Iraq	32.1	31.7
Sweden	8.4	3.7	Korea, North	38.0	39.1
Switzerland	3.6	−1.3	Laos	15.8	21.6
Austria	5.3	1.5	Madagascar	2.2	5.3
Italy	6.9	3.8	Mongolia	21.2	21.6
Mid-East			Mozambique	1.5	4.4
Israel	46.2	43.4	Nicaragua	27.8	28.7
Turkey	13.3	13.5	Poland	11.9	9.3
Jordan	19.7	19.8	Romania	10.5	8.1
Egypt	10.0	11.7	Somalia	8.9	12.0
Saudi Arabia	5.4	0.5	Soviet Union	16.3	13.3
Iran	11.4	11.0	Syria	30.9	30.4
Libya	16.7	19.8	Tanzania	2.7	6.1
			Vietnam	21.5	25.8
Africa			Yemen (South)	12.5	14.8
South Africa	2.3	0.9	Yugoslavia	10.9	9.3
Nigeria	1.6	2.5	Mean, 32 Marxist countries	13.3	14.1
Ghana	1.0	0.3			
Zaire	0.9	5.3			
Liberia	3.5	5.8	Mean, 109 Non-Marxist countries	6.1	5.9
Sudan	3.3	5.3			
Asia					
Japan	2.0	−2.0			
India	1.6	5.3			
Indonesia	1.7	3.7			

350

Table 5.2. (cont.)

Selected non-Marxist countries	Force ratio	Wealth-adjusted force ratio	Marxist countries	Force ratio	Wealth-adjusted force ratio
Asia					
Thailand	4.8	5.1			
Taiwan	27.2	25.8			
Australia	4.8	0.5			
Philippines	3.0	4.3			

Note: The force ratio is the number of active, full-time military personnel per 1,000 population (data are for 1982). The adjusted force ratio is based on the relationship between national wealth and the force ratio. Each country's figure represents the deviation of its actual force ratio from the force ratio it would be expected to have given its level of wealth.
Source: World Military Expenditures and Arms Transfers, 1972–1982, U.S. Arms Control and Disarmament Agency, 1984.

2. But it is oversimple dogma to argue that free trade *always* entails a boost in America's well-being. When Pacific economies develop new technical advances in goods that we previously produced at low cost, this dynamic change in comparative advantage most definitely will subtract from America's consumers' surplus from trade and thus from our average real incomes. Those Americans hurt are not merely the workers and factory owners in the export industries that have lost visibility; most U.S. incomes may have to come down to clear markets in the new equilibrium. That can imply a slowdown in the trend of mean real wage rates, or can even entail an outright decline.

I should add that the necessary drop in European real wage rates can be as great as or greater than the implied drop in American wages. There is perhaps some evidence that post-1973 European real wage rates have been even more inflexibly resistant than ours have been; this may help explain why we have been able to create more than 30 million new jobs in the last decade, whereas western Europe has barely been able to maintain the same total of jobs.

When noneconomists learn that dynamic free trade can hurt America's living standards, they have one first natural reaction: "Avoid free-trade's hurt by putting quotas and tariffs against the low-cost foreign imports."

Economists who are expert in the analysis of international trade cannot agree. Their system deduces that, on top of the new harm that innovation under free trade brings, there is likely to be superimposed a second harm from the protectionist measures. Yes, some old high-paying jobs can be subsidized into existing ones; however, the accompanying new market-clearing spread of American real wages in other places will average out to a lower overall standard of U.S. earnings. What holds for the factor of production labor can hold also for capital or for U.S. natural resources. That is why experts advise: "Don't react to decline in our effective productivity, brought about by innovation abroad, by gratuitously shooting ourselves in the foot through the device of import quotas."

Qualifications

That, in a nutshell, is basic trade theory. Are there no exceptions and qualifications? Yes, here are a few that are possibilities but that don't stand up as being significant under quantitative measurements.

1. If American firms have a lot of unexploited monopoly power, then some cleverly allocated modest tariffs might force foreigners to pay more for the products we alone can supply. Note that this does not suggest tariffs where lobbyists and senators are most eager to put them – namely on auto, steel, shoe, and textile industries, where the United States no longer has competitive viability much less unexploited monopoly power.
2. There is a new second argument associated most recently with the name of Dean Henry Rosovsky of Harvard University. Schumpeterian innovators, he points out, typically make large temporary profits in the time period when rivals have not learned to imitate their new productivity. However, the Japanese are alleged to collusively rob American entrepreneurs of these Schumpeterian rents from innovation by erecting "unfair" trade barriers. Professor Rosovsky in effect counsels: "An eye for an eye. Let's put on quotas as a bargaining chip to force Japan to play the free trade game fairly."

If we study the Rosovsky point, we shall ultimately find that it belongs with the earlier point alleging that America does have some monopoly power, in the sense that we can legislatively alter the mean terms of trade at which we sell our exports relative to the prices we pay for our imports.

Does America have great power over its international terms of trade? Under pure-competition theory, where rivals and potential rivals exist in many regions, the answer is, only within narrow limits.

Under realistic workable competition, where Fortune-500 companies here and abroad do learn by doing and where economies of large-scale production are important, one cannot be so dogmatically negative.

However, what is it that is actually being proposed by the protectionists? They have no way of calculating the maximal terms of trade as called for by

U.S. economic prospects and policy options

the "scientific tariff" of the advanced textbooks. In fact, they are not proposing tariffs or quotas for Schumpeterian infant industries and processes. Either they favor across-the-board surcharges against all Japanese exports, or against all Pacific-Basin exports; or, primarily, they favor ad hoc quota relief for old industries that have for a long time been losing market share – textiles, shoes, steel, autos, sugar, and so forth.

Almost all economic experts, here and abroad, will doubt that quotas on routine American manufacturers can succeed in a bootstrap operation of raising mean U.S. real incomes or in preserving them. A few experts do hold out hopes for an industrial policy. The late Lord Kaldor of the U.K. Labor Party was a rare theoretist who believed that U.K. protection would actually raise U.K. incomes. Miyohei Shinohara is a Japanese economist who has investigated how a MITI-like industrial policy might succeed in dynamically altering a nation's comparative advantages. Both on the liberal left in the American labor movement, and at that West Point of American capitalism – the Harvard Business School – there is a similar belief by Professor Bruce Scott and others, that abandoning free trade would have a useful role to play as part of a new American industrial policy.

To make more precise statements about the merits of free trade with technologically advancing Pacific Basin countries like Japan, we need to examine some simple models of trade with foreign innovation. We begin the discussion by considering the Ricardian model. Let our traditional export be good 1, which has unit labor costs here of a_1 and a_1^* in Japan. Good 2 has respective labor costs of a_2 and a_2^*, and good 3 has costs of a_3 and a_3^*. Good 3 is traditionally our import because we postulate the following initial comparative-advantage inequalities:

$$a_1/a_1^* < a_2/a_2^* < a_3/a_3^*. \tag{1}$$

It must depend on reciprocal demand whether good 2 is an import or an export for us. (If Japan begins with a relatively "small" population and labor supply, so that

$$L^*/L \ll 1, \tag{2}$$

it is probable that we do export good 2 initially.)

What is the effect of a Japanese innovation that lowers its a_3^*? Now Japan supplies our import good at lower real costs in terms of its labor; now its workers get an increased real wage in terms of good 3. Once Japan is big enough to supply *all* of our good-3 needs, competition will bid down the relative price of our import relative to the other goods that we do produce. This illustrates two principles:

> *Rule 1.* Innovations abroad in goods we continue to import tend to benefit Americans.

353

Rule 2. Such innovations will also benefit Japanese if, but only if, our demand for those goods is "sufficiently" elastic.

With more than two goods in the model, the full analysis of this becomes complicated. However, the above qualitative results can be illustrated well by the easy-to-manage case of two Ricardian goods that people everywhere spend their money on in the same fixed proportions (the Millian and Cobb-Douglas case). Suppose the two regions have comparable labor supplies in the sense that each is able to specialize completely as the sole producer of the good in which it has a comparative advantage.

In this case, both before and after the Japanese innovation, the regions keep as shares of combined income the respective fractions in which their own good attracts income. As long as this is the case, the Japanese innovation that raises *aggregate* real income must raise *each* nation's per capita income by the same percentage. Rule 1 is confirmed; and, in this case, so is Rule 2.

This Mill-Ricardo two-good case suggests some of the needed qualifications. When Japan is so small that it can't fill our entire needs for its export good, Japan faces infinitely elastic demand and we get *none* of the joint benefit from the innovation; this consequence is the limiting edge of Rule 1. When Japan is so large that we can't fill all its need for our export good, Japan's comparative costs determine all prices and our labor shares with its labor in getting higher real wage after the innovation, confirming both rules.

When the increased potential supply for her favored good causes people everywhere to spend a smaller fraction on it – as is the case when inelasticity of uniform homothetic demand prevails – increased plenty can be absolutely immiserating to Japan, confirming the contingent second part of Rule 2.

Are these conclusions robust under departures from Ricardo's labor-only model? Little that is unambiguous can be said about a truly general model involving any number of goods and factors of production, nonhomothetic taste differences among people by regions, and possibly negative income elasticities. However, even in a Heckscher-Ohlin world,[2] or a Viner-Ricardo-Samuelson-Jones technology like that in Samuelson,[3] there remains a presumption that the industry and region wherein an innovation takes place will have the prices of its goods cheapened; people elsewhere are probably benefited. People there may well benefit, save that inelasticity of demands for their goods may make the innovation entail a net loss to them.

The reader can work out the two-factor model in which every good in each place is producible by transferable labor there working with fixed lands specialized for each of the goods. Every good might be produced in some positive amounts in both places. With ignorable transport costs, each good is being exported by the region that is favored to concentrate on it. Now let Japan undergo an innovation that reduces its costs in one of its export goods. Presumably that cheapens it relative to other goods: The American land specific to that good will now have less labor working on it, and the U.S. real wage in terms of that good rises, whereas this land's real rent falls. The U.S. labor displaced from this industry gets spread over the other industries, thereby raising land rents there a bit and lowering U.S. real wage rates measured in terms of the other goods. There still remains a presumption that U.S. factors of production as a whole now earn a higher real income in toto. In Japan it depends on elasticities of demand whether the innovation has raised or lowered the remuneration of total factors. Unless inelasticity is great, there is a presumption toward a net Japanese gain. Gains, however, are unevenly distributed.

To the degree that the prices of other goods will have risen relative to Japan's new market-clearing wage, labor will be shifted to them, and their lands will share in the gain via higher land rents. (However, the reverse allocations between lands and labors in other industries could occur.)

How innovations abroad can harm our free-trade well-being

Now for the more subtle part of the problem, the part so often misunderstood by naive free traders:

> Rule 3. Innovation abroad that enables producers there to displace producers here who previously exported abroad (and provided for domestic needs here) will tend *to reduce American living standards*.

This displays the usefulness of the Ricardian three-good scenario. Suppose that, before the innovation, we produce good 1 and they produce good 3, and that both of us competitively produce good 2. In that case, the ratio of our real wage level to theirs, measured in any units – both in $, both in yen, both in terms of good i as numeraire – will equal the a_2^*/a_2 ratio of the borderline good produced in both places.

$$W/W^* = a_2^*/a_2. \tag{3}$$

Now introduce a small innovation in Japanese production of good 2, which reduces a_2^* a little. Until the cost reduction becomes so large as to drive out of existence *all* U.S. production of q_2, the relation (3) still obtains. Clearly, then, our real wage will fall when a_2^* drops!

Fall relative to the Japanese wage? Or fall absolutely? Actually, *both!* Here is why. As before, a unit of American work buys the same amount of good 1 (namely, a real wage of $1/a_1$). As before, the U.S. real wage in terms of good 2 stays at $1/a_2$. But now each American worker must work longer to get 1 unit of good 3 by importing. While both regions produce good 2, we must have:

$$W/P_3 = (P_2/P_3)(W/P_2) = (a_2^*/a_3^*)/a_2. \qquad (4)$$

From (4) it is clear that a reduction in a_2^* must reduce America's real wage expressed in terms of the good obtainable only by importing. Since the other real wages for the goods we continue to produce at home are unchanged, it is manifest that America's *overall real wage* has indeed been hurt by the Japanese innovation.

Warning: This hurt has nothing to do with induced transitional unemployment. All markets clear always. However, the real wage at which our labor market clears has been hurt by innovation abroad, which makes Japan more cost-competitive in goods we did previously (and perhaps still do) produce. Thus, Rule 3 is confirmed. QED.

A dramatic and simple redemonstration for how free trade can hurt us is provided by the two-good case where, prior to the innovation, $a_1/a_1^* < a_2/a_2^*$, and we export good 1 in exchange for imports of good 2 from Japan. Now let innovation reduce a_2^* so much as to convert the inequality into an equality. This means that there are *no* exploitable differences in advantage: The free trade equilibrium becomes that of self-sufficient autarky; our terms of trade for exports in relation to imports P_1/P_2 have dropped all the way to a_1/a_2 (and a_1^*/a_2^*), robbing us of *all* of our consumer's surplus from trade; by the same token, Japan's terms of trade, P_2^*/P_1^*, have risen from somewhere in the old (a_2^*/a_1^*, a_2/a_1) interval all the way to the top endpoint of a_2/a_1 – and at the same time the innovation gives Japan more of both goods to exchange at these improved terms. The dogmatic free trader who alleges that each and all *must* gain always is shown to be plain wrong.

The n-good case is, not surprisingly, considerably more involved; its details are included in an appendix to this chapter.

Reacting to free-trade's harm

Let one region (say, Japan) always play the free-trade game, always acting as if it is a price taker too small to affect competitive prices. Let us, after the innovation, try to use our monopoly power to offset the harm it may have brought to us. Does the United States have such monopoly power?

Yes. Even if each is a standardized good produced by many independent American and Japanese firms. As long as America has almost 25 percent of global product and Japan 10 percent, if our government acts in concert it should be able to move Japan on its competitive-reaction loci to a state of the system that improves American welfare. Usually a system of tariffs and quotas may not be the Pareto-efficient way for America to play the Mill–Edgeworth–Bickerdike game of "scientific protectionism." But it is one way.

U.S. economic prospects and policy options

Clearly, this ultrarational policy would never call for prohibitive tariffs and quotas that lead to U.S. self-sufficiency. Not-too-large tariffs are what is called for. Whether these are 10 percent or 50 percent tariffs must depend on the parameters of technology and of taste elasticities. Moreover, it is not clear whether the maximal gain achievable by this Machiavellian ploy is equal to a 1 percent increase in per capita U.S. living standards, or 5 percent, or a fraction of 1 percent.

Also, it is reasonably clear that Japan would not stand by and continue to adhere to the rules of the free-trade game if the United States is manifestly playing the role of what economists call the Stackelberg–Edgeworth one-sided duopolist. That tariff retaliation by Japan must presumably involve global deadweight loss, lowering what we can expect from maximally exploiting our monopoly power. Theoretically, *all* parties could end up worse than they would have done under doctrinaire free trade.

Whatever the merits of scientific protectionism, the current politics of would-be American protectionists is far removed from such abstractions. Old and stagnant industries, often with union-induced above-average wage scales, are the ones most likely to succeed in lobbying Congress for curbs on imports. Acceding to those desires can preserve some high-paying American jobs, but only at the cost of lowering the real wages elsewhere that clear the labor market and avoid self-imposed mass unemployment.

The story would be less simple if we postulated many corporations. Each produces goods at increasing returns, with marginal products rising with scale, $\partial^2 q/\partial L^2 \gg 1$. Laissez-faire leads under these conditions in America and Japan to multiple possibilities, in which each region might end with no predictable set of successful products.

Fair trade versus free trade

The economic theory of the seminar room and the learned treatises seems to be in another world from discussions in Congress and the newspapers. When imports from the Pacific Basin kill off American manufacturing jobs, that is assumed axiomatically to be an economic tragedy.

Most businessmen and politicians are ashamed not to pay lip service to free trade. Senator John C. Danforth of Missouri is a typical example, and was written up in the *Wall Street Journal* of December 2, 1986. He is upset when his constituents lose jobs in the shoe industry. He is not against really free trade. But he believes that the Japanese, while pretending to believe in free trade, in fact engage in unfair trade. They protect formally against imports of meat and citrus. Informally, they block bids by our telecommunications industries. They dump goods into our markets at below true costs. An elaborate system of reciprocity among Japanese corporations effectively excludes our exports from getting into the Japanese markets.

The net result is to make Danforth favor U.S. protectionism. Until the Japanese change their ways, as attested by a marked reduction in our bilateral trade deficit with Japan, people like Danforth would favor surcharges, tariffs, and quotas targeted against Japan and similar Pacific nations. Such protectionists also lend a friendly ear to proposals for "a new industrial policy."

My MIT colleagues Lester Thurow and Michael Piore, disturbed by what they see as a decimation of middle-class workers and sapping of vigor of the trade union movement, regretfully come out in favor of some interferences with free trade. The more liberal of our two parties, the Democrats, are at present more protectionist than conservative Republicans such as President Reagan.

There is some truth to the charge that Japan does impede some imports. It is a pity that naggings by friends like me get almost nowhere in persuading Japan to throw open her markets out of her own self interest. The Danforths would soon learn that the elimination of *all* unfair trade practices would still leave us with a large deficit on current account and trade.

Calling the bluff of protectionists would not convert them into free traders. The mayors of Pittsburgh and Detroit and the congressional delegations from those manufacturing regions would still want to protect their jobs from cost-cutting importers.

I must therefore rush on to discuss the basic economic causation of America's overvalued dollar and resulting trade deficit with Japan.

Basic trends

First, it is successful innovation and investment by Pacific Basin countries in bringing down costs of manufacturing that dictates a balance of payments problem for an advanced country like the United States with its reduced pace of productivity progress and its modest rate of private saving. Under floating exchange rates, the presumption would be for a declining dollar even if macroeconomic policy were optimal or tolerably good.

Second, United States macro policy in the Reagan years has been disastrous from the standpoint of the balance of trade. The single important factor raising real interest rates here and attracting demand for dollars on capital account is our colossal basic fiscal deficit. Rightist supply siders deny that "crowding out" of investment is possible. Neoclassical and post-Keynesian economics, however, recognize truth in the story that public fiscal thriftlessness compounds our low private thriftiness. Favorable tax incentives for investment – investment credits, fast depreciation, and so forth – reinforce the rise in market-clearing real interest rates. Financing the public debt competes with domestic investment needs for Americans' savings; eagerness of foreigners to cycle back their balance of payments surpluses perpetuates overvaluation of the dollar on current account as it alleviates the crowding out process here by having some of the crowding out of investment take place with respect to Asian and European domestic investments.

Robert Mundell long ago pointed out the therapy for such unbalance. America should raise taxes and cut expenditures to increase its overall saving and reduce its real interest rates; Japan and Germany should do the opposite, pursuing a looser fiscal policy and a tighter monetary policy.

Enlarged saving here and reduced saving there will call for less capital inflow into America. This means a downward floating dollar, and greater competitiveness in global production for American producers.

It is easy to diagnose these basics, but hard to implement the implied therapies.

Quantitative trends

Figures 5.1 to 5.4 provide a picture of U.S. international variables up through 1984. A glance at Figure 5.1 leads to a straightforward but superficial impression: During the 1980s the dollar floated upward, and at this same time our trade balance deteriorated drastically. This simple story accords with standard theories of international finance. Lerner–Marshall elasticities being orthodoxly favorable, appreciation of an exchange rate moves the balance of payments adversely.

An important corollary follows from this paradigm: To alleviate or reverse the deterioration of America's current account, somehow engineer a depreciation of the dollar and an appreciation of the yen and mark.

Other things being equal, one may agree with this thrust. Reality, however, is not so simple. Quantitatively, the "other things being equal" provisos of the elementary classroom have not been valid in the 1970–86 period. Irreversible accelerations in Pacific Basin productivities are an important part of the picture: Shifts of curves and not reversible movements along curves must be reckoned with. Therefore, it may well take a drop in the dollar exchange rate of more than its post-1978 rise of 40 percent to accommodate the greater pace of innovation ahead.

Figure 5.2 reminds us that we should be working with real exchange rates and not simply with nominal rates. Thus, H. S. Wainright, a Boston firm giving advice to Wall Street and one of the few practitioners of "rational expectationism" with a respectable forecasting performance, recently argued that the lire had depreciated more than the dollar and that the U.S. balance

124   Paul A. Samuelson

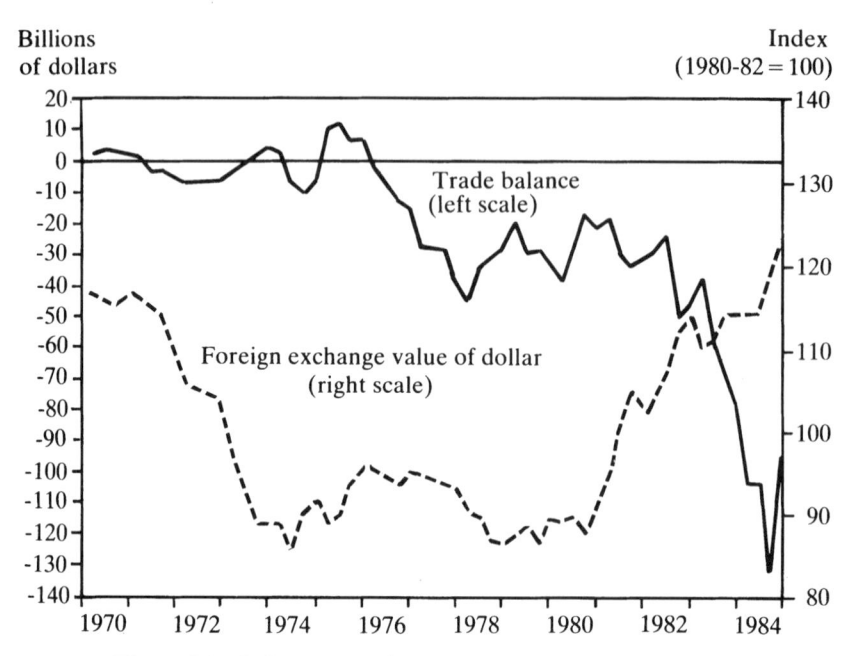

Figure 5.1 U.S. merchandise trade balance (seasonally adjusted annual rate) and weighted average real foreign exchange value of U.S. dollar (quarterly). *Source*: Data Resources Inc. and Morgan Guaranty Trust Co.

depreciated most. When the Italian price level rises faster than the American, experienced economists should know it is normal for a lire depreciation even when real exchange rates and real balances have not been changing at all.

Figure 5.2 reveals that in the crucial period of 1980–5, the real rise in the dollar averaged out to a bit less than its nominal rise, presumably because Japanese and German price levels were under slightly better control than our own.

Figure 5.3 confirms that interest rates in different countries tend to show common levels and common movements. During the first Reagan term, U.S. real interest rates did tend to move ahead of foreign rates, sucking in capital funds from abroad and suggesting to players in the futures markets that the dollar might be susceptible to a future fall in its relative level. Figure 5.3 could be augmented to show that the rise in U.S. real interest rates during the first half of the 1980s did help pull up real rates abroad.

Figure 5.4 both confirms and contradicts the thesis that expanding our rate of GNP growth tends to make the dollar depreciate. The Nixon–Burns boom of 1972 does cause the dollar to fall. The ensuing recession of 1974 does

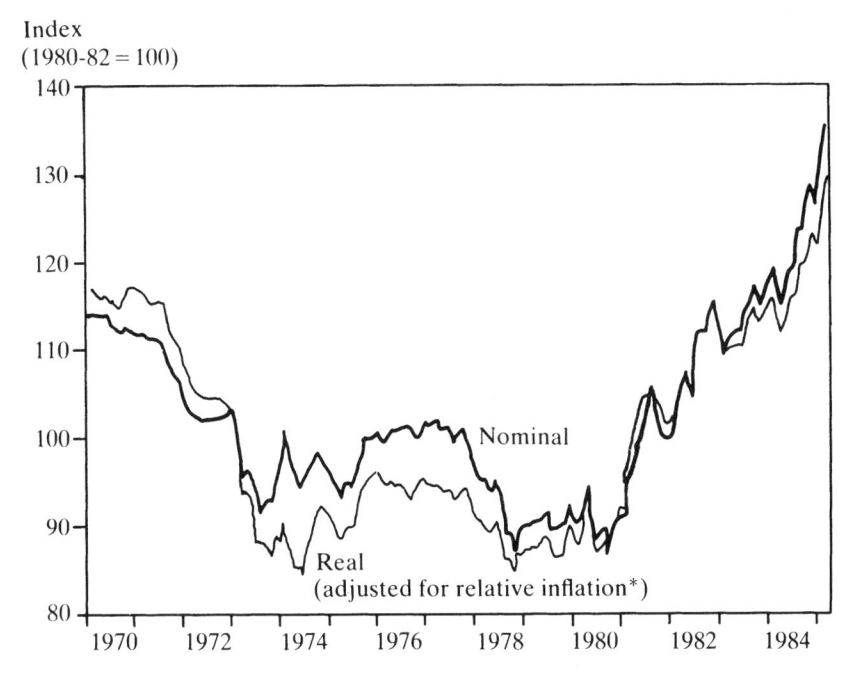

Figure 5.2 Weighted average foreign exchange value of U.S. dollar (in terms of 15 major currencies weighted according to bilateral manufactures trade, based on monthly averages of daily rates). *Source*: Morgan Guaranty Trust Co.
*Inflation measured in terms of wholesale prices of nonfood manufactures.

reverse its course. However, the rise of the dollar in the 1980s must be in answer to a different drumbeat since there was no concomitant oscillation in real GNP growth rates. Nor do we find in Figures 5.5 and 5.6 any extraordinary misbehaviors of price indexes or the money supply sufficient to account for the extraordinary rise of the dollar.

I must agree with Kazuo Ueda's analysis at the March 1986 conference in Tokyo sponsored by the National Bureau of Economic Research and Tokyo University. Among the long-term structural factors shaping our exchange rate are the differential saving tendencies of Americans and Japanese. The most notable change in these long-term tendencies was the drastic rise in the U.S. fiscal deficit between 1980 and 1982. This further lowered America's net saving and raised our market-clearing real interest rates.

The Reagan deficit, or if you will the Reagan–O'Neill deficit, did contribute to crowding out of investment here; and, by raising world interest rates, must also have been crowding out investment abroad as we absorbed on

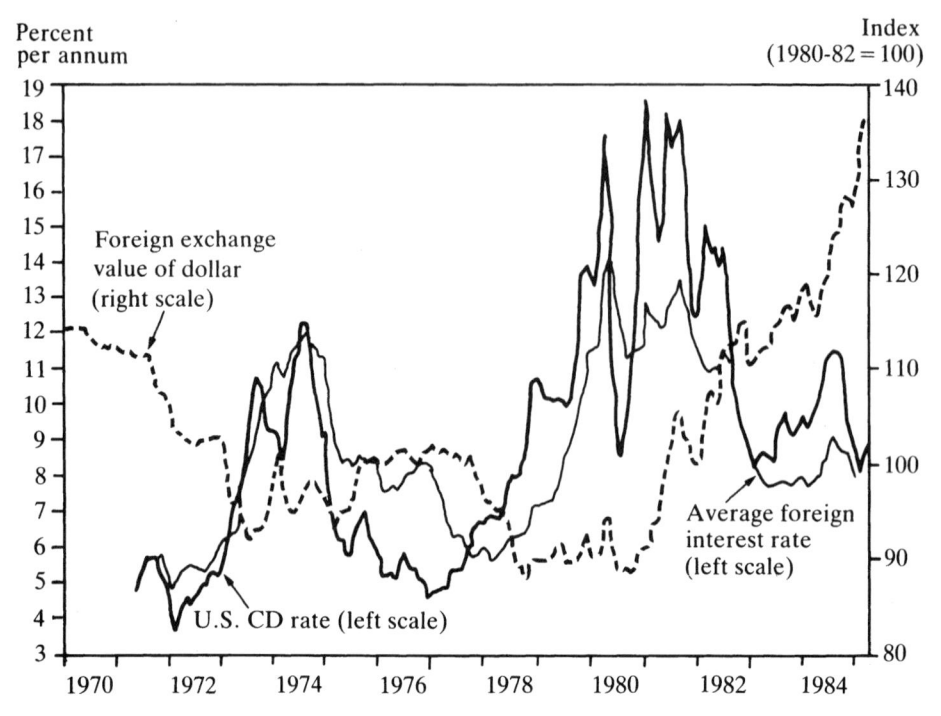

Figure 5.3 Three-month interest rates: United States and weighted average for four foreign countries, and weighted average nominal foreign exchange value of the U.S. dollar (monthly averages of daily figures). *Source*: Board of Governors of the Federal Reserve System and Morgan Guaranty Trust Co.

capital account foreigners' limited savings, diverting some of this away from financing capital formation abroad.

Current trends

The dollar has been floating downward relative to the yen and the mark ever since February 1985. After September 22, 1985, when the Group of Five met in New York to agree on official exchange-market interventions to help the dollar depreciate further, good progress has been made in reducing the degree of the dollar's overvaluation on current account.

Some economists dogmatically deny that a few tens of billions of dollars of stabilization operations can have any perceptible effect on markets that involve hundreds of billions of dollars of gross transactions. Other economists, like me, suspect that when the setting is right for the dollar to fall spon-

U.S. economic prospects and policy options

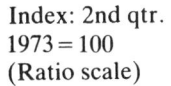

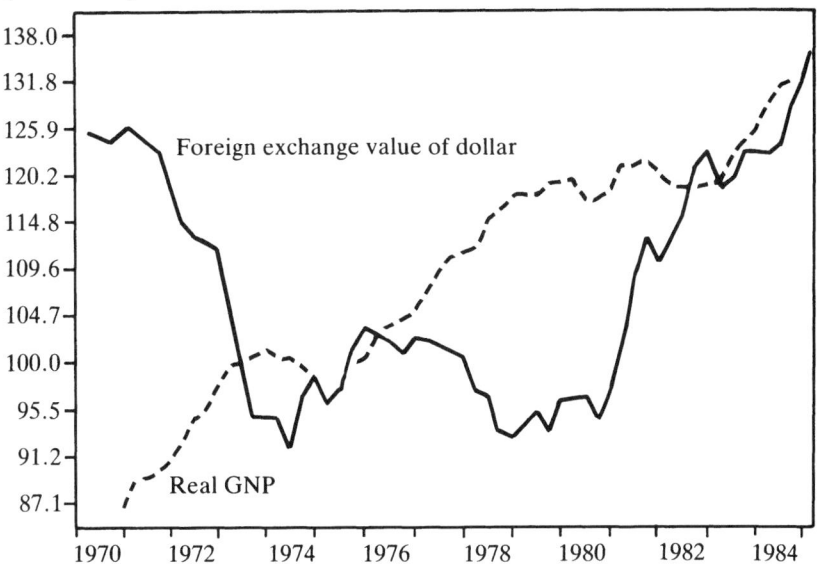

Figure 5.4 U.S. real GNP (seasonally adjusted) and weighted average real foreign exchange value of U.S. dollar (quarterly). *Source*: Data Resources Inc. and Morgan Guaranty Trust Co.

taneously, at just such a time the authorities have a window of opportunity. Then their limited pushes can speed up and accentuate the depreciation that is in accordance with economic fundamentals.

Still, I must confess to being pleasantly surprised by the degree and persistence of dollar weakness in the year after February 1985. Much of the credit, one suspects, was due to determined Japanese cooperation.

The Bundesbank and the German government were less enthusiastically cooperative. In private, Chancellor Helmut Kohl and his colleagues are quite pleased with Germany's current economic pattern. They are unwilling to risk present stability just because the tiresome Americans keep urging them to fire up their locomotive.

West Germany and the Common Market have less to fear from American resentment than perhaps the Japanese do. American public and Congressional opinion is resentful of the flood of imports from the Pacific Basin. Most of us economists, both in the United States and in Japan, have been urging that the most effective tactic against nascent American protectionism would be de-

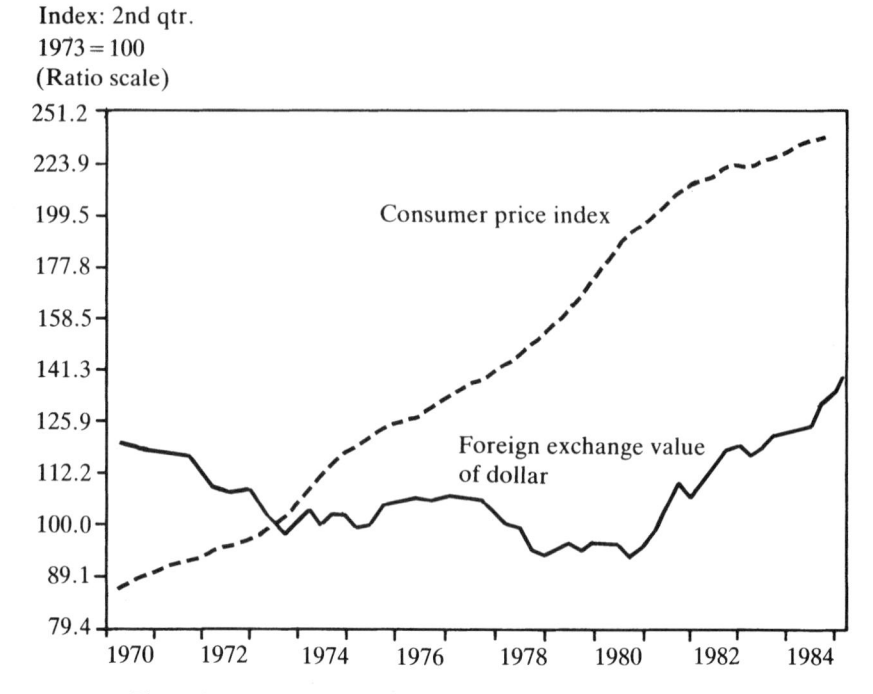

Figure 5.5 U.S. Consumer Price Index (seasonally adjusted) and weighted average nominal foreign exchange value of U.S. dollar (quarterly). *Source*: DRI and Morgan Guaranty Trust Co.

preciation of the dollar exchange rate. I believe the Japanese authorities have been persuaded to give this therapy a good hard try.

Repeatedly I have suggested that a powerful reinforcement to intervention operations would be informal capital controls designed to impede the automatic flow into dollar assets of the trade surpluses accruing to Japanese firms and investors.

I suspect that some of the 1985–6 success in raising the yen relative to the dollar has been due to strong moral suasion exercised by Japanese authorities on banks, insurance companies, corporations and institutional investors. I have no proof that this has been the modus operandi in the background. But it does seem plausible. In any case, some such forces need to be invoked to explain why relatively modest intervention operations were able to achieve such quantitative results.

If the goal of dollar depreciation has been so agreeably realized, cannot Japanese and American observers now breathe more easily? Hasn't protectionism been contained? Is it not reasonable to look ahead toward a substantial

U.S. economic prospects and policy options

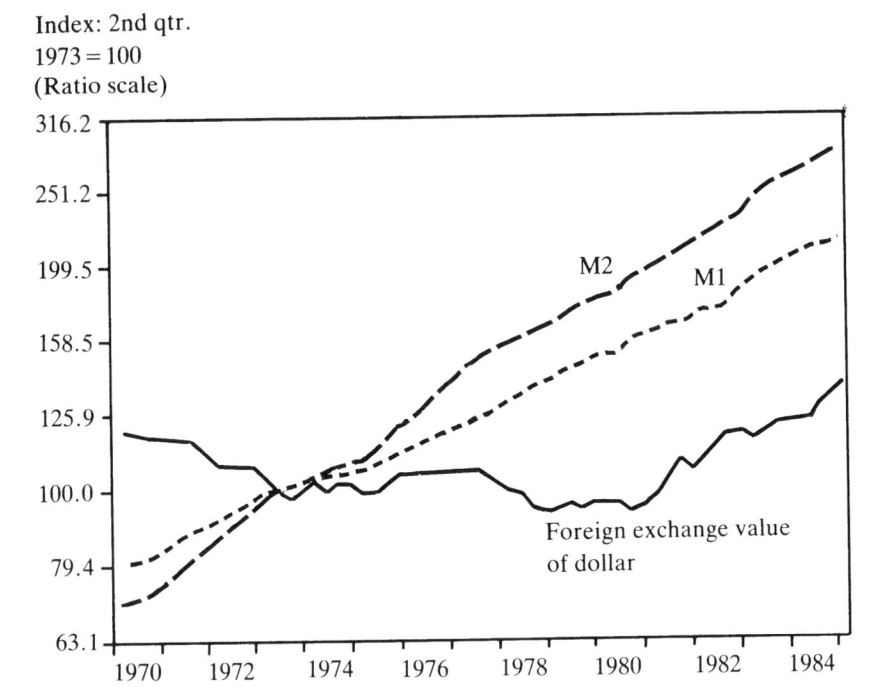

Figure 5.6 M1 and M2 (seasonally adjusted) and weighted average nominal foreign exchange value of U.S. dollar (quarterly). *Source*: Data Resources Inc. and Morgan Guaranty Trust Co.

reduction in the U.S.-Japanese bilateral trade deficit? Reckoning up the costs of the stabilization interventions, can't we conclude now that they are behind us, that the game was well worth its costs?

I have to warn against comfortable affirmative answers to these questions. The victory is not won. The game is not over.

Those Japanese investors who have been deterred from buying dollars by fear that the yen would fall further, once they are confident that the yen has reached a plateau around 160 to the dollar, may regain the courage to invest in Wall Street securities. Successful intervention to keep the yen's value high may have to be more than a one-time once-and-for-all operation.

The Nakasone government's engineered rise in Tokyo interest rates definitely did help the yen to appreciate in 1985. Against this must be reckoned Washington's disappointment that Prime Minister Nakasone stalwartly refused to embark on vigorous fiscal policy stimulus. Surely Japanese economists understand the important logic of Columbia University's Robert Mundell that I already mentioned.

130 Paul A. Samuelson

To sum up, the political fever for protectionism against Japan was a degree lower in 1986 than it was during spring and summer of 1985. (Recovery of control of the Senate by the Democrats late in 1986, realistically, must raise the chances of new protectionism.)

Median scenarios

There exist scores of alternative forecasts for the three years 1986, 1987, 1988. Professor Victor Zarnowitz of the University of Chicago has found empirically that the group of consensus forecasters does better than does any one chosen at random. Even if we try to identify the few single best forecasters in the group, it is unclear whether we can isolate any in whom one should place greater confidence than the whole group deserves.

Therefore, I have chosen from the October 10, 1985, *Blue Chip Indicators* the long-range projections presented in Table 5.3. Where the group has not estimated a variable, I have used and marked with an asterisk the December 1985 Wharton projections. (Late 1986 projections, I perceive, would tell a similar story.)

To illustrate the variability of such estimates, let me note how the highest 10 differ from the lowest 10 of the consensus forecasters on some key 1986–90 variables (Table 5.4).

The bottom line in Table 5.3 is literally "the bottom line." If our experts are right, the U.S. balance of payments problem will not be cured when President Reagan leaves the White House in January 1989. Nor will it be in sight of being solved, or even be on its way to being solved. And yet these experts are somewhat sanguine that

1. Some progress will be made in reducing our fiscal deficit.
2. Inflation will remain under good control.
3. The dollar will be floating downward in 1986–8.
4. No bad explosion of protectionism will have taken place.

A realistic outlook

I agree, in substance. A downward overshoot of the dollar will, I fear, be needed for several years if the dynamics of Pacific Basin innovation is to be fully offset. A drastic reduction in America's basic fiscal deficit will be required. The Federal Reserve will need to offset a new fiscal tightness fully and militantly.

Perhaps we face here one more case of economists' elasticity pessimism? However, going by the evidence and making eclectic use of prudent modern economic theory, we must face up to a continuing long-run problem with the

Table 5.3. Long-term U.S. projections

	1980	1981	1982	1983	1984	1985	1986	1987	1988
Real GNP, ann.gr.rate(%)	−0.3	2.5	−2.1	3.7	6.8	2.5	3.1	2.7	3.2
Inflation rate, CPI-all urban (%)	13.5	10.4	6.2	3.2	4.3	3.4	4.0	4.6	4.7
Unemployment, civ.rate(%)	7.2	7.6	9.7	9.6	7.5	7.2	7.1	7.1	7.0
Personal saving rate(%)	6.0	6.7	6.2	5.0	6.1	3.9	4.8	5.2	5.6
$ exchange rate (FRB:1973 = 100)	87.4	103.3	116.6	125.3	138.3	143.6	124.1	118.8	112
Auto sales (mi, with imports)	9.0	8.5	8.0	9.2	10.4	10.9	10.5	10.6	10.6
Housing starts (mi)	1.3	1.1	1.1	1.7	1.8	1.8	1.8	1.7	1.7
Federal surplus (NIA, Bil$)	−61.3	−64.3	−148.1	−178.6	−175.8	−190.7	−172.5	−142.8	−128
3-month Treasury rate(%)	11.4	14.0	10.6	8.6	9.5	7.5	7.6	8.0	8.1
AAA bonds (%)	11.9	14.2	13.8	12.0	12.7	11.4	11.2	11.1	10.8
Current account balance (Bil$)	1.9	6.3	−8.1	−40.8	−101.5	−134.8	−139.5	−127.1	−100

Source: From *Blue Chip Indicators,* October 10, 1985, p. 8; $ exchange rate and federal surplus are from *Wharton Quarterly Model Outlook,* vol. 4, no. 12 (December 1985), Table 1.1: 1988 estimates by Paul A. Samuelson.

Table 5.4. *1986–90 mean projections*

	Group average	High 10	Low 10
Real GNP growth	3.1	3.7	2.7
Price inflation	4.5	5.3	3.5
Unemployment	6.9	7.4	6.5

American balance of payments and with harmonious Japan–U.S. economic relations.

As I appraise the econometrics of the 1985–90 outlook for the United States and its trading partners, the U.S. deficit on current account will not heal itself by 1990. Even with a proper mix of macro policies here and abroad, improvements will be slow in coming. As a result, the rational odds of a protectionist blowoff in America must be put at no less than 1 in 2. Such an eventuality would be an economic tragedy – a tragedy for Japan and Asia, but also a tragedy for America's own well-being.

Appendix

n-good equilibrium

There are many goods in the world of reality. What is the minimal general equilibrium model that can justify the many Rules upon which our diagnosis and policy prescriptions are based?

The most manageable model is the two-region Ricardian one with tastes uniformly homothetic for all persons everywhere. These tastes can be summarized by the following "regular" first-degree-homogeneous utility function, $u[C] = u[C_1, \ldots, C_n]$, whose indifference contours are *strictly convex* and *smoothly differentiable*, are *insatiable*, and where something of every good is indispensable:

$$u[mC] = mu[C], m > 0 : \text{homotheticity} \tag{i}$$

$u[A] = u[B]$ and $A \neq B$ implies

$$u[\tfrac{1}{2}A + \tfrac{1}{2}B] > u[A] : \text{strict quasi-concavity} \tag{ii}$$

$$(\partial u[C_1, \ldots, C_n]/\partial C_j) = (u_j[C]) > 0 \tag{iii}$$

for $C > 0$: insatiability

For $A \gneq 0$ and $B > 0$, $u[B] > u[A]$: indispensability. (iv)

U.S. economic prospects and policy options

We are given positive vectors of regions' labor costs and labor supplies: (a_j), (a_j^*), (L,L^*). With transport costs zero and trade free of quotas and other impediments, the geographical pattern of production is determined by competition (save for inessential indifferences at various singular specifications of the above parameters). Competition also determines a unique vector of the world totals of production $(O_j + O_j^*)$ and, what is the same thing, the world totals of consumption $(C_j + C_j^*)$. Also uniquely determined are real price ratios (P_j/P_1) and equivalent (P_j^*/P_1^*) and the real wage ratio W^*/W, along with (P_j/W) and (P_j^*/W^*). The regional breakdown of $(C_j + C_j^*)$ into unique fractional shares $s(C_j + C_j^*)$ and $(1 - s)(C_j + C_j^*)$ is also uniquely determinate in the present model, which has balanced income effects that preclude multiplicity of equilibria.

The present model is simple because the world totals can be generated as a solution to the following maximum problem:
Subject to

$$\sum_1^n a_j Q_j = L, \sum_1^n a_j^* Q_j^* = L^*; Q_j \geq 0, Q_j^* \geq 0 \quad (v)$$

$$\text{Max } u[Q_1 + Q_1^*, \ldots, Q_n + Q_n^*]$$
$$Q_j, Q_j^*$$
$$= u[L, L^*; a_j, a_j^*] = u[L, L^*] \text{ for short.}$$

It can be shown that $u[L,L^*]$ is first-degree-homogeneous and concave, with positive partial derivatives that measure each region's real wage (expressed in the numeraire of u itself, $P_u = 1 = P_u^*$):

$$\partial u[L,L^*]/\partial L = W/P_u = w > 0 \quad (v')$$
$$\partial u[L,L^*]/\partial L^* = W^*/P_u^* = w^*.$$

The Kuhn–Tucker conditions for (v)'s maximum, expressed to take advantage of the goods' indispensabilities, yield the following first-order necessary-and-sufficient conditions for the competitive real prices and wages $(P_j/P_u = p_j = P_j^*/P_u^* = p_j^*; w, w^*)$:

$$u_i[Q + Q^*] = \text{Min}[wa_i, w^*a_i^*], \quad i = 1, \ldots, n \quad (vi)$$
$$= p_i = p_i^* > 0$$
$$Q_i (\text{Min}[wa_i, w_i^* a_i^*] - wa_i) = 0 \quad (vii)$$
$$Q_i^* (\text{Min}[wa_i, w_i^* a_i^*] - w^* a_i^*) = 0.$$

Conditions (v), (vi), and (vii) are sufficient to determine at least one positive solution for the unknowns $(Q_j, Q_j^*, p_j, p_j^*, w, w^*)$. A unique solution obtains for

369

the variables $(Q_j+Q_j^*, p_j = p_j^*, w, w^*, \Sigma_1^n p_j Q_j, \Sigma_1^n p_j^* Q_j^*)$. For particular values of the parameters, as when $n = 2$ and $a_2/a_1 = a_2^*/a_1^*$, or for L^*/L ratios that entail $wa_3/w^*a_3^* = wa_4/w^*a_4^*$, there can be an infinity of breakdowns of the $(Q_j + Q_j^*)$ vector into (Q_j) and (Q_j^*) specialization patterns that are inessentially different.

Once we know the equilibrium p's and Q's we can deduce the equilibrium values for the regional consumption vectors, (C_j) and (C_j^*), from the balance of trade relations:

$$(C_j + C_j^*) = (Q_j + Q_j^*) \qquad \text{(viii)}$$

$$(C_j) = [wL/(wL + w^*L^*)](Q_j + Q_j^*), \quad j = 1, \ldots, n \qquad \text{(ix)}$$

$$(C_j^*) = [w^*L^*/(wL + w^*L^*)](Q_j + Q_j^*).$$

Allowing capital movements will of course suspend (ix)'s balance of trade equality. But a model without transport impediments and tariffs is not one well designed to illustrate the deterioration of Japanese terms of trade that will be generated *endogenously* by Japan's running a chronic surplus on current account with America.

Remarks: Suppose that along with these *n freely* tradable goods, there were *m* nontradable goods $(y_1, \ldots, y_m)$ and $(y_1^*, \ldots, y_m^*)$. Then the device of a one-person maximizer would not work to generate the competitive general equilibrium. The same sacrifice in analytical simplicity would be introduced if some or all of these goods could be shipped in trade but at positive transportation costs. Thus, we might work with the 1954 Samuelson "iceberg" model in which export by us of y_j of good $n + j$ shrinks to $g_j y_j$ as $(1 - g_j) y_j$ "evaporates in transport" as the technical cost of shipment – where g_j is a fraction, $0 \leq g_j \leq 1$; and in which $g_j^* y_j^*$ of Japan's export of g_j^* reaches our shore. For some $(1 - g_j)$'s being positive, the one-maximizer trick would need elaboration.

The present general equilibrium can be tested for its comparative statical properties. Thus, a balanced halving in all Japan's (a_j^*) coefficients would be equivalent to doubling its L^*: That must increase *world* potential well being since

$$u[L, 2L^*] > u[L, L^*].$$

And, save in the singular case where a^* is proportional to a and there are no operative comparative advantages, such balanced innovations must raise U.S. per capita real income in the form of w or $\partial u/\partial L$ – for the reason that $\partial^2 u/\partial L \, \partial L^*$ is generally positive.

The two-good instance is easy to diagram. Figure 5.7 depicts the three possible cases: (a) where we and they are enough balanced in labor supplies

U.S. economic prospects and policy options

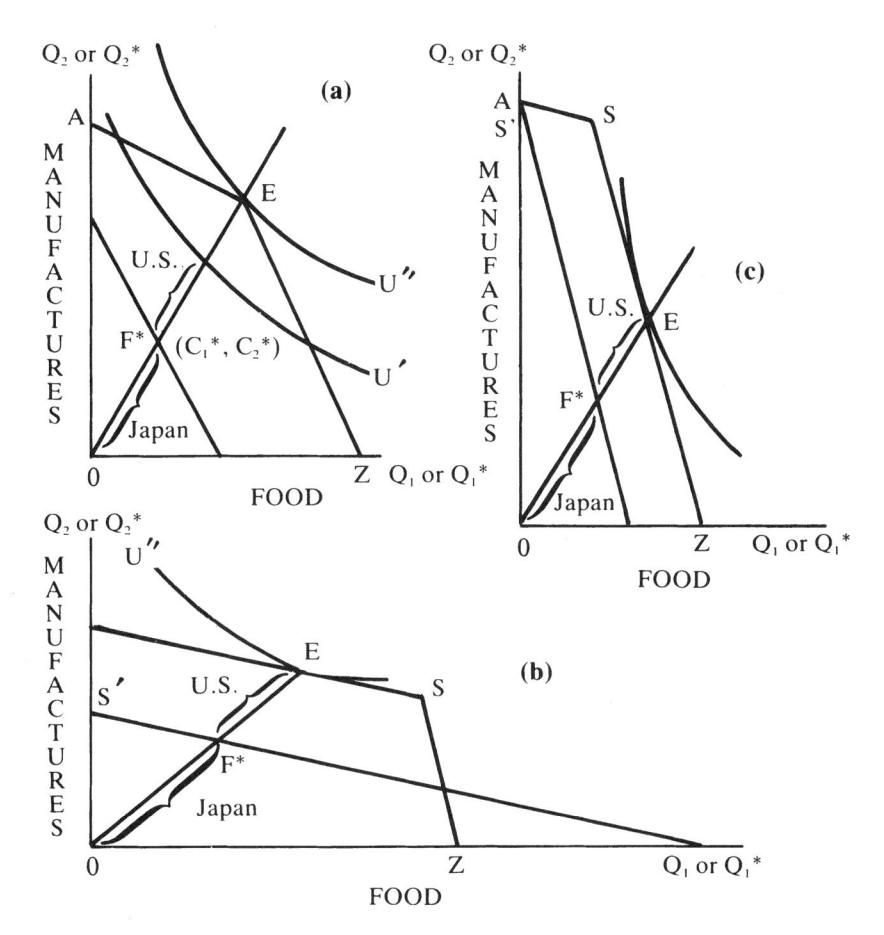

Figure 5.7 In (a) the United States specializes in food and Japan in manufactures, at E where the indifference slope is between the production cost slopes of regions. Japan's share of global E is at F^*, with U.S. share of F^*E. In (b), the United States produces both goods and its a_2/a_1 gives a price ratio equal to AS slope. In (c), Japan produces both goods and its a_2^*/a_1^* gives price ratio. Competition determines endogenously which one of (a), (b), or (c) obtains.

for each region to be producing only one good; (b) where Japan is so small as to require us to produce both goods; and (c) where it is the United States that is "small."

The three-good case requires three-dimensional geometry and can be left to motivated readers.

Notes

1. Table 5.1 builds on the elaborate University of Pennsylvania measurements of real incomes and purchasing-power-parities sponsored by the World Bank and the United Nations, and carried out by Irving Kravis, Robert Summers, Alan Heston, and others. (See Irving B. Kravis, Alan Heston, and Robert Summers, *International Comparisons of Real Product and Purchasing Power, United Nations International Comparison Project: Phase II,* Johns Hopkins University Press, 1978.) Their methodology corrects for the biases contained in the World Bank Atlas, which utilizes GNP estimates measured in local currencies deflated by current foreign exchange rates. In a year like 1985, when the yen appreciated by 20 percent, such crude purchasing-power-parity assumptions could exaggeratedly raise Japan's per capita real income from three-quarters of the U.S. income to almost 90 percent. By contrast, the Kravis team's methodology uses surveys of actual prices paid by Japanese and by Americans to deflate their respective nominal national incomes. If the yen/dollar exchange rate alters violently between two benchmark years, utilizing estimates of prices actually paid in each country eliminates spurious bouncing around of regional per capita real income ratios.

    I have included in Table 5.1 data on South Korea, West Germany, and various other countries that may be of interest. Of course any end-of-the-century projections must be hypothetical and would have to be based on imprecise guesses about future growth rates in Gross Domestic Products and in intercountry terms of trade.

2. A start at analyzing such an Adam Smith, Allyn Young, and Bertil Ohlin world has been made by Elhanan Helpman and Paul R. Krugman, *Market Structure and Foreign Trade: Increasing Returns, Imperfect Competitions, and the International Economy,* MIT Press, 1985, and I can refer the interested reader to that reference.

3. See Paul A. Samuelson, "Ohlin Was Right," *The Swedish Journal of Economics,* vol. 73, no. 4 (1971), pp. 365–84.

503

CHAPTER 2

THE PAST AND FUTURE OF INTERNATIONAL TRADE THEORY

Paul A. Samuelson

A Keynote Address is the windup for the main show. To help measure where you are going in the future, you need to survey previous history. I must say that reviewing past troops is a pleasant task at an international economics symposium.

If you've got it, flaunt it. Well, we in trade theory do have a lot to display. For, as I pointed out years back, the scientific corpus of international trade has led the way and broken the ground for the corpus of general economic science.

1. Thus, the first general equilibrium was not by Léon Walras. Sixty-five years earlier it was by John Stuart Mill—and in connection with international equilibrium, as John Chipman explicated long ago. When I began economics, Alfred Marshall was the Grand Emperor. But indeed his clothes were vastly overadmired. Still his genuinely finest garments were his curves of reciprocal international demand—the only part of his lifeworks in which a general equilibrium was truly achieved.

2. The great names in trade theory are the great names in general economic theory. Here are only a few: Ricardo. Mill, Marshall, and Mangoldt. Edgeworth and Pareto. Taussig, Viner, Haberler, Ohlin, Lerner, and Leontief. I stop short of the modern era.

3. With the names of Lerner and Leontief we are entering into that modern era. We've come a long way, baby, in these last 65 years, a time short enough to have been experienced in the academic lifetime of Gottfried Haberler, our venerable dean who still carries the flag for free trade.

I recently had occasion to eyeball the state of our art in the late 1920s. You would not believe how primitive that state was—how error ridden and superficial. Did Ricardo have two inconsistent theories as to where the terms of trade 'twixt Portuguese wine and English cloth must settle? Luigi Einaudi and James Angell believed he did. It took a Viner and a Sraffa to rebut that fallacy: at best Ricardo had *no* theory to determine where, within the cost limits, equilibrium price ratios would fall. Before Bertil Ohlin was 25, he did the great works that justified his 1977 Nobel Prize. But I could not believe my eyes when I reread his 1933 classic with a microscope and discovered that he indeed did believe it would be a contradiction for trade in goods to *fully* equalize factor returns!

4. To the omniscient graduate students of one age, the great pioneers of an earlier age seem veritably to be sleepwalkers. Dimwitted Aristotle who expected pennies to fall faster than feathers. Mystical Kepler who drew elliptical rabbits out of woolly hats. Befuddled Ricardo who thought he could get rid of land's contamination on *natural price* by concentrating on laborers who work at external-margin land or at intensive margins (that are allegedly not endogenous unknowns). If scientists on the revolutionary roads to Damascus are behind themselves, that is because they are also ahead of themselves.

When it sinks into the seminars and treatises on history of thought that the great classical economists never fully understood their own labor-land-time models—extrapolating from experience, I despair that this may take another century—the savants in *dogmengeschichte* will find us foreign-trade theorists already there waiting for them. (I snitch from the New Jersey mayor who said: I don't know where America is going, but when they get there, they'll find Newark waiting.)

I mean by this that Ricardo and Mill and Bastable, when they discussed the corn laws and not the high-fallutin' topics of the labor theory of value, clearly employed a 3-factor not a 1-factor or 2-factor paradigm. This was brought home to me when a decade ago I investigated what it was that Marion Crawford might have had to read in setting aright the famous post-1925 Australian case for a tariff. (I could have saved the many hours of library work that I reported on in the 1981 *Quarterly Journal* if I had remembered Dick Caves' magisterial review of the literature in his 1960 Harvard dissertation on *Trade and Economic Structure*.) What Caves and I found out was that, long before Heckscher, Ohlin, and Haberler broke the chains of labor-only comparative advantage models, Ricardo, Mill, Longfield, Bastable, Pigou, and

The Past and Future of International Trade Theory

Edgeworth had addressed the policy problems for foreign trade of non-labor factors of production.

5. Even though Samuel Johnson has said that Keynote Speakers are not under oath, I can claim for us:

> We in trade theory are the Green Beret élite troops of the profession. We lead the way and remove the landmines. If an Alan Turing concerns himself with when an equation system has a unique inverse solution in the large, you are not surprised that it is in connection with McKenzie-Gale-Nikaido expositions of factor-price equalization.
>
> If mathematical graph theory finds an application in economics, that is not surprisingly in connection with Ron Jones and Harvey Wagner investigations of multilateral arbitrage inequalities in spatial economics.
>
> The Robinson-Sraffa paradoxes on reswitchings and improved steady-state consumptions induced by *rises* in the interest rate—these find their deepest analysis by Steedman and Metcalfe in time-phased technologies that trade.
>
> With the regularity of Halley's Comet but at shorter periodicities, economists like Adam Smith, Friedrich List, Vilfredo Pareto, Frank Graham, Allyn Young, Will Baumol, Ralph Gomory, Paul Krugman, Elhanan Helpman, and Paul Romer rediscover the complications for competitive equilibrium occasioned by non-constant-returns-to-scale technology. (Despite help from Will Baumol and Paul Krugman, I still have not reached an intuitive grasp of Gomory's application of integer programming to U.S.-Japan specialization patterns in equilibrium.)

375

Indulge me now while I tell a scientist story. It even has the virtue of being true. Almost six decades ago, I was the first genuine economist in Harvard's top Society of Fellows. That was a heady honor. Among other things it meant that I was dinner companion with some famous scholars: Alfred North Whitehead, the philosopher; Willard van Quine, the logician; and Stan Ulam, the young Polish mathematician who was to reinvent the Monte Carlo method of calculating at Los Alamos and to originate the basic idea to make possible the hydrogen bomb. The point of this story was that I got to talk to America's first world class mathematician every two months, George Birkhoff, who discovered the Strong Ergodic Theorem and fathered Garrett Birkhoff. Alas, George had no small talk. He could talk about himself, but that was big talk—big with a capital B. Usually we spent the evening discussing who was a first-class mathematician. Present company excepted, that was virtually an empty set. George and Norbert Wiener had a love-hate relationship: each loved himself and hated the other; but there was a grudging respect.

By the time the cheese and salad arrived and the 1929 Burgundy was running out, we got down to fourth-class mathematicians or even $\sqrt{17}$-class chaps. One night in desperate boredom, I said: "I've just been reading Oliver Kellogg's *Potential Theory*. You knew him, didn't you?"

"Oh, Oliver was a very good friend. We played bridge together. Kellogg was, I think I can say, a second-class mathematician. But Oliver was a fool. He came to me around 1921 with a wonderful example: infinite potential capacitance at a point.

"I said to him: 'Oliver, don't breathe a word of it. Work it out.' The damned idiot went and mentioned it to Wiener and in two weeks Norbert had made a killing."

I don't know how this story affects you, but to young Paul A. Samuelson, it was like a kick to the pelvis. Isn't science a search for truth? Aren't we all companions in a common enterprise? If Leibnitz asks Newton a defined question, does not honor mandate an honest answer?

My story is not over. It has just begun. It is one of those tales where your listeners' reactions are more interesting by far than the anecdote itself. It is a virtual Rorschach blot. In 55 years I've collected reactions from half a hundred scholars. Since the hour is late, I'll tell you which I have thought to be the single most interesting one. It is the reaction of Harvard's George Mackey, who has contributed much to the mathematics of quantum theory and statistical mechanics. Here is what Mackey said:

> I agree that Oliver was a fool. For two reasons, and not because he desisted from being a Saint Francis who succored the poor and gave away his finest brain children. Norbert is a fast worker and I [Mackey] am a slow worker. It is indeed unfair that he should be given my credit merely for advancing by a week the time that science knows a new truth. But that is the secondary reason. The real fun in the creative game is in working out a thing for yourself and not having it handed to you on a platter. Fine problems are rare and it is a tragedy not to be able to solve one that has come your way.

Now what is my point? How, as they say in court, does this tie up with trade theory past or future?

It is because, to speak autobiographically, often by way of trade theory there have come my way some of my own most exciting researches. Ricardo's comparative advantage made me ready for linear programming before there was a linear programming. Thus, before there was a Dantzig linear programming algorithm, I wrote a paper showing how Stigler had to be wrong in thinking that Giffen's phenomenon could arise in the Least-Cost-Diet problem.

Again, it was from factor-price equalization that I was led to duality theory: to the Legendre Transformations of Physiocratic Ricardianism and the invariant Factor-Price Tradeoff Frontier 'twixt wages, rent, and the interest rate. Blessed problems, well-defined in useful context, have added to my consumer surplus from the direction of trade theory. Greater gifts can no scholar receive than important problems for us George Mackeys to work out.

Finally, T.N. Srinivasan reminded me of what I had already thought about when Ron Jones was speaking [see Chapter 7 below] about a *comparative advantage* approach to innovational leapfrogging.

My Junior Fellow friend, Stan Ulam, in his most charming manner, once challenged me, saying, "Paul, name me one proposition in the social science [in economics] that is both true and non-trivial." My 1938 reply was: "Ricardo's theory of comparative advantage. Using four numbers, as if by magic, it shows that there is indeed a free lunch—the free lunch that comes from not-previously-obvious geographical specialization that increases world potential production of all possible commodities." Again, trade theory leads our way.

A science seeks perfection and closure. But success brings dull complacency. To the degree that challenging problems remain to be solved, a science stays vital and exciting.

By this test, the theory of international trade is young and lusty. Our platter is full of delicious challenges. In science as elsewhere, it is better to travel than to arrive. And the papers in this volume attest that trade theory is very much on its way.

504

American and European Economic Divergences at Century's End
Paul A. Samuelson
University of Toulouse, France, May 9, 1996

I write often for the foreign press. That gives me ample opportunity to pontificate and nag. Thus, I have been telling the Japanese that theirs is the worst macro-managed economy in the 1990s: paralysis by the bureaucratic mandarins from the Tokyo University Law School, plus the chaos of the faction-ridden Diet, has perpetuated a completely unnecessary Japanese slump. And Japanese voters have passively acquiesced to the impasse.

None of that is your business or mine here today. But to sharpen my point and make it more persuasive to Japanese readers, here is how I framed the argument:

> You in Japan are now at the fork of the road. You must choose between the European pattern and the American pattern.
>
> If the Bank of Japan persists in speaking only kitchen German à la the *Bundesbank*, your GDP will grow only as slowly as Germany and France are now growing. And your unemployment rate, after we correct for Japanese ability to conceal disguised unemployment, will soar toward the double-digit percentages so typical of European Union Countries.
>
> I went on to write: On the other hand, there is the Nineties American pattern for you to follow. The United States was the first to recover from the global 1991 Gulf War Recession. For years we have surprised ourselves by outpacing the other leading countries of the world. Millions and tens of millions of new American jobs have been created *net* since the 1970s when worldwide productivity growth halved in the most advanced nations of the world -- a contrast with Europe's almost stagnant job total.
>
> And, I went on to boast, all this happened while our independent Federal Reserve got rid of the 1970s' stagflation and was keeping a steadying hand on the credit throttle. U.S. inflation in the 1990s remained contained at between two and three percent per annum for the official cost of living index. Since our best experts on the technical theory of index number construction tell us that the true rate of inflation is

maybe 1½ percent *less* than the overstated official index, American inflation behavior has pleasantly astounded us American economists.

We pinch ourselves and say, "What went right?"

Notice my intellectual arrogance when I leave the pages of learned journals on mathematical economics and write for the lay public. John Maynard Keynes could not have been more rashly self-confident when preaching to President Franklin Roosevelt in 1933 than was Paul Anthony Samuelson nagging away at the polite Japanese.

Actually, my overdramatic dichotomy between the American and European dichotomy backfired, as I came to realize. People get tired of being nagged and of being bullied by bilateral trade wars. Right now the U.S.-Japan marriage of 50 years ago has moved into an anti-honeymoon stage. I should have called a plan to rescue Japan by any other name than American: packaged as The Pacific Rim Plan it might have gone down better, and then Japan's present faint signs of genuine recovery might have come earlier.

Let me also admit that, although I may do a little low-keyed nagging during my French visit to Toulouse, policy prescription is definitely not the main purpose of this present lecture. Instead I want to grapple with analytical *diagnosis*.

How did our two continents come to diverge in macroeconomic and even microeconomic behavior? What part of that story was *volitional* rather than being *exogenously* dictated by trends of technology and politics?

Naturally I do not know all the answers. And where I do have guesses, they are mostly hypotheses that cannot be self-confidently proclaimed as attested scientific findings. I'll try to confess my doubts and maybes; but remember we are all children of God and Freud, all too prone to wishful thinking.

Let me start with America where my knowledge should be least deficient. The viewpoint I'll try to talk from will not be that of an American patriot but as a member of mainstream economic scholarship everywhere, pretending to be so-to-speak an observer from Mars.

The New Ruthless Economy

America began the 1930s as essentially pure Capitalism. I recall well this fact of my infancy and youth. But after the Great Depression and the New Deal, we went in and came out of World War II as a Mixed Economy--a welfare state much like Europe, Britain or even Sweden. America moved politically toward the Europe that traced its roots to Otto von Bismarck and Louis

Napoleon.

The early editions of my *ECONOMICS* were written just before my teacher Joseph Schumpeter died in 1950. He changed his brilliant mind considerably in the 15 years I knew him, and broadly I believe he agreed with my picture of the Fortune-500 corporations as possessing much "oligopoly power," both at home and abroad. They were not run by John Kenneth Galbraith's technostructure, but neither were they run by owner-managers. Berle-Means had corporate governance pretty much right in 1932. Managers with negligible ownership were secure and fairly autonomous in their jobs and policies because non-cohesive minorities characterized corporate shareowner democracy.

Trade unions had been unimportant in the America of the 1920s, having a foothold only in some AFL crafts. But after the Great Depression brought in Franklin Roosevelt's revolutionary New Deal, the Fortune-500 bought coexistence with their union and non-union workers by sharing some of the oligopoly rents with them. That is what was meant when my textbook first talked of good and peaceful industrial relations: white male blue collar workers in manufacturing enjoyed superior real wages in large and medium size American companies, who produced mostly only for our domestic market and who were secure in their hold on those markets.

To a remarkable degree by now our Fortune-500 companies have lost their absolute-monarch status within their niches. With the evaporation of their oligopoly power, these largest corporations have become constitutional monarchs who reign only so long as they do not autonomously rule. Why this change in basic economic structure?

The simple answer offered is that foreign competition has cut into the market power of the big three Detroit automakers; and into the power of U.S. Steel and Eastman Kodak. In the 1950s it was the Common Market miracles of growth that impinged on America and, according to this thesis nominating foreign competition as the prime mover, later it was Japan and such Pacific Rim tigers as Hong Kong, Singapore, Taiwan and Korea who eroded away the monopoly power of our largest firms.

This argument has merit but it is overly simple to impute the change mostly to new foreign competition. What is most persuasive politically to xenophobic protectionists is probably less than a third of the total explanation. New competition at home accounts for most of the change I am describing.

Steel rather than autos is most indicative. To start a fifth or ninth giant steel complex would have cost billions of dollars in the 1930s. That inhibited such threats to oligopoly power. But when technology changed, so that small electric furnaces using steel scrap could operate effectively with non-union labor, oligopoly power rapidly evaporated. Similarly, when trucks were invented, hundreds of thousands of independent drivers took away much of the business of the regulated railways with their strongly entrenched union restrictions on productivity.

As we look into the new century ahead, foreign competition will come increasingly into its own as a prime shaper of domestic market structure. There are more than a billion Chinese and Indians who work for one-tenth the European and North American real wage rates. Using mobile modern know-how, their productivity can assuredly be brought to within 25 percent of the best in the West. The same might be said for a quarter million people in what used to be the Soviet Union and its satellites. But when Europe arrives at wherever it is going, it will find America already there waiting.

Under a regime of future free trade, how can such a vast evening-up in effective GNPs fail to alter domestic patterns of competition drastically? America I discern has gone earlier and farther into the new pattern than as yet France, Germany, and Europe have. Partly that is because, contrary to historical reputation, America is a less protective country than the European Union generally.

Let me make a hasty but important digression. Neither Europe nor America are likely to be able to succeed by use of autarkical protectionism in restoring real rates of GNP progress back to the growth paces of the 1950s and 1960s. International politics may well be a zero-sum game. When Bismarck goes up, Louis Napoleon must go down. Not so with economic development. After a billion Chinese live better and longer, we Americans can still expect to enjoy in the first quarter of the twenty-first century a slowly rising standard of living at home. Economic history suggests--it can never prove anything--that going the route of isolationism and autarky hurts rather than helps the trend of average national affluence.

Now I return to the subject of the new Ruthless Economy. World wide there has been a trend back from an uncontrolled welfare state. Margaret Thatcher in Britain was an extreme case. But the same story applies in post-Reagan America and in most of Western Europe. Even Scandinavia, Australia, and New Zealand have been finally forced into more reliance on the market mechanism.

I am known as a do-gooder. But experience has persuaded me to speak of the *limited* welfare state, which knows it must ration the less-than-50-percent of the GNP that can be efficiently available to transfer-tax payments that mitigate the inequalities sure to be meted out by a market mechanism that lacks both heart and integrated brain.

One way to move toward the market is through privatization and deregulation. No longer can American unions count on the federal government as an ally that will by legislative force prevent corporations from breaking strikes by denying them the right to replace strikers *permanently* with willing non-union recruits.

What is the result of the new competition and the shift of voters toward the Right? In America we have witnessed the emasculation of trade unionism. At age 80 I see again what used to prevail when I was eight: few union members and scarcely any economic power possessed by collective bargaining and organized labor.

Time is scarce. Still I have to mention that nowadays corporate takeovers, mergers, and split-ups are epidemic. The CEOs of today know they can be fired tomorrow. And so it is down the line.

In the old days if you were an educated male in the corporate management bureaucracy, effectively you had lifetime tenure. As you aged and grew tired, your paycheck rose! All was supposed to even out on a lifetime basis, not on a month-to-month or year-to-year productivity basis. Berle-Means patterns of autonomous managers today seem gone forever. The gasoline that enables corporation raiders to run their races is, often, that they cast off corporate obligations toward employees' benefits and job security. This explains massive downscalings.

Here is the perfect example. American Tel & Tel announced its split up into three separate companies. Forty thousand employees are to be discharged. The stock market reacted by sending AT&T shares way up in price. Was it bad public relations to announce, along with the downscaling news, an increase of CEO's salary by millions of dollars? Main Street cared, but Wall Street didn't. This is the same AT&T that used to be regarded as the quintessential utility monopoly with the most bureaucratic of executive hierarchy.

In the ruthless economy all of us feel a new anxiety. At age 57 we Harvard Business School elite graduates may be retired with short notice. And maybe we'll never have another job unless we eventually condescend to be an assistant manager at a fast food McDonald's restaurant.

Explaining New American Macroeconomics

Most of what I have been talking about you would put in the category of microeconomics. That was not Maynard Keynes' specialty. But I have been Machiavellian in my exposition. My purpose has been to help you understand our sea change in macroeconomics since about 1975-80.

When I spoke of more than 30 million new U.S. jobs net

since then, did you think I was boasting and was being complacent? Let me set the record straight. The new jobs that Americans have been winning have tended to be mediocre rather than high-paying jobs. Average wages have been stagnating if not falling.

Inequality has increased in America since 1980. Property owners have gained a bigger share of the fruits of progress than have workers, especially unskilled and poorly-educated workers who lack human capital. Mind you, under the hypothesis I have been spelling out, these property profits and capital gains have not been the rents of monopoly and oligopoly positions. *Au contraire*, as we say in English. The perfection of competition has if anything improved. With the speed of light, computer-driven trading does arbitrage away many temporary aberrations attributable to ignorance.

Just when technological and market-structure trends exacerbate inequality, the political swing to the right reduces the mitigating income transfers from the state. That is positive fact and not normative complaint. There is even a sniff of paradox in the fact that, when the people need social insurance most, there is less of it available. And there will be even less in the future.

The overall share in the GDP of government programs does not yet fully reflect this basic change. That is because the entitlement programs for old age pensions and medical care, legislated in the past, become ever more costly as the population ages demographically and as scientific medicine becomes ever more elaborate and successful while at the same time being released from rationing by the purse.

The proper test is not to ask whether Ronald Reagan and his successor Republicans have cut down on the total of governmental expenditures. Broadly, they have not been able to do that. It is more illuminating to extrapolate beyond 1980 what the plausible trend in total government expenditure was at that time indicated. Then measure against this what the actual upward trend has been. I think you will conclude from this exercise that the conservative revolution has had a considerable measure of success in what matters to libertarians -- namely, the real total and scope of public control of America's resources is less than it was likely to be under pre-Reagan administrations.

America and Europe: Macro Opposites

Supply-side Reaganomics was not conservative macroeconomics. Instead of reducing budget deficits at high employment in the 1980s, its tax reductions enlarged deficits and made them chronic and structural by undertaxing the American people relative to their collective expenditure. Stupid madness? Not stupid if your sole goal is to reduce the scope of government no matter at what cost in making America, which has become un-thrifty at family and corporate levels, become net even less thrifty. Putting this tourniquet around the neck of continued government expenditures is the devil's recipe for making a low-saving society even more low saving.

At least the Reagan-Bush fiscal laxity contributed toward low American unemployment rates in the 1980s. Contrast this with the Continental pattern. Led by Germany and its austere *Bundesbank*, her neighbors who wanted to comply with the Maastricht timetable for a single European money and single central bank pursued overall macro austerity that created and froze in two-digit unemployment rates.

Since 1983 at least--and that is more than 14 years ago--we have been told that currency parity of the franc with the mark necessitated contriving an inflation rate in France less than the low rate in Germany. Temporary costs in terms of extra unemployment, we were told, would be temporary and moderate -- well worth the price of perpetual inflation-free prosperity cum balance-of-payments equilibrium.

This did not happen in 1983-1988. Or in 1988-1992. It still has not happened. But in the meantime longrun unemployment has grown and hardened in France. Recent statistics reported a 40 percent unemployment rate among youth under 25 years of age. And a quarter of these have been unemployed for more than a year. That bodes ill microeconomically for future French society. Basic skills are harder to learn and teach at 33 than at 23. And Satan does find work for idle hands to do.

I have failed to explain my message if you conclude that the fault is exclusively due to over-austere monetary and fiscal policy. Yes, in France these have been tight. And why? Ostensibly as necessary for Maastricht.

The European Union has been a great success, perhaps the most important creation of the last half century. It will be even more important in the future. But analysis shows that this has little to do with a European Parliament. Or with a future European central bank. Or with a future European currency based on pegged parities to the mark.

Remember I am speaking not as an American patriot. Nor as a post-Keynesian. Nor as a do-gooder. We in America can live well with a Maastricht that comes into existence if that should materialize. We can live as well with the present halfway house. Or with a Europe that evolves into floating parities and sliding pegs.

It is realism and basic economic analysis which cogently suspect that one European money is a pipedream between now and 2005. Yes, Europe might sometime start off with a common peg; but soon the U.K., Italy, and Spain will fall out of it. And better than 50-50 are the odds that the franc and the mark will themselves move divergently some time during the next decade. Avoiding that contingency by paying the high price of a stagnant decade is a game hardly worth the candle.

You may well reply: Yes, Professor Samuelson, you might prove right. But not making the attempt will, realistically, threaten even worse macro performance.

Before 1983 France often went through the gyrations of macro expansion, devaluation, and induced inflation without in the end achieving productivity progress and reasonably stable real GDP movements.

Those failures could turn out to be so again. Economics is not an exact science. At this point though, the American experience since 1980 may be suggestive and valuable.

America's Cowed Labor Market

The United States also had its bouts in 1950-1980 with stagflation and cyclical fluctuation. I used to envy Germany its "Phillips Curve" and wish that we in America could better avoid our wage-price price-wage spiral. Now the shoe pinches on another foot. I am happier in the 1990s with the mechanics of our labor market than with that of Europe.

Earlier I spoke of the ruthless economy. And of the trend back toward the market and toward limits on the welfare transfer state. Now I need to call attention to what might be called our cowed labor market. (I don't know how that translated into French. It is not mad-cow disease that is in question nor any kind of mad irrationality.)

Employers in America are tougher in bargaining, hiring, and firing than they used to be. Human charity and altruism is not what has changed. Rather it is: when you lack oligopoly power, continuing to follow your heart rather than head in human relations is a sure recipe for a short life of benevolence. After you have tapped out shareowners' wealth, the market action will have moved elsewhere anyway. Under modern market competition, social Darwinism is not a creed; nor is it public relations apologetics. Rather it is a reality.

As a humanitarian I lament that the markets for blue-collar, white-collar, and professional workers do not clear at full employment with nicely rising real wage rates and benefits. But still I would rather have people accept the jobs that can be there rather than hold out for better jobs that are just not there.

I give much causality credit for a decade of successful Federal Reserve monitoring of the real U.S. economy to the fact of America's cowed labor force. Contrast this with post-Franco Spain and its over 20 percent unemployment rates.

Right now our political parties fight over raising our minimum wage rate for $4.70 an hour to $5.60. Politically this is big news--a plus for Democratic voteseekers. Economically it is mostly only symbolic. Why? Our minimum wage rate has long been frozen far below median market wages. Your French minimum exceeds ours even though correctly calculated U.S. per capita affluence is distinctly above France's. That excess can hardly be a good thing for your stubborn youth unemployment problem; but I will not be dogmatic. America has a large number of black, Hispanic, and other minorities; therefore it could be the case that we can least afford high minimum wage rates. (Notice that I did not say "generous" standards: when too high they could end up being the reverse of generous.)

Conclusion

Let me wind up. Notice that I have been cautious in advising you in France to move to the American pattern in order to enjoy our scrumptious recent performance. Marie Antoinette said, "Let the poor eat cake." Such was not feasible cogent advice. I am an economics Ph.D., and my name is not Marie. If your labor movement turns class-conscious and aggressive in trying to raise its fractional share of a fixed total, trying to imitate the letter of our strategies might fail to achieve its fruits.

Economics is more than economics. It is political economy. What will the political market bear? Your political market, not ours. Can French democracy preserve minimal programs to alleviate suffering that accompanies a privatized and deregulated market economy, while at the same time restoring the sensitivity against cost and price-level inflation associated with unemployment slack in the system?

If so, the American pattern is there for you to emulate. And in America itself, if we lose the willingness of the population to accept moderate wage jobs when they are alone available, then the present American pattern will be lost to us and we might well move back to the 1970s era with too much of both unemployment and unpredictable price instability.

The divergence between our continents can be reversed by a reconvergence to a common pattern. My hope is that we not revert to Europe's structural high unemployment; but rather that we'll both come to enjoy America's recent good luck.

How Economics Has Changed

Paul A. Samuelson

I thought I had already paid my dues, and received my ample rewards, as far as the teaching of economics is concerned. But I did not reckon with so good a friend as Robert Solow. I can never get paid up on what I owe to him; and when he asked me to do him the favor of starting off your conference, it was inevitable that you should see me standing here before you.

I shall not pretend to preach on high school economics. In my day at Hyde Park High School in Chicago, the subject was not even taught. My first teacher at the University of Chicago, Aaron Director, was just as pleased. Jesuits like to work with virginal material, and in those pre-Galbraith days I was putty in Director's no-nonsense hands.

From what I hear in the senior common rooms, things have not changed all that much. College instructors go whole hours not brooding over what is taught by way of high school economics, and most would like to keep that terrain a curricular vacuum.

However, economic education is too serious a business to be left to university professors. There are still millions of people who will never get to college. And it could be the case—although I would not bet on it—that in the tender years of adolescence, the human brain is in an especially flexible and receptive state for learning to speak Hungarian or learning about present discounted values and foreign-trade multipliers.

About three decades ago, economics made a comeback in the high schools. And, for better or worse, I don't think you're going to be able to put the genie back into the bottle. Around 1960, Lee Bach dragged me, kicking and screaming, into curricular committees trying to decide what should be taught in the new renaissance. Each morning, the rock has to be rolled up the hill again, and here you all are struggling with the perpetual problem of curricular coverage.

It took money to keep the ball rolling. Was it my Boston neighbor Teddy Green who explained why he robbed banks—because that is where the money is? We get grants from business corporations and conservative foundations for economic education because that's where the money is. And what is the money offered for? Generally, to teach economic principles—sound economic principles.

Back in the 1950s, there was a move for on-the-job economics classes. Employees had to—er—volunteer to be inculcated with sound principles,

---

Paul A. Samuelson is a professor of economics at the Massachusetts Institute of Technology. This speech was the keynote address at the conference. © *1987 by Paul A. Samuelson.*

and none of this Keynesian claptrap. It was the good old times of Joseph McCarthy and the salad days of Bill Buckley, who sought in vain at Yale God and economic man. I was then even considered to be a dangerous radical. And my economics textbook was denounced as heresy.

What forever drove businessmen wild were people's responses on questionnaires when asked what fraction of each sales dollar went to profits. The American public would keep answering: 25 to 50 cents of each dollar goes for profits; the facts showed that the A&P and Sears got only a few cents of each dollar.

What was maddening was that, after workers stayed nights to learn economics, they still gave those same wrong numbers. There is something in the lay mind that keeps insisting that the lucky 5 percent of the population always ends up with 30 percent of the total swag.

How do we professionals gathered here draw the line between what is scientific economics and what is indoctrination? After we leave two days from now, we'll find no easy answers to that basic question.

For the rest of my brief remarks—before we throw the floor open for general discussion and questions—I am not going to talk further about high school economics. I teach federal judges economics, and, to tell the truth, if we knew what and how to teach those lay people, we'd know what should be in our college introductory texts and in the secondary school classrooms.

What I shall talk about—all too briefly, all too superficially—is how economics has been changing in my time. And, although I am longer in the tooth than all of you, as Rudy Vallee put it, "My time is your time. Your time is my time."

It was the tragedy of my teachers' generation that, as they grew older, economics grew more liberal, and even radical. It has been the comedy of my era that, as we grew older, our profession became more conservative. This was brought home to me around 1970 when I accepted a lecture engagement at the Las Vegas meeting of the Western Economic Association. I never encountered so unanimous a gang of free marketeers. It was a pleasure to see those fellows losing their chips at the rigged gambling tables.

Actually, the high-water mark of the New Deal tide came, probably, at the end of World War II. Keynesian macroeconomics had won the war and written the peace.

The timing is pinpointed for me by the incident of the 1945 pamphlet *Roofs or Ceilings*, a broadside against rent controls written by Milton Friedman and George Stigler. The brethren of our guild were outraged, and some literally wanted the American Economic Association to censure the capitalistic apologists. I had to defend this item as a labor of ideological love and not as the bullet from a gun for hire. Unfortunately, George informed me that, having written the pamphlet, the authors decided they might as well collect the market rent accruing to their effort.

I recall the incident not for the purpose of criticizing the scientific quality of the analysis, which was a finger exercise in Marshallian supply and demand. It is a story, not on the authors, but on the 1945 state of mind of our profession. By 1975, the loss of consumer's surplus from rent controls on flats was generally taken for granted.

Pareto efficiency is today all the rage. Since it is not easy to say things uncontroversial about distributional equity, let equity go hang.

Now that I have raised the topic, let me comment on how economists try to have their equity cake and eat it too. I met Carl Christ as he was finishing a 1958-59 Fulbright stint at Tokyo University. He had written a brief to abolish Japan's rent control. I inquired indelicately about the income redistribution thereby implied. "Oh," he said, on the run, "if that is an issue, all that needs to be done is to compensate all the losers out of the enhanced gains of the winners made possible by the efficiency of market-clearing rentals." I tell the complete story as it happened. I can also report I was once told by James Buchanan, truly an expert on public choice topics, that as a matter of principle he refused ever to go beyond Pareto optimality.

Mainstream economics reached its zenith of self-complacency around the time of Kennedy's Camelot. If our index of self-esteem peaked out at one hundred in 1965, by the late 1970s it had fallen to the vicinity of thirty-seven. As others thought less well of us economist scientists, we came to think less well of ourselves. Whoever takes credit for the sunshine of the Kennedy-Johnson expansionary decade must be prepared to be blamed for the stagflation of the 1970s.

To use Tom Kuhn's overdramatic terminology, it was not successes of a Galbraithian school that undermined mainstream economics—surely not new triumphs of Marxian economics, either in Eastern Europe or mainland China or New Left student quarters.

The paradigm of monetarism did score a few observational triumphs and an occasional high correlation coefficient in one or another Federal Reserve Bank of St. Louis reduced-form equation. However, it was not so much the arrival of a new and successful macroeconomic paradigm as it was the failure of any paradigm to deliver the goods of accurate predictions and efficacious policy prescriptions.

The fault, Brutus may say, was in the stars and not in our science. After 1965, the dilemma of stagflation descended on us with a vengeance. It is not physicians who are to be blamed for plague. But it does somewhat ill become trained astronomers to speak of faults within the stars that are not their faults.

In 1971 at the New School, my Gerhard Colm Lecture took as its text "Liberalism at Bay." I correctly identified all but one of the movements hostile to mainstream eclectic post-Keynsianism. What I could not have dreamed in advance was that these last fifteen years would see the birth of a new classical school that believes in full employment and neutral money, even in the short run of a few years. Like herpes, this condition caught us unawares. It began under the insidious title of *rational expectationism*, and it traveled on the false steam of efficient speculative markets. Every time a broker made money speculating on puts and calls by means of the Black-

Scholes formula, Robert Lucas and Robert Barro, and Tom Sargent were given a forward boost in respect to their new proposed paradigm.

As Schumpeter said long before Thomas Kuhn: you don't kill a theory with an aberrant fact. It takes a new theory to kill an old theory. So it was with Keynesianism. So it is with the new rational expectationism. It is a game with an interesting technique. All our brightest and best under forty are whoring after the new explorations.

Each year brings my office a couple of hundred National Bureau yellow-jacketed papers. Fifty of them test rational expectations. Forty-five report failure of the theory to pass those tests. The remaining few sometimes show weak agreement. But I expect the mail to keep coming on.

Actually, the 1980s have been hard on monetarism—and, if anything, hard on rational expectationism. Just today, in the *Wall Street Journal*, there is a piece by Milton Friedman in which he manages to interpret the most successful fine-tuning incident of our times (the Volcker Fed's contriving after mid-1982 the current Reagan recovery) into an indictment of fine tuning and a vindication of the wisdom of monetarism's inflexible rule concerning constant growth rate of some M or another.

Personally, I find unsettled times exciting times. It would be nice to have things work out perfectly in Camelot. But surely a little dull after a century or two?

From experience, I infer that some economics is better than some other. Kuhn was naively wrong in thinking that it all boils down to what school tie you've learned to wear. There is a reality out there that all too slowly reveals itself and forces the hand of the observing scientist.

The final word will be another lesson of experience. The shortcomings of a science—for example, a naive belief that the public debt doesn't count because we all realize we'll be paying taxes on it—more likely will be corrected from within than from without. Somehow it is easier, apparently, to learn from one's friends than from one's enemies. Scientists, like dogs, are only human too!

SYMPOSIUM: Federal Reserve Monetary Policy

Leaning Against What Inflationary Wind?

PAUL A. SAMUELSON

The U.S. economy is not on the verge of overheating at present. If and when that changes, it will be a good time to pump gently on the brakes. That time is not now.

After a dozen years of structural budget deficits and low private sector saving by U.S. families and corporations, economic history and economic science concur in the diagnosis that monetary policy rather than fiscal policy should be the major macroeconomic weapon for assuring a healthy 1993-96 recovery and for restoring the share of capital formation in the American economy.

The last five years will go down in the textbooks of economic history as a period of disappointing performances by central banks. America's central bank, the Federal Reserve, began the decade of the 1980s with a stellar report card. Under Chairman Paul Volcker, from 1979 to 1982, remarkable progress was made in wringing out of our economy the double-digit stagflation that had built up in the 1970s. Then in 1982 and 1983, as I shall describe for its peculiar relevance today, the Fed fired up the American locomotive in a prudent way, leading the United States and the global economies into a needed expansion.

Again, in the epoch when Chairman Alan Greenspan took over the helm from Paul Volcker, the nasty stock market crash of October 19, 1987 was brilliantly addressed by well-timed and judicious central bank support. What began as a potential worldwide disaster, fully as perilous as the October 1929 Wall Street Crash, by good policy and good luck was contained from being the prelude to serious recession.

Central banks perform poorly

That is the good news. Alas, future historians are forced to report that, after 1988, central banks have earned for their performances low marks.

In particular, the revered *Bundesbank* has brought on unified Germany a serious recession that it never expected to occur. Outside of Germany, directly and indirectly, the bias of the *Bundesbank* toward preoccupation with inflation to the neglect of real growth and unemployment has led to a lasting slump for Common Market and other European countries. In the end, the dream of a Maastricht Treaty that would unify the European economy was dashed by *Bundesbank* intransigence. Unemployment rates in

Nobel Laureate PAUL A. SAMUELSON is Institute Professor of Economics at the Massachusetts Institute of Technology. He presented this testimony before the Senate Committee on Banking, Housing and Urban Affairs, July 1, 1993.

Spain, Italy, and Ireland soared. Waiting upon the German credit expansion that never came, Britain, Italy, and Spain were forced out of the European Monetary Union. Countries like France that accommodated the *Bundesbank* have been penalized by double-digit unemployment rates. Sweden, with its interest rate forced temporarily up to a 500 percent annual rate in order to have the Kroner look the Mark in the eye, is a spectacle no sage ever expected to see again in the modern world.

The chimera of omniscient and independent central banks sadly contributed to the Bank of Japan's bringing on that dynamic society a serious stagnation of output. Where an Italy or a Spain face genuine international constraints, Japan's wounds have been self-inflicted and gratuitous. And in wounding herself, Japan has also wounded the U.S. bilateral imbalance with Japan, contributing significantly to the puny 0.7 of 1 percent annual rate of American real GDP growth in the 1993 first quarter. Were it not for involuntary piling up of inventory accumulation, our final real GDP would actually have been declining in 1993's first quarter.

Federal Reserve misdiagnosis

Alas, the Federal Reserve has shared in this central bank saga of acting too little and too late against macroweakness on Main Street, U.S.A. It can be said, soberly and with statistical significance, that the defeat of George Bush in 1992 and the Republican disappointments in the Senate and the House are the direct result of Federal Reserve misdiagnosis of the seriousness of the 1990-92 state of U.S. demand.

Yes, the Fed acted many times to help bring down short-term interest rates. Yes, those actions were important in the sense that, without them, our banks, corporations, and job-seekers would have been much worse off. But no, successive Open Market Committees did not act in time and in the degree called for by the current statistical indicators.

Why not? I do not think the nineteen persons who are entitled in any epoch to vote on the Open Market Committee are at this time less competent than in the past. Nor are they more poorly informed than the 50-odd consensus forecasters at our corporations, banks, and universities who publish current analyses and recommendations. All of these nineteen were appointed to office in the Reagan-Bush years. A significant minority of them have been candid in telling us that their regard was—and needed to be—solely to try to bring inflation down essentially to 0 or 1 percent per annum by 1995. (Some have quoted with approval and envy the charter of the *Bundesbank* which makes this the be-all and the end-all of that central bank.) Any jury of leading economists will, by majority vote, agree that only by contriving a weak U.S. economy like that of 1990-93 could one have a rational hope of approaching that 1995 inflationless state.

Main Street, U.S.A. has not in town meetings given the Federal Reserve such a monistic mandate. Nor has a committee of the two Houses, or a majority vote in either of the Houses.

I believe this to be important not as a matter of history or of general philosophy. It is important because the money market has every reason to believe—even without leaks to the press after Open Market Committee meetings—that this Federal Reserve (the only one we have) is only too prone to (1) *engineer* higher short-term interest rates, or (2) *countenance* such higher rates (a) at the first signs of a healthy real recovery—say, a 3.25 percent (annual) growth rate for two successive quarters, or (b) at the first signs of some acceleration of price-level indexes.

In 1958, within three months of the trough of the second Eisenhower recession, the Fed tightened interest rates to "stay ahead of the wave of the next inflation." The rest is history. The 1958-60 recovery was short and weak. John F. Kennedy was thereby able to defeat Richard Nixon and bring the Democrats back into the White House for eight years.

By contrast, consider mid-1982, when the 1981-82 recession did not end as expected. Chairman Volcker discerned a window of opportunity. Not only did Wall Street welcome his expansionary activism; it also approved of his ensuring that the recovery was a good one by risking some overdoing. When the expansion was assured, the Fed changed its tack. Doctrinaire monetarists condemned it as too much and too little. Eclectics, who understand stabilization theory, applaud ongoing corrections called for by new data.

I am not a pessimist who believes that we are in a vicious Kondratief downwave. I believe jobs can grow under prudent macropolicies. I believe that cutbacks in President Clinton's fiscal stimulus package should be the opportunity seized by the Federal Reserve for a pro-investment rather than a pro-consumption tilt to the U.S. GDP in this decade.

More than that, coordinating Federal Reserve monetary policy with austere fiscal deficit reduction can be the single most important path for the 1990s—a needed corrective for the irresponsible 1980s.

Let me close with an important caveat. Leaning against the wind of inflationary overheating is a vital duty of the Federal Reserve as a central bank. It goes along with the Fed's vital duty to lean against the winds of self-aggravating recession. The hardest task ahead for an intelligent and responsible Federal Reserve will be to distinguish between *microcaused* inflation, due to one-time supply shocks and tax changes, and *macrocaused* inflation, brought on by diminished slack in personpower and productive capacity.

On July 1, 1993, the weight of the evidence is against our economy as being one constrained by resource scarcity and on the verge of macroeconomic overheating. Later, when and if the weight of the evidence shifts, that will be the good time to pump gently on the brakes. That time is not now.

Paul A. Samuelson responds to questions for the record by Senator Donald W. Riegle, Jr.

Q. We are working now to lower our budget deficits, something that foreign countries have strongly encouraged in the past. Both of you [Henry Kaufman and Paul Samuelson] appear to be suggesting that we should now be asking other countries to lower their interest rates. How far do you think German and Japanese authorities should lower rates, and how much might we benefit?

A. America should seek to attain all or most of its needed short-term macrostimulus from Federal Reserve credit expansion—for the reason that, since 1981, our society has been on a consumption binge (private and public). Consequently, to address the deficiency of adequate domestic capital formation owned by Americans, for us the optimal stimulus mix involves budgetary austerity and compensatingly stimulative Fed policy.

For Japan, which is a high-saving society with an austere fiscal stance, our recommended advice ought to involve a larger recourse to deficit fiscal finance and less reliance on a balance-of-payments surplus for stimulus, and relatively less reliance on Bank of Japan credit stimulus. That kind of stimulus would tend to make investment in yen assets less attractive, thereby slowing down the appreciation of the yen needed to better balance Japan's bilateral and multilateral current accounts. (Some Bank of Japan easing is not precluded; still, the prime stimulus should be fiscal.)

For Germany, and the EC nations generally, *both* forms of macrostimulus are needed—in their own interest to tackle double-digit unemployment rates and slumping production, and in the interest of having European locomotives join in with the American locomotive to ameliorate the 1990-93 global recession.

Q. The Fed has had increasing difficulty interpreting its various monetary aggregates in recent years, to the point that the Fed appears to ignore them almost completely. Mr. Kaufman's testimony says that is appropriate. But if the Fed is not targeting monetary aggregates, what should they be targeting, and on what basis should we judge their success or failure?

A. In my reading of economic history and macroeconomic principle, it is never sufficient to build monetary policy on the basis of targets for one or several of M_1, M_2, or M_3 aggregates. I agree with Henry Kaufman that, particularly since 1980, reliance on M-targeting has produced and will yield erratic Fed actions. Behavior of the aggregates should be but one of several eclectic criteria for the best achievable policy of leaning against the winds of both adverse production trends and adverse price level trends. Stabilizing nominal GDP growth at the approximate growth potential of the economy, plus allowance for the residual price-level inflation that can be prudently curtailed only over a period of years—that criterion has an approximate and pragmatic role to play. However, in time of exogenous "supply shocks," and when public policy may bring once-and-for-all *micro*shocks to the price level (as from a new energy tax or a one-time step up in payroll taxes for medical care), then a delicate compromise between adjusting Fed policy to take partial account of such shocks and between nonaccommodating policy will be called for. There is no magic fine-tuning formula that can be decided on and announced to hold for the future. Always, the Fed needs to judge and balance the divergent trends of output strengths and of price level overheatings. After 1989, this Fed has shown nonoptimal bias toward preoccupation with ephemeral inflation accelerations. Central banks abroad—Germany and Japan—have been even more biased.

One holds the Fed accountable for understimulus in 1929-33 and 1990-93, and for overstimulus in, say, 1972-73. Always, one asks: Is the central bank making informed and responsible judgments about the levels and changes in manpower resources, in degrees of undercapacity operation, and in self-aggravating heatings-up of the price level? The *Bundesbank* notion that its *one* concern is price level stability and that it is an independent fourth estate of government has spread much mischief, around the world, and in Germany itself.

Q. On the face of it, the budget policy we are currently implementing over the next few years appears to be quite contractionary. Chairman Greenspan has argued that he believes it will not prove to be, because it will significantly lower interest rates enough to effectively offset most or all of the contractionary impetus. What is your view?
A. Economic history—in 1865-95 America, 1929-35 global economies, 1990-93 America, and the OECD economies generally—makes it doubtful that Chairman Alan Greenspan is correct to believe that *laissez faire* money markets will spontaneously equilibrate interest rates to offset any macrodrag from (a) post-cold war contraction of defense industries, (b) post-1980s restructuring of American industries after an era of debt leveraging, and (c) rapid strides abroad in competitive power to undermine many American sectors that used to possess comparative advantage in international trade.

What the American nation needs from Dr. Greenspan and his colleagues is a *credible* assurance like the following:

Without relaxing our vigilance and determination to act to offset significant macroinduced overheating of the U.S. economy, your central bank can be counted on to act to offset and compensate for depressing effects of foreign commerce, bank liquidity, industrial and defense restructuring, fiscal policy austerities for the long run, and gridlocks for the short run. The potency of monetary and credit weapons has not been used up, and the expansions that we would welcome if spontaneously occurring are not superior to expansions of the same macrostrength brought about by our prudent credit stimuli. When America is in special need of private capital formation domestically owned, we perceive a special role and importance for credit policies, and we agree that it would be a self-inflicted wound if America permitted austerity pressure on consuming to release resources from production to unemployment and excess capacities, rather than effectively to capital formation and prudently high employment.

Q. In recent years, high debt levels of households and businesses, and increased integration of the world's financial markets have led some to question the ability of the Fed to have a significant impact on the pace of the recovery. In your judgment, how much power does the Fed really have to stimulate the economy?
A. The many interest rate reductions achieved and/or tolerated by the Fed since 1990, although they have repeatedly been too little and too late, have had remarkably good effects on the U.S. economy. But for them, our banks and real estate markets would now be in shambles; but for them, the construction industry and durable goods spending would still be in

the doldrums and our 7 percent unemployment rate would be knocking on the two-digit doors of European unemployment rates. The present evidence, in comparison with 1930 or 1932 or 1938, argues strongly that the Fed will *not* (repeat *not*) "be pushing on a string." Nor will it be the case where "you can lead the horses to the tank of ampler credit, but you can't make them drink." In time of recession or prolonged weakness in a recovery, the authorities should not hesitate to contrive or countenance *negative* short-term *real* interest rates, if experience reveals that such are needed to induce greater private capital formation.

The Fed is not omnipotent. It lacks power and wisdom to "fine-tune" perpetual prosperity with zero price inflation. But its potential powers are still, on the evidence, vast, if deployed with vigor. The free market facts of life put squarely on the shoulders of the Federal Reserve the responsibility to lean against the prevailing winds of macromisbehavior.

Once the 1993-95 recovery is solidly assured, I will expect to join with other modern economists in testifying before congressional committees the desirability and necessity for Federal Reserve austerity to keep under optimal control the vigor and attained growth of the mid-decade American economy.

An Addendum:
Paul A. Samuelson's reflections on the Fed innovations of July 1993

My July 1 testimony and replies for the record to Senator Donald W. Riegle's four questions, alas, all too accurately foresaw the general tenor of Chairman Alan Greenspan's subsequent two July appearances before Congress. Let me comment on these new Federal Reserve developments.

Dr. Greenspan announced that the Fed is renouncing *monetarism* in the sense that it will no longer attach importance to controlling the M_2 growth rate (or any other M_j rate) as a primary weapon of macromonetary control. Some Chicago School and Shadow Open Market Committee members will recoil from this new mortal sinning. Not I. Neither neoclassical economic theory nor the weight of economic history seemed persuasive for those Milton Friedman dogmas. Were economics not a serious business, there would be much of the comic in this chapter of Federal Reserve rationalization. (If your rifle shots miss your target, move your target to where the shots have been hitting. After missing last year's announced 2-6 percent target range for M_2 growth, this year it named 1-5 percent. Realizing that it would be criticized in the not unlikely event that it again missed, the Fed now repudiates *any* range. To please Congress's mandate on reporting such a range, it complies but with the warning that no meaning is to be attached to the exercise.)

Why the change? Because now M_2 is allegedly no longer usefully causal for the control of nominal GDP. Entering into the 1980s, Paul Volcker had, in Machiavellian fashion, promulgated monetarist targets that he never believed in—those being his only politically feasible way to tighten monetary brakes enough to kill off the stagflation of the 1970s. Arsenic and curses kill the neighbor's sheep: Two recessions of 1980 and 1981-82, along with *Pater Nosters* and monetarist verbiage, created the 11 percent unemployment that did the trick for Volcker at about the social cost that Arthur Okun, Robert Gordon, and James Tobin predicted in advance would be entailed.

The more things don't change the more they are alike. If Dr. Greenspan had some new researches

PAUL A. SAMUELSON wrote these remarks on July 28, 1993, subsequent to his congressional testimony.

showing that, around 1992-93, the stability of the demand for money and for the M_2 income velocity degenerated, it would have been useful to produce them. He did not do so, and the several studies I have seen adduce no blinding revelations of sudden monetarist nonoptimality. Occam's razor favors the hypothesis that the Fed rejected M_2 growth in the central range of 1-5 percent, because it correctly guessed that this might turn out to be incompatible with its tightening the screws on interest rates and "staying ahead of the wave of future inflation."

Interest rate targeting

Never give up the old love until you've lined up a new. In place of M_2 targeting, we are now told there will be *real interest rate targeting*. Have Governor Wayne D. Angell and the new Cleveland Fed President gone Keynesian-gaga—along with Chairman Greenspan and Vice Chairman Mullins? Not to worry. The innovation comes from other considerations.

Right now the inflation rate is about 3+ percent. The fed funds rate is also about 3 percent. When the real shortest interest rate is thus about zero, *there is nowhere for interest rates to go but up if you can merchandise the notion that economic law requires the real interest rate not to be negative.*

This, in a nutshell, is the floated new Fed dogma. Will it stand up to peer review refereeing for the *American Economic Review* or the *Economic Journal*? What would Alfred Marshall or Knut Wicksell or Irving Fisher make of it?

Ph.D. candidates could form a new gold rush to weigh the demerits and merits of the July 1993 dogma. What limits that stampede is the fear, the legitimate fear, that this stratagem was conceived in accordance with the accounting maxim: Cost or Market, whichever is lower. (1) The mid-1993 numbers on inflation cannot themselves warrant preemptive tightening of credit to ward off near-term inflation. (2) It is hard to sell the caper that one should act now to head off inflationary expectations—expectations based not on National Bureau leading indicators of inflation but rather on convoluted fears that such expectations will get formed unless one scotches them in advance. No doubt the Open Market Committee members divide into (1) those who subscribe to Napoleon's rule: Hang an occasional general just to encourage the others. Dampen an unheated economy to show your *bona fides*; and (2) those of the growling dog school: Talk wildly tough and you won't have to do anything because your enhanced credibility will do it for you.

It is rare for a Federal Reserve official to tip-off even Congress as to what the future will bring for interest rates. Departing from his usual caution and formal correctness, Chairman Greenspan warned that we should all realize that interest rates must rise in the future. His audiences did not construe this to be like a warning to Congress: You are all going to die. Nor did he cast other fatuities before Solons: Be assured that the future sometimes will bring a rise in interest rates, sometimes a fall, and sometimes a sideward movement.

A dogma is *a truth that cannot be questioned*—or tested by vulgar facts about OPEC prices, reserves of personpower, excess industrial capacities, and so forth. "The real interest rate must move into positive territory" is such a dogma.

I conclude therefore by prosaically puncturing the new balloon. Hans Christian Andersen employed a small boy to puncture the myth of the Emperor's new clothes. Better, I believe it would have been, to use an experienced elder to do that job. Certainly I qualify for the role of elder.

Dr. Greenspan and I both understand well that we can use Fidelity money market funds to serve our transaction and other monetary needs as well or better than currency and checking deposits do. We both understand that the higher interest rates earnable with safety on such assets *not* included in M_2 can and will materially affect M_2's velocity of circulation V_2. Every devotee of neoclassical economics will expect the constancies, recorded over time in *A Monetary History of the United States, 1867-1960* by Milton Friedman and Anna Schwartz, to be altered under different institutional conditions. The wonder is not how badly M_2 has correlated with $\Sigma P_j Q_j$ but rather why that correlation was so slow in unraveling.

Here is where the Greenspan dogma exposes its Achilles heel. How much should modern corporations and sophisticated persons have to pay to enjoy our convenient transaction assets? How much should we expect to earn on them? Almost without thinking, Chairman Greenspan knows the answer. In real terms we must not have to pay permanently *any* net amount for our holding of liquid assets which statistical studies show have the best hedging covariance with unexpected inflation. Instead, those most liquid, short-term balances must assuredly have a sizable positive nominal yield. How sizable? That nominal yield must exceed the inflation rate by enough to ensure a positive real return on these convenient inflation hedges. Unlike bond prices which drop when the price index inflates, and unlike equity prices which zagged downward in the 1950-90 period when price levels zigged upward, money market yields rise quickly with acceleration of inflation.

Elementary economic principle goes against Dr. Greenspan, as his old NYU textbooks will remind him. Worse is the evidence of economic history, that Mankind has, much of the time, maybe most of the time, had to pay something for the convenience of its cash balance. From 1933 to the *accidental* birth in New England of NOW accounts, which permitted modest interest yields on checking accounts, the mean growth in price level chronically exceeded the derisory (or zero) yield on M_1.

The Eleventh Commandment

Whence cometh this new Eleventh Commandment: *Thou must earn more than the inflation rate on thy most liquid assets?*

Not from economic science. Not from the groves of academe. Not from the mathematical rocket kids who dream up put-and-call hedges for Wall Street. I hope not from the tacticians of central bank public relations.

Does any of this matter? Yes. Often, in the course of business cycle stabilization, optimal control policy has necessitated periods of some duration in which the economy needed the monetary stimulus of negative real short-term interest rates.

Example: The production index fell 25 percent from the 1937 cyclical peak to the 1938 trough. It rose more than that in the recovery, and in the years before America was in World War II. In the years when the price index accelerated to 2 percent per annum or above, was it a mistake that treasury bills chronically bore yields of half a percent per annum and garnered negative *real* interest returns? According to the new dogma it was a mistake, even though the unemployment rate still hovered around 15 percent! What jury of mainstream economists would find a majority in favor of this?

Just as Paul Volcker was a rice convert, not a true convert, to monetarism in 1979, I suspect Alan Greenspan is not a true convert to the dogma of necessarily positive real interest rates. It is merely the tactical way of carrying forward the Federal Reserve's resolve to make progress toward a mid-decade inflation rate of 0-1 percent. At a time when the world is in slump, when banks are sweating out a real estate bust and a once-and-for-all increase in capital requirements, when cold war defense spending is in blessed decline, when dynamic Schumpeterian inroads are being made abroad on America's traditional lines of comparative advantage, when our fiscal house is being put back into order after the Reagan-Bush decade of structural deficits and balance-of-payments deficits—at such a time, the Federal Reserve has no mandate from the people, the Congress, or the White House to pursue a monistic campaign to depress inflation at any cost.

Yes, inflation containment is one basic goal of macropolicy. Yes, behavior of the (M_0, M_1, M_2, M_3... M_{17}) vector of money aggregates does have a role to play in good credit policy. Yes, budgetary austerity to curb America's consumption binge of the since-Reagan years does require compensatory Fed stimulus to ensure that released resources go into American-owned capital formation and not into idleness and excess capacity. Yes, the Fed will be there to lean against the wind of an overheating economy after slack evaporates in the wake of prudent and healthy growth.

No, the record of the 1989-93 Federal Reserve cannot inspire confidence that they are now on the right track or even striving to understand how that track ought to be defined.

I have known and admired Alan Greenspan as a savvy economist for more than a third of a century. He could be right that we are entering several quarters of annualized real GDP growth at more than 2.5 percent. When and if macroheating becomes a clear and present danger, it will indeed be his duty to lean against those winds by countenancing rising real and nominal interest rates.

What I am objecting to, in my own right, and as a mainstream economist, is taking such actions on the basis of a new shibboleth that is as badly anchored in economic law as the last half-dozen cooked up in the brief history of the Federal Reserve System.

507

ECONOMIC SCIENCE GRAPPLES WITH DILEMMAS
OF INTERNATIONAL FINANCE

Paul A. Samuelson

Robbins Memorial Lecture, Claremont College

January, 1991

When you give a name lecture, you fall into a standard pattern. For five or ten minutes you describe how distinguished the departed scholar was, how he was virtually a Renaissance man, and how honored you are to speak in his name. Then you settle into the substantive business of the evening and describe the latest findings in the domain of quarternions or *Drosophila* fruit flies.

Well, Lionel Robbins truly was a Renaissance Man. Besides being economic theorist, historian of economic doctrines, exponent of pro-capitalistic policies and attitudes, and circus manager of the great pre-war zoo of LSE whiz-kids in economic science, Lord Robbins was a peer of the realm, a Chairman of the *Financial Times*, board member of Covent Garden, the Tate, and the National Gallery, and architect of higher education reform in Britain. And he was a character in his own right. In particular Robbins was an important player in the game our Bologna-Claremont Conference dedicates itself to: the study of how international economic affairs ought to be conducted.

Therefore, I should alter the stereotyped pattern. After recalling good stories about Robbins, I can still keep him present in my various comments on what economic science can teach us about proper commercial policies and institutional reforms.

Lionel was a tall and handsome and impressive presence. Once during a polished Robbins lecture at Harvard, young Bob Solow whispered in my ear: "People who don't lecture like that should be shot."

Tjalling Koopmans agreed with James Mill that people should not write too well. As Koopmans put it: "One's ideas should go only so far as their own merit takes them." Well, in a profession where the crime of good writing is not widespread, Robbins produced gem after gem. The finest of course is his youthful 1932 book: *The Nature and Significance of Economics as a Science*. It said what needed saying: Factual knowledge cannot yield you ethical norms. Never mind that the young Lionel swallowed much

Austrian guff about *a priori* truths and the unimportance of measuring quantitative relationships. It is an author's goods--not his bads--that survive the Darwinian gauntlet of science!

Readers of Edmund Gosse's *Father and Sons* will relish Robbins's more gentle ordeal arising from being born to a fundamentalist Baptist family. I refer you to his 1971 *Autobiography of an Economist* which, like most memoirs, begins even better than it ends. Let me give a personal anecdote, slightly doctored up to help make the point about his ascension to the elite of the British class system.

Back in Marshall Plan days, Robbins was in Paris for an inflation commission. I encountered him at an economists' cocktail party, and encounter is the right word. In cutaway garb, he looked more distinguished than any person could possibly be. Stimulated by his polite and flattering interest, I became more and more animated--until in a crescendo of hyperventilated brilliance, I spilled all of my dry martini over his beautiful tailoring. Guilt-stricken, I proffered wrinkled Kleenex to sop up the flood. Lionel turned not one hair. "Think nothing of it, my dear Paul. Have no concern."

What could I say? As an amateur anthropologist, I opined this to Robbins. "On the plane from Boston to Paris, a colonial from the fringe of the British Empire moved from passenger to passenger to convey his unease concerning missing his further connection in Paris. His nervousness quite annoyed more than 50 people. And here you, Lionel, have put me completely at ease despite my gaucherie. There really is something to the English Empire Builder and his phlegm."

Lionel gently punctured my pretentious balloon saying, "Yes, Paul, that good public school I never went to did wonders for me."

I ration myself to only two more Robbins anecdotes. In 1948-1949 those experts in trade theory who were not busily engaged in refuting my factor-price equalization theorem were busily engaged in proving it. When I dined as Robbins's guest at the Reform Club, he struck his forehead and said: "You know, I believe that Abba Lerner wrote a paper for my seminar on that topic back in 1933. Better still, I think I can find it in my files." He could and he did. The rest is history--Robert K. Merton history-of-science history. Abba Lerner had completely forgotten it; Joan Robinson had completely forgotten that a criticism she made of my 1948 paper she had already made to Abba on his 1933 paper.

The story is important to illustrate what Robbins too little emphasized in his autobiography: namely, his role in spotting and encouraging such talents as R.D.G. Allen, Abba Lerner, John and Ursula Hicks, Nicholas Kaldor, Tibor Scitovsky, Frank Hahn, Will Baumol, and many others.

The last story was told to me by Carl Kaysen who visited LSE while on leave from the Harvard faculty. An eminent Establishment figure said at a dinner party, "The Bank of England grossly mishandled the 1930-1933 credit policy. You and I, Lionel, told them to expand more but they just wouldn't listen." As bystander, Kaysen reported: "In case you never heard an academic admit to error, Robbins replied: 'Give yourself all the credit you like but count me out. I was a crazy Hayekian deflationist at that time.'"

Now I shift quickly into the substance of trade policy. In those same 1930-1933 years, the young Robbins clashed with the famous Keynes over Keynes's depression abandonment of free trade. Robbins never later regretted that stand on principle.

As I review the debate, both antagonists had a point. Keynes did not advocate tariffs to reduce British imports; he wanted tariffs so that the U.K. could stimulate GNP by expansionary domestic measures and accompany the same total of imports by a fuller-employment economy. Once the pound fell off gold parity, Keynes got his heart's desire. And recent cliometricians have confirmed Seymour Harris's study of the 1931 Sterling depreciation: it did not act as a beggar-my-neighbor measure to rob others of jobs, but served to permit macro expansion enough to keep the Sterling Bloc good economic neighbors.

Counsel for Robbins can argue that it may be better to stand up for the shibboleth of free trade in season and out of season lest the few departures from it that could help welfare be swamped in the long run by the many departures that entail deadweight loss.

Let me move on to consider what features of recent international finance have proved to be surprising. I always tell my students: Study your surprises. Always look back; you may learn something from your mistakes. What would Robbins have expected in 1975-1991 that the facts betrayed? I made my little list and then asked a number of experts to nominate surprises. There was surprising agreement.

1. Most experts think the volatility of floating exchange rates exceeds that which they expected.

2. My re-reading of the late 1970's literature turned up virtually no predictions that America would massively shift into debtor status with chronic balance of payments deficits on current account. If I showed Lionel the 1960-1980 export and import totals, he could have extrapolated the 1982-1990 gigantic sea change in their difference.

3. Even Harry Johnson, not long dead, must be astonished in Valhalla that *real* exchange rates have moved almost fully in step with *nominal* exchange rates. Johnson's simplest paradigms assumed different changes in regional M stocks induced nominal exchange rates that left real exchange rates relatively invariant. That seems to be precisely what has not happened.

4. What did experts expect about elasticity-optimism and elasticity-pessimism? And what did the 1980s teach us on these matters? Robbins, as an eclectic on the Right of Center, would put considerable faith in elasticity-optimism. He could be forgiven for being puzzled by the amplitude of induced terms of trade shifts in the post-Bretton Woods epoch of floating exchange rates.

4. The Purchasing Power Parity doctrine, which was good enough for David Ricardo and Gustav Cassel, however tempting it might seem to Robbins the antiquarian, would have been bloody expensive to the speculator in foreign exchange who listened to the version of PPP espoused by Professor McKinnon of Stanford and by the London branch of Goldman Sachs. As the pragmatist Charles S. Peirce almost said, the test of truth of your scientific hypotheses is writ large in your IRS tax return, Schedule D, of capital gains and losses.

6. America has for half a century been a low-tariff economy. The free trade ideologues, whom Jacob Viner used to despair of, aver that free trade helps everyone everywhere and at all times. That is bad Ricardian economics. Sophisticated analysts know to predict that superior technological progress by Japan and

Germany in those goods that America used to have Ricardian comparative advantage in--such progress will lower U.S. real incomes and lower America's consumers' surplus from international trade. (See Sraffa's *Ricardo*, Volume 1, pp. 140-141, for Ricardo's recognition that a large improvement in England's productivity in wine would hurt Portugal absolutely.) Therefore a Lionel Robbins brought back to earth as Rip van Winkle ought to have been unsurprised by the relative stagnation in the 1970s and 1980s of American manufacturing real wages.

7. The 1980s taught the trade experts what they had forgotten to emphasize. Domestic capital formation in America will be crowded out if low private thriftiness and non-laughable Laffer full-employment budget deficits suck resources into producing incremental consumption goods. However, when more copious saving persists abroad in Europe and the Pacific Basin, the U.S. consumption goods splurged on can be produced abroad in extraordinary measure--so that the crowding out of our capital formation can be ameliorated or even avoided. *The resulting massive structural current deficit in the balance of payments is thus understood in terms of differential regional net savings rates.* And the sea-change transition from America as the largest creditor nation to America as the ever-larger largest debtor nation is seen to be in accordance with economic science and not a continuing mystery.

Tautologies do not need to be admired even though they do insist on being respected. But the interregional tautology that America's net investment must be matched by her net saving minus her current deficit does not tell us whether this takes place on yesterday's 133 yen to the dollar or at Dr. McKinnon's 199 yen to the dollar; or whether it takes place at 1980's real terms of trade or at 1991's altered terms.

8. How do I know what experts expected on New Year's Day 1980? Robbins was not alive to tell me in his Diary. The then current academic literature is fairly fresh in my memory. Best of all, I have an infallible method for finding where the jackass of science is to be found. Like the old farmer, I say to myself: "If I were a jackass, where would I go?" And going there, I usually find the animal.

So I examine my 1972 New York speech to the Swedish-

American Chamber of Commerce entitled, "International Trade for a Rich Nation." If you lack an ancient pedigree you must forge and fabricate new traditions. When the parvenu Nobel Award in Economics was created, the Federation of Swedish Industries tried to launch the idea of a Little Nobel Prize, in which pearls of more popular exposition on a current topic were to be cast before a business and bureaucrat audience. When my time came, that December week in Stockholm was an over-busy one and I had to decline the invitation. But, as it turned out, if Mohammed would not go to the mountain, the mountain would come to Mohammed. It was arranged that my discourse could be delivered later in New York before the Swedish-American Chamber of Commerce.

What does the anthropologist practicing content analysis find in that speech? In retrospect I have to deem it one of my better days. Here were some of the home runs hit.

A. I correctly perceived how overvalued the dollar had been in the 1959-1971 period and the likelihood that it would float downward in the years to come.

B. I correctly attributed this trend to the differential superiority in manufacturing productivity abroad--in the Pacific Basin and the Common Market as compared to North America.

C. I correctly spotted and extrapolated a trend toward erosion of some of America's consumers' surplus from trade as innovation abroad proliferated in industries where previously we had enjoyed comparative advantage.

I desist from further blowing of my own horn. In hindsight what did I miss?

While I correctly extrapolated what Kravis and Lipsey have since documented--the shift of our multinationals to maintain their world share by outsourcing their production--back in 1972 I worried whether America's great accumulation of creditor ownership abroad would put her at political risk of not receiving her contractual principals and incomes.

In short, I failed completely to foresee the 1980's fall-off in American thriftiness relative to thriftiness abroad and our resulting shift to debtor status. It was as if I had anticipated the Shakespeare play but had left out the character Juliet.

Why feel bad, you may say, for not being clairvoyant? A scientist is not supposed to be a soothsayer. There are some things one ought not to be able to predict. (The 1939-1959 reversal of the long-time decline in the Net Reproduction Rate is a good example.) Who in 1972 could have predicted the 1981 Reaganomics, in which the successful attempt to limit the growth of public expenditure by the device of reducing tax receipts would entail an important shortfall of revenues behind expenditures and an important increment in the fraction of NNP devoted to private-plus-public consumption? No one. (Indeed many still fail to understand the Greek scenario involving this tapeworm therapy.)

What I do consider a proper matter of self-reproach is my lack of 1972 recognition that our best theory of overall saving behavior--that of my neighbor Franco Modigliani based on life-cycle processes--would expect our society's reduced rates of demographic and productivity growth to lead to a lowered private saving rate in the 1980s. And maybe I should have been more alert sociologically to the erosions of modernism and affluence as they sap the bourgeois ethic and undermine both thriftiness and social altruism.

The sun is down and time is short. In hit-and-run staccato here are my own glosses on the eight aspects of science surprise.

1. How much is much exchange-rate instability? When Abraham Lincoln was asked how long a man's legs should be, he said: Long enough to reach the ground. When asked what stock prices would do, Baron Rothschild said: They'll fluctuate. When the late Henry Wallich asked me at the Fed whether I didn't agree that the dollar undergoes St. Vitus's dance, my frank answer was the Cole Porter one. Soybeans do it. The Dow Jones does it. Safe Treasury bonds do it. Why won't all God's children in the organized-market zoo do it--namely oscillate so that, in retrospect, economists will say the movement was excessive? Am I endorsing or impugning macro-efficiency of organized markets? Not if my lawyer did his job in auditing my wordings.

2. *Ex ante* ain't *ex post*. When economic science looks back on the sea change to debtor status, an orthodox Ricardo-Dornbusch-Fischer model can model the gross fats.

In 1964 I shocked my venerable teacher Gottfried Haberler. I said that comparative advantage theory tells us nothing about what the capital-movements components in the payments balance would be. Yes, a nation can even be undersold *in everything* without contradicting equilibrium. (Proof by enumeration. Contemplate a nation of playboys who inherited rich fathers.) Put into the Ricardo, et al. model the current deficits and it becomes neutral on whether the reduced-form exchange rates were appropriate to the reduced-form capital movements.

3,4,5. I must diagnose the severe swings in real exchange rates as endogenously induced and not as exogenous quasi-random walks. This must send Johnson and McKinnon back to the PPP drawing boards. It must cast doubt on extreme-elasticity-optimism in the effective Marshall-Lerner sense. But of similar importance, it casts doubt on Ohlin balanced-income-elasticities optimism in the transfer-of-capital context. The late Frank Graham would be pained by the cheekiness of modern facts. *C'est la guerre! C'est le science!*

PPP of Ricardo, Cassel, and Viner began, not as a theory of one price via arbitrage, but rather as the irreducible long-run germ of truth in the Quantity Theory of Prices. Under strong and unrealistic caveats about invariant real propensities and homogeneities, correct PPP applies to non-tradeables as well as tradeables. Kravis-Summers-Heston have documented that the dollar-rupee exchange rate stays in equilibrium when Professor Cassel as tourist can live at one-third cheapness on his diet of lentils and saris.

Science seeks precision where it can be found. Science must also seek to define imprecisions: both imprecisions in our knowledge and imprecisions that exist in the acts themselves. What the exchange rate will be has to depend on what our net foreign investment will be. I wrote *our* foreign investment but it is not something determined by us. Nor do the animal spirits of foreigners determine it. We, they, and the play of comparative advantage all interact in a kettle of chaotic processes--and I may be using the adjective in its Lorenz-Poincaré modern sense. No wonder I am wary over contemporary mixed economies making firm commitments concerning inflexible exchange rates. No wonder I am skeptical about confident forecasts of future exchange rates and balances.

6 and 7. When we go back with Haim Barkai (1990) and re-examine Britain's tragedy in the 1925 restoration of pre-1914 gold parity, we realize that from 1870 to 1914 (and again after

1918) the U.S. was doing to the U.K. what Japan has been doing to the U.S. in 1955-1991. Even if the U.K. had not spent her overseas wealth in 1914-1918, by 1925 the U.K. welfare state had lost much comparative advantage. The clock should have been rewound at a lower pound parity--particularly if the U.K. expected to pay for her imports by new export successes.

Granted that dynamic shifts in comparative advantage can hurt a nation's welfare. Can tariffs and quotas reverse this? Or are they cases where we react to a cold breeze from abroad by shooting our own feet? For a small region there is a presumption that protectionism is self-defeating and unproductive. For a nation with more than a fifth of global output, the issue is more complex. One suspects that politics will not find the existent second-best.

8. Herman Kahn used to ask us to think the unthinkable. Years ago I made a two-society Ramsey model in which a perpetual-lived Crusoe traded with a perpetual-lived Friday and in which Friday's rate of time preference was biased above Crusoe's. The result was perpetually increasing indebtedness. I buried the results in a lead safe and vowed never to think of it again. Lately I've felt some need to dig it up. Enough said.

Those who have kept awake will have spotted my game. I have an arsenal of economic tools. After being confronted with each new fact, I dig out one that fits the specimen in retrospect.

Do I remind you of someone in the following tale? A rival to William Shakespeare discovered that Will had a portable word processor. Every word of his works and the words of Lord Oxford came out of that word processor. So, in the dead of night, our aspirant to fame kidnapped from Shakespeare's house that magic word processor.

Everyone lived happily ever after. William S. reverted to his old goose quill. And all his rival had to do was to work out the software program that would bring out the words of his perfect new plays.

So it is in economic theory. We have models aplenty and can devise new ones *ad hoc*. All we need is the judgment and creative spark to put them together in reproduction of what it is that is out there staring at us. If we cannot stay ahead of the game, we must try not to fall too far behind.

RECURRING QUANDARIES IN INTERNATIONAL TRADE

Keynote Address by Paul A. Samuelson
Conference on International Finance Markets
The Center for Japan-U.S. Business and Economic Studies
in cooperation with The Sanwa Bank, Limited
New York University, 5-6 May 1988

A keynote speech at the beginning of a conference is like the overture of a musical composition. The melodies that are yet to come are given an initial sampling.

But there the analogy ends. We have five different papers, not one unified symphony with successive movements shaped by the same hand. I would be foolhardy to pretend to orchestrate their diverse themes into one presentation.

Nevertheless, before I even had the opportunity to read the papers, I knew that there remained a number of open questions on the agenda for analysis and discussion of international finance in the late 1980s.

Exchange Stability?

Always we have with us the query, "Whither the dollar and the yen?" In Cambridge, Massachusetts, where I sip my morning coffee, the conventional wisdom is that the dollar must fall.

If the dollar must fall, supposedly it will fall. Many a time my colleague Professor Rudi Dornbusch has predicted 100 yen to the dollar by the end of 1988. And, three miles up the river from MIT, Professor Martin Feldstein of Harvard has issued similar prophecies that have been known to move futures markets on quiet Friday afternoons.

Therefore, it was no surprise that there should turn out to be three papers on the present program dealing with the floating exchange rate system. Dr. Kazuaki Harada discusses Japan under the strong yen. Professors Robert Cumby and John Huizinga analyze the past predictability of exchange rates, real and nominal. Professor Yoshio Suzuki grapples with the future of the international monetary system: the dollar in this century took over the leadership role that the pound sterling enjoyed in the nineteenth century. As we approach the next century will Japan's chronic creditor status elevate her into a similar key status for the yen? They are not so sure at the Bank of Japan that this is an honor worth the costs and responsibilities it may entail.

The *Laissez-Faire* Presumption

A second recurring theme is that of free competition and its regulation. Back in 1776 Adam Smith's *Wealth of Nations* established the doctrine of the Invisible Hand. Where naive observers saw the anarchy and chaos of push-shove free enterprise, Smith (and Charles Darwin after him) saw a process of teleological equilibrium. Many buyers meet many sellers in the market place. Even when each person selfishly pursues his or her own self interest, Smith proclaimed that somehow the outcome was led--as if by an Invisible Hand--to achieve efficiently the maximum well being for all.

Adam Smith did not provide a cogent logical proof of what he seemed to be claiming. Nor did he really understand just what it was that he was proclaiming. Only after more than a century later did Vilfredo Pareto isolate the germ of efficiency that inhered in Smith's doctrine of the Invisible Hand. And it tells us something about how science really operates that Pareto himself did not quite apprehend the exact content of the doctrine of "Pareto optimality." Not until two decades after Pareto's death did welfare economists such as Abram Bergson fully clarify the issues.

No matter. What was murky to precise scholars was crystal clear to ideologues and politicians. Bastiat and other post-Ricardians perceived that *laissez-faire* was very heaven. A strong burden of proof was to be put against any regulatory interferences with *laissez-faire* and free private enterprise.

There is an ebb and flow in the tide of human customs. My infancy and adolescence witnessed in America's 1920s a new approach to a state of pure capitalism. Then came the Autumn 1929 Stock Market Crash. This was followed by the bank failures and bankruptcies of the Great Depression. All over the world the Smithian doctrines went into a discount. Glass-Steagall regulation of banking and Securities Exchange Commission controls over the stock market came into effect.

I recall this ancient history because last October's Black Monday in New York and Chicago has checked the tide of deregulation in the securities markets. The vaunted microefficiencies of the new option markets, of financial futures--which even involve options of options--are being subject to serious accusations of worsening the macrostability of these markets and jeopardizing the performance of the real economy as well.

It is a bit soon to expect that papers at a conference like this will offer light on this thorny issue of "circuit breakers" in time of crisis. But welcome it is to have Professor Aikyoshi Horiuchi's paper on Japan's peculiar pattern of "relationship banking." Just as a would-be mother-in-law does not turn to an auction market in the search for this year's mate, a Japanese corporation apparently does not wake up and say: "Today we need a billion yen to build our new factory. We'll canvass 35 banks for best bids on a mortgage." Adam Smith and Fischer Black would understand the uniformity of interest rates on loans of comparable riskiness that might emerge from such a regime. But that is not to be. Each Japanese corporation, we have to learn, has a sweetheart lead bank. She gets the business automatically--and like a Dutch Uncle, I mean a firm disciplinarian Aunt--she ensures that the loan is well thought out and is of the appropriate scale.

If all that sounds like another heaven to you, keep a sharp eye out that a Boone Pickens may not emerge from the woods or the China Sea to woo away the corporation from its customary guardian and significant other. And before the reforming state introduces new regulations and rules, evaluate carefully what the net of costs and benefits is likely to be.

Professor Shelagh Heffernan reports on changes taking place in Britain, the traditional land of the Old School Tie and the cozy networks of gentlemen. How should we analyze what will be the new effects of ongoing deregulation of the London market?

United States economists faced just such a puzzle when ceilings on interest rates for home mortgages were phased out. Their theoretical predictions turned out to be near the mark. When residential construction ceased to be subject to direct rationing, the strength of building as countercyclical stabilizer was attenuated. Interest rates fluctuated with greater cyclical amplitude once rationing by price rather than by fiat became the rule. Given freedom, the savings and loan institutions began to resemble the ordinary commercial banks.

As Kipling once said, "What do they know of economics who only economics know?" We shall have our final wrap-up session at tomorrow's lunch where Tetsuko Kondo shares with us the benefits of his experience as a Minister of State for Economic Planning and as important leader in the ruling Japanese party. When I was a young theorist, often I tended to be a little impatient with and patronizing towards practical men of affairs who led the world's activities. I have learned better. It is empirical reality that provides the lifeblood of an organic science. We should render to the academic tower what properly belongs to pure scholarship. But what can serve better than a tower as a base for the telescopes we thrust out at the real world shimmering beyond the classroom and seminar? My many years in Cambridge, Massachusetts have been enormously enriched because it is a station on the underground railroad that connects practitioners of political economy and academic researchers.

The late Paul Dudley White was the physician who nagged the world into giving up smoking, sedentary lounging, and high-cholesterol food goodies. When he was in his eighties he told me at a neighborhood party that it was his practice to lecture at Rotary Clubs all over the world. The fee he exacted was to be paid in pints of blood, not local currencies. That way he could test his hypothesis that everywhere, even in Third World backwaters, the upper classes were jeopardizing their longevity by too rich a diet.

I too exact my pint of blood. Mine is the dear price that you must listen to my views and prejudices on the day's burning issues.

Concerning deregulation and control on the Invisible Hand, mine is a pragmatic position. Most of the work of the GNP is best left to the marketplace. We have seen how ineffectively the Lenins, Stalins, Maos, Castros, and Ghandis organize an economy. But left to itself the market has no heart. It is not cruel, but the market is indifferent as to whether a needy child or a plump tycoon procures the sweetmeats and vitamins. A mixed economy can reap some of the advantages of both worlds when it acts by tax-and-expenditure programs to attenuate the inequality inherent in market capitalism.

Rules of the road, provision of jointly-useful public goods, zoning rules on externalities--all these too are part of the good society. We should squarely recognize that much of society's second guessing of the market involves some deadweight losses of inefficiency. But as my old libertarian teacher at the University of Chicago, Henry Simons, used to say: "Every good cause should be pushed beyond the point of zero costs; and it should be stopped only well into the region of diminishing returns, being pressed on to the point where its incremental benefit is matched by the incremental cost it entails."

Specifically where finance is concerned, markets have become more rational and at the micro level more efficient. The modern theory of finance, as much the product of business schools as of economics departments, is a magnificent scientific edifice--with impressive empirical confirmations in millions of statistical instances.

One of the uses that I make of this modern theory is to predict that the divergences in institutions and behavior between the Tokyo and the New York financial markets will erode away as time goes by. The process, I believe, has so far been pretty much on schedule.

Please note my use of the words "*micro* efficient." To my mind that should not be confused with "*macro* efficient." Nothing in the words of Scholes and Black, or Sharpe and Merton, Modigliani and Miller, or Mandelbrot and Samuelson can lead me to believe that market crashes and manias are a thing of the past. I side with Robert Shiller, James Tobin, Franco Modigliani, and Lawrence Summers that speculative markets are led by visible hands to perpetrate macro oscillations which serve no useful purpose.

Each issue must be decided on its own merits and not by dogmatic principle. The fast computer that facilitates tight arbitrage can enable an avalanche of sellers to move the stock indexes as much in a day as used to take a week or month. But shutting down those computers will not necessarily accomplish more good than harm. To repeat, each such issue must be studied by scientists to estimate on which side the merits are to be found.

5
Purchasing Power Disparities

The reasons why a Milton Friedman or a Friedrich Hayek favors floating exchange rates are not necessarily mine. Philosophically, I am at peace with either stable or flexible exchange rates. However, my reading of past experience and my diagnosis of how politics works makes me very leery of pegged exchange rates. Much of the talk about international coordination is not worth the paper it is written on. Its value is worse than zero; it is negative.

Hermam Göring used to say, "When I hear the word 'culture,' I reach for my gun." When I see the words purchasing power parity, I confess to an urge for a red pencil. This is so even though I have written more than most economists on that subject. I make the prophecy--and remember where you heard it first--that much harm will come to the world trading system from a naive preoccupation with what is called purchasing power parity.

As said in Dornbusch's definitive *New Palgrave* piece on "purchasing power parity," it has been variously treated as "an identity, a truism, an empirical regularity or a grossly misleading simplification." It is all of those things--and more, and less. A year ago when the dollar was worth about 200 yen Ronald McKinnon declared that to be the desired equilibrium goal, even though the U.S. current balance of payments was at its worst and purely because some calculations of geographic price indexes made 200-to-1 be the *ppp* par.

Actual price index ratios have waved systemically above and below such pars in recent decades. It is absurd to think that this reflects systematic deviations in the validity of the dogma of one world price everywhere for each good; or to think that definable rises and falls in degree of deadweight inefficiency correlations.

Remember that there are tradeable and untradeable goods. For untradeable goods with heavy transport goods it is quite compatible with efficiency for price to differ geographically. Kravis-Heston-Summers have shown how right Ricardo, Harrod, and Belassa were in predicting systematic deviations from puristic *ppp*.

When a debtor nation like the U.S. seeks to limit its trade deficits by depreciation, one expects the correction process to generate terms-of-trade changes that *ppp* literalists regard as unkosher. Therefore, the more an economist extols *ppp*, the more he justifies continuation of a pegged exchange rate regime that perpetuates existing unbalances.

I wish that time were longer so that this and other issues could be debated more thoroughly. One such issue is the compatibility of an efficient market with systematic movements of the exchange rate in a floating regimen. A GM share looks like a random walk in a perfect market, but that is consistent with the existence of efficacious forces of real supply and demand that keep one GM share and one Cadillac auto from being expected to stay more valuable than one future head of cabbage.

Perhaps in the oral discussions we can scratch the surface of these theoretical matters.

509

REALITIES FOR A FINE JUNE DAY
Harvard Business School Class of 1948 Reunion, 5 June 1993
Cambridge, Massachusetts

I hardly know what to say to this audience, for you are so to speak dinosaurs or dodo birds. The Class of 1948 is virtually an extinct species. By 2020 there will be no one left in the category I am talking about.

Do not panic, however. This is just my over-dramatic way of pointing out that yours is the last class that was not brought up on Samuelson's *ECONOMICS*. That textbook came out in the autumn of 1948 and only since then has post-Keynesian economics dominated macroeconomics and governmental policies in the Mixed Economies around the world.

I counted a lot of Jaguars, Maseratis, and Mercedes in the Business School parking lot. Evidently you have not done so badly in life and can cry all the way to the bank despite your lack of Keynesian grounding in economics. And to tell the sober truth the 150 nations in the world have not been performing so well lately in terms of inflation and unemployment rates as to obviate the question:

> If the Brand X textbook was so damned good and used so widely from Timbuktu to East Arizona Tech, then how come the world is in its lousy present shape?

It's that present lousy shape that I will talk about today.

> Where are we?
> How did we get here?
> What should be done in the 1993-1996 period to improve the U.S. and global economic performance for the short-run and long-run future?

I have advised several governments. Time and again I've testified before Congressional Committees, Royal Commissions, and the Federal Reserve Board. I may say that my volunteered counsel has been worth every bit paid for it.

Experience has taught me to leave politics and strategies to experts and stick to my own inexact science of economics.

> Diagnose the situation. Prescribe what ought to be done and, equally important, what ought not to be done.

That's the economist's main job.

Then, in a low-keyed way, we can all participate in the tactical discussion of compromise--trading off A for B, saving what can be preserved of C or D, avoiding E at any cost. Experience shows that free discussion of questions from the floor is the most valuable part of an hour like this. And we do plan to leave time for that dialogue.

Here is factual background.

Fact 1. The post-World War II epoch has been the greatest period of global GNP growth in all history. From 1950 to about 1975, Western Europe and Japan grew mightily to lower the American lead. It is hard to be the first rider in a bicycle race. But America also grew remarkably in the Age After Keynes. It is just that foreign economies grew even more remarkably. And, with some notable exceptions in Africa and Central America, the underdeveloped regions shared in the real progress.

Fact 2. If the computations are done right, you find that America still enjoys the highest per capita real GNP. Call us 100 and Japan scores at about 80, just below Germany, Switzerland, and France. By the year 2010 it may be a different story of course. Today our 5% of world population enjoys only about 22% of world output rather than the 35% that used to be our fraction.

Fact 3. It was not 100% capitalisms that showed up the communisms of Eastern Europe and Mainland China. It was post-1929 Mixed Economies or Welfare Societies that grew on broadly-shared terms.

Fact 4. When the miraculous third quarter of the twentieth century approached its end, suddenly all over the world there broke out a virulent slowdown of the rate of productivity advance. Few advanced nations escaped. In Germany and in Japan, and here in North America, there was a halving of productivity growth. So universal was it that a coldly objective scientist might be compelled to invoke sun spots as an explanation, but I resist that temptation.

More plausible as an explanation is the sudden five-fold increase in the price of OPEC energy. But that alone can't account for the persistent drag-down. I personally attribute great weight to the new disease of stagflation--which dates from 1969 to 1980, and which may like tuberculosis be returning in the 1990s. However, while that can explain 20% unemployment rates in Spain and double digit rates in Germany and France, it doesn't bear directly on the drop in full-employment growth potentials.

Often in science you just have to admit that good explanations are not attainable. It is a fact that much of World War II military research created great fallouts for electronic and computer industries. But that impulse is in the past; and abroad the easy imitations of American techniques may be part of history.

Fact 5. Ronald Reagan won by landslide in the second most important election of the century. (1932, which brought in FDR's

New Deal, was the first most important election. It ended the pure capitalism that I was brought up under.) The Federal Reserve, at the cost of the two recessions in 1980 and in 1981-82, brought two-digit stagflation down to a 3 or 4% annual rate. It was a non-fact in 1981 that America was then in a Dunkirk, in a state of ruin brought on by punitive taxation and crippling economic regulation. But that belief formed the basis for the Kemp-Stockman-Laffer supply-side Reaganomics. A more accurate reading of contemporary economic history suggested--at least it did to me--that when a welfare state is not limited, when as in Sweden as much as half the GNP comes to be channeled through the public tax and transfer system, then tax avoidance burgeons and the rate of progress begins to sputter.

Fact 6. Two opposite strands of conservatism economics--for short call them Lafferism and Friedmanism--conspired to create the Reaganomics that no seer had predicted in 1980. The Muse of History must have a sense of humor: as Hegel said, "History repeats itself. The first time as tragedy, the second time as farce." The most conservative President in 60 years presided over the most radical of structural budget deficits at full employment.

In 1980 America was the world's largest creditor nation, having built up since 1914 a patrimony of net foreign assets. By 1985, or 1986, our chronic balance-of-payments deficits had used up that patrimony; by 1993, we are the champion in-the-red debtor nation; and on the more optimistic projections, by the year 2000 we shall have intensified our net-debtor status.

In 1980, America's public debt had been brought down from its end-of-war twelve months worth of GNP to barely three months of GNP. Under-taxing relative to our spending during the Reagan-Bush years to the tune of 3-to-4 percent of GNP, we have propelled the public debt up to seven months of GNP and essentially with no end in sight. We are not yet at Italian, Belgian, or Argentine stratospheres; but all the projections show we are on the way.

I'll leave to the question period explanation of how this came to pass. Let me only say that we have eaten of the fruit of the tree of knowledge: low tax rates are delicious; 31% marginal income taxes beats 77% hands down. But of course we do want national defense and to honor the commitments to social security participants and those without disposable incomes.

Is the burden a hopeless one? No, it is a myth that America is at some limit of taxability, so that one more pfenning will break the camel's back. Germany and Japan, which outperform us, tax a larger fraction of GNP. America in the time of Eisenhower-Kennedy-Johnson-Nixon grew faster than we grew in Reagan-Bush-Clinton times, and did so with higher tax rates.

This brings me to one more fact, a crucial one.

Fact No. 7. America is a low-saving society. Private family

saving has been way down in the 1980s. Taiwanese save 25% of their incomes; Japanese save 18%; Germans save 14%; the dashing French, Italians, and Spaniards save 11%. In America we save 4%, 3%, or even 2% in some years. Private corporate saving has also dropped drastically in the United States. Add to low private thrift the negative thriftlessness of Laffer-Friedman structural deficits. That gives you the devil's recipe for a consumption-binge society, which must go abroad for savings to finance its capital formation, and which will be paying in the next century in the form of dividends and interest the fruits of that foreign-financed capital formation.

It's a free country. If we Americans of this generation want to rob our children and grandchildren, who's to stop us? What do we owe to posterity? What's it ever done for us? Maybe that's the way we want to crumble the cookie?

But when did we decide that? Providence will forgive President Reagan because of course *he* didn't know what he was doing. My point is a different one. There were no town meetings all over the land in which Americans studied the menu between future and present and decided to change what we had been doing from 1776 to 1980--and I include the 1929-1939 period of the Great Depression in this. Instead America sidled into the new syndrome through the back door. God will forgive us under the doctrine that we didn't know what we were doing. But still we shall have to sleep in the 1999 bed we have made up for ourselves.

Few understand the exact sense in which our structural deficit is an evil. Economists do not explain this well, and even when they do, Congress and the people can't keep in mind the complexities of the subject.

Presidents really don't like economics. They go whole hours not thinking about the subject. From many years of advising the Prince or the President, I've learned that only two topics can capture their interest:

> If you can say, "Sire, unless you do A and B, there will be a Great Depression," then he may stay awake, and if you are convincing, you may evoke some action.

> Or, if you can say, "Mr. President, unless you do C and D, inflation will accelerate toward and into two-digit annual rates," then you will get a hearing and maybe some action.

Everything else is a bore and a yawn. Well, I have to inform you that our structural deficit is an insidious thing. One cannot honestly say it will cause a 1994 recession. Or entail a 1995 inflation.

It is neither of these short-run things.

I can see glazed eyes in the audience. And a few yawns. You are bored. Why my fuss? Because continuance of the structural deficit does crowd out American-owned capital formation in favor of having resources go to current consumption. True supply-side economics--and I'm not talking about radical-right 1981 snake oil supply-side economics--says that earnings and living standards of us Americans will be the worse if the high-employment, non-Keynesian budget deficits are allowed to go their merry way.

Well, what to do about it? The Republicans have an easy solution: Solve it by cutting public expenditure programs. The Democrats have an easy solution: Solve it largely by raising tax rates.

The gridlock is not in Washington, within the beltway. Main Street America is where the impasse persists. As Pogo said, "We have met the enemy and he is us."

Much of President Clinton's travail comes from his lack of focus; his taste in haircuts; his tactical blunder in tackling the issue of gays in the military; his attempt to get more from the bottle of national resources than is contained within it. All this is true.

But a deeper diagnosis is that we people find it hard to like the messenger who brings us the bad news. And if the news is true news, we resent the messenger all the more.

In our bones we know that both higher tax rates and tighter spending limits ought to be in the cards.

I speak not as a pessimist but as a realist when I say that the Clinton troubles are Main Street troubles.

Would that it were true that a slash in capital gains rates would solve America's problems. Or that a ruthless pruning back on regulations would bring back Camelot's real growth rates of four percent per annum.

Only a lobbyist or a libertarian can believe in that.

It was President Truman who called for a one-armed economist. Not for him, the adviser who says," On the one hand this. On the other hand that."

My experience requires me to reply thus:

> With respect, Sir, you really cannot want a one-armed economist. For in economics, one-armed experts come in two varieties: those with a right arm only, and those with only a left. And then, Sir, you have to call in a two-armed eclectic like me to adjudicate between the zealots.
>
> My most precious trait is the important gift of "Maybe."

Notice I have not had the chance to speak of the 1990-91 recession or the disappointing 1991-93 recovery. If it is your pleasure, we can go into that--and more--during the question period that begins right now.

510

INFORMAL THOUGHTS ABOUT MACROECONOMICS
Paul A. Samuelson, 3 October 1997
Banca d'Italia, Rome, Italy

Back in the 1930-1950 period, macroeconomics was in political economy's central limelight. No wonder. The world suffered stock market crashes, the Great Depression, and then post-war inflations. The public naturally pays most attention to the pathologies that are affecting the body politic.

And in the shape of the Keynesian income-analysis Revolution, from inside economics came a new paradigm that seemed to have an important measure of success in solving some persistent social problems. Public esteem for economics went up in the Roosevelt and Kennedy days; and, as always is the case with scholars, our self-esteem shines moon-like by the reflected algebraic glory of popular acclaim.

That was the good side. After 1950 diversity proliferated in the methodology of macroeconomics. The potency that seemed lost for money in deep depression days of liquidity traps, and in wartime regimens of pegged interest rates, returned when more normal conditions returned. Although disagreement in a science is a sign of imperfection and incompleteness, disagreement does make for debate and liveliness within the academy. That kept the kettle boiling in macroeconomics long after microeconomics was returning to its traditional place at the head of the table where economists sit.

At the frontier of microeconomics there is a broad measure of agreement among modern mainstream economists. It would be laughable to speak of a pro-Debreu and an anti-Debreu School. But the same cannot be said of a Rational-Expectationist and an anti-Rational-Expectationist School in macroeconomics. Yes, we are all post-Keynesians now. But after you cut away inessential differences in terminology and self-proclaimed titles, there do remain genuine differences in the behavior equations employed tacitly or implicitly by different macroeconomists.

What I want to do here today is to confess to what I really believe about the validity of different macroeconomic notions. I am not going to try to prove that these heuristic conjectures are absolutely or approximately true. That would be too tall an order. On the other hand I have no right to expect you to accept any view of mine on the ground that I have earned the authority to be believed. No one deserves such an open-end bank account. At best I may be able to suggest hints as to why I come down where I do.

The Inexactness of Science

I believe it was some four decades ago that Tjalling Koopmans stepped into my MIT office. He said, "Paul, I have been granted a Sabbatical to think through some basic questions in economics. One opinion from you I would much appreciate. Where do you think we stand and in what direction are we moving in economics as far as our scientific ability to make accurate predictions?"

My reply was a cautious one: "As far as aggregate output and price-level forecasts are concerned, economists do have a better batting average than astrologers, psychics, brokers, Chairmen of the Board, or journalists. And now we do have better statistical data and get it on a more timely basis. Modern computers are facilitating our ability to analyze, simulate, and process such information. And the variety of our theoretical models encompasses and goes beyond that of our teachers and their teachers. I find it plausible that in the next ten or twenty years our *ex post* scorings of our *ex ante* quantitative forecast accuracy will show some gradual improvement.

"But I do not honestly think we are on a convergence path toward ever more stochastic precision. It is not merely that zero standard deviations are not in the future horoscopes of the real world. It is also that there are presumptively no *100%-stationary* probability processes that will characterize the future behavior of global and regional economies. Possibly we will seem to get just so far until, so to speak, a basic indeterminacy level will prevent us from getting significantly farther."

I fear Tjalling found my banalities just a little disappointing. But he also was of a cautious and eclectic temperament, and autobiographical experience had taught him that the laboratory precisions of his physicist days were not to be taken for granted in the social science realm of economics.

My answer to Koopmans missed some important points. Well-informed economists at the frontier of their art can guess pretty well about the general level of next year's basic variables: GDP, price deflator, savings ratios. But what they can tell an audience is pretty much *what is already discounted in the market*. No trader can make capital gains on their sensible scoop. Time and again when I have listened to a banking expert speak at an international conference, I had to yawn because what he was confiding to the audience I found already embalmed in the futures-market reports of that morning's *Wall Street Journal* and *Financial Times*. It is the news that has not yet broken whose knowledge will make you rich if only you could know it. The germ of truth in the notion of efficient markets and random walks was just becoming understood as Koopmans and I were then talking.

My first sermon in macro must therefore enjoin myself to be Eclectic with a capital E and Humble with a capital H.

At once I prescribe the antidote to my own banality. A wide open mind is an empty mind. I must try to be as eclectic as the recurring facts suggest but only that eclectic. No small order.

A Time to Remember and to Forget

I was a well-trained neoclassical economist at the University of Chicago. That was more a handicap than a help when thousands of banks were failing and millions of mortgages being foreclosed on. Along came the Model T Keynes *General Theory*. I kicked its wheels and at first had to reject it. As has been said, it lacked kosher micro foundations. Gradually I overcame my hesitations and came to use a sticky-wages income multiplier model to rationalize the U.S. 1930s world. At a time when the shortest Treasury Bill rate approximated to 3/8 of 3/8 of one percent, my earliest students understood my lectures on liquidity traps and the reduced potency of 1938 conventional Fed open-market purchases. It was my more recent grandchildren students who could not believe that such things were possible -- until, as a matter of brute fact, Japan in the 1990s came to work with short rates of only 1/2 of one percent.

By 1946 I had outgrown my Neanderthal-Keynes garments. My students now had to learn that Money Does Indeed Matter, which is different from Money *Alone* Matters. Naturally I became a disappointment to the Robinson-Kahn-Kaldor-Harrod crowd who shaped the out-of-date 1959 Royal Radcliffe Committee Report on Money.

An old friend asked me: "Is it true you've become a Monetarist?" In reply I quoted George Santayana, the Spanish philosopher brought up in the Catholic tradition, who had been asked, "Is it true that you have become a Protestant?" Santayana retorted: "Sir, I have lost my Faith. But not my Reason." At no date did I find Monetarism plausible.

Later editions of my textbook spoke of a Neoclassical Synthesis, in which both weapons of monetary *and* fiscal policy could alter real Q and P in the tautology $MV = PQ$. Changed facts in the U.S. and global economy changed my 1930s paradigm, and I suffered no ideological *angst* in changing my skin. As long as I kept the approbations of Tobin, Hansen, Okun, and Musgrave I purred like a cat. Too bad that Bob Eisner and Milton Friedman were strange bedfellows in rejecting from different directions my version of evolved Keynesianism.

Following upon the Kennedy Camelot, it became the fashion to say that Keynes was dead. But who was the new King? And what killed the old King? Was it a case of Tom Kuhn's revolution and counter-revolution in science? Did a new set of aberrant facts negate the Hicks-Hansen LM-SI paradigm and re-legitimatize Friedman's monetarist version of $MV = PQ$ paradigm? No. I was there. I can report on the mean-square-errors of all the post-Camelot forecasting models.

There was a fleeting instant in the early 1970s when a monistic lagged M model did moderately well at the Federal Reserve

Bank of St. Louis. Reality staggered randomly into the Friedman gun sights; and then it as randomly staggered out of those gun sights. The monetarist Citibank economics department added epicycles to the Friedman-Ptolemaic structures but to little avail: their forecasts always lagged changing reality. Finally Chairman Walter Wriston liquidated all of Citibank's economics department, kit and caboodle.

Alan Greenspan at his Townsend-Greenspan consulting firm continued to make do with Tinbergen-Klein macro modelling. And the Fed itself could not handle the facts better than with a Penn-MIT-Federal Reserve Bank model à la Modigliani, which of course got subjected to the Governors' own judgmental add-ons.

If there was no Kuhnian factual endorsement of this or that version of anti-Keynesianism, what did kill the beatification of Keynes? Here is my take on that. When the U.S.A. was achieving reasonably stable prices *cum* long expansions and short recessions, macroeconomics and post-Keynesians were popular. After the Vietnam War brought on demand-pull inflation, and in the 1970s OPEC oil shocks and repeated harvest failures solidified stagflation, Main Street and Wall Street became disillusioned with the magicians of macroeconomics. Who takes credit for the sun cannot escape getting blame for the rain. Ironically, economists let their own self-esteem rise and fall with their external Gallup-poll fan ratings.

Monetarism à la 1970 was never good neoclassical economics. A quasi-constant velocity makes no sense when what is defined as "money" varies from a zero-interest return to a 15% per annum 1978 money-market fund return. As soon as Dr. Friedman agrees to write $MV = PQ$ as $PQ/M = $ a rising function of the interest rate, he has caught up with the 1936 *General Theory* formulation of Liquidity Preference!

In my reading, what killed off monetarism was not its lack of intrinsic plausibility but rather the dramatic break in the M-Y regressions occurring between late 1970s and early 1980s. Who lives by the sword of a narrow empirical positivism perishes by that sword. Since nature abhors a vacuum, Robert Lucas's more interesting paradigm of rational expectationism piped the tune that attracted the disillusioned monetarists out of Hamlin.

Yesterday in my public lecture I dubbed the U.S. a ruthless economy with a cowed labor force. I explained the genesis of this from domestic and international competitive erosion of Fortune-500 oligopolism and from the rise of more ferocious forms of corporate governance. And I analyzed how such an economy would behave more like a Say's Law model and thereby be more amenable to central bank stabilizings. Some, but not most of America's closer approaches to Say's Law, I do believe are related to a subset of the notions underlying Lucas's New Classical School. (Example: people do learn in the longer run how not to be re-surprised in the short run. But that does not create a dynamic model which is real-variables neutral to policy changes and which behaves as if it approximates to some group Expected Value.) From 1983 to 1989 and thereafter were the Tokyo stock and land markets efficiently maximizing some definable thing--as would be the case of a rational single entrepreneur who sets *ex ante* control variables so as to maximize a definable Expected Utility while possessive of knowledge of the probability functions that she faces? I think it naive to believe that.

Before trying to answer questions from this audience, let me mention a paradox about the economic history of the last quarter century.

Since 1980, using only the tools of a 1965 intermediate macro textbook, you would have done better in achieving approximate forecasting and in prescribing policy than you would have done in the 1965-1980 years. However, if by contrast you tried to rely on alternative tools--culled from Friedman or Lucas or Pasinetti, and thereby providing you with genuine alternatives to the consensus mainstream macro models--then by my scorings of the 1980-1997 batting averages, the slightly old-fashioned and out-of-fashion tools were having a surprisingly good run.

It is not that I am satisfied with old-fashioned things. I welcome study of auto vector regressions, of cointegration models, of unit-root quasi-random walks. The fancier, the more delicious. But I am results-oriented, not elegance-oriented. Experience has taught me that nature does not act to give us data scatters that will answer definitively the questions we analysts need answers for. I must pool informal cross-sectional experiences and resort to Bayesian judgments that cannot be *proved* to be right. Where our knowledge still is inadequate, my guess is that progress will probably not come from grand new Kuhnian alternatives, but rather from detailed structural experimentation that tries to make a humane mixed economy less subject to deadweight losses of macro and micro types.

I hope I am wrong in this. How nice it would be to reap quantum leaps of progress from brilliant new theory discovery. But ever I push down the wishful-thinker dreamer inside me: Always welcome the new, but be merciless in auditing its pretensions.

One can accept some of rational expectationists' useful insights without having to swallow its more extreme and farfetched crotchets. Yes, one surprise may work well even though it is wrong to believe that the same surprise can be perpetrated on the same people repeatedly with the same favorable effects. But No, the dogma is false that all policy changes essentially affect only the price level and are impotent to alter real variables. Most of economic history, thoughtfully reflected on, rejects this as unlikely. Here is an example. Some time ago Robert J. Gordon studied how movements in total P×Q fluctuated *in toto* and broke that total down into the fluctuations in each of its P and Q components. What were the brute yearly facts? Two-thirds of the variability was in Q and only one-third in P over a century of American data. A similar tale would be told about business-cycle-length fluctuations although not so asymmetric and regular. At the level of pure theory, the 1936-39 real contrasts between a pegged-to-gold France and an opportunistically-depreciating Belgium accords with the non-Lucas expectations in the '70s or '80s. But of course an eclectic will understand that in almost a century of Latin American inflations much did accord with a Lucas orientation.

This is not academic. A bit back the Bank of Italy celebrated a birthday. Of course Governor Fazio spoke then about tenets of central banking. And Paul Volcker, no longer Fed chief, spoke too. Which one of them was more unrealistic about the importance for policy goals about concentrating *solely* on price-level goals? To my surprise, it was the American who sounded dogmatic and naive and monistic while the European, in the lines and between the lines, was more eclectic and balanced.

Now I ask you. Did the Paul Volcker of 1979-1989, who helped us break out of stagflation and into the better-run U.S. economy of the 1980s behave at all like what he was recommending at the Bank of Italy birthday party? Not at all. History will admire and applaud Volcker for the Machiavellian way he used monetarism arguments he never personally swallowed to gain political support for two back-to-back minor recessions necessary to break out of stagflation. And then in mid-1982 when the second recession was persisting uselessly long, Volcker glimpsed and took advantage of a window of opportunity to activistically initiate a long American recovery. His gamble worked out magnificently to the chagrin of the dissenting monetarists. I commend a Hippocratic Oath: Minimize the harm you do. All of us, including rational expectationists, can take that to heart.

The Emeriti Speak Out

Two Gods That Fail

Paul Samuelson

When the failed god of Marxian socialism gets replaced by the ancient god of libertarian laissez-faire, watch out, says this Nobel laureate.

Robert Heilbroner's *The Worldly Philosophers* has been a twentieth-century book of great influence. If it has not had more readers than Thorstein Veblen's *Theory of the Leisure Class*—and note my use of the word "if"—almost certainly more of its readers have survived to master its final page.

Most of mainstream economics is *not* "big-picture economics." Our journals and textbooks are full of the grimy details about inventory cycles or the deadweight losses incident to taxes and regulation. Besides, most big pictures are wrong. Joseph Schumpeter's notion, that it would be capitalism's very *successes* that would doom it to destruction, turned out to be a nice try but no cigar. Marx and Engels' ringing prose in the *Communist Manifesto,* on the occasion of its 150th birthday, defines a new poignancy for the lines "Workers of the world, unite. You have nothing to lose but your chains." Test that out in North Korea or on the histories of Mao's China and Lenin–Stalin's Soviet Union.

PAUL SAMUELSON is Institute Professor Emeritus, Massachusetts Institute of Technology. This article was originally presented as a speech in honor of Robert Heilbroner at the New School for Social Research, New York, November 12, 1998.

Years ago Arthur Koestler edited *The God That Failed*, whose chapters report the disillusionment of one true believer after another in the promise of Marxian prophecies under the impact of contemporary actuality. It would be boring sawing of sawdust to elaborate on that god that failed. More relevant to the present moment of global economic chaos is an antipodal-polar archetype. I am speaking about the god of pure *libertarian* capitalism.

Not a few people look on the cold war as a quasi-controlled laboratory experiment. Dempsey dueled with gigantic Firpo, the Wild Man from the Pampas. And Dempsey scored the final conclusive knockout. Period. Fini. Now we can move on to producing free energy by mastering control of nuclear fusion.

This is specious naïveté. Miracle-making 1945–90 Japan was never Friedrich von Hayek's laissez-faire Whig utopia. The defection of East Germany from the Soviet bloc was not occasioned by any new dramatic failure of its gross domestic product performance. When Mikhail Gorbachev released the Soviet grip on the East German population, they began to vote with their feet in a mass migration toward the Candyland to the west that they had long viewed on their TV screens.

The brute fact of crude economic history is that the mixed-market economy in the Age After Keynes did significantly outperform the communist societies in Europe and Asia. As Keynes said about another system, the market system, in its moment of worst 1930s pathology: *It is not aesthetic and it does not deliver the goods.* Exactly that held for pre- and post-Stalin Soviet Union, Maoist Cultural Revolutions, Tito's Yugoslavia, North Korea, Albania, Cuba, and all the utopias that transiently enchanted so intelligent and humane an expert as the late Joan Robinson.

In this piece for the Heilbroner Fest, I aim to deal with a medium-size picture infatuation. After the mixed economies recovered from their malignant and long-lasting slump of the 1930s, so-called economic science did make significant advances internally. Gradually, though, in very many societies, electorates have more recently been shifting away from the redistributional welfare state. Margaret Thatcher in Britain is indicative, as are Ronald Reagan in the United States and the oscillatory disintegration of the Roosevelt Democratic Party majority forged in the Great Depression crucible. Even in—nay, especially in—Scandinavian and other Social Democratic regions, the same trend away from democratic altruism was evident until recently. The welfare state, for better or worse, perforce seems to become the *limited* welfare state.

The dog wags the tail when we compare direction of causal influence from the lay public to academic economists' ideology—despite Keynes's assertion that men in authority are merely slaves of past zealots of the chair. (In my observations princes always get the advisers they deserve, as they select from a varied menu of flat-earthers. President Truman was dead wrong: It is the prince as much as the brain trusters who needs two arms. In our guild, one-armed economists divide between those with only a right arm or those with a left arm only; and then the wise prince will have a need for the eclectic two-armer to adjudicate between them. "One man with the truth is a majority." That is not a wise truth. It is an expensive joke.)

To discern and measure a discipline's trend, study its assistant professors. They will be around longer. While voters move away from altruism, savants grow in credulity about the self-stability of macro-market mechanisms. Thomas Carlyle's formula for laissez-faire was "Anarchy plus the constable." Today this has become "Laissez-faire and the independent central bank (preoccupied solely with price-level stability)."

Alas, dual stock and land bubbles bursting in 1990 created for Japan a decade of output stagnation reminiscent of Irving Fisher's ancient debt deflation models. In mid-1997, most of the rest of Asia went abruptly from sunny daytime to ghostly night in a magisterial display of *macro-inefficient* organized markets. International capital movements somehow were not led by an invisible hand to a definable Pareto optimality. Outside the still-prevailing oases of Main Street serenity in the United States and Western Europe, Russia and Latin America have been infected by the virus of the so-called Asian flu.

If rational expectationism or rule-bound monistic monetarism are realistic and potent doctrines, then the god of libertarian laissez-faire reigns intact. Do not, they say, let one storm panic you into any macro-activism. Things themselves will allegedly muddle through and, besides, activism can only systematically affect long-term price levels rather than sustainable macro-output and employment patterns. So it is argued.

Outside the seminar rooms, movers and shakers are becoming shaken in their faith that the god of libertarian laissez-faire cannot fail. Paul Volcker and Alan Greenspans dutifully pay lip service to the independent central bank boilerplate, but—like Mr. Dooley's Supreme Court, which "follows" the election returns—in 1982, 1987, 1998, Volcker and Greenspan have shown a proper concern for $Q(t)$ likelihoods even when $P(t)$ remained pacific. I hope that the rumor is true that the clerks at the new (Frankfurt) Central European Bank are furiously learning English at Berlitz night school courses and letting their Bundesbank German rust.

I conclude on a serious note. Why have the rational expectationists suddenly turned quiet? The ball is in the court of Lucas, Sargent, and other important contributors to the New Classical School. Are organized markets *macro-efficient* inside of modern mixed economies, as those economies *actually* are? What makes them so? What keeps them so? Are self-fulfilling "rational" bubbles (away from "fundamentalists' value") impossible? Or possible? And with what plausible theory about life tables of bubbles' expected duration?

As a pioneer in the elucidation of market *micro-efficiency*, I have always deemed it a duty to test whether and when a market participant can selfishly earn excess returns by discerning an "inefficient" pattern and acting to correct it. But what can an expert do when she (1) recognizes the general level of the market to be "overvalued" but (2) knows that she would lose her socks betting against the tape? Instead many affluent and experienced money managers, even while believing the market to be overvalued, "fear *not* to be *net* long in it!" Their mantra is "I hope we will not be the last getting out the door of the burning bourse when the inevitable turn hits." How should we reconcile this with chatter about warrantable Muth expectational means?

Rational expectationists on my reading list depart from the maxim that says, "If you must forecast, forecast often." For them generally, silence is golden. Alas, only when orbits and motions are simply periodic is the stopped clock right twice a day.

Like servomechanisms hunting out of control, voters can overshoot toward libertarian laissez-faire. Maybe social Darwinism provides its own cure. This possibility came to me when I recalled an old crude Otto von Bismarck joke. He is supposed to have proposed a solution for the alleged Irish problem: "Interchange the Dutch and Irish populations. Then the Dutch would make the Emerald Island bloom, while neglect of the Dutch dikes would take care of Dean Swift's Irish problem." A libertarian society that goes all the way might thus self-destruct—but personally I wouldn't count on this Pyrrhic solution.

Does the rejection of Newt Gingrich feed rational hope that fanatical libertarianism, by neglect of the common purpose, will self-destruct? Nothing is impossible in the social sciences. But who wants to be the guinea pigs in a costly experiment? And besides, who wants to wait for that long run in which some of us will already be dead?

To order reprints, call 1-800-352-2210; outside the United States, call 717-632-3535.

512

PAUL A. SAMUELSON

Foreword

Most people think of scientists as dull people who spend their time in doing boring things — things boring possibly even to themselves. That is not the view of us scholars. We deem ourselves lucky: the system pays us to do what we'd like to do for nothing. For pure pleasure, boring research beats playing tennis, or dancing, or eating at four-star restaurants. It ranks up there with teaching your child to tell time.

I am speaking, of course, about successful researchers. If you spend your life in the doomed quest for a proof of how to trisect an angle, there's not a lot to look back upon with nostalgia and pleasure. That explains why the biologist Peter Medawar could say that scientists narrow down to focus on *tractable* problems. It is the rational coward's way, just as those darn sensible rats are the first ones to leave the sinking ship.

Usually it is only elderly celebrities who get to publish their autobiographies. *Passion and Craft* is an exception in that it sought deliberately to recruit active scholars in the active phase of their lifetime career. Some sage has said, "Science advances funeral by funeral." (Actually it was the creator of quantum physics, Max Planck, in his own scientific biography; but I confess to having polished for English its more guarded German wording.)

Passion and Craft is both exciting and valuable. If you are at the beginning of a possible calling to scholarship and teaching, it can help you decide what career is truly best for you. And at any stage or station in life, reading what lively minds remember and want to say is fascinating and rewarding. In my experience a collection like this is not best read at one or two sittings. You wouldn't gobble up the best box of chocolates all at once. Stretch out the fun. Leave the volume on your desk or beside your bed and dip into it as fancy tempts you. Lest you lose track of the best parts, underline and make checkmarks. After all, it's *your* book.

No one has written a really successful novel about what makes a Newton or Darwin or Mozart or Keynes tick. Only Leibnizes or Wallaces or Beethovens or Adam Smiths will understand — and they will understand without having to read it in a book. (When Mozart was asked how old you had to be to write your first symphony, he replied: "eighteen." "But," came the protest, "*you* wrote your first one at eleven." "Yes," he replied, "but I didn't have to go around asking people when it was OK to do that.")

Passion and Craft is a collection of accounts about how successful younger economists do and have done their creative work. It is like the famous interviews in the *Paris Review* with authors and poets. Do they use ball pens or word processors? Do they revise endlessly like Balzac or write it all down perfect the first time like Verdi? (The style of Henry James was comparatively simple in his *first phase* when he wrote his drafts with a pen; later, because of writer's cramp, he came to dictate; when his catty brother William (the philosopher) was asked about H.J.'s famous second phase, he more or less averred: "There is no *second phase*. It's just that his new secretary leaves in all that guff." Bill never understood that Hank would have been bothered rather than pleased to write what would command his brother's approval.)

Who cares about another chap's work habits? Well, I do, even though it is late in the day to benefit from the account. And I did when I was just entering into my studies of economics. Wolfe Boy in the jungle goes whole hours not thinking about the best way to discover scientific breakthroughs. But we must not forget that Einstein and Bohr and Watson-Crick were all young once. Except for the chance encounter with the biography of some earlier scientist, they might have become violinists or brokers or plumbers rather than mere Nobel laureates.

Do I exaggerate? Maybe. Fifty years ago Paul de Kruif wrote *Microbe Hunters,* a sparkling vulgarization of the history of biological science. Its pages tell how Pasteur, searching for better fermenters of wine, stumbled on the Pasteur vaccines to keep alive children who are bitten by rabid dogs. He wrote about Lister's crusade for sterility in operating rooms and told how Jenner infected folk with cowpox in order to ward off the more virulent smallpox. In the same vein, and at about the same time, the novelist Sinclair Lewis wrote *Arrowsmith* to describe how Dr. Arrowsmith took a vow to work unselfishly toward the distant goal of new knowledge and the saving of lives. Those books sold well—even if not to the senior faculty. Hans Zinsser (author of *Rats, Lice, and History* and of his own exemplary scientist's autobiography, *As I Knew Him*) sniffed snobbishly at de Kruif and Lewis, writing, "When a real scientist reads Arrowsmith's prayer and oath, it makes him [sic] want to throw up."

Sorry. Zinsser was quite wrong. I have read short autobiographies of many Nobel Prize winners. A surprisingly large fraction of them report: "It was reading *Arrowsmith* or de Kruif or Darwin's aw-shucks autobiography for his grandchildren that first drew me into the realm of research and science." Once again we see how cynicism and sophistication are the enemies of enthusiasm. And it is enthusiasm that is the gasoline that drives us to accomplishment and to self-fulfillment. No medal or promotion or pay raise can stand comparison with self-fulfillment: that's the coin worth working for.

Shaw was wrong: Youth is not wasted on the young. Nor is it a matter of arteries and brain circulation. Thus the great Swedish economist Knut Wicksell didn't come into economics proper until he was forty: at forty-eight he had to take a Ph.D. in order to get his first chair. But still, at whatever chronological age, he had his glorious first decade of youth in the subject. And well into his seventies he wrote works that we still study today, works that of course benefited from contributions that younger Swedish and world economists (Heckscher, Ohlin, Keynes) were then making.

I must not quit without warning against a misunderstanding. Scholarship is not an invariable delight. Disappointments abound. Writer's block—this really means a period when nothing good occurs to one to write about—can occur and reoccur. Experimenters—empiricists in our case as economists—can more easily overcome this drought. Always there is something fascinating to investigate, describe, and measure. Charles Darwin, at his peak, took years off to describe barnacles. Small beer? Not to Charles D. or to his scholarly posterity. And his findings, in the end, contributed much to our understanding of the grand and abstract principles of evolution.

In my own case I fall back on the least unimportant problem left in my inventory of useful questions. Moving down curves of diminishing returns is the rational thing to do between great Schumpeterian shocks and innovations.

Autobiography has one advantage over biography. In a prior book edited by Michael Szenberg, *Eminent Economists: Their Life Philosophies,* as interesting as authors' claims for their successes were to my mind their confessions of failures and complaints that some of their genuinely important contributions have, as yet, not been given their due by contemporary scholars. That has the authenticity of real life.

And this leads to another, and final, correction that will be reassuring to neophyte scholars. A worthy contemporary of mine, who accomplished much that was unique, was hounded all his life by a sense of nonfulfillment. Why? His brilliant father, a noneconomist acquaintance of the brilliant Joseph Schumpeter, told him early in life: "If you can't be a Schumpeter, the scholarly game isn't worth the candle." What nonsense! Schumpeter himself was never the transcendental genius. The corpus of science does not trace to Nobel laureates and off-the-chart IQs. Science is a beehive to which we all add our bits. Carlyle's Great Man theory of History, to my mind and on the evidences of all experience, is a 10 percent truth — even less true in science and scholarship than it is in politics and war.

Fortunately young humans have evolved to believe in the worth of their works. If cave people had not developed a slight overestimation of their own achievements, they would never have survived in the incessant struggle for existence. One does one's best. One cuts one's losses. And satisfaction comes whether directly sought or not.

Book Reviews
Globalization and the Theory of Input Trade
by Ronald W. Jones
Cambridge, MA: The MIT Press, 2000, pp. x, 170.

*Paul A. Samuelson**

This is the eighth of the distinguished Ohlin Lectures. Over more than four decades Ronald Jones has earned the title of "the international trade experts' international trade expert." Articles and books leaping out from his pen overflow both with originality and that rare accompaniment "perfect-pitch" judgment. I hope those who listened to him in Stockholm brought along notebook and pencils, for this volume's seven chapters cover intricate new and *manageable* (!) scenarios involving—along with trade of finished outputs—also *trade of inputs*.

David Ricardo and Heckscher–Ohlin provisionally idealized regional exchange under the following rules of the game: finished goods can alone move abroad; inputs (labor only for Ricardo; labor and non-labor[s] for Heckscher–Ohlin) are frozen at home. Heckscher worked out that the equalization of real wage rates which unlimited immigration would induce might sometimes be alternatively achieved by free trade in finished goods. (I noticed recently that the 1892 Yale graduate student Irving Fisher sketched what could be a third model that defined trade *sans* any explicit mention of productive inputs. A person's *consumption good* created a cardinally measurable utility: $U(q)$, $U'(q) > 0 > U''(q)$. His/her *production* of that good engendered a measurable disutility function: $V(\bar{q})$, $V'(\bar{q}) > 0 < V'''(q)$. In autarky, if their respective unique competitive price ratio $p_2/p_1 = U'_2(q_2)/U'(q_1) = V'_2(q_2)/V'_1(q_1)$ differed between people or regions, then free trade in q goods would thereafter result in an equalization of p_2/p_1 everywhere, with improved net $\Sigma\{U_j(q_j) - V_j(q_j)\}$ everywhere and export goods in every case going from where they were relatively cheap in autarky to places where they had had dear prices. (Too clever by half this 1892 scenario of interior invisible-hand equilibrium?)

If everything could move freely and costlessly—wine, cloth, labor and technology itself—international trade would evaporate into a closed-economy scenario. If nothing can move across geographical boundaries, we are in autarky: two unrelated closed economies. Suppose Ricardo permitted only labor to move freely. In the models used with beginners to dramatize that, even when Portugal has *absolute* advantage in all goods so that both its autarky real wages (W/P_W and W/P_C) exceed England's, free migration would cause all England economaniacs to move to Portugal and we would be back to closed-economy paradigms. If both autarky real wage rates are equal, no-one would move and making trade possible would not induce any of it. In the remaining case, where autarky's W/P_W was higher in Portugal than in England while England's W/P_C was higher than Portugal's, populations would interchange so long as finished goods could not trade: topers would all end in Portugal; peacocks would end in England.

---

*Department of Economics, Massachusetts Institute of Technology, Cambridge, MA 02139.

© Blackwell Publishers Ltd 2001, 108 Cowley Road, Oxford OX4 1JF, UK and 350 Main Street, Malden, MA 02148, USA

Jones does not explicitly cite Sraffa's 1960 *Production of Commodities by Means of Commodities*. Sraffa makes Ricardo's labor-only model intertemporal, the goods that can trade are also by definition *inputs* that can trade. Even if regions A and B have identical technologies with the same $(L_j/Q_j, Q_{1j}/Q_j, \ldots, Q_{nj}/Q_j)$ choices, any difference in A's and B's equilibrium interest rates will generically induce unequal autarky price and wage ratios; that alone would induce geographical specializations and exchanges.

It is the unequal mobilities of goods and factors of production that makes a separate field of international trade necessary and possible. When everything can be freed from location, international trade evaporates into the closed-economy scenario; or, alternatively and equivalently, we can say that international trade has then become perfectly complete. Ricardo's labor-only story of Portugal and England producing and consuming wine and cloth can illustrate. Under autarky (including autarky of technical knowledge!) each isolated region has its idiosyncratic real wage rates and relative prices in terms of both (all) goods. No reason why not. If labor alone could move freely and costlessly, under Ricardo's rules *all* people would go to the dominantly more productive place. (Today, that sort of thing is actually trying to happen. Inertia and custom plus fiats limit the process.) Free trade in finished wine and cloth generically lessened the need or urge to migrate. (In the Heckscher–Ohlin model, where lands *ex definitione* cannot move, free trade hurts some localized laborers and helps some depending on their tastes between goods that use much or little of their regions' endowments of land.)

The simple 1817 story changes when, along with labor inputs, each of wine and cloth needs as input something of both wine and cloth, *à la* 1960 Piero Sraffa. (Neglect timing technology so that the interest rate can be initially ignored.) Autarky still generally leaves W/P_W and W/P_C different in both places when technologies differ. The 1817 Ricardo model has free trade generally raising one of this pair in each place while leaving the other unchanged. (The limiting case where free trade leaves one big country having to produce both goods leaves its real wage(s) at their autarky level while cheapening imports to the smaller place.)

The post-1960 Sraffa–Ricardo case (with intertemporal effects and interest rates initially ignorable) is a bit more complicated. In autarky both places must produce both goods. Unless P_W/P_C was the same in autarky, free trade will generate positive trade. When England can buy more cheaply by trade the wine it needs (needs both to produce cloth and to consume at the table), that could induce it to adopt a known wine-intensive technique to produce cloth (that had been uncompetitive in autarky). Likewise there can be possible induced technique change in Portugal's wine production under free trade. Now trade alone might raise W/P_W and W/P_C in *both* places. Still for Ricardo–Sraffa there exists a free-trade equilibrium P_W/P_C at level(s) dictated by consumer-tastes-demand functions *à la* 1844 John Stuart Mill or 1879 Alfred Marshall.

I predict that well into the century graduate students will be reading and benefiting from this magisterial sorting out of how trade movements in inputs modifies conventional received treatments of international exchange.

References

Fisher, Irving, *Mathematical Investigations in the Theory of Value and Prices*, Transactions of the Connecticut Academy (1892). Reprinted together with his *Appreciation and Interest* (1896), New York: A. M. Kelley (1961).

Marshall, Alfred, *The Pure Theory of Foreign Trade. The Pure Theory of Domestic Values*, privately published (1879). Reprinted in London, London School of Economics, Scarce Works in Political Economy, No. 1 (1930).
Mill, John S., *Essays on Some Unsettled Questions of Political Economy*, London: Parker (1844). Reprinted in *Collected Works of John Stuart Mill*, J. M. Robson (ed.), Toronto: University of Toronto Press (1963–85).
Ricardo, David, *The Principles of Political Economy and Taxation*, London: John Murray (1817). Reprinted in *The Works and Correspondence of David Ricardo*, P. Sraffa (ed.), with collaboration by M. H. Dobb, Vol. I, Cambridge: Cambridge University Press (1951).
Sraffa, Piero, *Production of Commodities by Means of Commodities, Prelude to a Critique of Economic Theory*, Cambridge: Cambridge University Press (1960).

Innovational progress sans thrift

Paul A. Samuelson[*]

Department of Economics, Massachusetts Institute of Technology, E52-358C, 02139-4307 Cambridge, MA, USA

Received 30 March 2001; received in revised form 7 February 2002; accepted 25 February 2002

Abstract

Federal Reserve Chairman Alan Greenspan seemed to succumb partially to the irrational exuberance that underlay the U.S. 1995–2000 Wall Street bubble: a specified step-up in total-factor productivity à la Schumpeter, centered in the high technology sector, was believed to accelerate long-term real GDP growth and equities' future total returns. Even without positive U.S. thrift, by 2020 when babyboomers' retirements exploded as a demographic revolution, technological progress could allegedly atone for the worsening of thrift traceable to the massive Bush tax cuts that had earlier received Greenspan's blessing. Here I spell out a 1912 Schumpeter scenario of "Progress sans Thrift" and show how it is unlikely to fulfill high-profit growth hopes of bubble speculators.
© 2002 Elsevier Science B.V. All rights reserved.

Keywords: Schumpeter's creative capitalist destruction; Wage rise sans profit-rate rise; Sans "human-capital" formation

---

In 1937, Alvin Hansen, newly arrived at Harvard, taught me about a J.S. Mill progressive steady state which, although it lacked conventional net savings and any tangible capital deepening, enjoyed rising real income from total-factor productivity growth alone. It merits attention today because only with it can I cogently rationalize Alan Greenspan's recent recantation of his opposition to a sizable Bush tax cut.

Greenspan at first warned against "irrational exuberance." Later he seems to have become a semi-convert to the "new economy" *zeitgeist* that fueled the 1995–2000 Wall Street bubble and the honeymoon Main Street economy. A tax cut would add to over-consuming by a US populace that already spends on consumption *all* of its wage and property return-after-tax income. And this at a time when looking ahead to 2020 we know that numerous baby boomers will be retired and prime-age workers will be few—so that

---

[✩] This was a lunchtime lecture at the 30 March 2001 Productivity Conference at the Japan–US Center of the New York University Stern School of Business.
[*] Tel.: +1-617-253-3362; fax: +1-617-253-0560.

0922-1425/02/$ – see front matter © 2002 Elsevier Science B.V. All rights reserved.
PII: S0922-1425(02)00008-7

American-owned capital will be presumptively short. However, if America does face a genuine and sustained acceleration of total-factor productivity in 2001–2020, then our existing tax structure might possibly raise more revenue than under-funded social security and medicare programs require. *Ergo*: it is safe to cut tax rates massively.

Neither Greenspan nor I can know whether America will enjoy technological change in the next dozen years at a rate *considerably above* the 1970–1994 average rate. Furthermore, the question arises: would such a Schumpeterian wave generate a rising trend for the profit rate and the real interest rate, growth trends so strong as to generate huge and non-optimal explosive fiscal surpluses?

Schumpeter's own 1912 theory of innovational development is guarded in its predictions on this matter. That is why today's lecture analyzes some Mill–Greenspan scenarios using Solow–Ramsey models. All are variants of the general case

$$q_t = C_t + \left(\frac{dK}{dt}\right)_t = F(L_t, K_t; T_t), \tag{1}$$

where

$$(L_t, K_t; T_t) = (\text{labor, capital; technology progress parameter}). \tag{2}$$

One assumes in neoclassical fashion

$$\left(\frac{\partial F}{\partial L}, \frac{\partial F}{\partial K}, \frac{\partial F}{\partial T}\right) > 0, \quad \left(\frac{\partial^2 F}{\partial L^2}, \frac{\partial^2 F}{\partial K^2}, -\frac{\partial^2}{\partial L \partial K}\right) < 0. \tag{3}$$

$$F(\lambda L, \lambda K; T) \underset{\lambda}{\equiv} \lambda F(L, K; T), \text{ constant returns to scale.} \tag{4}$$

A common example of Cobb–Douglas and Hicks-Neutral type, might be

$$q_t = e^{0.04t} K_t^{0.2} L_t^{0.8}. \tag{5}$$

For it, both wage rate and the interest rate, w_t and r_t would grow exponentially even if $(L_t, L_k) \equiv (1, 1)$, Mill's case.

$$r_t = r_0 e^{0.04t}, \quad w_t = w_0 e^{0.04t}. \tag{6}$$

A progressive tax system would certainly raise in revenue an ever-larger fraction of GDP for this case.

Now, let's review some relevant economic history. Since Newton's time w_t has indeed risen in real terms. However, despite the successive industrial revolutions and long Kondratief waves of innovations, real interest rates have followed a more meandering path. 1912 Schumpeter himself stressed high *transitory* profits of innovators *while* they enjoyed asymmetric special knowledge. But as others learn how to imitate new technologies, these rents of oligopoly erode away. My Eqs. (1)–(6)—and (7) and (8) to come—do *not* model Chamberlin oligopoly, but rather the longer-run *competitive* relationships.[1] On-line traders,

---

[1] When we do posit a steady-state continuing intensification of innovation, 1912 Schumpeter should expect some steady-state increment to property's share of GDP above my equations' marginal-productivity imputations—maybe one or two percent above a 20 percent fractional share for property?

439

and Dr. Greenspan, must not make the mistake of extrapolating, to the long-run steady state of brisk innovations, the fools-gold part of our recent speculative bubble.

Technical innovation does add to human welfare. But leaving go–go speculators aside, it does so primarily by competitively cutting costs, prices and transitory monopoly rents. Much of its contribution will constitute Schumpeter's "creative capitalist destruction." Year 2001 will not generate the taxable capital gains that accrued in 1999 and 2000. Even with a future soft landing, even with future continuing innovations, there will still be an attenuation of bubble-created inequalities and fiscal surplus.

To better portray realistic economic history, I replace Eq. (5)'s Hicks–Neutral Cobb–Douglas case by an alternative extreme case that plays down the role of the profit rate as the beneficiary of total-factor productivity growth. One hundred percent of the benefit from innovation can go to workers' wages when (1) there is zero complementarity between L and K; and (2) when technical change is solely of the 1948 Harrod labor-augmenting type. Now

$$q_t = e^{0.04t}\bar{a}L_t + \bar{r}K_t = e^{0.04t}\bar{a}L_0 + \bar{r}K_0,$$

(Mill's case of zero population and $\dot{K}$ growth). (7)

Now r_t and w_t follow contrasting trends:[2]

$$w_t = w_0 e^{0.04t}, \qquad r_t \equiv_t \bar{r}. \tag{8}$$

When it is future labor that is splashed primarily by future Edisons, on-line traders will be encountering lean pickings; and so will Modigliani lifecycle savers!

Reality may fall between the (5) and (7) poles. Furthermore, time may decimate a good deal of the BLS calculations of high 1995–2000 productivity. When amazon.com and AOL can burn up venture capitalists' antes, that counts in the dK/dt measurement. But in reality these burn downs were largely *failed capital formation*—what in 1931–1935 we derisively called "Hayeks"—and not genuine trees whose nuts (and trunks) can be munched on by retirees in 2020+.

The new Greenspan hunch may well turn out to be in significant degree partly fantasy of exaggerated wishful thinking.

---

[2] Since Eqs. (7) and (8) imply an ever-rising wage share in NNP, this scenario does violate Bowley's Law of approximate constancy of long-run relative shares (which has been the prime justification of Cobb–Douglas approximations). However, in my exposition of Mill's *thriftless* case, itself a departure from prior realistic economic history, much of the historical unrealism need *not* be attributed to the peculiar technology of (7)'s scenario, but rather to its unrealism of saving behavior compared to the past. As a pedantical, young Junior Fellow at Harvard, I was bothered by one thing in the Mill story of zero "thrift." Yes, net capital formation was zero in the sense of dK/dt. But when the total of NNP was rising for the same L and K, how could Irving Fisher, A.C. Pigou, and I agree that the total of "capital" was just being "maintained intact?" Before Theodore Schultz, Friedman-Kuznets or Gary Becker had published on "human capital," I knew of the definitive 1935 *QJE* article on that subject by J. Raymond Walsh, Taussig's left-wing protegee at Harvard. In Eqs. (7) and (8), all of productivity progress could tautologically be "due to" [sic] human capital—even though no one had to invest in it when it, so to speak, fell exogenously from Heaven and Newtonian brows. But in Eqs. (6) and (7) that empty "explanation" could not literally apply to rebut the constancy of real K input while its future discounted value stream does remain patently constant. I decided then to ignore terminology puzzles and stick to substantive content.

Further reading

Becker, G.S., 1962. Investment in human capital: a theoretical analysis. Journal of Political Economy 70, 9–49.

Friedman, M., Kuznets, S., 1945. Income From Independent Professional Practice. National Bureau of Economic Research, New York.

Harrod, R.F., 1948. Towards a Dynamic Economics: Some Recent Developments of Economic Theory and Their Applications to Policy. Macmillan, London and New York.

Hicks, J.R., 1932. The Theory of Wages. Macmillan, London.

Mill, J.S., 1848. Principles of Political Economy with Some of Their Applications to Social Philosophy, Vols. I and II. Little and Brown, Boston.

Pigou, A.C., 1935. Net income and capital depletion. Economic Journal 45, 235–241.

Ramsey, F.P., 1928. A mathematical theory of saving. Economic Journal 38, 543–559.

Samuelson, P.A., 1961. The evaluation of 'Social Income': capital formation and wealth. In: Lutz, F.A., Hague, D.C. (Eds.), The Theory of Capital, Macmillan, London. Reproduced as Chapter 27 in The Collected Scientific Papers of Paul A. Samuelson, Vol. 1. Cambridge, Mass., The MIT Press, 1966.

Schultz, T., 1961. Investment in human capital. American Economic Review 51, 1–17.

Schumpeter, J.A., 1912. The Theory of Economic Development. Leipzig, Duncker & Humblot. Trans. R. Opie. Harvard University Press, Cambridge, Mass., 1934. Reprinted, Oxford University Press, New York, 1961.

Solow, R.M., 1956. A contribution to the theory of economic growth. Quarterly Journal of Economics 70, 65–94.

Walsh, J.R., 1935. Capital concept applied to man. Quarterly Journal of Economics 49, 255–285.

441

515

2. The state of the world economy

Introduced by

Paul A. Samuelson (via satellite)

I will begin by discussing inflation, monetary stability and growth in the world economy.

I've lived a long life. And that means that I have witnessed a number of new ages and new final paradigms, the end of history, and I don't think that right now we're in a new revolutionary improvement in the behavior and expected future behavior of the mixed economy. A number of problems are behind us. But in economics, what goes around comes around. It's possible that when you've cured that last case of smallpox in Somalia, that smallpox goes into the history books. The problem of inflation control isn't like that at all. It's more like the containment of weight of an adult in an affluent society. Eternal vigilance is not only a price of liberty, but it's also the price of a slim figure. There are remarkable things going on in the economy because of computers. This has profound micro influences on economic history. When micro influences become large enough and bunch together, you have macro effects. However, even when you make corrections as best we can, for the inadequacy of our tools to measure productivity in what has become a largely service economy, there is not a sea change in the U.S. GDP statistics. The same is true for most of the world.

Similarly, I like to read the *Atlantic Monthly*, but I don't believe, when I look at the last issue, that the Dow-Jones is 33 percent undervalued compared to its fundamental value. The equity premium, no doubt, will decline over time, but the equity premium, like Tobin's q, will both rise and fall over time. So, we have been lucky, we have been more than lucky, because by a combination of unpredictable circumstances, we have at the head of the Federal Reserve a skillful and non-dogmatic, powerful chairman, and he has helped our luck. For a variety of political reasons, we've also had great luck in the U.S. economy. Nevertheless, by several different measures the private sector saving rate has been declining substantially since 1980, with a similar trend at the corporate level. By chance and by what I have to call good fortune, this is offset by a public sector surplus.

The U.S. economy, which I've followed very carefully edition by edition in my textbook, in my judgment behaves more nearly like a dream economy than used to be the case when the first edition was being written. I also think that the oligopoly power of the Fortune 500 U.S. corporations has ebbed away and has had profound effects upon corporate governance and the status of the union movement. So, America, and now I must give the credit to the American people, not to policy, have shown an amazing flexibility, being willing to accept new types of jobs. I attribute much of America's recent prosperity to this sea change in attitudes and behavior. But in my judgment, that is a fragile thing. It is something which has built up nicely in the 1980s and the 1990s, but is also something which can seep away in an overheated economy. That is why I've been a bit on the wrong side in the advice that I've been giving the U.S. authorities. It's advice, by the way, worth every penny that I've received in return for it, but I've been saying that one should be on the austere side in monetary policy. This, not because I've lost my do-goodism idiocies, I've still got them all, but because, what I'm trying to maximize is the sustained average of the performance of the economy, not just for today and tomorrow, but over the next five years. Well, mostly I've been wrong in that caution. I really can't say that it's a worse world because they didn't listen to me in this particular case. But, what I'm emphasizing is what does not exist in Germany today, for profound historical reasons, what does not exist in France, what does not exist in Spain, and what does exist in America, are profound sociological and political reasons for our economic performance. One of the worst dangers is that we ought not to risk losing this temporary agreeable behavior to generate a little extra current output. It's not a new paradigm. It's an approach toward an older paradigm which only imperfectly prevailed anywhere in economic history.

QUESTIONS

ROBERT MUNDELL: Paul, I'm glad to see you in such good form. I want to ask you a question about exchange rates. We have seen extremely high volatility of the dollar–yen rate, when the dollar went down to 78 yen in 1995 and then went way up to 148 yen. Now it's down again to not much more than 100. But we have also seen big changes in the dollar–euro rate and my question is about that and the future of the euro. When the U.S. expansion starts to slow down – and you've noted that this is one of the longest expansions on record and might be the longest when it is finished – the dollar should weaken, and speculation could lead to substantial diversification from dollars into the euro. Coupled with a very large build-up in the U.S. net debt position, combined with the current account deficit, do you think that there's going to be some need for management of the dollar–euro rate? Would you support a proposal for more explicit management of the dollar–euro rate?

PAUL A. SAMUELSON: First, a couple of points. I have to confess that I was completely accurate on the behavior of the euro after January 1, 1999 when it started. What I predicted was that nothing revolutionary would happen, but there would be a slow trend in one direction. Unfortunately, the algebraic sign which I predicted was wrong, because I thought there might possibly be a honeymoon effect that many people had hoped for. Italian interest rates came down towards German interest rates and so I thought there could be a psychological element favoring that movement. Well, that didn't happen. However, the fact that there should have been, over a period of nine months, that kind of fluctuation in the dollar–euro rate, to me is not surprising. Henry Wallich, who I thought was one of the best people that ever served on the Federal Reserve, asked me about the surprising instability of the post-Bretton Woods exchange rates. I said to him that I wasn't convinced it was surprising. When Baron Rothschild was asked what the stock market was going to do, he said it would fluctuate. Similarly, I said to Wallich that things fluctuate. What is a normal standard deviation to put in a Black–Scholes formula for option contracts on the euro–dollar rate? I expect there to be instability. There is no natural tendency for stability in exchange rate behavior, where the new rate would be some kind of fundamentally predictable real level, based on the terms of trade between countries. Further, terms of trades have fluctuated more than any of the writers that I was familiar with thought 30 years ago.

You ask is there going to be a need for management. That is an entirely different question. Interventions, you know from experience, but also could know from working out the numbers, that a nation can lose in three weeks, reserves that are substantial compared to what it's built up over years in trying to fight market forces. That's part of inescapable macro-inefficiency. So, I would be skeptical that, because, let's say the Japanese, for their recovery, would like the yen to depreciate. And let's suppose that [Treasury Secretary Robert E.] Rubin's policy is still in effect, but a strong dollar occurs because of the strong American economy. I always thought that at best, that was a little bit like King Canute blessing the incoming tide at the time, and I don't suppose that such a doctrine can be embedded in stone. I don't think that with fundamental forces going against the yen staying where it is, the yen may not depreciate. All the goodwill between two sub-cabinet people in the Japanese and American governments can muster up, even if they have the ear of the executive, are unlikely to make any lasting change. So interventions are very difficult.

Now, economists can dream up solutions to some of the worst problems in the world. And naturally, it will occur to them that in some situations we should go back to capital controls. I'm eclectic. I've been eclectic only part of my life. I was once very impatient with my teacher back in Harvard and I said, "Professor, the trouble with you is that you're so damned eclectic." And Gottfried [Haberler] said in his slow, humorous way, "Paul, how do you know mother nature isn't eclectic?" And there was my road to Damascus. Ever since, my credo has been, I've got to be as eclectic as the facts call for, but not be more eclectic than that. I need to remind myself that an open mind can be an empty mind. So there could be a time when some temporary recourse to capital controls would, after it's all over, been judged to have done more good than bad. I can tell you those times will be very rare. The good news from capital controls comes in early. The bad news and the bill, comes in afterwards. So for now, I don't want to get into the sliding peg. There is something of a contradiction in a perfect market where it is supposed that people can count upon daylight savings time, they've advanced on a putative future basis more or less known to everybody, and that this eases the disequilibrium and makes it a quasi-equilibrium situation. I think that sliding pegs stimulate all sorts of bets. A lot of the cleverness of the huge hedge funds comes from government. It's all a zero sum game, but it's always the government that's in the poker game, ready to lose a lot of money. Hedge funds can be pretty sure, over a certain interval, that they know the direction the next move will take, so the risk is generally minimal. I don't want to be dogmatic, but I think that anyone who is deeply skeptical about floating exchange rate systems and the few large currency blocks in the world and he thinks sliding pegs will increase stability, I think that faith might be exaggerated. I could be wrong, though.

AUDIENCE QUESTION: I wonder if you could elaborate a bit on your suggestion that financial markets are very efficient at the micro level, but very inefficient at the macro level. This certainly has an appeal as an intuitive explanation of events that we observe. On the other hand, on the theoretical level, it's not easy to see why the correct valuation of 30 underlying stocks should add up to an incorrect valuation of the average of them.

PAUL A. SAMUELSON: According to economic history, with the phenomenon of cumulative self-fulfilling prophecies, asset markets have bubbles. It's not a question anymore, the stock market is in a bubble. There's every theoretical reason, in terms of expectations, that if a movement gets started in one direction, either away from equilibrium, somehow defined, that that movement will continue. We know so much about bubbles, but the vital, single fact that we want to know, is the actuarial odds of how long it will last. And we have absolutely no handle on the theory of how long it will last, because it can always last as long again as it has already lasted. People think that the duration of Ponzi schemes is brief. There are only a certain number of new suckers in the world. That's profoundly wrong, because the old suckers who have been paid off, come back in as new suckers. And they're right to do so. I will tell one true story to illustrate this.

In the late 1970s, my dear colleague Franco Modigliani wrote an article where he argued that the Dow Jones index is grossly undervalued. It was about 750, and should be at least 1400. Well, you can't sell the Brooklyn Bridge unless you are a good story-teller, and Franco had a good story. He knew why the market was grossly undervalued. He said only an Italian would understand this. It's because people in the market do not understand the proper correction that should be made to price–earnings ratios for inflation. They think that stocks and bonds are essentially the same thing. As a result, anybody can tell you confidently when an upswing in inflation takes place what that will do to the yields of bonds. If you apply that same line of reasoning to stocks, then the 750 level in the late 1970s, when I was getting 18 percent on my Fidelity Investments overnight fund, and Milton Friedman was only invested in bonds, undervalued the stock market. Franco said what people don't realize is that price–earnings ratios implicitly appreciate with inflation. When you make that correction, then at least a doubling of the Dow Jones is justified.

Well, Paul Samuelson, always ready to be the helpful colleague, said to Franco: "Yes Franco, you're right, and it might even be that you're right for the right reason, but you know Franco, you could lose your shirt buying the Dow Jones, because it ought to be at 1400, but it's only at 750. When everybody is insane, it's folly to be wise." That's the difference between a macro attempt to correct a perceived inefficiency and a micro. And Franco said to me properly, "Paul, you don't have to teach me how to suck eggs, I know that, I'm not going out and investing my Grandmother's portfolio in stocks because the market's making this mistake." So, I think there are profound reasons why macro efficiency doesn't assert itself, and why perhaps there isn't even a trend towards it becoming more relevant.

Consider the Thai situation in the middle part of 1997. Earlier, every credit rating agency, Standard & Poor's, Moody's, and so forth, had given Thailand a very good rating. The previous year, the economy had grown in real terms at 6 percent. The previous five years, it had averaged nearer to 8 percent. Everything looked sunny. That's when the money was coming in. For a variety of reasons, and we don't really need to look for profound reasons, because we're dealing now with the economics of avalanches. It is a pistol shot in the Alps that causes a village to be submerged, or more correctly, the piling up of the snow which had been occurring and was present, made this possible. But for whatever reason, including the competition of the Chinese, the new guy on the block, in competition with the other emerging markets in the trade area, suddenly there was a change, and the money went the other way. South Korea had long been growing well by imitating exactly every virtue and every fault of the Japanese system. They had deep pockets, they had new technocratic bankers, they had the influence of not disinterested bureaucrats, and they were heavily invested in short-term borrowing. Of course the pistol shot in Thailand reached them. So, I don't consider it a mystery that the macro markets are capable of misbehaving. Rather, it seems to me that that's in accord with the realities of economic law, though it's different at the micro level.

This isn't the place to moralize, but somebody should be thinking about Long-Term Capital Management's investors – how it was that the best and the brightest, who thought they were making thousands of quasi-independent bets, hedged as well as is possible, ended up trying to balance a baseball bat as tall as the Empire State building. In fact, it grew to a number of people making essentially the same big bet. Of course when the word got around that LTCM was in trouble, they even had to ask for money, it wasn't hard to figure out exactly what the trouble was and all the bids to them dried up and a lot of vultures made money on their distress.

AL HARBERGER: Paul, I think the audience here would be very interested in your telling us your secret of eternal youth. You both look and sound very much the same as you did 20, 30, 40 years ago, and I think it's just wonderful.

My substantive comment is the following: some considerable time back, people thinking about macroeconomics thought in terms of structural models. We had little, mid-sized, and big structural models and they were a very important part of the way people viewed the world. What I seem to perceive, both in much of the profession's thinking and certainly in terms of policy authorities, both in the Fed and elsewhere, is a trend toward thinking of policy as a kind of a servomechanism. That we have an accelerator and a brake and a steering wheel, and we look at all of the evidence that's coming in day by day and week by week, and the policy authorities come to decisions about is this the time to use one, two or three of these instruments. Do you agree with this perception of a change in attitude? That's the first question. My second question is do you see any dangers for the future in this servomechanism type of behavior?

PAUL A. SAMUELSON: Let me think aloud. First let's talk about short-term forecasting purposes, and now I'm talking about what is a very dull business. At the non-profit organization and finance committees that I sit on, we don't even let people go through the process of briefing us on the outlook for the next 12 to 18 months. We all know pretty much what there is to be known.

Most of the banks have actually fired their short-term forecasters and they can subscribe to the modern equivalent of DRI and know what the simple odds favor. Those forecasts are not bad. They are better than Wall Street analysts. They are better than gypsy tea readers. But, what they tell you is not useful. I can remember, a few years ago I went to hear a representative of Citibank from London at a Copenhagen meeting and he told the inside story of what they expected to happen. I opened my *Wall Street Journal* and I looked at futures on the interest rates, and everything, and everything that he told us was already priced in the market. A very few people who I know, and it is surprisingly few, can over a long time period by their wits, good timing, and momentum make money investing.

Experience has shown that most of the useful models are not "M" [monistic] models. Citibank got burned badly. There was a brief time in the early 1970s when monistic monetarism, for a time didn't do too badly. But the reality which had staggered like a drunken sailor into the gunsights of that model moved and in this technological change in the financial securities markets and institutions, the constancy of any velocity of money figure (the ratio that measures what I have in my jeans and dictates my spending) to the level of nominal income flow. Velocity now and forever after now, a much more volatile thing. The simple-minded, almost Neanderthal consensus models did pretty well for a time, but these forecasters all turn over together, that's the only thing we can be sure about, and what they're sure about is why they were wrong on previous occasions. So I don't think there is anything in the technical advances that have been made in the macro literature, such as rational expectations and random walks [unpredictability] in technological progress which have useful lessons for the financial markets and for policy purposes. Maybe that's reassuring, because it means that we're not subject to a new regime we didn't have before. I do think that the easily accessed professional trading systems, that allow me to turn my portfolio over in an afternoon, literally is like putting a new powerful cannon in the hands of children. You know in the old days, if you had a demented kid on the farm, all he could do is torture the dog or do a little harm. Today, he just puts together a little fertilizer and he can blow up a huge skyscraper. When I go before St. Peter I'm going to have to answer for some of these financial advances.

Does online trading make markets more volatile? We don't know. We really do not know what happened on that Tuesday morning in 1987, a day after Black Monday [October 19, 1987]. There was an hour when essentially every market was closed down by the circuit breakers, and then the markets opened up again. Someday Alan Greenspan will write his memoirs and he'll reveal what he said to Banker's Trust and the other investment banks, but the 1987 crash is a very important element. I heard Alan Greenspan say in a private dinner at the Boston Federal Reserve that the market crash was just to cool things off a little. So I asked with so many people worried, why the Fed didn't raise margin requirements? This would be a shot across the bows of the ultra-bulls. Greenspan responded, "Paul, we don't know whether that'll end up doing good or otherwise." He added that how things worked out in the aftermath of the 1987 crash may itself have added 3000 points to the present value of the Dow Jones Industrial Average, because a lot of people learned a lesson that the cowardly people who sold after Black Monday ended up with big losses. I think I'd better stop there.

CHRISTOPHER JOHNSON: Hello Paul, this is Christopher Johnson of the Association for Monetary Union of Europe. I would like to put a question to you about the U.S. balance of payments. There's a rather disturbingly large deficit in the current account. Should we not be looking at this just as much in terms of the capital account, where of course mathematically there has to be a corresponding surplus in the capital account. The U.S. has always been known as one of the world's major capital exporters. A country like Mexico has a lot of investment from U.S. multinational companies. But, the inflow of capital into the U.S. is very much greater than the outflow. And this, of course, has turned on its head all the traditional views we used to learn in economics, maybe in earlier editions of your textbooks, that rich countries were capital exporters and the poor countries were capital importers. Well, the U.S. is certainly not poor. It's the world's richest country and the biggest importer of capital. One can see this as having pushed the rate of the dollar up. Everybody wants American assets, either factories or shares, and this of course has driven the current account into deficit. But, should we worry about this? Is this a natural and self-sustaining situation, a virtuous circle, where as long as Wall Street goes up, the U.S. can import capital, and people are very happy to hold dollars? In addition, does this mean that the risk of a Wall Street correction is going to be amplified by a reverse flow of capital as the world's investors take their profits and seek solace elsewhere in the euro, the yen or whatever? Maybe Mr. Greenspan is aware of this and that's why he doesn't want to be blamed for bringing about the correction on Wall Street by putting interest rates up too high. So, is this virtuous circle or is it really a precarious and worrying situation? Have we discovered perpetual motion, at least in the U.S. economy, so that it could go on forever being the world's fastest-growing economy and continue to import capital on the basis of that rapid growth, which will thereby be further fueled and encouraged?

PAUL A. SAMUELSON: One of the ways of saying things that are interesting is to say things that excite and scare people, and I consider that a cheap popularity which I should eschew. But, I do say all the time, and not to shock, that no country is too big to be immune to a run. I have written a lot for

Japanese, Korean and some Latin American newspapers, saying things there which I think should be said for them, but I'm really picky when I say things about the U.S. I don't think that it was an irrational view toward the end of the 1950s when more and more people abroad piled up assets here, because this was a safe haven with the U.S. dollar an undervalued currency. But there should become a point at which the flow could begin to go the other way. I can well imagine a situation, fortunately it's not realistically imminent, where a serious correction in America could become an algebraic down bubble. History is replete with them. When foreigners want to take more and more money out, maybe because the economy has recovered, or just for reasons of diversification, that's exactly the time when American money will flow out, too. If the euro is a better deal prospectively a year and a half from now, to financiers from Zurich and Frankfurt, it will also be a better deal for San Francisco and Chicago. And so yes, I think there is a potential problem.

I'm also confessing my arrogance, as one of my former students wrote a paper which was too well received by the assembled central bankers at the Kansas City Federal Reserve meetings. What was said there, and said more than once, was that the Federal Reserve should stick to one goal, the requisite price level stabilization, and not have an interest in the stock market. If they added that to the Federal Reserve charter it would not be a good rule. I don't think that in Japan in 1985, you could properly ignore those topics with my methodology and say, who cares about the speculative land boom and who cares about the speculative stock market boom because everybody was making money. That's why we should be concerned. I don't think the Federal Reserve must follow every sparrow that falls to earth, but they must follow the economy because the U.S. is not immune to a currency run. Now, that's a different thing from doing what I've heard criticized, that we're not on an M [money supply] standard anymore, we're on a stock market standard and the Fed appears to have a new duty to keep the stock market up. I don't think that's the actual duty, but they're interconnected. And when I examined that paper, which defended the view, every one of its theoretical simulations, that we should have a balance sheet approach on what debt growth does to lending, I agreed with it. But my spin on it would be that this makes it a problem, at least in the backrooms of the central banks of the world, to be worried about.

ROBERT SOLOMON: Paul, in your initial remarks when you used the term "capital controls" various people around the table here whom you can't see frowned. I thought perhaps you'd like to think about what is being discussed among those who are considering this so-called "architecture" of the international monetary system. The device that's being talked about most commonly is what's been used in Chile – a tax on short-term capital flows. This seeks to discourage volatility of short-term capital, but not to discourage capital flows in general, particularly long-term flows. This device has been supported by a man who used to be Undersecretary of the Treasury, he's now Secretary of the Treasury and I think you have a certain acquaintance with him. Do you have any comments on that?

PAUL A. SAMUELSON: In the first place, my acquaintanceship is a distant one. The Secretary of the Treasury [Lawrence H. Summers, who is Samuelson's nephew] was an undergraduate at MIT. He scrupulously avoided every course I ever gave and I scrupulously avoided giving him any advice on any matter, so there was a so-called Chinese wall between us. But I'll turn to me. I have a certain skepticism of "Tobin taxes" [taxes on short-term capital flows] to handle what some people might consider excessive turnover in mutual fund investing management. Putting a little sand in the gears, a little friction, a Tobin tax on transactions – I'm against that. Among other reasons, it's not that it's a crime, but it's a blunder, because this moves markets overseas. If in New York markets there's a tax on transactions and if American citizens are still free to go to any market in the world, you can be very sure that substitute markets will open up. Where Chile is concerned, this could be a more enforceable thing – a tax on short-term movements. Bob, you remember that for many years Switzerland paid very low interest rates on transitory balances and Switzerland was a safe haven for political and other reasons. And so there were in effect, some impediments of that kind.

The role that I would envisage as possible, and with something that could be salutary about it, would be like the recourse to circuit breakers in the stock market. We're not sure whether circuit breakers and up-tick rules for short sales make things better or worse. But, assuming that in the peak of the worst gale, they make things better, some short-term moratoria standstill fiats could be useful. The trouble with fiats, and I speak with good credentials as a liberal in the modern sense, is that they increasingly spring leaks. People learn the ways around them. They increasingly create inefficient allocations of resources and so they fall of their own weight, and when you do the postmortem, there's no law of conservation of harm – everything you gain from the capital controls, you lose – but, it could be worse than that.

Let's take the case of Malaysia. My teachers were always looking for controlled experiments performed by economic history. You know I'm very good at criticizing my teachers, because I was so preoccupied with them for a long time in my life. Belgium originally, after World War II, was a more open economy and you could get white flour rolls there, whereas Holland was controlled. And see how much better Belgium did in the late years of the 1940s than Holland did. Well, those are not good controlled experiments. But in my journalism, I've tried to see whether a strong case could be made that

451

those countries which have followed the IMF, Thailand for example, and South Korea, followed them full force. In comparison with those that have resisted, it's a no-brainer, less control was better. There are time periods when that's so and then there are time periods when it's going the other way. At the moment, the head of Malaysia believes that he can document that they are better off [with controls]. I think we should reserve judgment until nature tells us more.

JUDY SHELTON: Hello, Paul. I would like to go back to some comments you made about the Asian situation. You referred to the Thai baht in 1997, and I think the same analysis might apply to the Philippines, or Malaysia, or South Korea or Indonesia. I thought you were suggesting that a lot of very smart foreign investors, who thought they were putting money into productive opportunities in these countries, suddenly got wise and decided that they were not going to be productive and generate revenues so they pulled back. To me, that is in keeping with the idea of crony capitalism – suddenly realizing that these were not good investment decisions. To what extent would you say that the collapse in the exchange rates for those countries, the currency meltdown, contributed to the subsequent economic problems? That is, which was the driving force – did the currencies reflect these sudden changes in the economic expectations, or did they cause it? I wouldn't want to suggest speculators were villains, but maybe they were taking advantage of a very flawed system – a very unstable global currency system – and that also contributed to the economic downfall of these countries.

PAUL A. SAMUELSON: First, I have to say that the inextricably interconnected are foolish mistakes by speculators and investors, and structural flaws in the way of doing business. You all recall the degree to which we were preached to by the successful Japanese in the late 1980s, who had gone way beyond the Harvard Business School where you had to have a plan, an investment project, you had to have a stream of income. Under the business school system, nine out of ten potential projects are scratched and you pick the better ones. Well, instead of that, in Japan, decisions were made by consensus – a new, wonderful thing in a corporation.

I know how this wonderful decision by consensus worked. At one of our previous meetings in Claremont, California, an executive of a large Japanese automobile company was at the reception dinner. Probably his company had provided part of the funds. He told me that he was a very good head of this Japanese company because he was a person of two cultures. He said, "I am a Mexican, but I am an American executive and so I'm better prepared to deal with the Japanese." And I said, "You're the man I need then, you're an outside observer. Tell me how this decision making by unanimity and by consensus works." He said, "Here's how it happens: call all the people in the room and tell them what you're discussing, and they spend three or four hours trying to guess how I want it to come out. Finally, I get tired of that and so I tell them how it's going to come out and that's what decision making by consensus is." Now, I only jest to make a point. Japanese companies have deep pockets, and are unconcerned about their stock market value. That sounds like a good thing. But deep pockets, without detailed, rational business school kinds of calculations about investment projects, means you can make big mistakes and you can persist in those big mistakes for a very long time. And so, when people speak about Asian crony capitalism, the only thing that's wrong about that is to make it exclusively Asian, and also to make it exclusively capitalism. For example, in the Korean case, the government bureaucracy and politicians, and not necessarily disinterested politicians, with an independent banking system, are encouraging large corporations with no comparative advantage in innumerable diverse operations, to go deeply into debt, be deeply leveraged, on ephemeral projects that have no real reason to be active.

Now, to take Judy's question, in Thailand, there were a lot of marginal projects which made some economic sense and were profitable. Things looked great when money was coming into the country and the general availability of capital was strong. By the way, the money coming into the country came from the whole Western world and especially emerging market mutual funds. But investors weren't particularly well informed. What they were well informed about was the total return for the previous eight quarters of similar projects. A lot of projects that had some merit, lost merit alongside of those which never really had merit and would only in the end survive by being pooled with other things. This is evidence of a bubble economy, and it becomes pervasive. Then drastically between day and night, the bubble burst. Now, that's an over-simplified picture, because it isn't simply a bursted bubble and a return to equilibrium. The system is also always subject to [internal and external] shocks.

FAUSTO ALZATI: Hello Professor Samuelson. Neoclassical growth theory, essentially established by Robert Solow, predicts long-run convergence in per capita incomes between poor and rich countries. Now, we also know from historical evidence, that when countries share common economic rules, as let's say between the north and the south of the U.S. after the Civil War, that convergence takes place. Poor countries and poor regions grow faster and the gap between rich and poor tends to close. Now, if that is the case, wouldn't a movement towards unified currency areas, and eventually a single global currency, be a better solution for promoting growth than, let's say, floating exchange rates? If you agree with that proposition, what measures should be taken in the short run to promote this?

453

PAUL A. SAMUELSON: At the beginning, let me say that I don't think that it is a crucial matter whether a region or the world is on a single currency or whether you have coexisting, floating currencies for the basic problem of development. To an economic historian, the key feature of the last half of the twentieth century is the catch-up of much of the rest of the world with the primary position of America. My back of the envelope calculation when peace broke out in Europe and Japan in 1945 was that the U.S.A. had almost 50 percent of world GDP. Europe was devastated, Japan was devastated. In the next 25 years, the U.S. fraction of world GDP dropped from 45 percent to 40 to 35 percent to 30 to 25 percent to perhaps 20 percent of the world. This convergence didn't happen after World War I. And we economic theorists should be asking ourselves why Austria was such a basket case after World War I and contrast it with post World War II. That catch-up is not inexplicable. We speak of "miracles" and we can work out econometrically how much is due to the inputs, human capital, and to technological innovation. But we picture it as a bicycle race. The frontrunner, or a few frontrunners, break the wind for the rest. This is all in accord with Schumpeter's theory of innovation. It is to be noted that there isn't a single one of the bicycle riders in the back who had notably forged toward the front, and who then subsequently broke away ahead of the U.S. Do keep that in mind in understanding why an emerging market like China can be growing the way it has been growing, that there will be a time when we suddenly discover that the trees don't grow to the skies.

Consider the history of Argentina. Argentina has a currency board and can even formalize that and use the U.S. dollar as its currency. I would not add, in a guess of growth rates in Argentina, a half of one percent per year extra growth catch-up on the U.S. because of its currency board. I would guess that the rational things which can be done in Argentina, in quasi-imitation of the best things that are done in America and in Japan, are there under either a floating exchange rate or dollarized system. It is a question of the advantages and disadvantages of each system.

Now I'm going to talk about the euro. It's worked out about as the American skeptics thought would be the case. Europe is not one country. The situation in Ireland, in Denmark, in the Netherlands, and maybe even Spain is different from what the situation is in Italy, which is more like the situation in France and Germany. But Italy, which has in my judgment benefited a lot in its budget and a lot of other things by being a European Union member, but the price of that is that the central bank in Frankfurt isn't doing anything for the developing Italian situation and couldn't be doing the same right thing for Ireland, which, for example, may be overheating. This should not surprise anybody. That's what happened under the gold standard, and that's part of what a single currency system is like.

Take for example the U.S. 12 Federal Reserve districts that use a single currency. When [MIT Economics Professor] Olivier Blanchard studies business cycles, he doesn't find that West Virginia cuts its prices relative to the rest of the country and attracts industry that way. He finds an important part of the picture is differential migration. Few Americans live near where they were born. I exaggerate. But in Europe, I can go 12 miles and run into two dialects and maybe a different language and I don't see that there has been any special new equilibrating migratory behavior in the short nine months under the currency union. Over time, there may be. There are both economic laws operative in things as well as country-specific effects.

ROBERT MUNDELL: Paul, thank you from all of us at the conference for joining us. In thanking you, I am speaking in the role that would ordinarily have been performed by [deceased Claremont Graduate University Economics Professor] Randall Hinshaw, in whose honor and memory we are holding this conference. We thank you very much for an excellent contribution and we're all very pleased and happy to see you in such great form and wish you many more happy and fruitful years ahead.

Technical symposium

Pure theory aspects of industrial organization and globalization

Paul A. Samuelson[*]

Department of Economics, Massachusetts Institute of Technology, 50 Memorial Drive, Cambridge, MA 02142-1347, USA

Received 5 April 2002; received in revised form 23 April 2002; accepted 15 October 2002

Many of the truths that apply to the political economy of one country do apply also to a global economy involving trade between more than one nation state or region. Industrial organization is no exception to this banality. And also some of the principles—industrial organization or otherwise—appropriate to a single sovereignty fail when global exchange is involved.

Still there is a heretical sense to my suspicion that today's global economy has wiped away or ameliorated many of the IO problems that properly did concern the generation of my teachers. Let me explain this lucky fact.

Go back to read the first few editions of my best-selling economics primer. Those pages described well the US scheme of corporate governance and inter-firm patterns of competition. In that Berle-Means era of, say, 1930 to 1960, the Fortune 500 corporations did possess a measure of oligopoly power. You will recall the usual suspects. AT&T was the quintessential monopolist of local and long distance services. It was the ideal stock for widows and orphans to hold. No group, including management, possessed even one percent of all voting shares.

Nevertheless, the management in-group possessed virtual lifetime job security and unlimited power of decision making. What my chapters on labor and unions made clear was that some of any oligopolistic rents had to be divvied up with existing unions, or, as in the case of corporations like duPont, if militant unions were to be kept at bay or tamed into a company-union acquiescence, wages and fringe benefits had to be provided that would match those of similar unionized enterprises and which presumptively exceeded rates that would have "cleared" a truly competitive labor market. Industrial organization professors like Ed Mason at Harvard and labor experts like Sumner Slichter were in strong demand and as a dutiful textbook writer I dubbed what I have described to be good, enlightened labor relations.

[☆] The Journal will publish lectures and short papers by renowned administrators, statesman and scholars who have influenced economic policy. This paper is one of those series of policy papers.
[*] Tel.: +1-617-253-3368.

0922-1425/02/$ – see front matter © 2002 Elsevier Science B.V. All rights reserved.
PII: S0922-1425(02)00053-1

Joseph Schumpeter, by the way, had changed his early view that innovation would come primarily from independent innovators and came to declare that much of 1900–1950 real-income progress stemmed from these oligopolists. Had Schumpeter lived beyond 1950, one guesses he would today be soft rather than hard on Microsoft and such.

The 17th edition of Samuelson–Nordhaus is a sea change away from that of the 1948–1960 world. Why the vast erosion of oligopoly power and the new "what have you done for me lately?" de facto extinction of the old Berle-Means regimen of corporate governance?

Much, but not all, of the change surely traces to globalization. During my sixty years of teaching in New England, my students saw whole industries such as textiles and shoes go south, then go to Puerto Rico, Mexico, Japan, Taiwan, Korea, and now to India and China.

Widening of the market is the enemy of monopoly and oligopoly as these relate to economies of increasing scale and spreading of the overhead. Paradoxically, in the century when governments turned away from the laissez faire I lived through during 1915–1933, I sense that we have come closer to the truly competitive market with its Adam Smith Invisible Hand of Pareto optimality!

Old-time economists recognized this monopoly-tariffs tie-up in partisan political debates between Republican Party 19th century protectionists and Democratic Party pitches for lower tariffs and quota restrictions. During presidential campaigns, one heard repeatedly the slogan, "Tariffs are the Mother of Trusts."

Rich Ivy League student idealists who protest in the streets of Seattle do not understand the 21st century realities of freer trade and export-led miracles of emerging economy productivity growth. We can agree on that.

However, it is my duty to remind the zealots for ever freer trade that the new winds of comparative advantage do not always or usually improve the lot of everyone.

Consider, as we should do here, Japan's travails of 1989–2002. Yes, these do trace in part to bursting of two huge bubbles: P/E ratios of 200 in Tokyo and Osaka stock markets; and sky-high real estate prices for both land and skyscrapers in the late 1980s.

Yes, too little and too late macro- and micro-policies by the lawyer bureaucrats in government and at the Bank of Japan played their important role. And yes, the lifetime employment system of the large Japanese corporations contributed to inflexibility of Japan's recovery efforts.

However, I must point out an important relevant truth. If Japanese real incomes in the form of wage rates and other costs are today perhaps 30 percent above the relevant global competitive level, do look to gigantic China as one vital reason.

What Japan did earlier to many basic activities in America or Sweden or ..., China is now doing to Japan. And it is not only China. India and later-to-develop regions, where wage rates are still low, are increasingly competitive against well-educated ingenious Japanese labor and management.

Industrial organization experts patrol the beat to study how macro trends translate themselves out at the corporate firm and industry level. Globalization will throw up numerous new industrial organization problems to keep your guild members faced with new and challenging research problems.

457

A few theoretical aspects of deregulation

Paul A. Samuelson[*]

Department of Economics, Massachusetts Institute of Technology, 50 Memorial Drive, Cambridge, MA 02142-1347, USA

Received 5 April 2002; received in revised form 23 April 2002; accepted 15 October 2002

Abstract

Market economies devoid of all public regulation cannot be counted on to achieve either Pareto-all-optimal efficiency or a democracy's definition of distributive justice. Therefore, some regulative regimes can improve a society's importance, while some can be net counter productive. Finding a better golden mean between deregulation and positive regulation is the hard challenge facing the better society.
© 2002 Elsevier Science B.V. All rights reserved.

Keywords: Deregulation; Regulation; Reforms

Before recent deregulations of public utility energy operations, large organizations such as MIT self-generated some of their own energy needs. Pretty soon neighboring organizations such as Harvard and MIT, if their daily rhythms of energy use differed, would do contractual swaps. Money could pass hands, but it didn't need to. Over a day, or a month, or a year, some of the balances of liability would net out.

An economic theorist would ask: "What sets the money price of 2:00 a.m. electricity inside of MIT? And how would we reckon whether our co-generation effort was economically worthwhile?" (Actually, two decades ago a co-generation effort for all Harvard's hospitals was in the headlines as an unsocial activity, and when it was ignominiously aborted in midstream, it left a big hole in the Harvard endowment).

"A rose is a rose is a rose", said Gertrude Stein. Maybe so in poetry. But 2:00 a.m. kilowatts can no more be compared with rush-hour 5:00 p.m. kilowatts, than can five apples + three oranges be able to define eight units of anything meaningful.

Economic theory cuts the Gordian measurement knot by using *marginal cost* as *numeraire*. And indeed for some years, before public policy at the federal and state levels

---

[☆] The Journal will publish lectures and short papers by renowned administrators, statesmen and scholars who have influenced economic policy. This paper is one of those series of policy papers.
[*] Tel.: +1-614-253-3368.

0922-1425/02/$ – see front matter © 2002 Elsevier Science B.V. All rights reserved.
PII: S 0922-1425(02)00054-3

underwent its recent considerable deregulation, on a summer day, a Cambridge, Massachusetts computer nerd could latch onto a website to observe the minute-to-minute change in auctioned private energy prices. Thus, suppose it is a hot Boston day and air-conditioners are being turned on at the same time that TV viewers are honing in on the Red Sox game. Then, when auxiliary diesel generators are drawn into use, MC prices may soar to triple or double normal levels. Then suppose a cloud comes across the sky and brings some rain. Before your eyes you can see energy prices drop by 10 percent, even by 50 percent or more.

That is how competitive futures prices for wheat do gyrate on the Chicago Board of Trade. It is a far cry from the experience of Boston households who have since time immemorial been buying electricity at one government-regulated rate purporting to equate the utility company's annual revenues with its cost outlays, plus a state determined maximum proper rate of profit.

Ph.D.'s in economics understand all this. But we guys are rare nerds. To illustrate this, here is a true story. The doorbell rang one evening in my Belmont, Massachusetts suburban residence. An attractive couple aged about 20 asked Professor Samuelson to sign a petition requiring corporations to pay a higher kilowatt electricity rate than poorer consumers have to pay. I read their fine print and had to say, "I can't sign this". Genuinely surprised, they blurted out: "Don't you care about poor people's welfare? Professor X across town signed". X is a Nobel laureate and actually an admired friend. Nevertheless, I heard myself explaining pedantically, "It is because of my concern for the lower-income families that I refuse to sign. Economists' mathematical theory of the optimal second-best deduces that especially taxing high-elasticity-of-demand corporations, who can easily leave the system and self-provide, will harm the inelastic-demand family populace by throwing more of the total shared overhead burden on the shoulders of those least able to bear that extra burden". As the couple left, I could see they had just learned the lesson that economists do indeed seem to be odd nerds.

For a century, experts in economics and law have understood that problems of monopoly, oligopoly, and imperfect competition generally are complicated precisely because of the existence of overhead costs and the great discrepancies thereby implied between *average* costs and *marginal* costs.

Policy moves toward deregulation are fueled by this recognition. Besides, philosophers of libertarianism (who are also a different species of odd nerds) often subscribe to the simplistic rule: "More deregulation is always better than less".

Alas, empirical life is replete with examples where the half-way house of incomplete deregulation can be worse than either of the polar extremes of (1) *laissez faire* and (2) old-fashioned public utility law. California, a couple of years back, provided a horror story case to confirm the point.

In California, utility suppliers were freed to buy electricity from any cheapest source. But, at the same time, they still were legally bound to charge consumers a fixed rate much as used to be the case. Then came a US late-1990s boom. OPEC was able to raise world oil prices, thereby causing US price of natural gas to soar. New companies like, excuse the expression, Enron, rolled in the golden profits. Old utility companies who had to sell cheap and buy dear literally went bankrupt.

The voting public raged. The non-Ph.D. governor of California panicked. In desperation, the state tried to hedge by signing a fixed contract to purchase future oil at a quite elevated price. And then, what happened? Oil prices on world markets plummeted. The blackouts became a thing of the past. Voters felt as if first a Mack truck of energy inflation had run over them. Then back up over them came that Mack truck of deflation.

What went wrong with the economist experts' game plan? Almost everything. When oil and gas were scarce, higher price was supposed to persuade consumers to economize on energy use. Let the housewife do her weekly wash at 3 a.m. when marginal cost was low.

But why should she? Few residences had *smart* electricity meters that told the time their use of energy took place.

Worse than that. Economists' palaver was about spirited free competition. That is not what the Enron chieftains had in mind. Without e-mail communication between them, the few largest producers tacitly recognized that by holding back extra production, they could jack up prices above the true minimized marginal costs.

How do I know that? I do not. But, as Henry Thoreau said, circumstantial evidence can be strong—as when you find lake fish in your dairy's morning milk delivery.

Have we learned a lesson from history? Unfortunately, history does not tell us the kind of lessons that chemists can learn from controlled experiments. Enron will be remembered forever. But its misdeeds were many and various. Most of them were only remotely connected with the deregulation of utility rates. Top officers gave themselves obscene options to receive shares cheap. The company used off-balance-sheet swaps and loans to conceal losses and appear to show soaring profits. While their employees' pension fund was frozen into holding Enron stock, the top bureaucrats bailed out before the zero worth of the shares would become apparent.

To sum up, it is back to the drawing boards to seek a golden mean between deregulation and regulation; to outlaw conflicts of interest between auditors and their fee-charging consultants; to reduce monied interests' ability to purchase by gifts to political parties what their lobbyists want to have.

The list of needed reforms is long and intricate. Implementing many of them in our democracy is even more of a challenge. Who said economics has become an exact and perfected science?

The pros and cons of globalization

Paul A. Samuelson*

*Massashusetts Institute of Technology, MIT Department of Economics,
50 Memorial Drive, Cambridge, MA 02142-1347, USA*

Received 12 November 2004; received in revised form 30 November 2004; accepted 30 November 2004

Abstract

Analysis suggests that future freer globalized trade will (1) likely benefit both rich and poor regions, (2) probably give measured percentage gains to poor places that exceed those to rich places, (3) possibly exacerbate real income inequality between rich and poor, and more certainly (4) bring more lifetime uncertainty along with enlarged material gains. A backlash to freer trade, economic history suggests, will lead to weaker productivity advance, enhanced degree of monopoly, and to aggravated crony-capitalism and plutocratic lobbyist democracy.
© 2005 Elsevier B.V. All rights reserved.

JEL classification: A11; B2; C6; D3; D61; F11; F13

Keywords: Mills–Ricardo comparative advantage; Money–metric–utility; Win–win or win–loss or loss–win innovations

In August 2004, my article in the *Journal of Economic Perspectives* created more of a political stir than an analytical ferment. Out and out protectionists rejoiced that a devotee of free trade finally saw the light.

That is not my view of the matter. When economic experts, both from ivory towers and from the Federal Reserve and the CEA, were writing op-ed unqualified articles that seemingly proclaimed that all dynamic developments under free trade must help all nations—help them in the sense that in each place, gains of the new winners must exceed

---

[☆] The journal will publish lectures and short papers by renowned administrators, statesman, and scholars who have influenced economic policy. This paper is one of those series of policy papers.
* Tel.: +1 617 253 3368; fax: +1 617 253 0560.

0922-1425/$ – see front matter © 2005 Elsevier B.V. All rights reserved.
doi:10.1016/j.japwor.2004.11.006

the losses of the new losers—my credo of scholarly rectitude mandated that someone should set the record straight.

There was a second, minor reason, why I accepted the invitation of the *JEP* editor to publish my view of the matter. Long after both editions of my *Foundations* got published, I devised a novel useful tool for comparative statics of a social system involving along with Robinson Crusoe one or many Fridays. Stretching empirical exactitude, if I could posit an idealized population possessing uniformly identical *homothetic* demand structure, my concept of money–metric–utility could give a useful measuring rod for well-posed thought experiments exploring deadweight losses.

God is in the ad libs. So let me digress. A few years back, the distinguished mathematical biologist Joel Cohen—of Rockefeller and Columbia universities—surprised me. He said, "Paul, I envy you economists. Unlike you guys, we in biology have no solid yardstick." Much of my lifetime energies have gone to analyzing how treacherous are economists' metric index-number problems and other aggregative constructs that behave more like slippery spaghetti than like the standard meter bar in the Parisian laboratory.

Alerted to homothetic uniformity, I noticed that J.S. Mill, youthful genius, back a dozen years after David Ricardo enunciated comparative advantage, had jumped ahead of 1850–2004 utility analysis by cutting the Gordian Knot of demand theory with the manageable model that said: suppose each consumer always spends seven-tenths on food, one-tenth on warmth, and two-tenths on comfort. "Then I, J.S. Mill, can settle for the late David Ricardo just where the free trade P_{wine}/P_{cloth} price ratio will end up within the interval bounded by the respective Portugal autarky P_w/P_c ratio and the high England autarky P_w/P_c ratio."

Mill did not realize what I came to realize. All his free trade unknowns can, eschewing supply–demand prattle, be determined as maximizing roots of the Newtonian first-order conditions for maximizing the Geometric Mean of Global Consumptions. Why the Geometric Mean? Because the money–metric–utility defined by constant fractional shares of disposal income spent on each good does have for its money–metric–utility

$$C_1^{K_1} C_2^{K_2} C_3^{1-K_1-K_2} \cdot \text{QED}$$

Mill, like the Moliere character who did not realize he had been speaking prose all his life, was solving a Kuhn-Tucker non-linear concave programming problem. The readers and editors needed to know that.

One ad lib generates another. Adam Smith's Invisible Hand was proclaimed to achieve, solely from the avarice of selfish competition, the maximization of the well-being of all. From age 16 to 25 years, I badgered Frank Knight, Jacob Viner, Joseph Schumpeter, and Wassily Leontief to explain to me exactly what that "well-being" aggregate was. Later, the best I could do was to declare that *laissez faire* competition will attain Pareto Optimality *sans deadweight* loss.

On November 12, 2004, you can now be told: under uniform homothetic tastes, an Invisible Hand maximizes total money–metric–utility. But as Thomas Aquinas declared long ago, there is no damn normative content to this. Transferring some of that Platonic stuff from rich Croesus to poor Lazarus could still be a *desideratum* for some cult leaders. But as Davey Hume would remind us, *laissez faire* will never arrange that nor will it be governmentally ordained by unanimous vote.

Back to prosaic business. My 2004 point had not been newly arrived at. Before 1935, it had been ill understood by my generation of teachers. After, say, 1950, it had become old hat among the trade virtuosi. Free trade's potentiality does indeed always trump the potentiality of enforced autarkies. Dynamic changes in technology, if market viable, do improve globally potentialities. But they need not help everyone, need not help every nation in the sense that gains of their winners must always exceed losses of their losers.

My 2004 three-good America–China model encapsulated the distinction between (A) win–win new Chinese innovations versus (B) win–lose innovations. Bombay outsourcing was not at all my major preoccupation. My message was more subversive than that. 1955–1970 Toyota versus Ford–GM–Chrysler represented a perfect type B invention. Since the *JEP* editors put my three-good equations in the web ghetto, my two-good text had to overkill with a Chinese innovation big enough to wipe out *all* of America's pre-invention consumer surplus from geographical exchange. And, if strict *ceteris paribus* were stuck to, America would be reduced back forever to its most recent autarky.

The major lesson, from economic history and for economic-historian futurists, seems this:

> New free trade does more for not yet developed educatable people than it does for advanced industrial populations. But that does not condemn the latter to negative real-growth trends. If the Darwinian card shuffler deals out more A inventions than B inventions, both places can grow considerably in potentiality. However, within nations, inequality between the lower-income classes and the upper-income classes will probably be exacerbated by free trade globalization.

Why does *JEP* Samuelson not persuade Paul A. Samuelson to become anti-free trade? My experience and book learning induce in me the belief that a Balkanized global regime will net hurt the future per capita incomes of *both* the affluent and less affluent populaces. Most likely, under future free trade, the relative frequencies of type A and type B innovations will be in the range that continues to help the Sleeping Beauties and also the kissing Princes, albeit in reversal of the doctrine of Matthew:

> To him who hath not, shall be most given. When I read this to my Portuguese water dog, Deixa barked, AMEN.

PART VIII.

Miscellany

519

SCIENTIFIC CORRESPONDENCE

Nature, Vol. 347, 6 September 1990

The law beats Maxwell's demon

Sir--Maddox (*Nature*, **345**, 109; 1990) reverts to Maxwell's demon and subsequent discussions by Szillard and others concerning its practical use to circumvent the second law of thermodynamics and elude energy constraints. Can the demon in theory defend or resolve the Boltzmann paradox of purporting to deduce a macro time-symmetric one-sided increase in entropy from time-reversible microscopic differential equations?

The answer is no. If a demon could operate as described, the resulting microscopic differential equations are non-Hamiltonian. This is not so much because of some special violation of energy conservation, but rather because the observable particles going through apertures or being reflected from trapdoors obey new differential equations that are definite, but definitely not time-symmetric. There is no paradox to be resolved when time-asymmetric microscopic equations entail macroscopic measurements that are time-asymmetric.

To confirm that point, consider a frictionless trough containing two perfectly elastic balls and being bounded by perfectly elastic walls at each side. Before Maxwell's interfering, the balls proceed from their specified initial positions and velocities according to Newton's simplest law of non-acceleration--until a ball hits a wall or another ball. By definition of 'perfectly elastic' entities, approximatable in real-life experiments, a ball reverses in direction instantly without losing speed just when hitting a wall; two balls that collide, if of the same mass, instantaneously exchange their velocities. When averaged over all future time, each half of the trough has the same mean number of balls. (Their temperatures average out equal, so to speak.) Of course, the history of the specified system going backwards in time obeys precisely the same kind of Newtonian equations. Whatever statements I can make about 'mean temperatures' or about 'entropy' going forwards in time can be matched by a valid similar deduction going backwards in time.

But take Maxwell's demon. It changes linear differential equations such as $\dot{y}_1(t) \equiv 0$ and impulsive reversals of velocities at walls and collisions into nonlinear differential equations that are complicated only to write down. Let (-0, 1/2, +1) be respectively the values of a $y_1(t)$ when at the left wall, at the middle of the trough where the demon slides in Maxwell's trapdoor, at the right wall. Before the demon where the y_1 are away from the walls and are separated, they everywhere satisfy $\dot{y}_1 = f(\dot{y}_1,\dot{y}_2;y_1,y_2)$ where $f(,) \equiv 0$ for $y_1 \neq y_2$; and $0 < y_1, y_2 < 1$. Now, then y_1 is near the trapdoor and away from y_2, the demon will want to shepherd y_1 into, let us say, the left-hand corral. Effectively between collisions the demon replaces Newton's laws by its own new rules:

$$\dot{y}_1(t+) = D[\dot{y}_1(t-),y_1(t)]$$

where

$$D[\dot{x},x] = \dot{x} \text{ for } x \neq 1/2$$
$$D[\dot{x}, 1/2] = -\dot{x} \text{ for } \dot{x} < 0$$
$$= +\dot{x} \text{ for } \dot{x} > 0.$$

To convince oneself of the time-asymmetry of the demonized system, ask where the system had been a short time before observing both balls in the left-half corral with one moving just to the left of the trough's midpoint. One cannot say whether the last ball will have just been trapped, and therefore that it was recently at a positive y reading; or that the trapping might have happened a million years ago. The demonized system's differential equations are so time-asymmetric as to make them globally not uniquely time-invertible. Forwards in time the Maxwell scheme has uniquely defined trajectories.

Maddox may be right in thinking Maxwell's tongue was in his cheek, but his text has been mostly interpreted otherwise. At least Maxwell seems to have wanted to get people to think in terms of statistical mechanics by fabricating a contractual whimsy.

Paul A. Samuelson
Department of Economics
Massachusetts Institute of Technology
Cambridge, Massachusetts 02139, USA

Proc. Natl. Acad. Sci. USA
Vol. 89, pp. 1090–1094, February 1992
Applied Mathematics

Conserved energy without work or heat

(temperature equalization/Invariance Law/Abel's Functional Equation)

PAUL A. SAMUELSON

Department of Economics, Massachusetts Institute of Technology, Cambridge, MA 02139

Contributed by Paul A. Samuelson, October 28, 1991

ABSTRACT By merely observing the common empirical temperature that two like subsystems in contact reach, as a recordable function of their initial empirical temperatures and specific volumes, we can deduce logically a conserved energy function that depends only on empirical temperature and specific volume. What makes possible this offbeat 18th-century inference, quite free of any 19th-century concepts of "heat" or measurable mechanical work, is the Invariance Law of nature, whereby any four like subsystems must settle down to the same common temperatures regardless of which two-by-two pairings are made—so to speak, an "independence of path" property. Mathematically, the Invariance Law imposes Abel-like functional equations on the admissible functions. Remarkably, recourse to such temperature-equalization data renders it impossible to identify one constant in the energy function. By observing how two quite different substances come into equilibrium, or by utilizing "adiabatic slopes" at two points for one substance, or by observing its expansion into a vacuum, we can determine all its unknowns. Much of conventional expositions of the First and Second Laws seems derivable from the equation of state and the First Law's energy function.

A unit of a specified homogeneous substance is contained within exterior walls that are insulating, and are rigid so as to occupy a specified *specific volume*, $v = V/M$. We can infer that its empirical temperature is different from that of a similar unit mass when, after we connect the two subsystems by an inner wall that is noninsulating, both systems begin to display observable changes; for example, when the connecting wall is nonrigid (a piston), the respective volumes will change, until finally the combined system asymptotically settles down to a new uniform equilibrium temperature. Or, we can recognize by induced changes in the subsystems' respective pressures (p_1 and p_2) that initially there was an inequality in their temperatures ($t_1 \neq t_2$). Symbolically,

$$(t_1, t_2) \to (t^*, t^*), \quad [1]$$

where the final equilibrium t^* is an observable function of the system's initial values.

The present analysis will take the concept of empirical temperature to be understood. Our unit mass of the fluid, once both its specific volume and empirical temperature are specified, will have all its observable properties uniquely determined. (Gravitational and magnetic forces are supposed ignorable, as are all changes in various chemical masses.)

Two Passive Experiments

Our discussion will focus on two cases, where the unit masses become connected by an inner connecting wall that is either (*i*) rigid and noninsulating or (*ii*) nonrigid and noninsulating.

The publication costs of this article were defrayed in part by page charge payment. This article must therefore be hereby marked "*advertisement*" in accordance with 18 U.S.C. §1734 solely to indicate this fact.

In the first passive experiment (*i*), we observe symbolically the transformation

$$(t_1, v_1; t_2, v_2) \to (t^*, v_1; t^*, v_2) \quad [2a]$$

$$t^* = f(t_1, v_1; t_2, v_2) = f(t_2, v_2; t_1, v_1), \quad [2b]$$

where the four-variable f function is in principle empirically measurable.

In the second passive experiment (*ii*), involving a movable conducting piston, the *volume* of the total system is conserved even though v_1 may change at the expense of v_2. Final temperature must still equalize. Symbolically,

$$(t_1, v_1; t_2, v_2) \to \left(t^{**}, \frac{1}{2}v_1 + \frac{1}{2}v_2; t^{**}, \frac{1}{2}v_1 + \frac{1}{2}v_2\right) \quad [3a]$$

$$t^{**} = F(t_1, v_1; t_2, v_2) \equiv F(t_2, v_2; t_1, v_1). \quad [3b]$$

The f and F functions, arising from disparate experiments, must of course be different functions. However, they are closely related when v_1 is specified to equal v_2; then the experiments are found to be indistinguishable, with

$$f(t_1, v; t_2, v) \equiv F(t_1, v; t_2, v)$$

$$= f(t_1, t_2|v), \text{ or } f(t_1, t_2), \text{ for brevity.} \quad [4]$$

Some further, subtle, connections between the f and F functions will be described below.

Deducing a Conserved Energy Function

It is a law of nature, confirmable by measurement of simple passive calorimetric experiments, that *no matter in what order you combine four equal masses of the same fluid that are initially at different empirical temperatures* (t_1, t_2, t_3, t_4), *their final equilibrium* t* *will be the same*. This analysis builds on that Invariance Law.

When all four subsystems are restricted to have the same specific volumes, $v_1 = v_2 = v_3 = v_4 = v$, it is realistic and convenient to hypothesize the following testable restrictions on Eq. 4's observable $f(t_1, t_2)$ function:

$$f(t_1, t_2) = f(t_2, t_1), \text{ symmetry} \quad [5a]$$

$$f(t, t) = t, \text{ a mean.} \quad [5b]$$

$$f(t + \Delta t, t_2) > f(t, t_2), \quad \Delta t > 0, \text{ monotonicity.} \quad [5c]$$

For simplicity of first exposition, let the f function be not only continuous but also twice differentiable, so that there exist well-defined expressions

$$\partial f/\partial t_i, \ \partial^2 f/\partial t_i^2, \ \partial^2 f/\partial t_i \partial t_j, \ldots ; \ \partial f/\partial v_i, \ldots \quad [6]$$

The stated Invariance Law, by making it irrelevant whether we first pair (1, 2) and (3, 4) or pair (1, 3) and (2, 4), translates into an Abel-like functional equation on the $f(t_1, t_2)$ function:

1090

$$f(f(t_1, t_2), f(t_3, t_4)) = f(f(t_1, t_3), f(t_2, t_4)). \quad [7]$$

Since the 1820s, relations like Eq. 7 were known to imply the existence of a conserved energy function, $E[t]$, for which

$$E[t_1] + E[t_2] = E[f(t_1, t_2)] + E[f(t_1, t_2)], \quad E' > 0$$

$$f(t_1, t_2) = E^{-1}\left(\frac{1}{2}E[t_1] + \frac{1}{2}E[t_2]\right), \quad [8]$$

$$E[x] = y \leftrightarrow x = E^{-1}(y),$$

$$(d/dy)E^{-1}(y) = 1/E'[E^{-1}(y)] > 0.$$

See ref. 1 for discussion of *quasiarithmetic* means and proof that Eqs. 7 and 8 mutually imply each other.

From observable measurements of f and its derivatives, elementary calculus could deduce the necessary form that must be taken by

$$(E[t] - E[\bar{t}])/(E[\bar{\bar{t}}] - E[\bar{t}]) = J[t], \quad [9]$$

where $J[t]$ is a variant of the classical Joule internal-energy function deducible from the work and heat concepts of the classical First Law of Thermodynamics. Here $\bar{t}$ and $\bar{\bar{t}}$ are distinct empirical temperatures chosen as reference points by convention, so that

$$(J[\bar{t}], J[\bar{\bar{t}}]) \equiv (0, 1). \quad [10]$$

Expressions 8–10 are short for

$$E[t_1|v] + E[t_2|v] = 2E[f(t_1, t_2|v)] \quad [8']$$

$$(E[t|v] - E[\bar{t}|v])/(E[\bar{\bar{t}}|v] - E[\bar{t}|v]) = J[t|v] \quad [9']$$

$$(J[\bar{t}|v], J[\bar{\bar{t}}|v]) \equiv (0, 1). \quad [10']$$

For any specified v, the dependence on t of $E[t|v]$ and $J[t|v]$ can be shown to match exactly the dependence on t of Joule's true energy function $J[t, v]$. But the Joule function does *not* have

$$\partial J[\bar{t}, v]/\partial v \equiv J_v[\bar{t}, v] \equiv 0, \quad [11]$$

whereas, by contrast,

$$\partial J[\bar{t}|v]/\partial v \equiv J_v[\bar{t}|v] \equiv 0. \quad [12]$$

This last vanishing is a mere notational convention.

For each fixed v in $f(t_1, v; t_2, v)$, we can only identify $E[t]$ or $E[t|v]$ subject to an arbitrary origin function, $a(v) \gtrless 0$, and an arbitrary scaling (or unit) convention, $b(v) > 0$, in

$$E[t|v] = a(v) + b(v)C(t|v), \quad [13a]$$

$$a(v) \gtrless 0, \quad b(v) > 0. \quad [13b]$$

It will be shown presently that $C(t|v)$ can be defined by

$$A(t|v) = \partial \ln[-(\partial t_2/\partial t_1)_{f=c}]/\partial t$$

$$= (\partial^2 E[t|v]/\partial t^2)/(\partial E[t|v]/\partial t) \quad [13c]$$

independently of (t_2, v_2) in $f(t, v; t_2, v_2)$ and by

$$B(t|v) = \exp\left[\int_{\bar{t}}^{t} A(t'|v)dt'\right] = \frac{\partial E(t|v)/\partial t}{\partial E(t_2|v_2)/\partial t} \quad [13d]$$

$$C(t|v) = \int_{\bar{t}}^{t} B(t''|v)dt'', \quad [13e]$$

where $\bar{t}$ is an arbitrary reference.

Differing Initial Volumes

To explore further the identification of $E[t, v]$ for varying v, so that it is free of the arbitrary $b(v)$ function, we allow v_1 and v_2 to differ. Now f satisfies the generalization of Eq. 8,

$$E[t_1, v_1] + E[t_2, v_2]$$

$$= E[f(t_1, v_1; t_2, v_2), v_1] + E[f(t_1, v_1; t_2, v_2), v_2], \quad [14]$$

which can be solved for f as the three-variable function

$$f(t_1, v_1; t_2, v_2) = \Phi\left(\sum_{1}^{2} E[t_j, v_j], v_1, v_2\right) \quad [15]$$

$$-(\partial t_2/\partial t_1)_{f=c} = \frac{\partial f(t_1, v_1; t_2, v_2)/\partial t_1}{\partial f(t_1, v_1; t_2, v_2)/\partial t_2} = \frac{\partial E[t_1, v_1]/\partial t_1}{\partial E[t_2, v_2]/\partial t_1}. \quad [16]$$

Writing the middle ratio above as $B(t_1, v_1; t_2, v_2)$, by quadrature we determine E as

$$E[t, v] - E[\bar{t}, v] = \bar{b}\int_{\bar{t}}^{t} B(t', v; \bar{t}, \bar{v})dt' = \bar{b}C[t, v],$$

$$\bar{b} = E_t[\bar{t}, \bar{v}], \quad C[\bar{t}, \bar{v}] = 0, \quad C_t[\bar{t}, \bar{v}] = 1, \quad [17]$$

where $(\bar{t}, \bar{v})$ is an arbitrarily specified reference point and $E_t[t, v]$ denotes $\partial E[t, v]/\partial t$. Clearly $E[t, v]$ so far contains the arbitrary function of v, $E[\bar{t}, v] = a(v)$; but rather than allowing Eq. 13a's arbitrary scaling function, $b(v)$, Eq. 17 contains only the arbitrary constant $b(\bar{v}) = \bar{b}$. The $C[t, v]$ defined in Eq. 17 will agree with Eq. 13's $C(t|v)$ only for $v = \bar{v}$.

Remark: We deduce rather than assume the truth of Eq. 14's conservation of energy. It suffices to deduce that the following form of the Invariance Law holds: when four equal-mass subsystems are connected by rigid inner walls that are not insulating, we must observe the same final t^* equilibrium no matter the order in which inner-wall connections are made. Symbolically,

$$(t_1, v_1; t_2, v_2; t_3, v_3; t_4, v_4)$$

$$\rightarrow (t^*, v_1; t^*, v_2; t^*, v_3; t^*, v_4). \quad [18]$$

This holds even when $(v_1, v_2) = (v_3, v_4)$ and regardless of the way we pair up the subsystems in two stages, and it imposes on f the Abel-like (see ref. 2) functional equation

$$f(f(t_1, v_1; t_3, v_1), v_1; f(t_2, v_2; t_4, v_2), v_2)$$

$$= f(f(t_{12}, v_1; t_{34}, v_1), v_1; f(t_{12}, v_2; t_{34}, v_2), v_2)$$

$$= f(f(t_{14}, v_1; t_{32}, v_1), v_1; f(t_{14}, v_2; t_{32}, v_2), v_2), \quad [19a]$$

$$t_{12} = f(t_1, v_1; t_2, v_2), \quad t_{34} = f(t_3, v_1; t_4, v_2),$$

$$t_{14} = f(t_1, v_1; t_4, v_2), \quad t_{32} = f(t_3, v_1; t_2, v_2). \quad [19b]$$

What Pressure Equilibrium Further Entails

Beyond knowing the f function, we have knowledge of the F function from the second class of passive calorimetric experiments in which the interacting subsystems are connected by inner conducting walls that are not rigid. This F knowledge enables us to reduce the arbitrary function in Eqs. **13a** and **17**, $a(v)$ or $E[\bar{t}, v]$, to a linear function of v with one unknown arbitrary parameter. It will be shown that this unknown parameter is forever unknowable until we somehow go beyond merely passive, autonomous experiments on one substance.

The Invariance Law puts restrictions on F. Thus, consider four equal-mass subsystems: (t_i, v_i), $i = 1, 2, 3, 4$. Whether we (*i*) pair in a first step (1, 2) and (3, 4) and then combine the respective results or (*ii*) pair (1, 3) and (2, 4) in a first step and then combine their results, we must arrive at the *same* t^{**}. This imposes the vector functional equation

$$F\left(F(t_1, v_1; t_2, v_2), \frac{v_1}{2} + \frac{v_2}{2}; F(t_3, v_3; t_4, v_4), \frac{v_3}{2} + \frac{v_4}{2}\right)$$

$$= F\left(F(t_1, v_1; t_3, v_3), \frac{v_1}{2} + \frac{v_3}{2}; F(t_2, v_2; t_4, v_4), \frac{v_2}{2} + \frac{v_4}{2}\right),$$

$$\frac{1}{4}(v_1 + v_2 + v_3 + v_4) = \frac{1}{2}\left[\frac{v_1}{2} + \frac{v_2}{2}\right] + \frac{1}{2}\left[\frac{v_3}{2} + \frac{v_4}{2}\right]$$

$$= \frac{1}{2}\left[\frac{v_1}{2} + \frac{v_3}{2}\right] + \frac{1}{2}\left[\frac{v_2}{2} + \frac{v_4}{2}\right]. \quad [20]$$

This Invariance Law can be shown to suffice to put on F the following relations resembling Eqs. **8** and **14**:

$$E[t_1, v_1] + E[t_2, v_2] = 2E\left[F(t_1, v_1; t_2, v_2), \frac{v_1}{2} + \frac{v_2}{2}\right]. \quad [21a]$$

$$F(t_1, v_1; t_2, v_2) = \Psi\left(\sum_1^2 E[t_j, v_j], \frac{v_1}{2} + \frac{v_2}{2}\right), \quad [21b]$$

where Ψ is a two-variable function; and

$$-(\partial t_2/\partial t_1)_{F=c} = \frac{\partial F(t_1, v_1; t_2, v_2)/\partial t_1}{\partial F(t_1, v_1; t_2, v_2)/\partial t_2} = \frac{E_t[t_1, v_1]}{E_t[t_2, v_2]}. \quad [21c]$$

Why does Eq. **21a**, involving F, contain the same E function as did Eq. **14**, involving f? Rather than positing this as a further law of nature that can be affirmatively tested again and again, I suggest that the following (Eq. **22**) can be *deduced* from the Invariance Law applied in Eq. **23** to successive experiments involving both f and F in tandem:

$$\frac{\partial F(t_1, v_1; t_2, v_2)/\partial t_1}{\partial F(t_1, v_1; t_2, v_2)/\partial t_2} \equiv \frac{\partial f(t_1, v_1; t_2, v_2)/\partial t_1}{\partial f(t_1, v_1; t_2, v_2)/\partial t_2}. \quad [22]$$

Consider, for example, four initial subsystems of equal mass: $(t_1, v_1; t_2, v_2; t_3, v_1; t_4, v_2)$. Suppose they are arbitrarily paired in first-step F experiments: (1, 2) and (3, 4). Then connect *their* results in an f experiment, leading to a final t^*. We should observe exactly the same t^* if the first F experiment had involved (1, 4) and (3, 2); and still other combinatorials should also produce that same t^*. Thus, F and f must satisfy relations such as

$$f\left(F(t_1, v_1; t_2, v_2), \frac{v_1}{2} + \frac{v_2}{2}; F(t_3, v_1; t_4, v_1), \frac{v_1}{2} + \frac{v_2}{2}\right)$$

$$= f\left(F(t_1, v_1; t_4, v_2), \frac{v_1}{2} + \frac{v_2}{2}; F(t_3, v_1; t_2, v_2), \frac{v_1}{2} + \frac{v_2}{2}\right) \quad [23a]$$

$$F(t_1, v_1; t_2, v_2)$$

$$= F(f(t_1, v_1; t_2, v_2), v_1; f(t_1, v_1; t_2, v_2), v_2). \quad [23b]$$

Indeed, from Eq. **23b** we realize that knowledge of Eq. **2b**'s four-variable f function, and of Eq. **23b**'s three-variable $F(t, v_1; t, v_2)$ function, gives us knowledge of the four-variable function $F(t_1, v_1; t, v_2)$. [Because $F(t, v_1; t, v_2)$ does not generally equal t, the F function shares with the f function the property of in general not defining a *mean* of t_1 and t_2.]

Now we can use F data to narrow down the admissible arbitrary origin function of v, $a(v)$, in the following rewrites of Eqs. **17** and **21a**:

$$E[t, v] = \bar{b}a(v) + \bar{b}C[t, v] \quad [24a]$$

$$a(v) - 2a\left(\frac{\bar{v}}{2} + \frac{v}{2}\right) + a(\bar{v}) = G(v), \quad G(\bar{v}) = 0,$$

$$= 2C\left[F\left(\bar{t}, \bar{v}; \bar{t}, \frac{\bar{v}}{2} + \frac{v}{2}\right), \frac{\bar{v}}{2} + \frac{v}{2}\right] - C[\bar{t}, \bar{v}] - C[\bar{t}, v]. \quad [24b]$$

To deduce a functional equation that $a(v)$ must satisfy, we differentiate Eq. **24b**'s identity in v, to arrive at

$$a'(v) - a'\left(\frac{\bar{v}}{2} + \frac{v}{2}\right) = -C_v[\bar{t}, v] + C_v\left[F(\bar{t}, \bar{v}; \bar{t}, v), \frac{v}{2} + \frac{\bar{v}}{2}\right]$$

$$+ 2C_t\left[F(\bar{t}, \bar{v}; \bar{t}, v), \frac{v}{2} + \frac{\bar{v}}{2}\right]F_v(\bar{t}, \bar{v}; \bar{t}, v) = G'(v). \quad [24c]$$

This is of the general form

$$y'(x) - y'\left(\frac{x}{2}\right) = g(x), \text{ a known function.} \quad [24d]$$

The only continuous solution to Eq. **24c** must be of the form

$$a(v) = A(v) + \bar{a}(v - \bar{v}), \quad \bar{a} \text{ arbitrary} \quad [24e]$$

$$A(v) = \int_{\bar{v}}^{v} \sum_{k=0}^{\infty} G'(v'2^{-k} - \bar{v}2^{-k} + \bar{v})dv'$$

$$= \sum_{k=0}^{\infty} 2^k G(v2^{-k} - \bar{v}2^{-k} + \bar{v}). \quad [24f]$$

I owe thanks to my colleague Dan McFadden (Massachusetts Institute of Technology) for the explicit form of Eq. **24f**.

That the numerical value of $\bar{a}$ in the (Joule) energy function can never be determined from the passive f and F experiments is intuitively evident from the forms of Eqs. **14** and **21a**. Adding $\bar{a}(v - \bar{v})$ to any proposed $E[t, v]$ solution yields another E that is still a valid solution. QED.

So Far, But Not All the Way

We have now arrived as far as the passive experiments can take us—with Eqs. **13a** and **17** narrowed down to

$$E[t, v] = \bar{b}A(v) + \bar{b}C[t, v] + \bar{b}\bar{a}(v - \bar{v}). \quad [25]$$

With $\bar{a}$ not knowable, $E[t, v]$ fails to yield us full knowledge of the Joule energy function of the classical First Law.

What additional experimental observations could pin down $\bar{a}$ to the sole numerical value that would make our $E[t, v]$ agree completely with the classical $J[t, v]$ energy of Joule–Mayer–Helmholtz arrived at by external-work observations?

In the final sections I explore how utilizing *two* different substances in our experiments might enable us to estimate $\bar{a}$ numerically without measuring external work done on the system. However, as a stunt that justifies this paper's titular claim to avoid heat and work measurements, I finally suggest how the needed missing information could be arrived at from one-substance experiments merely by experimentally measuring the substance's "adiabatic" dp/dv slopes at two (t, v) points or by porous-plug experiments in which the substance expands into a vacuum without any change in energy.

For the first time we will want to be able to refer to the observable *equation of state* that relates observable pressure to observable (empirical temperature, specific volume):

$$p = P(t, v). \quad [26]$$

Also, it could be useful to know the dt/dv slope defined at any (t, v) point by a porous-plug experiment in which the substance is allowed to expand spontaneously into a vacuum and with no change in energy. Write

$$-(dt/dv)_{\text{porous-plug}} = \pi(t, v) = \frac{E_v(t, v)}{E_t(t, v)}. \quad [27]$$

Energy Closure from Two-Substance Contacts

From passive experiments on a single substance we have been able to determine the wide class of energy functions of Eq. 25, which include as a special case the classical Joule energy function but which differ from it by an arbitrary linear term in volume, $\bar{a}(v - \bar{v})$. Can using different masses of the substance help to pin down the true $\bar{a}$? Exploration would show why it cannot do so.

What about using passive experiments involving two quite different substances? This turns out to be more hopeful and still eschews recourse to concepts of "adiabatic" processes and "infinitely slow, reversible processes" involving mechanical "work" being done on the system's *insulated* external walls. I now show how use of a second, essentially different, substance may enable numerical determination of the $\bar{a}$ coefficient needed for our knowledge of conserved energy to be complete.

Boldface type will be used for the second substance. Corresponding to $(t, v, C[t, v], M, \ldots)$ for substance 1 will be $(\mathbf{t}, \mathbf{v}, \mathbf{C[t, v]}, \mathbf{M} \ldots)$ for substance 2, all being determinable by exactly the same logical and observational procedures. For brevity, we employ *unit* masses: M and $\mathbf{M}$.

Now the two different substances can be brought into contact by inner conducting walls that are either rigid or nonrigid, leading to the observable transformations

$$(t, v; \mathbf{t}, \mathbf{v}) \rightarrow (t^*, v; t^*, \mathbf{v}) \quad [28a]$$

$$t^* = \mathbf{f}(t, v; \mathbf{t}, \mathbf{v}) = q. \quad [28b]$$

Our notation does not imply equality of initial vectors, (t, v) and $(\mathbf{t}, \mathbf{v})$.

Alternatively, there is the *rigid* walls transformation

$$(t, v; \mathbf{t}, \mathbf{v}) \rightarrow (t^{**}, v^{**}; t^{**}, \mathbf{v^{**}}) \quad [29a]$$

$$t^{**} = F(t, v; \mathbf{t}, \mathbf{v}) = Q \quad [29b]$$

$$v^{**} = r(t, v; \mathbf{t}, \mathbf{v}) = R \quad [29c]$$

$$\mathbf{v^{**}} = \mathbf{r}(t, v; \mathbf{t}, \mathbf{v}) = \mathbf{R}. \quad [29d]$$

Warning: the old f and F functions must not be confused with the new, boldface $\mathbf{f}$ and $\mathbf{F}$ two-substance functions.

Our Invariance Law applies in a straightforward way to the two-substance functions, enabling us to deduce and/or verify the conserved-energy relations

$$E[t, v] + \mathbf{E[t, v]} = E[q, v] + \mathbf{E[q, v]} \quad [30a]$$

$$\bar{b}C[t, v] + \bar{b}A(v) + \bar{b}\bar{a}(v - \bar{v}) + \bar{b}\mathbf{c}\mathbf{C[t, v]} + \bar{b}\mathbf{c}\mathbf{A(v)} + \mathbf{bca(v - \bar{v})}$$

$$= \bar{b}C[q, v] + \bar{b}A(v) + \bar{b}\bar{a}(v - \bar{v}) + \bar{b}\mathbf{c}\mathbf{C[q, v]}$$

$$+ \bar{b}\mathbf{c}\mathbf{A(v)} + \bar{b}\mathbf{ca(v - \bar{v})} \quad [30b]$$

where $\bar{b}$ and $\bar{b}\mathbf{c}$ are scaling constants:

$$\bar{b} = E_t[\bar{t}, \bar{v}] \quad [31a]$$

$$c = \frac{\partial \mathbf{f}(\bar{t}, \bar{v}; \bar{t}, \bar{\mathbf{v}})/\partial \mathbf{t}}{\partial \mathbf{f}(\bar{t}, \bar{v}; \bar{t}, \bar{\mathbf{v}})/\partial t} \quad [31b]$$

$$\bar{b}\mathbf{c} = \mathbf{E_t[\bar{t}, \bar{v}]}. \quad [31c]$$

Similarly, for the $\mathbf{F}$ experiment, $(Q, R, \mathbf{R})$ are solutions of the triplet of implicit relations

$$E[t, v] + \mathbf{E[t, v]} = E[Q, v] + \mathbf{E[Q, v]} \quad [32a]$$

$$v + \mathbf{v} = R + \mathbf{R} \quad [32b]$$

$$P(t, R) = \mathbf{P}(t, \mathbf{R}), \quad [32c]$$

where $\mathbf{P(t, v)}$ is the second substance's equation of state just like the first substance's $P(t, v)$ in Eq. 26.

For any two or more initial $(t_j; v_j; \mathbf{t}_j; \mathbf{v}_j)$ points, $j = 1, 2, \ldots$, we can infer the following equalities from Eq. 32:

$$C[t_j; v_j] + A(v_j) + \mathbf{c}\mathbf{C[t_j; v_j]} + \mathbf{cA(v_j)}$$

$$- C[Q_j, R_j] - A(R_j) - \mathbf{c}\mathbf{C[Q_j, R_j]} - \mathbf{cA(R_j)}$$

$$= \bar{a}(R_j - v_j) + \mathbf{ca(R_j - v_j)}. \quad [33]$$

These are linear equations for the $(\bar{a}, \mathbf{a})$ unknowns. Their Jacobian determinant, $(R_1 - v_1)(\mathbf{R}_2 - \mathbf{v}_2) - (R_2 - v_2)(\mathbf{R}_1 - \mathbf{v}_1)$, should not vanish if the substances are truly diverse. Therefore, from the observable and inferable data, we should be able to deduce any substance's true energy function completely free of any arbitrary constants.

This completes our search. Since this last stage involved an element of black magic, competent mathematical physicists should vet my two-substance methodology. (Example: two substances *almost* alike ought to yield ill-conditioned linear equations. Also, two different gases, if they are almost ideal "perfect" gases, might well be useless for the present purpose. Actually, if there were a law of nature that makes the critical Jacobians *always* identically zero, that would be a strong and perhaps new law of nature.)

Fortunately, as the next section will show, very limited knowledge about *adiabatic slopes* for one substance can in any case enable our numerical determination of its $\bar{a}$.

And, by an alternative third experiment, the observable $(dt/dv)_{p-p}$ slope along the path of a porous-plug expansion into a vacuum can identify $\bar{a}$ numerically.

Digression on "Reversible" Processes

For the first time, contemplate mechanical work being done to move the insulated external walls of the one substance's unit mass. Without necessarily taking any measurement of the magnitude of the external work, imagine moving the walls ever more slowly so that the initial state of $(\bar{t}, \bar{v})$ ends in a different state. Experience confirms that, in the limit of ever slower wall movements, there can be identified a unique ("adiabatic") contour in the (t, v) plane through $(\bar{t}, \bar{v})$. In principle, the contour's unique adiabatic slope can be identified at any (t, v) point:

$$(dt/dv)_{ad} = \sigma(t, v), \qquad [34]$$

where σ is an observable function.

As a matter of terminology and definitions, we define our energy scale in "work units" and use the equalities

$$E[t, v] - E[\bar{t}, v] = \bar{\lambda}C[t, v] + \bar{\lambda}A(v) + \bar{\lambda}\bar{a}(v - \bar{v}) \qquad [35a]$$

$$E_t[t, v](dt/dv)_{ad} + E_v[t, v] = -P(t, v), \qquad [35b]$$

where P is the equation of state relating pressure to empirical temperature and specific volume (Eq. 26).

For any distinct $(\bar{t}, \bar{v})$ and $(\bar{\bar{t}}, \bar{\bar{v}})$, Eq. 35 implies that knowledge of $C[\bar{t}, \bar{v}] + A(v)$ and two adiabatic slopes, $\sigma(\bar{t}, \bar{v})$ and σ $\bar{\bar{t}}, \bar{\bar{v}}$, suffice to provide the following exact relations for the unknown $\bar{a}$:

$$\bar{\lambda} = -\frac{P(\bar{t}, \bar{v})}{C_t[\bar{t}, \bar{v}]\sigma(\bar{t}, \bar{v}) + C_v[\bar{t}, \bar{v}] + A(\bar{v}) + \bar{a}} = -\frac{P(\bar{\bar{t}}, \bar{\bar{v}})}{C_t[\bar{\bar{t}}, \bar{\bar{v}}]\sigma(\bar{\bar{t}}, \bar{\bar{v}}) + C_v[\bar{\bar{t}}, \bar{\bar{v}}] + A(\bar{\bar{v}}) + \bar{a}} \qquad [36]$$

$$\bar{a} = \frac{C_t[\bar{t}, \bar{v}]\sigma(\bar{t}, \bar{v}) + C_v[\bar{t}, \bar{v}] + A(\bar{v}) - C_t[\bar{\bar{t}}, \bar{\bar{v}}]\sigma(\bar{\bar{t}}, \bar{\bar{v}}) - C_v[\bar{\bar{t}}, \bar{\bar{v}}] + A(\bar{\bar{v}})}{P(\bar{\bar{t}}, \bar{\bar{v}})^{-1} - P(\bar{t}, \bar{v})^{-1}}. \qquad [37]$$

If we do already know the true $\bar{a}$, from two-substance data or whatever else, knowledge of a single $\sigma(\bar{t}, \bar{v})$ slope enables us to extrapolate to *any* $\sigma(t, v)$:

$$\sigma(t, v) = \frac{-P(t, v) - J_v(t, v)}{J_t(t, v)}$$

$$= \frac{-P(t, v) - \bar{\lambda}C_v[t, v] - \bar{\lambda}A(v) - \bar{\lambda}\bar{a}}{\bar{\lambda}C_t[t, v]}, \qquad [38]$$

where $\bar{\lambda}$ is the expression given in Eq. 36 and J is the true Joule energy function expressed in work units:

$$J(t, v) = \bar{\lambda}C[t, v] + \bar{\lambda}A(v) + \bar{\lambda}\bar{a}(v - \bar{v}). \qquad [39]$$

Here $\bar{\lambda}$ is understood to be that of Eq. 36.

From the porous-plug slope function of Eq. 27, $\pi(t, v)$, we could alternatively define $\bar{a}$ in Eq. 39's $J[t, v]$ by the relation

$$-(dt/dv)_{p-p} = \pi(\bar{t}, \bar{v}) = \frac{A'(\bar{v}) + C_v[\bar{t}, \bar{v}] + \bar{a}}{C_t[\bar{t}, \bar{v}]} \qquad [40a]$$

$$\bar{a} = \pi(\bar{t}, \bar{v}) - A'(\bar{v}) - C_v[\bar{t}, \bar{v}] \qquad [40b]$$

I conclude by only mentioning how Kelvin's absolute temperature can be defined without explicit mention of "heat" or Carnot concepts of efficiency once the $J[t, v]$ energy function is known. Let $v_1 = h_1(t)$, $v_2 = h_2(t)$ be the known equations of any two distinct *adiabats*. Then we can calculate at any empirical t

$$\Theta(t) = -\int_{v_1}^{v_2} P(t, v')dv' + J[t, v_2] - J[t, v_1]. \qquad [41]$$

It can be verified to be a law of nature that

$$\Theta(t)/\Theta(\bar{t}) = T \qquad [42]$$

is a new empirical temperature with the property of being the same no matter which two adiabats are used and no matter which substance is being observed. Such an empirical temperature is truly special and deserves the adjective "absolute". Knowing J, P, and a single adiabatic slope, we have no further need to talk about "reversible" processes to define T. Unlike our natural discovery of the E function, no early scientist could possibly have arrived at T by the unmotivated approach of Eq. 41.

Discussion

After Carnot, Kelvin, and Clausius, one understands and admires the structure of classical phenomenological thermodynamics. The point of the present investigation is to explore how by the time of Galileo, or certainly of Joseph Black, decades before the works of Carnot, Kelvin, Joule, and Clausius, a serendipitous researcher might have recognized and measured the conserved internal-energy function by which every substance is characterized.

Note that no explicit use had to be made of heat, work, line integrals, exact or inexact differentials, concepts of reversibility or irreversibility, or perpetual-motion machines.

To avoid misunderstanding, let me assert that no one before 1800 could be expected to have followed the path shown here to have been feasible. Science does not develop historically as it might have done: that is its way.

The logical puzzle presents itself. You never get something for nothing. If the impossibility of perpetual-motion machines is not postulated, what rabbit is put into the sorcerer's hat and at what stage?

I believe that the present basic Invariance Law is indeed by itself a kind of Impossibility Axiom. The order in which things happen is forbidden to make a difference, and that stipulation is a Carnot-like stipulation that there is a game out there that cannot be beaten. What will perhaps be unfamiliar if not novel is the use here of Abel-like functional equations to derive the testable restrictions on experimental data implied by the Invariance Law.

Over the years I benefitted from conversations with Profs. Edwin Bidwell Wilson and Percy Bridgman at Harvard University and with Joseph Keenan and Laslo Tisza at the Massachusetts Institute of Technology. My idiosyncratic explorations can be discerned in ref. 3. I owe thanks for editorial assistance to Janice Murray and to the Sloan Foundation for indirect support.

1. Aczél, J. (1966) *Lectures on Functional Equations* (Academic, New York), p. 287.
2. Abel, N. H. (1826) *Oeuvres Completes* (Christiana), Vol. 1, pp. 61–65.
3. Samuelson, P. A. (1966, 1972, 1977, 1982) *The Collected Scientific Papers of Paul A. Samuelson* (MIT Press, Cambridge, MA), Chaps. 42, 43, 44, 103, and 303.

521

ECONOMICS AND THERMODYNAMICS: VON NEUMANN'S PROBLEMATIC
CONJECTURE

Paul A. Samuelson
Massachusetts Institute of Technology, E52-383C
Cambridge, Massachusetts 02139, U.S.A.

Of the attempts to find analogies between thermodynamics and economies, there is alas no end. But the mathematical genius John von Neumann has earned the right to command our investigation when he suggests that his growth model (1945; earlier 1932 and 1937) defines a function

$$\text{Value of Inputs}_t / \text{Value of Outputs}_{t+1}$$

$$= \sum_{i}^{n}\sum_{j}^{m} p_i A_{ij} x_j \Big/ \sum_{i}^{n}\sum_{j}^{m} p_i B_{ij} x_j$$

$$= \phi(P,X) \tag{1}$$

whose "role seems to be similar to that of thermodynamic potentials in phenomenological thermodynamics." (1945, p.1)

Recently Andrew Brody (1989) has interestingly addressed the suggested relation and I shall attempt here to make further explorations. The goal is not to have economics shine brighter in the reflected light of physics's most perfected axiomatic system, but rather to guard against unwarranted pretensions.

Motivation

It is a fair bet that von Neumann was influenced by the following aspects of his $\phi(P,X)$ function.

1. Just as an economic system has a pair of conjugate vectors--in his case the *intensive prices* of n goods, $P = (p_1 \ldots p_n)$, and the *extensive quantities* of the m different activity levels, $X=(x_1 \ldots x_m)$--so does a Gibbs thermodynamic system have an *extensive vector of quantity magnitudes*, (specific volume, entropy,...) or (V,S,...) or more abstractly $(x_1 \ldots x_n)$, and a *conjugate vector of corresponding intensive forces*, (-pressure, absolute temperature,...) or (-P,T,...) or more abstractly $(y_1 \ldots y_n)$.

2. Von Neumann (1928) had already worked out two-person zero-sum game theory that involved each player's vector of conjugate mixed strategies: $(x_1 \ldots x_m)$ and $(y_1 \ldots y_n)$, $n \gtrless m$. The 1928 game theory involved saddlepoint or Min-Max properties and so did his growth model's ϕ function: namely, for $(\bar{P}, \bar{X})$ *equilibrium* vectors of the growth system and (P,X) arbitrary vectors, von Neumann could proclaim

$$\phi(P,\bar{X}) \leq \phi(\bar{P},\bar{X}) \leq \phi(\bar{P},X) \qquad (2)$$

Classical mathematical economics had primarily concerned itself with Min-Min, or what is the same thing with Max-Max, rather than with Min-Max. No doubt this was one reason why von Neumann, with and without his economist collaborator Oskar Morgenstern, used to proclaim that the social sciences would need a new kind of mathematics rather than rely on the post-Newtonian calculus that had been devised primarily to serve the needs of physics.

3. Brody (1989) spells out a possible third reason to motivate a connection between thermodynamics and the 1945 economics. If I interpret Brody (1989, pp. 145-6) properly, (2)'s first inequality corresponds to "..the first criterion of equilibrium: maximal entropy." The second inequality of (2) is "analogous in the Gibbs system to the dual criterion of equilibrium; minimal energy."

Doubts

On reflection some possible disquiet develops on these three suggestive points.

A. In thermodynamics, the intensive and extensive conjugate vectors have the *same* number of elements: $n=n$ rather than $n \gtrless m$, as in game theory, the growth model, Danzig linear programming, and Gale-Kuhn-Tucker concave programming. (Caveat: the number of *non-zero* p's and x's will not exceed Min(n,m).)

B. In Gibbs thermodynamics, as in classical mathematical economics, there is a basic role for Min-Min rather than initially for Min-Max. Gibbs (1873), his first thermo paper, builds on an (internal) Energy function that is convex (from below) in its arguments--in both of them individually and collectively:

$$\text{Energy} = U(V,S) \tag{3a}$$

$$-P = \partial U(V,S)/\partial V \text{ or } U_v(V,S) \tag{3b}$$

$$T = U_s(V,S) \tag{3c}$$

$$U_{vv}>0, \ U_{ss}>0, \ U_{vv}U_{ss} - U_{vs}U_{sv}>0 \tag{3d}$$

At once Gibbs's function $G(P,T)$ is definable by a Min-Min property
$$\underset{(V,S)}{\text{Min-Min}}\{U(V,S) + PV - TS\} = G(P,T) \qquad (4a)$$

We can verify that $-G(P,T)$ has the same properties in its arguments as $U(V,S)$ had in its; actually, U and $-G$ are "dual to each other." Corresponding to (4a) goes
$$\underset{P,T,}{\text{Min}}\{-G(P,T) + PV - TS\} = U(V,S) \qquad (4b)$$

Corresponding to (3) goes
$$V = G_p(P,T), \quad S = -G_T(P,T) \qquad (4c)$$
$$-G_{PP} > 0, \quad -G_{TT} > 0, \quad G_{PP}G_{TT} - G_{PT}G_{TP} > 0 \qquad (4d)$$

Corresponding to von Neumann's $\phi(P,X)$, for the case of $n=2=m$, we can now write the 4-variable thermodynamic function
$$U(V,S) + PV - TS - G(P,T)$$
$$= \Phi(-P,T,V,S)$$
$$= \Phi(y_1, y_2, x_1, x_2) = \Phi(Y,X) \qquad (5)$$

Unlike (2)'s Min-Max property, we translate from (4) the following symmetric Min-Min properties that any equilibrium $(\overline{Y}, \overline{X})$ must possess
$$\Phi(Y, \overline{X}) \geq \Phi(\overline{Y}, \overline{X}) = 0 \leq \Phi(\overline{Y}, X) \qquad (6)$$
Note the contrast between (6)'s inequality signs that point inward instead of showing the parallel Min-Max pattern of von Neumann's (2).

C. The analogy achieved for von Neumann's model with thermodynamics is evidently thin at spots. To dramatize this deficiency let me demonstrate how much closer is the thermodynamics isomorphism with classical mathematical economics, that scholars like Harold Hotelling (1932) were already working out just when von Neumann was first unveiling his growth model before Princeton's 1932 mathematicians. Hotelling had begun the duality developments later associated with R. Roy (1942), L. Court (1941), Samuelson (1938, 1947, 1953, 1960, 1962, 1965, 1972), R. Shephard (1953), D. Champernowne (1953); and Hotelling had also chanced already to use the terminology of a "potential function." I shall be cruelly brief in my exposition.

Classical Math Economics and Thermo

Define a firm's gross revenue as a concave function of its n inputs, $X = (x_j)$, which it buys at prescribed competitive prices, $Y = (y_j)$. Then

$$\underset{x_j}{\text{Max}}\{R(x_1,\ldots,x_n) - \sum_{1}^{n} y_j x_j\} = -R^*(y_1,\ldots,y_n) \quad (7a)$$

$$y_j = \partial R(X)/\partial x_j, \quad x_j = \partial R^*(Y)/\partial y_j, j=1,\ldots n \quad (7b)$$

Exactly dual to each other are $R(X)$ and $R^*(Y)$.

Now, in addition to von Neumann's ϕ and Gibbs's Φ, let's define Hotelling's

$$\Psi(Y,X) = R(x_1,\ldots,x_n) + R^*(y_1,\ldots,y_n) - \sum_{1}^{n} y_j x_j \quad (8)$$

Then, in *exact* analogy with thermodynamics, pre-Neumann mathematical economics does escape (2)'s parallel-arrowed Min-Max in favor of (6)'s Max-Max: namely,

$$\Psi(Y,\overline{X}) \leq \Psi(\overline{Y},\overline{X}) \geq \Psi(\overline{Y},X) \qquad (9)$$
$$\Psi(\overline{Y},\overline{X}) \geq \Psi(Y,X)$$

D. We are still left with the task of doing full justice to Brody's "maximal entropy" and "minimal energy" interpretations for (2). I shall return to this after we notice that other Legendre-transformation potential functions--other than Gibbs's U(V,S) and G(P,T)--do permit of some Min-Max interpretations. Perforce I must discuss Gibbsian "Enthalpy", H(P,S), and Gibbsian "Free Energy à la Helmholz", F(V,T).

E. Economists go whole afternoons not thinking about the intricacies of thermodynamics, and they prefer that way of life. However, if we are to do serious justice to the proposed topic we cannot just talk about thermodynamics; we must actually do some. Otherwise someone might get snowed by mere cocktail chatter.

Mixed Thermo Functions and Minimax

The Enthalpy and Free Energy potentials are defined respectively as follows:

$$\text{Enthalpy} = H(\overline{P},\overline{S})$$
$$= \underset{V}{\text{Min}}\{U(V,\overline{S}) + \overline{P}V\} \qquad (10a)$$

$$H_P(P,S) = V, \quad H_S(P,S) = T \qquad (10b)$$

Free Energy (Helmholz) = $F(\overline{V},\overline{T})$

$$= \underset{s}{\text{Min}}\{U(\overline{V},S) - \overline{T}S\} \qquad (11a)$$

$$F_V(V,T) = -P, \quad F_T(V,T) = -S \qquad (11b)$$

As yet still no thermodynamic Min-Max. So far only two separate single Mins. But now when we proceed to examine the convexity or concavity of H and F as functions, we find that they differ from the *uniform* convexity of U and -G assured in (3d) and (4d). We do find convexity in one variable and concavity in the other, which does smack of some kind of Min-Max.

Specifically, double differentiation does deduce from (3) and (10) and from (4) and (11)

$$H_{PP}(P,S) < 0 < H_{SS}(P,S), \partial(V,T)/\partial(P,S) < 0 \qquad (12a)$$

$$F_{TT}(V,T) < 0 < F_{VV}(V,T), \partial(P,S)/\partial(V,T) < 0 \qquad (13a)$$

From these opposite-signed curvatures, we can verify the respective saddlepoints

$$H(P,\overline{S}) - P\overline{V} - \overline{TS} \leq H(\overline{P},\overline{S}) - \overline{PV} - \overline{TS} \leq H(\overline{P},S) - \overline{PV} - \overline{TS} \qquad (12b)$$

$$F(\overline{V},T) + \overline{PV} + \overline{TS} \leq F(\overline{V},\overline{T}) + \overline{PV} + \overline{TS} \leq F(V,\overline{T}) + \overline{PV} + \overline{TS} \qquad (13b)$$

At last we have deduced in (12b) and (13b) a saddlepoint property in some thermodynamic functions. Does this confirm von Neumann's conjecture? Only minimally--in the following sense. Von Neumann's saddlepoint in (2) is a different species from the saddlepoints of (12b) or (13b), even though they belong to the same genus. In (2) the left-hand-most and right-hand-most expressions allow *half* the 2n variables to be freely variable; in (12b) and (13b), only half-of-half the 2n variables are permitted to be freely variable in the exterior expressions.

Actually, we are now alerted to a more fundamental mismatch between the von Neumann and Gibbs models. For von Neumann, after conventional normalization, there is *generically* a unique $(\overline{P}, \overline{X})$ equilibrium. Almost always, technology determines a mode of maximal growth that is a unique (normalized) $\overline{X}$ vector; almost always it determines a vector of relative prices that is a unique (normalized) $\overline{P}$ vector. For standard Gibbs or Hotelling we have parametric equilibria: for each of the n-fold infinity of possible $\overline{X}$ specified, there is a unique $\overline{Y}$ equilibrium; for each of the infinity of specified $\overline{Y}$, there is a unique $\overline{X}$ equilibrium; indeed, for each of the 2^n arbitrary ways of specifying a vector whose elements can be each *either one* of the pair (y_j, x_j), there is a unique equilibrium vector whose elements are the equilibrium values of the *other ones* of the various (y_j, x_j) pairs, $j = 1, 2, \ldots, n$.

In sum, after a tedious post mortem, we find that the purported von Neumann analogy between his growth model and classical thermodynamics is a limping analogy—a kind of a logical pun rather than a congruent isomorphism.

Meaning of Entropy Maximization

C. P. Snow, in a moment of enthusiasm, proposed as a test of whether one belonged to "the two cultures" the ability to understand and appreciate both Shakespeare and the Second Law of Thermodynamics. I fear the last is an over-stringent test for it would leave heaven underpopulated. Rarely do two scientists agree on how to resolve the paradoxes of time-symmetric microdynamic equations leading to time-asymmetric evolution in entropy. Fortunately, if we stick resolutely to phenomenological, macroscopic, classical thermodynamics, we sidestep deep issues.

Gibbs wisely took as his credo the words of Clausius:

> The Energy of the World is Constant.
> Its Entropy Ever Grows.

Time's arrow does not treat energy and entropy symmetrically: one is not maximized while the other is minimized; one is conserved as a constant while the other is being maximized, which is not quite the same thing as a Min-Max property.

Dr. Brody is not in error when speaking of minimal energy as a criterion of thermo*static* equilibrium. Thus, economists recognize the interchangeability of "An efficient demand allocation *maximizes* (ordinal) utility for fixed total income," and "An efficient allocation *minimizes* total expenditure for fixed utility attainment." In Samuelson (1960) I followed Gibbs's thermostatics and spoke of "minimizing total energy for fixed entropy." But neither Gibbs nor I were addressing time's asymmetric arrow when doing this. To elucidate the time-directional point, the present section is needed. (Interestingly, consumers-surplus economists after Dupuit (1849) anticipated the equal-area criterion that Maxwell admired so much in

Gibbs's treatment of super-cooled liquids near freezing point regions where van der Waal's kind of relation obtains.)

Figure 1 uses a Jevons-like and Edgeworth-like box diagram of economics to handle the following case. A unit mass of a vapor fills the inside of a rigid and insulated container: its temperature, if measured, would be found to be about 110° centigrade--above the boiling point. Its internal energy, if measured, would be found to be initially $\overline{U}_1$. A second similar unit mass is initially at 120° centigrade with a higher initial energy of $\overline{U}_2$.

Now let the two subsystems be connected by a conducting inner-wall, a piston. Their temperature difference disturbs the initial equilibrium: their temperatures finally settle to a common level, say at somewhere near 115°C; likewise they achieve a common pressure. By symmetry, they end up at equal energies and specific volumes. Symbolically, we have observed the spontaneous ("irreversible") transformation

$$(\overline{T}_1, \overline{U}_1, \overline{V}_1, \overline{S}_1; \overline{T}_2, \overline{U}_2, \overline{V}_2, \overline{S}_2) \rightarrow (T^*, U^*, V^*, S^*; T^*, U^*, V^*, S^*) \quad (14)$$

Because the external walls of the whole system are kept rigidly at the initial total volume, $\overline{V}_1 + \overline{V}_2$, and because the Law of Conservation of Energy says the initial total of energy is conserved at $\overline{U}_1 + \overline{U}_2$, we can write

$$\overline{V}_1 + \overline{V}_2 = V_1^* + V_2^* \tag{15a}$$

$$\overline{U}_1 + \overline{U}_2 = U(V_1^*, S_1^*) + U(V_2^*, S_2^*) \tag{15b}$$

Subject to the constraints of (15a) and (15b), Nature moves to maximize the new total of entropy:

$$\max_{V_j*, S_j*} \{S_1+S_2\} = S_1*+S_2* \tag{15c}$$

So long as U is a strictly convex function, the symmetry of the (15) system does assure a unique symmetric equilibrium. Since (15a) and (15b) give us only two relations for four variables, we pick up the needed two further relations from the vanishing of Newtonian derivatives. After elimination of Lagrange multipliers, these can be verified to be equivalent to the conditions of equal pressures and temperatures:

$$-U_V(V_1*, S_1*) = -U_V(V_2*, S_2*) = P* \tag{15d}$$

$$U_S(V_1*, S_1*) = U_S(V_2*, S_2*) = T* \tag{15e}$$

In Figure 1a the contours represent levels of equal total entropy. Figure 1b records how the symmetry point in the box diagram, whose sides respectively measure initial total volume and total energy ($\Sigma \overline{V}_j$ and $\Sigma \overline{U}_j$), does achieve a maximum of final entropy (ΣS_j*).

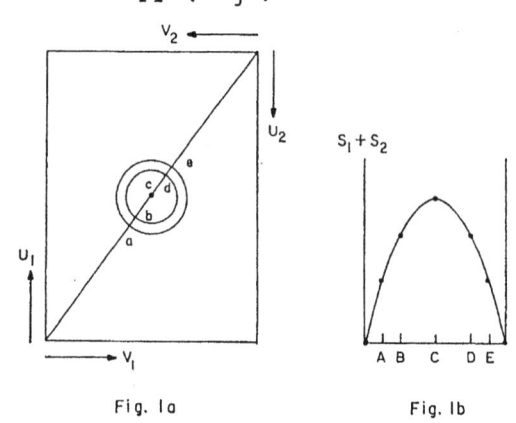

Fig. 1a

Fig. 1b

How Min-Energy Works Only for Thermostatics

The Max-Entropy conditions of (15) are seen to define a different final equilibrium from the following Min-Energy algorithm:

Subject to

$$\overline{V}_1+\overline{V}_2 = \hat{V}_1+\hat{V}_2 \tag{16a}$$

$$\overline{S}_1+\overline{S}_2 = \hat{S}_1+\hat{S}_2 \tag{16b}$$

$$\underset{V_j, S_j}{\text{Min}}\{U(V_1, S_1) + U(V_2, S_2)\} \qquad (16c)$$

$$= \hat{U}_1 + \hat{U}_2$$

This turns out to entail similar vanishings of Newtonian derivatives as before; after we eliminate the new Lagrange multipliers of this new problem, we do get (15d) and (15e), namely

$$-\hat{P} = U_V(\hat{V}_1, \hat{S}_1) = U_V(\hat{V}_2, \hat{S}_2) \qquad (16d)$$

$$\hat{T} = U_V(\hat{V}_2, \hat{S}_2) = U_V(\hat{V}_2, \hat{S}_2) \qquad (16e)$$

However, with the disagreement of the (15b) and (16b) relations, the systems (15a)-(15b)-(15d)-(15e) and (16a)-(16b)-(16d)-(16e) do differ and necessarily the deduced equilibria differ. Specifically,

$$S_1^* + S_2^* > \overline{S}_1 + \overline{S}_2 = \hat{S}_1 + \hat{S}_2 \qquad (17)$$

$$\hat{U}_1 + \hat{U}_2 < \overline{U}_1 + \overline{U}_2 = U_1^* + U_2^*$$

Dr. Brody's readers will realize that the alternative approaches cannot both correctly match Nature's true before-and-after scenario. But they and Gibbs's readers will also realize that where thermo*statics* is concerned, both approaches do lead to the identical (15d)-(15e) and (16d)-(16e). These last equilibrium relations are the only ones that are free of the initial condition's barred variables, and therefore they do correctly identify all of the $(V_1, S_1, U_1, -P_1, T_1; V_2, S_2, U_2, -P_2, T_2)$ states that would be self-perpetuating (which is the very notion of a thermostatic equilibrium!).

Non-convexity: Phase Transitions and Non-Local Maxima

Figure 1's simple story holds when isotherms in the *indicator diagram* of the (V,P) space are well-behaved monotonically falling. Gibbs was never one wantonly to break his silence: his 1873 paper was motivated to explain phase transitions 'twixt solid and liquid or liquid and gas. The U(V,S) surface Maxwell fabricated from Gibbs's recipe violated convexity so as to explain coexistence of ice and water at melting-point transitions.

Figure 2 plots on the (V,P) indicator diagram an isotherm that violates convexity of the U(V,S) surface. (It pictures what obtains for, say, H_2O near standard atmospheric temperature and in the range of a couple of degrees Celsius and below 0°C. To aid the reader's eye my curvilinear isotherm is drawn to consist of line-segments.)

The *isotherm abcdfghcde* has the anomalous rising branch of *fgh*, so that latitudes between *f* and *g* intersect it three times. Mother Nature, tolerating no local instabilities, in fact maximizes its total Entropy by replacing the anomalous isotherm with the "stable" *abcde* locus. Gibbs taught the delighted Maxwell that the *bc* freezing point, at which both the solid and liquid would coexist, had to come at the precise P level where the shaded triangular areas would be equal. Beyond C all is ice; before B all is water; 'twixt B and C both ice and water obtain, with just enough B-like molecules and C-like molecules to precisely fill the specified $\overline{V}_1 + \overline{V}_2$ total

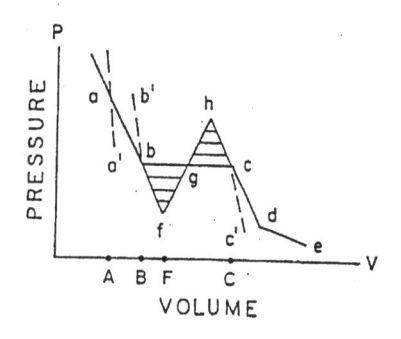

Fig. 2

volume. (A skilled experimenter can actually realize a "supercooled" liquid along the *bf* branch; but shaking or otherwise perturbing the equipment will destroy the globally unstable equilibrium in favor of the stable *bc* branch. The dashed loci--aa', bb', cc', ... represent the *adiabats*, steeper than the *isotherms* they touch in accordance with the LeChatelier principle of convexity.)

Hotelling economics varies the Gibbs story. For it, label the vertical axis p_1, and the horizontal axis x_1. Holding $(p_2,...)$ constant, the demand for x_1 will not be *abcde*. Rather will it be *ab* for p_1 above the *bc* level, and *cd* for p_1 below that level; at the critical level for competitive p_1 of *bc*, the end-points *b* and *c* will be indifferently tied, but the points between them will be avoided; the level at which the bifurcation takes place is determined by the same Gibbs-Maxwell rule of equal areas!

Qualifications

Dr. Brody is right to call attention to the fact that the techniques in mathematics useful to economists in the Debreu age involve inequalities like those pioneered by von Neumann (1928, 1945). It is appropriate to emphasize that Willard Gibbs himself peculiarly utilized inequalities. (I confine my remarks to his classical thermodynamics. His formulation of Newton-Lagrange dynamics in a manner reminiscent of Gauss's principle of least restraint is a related matter.)

Not for nothing am I the intellectual grandson of Gibbs (via his last protegé, E. B. Wilson, my Harvard master). Before the epoch of linear and concave programming and prior to the introduction of fixed-point theorems, my prewar explorations of revealed preference (Weak Axioms and such) dealt with $\Sigma \Delta p_j \Delta x_j$ and $\Sigma p_j \Delta x_j$ expressions that were in the Gibbsian mold.

My strategy was to take from thermodynamics not its dubious analogies of content but rather what it had to offer by way of common useful techniques of maximization and implied comparative statics. I have had to stress, and I take this occasion to reinforce the point, that there is no Energy whose magnitude is conserved in the universe of economics. There is no one Entropy total that gets maximized in the economic world. For profit-seeking firms and pleasure-pursuing consumers, a dollar *profit function* or a (ordinal) *utility* function has some of the properties that an Entropy function has for Clausius's domain.

Nicholas Georgescu-Roegen (1971) has sagely reminded us economists that the image of an hour glass (whose sands run out) may be a more appropriate logo than the image of a frictionless pendulum (whose equilibrium and conserved-energy is eternal). But the formalisms of Gibbs-Tisza thermodynamic potentials (and their Min-Min or Min-Max aspects) add naught to the Georgescu insight. As I wrote for the Yale 150th Birthday Convocation for Gibbs (Samuelson, 1990, p.266) eschewing the formalism of Equation (16) above, we capture in a simple way the fact that an economic equilibrium must run down if it depends indispensably on (say) a supply of copper, and if concentrated deposits of copper ore are finite and become exhausted in finite time. As soon as equilibrium displays *hysteresis dependence on the integral of all copper ever mined*, no steady state for Q* is possible at a positive level. Enough said.[1]

---

[1] For bibliographical reference, the formulation in (12b) and (13b) seems to be only implicit in the vast thermodynamic literature. What I have called Hotelling duality in (8) is actually borrowed from my 1960 homage to his *Festschrift*, and from my 1965 paper on "full duality." The new mathematics envisaged for economics by von Neumann involved, among other things, the topology of fixed points and all that. However, Gibbs's fruitful use of finite inequalities, which resembled my use of expressions like $\Sigma \Delta y_j \Delta x_j \leq 0$, (applicable to real variables or to integral variables), would have been justly deemed by him part of physics' "old mathematics."

References

Brody, A. 1989. "Economics and Thermodynamics," in M. Dore, S. Chakravarty, and R. Goodwin, eds., *John von Neumann and Modern Economics*. Oxford: Clarendon Press.

Champernowne, D. 1953. "Commentaries on J. Robinson on Capital," *Review of Economic Studies* 21, 107-35.

Court, L. 1941. "Invariable Classical Stability of Entrepreneurial Demand and Supply Functions," *Quarterly Journal of Economics* 55, 134-44.

Georgescu-Roegen, N. 1971. *The Entropy Law and the Economic Process*. Cambridge, Massachusetts: Harvard University Press.

Gibbs, J.W. 1873, 1873, 1876-78. Thermodynamics papers in *The Collected Works of J. Willard Gibbs*, Volume I. New Haven, Conn.: Yale University Press.

Hotelling, H. 1932. "Edgeworth's Taxation Paradox and the Nature of Demand and Supply Functions," *Journal of Political Economy* 40, 577-616.

von Neumann, J. 1928. "Zur Theorie der Gesellschaftsspiele", *Math. Annalen*, 100, 295-320.

_____. 1945. "A Model of General Equilibrium," *Review of Economic Studies* 13, 1-9.

Roy, R. 1942. "De l'Utilité, Contribution à la Theorie des Choix." Paris: Hermann.

Samuelson, P. 1947 and 1983. *Foundations of Economic Analysis*. Cambridge, Mass.: Harvard University Press.

_____. 1938. "A Note on the Pure Theory of Consumer's Behavior," *Economica*, N.S. 5, 61-71.

_____. 1953. "Prices of Factors and Goods in General Equilibrium," *Review of Economic Studies* 21, 1-20.

_____. 1960. "Structure of a Minimum System," in R. Pfouts, ed., *Essays in Honor of Harold Hotelling*. Chapel Hill: University of North Carolina Press.

_____. 1962. "Parable and Realism in Capital Theory," *Review of Economic Studies* 29, 193-206, particularly Appendix.

_____. 1965. "Using Full Duality to Show That Simultaneously Additive Direct and Indirect Utilities Implies Unitary Price Elasticity of Demand", *Econometrica* 33, 781-96.

_____. 1972. "Unification Theorem for the Two Basic Dualities of Homothetic Demand Theory," *Proceedings of the National Academy of Science, USA* 69, 2673-74.

_____. 1990. "Gibbs in Economics" in D. G. Caldi and G. D. Mostow, eds., *Proceedings of the Gibbs Symposium, Yale University 1989*. Providence, Rhode Island: American Mathematical Society and American Institute of Physics, 255-68.

Shephard, R. 1953. *Cost and Production Functions*. Princeton, N.J.: Princeton University Press.

ern Economics 1(1), 1-9, 1992

Factor-Price Equalization by Trade in Joint and Non-Joint Production

Paul A. Samuelson

Massachusetts Institute of Technology, Cambridge, MA 02139

Abstract

Sans joint products, relative factor prices do determine relative goods prices. Free trade in goods thus can hope to equalize factor returns when this relationship is monotone and therefore uniquely reversible. However, when joint production obtains, often the same relative factor prices can entail an infinity of relative goods prices depending upon the composition of tastes and demand. In consequence, trade's equalization of goods prices is compatible with factor-returns inequality. Generic and singular relationships are described.

1. Introduction

At the Fiftieth Anniversary of the Stolper-Samuelson Theorem Colloquium (1991) in Ann Arbor, I made the remark that when technology admits of the slightest amount of joint production, the factor-price equalization deduction will be spoiled even for regions that hardly differ in factor endowments—a marked contrast with the no-joint products case where *generically* factor-price equalization will occur. This caused some raised eyebrows. Not for the first time, Ronald Jones asked for explication.

The present purpose is to ruminate on some of the trade issues raised by jointness of production, issues hardly addressed in Samuelson (1948, 1949, 1953, 1962). My exposition will be heuristic and less than exhaustive. Mostly I shall be rehashing what is familiar in the intermediate textbooks.

2. No-Joint Products

Cases where wool and mutton or gasoline and heating oil are produced at the same time were discussed by Smith (1776), Longfield (1834), Mangoldt (1863), Marshall (1890), Sraffa (1960), and von Neumann (1945). Most well understood that changes in relative demands for the various by-products could generally alter their price ratios even when factor inputs and firm cost outlays were not changing. By contrast, single-product competitive firms had their goods prices more closely linked to factor prices. The Heckscher (1919), Ohlin (1933), Lerner (1952), and Samuelson (1948, 1972) insights into factor-price equalization from trade in goods came, essentially, from the perception that the goods-price and factor-price interrelation was a two-way transformation: besides the easy and generic factor-to-goods relation, $W \to P$, there was a more subtle inverse (local) relation, $P \to W$. Since idealized interregional trade equalized competitive P_i/P_j ratios, under interesting conditions this meant that trade would equalize W_r/W_s factor-price ratios; and thereby equalize, between regions with the same technical knowledge and not too disparate factor endowments, *all* W_s/P_j real returns!

A few axioms simplify the discourse. Constant-returns-to-scale technologies are to be instantaneous (time-free) and regionally uniform. Transport costs are zero for goods. Initially two factors (labor, L, and land, T) produce two goods (clothing, Q_1, and food, Q_2). To obviate demand complications, consumers everywhere have the *same homothetic* tastes (unitary income elasticities and common expenditure allocations in each price configuration). Until stage directions are given for factor mobility, total regional factor supplies are specified parameters. Perfect competition prevails.

3. Cases of Perfect Equalization

Under autarky, the region with relatively high endowment in the labor-intensive good, Q_1, will display the lower P_1/P_2 ratio and the higher production and consumption of clothing. If both regions are identical in $(L_1 + L_2)/(T_1 + T_2)$ endowments, a *singular* or nongeneric coincidence that can be expected to occur only on a set of L/T coefficients "of measure zero," autarky will fortuitously result in the same price ratio, same $(L_1/T_1, L_2/T_2)$ ratios, and same real factor returns $(W/P_j, R/P_j)$. Sans trade, world output (measured in the homothetics-tastes' real dollars-worth market basket of goods) would then fortuitously be already at the maximum that world factor endowments can produce, and no factor mobility or goods trade could serve a useful purpose in raising *world productivity* or altering *wage-rent shares anywhere*.[1]

One way to understand factor-price equalization by trade is to begin with regions A and B of exactly alike endowment intensity and implied fortuitous factor-price equalization under autarky. Now move some L from A to B, raising B's L/T endowment a bit above A's. Then trade alone, *sans* factor mobility, can generically raise world productivity fully as much as would migration of labor back from the land-sparse to the land-abundant region.

Theorem: *For small enough endowment disparities*, generically *trade alone can completely achieve all the welfare efficiencies of free migration; under free trade and free migration, labor will not move all the way to achieving geographical endowment uniformity; before that state is reached, the wage disparity needed to motivate further migrations will have sunk to zero.*[2]

All of the above about *perfect* factor-price equalization is known to hold for the no-joint-production world.

4. Incomplete Equalization

Now I leave perfect factor-price equalization for the vaguer case where trade in non-joint goods tends "qualitatively" to *lessen* divergences in factor prices stemming from *appreciable* Heckscher-Ohlin endowment disparities. In the two-good, two-factor case, let more and more of A's labor be initially settled in B. Then the autarky real wage (in *both* goods!) in A rises and rises, while in B's autarky it falls; for land rent the opposite happens.

Theorem: *Beyond some critical L/T endowment discrepancy, generically A will specialize completely in food (the land/intensive good) and B in clothing (the labor/ intensive good). Goods trade can no longer wipe out* all *of B's inferiority in real wage and A's inferiority in real rent. But trade will have* reduced *the factor-price discrepancies of autarky, as each region's specialization on the good using its*

493

abundant factor most does ameliorate the initial cheapness of that supra-abundant factor. Thus, when the goods differ uniformly in technical factor intensity, goods trade achieves some, but not all, of the potential improvement in world productivity that only factor mobility can achieve.

All of the above arguments rest upon the premise that factor intensities of the goods never interchange. What difference will reversals of factor intensities make?

5. Qualification: Factor Intensity Reversals

Figure 1, adapted from Samuelson (1949, p. 188), provides a definitive summary of the effect of goods trade on factor-price equalization in the two-by-two case.[3] At first the reader should concentrate on the top half of the graphs where clothing is labor-intensive and food is land-intensive: the graph duplicates my earlier literary findings.

Land-rich Region A has low autarky P_F/P_C ratio shown at a. Labor-rich B has slightly higher autarky P_F/P_C ratio at b. Under free trade these nearly alike regions still produce both goods; but A now exports food and B exports clothing, raising P_F/P_C in A and lowering P_F/P_C in B, as shown at the common intermediate equilibrium point e^*. A's high initial wage/rent at α drops to the common point ε^* of factor-price equalization; contrariwise, B's low W/R rises from β to the intermediate ε^*.

Region D, which is considerably more labor-rich than B (and A), does also have its W/R ratio raised by the free trade in goods—but its drop of P_F/P_C from d to e^* forces it to specialize only on clothing, and that prevents trade from *fully* equalizing its wage return up to the common level elsewhere: its post-trade δ^* is seen to fail to reach the common ε^* of the others; and, specializing only on clothing, it finds the FF curve becomes irrelevant for it. (The reader can pencil in above a a region with so little labor that, in free trade, it can afford only to produce food along FF, so that in consequence its high autarky W/R fails to drop all the way to ε^*.)

Now the reader can contemplate the lower half of the graphs, which portray a *reversal* of the labor/land intensities of the goods food and clothing. Note that FF is inside of CC only at the top; at the low W/R ratios of the bottom, it is CC that is inside FF! Along RR in the middle, the goods have essentially the *same* production functions. That is why the direction of a rise in P_F/P_C with a fall in W/R at top (along rdbe*a) reverses itself below the switch-points of RR (within which the price *ratio* is independent of *relative* factor prices).

For simplicity, let's suppose that free trade leads to the same e^* price ratio, whether we pool *all* the regions or deal only with the regions in each half of the diagram. Suppose Z, Y, and X had been the only regions in the world. The reader can trace in the bottom half the same story already told for the top half—but with roles reversed, so that clothing is the *land*-intensive good. Free trade again equalizes factor returns for the two regions, Z and Y, which are close enough together in endowment; but it goes only part way toward reducing in X the factor return of its abundant factor; X can succeed in using up all its endowment of its abundant factor (land) only by *specializing completely* along CC on the good which utilizes that factor most. And then for it no longer is there a $W \to P$ *vectoral* relation and no longer a *vectoral* (local) $P \to W$ relation.

With intensity reversal in the scenario, does free trade equalize returns for *all* regions that produce *both* goods? No, trade creates clusters of regions with equalized

4   Paul A. Samuelson

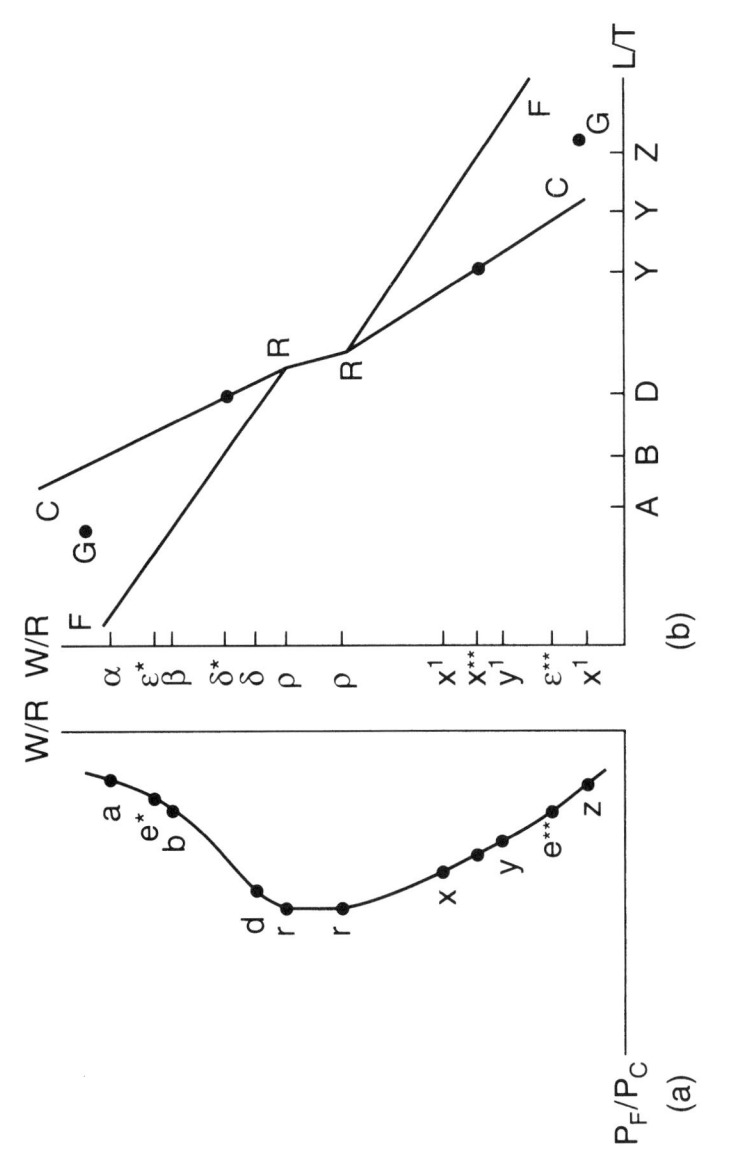

Figure 1. Goods Price Ratios and Factors Price Ratios

returns *within* a cluster, but with divergences *between* the clusters of *altered* factor intensities! The inverse, $P \to W$ relation is bifurcated when factor intensities are not axiomatized to be uniform and unchangeable.

The reader can explore the further case where only the two regions of A and Y exist, each from a different intensity regimen. What does the free-trade price ratio at e^* do to their ultra-divergent autarky factor returns when they are in *opposite* domains of factor intensity? Trade does not operate to move them to or toward a common W/R level. In Figure 1, *both* A and Y are seen to experience a *fall* in their W/R levels. Who can say whether their divergence has been attenuated at all![4]

According to Homeric legend one should never rehash an old story without improving on it. Here is a slight 1992 extension of 1949's Figure 1 to take account of the uniform-homothetic-demand axiom. Given those tastes, all regions with the same L/T endowment will have in autarky the same determinate factor-prices and goods-prices ratio. (This truth holds even when there are one or more domestic goods. *A fortiori* it holds for any number of goods in excess of two.) The reader can connect to the respective R points in 1(b) the points under the upper and lower letters G. This will give the new GRRG locus, which summarizes that autarky relationship.

If regions differed in tastes as well as in labor/land endowments, Figure 1's orderly relations between $a \geq b \geq \ldots$ and $A \leq B \leq \ldots$ could not be guaranteed. In other words, in the background to Figure 1 I already had used the GRRG locus.

Note that our diagrams depend by construction only on L/T *ratios* and not on absolute (L, T) magnitudes. Therefore, even if one specified uniform homothetic demand, one cannot hope to predict from this diagram alone where between two autarky P_F/P_C ratios the free-trade ratio will fall. Thus, if A's absolute endowments of (L, T) were very large compared to B's, the free-trade $(P_F/P_C)^*$ would be close to A's autarky price ratio. And, of course, if B were absolutely large relative to A, free trade would have to be near B's autarky pricing. It follows that homothetic tastes cannot narrow down the maximum endowment disparities that two regions can have and still come into factor-price equalization. The Samuelson (1948, Figure 2, p. 173) "L-shaped limits" still generally apply to indicate where factor-return equalization must be at best incomplete.

Having now completed the non-joint-products analysis, I turn to the contrasting case of joint production.

6. Joint Products: A Simple Counter Example

Suppose labor and land produce an intermediate stuff that can be transformed alternatively into (much gasoline, little kerosene) or (little gasoline, much kerosene). The archetype of this is the ("self-dual" and symmetric) neoclassical example of joint production.

$$\left[\frac{1}{2}(Q_1)^2 + \frac{1}{2}(Q_2)^2\right]^{1/2} = [\text{labor} \times \text{land}]^{1/2} = [LT]^{1/2} \quad (1)$$

Now, *sans* demand, we cannot infer from knowledge of W/R anything about what P_2/P_1 must be. And reciprocally, it is crucial for failure of factor-price equalization (absolute or partial) that we can infer nothing about W/R from knowledge of P_2/P_1!

Readers can substitute for the above technology a case of less symmetry, where the coefficients of $(Q_1)^2$ and $(Q_2)^2$ differ. Also, they can eschew smoothly differentiable neoclassical technology so that (à la Sraffa) only a few activities are possible rather than an infinity of them.

I do not mean to contend that *never* under joint products can there be mandatory exact factor-price equalization by trade. My point is that the *universal* theorem can no longer be maintained.

I conjecture that Ronald Jones and others may have the following kind of scenario in mind. Along with (1), posit joint-product technologies that replace $(LT)^{1/2}$ with $L^{1/4} T^{3/4}$ and $L^{2/3} T^{1/3}$. Then, if A has less L/T endowment than B does, A will move to use $L^{1/4} T^{3/4}$ and B will economize on its scarce factor of land by going to $L^{3/4} T^{1/4}$. Then at the least there will be a tendency under such joint production toward factor-price similarity (and even by coincidence or homotheticity, exact equalization).

Study of the special example of equation (1) will show that it involves essentially production by land and labor of a *single* intermediate product, which later produces joint products. When joint production happens to be singularly decomposable into single products (or, more robustly, can be envisaged as "close to" such singular cases), then all the single-product presumptions can be given their best chances. That I cheerfully concede.

However, my reason for expecting joint production *generically* to void the $P_2/P_1 \to W/R$ exactitude that *exact* factor-price equalization depends on goes back to Samuelson (1966), entitled "The Fundamental Singularity Theorem for Non-joint Production."

For brevity I can stick to the neoclassical case of unlimited activities, leaving the reader to work out the von Neumann-Sraffa equivalent. The *generic* two-by-two *production-possibility frontier* becomes

clothing = F(labor, land; food)

$$Q_1 = F(V_1, V_2; Q_2): \text{concave, first-degree homogeneous} \quad (2)$$

$$\text{wage} = W_1/P_1 = \partial F(V_1, V_2; Q_2)/\partial V_1 = F_1(V_1, V_2; Q_2) \quad (3)$$

$$\text{rent} = R/P_1 = \partial F(V_1, V_2; Q_2)/\partial V_2 = F_2(V_1, V_2; Q_2) \quad (4)$$

$$P_2/P_1 = -\partial F(V_1, V_2; Q_2)/\partial Q_2 = -F_3(V_1, V_2; Q_2), \text{ if } Q_i > 0;$$
$$\leq -F_3(V_1, V_2; Q_2) \text{ if } Q_2 = 0; \text{ and}$$
$$\geq -F_3(V_1, V_2; Q_2), \text{ if } Q_1 = 0 \quad (5)$$

Now my mathematical point is that *generically*, when joint production is not ruled out, there is no one-to-one $P_2/P_1 \to W_2/W_1$ relation such as is required for *exact* factor-price equalization (by goods trade alone between A and B regions with near endowments). Generically, there will not be the requisite straight-line rulings on (2)'s surface!

The non-joint products case has special features; and it holds, if and only if, crucial Jacobian expression(s) vanish. See Samuelson (1966, pp. 36–39ff) for rank restrictions on the 3×3 matrix $[F_{ij}(V_1, V_2; Q_3)]$ under single-good production. *Generically*, the degeneracy of rank needed for factor-price equalization is not to be expected.

Fortunately, I can be more guarded in my contentions about what a little bit of jointness of production does to the *robustness* of *partial* factor-price equalization from trade.

Theorem: *If a joint-production technology is not too different from a one-product scenario that does mandate a partial regional equalization of factor returns from goods trade alone, then this small degree of jointness in production need not emasculate the* partial *equalization effect.*

7. Conclusion

One should question the Heckscher-Ohlin presumption that real world trade is best understood in terms of a maintained convention that production functions in every region may be deemed uniform. Such a convention can bias the analysis, as when an Ohlin disciple attributes the low African productivity to the scarcity there of the vague variable "knowledge"—as if that were analytically similar to a scarcity of oil in Sweden.

Fortunately, however, the tendency of goods trade to compensate somewhat for endowments discrepancy, which is an exact theorem in the Heckscher-Ohlin paradigm, may possess robustness for less clear-cut world scenarios in which regional production functions are not too different.

Pure-theory models may be rarely *generic* in the exact mathematician's sense. But that does not mean that they must (or do) lack robustness for real-world insights. A seminal theory is singularly simple but serendipitously robust in illuminating a wide and important array of facts.

Notes

1. Remark: If food and clothing had the same land/labor "intensities" everywhere, that would also be a singular, nongeneric case, one of measure zero. Then autarky and free trade would have the same equilibrium price ratios, and zero (essential) trade would be mandated. Then the least bit of regional endowment disparity would create differences in real factor returns that could not be touched by goods trade. If the food and clothing production functions are "almost alike," the ability of free trade will be limited to substitute for labor mobility in modifying endowment disparities, in raising effective world productivity, and in attenuating factor-return differences. Nearly alike clothing and food factor intensities will tend to shrink the endowment disparities that can coexist with post-trade factor-price equalization.
2. The theorem can be validly extended to the case of more than two goods. We can go beyond the two-by-two case. Consider n goods and m factors, $m = 2 \leq n$, and still the theorem will hold. We can also let there be more than two factors, permitting $2 \leq m \leq n$. Begin with like factor endowments, $(V_2/V_1, \ldots, V_m/V_1)$ in A and B. Their common autarky $(P_i/P_1, V_{ji}/V_{1i})$ ratios will be unaltered by free trade, and real factor returns are geographically equal both before and after (zero!) trade. Now alter a bit the (V_j/V_1) endowment vector of B as compared to A by specifying that some subset of A's endowment vector had been resettled in B. Then, *generically*, trade alone can undo the small factor-price inequalities and world inefficiencies your perturbation had created for autarky. That is a sweeping n-by-m theorem that holds both before and after trade under uniform homothetic tastes.

If two regions differ only minutely in endowments and still each produces two freely traded goods, then generically their W/R ratios will be equal. If their separate non-traded goods face the same W/R ratio, their prices relative to the traded goods must be the same. Therefore, existence of non-traded goods does not alter the results that hold when all goods are freely tradeable.

3. Harry Johnson (1958, pp. 9, 18) first attributed this diagram to 1957 Roy Harrod. After various readers pointed out to him its 1949 origin, he made corrections in the Japanese translation of his works but forgot to alter his 1961 reprinting. Many of the genuine and

generic complexities addressed by Johnson (1958) fall away in the nongeneric world of uniform homothetic demand. Thus, in this latter case the two Johnson definitions become one: where a factor is defined to be relatively scarce in A as measured (1) by relative L/T *endowments* in A or B, or (2) by relative autarky factor-prices, W/R. See Figure 1 here for more on this.

4. Note on the vertical axis of 1b that the lower downward move of $y'\varepsilon^{**}$ actually happens to *exceed* in length the downward move from α and ε^*! But using the metric of W/R is arbitrary for meaningfully comparing pre- and post-trade factor returns by region. Why not use R/W, which could tell a different numerical story? Or use W/P_F? Or W/P_C? Or R/P_F? or R/P_C?

Remark: I believe there is a sense in which I can prove that free trade does diminish factor-return divergences for regions like A and Z that belong to reversed domains. *World aggregate output* (measured unambiguously in the homothetic-demand case by the real-dollar's-value market basket) is at a maximum for specified regional factor endowments *only* when real factor returns are perfectly equalized. For regions so far apart as A and Z, that perfection cannot be achieved by goods trade, *sans* some factor migration. Still I believe it is a general theorem—as in Samuelson (1962)—that free trade is Pareto-optimal compared to *autarky* in the sense that world output can but go up and thereby improve people's *potential* utility. This suggests that I propose as a device to define which of two configurations involves the lesser of "factor-returns divergence" the following: Configuration I has *more divergence* that II does if it yields *lower* world output. Then it is a theorem: Trade generically does lower factor-price divergence regardless of intensity reversals. QED. Warning: this new proposed measure of numerical factor-returns divergence is not calculable from these diagrams about *relative* variables. To calculate maximal world output we do need to know *absolute* (L, T) magnitudes. Also, remember that a single scalar measure of "world output" is possible only for the nongeneric case of uniform homothetic demand, save nontradeable goods.

Afterthought: Johnson (1958, pp. 27–28) has shown how free trade can widen numerical differences between the (W/F)s of two regions whose (L/T)s differ so much that there are two intersections of 1(b)'s curves on the interval between them. This worries me about my theorem. For, if it is valid, it implies that factor returns on one definition definitely diverge and on my new definition do at the same time definitely converge. My nose suspects the new!

References

Caves, Richard E., *Trade and Economic Structure*, Cambridge, Mass.: Harvard University Press, 1958.

Caves, Richard E. and Ronald W. Jones, *World Trade and Payments: An Introduction*, Boston: Little, Brown and Company, 1973.

Harrod, Roy, "Factor-Price Relations under Free Trade," *Economic Journal* 68 (1958):245–55. This recapitulates a 1957 Harrod lecture heard by Johnson.

Heckscher, Eli, "The effect of foreign trade on the distribution of income" in *Readings in the Theory of International Trade*. Selected by a committee of the American Economic Association. Philadelphia and Toronto: The Blakiston Company, 1950. Translated from *Ekonomisk Tidskrift*, University of Stockholm, 1919. For a new, unabridged translation see Flam, Harry and M. June Flanders, *Heckscher-Ohlin Trade Theory*, Cambridge, Mass.: MIT Press, 1991.

Johnson, Harry G., *International Trade and Economic Growth; Studies in Pure Theory*, London: Allen & Unwin, 1958.

Lerner, Abba P., "Factor prices and international trade," *Economica New Series* 19 (1952):1–15.

Longfield, Mountifort, "Lectures on Political Economy," first published in 1834, in R. D. Collison Black (ed.), *The Economic Writings of Mountifort Longfield*. New York: Augustus M. Kelley, 1971.

Mangoldt, H. von, *Grundriss der Volkswirtschaftslehre*, Stuttgart: Gustav Fischer, 1863.

Marshall, A., *Principles of Economics*, first published 1890, reprint of the eighth edition, London and Basingstoke: Macmillan, 1920.

Ohlin, Bertil, *Interregional and International Trade*, Cambridge, Mass.: Harvard University Press, 1933.

Samuelson, Paul A., "International trade and the equalisation of factor prices," *Economic Journal* 58 (1948):163–84.

———, "International factor-price equalisation once again," *Economic Journal* 59 (1949):181–97.

———, "Prices of factors and goods in general equilibrium," *Review of Economic Studies* 21 (1953):1–20.

———, "The gains from international trade once again," *The Economic Journal* 72 (1962):820–29. Reproduced as Chapter 62 in *The Collected Scientific Papers of Paul A. Samuelson*, Volume 2, Cambridge, Mass.: MIT Press, 1966.

———, "The fundamental singularity theorem for non-joint production," *International Economic Review* 7 (1966):34–41. Reproduced as Chapter 145 in *The Collected Scientific Papers of Paul A. Samuelson*, Volume 3, Cambridge, Mass.: MIT Press, 1972.

———, "Summary on factor-price equalization," *The Collected Scientific Papers of Paul A. Samuelson*, Chapter 161, Volume 3, Cambridge, Mass.: MIT Press, 1972.

———, (forthcoming) "Tribute to Wolfgang Stolper on the Fiftieth Anniversary of the Stolper-Samuelson Theorem." Speech delivered at Stolper and Samuelson Symposium, "Protection and Real Wages": A Golden Jubilee, University of Michigan, Ann Arbor, November 15, 1991. To be published in *Studies in International Trade Policy*, Ann Arbor: University of Michigan Press, 1992.

Smith, Adam, *An Inquiry into the Nature and Causes of the Wealth of Nations*, 1776, E. Cannan (ed.), New York: Modern Library, 1937.

Sraffa, Piero, *Production of Commodities by Means of Commodities*, Cambridge: Cambridge University Press, 1960.

von Neumann, John, "A model of general economic equilibrium", *Review of Economic Studies* 13 (1945):1–9.

THE ECONOMICS OF ALTRUISM[†]

Altruism as a Problem Involving Group versus Individual Selection in Economics and Biology

By PAUL A. SAMUELSON*

Heroes who help others will eliminate themselves in doing so, and their strains will tend to die out in the population. Contrariwise the DNA of selfish cads, who look out for themselves and elbow others away from nubile mates, will tend to proliferate at the expense of the altruists' DNA. All this will transpire even in situations where populations-*cum*-altruism can compete to extinction populations-*sans*-altruism.

I. Economists' Uneasiness with Altruism

Charles Darwin had already puzzled out this tendency for altruism to go extinct under the scenario of *individual* natural selection. Economists understand the paradox. The first pages of our elementary textbooks teach the *fallacy of composition*: what is best for each separately need not (on that account) be best or even good for *all*. Old hat to us was game theorists' *prisoner's dilemma*—in which each crook thinks to gain a light sentence by being the (sole) informer, but in which all will get the greatest punishment as a result.

Mesmerized by *Homo economicus*, who acts solely on egoism, economists shy away from altruism almost comically. Caught in a shameful act of heroism, they aver: "Shucks, it was only enlightened self interest." Sometimes it is. At other times it may be only rationalization (spurious for card-carrying atheists): "If I rescue somebody's son, someone will rescue mine."

I will not waste ink on face-saving tautologies. When the governess of infants caught in a burning building reenters it unobserved in a hopeless mission of rescue, casuists may argue; "She did it only to get the good feeling of doing it. Because otherwise she wouldn't have done it." Such argumentation (in Wolfgang Pauli's scathing phrase) *is not even wrong*. It is just boring, irrelevant, and in the technical sense of old-fashioned logical positivism "meaningless." You do not understand the logic and history of consumer demand theory—Pareto, W. E. Johnson, Slutsky, Allen-Hicks, Hotelling, Samuelson, Houthakker,...—if you think that is its content.

II. Hamiltonian "Inclusive Fitness" to the Rescue for Darwinists

Biological writers on individual natural selection, for clear thinking, had to purge from their expositions the teleology of Lamarckianism: giraffes' necks did not lengthen because their parents had to reach up in grazing. Similarly, biologists had to and purge away teleological explanations of altruism as needing to evolve lest the species become extinct.

Therefore, it was with some relief that the neo-Darwinian synthesis could appeal to kin selection and "inclusive fitness" as a basis for viable altruism in *individual* natural selection. Already, Darwin understood that the natural mother who perishes to save a child, or slaves to rear it, is exercising altruism of a kind that does have survival value in a competition between different genotypes *within* a species. *Her* kind of genes thereby proliferate. Sharpening the point quantitatively, J. B. S. Haldane said

---

[†]*Discussants:* Jack Hirshleifer, University of California-Los Angeles; Gary S. Becker, University of Chicago; Julio J. Rotemberg, Massachusetts Institute of Technology.

*Institute Professor Emeritus, Department of Economics, Massachusetts Institute of Technology, E52-383C, 50 Memorial Drive, Cambridge, MA 02139.

decades ago: "I will not die for a stranger or even for one brother. But I will for two brothers or eight cousins." In this paraphrased syllogism, he neither jokes nor requires that animals in the jungle must master the Mendelian algebra of particulate inheritance in order to behave correctly. His point is that those genetic strains whose mutations have preprogrammed them to behave in this specified way will eventually out-compete those strains lacking such mutations. W. D. Hamilton (1964) elevated a casual insight into the working doctrine of *inclusive fitness*. Cute ideas carry weight in science, but their impact is enormously amplified when combined with important facts. Hamilton's triumph was to elucidate why insect colonies can be expected to display the incredible cooperation that occurs among queen, drones, and others of the collective. Subject to haploid rather than diploid inheritance, fellow workers in the hive are much more closely related than are Prince Charles and Prince Andrew. Evolution toward altruistic cooperation is more powerful among wasps than among Windsors! No one need go through the Haldane soliloquy. Differentiable survivability creates the observable pattern, which is much like what would result from a consciously maximizing regimen. The teleology is only an "as if" teleology.

III. "Sexual Selection" versus Natural Selection

The issue of altruism is but one of many issues that can involve a conflict 'twixt *group* and *individual* fitness, and actually altruism gets more discussion than it deserves. In the *Origin of Species*, Darwin had carefully eschewed discussing man's role in evolution. Later he came out of the closet to discuss *The Descent of Man, and Selection in Relation to Sex*. Much of its wordage is concerned not so much with human evolution as with a variant to "natural selection" referred to as "sexual selection." The former concept had been to Darwin the familiar process where a more fit strain competes with a less fit strain and proliferates in the species to its own benefit *and* to the benefit of the species in its competition with other species. Sexual selection, by contrast, describes cases in which male birds evolve to have ever more elaborate tails, which may serve no functional use and indeed may degenerate into dysfunctional baggage; yet this odd process can even accelerate if females for whatever reason are preprogrammed to exercise mating choice toward ever-bigger tails.

Evidently Darwin regarded sexual selection as kind of a pejorative alternative to good old natural selection. In the latter, survival of the fittest was envisaged to possess a vague truth beyond mere "survival of the survivors." By contrast there is something perverse and pathological about sexual selection, in which what makes for *individual* fitness in the sense of differential survivability of genotypes within the species can be definitely conducive to *group* unfitness. Those tails thus can grow indefinitely until they cause the species to be rare or go extinct.

Orthodox biologists are like orthodox economists. When confronted by tensions between their paradigms and reality, they work to explain away the aberrations. Hence, there is a cottage industry in the writing of articles demonstrating that those long tails are useful; or that they are surrogates and markers for special fitness, so that he who can grow the longer tail is presumptively the bridegroom with the genes to produce more viable and numerous offspring. Sometimes the explanations are fitted retrospectively to the facts observed. Sometimes experimenters can glue longer tails on to control birds and observe whether this suffices to achieve extra popularity with choosy mates. Sometimes empirical observations can test whether the rationalizations lack objective merit.

IV. Lack of Coincidence of Group and Individual Fitness

The bottom line is that we face a hierarchy of levels of competition (and cooperation), and there is no a priori presumption that what conduces to victory at one level also conduces at another. Economists understand that much self-regarding behavior is socially harmful and that this lack of congruence is not a freak of rare paradox. In mathematical jargon, lack of congruence is *generic* and can "almost always" be expected to obtain in some degree. Coincidence of congruence is *singular*, lacking in "structural stability," and occurs for numerical parameters "of measure zero" in the space of possible parameters. Analogy in economics: constant returns to scale *sans* externality *cum* perfect competition singularly entails Pareto optimality of prices.

To illustrate, R. A. Fisher (1930 p. 141) beautifully deduced a tendency for there to be an equal number of male and female conceptions. His neat argument rests only on the fact that each generation has exactly the same number of mothers and fathers—exactly one of each per child.

It is a well-known fact that, in humans, the male force of mortality exceeds that for females at each age. Hence, the basic Fisher result of a balanced sex ratio at birth entails that individual selection makes for an *unbalanced* sex ratio at procreation ages. Such a result can reduce net fertility and group fitness. What is a different point, in species where redundant males are little but attractive nuisances, the Fisher mechanism prevents the species from attaining the optimal excess of females to males at ages of procreation. Again, what is optimal for group selection is not striven for in individual selection.

R. A. Fisher (1930) asserted his Napoleonic Fundamental Theorem of Natural Selection, which he modestly ranks with the Second Law of Thermodynamics. Fisher defines fitness as a specified species' realized rate of exponential growth. Fisher's theorem asserts that the proportions of different genotypes in the population—of AA's, aa's, and Aa's—must evolve so as to increase the species' rate of Malthusian growth, until variance of genotypes' fitness is reduced to zero and growth is maximal. Fisher's exposition is Delphic, but a reader can be forgiven for concluding that selection is evidently a *good* thing. I show elsewhere (1993) that, when you master the fine print, Fisher is seen to understand the Malthusian point that every species is constrained by the environment's limits and by competition with other species so as to have its ultimate growth rate go to zero rather than grow to a maximized positive value!

Darwin's evolution is indeed mere sound and fury, signifying nothing normative, rather than denoting a process of meaningful Spencerian triumph. Natural selection is not an empty tautology about survival of those who survive. It is a lawful process subject to shrewd predictions and testable refutations. But in general it does not act to maximize *any* scalar magnitude. Many of its subprocesses do eschew submaximal configurations, and some may approximate efficiency criteria, but the resultant of them all is only positivistic!

Sophisticated economists should be prepared for such an interpretation. Actual economic history departs from any definable geodesic. Wars, recessions, and party competitions remind us that life is not even Pareto-optimal—although some mutually advantageous transactions do get made.

Social Darwinism is a perverted borrowing from what can be validly established for biology. When I contemplate strong claims by a Richard Posner that law has evolved historically à la Pareto, or arguments that a Coase Theorem ensures that deadweight loss is at its feasible minimum, I fear that von Neumann and Morgenstern are spinning in their graves and Charles Darwin is wondering why he left his barnacles, pigeons, and earthworms.

An unsupported claim by an economist-Darwinist does not acquire validity from a cited analogy with evolution. Truth must find its own legs to stand on.

I must reiterate my 1985 AEA Convention warning on the important differences between genetic processes and economic or sociological processes. An economist writing on how a bear should hibernate works out why sleeping is more efficient than foraging when snow is deep.... He may find in a book the optimal properties of a bear or work them out. If it is a robot bear, he can imitate a Japanese model. Market competition may then eliminate in short time "less fit" robot bears. In genetics there is no thought, no linear programming, no imitation. The real bear, by trial and differential survivability over the generations, may come to resemble the computed-optimal bear, but it will be the last to know this. If genetic mutation of DNA is not serendipitously occurring, the evolved bear can well remain in a stable way far from the programmer's feasible best.

From this biological viewpoint, economists' discussions can be too cerebral. Thus, in repeated-game theory, the one-time Nash solution (in which both crooks tattle on each other), may perhaps be deduced to give way to the cooperative solution. In genetics, if the Nash solution holds once, it will hold forever in the absence of special mutation. There is no Lamarckian learning. (Does this contradict the first two-sister case of Theodore Bergstrom and Oded Stark's (1993) paper at this session? No. They *deduce* that natural selection will lead to cooperating sisters outnumbering defecting sisters. Note that this specific case is a version of strong kin selection where panmixia assumptions are irrelevant and where there happens to be no clash between individual Mendelian selection and altruism.)

V. Climax

Agree that I have demonstrated conclusively how selection (or "competition") at one stage can act independently of selection at another stage. Alas, poor Herbert Spencer. Genetic adaptation might work at cross purposes to species adaptation.

Now I want to demonstrate why group-adverse effects of individual selection, whatever their likelihood of occurrence, are biased to be unlikely of persistence by the actions of group selection.

Space does not permit explication of the mathematical rigor of the argument. For the record, here is a terse sufficient model. We have two or more species: $j = 1, \ldots, J \geq 2$. Each species has subpopulations of more than one genotype: $(X_{ij}) = (X_{1j} \ldots X_{Ij})$, where $I > 1$. The total population of any species will grow exponentially à la Malthus when environmental resources are amply redundant. The law of diminishing returns sets in when $X_j = \Sigma_1^I X_{ij}$ becomes appreciable, and a logistic S-shaped curve of growth occurs. When the species are similar, their summed population acts to swell each one's death rates. In the special model I call a Verhulst-Gause coupled logistic, one of the like species generally drives the others extinct: that is a deducible theorem of "competitive exclusion."

Add to this ecology the usual Mendel-Fisher-Haldane-Wright dynamics of particulate inheritance. For drama and simplicity, let Fisher's "fitness" grow autonomously while resources are redundant. We then have the simplest Verhulst-Gause paradigm for $[dX_j/dt, dX_{ij}/dt] = [\dot{X}_j, \dot{X}_{ij}]$, $j = 1, \ldots, J$,

(1a) $\dot{X}_j/X_j = r_j(X_{1j}, \ldots, X_{Ij})$

$$- \sum_{s=1}^{J} X_s / K_j(X_{1j}, \ldots, X_{Ij})$$

(1b) $\dot{X}_{ij}/X_{ij} = \partial r_j(X_{1j}, \ldots, X_{Ij})/\partial X_{ij}$

$$- \sum_{s=1}^{J} X_s / K_j(X_{1j}, \ldots, X_{Ij}).$$

Here $r_j(\cdot)$'s are homogeneous-first-degree functions that are quasi-concave and smooth: they measure growth potentialities when environmental scarcity is absent. The $K_j(\cdot)$ are assumed to be homogeneous-zero-degree functions; $r_j(x_{1j}, \ldots, X_{Ij})$ $K_j(X_{1j}, \ldots, X_{Ij})$ are the respective species "carrying capacities," when each is autonomous in the environment.

In Samuelson (1993), I show the following properties of (1a)–(1b): for $X_{ij}(0)$ all initially positive, independently of (1a)'s group selection, genetic evolution proceeds autonomously as $t \to \infty$ to a determinate asymptotic equilibrium. Only while resources are still superabundant will Fisher's fundamental theorem apply to maximize every species' exponential growth rate of $r_j(\cdot)$. Still, within any species, Darwin-Mendel genetic selection can hurt $K_j(\cdot)$ and worsen or extinguish the species' ultimate steady-state population. However, group competition, which leads in this model to one surviving species, will make it less likely that very many cases in which individual selection is grossly prejudicial to group selection will be observed in the living or fossil record. The mathematical model clinches the point.

VI. Conclusion

I believe that Gordon Tullock (1990) is in essential agreement with the heretical view I have long independently expounded. (I respect his 1993 report that insects in a hive may be less close than Hamiltonians count on—because queens often have multiple mates. But E. O. Wilson tells me that, once an elaborate cooperation has evolved, an impairing mutant will kill off its colony and eliminate itself: this selection among competing strains is much like group selection.) Herbert Simon (1990) presents an argument in which a mutation that enhances teachability, bounded rationality, and altruism survives to pursue altruistic cooperation—survives because its extra productivity more than offsets its quixotic rashness. When I try Simon's argument on hard-boiled naturalist friends, they in effect reply, "Arsenic and witchcraft kill the neighbor's sheep: how nice for witchcraft!" But then I trot out the present argument: "agreed that teachability can as often be on the same mutant gene as clear-sighted selfishness can be. So what begin as equally likely coincidences are trimmed by interspecific competition to biased likelihood that the Simon case will persist to be observed."

Species do compete. Species, like Aristotle, will eventually die. The dogma that group-selection arguments are somehow unclean evaporates under the light of reason and force of fact.

In L. J. Henderson's *The Fitness of the Environment* (1913) and *The Order of Nature* (1917), he called attention to the persistence of stable forms. One might try out individual and group selection as presumably independent dances. To exposit this, write $(+ -)$ for a case in which a species' new mutant displays superior individual fitness but lowers group fitness. (To allay Jack Hirschleifer's queries about coexistence of diverse genotypes, my argument does not depend on the nonmutants being entirely eliminated.) Then $(- +)$ is the case in which mutants lack individual survivability, but in which if they had proliferated it would have added to group fitness. Readers can interpret $(+ +)$ and $(- -)$. One can presume in the postulated case of independence that $(+ +)$, $(- -)$, $(+ -)$, and $(- +)$ are equally probable. What will be observed by vigilant recorders of nature will not, in the long run, be equal frequencies for the four cases! Hands down, $(+ +)$ will occur more often and last longer than $(- -)$; $(- -)$ and $(- +)$ are likely to exist only for transient periods, as most mutants that lack individual fitness are prone to die out fast. The $(+ -)$ mutants can possibly last long enough to be observed, but it is against the odds as it would require scientists to stumble onto observable data about species in the process of being fast elbowed out of existence.

In sum, group selection prunes from the record many of the perversities of individual selection. This is not God's will. It is merely the banality of mathematics and logic applied to survivability. Sophisticated economists will say, after the fact, "Of course."

REFERENCES

Bergstrom, Theodore C. and Stark, Oded, "How Altruism Can Prevail in an Evolutionary Environment," *American Economic Review*, May 1993 (*Papers and Proceedings*), *83*, 000–00.

Fisher, R. A., *The Genetical Theory of Natural Selection*, Oxford: Clarendon, 1930.

Hamilton, W. D., "The Genetical Evolution of Social Behaviour," parts I and II, *Journal of Theoretical Biology*, 1964, 7 (1), 1–52.

Henderson, Lawrence J., *The Fitness of the Environment*, Cambridge, MA: Harvard University Press, 1913.

_____, *The Order of Nature*, Cambridge, MA: Harvard University Press, 1917.

Samuelson, Paul A., "Frontiers in Demographic Economics—Modes of Thought in Economics and Biology," *American*

Economic Review, May 1985 (*Papers and Proceedings*), 75, 166–72.

——, "A Verhulst-Gause Model to Illustrate the Legitimate but Vulnerable Coexistence of Individual and Group Selections That Work at Cross Purposes," *Proceedings of the National Academy of Sciences*, 1993 (forthcoming).

Simon, Herbert, "A Mechanism for Social Selection and Successful Altruism," *Science*, 21 December 1990, *250*, 1665–9.

Tullock, Gordon, "The Economics of (Very) Primitive Societies," *Journal of Social and Biological Structures*, 1990, *13* (2), 151–62.

Facets of Balassa-Samuelson Thirty Years Later[*]

Paul A. Samuelson

Massachusetts Institute of Technology, Cambridge, MA 02139

Abstract

Prior to the important Penn studies of Kravis-Heston-Summers, statisticians relied on exchange-rate conversion estimates that would be correct only if naive Gustav Cassel versions of purchasing-power parity were true. By contrast, correct real-income estimates, using actual local prices and incomes, exhibit the systematic Penn effect: real per capita income ratios between poor and rich are systematically exaggerated by conventional exchange-rate conversions. Bela Balassa and Paul Samuelson, independently in 1964, explained why. And, as the Penn authors cited, David Ricardo and Roy Harrod had already similarly argued. It is shown here how subtle must be the theoretical analysis addressed by Jagdish Bhagwati and mainstream economists in tackling this problem.

1. Reflections

The teams of Irving Kravis (Kravis et al., 1978), Kravis, Alan Heston, and Robert Summers (1978, 1983), and Summers and Heston (1991) have documented in repeated Penn studies a fundamental economics fact. This K-H-S effect—or Penn effect—states that a rich country, in comparison with a poor one, will be estimated to be richer than it really is if you pretend that the simplified Cassel version of purchasing-power parity (PPP) is correct and if you use crude exchange-rate conversions to deflate the nominal total per capita incomes of the two countries. The greater their per capita real-income differentials truly are, the greater tends to be the resulting coefficient of bias. My title would gain in accuracy if it contained the names Ricardo-Viner-Harrod-Balassa-Samuelson-Penn-Bhagwati-et al.[1]

In World War I days several countries expanded their money supplies and thereby experienced price-level inflations. Gustav Cassel, like David Ricardo during Napoleonic War days, noticed that when a pair of countries experienced different degrees of general price elevation, the one with the greater record of inflation tended to have its exchange rate depreciated relative to the other. Cassel was thus led to enunciate what he called the purchasing-power parity doctrine: Exchange-rate levels and trends can be understood (and predicted) in terms of the relative price levels of nations.

Thus, consider the simplest case where all consumers, whether in the *Home* country H, or the *Abroad* country, A, have the same demand tastes at all income levels. Then, as my analytical appendix explicates, under simplified-tastes assumptions we know how to measure unambiguously the price levels of H and A, in terms of H's price vector $(P_j) = P$ and A's price vector $(P_j^*) = P^*$. Call these *exact* index numbers of price $\pi(P)$ and $\pi(P^*)$. Call the exchange rate giving the price in H currency of one unit of A's currency $E = 1/E^*$.

---

[*] I owe thanks to the MIT Sloan School of Management for partial support and to Janice Murray for editorial assistance. My debt to Robert Summers is great for extended discussions and to W. E. Diewert for wise counsel over the years.

© Basil Blackwell Ltd. 1994, 108 Cowley Road, Oxford OX4 1JF, UK and 238 Main Street, Cambridge, MA 0214, USA.

Then Cassel at his crudest asserts

$$E = \pi(P)/\pi(P^*). \tag{1}$$

This would hold in time series that include prewar, wartime, and postwar periods. It would also hold at *any* one time, cross-sectionally between and among all pairs of countries.[2]

In more guarded expositions of PPP, Cassel and others were more cautious. They would admit that competitive arbitrage *cannot* operate in the case of a nontradable good to keep its P_j price in H currency, relative to its P_j^* price in A currency, strictly equal to the ruling exchange rate. If nontradables violate the Law of One Price in the market, $P_j/P_j^* = E$, then market baskets of all goods cannot be guaranteed to have their price levels satisfy Cassel's equation (1). Hope was expressed that in the long run, inflation would be *balanced* with respect to different sectoral prices; therefore, if we can bet on the ratios of nontradables to tradables prices settling down at their predisturbance levels, then PPP (in this "relative" rather than "absolute" form) will be a useful guide as to where the equilibrium rendezvous for E is likely to tend. Speculators, like young Maynard Keynes, could thus hope to profit by selling the mark short relative to the dollar.

There is another unrealism about any $E = \pi(P)/\pi(P^*)$ absolute relation. If H and A have different tastes, their price levels cannot be measured by the same $\pi(\ )$ function applied to P and P^*. In general we at best will have $\pi(P)$ and $\pi^*(P^*)$. Now each region's index number of price involves different weighting; so even if P^* were strictly twice the P vector, it would not be true that PPP in the form $\pi(P)/\pi^*(P^*)$ gives a correct estimate of $E = 2$. PPP, critics say, is a mere tautology; and, worse, it is a tautology that is not even true! Economists cognizant of PPP's pitfalls would sometimes replace P and P^* *price* data by putative measures of regional *costs*, praying that costs will point to where equilibrium Ps will be later found.

An imperfect theory can sometimes be useful. Cassel and Keynes cautioned against a return to pre-1914 gold and exchange-rate parities, reasoning that P^*s in Britain and Sweden had risen more than Ps in America had; and therefore, factor prices being sticky, unemployment would result from overvaluing the postwar pound and kroner. The jury of history, I believe, sides with them and against Knut Wicksell, A. C. Pigou, and Edwin Cannan who prattled about national honor as mandating return to prewar pars and who belittled the macro real costs that would result from overvaluations. Moreover, subtle defenders (and critics) of PPP saw that by spatial arbitrage's *tautology*, tradables prices would accommodate *in advance* to expected return to prewar gold parities. Deceptively, PPP involving wholesale (largely tradables?) prices would give confirming $\pi(P)/\pi^*(P)^*$ estimates for whatever ridiculous nonequilibrium E fools in government could be expected to establish!

I have told the good news about PPP judiciously qualified. Offsetting is the bad news about economists who tried to use PPP as a guide even when substantive microeconomic changes had taken place between the previous putative equilibrium period and the new status quo. Thus, at a time in the 1980s when the actual yen-to-dollar exchange rate was 150 yen to the dollar, and when hindsight knew that 150 was on its way down to 110 or below, Professor Ronald McKinnon (1988) was publishing PPP cost estimates calling for a 200 yen-to-the-dollar equilibrium exchange rate. This was a palpable Casselian error resulting from an attempt to use an inadmissable *relative* form of the PPP dogma.

A palpable error resulting from attempting to use the *absolute* form of PPP was provided by the congressional testimony and writing of Professor Hendrick

© Basil Blackwell Ltd 1994

Houthakker (1962, 1963) arguing that the US dollar was overvalued in the 1960s relative to the German mark *for the reason that our American dollars could buy in Germany a desired basket of goods for less than it would cost in America.* Both Bela Balassa (1964) and Samuelson (1964) balked at this literal acceptance of Cassel's injudicious doctrine, which tried to defend PPP on the ground that (in my paraphrase):

What we'll pay for a currency depends on what it will do for us. If the cost of living is cheaper in Germany than in America, people will more and more buy there—until the augmented demand for marks and reduced demand for dollars will bid down the dollar and appreciate the mark, up to the point of new equilibrium where E = German cost of living/American cost of living. In sum, absolute PPP is the equilibrium condition determining where currencies will float to under nondirty floating. So to speak,

$$(dE/dt)/E = f\left[\frac{CoL}{CoL^*} - E\right]; \lim_{t \to \infty} E = \frac{CoL}{CoL^*} \text{ for } f[0] = 0 \text{ and } xf(x) < 0 \text{ when } x \neq 0 \quad (2)$$

In the years 1959–71 I happened to be in agreement with Houthakker's (1962, 1963) contention that the dollar was overvalued and, under Bretton Woods, the mark should be appreciated. (I had told President-Elect John F. Kennedy in 1960 that, ideally, his first act should be to depreciate the dollar and blame it on the previous rascals. That was not in the political cards and I sulked in the closet until the noneconomist John Connolly persuaded Richard Nixon in August 1971 to go off gold and end Bretton Woods. Two cheers, I said then and I say now.)

Whether Balassa felt the same way about the dollar, he did in no uncertain terms criticize Houthakker along the same lines as I did. In effect, Houthakker and Cassel were overlooking what came to be called the Penn effect, and which two earlier Penn scholars, Milton Gilbert and Irving Kravis (1954), had already documented for OECD countries. Balassa rightly observed that such a Houthakker-Cassel doctrine would mandate that every poor country appreciate relative to any richer country. And I will add, after they were to successfully defend the new gratuitous parities, the Penn effect would be likely to reassert itself! Following this Cassel dogma would entail perpetual currency revaluations for no good reason.

Here is a more defensible and possibly useful revisionist form of a *relative* PPP formulation for predicting how exchange rates will have to move to reduce disequilibrium. Suppose capital movements and exchange rates were earlier at equilibrium in a base period and the Penn effect made Cassel think PPP was violated by, say, the usual 40%. Now let an exogenous disturbance occur, as for example (1) a decrease in H's saving rate related to A's, with a resulting step-up in capital movements and (2) a depreciation of H's currency, and (3) a clear-cut observed step-up of the Penn correction to 50% from allegedly "normal" 40%. Then, if real incomes had putatively not changed much, one might hypothesize that there had been an overshoot (or undershoot) in the exchange rate and some betting odds for a subsequent correction in exchange rate in the direction of the hypothesized normal size of the Penn correction. Caution: use this notion with care; later I shall show why the Penn correction itself can be an *endogenous* variable rather than a preordained parameter resistant to changes in basic trends of tastes, technology, and thriftiness.

Wherein and why did Cassel err in believing implicitly that the Penn correction should be zero in equilibrium? The why is easy: he didn't think the problem through and his facile pen overstated his case. To be sure, if there did exist a large cadre of rentiers with their bags packed and no regional loyalties, the Cassel-Houthakker contention could actually become more nearly true. Then the empirical Penn effect

© Basil Blackwell Ltd 1994

would *not* obtain or be weakened. Indian wages would not rise to the British level after numerous retired Colonel Blimps newly demanded the services of Indian valets; but there would be some tendency toward lessening the geographical inequalities of factor returns—and this not for Heckscher-Ohlin reasons. However, the brute fact is that E in real life is not well approximated by $\pi(P)/\pi^*(P^*)$ approximations. There does exist out there a documentable Penn effect.

As mentioned, the size of the needed Penn correction (p.c.) ought to be an endogenous variable, affectable in the standard model of reparation payments of unilateral capital movements. I do not mean the Ohlin version where reparations from Germany to Britain are supposed to have no effect on the terms of trade; I have in mind the Keynes-Pigou-Taussig "orthodox effect" as finally worked out in Samuelson (1954), where reparations do induce some rise in British nontradables prices and some fall in German nontradables prices; and where there is a presumptive terms-of-trade secondary burden in the form of worsened German net terms of trade as a result of the unilateral payment.

Here is proof. Nontradables consumed in Germany drop somewhat as people there have less disposable income after paying reparations; nontradables consumption rises in Britain as their people use extra income to bid resources into nontradables production. Therefore, even if tastes are the same in both places for tradables, the relative drop in tradables resources for the receiver and rise in tradables resources for the payer can be presumed to bias the terms of trade against the payer. QED. Is it clear that the Penn effect for poor Germany and rich Britain could not be weakened by the reparations?

2. The Penn Correction Relations

I refer the reader to my analytical appendix where are described and analyzed the Penn systematic *correction functions*,

$$f\left(\frac{\text{true p.c. real income}^*}{\text{true p.c. real income}}\right)$$

or

$$f\left(\frac{y^*}{y}\right),$$

and

$$F\left(\frac{\text{exchange-converted p.c. real income}^*}{\text{exchange-converted p.c. real income}}\right)$$

or

$$F\left(\frac{y_e^*}{y_e}\right).$$

Before going into the Ricardo, Viner, Harrod, Balassa, Samuelson, and Penn purported theoretical rationalizations and explanation of the brute fact of the Penn effect, I can sum up its *description* in bare-bones terms.

It seems to be a verifiable fact that if one can rank goods $(1, 2, \ldots, m, \ldots, n)$ in order of their free tradability and approximation to the Law of One Price in One Market, rich countries tend to have higher per capita $(Q_1, \ldots, Q_n)$ than poor do on the average anywhere in the vector. But when Penn investigators construct statistical estimates of local price vectors and infer approximations to $(Q_1/Q_1^*, \ldots, Q_m/Q_m^*, \ldots, Q_n/Q_n^*)$, the nontradables toward the right of the vector do tend on the average to

© Basil Blackwell Ltd 1994

have lower ratios than do the tradable exports and imports towards the left. In brief, $Q_{\text{trade}}/Q_{\text{trade}}^* > Q_{\text{nontrad}}/Q_{\text{nontrad}}^*$ can be presumed to hold empirically—the BASIC FACT.

Conventional exchange-rate conversions would do a pretty good job for real-income comparisons if all goods were perfect tradables. They are least biased in estimating the true higher Q_j/Q_j^* ratios for the left-side tradables. They are most inadequate in approximating the low Q_{m+j}/Q_{m+j}^* ratios for the right-side nontradables. The *true* aggregate ratio should even-handedly average the higher Q_j/Q_j^* items with the lower Q_{m+j}/Q_{m+j}^* items; and Penn's estimates of *all* local ($P_1, \ldots, P_n$; $Q_1, \ldots, Q_n$) data enables their Geary (1958)-Khamis (1972) measures to approximate evenhandedness. Underweighting the nontradables where the rich are least strong therefore leads a Casselian exchange-rate conversion to that overestimate of their richness which long contaminated World Bank Atlas and other official data. Who could believe that, on a day when the yen appreciates 2% relative to the dollar, Japan's real income gains 2% on ours even though little that is substantive has changed at all?

Note that all this does not "explain" why a Q_j/Q_j^* for tradables tends to exceed a Q_{m+j}/Q_{m+j}^* for nontradables. It accepts that this is what the most careful statistical study will report when the rich and poor are compared. Note that I have so far said nothing about "productivities" in the two countries by sectors. Nor have I speculated about geographical real wage rates. Why this squeamishness? For the reason that, in general, a change in a region's tradable-exports productivities can even have a systematic perverse effect on some of its Q_j/Q_j^* ratios (particularly those of *imports*) and certainly cannot be expected to have numerically equivalent effects on the amounts consumed of tradable goods.

A reliable fact that is not provided with an explanation is better than a nice theory that helps explain and understand an *untrue* fact. Agreed. Agreed too that a reliable fact with a good theory to explain it is best of all—for the reasons that experience suggests that *it* will more likely *stay* reliable, and that a theory is good when it can warn us of what will negate an existing fact in the future.

Much of what Ricardo, Harrod, Balassa, or Samuelson say boils down to *repetition* of the brute fact of the Penn effect. Some of what is said, however, consists of specifying *sufficient* scenarios to create a Penn effect, along with explicit or implicit contention that these sufficient conditions have themselves been correct brute facts about economic history and geography. Thus, Jagdish Bhagwati (1984) adds to the discussion when he provides or emphasizes additional sufficient scenarios for some aspect of the Penn effect.

My own researches, published and unpublished, re-emphasize that sufficient conditions need not be necessary. (Note 1 illustrates a case where comparing poor Portugal with rich England involves no Penn effect at all!) Interesting conditions that are both necessary and sufficient, alas, are too unspecific to be much more than reiterated descriptions. As I shall show, sufficient scenarios abound that can entail anti-Penn effects. The Penn effect is important, but it is not an inevitable truth of economic history. True effects can deviate from stipulated approximations in different directions and in degree that varies exogenously and endogenously from case to case and epoch to epoch.

Here is what Kravis, Heston, and Summers (1978, p. 9) provide as a lead to understanding why the Penn effect that they document can be rationalized by economic theory: "... the ratio of real GDP per capita to exchange-rate converted GDP per capita [$(y^*/y)/(y_e^*/y_e)$ in present notations] ... falls as per capita GDP [or

y^*/y] rises. This phenomenon can be explained in terms of what may be referred to as a 'productivity-differential' model, which has been offered at various times by Ricardo, Viner, Harrod, and Balassa. The model turns on the impact of differences in the productivity gap between high- and low-income countries for traded and nontraded goods. International trade tends to drive the prices of traded goods, mainly commodities (but occasionally services), towards equality in different countries. With equal or nearly equal prices, wages in traded goods industries in each country will depend upon productivity. Wages established in the traded goods industries [sic] within each country will prevail in the country's nontraded industries' goods industries. In nontraded goods industries, however, international differences in productivity tend to be smaller.

"Consequently, in a high-productivity country high wages lead to high prices of services and other nontraded goods; whereas in a low-productivity country low wages produce low prices. The lower a country's income, the lower will be the prices of its home goods [untradables] and the greater will be the tendency for exchange-rate conversions to underestimate its real income relative to that of richer countries."

Digression. This is an excellent statement. However, it smacks a bit of the Senior-Taussig fallacy that somehow it is export industries that determine a region's wage rates; in fact, as Viner (1936) pointed out in a rare criticism of his teacher Taussig, simultaneous determination by nontradables and tradables takes place for the respective regional real-wage vectors (W/P_j). Also, as will be seen, productivity changes that raise Ricardian real wages in terms of an export good may well at the same time *lower* its real wage in terms of import goods as terms-of-trade changes may be induced. If $Q^*_{\text{trad}}/Q_{\text{trad}} < Q^*_{\text{nontrad}}/Q_{\text{nontrad}}$ and $P^*_{\text{nontrad}}/P^*_{\text{trad}} < P_{\text{nontrad}}/P_{\text{trad}}$ when $y^* < y$, this BASIC FACT is to be documented and if possible to be "explained."

To repeat, no one scenario can alone explain such a fact. Many different, and mutually exclusive, sufficiency conditions could lead to it. The Penn effect is an important phenomenon of actual history but not an inevitable fact of life. It can quantitatively vary and, in different times and places, trace to a quite different process, as we shall see.

3. Ricardo to the Test

The first authority cited by Kravis-Heston-Summers (1978, p. 9) is, of course, David Ricardo (Sraffa edition, 1951, p. 142; Dent edition, 1911, p. 187), who notes, "... the prices of home commodities [nontradables] ... are, independently of other causes, higher in those countries where manufactures flourish." Here is how Viner (1937, p. 315) seems to interpret this: "... non-transportable 'home commodities' ... according to him [Ricardo] would be higher in price in countries where the effectiveness of labor in export industries and therefore also the wages of labor were comparatively high."

To deduce this, Ricardo contemplates two countries (*Home*, or England; and *Abroad*, or Portugal) with the same populations and lands ($L = L^*$, $T = T^*$), the same (homothetic) tastes, and initially with the same technology. It will shorten my audit of Ricardo, if I make tradable cloth one manufacture and nontradable bricks another. It is immaterial if tradable wine is called a manufacture or not; and for brevity, I adhere to Ricardian labor theory of value with *no* scarce land. I can contrive for Ricardo initial labor productivities that begin the same in H and A for bricks. Initially, Portugal and England have offsetting superiorities in production of

© Basil Blackwell Ltd 1994

wine and cloth: L has productivity of two in cloth and one in wine; L^* has productivity of two in wine and one in cloth.

In autarky they are equally affluent, but with A enjoying relatively much wine and H enjoying relatively much cloth; in bricks they are equally well off if always consumers everywhere spend the same fraction of their income on wine and cloth—as, e.g., in a J. S. Mill model with 40% on wine, 40% on cloth, and 20% on bricks. (Warning: Mill's special tastes are easiest to analyze; however, more realistic homothetic tastes can qualify its over-sharp results.)

Just as Ricardo-Samuelson initial symmetry made autarky incomes equally affluent, under 1817–1829 Ricardo-Mill free trade, each will here be improved in the same percentage degree: the terms of trade P_{wine}/P_{cloth} will now be unity in both places; A alone produces cloth, exporting half to H; H alone produces wine, exporting half to A; each devotes 20% of home labor to bricks. Cassel will infer from exchange-rate conversion that A and H have equal real incomes per capita; the Penn team will arrive at the same (correct) result; no Penn effect expected when $y^*/y = 1$.

Suppose Ricardo to argue: Let H's productivity in tradables now double while A's is unchanged. Then it must be the case that H's nontradable becomes relatively expensive relative to its tradable export and A's nontradable stays relatively cheap relative to A's export tradable.

Those who invoke Ricardo as the anticipator of the Penn effect will presumably want to further argue: The described Ricardo scenario will, *by its logic*, entail the K-H-S effect documented in the Penn studies (and expected by Viner, Harrod, Balassa, Samuelson, Bhagwati, and others).

I have made the calculation and, alas, it is not that simple. Ricardo's own 1817 test case, in my note 1 version, if taken literally and completed in the J. S. Mill (1829, 1848) way, again leads to no geographical real-income differential (and hence no Penn effect is to be expected). However, the flourishing of manufactures in this numerical example lowers England's real wage in terms of the tradable wine and leaves P_{wine}/P_{bricks} quite unchanged.

Recall by contrast my note 1 where a new relative abundance of labor in England lowered its per capita income relative to Portugal's. Its "manufactures flourish" (because of augmented labor) and yet no rise in relative price of nontradable bricks is induced. Some flourishings of manufactures fail to produce (or explain!) a Penn effect.

It is unfair to hold Ricardo to a higher standard than modern writers. Harrod (1933, 1957) gives the best early analysis I know, one that is not bettered by 1964 Balassa-Samuelson (neither of whom knew of Harrod's work until the 1978 Penn citation). But in essence, Ricardo's terse analysis is in no way inferior to Harrod's. My point is that, 30 years after 1964, we must hold ourselves to a high modern standard.

4. Harrod's Prescience

Here are quotations from Harrod (1957). Note how far his analysis had reached. (My quotations are from his last edition, but I am not aware that it goes essentially beyond his 1933 text.)

"[Tradable goods] are in the main . . . raw materials and foodstuffs [plus somewhat-imperfectly competitive] differentiated manufactures and services such as insurance and securities-issuing" (pp. 53–54).

© Basil Blackwell Ltd 1994

"[Nontradables are] houses, fixed plant, railway services, public utility services and domestic services" (p. 55).

"[Tradables] have a common international price [converted into the *same* currency] ... except as, disturbed by transport costs and tariffs [and imperfections of monopolistic competition]" (pp. 56–57).

"[For nontradables] ... the theory of Purchasing Power Parity [calling for each currency, when converted into the other to have the power 'to purchase the same quantity of goods'] ... is no longer true" (pp. 62–63).

"Factors of production are like C goods [nontradables] in that there is no tendency toward a common international price level" (p. 63).

"... the sum total of all [factor] rewards must be proportional to the efficiency of a country ... in the output which she undertakes.... The level of rewards proper to a country [is] ... that which enables ... [tradables] to be marketed at world prices ... [while nontradables use up remaining resources, so as to have] prevailing reasonably full employment" (pp. 67–68).

"... [For tradables] these are common world prices. There is no world price level for C goods [nontradables, which are] likely to be more expensive in more efficient countries" (p. 75).

"... it may be observed that great differences between nation levels of efficiency are usually due either to differences in natural resources [Heckscher-Ohlin and 1984 Bhagwati] or to the difference in the degree to which scientific knowledge and capital have been applied to manufacturing processes. On the side of retailing, transport, and domestic service it is doubtful if differences in efficiency occur on so great a scale. Since gold rewards are proportional to efficiency in the output of tradable goods, highly efficient countries may find the gold cost of providing their C services [nontradables] in which proportional [productivity] economies cannot be made, higher than that in the less efficient countries" (pp. 60–61).

"The cost of living is compounded of [both tradables and nontradables]. The efficient countries will therefore tend to have a high cost of living" (p. 61).

"... the value of international goods [tradables] ... probably will [decline in the future] ... relative to a sample of all national goods [nontradables]" (p. 57).

It is hard to beat this. But clearly, Balassa (1964) did independently arrive at the same syllogisms and conclusions. In addition he could cite the statistical evidences of the early Penn scholars Milton Gilbert and Irving Kravis (1954).

5. Bhagwati's Two Scenarios

Bhagwati (1984) concentrates not so much on (what is here called) the Penn effect, but on the related problem of explaining why nontradable services tend to be cheaper in poorer countries. I begin with his second scenario: in it Heckscher-Ohlin identity of production functions obtains in rich H (I call it Portugal this time) and in poor A (England) for land-intensive tradable wine, for tradable cloth, and for nontradable bricks (or, better, personal services such as hair care, which is relatively labor intensive). He uses labor and capital where I am going to continue to use "labor" and "land": L and T for Portugal; L^* and T^* for England.

Begin with symmetric endowments in H and A. Autarky and free-trade equilibria are identical under common homothetic tastes; factor-price equalization is already attained:

$$(W/P_j) \equiv (W^*/P_j^*), \qquad (P_2/P_1 \quad P_3/P_1) = (P_2^*/P_1^* \quad P_3^*/P_1^*). \tag{3}$$

No Penn effect with $y^*/y = 1$. Services are equally dear in H and A.

Now let England's L^* alone rise a bit. This impoverishes her per capita real income a bit. But still it leaves factor prices equalized, albeit the world rise in labor cheapens the most labor-intensive goods *everywhere*. Still no Penn effect (as in my note 1). And, as yet, no second Bhagwati effect.

Raise L^* still more—until we are outside the cone of factor-price equalization. (In occasional confusion, Ohlin seems to have thought to be normal this case of necessarily only partial factor-price equalization.) When England becomes sufficiently land poor she won't be able to afford to produce any wine; she specializes in cloth; and of course produces her nontradable good. And with L^*/T^* sufficiently large, Portugal too comes to produce only land-intensive wine and the nontradable. England's drop in real W/P_{cloth} entails a further rise in Portugal's y/y^* as $P_{\text{wine}}/P_{\text{cloth}}$ rises everywhere.

Now Bhagwati achieves his desired proof of a relative cheapening of nontradable services in the poor country. On the basis of the specification that always hair care is more labor intensive than cloth production and cloth production is more labor intensive than wine production, he can deduce that large enough L^* relative to unchanged $(T^*; L, T)$ will necessarily lower all of $[(W^*/P_3^*)/(W/P_3), (P_3^*/P_2^*)/(P_3/P_2), (P_3^*/P_1^*)/(P_3/P_1)]$. We can also deduce that there will be the Penn effect: $y_e^*/y_e < y^*/y < 1$. QED.

Bhagwati recognizes that production functions are not the same everywhere among rich and poor societies. And he would readily agree that, if nontradables involved land-intensive activities (as in hunting), all the arguments would go into reverse. An anti-Penn effect would be observed and nontradables would be relatively *dear* in the overpopulated regions, $P_3^*/P_1^* > P_3/P_1$.

Now for Bhagwati's first scenario, which aimed to free the analysis from Ricardo's labor-only arithmetic of comparative advantage. Like Ricardo, Bhagwati (1964, 1984) wished to specify systematically different production functions for different goods in different places. Like Heckscher-Ohlin, he concentrated on two-factor cases: labor and land in my paraphrase of his labor and capital analysis.

He concentrates on Hicks' neutral technical progress, the special case where tradables *all* have the same production functions in H and A, save that in H *both* productive factors have their productivities augmented in the same quantitative degree for all tradables. By contrast, for nontradables the strong special assumption is made that H enjoys productivity progress over A (or, we may suggest, enjoys *less* Hicks-neutral advantage than is common among the tradables).

Bhagwati's First Scenario thus involves production functions

$$F_i[L, T] \equiv \lambda F_i^*[L, T], \qquad \lambda > 1, i = 1, 2,$$
$$F_3[L, T] \equiv \gamma F_3^*[L, T], \qquad 1 \leq \gamma < \lambda. \tag{4}$$

The author recognizes he has struck a hard Faustian bargain with the Devil, paying a high price in loss of generality in order to be able to handle a two-factor advance over Ricardo's labor-only technology.

Now Bhagwati stipulates that factor endowments are *not* too far apart. With

$L^*/T^* > L/T$, but $(L^*/T) - (L/T) \ll 1$, both places must produce some of both tradables along with their nontradable. Absolute real-factor returns in tradables cannot be equalized when Portugal enjoys Hicks-neutral productivity advantage in all tradables. But because of the Hicks-neutral definition, *relative* rent/wage ratios must be equalized for Heckscher-Lerner-Samuelson reasons!

$$\frac{W}{W^*} = \frac{R}{R^*} = \lambda > 1, \qquad \frac{P_2}{P_1} = \frac{P_2^*}{P_1^*}. \tag{5a}$$

$$\frac{W/P_1}{W^*/P_1^*} = \frac{R/P_1}{R^*/P_1^*} = \frac{W/P_2}{W^*/P_2^*} = \frac{R/P_2}{R^*/P_2^*} = \lambda > 1. \tag{5b}$$

$$1 < \frac{\lambda}{\gamma} = \frac{P_3}{P_i} < 1, \qquad i = 1, 2. \tag{5c}$$

For Mill's constant fractional-expenditures model, it can be verified that

$$y_e/y_e^* > y/y^* > 1. \tag{5d}$$

Thus, Bhagwati's First Scenario does succeed in entailing both the Penn effect and the dearness of nontradable services in affluent regions. However, it does so by invoking more special conditions than were ever envisaged by Ricardo, Viner, Harrod, Balassa, or Samuelson, or Penn. Along with low real-wage rates in the poor region—a realistic enough result—it deduces an implausible equally low real return for *any* nonlabor factor; and, as Professor Bhagwati warns, it requires that poor regions use the factors in the *same* proportion *everywhere* as the rich regions use them. And, as far as (5) goes, it entails dear nontradablès in the rich place *even if the nontradable* is *non*labor intensive and polar opposite to Bhagwati's "services."

If we raise L^*/T^* enough to go beyond the cone of *relative* factor-return equalization, this First Scenario is pushed in the direction of less unrealism. This blending of the two 1984 scenarios will entail that poor regions do generally tilt in the direction of becoming generally more labor intensive in production.

This general result can, fortunately, be heuristically suggested outside of the Lerner-Samuelson formalisms appropriate to the Heckscher-Ohlin specializations.[3] Thus, consider what is today called the Haberler-Jones-Samuelson technology of a transferable labor working with fixed lands specialized to each product (Gottfried Haberler, 1933; Ronald Jones, 1971; Paul Samuelson, 1971). In this manageable case, we have no hope of mandatory full factor-price equalization à la Heckscher-Ohlin. But still there is a deducible Penn effect if nontradables tend to be labor intensive and the poverty of regions is associated with their overpopulation.

6. The Leontief Paradox and Generalizations

Hicks neutrality is a very special case. Why not Harrod neutrality (or, what is the same thing, purely labor-augmenting change)? Why not *general factor-augmenting* change of the following type?

$$F_i[L, T] \equiv F_i^*[\alpha_i L, \beta_i T], \qquad i = 1, 2, 3, \tag{6}$$

where α's and β's can differ, and where $(\alpha_1 \ \alpha_2 \ \alpha_3)$ and $(\beta_1 \ \beta_2 \ \beta_3)$ can differ in any pattern?

The Leontief (1954) paradox enjoyed a certain vogue three decades ago. I will translate its (labor capital) inputs to the present $(L \ T)$ inputs and will not discuss the empirical validity of the Leontief findings. Here is my version.

© Basil Blackwell Ltd 1994

America, H, is more productive than Japan, A. But paradoxically its export goods are more labor intensive than its import goods are. How to explain this?

One hypothesis is that each of H's L is three times as effective as each L^*; but each of H's T is the same as each T^*. This will be recognized as perfect Harrod-neutral change, systematically differing from Hicks neutrality on the realistic proviso that all elasticities of substitution fall short of the Cobb-Douglas unity. Finally, agree that H's relative land endowment, T/L, does indeed exceed T^*/L^*, but in *less* than a *three*-fold way.

In *efficiency* units, written in boldface,

$$\frac{L^*}{T^*} < \frac{L}{T} = \frac{3L}{T}. \tag{7}$$

Even when such endowments are close enough together to have both countries produce both tradables, H will be "labor rich" and will concentrate more on Ricardo-Ohlin cloth than on Ricardo-Ohlin wine.

Agreed, we have duplicated Leontief's alleged pattern—now without paradox. What about the Penn effect? What about the relative dearness of Bhagwati's labor-intensive nontradable?

Within the cone of partial specialization only, American and Japanese land rents are equal. American wage rates are exactly triple those in Japan. Hence

$$(R/P_1 \quad R/P_2) = (R^*/P_1^* \quad R^*/P_2^*),$$
$$(W/P_1 \quad W/P_2) = (3W^*/P_1^* \quad 3W^*/P_2^*), \quad W/R = 3W^*/R^*,$$
$$P_2/P_1 = P_2^*/P_1^*. \tag{8}$$

If American superworkers are three times as tall as Japanese in *everything*, including services (!), then *all* $P_i/P_j = P_i^*/P_j^*$; Bhagwati's effect of relatively dear services in richer places is not at all realized.

However, what will get that job done is to assume that no one can be three times as good a barber or masseur as anyone else. In that case, in (6),

$$\alpha_1 = \alpha_2 = 3 > \alpha_3 \geq 1 = \beta_1 = \beta_2 = \beta_3. \tag{9a}$$

Then, Bhagwati's desideratum is achieved:

$$(P_3/P_2 \quad P_3/P_1) > (P_3^*/P_2^* \quad P_3^*/P_1^*), \quad \frac{W}{P_3} < 3\frac{W^*}{P_3^*}. \tag{9b}$$

We fail to contrive relatively dear services in rich H if we assume L/T in efficiency units exceed L^*/T^* by so much as to force H to produce no wine and A to produce no cloth. Now $(P_2/P_1)/(P_2^*/P_1^*)$ rises. If the nontradable is more labor-intensive than all tradables, we actually seem to get a reverse Bhagwati result since $(P_3/P_1 \quad P_3/P_2)$ will both be *less* than $(P_3^*/P_1^* \quad P_3^*/P_2^*)$! Remark: Harrod-neutral uniform productivity gain in H, accompanied by L/T in efficiency units much *less* than L^*/T^*, can thus achieve the Bhagwati and Penn effects. But such a scenario is precisely what Leontief contended was not in accord with the facts.

In summary, it would seem that Harrod's 1933 generality was the safest approach. Eschewing Ricardian labor-only technology, eschewing Heckscher-Ohlin identity of geographical production functions, while positing a presumption that tradables have differentially superior productivity in rich places compared to nontradables, the Penn effect is deduced to be likely. And if goods that are most labor intensive are hardest to reduce in technical costs, the presumption follows that services will remain relatively dear in the advanced societies.

Thus, generalize (6) to recognize a technical change parameter τ

$$F_i[L, T] = F_i^*[L, T; \tau_i], \text{ where } \tau_i > 0 \text{ and } \partial F_i^*/\partial \tau_i > 0. \tag{10}$$

If nontradables τ_3 is systematically less than tradables τ_1 and τ_2; and if F_3^* [ ] is more labor intensive than the tradables F_1^*[ ] and F_2^*, we get a presumption toward the Penn and Bhagwati effects without any Ricardo or Heckscher-Ohlin ballast.

7. A Purist's Qualifications and Qualms

The Penn team tries to measure GDPs. Most of my discussion here has concentrated on the economic theory of index numbers that is appropriate to only one (albeit important) component of GDP—namely, to private *consumption* items. Neglected are govermental use of resources. Neglected are issues having to do with capital formation and investment. In three papers, Samuelson (1950, 1954b, 1961) tried to comment on some aspects of all three components. Also, there does exist a Hicks-Bergson approach to index numbers, which, quite aside from public-sector and investment-sector components, does try to measure production capacity of an economy rather than the welfare of its representative citizen. That too is largely ignored here. See John Hicks (1948), Simon Kuznets (1948), Samuelson (1950), and Abram Bergson (1961).

A purist who ignores much cannot cogently cavil at the practical expedients employed by serious scholars on the Penn team. I cheerfully concede that. Still it may be useful to analyze in further depth what their expedients would mean for a purely consumption approach.

I have talked mostly about two countries: H and A, with y and y^*. Penn deals with dozens of benchmark countries and with many score nations. Mostly they have used the so-called Geary-Khamis algorithm for comparing multiple regions' real y's; see Robert C. Geary (1958) and Salem Khamis (1972). The European common market has more recently experimented with a so-called Eltetö-Köves-Szulc (or E-K-S) alternative approach to Geary-Khamis; see O. Eltetö and P. Köves (1964) and B. J. Szulc (1964). See also Samuelson (1974b, 1984) for discussions of these complicated matters; and any treatise on index numbers, such as W. E. Diewert and Alice Nakamura (1993).

From conversation with W. E. Diewert I learn that the E-K-S system does in effect postulate the uniform homotheticity (unitary income elasticities) that my U and U^* functions presupposed. Without such homotheticity, it is well known that a *unique* y^*/y metric ratio cannot be unambiguously inferred. (For each of the $\frac{1}{2}N(N - 1)$ pairs of countries, E-K-S forms Fisher's ideal index. Then an unweighted geometric mean of all these is the final E-K-S measure. Since Irving Fisher's ideal index is exact for the homothetic Buscheguennce-Alexander quadratic family of indifference contours, E-K-S is seen to posit uniform homotheticity.) The Penn group does not much care whether Geary-Khamis does or does not presuppose homotheticity. Whether or not it does may be almost an unanswerable question, since it is so highly mechanical an algorithm as not to be closely identifiable with any *exact and superlative* index formula.

Whether or not Geary-Khamis satisfies unitary income elasticities, when the Penn team applies to the same data both Geary-Khamis and E-K-S, they derive almost the same arithmetic result. So, for a reduced-form pragmatist, we might pretend Geary-Khamis approximates to homotheticity.

This produces a puzzle. Engel's laws of budget behavior are among economic science's oldest and best econometric findings. Definitely, they depart from unitary income elasticities. Food expenditure has income elasticity below unity. Recreational luxuries have income elasticity in excess of unity.

Samuelson (1974a, 1984) tries to grapple with the reality of nonhomotheticity. More realistic for a purist is perhaps to assume that US and India, and everybody, have the *same* nonhomothetic tastes that mimic Engel's laws. Admittedly that gives us an infinity of money-metric utilities—see Samuelson (1974b)—with somewhat different $y_{\text{India}}/y_{\text{US}}$ ratios. Two alternatives recommend themselves: for, say a 1994 $y_{\text{India}}/y_{\text{US}}$ comparison, use either the price ratios and Engel paths at India's 1994 consumption position, or use those at the United States' 1994 consumption position. With luck, the two estimates will not be too far apart numerically. And each may perhaps approximate to the E-K-S and Geary-Khamis numerical estimates. My brother Robert Summers tells me that several Heston-Summers numerical explorations have concurred with this common finding of index-number constructors.

In short, even a purist finds considerable reassurance in the actual econometric procedure.

The Penn studies have been invaluable not only for the empirical truths that they have discovered or documented, but also for their demonstration that many of the things economists take for granted as obvious truths are actually either wrong or questionable. As I reread Samuelson (1974a, 1984) I am made aware by the Penn studies of how vulnerable my discussions have been to these nontruths or half truths. Here are concrete issues.

A. G. B. Fisher (1939) in the last generation set forth the following hypothesis, which Colin Clark (1949) popularized: Economies go through three stages. First comes Agriculture. Then comes Manufacturing. Finally comes the third stage of a Service economy.

This thesis from Down Under—from New Zealand and Australia—suggests that farm foodstuffs have income elasticities that are *in*elastic. Luxury services—and one thinks of a valet's labor-intensive attentions—are the goods of income elasticity most above unity.

Every schoolchild knows this. But when Penn puts it to the test, after correcting for the dearness of services in the advanced societies, it finds that the real share of services is about the same fraction at all real-income levels. Grown-up schoolchildren like Drs. P. A. Samuelson and J. Bhagwati have no choice but to revise their expositions.

Actually, as the Penn researches illuminate, the category of "services" is a mixed bag. A service to a consumer, such as a beautiful FM broadcast of Mozart, may be produced from a Leontief viewpoint primarily by goods-manufacturing industry. On the other hand consider a consumer good such as an auto. A Leontief peek back into its stages of production might show most of the employees performing "service" functions—watching computers, programming lathes, and so forth. There are more things in modern Heaven and Earth than were dreamed of in the A. G. B. Fisher philosophy.

When you and I think of a nontradable and think of it as a labor-intensive service item, at first we find reassurance in the Penn finding that its category of most untradables does indeed tend to be relatively more labor intensive. However, when the group reminds us that one of the biggest components of *its* nontradables is

© Basil Blackwell Ltd 1994

"construction," we are unsettled. Yes, a skyscraper cannot be put on a barge and sold abroad. But still a skyscraper could be a bolted-together assemblage of hard goods: wires, bricks, ceramic sinks, fabricated plastic frames—all assembled by minimal on-site crews. What then is this category of "services," whose income elasticity to the consumer we are essaying to measure and which is allegedly labor-intensive?

Theorists like to walk away from real-world ambiguity. That is a fault. We should accord double pay to the empiricists who optimize the analysis of the ambiguity that is irreducibly there in the economic data. Hail then the Penn achievements over the many years. Even when I cavil at Penn's agnosticism on purists' homotheticity axioms, I remind myself that Penn focuses on more than metric real-income comparisons. A complete set of real-income accounts is their goal, and for *this* purpose no one yet has found better algorithms than those of the Geary type.

Analytical Appendix

A1. Notations

Write *prices* of goods and services (produced and/or consumed) as $(P_1 \ldots P_n)$ for the *Home* country (England or US); and as $(P_1^* \ldots P_n^*)$ for the *Abroad* country (Portugal or Japan). All prices are in the nominal currency of the region itself (in pounds or dollars, in escudos or yen). Write the *quantities* of goods (produced and/or consumed) as $(Q_1 \ldots Q_n)$ and $(Q_1^* \ldots Q_n^*)$. Nominal GDPs (or GNPs or, better, NNPs) are respectively $Y = \Sigma_1^n P_j Q_j$ and $Y^* = \Sigma_1^n P_j^* Q_j^*$. Write the market *exchange rate* for the *Abroad* currency in terms of *Home* currency as E (with $1/E = E^*$ being the price of a unit of *Home* currency in terms of a unit of *Abroad* currency). The *Abroad* income, converted to *Home* currency terms by means of the exchange rate, is simply $E\Sigma P_j^* Q_j^*$.

By definition of "exchange-rate estimated relative real incomes,"

$$\frac{Y_e^*}{Y_e} = \frac{E\sum_1^n P_j^* Q_j^*}{\sum_1^n P_j Q_j} \equiv \frac{\sum_1^n P_j^* Q_j^*}{E^* \sum P_j Q_j} \tag{1.1a}$$

If the respective labor populations are L and L^*, by definition of "exchange-rate estimated relative per capita real incomes," (y_e^*/y_e), become

$$\frac{y_e^*}{y_e} = \frac{EY_e^*/L^*}{Y_e/L}. \tag{1.1b}$$

True relative real incomes per capita will be denoted by y^*/y. The systematic differences between y_e^*/y_e and y^*/y are documented by the Penn studies and constitute the Penn effect that is to be numerically described and perhaps theoretically explained.

The Penn effect, or K-H-S effect, can be summarized in terms of present notations as requiring a correction function, or $f[\ ]$:

$$(y_e^*/y_e) = (y^*/y)f[y^*/y], \quad f[1] = 1, \tag{1.2a}$$

$$\begin{aligned} f[y^*/y] &< 1 \quad \text{if } y^* < y; \\ &> 1 \quad \text{if } y^* > y. \end{aligned} \tag{1.2b}$$

© Basil Blackwell Ltd 1994

$f[y^*/y] \equiv 1$, by notational consistency. (1.2c)

Special admissible examples for $f[z]$ could be z, z^2, $z^{1/2}$, $z^{|a|}$, or more general formulas. However, I have not explored an approximate fit for the various Penn empirical scatters.

It is to be understood that there is no "one true $f[z]$," in that y can exceed y^* for a great variety of reasons; e.g., H's L could have more and better land to work with; or it could have better technology; or ... and or.... Even if our sample were confined to *one* specified process of geographical development, were it to include a great continental economy like India, far removed from world centers, and at the same time include a poor region like Albania, located in the middle of Europe, even if y equalled y^*, why expect the realistic departures from ideal Cassel PPP conditions to be the same for them as for a comparison between Sweden and Norway?

In short (1.2a) needs to be rewritten to include an error or noise term in the relations scatter:

$$y_e^*/y_e = (y^*/y)f[y^*/y] + \text{Remainder}. \quad (1.2a')$$

The remainder component becomes particularly prominent when y^* and y are not far apart. Particularly when several advanced economies will come to achieve approximate real-income per capita equality with the US, we must expect y_e^*/y_e to scatter both above and below putative y^*/y. Indeed, the Penn authors report that the common practice of using the US as the reference *numéraire* in the y_e^*/y_e denominators leads to vulnerability, for the reason that ours is a special economy in various singular ways. One could imagine a decision to use a less singular leading region as *numéraire*; or even to use a "market basket" of such countries as the reference standard. (None of my observations are meant to be critical of the Penn researchers. In truth, it is they who best know the irreducible limitations in their data and approximations, and in anybody else's attainable data.)

Most countries studied by the Penn team are not "benchmark countries." For benchmark countries local investigators gather data on actual Ps in the respective nations, on P_jQ_j expenditure data, and for manageable subaggregates approximations to Q_j data. By use of Geary-Khamis functions, from these benchmark data, Penn estimates putative true y^*/y comparisons.

Since there obtains an approximate systematic pattern relating $y^*/y = z$ to $y_e^*/y_e = zf[z]$, the Penn team has a powerful tool to use to estimate from easily available z_e exchange-rate conversion data a useful approximation to true $y^*/y = z$ data. The appropriate "inverse" function to $f[z]$, written as $F[z_e]$, is formally defined as follows:

a. z and z_e, by hypothesis, grow and fall together.

b. ∴ elasticity

$$zf'[z]/f[z] > -1 \quad \text{or} \quad \frac{\partial \log z_e}{\partial \log z} > 0; \quad (1.3a)$$

c. $z_e = zf[z] \leftrightarrow z = z_e F[z_e]$, with (1.3b)

$$\left(\frac{\partial z}{\partial z_e}\right)\left(\frac{\partial z_e}{\partial z}\right) \equiv 1 \equiv (f[z] + zf'[z])(F[z_e] + z_e F'[z_e]). \quad (1.3c)$$

Of course this procedure ignores the Remainder in (1.2a'). When we allow for such, there follows the kind of relation used by the Penn team for nonbenchmark countries:

$$y^*/y \text{ est.} = [y_c^*/y_c]F[y_c^*/y_c] + \text{New Remainder.} \tag{1.4}$$

For numerical illustration, if $f[z] = z^\alpha$, then $F[z] = 1/z^{\alpha/(1+\alpha)}$. For $\alpha = 1/2, 1, 2$, $F[z_e] = 1/z^{1/3}$, or $1/z^{1/2}$, or $1/z^{2/3}$. When an empirical best fit is sought that will somehow minimize New Remainder in (1.4), the interrelationship between $f[z]$ and $F[z_e]$ will have to be appropriately modified.

A2. Unrealistic Cassel PPP Notions

If *all* goods were freely tradable sans tariffs or transport costs, competitive arbitrage would impose that the *price vectors* at *Home* and *Abroad*, (P_j) and (P_j^*), would be *strictly proportional in all n goods*:

$$\frac{P_j}{P_1} \equiv \frac{P_j^*}{P_1^*}, \quad j = 2, \ldots, n; \tag{2.1a}$$

$$\frac{P_j}{P_j^*} \equiv E, \quad j = 1, \ldots, n. \tag{2.1b}$$

Valid real-income comparisons could still not be made unambiguously between regions except in singular cases. If tastes *Abroad* differ from *Home* tastes, which ones shall provide the measuring rod for real incomes? Using the tastes of one of the regions, it could be that H has a higher per capita income than A—at the same time that A's real income is better than H's when we use the *other* region's tastes. We know these facts of life from index-number theory; see Paul A. Samuelson (1974a, 1984) in the present context.

I give Cassel rope to hang himself. Let's stipulate *identical* tastes by *every* individual in whatever country and at *however much nominal income* each has available to be spent at the prevailing price vector $(P_j) = P$ or $(P_j^*) = P^*$ as the case may be. With "uniform homothetic" tastes, we could contrive a commensurable measure of real income(s). Moreover, it is metric so that a doubling of real y or real y^* or a 1% increase in them is meaningfully defined and testable.

Our strong, singular axiom about tastes gives us for any region, or person, or group of persons, a common first-degree homogeneous real-income function: $U(Q_1, \ldots, Q_n)$ or $U(Q_1^*, \ldots, Q_n^*)$ as the case may be; and note that we never need distinguish $U(\ )$ and $U^*(\ )$, since U and U^* are here exactly the *same function*.[4]

Cassel never thought about the complexities of this analysis, but we can do it for him. With all goods *perfectly tradable* and tastes *perfectly identical*, under competition the (Q_j) and (Q_j^*) quantity vectors will themselves be perfectly proportional!—just as prices were:

$$Q_j/Q_1 \equiv Q_j^*/Q_1^*, \quad j = 2, \ldots, n; \tag{2.2a}$$

$$Q_j^*/Q_j \equiv U^*/U, \quad j = 1, \ldots, n. \tag{2.2b}$$

This is amazingly simple. We need only measure any one of the many goods and services in the two regions: if Q_{17}^*/Q_{17} is three, then Portugal enjoys *exactly* three times the real income of England; and if their populations and labor supplies are equal, Portugal's per capita real income is exactly three times that of England's! And we know this without having to estimate the $U(q_1, \ldots, q_n)$ function or to make the particular Geary-Khamis approximations!

Also, we solve our problem without caring whether the Cassel-Ricardo quantity theory of money and prices is exactly valid or is vitiated by brute facts.

A3. Manageable Models with Goods either Perfectly or Not at All Tradable

When (1) $P_{\text{nontrad}}/P_{\text{trad}} \neq P^*_{\text{nontrad}}/P^*_{\text{trad}}$, even if (2) tastes are uniform-homothetic in the two countries and (3) price ratios among tradables are exactly uniform, it will (4) no longer be the case that for perfect tradables quantities are proportional in the fashion of (2.2b) given above.

To a purist this is a devastating result. It means that all the discussants up until now have not been quite right in thinking that exchange-rate conversions, y^*_e/y_e, would give correct estimates of the "true y^*/y as far as 'tradable-goods contribution' to real welfare is concerned." Indeed, even when total real welfare is perfectly metric and definable, in general the purist will have to cavil at the notion of splitting *it* up into meaningfully measurable components: tradables contribution to it, and nontradables contribution to it.

Following the methodological precept divide and conquer, take the coward's way and concentrate on the singular case where homogeneous first-degree total $U[q_1, \ldots q_m, \ldots, q_n]$ is weakly separable into tradable and nontradable components, namely,

$$U[q_1, \ldots, q_m, \ldots, q_n] \equiv V[T, N] \equiv \lambda^{-1}V[\lambda T, \lambda N]$$
$$\equiv V[T(q_1, \ldots, q_n)N(q_{m+1}, \ldots, q_n)], \tag{3.1}$$

where T and N are themselves homogeneous first-degree concave functions in their respective tradable and nontradable vectors:

$$T(q_1, \ldots, q_m) \equiv \lambda^{-1}T(\lambda q_1, \ldots, \lambda q_m), \quad \lambda > 0; \tag{3.2}$$

$$N(q_{m+1}, \ldots, q_n) \equiv \lambda^{-1}N(\lambda q_{m+1}, \ldots, \lambda q_n), \quad N \text{ and } T \text{ concave.} \tag{3.3}$$

The Mill simplifying case is one convenient form for T and N, and was used in Samuelson (1984) for present purposes in the form of

$$U = (q_1^{k_1} \ldots q_m^{k_m})(q_{m+1}^{k_{m+1}} \ldots q_n^{k_n}), \quad \sum_1^m k_j + \sum_{m+1}^n k_j = 1, \quad k_j > 0. \tag{3.4}$$

In computations not presented here, I have also found it convenient to use CES functions of the form

$$V[T, N] = [(AT)^\alpha + (BN)^\alpha]^{1/\alpha}, \quad -\infty \leq \alpha \leq 1, \alpha \neq 0 \tag{3.5a}$$

$$= bT^\beta N^{1-\beta}, \quad \text{for } \alpha = 0; \tag{3.5b}$$

$$T \equiv \left[\sum_1^m (a_j q_j)^\beta\right]^{1/\beta} < -\infty \leq \beta < 1, \quad \beta \neq 0; \tag{3.5c}$$

$$N \equiv \sum_{m+1}^n [a_j q_j)^\gamma]^{1/\gamma}, \quad -\infty \leq \gamma < 1, \gamma \neq 0. \tag{3.5d}$$

Under weak separability, the valid realization of price-vector proportionality of type (2.1) will validly entail *for tradable goods*, $j = 1, \ldots, m < n$, the quantity-vector proportionality of type (2.2). Then the purist's qualms are set to rest as far as is concerned the perfection of exchange-rate conversions applied to the tradables themselves: perfectly valid is the estimate

$$\frac{T(q_1^*, \ldots, q_m^*)/L^*}{T(q_1, \ldots, q_m)/L} = \frac{E\sum_1^m P_j^* Q_j^*/L^*}{\sum_1^m P_j Q_j/L}$$

$$= \frac{Q_i^*}{Q_i}, \quad i = 1, \ldots, m. \tag{3.6}$$

What now produces a genuine Penn effect and has to be addressed by benchmark statistical studies is the distribution of N^*/N estimates that come from exchange-rate conversions dependent on $E/\Sigma_{m+1}^n P_j^* Q_j^*$ and $\Sigma_{m+1}^n P_j Q_j$ calculations involving no longer-proportional (P_{m+j}^*, P_{m+j}) and (Q_{m+j}^*, Q_{m+j}) nontradable vectors.

To grapple with the theory of this, I first touch on autarky estimatings, then on explicit facing up to nontradable goods.

A4. Measuring Per Capita Real Incomes under Autarky

Suppose no goods trade. All goods are *nontradable* under autarky. If we know L and L^*, and knew the respective (Q_j) and (Q_j^*) vectors, there would be no other way of comparing y^*/y (even under uniform tastes!) than to somehow discover the $U(\ )$ function and derive from it

$$\frac{y^*}{y} = \frac{U(Q_1^*/L^*, \ldots, Q_n^*/L^*)}{U(Q_1/L, \ldots, Q_n/L)}. \tag{4.1}$$

The Penn team lines up local investigators in various benchmark nations to gather data on sectoral (P_j) and (P_j^*) vectors; combining these with data on $P_j Q_j$ and $P_j^* Q_j^*$ expenditures, the Penn effort provides valuable information about the (Q_j) and (Q_j^*) vectors. If cross-sectional and time-series demand patterns can be pooled, Penn could make a stab at estimating even under autarky. Cassellian exchange-rate conversions would of course be quite unavailable under autarky conditions.

The real world is of course neither one of autarky nor of perfect tradability. It is somewhere in between, and we must study how to improve on crude exchange-rate conversions.

A5. How Nontradability Clouds the Picture

Suppose some or all of the goods need positive transport costs to move in trade between *Home* and *Abroad*. Perhaps the most easily manageable case is the iceberg model of Samuelson (1954). In this, some fraction of Q_j exported from *Home* to *Abroad* evaporates in passage. Call those nonnegative fractions that do survive $(b_1, \ldots, b_n)$. Then $(b_1^*, \ldots, b_n^*)$ will be the transport-cost survival fractions relevant to exports of Q_j^*s from *Abroad* to *Home*. The b_j and b_j^* need not be equal to one another, good for good, or equal for the same goods from different regions. Indeed, if $(b_1, \ldots, b_m)$ and $(b_1^*, \ldots, b_m^*)$, $m < n$ are identically one(s), and both $(b_{m+1}, \ldots, b_n)$ and $(b_{m+1}^*, \ldots, b_n^*)$ are very small fractions, we shall have the case beloved in the literature: then we have m goods perfectly or substantially *tradable*; and have

© Basil Blackwell Ltd 1994

$n - m$ nontradable goods. For the most part I go along with this expositional convention.

First, though, let's consider arbitrage limits in the general case, where some bs are not unity. How is the Cassel fable altered?

The equalities of (2.1) must be replaced by the following *duality inequalities* when transport costs are not zero. Assume the same E (and $1/E \equiv E^*$) prevails in the *Home* and *Abroad* market, as would be almost the case if gold were used as ultimate money *numéraire* and transporting gold from H to A and from A to H involved negligible transport costs. Then (2.1b) is replaced by

$$P_i/b_i \geq EP_i^* \geq b_i^* P_i, \quad i = 1, \ldots, n; \tag{5.1b}$$

$$0 = [(P_i/b_i) - EP_i^*] \text{ [Export of } Q_i \text{ from } H \text{ to } A];$$

$$0 = [b_i^* P_i - EP_i^*] \text{ [Export of } Q_i^* \text{ from } A \text{ to } H]. \tag{5.1c}$$

The reader can work out how (2.1a) price ratios and (5.1b) must be bounded by competitive arbitrage (even if gold were costly to transport). Generally, for any pair of goods, the bounds on the $(P_i/P_j)/(P_i^*/P_j^*)$ ratios away from unity widen to

$$(b_i^* b_j)(P_i^*/P_j^*) \leq \frac{P_i}{P_j} \leq \frac{P_i^*/P_j^*}{b_i b_j^*}; \tag{5.1a}$$

$$(P_i/P_j) = \frac{P_i^*/P_j^*}{b_i b_j^*} \tag{5.1c}$$

when A exports j and imports i, etc.; see Samuelson (1952, 1954a, 1957).

An interesting case is where all goods are "almost perfectly tradable" and *all* $(1 - b_j, 1 - b_j^*)$ are epsilon small. The Casselian equalities of (2.1) are *almost* exactly realized in (5.1).

Balassa-Samuelson discussants sometimes unnecessarily stipulate that trade is to be balanced, with capital movements negligible. In such a situation, so to speak half the almost perfectly tradables will be *Home*-export goods and half will be *Abroad*-export goods. Our export goods will tend to have lower prices here than *Abroad* (expressed in either currency); our imports will tend to have higher prices at *Home* than *Abroad*. One bias will tend to cancel the other under balanced trade.

Cassel's allegedly perfect PPP relation

$$E = \frac{\text{Home Price Level}}{\text{Abroad Price Level}} \tag{5.2}$$

will be exact (in a trivially tautological sense) when all goods are perfectly tradable, provided the index numbers of prices use the *same* goods weightings and formulas. Under balanced trade it will be almost exact when bs and b^*s are all near to unity, since the numerator's upward biases are well matched by the denominator's biases.

Capital movements need not be zero, even in equilibrium. We see that in cases favorable for y_e^*/y_e estimation, sizable capital investment by us would bias foreign prices upward. Therefore, even if they have the same nominal per capita incomes as we (expressed, say, in our currency), the high prices they face entail that y_e^*/y_e measures will overestimate their true y^*/y. If *Home* is the rich country, the *reverse* of the K-H-S effect will obtain when *it* has a large trade surplus. (Warning: when A reports high current Q^*s because of borrowings, there can be danger in regarding it as "enjoying" or "producing" high real income. When GNP and GDP differ, qualifications are in order.)

© Basil Blackwell Ltd 1994

220 Paul A. Samuelson

Although commentators on Penn studies find it useful to dichotomize between tradables and nontradables, virtually all of their data refer to partially nontradables. This makes their data gathering on local (P_j, P_j^*, Q_j, Q_j^*) all the more vital.

A6. Ricardo-Mill Exact 2-Good Models

The 1817 example of Portugal exporting wine while England exports cloth initiated comparative advantage theory. It can be useful to make the point that real incomes can only imperfectly be determined from knowledge about *productivities* alone. To adapt its story to the present purpose, add untradable bricks to tradable wine and cloth. And, in the 1829–1948 manner of J. S. Mill, posit that everyone always spends 40 cents of each dollar of income on cloth and 40 cents on wine, while the remaining 20% goes for bricks.

Begin in case 1 with $L = L^* = 100$; with each English laborer's productivity 2 in cloth, 1 in wine, and 1 in bricks; and with each Portugese laborer's productivity 2 in wine, 1 in cloth, and 1 in bricks. For $j = 1, 2, 3$, write (C_j) and (C_j^*) for respective consumptions of England and Portugal; (Q_j) and (Q_j^*) for their respective productions.

With this initial symmetry of technology, tastes, and endowments, case 1's free-trade equilibrium can be verified to involve

$$y^*/y = 1, \quad (C_1 \ C_2 \ C_3) = (80 \ \ 80 \ \ 20) = (C_1^* \ C_2^* \ C_3^*); \tag{6.1a}$$

$$\frac{P_2}{P_1} = \frac{P_2^*}{P_1^*} = 1, \quad (Q_1 \ Q_2 \ Q_3) = (160 \ \ 0 \ \ 20); \tag{6.1b}$$

$$\frac{P_3}{P_1} = \frac{P_3^*}{P_2^*} = 2, \quad (Q_1^* \ Q_2^* \ Q_3^*) = (0 \ \ 160 \ \ 20); \tag{6.1c}$$

$$U^* = U = (4/5)^{0.4}(4/5)^{0.4}(1/5)^{0.2}. \tag{6.1d}$$

Now, in case 2, let Harrod, Balassa, Samuelson, Bhagwati, and Penn specify a *doubling* of England's productivity in all tradables, while nontradables everywhere and goods in Portugal have no change in productivities at all. Surely this will make $y/y^* > 1$? And will it not entail a Penn effect? Seems like a no-brainer lay-down hand?

Exact calculation shows, however, the following new equilibrium for case 2:

$$y^*/y = 1, \quad (C_1 \ C_2 \ C_3) = (C_1^* \ C_2^* \ C_3^*) = (160 \ \ 80 \ \ 20); \tag{6.2a}$$

$$\frac{P_2}{P_1} = 2 = \frac{P_2^*}{P_1^*}, \quad (Q_1 \ Q_2 \ Q_3) = (320 \ \ 0 \ \ 20); \tag{6.2b}$$

$$\frac{P_3^*}{P_2^*} = 2, \frac{P_3}{P_1} = 4, \quad (Q_1^* \ Q_2^* \ Q_3^*) = (0 \ \ 160 \ \ 20); \tag{6.2c}$$

$$U^* = U = (8/5)^{0.4}(4/5)^{0.4}(1/5)^{0.5}$$
$$= (2^{0.4} \text{ or } 1.38) \times \text{previous common } U. \tag{6.2d}$$

No, the nation with new productivity in tradables has not gained at all on the stagnant nation. Why not? Because the abundance that productivity brings can weaken the innovating region's terms of trade. Here that induced effect completely compensates for the productivity improvement. And, naturally, where there is no rich and poor in this Ricardo-Mill instance, there is no Penn effect of biased exchange-rate conversions possible.

© Basil Blackwell Ltd 1994

Why this anticlimax? That is because we are in the over special, oversimple Millian tastes model of *invariant* fractional expenditures on goods. See (3.4) and (3.5b) above. When, say, general (3.1) were to apply here, and the elasticity of substitution between wine and cloth as a group and bricks were to be *less* than unity, *innovating England can then be punished for its technological prowess*. Then $y < y^*$!

However, let us go on in case 3 to *triple* rather than double the productivities of tradables in England, while staying always in the Ricardo-Mill rules of the game. Then England becomes so big as to become no better off after trade than under its (new) autarky. Portugal comes to get all the benefits of trade. However, lacking any benefits from enhanced domestic productivity, Portugal's y^* now falls definitely below England's enriched y. It is a legitimate task to see whether the Penn effect does or does not obtain.

The reader should check out my following equilibrium calculation for case 3:

$$P_2/P_1 = P_2^*/P_1^* = 2,$$

$$(P_3/P_1 \quad P_1/P_2) = (6 \quad 3) > (4 \quad 2) = (P_3^*/P_1^* \quad P_3^*/P_2^*); \tag{6.3a}$$

$$(Q_1^* \quad Q_2^* \quad Q_3^*) = (0 \quad 160 \quad 20); \quad (Q_1 \quad Q_2 \quad Q_3) = (400 \quad 40 \quad 20); \tag{6.3b}$$

$$(C_1^* \quad C_2^* \quad C_3^*) = (160 \quad 80 \quad 20); \quad (C_1 \quad C_2 \quad C_3) = (240 \quad 120 \quad 20); \tag{6.3c}$$

$$1 < y/y^* = \frac{(12/5)^{0.4}(6/5)^{0.4}(1/5)^{0.2}}{(8/5)^{0.4}(4/5)^{0.4}(1/5)^{0.2}} = (9/4)^{0.4} \approx 1.38; \tag{6.3d}$$

$$1 < y_e/y_e^* = \frac{1(240) + 2(120) + 6(20)}{1(160) + 2(80) + 4(20)} = \frac{600}{400} = 1.5 > 1.38. \text{ QED.} \tag{6.3e}$$

Yes, the Penn effect does obtain here. Yes, the "Bhagwati effect" (in the sense that the nontradable is relatively more dear in the richer country) does obtain here. But:

1. Is this really the Bhagwati effect, which contends that it is highly *labor-intensive* nontradables ("services") that are to be dear in the rich country? Bricks are *not* more labor intensive than cloth or wine for Ricardo. For 1817 Ricardo, *all* goods are equally labor intensive—namely, 100% labor intensive!

2. By contrast suppose in case 4 that L is increased three-fold from our initial specifications and *no* productivity alters from the original specification. To a Portugese observer, or to an observer from Mars who has no peek *into* the black box of England, the equilibrium $(P_2/P_1; P_2^*/P_1^* \quad P_3^*/P_1^* \quad P_3^*/P_2^*) = (2; 2 \quad 4 \quad 2)$ would look exactly the same as prevailed in case 3's example of a tripling of England's productivities in the tradables. However, on a per capita basis in England, its consumptions of tradables are worse now than they were in the original free-trade situation because of an uncompensated-for deterioration in her terms of trade, as P_1/P_2 halves in comparison with case 1's free trade. By contrast, now, on a per capita basis, Portugal's y^* is unchanged from its case 3 level, which was definitely better than in the case 1 status quo ante. England's increase in mere scale, while it hurt her terms of trade and initial y, definitely improved Portugal's terms of trade and y^*.

Now that Portugal is "the rich(er) region," does the Penn effect still obtain? What about one or another version of a Bhagwati effect? To provide precise answers, here is the equilibrium resulting from case 4's tripling of the English population *sans* any changes in productivities:

© Basil Blackwell Ltd 1994

$$(P_2/P_1 \quad P_3/P_1 \quad P_3/P_2 \quad W/P_1 \quad W/P_2 \quad W/P_3)$$
$$= (2 \quad 2 \quad 1 \quad 2 \quad 1 \quad 1); \tag{6.4a}$$

$$(P_2^*/P_1^* \quad P_3^*/P_1^* \quad P_3^*/P_2^* \quad W^*/P_1^* \quad W^*/P_2^* \quad W^*/P_3^*)$$
$$= (2 \quad 4 \quad 2 \quad 4 \quad 2 \quad 1); \tag{6.4b}$$

$$(Q_1^* \quad Q_2^* \quad Q_3^*) = (0 \quad 160 \quad 20); \quad (C_1^* \quad C_2^* \quad C_3^*) = (160 \quad 80 \quad 20); \tag{6.4c}$$

$$\left(\frac{1}{3}Q_1 \quad \frac{1}{3}Q_2 \quad \frac{1}{3}Q_3\right) = \left(\frac{400}{3} \quad \frac{40}{3} \quad \frac{60}{3}\right);$$
$$\left(\frac{1}{3}C_1 \quad \frac{1}{3}C_2 \quad \frac{1}{3}C_3\right) = (80 \quad 40 \quad 20); \tag{6.4d}$$

$$1 < \frac{y^*}{y} = \frac{(8/5)^{0.4}(4/5)^{0.4}(1/5)^{0.2}}{(4/5)^{0.4}(2/5)^{0.2}(1/5)^{0.2}} = (2)^{0.4}(2)^{0.4} = 4^{0.4} \approx 1.74; \tag{6.4e}$$

$$1 < \frac{y_e^*}{y_e} = \frac{(1)160 + 2(80) + 4(20)}{(1)80 + 2(40) + 2(20)} = \frac{400}{200} = 2 > 1.74 \approx \frac{y^*}{y}. \tag{6.4f}$$

Because 1.74 < 2, the Penn effect is shown to be present here. Because (4 2) ⩾ (2 2), nontradable bricks are dearer in rich Portugal (vis-à-vis cloth) than in poor England, agreeing with one version of a Bhagwati effect.

In sum, have our 1817 scenarios confirmed the received wisdoms of the Balassa-Samuelson traditions? Not quite.

The Penn findings are confirmed, but the Ricardo-to-Balassa "explanations and theoretical rationalizations" are brought into some doubt. For there are *no* differential productivities in case 4's last example that produced a Penn effect. Once again we are reminded that there are more valid sufficient conditions for that effect than were contained in the 1817–64 explicit literature of theoretical economics. Terms-of-trade effects temper, and can even negate, productivity effects.

To have a just appreciation of a theory you must have a just appreciation of its limitations. The brute facts documented by the Penn group are, in a sense, more illuminating and of wider scope than the traditional theory proffered to "explain" them. What comes through with flying colors in all my numerical scenarios is this.

The Penn effect is essentially an aspect of correct index-number theory. While exchange-rate conversions more or less correctly pick up the production increases in tradables, they fail to register the more disappointing production increases in non-tradables. Therein lies the essence and rationale of the realistic Penn effect. Exchange-rate conversions are unsound algorithms in cogent index-number theory. One sees this independently even of international trade. Within our great 50 states, who expects $1 to buy the same level of real goods everywhere? No one should. Penn's benchmark methodology, applied to Mississippi and Connecticut, would correct for the mistake of supposing that the former is as poor relative to the latter as would come from merely comparing relative per capita dollar incomes by states. Penn, with labor and intelligence, corrects for what a dollar can buy in each of the two places. And we are in their debt for getting things right.

Notes

1. To measure welfare or potential welfare per person, Penn and others deflate total income by total population (or, what is approximately a proportional thing, by countries' respective labor supplied: say L^* for Portugal and L for England in Ricardo's original 1817 wine-and-

cloth example). In the Heckscher-Ohlin (1919; 1924) development beyond Ricardo's labor-only model, we could imagine those goods producible out of labor and land: from L and T, and from L^* and T^*, by production functions said to be geographically the same in the usual Ohlin version. If factor endowments were identical, $L = L^*$ and $T = T^*$, total incomes would be identical: $Y^* = Y$; and so, by symmetry, would per capita $Y^*/L^* = y^* = Y/L = y$. Even incomes per acre would be equal: $Y^*/T^* = Y/T$ under such symmetric endowments. But now let Portugal have a bit more L^* and a bit less T^*. Factor prices will still be equalized by trade à la Ohlin: $W^* = W$, rentrate* = rentrate; also there is a critical choice of L^*/L and T^*/T such that total Ys are still just equal. But now Portugal has the higher Y^*/T^*; and England has the higher Y/L. Adding third and N Countries, their ordering of T/L ratios generates an ascending series of Penn per capita affluences; and a descending series of per acre real incomes. So long as wine is much more land intensive than cloth manufacture, within a broad range of T/L variation, factor-price equalization could be fully maintained. Moreover, we can add nontradables to our two tradables: e.g., manufactured bricks, very labor-intensive personal services, etc. What is worth noticing for future reference is this: the Penn effect is not to be expected when T/L changes are the sole changes and so long as T/L endowments stay within the cone of complete factor-price equalization!

2. The Penn effect is a clear violation of the crude form of the purchasing-power parity doctrine of Gustav Cassel (1916, 1918, 1983). It is a clear rebuttal of universal correctness of the Law of One Price for each and every good in a perfectly competitive, frictionless, geographical market. If transport costs and trade impediments were zero, and the exchange rate between the at *Home* and *Abroad* currencies was freely at E, then competitive arbitrage would enforce the one-price relation $EP_j^*/P_j = 1$ and $P_j^*/P_j \equiv P_k^*/P_k$, where P_j is the *Home* price, P_j^* the *Abroad* price. Under autarky "1" becomes anything from 0 to infinity. With low transport costs, we can count on $1 + \varepsilon$ or $1 - \varepsilon$, where ε is a small positive number.

Cassel made more than one error, along with his basically correct insight that after a dramatic *balanced* inflation there would be some tendency for the $(P_j/P_k, P_j^*/P_k^*)$ ratios to settle back near the preinflation magnitudes. The Penn effect refutes the Cassel contention that a dollar spent anywhere (after being converted to the currency of that place) buys the same level of well-being (which is equivalent to denying that PPP enforces equal costs of living everywhere as a condition of exchange-rate equilibrium). The Penn effect documents that "living seems cheaper in poor countries than in rich." "Earn in rich countries and retire to spend it in poor" makes some sense for frugal rentiers.

Haim Barkai (1993) documents some dithering on Keynes's part before the 1925 restoration of prewar gold parity. Had I had the wisdom in 1919–25 to question that restoration, I would have dithered in the same way: promising a *possible* future return to 1914; worrying about the danger to employment, exports, and production from a possibly overvalued pound; distrusting use of wholesale-price index numbers; and, I will add, sensing the Penn effect and how it would strengthen the testimony that the British cost of living would be too high if it did come anywhere close to the prosperous US cost of living!

3. If one learns to add 2 + 2 by using left fingers, one eschews the right hand. Bhagwati finds the Lerner diagram useful. As a matter of taste I prefer the 1949 Samuelson diagram (1949, fig. 1, note 1, p. 186). It illuminates why Bhagwati was tempted to use Hicks neutrality, rather than Harrod neutrality or some general case of factor-augmenting technical change. Only for strict Hicks neutrality is figure 1 free from the requirement that there be *identical* production functions in both regions for the tradables. The whole story of relative rather than absolute factor-returns equalization is cogently proved in figure 1. Lefthanders will no doubt prefer to formulate the proof for the Lerner diagram. Later Harrod-neutral or labor-augmenting change is handled; and also general factor-augmenting change.

4. Here is a brief sketch of how duality theory identifies the $U(Q_1, \ldots, Q_n) = U(Q)$ real-income function from observable inverse-demand functions connecting

$$(Q_j, P_j/Y) = (Q_j, \pi_j) = (Q, \pi). \tag{4.1}$$

$$[P_j/Y] = \pi = [D_1(Q), \ldots, D_n(Q)] = [\partial U(Q)/\partial Q_j]U(Q)^{-1}, \quad \text{because} \tag{4.2}$$

© Basil Blackwell Ltd 1994

$$\left[\frac{\partial(\pi_1, \ldots, \pi_n)}{\partial(Q_1, \ldots, Q_n)}\right] = [D_{ij}(Q)] \equiv [D_{ji}(Q)] \tag{4.3}$$

is a testably symmetric Jacobian matrix. Therefore, the following line integral of observables, independently of path of integration, gives

$$U(Q)/U(Q^a) = \exp\left[\int_c \sum_1^n D_j(q) \mathrm{d}q_j\right], \tag{4.4}$$

where c indicates any contour connecting the points Q^a and Q. QED. See Samuelson (1972) for more on Shephard-Samuelson duality.

References

Balassa, Bela, "The Purchasing-Power Parity Doctrine: A Reappraisal," *The Journal of Political Economy* 72 (1964):584–96.

Barkai, Haim, "Productivity Patterns, Exchange Rates, and the Gold Standard Restoration Debate of the 1920s," *History of Political Economy* 25 (1993):1–37.

Bergson, Abram, *The Real National Income of Soviet Russia Since 1928*, Cambridge, Mass.: Harvard University Press, 1961.

Bhagwati, Jagdish, "The Pure Theory of International Trade: A Survey," *The Economic Journal* 74 (1964):1–84.

———, "Why Are Services Cheaper in the Poor Countries?" *The Economic Journal* 94 (1984):279–86.

Cassel, Gustav, "The Present Situation of the Foreign Exchanges," *The Economic Journal* 26 (1916):62–65; 319–23.

———, "Abnormal Deviations in International Exchanges," *The Economic Journal* 28 (1918):413–15.

———, *The Theory of Social Economy*, New York: Harcourt, Brace & Co., 1983.

Clark, Collin, "Theory of Economic Growth," *Econometrica* 17 supp. (1949):112–14.

Diewert, W. E., and Alice Nakamura, eds., *Essays in Index Number Theory*, vol. 1, Amsterdam: North-Holland, 1993.

Eltetö, O., and P. Köves, "On a Problem of Index Number Computation Relating to International Comparison," *Statisztikai Szemle* 42 (1964):507–18.

Fisher, A. G. B., "Production, Primary, Secondary, and Tertiary," *Economic Record* 15 (1939):24–38.

Geary, R. C., "A Note on Comparisons of Exchange Rates and Purchasing Power Between Countries," *Journal of the Royal Statistical Society* 21 (1958):97–99.

Gilbert, Milton, and Irving Kravis, *An International Comparison of National Products and the Purchasing Power of Currencies*, Paris: OEEC, 1954.

Haberler, Gottfried, *Der Internationale Handel. Theorie der Weltwirtschaftlichen Zusammenhänge sowie Darstellung and Analyse über Aussenhandelspolitik*, Berlin: Verlag von Julius Spring, 1933; Alfred Steiner and Frederic Bentham, trans., *The Theory of International Trade with its Applications to Commercial Policy*, Edinburgh: William Hodge; New York: The Macmillan Co., 1936.

Harrod, Roy F., *International Economics*, London: Nisbet and Cambridge University Press, Cambridge Economic Handbooks, 1933; 2nd revised ed., Chicago: The University of Chicago Press, 1957.

Heckscher, Eli F., "The Effect of Foreign Trade on the Distribution of Income," *Ekonomisk Tidskrift* 1919; reprinted in H. S. Ellis and L. Metzler, (eds.), *Readings in the Theory of International Trade*, Philadelphia: Blakiston, 1949.

Hicks, John, "The Valuation of the Social Income: A Comment on Professor Kuznets' Reflection," *Econometrica*, n.s., 15 (1948):163–72.

Houthakker, Hendrick, "Should We Devalue the Dollar?" *Challenge* 11 (1962):10–12.

———, "Exchange rate adjustment," Compilation of Studies Prepared for the Subcommittee on International Exchange and Payments, *Factors Affecting the United States Balance of Payments*, Joint Economic Committee, 87th Congress; 2nd Session, 1962, pp. 297–304.

Jones, Ronald W., "A Three-Factor Model in Theory, Trade, and History," in J. N. Bhagwati, R. W. Jones, R. A. Mundell, and V. Jaroslav, (eds.), *Trade, Balance of Payments, and Growth*, Amsterdam: North-Holland, 1971, pp. 3–21.

Khamis, Salem H., "A New System of Index Numbers for National and International Purposes," *Journal of the Royal Statistical Society*, ser. A, 135 (1972):96–121.

Kravis, Irving B., Alan Heston, and Robert Summers, *International Comparisons of Real Product and Purchasing Power*, Baltimore: The Johns Hopkins University Press, 1978.

———, "The Share of Services in Economic Growth," in F. G. Adams and Bert Hickman, (eds.), *Global Econometrics: Essays in Honor of Lawrence R. Klein*, Cambridge, Mass.: The MIT Press, 1983, pp. 188–218.

Kravis, Irving B., Zoltan Kenessey, Alan Heston, and Robert Summers, *A System of International Comparisons of Gross Product and Purchasing Power*, Baltimore: The John Hopkins University Press, 1975.

Kuznets, Simon, "On the Valuation of Social Income: Reflections on Professor Hicks' Article, pt. I–II," *Econometrica*, n.s., 15 (1948):116–31.

Leontief, Wassily, "Domestic Production and Foreign Trade: the American Capital Position Re-examined," *Economia Internazionale* 7 (1954):9–38.

Lerner, Abba, "Factor Prices and International Trade," *Economica*, n.s., 19 (1952):1–15.

McKinnon, Ronald, "Monetary and Exchange Rate Policies for International Financial Stability: A Proposal," *The Journal of Economic Perspectives* 2 (1988):83–104.

Mill, John S., *Essays on Some Unsettled Questions of Political Economy*. London: Longman, Green, Reader & Dyer, [1829] 1844.

———, *The Principles of Political Economy*, London: Longman, Green, 1848.

Ohlin, Bertil, *Handelns Teori*, Stockholm: AB Nordiska Bokhandeln, 1924; Reprinted in English as *Interregional and International Trade*, Cambridge, Mass.: Harvard University Press, 1933.

Ricardo, David, *The Principles of Political Economy and Taxation*, London: J. M. Dent and Sons, 1911; also in P. Sraffa, (ed.), *Works of David Ricardo*, vol. 1, Cambridge: Cambridge University Press, 1951.

Samuelson, Paul A., "Disparity in Postwar Exchange rate," in Seymour Harris, (ed.), *Foreign Economic Policy for the United States*, Cambridge, Mass.: Harvard University Press, 1948; reproduced as ch. 64 in J. E. Stiglitz, ed., *The Collected Scientific Papers of Paul A. Samuelson*, vol. 2, Cambridge, Mass.: The MIT Press, 1966.

———, "International Factor-Price Equalization Once Again," *Economic Journal* 59 (1949): 181–97; reproduced as ch. 68 in J. E. Stiglitz, ed., *The Collected Scientific Papers of Paul A. Samuelson*, vol. 2, Cambridge, Mass.: The MIT Press, 1966.

———, "Evaluation of Real National Income," *Oxford Economic Papers*, n.s., 2 (January 1950):1–29; reproduced as ch. 77 in J. E. Stiglitz, ed., *The Collected Scientific Papers of Paul A. Samuelson*, vol. 2, Cambridge, Mass.: The MIT Press, 1966.

———, "Spatial Price Equilibrium and Linear Programming," *The American Economic Review* 42 (1952):283–303; reproduced as ch. 72 in J. E. Stiglitz, ed., *The Collected Scientific Papers of Paul A. Samuelson*, vol. 2, Cambridge, Mass.: The MIT Press, 1966.

———, "The Transfer Problem and Transport Costs, II: Analysis of Effects of Trade Impediments," *The Economic Journal* 64 (1954a):264–89; reproduced as ch. 75 in J. E. Stiglitz, ed., *The Collected Scientific Papers of Paul A. Samuelson*, vol. 2, Cambridge, Mass.: The MIT Press, 1966.

Samuelson, Paul A., "Intertemporal price equilibrum: A prologue to the Theory of Speculation," *Weltwirtschaftliches Archiv* 79 (1957):181–219; reproduced as ch. 73 in J. E. Stiglitz, ed., *The Collected Scientific Papers of Paul A. Samuelson*, vol. 2, Cambridge, Mass.: The MIT Press, 1966.

———, "The Evaluation of 'Social Income': Capital Formation and Wealth," in F. A. Lutz and D. C. Hague, (eds.), *The Theory of Capital*, London: Macmillan, 1961; reproduced as

© Basil Blackwell Ltd 1994

ch. 27 in J. E. Stiglitz, ed., *The Collected Scientific Papers of Paul A. Samuelson*, vol. 1, Cambridge, Mass.: The MIT Press, 1966.

——, "Theoretical Notes on Trade Problems," *The Review of Economics and Statistics* 46 (1964):145–54; reproduced as ch. 65 in J. E. Stiglitz, ed., *The Collected Scientific Papers of Paul A. Samuelson*, vol. 2, Cambridge, Mass.: The MIT Press, 1966.

——, "Ohlin was right," *The Swedish Journal of Economics* 73 (1971):365–84; reproduced as ch. 254 in H. Nagatani and K. Crowley, eds., *The Collected Scientific Papers of Paul A. Samuelson*, vol. 4, Cambridge, Mass.: The MIT Press, 1977.

——, "Unification Theorem for the Two Basic Dualities of Homothetic Demand Theory," *Proceedings of the National Academy of Sciences, USA* 69 (1972):2673–74; reproduced as ch. 212 in H. Nagatani and K. Crowley, eds., *The Collected Scientific Papers of Paul A. Samuelson*, vol. 4, Cambridge, Mass.: The MIT Press, 1977.

——, "Analytical Notes on International Real-Income Measures," *The Economic Journal* 84 (1974a):595–608; reproduced as ch. 210 in H. Nagatani and K. Crowley, eds., *The Collected Scientific Papers of Paul A. Samuelson*, vol. 4, Cambridge, Mass.: The MIT Press, 1977.

——, "Complementarity: An Essay on the 40th Anniversary of the Hicks-Allen Revolution in Demand Theory," *Journal of Economic Literature* 12 (1974b):1255–89; reproduced as ch. 208 in H. Nagatani and K. Crowley, eds., *The Collected Scientific Papers of Paul A. Samuelson*, vol. 4, Cambridge, Mass.: The MIT Press, 1977.

——, "Second thoughts on analytical income comparisons," *The Economic Journal* 94 (1984):267–78; reproduced as ch. 299 in K. Crowley, ed., *The Collected Scientific Papers of Paul A. Samuelson*, vol. 5, Cambridge, Mass.: The MIT Press, 1986.

Summers, Robert and Alan Heston, "The Penn World Table (Mark 5): An Expanded Set of International Comparisons, 1950–1988," *Quarterly Journal of Economics*, 106 (1991): 327–68.

Szulc (Schultz), B. J., "Indices for Multiregional Comparisons," *Przeglad Statystyczny* 3 (1964):239–54.

Viner, Jacob, "Introduction. Professor Taussig's Contribution to the Theory of International Trade," ch. I in *Explorations in Economics Notes and Essays in Honor of F. W. Taussig*, New York and London: McGraw-Hill Book Co., Inc., 1936, pp. 3–12.

——, *Studies in the Theory of International Trade*, New York: Harper & Sons, 1937.

525

FOREWORD

THE NEW LEFT is an important movement in the history of ideas. It is an important ideology in the political struggle for men's minds. It is the continuation of an important strand in the development of economics and the related social sciences, and represents a growing discontent on the part of students with what they are being taught in the universities.

Yet where can the open-minded reader go for a detailed discussion and evaluation of the basic tenets of the New Left? There of course are no shortages of tracts and treatises written by radical critics of the social order. And, if all you want are vituperative denunciations of any ideas newer than those of Herbert Spencer or Friedrich Hayek, there are plenty of books and Rotary speeches glorifying free enterprise and condemning atheistic communism. But no one, before Professor Lindbeck, has had the patience to collect together the various notions of the New Left, sift and analyze them, and finally to give an unsparing evaluation —involving both critique and acceptance—of their validity and limitations.

THE STRANGER AS JUDGE AND JURY
Thirty years ago, when the Carnegie Foundation sought to commission an objective study of America's racial problems, it turned to a Swedish economist, Gunnar Myrdal. Precisely because Myrdal came from a society that lacked our racial heterogeneity, he would be able, it was hoped, to arrive more nearly to objective truth. And so it turned out: *An American Dilemma* by Myrdal is not only one of the few

classics in the social sciences, but, in addition, it alerted us and the world to the fact that we were an unconscionably divided house, only superficially in a state of equilibrium. The fundamental decisions by the Supreme Court, the Civil Rights movement, the struggle toward integration—all of these things which have become commonplaces were foreseen in the Myrdal study.

Once before it was from the pen of an outsider that America came to know itself. Precisely because de Tocqueville was a Frenchman, rather sympathetic to much in the ancien régime that had vanished with the French Revolution and rather unsympathetic with the nascent notions of American individualism, he was able to discern and extrapolate the characteristic features of a new society. If I wish my face to be drawn as it is, I must not go to my lover. Nor to my enemy. Only what is seen for the first time can be perceived in its uniqueness.

But not any stranger can pen the likeness of a revolutionary movement. Political economy must be grateful that Assar Lindbeck happened to be a visiting professor at Columbia University in the academic year 1968–1969. The right man was at the right place at the right time. To economists, Professor Lindbeck needs no introduction. Appointed at a comparatively early age to the prestigious chair in international economics at Stockholm University, Dr. Lindbeck is one of the young turks in Swedish economics. His grandsires, so to speak, were the great Swedish economists of the First World War period, Gustav Cassel and, above all, the incomparable Knut Wicksell. (Wicksell, who wrote one of his books from jail, never hesitated to speak out in good causes however unpopular: his views against marriage, against the monarchy, against religion, and against a Swedish standing army on the Russian borders kept him from a university post until the age of almost 50; his view that the worker would gain more in real wages from a non-Marxist evolution of the Welfare State lost him popularity in other circles, a fact which inhibited him from speaking his mind not at all.) Lindbeck's immediate teachers were of that vintage generation of Swedish economists: Myrdal, Bertil Ohlin, Bent Hansen, Erik Lindahl, Erik Lundberg, Ingvar Svennilson—but really the list is too long to enumerate.

Assar Lindbeck, though, is his own man. As a schoolboy he saw with his own eyes the flirtations with Hitler's superrace doctrines to which some Swedes succumbed in the days of the successful *blitzkrieg*. No ancient doctrine of Swedish neutrality has kept this soldier in the army of humanity from criticizing, criticizing bitterly, the United States policies in Vietnam. Just as in this country most economists have been associated with the critics of the ruling elite, the business elite—favoring the Democratic programs of the New Deal, Fair Deal, New Frontier, and Great Society, rather than the rugged individualism of Herbert Hoover and/or Barry Goldwater or the moderated versions of Eisenhower and Nixon—it has always been my impression when visiting Sweden that most of the economists there have been rather critical of their own Labor government. Economists, apparently, tend to be perverse! Lindbeck, however, is one of the economists who has been a defender of the general policy of the Social Democrats, though a "friendly (sympathetic) critic" of many details. It is germane to mention this because, if you are too far away from a social movement, you rarely have the interest or the competence to appraise it. Every day of his life, a Social Democrat is fighting through in his own mind the great issues of egalitarianism and efficiency with which the New Left is now engaged. No wonder then that when he visited Cambridge, New York, and Berkeley, Professor

Lindbeck kept his ears open to hear what was being said; and kept his mind open to evaluate the sounds heard. Moreover, a scholar trained in the European tradition can, thank heaven, be expected to know a good deal about the writings of Fourier and Owen, Proudhon and Kropotkin, Marx and Engels, Luxemburg and Lenin, Sorel and Gramsci, along with the more recent writings of Baran, Sweezy, Mandel, Mills, Cohn-Bendit, and Galbraith. Hanging up a picture of Che in your dormitory room is only the first step on the way to understanding the laws of motion of capitalistic development.

THE TEXT BEFORE US
During his sojourn in the United States, Professor Lindbeck was able to try out his first drafts of this book on audiences in Cambridge, New York, and Berkeley. It says something for the complacency of American economics that, prior to Lindbeck's lecture at MIT, many of our graduate students had thought of the New Left as having something to do with politics, not with honest-to-goodness economics.

The Swedish version of this book was published in paperback form under the title, *Den nya vänsterns politiska ekonomi*. So resonant was the response, that the book was soon translated into Danish; and a Finnish translation is now in the works. This present expanded American version is not a translation from the Swedish, but an English text prepared by Professor Lindbeck.

Who ought to read this book? I fear that those who need it most are least likely to crack its pages. Those who believe that Milton Friedman's modernization of Adam Smith is all one can know or needs to know about economic policy will hardly be tempted to spend an afternoon studying Lindbeck's evaluations of notions about manipulated consumer preferences or decentralized planning. On the other hand,

I hope that those on the New Left will not be put off by Lindbeck's occasional tart critiques. De Tocqueville's strictures on America were at first resented, particularly where his shafts went to the heart; but in the end we gained more from his work than did the supercilious Europeans.

When Lindbeck points out that often the New Left manages to be critical *both of the market and of the bureaucracy,* and that it is a sign of immaturity or of sentimentalism to think you can have it both ways, he is as little likely to be as popular with the groups he comments on as Margaret Mead would be if she called to the attention of the citizenry of New Guinea the oddity of their refusal to sleep with their cousin's cousin, or their insistence upon doing nothing but that.

An active member of the New Left will, then, not read the book in the expectation that it will convince him of the error of his ways. He will read it in order to give his views that severe self-testing which, as John Stuart Mill reminded us in connection with the necessity for free speech, is a necessary condition for conviction.

But most of all one would expect the readers of this book to be those who, like its author, have still an open mind on these momentous issues. You don't have to be an econometrician to tie in to this discussion. You don't even have to be a student of economics. No diagrams or equations interrupt this reasoned conversation. To be sure, the non-economist will not polish off this text in the time that he can read *Love Story.* But he will, I am sure, learn more from these hundred or so pages and will be given more to ponder over than if he spends the weekend grappling with the prolix sermons of Charles Reich's *The Greening of America.*

To the New Left most of the currently fashionable economic textbooks look pretty much alike. Any of them would benefit from being assigned alongside of the present work. Just because *Pride and Prejudice* is assigned in school doesn't make Jane Austen a dull writer; just because a paperback appears on a compulsory reading list doesn't make its subject matter boring or irrelevant. I may add that some unconventional economic textbooks, written by those proud to call themselves radical economists, are now on the way. This Lindbeck book will not lose in usefulness in being assigned as collateral reading along with such new textbooks.

THE NEW CONSCIOUSNESS

Good wine needs no glowing introduction. But I think it is appropriate for me to point out that Lindbeck's discussion has a relevance that goes far beyond the New Left itself. The ideas he is examining are not the esoteric views of a small sect of the SDS or of Village bohemians. Every single notion that is fervently held by those revolutionaries zealous to reform the bone and marrow of contemporary society are endemic in the minds of all of our population under 30.

It is laughable to think of John Kenneth Galbraith, although he is often cited by the New Left, as a revolutionary; and there is no shortage of critics from the Left who regard him as an echo of Thorstein Veblen and an apologist for the new industrial state his pen describes. Still, the ideas of Galbraith have an importance today that exceeds any influence Veblen had during his lifetime or since his death. For a better parallel you must turn to the role that R. H. Tawney played in converting the minds of educated Englishmen away from the Tory–Liberal dichotomy and toward a fundamental rejection of the acquisitive society. Alert Americans, before they have arrived in college as freshmen, have already read *The Affluent Society* and sampled *The New*

Industrial State. This helps explain why Ralph Nader is one of the most important men in America today. The fact that he is so is a reflection of a deep distrust of the business establishment and a similar suspicion of the government itself. This is not a passing mood which will evaporate once the Kent State killings are forgotten and a Vice President Agnew stops shooting off his mouth.

It is true that the campuses have been quieter in some years than in others. It is true that the ending of the Vietnam war will remove some of the deeper resentments of the younger generation. But to think that opinions have now reverted back to the hopeful days of John F. Kennedy is as naive as it used to be to think in the later 1930s that, once the economy had gotten its second wind following a malignant depression, the American mind had returned to the verities of Calvin Coolidge and Alfred Sloan.

Look at Lindbeck's contents page and purge your mind from any interest in the New Left as such. Concern about the quality of life is not the monopoly of a radical fringe. Or consider that tendency to reject both bureaucracy and the market as coordinator of resource allocation. Whatever its consistency, this strikes a resonant response all across the political spectrum. When Professor Lindbeck points out that the most elementary tools of supply and demand will correctly predict the inequities and inefficiencies to be expected from rent controls in the city, he will raise the hackles of every college student in the land— which is all the more reason why he should be read. When Lindbeck points out that Galbraith's model of quasi-absolute corporation monarchs, who tell us what to want and buy, lacks a determinative theory of how this one particular group of 200 giants happened to stake out claims to the areas they inhabit, the orthodox general-equilibrium theorist must hang his head in shame that he had not paid the

Galbraith system the compliment of taking it sufficiently seriously to have noted this lacuna in it; and, of course, no Marxian methodologist will be fobbed off with a model that simply has some group or agents having the ability to get what they *want* to get.

I could go on pointing out new insights that Lindbeck has put forth. And since no two people can be expected to give the same emphases in fields that are controversial and subtle, I daresay I could differ with some of the author's judgments—strictures against the critics that strike me as too strong, concessions to their arguments that strike me as gratuitous. Such tasks can be left to the future, to those polemicists who will spring up from both the Right and the Left to denounce the author for his findings.

Let me merely conclude by calling attention to Lindbeck's important discernment that one of the most notable things that is new about the New Left is its dominance by what may be called the university mentality—by youth. But before doing so, I think one disclaimer should be made. Professor Lindbeck is discussing the New Left and what I have called the "modern consciousness." He is not at all purporting to discuss that narrower movement which is called *radical economics*. Within American universities today the radical economists constitute an important trend. At Harvard, names like Samuel Bowles, Arthur MacEwan, Herbert Gentis, Thomas Weisskopf, and Stephen Marglin stand for something new under the sun. Elsewhere, at The New School for Social Research, American University, Stonybrook, Cornell, Stanford, the public universities of California, names such as Michael Hudson, Stephen Hymer, Edward Nell, Thomas Vietorisz, James Weaver, Michael Zweig, Douglas Dowd, John Gurley, James O'Connor, Robert Fitch, and Mary Oppenheimer represent to one familiar with the domestic scene in academia a serious research movement from which much will be heard in the future. The fact that other leading universities do not have members of the URPE on their mastheads does not mean that at those universities there is not among the students, both graduate and undergraduate, a growing interest in alternative economics to that of the standard textbooks. Since the time of Professor Lindbeck's visiting professorship in America, this movement has grown in numbers and importance. It was appropriate, however, for Professor Lindbeck to desist from judging a research effort that is just beginning; later, when the fruits of these studies begin to pile up, it will be inexcusable if the American economics profession does not give them the attention, and praise and critiques, that their quality and seriousness merit.

FROM THE JUNIOR COMMON ROOM

Who shall lead the revolution? Many answers have been given. The downtrodden worker himself. But not by himself, necessarily: with the help of the intellectual bourgeoisie. Or, in Lenin's reformulation, the professional agitator and revolutionist must be counted upon to shape the spontaneous consciousness of the downtrodden proletariat, sheltering them from the temptations of revisionist reform and cooling off the premature enthusiasms of disastrous utopianism.

Now Marcuses and Goodmans and Reichs have come forward to say to university youth: Who shall lead? It is *you* who shall lead. Upon reflection, the message is found to have merit in the ears of their listeners. Indeed, who is the most repressed by modern society? Who is most learned and least tainted with the rottenness of the older generation? The questions answer themselves.

I exaggerate, but I do not jest. The Marxian strategy of trying to understand the development of ideology and history out of the material conditions of production and class structure of society leads to fruitful hypotheses in this area. Youth, college youth, do not form a class in the conventional Marxian sense; but they do live under conditions peculiar to themselves, with a distinguishable economic base. And all *a priori* theories aside, one must accept the facts of experience: it was youth who formed the spearhead of the civil rights movement in the South. When white liberals were no longer welcome there, the action moved toward opposition, passive and active, to the Vietnam war. The fortress of the university itself came under siege in the name of "participatory democracy." The unmaking of a President, LBJ, was the fruit of work by young people in the New Hampshire campaign of Eugene McCarthy.

There is nothing new about this except in America. Abroad, the campus has always been the seedbed of social change. Korean and Indonesian governments have toppled when students shook the tree. The Japanese are great imitators of Western technology, but where radical activity on the part of students is concerned, and, for that matter, interest in Marxism on the part of the faculty, the Japanese have long been in the van. When the long-suffering students in Paris—now there *is* an exploited group—erupted in 1968, they very nearly brought down the de Gaulle government.

A class is formed as much by pressures from without as from within. Persecution of the Jews helps to maintain their group cohesion. By this test, students have come to form a distinct class. Students today elicit an enormous amount of hate, not merely from the hard-hat workers, but from the populace at large. When those over 30 meet for innocent merriment, their conversation about youth always involves the ominous pronoun "they." Over her third martini, the anxious dowager asks nervously: "Is it true that they smell?" What orgies of sexual pleasure are not imputed to the integrated dormitory life? TV coverings of Woodstock festivals and Washington marches keep alive the image of the bearded and long-haired barbarian within our midst.

How can students be both against bureaucracy and against the market, the objective stranger asks. The only alternative is utopian self-sufficient kibbutzim. Yes, indeed it is. Students are not out to make the universities like life; they wish to make life like the university, the nearest thing to the kibbutz one will ever know. Read *Walden* and you will realize that Thoreau was able to lead the good life there precisely because the rest of the world provided him with the library books and the sustenance that could not be grown on the shores of Walden Pond. Read Fred Skinner's *Walden Two*, and try to draw up the balance sheet and income statement of his utopian colony. I defy you to show that it can continue to exist as a viable economic entity without monthly allowance checks from parents outside the community.* If simple living and intelligent goodwill could solve the economic problem, poverty in East Pakistan or Haiti would soon be a thing of the past. So it is within

---

*Since writing these lines, I have come across a most delicious illustration of the rentier psychology that underwrites—oh happy word—the Ivy League mind. Dwight Macdonald, that doughty graduate from the Trotskyist ranks, was asked at Yale what he thought of Galbraith's complaint that Reich's Consciousness III was unconscious of its own economic base.

> *Macdonald:* . . . I think Galbraith's reaction ["Who's going to mind the store?"] is philistine. It reminds me of people who criticize anarchism by saying, "But who's going to collect the garbage?" Incidentally, Fourier had a very interesting solution to the garbage problem in his utopia. His idea was to have it collected by *les petites hordes*—children love to play with dirt, so let them enjoy themselves in this way. . . .

Marie Antoinette is alive and well, living in Mayor Lindsay's New York!

the university. The commissary provides the bare minimum of nutrition. (That's all it provides!) Clothing is no item of expense in an era of bluejeans and bell bottoms. Where there is a sense of community and sharing, housing space becomes no problem at all.

But, you will object, many students still work their way through school, in whole or in part. True, but the number is way down: the night school is one of the casualties of the modern age. Even a state university must look beyond its own student body for switchboard operators and maintenance workers. And the places in which the students by and large must depend on themselves for subsistence, by contrast with the elite universities of the Ivy League, serve to reinforce the point being made. I have been struck when lecturing at commuter schools, such as Suffolk University in Boston or the Chicago campus of the University of Illinois or vocationally minded places like the University of Cincinnati and the Rutgers Graduate School of Business, that I am in a different world from my usual milieu of MIT, Harvard, or Yale. Indeed, the University of Illinois at Urbana differs less from Princeton than it does from the Chicago campus. To appreciate the difference you must talk with the recruiters sent out each spring by corporations to interview prospective graduates for possible jobs as junior executives. One of the questions that businessmen often put to an academic teacher is the wistful query: "Why are we in business so disliked? What can we do to change our image?"

For my thesis it is not necessary that more than 10 to 20 percent of the student population undergo a change in consciousness. Most of the world never changes but continues in the ways of their parents. So it was throughout the period of the opening up of Japan to the outer world. So it was in Czarist Russia, through the 1905 revolution and right up to the 1917 transformation: reading the novels of Russian life and the letters of political exiles gives a completely biased picture of what the bulk of the population is thinking and doing; but it gives you a useful picture of what the pace-setters of ideology and opinion are thinking about the future.

A reader of Lindbeck will be prepared to understand how important the movement connected with Ralph Nader has become. It is not primarily hippies or activists who mutter, "Right on," when Nader's legions castigate General Motors for contrived obsolescence through frequent model changes; if it were, General Motors would be much less worried. What many of the readers of *Time* magazine think today, the antitrust division of the government may come to think and act upon tomorrow. Therein lies the power of ideas.

To the reader about to sample the Lindbeck vintage, I say "skoal!"

PAUL A. SAMUELSON

MIT
June, 1971

On just how great 'great books' are

Paul A. Samuelson

Joseph Schumpeter used to tell his Harvard classes that, to achieve fame, books are better than articles. Edgeworth and Marshall were his proofs, but by then the example had already misfired. In the front trenches we took Marshall's three tomes for granted; it was Edgeworth we excavated to understand Pareto Optimality, second-best taxation, non-constant scale returns and firm sizes, von Stackelberg asymmetric duopoly and game theory, the analytics of many-good many-countries comparative advantage, *core* theory and much else.

Besides, life came to teach me that great books usually turn out to be great busts. I am referring to *The Decline of the West, The End of History,* the *Communist Manifesto,* and *Das Kapital,* Volume I, or *The Road to Serfdom.*

Schumpeter's own special prophetic twist was no exception. Capitalism was doomed, he prophesied, but not so much from its weakness as from its genuine successes and, in consequence, socialistic communism was inevitable and would work out to be tolerably effective. What reading of 1920–2000 history confirms *that* schemata? To my mind one great 1945 Hayek article outweighs in the balance his 1931 *Prices and Production* with its Andy Warhol moment of celebrity or Hayek's 1944 prediction that each humanitarian step against *laissez-faire* is a slide down the slippery slope to Stalin-Mao and Pol Pot serfdom. Every author has a call option on vindication but in the first half-century of life for *The Road to Serfdom* the realities of post-Roosevelt America, post-Thatcher–Blair UK, post-Palme Sweden and Hayek's own Austria have not yet brought this book's options' market value back up to its original exercise price.

Great books are full of *algebraic* knowledge. Negative knowledge compares as badly with ignorance as ignorance compares with tested-out knowledge. Do not believe that those items on the menu that you don't order can't hurt you. In the history of ideas it is a book's *innuendo* that constitutes its positivistic cash value. One-line Malthus lives forever; his qualifications are on file in the dustbin of history. I say dig into the files.

'Oh, that my enemy would write a book.' This is an unworthy wish to be able to do the enemy in by cogently rebutting his faulty syllogisms and biased empirical nominations. Yet I will second its motion for a quite different reason. Experience teaches you that you have more to learn from the enemy than the friend. Friends only echo back to us what we already believe (which may be right or wrong). Charles Darwin was so great because he pre-empted for himself the investigation of arguments *against* his own theses – and this long before Karl Popper!

In terms of human sympathy, I reverse the unworthy saying to read: 'Would that my friend would *not* write a Great book.' Poor Schumpeter. The actuary in the sky gave him but two decades at Harvard. Most of his extra-curricular energies during the first of these he squandered on his 1939 two-volume *Business Cycles*. Instead of going far beyond the heuristic insights of his youthful 1912 classic on development, it was stillborn as an anti-climatic failure: a tale of Kondratieff, Juglar and Crum–Kitchin periodicities that never caught on even with the Sunday rotogravure pages; and a paean to the creative catharsis of a depression that was actually decimating aggregate production and eroding away Solow total-factor productivity.

Cleo's perverse sense of humor is even handed. Maynard Keynes's big book of the 1920s, his 1930 *Treatise on Money*, was a sterile flop to both friend and foe wherever its novel fundamental tautologies were concerned. Only by undeserved good luck did the occurrence of the great 1929–33 depression induce in and from him the incomparable 1936 *General Theory*. This book's numerous imperfections ultimately got sorted out, but primarily by use of its own new paradigms. Double and triple luck that sometimes favours genius.

Consider Newton's great *Principia*. Virtually nobody even in its own time really read its Latin and calculus proofs disguised in dead geometry. Nor had they need to do so. Enough to know it was there. And what was the 'it' that was there? Two short pages of differential equations of accelerations proportional to the inverse square of the distances between N point-mass objects – that was what Henri Poincaré needed to build his new methods in celestial mechanics and from which modern chaos theory was able to qualify Laplace's boast that he could rationalize the deterministic future and the deterministic past.

All Nobel Prizes are equal. But none exceeds the 1961 Medicine and Physiology prize to Crick-Watson for their double helix model of DNA. Jim Watson's 1968 *Double Helix* book is a telling cartoon about how some science actually gets done in real life. However, the microbiology work that evoked the prize from the Stockholm Karlinska Institute and launched a million research ships was a short, laconic article in 1953 *Nature*.

Economics is not physics. It is not evolutionary genetics or Gibbsian thermodynamics. It is not exact art; nor do its evolutionary trends suggest convergence toward exact or exact-stochastic art. But that does not mean that it – or any human or organic discipline – is blessed or cursed with special powers or limitations.

Apropos my present point. I end near where I began with the contrast between Edgeworth and Marshall. Since their time, within one academic lifetime, the modern edifice of finance theory was conceived, delivered and came of age; it also was predictably opposed by respected elders of our congregation. One of its great books, the 1959 Cowles Monograph by Harry Markowitz on optimizing mean-variance quadratic programming algorithms for 'efficient' portfolio diversification, has changed how thousands of real-world practitioners operate in a way that no work of Pigou, Samuelson or John Doe has ever done. We would be the poorer had this handbook never been patiently spelled out. But the essential essence of it was already in the 1952 *Journal of Finance* article write-up of Markowitz's University of Chicago Ph.D. thesis, an item that initially met with less than universal admiration from its academic examiners. As Max Planck noticed, science does progress funeral by funeral.

References

Crick, Francis H. C. and Watson, James (1953). A structure for deoxyribose nucleic acid. *Nature*, 171: 737–8.
Edgeworth, Francis Y. (1925). *Papers Relating to Political Economy*, vols I, II and III. London: Macmillan for the Royal Economic Society.
Fukuyama, Francis (1992). *The End of History and the Last Man*. New York and Toronto: The Free Press.
Hayek, Friedrich von (1931). *Prices and Production*. London: G. Routledge.
Hayek, Friedrich von (1944). *The Road to Serfdom*. Chicago: University of Chicago Press.
Hayek, Friedrich von (1945). The use of knowledge in society. *American Economic Review*, 35: 519–30.
Keynes, John Maynard (1930). *A Treatise on Money*, vols I and II. London: Macmillan.
Keynes, John Maynard (1936). *The General Theory of Employment, Interest and Money*. London: Macmillan.
Laplace, Pierre Simon (1798–1823). *Traité de mecanique celeste*, Books 1–7. Paris: Echez J. B. M. Duprat.
Lorenz, Edward N. (1993). *The Essence of Chaos*. Seattle: University of Washington Press.
Markowitz, Harry M. (1952). Portfolio Selection. *Journal of Finance*, 7: 77–91.
Markowitz, Harry M. (1959). *Portfolio Selection, Efficient Diversification of Investments*. Cowles Foundation Monograph 16. New Haven and London: Yale University Press.
Marx, Karl (1848). *Manifest der Kommunistischen Partei*. Written in collaboration with Friedrich Engels. In English: *Manifesto of the Communist Party*. New York: International Publishers, 1948.
Marx, Karl (1867). *Das Kapital*, vol. I. Chicago: Charles H. Kerr and Company, 1909. Hammonsworth: Penguin Books, 1976.
Newton, Isaac (1687). *Philosophiae Naturalis Principia Mathematica*.
Poincaré, Henri (1892–99). *Les methodes nouvelles de la mecanique celeste*. Paris: Gauthier-Villars et fils.

Marshall, Alfred (1890–1920). *Principles of Economics.* London: Macmillan.
Marshall, Alfred (1919). *Industry and Trade.* London: Macmillan.
Marshall, Alfred (1923). *Money, Credit and Commerce.* London: Macmillan.
Schumpeter, Joseph (1939). *Business Cycles,* vols I and II. New York: McGraw-Hill.
Schumpeter, Joseph (1912, 1934). *The Theory of Economic Development.* Leipzig: Dunder & Humboldt. Translated into English by R. Opie. Cambridge, Mass.: Harvard University Press.
Spengler, Oswald (1939). *The Decline of the West.* New York: Alfred A. Knopf.
Watson, James (1968). *The Double Helix, a personal account of the discovery of the structure of DNA.* New York: Atheneum.

Coeditor's Foreword

Reflections on How Biographies of Individual Scholars Can Relate to a Science's Biography

Paul A. Samuelson

This book adds up to more than the sum of its parts. When W. Somerset Maugham opined that "to know one country you must know two countries," he was saying in a different way that 1 + 1 can exceed 2. Adam Smith and Allyn Young categorized this as "increasing returns to scale."

When a discipline—economics, chemistry, or acupuncture—is in a dynamic stage of rapid growth, its up-front cyclists care little whether it was Newton or Leibniz who "invented" the calculus. The economics profession is in such a dynamic stage of rapid growth, as made clear by the interviews in this book. The book permits us to step back and view the whole of the field in a revealing context that otherwise is easily missed in the narrow focus of individual expert researchers. The twenty-first century's go-getters in economics go whole hours ignoring what more John Bates Clark did for marginal productivity theorizing, than Johann Ludwig von Thünen had not already done.

This helps explain the historical fact that the role in the graduate curriculum once played by "History of Economic Thought" has eroded down to a narrow cadre of learned experts. An unearned snobbery ensues, as is well illustrated by Bernard Shaw's canard: "Those who can, do. Those who can't, teach." Good history of science deserves a nonzero weight in the university curriculum. The dynamic growth in individual subfields of the economics profession needs to be supplemented by overviews of the whole, not just as the sum of its normally separated parts. This book provides such a view of the whole of the modern field of economics and the connection of that whole with the life experiences of famous economists whose work was seminal to the field.

Returning to the theme of how multiplicity of cases can be fruitful, let's test an alleged dictum of Socrates: "The unexamined life is not worth living." When I once read an excellent book about the principal philosophers, all the usual suspects were there: Spinoza, Kant, Hegel, Wittgenstein, Russell, ... My inductive finding was that Socrates had it completely wrong. An unhappier gaggle of misfits could hardly be imagined. Suicides abounded, melancholies persisted, celibacies and divorces competed for frequencies. A vulgar explanation would nominate as a common cause that the study of philosophy destroys the joy of life. Perhaps a better explanation would be that becoming an orphan early, or being born dyslexic, et cetera, predisposes one to choose philosophy over being a cheerful bartender. Acquiring an objective and insightful overview of the whole in any area of understanding is important, but less easily and enjoyably acquired than the skills of a bartender.

I return to economics and to economists, and to the question of why the profession's directions have evolved in the manners evident from this book. A major conservative economist once explained that a source of his antipathy to government traced back to the defeat of his southern ancestors by a larger north economy. Here is a similar factoid. Joan Robinson once wrote that her opposition to having the U.K. enter the European Market was due to the fact that she "had more friends in [Nehru's] India than on the continent." Yes, it is a banality that personal piffle can affect ideology. But can we take autobiographical judgments as most accurate judgments? The Robinson I knew could well have thought back in the 1960s that her kind of post-Fabian socialism would flourish better in India than on the continent. And, alas, she may have been right in so thinking.

Published scientific research, by its very nature, is designed not to identify any personal motives of the authors. In understanding what is in this revealing book, need we be concerned with the personal motives for the directions taken by these eminent economists? If so, is this interviews format the best way to gain insight into those motives?

I conclude with an unworthy hypothesis regarding past and present directions of economic research. Sherlock Holmes said, "*Cherchez la femme.*" When asked why he robbed banks, Willie Sutton replied, "That's where the money is." We economists do primarily work for our peers' esteem, which figures in our own self-esteem. When post-Depression Roosevelt's New Deal provided exciting job opportunities, first the junior academic faculties moved leftward. To get back ahead of their followers, subsequently the senior academic faculties shoved ahead of them. As post-Reagan, post-Thatcher electorates turned rightward, follow the money pointed, alas, in only one direction. So to speak, we eat our own cooking.

We economists love to quote Keynes's final lines in his 1936 *General Theory*—for the reason that they cater so well to our vanity and self-importance. But to admit the truth, madmen in authority can *self-generate* their own frenzies without needing help from either defunct or avant-garde economists. What establishment economists brew up is as often what the Prince and the Public are already wanting to imbibe. We guys don't stay in the best club by proffering the views of some past *academic* crank or academic sage.

Indeed, this book adds up to more than the sum of its parts. It provides a rare overview of the economics profession in a manner that reveals the relevancy of the personal motives and experiences of some of its leading modern contributors.

7

An Interview with Paul A. Samuelson

Interviewed by William A. Barnett
UNIVERSITY OF KANSAS
December 23, 2003

It is customary for the interviewer to begin with an introduction describing the circumstances of the interview and providing an overview of the nature and importance of the work of the interviewee. However, in this case, as Editor of this journal, I feel it would be presumptuous of me to provide my own overview and evaluation of the work of this great man, Paul Samuelson. The scope of his contributions has been so vast (averaging almost one technical paper per month for over 50 years) that it could be particularly difficult to identify those areas of modern economic theory to which he has *not* made seminal contributions.[1] In addition to his over 550 published papers, his books are legendary. He once said: "Let those who will—write the nation's laws—if I can write its textbooks."

Instead of attempting to provide my own overview, I am limiting this introduction to the following direct (slightly edited) quotation of a few paragraphs from the Web site, *The History of Economic Thought*, which is maintained online by the New School University in New York[2]:

> Perhaps more than anyone else, Paul A. Samuelson has personified mainstream economics in the second half of the twentieth century. The writer of the most successful principles textbook ever (1948), Paul Samuelson has been not unjustly considered *the* incarnation of the economics "establishment"—and as a result, has been both lauded and vilified for virtually everything right and wrong about it.

Reprinted from *Macroeconomic Dynamics*, 8, 2004, 519–542. Copyright © 2004 Cambridge University Press.

Samuelson's most famous piece of work, *Foundations of Economic Analysis* (1947), is one of the grandest tomes that helped revive Neoclassical economics and launched the era of the mathematization of economics. Samuelson was one of the progenitors of the Paretian revival in microeconomics and the Neo-Keynesian Synthesis in macroeconomics during the post-war period.

The *wunderkind* of the Harvard generation of 1930s, where he studied under Schumpeter and Leontief, Samuelson had a prodigious grasp of economic theory, which has since become legendary. An unconfirmed anecdote has it that at the end of Samuelson's dissertation defense, Schumpeter turned to Leontief and asked, "Well, Wassily, have we passed?" Paul Samuelson moved on to M.I.T. where he built one of the century's most powerful economics departments around himself. He was soon joined by R.M. Solow, who was to become Samuelson's sometime co-writer and partner-in-crime.

Figure 7.1 Paul A. Samuelson.

Samuelson's specific contributions to economics have been far too many to be listed here—being among the most prolific writers in economics. Samuelson's signature method of economic theory, illustrated in his *Foundations* (1947), seems to follow two rules which can also be said to characterize much of Neoclassical economics since then: With every economic problem, (1) reduce the number of variables and keep only a minimum set of simple economic relations; and (2) if possible, rewrite it as a constrained optimization problem.

In microeconomics, he is responsible for the theory of revealed preference (1938, 1947). This and his related efforts on the question of utility measurement and integrability (1937, 1950) opened the way for future developments by Debreu, Georgescu-Roegen, and Uzawa. He also introduced the use of comparative statics and dynamics through his "correspondence principle" (1947), which was applied fruitfully in his contributions to the dynamic stability of general equilibrium (1941, 1944). He also developed what are now called "Bergson–Samuelson social welfare functions" (1947, 1950, 1956); and, no less famously, Samuelson is responsible for the harnessing of "public goods" into Neoclassical theory (1954, 1955, 1958).

Samuelson was also instrumental in establishing the modern theory of production. His *Foundations* (1947) are responsible for the envelope theorem and the full characterization of the cost function. He made important contributions to the theory of technical progress (1972). His work on the theory of capital is well known, if contentious. He demonstrated one of the first remarkable "Non-Substitution" theorems (1951) and, in his famous paper with Solow (1953), initiated the analysis of dynamic Leontief systems. This work was reiterated in his famous 1958 volume on linear programming with Robert Dorfman and Robert Solow, wherein we also find a clear introduction to the "turnpike" conjecture of linear von Neumann systems. Samuelson was also Joan Robinson's main adversary in the Cambridge Capital Controversy—introducing the "surrogate" production function (1962), and then subsequently (and graciously) relenting (1966).

In international trade theory, he is responsible for the Stolper–Samuelson Theorem and, independently of Lerner, the Factor Price Equalization theorem (1948, 1949, 1953), as well as (finally) resolving the age-old "transfer problem" relating terms of trade and capital flows, as well as the Marxian transformation problem (1971), and other issues in Classical economics (1957, 1978).

In macroeconomics, Samuelson's multiplier–accelerator macrodynamic model (1939) is justly famous, as is the Solow–Samuelson presentation of the Phillips Curve (1960) to the world. He is also famous for popularizing, along with Allais, the "overlapping generations" model which has since found many applications in macroeconomics and monetary theory. In many ways, his work on speculative prices (1965) effectively anticipates the efficient markets hypothesis in finance theory. His work on diversification (1967) and the "lifetime portfolio" (1969) is also well known.

Paul Samuelson's many contributions to Neoclassical economic theory were recognized with a Nobel Memorial prize in 1970.

Barnett: As an overture to this interview, can you give us a telescopic summary of 1929 to 2003 trends in macroeconomics?

Samuelson: Yes, but with the understanding that my sweeping simplifications do need, and can be given, documentation.

As the 1920s came to an end, the term macroeconomics had no need to be invented. In America, as in Europe, money and banking books preached levels and trends in price levels in terms of the Fisher–Marshall $MV = PQ$. Additionally, particularly in America, business-cycles courses eclectically nominated causes for fluctuations that were as diverse as "sunspots," "psychological confidence," "over- and underinvestment" pathologies, and so forth. In college on the Chicago Midway and before 1935 at Harvard, I was drilled in the Wesley Mitchell statistical descriptions and in Gottfried Haberler's pre-*General Theory* review of the troops.

555

Read the puerile Harvard book on *The Economics of the Recovery Program*, written by such stars as Schumpeter, Leontief, and Chamberlin, and you will agree with a reviewer's headline: Harvard's first team strikes out.

Keynes's 1936 *General Theory*—paralleled by such precursors as Kahn, Kalecki, and J.M. Clark—gradually filled in the vacuum. Also, pillars of the $MV = PQ$ paradigm, such as all of Fisher, Wicksell, and Pigou, died better macroeconomists than they had earlier been—this for varied reasons of economic history.

Wicksell was nonplussed in the early 1920s when postwar unemployment arose from his nominated policy of returning after 1920 back to pre-1914 currency parities. His long tolerance for Say's Law and neutrality of money (even during the 1865–1900 deflation) eroded away in his last years. For Fisher, his personal financial losses in the 1929–34 Depression modified his beliefs that V and Q/V were quasi constants in the $MV = PQ$ tautology. Debt deflation all around him belied that. Pigou, after a hostile 1936 review of *The General Theory* (occasioned much by Keynes's flippancies about Marshall and "the classics"), handsomely acknowledged wisdoms in *The General Theory*'s approaches in his 1950 *Keynes's General Theory: A Retrospective View*.

I belabor this ancient history because what those gods were modifying was much that Milton Friedman was renominating about money around 1950 in encyclopedia articles and empirical history. It is paradoxical that a keen intellect jumped on that old bandwagon just when technical changes in money and money substitutes—liquid markets connected by wire and telephonic liquid "safe money market funds," which paid interest rates on fixed-price liquid balances that varied between 15% per annum and 1%, depending on price level trends—were realistically replacing the scalar M by a vector of (M_0, M_1, M_2, ..., M_{17}, a myriad of bonds with tight bid-asked prices, ...). We all pity warm-hearted scholars who get stuck on the wrong paths of socialistic hope. That same kind of regrettable choice characterizes anyone who bets doggedly on ESP, or creationism, or.... The pity of it increases for one who adopts a simple theory of positivism that exonerates a nominated theory, even if its premises are unrealistic, so long only as it seems to describe with approximate accuracy some facts. Particularly vulnerable is a scholar who tries to *test* competing theories by submitting them to *simplistic* linear regressions with no sophisticated calculations of Granger causality, cointegration, collinearities and ill-conditioning, or a dozen other safeguard econometric methodologies. To give one specific example, when Christopher Sims introduces both *M and an interest rate* in a multiple regression testing whether M drives P, Q/V, or Q in some systematic manner congenial to making a constant rate of growth of money supply, M_1, an optimal guide for

Figure 7.2 New York, February 19, 1961. Seated left to right, participating guests who appeared on the first of The Great Challenge symposia of 1961: Professor Henry A. Kissinger, Director of the Harvard International Seminar; Dr. Paul A. Samuelson, Professor of Economics at MIT and President of the American Economic Association; Professor Arnold J. Toynbee, world historian; Admiral Lewis L. Strauss, former Chairman of the Atomic Energy Commission and former Secretary of Commerce; Adlai E. Stevenson, U.S. Ambassador to the United Nations; and Howard K. Smith, CBS news correspondent in Washington, moderator of the program. The topic: "The World Strategy of the United States as a Great Power."

policy, then in varied samples the interest rate alone works better without M than M works alone or without the interest rate.

The proof of the pudding is in the eating. There was a widespread myth of the 1970s, a myth along Tom Kuhn's (1962) *Structure of Scientific Revolutions* lines. The Keynesianism, which worked so well in Camelot and brought forth a long epoch of price-level stability with good Q growth and nearly full employment, gave way to a new and quite different macro view after 1966. A new paradigm, monistic monetarism, so the tale narrates, gave a better fit. And therefore King Keynes lost self-esteem and public esteem. The King is dead. Long live King Milton!

Contemplate the true facts. Examine 10 prominent best forecasting models 1950 to 1980: Wharton, Townsend–Greenspan, Michigan Model, St. Louis Reserve Bank, Citibank Economic Department under Walter Wriston's choice of Lief Olson, et cetera. When a specialist in the Federal Reserve system graded models in terms of their accuracy for *out-of-sample* future performance for a whole vector of target macro variables, never did post-1950 monetarism score well! For a few quarters in the early 1970s, Shirley Almon distributed lags, involving $[M_i(-1), M_i(-2), \ldots, M_i(-n)]$, wandered into some temporary alignment with reality. But then, outfits like that at Citibank, even when they added on Ptolemaic epicycle to epicycle, generated monetarism forecasts that diverged systematically from reality. Data mining by dropping the M_i's that worked worst still did not attain statistical significance. Overnight, Citibank wiped out its economist section as superfluous. Meantime, inside the Fed, the ancient Federal Reserve Board–MIT–Penn model of Modigliani, Ando, et al. kept being tweaked at the Bank of Italy and at home. For it, M did matter as for almost everyone. But *never did M alone matter systemically, as post-1950 Friedman monetarism professed.*

It was the 1970s supply shocks (OPEC oil, worldwide crop failures, ...) that worsened forecasts and generated stagflation incurable by either fiscal or central bank policies. That's what undermined Camelot cockiness—not better monetarism that gave better policy forecasts. No Tom Kuhn case study here at all.

Barnett: Let's get back to your own post-1936 macro hits and misses, beliefs, and evolutions.

Samuelson: As in some other answers to this interview's questions, after a struggle with myself and with my 1932–36 macro education, I opportunistically began to use *The General Theory*'s main paradigms: the fact that millions of people without jobs envied those like themselves who had jobs, while those in jobs felt sorry for those without them, while all the time being fearful of losing the job they did have. These I took to be established facts and to serve as effective evidence that prices were not being *un*sticky, in the way that an auction market needs them to be, *if full employment clearing were to be assured*. Pragmatically and opportunistically, I accepted this as tolerable "micro foundations" for the new 1936 paradigm.

A later writer, such as Leijonhufvud, I knew to have it wrong, when he later argued the merits of Keynes's subtle intuitions and downplayed the various (identical!) mathematical versions of *The General Theory*. The so-called 1937 Hicks or later Hicks–Hansen IS–LM diagram will do as an example for the debate. Hansen never pretended that *it* was something original. Actually, one could more legitimately call it the Harrod–Keynes system. In any case, it was isomorphic with an early Reddaway set of equations and similar sets independently exposited by Meade and by Lange. Early on, as a second-year Harvard graduate student, I had translated Keynes's own words into the system that Leijonhufvud chose to belittle as unrepresentative of Keynes's central message.

558

Just as Darwinism is not a religion in the sense that Marxism usually is, my Keynesianism has always been an evolving development, away from the Neanderthal Model T Keynesianism of liquidity traps and inadequate inclusion of stocks of wealth and stocks of invested goods, and, as needed, included independent variables in the mathematical functions determinative of equilibria and their trends.

By 1939, Tobin's Harvard Honors thesis had properly added Wealth to the Consumption Function. Modigliani's brilliant 1944 piece improved on 1936 Keynes. Increasingly, we American Keynesians in the Hansen School—Tobin, Metzler, Samuelson, Modigliani, Solow, . . . —became impatient with the foot-dragging English—such as Kahn and Robinson—whose lack of wisdoms became manifest in the 1959 Radcliffe Committee Report. The 1931 Kahn that I admired was not the later Kahn, who would assert that the $MV = PQ$ definition contained bogus variables. Indeed, had Friedman explicitly played up, instead of playing down, the key fact that a rash Reagan fiscal deficit could raise V systematically by its inducing higher interest rates, Friedman's would have been less of an eccentric macro model.

I would guess that most MIT Ph.D.'s since 1980 might deem themselves *not* to be "Keynesians." But they, and modern economists everywhere, do use models like those of Samuelson, Modigliani, Solow, and Tobin. Professor Martin Feldstein, my Harvard neighbor, complained at the 350th Anniversary of Harvard that Keynesians had tried to poison his sophomore mind *against saving*. Tobin and I on the same panel took this amiss, since both of us since 1955 had been favoring a "neo-classical synthesis," in which full employment with an austere fiscal budget would *add to capital formation* in preparation for a coming demographic turnaround. I find in Feldstein's macro columns much the same paradigms that my kind of Keynesians use today.

On the other hand, within any "school," schisms do tend to arise. Tobins and Modiglianis never approved of Robert Eisner or Sidney Weintraub as "neo-Keynesians," who denied that lowering of real interest rates might augment capital formation at the expense of current consumption. Nor do I regard as optimal Lerner's Functional Finance that would sanction any sized fiscal deficit so long as it did not generate inflation.

In 1990, I thought it unlikely ever again to encounter in the real world liquidity traps, or that Paradox of Thrift, which so realistically did apply in the Great Depression and which also did help shape our pay-as-you-go nonactuarial funding of our New Deal social security system. In economics what goes around may well come around. During the past 13 years, Japan has tasted a liquidity trap. When 2003 U.S. Fed rates are down to 1%, that's a lot closer to 0% than it is to a more "normal" real

Figure 7.3 From left to right at back: James Tobin and Franco Modigliani. From left to right in front: Milton Friedman and Paul A. Samuelson. All four are Nobel Laureates in Economics.

interest rate of 4% or 5%. Both in micro- and macroeconomics, master economists know they must face up to *nonstationary time series* and the difficulties these confront us with.

If time permits, I'll discuss later my qualified view about "rational expectations" and about "the New Classicism of Say's Law" and neutrality of money in effectuating systemic real-variable changes.

Barnett: What is your take on Friedman's controversial view that his 1950 monetarism was an outgrowth of a forgotten subtle "oral tradition" at Chicago?

Samuelson: Briefly, I was there, knew all the players well, and kept class notes. And beyond Fisher–Marshall $MV = PQ$, there was little else in Cook County macro.

A related and somewhat contradictory allegation by David Laidler proclaimed that Ralph Hawtrey—through Harvard channels of Allyn Young, Lauchlin Currie, and John H. Williams—had an important (long-neglected) influence on Chicago's macro paradigms of that same 1930–36 period. Again, my informed view is in the negative. A majority of the Big Ten courses did cite Hawtrey, but in no depth.

Before comparing views with me on Friedman's disputed topic (and after having done so), Don Patinkin denied that in his Chicago period of the 1940s any trace of such a specified oral tradition could be found in his class notes (on Mints, Knight, Viner), or could be found in his distinct memory. My Chicago years predated Friedman's autumn 1932 arrival and postdated his departure for Columbia and the government's survey of incomes and expenditures. I took all the macroeconomic courses on offer by Chicago teachers: Mints, Simons, Director, and Douglas. Also in that period, I attended lectures and discussions on the Great Depression, involving Knight, Viner, Yntema, Mints, and Gideonse. Nothing beyond the sophisticated account by Dennis Robertson, in his famous *Cambridge Handbook on Money*, of the Fisher–Marshall–Pigou $MV = PQ$ paradigm can be found in my class notes and memories.

More importantly, as a star upper-class undergraduate, I talked a lot with the hotshot graduate students—Stigler, Wallis, Bronfenbrenner, Hart —and rubbed elbows with Friedman and Homer Jones. Since no whisper reached my ears, and no cogent publications have ever been cited, I believe that this nominated myth should not be elevated to the rank of plausible history of ideas. Taylor Ostrander, then unknown to me, did graduate work on the Midway in my time and has kept copious notes. I have asked him and Warren Samuels to comb this important database to confirm or deny these strong contentions of mine.

Having killed off one 1930s Chicago myth, I do need to report on another too-little-noticed genuine macro oral tradition from the mid-1930s Chicago. It is not at all confirmatory of the Friedman hypothesis, and is indeed 180 degrees opposed to that in its eclectic doubts about simplistic monetarism. Nor can I cogently connect it with a Young–Hawtrey influence.

You did not have to be a *wunderkind* to notice in the early 1930s that traditional orthodox notions about Say's Law and neutral money were sterile in casting light on contemporary U.S. and global slumps. Intelligently creative scholars such as Simons and Viner had by the mid-1930s learned something from current economic history about inadequacies of the simple $MV = PQ$ paradigm and its "M alone drives PQ" nonsequitur.

Keynes, of course, in shedding the skin of the author of the *Treatise*, accomplished a virtual revolution by his liquidity preference paradigm, which realistically recognized the *systematic* variabilities in V. Pigou, when recanting in 1950 from his earlier bitter 1936 review of *The General Theory*, in effect abandoned what was to become 1950-like monistic Friedmanisms.

Henry Simons, to his credit, already in my pre-1935 undergraduate days, sensed the "liquidity trap" phenomenon. I was impressed by his reasonable dictum: When open-market operations add to the money supply and at the same time *subtract equivalently* from outstanding quasi-zero-yielding

Treasury bills that are *strong money substitutes*, little increase can be expected as far as spending and employment are concerned. Note that this was some years before the 1938 period, when Treasury bills came to have only a derisory yield (sometimes negative).

Experts, but too few policymakers, were impressed by some famous Viner and Hardy researches for the 1935 Chicago Federal Reserve Bank. These authors interpreted experience of borrowers who could not find lenders as a sign that during (what we subsequently came to call) "liquidity trap times" money is *tight* rather than loose: Safe Treasury bills are cheap as dirt just because effective tightness of credit chokes off business activity and thereby lowers the market-clearing short interest rate down toward the zero level. Hoarding of money, which entailed slowing down of depression V, is then not a psychological aberration; rather, it is a cool and sensible adjustment to a world where potential plenty is aborted by failures in both investment and consumer spending out of expectable incomes (multiplier and accelerator, rigidity of prices and wages, et cetera).

Go back now to read Friedman's article for the 1950 *International Encyclopedia of the Social Sciences*, where as an extremist he plays down (outside of hyperinflation) the effects of i (the interest rate) and fiscal deficits on V, to confirm that this Simons–Viner–Hardy Chicago oral tradition is not at all the one he has for a long time claimed to be the early Chicago tradition. (In his defense, I ought to mention that Friedman had left Chicago for Columbia by the time of the Viner–Hardy publications.) The commendable 1932 Chicago proclamation in favor of expanded deficit fiscal spending was itself a recognition of the limited potency of $\partial(PQ)/\partial M$. In terms of latter-day logic, a consistent Friedman groupie ought to have refused to sign that 1932 Chicago proclamation. Meantime, in London, Hayek's 1931 *Prices and Production* had converted the usually sensible Lionel Robbins into the eccentric belief that anything that expanded MV or PQ would only make the Depression worse!

Barnett: You first surfaced as a comer at the University of Chicago. What is your final take on your Midway days?

Samuelson: I was reborn when at age 16 on January 2, 1932, 8:30 a.m., I walked into a Midway lecture hall to be told about Malthusian population. At the zenith of Hutchins's New Chicago Plan, I got a great education in width: physical, biological, and social sciences topped off by humanities.

January 2, 1932, was an auspicious time to begin economic study for two unrelated reasons. The Great Depression was then at its nadir—which attracted good minds into economics and which presented exciting puzzles needing new solutions. The Chicago Midway was a leading center (maybe *the* leading center) for neoclassical economics, and I

Figure 7.4 From left to right, at the University of Chicago Centennial, 1991: Rose Director Friedman, Milton Friedman, Paul A. Samuelson, and George Stigler.

found exciting Frank Knight, Henry Simons, Jacob Viner, and Paul Douglas. My very first teacher, Aaron Director (now around 100), I liked as an iconoclastic teacher. He was the only man alive who could (later) speak of "my radical brother-in-law Milton Friedman." Long without Chicago tenure, his bibliography was epsilon. But without any database, he was a primary creator both of the second Chicago School—of Friedman, Stigler, Becker after Knight, Viner, Douglas, Schultz, Nef, and Simons—and present-day antitrust inactivism.

What incredible luck, while still adolescent, to stumble onto the subject that was of perfect interest to me and for which I had special aptitudes! What work I have done has been for me more like play. And always I have been overpaid to do it.

Director's published works are nearly nil, but his was later a major influence on (or against?) antitrust policy, and his stubborn iconoclasm had a significant role in creating the Second Chicago School of Friedman, Stigler, Coase, and Becker. (See the Stigler autobiography.) Since I entered college before graduating from high school, I missed the 1931 autumn quarter during which the Social Science Survey 1 curriculum surveyed economics popularly. As a makeshift, I was put into an old-fashioned, beginners' course that was being phased out. Slichter's *Modern Economic Society* was Director's assigned text, even though he did not speak well of it. (The following quarter, Lloyd Mints carried on with Richard Ely's best-selling *Outline of Economics*, with micro theory largely by Allyn Young.) Director's best gift to me was his unorthodox assignment of Gustav Cassel's *Theory of Social Economy* chapter on "the arithmetic of pricing," as stolen by Cassel from Walras. Few knew in those Model T days about the mathematics of general equilibrium in economics.

But it was Henry Simons, Frank Knight, and Jacob Viner who most influenced my mind. I may have taken more different economics courses at Chicago than anyone before 1935. Certainly, I was overprepared when entering the Harvard Graduate School in 1935. I also carried the baggage of excessive admiration of Frank Knight until time eroded that away.

The best that Knight told us in those days was that in rare depression times, inexplicably Say's Law and market clearing somehow didn't obtain temporarily. Most of the time, normalcy would serendipitously return and maybe then we could live happily ever after. Maybe. Meantime the only present choice was between communism and fascism. And for himself, Knight would not choose the latter. Later, understandably, he recovered from that failure of nerve and reneged on his circulated text. Somewhere in my files will be found a copy of his doomsday text.

This explains the second reason why 1932 was a great time for an eager teenager to enter economic study. Our subject had myriads of challenging open problems—problems that mathematical techniques could throw light on, and also close out. I once described this as being like fishing in a virgin Canadian lake. You threw in your hook and out came theorem after theorem. Viner is a useful example. He was a great economist, and perhaps the most learned one on the 1931 globe. He was also a subtle theorist. With suitable training at McGill and Harvard, Viner could have been a leading mathematical economist. However, Stephen Leacock and Frank Taussig taught him no mathematics at all. This made him fearful of acne-age students like me and our generations, who seemed to provide him with painful competition. (To do Viner justice, let me state that the 1930s graphics of trade theory by Lerner, Leontief, me, and Meade was in its essence already in a 1931 LSE Viner lecture, that the young Lerner would probably have attended.)

I carried a stout staff in the fight to lift the level of mathematical techniques during the second third of the twentieth century. But an evolving science does not wait for any one indispensable genius to arrive.

Others in plenty would have come along, trained by Hotellings, Evanses, and Frisches to accomplish that overdue task.

Although I've had an acquaintanceship with scores of leading world mathematicians and physicists, I've been surprised at how little help I've been able to garner from presenting orally some unsolved puzzles to them. I should not have been surprised. It is not that a Birkhoff, or Quine, or Ulam, or Levinson, or Kac, or Gleason was incapable of clearing up my open questions. Rather, it is the case that a busy mathematician has no motivation to waste his (or her) time getting intuitively briefed on someone else's models in the idiosyncratic field of mathematical economics. Fortunately, access to the good Harvard and MIT libraries enabled one to ferret out needed book expositions. And it was my good luck that Harvard's E.B. Wilson, only protegé of thermodynamicist Willard Gibbs, provided essential hints that helped in the development of revealed preference and the anticipation of the inequalities techniques in post-1945 economics programming.

Barnett: For some months in 1936 at Harvard, legend reports, you resisted conversion to Keynes's *General Theory*. Any truth in that?

Samuelson: After 1936 February, when copies of *The General Theory* arrived in Cambridge, I did struggle with my own initial criticisms of the book; and I suspect my begrudging acceptance of the Keynesian revolution in paradigm was importantly the result of Henry Simon's remark about short-term bonds as a substitute for M, when the interest rates are low. I was influenced by that, plus my earlier recognition that prices and price levels are sticky, and therefore neutral money and Say's Law lose realism. I knew 100 people without jobs in 1931–34 and 100 with jobs. The groups would never voluntarily change places: the latter felt very lucky. The former, about equal in ability, felt unlucky. That's not what happens when auction markets equate supply and demand.

Timing is everything. My Society of Fellows 1937–40 prewar leisure enabled the publication in 1948 of *Foundations of Economic Analysis*. Groups of youngsters all over the world joined to master its fundamentals. Not until 1983 did I prepare an enlarged edition with terse exposition of post-1947 developments. Why did this better book sell so poorly in comparison with its predecessor? It was because practitioners everywhere had become so much more sophisticated by the end of the century. Schumpeter would say: Monopoly profits are bound to erode away, as knowledge spreads, which is a good thing.

Barnett: So why did you leave Chicago for Harvard?

Samuelson: Given my volition, I would never have left Chicago, but a new Social Science Research Council Fellowship, awarded to the eight most promising economics graduates, bribed me to go to a different university. The effective choice was between Harvard and Columbia. Without exception, my Chicago mentors advised Columbia. By miscalculation, I opted for Harvard, not even knowing that it was about to move out of lean seasons, thanks primarily to the European immigrants Schumpeter, Leontief, Haberler, and also later Alvin Hansen.

Three years later, at Harvard, I did thank providence for my hegira *away from* the Midway—where I would have missed out on three great twentieth-century revolutions in economics: the mathematics revolution, the imperfect competition revolution, and the Keynesian effective-demand revolution. I deplore adversary procedures in the healthy evolution of a scientific discipline. Remaining at dogmatically conservative Chicago or accepting its lucrative 1947 professorship would have made me more radical than I wanted to be. For my temperament, serenity would be much more fruitful than the stimulus of polemical debate. I speak only for myself.

Barnett: Franco Modigliani, in his interview in *Macroeconomic Dynamics* [see Chapter 5], stated that he was discouraged from pursuing an offer early in his career from Harvard University by its Economics Department chair, whom Modigliani characterized as anti-Semitic and xenophobic. When you acquired your Ph.D. from Harvard as an A+ student, having produced one of the most extraordinary dissertations of all times, you were offered a position by MIT, but not by Harvard. Do you believe that the prejudices of the Harvard department chair at that time had a role in Harvard's enormous mistake in that regard? If not, why did they fail to hire you immediately upon receipt of your Ph.D.?

Samuelson: Anti-Semitism was omnipresent in pre-World War II academic life, here and abroad. So, of course, my WASP wife and I knew that would be a relevant factor in my career at Harvard. But by 1940, times were changing. Perhaps I had too much of William Tell's hauteur in my personality to ingratiate myself with the circles who gave limited weight to merit in according tenure. When MIT made a good offer, we thought this could test whether there was great enthusiasm for my staying at Harvard. When Harvard's revealed preference consisted of no majority insistence that I stay, we moved three miles down the Charles River. (My Mark Perlman *Festschrift* piece provides a memoir of an earlier "politically incorrect" age.)

In retrospect, that was the luckiest decision I ever made. In less than a decade, postwar MIT developed into a powerhouse in frontier economics. The Ivy League snared future Rhodes scholars. Our magnet attracted most of the NSF Fellows in economics.

Barnett: Tell us about Harvard in the 1930s.

Samuelson: Hitler (and Lenin) did much for American science. Leontief, Schumpeter, and Haberler brought Harvard to life after a lean period. Alvin Hansen was for me an important influence. Outside of economics, both in the physical sciences and the medical–biological sciences, the U.S. dominates. Actually, toward the end of World War II, when victory was no longer in doubt, I was lent by the Radiation Laboratory to help the Vanevar Bush Secretariat draft *Science, the Endless Frontier*. Biochemist John Edsall (Harvard), Robert Morison (physiologist at the Rockefeller Foundation), and I did a lot of the drafting—of course under the instruction of I.I. Rabi, Edwin Land, Olivier Buckley (head of Bell Lab), and other members of Bush's appointed committee. Against some resistance, what emerged was beyond my fondest hopes: an NSF (inclusive of the social sciences), a vastly expanded NIH, rather than a nominated plan to give every U.S. county its population quota of dollar subsidies for research.

Barnett: As you have mentioned, Hitler was responsible for an extraordinary migration of many of Europe's greatest economists to the United States, including Koopmans, Leontief, Schumpeter, Marschak, Haberler, and Kuznets, along with most of the Austrian School of Economics. They in turn helped to attract to this country other major European economists, such as Hurwicz, Debreu, Theil, Bhagwati, Coase, and Fischer. But it is widely believed in much of the world that the United States no longer has the clear political advantage for scholars over Europe that existed at that time, and in fact there is now an increase in the number of American students deciding to study in Canada. Is America in danger of losing its intellectual comparative advantages for economists to other countries?

Samuelson: I do not discern any trend toward foreign out-competition of U.S. science. Sole reason: our predominant real GDP, and the brain drain *to us* it has induced.

Barnett: Your research from the beginning has shown exceptional influence from the physical sciences, and you mention the work of physical scientists extensively throughout your research, as you did in your famous *Foundations*. How did you become so heavily influenced by physical scientists? Did you study their work at some point in your education?

Samuelson: I would be rash to ignore analytical sciences outside of the social sciences. But I would be stupid, if out of "physics envy" or snake oil salesmanship, I would inject into economic theory analytical mathematics that fit only gases and liquids. In my writings, I have criticized wrong analogies to physics by Irving Fisher (whom I admire as a superlative American theorist). Even the genius of von Neumann has not escaped my critical auditings. I have given only qualified approval to

Marshall's hope for a more *biological* and less *physical* approach to future economics. But that has not aborted my writings in demographical genetics, not all unqualifiably admiring of R.A. Fisher's genetical writings. Maybe someday, future Philip Morowskis or Roy Weintraubs will better fine-tune their nuances.

Barnett: Throughout your career, you have tended to have your "finger in every pie" within the field of economics. But at the present time, it is difficult to think of any economists who are "generalists" in such a total sense. To be influential in any area of economics requires a degree of specialization that virtually rules out broad influence throughout the field. Is that because of the dramatic expansion of the field and its growth in both breadth and depth, or is it because we don't yet have another young Samuelson on the scene?

Samuelson: If only because of the explosion of total numbers of academic and nonacademic economists, no young Samuelson today could hope to be the kind of generalist that I used to be. Remember I got a young start. I was a fast and voracious reader who turned the pages of *all* the newly current exchange journals at Harvard's *Quarterly Journal of Economics* office. The micro tools that worked in general theory also worked in trade theory. With some help from me, post-Keynesian macroeconomics lent itself to complete general equilibrium techniques. Post-Fisher pure finance theory was poised to explode. Since probability was a passion with me, the banal statistics taught at Harvard naturally spurred me on to Fisher, Neyman–Pearson, and Wald–Savage further developments.

Having a facile pen helped. Before MIT Chairman Ralph Freeman drafted me to author an elementary text, I wrote for *New Republic* and other publications. Hansen brought me into Washington New Deal circles.

Barnett: The economics profession widely was in error about the consequences of the Second World War. It is well known that a large percentage of the economics profession, including you in an article in the *New Republic*, expected an economic collapse at the end of the war. There were a few exceptions, such as Alvin Hansen and Sumner Slichter. Why did so many economists expect the economy to perform badly at the end of the war? In retrospect, it is difficult to understand why that would have been believed, especially in the United States.

Samuelson: Often I've stated how I hate to be wrong. That has aborted many a tempting error, but not all of them. But I hate much more to *stay* wrong. Early on, I've learned to check back on earlier proclamations. One can learn much from one's own errors and precious little from one's triumphs. By September of 1945, it was becoming obvious that oversaving was not going to cause a deep and lasting postwar recession. So then and there, I cut my losses on that bad earlier estimate. Although Hansen was wise enough to expect a postwar restocking boom, it was his and Keynes's teachings about declining investment opportunities that predisposed my activist contemporaries to fear a post-peace depression. Aside from Hansen and Slichter, Willy Fellner and W.W. Woytinski taped things right: Accumulated saving from the way we financed the war and rationed resources, plus lust for long-delayed comforts and luxuries, were the gasoline that shifted resources from war to full-employment peacetime uses. I knew that argument but did not know what weight to give to it. (Scores of older economists were optimists about 1946 full employment. But if their only support for this view was a dogmatic belief in Say's Law, they [Knight is an example] carried little weight with me.)

Mention should be made of another mid-1940s Samuelson error. I judged that the market-clearing real interest rate level would be 3% or less. That big mistake of course correlated with the earlier unemployment error. I was too stubbornly slow in cutting my losses on that hunch.

Barnett: You were an important adviser to President John Kennedy. To this day, politicians of both major political parties tend to point to Kennedy's economic policy for support of their agendas. To what degree were those policies influenced by you, and who else played a role in those economic policies?

Samuelson: With great reluctance, I let Senator John F. Kennedy recruit me to his think tank. From nomination date to inaugural day I became his chief economic advisor. Our styles and chemistries clicked. I've never regretted staying out of Washington for two reasons: (1) Research is my true love. (2) The CEA team of Heller, Tobin, and Gordon was the greatest ever. (I did help pick them.) Only when they needed my extra heavy lifting from Cambridge did I weigh in.

Barnett: How did you become a mathematical economist? Legends proliferate that you began in physics, or mathematics, and then levitated down to economics.

Samuelson: The truth is that, although I did have aptitude for school math, it was only early in my economic studies that I realized how useful more, and still more, math would be for the puzzles my generation would have to face.

Beulah Shoesmith, spinster, was a famous mathematics teacher at Hyde Park High School near the University of Chicago. A number of scientists came from her workshop. Two of the eight recipients of the 1996 Medal of Science had been her pupils, as were Roy Radner and my brother Bob Summers. I took the many courses offered: advanced algebra, solid geometry, and (boring, surveyor-like) trigonometry. However, in the old-fashioned curriculum, neither calculus nor analytic geometry was considered to be a precollege subject—a terrible mistake. So, after my freshman college year, I hurried to make up for lost time.

Aside from mathematics coursework, I was to a considerable degree self-taught. (When I thought determinants were boring, graduate student George Stigler showed me the big ones Henry Schultz assigned. That wised me up.) Before I knew about Lagrange multipliers, I had worked out the Stackelberg improvements on the Cournot–Nash solution to duopoly. In working out a theory of the circulation of the elite, I discovered matrix multiplication before I knew about matrices—Markov, Frobenius, or Minkowski. I took or audited, at Chicago or Harvard, useful courses from Barnard, Graves, George Birkhoff, Hassler Whitney, Marshall Stone, and especially Edwin Bidwell Wilson. E.B. had been the only protégé at Yale of Willard Gibbs. Since I was Wilson's main protégé, that makes me kind of a grandson to Gibbs.

Fortunately, I was enough ahead of my contemporaries in economics that I had all the time in the world to spend in the library stacks on mathematics. Never did I reach a limit to usefulness of more elaborate mathematics. My economic problems dictated where my math preoccupations should go—not vice versa. Of course, it was Edgeworth, Walras, Pareto, Gibbs, E.B. Wilson, Griffith Evans, Frank Ramsey, Bowley, R.D.G. Allen, Hicks, Frisch, Lotka, Leontief, and von Neumann who were my masters. I'm afraid that I was a captious pupil, often stubbornly critical of my betters. (Example: von Neumann's foundations for cardinal utility in stochastic Laplacian choice begged the issue of the Ramsey–Marschak–Savage–Debreu independence axiom by burying that in his zeroth axiom. Worse, he stubbornly ignored all of his critics.)

At Harvard [1935–40], economists learned little statistics, except in E.B. Wilson's small seminar. Outside Schultz's specialized graduate course, the Chicago economics curriculum had been little

Figure 7.5 Paul Samuelson with Bill Clinton in the White House.

Figure 7.6 Paul Samuelson (front left) with Jerome Friedman (Nobel Prize in Physics), Theodore Schultz (Nobel Prize in Economics), James Watson (Nobel Prize in Biology), and George Stigler (Nobel Prize in Economics) at the University of Chicago Centennial, 1991.

better. In the early 1930s, I had to read, on my own, Thurstone's little potboiler to learn about the rudiments of statistics. Only at Columbia was Hotelling teaching 1920–30 R.A. Fisher. Of course, all this changed rapidly once Wald, Feller, Tukey, and Savage entered the scene.

Barnett: How can we relate your Stolper–Samuelson work, and your later Heckscher–Ohlin–Samuelson research to the present revolts against globalization? Can this trend among some of the world's youth be viewed as opposition by the political left to the implications of your work on trade?

Samuelson: Trade is confirmed to be a substitute for massive immigration from poor to rich countries. U.S. labor has lost its old monopoly on American advanced know-how and capital. U.S. total real GDP has net gained [1950–2003] from foreign export-led growth in Pacific Asia and the EU. However, free trade can also systematically affect U.S. wages/ GDP share and overall inequality. My little Nobel Lecture ["International Trade for a Rich Country," lecture before the Swedish–American Chamber of Commerce, New York City, May 10, 1972: Stockholm: Federation of Swedish Industries pamphlet, 1972] pointed out that a rich place *can lose net* when a poor one newly gains *comparative* advantage in activities in which previously the rich county had enjoyed comparative advantage. Free trade need not help *every*body *every*where.

Barnett: Do you have views and reactions to the "rational expectations" approach and real-business-cycle theory? In the dialogue between James Tobin and Robert Shiller in *Macroeconomic Dynamics* [moderated by David Colander; see Chapter 16], Tobin stated that real-business-cycle theory is "the enemy." In contrast, as is seen in much of the published research appearing in this journal, the use of rational expectations theory (sometimes weakened to include learning) and stochastic dynamic general equilibrium theory is common within the profession among macroeconomists of many political views.

Samuelson: Yes, but a lot of different things are loosely related to the words "rational expectations." One extreme meaning relates to "the New Classical doctrine," which alleges in effect that Say's Law does obtain even in the short run. I do happen to believe that the U.S. economy 1980–2003 behaves nearer to Say's Law's quasi full-employment than did the 1929–60 U.S. economy, or than do say the modern French and German economies. But this belief of mine do not necessarily require a new Lucas–Sargent methodology. Sufficient for it is two things:

(1) The new 1950–2003 freer global trade has effectively intensified competition with U.S. labor from newly trainable, low-wage Pacific Rim labor—competition strong enough effectively to emasculate the powers of American trade unions (except in public service and some untradeable goods industries). Nowadays every short-term victory by a union only speeds up the day that its industry moves abroad.

(2) There has been a 1980–2003 swing to the right among voters, whose swing away from "altruism" is somewhat proportional to the *time elapsed* since the Great Depression and since the U.S. government's effective organization for World War II's "good" war. As a result, trade unions no longer benefit from government's help.

A "cowed" labor force runs scared under the newly evolved form of ruthless corporate governance. In contrast to Japan, when a U.S. CEO fires redundant workers quickly, Wall Street bids up the price of the firm's shares.

Another weak form of "rational expectations" I agree with. "Fool me once. Shame on you. Fool me twice. Shame on me." Economic historian Earl Hamilton used to agree with the view that, when New World gold raised 1500–1900 price levels, nominal wages tended systematically to lag behind. Kessel and Alchian had a point in suspecting that people would at least in part learn to anticipate what has long been going on. I concur to a considerable but limited degree.

Some rational expectationists overshoot, in my judgment, when they exaggerate the "neutrality of money" and the "impotence of government to alter *real* variables." Friedman's overly simple monetarism à la 1950, was criticized from his left for its gross empirical errors. What must have cut him more personally would come from any Lucas follower who accused Friedman of *fallaciously* predicting that mismanagement of M in $MV = PQ$ was capable of deep real damage rather than of mere nominal price-level gyration.

Modern statistical methodology, I think, benefits much from Lucas, Sargent, Hansen, Brock, Prescott, Sims, Granger, Engle, and Stock–Watson explorations and innovations. But still much more needs to be analyzed. Strangely, theory-free vectoral autoregressions do almost as well. Also, variables that pass Granger causality tests can seem to perform as badly in future samples as those that fail Granger tests. And, still the nonstationariness of economic history confounds actual behavior and necessarily weakens our confidence in inferences from past samples.

This does not lead me to *nihilism*; but hopefully, only to *realism*, and, à la Oliver Twist, to urge for *more* research.

At many a Federal Reserve meeting with academic consultants, there used to be about one rational expectationist. So unuseful seemed their contributions and judgments that the next meeting entailed a new rational expectationist. And each year's mail would bring to my desk a few dozen yellow-jacket manuscripts from the National Bureau, purporting to test some version of rational expectationism. Many were nominated for testing; few passed with flying colors the proposed tests. I continue to live in both hope and doubt.

In some quarters, it is a popular belief that macroeconomics is less scientific than micro and less to be admired. That is not my view. I think macroeconomics is very challenging, and at this stage of the game it calls for wiser judgments. A lively science thrives on challenges, and that is why I transfer a good deal of my time and energy from micro to macro research. Probably as a syndicated columnist, I have published at monthly intervals a couple of thousand different journalistic articles. Maybe more. My aim is not to be interesting but rather, as best as I can, not to be wrong. When my conjecture is still a conjecture, I try to mark it as such. My notion of a fruitful economic science would be that it can help us explain and understand the course of actual economic history. A scholar who seriously addresses commentary on contemporary monthly and yearly events is, in this view, practicing the study of history—history in its most contemporary time phasing.

NOTES

1. Perhaps those rare exceptions might include game-theoretic and topological models and maybe the recent literatures on complex unstable nonlinear dynamics, sunspots, and incomplete markets. But I would not be surprised, if he were to correct those speculations as misperceptions, if I were to ask.
2. The current URL of that Web site is http://cepa.newschool.edu/het/home.htm

4

Advance of Total Factor Productivity from Entrepreneurial Innovations

Paul A. Samuelson

Joseph Schumpeter (1883–1950), my Harvard mentor, won early fame for his 1912 *Theory of Economic Development*. However, during the fifteen years I was his Cambridge neighbor, it was Maynard Keynes (1883–1946) who, by general agreement, earned the reputation of being the greatest economist of the twentieth century. The primary reason for this was that the great global depression of 1929–1935 desperately needed a new macro paradigm like Keynes's 1936 *General Theory*.

I believe there was a grain of truth in the innuendo that Schumpeter experienced some scholarly jealousy of Keynes's celebrity. Like the entrepreneurs he praised, Schumpeter possessed a competitive personality. Because the Muse of History has an ironic sense of humor, now in the twenty-first century, Schumpeter's fame (and his citation frequency) exceeds anything he enjoyed during his lifetime, including my colleagues here who cite him authoritatively in their explorations of entrepreneurship.

It would be useful for the few surviving members of the Schumpeter Circle to record the evolutionary nuances of change in Schumpeter's own late-in-life thinking. For example, when first in September 1935 I entered his Harvard Yard graduate classroom, Schumpeter was still stressing *youthful* innovators. He then seemed to doubt that a General Electric or a Bell System Laboratory could succeed in staying at the frontier of technical and know-how discovery. But later, contemporary economic history converted him to the view that the great oligopolies of the Fortune 500 corporations deserved most credit for progress in mid-twentieth-century total factor productivity.

Has the Muse of History once again pulled the rug out from under human prophets? During World War II and its aftermath, public spending – at the Pentagon, Office of Naval Research, RAND, NIH, NSF, and so on – spawned the Silicon Valley's and Route 128's decentralized high- and low-tech venture-capital innovative firms. It was not so long ago that academic acquaintances when inventing new technology received (and expected to receive) nought in the way of monetary remuneration.

That was then, and now is now. Paradoxically, the Fortune 500 has become a revolving door bereft of much of the former oligopoly powers that it once had to share with militant trade unions. The credit or blame for that traces much to the miracle post-1950 imitative export-led growth spurts of the European Union, Japan, Hong Kong, South Korea, and Taiwan. Outside of public government employment, every union "victory" was actually a pyrrhic defeat that only accelerated the advent of global production outsourcing and factor price equalization.

No one predicted this revolutionary geography tilt toward factor price equalizations in either the *Economic Journal* or the *American Economic Review* before 1950.

Probably, scholars will write much about the role of individual innovators for this conference hosted by the Max Planck Institute of Economics and the Kauffman Foundation for Entrepreneurs. I hope and expect that there will also be recognition of *group* contributions to scientific and engineering discovery. In my limited space here, I will mostly address the evolution of economists' thinking about how "total factor productivity" grew historically and is likely to continue to grow. Society's interest in entrepreneurial innovation centers on what it does and can continue to do to enhance *total* factor productivity and thereby real standards of living. Economic history reveals that real wages are driven upward by improved technical and know-how productivity. This truth does not deny that sometimes it is owners of property rather than owners of labor who benefit the most from improving total factor productivity.

4.1. Thumbnail Sketches of Economists' Grappling with Technical Change

Modern economics can be said to go back to the Scottish Enlightenment of 1750–1850. Before and after Adam Smith's *Wealth of Nations* (1776), economic scholars were somewhat obsessed by the "law of diminishing returns." That is why Thomas Carlyle, no economist, called political economy "the dismal science." Robert Malthus (1799) epitomized this fear of diminishing returns, even before the 1812 formalized defining of that classical returns law by West, Malthus and Ricardo.

The sweep of post-A.D. 1000 economic history undergoes a sea change around 1700. For reasons not yet fully understood, China's average level of technical productivity exceeded that in Europe around 1000 A.D. Just why China's real growth subsequently fell behind that of Europe is not clear. Such change in economic fortune is not unheard of; countries in the cradle of civilization are (except for the luck of oil wells) in the lower ranks of the Penn Tables of National Per Capita Well-being (purchasing power corrected).

By 1450 it was probably the Dutch who enjoyed the greatest world per capita real income, due much to their post-Columbus New World colonies. Only after what I like to call the epoch after Newton did Britain surpass the Dutch in enjoying the globe's highest per capita real income. Then, around 1900, America, Britain's one-time colony, swept past its motherland in average individual affluence.

During that same Bismarck era, Germany sought energetically to become Britain's equal. Certainly it was the outburst of scientific creativity in Wilhelmine universities that helped propel Germany into comparability to the United States and the United Kingdom. Indeed, the number of Nobel Prizes awarded to Germans between 1901 and 1933 was substantial; this number fell after Hitler came to power and has yet to return to prewar levels.

4.2. The Age of Scientific Discovery

More important than China's relative decline or the declines of the Dutch and the British is one striking fact about the documentable productivity wage rates of A.D. 1250 to 2006. Successive editions of Samuelson's introductory economics textbook contained perhaps the most interesting and most important graph of historical real wage growth in western Europe. (See, e.g., Samuelson-Nordhaus, 1995, p. 669, Figure 32.2.) Its story is striking.

Prior to 1700, wages *merely oscillate trendlessly*. A "little ice age" would show a general drop in Britain's real wages, followed by a recovery. But after 1700 – the age after Newton – the march of science mandated a steady rise in real wages per capita, strongest in Western Europe but discernible elsewhere globally. This has to be interpreted as both result and cause of entrepreneurial know-how and practice. In the Darwinian historical record, it stands out as a new thing under the sun. Yes, Malthus had been right to worry about diminishing returns due to excessive human fertility.[1]

Paradoxically, the classical economists of the 1750–1870 period were slow to understand their own industrial revolution. Adam Smith's excellent library was light on books describing major advances in steam, iron, steel, and coal, plows, and horse harnesses – to say nothing of contemporaneous inventions in textile spinning and weaving. Smith rightly discussed how the divisions of labor could expedite pin manufacture manifold times. But, it was the seeming triviality of the pin that added his example's drama.

Science and industrial practice were in a two-way interaction. As has been said, Watt's steam engine did as much for the science of thermodynamic heat as science did for Watts. The same was to happen again and again: Faraday's lab findings about magnetism and electricity generated power manufacturing. High-tech nineteenth-century industry fertilized post-Faraday inventors such as Maxwell, Hertz, and Marconi.

John Stuart Mill (1806–1873), in the middle of the Victorian nineteenth century, could nevertheless still come to false results, such as "it is doubtful whether invention has ever lightened the burden of the working classes." This from Mill, the wisest of the Enlightenment's philosophers. Stanley Jevons (1835–1882), a brilliant polymath, despaired that the coal mines of Britain would soon decline.

By contrast with the pessimism of Malthus, Mill, and Jevons, Karl Marx went to the opposite extreme. In their revolutionary 1848 *Communist Manifesto*, Marx and Engels proclaimed that all human kind could *already* enjoy a good standard of living if only the capitalists' market system could be abolished. Workers allegedly had nought to lose but their chains. Technical know-how could allegedly run itself; this at a time when nineteenth-century life expectancies were less than half of those of the present century.

The duel between innovation and diminishing returns is a never-ending one. Environments are limiting and fragile. What once were rich stores of Minnesota ores and Texas oils are now depleted. Moreover, science itself creates some new perils, perils that can be ameliorated only with new scientific and engineering discoveries.

In Schumpeter's view an Edison or a Pasteur made possible Henry Fords and J. Pierpont Morgans who can organize successful new products and

---

[1] Charles Darwin reported that reading the economist Malthus had provided him with the "Eureka" moment when he realized how evolution by competitive natural selection had to be the key to biological understanding. But if Malthus had looked out his library windows he would already have seen powerful trends toward increasing productivity trends.

services. Wal-mart's Sam Walton is in the Schumpeter Hall of Fame. Even the avid imitators, who brought, by stealth, spinning and weaving to New England or who import from Detroit to Nagoya the arts of auto-making are, to the 1912 Schumpeter, heroes.

4.3. Technical Economic Paradigms

I fast forward in time to Senator Paul Douglas (1892–1976), onetime professor at the University of Chicago, my alma mater, who received the prestigious Hart Schaffner Prize for his statistical measurements of early twentieth-century macro production functions. Douglas (1934) compiled a time series of total U.S. labor supply. He also built up, by statistical estimate, a time series of "capital" – plants and equipment, for example. Using official aggregate U.S. production index data for the same sample time span, Douglas used simple regression correlation methodology, and came up with the formula:

U.S. Production Q is the following mathematical function of U.S. Labor L and U.S. "capital," K:

$$Q_t = 1.01 L_t^{75} K_t^{25}, \quad 1899 < t < 1922 \qquad (1)$$

Douglas was audacious. Douglas was applauded. Also Douglas was criticized. If Nobel Prizes in economics had existed then, Douglas probably would have won one during my 1933–1934 junior year on the Chicago Midway.

I skip over many important debates. For example, L_t and K_t moved so closely together in this sample period, that a relationship like $bL^{1/2}K^{1/2}$ or $bL^{3/4}K^{1/4}$ could have given a goodness-of-fit coefficient only a bit lower than those Douglas reported.

When I left Chicago to enter Harvard's post-1935 graduate school, inevitably my new teacher Schumpeter lectured critically on the Douglas breakthrough. I paraphrase Schumpeter thus:

It is almost a *reductio ad absurdum* to ignore those vital changes that were going on in the first third of the twentieth century. Ford's assembly line. Truck competition to the railroads. Urban and rural electrification. Clearly $F[L_t, K_t]$ ought to have been replaced by $F[L_t, K_t; t]$ so that $F[L_{1922}, K_{1922}; 1922]$ would be materially greater than $F[L_{1899}, K_{1899}; 1899]$ even when the input pairs of $F[L_{1899}, K_{1899}]$ and $F[L_{1922}, K_{1922}]$ had not been too far apart.

Dynamic sciences advance by testing and correcting themselves. After the mid-1950s Robert Solow of Harvard and later MIT won a Nobel Prize

579

by generalizing and correcting Douglas's pioneering efforts. Using cross-sectional data on wages and capital returns, Solow (1957) improved on Douglas's simple estimation regressions by bringing in yearly data on profit/wages sharing. Now for the 1909-1949 timespan Solow modified Douglas's earlier $bL^{3/4}K^{1/4}$ by the kind of exponential growth factor that Schumpeter had been looking for. Here is Solow's new approximation:

$$Q_t = (1.015)^t L_t^{5/8} K_t^{3/8} \qquad (2)$$

The factor $(1.015)^t$, representing 1.5% per year growth in total factor productivity, Solow called the innovational "residual." He reminded us contemporary economists that, as important as growth in (K/L) is to boost real productivity wage rates, so too is the residual that traces to innovations in know-how and practice. This "residual," Solow proclaimed, demonstrated that much of post-Newtonian enhanced real income had to be attributed to innovational change (rather than, as Douglas believed, being due to "deepening" of the capital/labor K/L ratio).

This is part of the reason why the 1912 Schumpeter came to be vindicated in the economic literature of the last half century.

Despite the divergent views of Malthus, Mill, Schumpeter, or Solow, if the Max Planck Institute and the Kauffman Foundation on Entrepreneurship were to nominate an honor roll for scholars who advanced our understanding of entrepreneurship, *all* their above names would deserve to be included in that Pantheon.[2]

4.4. Postwar Convergent Trends of Regional Factor Price Returns

All my above words about a single country's production apply as well to postwar 1950 economies intimately engaged in foreign exports and imports. Already, prior to Douglas or Solow, the Swedish economists Eli Heckscher (1879–1952) and Bertil Ohlin (1899–1979) discussed how and why the exchange of goods between different countries could diminish (or even wipe out) differences in their wage and profit returns much the same way that migration of people do.

When Japan's educatable low-wage population imitatively borrowed American and European know-how, it transformed its poor Asian society

---

[2] The cream of the jest is that the same Mill who belittled past inventions did in his classic 1848 *Principles* sketch a progressing society that depended not at all on net accumulation of saved capital. The funds to replace old capital could go into improved tools, and so forth, ad infinitum.

via export-led growth into a progressive advanced economy. Most economists were too slow to apprehend how globalization would be the leitmotif of the last half century.

Am I writing about the past economic history? Yes. But my words apply as well to the coming half-century, from 2006 to 2056. Just as South Korea or Taiwan or Singapore could follow in Japan's footsteps, two billion people in China and India will be able to do so too.

Not all will be sweetness and light. Schumpeter spoke of "creative capitalist destruction." Competitive market systems have no mind and no heart. Often when technical innovations expand *mean* or *average* real incomes, at the same time they may widen the gap between rich and poor – that is, between those blessed with energy, education, cleverness, and early family support versus those who by whatever combination of nature and nurture were condemned to a lower quality of life.

In addition, science's enhanced harvest of present-day globalized plenty contributes to air and water pollution, to future exhaustion of non-renewable resources, and perhaps even to terrorism and guerrilla warfare.

Going beyond factual and objective logic and empirical knowledge, we ought to remind ourselves that science itself offers us more than enough in new enlarged resources for democratic communities to be able to tackle successfully programs to limit ecological deterioration and political anarchy.

4.5. Conclusion

To sum up, economics and humanity have need for both a Keynes and a Schumpeter. Creative capital destruction can be limited by means of humane mixed economy transfers to the losers from those who are winners. Laissez-faire, by itself, will not and cannot heal the most grievous wounds of inequality that globalization will entail.

In democracies it is the voters' choices that must count. If the dynamic forces that accelerate globalized growth do, at the same time, erode electorates' feeling of altruism, then what both Schumpeter and Keynes helped to contribute – accelerated real growth and less unstable business cycles – will unequally bless our future progeny.

References

Douglas, Paul H. 1934. *The Theory of Wages*. New York: Macmillan.
Heckscher, Eli. 1919. "Effects of Foreign Trade on Distribution of Income." *Ekonomisk Tidskrift*. Reprinted in H. S. Ellis and L. Metzler, eds., *Readings in the Theory of International Trade*. Philadelphia: Blakiston, 1949.

Jevons, William S. 1865. *The Coal Question*. London: Macmillan.

Keynes, John M. 1936. *The General Theory of Employment, Interest and Money*. Reprinted in *The Collected Writings of John Maynard Keynes*, vol. 7. London: Macmillan for the Royal Economic Society.

Maddison, Angus. 1991. *Dynamic Forces in Capitalist Development: A Long-Run Comparative View*. Oxford and New York: Oxford University Press.

Maddison, Angus. 2003. *The World Economy: Historical Statistics*. Paris: OECD.

Malthus, Thomas R. 1789. *An Essay on the Principle of Population*. Reprint. London: Macmillan, 1926.

Marx, Karl H., and Friedrich Engels. 1848. *Manifest der Kommunistischen Partei*. Translated into English as *Manifesto of the Communist Party*. New York: International Publishers, 1948.

Mill, John Stuart. 1848. *Principles of Political Economy, with Some of Their Applications to Social Philosophy*. London: John W. Parker.

Ohlin, Bertil G. 1933. *Interregional and International Trade*. Cambridge, Mass.: Harvard University Press.

Samuelson, Paul A. 1949. "International Factor-Price Equalization Once Again." *Economic Journal*, 59, 181–197.

Samuelson, Paul A., and William D. Nordhaus. 2005. *Economics*, 18th ed. New York: McGraw-Hill/Irwin.

Schumpeter, Joseph A. 1934 (1912). *The Theory of Economic Development*. Cambridge: Harvard University Press.

Smith, Adam. 1776. *An Inquiry into the Nature and Causes of the Wealth of Nations*. E. Cannan, ed. New York: Modern Library, 1937.

Solow, Robert M. 1957. "Technical Change and the Aggregate Production Function." *Review of Economic Statistics*, 39, 312–320.

PART IX.

Biographical Writings

The 1985 Nobel Prize in Economics

PAUL A. SAMUELSON

Franco Modigliani of the Massachusetts Institute of Technology was awarded the seventeenth Nobel Prize in economics. This choice was widely applauded since Modigliani has been a versatile and deep contributor to modern economics for 40 years.

Two countries can take pride in his being honored: Italy, from which he fled as a young victim of Mussolini's racial persecutions and whose postwar policy problems he has attentively researched; and the United States, where he received his Ph.D. training (at the "University in Exile," the New School for Social Research) and where he has held many university chairs.

More than 40 years ago, when Modigliani was only 25, he wrote a seminal article setting Model-T Keynesianism on its modern evolutionary path and probing its microfoundations in rigid, nonmarket-clearing prices (*1, 2*). Although neither this paper nor his 1963 classic (*3*), which set the pattern for today's post-Keynesian eclecticism, were mentioned in the citation of the Swedish Royal Academy of Science, they form the basis for the Federal Reserve Board–MIT–Penn forecasting and policy model that has long been useful in framing Federal Reserve monetary policy. As an MIT colleague documented at a September 1985 conference at Martha's Vineyard attended by scholars from all over the world to honor Modigliani, the best state of the macroeconomic art in these days after "monetarism" and "the new classical economics" of the rational expectationists, calls for a paradigm that is a natural evolution from those 1944 and 1963 classics (*4*).

Franco Modigliani shares one characteristic with his older countryman, Enrico Fermi. Fermi, also a refugee from Mussolini's Italy, was a doubly great physicist. In addition to being a great theorist, Fermi had the rare quality of being a brilliant experimentalist. Modigliani is recognized as an outstanding economic theorist. At the same time he insists on measuring empirical behavior patterns econometrically, refusing others all the pleasures of quantitative testing of his own novel hypotheses. Before he had ever heard of Karl Popper, Modigliani was already practicing the advice that a scholar should be his own most stringent critic. It is good for science; it is good for self-protection; besides, it is good fun.

In a field known for its voluble talkers, Modigliani is one of the fastest—quick off the mark in the short sprints, but ahead of the pack also for the long jog. Stealing a line from Sydney Smith's conversation with Thomas Babington Macaulay, I used to utter the mock complaint, "Franco, when I am dead you will be sorry you never heard the sound of my voice." Actually, as we both know, this is quite untrue. Economists from all over the world, and not least young scholars from Italy, bring their problems to Franco Modigliani. He is slow to digest the issues because he insists on fundamental understanding at every stage of the examination, avoiding facile handling. (Once, referring to a world-famous scholar, Modigliani said to me, quite guilelessly, unselfconsciously, and truthfully, "He's *deep*—like me.") Although known to be a lover of argument, Modigliani is also known as one who never argues for victory, but rather for truth. That is why, at 67, he remains a Mecca for both young and established researchers.

The Life-Cycle Saving Model

Modigliani has many brain children to his credit. All of a scholar's children are equal, but in my view the jewel in the Modigliani crown is his life-cycle hypothesis of saving, developed in collaboration with Richard Brumberg, a scholar who died young (*5*). The Royal Academy of Sciences agreed and mentioned it first in their official citation announcing the award.

I believe it to be the best single explainer, across time and space, of saving and investing behaviors and their responsiveness to various policy programs. From its deceptive simplicity, novel and testable expectations emerge. Here is how it goes.

Most of us will live beyond our prime earning years. So we must save when in our prime to accumulate the assets on which we will live in retirement. In the purest life-cycle model, when the end comes we'll die broke.

Simple stuff? They give prizes, you will ask, for that? Yes, so simple as to be fundamental. And the insights gained are far from simple or obvious. Suppose population ceased to grow (as in Denmark or the Germanies). Suppose productivity improvements that raise real incomes virtually cease (as happened from 1973 to 1980 much over of the globe). A life-cycle system without growth involves zero net saving and investment: saving of the young is canceled by dissaving of the old. Modigliani gets us to focus on the right questions. Growing nations save much, stagnating nations save little—a different hypothesis from "rich people save much, poor people little."

Science says: Let them who can be clever. What counts is which clever theory fits and predicts the observable facts. On this score Modigliani wins hands down. Early Americans, though poor, saved much; we affluent moderns save little. The fast-growing Japanese and Germans save much; the French and Italians, allegedly so romantic and carefree, have high saving rates between those of Japan and the United States.

An inexact science like economics benefits enormously from theoretical models that are themselves only partially accurate. Ten physiologists could make their reputations disproving aspects of Claude Bernard's seminal theories. Fifty economists win fame by finding exceptions to Modigliani's life-cycle paradigm. Leading that pack is Franco Modigliani himself. (Not knowing when we will die, we leave bequests willy-nilly. Some classes do dance to the bourgeois drumbeat and plan for their posterity's economic needs.)

Indifference of Leveraging

Modigliani has contributed both to the macroeconomics of business cycles and inflation and to the microeconomics of relative prices and rational decision-making. The 1985 award explicitly cited

---

The author is Institute Professor Emeritus at the Massachusetts Institute of Technology and Gordon Y. Billard Fellow at the Alfred P. Sloan School of Management, Massachusetts Institute of Technology, Cambridge 02139. He received the 1970 Nobel Prize in Economics.

a second line of his work, that dealing with "efficient-market" analysis and leading to the 1958 Modigliani-Miller theorem concerning the neutrality of corporate leveraging (6).

Some companies float bonds as well as stocks; some eschew debt and any such "leveraging." The conventional wisdom before 1958 was that, depending on the growth prospects and intrinsic variability of your industry and product line, your corporation should ideally borrow a certain optimal fraction of its total capital needs. The canny board of directors that achieves this golden leveraging ratio lifts, so to speak by its own bootstraps, the total market value of its owners' shares. The lazy or stupid management, which either stays zero leveraged or overleverages, loses prospective wealth and, in a cruel competitive world, may in the long run be forced out of office.

Merton Miller and Franco Modigliani argued otherwise. "Chicken legs and breasts can be separately packaged at the supermarket: the values of each such package must add up closely to the value of whole chickens. Otherwise consumers can do their own packaging." Similarly, Modigliani and Miller showed that firm A, with much debt and its entailed riskiness of common-stock earnings, cannot command a premium from risk-tolerant investors. Why not? Those investors can buy a zero-debt company on borrowed funds (margin purchases or collateral loans at the bank) and can produce with no premium that same attractive pattern of leveraged high-mean-return-cum-high-volatility. Similarly, no firm can win a premium by having a clean debt-free balance sheet. Private investors can put half their assets in leveraged stocks while keeping the other half in safe overnight deposits: that way they duplicate for themselves (premium free) whatever the clean balance sheet can produce. Conclusion: to a first approximation, total value to the owners of a company is invariant, independent of the degree of leverage, because investors can do for themselves, or undo for themselves, whatever leveraging can accomplish.

More important than deductive syllogizing is empirical testing, which showed that the alleged advantages of optimal leveraging could not be factually identified. Also important are deviations from the theory's axioms, such as recognition of how bankruptcy events can alter the simplicity and sweep of the proposition. Gratifying are corollaries, such as the 1961 Miller-Modigliani theorem that the percentage payment of earnings as dividends will not affect a stock's valuation.

We live in an age of accelerated corporate borrowing. This explosion in leveraging is in accord with the Modigliani-Miller theory: taxes aside, leveraging is neutral; inasmuch as deductability of debt interest from corporate taxation is patently favorable to borrowing, the 1960–1986 trend toward debt confirms the Modigliani-Miller analysis. We are left, though, with the puzzle: why do firms pay dividends to taxpaying shareholders? Why not buy back shares more than corporations actually do?

Self-Falsifying Prophecy?

Although a critic of the new Lucas-Sargent school of rational expectationism, Modigliani is himself a founder of rational expectationism (7). In a 1954 tour de force, written with Emile Grunberg, he contributed a solution to the old problem of whether correct prediction is a self-contradictory impossibility (8).

Here is how the late Oskar Morgenstern put the issue in a 1928 publication that led ultimately to his collaboration with John von Neumann on *The Theory of Games and Economic Behavior* (9). The diabolical Professor Moriarty pursues the incomparable Sherlock Holmes. Holmes boards in London the Dover train that makes an intermediate stop at Canterbury. Moriarty can just catch his prey in Dover if he flies a geodesic to there; however, if the quarry

Franco Modigliani

anticipates that fate and gets off in Canterbury, the gambit will fail and Moriarty will rue that he did not aim for Canterbury and victory there. We seem to be in the regression, What does A think B thinks A is thinking . . . ?, and so forth, seemingly endlessly. Morgenstern concluded that perfect prediction is impossible, since knowing it must alter it.

Now the white knights Grunberg and Modigliani come to the rescue of the logical possibility of perfect prediction. Here is how they would treat the case of a never-published Gallup poll that can correctly predict the fraction of votes, x, that Ike will get while Adlai gets $1 - x$. Provided no one is apprised of this datum, the election will (by hypothesis) yield an actual outcome fraction that equals the predicted fraction: $x' = x$. No Morgenstern problem yet. Suppose now that the Gallup fact of x is announced to the electorate. Then there may be a bandwagon effect: when $x > 1/2$ is announced, impressionable voters shift over to the front runner Ike and the result is actual $x' >$ predicted x. In this case, no correct prediction by candor is possible. Or, suppose there is an "underdog" effect, which is the reverse of a bandwagon effect: now when x is announced greater than 1/2, some voters pity Adlai and the shift of their votes makes actual $x' <$ predicted x. Again, candor destroys omniscience.

Grunberg-Modigliani (8) cut the Holmes-Moriarty knot thus. Stipulate that there is a knowable law (never mind *how* it is knowable), which specifies what actual x' will be for each pair of poll-finding x and *reported*-finding y:

$$x' = \text{known continuous function of } (y; x)$$
$$= f(y; x); 0 \leq [x, y, f(y; x)] \leq 1$$

Then they conclude, "Whatever the x finding that occurs, there is always a calculable y report that will be a self-fulfilling prophecy with actual $x' =$ published-prediction y."

The proof is trivial, a one-dimensional application of L. E. J. Brouwer's 1912 fixed-point theorem. (Doubters can try to move from a square's left wall to its right wall, never taking pencil off paper, and avoiding ever touching the square's diagonal.)

As the authors stress, the continuity assumption is basic to the demonstration. Thus, suppose that the variables (x, y, x') must be rational numbers (as literally they must be if the electorate is finite in number). The above square then is replaced by a lattice of nails lined up in the same number of rows and columns.

Can we tie a long red string around a specified nail in each column, and end up with a path for the string made up of line segments—a path that traverses from the first left-hand column to the last right column, without ever touching any nail in the diagonal of the lattice? Of course we can; and in a stupendous number of ways. Indeed if we knot our string around each column's nail selected at random, the odds are better than one-third that the resulting x will never equal the reported y [the exact probability being almost exactly $e^{-1} = (2.73 \ldots)^{-1}$]. The 1928 Morgenstern point thus can still be a worry.

All this relates to rational expectationism, à la John Muth and others, as follows. A rational-expectation equilibrium time-profile of economic variables must be such that, if everyone were apprised of it, they would together all recreate exactly that profile. Hail to the Carnegie-Mellon workshops of the 1950's where Herbert Simon, John Nash, Abraham Charnes, William Cooper, John Muth, Charles Holt, Albert Ando, and Franco Modigliani made intellectual history with the perceptive support of Dean George Leland Bach.

Ad Hominem Matters

Hitler and Mussolini enriched American science. Along with Einstein, Weyl, Bethe, Ernst Mayr, von Neumann and so many others in the natural sciences, they presented us with such economists as Joseph Schumpeter, Wassily Leontief, Jacob Marschak, Gottfried Haberler, and Abraham Wald. Modigliani, by his youth, was at the end of this illustrious migration. By good luck, Jacob Marschak and Hans Neisser at the New School enabled him to land on his feet running. Great universities—Chicago, Illinois, Carnegie-Mellon, Northwestern, MIT—recognized his merits and he repaid their perspicuity. Every scholarly honor came his way, and fittingly early—presidencies of the American Economic Association, the Econometric Society, the American Finance Society, and so forth. Not only have governments benefited from his wisdom, but in addition he has helped universities and academies recognize undervaluations in Wall Street.

Still, there is one remarkable feature in Modigliani's scholarly profile. No lone scholar he; instead, dozens of his most famous contributions have been with joint authors, bearing such bylines as Modigliani-Ando, Modigliani-Brumberg, Modigliani-Grunberg, Modigliani-Miller, Modigliani-Samuelson, Modigliani-Drèze, and Modigliani-Papademos. No one doubts Franco Modigliani's autonomous originality; all envy his ability to raise his own productivity and that of others by intense and joyful collaboration.

REFERENCES AND NOTES

1. F. Modigliani, *Econometrica* 12, 45 (1944); reprinted in (2).
2. A. Abel, Ed., *The Collected Papers of Franco Modigliani* (MIT Press, Cambridge, MA, 1980).
3. F. Modigliani, *Rev. Econ. Stat.* 45, 79 (1963); reprinted in (2).
4. S. Fischer, in *Macroeconomics and Finance: Essays in Honor of Franco Modigliani*, J. Bossons, R. Dornbusch, S. Fischer, Eds. (MIT Press, Cambridge, MA, in press).
5. F. Modigliani and R. Brumberg, in *Post Keynesian Economics*, K. K. Kurihara, Ed. (Rutgers Univ. Press, New Brunswick, NJ, 1954), pp. 388–436; reprinted in (2), along with other publications by Modigliani, and by Albert Ando and Franco Modigliani, on the life-cycle model.
6. F. Modigliani and M. H. Miller, *Am. Econ. Rev.* 48, 261 (1958); M. H. Miller and F. Modigliani, *J. Business* 34, 411 (1961); reprinted in (2).
7. For a sketch of competing paradigms in modern macroeconomics—post-Keynesian eclecticism, monetarism, and the new classical rational expectationism—see P. A. Samuelson and W. D. Nordhaus, *Economics* (McGraw-Hill, New York, 1985), part 3.
8. E. Grunberg and F. Modigliani, *J. Pol. Econ.* 62, 465 (1954); reprinted in (2).
9. J. von Neumann and O. Morgenstern [*The Theory of Games and Economic Behavior* (Princeton Univ. Press, Princeton, NJ, 1944), pp. 176–178] described the Holmes-Moriarty problem and referred to earlier work by Morgenstern.

44

JACOB VINER

1892-1970

PAUL A. SAMUELSON

JACOB VINER spent more than half of a long academic career at the University of Chicago. It was during this time that Lionel Robbins of the London School of Economics declared Viner to be the most learned living economist. Yet I doubt that very many of my five thousand fellow undergraduates of 1935 had even heard of him—a fact that tells you something about the chasm that prevailed in the Hutchins University between the graduate schools and the undergraduate student body.

At the frontier of economic science Jacob Viner was very well known, respected, and—let us acknowledge it—feared. He was regarded as a ferocious critic, who cleaned the Augean stables of error. And far from the Midway the legends of his ferocity in the seminar room were told and retold in senior common rooms wherever economists gathered. Mostly the good stories were true stories. Because of Chicago's quarter system, both Frank Knight and Viner would often offer advanced seminars in the summer, and postdoctoral economists from around the world would brave the Midwest heat to sit before their blackboards and absorb their radiated genius. It was the closest approach to the German custom in which scholars trooped from university to university sampling the cafeteria offerings of the *Gelehreten*. When an Evsey Domar or a Robert Triffin experienced the Vinerian Socratic method firsthand, the experience was indelible and got reported widely throughout the profession.

· I ·

Before I describe Viner the teacher, let me recall his career. He was born and went to school in Montreal before the First World War. Quebec was then a divided society: the English-speaking Establishment ruled the roost and the French-speaking majority were an underclass. Children of immigrant Jews were marginal in that bigoted universe. I have heard Viner say that in all his years in the Montreal public schools he was never taught a word of French. At McGill University Stephen Leacock was Viner's teacher. Yes, the humorist Leacock, who by his pupil's testimony was a stimulating lecturer on the politics of empire if not on economics. Fortunately J. C. Hemmeon, a dour Scot, did teach Viner some of the niceties of neoclassical economics. The McGill of Osler and Rutherford must have been at its high noon in those Edwardian years. It was still sending top students to the Harvard of my day in the 1930s. We used to joke that the best American economists were Canadians: Simon Newcomb, Jacob Viner, Frank D. Graham, John Kenneth Galbraith, William Vickrey, Lloyd Reynolds, and Harry Johnson to name just a few.

Viner's brilliance must have been recognized (and resented!) from the beginning. But as with Sherlock Holmes who had a more brilliant brother Mycroft, Jacob had a more brilliant older brother who became a distinguished Canadian physician. He used to tease his younger brother, saying: "The trouble with you, Jake, is that you have the sense of humor of Hemmeon and the economics of Leacock." Viner spent a couple of years in the Harvard Graduate School during a dry season there. He had a low opinion of his fellow graduate students. Frank Taussig, leading scholar in Ricardian theories of international trade and dean of American economists, spotted Viner's talent. For the rest of his life Viner was known as Taussig's favorite pupil and it was from him that Viner got his Socratic manner in the seminar room. Jacob may have been the Sheik's favorite but that did not get him a permanent appointment at the Harvard of President Lowell: many an Esau walked before him in the academic procession.

It says something for the post-Harper University of Chicago that Viner was called to a rung on the ladder in the economics department there. Indeed, a decade later, in the late 1920s when the economics department at Chicago was contemplating recruiting the budding econometrician Henry Schultz, Viner and Paul Douglas persisted even after being told that President Max Mason did not care for Jews. Quite aside from any ethnic impediments, Viner was not one to suffer mediocrities gladly and must have irritated the Bullocks, Carvers, and Gays who were Taussig's rivals. For it was as late as 1922, when Viner was already world-famous, had written a classic thesis on the Canadian balance of payments, and had returned to Cambridge to defend it orally and accept his doctorate, that Taussig had to cancel the elaborate dinner he had planned in celebration—because

589

Jacob Viner was flunked in his final orals! (When he was a visiting Taussig Research Professor at Harvard during his retirement years from Princeton, I heard him say: "I deserved to flunk." What cant. Only Allyn Young in that assembled conclave was fit to kiss the hem of Viner's crimson robe. This reminded me of the account I heard from Professor John Black's lips about the famous flunking of Harry Dexter White at his generals orals in the Harvard of the late 1920s: "Harry White dominated every seminar and economic discussion group. But every bully is a coward at heart. At his generals *we* were asking the questions, and we flunked him.")

While Viner was climbing the ladder at Chicago, he began what was to be a long and distinguished career as editor of the *Journal of Political Economy,* Chicago's journal that came to surpass in prestige and influence Taussig's *Quarterly Journal of Economics* and the official *American Economic Review.* Later, around 1927, Viner was one of those who worked hard to recruit Frank Knight. (Knight, reliable rumor relates, ignored Harvard's whistle to come replace Allyn Young: Knight disapproved of how Mr. Lowell had handled the Sacco-Vanzetti investigation!) Knight and Viner were long listed as co-editors of the *JPE:* it was a good team but Viner did most of the work, just as Harry Johnson did in later similar arrangements. (Work goes to those who don't lock the doors.)

· II ·

Now I enter on delicate ground. The University of Chicago economics department, like Gaul, was divided into parts. Knight and Viner were the theorist patriarchs and rivals. Paul Douglas was the more-than-token liberal. Henry Schultz represented the wave of the future in econometrics and mathematical economics. Henry Simons, critic of the regulated state and advocate of redistributive income taxation, was in Knight's camp. Although Aaron Director began in the Douglas workshop, his heart was with Knight. Indeed Frank Knight was the irresistible Pied Piper. For five years—from the time I was sixteen until I was twenty-one—I was bewitched by Knight. The cream of the graduate school—a Stigler, Friedman, Wallis, Homer Jones, or Hart—downplayed the Vinerian sagacity and erudition. Schultz, an earnest pioneer who lacked in self-confidence and brilliance, was, I fear, patronized by the arrogant youth of the day; that did not add to his serenity or sureness of judgment.

Internal rivalry and incivility is a scenario seen a hundred times in the universities of Europe. The picture it presents is never a pretty one. Out of diversity there usually does not arise scientific fruitfulness. Too often from dissension comes polarization and the waste heat of friction. As an undergraduate I lived through it all with, so to speak, a foot in four camps. Later as a friend and visitor, two or three times a year I watched the pot boiling. I have been the confidant of half-a-dozen generations of Chicago economists, with most of the traffic coming of course from those with oxen they deemed recently gored.

Let me merely report that Frank Knight was not the easiest chap to live with. He had no guile but was quite unaware of what his frankness entailed. Like Joan Robinson, he constantly exploded. To the two of them everything was absurdly simple or simply absurd. Even Henry Simons, Knight's ally and disciple, complained to me bitterly. Paul Douglas of course had reason to complain, something that Knight found astonishing. Being the father of a large brood, I am an expert on children's quarrels: it is absolutely pointless to try to determine who was first at fault. Let me only say that Jacob Viner, never known for his diplomacy or sweetness, was something of a saint in getting along with Knight. (Only in his eighth decade did Viner permit himself to say privately: "I always felt we should have treated Frank as if he were on the verge of a nervous breakdown in the 1930s. His financial problems and concerns about the disintegrating world economy and society were an important part of the picture.")

Although Jacob Viner had the reputation of a conservative economist who defended the orthodoxies of neoclassical and classical economics, he played a role of modest importance in Franklin Roosevelt's New Deal. Henry Morgenthau, Jr., secretary of the treasury, was no great intellect but he came to have respect for Jacob Viner. Through Viner, Harry Dexter White was called from Lawrence College in Wisconsin to begin his Napoleonic rise in the Treasury. Indeed not a few Chicago students of Viner, who were identified in the McCarthy hunts as communists or fellow travelers, were recommended by Viner. This occasioned some snickers among Chicagoans who were critical of Viner on fine points of doctrine, but who should have had reason and experience to know that Jacob Viner was a center to right-of-center thinker and actor. (If the probability was one-tenth that A. C. Pigou, Alfred Marshall's protégé at Cambridge and Keynes's post-1933 antagonist, was the Fifth Man in Britain's spy ring, it was epsilon that Viner was ever a radical of any sort. Viner agreed with the majority of economists who deplored Roosevelt's devaluation of the dollar. Today's majority sides with Roosevelt.)

Actually, Viner's heresies in 1931 were to advocate with his Chicago colleagues a deliberate program of deficit spending to temper the Great Depression; and, pragmatically, he espoused a version of the quantity theory of money and prices that gave interest rates and confidence roles to play in determining the velocity of circulation of money and that treated output as an endogenous unknown in the truism of exchange MV = PQ. Postwar workshops in money finally did catch up with the Vinerian platitudes.

This brings me, finally, to Jacob Viner's place in "the Chicago school." Yes, there is a Chicago school in economics despite occasional disclaimers that all reasonable scholars believe in the same truth. Indeed, the data require us to recognize two Chicago schools. The first Chicago school was that of Knight, Viner, and Simons. It advocated use of the market, but recommended redistributive taxes and transfers to mitigate the worst inequalities of the laissez-faire system. It pragmatically favored macroeconomic policies in the areas of credit and fiscal policies to attenuate the amplitude of cyclical fluctuations. It endorsed antitrust policies to improve competition and favored utility regulation where competition was severely compromised. If time is short, call it the Knightian Chicago school. Without question, Viner belonged to it even if he was more pragmatic and less dogmatic than some of his colleagues.

The second Chicago school ought properly to be associated with the names of Milton Friedman, George Stigler, Aaron Director, and Gary Becker. Call it the Friedman Chicago school for short. It has lost the Simonsian imperative to use the tax system to modify economic inequality and has reverted to Adam Smith's view that most attempts by government to improve on the effectiveness of competition will only make matters worse. Viner has not gone on record with his assents and dissents. As a third Chicago School is gestating in the workshops of Robert Lucas's rational expectationism, one can conjecture what Viner's discontents would be with strong hypotheses of quick convergence to neutral-money homeostasis.

· III ·

The New Palgrave: A Dictionary of Economics (1987, vol. 4, 812–14) contains a fine piece by Henry W. Spiegel on Viner's contributions to economics, and I refer the reader to it. Worth quoting from it is the account of a little-known Viner item of 1921 that essentially anticipated the Sraffa-Robinson-Chamberlin paradigm of imperfect competition.

> Five years ahead of Sraffa, six years ahead of the publication of Joan Robinson's and Edward Chamberlin's books on the subject, Viner developed here, in a short paragraph, the outlines of the theory of monopolistic competition. He writes of inflexible prices, "differentiation" of products, advertising, non-price competition and other

characteristics of markets that are neither fully competitive nor completely monopolistic. In such markets producers may succeed in creating a special demand for their products. They can then to some extent determine prices independently of the prices charged by their competitors and still maintain their sales.

Jacob Viner earned a top reputation as an economic theorist in the Marshallian tradition of neoclassical economics. Along with Bertil Ohlin of Sweden and Gottfried Haberler of Austria and Harvard, Viner played a key role in advancing theory of international trade a quantum jump beyond the Ricardo-Taussig paradigm of comparative labor advantage. An erudite historian of economic thought, Viner was without peers in the history of the theory of international trade. His *Studies in the Theory of International Trade,* published in 1937, is a masterpiece, both as history of the subject and as definitive synthesis of the subject at the threshold of the Lerner-Meade-Samuelson-McKenzie-Jones-Chipman-Mundell-Kemp era.

Viner's article on "Cost Curves and Supply Curves" of 1931 gained him earned and inadvertent fame. Marshall had neglected to relate closely the theory of the firm to the supply of the competitive industry. Viner did well what needed doing, as Joan Robinson and Edward Chamberlin did a couple of years later in connection with imperfect competition. The new Appendix, added by Viner when the 1931 item was anthologized, shows how around 1940 he and Joan Robinson were getting a glimpse of the general equilibrium that transcends Marshall's partial equilibrium. Viner's contretemps with his mathematician draftsman Y. K. Wong, over the long-run *envelope* to his descending U-shaped curves, brought the inadvertent fame that was in part bittersweet. Among the article's many gems is Viner's so-called Pure Ricardian case, where a good is produced by an industry that uses specialized land and transferable labor—the manageable case known today in the literature on international trade as the Haberler-Jones-Samuelson technology. (Incidentally, Viner here is in effect showing up the root fallacy in Piero Sraffa's 1926 classic article, which purported to prove that only constant-cost industries are compatible with the logic of Marshall's partial equilibrium; fortunately this fallacy that bewitched six decades of pedants is accompanied by Sraffa's correct vision of decreasing-cost firms kept in equilibrium by facing market demand curves such that they can sell more of their product only by accepting a lower net price for it. As mentioned already in *Palgrave,* Viner and Chicago colleagues such as J. M. Clark and Theodore Yntema were comfortable with such notions long before Robinson and Chamberlin wrote their classics.)

One can only sample Viner's fabulous learning. Friedrich Hayek, Eli

Heckscher, and possibly Lionel Robbins were the few contemporaries in his league. In 1972, William Baumol gave some flavor of Viner's erudition in his memoir on the Princeton years. Aaron Director and Lloyd Mints, if they found an old item in Harper Library that didn't show a checkout slip with Viner's name on it, would confront him with glee; almost always he would reply, "I read that in the stacks standing up." For years Viner bought rare books for Harper Library, in jovial competition with such collectors as Piero Sraffa, Edwin Cannan, and H. S. Foxwell, each of whom would kill for a newly discovered letter of Ricardo.

I lack competence to judge the material Viner worked on in his last twenty-five years at Princeton. What was put in publishable state was apparently only the tip of a weighty iceberg. From the beginning Viner was much of a perfectionist. Some of his great Chicago lectures he for some reason never chose to publish. (His recent editor, Dr. Douglas Irwin of the Federal Reserve research staff, has spoken of a paper that was revised in some degree without authority by the journal that published it. And for that reason Viner excluded it from his list of publications.) As he grew old, Viner seems to have succumbed to a scholarly disease more virulent than arthritis or osteoporosis—increased reluctance to publish material regarded as incomplete only by himself.

As an elder statesman Viner gave out sage judgment and advice. His human wisdom and his reputation for that is illustrated by the advice he gave when the London School of Economics authorities asked what should be done with the papers and correspondence of Edwin Cannan. Since that irascible Scot treated the great minds of the past like schoolchildren, rather untalented schoolchildren, one can guess the terms in which he recommended his own students. After sampling the trove, Viner advised: "Burn them."

Back in the 1950s, the great foundations sent economists like Viner, Haberler, and Robbins to lecture in Brazil and Argentina. They cast their pearls before small audiences, while in nearby halls, so to speak, such Marxists as Paul Baran and Paul Sweezy lectured to the plaudits of hundreds. Clio must smile at the spectacle of present-day South American governments that are trying to limit past economic damages by applying the Viner-type wisdoms to their developmental problems.

I should mention that Viner did original work on patterns of imperialism, documenting the naiveté of the fashionable view that business interests generally succeed in manipulating the powers of the state for their selfish interests. Eugene Staley, as Viner's student, showed how it was often the flag that manipulated trade rather than vice versa. While at Princeton Viner did do pathbreaking analysis of customs unions, going beyond his precocious 1923 classic on dumping.

Brevity requires that I sample Viner's originality as a theorist: with respect to his valid polemics in favor of an eclectic merger of utility and real-cost elements in value theory; and with respect to his foreign-trade innovations.

Knight, Haberler, and Robbins underplayed real-cost determinants of price in the Austrian manner of opportunity cost and derive utility. (For a time Knight seemed even to defend a Sraffian-like paradigm that left relative prices invariant to shifts in consumers' demand patterns.) As Edgeworth had done in the 1890s in rebutting Böhm-Bawerk, Viner took the general position of Marshall and Walras: when factor supplies are variable, and labor is not indifferent between working for an hour on food or on clothing, then the Austrian position is shown to be oversimple. Of course, Viner was sitting in the poker game with four aces and in the end his opponents gave way, grew silent, or copped a Stiglerian plea that they were 93 percent free of error.

Viner's eclecticism with respect to a modern theory of value contrasts with his longtime effort to defend Taussig's use in international economics of Ricardian technologies that involved labor as the only input of production. Tom Kuhn, the methodologist of revolutions in science, should savor the contrasting styles of Ohlin and Viner: along with Haberler they both arrived at essentially the same general equilibrium model; but Ohlin did so claiming great novelty for his own innovations, while Viner always played down the departures from the previous status quo. Both were right—and wrong. Baumol and Ellen Viner Seiler (Viner's daughter), in their biography of Viner in the *International Encyclopedia of the Social Sciences* in 1979, attribute Viner's being overshadowed by Haberler and Ohlin to his eschewing the oversimplifications of the opportunity-cost dogma. That does not quite hit the nail on the head. Viner did present in a lecture at the London School of Economics in January 1931 the canonical trade diagram involving indifference contours and a concave production-possibility frontier. But he did not publish it for half a dozen years, leaving to A. P. Lerner the garnering of fame that eclipsed both Ohlin and Haberler.

Like a glassblower or hand-weaver, Jacob Viner was a victim of technical obsolescence. He lacked training in the mathematics that was to sweep the realms of economic theory. Being sensitive, he well realized this and let it become something of a King Charles's head. That is why, I believe, after the age of forty-five he disengaged from competition at the frontier of mainstream economics. He had much company in the generation of my teachers: their presidential addresses to the American Economics Association bristle with complaints about the over-mathematization of economics.

· IV ·

It is proper to conclude with an account of Jacob Viner as the toreador of the graduate seminar room. When the *Journal of Political Economy* asked me to write an obituary of Viner's Chicago days, I was in a quandary. *Nihil nisi bonum* was not Viner's own credo, but rather *nisi verum*. And my sister-in-law Professor Anita Arrow Summers of Pennsylvania, who registered in one of his last courses at Chicago, insisted that posterity deserved an accurate testimony. But, on the other hand, I kept thinking of the surviving Frances Viner, and her natural sensibilities. In the end I tried to compromise between verisimilitude and affectionate memory. When I received no comment on the reprint sent to his guileless widow, I at first had misgivings that I had overshot the mean; but, as I later learned, Frances was in a terminal illness and the issue was moot. As I reread my words of almost two decades back I doubt that I can do better than paraphrase them here.

The problem resides in the fact that the Viner who was so stimulating was also the teacher who caused not only young maidens to burst into tears but also battle-hardened officers from two world wars. Here is an abridgement of the account which I wrote in 1972.

> Viner was my teacher, I heard many lectures by Knight and had chances to talk to him. However, it was chance of the draw that the famous 301 graduate course in economic theory, which oscillated between Frank Knight and Jacob Viner, happened to be given by Viner in the winter quarter of 1935, my senior year and just after I had learned Marshallian economics from Paul Douglas. It was no easy matter to get into Viner's course (and, as we shall see, still harder to stay in it). For an undergraduate it was still harder, but Paul Douglas said he would write a letter on my behalf, reporting that I was somewhat "cantankerous" but a good bet.
>
> Fortunately for me, Viner had just returned from his tour of duty in Morgenthau's Treasury and must have been in an indulgent mood. With about thirty-five other aspirants, who I recall included Martin Bronfenbrenner and Warren Scoville, we lined up around a huge seminar table on the ground floor of the then new Social Science

Research Building. Viner appeared, holding our names on index cards; and after a speedy inquisition, five of us were found wanting in previous preparation or motivation. But that was only the beginning.

My impression of Viner never changed from that first glimpse. He was short and intense, like a bantam cock. His upper lip, usually bedewed by a bead of moisture, curled in what seemed half a smile. In my imperfect memory his hair was then reddish, and his complexion matched. His suit coats were on the short side and his posture was not that of a West Point cadet. How I remember anything about his person I do not know, since every eye in the room was fastened upon the diabolical deck of index cards in his hands through which he shuffled nervelessly. To be scrupulously honest, subsequent legend has contaminated my account. I was too innocent to be nervous. In contrast to the graduate students present, I had nothing at stake. But for them their whole careers and professional futures were in jeopardy each time he riffled through the cards.

Viner was a student of Frank Taussig, the master of the Socratic method. Taussig played on his classes as Pablo Casals played on his cello. He knew which idiot would botch up Ricardo's trade-off between the profit rate and the real wage; he knew which showoff student had to be kept out of the classroom verbal interaction lest he short-circuit the dialogue.

Viner added one new ingredient: terror. Members of the seminar sat tensely around the table, and when the name of the victim was read off the cards, you could almost hear the sighs of relief and the slumping back into chairs of those who had won temporary respite. Indeed, the stakes were high. Three strikes and you were out, with no appeal possible to any higher court. And this was no joke. I remember an able graduate student who, having failed to give an acceptable answer on two previous occasions, was told by Viner: "Mr. ——, I am afraid you are not equal to yourself or this class." This man barely managed to retrieve his position at the final moment. When one victim alibied, "I am beyond my depth," Viner is supposed to have said, "Sir, you drown in shallow water." If a graduate student was refused admittance to 301, the basic course in theory, he had no choice but to drop out or to transfer to the slums of political science or sociology. (Years later when I discussed with Jack Viner the legend of his ferocity, he said that the department had given him the function of screening the candidates for higher degrees. It was not work for which he was ill-equipped.)

What shall I say about the course? By reputation it was considered the best course in economic theory being given in the America of those days. On reflection, I think it probably deserved that accolade [this in 1972]. To my regret, the notes that I took for Viner's course, if they still exist, are not in any location known to me. But that is perhaps just as well, for Viner was vehement in his belief that it was a sacrilege to take skimpy notes from a course and present it to the world as a fair sample of the course's quality. To his indignation, a student had done just that around 1930, and a mimeographed copy of the notes was on deposit in Harper Library. In 1935 the course that I took was somewhat better in scope and coverage from the version presented in 1930. To buttress his sensitivity on this point, Viner made reference to Wesley Mitchell's famous course at Columbia. Without authorization, a student circulated rather elaborate mimeographed notes (which, subsequent to my conversation with Viner, were published by Augustus Kelley). Viner had read these notes and reported that their content was extremely disappointing, a fact he blamed on the unauthorized paraphraser, not on the quality of Mitchell's thought. It was an uncharacteristically gentle verdict *I* thought.

Viner put considerable store on the historical development of the subject. Since this was my first graduate course, I did not know there was any other way to do it. Viner made clear at the beginning that he would not be covering the latest wrinkles in the theory of imperfect or monopolistic competition. However, since Viner himself, along with his student and colleague Theodore Yntema, had independently discovered the marginal cost-marginal revenue conditions for maximization of an imperfect competitor's profits, much of what was contained in the Chamberlin and Robinson treatises was adequately covered. Although I had the best undergraduate education in economics that opportunity could provide anywhere at that date, only once and there in Viner's graduate course was I exposed to the mysteries of indifference curves and the production-possibility frontier; this latter under the heading of Pareto's "production indifference" curve. In the first minute of the course Viner made clear that a proper prerequisite for it would be knowledge of the calculus. But that, since the instructor lacked the qualification, he would waive it for the rest of us. Jacob Viner was a respecter of mathematics, but also both critical and defensive about it. Let me make clear that Viner possessed in superlative degree what might be called *native* mathematical ability.

In writing these reminiscences of Viner as a teacher at Chicago I have consulted a number of eminent scholars who took his graduate courses both before and after the 1935 term I have spoken of. One view is that he mellowed over the years. A psychologist will be amused to learn that the Viner of 1946 at Princeton was "mellow" and the Viner of 1946 at Chicago was "unmellow." Saul must have become

Paul on the Pennsylvania Limited! The truth is that he used a teaching technique which to the best students was inordinately stimulating. I could quote testimony after testimony to this effect. I myself found his course enormously stimulating. Evsey Domar, who took it in 1940, tells me it was the best course he has even taken, and in part because of Viner's challenging manner. Martin Bronfenbrenner, who took many of Viner's Chicago courses, recalls that it was customary to sit in on the same course year after year because of the new insights to be gleaned.

After I left Chicago I learned that I was something of a teen-age legend myself in Viner's course of that year. Legends grow on legends. So let me set the record straight. The prosaic fact is that Viner had the custom of coming to class with complicated diagrams to be copied on the blackboard. Such transcriptions are notoriously subject to minor errors in which curves intersect on the wrong side of axes, and so forth. Fools rush in where angels fear to tread, and so it was left to the only undergraduate in the course to point out such occasional petty aberrations which detracted nothing from his evident erudition and keenness. Once Viner was a bit slow in providing a reference for Wicksteed's view of supply curve as a reserve demand curve. Always ready to do my boy scout's good deed of the day, I piped up: "Schultz's book on sugar demand deals with that." He threw his chalk down on the desk in annoyance I can now well understand.

Few of us like to be wrong. Jacob Viner, consummate scholar that he was, and meticulous in his knowledge of the literature, was no exception in this respect. Yet I would argue that it is the occasional errors of geniuses like Viner which make the reputations of mere mortals, and which also seminally advance the body of science. Who in economics would remember Dr. Wong if his memory had not been perpetuated by his correcting of Viner's long-run cost-curve envelope? Precisely because Viner was so Jovially impervious to error, the economics profession got a modicum of *Schadenfreude* at his expense over the envelope incident. Certainly he had no need to be sensitive about it. Indeed I later identified what I called the deeper Viner-Wong envelope theorem in a 1929 Viner review of Cannon. By 1935 Viner reported to the class that Wong had been right in their dispute in 1931 and he, Viner, had been wrong, mathematically and economically. "But" he said to me privately, just as the hour chimes had rung, "although there seems to be some esoteric mathematical reason why the envelope cannot be drawn so that it passes smoothly through the declining bottoms of the U-shaped cost curves, nevertheless I can do it." "Yes," I replied impishly, "with a good thick pencil, you can do it."

Now for a few second thoughts in 1990 on these 1972 formulations.

1. By 1935, Viner's 301 was probably not the best that America could then offer. Schumpeter's unsystematic Harvard lectures that I heard in the fall of 1935 referred to the future of our subject, not its past.

2. The Socratic method of Taussig was a bad pattern for the twenty-one-year-old Viner to emulate. It was a slow, slow, very slow procedure —appropriate for a science in its degenerate stage when no fundamental problems are deemed to admit of a definitive answer. Also, I learned with surprise from Paul Douglas's autobiography that he found the sweet old Taussig I knew to have been a seminar bully around 1915 when Douglas took his famous Ec 11 as a visitor from Columbia. Alas, Viner learned more from Taussig than I had realized. Taussig's Socratic method was grossly overpraised in my Harvard times. My friends Abram Bergson and Alice Bourneuf, from their own experience, told me not to believe all I heard. And, as I said in 1972, Taussig himself told me that his Ec 11 was overrated in his post-1919 years.

3. Screening out unpromising recruits to the graduate economics program, like dusting for athlete's foot, is I suppose a necessary activity. But how weak must be the statistical power of a procedure that uses as evidence against you your inability to respond quickly to vaguely defined questions, in an atmosphere of fright. That way one might lose a John Hicks and gain a J. R. McCulloch.

Some outsiders have looked at the University of Chicago as a jungle red in tooth and claw. That has always been an exaggeration. Yet when I used to wonder how Hutchins's university stayed so near the top after John D. Rockefeller had put it on its own, I decided that part of the story was that Chicago was a premature meritocracy. It was the kind of place where long-time teachers were finally refused permanent tenure; where, let it be said, colleagues occasionally fought over priorities and plagiarisms; and where a professor of economics or physics might receive five to eight times what some professors of classics would be paid. (When Hirofumi Uzawa left Chicago for Tokyo University, his yearly salary there barely matched his monthly salary on the Midway.)

History may be written by survivors but science is fabricated by overachievers. One understands why Jacob Viner, at the peak of his prime, would reveal a preference for the green lawns of Princeton. His children lived in the East. Along with Knight and Harry Gideonse, Viner played an important and honorable role in opposing the Machiavellian Robert Hutchins, surely a tedious distraction for a creative scholar. Frances and

Jacob Viner were not entranced by the Chicago social circle or entrapped by collegial friendships. At Princeton they did live happily ever after. (Frances Viner was a much loved extrovert, as hinted at by the following anecdote. At Princeton's retirement dinner for Viner, Frances spoke about his alleged helplessness: "Why, if I broke my leg in the basement, two people would starve to death. I in the basement and Jack upstairs in his study." With quick wit, Viner replied: "I had a colleague who cut his leg chopping kindling wood in the basement. I told him: 'That's what you get for doing woman's work'.")

Jacob Viner departed from Chicago with honor and without rancor. He had paid his dues and helped to make economists remember his Midway as Camelot.

532

Irving Fisher 1867-1947

Before 1930 American economics fell under the shadow of British economics. We spent much of our time reading the words of Alfred Marshall, F.Y. Edgeworth, A.C. Pigou, Maynard Keynes, and such older writers as Adam Smith, David Ricardo, John Stuart Mill, and Stanley Jevons. The various German historical-school writers were not much studied or translated, although the great Austrians Carl Menger and Eugen von Böhn-Bawerk were early translated and well read. Léon Walras and Vilfredo Pareto were only minor exceptions to the Anglo-Saxon dominance--minor for the reason that the generation of my teachers (Frank Knight, Jacob Viner, Paul Douglas, Edward Chamberlin, and even Joseph Schumpeter) were not very proficient in mathematical analysis. Because Gustav Cassel wrote in fluent English and dealt with major topics of finance, he escaped the neglect that was accorded to his untranslated Scandinavian colleagues: Knut Wicksell, Eli Heckscher, and David Davidson.

Fads and fashions rule in science as in art. An Impressionist painter from Paris receives more fame than one from St. Petersburg or Denver; a composer in Vienna or Munich had a definite advantage in the nineteenth century over a musical talent in Bristol or Osaka. If one objectively surveys economic treatises on important topics, written before 1930, a count of authorities cited by German and American authors would reveal that their two native literatures actually deserved more credit than economists then generally recognized.

In particular, a few American economists--usually the same few--possessed international reputations. The names of John Bates Clark, Francis Walker, Henry George, Thorstein Veblen, and Frank Taussig come to mind. (Even Friedrich List might be given a New World connection, in that his peculiar protectionist doctrines were nurtured by his earlier years of sojourn here.) The name of Irving Fisher would barely appear on any short list of American economists drawn up when I first began my economic studies some 60 years ago. Although Fisher was then near the pinnacle of his lifetime repute, he would probably have been lumped together with such minor luminaries as Frank Fetter, Wesley Mitchell, Allyn Young, or Thomas Nixon Carver.

My point is that each generation must rank anew its past scientific heroes. Informed scholars writing today would put Irving Fisher at, or near, the very top of historic American economists. As James Tobin, Yale's great contemporary scholar, puts it unqualifiedly in his splendid 1987 *New Palgrave Dictionary of Economics* biography: "Fisher is widely regarded as the greatest economist America has produced." And out of Fisher's many fields of scholarly contributions, his innovations in the realm of capital and interest would command the most superlative praises.

It is appropriate therefore that the 1906 masterpiece, *The*

Nature of Capital and Income, should be included in any set of economic classics. It set the stage and defined the nomenclature for Irving Fisher's great synthesis of interest theory--his 1907 *Rate of Interest*, and its 1930 revised edition under the title of *The Theory of Interest*.

As a personality and character, Irving Fisher commands considerable interest. He was the quintessential Protestant intellectual in the four decades before and after 1900. Son of a poor minister, he worked his way through Yale and rose by merit into the American elite. He became rich the old-fashioned way: by marrying an heiress. But he earned a second fortune as a Schumpeterian innovator who pioneered a visible index system for filing. Alas, these and the third fortune he acquired by speculation in the bull stock market of the 1920's, were all lost after 1929 when Wall Street crashed. He died broke at 80, bitter that the nation would not adopt his monetary proposals for stabilizing the price level and taming the oscillations of the business cycle.

An economist who loses big in the stock market! That is a sad sight. Philistines would ask: "If you're so smart, why aren't you rich?" One reason I suspect for the overvaluation that David Ricardo has enjoyed in comparison with his superiors--Adam Smith and J.S. Mill --was the fact that he was a self-made millionaire in the London stock market. John Maynard Keynes needed no boost to his earned brilliance as an economist, but it certainly did not hurt his reputation that he made fortunes for King's College, a great insurance company, and for his own account. The several hundred economists I have known around the globe averaged better than historians and physicists as canny investors, but their outcomes have been distributed in log-normal distribution about a mean that stands little above the general average. (Modern efficient-market theory explains why this is much in line with what is to be expected.)

Fairly or not, one reason for Fisher's not being recognized at his true scientific worth was his publicized failure in personal finance. A second reason was Fisher's inveterate do-goodism. After his bout with tuberculosis around the turn of the century when he was sentenced to an extended sojourn in a sanitarium, Fisher became a health fanatic. He crusaded against alcohol and cigarettes. He agitated (1915) for fresh air, thorough chewing of food, vitamins and vegetables, exercise, weight control, and was a pioneer in promoting annual medical examinations. To a sophisticated admirer of Fisher's science--Joseph Schumpeter--his do-goodism was almost laughable, as were Fisher's schemes to stabilize the price level by formula compensations in the weight of gold contained in the dollar or pound, and his monetary activism to offset the cyclical "dance of the dollar" and its induced "debt-deflation" syndromes of bankruptcy. Never mind that modern physicians espouse most of Fisher's health nostrums and that the post-Keynesian era has made macroeconomic stabilization the general custom, Fisher's scientific standing was obscured by the reception of his reformist activities. (One major exception must be noted because it stems from Fisher's present treatise on capital theory. In the tradition of J.S. Mill and A.C. Pigou, but with his own added novelties, Fisher (1937) opposed the taxation of income as involving avoidable deadweight loss from "double taxation of saving"--avoidable by embracing instead the taxation of a person's *consumption*, which Fisher insists is the only proper definition of income.)

Before concentrating on Irving Fisher's central scientific achievement in the area of capital and interest, I must briefly sketch his several major breakthroughs in other areas of economics.

Pure Walrasian theory. Fisher's great 1892 Ph.D. dissertation on value and price represented a belated, but independent, discovery of the general equilibrium of supply and demand. Alas, he was born too late to share with Jevons, Menger, Walras and Edgeworth the glory in bringing about the neoclassical revolution. But, working with Yale's great Willard Gibbs, Fisher did create a masterwork in value theory, replete with hydraulic analogue models and inclusive of goods with non-independent utilities.

Although Fisher realized that there was no need to measure the consumer's utility as a determinate function of the vector of goods consumed, he had a burning interest in defining such exact cardinal measures of utility. Before Ragnar Frisch, and as a mentor for the young Frisch, Fisher (1927) recognized how from $(P_1,...,P_n; q_1,...,q_n)$ observations of consumer's demand, if those demands were generated by the maximizing of *additive* independent utilities-- $\Sigma_1^a f_j(q_j)$, or even $F(q_1,...,q_n) + G(q_{r+1},...,q_n)$--the econometrician could identify the $[f_j()]$ functions, or the $F(,...,)$ and $G(,...,)$ functions. Schumpeter admired this tour de force, perhaps excessively.

Quantity theory of money and prices. Irving Fisher's 1911 *The Purchasing Power of Money* is the most comprehensive exposition of neoclassical price-level macroeconomics: $MV = PQ$, and all that. Alfred Marshall in Cambridge had pioneered similar ground, as his pupils Pigou and Keynes were later to do. The young Keynes unfairly downgraded Fisher's monetary contributions, dubbing his V velocity as more "mechanical" than Marshall's reciprocal velocity $1/V$. Today we recognize their equivalence. And, most important of all, *after* Keynes's 1936 *General Theory of Employment, Interest and Money*, we realize that Fisher, Marshall, and the young Keynes overlooked the crucial importance of the interest rate foregone by the holders of plentiful cash balances in their deciding on optimal V velocity. (In sum, when we rewrite the Quantity Equation as $PQ = MV(r)$, where V is a rising function of the interest rate--$dV/dr > 0$--a Milton

3

Friedman becomes an unconscious private in the army of Keynesian liquidity preference!)

Index numbers and econometric methods. Both in 1911 and more encyclopedically in his 1922 book *The Making of Index Numbers*, Fisher studied, empirically and axiomatically, how best to measure a price level between times and places. His ideal index number, the geometric mean between Laspeyres's base-weighted index and Paasche's terminal-weighted index, $[\Sigma P^t Q^0/\Sigma P^0 Q^0]^{1/2} [\Sigma P^t Q^t/\Sigma P^0 Q^t]^{1/2}$, ranked high in terms of his many proposed tests. Later work by Könus, Haberler, Staehle, Frisch, Leontief and Diewert replaced the purely statistical approach of Edgeworth, Walsh and Fisher--replaced it by the attempt to measure how much more money income it would take at the prices of P^t to buy the same level of well-being as the money income of time 0 had been to buy at the P^0 prices.

Fisher also pioneered in the 1920's the technique of "distributed lags"--as for example in estimating from past price-level changes what people now expect the future rate of inflation will be. That way Fisher, advancing beyond Henry Thorton, Wicksell and Marshall, was able to define and measure the "*real* rate of interest" as "the money or nominal rate of interest minus the percentage rate of inflation."

It was Irving Fisher, together with Joseph Schumpeter and the impassioned Ragnar Frisch, who were the key trio in founding the Econometric Society around 1930. Although econometrics today is usually interpreted to mean statistical economics, originally it had a wider meaning: the use of mathematics in advancing economic theory and empirical quantitative measurement of economic magnitudes.

* * *

I must now turn to Irving Fisher, the single greatest contributor to the theory of capital and interest. Böhm-Bawerk in the 1880's had written his three-volume treatise on (1) the different historical theories of interest and their shortcomings, (2) his own "positive" theory of capital and (3) his rejection of all criticisms of the Böhm-Bawerkian edifice. The young Fisher, by expositing mathematically an exact model of intertemporal equilibrium, sorted out what was correct and central to Böhm's paradigm. Instead of being grateful to Fisher, Böhm resented even more than rejection of his theory any purported improving upon it!

Posterity passes judgments on all debates. The merits and defects of non-mathematical economics are well revealed by Böhm-Bawerk's polemics. Thanks to Fisher's patient and lucid expositions, it is his models that have carried the day. Even the critiques of neo-classical capital theory by Sraffa or Joan Robinson have to be formulated in terms of Fisher's "present-discounted-values" and "rates of return over cost."

It is the present classic that provides the tools of intertemporal analysis: taxonomic accountancy and economics, as well as market-clearing equilibrium conditions.

After Fisher's 1907 *The Rate of Interest*, its author came to be known as an adherent of the "impatience school" of interest--akin to Frank Fetter and the earlier-day Nassau Senior. The eclectic Irving Fisher had only his own expositional emphasis to blame for this one-blade-of-the-scissors distortion of his actual viewpoint. In the 1930 rewrite of the 1907 work, entitled *The Theory of Interest*, Fisher clarified that his was a general clearing-of-intertemporal-markets approach. His new subtitle nicely rectifies the balance: *The Theory of Interest: As Determined by Impatience to Spend and Opportunities to Invest*. Along with Böhm's rational and irrational asymmetric time preference goes nature's technological tradeoffs of x future units of chocolate for each one unit of chocolate not consumed today. (Incidentally, the guns-or-butter production-possibility frontier that my textbook made ubiquitous in the modern age traces back to 1907 Fisher, filtered through the subsequent writings of Barone, Haberler, Lerner and many others. In connection with the time-phased problem of interest theory, today's textbook diagram of the Fisher type, with its curves' vertical biases vis-à-vis the 45° line of time symmetry, is more illuminating about Böhm's three causes of interest than tens of thousands of that master's literary words.)

Figure 1

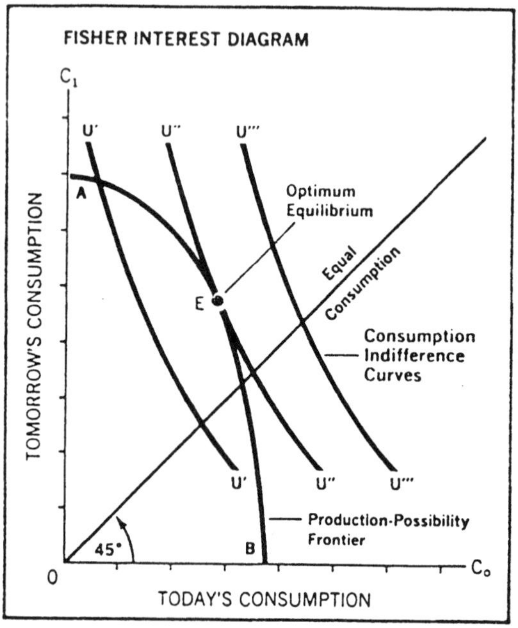

Fisher's triumphs in the realm of theory are actually used in the real world of economics. Thus, all over the world money managers seek *optimal investment portfolios* using the "discounted-dividends" model that John Burr Williams adapted from Fisher's concept of present-discounted-value in Williams's classic 1938 *Theory of Investment Value.* Similarly, business firms have been doing their capital budgeting by the sophisticated adaptations that the economist George Terborgh made for members of the trade association for manufacturing equipment: the optimal time to replace equipment and similar problems of Hotelling-Fisher type are solved by practitioners all over the world.

Many of my own early articles on capital theory were rediscovering concepts already in Fisher's turn-of-the-century books, alas not assigned to me by my Chicago and Harvard teachers. I had to insist, late in the day, that investors ought to concentrate on *total return*: the sum of dividend (or coupon) yield and (algebraic) capital gains. As late as the 1930s, economists such as Frederick Macaulay and I published Fisher-like formulae for variable rates of interest and discounting. Before Keynes's 1936 "marginal efficiency of capital" came Fisher's (marginal) rate of return over cost.[1] Long before the Sraffa-Pasinetti "reswitching" discussions, Fisher had pointed out the possibility of *multiple* real roots in present-discounted-value calculations.

Being a general equilibrium model of multi-period price clearing, Fisher's system has no need for any construction that relies on a scalar measure of aggregate capital, as was pointed out by Robert Solow in his 1963 De Vries lecture, *Capital Theory and the Rate of Return.* On the other hand it can accommodate useful special cases such as (1) the Ramsey-Solow one-sector model that Joan Robinson

---

[1] Economists used to debate in the 1930s whether a rational decision maker should maximize the present-discounted value of an investment process; or, instead, should maximize its "internal rate of return," defined as the interest rate that discounts its summed receipts to its summed costs. Under perfect competition, where you can borrow and lend indefinitely at the specified market interest rates, Fisher's PDV criterion is indisputably correct. Under imperfect competition or uncertainty as to relevant interest rates for different degrees of borrowing or lending, neither of the above criteria is exact; one's own subjective rates of time preference no longer cancel out of the decision solution when perfection of competition is denied; then a complex problem in dynamic programming may be unavoidable, and even integer programming may be needed in cases of coarse and lumpy variables.

called LEETS (STEEL spelled backwards): Consumption + Net Investment = Function of Labor and Capital:

$$C + \dot{K} = F(K,L) = Lf(K/L), f' > 0 > f''$$
$$\text{interest rate} = \partial \dot{K}/\partial K = f'(K/L).$$

(2) The century-and-a-half old capital model of Thünen is also admissible, in which labor alone produces a capital good that, together with other labor, can produce consumption. This 2-sector model involves

$$C = F(K, L - a\dot{K} - a\delta K),$$

where δ is the rate of exponential depreciation of the capital good and a is the cost in labor of one new capital good.

(3) The multi-good input/output model of Leontief and Sraffa, in which goods are produced by labor and raw materials of themselves, fits precisely into the Fisher framework.

Science never ends with one great scientist's innovations. After Fisher's works of 1896-1930, John von Neumann (1945) presented his model of time-phased general equilibrium. Its technology involves production of goods out of goods (and, possibly, out of primary-factor inputs like labor and capital), and it admits of joint products. It can accommodate *any* time-phased economic process and, had it been available in the days of Böhm, Wicksell, J.B. Clark, and Frank Knight, it could have settled or aborted many a famous polemic. Fisher grappled in this book (Chapter XVI) with the analysis of what we today call stochastic uncertainty. Recent generations of economists have carried forward his pioneering efforts and created the valuable modern theory of finance. As an example, for the *Festschrift* for Leonid Hurwicz, Samuelson (1986) generalized the Williams discounted-dividend evaluation of securities to the stochastic realm, deducing that the resulting capitalization time-series would not be a random walk or a martingale in an efficient market. (In order that a security's total return be a white-noise random variable with no excess *mean* return, its market price must be a red-noise process with negative auto-correlation and with future price being expected to rise when a run of low past dividends makes likely a run of high future dividends.)

Modern portfolio theory could take Irving Fisher as its patron saint, with his picture smiling down blessings on the portraits of Bachelier, Keynes, Musgrave-Domar, Tobin, Markowitz, Linter, Sharpe, Mandelbrot, Black-Scholes, Fama and other heroes.

"I *will* be a great man," Fisher wrote to his wife from his

7

sickbed. For such a designation, many are called but few are chosen. Irving Fisher fulfilled his vow. He was a great economic scientist and generations of scholars owe him a debt that grows with compound interest.

Selected Works of Irving Fisher

1892 *Mathematical Investigations in the Theory of Value and Prices*. New Haven, Connecticut: Connecticut Academy of Arts and Sciences, *Transactions*, 9. Reprinted, New York: Augustus M. Kelley, 1961.

1896 "Appreciation and interest," *AEA Publications* 3(11),331-442. Reprinted, New York: Augustus M. Kelley, 1961.

1906 *The Nature of Capital and Income*. New York: Macmillan.

1907 *The Rate of Interest*. New York: Macmillan.

1911 *The Purchasing Power of Money*. New York: Macmillan.

1915 *How to Live*, with E.L. Fisk. New York: Funk and Wagnalls.

1922 *The Making of Index Numbers*. Boston: Houghton Mifflin

1927 "A statistical method for measuring 'marginal utility' and testing the justice of a progressive income tax." In *Economic Essays Contributed in Honor of John Bates Clark*, J.H. Hollander, ed. New York: Macmillan.

1930 *The Theory of Interest*. New York: Macmillan.

1937 "Income in theory and income taxation in practice," *Econometrica* 5, 1-55.

Bibliography

Böhm-Bawerk Eugen von. *Capital and Interest: A Critical History of Economical Theory*, Vol. I, 1884. *Positive Theory of Capital*, Vol. II, 1889. *Criticisms and Excursi*, Vol. III, 1890. South Holland, Illinois: Libertarian Press. American translation, 1959.

8

Keynes, John Maynard, 1936. *The General Theory of Employment, Interest and Money.* London: Macmillan.

Leontief, Wassily. 1941. *The Structure of the American Economy, 1919-1929.* Cambridge, Massachusetts: Harvard University Press.

Macaulay, Frederick Robertson. 1938. *Some Theoretical Problems Suggested by the Movements of Interest Rates, Bond Yields, and Stock Prices in the United States since 1856.* New York: National Bureau of Economic Research.

Samuelson, Paul A. 1970. *Economics*, 8th ed. New York: McGraw-Hill book Co., 587.

_____. 1972. "Irving Fisher and the Theory of Capital," in W. Fellner, et al., eds., *Ten Economic Studies in the Tradition of Irving Fisher.* New York: John Wiley & Sons.

_____. 1986. "Stochastic Land Valuation: Total Return as Martingale Implying Price Changes--a Negatively Correlated Walk." Speech, 19 January 1984, University of California, San Diego. Reproduced as Chapter 327 in *The Collected Scientific Papers of Paul A. Samuelson*, Vol. 5, 1986. Cambridge, Massachusetts: The MIT Press, 527-536.

Solow, Robert M. 1963. *Capital Theory and the Rate of Return.* De Vries Lecture. Amsterdam: North Holland.

Sraffa, Piero. 1960. *The Production of Commodities by Means of Commodities, Prelude to a Critique of Economic Theory.* Cambridge, U.K.: Cambridge University Press.

Tobin, James. 1987. "Irving Fisher (1867-1947)" in *The New Palgrave, A Dictionary of Economics*, Vol. 2, 369-376. London: Macmillan Press, Ltd.

von Neumann, John. 1945. "A model of general economic equilibrium," *Review of Economic Studies*, XIII, 1-9.

Williams, John Burr. 1938. *The Theory of Investment Value.* Cambridge, Massachusetts: Harvard University Press.

533

AN ECONOMIST'S ECONOMIST
by Paul A. Samuelson

The New York Times, 23 June 1987

Cambridge, Mass. To help others understand next year's world economy, I must tell a story about our lamented economist, Walter W. Heller, who died not long ago.

Einstein liked sailing on a lake outside Berlin. It helped him to think, and to think about what experimentalists should measure. Every hour he saw two ferry boats pass each other in the middle of the lake. Both boats, he noticed, carried horseshoes. "Why do they have that horseshoe?" he once asked the eastbound skipper. "It's for good luck–to bring the wind to my back."

Einstein was amused. "Does it make good sense that two horseshoes can make the wind blow both ways at the same time?"

"Oh, I know it makes no sense. But I understand the horseshoe is so powerful that it works even without making good sense."

The story reminds me of a famous debate at New York University between the monetarist Milton Friedman and Mr. Heller, the eclectic post-Keynesian. Held near Wall Street, the dramatic debate attracted an overflow crowd and, I was told at the time, was deemed a draw. As Casey Stengel said, "You could look it up."

One of my investment banker friends was there, so I sought to learn from the customer's mouth just how things had really gone. My guinea pig from Wall Street reported: "Heller made better sense, but Friedman had mountains of evidence."

Alas, in the non-experimental science of economics, evidence is often in the eye of the author. For example, the fashionable view of the 50's was that the "velocity," or rate at which money is spent, is so unpredictable that the Federal Reserve should never try to manipulate the money supply to combat inflation and recession. Rather, the belief was that the Fed should freeze the growth rate of the money supply forever. In the 80's that monetarist dogma is perceived by the outgoing chairman of the Federal Reserve Board, Paul A. Volcker, and the prospective chairman, Alan Greenspan, to have oceans of evidence against it.

Nevertheless, when I met Mr. Heller at a meeting of the Congressional. Budget Office just five days before he died, he whispered to me between the acts: "Every time Sprinkel briefs the

611

White House Staff on its certitudes, the snickers can be heard all the way to Capitol Hill. But monetarism is not as bad as conservatives and liberals today believe." (Beryl Sprinkel is chairman of the President's Council of Economic Advisers.)

We agreed that as canny old Walter Stewart, an early Federal Reserve economist, testified to the MacMillan committee on macroeconomic policy in 1930: "You should teach the quantity theory of money in season and quit – not because it is a universal truth but because, when it is in season, its message is so very precious."

Mr. Heller was a both-sides-of-the-street Keynesian. He persuaded President John F. Kennedy to cut tax rates during the depressed early 60's. History is grateful. But also, after his return to academic life, Mr. Heller warned President Lyndon B. Johnson that the Vietnam buildup, imposed on a fully-employed American economy, mandated an increase in tax rates.

When a TV panelist asked Mr. Heller whether he was not inconsistent, he replied with that ready wit that made him so effective on the lecture circuit: "I blow on my hands to warm them up. That doesn't keep me from blowing on my soup to cool it down."

A principled exponent of temporary fiscal deficits to check persistent slumps, Mr. Heller warned Congress and President Reagan in 1981 that supply-side economics would not work and that tax cuts would produce a vast permanent budget deficit. Again, subsequent history bore him out. Mr. Heller's economics was not that of a dismal science. But he was never afraid to call a spade a spade and a boob a boob.

For 30 years, whenever writing on policy matters for an American audience, I have relied on Mr. Heller's writings, speeches and phone conversations for information and wisdom. From now on we shall have to go it alone.

All alone? No. We have the memory of a great policy economist. I shall have to pause in my penmanship and ponder, What would Walter advise now? The tactic may not be as powerful as a horseshoe, but I expect it to help a little bit in our inexact science of political economy.

Robert Solow: An Affectionate Portrait

Paul A. Samuelson

The great Cambridge mathematician G. H. Hardy summed up his scholarly worth with the assertion: "I collaborated with Littlewood." When I meet up with St. Peter in Heaven it will be my boast, "I collaborated with Bob Solow."

Solow is the consummate economist's economist. He does everything well and with apparent ease. What Ty Cobb was to baseball, Solow has been to our generation of economists. But with this difference. Cobb had a will to win that never let up. Solow acts as if he has nothing to prove. And what is most remarkable, as a youngster long before his merits had become clear to all, he displayed the same relaxed approach to economic science and academic life. The subjects of probability and mathematical economics he found to be the most fascinating things in life; and if you did not share this view, young Bob could only feel sorry for you. As an anthropologist who has spent a long lifetime observing achieving scholars and scientists, I can report how rare this relaxed approach is and how great must be the natural abilities of anyone with it who nevertheless attains the highest rung of the ladder.

I once said to Solow, "Bob, you are perfect except for one thing. You don't play tennis." Instead of reminding me that I don't ski, sail, play chess, and after the age of 40 row for Balliol, Solow merely smiled.

Meritocracy

My teachers were of the earlier American generations who came largely from farms and small towns. Frank Knight and Wesley Mitchell were typical specimens.

■ *Paul A. Samuelson is Professor of Economics, Massachusetts Institute of Technology, Cambridge, Massachusetts.*

Today Nobel winners in physics or medicine are more likely to come from the Bronx High School of Science. Even in my time, when the MIT graduate school was first becoming able to attract the most promising graduating seniors, they turned out to come from small colleges or large state universities distributed fairly randomly among geographical regions. Not so nowadays. I notice in recent years that the nation's NSF fellows tend to come from the dozen elite universities, as our meritocracy begins to do its sortings at an earlier age. A Ripon College in Wisconsin today has fewer weak students in its freshman class; but also those neighboring young stars whom it used to attract tend often to be lured away to Madison or Princeton or New Haven. The same tends to be true of the University of Buffalo or of Cincinnati.

Solow is a case in point. After Harvard learned how to locate Jim Tobin from Urbana, it discovered New York City. This is all summed up nicely in a conversation I eavesdropped on from my MIT office next to Solow's. After an eager Harvard visitor had mined Solow for information about a senior's honor thesis, I heard him say: "Excuse me, sir, can I ask you a personal question? I collect accents, sir. And, sir, I have you figured as Brooklyn filtered through Harvard." Bingo.

War and Peace

Precocious academics are a dime a dozen. Bob Solow was precocious. (His mother tells the story that, bored with the pace at which his class learned to read, Bobby proceeded to read upside down. It reminds one of the unusual case when overnight a schoolchild's IQ halved. The economist Emile Despres grew so tired of having his test prowess discussed that he was discovered to be reversing his answers on every other quiz question.) Nevertheless, as an economist Solow was not notoriously an early bloomer.

Table 1
Works by Robert M. Solow cited in this essay, listed in chronological order.

[1] "On the Dynamics of the Income Distribution," doctoral thesis, Harvard University, 1951.
[2] "On the Structure of Linear Models," *Econometrica*, January 1952, 20, 29–46.
[3] "Balanced Growth Under Constant Returns to Scale" (with Paul A. Samuelson), *Econometrica*, July 1953, 21, 412–424.
[4] *Linear Programming and Economic Analysis* (with Robert Dorfman and Paul A. Samuelson). New York: McGraw-Hill, 1958.
[5] "Analytical Aspects of Anti-Inflation Policy" (with Paul A. Samuelson), *American Economic Review*, May 1960, 50, 177–94.
[6] "Capital Labor Substitution and Economic Efficiency" (with Kenneth Arrow, Hollis Chenery, and Bagicha Minhas), *Review of Economics and Statistics*, August 1961, 43, 225–50.
[7] *Capital Theory and the Rate of Return*. Amsterdam: North-Holland, 1963.
[8] "The New Industrial State or Son of Affluence," *The Public Interest*, Fall 1967, 108.
[9] "The State of Economics: The Behavioral and Social Sciences Survey: Discussion," *American Economic Review*, May 1971, 61, 63–65.
[10] "Comments From Inside Economics," in Klamer, Arjo, Donald McCloskey, and Robert M. Solow, eds., *The Consequences of Economic Rhetoric*. Cambridge: Cambridge University Press, 1988.

Robert M. Solow

For one thing he liked to play horseshoes with the townies who lived around Harvard's Dunster House rather than split hairs with the virtuosi in the Junior Common Room. (In those days that section of Cambridge was called Kerry's Corner. Not only did you have to be Irish to live there, but if you didn't hail from County Kerry the neighbors would move your furniture out.)

For another thing there came along World War II. Most who entered Harvard in 1940 could delay military involvement and arrange for national service via various officers' training schools. A student like Solow could easily have been tapped by Harvard's Edward Mason for the OSS, or recruited for one or another cryptographic think tank. Solow quietly enlisted, serving through the Italian invasion as a spotter in small planes for artillery guidance. He refused promotion beyond the rank of sergeant, wanting to return as soon as possible to his Radcliffe fiancée Barbara (Bobbie Lewis).

Hegira Down the Charles

Several hundred veterans descended on the Harvard graduate school in economics. I wish I could take credit for having spotted Solow as the pick of the litter. It was my colleague the statistician Harold Freeman who came to me in the spring of 1949 and said, "I understand Robert Merton Solow is the best of Leontief's students. Why don't we try to get him for MIT?" It was surprisingly easily done. Although Schumpeter, Paul Sweezy, Richard Goodwin and Leontief knew Solow's caliber, no effective finger was lifted on his behalf. (Goodwin and Sweezy were themselves on the way out, but in their case the excuse could be made that political bigotry had some role to play.)

MIT competed unfairly. Not that we offered a salary no yuppie could refuse: instead our Department Head accepted the pittance that Solow had diffidently suggested. MIT appointed Solow before he had a Ph.D. (just as it had done with me a decade earlier). Also, we agreed to give him an initial leave of absence—unpaid!—to study mathematical statistics under the great Abraham Wald at Columbia. The academic year 1949–50 in New York City was a great one for both Bob at Columbia and Bobbie at the New York Fed: the statistics vacuum that Cambridge had not abhorred was replaced by intimate acquaintanceship with Wald's masterly foundations of stochastic inference, and lifelong friendships were made with the leaders of American mathematical statistics.

Solow's own Harvard thesis (1951) dealt with dynamic processes of income distribution. It naturally won the David Wells Prize for best dissertation of 1951. But Solow never received the princely emolument of $500. Arthur Marget in the late 1920s had pocketed the prize but never crashed through with the revised version of his winning thesis. Therefore, by my time and thereafter, the once-bit Harvard authorities had stipulated: no publishable MS, no $500 prize. Unfortunately Solow's perfectionism inhibited him from undertaking the revisions he deemed needed, with the result that for many years the work enjoyed a considerable private circulation via library loan. I toyed for a time with the thought of stealing the author's copy and having the Harvard University Press publish it in book form without the author's knowledge, but nothing ever came of that impulse.

The first decade at MIT proved to be a fruitful one for the newest assistant professor. Among my favorites in his list of publications were his magisterial summary of the properties shared by Perron–Frobenius and Markov matrixes, in their *input/output* and Metzlerian *multiplier* economic applications; also the 1953 generalized growth iterations that turned out to turn up in the most diverse economic models.

The Nobel authorities have properly singled out Solow's 1956 theoretical growth model and his 1957 econometric measurements of that model. Fermi-like, Solow scored a grand slam, covering both theory and empiricism. This work revived Paul Douglas's production-function measurements. Colinearity in the historical trends of labor and capital inputs had made it impossible for Douglas to identify the separate contribution of technical change. By the neat device of employing observable profit/wage shares, Solow was able to perform the identification task: to a good approximation, there could be estimated a constant trend of disembodied exogenous technical progress—so to speak the "residual" that could explain half of the enhanced productivity previously imputed primarily to the stock of capital. Suddenly illumination was provided for the concept of "total-factor" productivity, which econometric historians like Moses Abramovitz, John Kendrick, and Simon Kuznets had devised to correct the simplicities of traditional measures based solely on gross labor productivities. Although the Cobb–Douglas functional form with unitary elasticity of substitution and constancy of distributive shares fit Solow's sample tolerably well, later (with Arrow, Chenery, and Minhas) Solow pioneered the CES specification involving a common elasticity of substitution that could be any nonnegative number. (As in the cases of Newton and Leibniz or Darwin and Wallace, unknown to Solow were independent experiments with the CES form on the part of Abram Bergson, of H. D. Dickinson, and of David Champernowne.)

Joan Robinson generated cogent doubts about the admissibility of reducing vectors of heterogeneous capital to aggregates describable by a scalar magnitude. The debates between Robinson and Solow[1] did them both credit, even though it may be confessed that some observers succumbed to the law of diminishing marginal utility. As a not disinterested participant, it is as well for me to leave it at that.

Teacher and Publicist

At this time there is no need to review the many scholarly works in such diverse fields as resource economics, urban economic modeling, incomes policies and much else. Let me put in the record how witty Robert Solow has always been as a conversationalist, lecturer, and writer. Indeed, Solow's good-tempered but incisive review of Galbraith's "Son of Affluence" cost him for a year or two a treasured friendship. But it says something for the civility of the pre-1960 generation of economists that someone of Solow's New Deal ideology could forge a warm intimacy with a stalwart of the second Chicago School like George Stigler. In a famous Cook County debate on wage-price controls, Solow declared, "What Sydney Smith said to Thomas Babington Macaulay, I say to you, Milton: 'I wish, Babington, I was as sure of anything as you are of everything.'" No offense was taken from this by the sage who elsewhere observed: "One man and the truth is a majority."

Lest one fall into the misperception of Robert Solow as a bland yea-sayer to every passerby, the reader will want to look up Solow's debate with his good friend Jack Gurley on new-left radical economics; and his rhetorical reactions to Donald McCloskey's thesis of rhetoric in economics.

When you say a scholar is brilliant, that is usually assumed to mean she or he is flakey. And, as I review the troops, I see there is enough truth in the stereotype to keep it alive. Solow is an exception. As with the late Arthur Okun, people seek his advice not because they agree with his eclectic post-Keynesian ideology but because his knowledge and respect for evidence makes his long-run batting average useful to a Japanese mutual fund, a regional Federal Reserve Bank, or scientific advisory committee of a major car producer. When one observes how he fits all this into a scientific program, while lecturing to hundreds of non-economist undergraduates and doing the dishes, one wonders what Alfred Marshall used to do with all that spare time Mary Paley Marshall made available to him.

A psychobiographer might speculate that had RMS been six inches shorter his bibliography would have been two feet longer. A good story to illustrate his lack of self-importance was told to me by Walter Heller, chairman of the all-star Camelot

---

[1] In his de Vries lectures on the *Return to Capital*, Solow preferred to finesse the issue of measuring capital by employing Irving Fisher's general equilibrium approach of intertemporal substitutions between vectors of produced inputs and outputs.

Council of Economic Advisers. (Heller, James Tobin, and Kermit Gordon were its elder statesmen in their early forties: its second rank had to settle for Kenneth Arrow, Art Okun, and Robert Solow! I was the out-of-town *éminence grise* who played Esther to King John F. Kennedy, usually from Scheherazade scripts written to CEA tunes.) Heller had been asked to revise and bring up to date an old encyclopedia article on the gift tax, a task just not compatible with the brutal midnight hours worked by the CEA. "Let Robert do this," Heller scribbled on the item to be revised. As Walter reported to me, "To my surprise the next day I saw on my desk an up-to-date manuscript much better than my original version. When I asked who had done it, I was embarrassed to learn that my secretary had given it to the wrong Bob, not to the youngest recruit on the civil service ladder. I hastened to apologize but Solow merely said, 'It was fun to do, and I learned a lot doing it.'"

Walter Heller used to say, "Behind every successful man, you'll find a surprised mother-in-law." Keeping steps with Bob Solow has always been Bobbie Solow. Her own career in economic history simmered on the back burner when they both brought up three children out in the wilds, but sure now Barbara Lewis Solow is a leading authority on Irish development and the dynamics of emancipation from serfdom and slavery.

No One is Perfect?

Undiluted praise, however deserved and however fulsome, soon bores. I must therefore make the effort to find, or invent, a wart or two just to add to the verisimilitude of my portrait. I take my cue from the pre-puberty Niels Bohr. The great Danish physicist had for a younger brother the great Danish mathematician (and soccer player) Harald Bohr. The two brothers, we learned from biography, were very close and very fond of each other. Harald was as extrovertish and sparkling as Niels was inarticulate and reserved. One day Harald said to his older brother: "Let's take turns slamming each other. You say something critical about me, and I'll say something critical about you. It'll be lots of fun."

"Oh, I couldn't do that."

"Not even for me? To give me pleasure? Please, pretty please."

"Oh, all right. But you go first."

"Niels, the trouble with you is you mumble and never know when you start a sentence how it's going to end. No one can understand you, yourself least of all. There. Now it's your turn. Now you slam me."

"I couldn't do that."

"But you promised. So you must say something bad about me."

"Well...well, Harald, you have a string on your coat lapel."

If I try extra hard, the only possible string I can find on Robert Solow's waistcoat is his occasional tendency to dispose of some unlikely contention by rational expectationists with a devastating wisecrack. I admit it is often ludicrous to act as if aggregate markets clear within periods as short as a year or two and that it is not without humor to hear a grown scholar allege that each new tax reduction will cause us to save more against the day when our children will be taxed to meet the entailed deficit. My point, though, is that a wisecrack does not a science build. The refutation of unrealistic paradigms will come from prosaic scientific researches, and even from investigations carried on by rational expectationists themselves. It is not elder statesmen's wisdoms that kill off a young whippersnapper's foolishnesses, but rather another whippersnapper's regression data.

But what is it I am saying and preaching? It is precisely what I have learned over the years by eavesdropping through Solow's office door. Our forty years together have passed as if but a day. Like Oliver Twist I look forward to forty more, and can say with Wordsworth that this would be "very heaven."

■ *I owe thanks for my post-doctoral fellowship to MIT's Sloan School of Management, and for editorial assistance to Aase Huggins (a treasure shared by Solow and me).*

References

Douglas, Paul H., *Theory of Wages.* New York: Macmillan, 1933.

Moore, Ruth, *Niels Bohr: The Man, His Science and the World They Changed*, 1st edition. New York: Knopf, 1966.

Robinson, Joan V., *The Accumulation of Capital.* London: Macmillan, 1956.

Paul A. Samuelson

Galbraith as Artist and Scientist

1

Years ago in a pastoral lecture to brethren in the economics game, I said that whereas non-economists may take Kenneth Galbraith too seriously, we insiders pay Galbraith too little attention. As usual in my writings, I may have been only half right.

Certainly students come into our freshman classes already knowing the name of John Kenneth Galbraith — his *Affluent Society* and *New Industrial State*. If Shelley was right that poets are the unacknowledged legislators for the world, then he who writes society's legends is even more important than those who draft its laws, charters, and Ph.D. dissertations. Long before Vilfredo Pareto reaches students' minds with the doctrines of efficiency and deadweight loss, John Kenneth has already been there with his gestalt of the Fortune-500 corporation.

John Jay Chapman opined that what a man from Mars would observe on earth came closer to a Wagnerian opera than an Emerson essay. Certainly what the Martian saw in earthly markets would look less like a Walras-Debreu system of equilibrium than a Galbraith-Schumpeter picture of corporate bureaucracy.

Even a new doctor of philosophy from Chicago labors in the vineyard to find proper microfoundations for macroeconomics. Those are code words for dissatisfaction with the paradigm of perfect auction markets of purely competitive type. The National Bureau of Economic Research, from its aerie on holy ground halfway

620

between Harvard and MIT, issues forth each year a hundred manuscripts testing the hypothesis of rational expectationism and scarcely a one fails to reject its null hypothesis.

You will conclude, "Galbraith has won out in the Darwinian struggle for survival of ideas." It would be naive to think so, and would betray a lack of sophisticated understanding of how Kuhnian science develops.

Sinclair Lewis recirculated the words, "When fascism comes to America, it will come in the guise of anti-fascism." Similarly, orthodox mainstream economics arrives at its own version of Galbraithism without ever admitting agreement to his contentions. Indeed, if the simple truth were told, the process of absorption is genuinely unself-conscious and non-Machiavellian.

How is this possible? Very easily, and you can count the many ways. A George Stigler is hardly a Galbraithian. Rather he is a card-carrying founder of the Second Chicago School — not the First Chicago School of Frank Knight, Henry Simons, and Jacob Viner, but that of Aaron Director, Milton Friedman, and George Stigler. When you read Stigler's fascinating and breezy autobiography, *Memoirs of an Unregulated Economist,* you learn that his own most important contribution to economic science involved discovery of the crucial role for markets of "information." Prices fail to be glued to marginal costs because of the costs connected with search and information. We are carried back, not to the Jevons and Walras *Weltanschauung* of competitive capitalism, but rather to the vision of Carl Menger and Kenneth Galbraith!

When I walked into Joseph Schumpeter's classroom in 1935, he described the real world in non-Walrasian terms. At that period he believed that General Motors reigned on borrowed time. By the time of his death in 1950, Schumpeter had changed his vision: General Motors and General Electric had mastered the technology of staying on top, but the deviations of their behavior from Marshall-Cournot equality of marginal cost and price was of secondary importance. If competition was imperfect, it was workably efficient. Zealous trust-busting would do more harm than good. The label on the Pepsi Cola bottle is not that on the Coca-Cola bottle, and the labels on the Schumpeter-Stigler goatskins do not carry the letters JKG; still the wines are of the same vintage and demonstrably different from the Walras-Debreu grapes.

Perhaps the ultimate triumph is when your target is converted without realization.

2

Needless to say, the notions of JKG have altered exogenously and also in response to the findings of mainstream economics.

Affluence is seen to be less imminent than in the 1950s. Wasteful *public* expenditure remains a problem. Countervailing power from downstream and upstream competitors is seen to be secondary to rivalry by rivals. K-Mart has trimmed Sears down to size more than have any unions of retail clerks or retail clients. Trade union power, and that of their top officials, has been limited more by imitative manufacturing in the Pacific Basin than by Taft-Hartley and antilabor legislation. Internationalization of markets has done more to keep competition workable than has the promotion of antitrust regulation. Just after Schumpeter began to believe in the permanency of corporate residents on the top floors of capitalism's hotel, every oligopolist began to compete in every other oligopolist's markets domestically and abroad. If a Paul Sweezy doubted in the prewar world that a fifth rival to the existing steel giants could secure the needed initial finance, at century's end viability obtains for innumerable small-scale producers of steel in electric furnaces and with nonunion labor. The members of the class of Galbraithian technocrats alternately cringe at the power of the purse and the ballot box and tyrannize their subordinates. Each new edition of my *Economics* and the Samuelson-Nordhaus *Economics* has had to move further away from the Berle-Means paradigm of corporate-bureaucrats-in-the-saddle and shareowners-*sans*-power. A Harold McGraw shivers when a Boone Pickens is on the prowl. Minority battles minority, and uneasy sleeps the head that wears the corporate crown. Investment bankers no longer run the roost as in days of yore, but they are back in the Temple to pick up fees putting the cogs together and taking them apart.

3

Had Schumpeter lived to observe the four decades after 1950, I suspect he would have moved at least a small way back toward his earlier view on how limited are the powers of the giant corporations. In any case, I believe that Galbraith would do well to realize how much like constitutional monarchs his dinosaurs are: they reign only so long as they do not rule. The history museums are full of the fossil bones of Montgomery Ward, International Harvester, American-Nash-Studebaker Motors; GE of today has only a historical connection with the General Electric that used to make our fans, toasters, and turbines. When I gently protest that JKG lacks proper respect for the market, I refer not at all to his failure to worship Adam Smith's Invisible Hand and Pareto's elimination of deadweight loss. All that concerns ideology, and it is the bigger game of positivistic science that my gunsights are trained upon.

Let me connect up, as they say in court, with Gorbachev's attempted *perestroika* (restructuring) for the Soviet Union. Youngsters of my generation used to read the debate between Lerner-Lange and Von Mises on economic planning in a socialist state. We decided that L-L won decisively. Mises erred logically and empirically in denying that economic optimality could be even defined in the absence of markets (a position already refuted by Barone, Pareto, Wicksell, and Fred Taylor). By instructing bureaucrats to *play the game* of being price takers in auction markets, a totalitarian state could equal or surpass the efficiency of laissez-faire capitalism, achieving all the needed equalities between prices and marginal costs (and, indeed, relative marginal utilities).

That was the state of the debate in, say, 1939. But by 1989 connoisseurs realize that it was really Hayek and Schumpeter who were the winners of the debate. Even if the constant-returns-to-scale conditions conducive to perfect competition were fulfilled in the Communist state — a contra-factual premise — Lerner-Lange need to address a problem they have ignored: how are the bureaucrats to be motivated to actually do what L-L's rules of the game want them to do? *Sed quis custodiet ipsos Custodes?* Why shouldn't they use the monopoly powers L-L admit *they* always have? Why expect them to ignore such powers? This game-theoretic line of argument leads remorselessly toward having the planners not *play-act* the game of market competition but actually instead be the entrepreneurs who personally risk losses and seek gains.

At this point Hayek plays his trump card: knowledge is incomplete, fragmented, and ever-changing. Only with free entry of any would-be rival can *dynamic intertemporal*–Pareto efficiency be approximated and maintained. A Wriston may be as fallible as a Lysenko, but no one needs permission in a market mechanism to slay a Sewall Avery or a Walter Wriston; the jungle of bureaucracy and politics has its own Darwinian processes, but *there is no Bergsonian theorem that its mechanisms are eliminative of deadweight loss.* Lenin, on the eve of the October Revolution, believed wrongly that scarcity would wither away if man's institutions were not vile; only "the rule of three" would be needed to unleash technology's abundance once capitalism's centralized bastions fell to the revolutionists; "electricity plus democracy equals communism" is his romantic formula for a brave new world in which gold would be relegated to the construction of toilet seats. Eight decades later an economist in Hungary or East Germany, to say nothing of Moscow or Beijing, will despair that such romanticism was once taken seriously. Henry George, Bernard Shaw, and Joan Robinson imagined that whatever the problems of creating the golden-rule stationary state, once created it could maintain itself with all returns to property expropriated for the workers. Reality is more stubborn. As with the second law of thermodynamics, Schumpeter's stationary state runs down into disorder from the first instant of its creation. No one-time winding of the clock can outlast the day of its birth.

A real-thing (rather than a play-acting) Lerner-Lange system makes socialism reap the virtues of markets only by its reverting back to becoming capitalism. Gorbachev and Deng may not desire unemployment, bankruptcies, and inflation, but that is the road logic is taking them down.

Schumpeter spoke unemotionally of capitalism as "creative destruction." That is a euphemism for the system's cutting its losses. When we observe South Korea, Taiwan, and Singapore in the 1970s — and the rise and fall and persistence of the Chicago Boys in Chile during the 1980s — we realize that *glasnost* is no causal condition for *perestroika;* perhaps it is even the reverse. Demand-pull suppressed inflation is the specific disease of the halfway house between mindless "centralized planning" and mindless "free markets."

Logically, there is a way out of the dilemma. But it is not a prospect pleasing to Marx, Engels, Lenin, Trotsky, Mao, or even Beatrice Webb. And it would come as something of an anticlimax to Schumpeter and Galbraith — but not to Franklin Roosevelt or Maynard Keynes.

I refer to the mixed economy of the mainstream economists. For most of the year's work it relies on the market and not on governmental factories or planning agencies. But the extremes of laissez-faire inequality are tempered by the mutual reinsurance transfer payments of the fiscal-welfare system. And the extremes of macroeconomic instability are attenuated by discretionary central-bank and budget policies. (Robert Lucas has a statute in its Pantheon, not because rational expectations are rational or realistic, but because the constraints on policy ambitions are real, systematically changing, and need studying!)

Shaw said the trouble with capitalism is that, like Christianity, it has never really been tried. I have to admit that the trouble with the New Deal is that the citizenry do not display a consistent passion for achieving their New Jerusalem and that economic science lacks full understanding of its entailed trade-offs.

4

Political economy is an art as well as a science. John Kenneth Galbraith has always been a creative artist in formulating theories of the social world. His fabrications constitute the stuff of economic science.

536

Tribute to Nicholas Georgescu-Roegen on his 85th Birthday
Paul A. Samuelson, MIT, 1990

Nicholas Georgescu-Roegen is a great mathematical economist. Each time I go to consult one of his books--which is done often--I notice that Georgescu comes there on the shelf right next to Gauss. And I think there is something proper in this.

For Georgescu-Roegen is more than a mathematical economist. He is as well a humane, deep, and wise philosopher. It was a regret of the great Joseph Schumpeter, a regret that he carried to his grave, that his proposed collaboration with the young Georgescu-Roegen on a definitive economic treatise could not take place because of Nicholas's patriotic urge to return to the pre-war Romania that had nursed his genius. It was not only Schumpeter's loss, it was a loss to the budding science of political economy.

My own first contact with the Master came in Schumpeter's famed Harvard Ec 11 seminar: I was a beginning graduate student fresh from the Chicago of Frank Knight, Jacob Viner, and Henry Schultz. Georgescu was a young god who walked and talked and joked with such gods as Wassily Leontief, Joseph Schumpeter, Gottfried Haberler, Edwin Bidwell Wilson (Willard Gibbs's last protegé and polymath in his own right), and Nicky Kaldor (visiting Rockefeller fellow from the LSE). The stately Frank Taussig, dean and *éminence gris* of American economics, turned to Georgescu and Wilson for adjudication when the young Milton Friedman wrote for the *Quarterly Journal of Economics* his maiden article criticizing the venerable A.C. Pigou of Cambridge. (Score 1 to 1: Pigou was not wrong; Friedman's generalization was of value in its own right.)

For this issue of a mathematical journal dedicated to the 85th birthday of Nicholas Georgescu-Roegen, it is permissible for me to neglect his fertile contributions to economic history and political development, in favor of a few mathematical topics that his work has resolved. Even here, I shall be forced to ignore his contributions to statistical theory; and also his mathematical resolution of deep production-function processes.

1. *Consumer demand theory.* When interested at 21 in the mathematics of consumer demand theory, my mind was blown away by the first diagram in Georgescu's 1936 *QJE* article (p. 145 in his 1966 collected papers). For the first time I sensed the nature of the *integrability conditions* problem that Pareto had grappled with, only to be gently criticized by the great geometer Vito Volterra. R.G.D. Allen and J.R. Hicks were in need of Georgescu-Roegen's deep understanding of Pfaffian differential expressions. Connoisseurs appreciated Georgescu-Roegen even if the common run of economists failed to appreciate the *tour de force*.

2. *Topology and separable independence.* Gerard Debreu is properly praised for applying abstract topology to the problem of

additive separability--as when you act to maximize a total utility that is the sum of one-variable functions of your respective consumptions of tea, cloth, and ballets $\Sigma_1^3 f_j(x_j)$; or when you invest to maximize the Laplacian moral expectation $\Sigma_1^2 P_j U(M_j)$, where P_j is the probability of your ending with M_j of money. Debreu deserves his notice. But it is a matter of reproach to our profession that Georgescu-Roegen's earlier article in the 1954 *Southern Economic Journal* has not received its proper due. For there he dealt definitively with the deeper problem of the 2-good case's topology.

   3. *The economy as an hourglass rather than a pendulum.* As long as the words "entropy" and "economics" are remembered, the name of Nicholas Georgescu-Roegen will be remembered and honored. In one apt *Gestalt* he changed our way of looking at the universe. Classical economics, whether mainstream or otherwise, takes for its logo the image of a pendulum, one that oscillates forever in steady-state equilibrium. So to speak, the First Law of Thermodynamics reigns in the primers and monographs of economics. The Clausius-Boltzmann-Georgescu Second Law is brought home to us by Georgescu's pithy insistence that economic life is essentially an hourglass and not an unchanged pendulum. As the sands fall irreversibly into the lower chamber, the entropy of the world increases. As industrial America taps the rich mines of concentrated natural resources, dissipating to everywhere the copper seams of the Mesabi range, entropy remorselessly increases.

   One does not have to slavishly worship classical physics to the exclusion of evolutionary biology. Nor need one ape the precise formalisms of Clausius-Gibbs phenomenological thermodynamics. Before Georgescu economists would describe Ricardo's steady state by

$$Q = F(L,T,K) = C + dk/dt$$
$$(L,T,K,dk/dt) = (\overline{L},\overline{T},\overline{K},0)$$
$$= \text{(labor, land, capital, zero investment)}.$$

But once Ricardo remembers that the cost of getting a unit of copper from his exhaustible mines rises as the integral of past mined copper rises, we end up with

$$C + dk/dt + x = F[L,T,K,\int_{-\infty}^{t} x(t')dt'].$$

2

Now, with $\partial F[y_1,y_2,y_3,y_4]/\partial y_4 < 0$, Georgescu-Roegen demonstrates that no positive stationary state is possible.

A simple truth? Yes, simple after untruth and truth were separated for us by sage reason.

To Nicholas Georgescu-Roegen I lead the chorus:

Hail Master! Hail Sage!

Paul A. Samuelson
MIT, Cambridge, Massachusetts

SCHUMPETER, JOSEPH ALOIS (Feb. 8, 1883-Jan. 8, 1950), one of the dozen leading economists of the first half of the twentieth century, was born in Triesch, Moravia (now Czechoslovakia), the only child of Joseph Alois Schumpeter, a cloth manufacturer, and Joanna (Grüner) Schumpeter, the daughter of a physician. The father died when Schumpeter was only four, leaving him the adored object of the beautiful and ambitious mother whom he in turn adored. When Schumpeter was ten, his mother married Lt. Gen. Sigismund von Kéler, commander of Emperor Franz Joseph's Viennese forces. This elevation from the middle class to the aristocracy left a permanent mark on Schumpeter's *weltanschauung*. In part he could be objective about the merits of capitalism and what he yet regarded as its certain demise, because by the end of World War I he felt that his own world was already permanently gone. A man may lose perspective about his own home; but who will fail to notice the defects of a boardinghouse? One wonders how the precocious Schumpeter was received at the aristocratic Theresianum Gymnasium, where the Viennese gentry were schooled. What did they make of the *wunderkind*?

As was customary, the young scholar in economics took a law degree at the University of Vienna (1906). He practiced law briefly in Cairo soon afterward. It was in this period that he was the well-rewarded advisor of a princess and the proud owner of a racehorse. But economics was his true love, and in the Vienna seminars of von Böhm-Bawerk and von Wieser, his quality was soon recognized. Since such brilliant Marxists as Otto Bauer and Rudolph Hilferding were also in those seminars, it was no accident that Schumpeter studied and, in his own patronizing way, admired Karl Marx.

By the time he was twenty-five he had written his first book. At twenty-six he become professor at Czernowitz, a rather exotic outpost on the Russian-Rumanian frontier of the empire. By twenty-eight he was professor at Graz, only three hours from Vienna; perhaps because he was regarded as more brilliant than sound, the man whom Gottfried Haberler of Vienna and Harvard has called "the greatest Austrian economist of his generation" was never offered a chair at the University of Vienna. And this despite the fact that he was not Jewish--as he sometimes felt it necessary to make clear.

Invited presumably by his old classmate Otto Bauer, Schumpeter served as finance minister (1919-1920) in the post-World War I Austrian socialist government. To use his kind of phrase, this was not a good performance: the Austrian crown followed the Hungarian crown down the drain; if there was no one to blame for what is a common occurrence after a lost war, Schumpeter provided the convenient scapegoat. A brief career as head of a small bank also ended with that bank's demise. Those who knew Schumpeter would have been surprised if he had been a cool, deft, and solid politician and financier. Later, at Harvard, he carried little weight in the university at large; within the department of economics he was often his own worst enemy at committee meetings, expressing his contempt for academic red tape by giving A's to idiots and perversely espousing unpopular causes, whatever their merits.

Ready to leave Austria, Schumpeter in 1925 accepted a call to the public finance chair at Bonn. There he attracted excellent students--among them, Hans Singer, Erich Schneider, and Wolfgang Stolper. There he also annoyed German official opinion by writing publicly that of course Germans could pay reparations if they wanted to. When his old Austrian classmate Emil Lederer received the chair at Berlin, Schumpeter decided to accept the Harvard invitation that Frank Taussig had been pressing on him since his visiting professorship in Cambridge in 1927. He arrived at Harvard in 1932, to stay.

Schumpeter in 1925 married Annie Resinger, the twenty-one-year-old daughter of the caretaker of the Viennese apartment house where his mother lived. It was the romantic love of his life: he had sent her to schools in Paris and Switzerland to groom her to be his wife. But she died in futile childbirth within a year of their marriage, and ever after he paid homage at her grave in Bonn. The death of his mother that same year was a double blow. He was never the same man. But by his own peculiar theory, pressed upon his graduate students, marriage is a subtraction from the vital energies needed for creative scholarship. So perhaps he was blessed. After Schumpeter moved to Harvard, he lived with the elderly widower Taussig until Aug. 16, 1937, when he left this blessed state to marry Elizabeth (Boody) Firuski, the divorced wife of a radical bookseller. It was an agreeable marriage. Elizabeth Schumpeter was an economic historian in her own right. Their large, well-appointed Cambridge house and well-run Berkshire estate provided a good environment for what was actually a most important decade of Schumpeter's scholarly life.

Clearly Schumpeter lived up to his own Carlylean view that it is great men who make great history, great scholarly breakthroughs, and great entrepreneurial profits. And he partially lived up to his obsessive view that only in youth does one have great ideas, so that the roots of important original achievements, especially those of a theoretical nature, can almost always be found in the third decade of the lives of scholars, "that decade of sacred fertility." Newton's calculus and universal gravitation correspond to this timetable, as do Einstein's Brownian motions, special relativity theory, and photoelectric effect; but what Einstein himself regarded as his deepest and most significant contribution, general relativity, did not arrive until he was a doddering senior of more than thirty-five. Although Schumpeter by thirty-one had received an honorary degree from

2

Columbia (where he had been an exchange professor in 1913-1914 and had seen the first of his only two football games), much of his most lasting work was probably that done in the last decade of his life.

On the surface gallant, gay, urbane, and vivacious, Schumpeter was nevertheless a somewhat sad man. His first marriage was in 1907 to an Englishwoman, Gladys Ricarde Seaver, twelve years his senior and daughter of a Church of England dignitary; it seems not to have been a happy match and was terminated de facto by World War I. That the official divorce did not occur until 1920 may possibly have been related to his then being a nominal Roman Catholic. Later he listed himself as a Lutheran, but his friends detected no religious interests; his funeral services were Episcopalian.

Despite his gallantry and his frivolous facade--both were legendary--Schumpeter was actually a driven scholar. He worked days, nights, and weekends. Each day he graded himself ruthlessly in his shorthand diary. There was an insecurity in his nature, perhaps typical of a precocious only child, with Napoleonic aspirations. He was a showman who strove to be number one, and number one forever. The triumph of John Maynard Keynes, few of Schumpeter's friends and students doubted, depreciated in Schumpeter's mind his own undoubted achievements. There may have been something of envy in his criticism of Keynes for an excessive preoccupation with policy, the same criticism that Schumpeter made of Ricardo.

If Schumpeter had died on the verge of his fiftieth birthday when newly arrived at Harvard, he would be remembered primarily as the *enfant terrible* of the Austrian school, who had the bizarre notion that the interest rate would be zero in the stationary state and who put great stress on the importance of the innovating entrepreneur both for business cycles and for capitalist development generally. Fortunately, in the final phase of his career, Schumpeter wrote his seminal *Capitalism, Socialism, and Democracy* (1942), which far transcended mere economics in its historical, political, and sociological insights. And at his death, in Taconic from a cerebral hemorrhage in his sleep, he left behind the magnificent torso of his posthumously published *History of Economic Analysis* (1954), a magisterial work that, for all its incompleteness and patronizing pretensions, will long stand as an inimitable monument of scholarship. During these same fruitful years at Harvard, Schumpeter's earlier works in German, not well known in the modern age of Anglo-Saxon illiteracy, were gradually translated: his 1911 classic, *The Theory of Economic Development*; his brief 1914 history of doctrines; his graceful biographical essays on economists; his work on imperialism and sociology. In 1939 he received an honorary degree from Sofia. And it was in this period that he had a host of students who were later to become leaders in American economics: they sat around his lecture rostrum in the hundreds and were bedazzled, stimulated, and occasionally informed by his brilliant, extemporaneous, and florid discourse. He founded no school because he had no school to found. But in 1948 he was elected president of the American Economic Association, the first of many economists who came to America only in their scholarly maturity. Only death kept him from being the first president of the newly founded International Economic Association.

A scholar's lasting fame comes from his contributions. Schumpeter first achieved notice in his early twenties for work of a methodological character, in which he praised the mathematical method in economics and found merit in turn-of-the-century American contributions, particularly the stationary-state notions of John Bates Clark. Then in his late twenties, he developed his theory of dynamic development and business cycles: in the absence of innovation, he claimed the system would gravitate down to a steady-state circular flow, in which the rate of interest would be zero (a low rate of interest would have avoided controversy and sufficed for his model). The importance that he attached to circular-flow equilibrium accounts for his immense admiration for Léon Walras, who in the last quarter of the nineteenth century established once and for all the concept of general equilibrium in economics; for his inordinate admiration for the physiocrat François Quesnay, who sketched a *tableau économique* of circulation between economic classes; and for his admiration of Marx's models of steady and expanded reproduction and of Marx's grandiose vision of supplying a Newton-Laplace dynamics of historical stages of development. Schumpeter's stationary state provides the backdrop and contrast for the dynamic entrepreneurial innovation that he considered to be the essence of capitalism. "A gale of creative destruction" characterizes the market system, and coupled with inflationary financing by newly created bank money, this provided him with a theory of the business cycle and of long-term development.

Except for a tendency to overshoot equilibrium, the capitalistic system was in his view inherently economically stable, even though politically and sociologically inevitably unstable, as its very successes would make this unlovable system unloved by its affluent offspring. This early prophetic strain of capitalism as dying not from Marxian malignancies but from Freudian self-hate and excess rationality was reasserted in *Capitalism, Socialism, and Democracy*: although the prophecies there concerning the limited effectiveness of capitalism in an oxygen tent and the inevitability of socialism were refuted by the history of the post-World War II period, the alienation of students and intellectuals and the confrontation of the late 1960's confirmed his insights. His perception of intellectuals as ineffective troublemakers served, as in the case of Pareto, to build up his contempt for the spineless bourgeoisie and led him toward certain shoals of fascistic thought, albeit not crude fascistic thought. The disillusionment of World War II, which he long thought Germany would win until he began to think that Russia would be the only real victor, may have interacted with his disappointment over the failure of his two-volume *Business Cycles* (1939) to attract much attention. Indeed, the nature of the business cycle was changing in the post-Keynes era, and the number of epicycles introduced by Schumpeter, in the form of forty-month minor cycles, eight-year major cycles, and half-century-long Kondratiev waves, began to smack of Pythagorean moonshine; nor did his fancy concepts, borrowed from Ragnar Frisch, of equilibria and cycle stages defined by inflection points ever catch on.

Although Schumpeter would have wished to be remembered most for some brilliant and basic breakthrough in economic analysis, it seems just as well that he devoted the last part of his career to insightful social prophecy and to recording his tremendous erudition on past economic thought in his massive *History of Economic Analysis* (1954). Although the manuscript was incomplete, his widow was able to edit it for publication in the few years by which she survived him. It is a unique reference work, one that concentrates not so much on general reform movements and philosophies as on the development of economic analysis itself. Here Schumpeter's almost mindless tolerance of differences in vision proved to be a great virtue. If some sympathetic follower were to prune and complete this great work, it would provide Schumpeter's most lasting memorial.

[A complete bibliography of Schumpeter's many writings appears in the *Quart. Jour. Econ.* (1950). Seymour Harris, ed., *Schumpeter: Social Scientist* (1951), contains twenty biographical eulogies and evaluations, notably one of Gottfried Haberler, R.V. Clemence and Francis S. Doody. *The Schumpeterian System* (1950), provides an evaluation of Schumpeter's economics; see also the sixtieth birthday *Festschrift* "Essays in Honor of Prof. Joseph A. Schumpeter," *Rev. of Econ. Stat.*, Feb. 1943, and the W.F. Stolper article on him in the *Internal. Encyc. Social Sci.*, vol. XIV (1968). Also noteworthy among Schumpeter's books, other than those mentioned in the text, are *Ten Great Economists from Marx to Keynes* (1952); *Essays*, Clemence and Doody, eds. (1951); *Imperialism and Social Classes* (German, 1919, 1927; English, 1951); *Economic Doctrine and Method* (German, 1914; English, 1954); and his first book, *Das Wesen und der Haupinhalt der theoretischen Nationalökonomie* (1908).]

Paul A. Samuelson

1991 Afterthoughts on Schumpeter

This 1974 biographical piece was a lost item until its citation in Robert Loring Allen's 1991 two-volume Schumpeter biography enabled me to locate it for inclusion in Volume 6 of *The Collected Scientific Papers of Paul A. Samuelson*. Now that the Allen work has been supplemented by Richard Swedberg's [1991] Schumpeter biography and by a lengthy 1991 personal biography in an anthology of Schumpeter's collected papers on economic sociology, some earlier surmises that I had not dared to articulate have been confirmed.

1. Schumpeter kidded himself in thinking that his widowed mother's marriage to retired Lieutenant Field Marshall Sigmund von Kéler had elevated him to the aristocratic circles of Viennese First Society. Always he was a presumptuous outsider and a bumptious one. This would be comical if it were not pathetic. (The editors of the *Dictionary of American Biography* had prevailed on me to eliminate some words pointing out that Schumpeter lacked the superficial graces of the truly overbred, mindless nobility; if he forgot that more than half his genes were Czech, the matchmakers at Court were unlikely to.) A deep underground social insecurity is further betrayed in the outline for Schumpeter's novel about a brilliant hero of the noblest blood intermingled with the most brilliant and exotic. Shades of Walter Mitty!

2. This is not the place to review the excellent Allen and Swedberg books. I must content myself with a grave warning. Almost everything we know about Schumpeter's personal life is quite uncertain. (Exceptions are the elaborate Schumpeter diaries transcribed from German shorthand by the late Erica Gerschenkron.) There was a strong element of Baron Munchausen in Schumpeter's nature and water cannot rise above its own source--by which I mean that most data gleaned by biographers from interviews and correspondence with Edward Mason, Gottfried Haberler, Toni Stolper, Paul Rosenstein-Rodan, Wolfgang Stolper, Redvers Opie or Paul Samuelson themselves trace to stories Schumpeter had told them. There is little evidence that tests or confirms the best of these stories, and considerable evidence that belies some of them. Von Kéler was not top dog in the Vienna command. Annie, Schumpeter's second wife, was not sent to Paris by him to be educated as his bride-to-be: she was a maid there. Moreover, water can fall below its source--as in the numerous testimonies of Paul Rosenstein-Rodan, whom affectionate friends remember as Baron Munchhausen's older brother. To weigh Haberler evidence 1-to-1 with Rodan evidence is simply ludicrous.

When my generation knew from their own senses that Schumpeter's third wife, Elizabeth Boody, did not at 39 convey an impression of superlative past pulchritude, what can readers make of

Dr. Allen's words on the subject? It certainly does not add to the credibility of his claim that Schumpeter's first wife Gladys was "stunningly beautiful." If she was indeed "the daughter of a high dignitary of the Church of England," the evidence for this fact ought to have been easy to come by.

We really do not know at how many "good English clubs" Schumpeter took lunch during his year in Britain. Or how many hunt balls and weekend parties he attended. When Schumpeter told me he had champagne breakfast and rock pheasant with Edgeworth at All Soul's, I have to wonder about the assertion that it was Marshall who invited him to breakfast. The Mary Paley Marshall who would not let Böhm-Bawerk call on the Great Man on a visit to the Tyrol--can we believe she would open the morning door to the bold young student? Having heard from his lips many amusing stories that strain credulity--hinting at playing footsy-footsy with the young Joan Robinson in a rose garden--I beg leave to reserve judgment. About most of the legend we just do not know. And the biographer cannot know on the basis of the evidence that is shared with the reader. (When Schumpeter said he mistook the young lady who answered Foxwell's door for the Professor's daughter instead of his wife, is this but an echo of his account concerning Walras's assuming Schumpeter was the son of the great writer?)

3. Science fiction may cut very close to the bone--as when Allen speculates that Frau von Kéler sought divorce Austrian style after 13 years of marriage to the seventy-eight-year-old Field Marshall, having consummated her plan to use him to acquire for young Josef an aristocratic education and entrée into the best circles. Maybe so. But it would be better to raise the question and leave it at that. When science fiction becomes confused with science fact, the mischief is done.

4. I conclude by observing that the new data unearthed about Schumpeter's life do on the whole bear out one's cautious extrapolations. His virtues and faults were all part of an indecomposable pattern.

Schumpeter did, in spite of himself, make the most of his biblical talent. Being incapable by training and capacity of creating a revolutionary paradigm within microeconomics or macroeconomics, he had to settle for being a prophet and an omniscient historian of economics and of economists. Like Bernard Shaw's writings, Schumpeter's every page sparkles with lively images and original wordings. This depressed human being added much to the gaiety and vision of his times. I was glad to know him even though aware of certain imperfections and non-optimalities.

7

References

Allen, Robert Loring. 1991. *Opening Doors: The Life and Work of Joseph Schumpeter*, Volume I: Europe; Volume II: America. New Brunswick, New Jersey, Transaction Publishers.

Frisch, Helmut, ed. 1981. *Schumpeterian Economics*. London, Praeger Publishers.

Heertje, Arnold, ed. 1981. *Schumpeter's Vision: Capitalism, Socialism, and Democracy After 40 Years*. London, Praeger Publishers.

Schumpeter, Joseph A. Richard Swedberg, ed. 1991. *The Economics and Sociology of Capitalism*. Princeton, New Jersey, Princeton University Press.

Swedberg, Richard. 1991. *Schumpeter--A Biography*. Princeton, New Jersey, Princeton University Press.

GOTTFRIED HABERLER (1900–1995)

Paul A. Samuelson

Haberler's life spanned the twentieth century. He was the last of the famous Austrian School: Carl Menger and his two disciples Eugen von Böhm-Bawerk and Friedrich von Wieser began it; Ludwig von Mises and Joseph Schumpeter led its second generation; Haberler out-lived Friedrich von Hayek, Fritz Machlup, Oskar Morgenstern, Abraham Wald, Gerhardt Tintner, and the many other expatriates who enriched British and American economics. Gottfried knew them all, save for Böhm-Bawerk who had died in 1913. Although Wieser was Haberler's direct teacher, Böhm-Bawerk's writings influenced him much.

He was born into the *grande bourgeoisie* of the Hapsburg Dual Empire meritocracy, with ancestors on both sides who were bankers, lawyers, and high public officials. Haberler, who dropped the *von* shortly after his permanent move to Harvard in 1936, was both a hereditary knight of Austria and a baron of Liechtenstein. Just too young to serve in World War I, Haberler got an early start in economics at the University of Vienna. His maiden article was a 1925 critique of Schumpeter's theory of money, with its core built on a $\Sigma pq = MV$ identity (where V is 'income velocity'). This motivated Haberler's 1927 dissertation, *Der Sinn der Indexzahlen*: eschewing the formalisms of Irving Fisher's (1922) approach to define P and Q in a $PQ = \Sigma pq$ relation, Haberler pioneered in what we today call the *economic* theory of index numbers: he defined P in terms of what percentage change in income would be needed (between say, 1920 and 1925) to enable you to attain the same level of indifference in 1925 as had been attained in 1920. Like Könus and other earlier writers and like such later writers as Bortkiewicz, Staehle, Frisch, Leontief, Afriat, Samuelson-Swamy, Pollock, and Diewert, the young Haberler realised that the true P need not be bounded by

$$P_{\text{Laspeyres}} = \Sigma P_{1925}\, q_{1920}/\Sigma P_{1920}\, q_{1920} \quad \text{and by}$$
$$P_{\text{Paasche}} = \Sigma P_{1995}\, q_{1995}/\Sigma P_{1920}\, q_{1995}.$$

(Wherever demand is non-homothetic, so that income elasticities are not everywhere unity, there always could happen that P escapes those bounds – as post-1926 writings clarified.) It is interesting that Haberler was reluctant in later trade analyses to introduce indifference contours along with his *substitution frontier*, despite the fact that his 1927 thesis had to rely on the meaningful existence of the indifference contours of individual ordinal utility. (When Haberler expressed agnosticism on indifference curves in his 1936 Harvard class, I cheekily retorted: 'In that case your 1927 thesis was all wrong'. Brooding on the staircase over my own remark, I was led in a flash to my 1938 theory of revealed preference. That was not the last time I incurred important debts to Professor Haberler – or to 'Gottfried' as I learned to call him.)

My earliest papers were read before publication by Professors Schumpeter and Haberler. (Some of them were term papers for Harvard graduate courses.) Schumpeter returned my drafts with enthusiastic exclamation points and flowery praise. But it was Haberler who went over them paragraph by paragraph, with detailed pencil markings suggesting revisions and queries. Praise is sweet to young authors' ears. But comprehension is even more valuable. That is why – along with Jacob Viner, Henry Simons, Frank Knight, Paul Douglas, and Aaron Director at Chicago; Wassily Leontief, Edwin Bidwell Wilson, Edward Chamberlin, and Alvin Hansen at Harvard – I always included Haberler as an important master; and on the occasion of his 94th birthday I belatedly told him so.

More important than their personal contacts are scholars' writings. Gottfried Haberler was always more conservative than I, and ever less mathematical. I have discovered empirically in life that you learn less from those who agree with you than from those intelligent analysts who are critical. Water cannot rise above its own source. Since I was raised by jesuits of the Chicago School, zealots of the libertarian faith had little to offer me in the way of benefit. However, since scarcity produces value, Gottfried Haberler was especially useful as both sounding board and analyst.

After I had left Harvard and was a rising star at MIT, I once expostulated: 'Gottfried, your trouble is that you are so damnably *eclectic*'. He countered tellingly, 'Paul, how do you know mother nature is not eclectic?' That was a blow to the solar plexus – a moment of epiphany. (I did not then know the important dialogue between Albert Einstein and Neils Bohr concerning the ultimate validity of quantum mechanics' *probabalistic* foundations as against classical *deterministic laws*. Einstein: 'I cannot believe that God plays with dice'. Bohr: 'And who are we to tell him his business'?)

After much pondering I formulated for myself the following creed:

Be as eclectic as empirical experience suggests is necessary.

But be no more eclectic than the data seem to require. An open mind can be an empty mind. What science can at best bring to us is the ruling out, as both implausible and testably unlikely, the myriad of *possible* things that *could* obtain.

Such a creed is of course easier to verbalise as a goal than to live up to in a fruitful way.[1]

John Chipman (1987), in *The New Palgrave*, gives a masterful summary of

---

[1] Einstein began as a disciple of Ernst Mach. In the spirit of what was to be dubbed logical positivism, his theories of special relativity, photons of light, and brownian motion were economical renderings of the testable fact. Repeated success breeds self-confidence and even hubris. Yet, when he expressed scorn for alleged experiments that seemed to contradict special relativity, this betokened more than arrogance. Analysis confirmed that it would be hard to conceive of a consistent reality that violated both Galileo–Newton and Lorenz transformations. The luck Einstein enjoyed in 1903–15 from following his deductive hunches somewhat soured in the last half of his life when the mainstream of physics advance turned away from his attempts at a comprehensive paradigm that would unify smallest scale and largest scale matter. Aloofness is not for eclectics.

© Royal Economic Society 1996

Haberler's analytical contributions. They can be put into three categories: (1) trade theory; (2) macroeconomics; and (3) economic policy and methodology. Before he was 30, Haberler worked at the frontier of world economic science. As a 1927–29 Rockefeller Fellow he visited Britain (primarily at the London School of Economics), and visited America (primarily at Harvard, where later in 1931–2 he was a visiting lecturer). Someone at the Rockefeller Foundation must have been doing something right then: Frisch, Ohlin, Myrdal, Lundberg, Balogh, Haberler, Machlup, Kaldor, Palander, Georgescu-Roegen, and other great names received such fellowships. And Rockefeller grants, small in today's metric but then momentous, started modern economics going in Stockholm, Oslo, Paris, and elsewhere. (Gottfried was known, affectionately known, as one who made a dollar go a long way. The year that Tommy Balogh lost money on his Rockefeller travels, legend has it, was a year when Gottfried accomplished net saving.)

I. HABERLER AS TRADE THEORIST

Haberler's merited call, to move from the League of Nations in Geneva to Harvard, arose from his 1930–3 breakthrough in international trade theory. This advance can be measured by comparing Taussig's superb 1927 trade text based solely on Ricardian labour costs with Haberler's 1933 *Theory of International Trade with its Applications to Commercial Policy*. By a pioneer discovery of the tool today called the *production-possibility frontier* (or opportunity-cost transformation locus), Haberler's 1930 model could handle multi-factor technologies with land, produced capital goods, and heterogeneous categories of labour inputs. The time was overdue for trade theory to catch up with general equilibrium theory that goes beyond crude embodied labour contents. Before 1930 Irving Fisher (1907) and Enrico Barone (1908), along with Vilfredo Pareto (1897), had glimpsed such a geometrical substitution locus; and by 1925 the young Ohlin had combined Walras with Heckscher and Cassel to break out of the Ricardo-Taussig labour-only straightjacket. But you misunderstand how science advances if you fail to recognise the originality involved in turning mere hints into completed paradigm of analysis. So to speak, after reading Haberler, Heckscher and Ohlin could have better understood the depths of their own great innovations. And the same goes for Jacob Viner, who had arrived by 1931 at what Lerner, Leontief, Meade, and Samuelson-Stolper were to use as a springboard for the modern theory of international trade and finance.

Already by 1930 Haberler perceived an important point he returned to twenty years later. Free trade may not be optimal if the economy stays with some sticky prices. But it is a fallacy to believe that stickiness of a factor supply – as when folks fail to migrate fast enough to equalise wages in the North and South – will impair the presumptive efficiency case for free trade. In sum, the case for free trade does not have to rely on strict factor immobility between regions and strict factor mobility within each region, a truth which contradicts a rich literature of fallacies.

© Royal Economic Society 1996

Today's readers of what is now history, as for example debates between Haberler and Viner as to whether opportunity cost can supersede classical real costs of Mill and Marshall, may want to know which is the winner of the duel. Actually we cannot fully understand the value of a theory or paradigm until we understand its limits and qualifications. Haberler did admit in the end, just as Böhm had had to do in 1890s polemics with Edgeworth, this: as soon as some productive factors are not *indifferent* between producing guns or butter, then no *pp-frontier* will exist to provide tangent slopes that identify P_{guns}/P_{butter} price ratios. Haberler's main point will still stand: when Island A trades freely with B, *both* end up better off than *under autarky* — even when scarce land complicates a labour-only picture.[2] Haberler could, and did, maintain that his 1930 tools had important relevance as *approximations* and in any case moved the analysis nearer to correctness.

Posterity also has its smug afterthoughts. By 1940 one could do better in praising free trade than the 1930 claim for it that it maximised some vaguely-defined *aggregate output*. And Haberler himself no doubt came to wince at early expositions that seem to say that *every* participant is at a maximum under free trade. As he knew, removing tariffs can help some and hurt others; and putting on a small ('optimal') tariff could conceivably improve *all in one* country over their previous free trade utility.

I shall reserve for the section on Haberler's policy wisdoms further discussion of his trade theory contributions.

In the realm of positivistic trade analysis, mention though should be made of his postwar analyses of the partial-equilibrium supply and demand graphs used by Taussig, Schüller, Birckerdike, Joan Robinson, and other standard writers. Outstanding were his summings up on the purchasing-power-parity doctrine.

II. HABERLER AND MACROECONOMICS

At the League of Nations in 1934–6, Haberler was commissioned to survey the state of macroeconomic analysis. (Jan Tinbergen had a parallel assignment to survey and test the status of econometric models, a pioneering anticipation of the Lawrence Klein, Otto Eckstein, and Franco Modigliani forecasting macro models.) *Prosperity and Depression* (1937) provided a definitive critique of various business cycle theories. The first edition does nicely record in amber the pre-*General Theory* state of the art. The successive five editions provide the economic paleontologist with a judicious consideration of the post-Keynes debates. Herbert Furth, Haberler's brother-in-law and admirer at the Federal Reserve, wrote (when they were both in their nineties) that Haberler's macroeconomics

---

[2] As Viner threw his stone he ought to have realised it could ricochet and destroy his own Ricardian theory. When labour alone is needed to produce goods, differences in irksomeness from working to produce wine and cloth, destroys the Ricardo–Viner equality of $P_w/P_c =$ (labour embodied in a unit of wine)/(labour embodied in a unit of cloth). Does that vitiate Ricardo's normative case for free trade over autarky? No, as was shown in Samuelson (1939): one proves that, every single person is (if anything) worse off refusing to trade at all than when choosing to trade something positively; this theorem applies even when the new 1930 *pp-frontier* does not exist, either for Haberler or for Viner-Ricardo!

© Royal Economic Society 1996

was perhaps more noteworthy in the history of economic thought than even his trade innovations. We need not address that question. As Gottfried might say; 'If chocolate is good and herring is good, then how good must be herring and chocolate!'

Today there are new doubts about the meaningful existence of business cycles. Statisticians write of cointegration, random walks, and unit roots. The old farmer's almanac of cycles, recorded at the pre-war Natural Bureau of Economic Research à la Wesley Mitchell and Arthur F. Burns, lives on but perhaps not at the cutting edge of today's statistical macroeconomics.

Haberler himself divided each putative cycle into phases of *advance* and phases of *decline*: each are punctuated by *upper and lower turning points*. He distinguishes between different theories and theorists: for example, monetary theorists such as Hawtrey or Fisher (or, later, Friedman); psychological theories, such as those of Bagehot and Pigou; exogenous theories, whether of sunspot or agricultural or innovational type; endogenous mechanisms of cumulative spirals, resonances, and damping (à la J. M. Clark, Frisch, or Tinbergen). In particular, categories of over-saving or of under-investing or of under-consuming are put under the Haberlerian microscope. Although originally an Austrian, by his thirties Haberler is a player on the world scene who does not hesitate to find serious faults in Hayek's once fashionable 1931 *Prices and Production*, with its identification of the Great Depression as a contraction of the triangular time structure of production – brought on by excessive M creation and to be made only worse by fiscal deficits that stimulate consumer spending.

By ardent Keynesians such as Richard Kahn or Joan Robinson, Haberler was regarded as a philistine enemy. In some expressions Haberler could be interpreted as saying that what was true in *The General Theory* was not new and what was original was not true. But if you read his many writings on Keynes, you see that he concedes much merit and novelty of emphasis to Keynes. See Haberler (1947) for his postmortem on *The General Theory*, a judicious critique. I find it much superior to his initial methodological critique of the multiplier in Haberler (1936), which fails to perceive that Keynes's $\Delta Y/\Delta I = 1/[1-(\Delta C)/(\Delta Y)]$ multiplier is not intended to be the entailment of the *definitional* identity $Y \equiv I + C$; rather Keynes explains clumsily that he is describing a paradigm in which sustainable equilibrium is illustrated by the hypothesis that C is a measurable and tested function of income, $C = f(Y)$, $0 < f' < 1$, *ceteris paribus*. By 1947 Haberler gives even too much credence to the importance of income as a determinant of C, as compared to other variables, such as wealth. Haberler admires Franco Modigliani (1944) for his emphasis on the importance of wealth and of price-and-wage rigidities in 1936 Keynes; and the Modigliani he admires, by contrast to Haberler, regards Keynes as the greatest economist of the century and perhaps of all time. *Verbal* differences still abound among economists! Haberler can rightly say that he enunciated before Pigou the Pigou effect – whereby at low enough price levels, outputs demanded out of fixed stocks of (outside) M can always effectuate full employment. Bully for him (and for Wassily Leontief who mentioned this effect to his Harvard

© Royal Economic Society 1996

seminar immediately on reading *The General Theory* hot off the press). But future historians of science will judge that only in terms of Keynes's complete system can one understand the weaknesses of its 1936 Model T formulations. That's what constitutes greatness in my book.

III. HABERLER AS POLICY ANALYST

Throughout six decades of publishing Haberler was a remarkably consistent advocate of free or freer trade. He recognised the few valid cases for protection, which had primarily been worked out by mainstream economists of 1810–1995. Thus, a small optimum tariff could conceivably improve a country's terms of trade and welfare. Thus, a serendipitous temporary aid to an infant industry might in the end have a net benefit. Thus, under increasing returns to scale, the sustainability of competitive equilibrium could be impaired under free trade. Thus, *external* economies create a presumptive possibility for fruitful public policy. In the end, as he weighed the risks and quantitative advantages of each departure from free trade, he tended to put the burden of proof against quotas and tariffs. Although a sincere believer in the possibility of a *wert-frei* economic methodology, his lawyer-like argumentation in favour of nineteenth century Manchester liberalism did not seem wholly divorced from all ideological elements. Where he differed with run-of-the-mill conservatives was in the depth of his factual expositions and analysis. And he made two important advances in changing his mind: he came to favour flexible, floating exchange rates over pegged gold parities, and he feared repressed inflation more than open inflation. Both changes were to give market mechanisms a better chance.

Two other judgements illustrate his great good sense. He admired Milton Friedman and he thought money mattered much; but his reason and experience could not convince him to become a 'monetarist'. Also, he saw merit in arguments by rational expectationists that the use of policy surprises lose their potencies the more they are used. But he considered it implausible to believe that the resultant of diverse judgements by the many people with variable endowments of resources and information will somehow follow a meaningfully coherent and testable model that agrees with some mathematical expectation. Such a view, he feared, bordered on superstition.

For this occasion I want to call attention to Haberler's thesis that economic development stood to benefit from adhering to market disciplines. In the 1950s and 1960s the Rockefeller and Ford Foundations would send Viner and Haberler to places like Brazil and Argentina to lecture on development. Each would address audiences of perhaps 30 to 50 older local experts. At that same time younger and more leftist economists – Paul Sweezy and Paul Baran provide examples – would be lecturing to overflow audiences of university students. Following the banner of Raoul Prebisch from *The United Nations for Latin America*, there existed widespread enthusiasm for policies of 'import substitution'.

When Stendahl's novels failed to achieve popularity, he remained convinced that posterity would accord him his due. Haberler likewise remained a

© Royal Economic Society 1996

meticulous and polemical critic of views on development associated with such names as Gunnar Myrdal, Hans Singer, Nicholas Kaldor, and much of the active writers on economic development.

Typical of Haberler's repeated analyses of what he called fallacies among development economists was the piece he wrote in the last half of his ninth decade: *Liberal and Illiberal Development Policy* (1987, 1992). One advantage of living long is that economic history may wander in your direction of diagnosis and you can indulge freely in 'I told you so'. When Haberler tallied the evidence of evolving economic history, he came down increasingly hard against the Myrdal view of a vicious circle in which the rich regions gained and what they gained was at the expense of the poor ones. The pessimistic prophecies about an inexorable deterioration of the terms of trade against agriculture, as he weighed the facts and arguments, were not confirmed by recent and ancient history. Once it was popular to believe that poor regions, dazzled by 'the demonstration effect of advanced countries' affluence', were doomed to have low savings and be stuck forever in a poverty trap. Instead the Modigliani Lifecycle model correctly predicted strong saving out of successfully growing incomes.

Singapore, Taiwan, Korea, and Hong Kong confirmed the Krueger–Bhagwati belief in the optimality of *export promotion* as against *import substitution*. Basket cases of botched planning were repeated in Africa, Asia, and Latin America. Although Haberler supported Keynesian macro activisms to fight industrial depressions, he judged it ludicrous to believe that the typical underdeveloped country experienced its overt and disguised unemployed because of over-austere monetary and fiscal policy. Once but a minority voice arguing against the mainstream, by the Age After Gorbachev Haberler had become a voice of the mainstream. He did not have to change. The Mississippi River so to speak veered decisively in his direction. And the remarkable performance of Chile's democracy following upon the retirement of its military dictatorship raises hopes that market mechanisms can be combined with mixed-economy public policies to form both an efficient and a humane society. Typical of Haberler would be his special emphasis on a Limited Welfare State, which renders unto the market the vast preponderance of resource allocation and production.

IV. HABERLER, THE PERSON

Gottfried was low-keyed, with a quiet sense of humour. (In a famous Federal Reserve seminar, he introduced his prolific Harvard colleague Seymour Harris with the famous words: 'No need to introduce Seymour Harris. Those who are not busily engaged in reading his 50 books on economics are busily engaged in writing them.' He liked to repeat Friedrich Lutz's aphorism: 'That Dr Harris cannot hold his ink.')

From a letter to him from his sister in Liechtenstein, not long before his death, came the surprising news that in high school Haberler had been expelled for writing that a certain Viennese publication was nothing but a piece of trash. At his new Gymnasium, Gottfried established his intellectual superiority – so

© Royal Economic Society 1996

much so that his father could say on his deathbed: 'Much will come of Gottfried.' Much did.

Jobs in post-World War I Vienna economic circles were scarce. Gottfried's was found at his maternal uncle's bank. On the second day, when he picked up his coat and hat, he left behind the laconic message: 'I'm not coming back. I really don't like it here.'

Most Austrian expatriate economists relished gossip. Gottfried was no exception. But it is hard to imagine a greater contrast than between him and the extroverted, vivacious Joseph Schumpeter or Fritz Machlup. But always Gottfried was on the best of terms with each of them. At the same time that Haberler shared conservative views with Ludwig von Mises, Friedrich von Hayek, Milton Friedman, and George Stigler, he may have been friendliest in personal terms with the late William Fellner and Governor Henry Wallich of the Federal Reserve, intellectual conservatives of eclectic type.

At the Harvard office of the *Quarterly Journal* Haberler would leaf through all the exchange journals. He read widely about twentieth century trends in physics and science. Gottfried and his wife Friedl were a hospitable couple in their Mercer Circle and Shady Hill homes in Cambridge, Massachusetts. Having no children, they outlived a succession of dogs who carried the whimsical names of German literary figures. By his midthirties, it was apparent that Haberler's hearing was deteriorating. One never knew whether his delay in using a hearing aid was due to vanity or stubborness. But from early on his ability to read lips was remarkable. On balance developing deafness turned out to be no important subtraction from a long and fruitful scholarly career.

The quarter-of-a-century Haberler spent in Washington at the conservative American Enterprise Institute after becoming emeritus at Harvard appeared to have been a delightful Indian Summer. To me it was a matter of regret that Gottfried Haberler did not share a Nobel Prize with James Meade and Bertil Ohlin – or alternatively with Jacob Viner. Those who miss out on the baubles of science average out every bit as worthy as those upon whom capricious chance shines. Haberler's dozens of books, hundreds of research papers, and scores of graduate students give the only kind of immortality that any scholar can aspire to.

Massachusetts Institute of Technology

REFERENCES

Barone, E. (1908). *Principi di economia politica*. 1st of 7 editions. Rome: Sampaolesi (1929).
Chipman, J. S. (1987). 'Haberler, Gottfried.' In *The New Palgrave A Dictionary of Economics* (J. Eastwell, M. Milgate and P. Newmann ed.), pp. 581–2. London: Macmillan.
Fisher, I. (1907). *The Rate of Interest*. New York: Macmillan.
Fisher, I. (1922). *The Making of Index Numbers*. Boston: Houghton-Mifflin.
Haberler, G. (1925). 'Kritische Bemerkungen zu Schumpeters Goldtheorie. Zum Lehrte von "objektiven" Tauschwert des Goldes.' *Zeitschrift für Volkswirtschaft und Sozpolitik N.F.*, vol. 4, pp. 647–68. Berlin: Springer-Verlag. Translated (1985) as 'Critical notes on Schumpeter's theory of money – The doctrine of the "objective" exchange value of money'. In (A. Y. C. Koo, ed.), *Selected Essays of Gottfried Haberler*, pp. 531–52. Cambridge, Mass.: MIT Press.
Haberler, G. (1927). *Der Sinn der Indexzahlen*. Tübingen: J. C. B. Mohr.

© Royal Economic Society 1996

Haberler, G. (1933). *Der internationale Handel. Theorie der weltwirtschaftlichen Zusammenhänge sowie Darstellung und Analyse der Aussenhandelspolitik*. Berlin: Julius Springer. Translated (1936) (revised by the author) as *The Theory of International Trade with its Applications to Commercial Policy*. London: William Hodge & Co.

Haberler, G. (1936). 'Mr. Keynes' theory of the multiplier: a methodological criticism.' *Zeitschrift für Nationalökonomie*, vol. 7, pp. 299–305. Reprinted (1944) with revisions in *Readings in Business Cycle Theory*, pp. 193–203.

Haberler, G. (1937). *Prosperity and Depression*. Geneva: League of Nations.

Haberler, G. (1947). 'The General Theory.' In *The New Economics, Keynes' Influence on Theory and Public Policy* (S. Harris ed.) pp. 161–80. New York: Alfred A. Knopf.

Haberler, G. (1987). 'Liberal and illiberal development policy.' In *Pioneers in Development*, 2nd series (G. M. Meier ed.). New York: Oxford University Press for the World Bank. Reprinted (1992), in *The Journal of International Trade & Economic Development*, vol. 1, pp. 69–99.

Hayek, F. von (1931). *Prices and Production*. London: George Routledge & Sons.

Keynes, J. M. (1936). *The General Theory of Employment, Interest, and Money*, London: Macmillan.

Modigliani, F. (1944). 'Liquidity preference and the theory of interest and money.' *Econometrica*, vol. 12, pp. 45–88.

Pareto, V. (1897). *Cours d'economie politique*. Lausanne: Rouge.

Samuelson, P. A. (1939). 'The gains from international trade.' *Canadian Journal of Economics*, vol. 5, pp. 195–205.

Taussig, F. W. (1927). *International Trade*. New York: Macmillan.

© Royal Economic Society 1996

Proceedings of The Gibbs Symposium
Yale University, May 15–17, 1989

Gibbs in Economics

PAUL A. SAMUELSON

My title is not commutative. Economics in Gibbs would be like the case of that minimal treatise "snakes in Ireland."

True, I could trace some farfetched elements of economics connected to Gibbs. His *Equilibrium of Heterogeneous Substances* did advance chemistry and chemistry is a part of the gross national product. Like William Shakespeare who (if he did live) was an astute investor, Willard Gibbs inherited $30,000 in the 1860s and bequeathed $100,000 at his death in 1903, the difference hardly being attributable to savings out of the salary that Yale paid him only part of the time. (Conservative loaning out at contemporaneous interest rates and Yankee plain living, rather than any Maxwellian demon, accounted for this adequate performance.)

It is a matter of record that Gibbs always voted for Republican presidential candidates. Always? Well, almost always. His voting for Grover Cleveland is an exception that does not disprove the rule since Cleveland, to the perceptive eye, was a closet Republican. We know how Gibbs would reduce today's Reagan–Bush deficit, when we recall that he disposed of the surplus funds allocated the governmental commission on electricity by quietly returning them to the U.S. Treasury.

My task today is to describe some of the influences of Gibbs and his systems on modern economics. My title could just as aptly have been: *The Gibbs Circle in Economics.* It would of course have begun in New Haven with Irving Fisher being at its epicenter. Edwin Bidwell Wilson, Gibbs's last protégé, transported his tradition to Massachusetts Institute of Technology (MIT) and Harvard. (Lawrence J. Henderson, Harvard physiologist turned philosopher and zealot for Pareto's sociology, was not quite an economist but he did proselytize for Gibbsian equilibrium in blood and elites.) Wilson ("E. B." we called him to distinguish from E. Bright Wilson, Jr.) was my master, first among equals. Through his lineage I could claim Gibbs as my grandfather; and when my first Ph.D. student Lawrence Klein came to generalize the LeChatelier principle to quadratic forms of statistical variances, this Nobelist could claim rights to the apostolic succession.

© 1990 American Mathematical Society
0-8218-0157-0 $1.00 + $.25 per page

Thermodynamics, like economics, has always had strong Scottish roots. Both subjects benefitted from French researchers and also from German investigators. More idiosyncratically, there was long in the low countries—Holland and Belgium—a strong school of thermodynamicists. At least two Nobel laureates in economics show the Gibbsian influence: Jan Tinbergen, first winner of the Alfred Nobel Award in economics, was a protégé of the Ehrenfests; the late Tjalling Koopmans of Rotterdam and Yale similarly began study as a physicist, with an approximation law to his credit that still after fifty years is employed by quantum physicists.

As will become apparent, I have limited tolerance for the perpetual attempts to fabricate for economics concepts of "entropy" imported from the physical sciences or constructed by analogy to Clausius–Boltzmann magnitudes. The monthly mail still brings grandiose schemes to replace the dollar as a unit of value by energy or entropy units. Superficial knowledge of thermodynamics, brought into contact with ignorance of economics, cannot even in the presence of the catalyst of noble intentions beget stable equilibrium of useful products. That is not a tautology, merely a finding of fifty-five years of reading the morning mail.[1]

The benefit to theoretical economics, it will be shown, comes from discerning the *mathematical isomorphisms* between the maximum-minimum systems of thermodynamics and the cost-profit-utility systems of classical Walras–Debreu economics. I learned from Professor Arnold in the proceedings of this Gibbs celebration at Yale that fifty years ago the prose I was speaking was that of *contact structures*. (I may add, as a personal but idiosyncratic note, that Gibbs's work on statistical mechanics—which is clearly distinguishable from his earlier writings of phenomenological macroscopic thermodynamics—has involved many enjoyable overlaps with my own economic explorations in stochastic processes. Thus, recently I tried to model a theory of the asymptotic approach of the income distribution to an ergodic state; when the very rich and poor are more risk averse than the middle classes, the system evolves into an ergodic Markov state; still it displays all the Loschmidt–Poincaré–Zermelo paradoxes of being truly time-symmetric!)

Physicists go whole hours not thinking about economics. Let me therefore focus first on the personal legends and myths connected with Gibbs, and worthy of being addressed at a birthday party like this one.

---

[1] Nicholas Georgescu-Roegen is an exception who argues cogently that the image of an hourglass is more appropriate for economics than that of an undamped pendulum. Connoisseurs, such as Joseph Schumpeter and Wassily Leontief, have properly admired the width, depth, and originality of Georgescu's scholarship and it may be hoped that the Swedish Royal Academy of Sciences may yet see the light (cf. Georgescu-Roegen 1966, 1971). My text's remarks are not intended to be critical of use by such econometricians as Henri Theil of information-entropy magnitudes of the form $\sum_j X_j (\log X_j)$: no physicism is involved in such measures of partitioned variability.

647

Genius as neglected Yankee. William James sounded early the recurrent note of Willard Gibbs as lone American genius, unappreciated and neglected by Yale. James wrote in what Gibbs's biographer Muriel Rukeyser quoted up front:

> 'They laugh best who laugh last.' Wait till we're dead twenty years. Look at the way they're now treating poor Willard Gibbs, who during his lifetime can hardly have been considered any great shakes at New Haven.

Almost fifty years ago Muriel Rukeyser (Rukeyser 1942) embalmed this view in excitable prose. I can recall how indignant people like Wilson and Henderson were over what they regarded as presumptuous gush. (Whether the biographer's crime was greater for being a woman, a poet, or a New Yorker, I could never identify.) I recall then falling in with this scientist-Brahmin view. Now that I have picked up the book for the first time in decades, I find it to be not a bad book. The official biography by Gibbs's own student Wheeler is of course more accurate and informed on many matters: still the Wheeler work is a late-in-life effort, prompted by filial duty and the urgings of Wilson *et alii* to counter the Rukeyser legends; in 1989 I find the two works complementary rather than antithetical.

Gibbs's crime as a scientist was being ahead of his time and place. He felt no urge to write or to claim priority for scientific innovation. Only when something badly needed to be done, did Gibbs do it—and then so compactly as to be almost incomprehensible. Gibbs, like Mendel, did publish in an obscure journal, the *Transactions of the Connecticut Academy*, but New Haven was never as remote as Timbuctoo.

By his own admission Gibbs, who over multiple decades taught only advanced courses and to minuscule enrollments, had but six students adequately prepared to follow his lectures. Yet he never was tempted to offer more elementary versions that might remedy the gaps. It is an actuarial accident that Gibbs died while Wilson was away in Europe. Had Gibbs lived to be the proverbial three score and ten, quite possibly Wilson might have done for other subjects in the Gibbs oral tradition what he did in writing up a publishable exposition of Gibbs's vector analysis. What a nice precursor to Courant-Hilbert, Sommerfeld, and Laudau-Lifshitz would have been Gibbs-Wilson, *Thermodynamics*, Gibbs-Wilson, *Electricity, Light and Magnetism*, Gibbs-Wilson, *Orbits, Least Squares, and Probability*, Gibbs-Wilson, *Waves*.

Can so reserved, nay repressed, a person as Willard Gibbs have been a truly happy man? Whatever the a priorisms of Kinsey Institute researchers, his kinfolk reported, "Yes." We shall never know for sure. And, as Wittgenstein did not refrain from saying, on that which we cannot speak we must perforce be silent.

Both biographers of those earlier decades violate the Marquis of Queensbury rules for modern biography, according to which you must not speculate as to what was in your subject's mind unless you can supply evidence for your supposition. We know less about Gibbs's not serving in the Civil War than we do about the similar cases of Henry Adams, Henry James, and William James or about the opposite case of Oliver Wendell Holmes, Jr., who gloried in the risks of serving. Perhaps Wheeler is right that but for frailty of health Willard would have rushed to defend the Union, but we do not know that. Did the young Gibbs have tuberculosis, that nineteenth century affliction of Mill, Elizabeth Barrett, Clifford, D. H. Lawrence, and Irving Fisher? We may still be able to learn more about that, but as yet we do not know. We do have reason to doubt the legend that Gibbs's overworking on his *Statistical Mechanics* was what shortened his life. The family denied that, and sudden obstruction of the bowel is not an ordinary symptom of intellectual overexertion.

Certainly Gibbs's intimates and peers believed that he was content to have the good opinion of the contemporary scientists *he* admired: above all Maxwell sang Gibbs's praises and spread his fame, as did Rayleigh, J. J. Thomson, and Kelvin. In the polemics that Tait forced on Gibbs in connection with quaternions versus various vector and multiple Grassmann algebras, Gibbs stood his ground coolly and cogently and has been well rewarded by history. The lifelong serenity Gibbs displayed, if it was not effortlessly spontaneous, could well have been an optimal adaptation to the constraints of health and temperament. What is the operational difference?

With Gibbs being a rentier living off a parental inheritance and being a brother tied down to the New Haven neighborhood where he had been born and educated, the president and dean of Yale needed no elaborate von Neumann theory of games to work out Gibbs's maximal reserve price of a zero stipend.

Yes, this was indeed a scandal. Still I was interested to learn recently[2] that Gibbs was not the sole academician similarly exploited by the nineteenth century Yale. The economist Arthur T. Hadley, later to be Yale president, seems also to have started out at a zero salary. Henry W. Farnam, another early Yale professor of economics, began at that same austere wage level, as did John C. Schwab. All these were inbred Yale appointees and only Farnam could be deemed rich. A social structure that chose to depend on inherited or married wealth would have to be prone to genteel stagnation. (I can remember that, even in my time, many New England college communities engaged in elaborate ceremonies of black tie dinners, card exchanges, and

---

[2] See William J. Barber, *The fortunes of political economy in an environment of academic conservatism : Yale University*, in Breaking the Academic Mould: Economists and the Higher Learning in the Nineteenth Century (W. J. Barber, ed.), Chapter 6. For salary data see particularly pp. 154–158. Yale seems not to have been a happy ship in the last decades of the century. The pugnacious William Graham (Billy) Sumner taught social Darwinism, to the displeasure of the ordained president Noah Porter. General Francis Walker, who had headed the 1870 census, felt isolated in the Scheffield Scientific School and fled to the presidency of MIT. Coit Gilman, frustrated in the attempt to make Yale a great graduate school along German lines, left to head the University of California and shortly thereafter to realize his dream in innovating Johns Hopkins. Gilman's call to Gibbs came on the advice of top English physicists but undoubtedly he knew Willie Gibbs in New Haven and at Yale.

lifestyles that presupposed some investment income. When President Eliot unilaterally appointed to the Harvard faculty the economic historian Edwin Gay, all that he noted for the official record were the words: "Wife has independent income. They live on it.")

The two disciples. On the beat assigned to me, mathematician E. B. Wilson and economist Irving Fisher were the nearest to Gibbs. Temperamentally these two were not alike. Both share the property of being temperamentally different from Gibbs, whom each admired and loved. Wilson was as loquacious as Gibbs was taciturn; if anybody could have gotten near to Gibbs in a scholarly way during the final 1899–1902 years, it would have been Wilson. And we are grateful for the brief letter Gibbs sent to Wilson in Paris just a month before Gibbs died. Until rereading Wilson's 1931 Gibbs Lecture, reminiscing about Gibbs as teacher and colleague, I had forgotten how few were their actual contacts outside the classroom. Even Wilson's famous write-up of Gibbs's vector analysis was done with the explicit understanding of no participation or vetting on the part of Gibbs.

When I first knew Wilson he was about as old as Gibbs had been when Wilson first knew Gibbs. My age was almost that which Wilson's had been. As one of a few good students, I was able to talk to Wilson for an hour after each lecture—on any and every subject. E. B. Barkis would have been willing in 1899, but Gibbs did not do that sort of thing, period.

Wilson's merits are in danger of being lost in the mists of history and so it is appropriate to devote some words to him here. A number of Gibbses first went to Harvard before our Gibbs and his father went to Yale. Wilson's forebears went to Yale until he went to Harvard, graduating in 1899 at the age of twenty with the alleged designation of *summa summorum cum laude*. By miscalculation he went to the Yale Graduate School. Gibbs turned out to compensate for Yale's inadequacies in pure mathematics; this pushed Wilson toward mathematical physics and, in the end, toward many novel fields. He wrote the first studies on stability of an airplane and contributed to the following areas: psychometrics (principal components and generalized Spearman–Thurston factor analysis), population analysis and actuarial statistics, Fisherine mathematical statistics, and mathematical economics.

MIT called Wilson from Yale. At MIT he headed mathematical physics, wrote his serviceable and durable *Advanced Calculus*, and was drafted to be the acting president in the early 1920s. Then President Lowell called him to be the dean of what is now the Harvard School of Public Health. Each spring he taught in alternate years a seminar in mathematical economics and mathematical statistics, and I was one of the small contingent of economists who benefitted from his broad knowledge and wry wit.

E. B. was the only intelligent man I ever knew who liked committee meetings. He headed the Watchdog Committee that Harvard set up to monitor its new venture into sociology à la Sorokin, Parsons, and Merton. He headed the National Social Science Research Council.

Wilson knew where all the bodies were buried in American academic life. It was he who led the successful vendetta to negate President Lowell's call to Raymond Pearl of Johns Hopkins: in the history of academic freedom, this stands in the annals as the sole case of a pocket veto by the Board of Overseers against a Harvard academic appointment. To pump Wilson about the threatened Overseers' veto of John Kenneth Galbraith's appointment after World War II, I innocently asked Wilson, "How often are academic appointments at Harvard superceded by Board refusals?"

"Once every thirty-seven years," he replied. "Only once though for religious reasons."

My ears pricked up. "In the nineteenth century a historian was refused," he continued.

When I inquired as to the heterodoxies that were his impedimenta, Wilson said dryly: "He was a Unitarian. Some felt there were getting to be too damned many of them."

When Wilson was on leave from Yale to study under Poincaré and others, Gibbs indicated to him that he intended to redo thermodynamics in terms of *finite* rather than continuum methods; alas, on Wilson's return to New Haven after Gibbs's sudden death, no trace of such intentions could be found in his skimpy files. (Could Gibbs have had any intimations of quantum mechanics à la Planck? The weight of the evidence seems against it, even though his remarks show that he was bothered by ambiguities in the number of degrees of freedom involved in kinetic models.)

One yearns for explicit Wilsonian reports on how Gibbs felt about Maxwell's demon; about the Loschmidt–Poincaré–Zermelo critiques of Boltzmann in connection with time-reversibility of micro Hamiltonian systems and time-asymmetric growth of macro measures of entropy; about the pre- and post-Michelson demonstrations concerning the invariance of the speed of light in all directions through the "ether." While we are yearning, we can lust for Gibbs's reactions to modern *chaos* theory, Birkhoff–Neumann ergodic theories, and Ehrenfest flea-dog models of statistical mechanics.

Irving Fisher. Despite his tendency to be a do-gooder and faddist, Irving Fisher[3] is now recognized as having been America's first great economic theorist, now eclipsing Henry Carey, Henry George, Thorstein Veblen, John Bates Clark, and Frank Taussig. Fisher's greatest scientific contribution was not in the 1891 thesis that Gibbs helped supervise, but rather came in the 1896–1906 decade when he wrote on capital theory. His 1891 Yale Ph.D. thesis on the theory of values and prices was a classic memoir on mathematical economics. From 1896 to 1907, and culminating in 1930, Fisher created neoclassical capital theory. His macroeconomic writings made him a founder of

---

[3] Readers interested in Fisher are referred to his son's revealing autobiography (Fisher 1956); and to the Yale centenary lectures on Fisher (Miller 1967).

651

the modern quantity theory of money prices, and from 1911 until his death in 1947, Fisher was a principal analyst of business cycle fluctuations and an activist prescriber of stabilization policies. A founder with Joseph Schumpeter and Ragnar Frisch of the *Econometric Society*, Fisher pioneered in statistical index-number research and empirical time-series analysis.

Besides these solid contributions to economics, Fisher devised an ingenious map projection; he wrote a runaway best-seller on hygiene (fresh air, thorough chewing of food, teetotalism, exercise, and much else). He promoted the League of Nations, Prohibition, and the 1920s bull market in Wall Street. He cogently rejected taxation of income as involving deadweight distortion of saving as compared to taxation of consumed income. The pattern of economic textbooks that I inherited in 1948 was in some degree set by him in 1911. The son of an impecunious minister, Fisher was the academic star of his Yale class, outshining even his classmate Henry Stimson and getting tapped for Skull and Bones.

Fisher loved and admired his teacher Gibbs. Gibbs supervised few theses but he did supervise Fisher's. Gibbs's influence was somewhat remote; but we see his fine hand in Fisher's discussion of integrability conditions on preference functions and Fisher's demonstration that any metric stretching of the utility function would be admissible. (Surprisingly, the same Fisher later gratuitously proposed that income taxation be geared to one particular metric of utility—that one inferable from price-consumption demand data under the hypothesis that different goods had *independent* utility functions that could be added together.)

Fisher married one fortune and by his invention of a visible card-index filing system earned a second one. He augmented both in Wall Street's bull market, only to lose all in the 1929 Crash and its aftermath. He would have lost a third fortune, that of his sister-in-law, the president of Wellesley College, if not deprived of the opportunity. He died broke, owing Yale on his house mortgage. When I used to visit Yale, Fisher's name was mud with those who asked: "If you're so smart, why ain't you rich?"

When Fisher was still flush, it was he who financed reproduction of Gibbs's collected papers in two volumes. Although Fisher's hunger for fame drove him from mathematics to economics, he ever praised the virtues of his beloved mentor Willard Gibbs.

Although the two men differed as day and night in personality, Fisher and Gibbs had one thing in common; they were born too late. Fisher was born fifteen years too late to attain the golden fleece in economic value theory. Jevons, Walras, Menger and Edgeworth had arrived at the North Pole before Fisher got there in 1891. Fisher just could not stand not to be a great man. His son's worshipful biography (I. N. Fisher 1956), quotes him as writing to his heiress financée, "I will be a great man." Over a long life Fisher spread himself thin over a great variety of causes and fads, becoming in the end almost an object of derision.

Gibbs too was born some decades too late to be a founder of basic thermodynamics. Carnot, Joule, and Clausius had done the job before Willie was old enough to vote. That he recognized this is shown in his obituary words on Rudolph Clausius, in *Collected Works* (Volume 2, 1931, Chapter XX, especially p. 262) where he quotes Maxwell's 1878 characterization of thermodynamics as "a science with secure foundations, clear definitions, and distinct boundaries"; and states categorically that "it might have been said at any time since the publication of that (Clausius 1850) memoir, that the foundations of the science were secure, its definitions clear, and its boundaries distinct." (Incidentally, note the chaste beauty of Gibbs's English style. In his Clausius obituary, after praising Carnot, James and William Thomson, and Joule, Gibbs put Rankine in his place with the wry sentence: "Meantime Rankine was attacking the problem in his own way, with one of those marvelous creations of the imagination of which it is difficult to estimate the precise value." Gibbs's responses to the shrill Tait are similarly delicious.)

Martin Klein (Klein 1978), in commenting on Gibbs's "scientific style," cogently points out that Gibbs started in his first 1873 writings on thermodynamics from an unconventional base: he took absolute temperature, entropy, and (internal) energy for granted as variables just as anyone takes pressure and volume for granted as variables. Modern treatises, like that of Guggenheim, do the same (much to the displeasure of a Clifford Truesdell who grants only a Gibbs the license to ignore the understructure of his concepts). Gibbs was, so to speak, a premature no-nonsense Machian. He was not so much concerned with the history of how we come to know what we scientists know, as with summarizing in the most compact way what there is that is knowable. Actually, when Gibbs came to lecture to beginners in thermodynamics, we know from Wilson's survey of students' lecture notes that it took Gibbs all of the course to establish that which is behind Gibbs's 1873 geometric surface built on

$$d(\text{Energy}) = dE = -(\text{pressure})d(\text{volume}) + (\text{absolute temp.})d(\text{entropy})$$
$$= -pdV + tdS.$$

I have a vague recollection that Gibbs did not know until soon *after* 1873 that Massieu had anticipated the concept that a single knowable function (and its derivatives) could summarize *all* the information knowable in thermodynamics.

Unlike Fisher, Gibbs showed no concern for his own achievements and reputation in science. He proceeded to do that which by 1873 had not yet been done, extending to pairs of conjugate variables, such as (chemical mass, chemical potential) the appropriate generalizations of Carnot–Clausius thermodynamics. His *Equilibrium of Heterogeneous Substances* is the resulting masterpiece, written so economically as to cover much that was not rediscovered or understood for decades to come. Max Planck, like Gibbs, came a little late to the feast. Fortunately, Planck stumbled in 1900 on the quantum phenomenon and thereby earned imperishable fame. And Gibbs too earned fame as Johnny-come-early with his truly original and elegant *Statistical Mechanics*.

How thermodynamics impacts economics. What can the equations of steam engines have to do with the theory of economic equilibrium? There is very little direct connection. Therefore, I can sympathize with those critics who regard economic science as pretentious if it tries to add a cubit to its own stature by employing the hocus pocus of the Newtonian calculus borrowed from thermodynamics.

Actually, the analogies are misunderstood. As already indicated, I have come over the years to have some impatience and boredom with those who try to find an analogue of the entropy of Clausius or Boltzmann or Shannon to put into economic theory. It is the *mathematical* structure of *classical* (phenomenological, macroscopic, nonstochastic) *thermodynamics* that has isomorphisms with *theoretical economics*. In both cases a set of state extensive variables $(x_1, \ldots, x_n)$ is involved; but there is no reason why the prices and quantities of factors and goods, and the profit or utility functions of economics, should have any meaningful correspondences with the *intensive* force variables and *extensive* quantities that physicists call (pressure, volume), (temperature, entropy), (chemical potential, chemical mass).

Far from enhancing my own reputation with peers or with gullible amateurs by employing in economic analyses the abracadabra of physical science[4], I have risked acquiring a reputation for abstractness and posturing. I have done so simply because of the fruitfulness imparted by the shared mathematical structure. The LeChatelier principle, neither as applied to bicycle pumps nor to short versus long run elasticities of demand, has aught to do with teleology — as a system allegedly "strives" to relieve the stresses on it. Instead, the LeChatelier principle is a humdrum Jacobi theorem about the ratio of certain principal minors in the symmetric and definite determinants associated with a *minimum system* and it belongs to both subjects.

My own work has been as much interested in elucidating the differences as the likenesses between classical mathematical economics and thermodynamics. Thus, the *energy function* of Joule is measurable directly whereas the

---

[4]Alfred Marshall, writing at the turn of the century in England when Darwinism was in the air, proposed that *biological* models ought increasingly to displace *physics* models in economics. Periodically since then, similar notions have surfaced among economists dissatisfied with mechanistic economics and mathematical methodology. The late Jacob Viner, of Chicago and Princeton, and Earl Beach, of McGill, have been promoters of some kind of biological approach. Paradoxically, however, the great breakthroughs in molecular biology have come from using the mathematical modellings imported from chemistry and physics. Moreover, the formal genetic models of such neo-Darwinists as R. A. Fisher, J.B.S. Haldane, and Sewall Wright turn out to be similar to the modelings of modern economics. Altruism in terms of "inclusive fitness" and other concepts of sociobiologists W.D. Hamilton and E.O. Wilson, reads almost like University of Chicago parables of economics!

(nonstochastic) *utility function* of a post-Paretian can be given an infinity of different monotone stretchings without altering any invariantly-measurable magnitude. (There is no Kelvin absolute utility; even in the stochastic context, the cardinal utility function whose expected value is maximized by a von Neumann–Laplace adherent has no Kelvin Absolute Zero invariant.) Yes, minimized dollars of cost confront economists much as minimized energy confronts physicists. No, there is not in economics a conjugate variable anything like a Kelvin Absolute Metric of Temperature. Clausius was able to define for physics a metric of entropy so as to make it meaningful to speak of an *adiabatic contour* that is "exactly halfway between" two prescribed *adiabats*. No variable useful for Walras–Debreu economic equilibrium systems corresponds to this entropy concept.

If this were a conference of mathematical economists I would enlarge on how Legendre transformations like those of Gibbs, Helmholz, and Massieu occur in the theory of economic rationing and in what we call duality theory of production and utility. But to do that would be to subject you to the abuse of a captive audience. Also it would be presumptuous of me to bore you with my reflections as an economic theorist on what would seem a possible natural approach to axiomatizing classical macroscopic or phenomenological thermodynamics.

For the written record, where every reader is free to turn the page, let me only sketch one way of looking at the existence of an internal energy function for a specified fluid substance. Within a rigid and insulating external wall there is contained a unit mass of some gas such as H_2O or O or H or .... Imagine this mass subdivided into two equal masses, each in its own rigid and insulating walls. Initially, each part will have its own pressure and (specific) volume: (p_1, v_1) and (p_2, v_2), where these vectors can begin quite unequal. Now let us join the parts by an internal wall that is rigid but is no longer insulating. To save your time, consider only the special case of equal volumes: $v_1 = v_2 = v$. What were previously unequal pressures (because what we can define as empirical temperatures, t_1 and t_2, started out being specified as unequal) will now be observed to settle down to a common (temperature and) pressure. Symbolically

$$(p_1, v; p_2, v) \to (p^*, v; p^*, v)$$

where

$$p^* = P(p_1, p_2 | v)$$

is a three-variable function well defined by empirical observation. On reflection this P function will be perceived to be a symmetric (generalized) *mean*

$$P(p, p|v) \equiv p, \qquad P(p_1, p_2|v) \equiv P(p_2, p_1|v).$$

655

Empirically, it is strictly monotone-increasing

$$\min(p_1, p_2) \leq P(p_1, p_2|v) \leq \max(p_1, p_2)$$
$$\partial P(p_1, p_2|v)/\partial p_i > 0, \quad i = 1, 2.$$

Now we can infer the existence of an energy function, essentially unique except for arbitrary unit of scale and arbitrary origin at each v.

> Axiom of Invariance: Consider the unit mass divided into 4 subsystems of equal masses and volumes: $(p_1, p_2, p_3, p_4|v)$. Let the pair $(p_1, p_2|v)$ be brought into contact and the pair $(p_3, p_4|v)$ be also in separate contact, each resulting respectively in p_{12}^* and p_{34}^*. Then bringing these two into final contact will be observed always to lead to the same p^* as would have resulted from bringing all 4 parts into simultaneous contact. And similarly for *any* possible initial pairings.

This axiom is a testable law of nature not an artifact of thought. It is never experimentally refuted. From it, by methods of the mathematics of functional equations that go back to Abel in the 1820s, modern mathematical economists deduce that a conserved energy function exists of the form $p^* = P(p_1, p_2|v)$ iff there exists an $E[p|v]$ function such that

$$E[p_1|v] + E[p_2|v] = E[p^*|v] + E[p^*|v]$$
$$= 2E[P(p_1, p_2|v)|v]$$

where

$$P(p_1, p_2|v) = E^{-1}\left(\frac{1}{2}\sum_1^2 E[p_j|v]\right)$$

where $E^{-1}(\ )$ is the inverse function defined by $E[x|v] = y \leftrightarrow x = E^{-1}(y|v)$.

In terms of mathematical functional equations of the Abel type, when we ignore for notational brevity the common variable v, this axiom stipulates

$$P(P(p_1, p_2), P(p_3, p_4)) \equiv P(P(p_1, p_3), P(p_2, p_4)).$$

When P is a twice-differentiable function, we can constructively infer $E[p|v]$ from P observations, namely

$$-(\partial p_2/\partial p_1)_{p^*} = \frac{\partial P(p_1, p_2|v)/\partial p_1}{\partial P(p_1, p_2|v)/\partial p_2}$$
$$= \frac{\partial E[p_1|v]/\partial p_1}{\partial E[p_2|v]/\partial p_2} = \mathbf{A}(\mathbf{p_1, p_2}|\mathbf{v})$$

an observable invariant function. Likewise

$$\frac{\partial^2 E[p|v]/(\partial p)^2}{\partial E[p|v]/\partial p} = \frac{\partial \log A(p, p_2|v)}{\partial p}$$
$$= \mathbf{B}(\mathbf{p}|\mathbf{v})$$

an observable invariant function (that is independent of p_2).

By double quadrature we may infer $E[\ ]$'s most general form involving two arbitrary functions of v:

$$E[p|v] = a(v) + b(v) \int_{\overline{p}}^{p} dq \left\{ \exp \int_{\overline{p}}^{q} dz[\mathbf{B}(z|\mathbf{v})] \right\}$$

$0 \lessgtr a(v)$ = specified $E[\overline{p}|v]$ at reference $p = \overline{p}$

$0 < b(v)$ = specified $\partial E[p|v]/\partial p$ at reference $p = \overline{p}$.

Is this black magic or is it only an economist's way of observing that there is no free lunch in the form of a perpetual motion machine of the first kind? You decide.

A kind of heat death? Let me close on a serious note. Nicolas Georgescu-Roegen has well said that the logo for economics should be an hourglass and not a frictionless pendulum. To model this insight, I ignore the niceties of primers on thermodynamics. Instead I contrast two economic models.

In Model 1, a stationary population working on specified land (exposed to the sun's energies) produces a steady state of consumable output of bread. That is the orthodoxy Georgescu-Roegen wants to go beyond.

Model 2 is like Model 1 but to produce our daily bread we need, along with labor and land, an input of copper. Copper can be mined by labor but the faster you mine its limited seams the greater your incremental labor cost; and, the more you have depleted the mine of rich copper veins inherited from way back, the greater the needed labor.

It must be obvious without writing down the system's equations that no steady state of positive bread consumption is possible with a specified constant total of labor and land. The more copper that has been dissipated in the past from its rich seams, the more labor must be switched out of bread production. The system runs downhill in bread production as, so to speak, the entropy of dispersed copper concentrations grows. (If copper has no effective substitutes, the addition of produced capital goods to the model does not change its declining fate at all.)

Admittedly no steady state is possible in this Club-of-Rome model of exhaustible resources. The ball, however, is in the court of those who believe that Clausius–Gibbs formulisms can give us more insights than are already in this ad hoc model.

Conclusion. The house of science has indeed many mansions. And it has many inmates too. The personality of Willard Gibbs differs in a fascinating way from that of James Watson, or Isaac Newton, or the Marquis de Laplace, or Vilfredo Pareto—and I pick my names advisedly and guardedly.

William James was right. Gibbs, who did not particularly care, gets the last laugh in that 150 years after his birth we discuss how he drove his sister's buggy to marketing because her husband was the important librarian of Yale.

We do this because "such work as that of Clausius [and Gibbs] is not measured by counting titles or pages. His true monument lies not on the

657

shelves of libraries, but in the thoughts of men, and in the history of more than one science" (Gibbs 1931, p. 267).

REFERENCES

R. Clausius. 1850. *Poggendorff's annalen.*

Irving Norton Fisher. 1956. *My father Irving Fisher.* New York: Comet Press Books.

Nicholas Georgescu-Roegen. 1966. *Analytical economics.* Cambridge, MA: Harvard University Press.

———, 1971. *The entropy law and the economic process.* Cambridge, MA: Harvard University Press.

J. Willard Gibbs. 1902, 1931. *The collected works.* New York: Longmans, Green & Co.

Martin J. Klein. 1978. *The scientific style of Josiah Willard Gibbs,* in Springs of Scientific Creativity: Essays on Founders of Modern Science (R. Aris, H. T. Davis, and R. H. Stuewer, eds.). Minneapolis, MN: University of Minnesota Press.

John Perry Miller. 1967. *Irving Fisher of Yale,* in Ten Economic Studies in the Tradition of Irving Fisher (William Fellner, et al., eds.). New York: John Wiley & Sons.

Muriel Rukeyser. 1942. *Willard Gibbs.* Garden City, NY: Doubleday, Doran & Co.

Lynde Phelps Wheeler. 1951. *Josiah Willard Gibbs, the history of a great mind.* New Haven: Yale University Press.

Edwin Bidwell Wilson. 1931. *American scientist.*

DEPARTMENT OF ECONOMICS
MASSACHUSETTS INSTITUTE OF TECHNOLOGY
CAMBRIDGE, MASSACHUSETTS 02139

2 Remembering Joan

Paul A. Samuelson

1 INTRODUCTION

Throughout my lifetime as an economist Joan Robinson was always there at the frontier of science. We began together in 1932: I as a student at Chicago; she in her first publishing phase. Many times, in print and elsewhere, I expressed the considered opinion that the corpus of her work richly deserved a Nobel Prize.

For half a century after 1932, Joan Robinson contributed to every major field of political economy. The 1933 Robinson and Chamberlin classics in imperfect competition nicely complemented each other. The first intimation we outsiders had that Keynes (with the help of the 'Circus' which included Richard Kahn, Joan, Austin Robinson, Roy Harrod, James Meade, Piero Sraffa, and others) was forging a theory of output as a whole, came from Robinson (1933b). As an escape from the war and a digression from her nascent Marxian studies, Joan wrote her famous analysis of rising supply price, (Robinson, 1941), which was the first case of a scholar in the Marshallian tradition breaking through to sight the great Pacific of general–equilibrium analysis. I know how original this work was since Wolfgang Stolper and I were at the same time pursuing similar paths in connection with Stolper and Samuelson (1941). Joan's work on foreign exchange rates and the terms of trade, Robinson (1937), was the first quantum jump in that subject since C. F. Bickerdike (1920): before 1937 we all believed that depreciating a currency would, in stable equilibrium *necessarily* depreciate its terms of trade – a logical misapprehension.

Joan's education was as innocent of Marxian instruction as of mathematics. It was only the former that she considered a deprivation. She wore her lack of mathematical knowledge proudly: 'If you don't have it, flaunt it,' that was her motto. 'You think the Emperor has clothes? You think that Euler's Theorem is heap big stuff? Well, let this honest child tell you that ordinary glands are showing through, and all that is needed for competitive factor prices to exhaust market revenues is that total market demand be large enough to be served by numerous replicated firms.'

James Mill and the late Tjalling Koopmans considered it a sin if scholars wrote too well. That brought unearned importance to their offerings. If this be a sin, it is not a sin run rampant in economics. But Joan Robinson, before the seat of judgment of St Peter, would have to plead guilty to flagrant abuse of the art. Eschewing jokes and elegant rhetoric, in plain forceful prose she explicated complex relationships and seduced readers' belief. She could even make 'reswitching' in capital theory exciting, offering it as a lifeline to generous-minded Indians, Italians, and East Anglians feeling buried under the Leviathan of topological proofs that market capitalism delivered the goods of Pareto optimality.

Joan's *An Essay on Marxian Analysis* (1942) marks the division between (1) her early work in the mainstream tradition of post-Marshallian orthodoxy and of Keynesian macroeconomics and (2) her later work in post-Keynesian distribution theory and in Sraffian capital theory. Particularly her work in the foundations of capital theory I regard as valuable and constructive. A Nobel Prize to Joan Robinson alone, or to the pair Robinson–Sraffa, or Robinson–Harrod, or Robinson–Kalecki, or Robinson-Kaldor, I would judge to have been well deserved. And in making this evaluation, I give zero weight to the desirability that a female scholar should receive such an award.

The Marx essay deserves comment in its own right. And also for the light it casts on Joan's developing viewpoints.

2 MARXIAN STUDIES

St Paul's School and Girton College were silent on Marx. Maynard Keynes, whom Joan admired and only later was to patronize, regarded Karl Marx as a waste of time. Before World War II Robinson seems to have been ignorant of Marx's economic works. Robinson (1937, final essay) is a patronizing criticism of John Strachey's superficial use of Marxian patter to predict capitalist depression and to reject Hayekian orthodoxy: Marxians, it appeared, were guilty in Joan's eyes of not knowing elementary Model T Keynesianism.

By 1941 Robinson had mastered the three volumes of *Capital* and some of the Marx–Engels correspondence. (At that date no one knew the 1858 *Grundrisse*, and few had studied the early 1840s writings of the Marx who had not yet become a Marxian.) Joan's admiration for Michal Kalecki, whose originality in independently discovering Keynesian effective demand she if anything exaggerated, I suspect played a role in her investigating Marx.

Robinson pays Marx the compliment of taking him seriously as a scholar. This means no condemnation or praise for subversiveness. It means no patronizing or condescension. It means no reverence as to a sage or a God. She has somewhere expressed her impatience with mindless idolators of the Master who, if asked whether Marx's constant capital is a stock or a flow, reply that Karl Marx was a genius. By her code one must never encounter error or obscurity in *Capital* without calling it by its name; and never fail to hail greatness.

The Robinson *Essay* is an unsparing critique of Marx's paradigm, redeemed by the author's evident approval of Karl Marx and wholehearted rejection of capitalistic apologetics. In commemorating the centennial of *Capital*, Volume I, I said in effect, 'with Joan Robinson as a friend, Karl Marx had no need for an enemy'. (Samuelson 1967, p.622). Robinson then, and ever, rejected Marx's labor theory of value and his *uniform rate-of-surplus-value* (or of rate-of-*exploitation*) paradigm: even in socialism, making labor values determine the price ratio of land-intensive wheat to labor-intensive sugar beets was shown by her to be foolishly inefficient; not yet, apparently, could she show that a Sraffian system with price ratios made to be proportional to embodied (undated!) labor would lead to a similar gratuitous intertemporal inefficiency at profit rates conducive to switch points. What Joan Robinson began in 1942, the purification of Marxism *from within* the camp, has been continued by Ian Steedman's *Marx After Sraffa* (1977), by the many writings of John Roemer, and by a number of other modern Marxians.[1]

Robinson believes it is absurd for Marx to aver that labor is alone productive and that capital goods are not. Marx should recognize that such goods are productive: all Marx needs for his ethical message is that *ownership* of capital by capitalists is not productive. She is scathing – too scathing – on the Marshall–Senior apologetics which try to justify interest as the return to compensate for *waiting* in the part of savers. (It is interesting that, for a socialist state, Robinson then and ever afterwards did perceive the need for current generations to abstain from consuming in the interests of higher consuming by later generations. At MIT in reply to a questioner from an LDC, Joan in 1962 suggested that planners in a poor country ought first to use their limited resources for high-yield projects; after those had been exploited, and as resource availability improved, planners would naturally move down to lower-yield projects. God in heaven will forgive Joan for this neoclassical heresy, for at the moment she did not quite realize what she was saying. But on the issue of Wall Street's usefulness, Robinson never deviated into heresy.)[2]

The *Essay* devotes a short chapter to demolishing Marx's demonstration of a law of the declining rate or profit. Gross output (of an industry or a society) is broken down into Wages + Capital costs + Surplus = $v + c + s$. She then exposes as an empty tautology the syllogism:

> If the *rate of exploitation* is somehow constant (s/v is unchanged); and if the *organic composition of capital* rises ($v/[c+v]$ is down); then the *rate of profit* must fall ($s/[c+v] = [s/v][v/(c+v)]$ has to be down).

This tautology she differentiates from the neoclassical 'deepening of capital', in which a rise in Clarkian K/L must reduce the marginal-product-of-capital rate of return or of profit $-s/[c+v] = \delta Q/\delta K$ to be a declining function of K/L. Not yet does she express her post-1952 condemnation of platonic aggregate capital; not yet does she articulate Sraffa's demonstration that lower profit rates can accompany *lower* ratios of aggregate capital to aggregate labor, but we see already in 1942 a mind ready to be skeptical on this subject.

For an instant, I thought I glimpsed in Robinson's exposition (Robinson, 1942, pp.42–6) an early recognition[3] of the 1950's *factor price*, or (real-wage, profit rate), *tradeoff frontier*. How can the profit rate fall if (as Marxians believe) the real-wage rate does not rise? Unfortunately, as our hopes are raised that she understands, Robinson wrongly concedes (p.44) that the competitive profit rate could fall provided $\delta Q/\delta$ capital falls fast enough. (I once suggested she correct this blemish in any new edition; but she had apparently forgotten the point and the slip remains in the *Essay*'s 1967 second edition.)

Conceding defects in Marx's analysis, we should not deny too much. Even in the most complicated Sraffa–Neumann model, when a stationary workforce goes from a non-golden-rule technology to a golden-rule equilibrium configuration, the rate of profit does have to fall (while, to be sure, the real-wage rate does rise). Reswitching does not vitiate this germ of truth concerning 'capital deepening'.

We can provide an out for Robinson if we suppose her not to be dealing with competition. Most of the Marx-Morishima relationships of M. Morishima (1973), like those of Piero Sraffa (1960), lose relevance and content if *constant returns to scale* is specifically denied. Early on (Robinson, 1942, p.4) she attributes to Marx the view that concentration of capital in ever larger concerns, forced on by the development of technique, turns the capitalists towards the anti-social practises of monopoly. The $c+v+s$ paradigms of Marx, Ricardo, and Sraffa never grapple with these increasing-returns analytical issues. Robinson (1942, pp.3–4) never explains why workers should be forced below their pre-capitalism real income levels by the following developments, which make no mention of land enclosures, of expropriations of peasants' capital, of profit rates elevated by capitalistic encroachments or by capital-favoring inventions. She writes:

> But the workers, who under the compulsion of capitalism produce the wealth, obtain no benefit from the increase in their productivity power. All the benefit accrues to the class of capitalists, for the efficiency of large-scale enterprise breaks down the competition of the peasant and craftsman, and reduces all who have not property enough to join the ranks of the capitalists to selling their labour for the mere means of existence.

Aside from the problem of reconciling this with history, as game theory it is primitive. It reminds me of a time when MIT graduate students listened with disdain to the claim of Professor Stephen Marglin of Harvard that the factories of the industrial revolution neither increased workers' productivity nor their real wages but served merely to render them more docile. Our von Neumann sophisticates found this hard to reconcile with the existence of a blocking collusion by workers who merely stay at home and buy raw materials at their unchanged competitive scarcity.

3 CONSTANT RETURNS?

Among Robinson's patron saints are Keynes, Kahn, Kalecki, and Sraffa. To Americans, Sraffa (1926) is one of several important articles of the mid-1920s that initiated the monopolistic competition revolution. To Joan it is the grand progenitor of that revolution. Two different themes are argued by Sraffa.

The first theme is substantive. Real-life firms do face sloped demand curves. They definitely cannot sell all the q they wish at some p that is named by the perfect-competition market. By incurring promotion and advertising costs, they can entice new customers and widen *their* market. By lowering their p, they may coax out some new q sales from consumers and divert some q sales from rival firms. All this is realistic – nearly trite. Marshall was, of course, aware of it; but he muddied the waters for his disciples by pretending that all this was still *competition* theory. Since these firms we are talking about can well enjoy declining marginal cost curves, Marshall persisted in the nonsense that decreasing MC phenomena – increasing returns to scale – were compatible with perfect competition. Sraffa (1926) in a common-sense way emphasizes that all this is imperfect and not perfect competition. Sraffa's task is well done. His Marshallian audience needed for him to do it. But there is nothing earthshaking or, by 1926, even original in this Sraffian message. All the treatises on industrial organization from the 1890s to 1930 took for granted what Sraffa was neatly expressing. J. M. Clark (1923) had tried to provide analytical insight concerning the breakdown of perfect competition, by invoking the economics of increasing-return-to-scale ('of overhead costs', Clark called it). Edward Chamberlin (1933), a pupil of the author Allyn Young (1928), never ceased to emphasize this technical returns background of product differentiation and oligopoly.

A youngster in his twenties does not gain Byronic fame and a life fellowship at a Cambridge college by polishing up a neat description of realistic markets. The second theme in Sraffa (1926) was the one that commanded the admiration of Keynes and readers of the *Economic Journal*. It is purely definitional and analytic, a first exercise in the history of economic thought – that area in which Sraffa's Ricardian studies were to win him imperishable fame.

This second Sraffian theme deals with what Marshall's partial equilibrium should 'really' have called for. Alfred Marshall, it will be recalled, was at the peak of his fame when he died in 1924. Two-thirds of a century later, after the Anglo-Saxon world had come to digest the contributions of Leon Walras, Knut Wicksell, and Irving Fisher, it is realized that Alfred Marshall's reputation – deservedly great – was overrated in the 1900–30 period. If the world excessively overvalued Marshall, Oxbridge outrageously treasured his writings. A. C. Pigou, as successor to Marshall's Cambridge chair, protected his memory like a watchdog (and, in consequence, Pigou's own great originality was never properly recognized).

J. H. Clapham, another Marshall pupil and an eminent economic historian, was the one who initiated the so-called 'cost controversy' that brought the Anglo-Saxon literary tradition almost up to where A. A. Cournot (1838) had arrived a century earlier. Clapham (1922) spoke of those 'Empty Economic Boxes': it was a scandal, he suggested, that economists could not empirically allocate industries to one or another of Marshall's box of (1) increasing-cost industries, (2) decreasing-cost industries, and (3) constant-cost industries.

Sraffa's second theme was the bombshell that the only category compatible with Marshallian partial-equilibrium analysis of competition was, after all, the constant-cost case. This Sraffian theme is simply wrong. But, as far as I can recall, no one has explicated the error of his reasoning and conclusion. Actually, Robinson (1941), an article that I mentioned earlier with admiration and which elicited praise from the hypercritical Jacob Viner,[4] lays out clearly how misled a reader of Sraffa (1926) would be to deny the existence of important competitive industries that produce under rising marginal costs.

Robinson (1941) demonstrates, without apparently ever connecting up its analysis with Sraffa (1926), that the box of increasing-cost competitive industry is indeed not an empty one.[5]

The writers that Sraffa knew well, Smith and Ricardo understood from the beginning that a shift of demand towards hill-grown wine and away from plain-grown rye would raise the price of wine (relative to the wage and the price of rye), a deviation from the 1926 presumption of horizontal *SS* supply curve. Ricardo was able to forget this two-factor-costs-in-price truth in favor of the erroneous doctrine that unit labor costs alone determine price ratios in a time-free system by the bogus device of supposing that he could get rid of the complication of rent by concentrating on production at the external margin of rent-free land. When Piero Sraffa came at last to write the introduction to his edition of Ricardo's *Principles*, Sraffa (1951, p.xxiii), I was incredulous to read that so sophisticated a mind blandly accepted this fatally flawed error of Ricardo: if Sraffa did not himself realize that *where the external margin falls is itself an endogenous variable dependent on consumers tastes for corn and services*, the scandal is all the greater. That the many solemn reviewers of Sraffa's great Ricardo edition pass over the matter in silence is further occasion for surprise.

An essay remembering Joan must inevitably involve remembering Piero, Nicky, Luigi, and many others. It is rewarding to discern in Sraffa's 1926 preoccupation with the constant-cost case (1) his nostalgia for the classical writers before and after Ricardo; (2) his lifelong interest in Marxian analysis;

and (3) a foreshadowing of his 1960 classic input–output model, which we know he began shortly after 1925 and resumed only in the 1950s after his long confinement with Ricardo's works had been relieved by the parturition of publication. Robinson held Sraffa uniquely in respect.

Where Joan's own work of the 1950s and 1960s is concerned her blueprint technologies of the *Accumulation of Capital* eschew the special complications involved in increasing-returns-to-scale technologies. Joan and Piero may not have much liked the Egypt of constant-returns-to-scale, but it was not vouchsafed for them to pass in their lifetimes into the Canaan of increasing returns to scale.[6]

4 PERSONALITIES

Until the end of World War II Joan Robinson was still a name in print to me. She was an admired authority but a little distrusted for her enthusiasms. My Harvard friend Sidney Alexander, who was just about Keynes's last tutee in Cambridge, passed on to me the aphorism he distilled from his King's College experience: 'To Joan everything is either absurdly simple or simply absurd.'

One reason I chose to go to Harvard for graduate work in 1935 was my admiration for Edward Chamberlin's *Theory of Monopolistic Competition* (1933). Taking his so-called advanced course in the fall of 1935 deflated my esteem for him. What completed the operation was his comment on the margin of the term paper I wrote for his course. It was a very good paper for the time – my fellow student Robert Triffin assured me of that. But what really browned me off was the fact that Chamberlin's only remark on my paper was a pencilled in 'Good' next to a paragraph in which, while criticizing some implicit theorizing in passages from Joan's *Economics of Imperfect Competition* (1933a), I referred to her cheaply as Madame Robinson.

For Americans of my time Joan Robinson was a fascinating figure. Women economists were rare enough. Great ones could be counted on one thumb. Once at the old Merle, the coffee shop across from Widener library where Schumpeter and the in-crowd of Harvard economics gathered for gossip, I asked Joseph Schumpeter: 'How old is Joan Robinson?' That wicked raconteur replied ungallantly: 'I am over 30. She is over 30.' (Actually he was then about 53, she 33.)

I went on rashly and in evident bad taste: 'Is Joan Violet pretty?' Schumpeter in his best mock-Viennese caddishness replied: 'Let me put it this way, my dear Samuelson. Joan Robinson is the kind of person one would kiss in an English garden.' I recount this childish tale of not-kiss-and-tell only because it involves scholars with a permanent niche in the pantheon of economic science. Underneath the veil of his Viennese gaiety, Schumpeter gave, I thought, an impression of sadness in those days of his widowerhood prior to his final marriage with Elizabeth Schumpeter, the American economic historian.

5 FACTOR–PRICE FLAP

When I wrote my obituary of Keynes, Samuelson (1946), Joan Robinson wrote to me to express her wonder that an outsider could have discerned so accurate a picture of the *General Theory*'s genesis. Our intense correspondence began, however, after my 1948 article on factor–price equalization appeared. Parallel with her epistolary dialogue, I carried on a separate discussion with Richard Kahn. (All British economists seemed to take time out in 1948 to object to factor–price equalization. Both A. C. Pigou and (Sir) Donald McDougall wrote refutations for the *Economic Journal*, which had reached the stage of galley proofs before being withdrawn by their authors.[7] Jan Tinbergen (1949), James Meade (1950), S. F. James and I. Pearce (1952), Roy Harrod (1958), and D. Gale and H. Nikaido (1965) were only some of the reactors to the 1948–9 factor-price papers.

One of the valid points I remember Robinson's letters dealing with went like this: for the case where both goods always involve the same factor proportions, free trade in goods can't prevent the region with higher labor/land endowments from enjoying higher real rents and lower real wage rates. Samuelson (1948) had only belatedly stressed the important axiom that food was to be *uniformly* more land-intensive than clothing; not until Samuelson (1949, pp.188, 192) was this key aspect of the syllogism sufficiently stressed.

The factor–prices incident gained in international interest because, during my autumn 1948 sojourn in London, Cambridge, and Oxford, Lionel Robbins as my dinner host at the Reform Club said: 'I think that Abba Lerner, when he was my LSE student around 1933, wrote a paper on factor–price equalization much like your 1948 *EJ* paper. And I think I can locate a copy in my files.'

Robbins' memory was accurate. And, since A. P. Lerner had forgotten completely that he had ever written such a paper, it was the happy chance that Robbins did have a file copy that made possible publication of the classic Lerner (1952), which beautifully paralleled my independent effort.

Lerner was not the only forgetful scholar. There appeared in his 1933 manuscript a footnote thanking Mrs J. Robinson for pointing out the failure of factor-price equalization in the singular case of identical factor intensities. Joan had quite forgotten all this and her mind generated fifteen years later in our correspondence the same logical objection that had occurred to her earlier. With the voracious memory that I had in those days, I found such Lerner and Robinson absentmindednesses astonishing.

When my Guggenheim fellowship finally brought me to King's College, I enjoyed the delicious privileges of the don in the *ancien régime*, living in the comfortable rooms of old Professor Reddaway (Brian's father, the expert in Polish history) and walking through the Backs conversing with Piero Sraffa. Richard Kahn was the gracious host who arranged all things. As Bursar of King's and Executor to Keynes' estate, Kahn kept me from starving in postwar Britain by his hospitality at the Cambridge Arts Theatre Restaurant. (A woman at a neighboring table, past the first bloom of youth, rather annoyed me by her loud chatter. Imagine my surprise when she rose to grasp Richard by his lapels and asked: 'Darling can I afford a new fur coat?' He nodded gravely and proceeded to puncture the bubble of scandal by introducing me to Lydia, Keynes's ballerina widow.)

The big evening came when I was invited to Kahn's rooms, as I thought to discuss factor–price equalization. It was to be a seminar *pour trois*, it seemed, when Joan Robinson appeared in what looked at first to be red-orange pyjamas, but which I worked out to be some kind of Indian jodhpurs that would have graced a Harvard academic processional.

After providing whisky and the only ice cubes then obtainable in the other Cambridge, Richard was not to be seen. When Joan began speaking of factor intensities, I dragged my heels, suggesting that we delay until Kahn's return. Finally, it dawned on me that this was to be a dialogue and not a threesome. Since Kahn's letters had been no less creative than Robinson's, I found such self-effacement remarkable. For a long time I was overly gullible to gratuitous gossipings that gave Richard Kahn enormous credit for good things that appeared under the signature of John Maynard Keynes and J. V. Robinson. The number of those who can testify cogently on this matter are, alas, shrinking.

In any case, we had a good talk. Since I was sitting with a poker hand containing four aces, the whisky tasted exceptionally good. Sure enough, at about 11 p.m., Richard Kahn returned with a fresh supply of ice cubes and the memorable evening came to an end.

A second time I missed my cue with Richard. He mentioned to me: 'I think if you were to go to Pigou's rooms around four tomorrow he'd be in.' Two days later, Kahn asked me why I hadn't kept my appointment with Pigou. Knowing how reclusive Pigou was reputed to be, I had not understood that a command was being given. The next day I did get admitted to the old rooms of Clapham where Pigou chose to live after his heart began to act up.

I recall Pigou as sitting in an old robe, and complaining that he was going gaga with age. Actually, he was a deal younger than I am now and I thought that the articles he couldn't stop writing were worthwhile in their own right. One foolish conversational gambit by me I have to report. Looking at the picture of a handsome young oarsman on Pigou's mantle, I asked fatuously, 'Is that Frank Ramsey?' 'Good God, no,' Pigou replied.

I am glad I got to Cambridge in its 1930–55 prime. That was something of a highwater mark, nipped if not in its bud then in its blossom, by the internecine warfare between the Kahn–Robinson–Sraffa–Kaldor and the Dennis Robertson factions. Richard Stone stayed aloof. Harry Johnson managed still to be on polite terms with both parties but it was a tightrope that impatient souls could not continue to walk. Observing life in Cambridge made me happy I had refused an earlier call to a chair in Chicago. I realized that the adversary procedure may possibly work for the law, but is an inefficient and unpleasant way of doing science. I've never changed my mind on this.

One last anecdote.[8] To josh Joan, I said we Americans took an unfair advantage over the English: we were able to read both English and American. She replied that one would want to benefit from the American literature but where in that vast terrain would one know where to begin? My mentioning of the *AER* exhausted this unprofitable topic.

6 AGNOSTICISM

Joan Robinson to the end of her life lacked a theory of the distribution of income. I do not say this lightly. It was a conclusion I resisted for many years. Yet, when I wanted to reproduce her verbatim views on the subject in a book of *Readings*, a search through all her writings – no mean task in itself – turned up no quotable passages, nor even brief ones.

I was therefore not surprised when I read Maurice Dobb's last book (Dobb, 1973), on theories of value and distribution, to see that he went to his grave regretfully conscious that it was impossible to specify how the shares of rent, profit, and wages were determined under capitalism; and *a fortiori* impossible to explain the Gini and Pareto statistics or the distribution of incomes among the poor and the rich.

Nicholas Kaldor, of course, differed in this respect from Joan. As his readers used to quip, in any month Kaldor had at least one theory of distribution. Similarly, readers were never in doubt about Luigi Pasinetti's neo-Keynesian model of distribution. Robinson did share with these authors Harrodian and Kaleckian macroidentities such as

natural growth rate = saving rate ÷ capital/output ratio
  = saving rate of capitalists × profit rate

But Robinson repeatedly insisted that golden-age exponential paths were only classroom idealizations with no possible real-life applications. And I can recall no writing in which she expressed agreement with Kaldor's mid-1950s infatuation with full-employment equilibrium and with the relevant view in Kaldor (1956) that Keynes's *Treatise* and not his *General Theory* was the great breakthrough.

For more than a century of history, each 1 per cent variation in nominal

GNP (or PQ) has involved about $\frac{1}{3}$ of 1 per cent change in P and a $\frac{2}{3}$ of 1 per cent change in Q: suppose Kaldor's model were realistic, in which autonomous change in investment alters the wage–profit shares of income just enough to evoke full-employment saving (from unthrifty workers and thrifty capitalists) of exactly enough to match whatever the autonomous investment is; then Q's percentage change should be virtually zero and P's change virtually 1 per cent. Curiously, just when President Eisenhower was enjoying three recessions within his two four-year terms, Dr Kaldor was proclaiming the demise of the business cycle and of underemployment equilibrium. Robinson sensibly refrained from joining in that waltz.

During the short segment that I could stand of Solow's debate with Joan Robinson at the 1970 World Econometric Congress in Cambridge, I did hear her commit herself to a definite theory of what determines a society's wage-share: it is the militancy of bargaining by the laboring class, through formal unions or otherwise, that can elevate real-wage rates and depress the aggregate of profits, she seemed to be saying on that occasion. I almost doubted the correctness of my hearing, because of my reluctance to attribute to so sophisticated a scholar so simple a view. But actually, in preparing this memoir, I note in Robinson (1965, pp.179–80), an earlier echo of this same bargaining-power theory, namely

> we find (1953) a low share of wages (corresponding to a high rate of exploitation) in manufacturing industry in countries like Cost Rica (less than 20%), Turkey (30%), Japan (40%) and a relatively higher share in Australia, Finland and UK (58%) and only slightly less in the USA (55%) ... [These] figures ... certainly suggest that the rate of exploitation depends far more upon the bargaining power of the workers than upon the rate of profit and the capital/labour ratio ...
>
> ... All this seems to justify Marx's conception that the rate of exploitation is a more fundamental relationship than the rate of profit.

If Joan believed that society obeys a Sraffa input – output model with but one possible set of techniques – fixed (a_{ij}) coefficients and fixed direct-labor coefficients $(a_{01} \ldots a_{0n})$ – then the interest rate could be anything from its maximum to zero, with the wage-share going from a zero share to a share of unity. This bargaining notion, however, does not so much answer a puzzle as create one. What was the purpose of her sheaf of blueprints in the *Accumulation of Capital* if not to deny the adequacy of a one-technique view of the world?

Momentary lapses into so narrow and special a view of fixed-coefficients would rationalize her simple view that, since existing capital is already here, its owners can safely be expropriated of any profit income the market accords it. However, if socialist societies can benefit from having more of a great variety of capital goods, that basic technological property ought to characterize capitalist and mixed economies. Not only is there the problem of motivating the expropriated capitalists to maintain existing capital goods intact, there is also a tremendous *informational* problem in every society. In the absence of markets, thousands of heterogeneous capital items will not get themselves, and keep getting themselves, rationed properly in an automatic way: effective technology can erode and disappear as well as be born.

If Robinson were to specify for a many-sector economy the many alternative blueprint activities that she herself envisages, most societies observed in history or nowadays are far from the golden-rule endowments of heterogeneous inputs that give a stationary population maximal *per capita* consumption. A zero rate of profit could not sustain the currently observed non-golden-rule vectors of inputs and outputs.

The positivity of competitive interest rates, with all that this implies for a wage-share of less than 100 per cent of national income, thus seems genuinely to be a result of scarcity of capital(s). Very poor regions are especially poorly endowed with the elements in their vectors of heterogeneous capital goods and of natural resources. That ought, one would think, to be cogently related to the gross inequalities of wage and property incomes that so often are reported in poor regions. In stressing this role of economic law, as against the role of economic power, I am, of course, cognizant of all the Sraffian complications. Reswitching can occur, so that a simple identification of more-roundabout, more-mechanized, more-time-intensive configurations with lower market interest rates is in general not valid.

To me, the facts of twentieth-century history, to say nothing of experience in earlier times, suggest how stubborn rather than loose are the market forces constraining what real wage gains can be secured by militant collusions to limit labor supplies. Thus, when the populist dictator Juan Perron tried many decades ago to raise wage rates quickly by 40 per cent, he did not succeed in materially raising the mean Argentine *real*-wage on a sustained basis. Inflation, unemployment, and other reactions to higher nominal wage rates characterized this and innumerable other similar incidents in history. No 1-technique Sraffa hypothesis could convincingly cover those facts of real life.

7 A SIMPLIFIED THOUGHT EXPERIMENT

At this point I am not arguing that Joan should take up with marginal-product notions of the simplest Clarkian type. My point can be made within the framework of a von Neumann–Sraffa technology where $\delta Q/\delta K$ coefficients are not everywhere definable for the system.

Let me begin with what may be called the case of *ultra-surrogate* capital. There are n sectors (perhaps n equals 100). Each produces a heterogeneous good to be consumed or used as an input in the many industries. To conserve space, I'll ignore the durability of the diverse inputs. Each industry may well have dozens of different techniques that convert direct-homogeneous-labor and the heterogeneous inputs into the respective goods: Robinson's book has many pages of blueprints, adjacent technologies being close to each other and spanning diverse input ratios for $(Q_{ij}/L_j, Q_{1j}/Q_{2j})$.

What makes my scenario a Santa Claus case of *ultra*-surrogate capital is the very special assumption that *all* industries are posited to happen to have *exactly the same choices of blueprints*. This is a much stronger and more special axiom than what is involved in Marx's case of 'equal organic compositions of capital(s)'. What makes the ultra simplification worth examining is that, despite the heterogeneity of the capital items themselves, and despite the lack of smooth differentiabilities of the production functions with the implied illegitimacy of marginal products and $\delta Q_i/\delta Q_{ij}$ terms, a Joan Robinson could find in the ultra-surrogate capital model a manageable supply and demand model of income distribution. Her bogey of a razor's edge for Harrod's model evaporates into something close to the Solow–Meade non-exponential growth paths. No neoclassical faking or cheating, of the kind that Robinson abhorred, is involved within the ultra rules of the game. Also, the complications of the Hahn Problem (Hahn, 1966) which Joan perceived as the problem of consistent expectations in a world not growing in balanced exponentials, are made manageable in this special Santa Claus case.

If Joan were given this ultra model as a Tripos problem, she could discern how it would develop under the Marx–Kalecki hypothesis that all profits are saved and all wages are consumed; or under the Harrod hypothesis of a constant fraction of all net income saved; or under a Kalecki–Harrod–Kaldor blend in which the constant fraction s_w of wages are saved and the constant fraction s_r of profits are saved; or under the oft-observed life-cycle saving patterns of Modigliani (1986).

The advantage of this model is that it can be regarded as neo-Keynesian rather than neoclassical. It will accommodate to post-Keynesian macroidentities while exhibiting a macrodistribution of income that is truly the resultant of all the micro-supply-and-demand relations of the separate markets. At the same time that Kalecki could apply his saving insights to the model, a Walras or Wicksell could do the same.

I shall describe only two scenarios of the model. In the Pasinetti (1962) 2-caste version, let caste 1 be non-workers who always save the positive fraction s_1 of their profit incomes. The rest belong to caste 2, people who both work and earn profit on their past saving: these people save the positive fraction s_2 of their net income from whatever source it may come.

Begin the *ultra* technology with society having sparse elements of every heterogeneous good, sparse relative to the existing labor force which we can take to be growing very slowly at the exponential rate $(1+g)^t$. Early on there could be labor redundancy and low imputed market real-wages; or, if low-

671

productivity direct-labor methods always exist, early on real-wages could be very low and the profit very high. Given early initial *per capita* capitals very sparse and several alternative techniques feasible, with the s_1 saving coefficient large, the ultra model will begin with the heterogeneous capitals growing faster than labor. In the ultra case, the profit rate falls and the real wage rises as capital(s) meaningfully 'deepen'. The process is slow and people understand it to be going on. In this stage the observed profit rate at the successive switch points reached can be considerably higher than g/s_1. If the profit rate, $r(t)$, should drop down to g/s_1 and if s_2 is less than s_1 times the wage-share of income at that profit level, the system could stay forever in a primal Pasinetti equilibrium with only widening of capital going on and both castes having wealth growing at the same $(1+g)^t$ rate.

If the profit rate g/s_1 brings for low g a wage-share such that $s_2 >$ (wage-share) times s_1, capital will continue to deepen because of caste 2 saving. Indeed, this could result in a profit rate that goes foolishly below the golden-rule of g and becomes even virtually zero.

What is the moral of the simple ultra scenario? It provides a case that can lack all neoclassical marginal products (or partial derivatives) and yet give for Robinson and Dobb a determinate supply-and-demand micro handle on distributive factor shares at *all* times – including the special long-run macro asymptotes that would hold if certain simple macro saving propensities could be validly hypothesized. In the ultra model, when effective labor supplies depart systematically from simple exponentials, the micro foundations of distribution still hold firm even when macro theories cease to apply.

Consider the gross facts of present-time experience. In the 1980s, there are no Harrodian natural rates of labor-supply growth that display constancies. But if we calculate approximate constants estimated for OECD nations, we find them to be little above zero. Demography is stagnant and post-OPEC productivity sluggish. At the same time, real interest rates are unprecedentedly high in the 1980s. I cannot glean much help from macrodistribution models to rationalize these trends. Robinson, while spurning micro models, seems to have done well to remain agnostic concerning post-Keynesian theories of distribution.

The second scenario for the ultra technology could be one that Cassel or Ramsey might have more interest in. Suppose we are all born into a clan that lives forever in unchanged population size. Suppose clan saving behavior acts to maximize the integral of all future utilities from final consumption, but with all future utilities systematically discounted at the subjective rate $(1+R)^{-t}$. Then even though there are no partial derivatives of the marginal-productivity type, the ultra system will have the following properties:

If it begins with sparse *per capita* stocks of heterogeneous capital goods, people will save: the deepening of capital thus induced lowers the objective own-rate-of-interest of the heterogeneous capital stock(s), $r(t)$, until as $t \to \infty$ we observe $r(t) \to R$ from above. Etc.

A similar but more complicated story holds when we drop the ultra-surrogate singularities and still deal with a von Neumann system whose alternative techniques are many but are still only finite in number. When Robinson decided no one could analyze non-steady states of capitalistic development, she abdicated from the only game in town – the one spelled out by economic history.

8 JOAN ROBINSON, LEFTIST

Superficially, but only superficially, Robinson was easy to classify. She rejected perfect-competition Hayekianism. She rebelled against Marshallian Say's-Lawism in favor of *General Theory* Keynesianism. She successively waxed enthusiastic about Stalin's Soviet Union; Mao's China; North Korea; Castro's Cuba; American students' new leftism.

The above paragraph fails to convey her independence of mind. Joan wore no man's collar (or woman's either). I once remarked to an old Cambridge hand that she must think well of another leftist scholar there. He corrected me: 'Oh no, she is contemptuous of him as a lackey of the Party Line.' I stood corrected.

A Polish scholar once volunteered to me: 'I love that woman. When she visited Poland all the brass turned out to give her the royal treatment. Replying to the toasts and fine words, she proceeded at once to the forbidden topic that all of us were thinking about, saying, "Why are we wasting our time on these matters when the workers in Posen are rebelling? What is the reason for that?" We young people revered her for that.'

By temperament Joan was, apparently, mercurial. I happened to be in Cambridge in the spring of 1952, on my way home from the famous Paris colloquium on risk. She had just returned from the Moscow conference orchestrated for scholars by Oskar Lange, by then a stalwart of the Polish apparatus.[9] Robinson was on a high. The return of a lost wallet with its currency gone but its papers intact was deemed by her evidence of a new spirit of mankind under (Stalin's) socialism. After Joan's enthusiastic lecture to a Cambridge audience on her Sydney-and-Beatrice-Webb visit to utopia, an undergraduate asked: 'But, what about the alleged plot of Jewish doctors to kill Joseph Stalin?' Robinson, no bigot, could only rebut with a *tu quoque*: 'And how about your lynchings in the South?'

Although she was no member of the Bloomsbury set, her reply to a *Commentary* survey on whether Britain should join the Common Market had echoes in it of E. M. Forster. Having more friends in the Third World than in Europe, she asked why then should she favor the move.

As far as I can recall, she never lost her heart to Albania. But it says something for her kindliness that she could, even momentarily, admire North Korean totalitarianism and take seriously allegations of 18 per cent per annum trends of real growth there. In her 1964 view, but for the black-out in South Korea of news of progress in the North, spontaneous immigration would explode from South to North!

At those times in the late 1950s when we now know the Great Leap Forward was being followed by the greatest economic distress – including famine that may have killed tens of millions of people – the testimony of her eyes told of bonny people in the streets. While criticisms of the cultural revolution were growing in the West, she told me pointedly that it would be good for sedentary professors to lead a more active life in the countryside.

Like my old teacher in Schumpeter's classroom, Paul Sweezy, Joan Robinson became successively disillusioned with the perversions of socialism perpetrated by the bureaucracies of Eastern Europe and elsewhere. 'True socialism' was her first and ever love, not the pretenders who took its name in vain.

Who is to say her value judgments were wrong, or other than noble? What I regret is the loss of her keen mind in helping understand and improve the trend of mixed capitalism. Reswitching captured and emasculated a whole generation of economists in East Anglia, Italy, and India. If only they could have spent six days of the week on researching the causes of stagflation, productivity slowdowns, and of waxing natural-resources fortunes, and only Mondays on input–output matrices!

I had Joan Robinson in mind when one edition of my *Economics* improved on John Morley's aphorism, 'Where it is a duty to worship the sun, the laws of heat will be ill understood.' The laws of heat will also be poorly understood where it is a duty to hate the sun.

Joan Robinson came to have a profound distaste for American society. She would have smiled grimly at Laski's quip: 'America is the only society that has managed to go from savagery to decadence without passing through civilization.'

Because it reflects an important strand in her thinking, I reproduce in its entirety the letter she wrote to my dear colleague, Harold A. Freeman, an eminent statistician who wrote in his retirement a 1979 book documenting the evils of American capitalism, *Towards Socialism*.

29 October 1979

Dear Professor Freeman

I was absolutely amazed that such a sensible book could be written in the Economics Department at MIT. How did you hit it off with Samuelson and company?

Your statement of the case is very clear, but the 'towards' seems rather Utopian! The obstacles now are formidable.

I thought perhaps that section 14 is too optimistic. It implies that once Socialism is installed people will become enlightened and cooperative, but Socialism, particularly in United States, will have to cope with a pro-

foundly corrupted society and a great deal of neurosis and sheer wickedness.
Wishing you the best success,
Yours
JOAN ROBINSON

9 WHAT THE CAPITAL CONTROVERSY TAUGHT ME

Onlookers like high drama. Controversy between the two Cambridges – with Joan Robinson against Robert Solow, or against Robert Solow and Paul Samuelson – captures economists' attention.

But then, after a time, the crowd's enthusiasm ebbs. The action moves elsewhere: to Friedman's monetarism versus Tobin's eclectic post-Keynesianism; or, to descend from the sublime to the ridiculous, radical-right supplyside economics grabs the limelight.

On one of Joan Robinson's return visits to Cambridge, Massachusetts, as she explicated the intricacies of Wicksell effects, one of the radical students stomped out of the room muttering loudly 'A plague on both your houses.' More serious researchers resolved their perplexities one way or another concerning the intricacies of time-phased systems and wanted to move on to new frontiers.

Joan Robinson complained of deaf adders who would not hear. I don't know whether she determined that I just could not understand her message, or whether she decided that perversely I chose to disregard it. For my part, I read all her writings and did not find the calculus of time-phased systems a transcendental mystery. That part of my work dealing with equilibrium paths of heterogeneous capital vectors I never expected her to read, any more than I expected my good friend and mentor, Alvin Hansen, to spend his sixth and seventh decades swotting the intermediate mathematics involved in my accelerator–multiplier models or in Richard Goodwin's autorelaxation limit cycles.

Something precious I gained from Robinson's work and that of her colleagues working in the Sraffian tradition. As I have described elsewhere, prior to 1952 when Joan began her last phase of capital research, I operated under an important misapprehension concerning the curvature properties of a general Fisher–von Neumann technology.

What I learned from Joan Robinson was more than she taught. I learned not that the general differentiable neoclassical model was special and wrong, but that a general neoclassical technology does not necessarily involve a higher steady-state output when the interest rate is lower. I had thought that such a property generalized from the simplest one-sector Ramsey–Solow parable to the most general Fisher case. That was a subtle error and, even before the 1960 Sraffa book on input-input, Joan Robinson's 1956 explora-

675

tions in *Accumulation of Capital* alerted me to the subtle complexities of general neoclassicism.

These complexities have naught to do with *finiteness* of the number of alternative activities, and naught to do with the phenomenon in which, to produce a good like steel you need directly or indirectly to use steel itself as an input. In other words, what is wrong and special in the simplest neoclassical or Austrian parables can be completely divorced from the basic critique of marginalism that Sraffa was ultimately aiming at when he began in the 1920s to compose his classic: Sraffa (1960). To drive home this fundamental truth, I shall illustrate with the most general Wicksell–Austrian case that involves time-phasing of labor with no production of any good by means of itself as a raw material.

As in the 1893–1906 works of Knut Wicksell, translated in Wicksell (1934, Volume I), let corn now be producible by combining (labor yesterday, labor day-before-yesterday, etc.):

$$Q_t = f(L_{t-1}, L_{t-2}, \ldots, L_{t-T}) = f(L) \tag{1}$$

$$Q = f(L_1, L_2, \ldots, L_T) \quad \text{in steady states} \tag{2}$$

$$= L_1 f(1, L_2/L_1, \ldots, L_T/L_1), \quad \text{1st°-homogeneous and concave} \tag{3}$$

$$= \sum_1^T L_j (\delta f(L)/\delta L_j), \quad \text{Euler's theorem} \tag{4}$$

$$\delta f/\delta L_j = f_j(L), \quad \delta^2 f/\delta L_i \delta L_j = f_{ij}(L) \quad \text{exist for } L \geq 0 \tag{5}$$

$$f_j > 0, \quad (z_1 \ldots z_T)[f_{ij}(L)](z_1, \ldots, z_T)' < 0 \text{ for } z_j \neq bL_j > 0 \tag{6}$$

Nothing could be more neoclassical than (1)–(6). *If* it obtained in the real world, a Sraffian critique could not get off the ground.

Yet it can involve (a) the qualitative phenomena much like 'reswitching', (b) so-called perverse 'Wicksell effects', (c) a locus between steady-state *per capita* consumption and the interest rate, a (i,c) locus, which is *not* necessarily monotonically negative once we get away from very low i rates. This cannot happen for the 2-period case where $T=2$. But for $T \geq 3$, all these 'pathologies' can occur, and there is really nothing pathological about them. No matter how much they occur, the marginal productivity doctrine does directly apply here to the general equilibrium solution of the problem of the distribution of income.

Remarks. What eternal verities do always obtain, even when corners in the technology make derivatives $[\delta Q_j/\delta L_j, \delta Q_j/\delta Q_{ij}]$ be somewhere undefined? Always, it remains true:

(a) To go from an initial sub-golden-rule steady state to a maintainable golden-rule steady state of maximal *per capita* consumption, must involve for

society *a transient sacrifice of current consumptions* ('waiting' or 'abstinence' à la Senior, Böhm, and Fisher!).
(b) For non-joint-product systems, there is a steady-state trade-off frontier between the interest rate and the real-wage (expressed in terms of any good).

This monotone relation between $(W/P_j, i)$ was obscurely glimpsed by Thünen and other classicists and by Wicksell and other neoclassicists. But the *factor-price trade-off frontier* did not explicitly surface in the modern literature until 1953, as in R. Sheppard (1953), P. Samuelson (1953), and D. Champernowne (1954). One can prove it to be well behaved for (1)–(3), or any convex-technology case, by modern duality theory. Before Robinson (1956), I wrongly took for granted that a similar monotone-decreasing relation between $(i, Q/\Sigma_1^T L_j)$ must also follow from mere concavity – just as does the relation $-\delta^2 C_{t+1}/(\delta C_t)^2 = \delta i_t/\delta C_t > 0$. But this blythe expectation is simply wrong! I refer readers to my summing up on reswitching: Samuelson (1966).

I realize that there are many economists who tired of Robinson's repeated critiques of capital theory as tedious and sterile naggings. I cannot agree. Beyond the effect of rallying the spirits of economists disliking the market order, these Robinson–Sraffa–Pasinetti–Garegnani contributions deepen our understanding of how a time-phased competitive microsystem works.

10 FINALE

The life of science is performed on a stage. The same actors come and go for a while. New scholars emerge. Each scholar someday drops out permanently.

Great scholars leave their mark on the drama of accumulated scholarship. Joan Robinson will be long remembered for her originality and breadth – and for the person she was.

Notes

1. During the bad McCarthy years of the 1950s, Joan Robinson once said to me: 'I understand it is a dangerous and reportable act to buy my *Essay* in a Washington, DC bookstore – even though the book is, after all, a critique of Marx!' My 1967 remark about Robinson as a friend had reference to Robinson (1965, pp.154–5): 'The prediction of "growing misery" for the workers under capitalism ... today has been obviously falsified. ... This error, like Jesus' belief that the world was shortly coming to an end, is so central to the whole doctrine, that it is hard to see how it could have been put afloat without it ... "You [workers] have nothing to lose but the prospect of a suburban home and a motor car" would not have been much of a slogan.'
2. See Robinson (1965, p.410) for '... there is one point on which I agree with him [Solow] – that the notion of factor allocation in conditions of perfect competi-

677

tion makes sense in a normative theory for a planned economy rather than in a descriptive theory for a capitalistic economy, and that the notion of the marginal productivity of investment makes sense in the context of socialist planning.'

3. Often one found in Robinson's writings prescient insights. Browsing through an early collection of her papers, I spotted what was essentially a statement of the Nonsubstitution Theorem.

4. J. Viner (1931) is the famous article in which the mathematical draftsman Y. K. Wong corrected Viner's boo-boo concerning the envelope to the U-shaped cost curves, insisting that Viner should make the envelope's slope negative where it touches tangentially the short-run Us that are still falling. In Viner (1931) there is the 'pure Ricardian case' – today often called the Jones–Samuelson or Ricardo–Viner–Samuelson–Jones case: in this case, each good requires transferable labor and a land specific to itself; here an expansion of demand for such a good (burgundy wine, for example) *must* raise its relative price – a clear negation of any Sraffian contention that only constant costs are truly compatible with perfect competition. Cf. Ronald Jones (1971) and Samuelson (1971a).

5. A close reading of Sraffa (1926) suggests a technical defence for Sraffa. The increasing-cost box, if not empty, is 'almost empty' in that the cases where it occurs are alleged to be unimportant. Will this wash? From the standpoint of the mathematical theory of what is generic and what is singular – of what is 'almost always' the case in the space of all possible (labor/output, land/output) coefficients, constant costs is the singular case that is as rare as Marx's configuration of 'equal organic compositions of capital'. Counsel for Sraffa can retreat to a different defensive tack: Sraffa is not so much denying the empirical relevance of competitive increasing costs, as he is pointing out the limitations of Marshall's *partial* equilibrium methodology. You might object: 'Outside East Anglia in the flapper age who cares all that much about Marshall's idiosyncratic constructs?' The answer is that we economists everywhere did take Marshall seriously in every respect; and so any cogent comment by Sraffa on the matter would indeed be important for the time. But, substantively, would a Sraffian claim be correct, that constant costs are appropriately handled by partial equilibrium paradigms while increasing costs are not? In its own right, the claim cannot be sustained. Increasing costs can be rigorously handled in certain special models by Marshallian-cross diagrams – as can be seen in Samuelson (1971b); and, conversely, it is not correct that the general constant-cost case can dispense with Walras–Pareto general–equilibrium methodology and be adequately handled by partial–equilibrium techniques. *Remark*: I have ignored completely the topic of 'externalities'. These can be important in their own right but they were red herrings that befuddled the post-Clapham polemics of the Marshallians.

6. Scholars more learned in the genesis of Marx's thought than I am will know that, when the young Marx was fumbling towards an understanding of economics, he entertained the notion of a normal price for a good around which its supply-and-demand oscillations would take place. At first he resisted, I am given to understand, the hypothesis that labor costs alone determined this normal level of price. Had he stayed in such a viewpoint, Marx would not only have been near to the Marshall to come (and the Walras!) but also would have been in general agreement with Smith's eclectic wage + rent + interest resolution of competitive price. Anti-Marxians and Marxians do not sufficiently realize how many tens of thousands of words Marx devoted to criticizing this Smithian 3-component resolution of price. Robinson (1965, p.12) reads Sraffa (1960) 180° backward: Sraffa's dated-labor resolution, which in matrix terms says

$P = Wa_0[I + a(1 + i) + a^2(1 + i)^2 + \ldots]$, is a vindication of Smith's value-added approach and not a 'rejection' of it. Paradoxically, Marx's Volume II tableau of reproduction, without his realizing it, gives the simultaneous-equation vindications for Smith's resolution: ignoring fine points connected with differences in sectors' organic composition of capital, in matrix terms it says $P(Q - aQ) = WL + i(PaQ) = Wa_0Q + i(PaQ)$, where by convention the wage is defined to be paid *post-factum*. It is trivial to add land and rent to this Smith-Sraffa system. V. Dmitriev (1898) was the first to dot the i and cross the t of this vindication of Smith.

7. Pigou amused Kahn by saying, 'Samuelson's argument, which seems to have more merit than I at first believed, should be vetted by a mathematician.' 'But', responded Kahn (somewhat generously), 'Samuelson is a mathematican.' To which, the sexagenarian Pigou replied, 'I mean a good British mathematician.'

The joke evolved into romance. The great A. W. Turing, of Turing-machine Godel-like fame, was a chess partner of Pigou and looked into the matter. He pointed out for me, correctly and usefully, that a vector transformation, $y = f(x)$, with everywhere one signed, $\det[f'(x)] \neq 0$, could have a multivalued inverse $f^{-1}(y)$ – as in the case of the complex-number equation(s) $e^x = 1$. All this led in the end to the Gale-Nikaido breakthrough on univalent functions – as in Gale-Nikaido (1965), L. W. McKenzie (1955, 1967), I. Pearce (1959, 1967), Samuelson (1949, 1953, 1967).

8. When I was introduced to Provost Sheppard of Kings, he inquired where I had come from. On learning that I had just been in Oxford, Sheppard replied: 'Quite proper. As the old Baedekker says: "Oxford and Cambridge – if time is short, skip Cambridge."'

At Oxford I lived in what was then called Halifax House, but which for a century had been an Anglican nunnery. Its walls had collected the frigidities of a full century and I was the coldest Yank in Britain. During my sojourn there double tragedies struck Oxford: Magdalen budgetary pinch cost it the waiting staff, and All Souls for the first time since the Middle Ages stopped brewing its own beer.

9. I believe no American accepted Lange's invitation, and seem to recall being told by Harvard's Edward Mason that he had refused at the suggestion of the State Department. The apolitical Herman Wold of Uppsala attended, grateful for the rare opportunity to meet again with the great mathematician Kolmogorov.

References

Bickerdike, C. F. (1920) 'The Instability of Foreign Exchange', *Economic Journal*, 30 (March): 118–22.
Chamberlin, E. H. (1933) *Theory of Monopolistic Competition* (Cambridge, Mass.: Harvard University Press).
Champernowne, D. G. (1954) 'The Production Function and the Theory of Capital: A Comment', *Review of Economic Studies*, 21(2): 112–35.
Clapham, J. H. (1922) 'Of Empty Boxes', *Economic Journal* 32 (September): 305–14.
Clark, J. M. (1923) *Studies in the Economics of Overhead Costs* (Chicago: University of Chicago Press).
Cournot, A. A. (1838) *Researches into the Mathematical Theory of Wealth*. English translation (1897).
Dmitriev, V. (1898, 1902, 1974) *Economic Essays on Value, Competition, and Utility* (London: Cambridge University Press).

Dobb, M. H. (1973) *Theories of Value and Distribution Since Adam Smith* (Cambridge: Cambridge University Press).
Freeman, H. A. (1979) *Toward Socialism in America* (Cambridge, Mass.: Schenkman).
Gale, D. and H. Nikaido (1965) 'The Jacobian Matrix and Global Univalence of Mappings', *Mathematische Annalen*, Bd. 159 (Heft 2): 81–93.
Hahn, F. H. (1966) 'Equilibrium Dynamics with Heterogeneous Capital Goods', *Quarterly Journal of Economics*, 80 (November): 633–46.
Harrod, R. F. (1958) 'Factor–Price Relations under Free Trade', *Economic Journal*, 68 (June): 245–55.
James, S. F. and I. F. Pearce (1952) 'The Factor–Price Equalisation Myth', *Review of Economic Studies*, 19(2): 111–20.
Jones, R. W. (1971) 'A Three-Factor Model in Theory, Trade and History', in *Trade, Balance of Payments and Growth*, J. N. Bhagwati *et al.* (eds) (Amsterdam: North-Holland), pp.3–21.
Kaldor, N. (1956) 'Alternative Theories of Distribution', *Review of Economic Studies*, 23(2): 83–100.
Lerner, A. P. (1952) 'Factor Prices and International Trade', *Economica*, 19 (February): 1–15.
Marx, K. (1867, 1885, 1894) *Capital.* Vols. I, II, III. (Hamburg: Verlag von Otto Meissner).
McKenzie, L. W. (1955) 'Equality of Factor Prices in World Trade', *Econometrica*, 23 (July): 239–57.
McKenzie, L. W. (1967) 'The Inversion of Cost Functions: A Counterexample', *International Economic Review* 8 (October): 271–85.
Meade, J. E. (1950) 'The Equalisation of Factor Prices: The Two-Country Two-Factor Three-Product Case', *Metroeconomica*, 2 (December): 129–33.
Modigliani, F. (1986) 'Life Cycle, Individual Thrift, and the Wealth of Nations', *American Economic Review*, 76(3) (June): 297–313.
Morishima, M. (1973) *Marx's Economics: A Dual Theory of Value and Growth* (Cambridge: Cambridge University Press).
Pasinetti, L. (1962) 'Rate of Profit and Income Distribution in Relation to the Rate of Economic Growth', *Review of Economic Studies*, 29 (October): 267–79.
Pearce, I. (1959) 'A Further Note on Factor-Commodity Price Relationships', *Economic Journal*, 69 (December): 725–32.
Pearce, I. (1967) 'More About Factor Price Equalization', *International Economic Review*, 8 (October): 255–70.
Robinson, J. (1933a) *Economics of Imperfect Competition* (London: Macmillan).
Robinson, J. (1933b) 'The Theory of Money and the Analysis of Output', *Review of Economic Studies*, 1 (October): 22–6.
Robinson, J. (1937) *Essays in the Theory of Employment* (London: Macmillan).
Robinson, J. (1941) 'Rising Supply Price', *Economica*, NS 8 (February): 1–8. Also *Collected Economic Papers*, Vol. II (Oxford: Blackwell).
Robinson, J. (1942) *An Essay on Marxian Analysis* (London: Macmillan).
Robinson, J. (1952) *The Rate of Interest and Other Essays* (London: Macmillan).
Robinson, J. (1956) *The Accumulation of Capital* (London: Macmillan).
Robinson, J. (1965) *Collected Economic Papers*, Vol. III (Oxford: Blackwell).
Samuelson, P. A. (1946) 'Lord Keynes and the General Theory', *Econometrica*, 14 (July): 187–200. Also (1966) chapter 114 in Vol. 2 of *Collected Scientific Papers of Paul A. Samuelson* (Cambridge, Mass.: MIT Press).
Samuelson, P. A. (1948) 'International Trade and the Equalisation of Factor Prices', *Economic Journal*, 58 (June): 163–84. Also (1966) chapter 67 in Vol. 2 of *Collected Scientific Papers of Paul A. Samuelson* (Cambridge, Mass.: MIT Press).

Samuelson, P. A. (1949) 'International Factor–Price Equalisation Once Again', *Economic Journal*, 59 (June): 181–97. Also (1966) chapter 68 in Vol. 2 of *Collected Scientific Papers of Paul A. Samuelson* (Cambridge, Mass.: MIT Press).

Samuelson, P. A. (1953) 'Prices of Factors and Goods in General Equilibrium', *Review of Economic Studies*, 21(1): 1–20. Also (1966) chapter 70 in Vol. 2 of *Collected Scientific Papers of Paul A. Samuelson* (Cambridge, Mass.: MIT Press).

Samuelson, P. A. (1967) 'Marxian Economics as Economics', *American Economic Review*, 57 (May): 616–23. Also (1972) chapter 152 in Vol. 3 of *Collected Scientific Papers of Paul A. Samuelson* (Cambridge, Mass.: MIT Press).

Samuelson, P. A. (1971a) 'Ohlin Was Right', *Swedish Journal of Economics*, 73(4) (December): 365–84. Also (1977) chapter 254 in Vol. 4 of *Collected Scientific Papers of Paul A. Samuelson* (Cambridge, Mass.: MIT Press).

Samuelson, P. A. (1971b) 'An Exact Hume–Ricardo–Marshall Model of International Trade', *Journal of International Economics*, 1 (February): 1–17. Also (1972) chapter 162 in Vol. 3 of *Collected Scientific Papers of Paul A. Samuelson* (Cambridge, Mass.: MIT Press).

Sheppard, R. W. (1953) *Cost and Production Functions* (Princeton NJ: Princeton University Press).

Sraffa, P. (1926) 'The Laws of Returns under Competitive Conditions', *Economic Journal*, 36 (December): 535–50.

Sraffa, P. (1951) (ed.), *The Works and Correspondence of David Ricardo*. Vol. I, *On the Principles of Political Economy and Taxation* (Cambridge: Cambridge University Press).

Sraffa, P. (1960) *Production of Commodities by Means of Commodities* (Cambridge: Cambridge University Press).

Steedman, I. (1977) *Marx after Sraffa* (London: NLB; also (1981) London: Verso).

Stolper, W. F. and P. A. Samuelson (1941) 'Protection and Real Wages', *Review of Economic Studies*, 9 (November): 58–73.

Tinbergen, J. (1949) 'The Equalisation of Factor Prices Between Free-Trade Areas', *Metroeconomica*, 1 (April): 39–47.

Viner, J. (1931) 'Cost Curves and Supply Curves', *Zeitschrift für Nationalökonomie*, 3, 23–46, reprinted (1959) in *The Long View and the Short*, J. Viner (Glencoe, Il.: The Free Press).

Wicksell, K. (1893–1906) *Lectures on Political Economy*, Vol. 1 *General Theory*. English translation (1934) (New York: Macmillan).

Young, Allyn (1928) 'Increasing Returns and Economic Progress', *Economic Journal*, 38 (December): 527–42.

THE FITNESS MAXIMIZED BY THE CLASSICAL CANONICAL ECONOMY: A THEME FROM HOUTHAKKER AND R.A. FISHER

PAUL A. SAMUELSON
Massachusetts Institute of Technology
77 Massachusetts Avenue, E52-383C
Cambridge, Massachusetts 02139
U.S.A.

ABSTRACT. Stimulated by a 1956 biology paper of Hendrik Houthakker that mentions the R.A. Fisher paradox in which allegedly a species ever grows in fitness up to the instant of its extinction, I here define a new fitness function for classical economics, namely the system's Virtual Rent. Using my 1978 Canonical Classical Growth Model (for a subsistence-wage-and-subsistence-profit-rate system), I specify for it a Liapunov function of Virtual Rent that is shown to necessarily increase on each growth trajectory. No paradoxes are entailed, since *exogenous* shocks are permitted to raise or lower Rent.

1. Portrait of a Scholar

Originality, depth, and versatility --those are the marks of a master scholar. Hendrik Houthakker started off with a bang: A big bang. Reckoning stages of life in fractions of a century -- as I have come to do -- this young and unknown Dutchman resolved a long-standing challenge before he reached his second quarter century. Houthakker (1950) proved that the Strong Axiom of Revealed Preference -- whereby no chain of situations could occur in which "B was revealed to be worse than A, C revealed to be worse than D,...Z to be worse than Y, and yet A showed itself worse than Z" -- did indeed suffice to rule out non-integrability of preferences.

In England, if you were a Triple First at Oxbridge, no matter if afterwards you remained a curate in remote Devon, your reputation was made for life. So it is for the first scholar to prove the ergodic theorem or, heaven forbid, refute the Riemann hypothesis. Hendrik Houthakker, however, could not stop at the beginning and keep creativity down. Avoiding the well-trodden paths, he has again and again struck out in his chosen directions. I have particularly admired his theoretical and empirical pioneering, with James Tobin, in the analysis of postwar rationing [Houthakker and Tobin (1951, 1952)]. It was his *Econometrica* formulation of duality theory for demand under constraint that reawoke my fascination with that topic [Houthakker (1960), Samuelson (1953, 1960, 1965)]. Even old subjects like Ricardian comparative advantage and Purchasing-Power-Parity reflect with new lights from his pen [Houthakker (1962, 1976; 1978)]. And of course there are his important researches on normal backwardation in commodities futures, on durable-goods demand, and on energy scarcity.

L. Phlips and L.D. Taylor (eds.), *Aggregation, Consumption and Trade*, 9–19.
© 1992 Kluwer Academic Publishers. Printed in the Netherlands.

I peruse hundreds of scientific articles, benefitting from almost all of them -- a remarkable testament to the cleanness of refereeing in economics, and an agreeable contrast with the sad tales about plagiarism and experimental fraud in contemporaneous areas of biological research. But rarely do I consciously envy a paper, wishing that I might have conceived it. Houthakker is one of the narrow circle of writers who especially captures my admiration, which is all the more remarkable in that I am ideologically usually more of a bleeding-heart liberal than he is. An instance is Houthakker (1955), in which he analyzes a production model that involves fixed coefficients at every point in space but whose envelope-integrals reproduce for totals of inputs and output smooth relations of the neoclassical type. [All this is an original development of Ricardo's model of land economics, and is in the same spirit as the paradigm of Bensusan Butt (1960) in macro growth theory.]

No need to go on with unfaint praises. As homage to Houthakker, I want to pick up on a sentence of his that I read in a working paper he gave at a summer Stanford workshop in Tokyo of the 1950s. The paper was on evolution and antedated the post-sociobiology fads among economists. See Houthakker (1956) for what I believe is the final draft of the Japanese working paper.

The words that caught my eye are found in Houthakker (1956, p. 186):

> ...biologists tend to use the word "advantage" quite freely, and usually in the sense of something which promotes survival. This may easily lead to paradoxical results; thus R.A. Fisher [1930] in his *Genetical Theory of Natural Selection* maintains that evolution leads to an increase in fitness, which he defines as the chances of survival, from which it follows, oddly enough, that a species has the best chance of survival just before it becomes extinct.

The last view, attributed to Fisher, did seem to me paradoxical. After 1970, when the Swedish Royal Academy of Sciences bestowed on me the illusion of omniscience and infallibility, I determined to study enough biology to master Fisher's "Fundamental Theorem on Natural Selection," which its founder (1930, p.39) modestly equates with the Second Law of Thermodynamics, each holding "supreme position" (respectively in the biological sciences and among the laws of [physical] nature). I should confess at the beginning that Fisher's exposition is so non-optimal as to leave his interpreters in disagreement as to what he meant by his Fundamental Law. (Indeed, the distinguished geneticist James F. Crow confided to me that, only *before* he understood Fisher, did he regard the theorem as *fundamental*.)

There is no way that I could, in limited space, give economist readers any feel for Fisher's so-called Fundamental theorem. It will suffice if I relegate to a footnote one trivial instance of it,[1] and merely sum up its relevance for the present purpose as follows:

Fisher (1930) and Sewall Wright (1971) sometimes can analyze the differential equations of genetic demography with the help of Liapunov-like functions:

(1a) $$dx_j/dt = f^j(x_1,...,x_n), \quad j = 1,2,...,n,$$

where the f^j functions are such that there exists a non-negative Liapunov $L(x_1,...,x_n)$ function such that

(1b) $$dL(x_1,...,x_n)/dt = \sum_j [\partial L(x_1,...,x_n)/\partial x_j] f^j(x_1,...,x_n) < 0$$

(1c) $$L(x_1,...,x_n) = 0 \text{ only for } (x_1^*,...,x_n^*), \text{ the root of}$$

$$\partial L(x_1,...,x_n)/\partial x_j = 0, \; j = 1,...,n$$

and of

(1d) $$f^j(x_1,...,x_n) = 0,$$

so that

(1e) $$\lim_{t \to \infty}[x_j(t), L(t)] = [x_j^*, 0].$$

Actually, Fisher has not even fabricated a genuine paradox concerning fitness's growing until just before the species goes poof and disappears. If the above system refers to n=6 and ecological equilibrium between the number of genotypes of two diploid species, what destroys the old x^* equilibrium is some new exogenous mutation or some new exogenous change in the environment: After such a perturbation, any possible *old* relation between genetic variance and growth in fitness is impulsively abrogated -- leaving no paradox and only the malaise of an obscurely written treatise.

---

[1] Imagine two subsets of a species, each growing at exponential rates a_1 and a_2: $a_1 > a_2$, $N(t) = \sum_1^2 (c_j e^{a_j t})$. Then Fisherine "fitness" is defined as $N'(t)/N(t) = m(t) = \sum_1^2 (c_j e^{a_j t}) a_j / N(t) =$ Mean <a's>. By tautological differentiation,

$$m'(t) = \left[\sum_1^3 (c_j e^{a_j t}) a_j^2 / N(t)\right] - \left[\sum_1^2 (c_j e^{a_j t}) a_{ij} / N(t)\right]^2$$
$$= \text{Var} \langle a\text{'s}\rangle$$

The equality of the Change in Total Growth Rate to the Variance of the Part's Growth Rates is trivial next to the Second Law of Thermodynamics and, in this form, doesn't even involve biology! See Nagylaki (1991) for more meaningful versions of Fisherine selection.

My present analysis discovers exactly what it is that the classical canonical growth model of Ricardo -- and of Smith, Mill, and Marx -- can be conceived of as maximizing. As these writers dimly glimpsed, some variant of land rent is maximized in such a subsistence-wage-and-subsistence-profit model. Here our mathematics pins down precisely what definition of "rent" is teleologically made a maximum by the classical behavior equations, both (1) *ultimately* after any technical innovation or any change in saving and procreating parameters and (2) *at every time instant* during the transition period to long-run equilibrium.

The novelty is in identifying and specifying the existent Liapunov function for which the canonical classical dynamical paths are gradient climbing motions.

2. What the Classical System Maximizes

When Columbia University celebrated its Two-Hundredth birthday in 1954, Sir Dennis Robertson spoke from the text: "What Does the Economist Economize?" Few guessed in advance that the Robertsonian minimand was Love, which being so rare needed to be husbanded so preciously.

Smith and Ricardo were hardheaded sons of the Enlightenment with DNA that runneth not over in sentimentality. Their shared growth paradigm did however act as if to maximize something. One of the virtues of the *canonical classical growth model* (of Samuelson, 1978) was that it encapsulated the core common to Smith, Ricardo, Mill, and Marx [as Samuel Hollander (1980, 1987) has extensively documented]. As a further virtue, the canonical classical model is shown here to identify just how the old notion -- that technological progress and supply adjustments of population and capital act teleologically to maximize "total rent" -- needs to be sharpened to the *maximization in both the longest run* and also *in the transitions to equilibrium* of "Virtual Rent as total product left over after the factors of labor and capital were to be paid their equilibrium real subsistence wage and profit rates." (The *exact* wording is vital.)

It will shorten the exposition if we contemplate classical subsistence-wage of labor and classical subsistence-profit-rate grafted on to a regular 3-factor technology of post-1848 type. Motivated readers can duplicate *all* of the present qualitative features in a discrete-activities technology of the von Neumann and Sraffa type that early writers could handle by numerical examples. (What is special about the present model is its restriction to the axiom that there exists but a *single* producible good that can serve as an input.)

3. The Canonical Growth Model

Assume a homogeneous land of fixed positive supply, $\overline{T}$. Assume a homogeneous labor supply of L; the growth rate of population is dL/dt or $\dot{L}$. The supply of the produced good is K, with net investment or capital accumulation of dK/dt or $\dot{K}$.

The totals of the three factors, $(\overline{T},L,K)$ or (V_0,V_1,V_2), produce society's output(s), which includes both a consumption good like corn and net capital formation like $\dot{K}$ or $\dot{V}_2$. In inessential aggregation à la Ramsey (1928), we write

(2) $\qquad$ consumption + net c.f. = $C + \dot{V}_2 = Q(\overline{V}_0, V_1, V_2)$.

685

The real return of land is rent, written as R or w_0. The real wage of labor is w_1. The rate of profit (or of interest, they are the same *sans* uncertainty) is w_2. Both a 1776 Smith and a 1900 Wicksell would expect a factor's return of w_i to be depressed when its supply of V_i is higher. How does a change in V_j affect the w_i return of V_i? The 1900 answer would be more definite and catholic than the answer of 1776, 1817, 1848, or 1867. By this century economists realize that more V_0 of land could possibly *lower* labor's w_1 wage if land and labor, instead of being "complementary", were "competing factors"; and so forth for any one i and j pairing of the three factors. Classical writers seem implicitly to assume all three factors to be complements. More labor tilling the same corn acres are supposed to induce higher land rent of w_0; when doses of capital and labor have more acres to work on, their composite return goes up; the w_1 wage could be forced way down if needed capital is short enough in supply; etc. Actually though, there are plenty of passages in the classic texts where horses and men are strongly competitive in their factor returns, and the same can occur for land and produced goods. Here I therefore admit all feasible patterns of complementarity. See Samuelson (1991) for a modern version of the canonical model.

What is peculiarly *non*-neoclassical is the following subsistence-driven supplies of V_1 and V_2, with $dV_i/dt = \dot{V}_i$ each being a function of $w_i - \bar{w}_i$ deviations, the differences between market returns and needed subsistence returns specifiable as $(\bar{w}_1, \bar{w}_2)$,

(3a) $$\dot{V}_i / V_i = g_i f_i[w_i - \bar{w}_i], \quad i = 1,2$$

(3b) $$g_i > 0, \ f_i[0] = 0, \ f_i'[0] = 1 \text{ by convention}$$

(3c) $$f_i'[x] > 0 \text{ so that } x f_i[x] > 0 \text{ for } x \neq 0.$$

(3c)'s final sign-preservng property for $f_j[x]$ and x is vital for what is to come; g_1 and g_2 are parameters relevant to speeds of dynamic adjustments.

Adjoining to (2) and (3) a 1900 Wicksellian 3-factor marginal-product paradigm, we write

(4a) $$w_i = \partial Q(\bar{V}_0, V_1, V_2)/\partial V_i = Q_i(\bar{V}_0, V_1, V_2), \quad i = 1,2$$

(4b) $$w_0 = \left[Q(\bar{V}_0, V_1, V_2) - \sum_1^2 w_j Q_j(\bar{V}_0, V_1, V_2) \right] / \bar{V}_0.$$

Rent as a classical residual is given in (4b), in the classical Ricardian fashion. Constant returns to scale implies

(5a) $$Q(\bar{V}_0, V_1, V_2) \equiv \bar{V}_0 Q(1, V_1/\bar{V}_0, V_2/\bar{V}_0).$$

I assume $Q(1, V_1, V_2)$ is to be strictly concave in (V_1, V_2), twice differentiable, strictly-monotone-increasing, with $Q_i(1, V_1, V_2) \to \infty$ as $V_i \to 0$, and $Q_i \to 0$ as $V_i \to \infty$. These regularity conditions suffice to make the relations of (4) uniquely invertible in the positive orthant

14

(5b) $$0 < (V_0\ V_1\ V_2) \longleftrightarrow (w_0\ w_1\ w_2) = 0.$$

Substituting (4) into (3) gives us two differential equations in the two unknowns, $(V_1\ V_2)$.

(6a) $$\dot{V}_i/V_i = g_i f_i [Q_i(\bar{V}_0, V_1, V_2) - \bar{w}_i], \quad i = 1,2.$$

The sole stationary point of this dynamical system must occur at $(V_1^*\ V_2^*)$, the unique vector root of the stationary maximum conditions:

(6b) $$Q_i(\bar{V}_0, V_1, V_2) - \bar{w}_i = 0, \quad i = 1,2.$$

The following global stability property will be proved for (6):

Theorem:

(a) From any positive initial $(V_1^0\ V_2^0)$, the canonical classical system of (6) will, under our stipulated assumptions, converge asymptotically to the unique equilibrium state that maximizes Virtual Rent,

(7a) $$L(\bar{V}_0, V_1, V_2) = Q(\bar{V}_0, V_1, V_2) - \sum_1^2 \bar{w}_j V_j.$$

Thus

(7b) $$\lim_{t \to \infty} [L\ V_1\ V_2\ w_1\ w_2\ w_0] = [\text{Max} L\ V_1^*\ V_2^*\ \bar{w}_1\ \bar{w}_2\ w_0^*],$$

where

$$\underset{V_1, V_2}{\text{Max} L} = \underset{V_1, V_2}{\text{Max}} [Q(\bar{V}_0, V_1, V_2) - \sum_1^2 \bar{w}_j V_j],$$

(7c) $$= Q(\bar{V}_0, V_1^*, V_2^*) - \sum_1^2 \bar{w}_j V_j^*,$$

where $(V_1^*\ V_2^*)$ is the unique vector root of

(7d) $$\partial Q(\bar{V}_0, V_1, V_2)/\partial V_i = \bar{w}_i, \quad i = 1,2$$

and

$$w_0^* = \left[Q(\bar{V}_0, V_1^*, V_2^*) - \sum_1^2 \bar{w}_j V_j^*\right]/\bar{V}_0$$

(7e) $$= [\text{Max} L]/\bar{V}_0.$$

(b) A technological innovation that is mandatorily viable in the long run must, in the canonical subsistence model, create a higher Long-run Rent, $L^* = \text{MaxL}$ than in the status quo ante. The viable innovation may raise or lower total real wages, raise or lower total real profits, raise or lower output Q^*, raise or lower long-run V_1^* or V_2^*. [Ricardo was right in asserting that new machinery could depress Q^* and depress Labor*, even though his neoclassical critics, egged on by Wicksell, denied this prior to 1988! See Samuelson (1988, 1989).]

(c) Along the transitional path to the new $(V_1^* \; V_2^*)$ rendezvous called for by any once-and-for-all innovation, Virtual Rent (but not necessarily *actual* short-term Rent) is constantly rising. (In this sense, Virtual Rent is so to speak a measure of Darwinian "fitness" that Darwinian competition ever maximizes in the canonical model -- a subtlety apparently not hitherto noticed. Once the Darwinian adjustment has been fully realized, a new technological shock will without paradox lead to a new climbing path toward a new MaxL.)

Lest any reader suppose this theorem to be a mere tautology not requiring proof, or to be an obvious banality, one must realize that modifying the classical hypothesis about a subsistence wage rate in the direction of *neoclassical exogeneity of the population supply* would demote Rent from its classical primacy and would permit a viable innovation to raise or lower rent and lower real returns of any subset of factors. With ingenuity new Darwinian fitnesses might be formulated for neoclassical models of generality, but the worth of the whole game depends on whether the contrived description has a natural simplicity that improves our description and understanding of the specified system.

That a unique long-run equilibrium obtains for $(V_1^* \; V_2^*)$ follows from (5)'s strong curvature properties specified for the production function Q. That L^* is indeed Maximized (long-run) Rent follows from (4)'s marginal-product interpretation of competitive pricing. (In a discrete technology, the proof is more intricate.)

To prove the long-run comparative dynamics of (b), I can cite the basic factor-price-tradeoff theorem of Samuelson (1975), which asserts that, in the absence of joint products, a time-phased competitive system will have for each profit rate a *convex* trade-off relation between all real factor returns of primary factors (land, labor,..), whatever be the good used as *numeraire*:

(8) $\quad\quad\quad\quad T(w_1, w_2 ..., w_n) + w_0 = 0,$

where $\partial T/\partial w_i > 0$ and T is a *quasi*-concave function.[2] In the present case of a continuous-time 1-produced good formulation, T by duality theory must more specially be a strongly *concave* function. For n+1=3 and $(w_1 \; w_2)$ frozen at their long-run subsistence levels, $(\bar{w}_1 \; \bar{w}_2)$,

---

[2] Morishima (1989, p. 72 *ff.*), gives a non-optimal account of my writings on Marx and on Ricardo, where this theorem is concerned. When Marx deals with competitive models where labor is the only primary factor, I was right to insist that he could not validly have simultaneously a Law of Declining Rate of Profit and a law of immiserating real wage rate. Where Ricardo deals with *two* primary factors, labor and land, I have been right to assert that any two of $(w_0 \; w_1 \; w_2)$ could fall in time.

to viably force its way into long-run existence an innovation must shift $T(\bar{w}_1,\bar{w}_2)$ upward, thereby indeed raising w_0^*. *QED.*

To prove the novel result of (c), namely that dL/dt is positive on a transitional climb of the canonical fitness hill, we calculate

$$dL/dt = \sum_1^2 [\partial L(\bar{V}_0,V_1,V_2)/\partial V_j]\dot{V}_j$$

(9)
$$= \sum_1^2 [w_j-\bar{w}_j]g_jf_j[w_j-\bar{w}_j]V_j > 0 \text{ by (3b) unless } (w_j) = (\bar{w}_j). \text{ QED.}$$

Figure 1 sketches how the global convergence to equilibrium cannot involve spiral convergence corresponding to complex characteristic roots of the system's locally-linear approximant. The quasi-circular contours of Virtual Rent define the top of the hill at E. The paths of approach to E must cut those rent contours in a quasi-perpendicular, or quasi-transversal, fashion. Actually, the paths off aEa' must swerve penultimately toward the "turnpike path" AEA', defined by the system's least-negative real latent root in the locality of equilibrium.

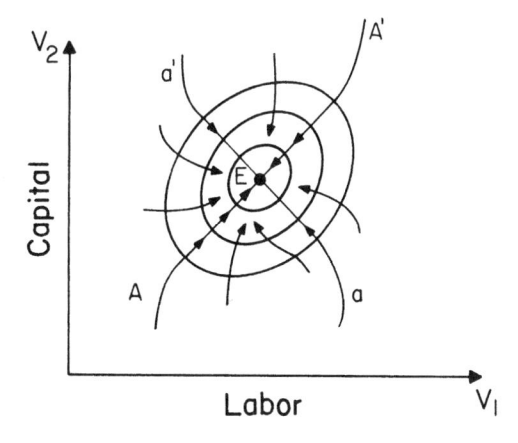

Figure 1. Dynamic "Rent" Growth

Remark: If we reverse the classical writer's presumption that labor and capital are "complements", and make them "rivals," the diagram will go through a mirror-like reorientation that makes AEA' a curve running northwestward rather than northeastward.

I must conclude with a warning. Actual rent, $w_0(t)$, can diminish in the short run even though Virtual Rent must always increase. This subtlety eluded the classical writers and, I fear, modern commentators on them.

Here is an example. Let some temporary shock start the system off with a surfeit of both $(V_1\ V_2)$. Then $\dot{w}_0$ of rent begins above w_0^* equilibrium. As $(V_1\ V_2)$ both fall, $w_0(t)$ falls. QED. (How to reconcile this with an ever-rising Virtual Rent? Rent differs from Virtual Rent by the expression $\sum_1^2 [\bar{w}_j - w_j(t)]V_j(t)$. Since both factors in each of these terms begin as declining, this sum drops more than L rises.) Here is another, similar, example. Science derives an invention that strongly favors land. Rent has immediately risen, while $(w_1\ w_2)$ have immediately fallen. The ensuing drops in both $(V_1\ V_2)$ take away some of the first rise in w_0. Warning: new w_0^* cannot end up *below* the prior w_0^*. If you plot the new contour of (8)'s $T(w_1,w_2)$, for the old w_0^*, it will have shifted outward; when the old $(\bar{w}_1,\bar{w}_2)$ point is reattained, it will now fall on a contour of (new w_0^*) that is greater than the (old w_0^*). QED.

Acknowledgments

For editorial assistance I owe thanks to Janice Murray, and for partial support to my Gordon Y Billard Post-doctoral Fellowship at the MIT Sloan School of Management.

I have appended to the list of References various relevant citations from earlier writings. It is gratifying that the techniques of more than half a century ago, in *Foundations* (1947, 1983) and elsewhere, should have applied so neatly to the present problem. Also, in Samuelson (1991), there is an elaboration of the comparative statics and dynamics of the classical canonical growth model, a task that would seem overdue in view of the non-optimal state of the classical literature and of the present-day commentaries on it.

REFERENCES

Butt, D.M. Bensusan (1960), **On Economic Growth: An Essay in Pure Theory**, Oxford University Press, London.

Crow, James F. and Kimura, Motoo (1970), **An Introduction to Population Genetics Theory**, Harper and Row Publishers, New York.

Fisher, R.A. (1930), **Genetical Theory of Natural Selection**, The Clarendon Press, Oxford; see particularly chapter 2.

Hollander, Samuel (1980), 'On Professor Samuelson's Canonical Model of Political Economy', *Journal of Economic Literature*, Vol. 18, 559-74.

Hollander, Samuel (1987), **Classical Economics**, Basil Blackwell, Oxford.

Houthakker, Hendrik (1950), 'Revealed preference and the utility function', *Economica*, New Series, Vol. 17, 159-74.

Houthakker, Hendrik and James Tobin (1951), 'The effects of rationing on demand elasticities', *Review of Economic Studies*, Vol. 18, 140-53.

Houthakker, Hendrik and James Tobin (1952), 'Estimates of the free demand for rationed foodstuff', *Economic Journal*, Vol. 62, 103-18.

Houthakker, Hendrik (1955), 'The Pareto distribution and the Cobb-Douglas production function in activity analysis', *Review of Economic Studies*, Vol. 23, 27-31.

Houthakker, Hendrol (1956), 'Economics and biology: specialization and speciation', *Kyklos*, Vol. 9, 181-87.

Houthakker, Hendrik (1962), 'Exchange Rate Adjustment', *Factors Affecting the United States Balance of Payments*, U.S. Joint Economic Committee, Washington, D.C.

Houthakker, Hendrik (1976), 'The Calculation of Bilateral Trade Patterns in a Ricardian Model with Intermediate Products and Barriers to Trade', *Journal of International Economics*, Vol. 6, 251-88.

Houthakker, Hendrik (1978), 'Purchasing Power Parity as an Approximation to the Equilibrium Exchange Ratio', *Economics Letters*, Vol. 1, 71-75.

Morishima, Michio (1989), **Ricardo's Economics: A General Equilibrium Theory of Distribution and Growth**, Cambridge University Press, Cambridge, U.K.

Nagylaki, Thomas (1991), 'Error bounds for the fundamental and secondary theorems of natural selection', *Proceedings of the National Academy of Science*, 88, 2402-06.

Robertson, Dennis H. (1955), 'What Does the Economist Economize?' in Robert Lekatchman (ed.), **National Policy for Economic Welfare at Home and Abroad**, Doubleday & Co., Garden City, N.J.

Samuelson, Paul A. (1938), 'A note on the pure theory of consumer's behavior', *Economica* New Series Vol. 5, 61-71.

Samuelson, Paul A. (1947, 1983), **Foundations of Economic Analysis**, Harvard University Press, Cambridge, Massachusetts.

Samuelson, Paul A. (1953), 'Prices of Goods and Factors in General Equillibrium', *Review of Economic Studies*, XXI(1), 54, 1-20. Reproduced as Chapter 70 in *The Collected Scientific Papers of Paul A. Samuelson*, Vol. 1, 1966, The MIT Press, Cambridge, Massachusetts.

Samuelson, Paul A. (1960), 'Structure of a Minimum Equilibrium System' in Ralph W. Pfouts, ed., *Essays in Economics and Econometrics: A Volume in Honor of Harold Hotelling*, University of North Carolina Press, Chapel Hill, pp. 1-33. Reproduced as Chapter 44 in *The Collected Scientific Papers of Paul A. Samuelson*, Vol. 1, 1966, The MIT Press, Cambridge, Massachusetts.

Samuelson, Paul A. (1965), 'Using Full Duality to Show that Simultaneously Additive Direct and Indirect Utilities Implies Unitary Price Elasticity of Demand', *Econometrica*, Vol. 33, 4, 781-96. Reproduced as Chapter 134 in **The Collected Scientific Papers of** Paul A. Samuelson, Vol. 3, 1972, The MIT Press, Cambridge, Massachusetts.

Samuelson, Paul A. (1975), 'Trade Pattern Reversals in Time-Phased Ricardian Systems and Intertemporal Efficiency', *Journal of International Economics*, 5, 309-63; see particularly p. 342 *ff*. Reproduced as Chapter 251 in **The Collected Scientific Papers of** Paul A. Samuelson, Vol. 4, 1977, The MIT Press, Cambridge, Massachusetts.

Samuelson, Paul A. (1978), 'The Canonical Classical Model of Political Economy', *Journal of Economic Literature*, 16, 1415-34. Reproduced as Chapter 340 in **The Collected Scientific Papers of** Paul A. Samuelson, Vol. 5, 1986, The MIT Press, Cambridge, Massachusetts.

Samuelson, Paul A. (1980), 'Noise and Signals in Debates Among Classical Economists: A Reply', *Journal of Economic Literature*, 18, 575-78. Reproduced as Chapter 341 in **The Collected Scientific Papers of** Paul A. Samuelson, Vol. 5, 1986, The MIT Press, Cambridge, Massachusetts.

Samuelson, Paul A. (1988), 'Mathematical Vindication of Ricardo on Machinery', *Journal of Political Economy*, Vol. 96, 274-82.

Samuelson, Paul A. (1989), 'Ricardo Was Right', *Scandinavian Journal of Economics*, Vol. 91, 47-62.

Samuelson, Paul A. (1991), 'The Classical Canonical Model in Modern Garb: Comparative Statics and Dynamics', unpublished working paper, Massachusetts Institute of Technology, Cambridge, Massachusetts.

Wright, Sewall (1977), **Evolution and the Genetics of Populations, Volume 3, Experimental Results and Evolutionary Deductions**, The University of Chicago Press, Chicago.

LEONTIEF'S 'THE ECONOMY AS A CIRCULAR FLOW': AN INTRODUCTION

PAUL A. SAMUELSON

It was Wassily Leontief who said that a scientist's first work, like a person's first love, is of key importance. However, in his own case, Leontief has never grown old; and having been incredibly precocious, Leontief's beginnings must be traced back to adolescence and childhood in Petersburg, Petrograd and Leningrad. Still the scientist is his major work, and this translation of Leontief's 1928 *The Economy as a Circular Flow* sounds the first note of the overture to his *Ring* of Input–Output.

A 22-year-old, working in Kiel but out of the Berlin stable of Bortkiewicz, Wassily labored on his own. Except for perfunctory references to Irving Fisher, Jevons and Böhm-Bawerk, he seems not even to have mentioned such obvious works as Quesnay's *Tableau Economique,* Marx's Tableaux of Steady and Expanded Reproduction (appearing in *Capital's* little-studied Volume 2 of 1885), or the virtually unknown 1898 Russian essay of Dmitriev with its vindication of Adam Smith's resolution of all income into the values-added of wages, land rents and profit–interest. Of course he did not refer—nor could he have before 1960—to the tentative researches, then being done in Cambridge by 30-year-old Piero Sraffa, on the intricacies of production of commodities by means of commodities.

A historian of science like Robert K. Merton, knowing about Newton and Leibniz and about Darwin and Wallace, would expect that somewhere a Leontief and a Sraffa would be *independently* discovering at about the same time the theory of input–output.[1] If Wassily did not know Piero in 1928, Piero did not know Wassily. What is more interesting—and it tells us much about the two personalities—in the half century that followed neither one seems ever to have referred explicitly by name to the other. The tub of genius stands on its own bottom!

A new embryo contains the future organism, but not even the most discerning eye can see in the constellation of early cells the beautiful baby that is to come. Reviewing the present translation, one sees a considerable gap between it and the 1936 paper my Harvard teacher published in the *Review of Economics and*

Address: Massachussets Institute of Technology, Cambridge, MA, USA.

[1] Neither Leontief nor Sraffa knew that, in 1928, the 24-year-old John von Neumann was perfecting his model of a two-person zero-sum game—a model whose duality and saddlepoint properties pointed him toward his general equilibrium growth model (of 1932, 1937 and 1945) with its considerable overlap with input–output and linear programming analysis. As Merton knows, good things in science often come in threes.

Statistics. (Since Wassily, like Joseph Schumpeter, rarely lectured at Harvard on his own current researches, I had to learn about input–output on my own—much as I had to puzzle out for myself Schumpeter's curious 1911 theory about the necessity of a zero interest rate in circular-flow equilibrium *sans* developmental innovations.)

This 1928 maiden voyage includes nothing in its ballast of what has always been a hallmark of Leontief's research: nothing of manageable empirical measurement. No mother would be confused between her baby gorilla and yonder baby chimpanzee. In embryo, when all mammals begin superficially alike, the resemblance is much greater. Therefore, the Sraffian paradigms that remained forever innocent of empirical investigation started out more closely resembling the 1928 Leontief formulations than did the ultimate 1960 classic, *The Production of Commodities by Commodities*. Oddly, the 1928 non-mathematical Italian began more with algebra and formal mathematics than did the *wunderkind* of mathematical economics. The present article contains no matrix, much less a determinant. It is, so to speak, primarily taxonomic and topological. The pioneer is carving out a new language, prior to composing a scientific poem in that language. Directed arrows connect points A, B, C and D with each other, depicting flows of cash or more basically the temporal production of outputs from earlier-time application of inputs. The coal needed last period to make this period's coal was preceded by the smaller fractional total of day-before-yesterday's coal needed for yesterday's coal—and so on in what is implicitly a converging geometric progression of scalar or matrix type. What in 1958 Dorfman–Samuelson–Solow dubbed Leontief–Cornfield and Gaitskill infinite series are already glimpsed in 1928 by the bold pioneer. The formal cases of Perron–Frobenius non-negative matrices that are or are not *decomposable* and *cyclic* are sketched with a broad brush. The blackboard is prepared for the time-phased production functions, in which output of a good at time $t + 1$ depends on inputs at time t of labor, and of different raw materials and produced factors (including, possibly, input of the good itself). To make his model empirically identifiable, Leontief approximated reality by the special assumption of a single set of techniques (fixed technical coefficients of labor a_{0j} and of produced inputs a_{ij}) and by aggregation into at first a dozen sectors and ultimately into several hundred.

The rest is history. Indicative planning for peacetime reconversion. Planning for growth and development. Estimating the impacts of OPEC energy shocks. These and scores of similar policy applications and econometric measurements have been the harvests of Leontief's research groups at Harvard, the US Bureau of Labor Statistics and at NYU (well into his ninth decade of life!).

The public at large thank Wassily Leontief for his Nobel-class research findings. The guild of professional economists blesses him for his brilliant, deep and many scientific breakthroughs. His pupils, colleagues and friends appreciate Wassily Leontief for his creative productivity, serene integrity and generous kindnesses. By shear good luck I met my Master young and have coasted along ever since on the impulse of his wisdom and knowledge.

REFERENCES

DORFMAN, R. SAMUELSON, P. and SOLOW, R. (1958). *Linear Programming and Economic Analysis.* McGraw-Hill, New York.

DMITRIEV, V. K. (1898). 'The Theory of Value of David Ricardo', in D. M. Nuti (ed.), *Economic Essays on Value, Competition and Utility.* Cambridge University Press, London.

LEONTIEF, W. W. (1928). 'The Economy as a Circular Flow', *Archiv für Sozialwissenschaft und Sozialpolitik,* **60,** 577–623.

—— (1936). 'Quantitative Input and Output Relations in the Economic System of the United States', *Review of Economics and Statistics,* **18,** 105–25.

—— (1941). *The Structure of the American Economy, 1919–1929.* Harvard University Press, Cambridge, MA. The 1951 Oxford University Press second edition is an expanded version.

MARX, K. (1885). *Capital.* Volume 2.

QUESNAY, F. (1758). *Tableau Oeconomique* (so-called 'first edition' as reproduced and translated in Appendix A of Kuczynski and Meek, 1972, *Quesnay's Tableau Economique.* Macmillan, London).

SRAFFA, P. (1960). *Production of Commodities by Means of Commodities.* Cambridge University Press, Cambridge.

VON NEUMANN, J. (1928). 'Zur Theorie der Gesellschaftsspiele', *Math. Annalen,* **100,** 295–320.

—— and MORGENSTERN, O. (1964). *The Theory of Games and Economic Behavior.* John Wiley, New York.

12

Homage to Chakravarty: thoughts on his lumping Schumpeter with Marx to define a paradigm alternative to mainstream growth theories

Paul A. Samuelson

Sukhamoy Chakravarty was a great economist. I did not write "a great *Indian* economist," but of course he was one of the giants of his Indian generation. Alas, considerable as were his published contributions to economic science, we must feel that fate deprived us of the full potential that his friends and colleagues believed him capable of.

Here are a few reasons for our regrets. First, bad health limited both his life span and the fullness of his activities. This was not all loss: when John Maynard Keynes's health would turn bad in the 1930s, he would be forced to spend more of his time at Cambridge University and his scientific output thereby benefited; similarly Chakravarty's temptations to depart from contemplative scholarship may have lessened in consequence of chronic hypertension. Still, on a net basis, bad health must have deprived us of Chakravarty's potential contribution much as was the case with the brilliant Lloyd Metzler after his tragic brain tumor in 1951.

Second, Chakravarty as an Indian patriot was drafted into government service at the highest level as a member of planning commissions and as personal advisor to Prime Ministers Indira Gandhi and

Rajiv Gandhi. One of the purposes of effective economic science is to provide counsel for society. But, as testified by the descent of Swedish economics from the transcendental heights of Wicksell, Cassel, Heckscher, Ohlin, Myrdal, Lindahl, Svennilson, and Lundberg to its latter day excellence, the creative advance of political economy as a discipline is hampered by concentration over extended periods of time on public and commercial activities. That involves living off capital. It is worse than that. A high advisor must be a team player, arguing against a mixed bag of policies behind shut doors but closing ranks and being circumspect in public utterances and in scientific publications. The economic policies in India, all agree as they look back upon the history, have not been so sophisticated and sage as to require no misgivings. Warren Hastings said in self-defense when accused of nonoptimal governing in India: "When I consider my opportunities, I marvel at my moderation." A brain truster for Indian governments of recent decades sometimes must have recourse to lame arguments that political feasibility had been such that policies actually promulgated were the best the political traffic could then bear. And always there is the insidious danger that one's paradigms may get bent toward fashions that turn out to be losers in the Darwinian jungle of economic science. Did Chakravarty bet on the wrong trends in political economy of the last half of the twentieth century?

A third handicap possibly limiting Chakravarty's realization of his full potential stems from his being confined in most of the last three decades largely to India itself, some thousands of miles away from the strong European and North American centers of lively economic advance. As with Trevor Swan in Australia and Hirofumi Uzawa in Japan, Chakravarty had plenty of the solitude that makes for originality. But too much of that good thing, experience shows in economics and in other disciplines, can lead to a lack of direct participation in frontier debate and critical interchange.

A Ramanujan blessed with good health and accommodated to Saville Row tweeds – can we doubt? – would have produced more mathematics of genius at Oxbridge in the 1913–19 years than the actual scholar of history was able to. The great astrophysicist, S. Chandrasekhar, never returned permanently to India after leaving it at age 20 in 1930. He had good offers; but, comparing conditions for serene research, he decided to stay at the University of Chicago. The revealed preferences of Bhagwati, Sen, Srinivasan, and others of

697

Chakravarty's generation to accept permanent appointments in the West have similarly helped world science at India's expense. And it has at the same time contributed to their own research accomplishment. Chakravarty chose to forgo such opportunity. Perhaps this partially explains why some of his writings of the 1980s bear resemblance to topics and treatments of earlier days.

Here I shall concentrate on Chakravarty's R. C. Dutt Lectures on Political Economy, which are too little known in the West (see Chakravarty, 1982). They bear the provocative title *Alternative Approaches to a Theory of Economic Growth: Marx, Marshall and Schumpeter*. Peculiarly in the India of colonial days and of early independence, a Laski-like popularity of chic Fabianism prevailed. This is not a trend for me to deplore. The world does not particularly need local Friedrich Hayeks and Milton Friedmans on every subcontinent. Since Sukhamoy Chakravarty was so deep and sage a mind, we can benefit by appraising critically his notions for alternatives to mainstream economics. Here is a selective paraphrase of characteristic interpretations in Chakravarty (1982) and other writings late in life.

1 He contrasts two main systems of growth and development. First there is the mainstream viewpoint associated with J. S. Mill and Alfred Marshall. Second there is the alternative analysis stemming from Marx and Schumpeter. Both of these have as common ancestors the classical models of Adam Smith and David Ricardo. This classical trunk is described as bifurcated into the branches of Mill and of Marx.

2 Chakravarty, while respecting useful elements in the mainstream branch, pretty clearly wishes to defend the alternative branch in these current years when planning has become a dirty word and when the ideology of *laissez faire* has been making a strong comeback.

3 He is distinctive in picking Mill as the first of the mainstream writers, removing him from the usual classical trio of Smith–Ricardo–Mill and using Mill rather than the neoclassical triad of Jevons–Menger–Walras as the Abraham of the modern mainstream genealogy. Also Chakravarty is distinctive in selecting Marshall as the prototype of neoclassical growth theorists rather than naming a committee of Knut Wicksell, Eugen von Böhm-Bawerk, J. B. Clark,

Homage to Chakravarty

and Vilfredo Pareto to represent the neoclassical school. Chakravarty realizes that he is being idiosyncratic in giving Joseph Schumpeter pride of place beside Karl Marx, and knows he must argue his contention before his Marxian contemporaries. And, I would add, before the mainstream crowd.

4 At this point it is worth enumerating some of the features Chakravarty approves of in the Marxian paradigm.

(a) Marx, both in Hegelian and non-Hegelian terms, has a theory in which change from *laissez faire* capitalism is a natural expectation. Although Chakravarty points out explicitly that Marx has no clear-cut unambiguous paradigm of the collapse of capitalism, Marx does specify important aspects purporting to explain the laws of motion of the mid-nineteenth-century economy.

(b) Chakravarty cites with approval Marx's basic notion of a "surplus" as characterizing the mode of production in the bourgeois society. Exploitation of non-capital-owning labor by the capitalist owners of capital is regarded as a central feature of capitalism's evolution. *Capital*'s 1867 paradigm of *surplus value* (*mehrwert*), which an analyst like me dismisses as a gratuitous detour into unrealism and a swamp of *non sequiturs*, seems to be regarded more favorably by Chakravarty. (In many of his writings defensive of the general philosophy of planning that pervaded the Indian programs of his time, Chakravarty deplores the pressures holding down real wages in the market guided takeoffs espoused for Korea, Taiwan, Singapore, Hong Kong, or Chile by economists like Peter Bauer, Ann Krueger, Hia Myint, and even Ian Little. By contrast, despite their imperfections, the prescriptions for a democracy like India by P. C. Mahalanobis, Charles Bettelheim, Nicholas Kaldor, and other deviates from the mainstream are well tolerated by Chakravarty.

(c) Although Keynes himself receives little explicit attention in the Dutt Lectures, Chakravarty values in Marx an appreciation of the "realization problem" that capitalism must sometimes face. Keynes, Malthus, Sismondi, Rodbertus, Rosa Luxemburg, Hobson, and other under-consumptionists are by no means in perfect agreement with Marx's views on the subject. But neither is Marx in perfect agreement with J. B. Say, James Mill, [Robert Lucas,] and neoclassical believers in a version of Say's law that insists upon the impossibility of a problem of general overpro-

699

duction and of unmaintainable full employment. As will be seen, although Chakravarty attempts to link up Schumpeter and Marx in various dynamic respects, he admits that Schumpeter is more a devotee of full employment economics than Marx is – and Chakravarty clearly lauds Marx for his difference in this regard.

Why "Mill–Marshall"?

Generally, wherever Chakravarty refers to a Mill–Marshall conventional approach, I find myself substituting for it a "mainstream" approach. This is not a matter of importance but it deserves some discussion.

John Stuart Mill used to be underrated as merely an eclectic expositor of the doctrines original with Smith and Ricardo. Marx naturally denounced Mill as a vulgar bourgeois economist. Mill and Marx were contemporaries and Marx was hard on all contemporaries – Mill, Proudhon, Rodbertus, Lasalle. . . . Had mastoid infection spared David to live three extra decades after 1823, one suspects Ricardo would have cut a less favorable figure in Karl's writings. Jevons also had his phobia against Mill. Even Marshall, who mathematized Mill, disliked Mill's feminist sympathies. And Schumpeter, characteristically, patronized Mill for his competence – much as he patronized Smith and Marshall.

Today we know better: Mill and Smith rise in the esteem of connoisseurs as Ricardo's over-blown shares fall on the bourse of antiquarians' rankings. Whatever excellence Mill is guilty of, he cannot be convicted of being neoclassical in the fashion of Gossen, Jevons, Menger, Walras, Wicksteed, Fisher, and Wicksell. Chakravarty may be right that Mill does not give increasing returns the emphasis that Smith did or that Bertil Ohlin and Allyn Young were to do. But in this respect Mill shows no retreat from Ricardo. Moreover, the passages in Marx that hint of monopoly formation as capitalism ripens and decays, they are quite distinct from Marx's theoretical analyses bearing on *mehrwert* equalization versus profit-rate equalization, on the transformation problem, on the tableaux of reproduction, on the laws of decline in the rate of profit, or on the immiseration of wage earners.

My own reading of the classicals – Smith, Malthus, Ricardo, Mill, Marx[1] – found in them essentially one and the same canonical model of growth (see Samuelson, 1978). Where Mill is not identical with Ricardo, he is not inferior. And the same can be said in comparing Mill with Marx.

During the nineteenth century that saw world population double and European population quadruple while life expectancies and real wage rates rose, the time was overripe for a *post*-Mill² bifurcation that would jettison the near-empty and out-moded classical paradigm of "*subsistence* real wages." I suppose agreement with this would require Chakravarty to replace his dichotomy of Mill–Marshall and Marx–Schumpeter with the dichotomy of mainstream economists versus Marx–NeoKeynes–Sraffa economics.

I am only half done with my carping. A teacher in India of Chakravarty's earliest teachers would naturally think of Alfred Marshall as the quintessential mainstream economist. (So, in lesser degree, would the teachers of my American teachers.) But for thirty-five years now Marshall has been old hat. Nor was he ever much on growth theory as such. An Englishman like John Hicks was much more influenced by Wicksell than by Marshall and it is laughable to explain this away by Hicks's LSE residence. The juvenilia of Marshall in J. K. Whitaker (1975) were not remarkable, compared with writings by other contemporaries, in their treating population and technology trends as largely exogenous and in their emphasis on the need to divert resources from current consumption to capital formation tangible and human.

Where does Schumpeter belong?

If I had to give two names to *mainstream* growth theory, I suppose that I might select instead of Mill–Marshall names like Wicksell–Schumpeter or Kuznets–Solow. This leaves Sukhamoy and Paul jousting over which side of the grand-bifurcation line Schumpeter is to be found.

My principal task in the present chapter will be to conduct with the shade of Chakravarty a respectful debate concerning where Schumpeter does fit into the picture. As one of the diminishing tribe of surviving Schumpeter pupils, I owe it to the memories both of Chakravarty and of Schumpeter to record my judgments on the proposed linking of Schumpeter with Marx.

And now is the time to provide this fresh evaluation of Schumpeter's schema when Robert Loring Allen (1991) and Richard Swedberg (1991a,b) have provided us with fresh biographical material from Schumpeter's own diaries. My guess that the 52-year-old Schumpeter I first met in 1935, for all his gaiety and bravado, was a sad person is more than confirmed; indeed the diaries reveal him to have been a seriously depressed personality under the surface. And although he made no bones about his conservatism in politics, I don't think that any of us realized quite how conservative he really was at heart – a finding that cuts for me rather than for Chakravarty. Schumpeter went along with the popular belief that the mass of people are led by wishful thinking into expecting to happen what they *want* to happen. But as I have noticed in life, among sophisticated people like Schumpeter, all goes into reverse: what they would hate to have happen, they paranoidly expect to happen. Schumpeter's views about the inevitability of socialism reflected in part a shallow understanding of American politics – as, for example, in his stimulating and provocating *Capitalism, Socialism and Democracy* (1942). Schumpeter's hatred of Franklin Roosevelt – and his fear of Roosevelt – bordered on the pathologic.

Of all the points I shall try to make in this chapter, I believe the most important one is this:

> It is a grave misinterpretation to link Schumpeter together with Marx, either as forming a paradigm that is an alternative to mainstream paradigms of Mill–Marshall and others (Hayek, Solow, Samuelson, Debreu, . . .) or as being *two scholars who truly share basic insights*.

I am of course aware that Schumpeter has in many places articulated words of praise and admiration for Karl Marx. But I and other of his students found this puzzling since in neither his lectures nor his writings could we identify the reasons for this admiration. It would be an evasion for us to write it all off as typical Schumpeterian empty praise – as when he would introduce to Harvard audiences with flowery compliments the Mises he looked down on and the Hayek whom he considered overvalued. Somehow his respect for Marx was more long-lasting and seemed genuinely sincere. Despite repeated investigations I never could find the answer to the puzzle.[3] Indeed in the end the evidential record requires me to conclude that, even if under hypnosis Schumpeter were to insist on the genuineness of his admiration for Marx, careful comparison of how the two writers would interpret dozens of different questions and processes will reveal that Schumpeter's answers are 180° different from Marx's – and the differences are generally precisely those differences that neoclassical pedants have with Marxian writers. Pragmatically what counts is not a scholar's rhetoric but rather his substantive hypotheses and descriptions.

Let me contemplate one such issue. Chakravarty (1982, pp. 14–15, 23–4, 40, n. 10) correctly makes much of Marx's qualms about Say's law and the inevitability of full employment. And he does not fail to notice certain ambiguities if not self-contradictions in Marx concerning this matter: under-consumptionists like Rodbertus are chided by Marx, and Marx's own Tableaux of (Expanded) Reproduction accommodate continued saving by capitalists without disturbance to equilibrium; on the other hand, Marx does speak derisively of the childish babble about Say's law, and worries much about cyclical breakdowns in the "realization" process. Schumpeter, as Chakravarty himself points out, was essentially a full employment economist – an anti-Keynesian even before there was the 1936 *General Theory*. Only compare the contradictory reactions of Marx and Schumpeter to Ricardo's belated sections on machinery and its likely harm to wage earners!

If two prophets differ on each essential doctrine of theology, how can they be lumped together as being of the same religion? Chakravarty concentrates on what he perceives to be their common dynamic vision. But is it the *same* dynamic vision? Newton had his mechanics. Aristotle had his mechanics. I would never speak of an Aristotle–Newton paradigm if Aristotle believed that a cannonball needed new pushes to keep flying while Newton believed that new pushes would only serve to accelerate or decelerate its continued motion. There is only one night sky, but Ptolemy and Copernicus are not one. Marx believed that capitalism's contradictions would somehow entail its demise and cause it ultimately to be succeeded by communism. Schumpeter believed the capitalistic system to be *economically stable*: between bursts of innovation it had a rendezvous with a circular-flow equilibrium (involving a zero interest rate); but quasi-endogenously caused clusters of innovation, amplified by a money-creating banking system, will constantly engineer economic growth and development (generating unavoidable business cycles that, often, unnecessarily overshoot and engender unnecessary waves of unemployment and inflation).

Schumpeter's theory of an inevitable progression from capitalism to socialism *is not based on his economics but rather on his sociology*, according to which the very successes of rational capitalism will undermine the irrational feudal traditions that might forestall its decline.

Schumpeter's essential brief is an apologetics for Walras–Mill economics once it is made to be dynamic – not an indictment.

My final summing up finds Marx essentially lacking in a cogent model that helps explain the inequality of capitalism and the laws of motion of the economic system. But what we may call his innuendo about the future of capitalistic dynamics undoubtedly constitutes in his eyes and those of his followers an indictment of mainstream economics (1840–84, and by extrapolation 1885–1992). By contrast Schumpeter admires and commends what markets accomplish, statically and dynamically.

I ought to add my considered opinion that, although Schumpeter's differs from Marx's unsatisfactory dynamics, his own different dynamics is also fundamentally flawed. This is not the place to document in detail this damning verdict but here are a few suggestive hints.

1 As argued in Samuelson (1981), by the trick of defining capitalism too narrowly and socialism too broadly, Schumpeter achieves the empty accomplishment of an almost tautological deduction that capitalism must die and be succeeded by socialism. Events since his death in 1950 quite disconfirm his prophecies of 1919, 1928, 1942, and 1949. Schumpeter's bland blessing of socialism's viability does not prepare us for the post-1970 swing toward the market, nor for the travails of the Soviet and Chinese systems. Schumpeter fell in love with his own 1911 theory of development, and somehow convinced himself that capitalism by its nature could not be stationary (*or steadily growing* in trend).

2 Schumpeter's non-developmental core of pure economics is itself gratuitously flawed. He never reasoned well about the zeroness of the rate of interest in stationary long-run equilibrium. (If land with permanent income is to be traded between overlapping generations endowed with only finite life spans, it is hard to envisage its being bid to *infinite* value, as a zero Schumpeter interest would require.) Indeed, I believe that in the last twenty years of his life Schumpeter came to suspect his own youthful thesis, but like Bre'r Rabbit he preferred to say nuffin' on that score. Capitalism as a

system relying on competitive markets would, in any case, be perfectly viable whether its equilibrium interest rate were or were not to have a rendezvous with zero; but neither the evidence of economic history nor the best theories of modern economies predispose us to believe in a trend towards euthanasia of the rentier. Recall that Schumpeter was always patronizing toward Cassel's *Theory of Social Economy* (1918), dismissing it as being exactly what continental economists could handle. But actually, Cassel's (Harrod–Domar!) model of a system that grows progressively through capital accumulation and technical change is nearer to a correct *historical* account of growth and development trends than are Schumpeter's 1911 or 1938 scenarios. And Cassel's view of the business cycle and technical change is in no way inferior to Schumpeter's. (I add that Cassel is no hero of mine, but he deserves not to be underrated. See Samuelson (1993) for my views on Cassel and on Schumpeter's valuations of him.)

3 Schumpeter unnecessarily overemphasized the importance of *bank creation of money* in initiating business cycles and financing venture capital. If much of European gross national product went through market pricing before 1790, and even if there had been less M-creation by pre-1790 banks, it would be absurd for Schumpeter to try to date the genesis of capitalism to only the end of the eighteenth century. Schumpeter's toy boat carried a deal of gratuitous ballast (as Schumpeter (1946, pp. 184ff.) admits).

4 I delight in the new boom for Schumpeter shares. His personality, literary style, and bold speculations merit our rereading him. His prophecies, right or wrong, are interesting and *ex ante* they were not absurd but merely mistaken. And this is quite aside from his solid writings as a historian of economic analysis and of intellectual thought. Moreover, especially at a time when Poland, Hungary, Czechoslovakia, and the erstwhile Soviet republics are trying to find a path from bureaucratic command to a market system, Schumpeter's emphasis on capitalism as "creative destruction" (a process for ruthless cutting of losses) is indeed important.

But having said that, one must also note various spurious reasons for a vulgar popularity of Schumpeter. Keynes is dead, long live Schumpeter. (Indeed Keynes is dead and 1933–40 model T Keynesianism served its purpose and deserves its honored place in the museums and in the insides of 1992 Mercedes–Cadillac retooled

705

neo-Keynesian versions. But whatever will end up being valid in Robert Lucas or Edmund Phelps is not to be found in 1911 or 1942 Schumpeter.)

Furthermore, in a technical season when the general run of scholars feels oppressed by the rigors and minutiae of mathematics and econometrics, there will always be a derived demand for soft discussions concerning what differentiates the innovator from the inventor and the provider of capital. If Chakravarty and I want to analyze seriously Smith–Ohlin–Young increasing returns to scale, we cannot look to tomes by Marx and Schumpeter but rather must study J. M. Clark, Chamberlin, Paul Krugman, and Paul David. The Schumpeter who first lectured to me in 1935 did not believe that *Fortune 500* giants could stay creative and viable. By 1940 he had a mind change and was prepared to believe that oligopolies could learn to stay creative in competitive innovating and technical research. No Schumpeter I ever shared a drink with feared Galbraithian monarchs as having enough monopoly power to sap capitalistic vigor!

Chakravarty, polymath and sage

My main task, that of analyzing where Schumpeter belongs along the Marx–Walras continuum, is done. It would require a deeper and wider paper to appraise in a friendly but objective way whether a Chakravarty or a Samuelson can find in the post-Sraffian and Marxian literatures genuinely useful corrections or supplements to the dominant post-neoclassical literature.

I have enumerated before the important sources of wealth-and-income inequality from (a) natural resource holdings (Paul Getty, Sheikh Smith), (b) Schumpeterian innovation (Hewlett and Packard, Edwin Land, Henry Ford), (c) Knightian uncertainty (Warren Buffett, Michael Milken, real estate developers), (d) human capital (university-educated subclasses), and (e) organized crime and political dictators (Capone, King Saud). What will strike the reader of Karl Marx's dozen volumes, and the literature spawned from them, is that we are given no understanding of the data on Gini distributions or on the Forbes lists of the top 400 in global affluence by the Marxian calculus of *mehrwert*, the elucidation of the transformation problem from values to prices, or the laws of declining profit and immiseration of the working classes! It is a loss that, now, I cannot look forward to talking to Sukhamoy on a hundred topics like this.

Arthur Spiethoff has spoken of the miracle that the young Schumpeter, who before he was 30 had written a great work on development and a learned treatise on doctrinal history, was so to speak born omniscient. Before Sukhamoy came to the Massachusetts Institute of Technology from Calcutta and Rotterdam, already he knew everything. At least everything that I might want to know. The Hegel dialectic and Hamiltonian conservation of energy. How Locke related to Erasmus. At any round seminar table, where Chakravarty sat was the head of the table! So, inevitably, his death leaves us impoverished.

But right at this time our loss is especially great. When Einstein distrusted quantum mechanics as not providing the ultimate explanation, Max Born bemoaned to him that his generation had to carry on without their leader. Right now when the Soviet Union has disintegrated and Eastern Europe is bolting toward the market, humane economists with misgivings about *laissez faire* outcomes face a crisis, external and internal. Can social Darwinism (or Spencerian) after all be the wave of the future and the *desideratum maximorum*? We could use from Sukhamoy Chakravarty counsel in traversing the new shoals of passage. Has there really been a high-noon showdown in which *pure* capitalism outperformed *pure* socialism? Or was the triumph a triumph of the mixed economy over bumbling bureaucracies? Were Mises and Hayek right that such bumbling is *generic* not singular? Were Lerner and Lange the romantic dreamers? Ideological preferences by the like of Galbraith or Friedman cannot validly pronounce on these vital questions and the wisdom of a Chakravarty was never more in need than at the present hour.

Now, in his memory, we must work away at providing our own answers.

Notes

1 At many places Marx deals with land scarcity and rent. Nevertheless, he despised Malthus and disliked explanations of poverty attributable to technological and geological necessity or to excessive birthrates; he preferred explanations that emphasized exploited labor and the class struggle. Therefore most of his million-odd words relevent to a coherent theory of growth are at best explicated by a version of the canoni-

cal classical models that omits land scarcity (and would tolerate asymptotic exponential growth of populations held down to near-subsistence real wages).

2. In Samuelson (1970) I tried to explain to myself why Schumpeter admired Marx. In the end I failed. Again, for the present chapter I chased down in *The History of Economic Analysis* (1954) every Schumpeter reference to Marx. My notes show it to be thin stuff: much roll of drums and blare of trumpet; few heard melodies. My finding could only be expressed in the old doggerel, with meaning inverted and Dr Marx substituted for Doctor Fell:

> I really love thee, Doctor Fell.
> The reason why I cannot tell;
> But this alone I know full well,
> I really love thee Doctor Fell.

Chakravarty (1982, p. 24, n. 25) is acute to quote from Schumpeter's 1937 preface for the Japanese translation of *Theory of Economic Development*.

> It was not clear to me at the outset . . . that the idea and aim are exactly the same as . . . underlie the economic teachings of Karl Marx . . . precisely a vision of economic evolution as a distinct process generated by the economic system itself.
>
> (see Schumpeter, 1951, p. 160)

As I put it to myself, "Joseph Alois Napoleon, it turned out, in the end admired Karl for his *chutspah* in aiming at a Napoleonically ambitious (if faulty) schema. But, he believed, it was Joseph and not Karl who was the real Napoleon!"

3. Marx called religion the opiate of the masses, evoking from Raymond Aron the aphorism that Marxism is the opiate of the intellectuals. One modern Marxism fad, according to my post mortem, *dulls* understanding of the laws of motion of capitalism by professing to find distributional profundity in the notion of "surplus" under modern modes of production. I cannot concur with Chakravarty's finding fault with Marshall for dropping this standpoint. When past societies became depopulated, that did not mean that their interest rates had to be zero or negative in their final stages! There is no scientific explanatory power for the quantitative degree of inequality for income and wealth among the 4 billion global inhabitants whose real wages are above physiological subsistence levels from the fact that post-Newtonian science has lifted mean incomes above physiological or meaningful definitions of subsistence. Marshall never dropped what was never in Smith or Ricardo. Put in our language, Ricardo's distribution theory was a supply-and-demand analysis of how changing labor-cum-capital goods, relative

to inelastic natural resources, alter market interest rates, wage rates, and rent rates. The mumbo-jumbo of "surplus" adds no iota of insight into the process. And its relevance for the process in which societies die of starvation is understandable only in the supply-and-demand terms that a Marshall or Wicksell uses.

References

Allen, Robert Loring 1991: *Opening Doors: The Life and Work of Joseph Schumpeter*. New Brunswick, Transaction Publishers.
Cassel, Gustav 1918: *Theoretische Sozialökonomie*. Leipzig: C. F. Winter. Translated into English as *Theory of Social Economy*. New York, Harcourt Brace, 2nd edn, 1932.
Chakravarty, Sukhamoy 1959: *The Logic of Investment Planning*. Amsterdam: North-Holland.
—— 1982: *Alternative Approaches to a Theory of Economic Growth: Marx, Marshall and Schumpeter*, R. C. Dutt Lectures on Political Economy, 1980. Calcutta: Centre for Studies in Social Sciences.
Samuelson, Paul A. 1970: A foreword: Schumpeter and Marx. In Alexander Balinky, *Marx's Economics: Origins and Development*, Lexington, MA: D. C. Heath.
—— 1978: The canonical classical model of political economy. *Journal of Economic Literature*, 16, 1415–34.
—— 1981: Schumpeter's capitalism, socialism and democracy. In A. Heertje (ed.), *Schumpeter's Vision: Capitalism, Socialism and Democracy after 40 Years*, New York: Praeger.
—— 1993: Gustav Cassel's scientific innovations: claims and realities. *History of Political Economy*, forthcoming.
Schumpeter, Joseph A. 1934: *Theory of Economic Development*. Cambridge, MA: Harvard University Press. English translation of the 1911 German classic.
—— 1942: *Capitalism, Socialism and Democracy*. New York: Harper & Row.
—— 1946: Capitalism. In Richard V. Clemence (ed.), *Essays on Entrepreneurs, Innovations, Business Cycles, and the Evolution of Capitalism*, Reading, MA: Addison-Wesley.
—— 1951: *Essays on Economics Topics of J. A. Schumpeter*, edited by Richard V. Clemence. Port Washington, Kennikat Press.
—— 1954: *The History of Economic Analysis*, edited by E. Boody Schumpeter. New York: Oxford University Press; London: George Allen & Unwin.

Swedberg, Richard 1991a: *Joseph A. Schumpeter, His Life and Work.* Cambridge: Polity Press.
—— (ed.) 1991b: *Joseph A. Schumpeter, The Economics and Sociology of Capitalism.* Princeton, NJ: Princeton University Press.
Whitaker, J. K. (ed.) 1975: *The Early Economic Writings of Alfred Marshall 1867–1890.* London: Macmillan.

CHAPTER 25

TRIBUTE TO WOLFGANG STOLPER ON THE FIFTIETH ANNIVERSARY OF THE STOLPER-SAMUELSON THEOREM

Paul A. Samuelson

The British mathematician G.H. Hardy summed it all up: "Well, I've lived a good life. I have collaborated with Littlewood and Ramanujan." Indeed the Trinity mathematician reported that the one romance in his career had been his discovery of Ramanujan's genius in a letter that came over the transom, his success in bringing Ramanujan to England before his early death, and their historic collaborations.

Well, I have had a good life. I've collaborated with Stolper—and Solow and Modigliani. None was more fun than our exciting progress after Wolfgang brought to me his seminal insight. "How can Haberler and Taussig be right about the necessary harm to a versatile factor like labor from America's tariff, when the Ohlin theory entails that free trade must hurt the factor of production that is scarce relative to land?"

The rest is history. So fundamental a point is obvious in retrospect but the earth moves when first you hear it. "You have something here. Work it out, Wolfie," I said. He worked it out. But suddenly, like all breakthroughs, the analysis opened up a new continent. The newly married Stolpers and Samuelsons lived on the same Ware Street in earshot of Harvard Yard's bells. We talked about new puzzles when we met, and each week a surprising lemma knocked on our brains' door. Was it really possible and mandatory that free trade raise the American land/labor ratio in both food and clothing!

I have always insisted I was the midwife, helping to deliver Wolfie's brain child. Eventually Stolper turned stubborn, saying he could not conscientiously take sole credit for what had involved a fruitful collaboration. I yielded gracefully, understanding that I was the junior partner but that the senior partner might never feel completely comfortable under any other arrangement.

Never was there a more harmonious conception. Gilbert & Sullivan were never like that: always, Sullivan felt as if he were slumming in the lucrative partnership with the vulgar Gilbert. Even the great physics pair of Yang and Lee ceased to be friends in consequence of priority disputes over the Violation of Parity Conservation. I shall digress to speak of an equally famous *contretemps*. When James Watson's *Double Helix* was first written, the Harvard University Press turned it down under its original title of *Honest Jim*. Harvard feared a law suit from Sir William Bragg, the head of Cambridge's lab. I was one of many who read the MS. "Publish it," I advised the Head of the Press. "Publish it as it is. If a man will write such an account of cutthroat competition in science, let it get embalmed in the record." Harvard was chicken and missed publishing this single greatest chronicle of a fundamental science breakthrough. But it was not Bragg who was offended. Actually Bragg wrote a Foreword for the book. And most people have thought that it was the dead Rosalind Franklin whose accomplishment was most slighted by the account of how Crick and Watson one-sidedly benefited from her crystallography x-rays of helix structures. But at the time I mentioned to Watson the view that it was Crick who might take major offence. "I don't know whether the discovery was a 50-50 affair, but to me the account conveys a suggestion of Watson 55 and Crick 45." And for years Crick and Watson were not on their old intimate terms.

Stolper-Samuelson has always been quite a different matter. Naturally, therefore, I was puzzled some 25 years ago when Katherine Ruggles Gerrish, Assistant Editor of the *Quarterly Journal of Economics* and an old friend, called me on the telephone to ask where "my polemic with Stolper" had been published. "I know of no quarrel with Wolfgang. How does your *QJE* author describe it?" I laughed when she read out to me the words: "According to the Stolper-Samuelson argument...." Our English language has its delicious ambiguities. If anything, the junior partner has been accorded too much credit. This is in accordance with Robert K. Merton's "Matthew Effect" in the history of science: *To him who hath shall be given.*

In Europe there is a custom of celebrating 50th anniversaries of a scholar's Ph.D. thesis. Preserved in the record is what Niels Bohr said to Wolfgang Pauli and to Paul Ehrenfest on his way to attend the 50th Birthday Party for Hendrik Lorentz's doctoral dissertation. By coincidence 1991 is the birthday of my own 1941 Harvard thesis, *Foundations of Economic Analysis*. How nice to be given two birthdays in one year. It reminds me of what my mother-in-law said after 18 people visited her in the nursing home on her ninetieth birthday, "That is the way it should be every day!"

As yet, I have not seen the texts of any of today's lectures. I can guess that some will speak of Stolper-Samuelson theorems, Rybczynski's Lemmas, duals to the S-S theorem, and such like things. And that is as it should be. But now that I focus anew on our 1941 opus, I perceive that what it represents is something that quite transcends mere international trade. Our 1941 child registers the quantum jump from Marshallian *partial* equilibrium in economic theory to *general* equilibrium. The whole post-1941 literature is different in a way that can be appreciated only by those of us who were brought up in the *Ancien Régime*.

But, you will say, Léon Walras discovered general equilibrium in 1874–78; and Vilfredo Pareto perfected it in 1894–98. Yes, yes. And I will add, Bertil Ohlin's 1933 trade classic has a general equilibrium appendix that goes beyond Walras, Cassel, Schlesinger, and Wald. (Bertil Ohlin's 1924 Swedish thesis has just been translated by Harry Flam and June Flanders for the MIT Press—along with an unabridged version of Eli Heckscher's classic 1919 article. Already by age 25 Ohlin had done all that brought him a deserved Nobel Prize in 1978.)

What put general equilibrium, so to speak, on the undergraduate classroom map after 1941, was bringing it out of the realm of n+m equations and n+m unknowns to the beautifully simple diagrams of land and labor, cloth and corn. Finally a *manageable* general equilibrium system—one with texture and content—was at hand. Never again could an Ohlin not understand his own system, as when he denied the logical possibility of perfect factor-price equalization!

Stolper-Samuelson was an overture to a symphony that has never stopped playing. But always there are overtures to overtures. On this occasion I must call attention to an unconscious influence that was operating on us back in 1940—operating at least on Paul if not on Wolfgang.

Wolfgang has recalled that my late wife Marion Crawford did on occasion serve as ammanuensis for our joint draftings. Indeed there must exist somewhere in Marion's clear handwriting drafts of my *Foundations* and early mathematical articles, some of them dictated while driving at cruising speed between Cambridge and Berlin, Wisconsin. As readers of the 1941 paper will remember, we were conscientious in seeking earlier anticipations of our analytical relationships between the production-possibility frontier and the Stolper-Samuelson production box diagram. The pickings were very slim indeed. We could find many imprecise statements about the optimality of free trade, but only in one unrelated Benham item were we able to find crisp remarks about relative factor intensities of corn and cloth and mandatory induced shifts in their terms of trade under relative-output shifts.

Today I could add a 1941 classic by Joan Robinson on rising supply prices. But at the time of gestation of Stolper-Samuelson that had not yet appeared. Nor had Viner's 1950 similar supplement to his classic 1931 piece on cost curves and supply curves by then appeared, even though he tells us that by 1938 he had glimpsed the essential point. (In 1991 I have retrieved a 1930 Harrod reference that would be relevant and which for three decades I had lost track of. And of course no one before Lionel Robbin's 1950 rediscovery in his files of Abba Lerner's lost 1933 term paper on factor price equalization even had any notion of that classic's existence.)

But we did twice refer conscientiously to Marion Crawford's celebrated term paper on the Australian case for a tariff on labor intensive imports, calculated to raise that land-rich country's population and real wage rate. I can refer interested readers to my 1989 post mortem on that Crawford Australian breakthrough. I ought to add now what I failed to stress earlier, that my unconscious mind must certainly have benefited enormously in 1940–41 from knowledge of Marion's 1939 *QJE* findings.

This is the occasion to do justice to that influence. The point goes beyond Stolper-Samuelson and international trade theory. Indeed, as I shall explain, I have come to realize that the whole antiquarians' literature on the essence of classical economics à la Smith, Ricardo, and Mill is long overdue for a drastic revision of interpretation.

Let me explain what Marion Crawford Samuelson made explicit. Ricardo did not contemplate a labor-only model such as he and we use in simplest comparative-advantage paradigms. At a minimum, the classicals and the 1925 Australian economists had to deal with a labor and land model, in which an agricultural good used both inputs while by contrast a second good required only labor. I am going to skip over the complication of time-phasing, which Ricardo in some moods admitted did require qualifying his labor-theory-of-value. His grudging admissions in this regard, despite Stigler's defenses of Ricardo as having a "93% labor theory of value" are grossly inadequate: but that is another story and not one treated in the Australian or Stolper-Samuelson literature.

Without the Stolper-Samuelson box diagram, Marion Crawford could handle the p-p frontier of the 2 good case where one of them utilized only labor. That could have provided Joan Robinson, Jacob Viner, Roy Harrod, Stolper-Samuelson, and indeed Heckscher-Ohlin with a manageable analysis for unambiguous classroom explication. (Remark: The Haberler-Jones-Samuelson 1974 model of labor as the only transferable input intersects with the S-S box-diagram in this singular Crawford instance.)

I doubt not that my midwifery benefited from this unconscious source. What surprises me was my dullness in not benefiting more explicitly from this same source. Commentators on Smith-Ricardo-Mill—such as Mark Blaug, Samuel Hollander, and scores of lesser lights—will at the end of the day realize that their Sraffian expositions of natural prices set by horizontal classical ss curves can never validly characterize the classical system as it was actually debated in discussion of the Corn Laws. Malthus and Ricardo were far better in their applied economics than they were in their articulated notions about value and distribution theory. Their gap behind Mill and Jevons and Walras was less than they would have been proud to insist upon. Alas, David Ricardo never really understood "his" own system.

The hour is late. Enough of dry substance. Let me conclude with some fond remembrances of Wolfgang Stolper.

When I came to Harvard, he exuded unconscious charm. European charm. Stolper was Cambridge's link with Schumpeter's days at Bonn. I can recall Wolfgang's indignation when his complaint about

715

the warmth of the Mosel wine served him was met by a waiter who returned with an ice cube plunked down into the wine glass. If Wolfgang had asked that same waiter to cut his Cuban cigar, no doubt he would have returned with two equal pieces.

In 1938 Wolfgang returned from summer vacation with his beautiful Swiss bride. To European eyes America presented many strange features worth commenting on. In his gentle way, Wolfgang suggested: "Vögi, ride with the punches. It's really not polite to comment on each perceived difference." Therefore, when the terrible Hurricane of 1938 hit us, Vögi observed urbanely: "Your usual autumnal disturbance, I presume?" Once Vögi Stolper complained to me that Wolfgang had bought a cigarette rolling machine. "What's so terrible about that?" I asked. She had to explain: "But Wolfie doesn't smoke cigarettes."

Wolfgang knew Hitler's evil and was an interventionist in the pre-war debate with isolationists. The late Dick Slitor, who was to have an important career at the U.S. Treasury, shared a tutorial suite in Leverett House with Stolper. I was friend to both of them and they argued incessantly. To patch things up, I took Stolper aside and said: "Look, don't argue every point with Dick. Let's face it. He's a character, a strange guy." "What do you mean he's a strange guy?" "Well, just as an example, Dick Slitor shampoos his hair every day." "What's the matter with that?" Wolfie asked. "I shampoo my hair every day."

I am sure Wolfgang thought me a crude American. For one thing I never knew the proper temperature at which a Riesling should be served. For another I once revealed an unbelievable gaucherie. In those days we had short-lasting 78 classical records. You were always having to get up to change the record. Then semi-automatic record changers arrived on the market. You had to get up only half as often. I made the mistake of revealing to Wolfgang that I saved effort by listening to Beethoven's Sixth Symphony in the following order: First, the first movement. Then the third movement. Then the fourth movement. And then the second movement. He was incredulous. Just as incredulous as Bob Bishop used to be when I did not lay down the bridge hand seven steps ahead of its inevitable ending. I realized that Wolfgang Amadeus and Wolfgang Friedrich must use a different half of the brain than I did when listening to music.

Wolfie also had a better grasp on theology than I did. Yes, my calculus was better than his but on the exact meaning of Grace his was the more expert opinion. One thing we did have in common was our affection and respect for Schumpeter. Mine was great, his was unbounded.

That was a magic pre-war world in the Harvard Yard. And no one is preserved more perfectly in the amber of my affectionate memory than Wolfie Stolper—friend and collaborator.

TRIBUTE TO JAN TINBERGEN: ONE EXACT MATCH FOR ECONOMICS AND PHYSICS

*Paul A. Samuelson**

ABSTRACT

Jan Tinbergen, like Tjalling Koopmans, began as a Physicist until economics tempted him away. As homage to him I provide an immigration model in economics that matches closely a thermodynamics model which equalizes subsystems' temperatures and pressures: both models' positivistic facts are deducible from an isomorphic maximization model.

Jan Tinbergen of Holland was a great and creative economist who fittingly was awarded a Nobel Prize in economics (along with Ragnar Frisch of Norway) the first year that such a prize was established. He lived a long life, and devoted himself throughout to public service. In 1969, at the time of his Stockholm triumph, I called him a "humanist saint" in an adulatory *Newsweek* column.

Tinbergen came from a free-thinking socialist background. (His brother Niko also won a Nobel Prize, this time in biology for his pioneer writings in ethology.) Early in this century friends of the working class regarded alcoholism as the curse of the poor and all his life Jan remained a teetotaler. Tinbergen was prolific in a wide variety of economic areas. But perhaps his reputation was most elevated in the econometrics and the mathematics of dynamic macroeconomic systems. The leading private forecasting groups today—Data Resources, Inc., Wharton, University of Michigan model, ... —still utilize Tinbergen's essential macromodeling paradigm of the late 1930s. But Tinbergen was also a deep microeconomist.

---

*Institute Professor Emeritus, Massachusetts Institute of Technology, Cambridge, Massachusetts; LTCB Visiting Professor of Political Economy, Japan-U.S. Center, Stern School of Business, New York University, New York, USA.

[1]

In homage to this great scholar, I wish briefly to write about some microeconomic matters that were congenial to his interests and talents. I begin at the personal level, calling attention to his mathematical style that I found to be not dissimilar to my own. Then in honor of Jan Tinbergen I try to bring some rigor into the much maligned and much confused relationship between 1996 theoretical economics and that most deductive branch of classical physics, namely phenomenological thermodynamics (à la Carnot, Kelvin, Clausius, and Gibbs).

I. TINBERGEN AND FACTOR PRICE EQUALIZATION

Here is a historical anecdote, accurately remembered by a participant. In the late 1940s, as a moonlighter, I taught trade theory to future diplomats at Tufts University's Fletcher School of Law and Diplomacy. Using Paul Ellsworth's competent intermediate text, I discovered that my explication of Bertil Ohlin's factor-price-equalisation-by-trade was logically unsatisfactory. It turned out that Ohlin never quite correctly understood his own theory as bequeathed to him by his teacher Eli Heckscher. In the end I wrote the 1948 *Economic Journal* article that initiated a new phase in the factor equalisation story. (It was later learned that Abba Lerner as a student had already covered much the same ground in a 1933 LSE course paper for Lionel Robbins. Everyone, including Lerner, had forgotten the topic, until the 1948 paper tweaked Robbins' memory and led to rediscovery of the 1933 manuscript, which first saw print in 1952.)

The 1948 paper led to considerable excitement, to correspondences of protest from such as Joan Robinson and Richard Kahn, and to attempted rebuttals by A.C. Pigou and by Sir Donald McDougall, which were subsequently withdrawn only at the page proof stage. Evidently my own exposition could not have been optimal first time out. My present point is that the first economist to submit to me an adequate proof of my indisputably true theorem was Jan Tinbergen. Like me he realized that manipulating $a/b = c/d$ expressions of comparative costs would never be enough.

No matter how slow or befuddled you or I may be, our mathematics will, from its own logic, point the correct way. From personal conversation with Jan in the Hague during September 1948, I learned that it was partly as a result of his initial training in physics that the true light dawned on Tinbergen. Let me paraphrase his explanation.

Normally, when Portugal gets more land that is especially suitable to wine producing, we expect that increase in factor supply to lower its land rent relative to the land rent in the England that has had no change in supply. This normal presumption is like the expectation that touching a cold body with a hot body

© Indian Journal of Applied Economics, 1996

will raise the cold body's temperature. However, suppose the cold body is ice that is already at the temperature of freezing. Touching it with a small hot body must at first only melt *some* of the ice, while leaving its mixture of ice and water at the same temperature of freezing. This, Tinbergen went on to say, is what must happen when you begin with a small island surrounded by a huge continent with the same land/labor endowment. Both places produce both goods. Adding a bit of land to the island can leave the rent/wage ratio uniform everywhere. Why? Because the island absorbs the new land by upping its land-intensive good a bit at the expense of its labor-intensive production. So to speak, its ratio of ice to water can change enough to absorb the exogenous shock. (Of course, new land anywhere must slightly lower the world rent/wage ratio, but generically it does so at first *equally* in both places—until the directly affected island has given up *all* production of the labor-intensive good; after one of the ice-water mixture has vanished, you do expect a rise in temperature and, correspondingly, a bigger drop in the island's final rent than in the continent's rent. Q.E.D.)

I leave this *curiosum* with the Delphic remark that the physics analogy served the good purpose of softening up Tinbergen to accept the truth of necessary factor-price equalization when two places with like technologies are near enough alike in their labor/land endowments. But, in exact logic, the analogy is alas faulty. Nothing in the wine-cloth: labor-land story involves the *special* property that ice and water have at the freezing point; there is nothing like a *latent heat of melting* in the economics! My present exposition will strive for no *near*-analogies, instead seeking *exact isomorphisms* between the physics and the economics.

II. THE DUTCH CONNECTION

The stage has been set to describe how Jan Tinbergen gravitated into economics from physics. He began in physics under the brilliant Leiden physicist Paul Ehrenfest. Tanya Ehrenfest, a thermodynamicist in her own right, was also his mentor—particularly in the years of her widowhood after Paul's tragic suicide. (Despair over Hitler, frustration over the non-deterministic foundations of quantum mechanics, and grief over a handicapped child may have played a part in the too-early death of this brilliant Viennese student of Boltzmann and confidant of Albert Einstein.)

The point for us is that Tinbergen was no physicist manqué but rather a promising scholar who could not resist the analytical and humanitarian temptations of economics. In this he resembled his younger countryman Tjalling

© Indian Journal of Applied Economics, 1996

Koopmans, a promising protegé of the eminent Dutch physicist H.A. Kramers. Koopmans also could not resist the ethical and analytical pull of economics, and in 1975 he received a deserved Noble Prize in economics. On the day that award was announced, I happened to be at a Harvard cocktail party with distinguished chemists and physicists. More than one asked me: "Is that the Koopmans of 'Koopmans' Theorem' in Quantum Mechanics, an approximation that some of us still use some forty years later?" It was indeed the same person.

To avoid being misunderstood I ought to add that Tinbergen had devised an analytic proof of the equalisation theorem. And that, which alone is of substantive scientific merit, had nought to do with any kind of physics or mechanics at the literary or mathematical level.

I must report one more revealing conversation with Tinbergen. The subject of linear programming had beginnings and rebirths during World War II, thanks to George Dantzig, Tjalling Koopmans, and the Soviet mathematician Leonid Kantorovich. It linked up also with the equalities-inequalities of von Neumann's 1928 two-person zero-sum game theory. By 1950 most of its essential perfectings had already been accomplished and economists like Tinbergen were making increasing use of modern programming paradigms. (The Ricardo-Mill comparative advantage theory of 1817 and 1829 had already been an unselfconscious example of parametric linear programming!)

In the mid-1950s when Jan spent a sabbatical year at Harvard, he confided in me that, generally when a new problem or consideration came up in programming matters, he found it congenial to work out first the smooth neoclassical version of the problem by the usual Newtonian calculus techniques. Then when he saw how things ran in this mode he would be better prepared to understand its literal linear programming version involving a finite number of feasible techniques.

I could well understand this even though I lacked his years of maturity. Thus, in my original 1949 treatment of the Nonsubstitution Theorem applicable to the Leontief (and 1960 Sraffa) input-output system, I deliberately first tackled the neoclassical case where an infinity of substitutions were specified to be feasible. The familiar counting of equations and of endogenous unknowns was validly applicable; and despite the understood complexities and treacheries introduced when the contemplated relations are known to be nonlinear, my published 1951 proof adequately covered both the discrete and the continuum cases. Besides, the great Berkeley mathematician Stephen Smale was about to give economists back legitimacy of the calculus under provisos that exceptions which occur "almost never" (in the sense of measure theory) are to be explicitly

© Indian Journal of Applied Economics, 1996

allowed for.

As a final word in this connection, let me mention a common misunderstanding in the Sraffa-Robinson literature. Joan Robinson's concerns about misuse of aggregate capital scalars, I think, were admirable. And it is a pity that we never got from Piero Sraffa meaningful content for his proposed critique of (neoclassical) *marginalism*. As a result the impression became widespread among some Sraffians that: (1) realistic denials of various common neoclassical dogmas do occur in specifiable discrete technologies; and (2) that these demonstrable denials served to rule out and discredit the Clarkian use of smooth marginal products. Actually, however, (2) does not follow logically from (1): the important departures from the apologetics of classical and neoclassical economists, one learned belatedly, occur as well in vectoral-capital smooth ("marginal productivity") models with "non-spurious margins" as they do in finite-activities discrete technologies.

III. THERMODYNAMICS AND ECONOMICS AT LAST

This long introduction was of interest for its own sake and now I turn to what would have interested Tinbergen the one-time physicist turned economist. Most analogies between those subjects, as when an "entropy" is proposed for economic theory, are faulty and ill-informed. (I shall not cover the special and interesting writings of the late Nicholas Georgescu-Roegen: emphasizing that all high-content deposits of scarce and useful materials ultimately get dispersed, Georgescu stressed the superiority for economics of the logo of the irreversible hour glass that goes toward empty over the logo of the forever-swinging pendulum.)

With eclectic aplomb economist amateurs stumble from "entropy" to "energy," one or another of which is thought to correspond with economists' utility or economists' something-or-other. My old Master Joseph Schumpeter possessed a shaky acquaintance with exact theories of mechanics but still he delighted in harmless babble about "potentials" in economics. Even the great genius of John von Neumann wrote loosely about analogies between game-theory minimax formulations and Gibbsian definitions of energy, enthalpy, Helmholtz free energy, and other species in the genus of thermodynamic Legendre Transformations. However, serious investigation into the matter has shown how little and much there was in the parallel. See Brody (1989); Samuelson (1992).

Philip Mirowski (1989) has written on what earlier mathematical economists owed, or thought they owed, or Mirowski thought they owed, to an "energetics" phase in historical theoretical physics. It is not my purpose to pronounce on his misses and hits. But I owe a duty to readers to report that the Mirowski texts, under auditings, appear to be replete with erroneous passages. *Liceat emptor.*

My task here is not to summarize how economic and physics theories interrelate, if at all. It is the humbler one to try to specify one model in each that, when paired and compared, are analytically isomorphic to each other. Humble or proud the effort may be, but still the task was not a simple one. And the paired models that I do present have never to my knowledge been meticulously specified, described, and compared. And even they had to be a bit inelegant and contrived in the pursuit of the goal of *almost complete* parallelism.

How can it be that one who has written so often on things like LeChatelier's Principle and the like can assert that he has not accomplished long ago and many times what is here assayed in this homage to Tinbergen?

The answer is so simple as to be anti-climatic. My previous writings have not tried to improve on economics by use of concepts in physics; or, perish the thought, hoped to improve on physics by importing subtleties of mathematical economics. Instead I have looked for mathematical methods—theorems about co-factors of definite determinants and such like—that occur in the two different applications. Now, here, I am as interested in identifying what *cannot* be common to the two valid applications as in what can be.

IV. A MIGRATIONS SCENARIO

Begin with economics. Two islands are alike in their endowment of unit acreage. (Later two flasks of the same gas will be alike in their endowment of unit mass of some substance.) *Land* works in each place with *Labor* and (simple, *scalar*) *Kapital*—$(A; L, K)$—to produce a single corn Product, q. Identical technology gives all places the same production function: it may be smoothly differentiable in the neoclassical fashion; or, in the fashion of Sraffa and von Neumann, it can involve several discrete alternative techniques.

Here is the specified production function.

$$\text{corn} = q = F(A, L, K) \tag{1a}$$

$$= AF(1, L/A, K/A), \text{ constant returns to scale} \tag{1b}$$

$$= F(L, K) \text{ for } A = 1. \tag{1c}$$

© Indian Journal of Applied Economics, 1996

Doubling Labor and Kapital, on fixed acres of Land, less than doubles corn Output: more specifically the classical *law of diminishing returns* specifies that, on fixed Land, $F(L, K)$ is to be *strictly concave* (from below) in (L, K). In a neoclassical context, for positive (L, K), both $\partial F/\partial K \equiv F_L(L, K)$ and $\partial F/\partial K \equiv F_K(L, K)$ are *positive marginal productivities*. In a 1-sector context I assume:

$$q = \text{consumption} + \text{net Kapital formation} = C + (dK/dt) \tag{2}$$

In our simplest scenario let there be two (or more) islands each with unit acreage of Land. $(L_1\ K_1)$ can differ from $(L_2\ K_2)$ in either or both variable-factor endowments. Indeed, if Isle 1 has more L_1 than Isle 2 has L_2 while $K_1 = K_2$, then definitely the *wage rate* of the plentifully supplied factor will be lower there. From free *internal* domestic competition

$$w_1 = \partial F(L_1, K)/\partial L_1 < w_2 = \partial F(L_2, K)/\partial L_2 \quad \text{for} \quad L_1 > L_2. \tag{3a}$$

Such is the dictate of Darwinian competitive arbitrage as an oversupply of Labor$_1$ bids down its market-clearing factor price w_1.

What happens to the *interest rate* r_1 that must equate in equilibrium to the domestic market-clearing marginal product of Kapital? That must depend on whether, in the presence of fixed Land, the Labor and Kapital are technical *complements* or *rivals* to each other: for $L_1 > L_2$ and $K_1 = K_2 = K$,

$$r_1 = \partial F(L_1, K)/\partial K \gtreqless r_2 = \partial F(L_2, K)/\partial K \tag{3b}$$

depending respectively on whether

$$\partial^2 F(L, K)/\partial K\,\partial L \equiv F_{LK}(L, K) \equiv F_{KL}(L, K) \gtreqless 0. \tag{3c}$$

We need to contemplate four different possible scenarios of competitive international factor mobility.

Scenario 1. Neither L nor K can move from one Isle to the other.

Scenario 2. Both L and K can move perfectly freely.

Scenario 3. K alone can move and will do so until $r_1^* = r_2^* = r^*$; $(\overline{L}_1, \overline{L}_2)$ stay fixed and $(w_1^*\ w_2^*)$ end up generally unequal.

Scenario 4. L alone can move and eventually $(w_1\ w_2) \to (w^*\ w^*)$. With $\overline{K}_1 \neq \overline{K}_2$, $r_1^* \neq r_2^*$ generally. (Since Scenarios 3 and 4 are similar in logic, each involving a mobile and an immobile factor, I leave Scenario 4 to the reader to work out.)

© Indian Journal of Applied Economics, 1996

Here are the Scenario 1 equilibrium equations for the unknown (w_1^* w_2^*; r_1^*, r_2^*), written in terms of the specified ($\overline{L}_1 \overline{L}_2$; $\overline{K}_1 \overline{K}_2$):

$$r_j^* = F_K(\overline{L}_j, \overline{K}_j), \quad j = 1, 2$$

$$w_j^* = F_L(\overline{L}_j, \overline{K}_j). \tag{4a}$$

Generally, an abundant endowment of a factor will depress its relative factor price:

$$\text{if } \overline{L}_1 = \overline{L}_2 \text{ and } \overline{K}_1 > \overline{K}_2, r_1^* < r_2^*. \tag{4b}$$

If L and K are technical *complements* (rather than being rivals), $F_{LK} > 0$, (4b) will enable us to predict that $w_1^* > w_2^*$. Generally, under (4b),

$$\text{sign}\{F_{LK}\} = \text{sign}\{w_1^* - w_2^*\}.$$

Scenario 2 has the following equations determining the equilibrium values of ($L_1^* K_1^* w_1^* r_1^*$; $L_2^* K_2^* w_2^* r_2^*$):

$$w_j^* = w^*, r_j^* = r^*, \quad j = 1, 2$$

$$w^* = F_L(L_j^*, K_j^*), \quad r^* = F_K(L_j^*, K_j^*)$$

$$L_1^* + L_2^* = \overline{L}_1 + \overline{L}_2, K_1^* + K_2^* = \overline{K}_1 + \overline{K}_2. \tag{5a}$$

By symmetry, we deduce from (5a) that full factor mobility must iron out *all* differences in factor endowments:

$$w^* = F_L\left(\frac{1}{2}\overline{L}_1 + \frac{1}{2}\overline{L}_2; \frac{1}{2}\overline{K}_1 + \frac{1}{2}\overline{K}_2\right),$$

$$r^* = F_K\left(\frac{1}{2}\overline{L}_1 + \frac{1}{2}\overline{L}_2; \frac{1}{2}\overline{K}_1 + \frac{1}{2}\overline{K}_2\right)$$

$$L_1^* = L_2^* = \frac{1}{2}(\overline{L}_1 + \overline{L}_2),$$

$$K_1^* = K_2^* = \frac{1}{2}(\overline{K}_1 + \overline{K}_2). \tag{5b}$$

Scenario 3 has the following equations for equilibrium ($w_1^* r_1^* K_1^*$; $w_2^* r_2^* K_2^*$):

$$r^* = r_j^* = F_K(\overline{L}_j, K_j^*), \ j = 1, 2$$

$$w_j^* = F_L(\overline{L}_j, K_j^*)$$

$$K_1^* + K_2^* = \overline{K}_1 + \overline{K}_2 \tag{6a}$$

If $\overline{L}_1 > \overline{L}_2$, sign $\{K_1^* - K_2^*\}$ = sign $\{F_{LK}\}$. \hfill (6b)

The reader who seeks to work out Scenario 4 can use the (6) relations with L and K variables interchanged.

To sum up on our economic scenario of factor mobility and immobility: competitive arbitrage and self-interest, with no trace of physics methodology, guides the pre- and post-Smith writers on this economic model.

Smith's vague doctrine of an Invisible Hand hints by innuendo that all these *positivistic* behavioristic relations may be capable of being rationalized by some *maximizing* model. By the time of *Foundations of Economic Analysis*, Hotelling (1932) and later writers converted this innuendo into a demonstrable truth.

The relations of Scenario 2's (5) can now be shown to be equivalent to the following maximization problem:

Subject to initial global endowment totals, reallocate factor supplies by region so as to *maximize global production* (of corn):

$$\text{Subject to } L_1 + L_2 = \overline{L}_1 + \overline{L}_2, \ K_1 + K_2 = \overline{K}_1 + \overline{K}_2, \tag{7a}$$

$$\text{Max} \ (q_1 + q_2) = \underset{L_j, K_j}{\text{Max}} \ [F(L_1, K_1) + F(L_2, K_2)] \tag{7b}$$

$$= 2F\left(\frac{1}{2}\overline{L}_1 + \frac{1}{2}\overline{L}_2, \frac{1}{2}\overline{K}_1 + \frac{1}{2}\overline{K}_2\right) \tag{7c}$$

$$w^* = F_L\left(\frac{1}{2}\overline{L}_1 + \frac{1}{2}\overline{L}_2, \frac{1}{2}\overline{K}_1 + \frac{1}{2}\overline{K}_2\right) = w_1^* = w_2^*$$

$$r^* = F_K\left(\frac{1}{2}\overline{L}_1 + \frac{1}{2}\overline{L}_2, \frac{1}{2}\overline{K}_1 + \frac{1}{2}\overline{K}_2\right) = r_1^* = r_2^* \tag{7d}$$

Scenario 3's case, where Kapital is alone mobile, leads to Max $\{q_1 + q_2\}$ subject to immobile Labor supplies and self-motivated free Kapital movements: namely,

Subject to $\quad L_1 = \overline{L}_1, L_2 = \overline{L}_2, K_1 + K_2 = \overline{K}_1 + \overline{K}_2$ (8a)

$$\underset{K_1, K_2}{\text{Max}} \ [F\ (\overline{L}_1, K_1) + F\ (\overline{L}_2, K_2)] \tag{8b}$$

$$= F\ (\overline{L}_1, K_1^*) + F\ (\overline{L}_2, K_2^*) \tag{8c}$$

where K_1^* is the root of

$$F_K\ (\overline{L}_1, K_1^*) = F_K\ (\overline{L}_2, \overline{K}_1 + \overline{K}_2 - K_1^*) = r_1^* = r_2^*. \tag{8d}$$

We can solve (8) for its unique K_1^* root and its implied unique (w^*, r^*) roots.

The next section shifts gears abruptly to the world of elementary physics, light years away from prosaic economics.

A PHYSICS ANALOGUE

Parallel logical structure underlies the following model of post-1840 classical thermodynamics. Parallel to separable economic regions are separable enclosed-in-walls volumes that each contain the same mass of a homogeneous fluid: it may be oxygen gas; or, alternatively, nitrogen; or H_2O vapor. The equal masses of the substance correspond to equal land acreages in the different economic regions. By having each subsystem of fluid be surrounded by *rigid* and *insulated* inner walls, we create the equivalent to *immobile* Labor and Kapital. Result: initial temperatures and pressures of the subsystems can stay permanently unequal.

Now remove the insulation from the inner walls connecting the two subsystems. Then the *temperatures* will move toward equality. ("Temperature" can be measured by different empirical scales: Fahrenheit or Celsius or Kelvin Absolute; by an alcohol or a mercury "thermometer." For brevity I use Kelvin Absolute to write down relations such as $(T_1 = T_2 > 0, T_1 > T_2 > 0)$ or $(1/T_1 = 1/T_2; 1/T_1 < 1/T_2)$. Every substance can in principle have its Kelvin Absolute temperature, T, be measured unambiguously.) To have $(1/T_1\ 1/T_2) \to (1/T^*\ 1/T^*)$ is *logically* just like having $(r_1\ r_2) \to (r^*\ r^*)$ when Kapital is permitted to be freely mobile.

Further, one can change the scenario to make the connecting wall between the separate subsystems be *at the same time both non-insulating* and *non-rigid*. Then, even though no mass can travel through the wall from one subsystem to the other, we will observe that initially divergent temperatures and pressures do both converge asymptotically to equality: $(1/T_1\ 1/T_2; p_1\ p_2) \to (1/T^*\ 1/T^*; p^*\ p^*)$, paralleling the economic Scenario 2 where $(r_1\ r_2; w_1\ w_2) \to (r^*\ r^*; w^*\ w^*)$.

© Indian Journal of Applied Economics, 1996

So far I have been an operationalist logical positivist parsimoniously describing the testable and observed facts without offering any deductive theory to "explain" and help "understand" the facts. That roughly agrees with the historical stages of thermal science.

In economics, pre-Smithians such as David Hume grasped the notion that [Darwinian] competitive arbitrage, and nothing else, could guarantee the factor-price equalization(s) entailed by spontaneous factor migrations. Self interest did the trick. And we've seen Smith's vague notion of THE INVISIBLE HAND hinted that mindless competition would effectuate *maximization* of something identifiable. The virtue of Equations (7)-(8) is that they permit by extrapolation knowable answers to what would occur when *new* economic experiments were to be performed (even for the first time!).

Similarly, in physics long before 1840, the bare facts of pressure equalization and temperature equalization were known prior to Rudolf Clausius's discovery (c. 1850) of an identifiable "entropy" magnitude that does get itself maximized in Mother Nature's spontaneous processes. Hume and Smith and Turgot could not have known of physics laws that were unknown to physicists of their respective times.

In the economics case, Whig historians now know that the *world* total of *corn* production is maximized when perfect Kapital and Labor mobility of migration equalizes wage rates and interest rates globally. And they understand that, freeing up Kapital mobility while immobilizing Labor regionally will give *maximal world corn output* subject to the constraint of localized Labor supplies.

In the physics case, after Helmholtz (and Mayer and Joule and Kelvin) and Clausius sorted out the First and Second Laws of Thermodynamics, the bare facts of (temperature pressure) equalizations and non-equalizations could be rationalized, tested, and predicted from Clausius's dictum:

The Entropy of the world increases;
Its Energy is conserved.

The heroes of neoclassical economics—Thünen, Gossen, Jevons, Walras, Menger, Clark, Marshall, Fisher, Wicksteed, Wicksell, Pareto, . . .— textual analysis shows, in no case arrived at their economic novelties by attempted analogy with this kind of physics. Irving Fisher was best situated to have done so but his *ex post* attempt to draw the kind of parallel that is presented in this Tinbergen tribute was cursory, casual, and non-cogent. (This is not intended to be critical. When T.S. Eliot was told, "We know more than the ancients," he replied. "Yes, and it is the ancients that we know." Poets are given to half-truths!)

© Indian Journal of Applied Economics, 1996

I am writing for economists not for physicists and erudite historians of science. Therefore I may skip important details and provide a minimal exposition of how in physics, as in economics, a bare facts story about positivistic convergences of temperatures and pressures can be rationalized as a deduction from a specifiable maximizing algorithm. My formulation aspires to bring out exact *deductive* analogues with the economic scenario of migration; but I shall not force the analogy, instead pointing out some essential differences.

Clausius, Gibbs, and Planck established that for each fluid there can be identified (and tested) an internal *Energy* magnitude, an internal *Entropy* magnitude, its *Mass*, its Absolute Kelvin *Temperature*, its absolute and specific *Volume*, and its *Pressure*. Choosing from the multiplicity of thermodynamic notations, I use here for these: (E, S, M, T, V, p). And going beyond mere *differences* in Energy or Entropy levels, I concentrate on extensive E and S measures that grow proportionally with the other extensive variables of the problem (thereby ruling out mere scale effects). Instead of employing the common notations for thermodynamic functions, I shall use the same $F(\ ,\ .)$ function that served for economic output-and-input relations, but I take care not to impose anything on physics that is not well known to hold in its domain.

Paralleling $q = F(A, L, K)$ in economics, I write

Entropy $\equiv S = F$ (Mass, Energy, Volume) (9a)

$\equiv F(M, E, V)$

$\equiv MF(1, E/M, V/M)$, 1st-degree-homogeneity (9b)

$\equiv F(E, V)$ for $M \equiv 1$ (9c)

where $F(E, V)$ has all the concavity, monotonicity, and smoothness specifications that held in economics and will hold in physics when stable regularity equilibria do obtain.

The partial derivatives of the Entropy function do determine the intensive *Absolute Temperature* and *pressure* as follows:

$$1/T = \partial F/\partial E \equiv F_E(E, V) \equiv (\partial S/\partial E)_V$$

$$p = -(\partial E/\partial V)_S \equiv TF_V(E, V). \qquad (10)$$

For Scenario 1, where the connecting wall is both *rigid* and (perfectly) *insulating*

© Indian Journal of Applied Economics, 1996

$$1/T_1 = F_E(E_1, V_1) \neq F_E(E_2, V_2) = 1/T_2 \tag{11a}$$

$$p_1 = T_1 F_V(E_1, V_1) \neq T_2 F_V(E_2, V_2) = p_2 \tag{11b}$$

This exactly parallels economics Scenario 1 with no factor mobility at all and with unequal (w_j, r_j)'s.

For Scenario 2, we get the benefit of a Max-Entropy formulation. Now, subject to

$$E_1 + E_2 = \overline{E}_1 + \overline{E}_2, \text{ conservation of total energy} \tag{12a}$$

$$V_1 + V_2 = \overline{V}_1 + \overline{V}_2, \text{ imposed fixed } total \text{ volume} \tag{12b}$$

$$\text{Max} \{S_1 + S_2\} = \underset{E_j, V_j}{\text{Max}} \{F(E_1, V_1) + F(E_2, V_2)\} \tag{12c}$$

$$= F(E_1^*, V_1^*) + F(E_2^*, V_2^*) \tag{12d}$$

$$= 2F\left(\frac{1}{2}[\overline{E}_1 + \overline{E}_2], \frac{1}{2}[\overline{V}_1 + \overline{V}_2]\right). \tag{12e}$$

From (12d) one deduces the remarkably simple (12e). It is the only admissible solution of the implied maximizing relations (12a, b, f, g) which are seen to be symmetric in structure and subject to concavity: for $j = 1, 2$, the first-derivative conditions are

$$F_E(E_j, V_j) = (1/T)^* = 1/T_1 = 1/T_2 \tag{12f}$$

$$F_V(E_j, V_j) = p^*/T^* = p_1^*/T^* = p_2^*/T^*. \tag{12g}$$

Scenario 3 parallels its economic analogue with the following maximum-problem determination of $(E_1^* E_2^* 1/T^* p_1^* p_2^*)$. Connecting the subsystems by a thermal-conducting inner wall permits Energy to flow from the warmer to the cooler volume, while at the same time the still-rigid walls keep $(\overline{V}_1 \overline{V}_2)$ the same. Now

Subject to

$$E_1 + E_2 = \overline{E}_1 + \overline{E}_2, \tag{13a}$$

$$\text{Max} \{S_1 + S_2\} = \underset{E_j}{\text{Max}} \{F(E_1, \overline{V}_1) + F(E_2, \overline{V}_2)\} \tag{13b}$$

© Indian Journal of Applied Economics, 1996

$$= \underset{E_1}{\text{Max}} \{F(E_1, \overline{V}_1) + F(\overline{E}_1 + \overline{E}_2 - E_1)\} \quad (13c)$$

$$= F(E_1^*, \overline{V}_1) + F(\overline{E}_1 + \overline{E}_2 - E_1^*)$$

where E_1^* is the unique root for E_1 of the maximum relation

$$F_E(E_1, \overline{V}_1) - F_E(\overline{E}_1 + \overline{E}_2 - E_1) = 0 = 1/T_1^* - 1/T_2^*. \quad (13d)$$

Thus,

$$(1/T_1\ 1/T_2) \to (1/T^*\ 1/T^*) \quad \text{as} \quad t \to \infty. \quad (13e)$$

The reader will not be able to work out a Scenario 4 for the physics. Why not? Because there is no way possible to keep the $(\overline{E}_1, \overline{E}_2)$ energies immobilized in their initial configuration(s) while a flexible piston ends the rigidity of the connecting interwall. My analogy is good, so to speak three-fourths of the way. But it limps in this case. Likening $(V_1\ V_2)$ to $(K_1\ K_2)$ does work fine. But relating $(E_1\ E_2)$ to $(L_1\ L_2)$ is a stretch. Labor supplies can change regionally while being forced to conserve total world Labor: it is our story and we issue economic stage directions to make it happen. The conservation of total energy is not a matter of expositional stage directions. In physics it is an inescapable constraint! (The young Einstein said that, to fit the facts he would give up every inherited law of physics—but the last one he would be willing to sacrifice would be the Law of Conservation of Energy. I think this was because he could not conceive of a general theory that would work while permitting perpetual motion machines of various kinds. By contrast, Niels Bohr in quantum mechanics did, for a fortnight, contemplate a model in which energy need not be conserved. Soon he cut his losses on that exploration.)

In economics I have always been loathe to swallow *ex ante* proposals (like that of Kalecki in the 1930s requiring dynamic oscillations to be neither damped nor anti-damped) which impose on economic facts analogues to the First Law of Thermodynamics. (For fabricated programming trajectories, deduced conserved integrals of motion are a different matter.)

Let me sum up. The migration-of-factor scenarios of economics have here been successfully framed so as to follow the same kind of equilibrium equations as do obtain in the simplest of thermodynamics systems involving interconnected temperatures and pressures. I believe Jan would have understood and enjoyed this repast cooked up in his honor.

© Indian Journal of Applied Economics, 1996

References

Brody, Andrew, "Economics and Thermodynamics," in M. Dore, S. Chakravarty, and R. Goodwin (eds.), *John von Neumann and Modern Economics*, The Clarendon Press, Oxford, 1989.

Dantzig, George, "The Programming of Interdependent Activities: Mathematical Model," in Cowles Commission for Research in Economics, T.C. Koopmans (ed.) *Activity Analysis of Production and Allocation*, New York, John Wiley & Sons, 1951.

Ellsworth, Paul T., *International Economics*, The Macmillan Co., New York, 1938.

Georgescu-Roegen, Nicholas, *The Entropy Law and the Economic Process*, Harvard University Press, Cambridge, Mass., 1971.

Heckscher, Eli, "The Effect of Foreign Trade on the Distribution of Income," *Economisk Tidskrift*, 21:497-512, 1912. Reprinted in *Readings in the Theory of International Trade*, Blakiston, Philadelphia, 1949.

Hotelling, Harold, "Edgeworth's taxation paradox and the nature of demand and supply functions," *Journal of Political Economy*, 40:577-616, 1932.

Kalecki, Michal, "A Macrodynamic Theory of Business Cycles," *Econometrica*, III: 327-52, 1935.

Kantorovich, Leonid, *Matematicheskie metody organizatsii i planirovaniia proizvodstva*, State Publishing House, Leningrad, 1939. Translated as "Mathematical methods of organizing and planning production," *Management Science*, 6:363-422, 1960.

Koopmans, Tjalling, "Optimum Utilization of the Transportation System," in *Proceedings of the International Statistical Conference, 1947*, Vol. 5, Washington, D.C., 1947. Reprinted as Supplement to *Econometrica*, 17, 1949.

Leontief, Wassily, *Studies in the Structure of the American Economy*, Oxford University Press, New York, 1941. Enlarged edition, 1951.

Lerner, Abba P., "Factor prices and international trade," *Economica*, N.S., 19:1-15, 1952.

Mill, John Stuart, *Essays on Some Unsettled Questions of Political Economy*, Parker, London, 1829, 1844.

Mirowski, Philip, *More Heat than Light: Economics as Social Physics, Physics as Nature's Economics*, Cambridge University Press, Cambridge, 1989.

Ohlin, Bertil, *Interregional and International Trade*, Harvard University Press, Cambridge, Mass., 1933.

Ricardo, David, *The Principles of Economics*, 1817, in Piero Sraffa (ed.), *The Works and Correspondence of David Ricardo*, Vol. 1, Cambridge University Press (for the Royal Econometric Society), Cambridge, 1951.

Robinson, Joan, *The Accumulation of Capital*, Richard D. Irwin, Inc., Homewood, Illinois, 1956.

Samuelson, Paul A., *Foundations of Economic Analysis*, Harvard University Press, Cambridge, Mass., 1947. Enlarged Edition, 1983.

Samuelson, Paul A., "International trade and the equalisation of factor prices," *The Economic Journal*, 58:163-84, 1948. Reproduced as Chapter 67 in *The Collected Scientific Papers of Paul A. Samuelson*, Vol. 2, The MIT Press, Cambridge, Mass., 1966.

Samuelson, Paul A., "International factor-price equalisation once again," *The Economic Journal*, 59:181-97, 1949. Reproduced as Chapter 68 in *The Collected Scientific Papers of Paul A. Samuelson*, Vol. 2, The MIT Press, Cambridge, Mass., 1966.

© Indian Journal of Applied Economics, 1996

Samuelson, Paul A., "Abstract of a Theorem Concerning Substitutability in Open Leontief Models," Chap. II in Cowles Commission for Research in Economics, T.C. Koopmans (ed.) *Activity Analysis of Production and Allocation*, John Wiley, New York, 1951. Reproduced as Chapter 36 in *The Collected Scientific Papers of Paul A. Samuelson*, Vol. 1, The MIT Press, Cambridge, Mass., 1966.

Samuelson, Paul A., "Two Remarkable Men," *Newsweek*, November 17, 108, 1969.

Samuelson, Paul A., "Economics and Thermodynamics: von Neumann's Problematic Conjecture," in R. Selten (ed.) *Ratinal Interaction, Essays in Honor of John C. Harsanyi*, Springer-Verlag, Berlin, 1992.

Smale, Stephen, "Dynamics in General Equilibrium Theory," *American Economic Review*, 66:288-94, 1976.

Sraffa, Piero, *The Production of Commodities by Means of Commodities*, Cambridge University Press, Cambridge, 1960.

Tinbergen, Jan, "The Equalisation of Factor Prices Between Free Trade Areas," *Metroeconomica*, I:40-47, 1949.

Tinbergen, Jan, *Statistical Testing of Business Cycle Theories*, Vols. I and II, The League of Nations, Geneva, 1939.

von Neumann, John, "Zur Theorie der Gesellschaftsspiele," *Mathematische Annalen*, 100: 295-320, 1928.

von Neumann, John, Über ein Ökonomisches Gleichungssystem und eine Verallgemeinerung des Brouwerschen Fixpunktsatzes, in Karl Menger (ed.), *Ergebrisse eines mathematische Kolloquiums*, 8, 1937. Translated as "A model of general equilibrium," *Review of Economic Studies*, 13:1-9, 1945-46.

von Neumann, John and Morgenstern, Oskar, *Theory of Games and Economic Behavior*, John Wiley & Sons, New York, 1944.

© Indian Journal of Applied Economics, 1996

Gustav Cassel's Scientific Innovations: Claims and Realities

Paul A. Samuelson

1. Contamination of the Record

H. L. Mencken, as a prank, published the notion that it was President Martin Van Buren who first introduced a bathtub into the White House. Despite determined denials and published notices, never could the record be cleared of this erroneous allegation. Gustav Cassel did not— repeat, not—anticipate the key notions of what has come to be called "the theory of revealed preference." But because Hans Brems (1989) or Herman Wold and Lars Juréen (1953) can be construed to have asserted that he had done so, and despite the demonstration of Lars Pålsson Syll (1993) that Cassel had never done so, until the end of time there will, I fear, remain confusion about Cassel's alleged priorities.

As an optimist I shall try to clarify the issues. More constructively I can exposit what are the relations between (a) conventional *utilitarian* theories of demand à la Bentham, Walras, Edgeworth, Marshall, Fisher, Wicksell, etc.; (b) *ordinal* utility paradigms à la Pareto, Fisher, W. E. Johnson, Slutsky, Antonelli, Hicks-Allen, Hotelling, Samuelson, Wold, etc.; (c) "revealed *demand* paradigm" of Cournot, Cassel, etc.; (d) "revealed *preference* paradigm" of Samuelson, Houthakker, Afriat, Varian, etc.; (e) most-*general* revealed-preference calculus of Pareto, Arrow, etc. Just to complete the story, I shall finish with various remarks about Gustav Cassel, the man, the scholar, and the public figure.

Correspondence may be addressed to Professor Paul Samuelson, Department of Economics, E52-383C, Massachusetts Institute of Technology, Cambridge MA 02139-4307.

2. Standard Utility Equilibrium

How would Marshall, Wicksell, and Fisher handle the consumer-demand problem when they contemplated several individuals who each face the prices of, say, three goods, and where consumers got their spendable incomes from the pricing the competitive market put on their endowment of primary productive factors? *All* schools would write demand functions for *each* consumer as

$$q_j^* = f^j(p_1, p_2, p_3; I), j = 1, 2, 3;$$
$$\sum_1^3 p_j f^j(p_1, p_2, p_3, I) = I \tag{1}$$

where for the schools (a) and (b) (q_1^*, q_2^*, q_3^*) are the utility-maximizing roots of the calculus problem

$$\underset{q_i}{\mathrm{Max}} U(q_1, q_2, q_3) \text{ subject to } \sum_1^3 p_j q_j = I. \tag{2}$$

The first-order conditions for this maximum, written in a way to please both schools (a) and (b), would be

$$\frac{\partial U[q_1, q_2, q_3]/\partial q_i}{\sum_1^3 q_j \partial U[q_1, q_2, q_3]/\partial q_j} = \frac{p_i}{\sum_1^3 p_j q_j} = \frac{p_i}{I},$$
$$i = 1, 2, 3. \tag{3}$$

To use modern language, if a standard $U(.)$ is strictly *concave* (or even strictly quasi-concave), the consumer's demand will be unique as the three independent equations of (3) have a single root in the three unknown q's.

Cassel had a point in 1899 when he protested that the "facts" of (1) did not give us an objective utility function $U[q_1, q_2, q_3]$. He was as naive as a babe about the truth that an infinite class of identifiable *indicators* of utility can be recovered from the equation (1) data if the consumer does have a consistent set of "wants" (a word Cassel often *did* feel obliged to use!). It was Pareto (1909) and Slutsky (1915) who grappled with this latter problem—with limited mathematical success by Pareto. Later R. G. D. Allen, Hicks, Hotelling, and a crowd of us

735

cleared up those problems. Cassel was alive but never seems even to have heard of the problem. (Hicks and Allen [1934] used observable "marginal rate of substitution" to avoid using even one inferable *indicator* of utility; Hicks [1939] relapsed into *ordinal* utility usage.)

3. Revealed Preference Gets Born

Around 1937 or 1938, when my teacher Gottfried Haberler objected even to indifference curves (but persisted with *his* economic theory of index numbers), I perceived that one could indeed analyze the "revealed *demand* functions" of equation (1) by use only of the two (or more) finite (p,q) points of index-number theory. No Newtonian derivatives were needed, no marginal rate of substitution slopes, and not even *ordinal* indicators of utility. One did not even have to use the binary choices "I *like* goods-combination *A better* than *B*; or I am indifferent between *A* and *B*." My 1938-coined "Weak Axiom (of 2-situation, Binary Preference)"—which said, "If *B* could have been bought in the *A* situation but was definitely not, then it must not *also* be the case in the *B* situation that '*A* could have been bought but was definitely not.' "—would behavioristically do the job in the 2-good demand case.

Thus, Cassel's revealed-*demand* approach, which was quite empty of any useful comparative-statical properties (such as proof that $\partial q_i/\partial p_i$ was negative or averaged out negative), never before or after 1938 grappled with the search by all the other schools for testable hypotheses that consumer's demand must meet. Cassel never remotely heard about or thought about these logical niceties and methodological subtleties. Nor are Brems (1989) or Wold and Juréen (1953) seen to allege that he did. Thus Brems cogently alleges that Cassel took a revealed-*demand* approach, but then indulges in the pun of mislabeling this to be a "revealed *preference* approach."

Some erudite authors have asked why I did not in 1938 cite the earlier use of my "Weak Axiom" in the Abraham Wald (1935) proof of the existence of an equilibrium in a Walras-Cassel-Schlesinger model. My cheerful answer would have been: "Not until years after 1938 did I ever hear of Wald's German text in Karl Menger's Viennese mathematics colloquium." However, my deeper answer ought to have been: "Samuelson's 1938 Weak Axiom, although it does contain the expression '$\sum_1^3 \Delta p_j \Delta q_j < 0$' that was also contained in Wald's

1935 hypotheses, is quite a different animal. Wald's relation is not the Samuelson Weak Axiom." A terminological quibble? Not at all, as a footnote will explain.[1]

Needless to say, the Cassel who never dreamed of 2-goods preference niceties never remotely dreamed of the 3-goods complexities involved in the "integrability" issues addressed by Antonelli, Fisher, Pareto, Volterra, R. G. D. Allen, G. C. Evans, Hotelling, Georgescu-Roegen, Wold, Samuelson, and Houthakker. Gustav Cassel made many claims for originality—indeed more than can be substantiated—but he never claimed title to "revealed preference," by name or by substantive content.

Before leaving the 2-good case of the pre–Houthakker theory, let me clarify some possible misunderstandings. For $n = 2$, revealed preference provides *all* the comparative-statics properties of equation (1)'s demand functions that are entailed by the utilitarian or ordinal-utility paradigms of (a) and (b) above. And it adds no new restrictions on the observable facts. Aside from delighting a Watsonian behaviorist, a Bridgman operationalist, or a prewar logical positivist, it provides an economical way of testing or refuting the hypothesized deductive theory: no delicate measurements of Newtonian partial derivatives are, in principle, ever needed. As a young enthusiast in the 1938–47 period, I set considerable store on this exclusion of other than finite, *discrete* (p, q) observations. That was "revealed preference theory" in its strict and narrow sense.

---

1. For explication, consider an equivalent form of (1): $q_j = f^j(p_1/I, p_2/I, p_3/I; 1) = f^j(\pi_1, \pi_2, \pi_3)$. Ignoring the awkward Schlesinger-Wald functions that write the price vector as a function of the quantity vector rather than vice versa, a 1935 Wald reader would translate his relation to be this: the f's are restricted to satisfy, for (π_j^a) and (π_j^b) distinct points:

$$\sum_1^3 (\pi_j^a - \pi_j^b)[f^j(\pi_1^a, \pi_2^a, \pi_3^a) - f^j(\pi_1^b, \pi_2^b, \pi_3^b)] < 0. \tag{*}$$

By contrast, in 1938, I prescribe for (1)'s f functions subject to

$$\sum_1^3 \pi_j^a[f^j(\pi_1^b, \pi_2^b, \pi_3^b) - f^j(\pi_1^a, \pi_2^a, \pi_3^a)] = 0, \tag{**}$$

$$\sum_1^3 (\pi_j^a - \pi_j^b)[f^j(\pi_1^a, \pi_2^a, \pi_3^a) - f^j(\pi_1^b, \pi_2^b, \pi_3^b)] < 0. \tag{***}$$

For "homothetic" demand, where income elasticities are *all unity*, 1935 and 1938 would be the same. But neither author limited the analysis to that singular case. In general, a pair of my observed points can violate the 1935 equation (*)—so long as they do not happen singularly to satisfy (**). As applied to my f's, Wald's (*) would even rule out the (admissible!) Giffen Paradox and the frequently met case where one of two goods has negative income elasticity! Finally, Wald's is a specified artifact to permit proof of an elegant special result; the 1938 Weak Axiom is naturally motivated by any rational person's binary-choice behavior.

Running parallel with this narrower preoccupation were my articles and *Foundations* researches on "exactly what is revealed about the slopes and higher derivatives of the observable demand functions that are entailed by a maximizing consumer?" No longer could critics say: "Bah, *whatever* people do is what pleases them most." After Slutsky, we could prove what Cassel took for granted as true: for example, if I rationally buy more tea when I get more income, then indeed a rise in its price will kill off some of my demand for tea.

Warning. The 1938 theory does not require that indifference contours be convex to the origin. They can be anything. Where they are concave, no preference will be revealed under competition. Demand will bifurcate and jump. Why not? As a heuristic explorer, I did sometimes simplify by positing standard convexity; sometimes I tried to be general. As I reread my *Collected Papers*, I sympathize with the reader of the 1930s and 1940s who tried to achieve exact understanding.[2]

Warning. Standard revealed preference *always* presupposes straight-line budget constraints or *linear* hyperplanes. Its logic differs from the bimodal Aristotelian logic ("excluded middle") of general binary

---

2. Between 1938 and 1947, and since then as Pålsson Syll (1993) points out, I have been scrupulously careful not to claim for revealed preference theory novelties and advantages it does not merit. But Pålsson Syll's readers must not believe that it was all redundant fuss about not very much. (a) It was a program of research that had to establish where it overlapped and differed from previous theory. In history, revealed preference "revealed" how to complete its predecessor doctrine. (b) It (under Houthakker's augmentation) established the exact and complete testings that *finite* (p_j, q_j) data had to pass if a price taker did possess coherent preferences. By contrast, Henry Schultz (1938) and others in the post–Hotelling tradition had to estimate functional forms from demand data and then test on their calculated cross derivatives whether "integrability conditions" held. (c) When a Slutsky or a 1939 Hicks used any one of an infinity of utility indicators as a maximand, they implicitly ruled out lexicographic orderings—which revealed preference had no need to do. (d) A modern reader must not suppose that earlier careful readers of Herman Wold or other admirable innovators were in a position to understand the relationships between *narrow* revealed preference and standard 1939 preference theory. (e) When a commentator links Cassel's revealed-demand approach with the similar approach of Cournot (1838), in light of Cournot's deservedly high reputation that would seem to be a compliment. However, Jacob Viner (1937, 586–89) gives a harsh review of where this approach led Cournot in his normative analysis of trade relations. (f) Pålsson Syll does well to differentiate Cassel from such earlier innovators as Antonelli, Fisher, Pareto, W. Johnson, Slutsky, Hicks-Allen (and I may add Edgeworth). But in connection with enunciating testable (P_j, Q_j) theorems, this is a mixed bag. Slutsky (1915) succeeded in what Pareto attempted in the early 1890s; but before Pareto began serious study of economics, G. B. Antonelli (1886) had presented non-finite-point reciprocity conditions that $(P_j/P_1, q_j)$ data must directly satisfy. And one could cite a succession of writers on the economic theory of index numbers—Könus, Staehle, Haberler, Leontief, Frisch, Pigou, J. M. Keynes, and so on—who are direct inspirers of (narrow) revealed preference.

choice theory. That is why I earlier distinguished (narrow) "revealed preference theory of Samuelson-Houthakker" from "*general* preference calculus" of the type Arrow (1959) and Houthakker have elsewhere analyzed. In the former standard scenario, A is never "indifferent" to B; and it can well be the case that "neither point is revealed to be worse than the other."

To complete the non-Casselian story, it was the young Hendrik Houthakker who, on his 1950 maiden voyage, completed the n-good story. He augmented the 2-position relations of the Weak Axiom with the Strong Axiom as applied to any number of pairs of positions. The Strong Axiom says in effect: If point A is "revealed" to be "better" than B, and B "better" than C, and C "better" than D, ... and D "better" than Z, then it must not be the case that Z is "revealed to be better than A." If the Weak and Strong Axioms are always satisfied by equation (1)'s demand functions for all observations, then a Wicksellian can employ (an infinity of) objective utility functions and be immune to the Casselian objections. Thus, had Cassel truly anticipated revealed preference theory, his 1899 program would have self-destructed at its beginning—like the Wasa that sank in Stockholm Harbor, before the King and Court, on its maiden voyage in the seventeenth century.

4. Cassel, Warts and All

Having documented so to speak that the White House did have bathtubs before Van Buren's time, let me comment on Gustav Cassel.

I once said that Cassel, having been overpraised by the public in the century's first quarter, thereby came to be undervalued in modern times. Brems quotes that correctly. But I should have given a stronger reason for his fall from favor with scholars. Cassel had grave personal and scholarly defects. Yes, Schumpeter praised him. But Schumpeter's fulsome praise is often faint praise; when he said Cassel's text was just right for Europe, that reflected his low opinion of Continental economics. Cassel had Napoleonic pretensions. Like some moderns, Cassel was often in error but never in doubt. He was notorious for never properly acknowledging earlier priorities. Schumpeter aptly used to say: "Cassel is 10 percent Walras and 90 percent water." When the young Ohlin acknowledged that his brilliant trade theory of 1924 and 1933 was a combination of Heckscher and Cassel, Cassel as his adviser tried to get him to cut out the Heckscher ballast.

I am told that Cassel's Swedish autobiography of 1940–41 is self-incriminating on all these enumerated faults. I will add once again a story I heard from the lips of Hans Christian Sonne, the merchant banker who angelled the American National Planning Association and entrepreneured our 1961 *Commission on Money and Credit*. Cassel dined at the house of Sonne's father in Denmark not long after the First World War. A fellow guest mentioned that a young researcher had just disproved Cassel's demonstration that the 1865–1914 price level exactly mirrored the cumulative trends of gold production, à la the Quantity Theory. To the question, "What are you going to do about it?" Cassel is supposed to have replied in much the following terms: "I have a worthless son-in-law whom I have supported in theological studies. Just as he is in sight of ordination, he comes to me with the news that he has lost his faith. My advice to him is 'Just carry on as if nothing had happened.' And that's my answer to your question. I am going to carry on as if nothing had happened."

Very well. We understand half the story—why Wicksell disagreed with Cassel, and much else. But why do I now call Cassel underrated? Whether he is quite of Wicksell's stature, he was in absolute terms a creative scientist. Brems and Wicksell are right that he had a flair for quantitative statistical relationships, but more than that Cassel was an important theorist. Perhaps he deserves more than the *New Palgrave* patronizing notice (Gustaffson 1987).

The older generation of Cassel and Heckscher were conservative in politics. But they correctly favored countercyclical central bank policy to moderate the business tides and the Great Depression. They were leagues ahead of 1992 Milton Friedman or Robert Lucas. Cassel, like Wicksell, was an independent progenitor of marginal-cost pricing in public utilities, railroads, and situations of imperfect competition.

After achieving some competence in mathematics, Cassel in few years mastered a persuasive and lucid style in Swedish, German, French, and English. Several early books brought him international recognition. His insistence on the role of the interest rate in a socialist society would play well in today's Eastern Europe. His Senior-like interest theory puts stress on Modigliani life-cycle factors. (On the other hand, his specific view of a definite long-run plateau for the interest rate—determined at a critical level where people in the affluent stage of their life cycle choose between eating up their capital by use of life annuities or bequeathing it at death—lacks both theoretical plausibility and econometric support. Also, his replacement of the ambiguity of a "capital magnitude" by the ambiguity of a "capital disposal" concept robs Peter to avoid robbing Paul.) Brems (1989) nicely resurrects and mathematizes Cassel's anticipation of Hotelling's economics of exhaustible resources as it involves the interest rate.

Cassel borrowed from Ricardo as well as from Walras, also without acknowledgement or remorse. His important Ricardian doctrine of "purchasing-power parity" still lives on in the many slippery forms Cassel gave it. (To my taste it is not primarily, or simply, a tautology of *spatial* price arbitrage; rather its deepest content is the germ of truth at the international level inherent in the Quantity Theory notion that at the longest run it is only *relative* prices and prices *relative to the total money stock* that matter.)

Cassel deserves highest marks for having already in 1918 what is essentially the exponential growth model of Harrod-Domar. By hindsight, we recognize it as an accelerator-multiplier model. (Remark: although 1917 J. M. Clark is usually given credit for the accelerator, Hawtrey in 1913 had done much that Cassel was soon to do; also Bickerdike and Aftalion definitely glimpsed the principle of acceleration. Harrod, like Cassel, thought himself to be the first to combine the accelerator and multiplier into a Keynesian growth model.) By a quirk of fate, Cassel's growth model was a stone thrown into the pool of economic science that had virtually no pre–World War II ripples. It was of course a full-employment model with no aspects of Keynesian effective demand in it. Some have wondered why Cassel's growth system did not influence von Neumann's model of general equilibrium growth. But Cassel's is an *open* model with discretionary consumption and saving, with wage level set by scarcity of labor supply; by contrast, von Neumann's is a closed model with no discretionary consumption, or above-subsistence wages; I would be astonished if a mathematician who turned the pages of the Cassel book could even notice in it the growth model.[3]

---

3. In this article's circulated first draft, I gratuitously attributed to Brems (1989) the claim that Cassel's exponential growth paradigm anticipated the input-output models of Leontief, Sraffa, and von Neumann. For this, I apologize. Even Cassel's student Ohlin, when he improved on the assumption of fixed a_{ij} coefficients in 1924 and 1933, never introduces any *input*-output structure of the type "input of coal to product iron." I should mention that Ohlin's versions of Cassel-Walras, in their strong neoclassical versions of tastes and technology where all variables are indispensable and never satiate, could ignore modern inequalities and zero prices; under homothetic, uniform tastes, the equilibrium could be assuredly

I call attention to another Cassel felicity. Patinkin rightly faults his textbook's invalid dichotomy between absolute and relative prices. The 1932 edition text is as bad in the Patinkin scorebook as the 1918 or 1923 text. But, as discussed recently in Samuelson, Patinkin, and Blaug 1991 (150–56), the discussion in the popular lectures of Cassel (1925, chap. 2) does correctly avoid the illegitimate dichotomy: Patinkin grants that Cassel's 1925 words are quite consistent with an irreproachable Quantity Theory formalism involving *real* relations determined by *real* (P_j/M, W_i/M) variables only—so that the resulting Walras system is never decomposable into a mystical "barter system" plus a Quantity Equation of exchange. Chalk one up for 1925 Gustav Cassel!

I turn now to the famous review by Wicksell ([1919] 1934) of Cassel's textbook and lifework. Wicksell remained radical and bohemian. Cassel was increasingly conservative and rose in the establishment.[4] Success came hard and late for Wicksell. To Cassel it came easy and early. Wicksell got his Lund chair after Cassel withdrew his name from the competition. But this, apparently, was not so much a gesture of chivalry as the result of the recognition that Wicksell would be the winner. In any case, Cassel soon got a more congenial Stockholm chair in the capital metropolis. He wrote for banks, and like Heckscher and Ohlin, contributed hundreds and hundreds of newspaper articles. Cassel was adviser to the League of Nations and was a much-quoted authority.

Wicksell's was the ultimate revenge, as he secured posthumous fame both in Sweden and abroad as a great neoclassical scientist. Even vis-à-vis Alfred Marshall, Wicksell's terms of trade have risen in this century. In his old age retirement and on the occasion of the 1918 publication of Cassel's textbook, Wicksell wrote: "On various grounds, mostly personal, I have never undertaken a public criticism of . . .

---

unique. When Gödel heard the Wald seminar, he asked naively why people were not given incomes determined by their factors' prices—precisely as Cassel and Ohlin specified and contrary to the inferior model that the Viennese banker Karl Schlesinger (1935) assigned to Wald.

4. Here is evidence on Cassel's early elevated social position. At the 1970 Nobel festivities when I had my personal interview with the erudite and popular King Gustavus VI, he said to me, "I had an economics tutor [that would have been at the century's beginning], but you wouldn't know his name." "Try me," I said. It was Gustav Cassel. (It is permissible now to repeat the King's further words.) "I have a theory about economics but I wouldn't dare to express it." "Go on," I said. "I think we're all spending too much money these days." As the twig is bent, so grows the tree.

[Cassel's post-1899] work. If I delayed much longer, it might be too late for either or both of us" ([1919] 1934, 219–20).

In his long review, Wicksell does score many weighty points about Cassel the polemicist and oversimplifier (see for example Wicksell [1919] 1934, 248, para. 2, where Wicksell anticipates the 1919 Heckscher doctrines of factor-price equalization by trade!). But the score is by no means one sided. Wicksell always exaggerated the importance of land scarcity for twentieth-century Europe, just as Cassel soft-pedaled it. Was Cassel wrong? Was Wicksell right to reject out of hand Cassel's growth model, especially in view of possible land-saving innovations? Should Wicksell ([1919] 1934, 248, para. 3) have held *against* Cassel his anticipation of modern *golden rule* theory? Or awarded Cassel applause? Again, it was land that hypnotized Wicksell.

On the present topic, Cassel's insistence on eschewing utility in favor of positivistic demand functions, what is my scoring? Definitely mixed. To make interpersonal welfare-economic policies, one does need ethical norms. But before the works of Abram Bergson (1938) and John Harsanyi (1955), Cassel and Wicksell were in good company in being confused about the kinds of utility or preference mathematics needed. Cassel is ignorantly provocative where Wicksell is cautious. But Wicksell had not digested the Pareto and Slutsky ordinal utility paradigm that sufficed in (b) above to generate a useful positivistic demand theory of equation (1) above. Also, Cassel's caviling about the infinite divisibility of goods cuts neutrally across the utility polemics.

As a final task, I want to benefit from the Pålsson Syll commentaries on development of Cassel's anti-utility expositions over the years. Cassel began in 1899 determined to be provocative. After 1924, perhaps under criticism from his pupil Myrdal,[5] Cassel weakens a bit, insisting that economics does not need psychological utility apparatus but claiming not to oppose its (redundant?) analysis. On the other hand, a

---

5. It came as a surprise to me that the brash and radical Gunnar Myrdal was Cassel's favorite pupil. Sissela Bok's biography of her parents describes the intimacy between the older Cassel family and the Myrdal family. After a few years of what we would call graduate study in economics, Gunnar issued for the younger generation a declaration of independence from Heckscher and the older generation and from the cherished objectivist certainties of neoclassical economics. Not only did Myrdal's career survive, but when the impatient Myrdal told Gustav that the time had come for Cassel to yield his chair, the 67-year-old did so! I repeat again their famous dialogue. Cassel: "Don't be so independent, Gunnar. Remember your promotion depends on us older scholars." Gunnar: "Yes, but remember it is we younger scholars who will be writing your obituaries." See the obituary of Cassel in Myrdal 1945.

few Pålsson Syll quotations from Cassel's 1938 edition seem more dogmatic to me than those in the 1932 edition.

I have mentioned that the Swedish autobiography of Cassel (1940–41) shows little remorse, or regression toward the mean of modesty. I understand that a Swedish biography of Cassel, by his secretary, alibis for his scholarly borrowings by blaming it on his hatred for his father, which Freudianly caused him to forget from whom he had learned in his youth. If that trauma was responsible, it lasted a lifetime.

In recent times, Samuelson (1987, 1988, 1991) has been an exponent of Whig History in *Dogmengeschichte*. The past is usefully viewed and ordered in terms of the latest cumulative contents of economic science. Aside from the manifest dangers of self-indulgence and complacency in such a viewpoint, we see in the writings of Cassel, Brems, and Pålsson Syll how demanding must be analyses in this area *if we are to get history right—get it as it really was.*

References

Antonelli, G. B. 1886. *Sulla Teoria matematica della economia politica*. Pisa: Nella Tipografia del Folchetto.

Arrow, Kenneth J. 1959. Rational Choice Functions and Orderings. *Economica*, n.s. 26.102:121–27.

Bergson, Abram. 1938. A Reformulation of Certain Aspects of Welfare Economics. *Quarterly Journal of Economics* 52.2:310–34.

Bickerdike, C. F. 1914. A Non-Monetary Cause of Fluctuations in Employment. *Economic Journal* 24.95:357–70.

Bok, Sissela. 1991. *Alva Myrdal*. Reading, Mass.: Addison-Wesley.

Boulding, K. E., and G. J. Stigler, eds. 1953. *Readings in Price Theory*. London: Allen & Unwin.

Brems, Hans. 1989. Gustav Cassel Revisited. *HOPE* 21.2 (Summer): 165–78.

Cassel, Gustav. 1899. Grundriss einer elementaren Preislehre. *Zeitschrift für die gesamte Staatswissenschaft* 55:395–458.

——— .1903. *The Nature and Necessity of Interest*. London and New York: Macmillan.

——— . [1923] 1932. *Theory of Social Economy*. London: E. Benn.

——— . 1925. *Fundamental Thoughts in Economics*. New York: Harcourt Brace.

——— . 1940–41. *I förnuftets tjänst (In the Service of Reason)*, 2 vols. Stockholm: Natur och Kulter.

Clark, John M. 1917. Business Acceleration and the Law of Demand: A Technical Factor in Economics Cycles. *Journal of Political Economy* 25.3:217–35.

Cournot, A. A. [1838] 1927. *Researches into the Mathematical Principles of the Theory of Wealth*, translated 1927. New York: Macmillan.
Domar, E. D. 1946. Capital Expansion, Rate of Growth and Employment. *Econometrica* 14.2:137–47.
Georgescu-Roegen, Nicholas. 1936. The Pure Theory of Consumer's Behavior. *Quarterly Journal of Economics* 50.3:545–93.
Gustaffson, Bo. 1987. Gustav Cassel. In vol. 1 of *The New Palgrave: A Dictionary of Economics*, edited by John Eatwell, Murray Milgate, and Peter Newman. New York: Stockton.
Harrod, R. F. 1948. *Towards a Dynamic Economics*. London: Macmillan.
Harsanyi, John C. 1955. Cardinal Welfare, Individualistic Ethics, and Interpersonal Comparisons of Utility. *Journal of Political Economy.* 63.4:309–21.
Hicks, John R. 1939. *Value and Capital*. Oxford: Clarendon.
Hicks, John R., and R. G. D. Allen. 1934. A Reconsideration of the Theory of Value. Parts 1–2. *Economica* n.s. 1.1:52–76 and 1.2:196–219.
Hotelling, Harold. 1931. The Economics of Exhaustible Resources. *Journal of Political Economy* 39.2:137–75.
———. 1932. Edgeworth's Taxation Paradox and the Nature of Demand and Supply Functions. *Journal of Political Economy* 40.5:577–616.
———. 1935. Demand Functions with Limited Budgets. *Econometrica* 3.1:66–78.
Houthakker, Hendrik S. 1950. Revealed Preference and the Utility Function. *Economica* n.s. 17.2:159–74.
Myrdal, G. 1945. Gustav Cassel in Memoriam. *Ekonomisk Revy* 2:3–13. Translated in 1963 by Göran Ohlin in *Institute of Economics and Statistics, Oxford* 25.1:1–10.
Pålsson Syll, Lars. 1993. Cassel and Revealed Preference Theory. *HOPE*, this issue.
Pareto, Vilfred. [1909] 1971. *Manual of Political Economy*. New York: Augustus Kelley.
Samuelson, Paul A. 1938. A Note on the Pure Theory of Consumer's Behavior. *Economica* n.s. 5.1:61–71. Reproduced as Chapter 1 in *The Collected Scientific Papers of Paul A. Samuelson*, 1966, MIT Press, Cambridge.
———. [1947] 1983. *Foundations of Economic Analysis*. Cambridge and London: Harvard University Press.
———. 1950. The Problem of Integrability in Utility Theory. *Economica* 17.68:355–85. Reproduced as Chapter 10 in *The Collected Scientific Papers of Paul A. Samuelson*, 1966, MIT Press, Cambridge.
———. 1968. What Classical and Neoclassical Monetary Theory Really Was. *Canadian Journal of Economics* 1.1:1–15.
———. 1987. Out of the Closet: A Program for the Whig History of Economic Science. *History of Economics Society Bulletin* 9.1:51–60.
———. 1988. Keeping Whig History Honest. *History of Economics Society Bulletin* 10.2:161–67.

Samuelson, Paul A., Don Patinkin, and Mark Blaug. 1991. On the Historiography of Economics: A Correspondence. *Journal of the History of Economic Thought* 13.2:144–58.

Schlesinger, Karl. [1935] 1968. On the Production Equations of Economic Value Theory. In *Precursors in Mathematical Economics: An Anthology,* edited by William Baumol and Stephen Goldfeld. London: The London School of Economics and Political Science.

Schultz, Henry. 1938. *The Theory and Measurement of Demand.* Chicago: The University of Chicago Press.

Schumpeter, Joseph. 1954. *A History of Economic Analysis.* New York: Oxford University Press.

Slutsky, Eugen. 1915. Sulla teoria del bilancio del consumatore. *Giornale degli Economisti e Rivista di Statistica* 51 (July): 1–26. Translated as On the Theory of the Budget of the Consumer, in Boulding and Stigler, 1953.

Viner, J. 1937. *Studies in the Theory of International Trade.* New York: Harper & Brothers.

von Neumann, John. 1937. Über ein Ökonomisches Gleichungssystem und ein Verallgemeinerung des Brouwerschen Fixpunktsatzes. *Ergebnisse eines Mathematichen Kolloquiums* 8. Translated in 1945 as, A Model for General Equilibrium, *Review of Economic Studies* 13.1:1–9.

Wald, Abraham. 1935 and 1936. On the Unique Non-Negative Solvability of the New Production of Equations (Parts I, II). In *Precursors in Mathematical Economics: An Anthology,* edited by Willliam Baumol and Stephen Goldfeld. London: The London School of Economics and Political Science.

Wicksell, Knut. [1919] 1934. Professor Cassels nationalekonomiska system. *Ekonomisk Tidskrift* 21:195–226. Translated as Professor Cassel's System of Economics by S. Adler as Appendix 1 to vol. 1 of *Lectures on Political Economy* by Knut Wicksell. New York: Macmillan.

Wold, Herman, and Lars Juréen. 1953. *Demand Analysis: A Study in Econometrics.* New York: John Wiley & Sons; and Stockholm: Almqvist & Wicksell.

Piero Sraffa (1898-1983)
Paul A. Samuelson
Corriere della Sera, 1983

Piero Sraffa was one of the great economists of the century. His fame was based upon few publications, but their quality was so high as to make up for their infrequency and brevity. Aside from Sraffa's contribution to political economy, he achieved a position in the history of ideas through his influence on the great philosopher Ludwig Wittgenstein.

Piero Sraffa, while still a young Italian visitor to Britain, attracted the interest of John Maynard Keynes at Cambridge University. He was made a lifetime Fellow of Trinity College on the basis of one fundamental article (which was itself a translation and development of an earlier paper written in Italian). During his more than half-century academic career at Cambridge, Sraffa gave virtually no lectures. He never attended routine scientific conferences. His seminar for graduate students consisted primarily of their reading papers to each other. For a brief period of time Sraffa was Director of Research at Cambridge; but, since the position required him to be up and about a couple of mornings in the week, at his own request he was moved down to be Assistant Director of Research, in which capacity he constituted the whole of the research department.

A wasted life, you might be tempted to conclude on the basis of my description? If so, you show that you do not understand the nature of brilliant scholarly achievement. Great ideas are very rare indeed. They come as gifts from the gods to prepared minds, and are not the result of burning the midnight oil. The late Harry Johnson, to take the example of a superlative scholar of the type different from Sraffa, had more papers in proof when he died than Sraffa published in his whole lifetime. But not one of the Johnson papers, excellent as they each were, would be greatly missed if it had never been written, whereas scarcity itself imparts value and there is no scrap from Sraffa's pen that we would not be loathe to lose.

When the encyclopedias record Piero Sraffa's contributions to economics, they will list them under at least three headings. First, Sraffa was a contributor to the *monopolistic competition revolution* that we associate with the names of Joan Robinson, Edward Chamberlin, and other writers of the 1930s. Second, Sraffa was the incomparable editor of the complete works and letters of David Ricardo. Third, and this came as an unexpected bonus toward the close of Sraffa's active academic career, Sraffa's modern classic appeared under the title, *The Production of Commodities by Means of Commodities*.

The personality and lifetime incidents of a scholar count as nothing in comparison to his scientific innovations. But before describing and evaluating those scholarly achievements of Piero

Sraffa, let me devote a few words to his personal biography. In a sense Piero Sraffa led an existence that would be hard to imagine outside a world of capitalism and private property. In Marxian terms, subsistence is provided out of surplus value to students who do not toil in the fields nor spin in the factories, but instead think deep thoughts and rummage in the library. Figuratively speaking, the profits that Friends of Cambridge University like Maynard Keynes were able to wrest out of the marketplace and give to that university were what made Sraffa's great intellectual achievements possible. (My old teacher Joseph Schumpeter, who had met the brilliant Sraffa in the early 1920s, I seem to recall described him as bearing the burden of being a spoiled rich man's son; but, since Sraffa's father was a professor, I do not know whether Schumpeter had warrant in making that description.) A vulgar version of the materialist determination of history, according to which the lackeys who live off surplus value lick the hands that feed them and become apologists for the capitalistic order, would misfire as applied to Piero Sraffa. As is well known, he was a friend and benefactor of Gramsci, one of Italy's great communist martyrs. Although Sraffa's writings are apolitical, his frame of mind was deeply critical of capitalism and of neoclassical doctrines purporting to provide it with intellectual apologetics. This showed itself in the implicit, and sometimes explicit, criticisms that Sraffa made of the marginal productivity notions that were orthodox before and after his time. But it also showed itself in his basic set of mind. During the cold war of the late 1940s Piero Sraffa once asked me as an American whether my government really believed that Britain would agree to serve as an airfield for the United States. On still another occasion when we were walking through the beautiful Backs of Cambridge, the sophisticated Sraffa amazed me by defending the curious notion in Marx (and in Adam Smith's concept of "productive labor") that services are not productive and only material goods that you can kick and insure are really productive.

    The late Michael Kalecki of Poland used to tell the story that he went to England to find out what an English gentleman was really like. But in all his travels there he was able to encounter only two English gentlemen--one of whom was a communist and the other an Italian! Kalecki was referring to Maurice Dobb and to Piero Sraffa, and as far as ideological sympathies are concerned, one is not sure that he could not have spoken of two communists. As kind of a hidden life Sraffa continued to follow with interest the obscure political maneuverings of continental left-wing groups.

    Piero Sraffa had a handsome, if sad, face: great brown eyes; lean, swarthy cheekbones; iron-gray, close-cropped hair. His countenance was anything but that of an English blond, although a gentleman he was. I am the more conscious of his appearance because he was a double for the Italian doctor from Gary, Indiana, who brought me into this world and for whom I am named. Although from Turin, Sraffa had to my eye the expressive gestures of the South of Italy; and one can believe the legend that attributes Wittgenstein's new second philosophical stage to a query put to him in a railroad station by Piero Sraffa, in which Sraffa made a Sicilian gesture and asked Wittgenstein how that fitted in with his theory of language and tautology.

Sraffa, in my opinion, might well have earned a Nobel Prize on two accounts. His editing of the published and unpublished writings of David Ricardo is itself a work of art. Like many great works of art it was done over a long period of time. Keynes and the Royal Economic Society expected the finished work to be ready not long after 1930. Sraffa even bought the paper for it before the outbreak of World War II. The century was more than half over before the last volume left the editor's desk. Some explanation for the delay can be found in Sraffa's desire to include every scrap of letter, every laundry list of the master. Often, and thanks to Sraffa's detective work, new letters did continue to be found. But beyond that, the editor's perfectionism led to endless delays. When his secretary aged in his service and was forced by the passage of time to move on to marriage, Sraffa's progress was blocked by her not being there in the room while he worked. He found, however, that if Maurice Dobb would sit in the room, that was a partial substitute and with Dobb's editorial help the job finally got done. (Dobb's autobiography reveals that it was actually he, Dobb, who wrote the introduction to Ricardo's volume of *Principles*, a claim that ought to be investigated and audited by Lord Kahn or some other contemporary of Sraffa at Cambridge.)

When Samuel Johnson was told that it took the whole French Academy to collect the vocabulary of the French language while he as a single person was constructing his great dictionary, Johnson replied: As forty is to one, so is an Englishman to a Frenchman. When we observe the platoons of Yale scholars and coveys of computers needed to edit the papers of Horace Walpole and of James Boswell, we appreciate the perfection of Sraffa's editing of Ricardo. The harvest was well worth waiting for. And it was fruit without blemish.

Piero Sraffa would also have merited a Nobel Prize in his own right or along with Joan Robinson or with Wassily Leontief, for his work on time-phased systems of input-output. He began what became *The Production of Commodities by Means of Commodities* in the late 1920s. He put the work aside to finish off the Ricardo editing. When he picked up the thread again in the 1950s, he told me,

"Nothing has changed in the field of capital theory." Actually, one cannot agree that this was so. But the science of economics would have been much the richer if Knight, von Neumann, Leontief, Koopmans, Robinson, and other scholars of my generation had had available to them the results of Sraffa's investigations. By 1960, linear and nonlinear dynamic programming had independently rediscovered the hard way much of what was original with Sraffa.

Sraffa's positive findings were important for the neo-Keynesian critique of marginalism. In particular, although his simultaneous equation formulation of price determination in a sense refuted Karl Marx's purported paradigm of equalized surplus value and defended Ricardo's classicism along the same lines that Dmitriev and Bortkiewicz were to do at the turn of the century, Sraffa's exposition made clear that changes in the profit rate could move the price ratio between two goods both upward and downward and thereby make it possible for a given choice of technique to be optimal at both a high and a low rate of interest. Although Irving Fisher had noted the same reswitching phenomena, Sraffa provided Robinson, Pasinetti, and Garegnani with unmistakable proof that Clarkian neoclassical models were oversimplified in thinking that waiting and abstinence invariably lowers the rate of interest and in doing so raises the level of society's consumption. Sraffa's finding filled a deep ideological need for the critics of the market order and met with a resonant effective demand.

Those of us who worked in think tanks during World War II will remember that a puzzle concerning how to identify a false weight coin swept that intellectual establishment. It wasted so much valuable time that the suggestion was made that we should drop the puzzle on the enemy's research establishment, setting back their war effort by countless years. I sometimes think that reswitching and all that was the capitalistic devil's way of sterilizing a generation of radical economists. Students and scholars from England, India, and Italy have in considerable numbers had their energies and attention turned away from the study of inventories, national income, and scarcity pricing--and from study of the laws of motion of capitalism and the mixed economies--in order to manipulate the matrices and vectors of the Marxian and mainstream paradigms. If I am at all near the mark in this sad indictment, Piero Sraffa will have to receive much of the credit for this development. All of which proves what had already been demonstrated in the case of the magnificent Isaac Newton, that not all of the heritage of a great scholar is an unmixed blessing.

Political economy shall never forget the brilliant if repressed image of Piero Sraffa, gentlemen and scholar.

548

KNUT WICKSELL

Knut Wicksell (1851-1926) was not only Scandinavia's leading economist of all times. In addition, following his death more than sixty years ago and the translation into world language of his numerous writings, Wicksell's reputation as a great economic scientist had elevated him into the inner circle of immortals--into the Valhalla of Adam Smith, Léon Walras, and John Maynard Keynes.

Wicksell was a preeminent architect of neoclassical microeconomics. His first book, *Über Wert, Kapital und Rente* (1893) combined Böhm-Bawerk's theory of capital with the mathematical equilibrium models of Jevons, Walras, and Pareto. And among the creators of the marginal productivity theory of distribution, Wicksell ranks with John Bates Clark, Wicksteed, and Walras. (Even the so-called Cobb-Douglas production function, Output proportional to $(\text{Labor})^k(\text{Capital})^{1-k}$, which has been so famous in econometric research since its 1930s advocacy by Paul Douglas, had already been discovered and used several times by Wicksell at the turn of the century.) The three Swedish editions and the German edition of his *Vorlesungen*, Volume I, elaborated on his contributions to microeconomics. When translated into English in 1934, these *Lectures on Political Economy* were recognized to surpass Alfred Marshall's *Principles of Economics* (1890, 1920, 1961) in depth, relevance, and freshness. As an example, the whole post-Hicks discussions of the distributive impacts of technical change trace back to Wicksell.

Ten years after Wicksell's death it was for his macroeconomics that he was primarily renowned. His *Geldzins und Güterpreise* (1898) was translated in 1936 by Richard Kahn under the title *Interest and Prices*; and the various editions and translations of his *Vorlesungen, Volume II: Money* developed and generalized Wicksell's vision of the cumulative process in which the central bank engineered an upward trend in the money supply and the price level by a stubborn policy of bidding the market rate of interest down too low, forcing it below the "natural" (microeconomic) rate of interest. (Numerically, Wicksell assumes that real saving and investment decisions would mandate, say, a five percent per annum interest rate when the price level is stable. If the central bank will lend freely at four percent, so many borrowers will be forthcoming as to require it to print new money at some steady percentage rate of growth. As a believer in the Quantity Theory of Money, Wicksell would expect a permanent growth rate in the money supply to effectuate an equivalent growth rate in the price level--let's assume that both are at a two percent per annum rate. Under balanced inflation and unchanged full-employment, the *natural* rate of interest of five per cent in *real* terms would become in *nominal* terms an interest rate of seven percent [equals 5% + 2% inflation premium]. So even if the central bank were to bid up the market rate of interest above its initial four percent, say to six percent, the money supply would keep growing chronically at a fixed annual percentage. Only when real market rates and real natural rates are equal--as at five percent each--can we expect the money supply neither to grow nor decline and the price level to remain stable.)

Today we realize that this Wicksell macroeconomic theory is anything but Keynesian in the 1936 sense of Keynes's *General Theory of Employment, Interest and Money* with that paradigm's emphasis upon a theory of unemployment equilibrium. Wicksell's model is essentially a full-employment theory, involving a price level whose trend is determined by the trend in central-bank money supply.

Wicksell's cumulative process gave rise to spirited Swedish debates as to how exactly to define long-term equilibrium. Did it involve indispensably a notion of stationary price level? David Davidson, Wicksell's esteemed older colleague, argued that an epoch of technical improvement should result in the price level declining in tune with real cost reductions, extending to all consumers the benefits of higher real incomes procurable with their unchanged nominal income aggregates. Wicksell, rather dogmatically, defined price-level stability as the *desideratum* (but, since he on the whole believed in Say's Law, it is not evident why he should have disagreed so strongly with Davidson). The generation of Swedish economists after Wicksell, Davidson, Cassel, and Heckscher--Myrdal, Lindahl, Ohlin, Lundberg,....--spent much ink and time trying to grapple with Wicksellian equilibrium of saving and investment and of the natural and market rates of interest. To moderns of the New Classical School--Robert Lucas, Thomas Sargent, and rational expectationists--those nice distinctions lack much substantive significance. And for inheritors of the Keynes tradition, those discussions also seem not to focus on essentials.

Because Wicksell gives a non-mechanical discussion of the Quantity Theory of Money and Prices, some of his followers convinced themselves that he repudiated the Quantity Theory. This he did not do, instead supplying the MV = PQ tautology with a theory of how the supply of M is driven upward or downward by a positive or negative sign contrived by the central bank for the factor {natural interest rate *minus* market interest rate}. Wicksell, like Marshall, Irving Fisher, or Milton Friedman today, was content to regard Q as approximately constant near its full employment level; and to regard the velocity of circulation of money, V, as nearly constant or at most weakly affected by the nominal interest rate.

There is thus something of a paradox in his pre-war reputation as a macroeconomist as I describe it in *The New Palgrave: A Dictionary of Economics* (Samuelson, 1987):

3

A decade after Wicksell's death in 1926, it was his saving-investment macroeconomics that economists most prized. All Scandinavians were neo-Wicksellians in the interval between Keynes's *Treatise on Money* (1930) and *The General Theory of Employment, Interest and Money* (1936): on the continent, Austrians such as Ludwig von Mises, Friedrich von Hayek, and Gottfried von Haberler thought in the same mode; in America, the young Alvin Hansen was a Wicksellian fellow traveller in the period before his trek on the road to the Damascus of Keynes's *General Theory*. Although neo-Wicksellianism did weaken faith in Say's Laws, not much of it lives on in present-day economics. Now we realize that Gunnar Myrdal and Erik Lindahl were not anticipating in their Wicksellian debates of the early 1930s any general theory of *output as a whole*. Like the *Treatise on Money* and Dennis Robertson's monetary paradigms, their primary focus was on the *price* level as the macro-variable of their equilibrium theory. True, Bertil Ohlin and Ragnar Frisch wrote presciently about induced changes in aggregate output as the Great Depression deepened and as efficacious fiscal and monetary policies were advocated. And in this they were mindful of Wicksell's grapplings with macroeconomics.

For the Stockholm School around 1935, it was a fruitful mistake that they made in misinterpreting Wicksell's macroeconomics. See Ohlin (1937).

I should add that Wicksell's writings around the end of World War I confirm the orthodoxy of his macro views. He rashly advocated a rollback of the Swedish price level to its pre-war level by a policy of restoring 1914 gold parity of the Swedish crown. He convinced himself that fairness demanded it. And, worse, he foolishly minimized the transient unemployment and recession that would be entailed if Sweden followed his advice.

Before turning to the fascinating personality of Knut Wicksell, I should say a few words about his *Finanztheoretische Untersuchungen nebst Darstellungen und Kritik des Steuerwesens Schwedens* (1896), which is being reissued in the present beautiful edition. This work was undertaken when its author was well into his fifth decade, still jobless, and in need of the union card of a Ph.D. thesis. His genius could not help but make this a classic whose categories for public finance are still preserved in our generation's masterful treatise, Richard A. Musgrave's *Theory of Public Finance*

(1959).

Here are only a few of the gems in this work.

1. Wicksell stresses on value-judgment grounds of ethics the merits of progressively-graduated income taxes as against the indirect taxes on commodities then important in Scandinavia.

2. Like Gustav Cassel after him, Wicksell stresses the normative virtues of *marginal*-cost pricing for railroads and public utilities.

3. Most important is Wicksell's model of *voluntary-exchange* taxation. Austrians like Karl Sax had tried to apply to public goods of government the same marginal utility calculus that applied to private goods. Wicksell seeks to sharpen the analysis. So to speak, he begins with private goods like food and clothing, each partitionable among individuals so that the more citizen A gets the less is left for B to get. Provided constant returns to scale prevails technologically, Wicksell realizes that perfect competition can give a supply-and-demand market solution to (a) how much A and B will wish to work, and (b) how much of food and clothing will be produced and be purchased by A and B.

As a utilitarian, Wicksell realizes that any excessive earning capacity and consumption by A under *laissez-faire* in comparison with B can be corrected by transfer-taxation-*cum*-grants from A to B, imposed non-voluntarily by democracy on each of the citizenry. In Wicksell's eyes, the Invisible Hand of Adam Smith's *laissez-faire* needed the helping hand of redistributive taxes-transfer before individuals' marginal utilities could be deemed ethically commensurable.

But what about a public good, like concerts in the park or police protection? Wicksell in effect proposes that it is in the interest of A and B to agree on that sized program which accords to each a relative marginal utility that in some sense, summed up over all citizens, comes into equality with the marginal cost of the public good in question that they enjoy in common. A voting rule of unanimity gives us, for example, a two-platoon police force and every-other-Saturday jazz concerts rather than our agreeing to settle for more private food and private clothing.

Even in Scandinavia unanimity is hard to achieve. Erik Lindahl, a follower of Wicksell after that sage's retirement from Lund University to Stockholm, developed in his 1919 Ph.D. thesis, (Lindahl 1919), a more specific diagrammatic version of this Wicksell-Lindahl model of public goods. Learning of this from Musgrave's 1939 Harvard thesis, (Musgrave 1939), and benefitting from the Howard Bowen (1943) analogy between voting by voters and demanding by consumers, Samuelson (1954, 1955, 1958, 1969) formalized the Pareto-optimality properties of such a public-and-private goods' general equilibrium. Whereas Wicksell and Lindahl had worried too little about the temptation for all the citizens to *conceal* their respective true desires for the public goods--this in the interest of "a free ride"--I was probably too pessimistic about the problem of motivating people to reveal their genuine preferences for the public good in question. After 1977 Groves and Ledyard and other writers described in Ledyard (1987) have discussed some incentive-compatible algorithms that society might use to encourage people to reveal their true relative marginal utilities.

Again, we are led to admire the genius of Wicksell.

Wicksell and the Victorian Era

A century ago the nature of economic science was profoundly affected by the diversity of different geographical languages. Most of the words on economics that Wicksell wrote were written in Swedish. He had a certain monopoly access to the readers of that land and of bordering Denmark and Norway. But he paid a steep price for this, in that the vast rest of the world knew nothing of these writings in an obscure northern tongue.

Fortunately, Wicksell's major works were written in German or, as in the case of his *Lectures*, were soon translated into German. German at the turn of the century was the pre-eminent language of science. (When it used to be said that only a dozen people understood Einstein's theory of relativity, it could have been even more accurately claimed that virtually all of them were German.) Still Wicksell's great works probably sold only a few hundred copies each. As far as the narrow discipline of economics is concerned, Wicksell's influence on the world, though, might have been much greater if by accident English had been the non-Swedish language in which Wicksell had written. Certainly Carl Menger and Léon Walras and Vilfredo Pareto failed to be accorded the fame that their transcendent originality merited because by bad luck their works never achieved timely translation into English. Eugen von Böhm-Bawerk on the other hand suffered no such neglect because of the happenstance that William Smart promptly provided good translations of Böhm successive volumes.

With the benefit of hindsight we may perhaps perceive a paradox. Sometimes fame delayed is fame enlarged. Had Wicksell's originalities leaked out gradually in the years before 1920, there so to speak could not have been that renewal and extending-of-lifetimes of their copyrights that took pace when suddenly in the 1930s they became known by translation. Just as Darwin's Mother Nature augments the variability of organisms that makes for greater eventual fitness by contriving the isolating mechanism of speciation on detached islands, so there may have been advantage a century ago when the isolating barrier of language permitted there to arise and coexist somewhat differentiated scientific traditions. Better than to add to a James and John Bernoulli another Daniel and Nicholas writing in Latin and German, would be to have a French-writing LaGrange and an English-writing Hamilton?

Whatever the merits or demerits of past and present patterns, the die is cast. Were a Knut Wicksell to arise today in Götenberg or Osaka, or for that matter in Heidelberg or Paris, she or he would undoubtedly publish in the *American Economic Review* or the *Review of Economic Studies*. By electronic mail, any new theorems of non-substitution or factor-price equalization will speed through the scientific communities on whatever continent they may reside with the speed of light. No time is lost--even if that means that sometimes we shall be all making the same mistake together.

Wicksell the Man

Non-Swedes like myself regarded Wicksell as something of a saint. The arrogance and self-centeredness of his great Scandinavian rival, the conservative Gustav Cassel, made the halo around Wicksell's head glow all the more brightly. Here was a genius who worked alone until age 50 when, finally swallowing his anti-monarchy qualms, he succeeded in getting a chair at Lund University. Always, he perceived the depths and difficulties of a problem and shared with readers his uncertainties about its solution. Finally, after death, his true worth came to be appreciated by economists of every language.

Aside from being a wise scholar and scientist, Wicksell was a moral force striving for a more egalitarian society. He was an early architect for the welfare state of mixed economy. And yet his warm heart never ignored the reason of his cool scientific head. In the early decades of the century when Marxism had great appeal among the working classes of Europe, Wicksell resolutely examined and rejected Marxian paradigms and policy recommendations even at some cost to his own immediate popularity and influence. Instead, foreshadowing the post-Roosevelt New Deal and Sweden's own Middle Way of the 1930-1980 epoch, Wicksell recommended primary use of decentralized market competition, but with distributive taxation and transfer programs to reduce the inequities entailed by a *laissez-faire* capitalism.

The above idealized portrait has some truth. But after appearance of the splendid 1956-1958 biography of Wicksell by Torsten Gårlund, the foreign world came to realize that the realistic picture was a more complicated and interesting one.

Wicksell, we learned, was something of an agitator and crank. He had an inner need to speak out on unfashionable issues. After a youthful phase of religiosity, he reacted into a violent atheism. The cause of birth control and population limitation became something of an obsession with him; and this at a time in European history when technology, migration, and family planning were beginning to weaken the importance of the law of diminishing returns and of land scarcity for the advanced economies. It goes without saying that Wicksell was a pacifist. But few pacifists would urge turn-of-the-century Sweden not only to abandon an all-defensive army but even to annex itself with totalitarian tsarist Russia both to save on the budget and to civilize that barbaric society by boring from within. Wicksell was an ardent republican. But few anti-monarchists would, while still without an academic post at almost the age of 50, jeopardize being appointed to the chair that his family needed for its financial survival by his inability to apply to the King for the appointment. How many free thinkers, deep in their sixth decade of life, have a burning need to utter blasphemous remarks about virgin births in order to achieve martyrdom in prison?

This revised photograph of the hero has a romantic, even Strindberg-like, sheen to it. But where does the line get drawn between selflessness and self-indulgence? Gustav Cassel deserved reproach from contemporaries for his Napoleonic pretensions and right-wing claims. But is not politeness to such an antagonist sometimes a more effective weapon than rudeness? Besides, on some of the scientific issues that divided Wicksell and Cassel, Cassel was not necessarily wrong. Cassel and Keynes correctly criticized any attempt after World War I to roll back price levels and exchange parities to 1914 antebellum levels. Wicksell's opposing belief in money's neutrality I must suspect to involve dogmatic stubbornness and the psychological willfulness given rein to over a lifetime. Again, had Cassel not been willing to ignore Wicksell's *bète noir* of limited natural resources and diminishing returns, Cassel could not have so brilliantly anticipated at the time of World War I the celebrated accelerator-multiplier 1940s growth model of Harrod and Domar. Also, where description of the long-term evolution of the price level is concerned, who is to say that a Casselian approach based on estimating the exogenous (and endogenous) trends of the vector of money supplies may not be just as fruitful as a Wicksellian approach couched in terms of the central bank's manipulation of market rates of interest?

I cannot regret that Knut Wicksell was other than a plasterboard saint. Or that he differed so much as a personality from Stanley Jevons, Francis Edgeworth, Maynard Keynes, or Joseph Schumpeter. He paid for his idiosyncracies and in the end his star did prevail. The lack of dogma of his writings serendipitously enabled Ohlin and Lindahl and my generation of economists to go beyond his own scientific achievements.

Today when I read Alfred Marshall and J.B. Clark I am savoring Victorian antiquarianisms. It says something however for the genius of Wicksell, Thünen, and Cournot that when I read those writers I feel myself to be engaged in pushing forward the frontier of economic science and knowledge here and now at the end of the twentieth century.

References

Bowen, H.R. 1943. "The Interpretations of Voting in the Allocations of Economic Resources," *Quarterly Journal of Economics* 63, November, 27-49.

Cassel, G. 1923. *Theory of Social Economy*. London: T.F. Unwin. English translation of *Theoretische Sozialokonomie*; 1914, and several later German editions.

Gårlund, T. 1958. *The Life of Knut Wicksell*. Stockholm: Almqvist & Wiksell, English translation of fuller 1956 Swedish version.

Keynes, J.M. 1930. *A Treatise on Money*. Reprinted in *The Collected Writings of John Maynard Keynes*, Vol.V, 1971. London: Macmillan for The Royal Economic Society.

Keynes, J.M. 1936. *The General Theory of Employment, Interest and Money*. Reprinted in *The Collected Writings of John Maynard Keynes*, Vol. VI, 1973. London: Macmillan for The Royal Economic Society.

Ledyard, J. 1987. "Incentive Compatibility," in *The New Palgrave: A Dictionary of Economics*, Vol. 2, eds. J. Eatwell, et al. London: The Macmillan Press Ltd.

Lindahl, E. 1919. *Die Berechtigkeit in der Besteuerung. Analyse der Steuerprinzipien auf der Grundlage der Grenznutzentheorie*. Lund: Gleerup and H. Ohlsson.

Marshall, A. 1890, 1891, 1895, 1898, 1907, 1910, 1916, 1920, 1961. *Principles of Economics, An Introductory Volume*. London: Macmillan and Co.

Musgrave, R.A. 1939. "The Voluntary Exchange Theory of Public Economy," *Quarterly Journal of Economics* 53, February, 213-237.

Musgrave, R.A. 1959. *The Theory of Public Finance*. New York: McGraw-Hill.

Ohlin, B. 1937. "Some Notes on the Stockholm Theory of Saving and Investing," *Economic Journal* 87, March and June, 53-69 and 221-240.

Samuelson, P.A. 1954. "The Pure Theory of Public Expenditure," *The Review of Economics and Statistics*, 36, November, 387-389. Reproduced as Chapter 92 in *The Collected Scientific Papers of Paul A. Samuelson*, Vol. 2, ed. J. Stiglitz. Cambridge, Mass.: MIT Press, 1966.

_____. 1955. "Diagrammatic Exposition of a Theory of Public Expenditure," *The Review of Economics and Statistics*, 37, November, 350-356. Reproduced as Chapter 93 in *The Collected Scientific Papers of Paul A. Samuelson*, Vol. 2, ed. J. Stiglitz. Cambridge, Mass.: MIT Press, 1966.

_____. 1958. "Aspects of Public Expenditure Theories," *The Review of Economics and Statistics*, 48, November. 332-338. Reproduced as Chapter 94 in *The Collected Scientific Papers of Paul A. Samuelson*, Vol. 2, ed. J. Stiglitz. Cambridge, Mass.: MIT Press, 1966.

_____. 1969. "Pure Theory of Public Expenditure and Taxation," in *Public Economics: An Analysis of Public Production and Consumption and their Relations to the Private Sectors: Proceedings of a Conference Held by the International Economic Association*, eds. J. Margolis and H. Guitton. London: Macmillan. Reproduced as Chapter 172 in *The Collected Scientific Papers of Paul A. Samuelson*, Vol. 3, ed. R.C. Merton. Cambridge, Mass.: MIT Press, 1972.

_____. 1987. "Wicksell and Neoclassical Economics," in *The New Palgrave: A Dictionary of Economics*, Vol. 4, ed. J. Eatwell, et al. London: Macmillan.

Wicksell, K. 1893. *Über Wert, Kapital und Rente*. Jena: Gustav Fischer. Translated as *Value, Capital and Rent*, 1954. London: George Allen & Unwin. Contains Wicksell bibliography.

_____. 1896. *Finanztheoretische Untersuchungen nebst Darstellungen und Kritik des Steuerwesens Schwedens*. Jena: Gustav Fischer.

_____. 1898. *Geldzins und Güterpreise besimmenden Ursachen*. Jena: Gustav Fischer. Translated by Richard

Kahn as *Interest and Prices: A Study of the Causes Regulating the Value of Money*, 1936. London: Macmillan.

_____. 1934. *Lectures on Political Economy, Volume I. General Theory.* London: Routledge and Kegan Paul. Translation of 1901 and later Swedish and German editions of his microeconomics *Vorlesungen*.

_____. 1934. *Lectures on Political Economy, Volume II: Money.* London: Routledge and Kegan Paul. Translation of 1906 and later Swedish and German editions of his macroeconomics *Vorlesungen*.

Uhr, C.G. 1987. "Wicksell, Johan Gustav Knut (1851-1926)" in *The New Palgrave: A Dictionary of Economics*, Vol. 4, eds. J. Eatwell, et al. London: The Macmillan Press. An excellent biography and scientific evaluation.

Some Memories of Norbert Wiener

Paul A. Samuelson

Norbert Wiener came to MIT in the 1920s when it was primarily a practical engineering school. Only later, after Karl Compton's presidency, did science begin to realize its high potential here.

It was Vannevar Bush in electrical engineering who was Norbert's chief sponsor. Bush was a hands-on engineer with originality and drive in constructing what today would be called analogue computers—as for example Bush's MIT differential analyzer that serendipitously was available to grind out ballistic tables during World War II. Few geniuses in pure mathematics had the feel for physical models that Wiener did, and this made the Wiener-Bush team a fruitful one. Otherwise, they were something of an odd couple: Bush, the practical and laconic Yankee tinkerer, and Wiener the myopic parody of an absent-minded professor. It helped that electrical engineering in those pre-Laplace-transform days was unevenly heuristic and overdue for an infusion of Wiener's kind of rigor.

The mathematics department that Norbert joined was a highly uneven one also. Like so many departments of MIT at that stage, it was largely a service department rather than being a center of research at the frontier of the American mathematics profession or a magnet for the best graduate students. Wiener, Struik, Phillips (in applied math and thermodynamics), Wiener's brother-in-law Philip Franklin, others, and for a brief period Jesse Douglas, gradually changed that. But it was a slow evolution. It did not help that Norbert Wiener was said to be a poor teacher for elementary students of mathematics. My own experience in hearing Norbert lecture cannot gainsay that reputation.

What I have been saying is not novel and is well-known history. It may be added that Norbert came to MIT because he did not get tenure in the Harvard mathematics department of George Birkhoff, Osgood, Graustein, Julian Coolidge, and other worthies. With the knowledge of hindsight, one wonders whether Wiener's life accomplishment could have turned out as great in an alternative run of history in which Wiener did receive tenure at Harvard. MIT was an interesting niche for one with Wiener's powers, and being in Cambridge, Massachusetts, brought him the same contacts with world mathematics no matter exactly where on the Charles River he hung his hat. Nonetheless, the exodus from Harvard dealt a lasting psychic trauma to Norbert Wiener. It did not help that his father was still a Harvard professor (albeit, it must be said, a marginal one in Slavic languages), and that Norbert's mother regarded his move as a cruel comedown in life.

Edwin Bidwell Wilson, mathematical physicist and Acting President of MIT before he became Dean of Harvard's School of Vital Statistics, was the principal

---

1991 *Mathematics Subject Classification.* Primary 01A60.

© 1997 American Mathematical Society

person who talked me into coming to MIT at a later date. And one of the persuasive arguments he used was that his own earlier move to MIT after being Willard Gibbs' heir at Yale, plus Wiener's move to MIT, illustrated how promising this new environment could be for a scholar's development. Wilson proved to be a good prophet. But when I observed how Norbert Wiener's resentments against Harvard poisoned his lifetime serenity, I was able to benefit from his example and enjoy a long career of friendship and stimulus from the many Harvard economists who were my teachers, contemporaries, and students. It helped of course that Harvard did for me what it never did do for Wiener, namely later woo with offers of chairs, appointments to Ad Hoc and Visiting Committees, and awarding of honorary degrees and other honorific baubles. Norbert should have realized that creating well is the very best form of revenge.

Wiener created well. But having been a wunderkind with a force-feeding father, no accomplishments could be great enough to bring him serenity and fulfillment. Leo Wiener wrote, in the old *Colliers* magazine, that any good teacher could turn a broomstick into a genius. Norbert always felt like that broomstick. When he climbed mathematics' highest hill, he yearned for far-off peaks in biology. Professing to despise praise and vanity, if Norbert encountered me in the halls of Building Two, he would ask whether his name was in the book under my arm. I would open it to the index and solemnly report that Wiener was not included in the W's. Sometimes "cybernetics" was found among the C's and I thought it rather sad that this is what most people came to remember him by.

Norbert thought more about Harvard than Harvard thought about him. But I can testify from personal experience of dining with Dean George Birkhoff about once in every eight weeks at the Society of Fellows during 1937–1940 that Birkhoff talked much about Wiener's rival efforts in connection with then hot ergodic theory and much else. More about this later. The love-hate relation is a cold-fusion state.

Because I know that Robert Merton will be giving you a full description of how modern finance theory benefits from Norbert's brainchild that we call a Wiener Probability Process, I can with better conscience concentrate here on what can't be read in books, namely on Norbert Wiener's personality as his MIT colleagues knew him and on his interactions with scholars throughout the many disciplines bordering on mathematics.

My acquaintanceship with Wiener was confined to the years between 1937 and his death in 1964. Two score MIT people knew him more intimately than I ever did—but I was a sponge for Wiener stories, many of them filtered through Norman Levinson and Harold Freeman, and those who knew him best are for the most part dead by now.

Norbert titled the first installment of his autobiography Ex-Prodigy, but in plain truth he never graduated out of the phase of brilliant prodigy into sage and mature rotarian. He was lovable and generous and deservedly aware of his achievements. But at the same time he was insecure and sensitive. There ever remained something child-like in his personality and he was not able to see himself with other people's eyes. Mathematicians do not have to be regular guys, which gave him all the rope he could use to be Norbert Wiener. (Once at tea in Princeton's Fine Hall, I commented on the varied types to be seen among the mathematicians present. No one was insulted and all cheerfully agreed. To clinch the point, one recalled that during the previous week a stranger had barged in displaying evident signs of being lost and disoriented. When asked what the mathematician he sought was like, the reply was: "There's nothing unusual about him."'" In a chorus, all present said, "You mean Al Tucker." And it was indeed A. W. Tucker he was there to see. No one ever mistook Norbert for an Al Tucker.)

His was an isotropic personality. From every angle of vision there was something idiosyncratic about Norbert Wiener. At a young age, he wore a beard when only sailors and ancient scholars did. Often he walked down the corridors puffing on a fat cigar. His skin was red-veined as if he were not going to live the many decades of his actual life expectancy. He toed out in a duck walk. And yet, like unathletic Harold Laski, he would often climb steps two at a time. His post-cataract nearsightedness was proverbial; in those days, removal of cataracts left you with tunnel vision and glasses that looked like the bottom of beer bottles. To see Norbert at the wheel of his car sent geese and pedestrians into panic. Although we both lived in Belmont, my late wife forbade me ever to accept a lift home from him.

Tales of Wiener's absentmindedness were uncountably infinite. Many of them I had heard about local luminaries from Ripon College, Wisconsin or Texas Tech in Lubbock, Texas. Example: "When we met, was I walking toward the Faculty Club or away from it? For in the latter case I have already had my lunch." Just because other Mr. Chips(es) in a dozen different places were attributed with the same stories that were said to be Wiener stories, does not preclude that they were independently true about him. Even Darwin had his Wallace.

But here is a tall tale about Norbert that I never heard elsewhere. One afternoon he is supposed to have arrived at his Belmont house, only to find that his key would not fit. After repeated fumbling, he turned nearsightedly to urchins playing in the street to say: "Can you show me where the Wieners live?" One little girl replied: "Follow me, Daddy. Mommy sent me here to point the way to our new house."

Mathematicians are often good chess and bridge players. Norbert was a proverbial exception. Once Hardy said to Littlewood his co-editor: "If a chap could write this submitted paper, why would he?" The mystery was why one who played chess or bridge so atrociously would do so. Yet in some decades, Norbert was a frequent bridge player at the MIT Faculty Club after lunch. Any colleague with a bright child who needed boosting for his ego could bring him to wipe Norbert out at chess. The first time Wiener played chess at Rand, his style was so eccentric that a master thought the great Wiener must have some deep and novel gambits, and thinking that, he is supposed to have lost to Wiener. Lost, of course, only once. A middle-aged business executive attending MIT as a Sloan Fellow, after playing chess with Norbert asked him: "Professor Wiener, how can you be so great a mathematician and so lousy a chess player?" Wiener replied cheerily (and with some profundity): "In chess you're only as good as your worst move. In mathematics you're as good as your best move." Wiener's best was very great.

There is another legend that can use gentle debunking. At every math talk, the visiting lecturer had hardly stated his problem before Norbert went noisily to sleep. That is fact. Here is the legend. After the speaker developed the apparatus for his solution but had not yet presented his answers, Norbert would noisily awaken and announce the complete solution, often with insightful generalizations. I cannot testify concerning the pre-1933 Wiener, but in World War II and postwar days, it was even money whether his off-the-cuff contentions were correct. This was not a sign of fallibility, but a matter of personality: a Willard Gibbs would have ventured no opinion until being virtually certain; Wiener was more explorative and

763

chance taking. Of course, it was quite another matter when he buckled down and concentrated on his own innovative researches.

G. H. Hardy admired Wiener's depth in Fourier analysis and would have him lecture to his own Cambridge students. He found it especially remarkable when Wiener brought to pure mathematics the practical terminologies of engineering—white noise and all that jargon. Wiener in turn used to say: "Hardy is a mathematical snob with his professed disdain for any practical usefulness from pure mathematics. However, Hardy earned the right to be a snob and if you are a Hardy you too can be a snob."

It was Hardy who is supposed to have expedited Norman Levinson's achieving tenure at MIT. During a celebrated mid-1930s visit to MIT, Wiener is supposed to have told Hardy that anti-semitism was blocking Levinson's overdue promotion. On the next occasion of an opportunity to talk to President Compton, Hardy said: "I didn't realize that MIT is a denominational seminary." "But indeed it is not. What could give you that odd notion?" Compton asked. Hardy drove home his point: "Then how come the young Levinson with his international reputation in mathematics can be held back because of his religious affiliation?" The rest was history.

Some famous visitors were drawn to MIT because of Wiener. Paley, Hopf, the quantum physicist Born, and many more. Actually, Norbert believed that he had been an early anticipator of the Heisenberg Indeterminacy Principle, when he pointed out that you just cannot play a fast gig in the lowest-frequency range of the organ. (When I asked various Nobelists what they thought of this claim, they only smiled amiably. "Success has a thousand fathers. Failure is an orphan." Jack Kennedy said that; or Ted Sorenson did for him; or Count Ciano, Mussolini's rascal of a son-in-law wrote it in his war time diary. "Credit adds up to more than 100 percent," I learned from graffiti on the Gary, Indiana school walls.)

Wiener was a premature perceiver of the phenomena of fractals. He liked to quote Swift on fleas that had smaller fleas to prey on them, and so proceed to ad infinitum. A pioneer with R. A. Fisher and Shannon on perceiving measures of information, Wiener liked to ask, "How much information is there in that tape that the monkeys in the British Museum type out and that turns out to contain a patch flawlessly duplicative of the many volumes of the 11th edition of Encyclopedia Britannica?" If you answered, "zero information", he was a tad crestfallen. Long before Ed Lorenz zeroed in on strange attractors and deterministic chaos, I heard Norbert expatiate on the irreducible unpredictability of where autumnal hurricanes would strike because of the inevitable sensitivity to uncertain initial conditions.

Probably neither Wiener nor Kolmogorov knew anything of the early tradition in economic statistics of time series analysis à la Yule, Walker, Wold, or Frisch. But Wiener's classic work on generalized harmonic analysis set the stage for his wartime Yellow Peril manual on optimal separation of signal from noise. Unfortunately, it was too little realized by economists how germane these researches could have been for further progress in time series prediction. Wall Street never did beat a track to Norbert's door in search of help to augment pelf, but it could have done them no good to have tried—for he issued papal bulls to the world warning one and all that his brain children were not for sale to avaricious capitalists. You could hear his complaints as far away as Central Square when he accused Bell Lab of patenting one of his Paley Wiener theorems.

764

George Birkhoff was a notoriously competitive scholar. He needed little coaxing from me at our dinner conversations to spend the evening discussing who were first class, second class, third class, and even fifth class mathematicians. Not infrequently Wiener's name would come up as when once I recalled him saying: "Norbert did it again at the Joint Seminar. He was able to roll out the Weak Ergodic Theorem from the Fundamental Theorem of the Calculus." Thus, the hours passed happily from one odd month to another. But on one evening the law of diminishing returns was operative. That afternoon I had been reading Oliver Kellogg on Potential Theory. So I thought to say to Birkhoff: "You must have known Kellogg."

"Yes, indeed I did, he was a good friend and we played bridge. I think I can say he was an able man—a second class mathematician. But Oliver was a fool."

"Oh, how so?"

"Some years back, Kellogg came to me with a happy example of infinite potential at a point. I said to him, 'Oliver, you've got something important there. Work it out and don't breathe a word of it to anyone.' But Kellogg was a fool. He told Norbert Wiener about it and in three weeks Norbert had made a killing."

I only tell the story as it was told to me. Never had I been so disillusioned. I was only 22 at the time and believed we were all objective scientists working toward a common Holy Grail. For years I would retell the story. And, actually, it served as a Rorschach blot in that people's reactions to the story were more interesting than it itself was. A score of years later in *I Am a Mathematician*, Wiener's account of the incident is not quite congruent with my version above. But the details are not critical. The story is not so much a story about Kellogg as about both Birkhoff and Wiener. But the aspect I treasure most is that reaction to the story I got from a nameless world-famous mathematician. It goes thus.

"I agree that Kellogg was a fool, and for two reasons I wouldn't have done what he did. The first is minor: I am a relatively slow worker and Norbert was very fast. It's unfair to one's vanity that mere speed should gobble up all the fame.

"However, the important reason is quite different. All the fun in science is working a thing out for yourself. We shoot the guy who tells us how the Whodunnit ends. To deliberately give away to someone else the puzzle that you might yourself enjoyably solve is criminal. And it doesn't advance science with a capital S to have a result this month rather than next."

Elsewhere on the program, Wiener's views on automation and unemployment are sure to be addressed. On the basis of experience and plausible *a priori* reasoning, economists have learned not to expect from brilliant hard scientists much in the way of economic paradigms that are both new and true. Albert Einstein was a great physicist, but if we put John von Neumann's stature as an economist at 100 and Vito Volterra's at 40, Einstein weighs in at five on a scaling that is constrained to the non-negative number system. Judged by his peak performance, Bertrand Russell earns for himself a 35. Even on occasions like this, where, as Dr. Samuel Johnson observed, speakers are not "under oath", Wiener ranks well among those in the universe of natural science and mathematics.

However, there is an orthogonal metric in terms of where scholars as humans are to be ranked. I illustrate it by paraphrasing what a biographer of my great teacher Joseph Schumpeter once confided in me. This distinguished Swede said, "Schumpeter was great in new ideas, in breadth of knowledge too, and was a great stylist. But I have to ask myself:

"Was Schumpeter a good man in the sense of caring about the welfare of people? Alas, at the end of the day, I cannot affirm that he was."

On this occasion I am prepared to go under solemn oath and affirm that Norbert Wiener was indeed a good man.

INSTITUTE PROFESSOR EMERITUS, DEPARTMENT OF ECONOMICS, MASSACHUSETTS INSTITUTE OF TECHNOLOGY

Gottfried Haberler As Economic Sage and Trade Theory Innovator

Paul A. Samuelson

Gottfried Haberler is just as old as the Twentieth Century and he has been one of the few most valuable economic scholars of that epoch. In international trade theory he has been a giant among giants. But mere microeconomics cannot contain his originality: his *Prosperity and Depression* has been the definitive study of business cycles, both pre- and post-Keynesian; before there was a Pigou-Effect, or a perceived need for one to work toward clearing the labor-employment market, Haberler had clearly formulated the mechanism whereby a downward floating wage-price level would raise the real worth of the community's holding of outside money and thereby enhance consumption spending enough to restore full employment and a balance of saving and investment there.

Portrait of the Scientist

Haberler has been a prolific researcher, contributing important books and articles over a period of almost seven decades.[1] He has taught generations of leading economists at Harvard: their roster reads like a Who's Who in modern economics. Although he was asked to stay on teaching at ages beyond those normal for his generation, in the years of emeritus status Gottfried Haberler began a new productive life as a policy researcher at the Washington, D. C. American Enterprise Institute.

Von Thünen asked that his $\sqrt{ap}$ formula for the natural wage be put on his tombstone. I want my mausoleum to include the words: Gottfried Haberler was his teacher. When I first knew him, I was turning just old enough to vote and he was 36 years of age. I can see his tall figure walking across the Harvard Yard, briefcase in hand; his broad forehead marked him as a professor and, except on the tennis court, he did not seem young to me. But then time stood still: I grew older; new generations of students strode the Harvard Yard; but Gottfried Haberler changed not at all. It was more miraculous than the case of Oscar Wilde's Dorian Gray. For, although Gray's countenance remained impervious to time's hand, we know that inside beauty was giving way to decay. Not so with Haberler. For him there has never been an inside and

---

[1] A Haberler bibliography of publications up to 1979 is given in the valuable 1985 MIT Press book edited by Anthony C. Koo, *Selected Essays of Gottfried Haberler*. This contains English translations of his 1930 German masterpiece and of other important articles, and I commend it to economists.

an outside. Always he has been of one piece. What you see is what you get. No trimming to fad and fashion. No striving for elegant exoticism or paradox. No compromising for policy effectiveness or jockeying for personal power and influence.

As I shall argue, eclecticism has been Gottfried Haberler's strong suit. But do not think that this belies adherence to firm principle. All too often an open mind is an empty mind. Gottfried Haberler is more stubbornly consistent than almost anyone I know. None the less, unlike some of his contemporaries on the conservative right, he has been receptive to new experience; and, through a filter of caution, Haberler has absorbed new theoretical innovations and paradigms, selectively accepting those subsets of them that seemed realistic and relevant.

Economists know that it is scarcity that enhances value. By this test, Haberler can be judged to be priceless as one of the few intelligent conservatives of our profession, one of the few who has engaged in weighing the merits and demerits of competing views and paradigms.

Consider the contrast of temperaments between him and his older countryman Ludwig von Mises. Our profession owes Mises much – for his early contributions to monetary theory and his forceful advocacy of market individualism. But quiet and scholarly debate was never Mises's strong suit. He exploded rather than ruminated. He was well constituted to lead an ideology and, in a dry season for Manchester liberalism, his followers kept the faith alive.

Consider also the contrast between Joseph Schumpeter and his younger friend Gottfried Haberler. Schumpeter sparkled. He threw out ideas and criticisms. The big picture was his focus. Schumpeter and Haberler were both critical of the Keynesian Revolution. But it was Haberler who concentrated on its contents, weighing and judging its constituent parts. The world needs both its Schumpeters and its Haberlers. I can add my personal testimony in favor of that proposition since both were my teachers and I benefitted much from their complementary virtues.

Portrait of the Man

Before I get down to the business of surveying Haberler's economic originalities, I must devote a few words to the scholar as a person. America was the beneficiary in the age of Hitler of a virtual treasure trove of great scholars from Europe. Einstein and Fermi in physics, Wald and von Neumann in mathematics, are typical names. Some of these came before Hitler took over their countries. Some were Jews by Nazi standards. Some were married to Jews. Some were merely attracted by a new and more prosperous land where the shadows of bigotry and war were less threatening.

Economics, like the more exact sciences, benefitted from this great brain drain. Haberler was one of the many Austrian economists who enriched Anglo-Saxon economics. Rosenstein-Rodan, Schumpeter, Hayek, Machlup, Tintner, Morgenstern, Mises, Kaufman, and Gerschenkron are a few of an illustrious roster (listed by approximate date of leaving the Continent). In this connection I must retell an amusing conversation. Once when Chancellor Franz Vranitzky was still Finance Minister of Austria, I asked him innocently why the Austria that seemed to do so badly after World War I was doing so well economically in the post-World War II period. He answered mischievously (and with a wink to indicate that he was only

311

joking): "You don't suppose it is because we exported to America all those economic teachers of yours?"

These Austrian émigrés were a brilliant and amusing lot. A few of them lived up to the musical comedy image of the gallant Viennese cavalier. Most of them were fond of coffee-house gossip, some of it occasionally acerbic. Gottfried was the most kindly and gentle of the group. He helped people get jobs; he recruited help for Europeans destitute in the immediate aftermath of the War. I cannot count the hours he spent in reading carefully my manuscripts and offering useful revisions for them.

Haberler was remarkably catholic in his friendships. Sometimes Mises would castigate him as a radical for not denouncing heresies. Haberler was understandably partial to productive scholars whose conservatism sometimes made them unpopular. I am sure he tried to arrange a professorial call from Harvard to Milton Friedman. Early on he told me: "George Stigler is a coming star." (Since Stigler was my graduate-student mentor in my Chicago undergraduate years, I quite agreed.) If Arthur F. Burns was ever belittled in catty Cambridge conversation, Gottfried stood up for him. He and Willy Fellner were exceptionally companionable, especially in their so-called retirement years in Washington.

Finally, I recall his broad intellectual interests. He kept up on the latest in logical positivism, and related it to Robbins/Mises a priorism and to methodological writings of Felix Kaufman and Terence Hutchinson. Percy Bridgman on operationalism and Arthur Eddington on a priori deduction of the exact contents of the physical world – all this was grist for his active mind. His German and English prose was as distinct from, say, Schumpeter's as mine is from Faulkner's or Joyce's. The homes of Friedl and Gottfried – on Shady Hill Square and Mercer Circle – were reknowned for their hospitality, and my first acquaintance with world-famous visitors often came at their parties.

Gottfried Haberler enriched American scientific life and he deserved the recognitions and rewards that our society bestowed on him.

Haberlerian Macroeconomics

Haberler arrived at Harvard in 1936 by way of the League of Nations. The first, pre-Keynesian edition of his great treatise on business cycles was essentially completed during his Geneva sojourn. In Cambridge, Massachusetts he digested Keynes' *General Theory* and reacted to it in the second and later revisions of *Prosperity and Depression*. Embalmed in those valuable "Before" and "After" versions the student of the history of economic ideas can find testimony of the great impact of the *General Theory*. Later, in Haberler's contribution to Seymour Harris's 1947 *New Economics*, he reaffirmed his contention that much which was new in the *General Theory* was not generally valid. Indeed Haberler's 1947 text seems to proceed on the tacit premise that money's velocity of circulation is so inelastic to variations in the interest rate as to negate the usefulness of Keynes' liquidity preference – an odd premise, I must think, for a neoclassical economist to apply to utility-maximizing individuals.

A modern day Robert Lucas denies the Keynesian Revolution by positing that the labor market quickly clears and money is neutral (having systematic effects only on the price level). The pre-Keynes Haberler never believed that in his business-cycle writ-

312

ings, nor does he in his contemporary post-Keynes macro writings. In the sense of Tom Kuhn's *Structure of Scientific Revolutions* the paradigm Keynes uses differs from that of Say, Walras, and Debreu very much in the way that the Planck/Schrödinger paradigm of quantum mechanics differs from classical Newton/Hamilton dynamics. Thus, the multiplier writings of Kahn and the multiplier-accelerator articles of Clark/Frisch/Harrod/Domar/Samuelson are methodologically distinct from Mill's international economics or Marshall/Menger micro-economics. Haberler's pre-Keynes cycle writings are more in the spirit of the Harrod/Keynes methodology than the Marshall/Menger. So, I might interpret him to be saying, the "revolution" had already occurred before Keynes' 1936 work. However, Spiethoff, Robertson, Tugan-Baranowsky, Mitchell, and the other writers on cycles wrote down no complete model alternative to the Walrasian one. Their insights were empirical and ad hoc; their deductive analyses were partial and intuitive. Only after the Keynesian Revolution could a Pigou know how to introduce a *Haberler-Pigou Effect* into the macro model so as to deduce a long-run validity for Say's Law.

Haberler and I can agree that there are valuable insights in the rational expectational or new Classical paradigm; can agree that they are more valuable in 1990 than in 1930 or 1938, and are more valuable in the long- than in the short-run. But we can both agree that Lucas/Sargent constructs fail to pass the empirical tests of short-term verisimilitude, and that they fail because of the measure of validity that still obtains for the various Keynesian behavior equations. (Example: in Ramsey/Arrow complete temporal systems, intermediate swings in income should not induce the swings in consumption spending that repeated statistical testing reports as actually occurring. Speaking for myself, I am more surprised by the degree of Keynesian truth that economic history displays than its untruth. When Einstein said to Bohr in their debates on quantum methodology: "I do not believe that God plays dice," Bohr gave the proper reply: "Who are we to tell Him His business?" Like Margaret Fuller, we must accept how the cookie crumbles.)

Breaking Out of Labor-Only Comparative Advantage

My main assignment is to review Haberler's magnificent innovations in trade theory. He arrived in economics at a time when Ricardian comparative advantage was still a prisoner to the over-simplified Labor Theory of Value. Taussig's *International Trade* of 1927 nicely codified the Ricardian model, but leading trade experts such as Luigi Einaudi and James Angell still persisted in reading error into Ricardo's own formulation – as Jacob Viner and Piero Sraffa then had to rebut.

Three heroes advanced the pure theory of trade around 1930: Haberler (1930, 1933), Viner (1930, 1937), and Bertil Ohlin (1924, 1933). Each worked quasi-independently. Ohlin's brilliant 1924 thesis was buried in Swedish, with innovations not to be known widely until the 1933 American publication of his great book. Viner, as Taussig's prize pupil, fought a rear-guard defense of the labor theory, but in spite of himself had to go beyond it along lines parallel to Haberler's. Haberler's imperishable contribution was to grapple with non-labor inputs by the ingenious use of society's production-possibility frontier (or opportunity-cost transformation function).

313

I cannot do better than quote part of a paragraph from John Chipman's masterly article on Haberler in the *New Palgrave Dictionary for Political Economy* (1987, Volume 2, 581):

". . . Haberler's most significant contribution was his (1930) reformulation of the theory of comparative cost, which revolutionized the theory of international trade. Prior to this paper, the Ricardian theory still held sway . . . Haberler introduced the production 'substitution curve' (now usually known as the production-possibility frontier), allowing for several factors of production, and taken to be concave to the origin as a result of diminishing returns. This laid the foundations for Ohlin's theory, as well as Lerner's and Samuelson's . . . Haberler's independent discovery – and the use to which he put it – is what transformed the theory of international trade. Haberler also introduced the concept of a 'specific factor' – one that is completely immobile among industries."

Measuring all costs in terms of the single input of labor, and thereby disregarding the role in production of land, natural resources, and produced inputs cannot do justice to reality and economic history. It does not do justice to the actual discussions and insights of the classical economists themselves. (Ricardo and Mill knew the crucial role of land in the policy issues of the Corn-law tariffs on imported grain.) It does not do justice to the post-1870 multi-factor theories of value that all mainstream economists believed in. For Frank Taussig and Jacob Viner to be fighting in 1929 for Ricardo's labor-only comparative cost was therefore futile. Haberler's concave production-possibility frontier could handle the multiple-factor case and the Taussig/Viner defense collapsed as not needed. (Viner himself used the Haberler construct in a notable LSE lecture that presumably pre-dated Abba Lerner's famous papers on the diagrammatics of trade. Wassily Leontief and James Meade also did, as did Wolfgang Stolper and I. It was an instant conquest.)[2]

The 1930 Classic

Haberler early and late stressed the normative merits of free-trade policies. In Ricardo's labor-only world, under specified total labor supplies in two countries and simplified 2-good scenarios, each region has a straight-line p-p frontier. In the general case where the respective frontiers differ in slope, geographical specialization can produce the autarky totals of the two goods with less of labor in both places. That is the Pareto-optimal (1950 terminology) magic of free trade – even though neither 1930 Haberler nor his predecessors precisely puts it this way, clearly he sees this intuitively.

---

[2] Irving Fisher had used substitution-transformation frontiers in his 1907 work on the rate of interest. Pareto spoke, I believe, of "production indifference curves". We know today, thanks to researches of Machesi and Thweath that Barone's 1908 Italian elementary text had carried a trade diagram with a (perversely shaped) production frontier. Bertil Ohlin's 1924 Swedish thesis had already embraced the multi-factor Walras/Cassel model of his famous 1933 Harvard Press book: that model would yield results isomorphic with Haberler's if Ohlin had left the realm of n goods and m factors for a graphical exposition of two goods and two factors, but he seems never to have done that at the formal level (a pity!). Robert K. Merton, as a historian of science who knows well the multiple-simultaneous discoveries of Newton/Leibniz and Darwin/Wallace, would award highest marks to Haberler for his degree of independence in discovery and so would I.

What Haberler wants to do in 1930 is demonstrate that a similar argument holds when the goods use labor and non-labor inputs. With specified totals of regions' labor and land, each indifferent between use in one industry or the other, p-p frontiers are definable for each place: now they are concave to the origin. In effect Haberler sees and makes persuasive the following: whatever world totals of the goods were produced under autarky, under free-trade's specialization they could be technologically produced with less of every factor total in both places; what is the same thing, more could be produced of every good under free trade using only the specified localized totals of the factors. Warning: After free trade it is well known that the market equilibrium could involve a smaller total of some good's output and a larger total of the other(s). It is still provable – but not by any living 1930 author – that there exists a pattern of post-free-trade transfer bribes that could make everybody (or every region's "representative" person) better off than under autarky. We must give the 30-year-old author high (but not highest) marks for the vague but perceptive words (Haberler/Koo, 1985, 7):

> "... in one or both participant countries ... [free trade can] increase [one] output at the expense of the other good. This does not, however, yield an argument against free trade. For the output reduction of the one good will be overcompensated by the output expansion of the other – in the evaluation, that is, of both economies as manifested by the direction of their demand."

Although I did not know this passage, several of my articles written years later were devoted to clarifying the germ of truth contained herein. Also, it is a venial sin to claim too much in 1930: unilateral free trade by a large country can be improved on by a Mill/Edgeworth/Bickerdike "scientific not-too-large tariff", a truth I rediscovered as a graduate student only to be told by Professor Haberler that Edgeworth and Bickerdike had already glimpsed it.

Positivistic Equilibrium

The 1930 author did not apply his new p-p f tool to establishing positivistic trade equilibrium. He left that for Lerner, Leontief, Viner, Meade, and others to do. It will be useful for me to sketch a contrafactual historical exposition that Haberler did not present but which his 1930 progress brought within his ken.[3]

---

[3] At this late date one comment can be made on the titanic debate between Viner and Haberler concerning the generality of Austrian opportunity-cost doctrines. Suppose we test this on a food-clothing example, each producible by male labor and (distinguishable) female labor. If the supplies of labors vary with their respective real wage rates, Böhm-Bawerk's pretension to novelty do need to be qualified – as he grudgingly conceded. But still, as Haberler later correctly quotes me as contending, there remains some ceteris paribus usefulness to the opportunity cost frontier diagrammatics. But what is left in the following realistic cases adduced in the 1980s by Edgeworth to deflate Böhm's pretensions? Let both men and women not be indifferent between working in the food and the clothing industries; instead let their labor supplies to each industry depend on relative prices and the relative wage rates paid for each gender in the different industries. Then, alas, Viner is right to insist that the new 1930 tools do not work. Then Haberler and Viner must both levitate to Ohlin's Walrasian general equilibrium of localized production, and so must we all.

315

1. By assuming every dollar and mark gets spent the same way everywhere, Haberler could have rigorously plotted (homothetic) indifference contours on one diagram. Each indifference contour is a radial-scale blow up to some one contour, so that the Engel paths generated by alterations of income and unchanged prices are straight lines fanning out from the origin. By thus idealizing more complex reality, the author avoids all problems of aggregation: the representative consumers for all regions all have the same tastes and relative demands; indeed, for this case, we have a firm metric of real psychic income or product, as proportional to the distance that any contour is from the origin; this real (composite) output is a first-degree-homogeneous function of the two goods consumed! Now, normatively, 1930 Haberler can assert that his free trade raises the global real product available for the world's citizenry compared to autarky, and in fact achieves the maximum total of it feasible from the specified totals of the localized factor supplies. This dramatizes what the 1930 exposition omitted: not only does free trade optimize global production totals, it ensures that exchange will partition those totals in an Edgeworth-Pareto optimal way – so that no one person's wellbeing can be augmented except at the expense of some other person's well being.
2. On the same diagram, as Leontief later suggested, both production-possibility frontiers could be superimposed. For each region's frontier, at each point its tangent line defines a pointed exchange vector whose heel is tangent to the production locus and whose toe is tangent to an indifference contour.
3. As Haberler's reader scans all parallel exchange vectors for the two regions, she finds topologically the existent one-and-only pair whose lengths are exactly equal and opposite. The equilibrium terms of trade are given by that unique common slope. The geographical localization of production is given by the two vector heel points. Each nation's basket of consumption goods is given by its respective vector toe point. The vectors themselves demarcate the balance-of-payments equilibrium, both in aggregate value equivalence and in detailed micro breakdown. (As a bonus, half a decade before Abraham Wald's proof of existence of a Walras/Cassel/Schlesinger equilibrium, Haberler's reader is shown a rigorous case. Because Wald's so-called Weak Axiom is devoid of economic content when demands are not rigorously uniform-homothetic, no essential singularity is involved in this diagrammatic simplification: and, in the case of zero transport costs, topological complexities can be replaced by a simple proof that the maximum of global output is attainable by the free-trade algorithm – and uniquely under Haberlerian curvature specifications.)
4. Had the 1930 author used this model, he would have found that – in the absence of consideration of transport impediments that make certain goods untradeable or less-tradeable – Ohlin's view on the transfer problem was better than Keynes's; and the Thornton/Mill/Marshall/Pigou/Taussig presumption that a transfer will hurt the terms of trade of the paying country is not clearly preferable [Haberler/Koo, 1930, 134] to the agnostic view of Ricardo/Hollander/Ohlin that there is no presumption concerning the direction of transfer-induced effects on terms-of-trade. (In the diagram I described, no relative prices are changed by a unilateral transfer; more generally, when we consider all possible patterns of income elasticities of each country's good of comparative advantage as equally likely, all effects are

equally likely. The described example rids the transfer literature of any mumbo-jumbo of transferred abstract-purchasing-power and keeps the discussion in micro terms as in my transfer-problem writings of the 1950s. Actually, Haberler's own expressed 1930-1 logic on the transfer problem is more Ohlinish than it is Thornton-Keynesish.)

Final Tribute

A birthday party blesses the birthday boy. But it blesses his friends and admirers too. The occasion of Gottfried Haberler's 90th Birthday led me to reread his many and unique papers. This made me feel young again. Only the peaks of his icebergs could I mention here. They soar to the Heavens.

Hail Apollo!

Wickselll and neoclassical economics. Knut Wicksell was long known as Scandinavia's Alfred Marshall, the leading economist of that region, whose microeconomics married Böhm-Bawerk's time-phased interest theory with Walras's mathematical general equilibrium. His macroeconomics was thought to foreshadow Keynes's 1936 *General Theory*, even though it emphasized that the discrepancy between investment and saving is the cause merely of an inflationary trend in the general price level.

Usually when a great economist is translated into English, reputation is deflated. Not so with Wicksell: the 1930s appearance of his 1898 *Interest and Prices* (Wicksell, 1936) and of his *Lectures on Political Economy*, Volume I ('micro') and Volume II (money), which appeared in Swedish and German editions between 1901 and 1928 and was translated into English in 1934 (Wicksell, 1934), sent his reputation soaring over his neoclassical contemporaries, Alfred Marshall in England and his great Swedish rival Gustav Cassel. Just below the pure-theory throne of Léon Walras sits Knut Wicksell: anyone who reads Hicks's seminal *Theory of Wages* (1932) will realize that Wicksell brings analysis to bear on the recurrent problems of our own age: as an example, his explication of how technical innovation can affect the distribution of income and the real-wage level is a quantum leap in sophistication over Ricardian and Marxian paradigms.

A decade after Wicksell's death in 1926, it was his saving–investment macroeconomics that economists most prized. All Scandinavians were neo-Wicksellians in the interval between Keynes's 1930 *Treatise on Money* and *The General Theory of Employment, Interest and Money* (1936): on the continent, Austrians such as Ludwig von Mises, Friedrich von Hayek, and Gottfried von Haberler thought in the same mode; in America, the young Alvin Hansen was a Wicksellian fellow traveller in the period before his trek on the road to the Damascus of Keynes's *General Theory*. Although neo-Wicksellianism did weaken faith in Say's Laws, not much of it lives on in present-day economics. Now we realize that Gunnar Myrdal and Erik Lindahl were not anticipating in their Wicksellian debates of the early 1930s any general theory of *output as a whole*. Like the *Treatise on Money* and Dennis Robertson's monetary paradigms, their primary focus was on the *price* level as the macrovariable of their equilibrium theory. True, Bertil Ohlin and Ragnar Frisch wrote presciently about induced changes in aggregate output as the Great Depression deepened and as efficacious fiscal and monetary policies were advocated. And in this they were mindful of Wicksell's grapplings with macroeconomics. But, as Don Patinkin (1982) has documented, these sage writers articulated no formal paradigm of effective demand comparable to that of the 1936 *General Theory* (or of Michal Kalecki's concomitant partial formulation of an aggregate–output model).

Before concentrating on the Wicksellian microeconomics that moderns see as the jewel in his crown, I should devote a few words to Wicksell's macroeconomics. Wicksell affirmed, rather than denied, that germ of truth in the Quantity Theory of Money and Prices which holds that raising in balance *all* nominal prices of goods, services and assets can leave all *real* supplies and demands and all relative prices intact. Actually, Wicksell's own theory of the business cycle was not a saving–investment analysis but rather an exogenous-shock theory emphasizing the innovations and technical changes that were emphasized by Joseph Schumpeter, Arthur Spiethoff, Gustav Cassel, and by the young Dennis Robertson and young Alvin Hansen. Wicksell's image of a rocking horse, which can be set into quasi-periodic motions even by random hammer blows, was later revived to good effect by Ragnar Frisch and Jan Tinbergen.

Wicksell's saving and investment paradigm was essentially a theory of how the total supply of money will be driven secularly upward or downward by a Central Bank that insists on setting the market interest rate persistently below the *real* (or 'natural') interest rate defined neoclassically by the system's time-phased technology and time-phased consuming preferences. If M grows secularly at 5 per cent per year above the trend growth rate of output – because of persistent perverse pegging of the market interest rate too low – then P in aggregate PQ grows at about 5 per cent with Q limited (over the business cycle) to about its same approximation to high-employment potential-output. In opposition to Wicksell's insistence on the goal of stability for the price level, his great Swedish contemporary David Davidson espoused a price level that fell proportionately to society's gain in productivity, an arguable thesis if we put aside pragmatic frictions. The Wicksell who uncharacteristically made a fetish of honouring prewar 1914 price levels could with only poor consistency make light of real-world frictions.

Wicksell's device of an interest rate specified by the bank-credit system was perhaps 'too clever by 'arf' and did mischief later in delaying decay of the Model T Keynesianism that dogmatically downplayed the potency of M-changes to affect real Q. The middle-aged Bourbons who fabricated the Radcliffe Committee Report in Britain (Radcliffe, 1959), with its antiquated refusal to forget about great-depression liquidity traps, had their minds frozen in their salad days of 1936–39 along Wicksellian modes of thought in which halvings in the general price and wage level merely halved the total money supply – and in which singular versions of the Keynesian systems were invoked, implicitly or explicitly, that hypothesized the near-vanishing of $\partial(MV)/\partial M$.

For a neoclassical economist, the time to be born was by 1840, the epoch of Jevons, Walras and Menger. Vilfredo Pareto, Marshall, Wicksell and Cassel came too late for the feast – to say nothing of A.C. Pigou, Frank Knight and Jacob Viner. Besides, Wicksell was a late bloomer, whose degree in mathematics was followed by a bohemian existence of preoccupation with anti-religion, anti-sexual puritanism, anti-alcoholism, anti-monarchism and anti-militarism. Just as birth control was beginning to catch hold in Europe, Wicksell was obsessed with Malthusian overpopulation and the law of diminishing returns.

By good luck and genius, this self-taught and unemployed post-Doc wrote in his forties a splendid synthesis of Böhm-Bawerk's capital theory with Walras's general equilibrium. See *Über Wert, Kapital und Rente* (1893), translated as *Value, Capital and Rent* (1954), in which Wicksell builds a Jevons–Böhm model where output is increased when the time interval is enlarged between application of inputs and harvest of output. This marginal-productivity-of-time paradigm for a positive interest rate is second in importance only to Irving Fisher's 20th-century general equilibrium reformulation of Böhm-Bawerk's insights.

Only for singularly special technologies is it true that the interest rate equals the derivative of the value of total output with respect to the value of total capital, $\partial(\Sigma PQ)/\partial(\Sigma PK)$ – as Wicksell pointed out with reference to the technology of maturing wine. (His accusation (Wicksell, 1954, pp. 141–2) that Thünen erred on this point is refuted in Samuelson's (1983, Equation A11) demonstration.) Such a discrepancy between the interest rate and this derivative is called a 'Wicksell effect' in the modern literature. Recognizing Wicksell effects is important to correct over-simple neoclassical parables, yes; but this is not to agree with the frequently met notion that, in consequence, the steady-state interest rate of perfect competition can lack *intertemporal Pareto-optimality* when Wicksell effects are present. Actually, no matter what 'reswitchings' or Wicksell effects are present, the competitive equilibrium does support *intertemporal production-and-consumption 'efficiency'*.

Fruitful critiques have been made in our time by Joan Robinson (1956) and Pierro Sraffa (1960) of the simple parable that lower steady-state interest rates *must* be associated with 'more-roundabout' modes of production. What remains intact is only this: (1) if a stationary population is endowed with capital goods that cannot support a golden-rule state of maximal per capita consumption, it can evolve into that golden-rule state *only by transiently sacrificing some current consumption in return for permanently enhanced consumption*; (2) for each specified interest rate, there is a convex tradeoff frontier between steady-state real factor prices (real wage, real rent of land, etc.), and any increase in that interest rate must shift downward that tradeoff frontier.

This first 1893 work illustrates Wicksell's virtues: his generosity in recognizing contributions of others; his confession that specified problems remain unsolved, or fail to be solved to the satisfaction of his scientific conscience; his depth of insight into the essence of an economic situation. Four decades before the mathematician Abraham Wald used inequalities and zero prices to ensure existence of a competitive equilibrium, Wicksell (1893, p. 84, n.1) adumbrates the duality equalities-inequalities that common sense of economics requires. Wicksell (1934, pp. 180–81) gives pictures and words of a 'switch point', where two different activities that are coexistable are combined in any weighting just as ice and water coexist in any proportions at the freezing point. In his seventy-third year, Wicksell (1954) works out how fixed capital can be added to the Austrian models of circulating capital, an exposition that could be improved on only if he had replaced straight-line depreciation by the more convenient exponential depreciation.

Wicksell was an important creator of the neoclassical theory of the distribution of income according to the principles of marginal productivity. His work postdated J.B. Clark's breakthrough of the late 1880s; Phillip Wicksteed's conscious articulation in the early 1890s of first-degree-homogeneous production functions whose marginal products do exactly 'exhaust' the output; Léon Walras's mid-1890s generalization to infinite-many substitutable techniques of production, from his first edition's single technique and his second edition's finite-number of activities, a generalization that Walras could achieve only with the prior help of Pareto and Enrico Barone. If 'marginalism' is the essence of neoclassicism – and it is surely one important component – then Wicksell forms a trio with Johann Heinrich von Thünen (1826, 1850) and J.B. Clark (1899) as an archetypal neoclassicist.

Moreover, Wicksell's turn-of-century marginal productivity utilized the macromodel methodology of his 1893 capital theory: a simple general-equilibrium for society is envisaged with a single good and its production function. This is not macroeconomics in the modern Keynesian sense involving general price levels and elements of effective demand (the sense in which, up until now in this article, the word macroeconomics has been used). Rather, it is macroeconomics in the secondary sense that the word connoted in the mid-1940s when it early appeared in the literature: the sense of Cobb–Douglas aggregate production functions; the sense of a Clarkian aggregate produced by aggregate labour and one idealized total of homogeneous capital. Indeed, the so-called 1927 Cobb–Douglas production function, $Q = L^k C^{1-k}$, was already buried in Wicksell's earlier writings of the Victorian era. (See also Wicksell, 1934, pp. 125, 286.)

David Ricardo shocked his followers and contemporaries with a new chapter in the last edition of his *Principles*, which asserted that invention of machinery could harm wages and cause total production of society to shrink. A Wicksellian exposition, in which $Q(L, C)$ denotes output and $\partial Q(L, C)/\partial L$ denotes the real wage, clearly exposes the possibility that a viable invention which raises Q for fixed L and C can most certainly lower absolute $\partial Q(L, C)/\partial L$.

Uncharacteristically, Wicksell (1934, p. 137) blundered in falsely accusing Ricardo of error: under Ricardo's classical hypothesis that labour supply adjusts to keep the real wage near a constant level of subsistence, total Q could indeed be induced to shrink by a technology parameter's shift that lowered $\partial Q(L, C)/\partial L$ – as when raising the technical parameter T somewhat above unity near $(L, C, T) = (1, 1, 1)$ definitely does depress Q in $Q = 1.5(T-1)C + T^{-1}(LC)^{1/2}$ when the real wage is kept constant by downward adjustments of the labour supply.

Wicksell has good company in making this error: such eminent modern economists as Nicholas Kaldor and George Stigler, rightly impressed with the Pareto-optimality of competition's Invisible Hand in selecting viable inventions, wrongly infer that Ricardo's asserted drop in Q would contradict this Pareto Optimality and hence wrongly judge that there has to be an error on Ricardo's part. Since Ricardo is envisaging an induced drop in L, he is correct to assert that Q may well be decreased by the invention.

Of all the neoclassicists Wicksell is the most humanitarian, the least conservative. During his sixth decade of life he went to jail for the crime of blasphemy. A friend of the *avant garde* August Strindberg, Knut Wicksell espoused redistribution from rich to poor at whatever cost to his own career. No writer of the Edwardian age came closer to the New Deal ideology of 1933–65 and to that of modern social democracy than did Wicksell. Yet, using the words '... the Hegelian darkness – and conceit of Karl Marx ...', Wicksell (1893, Preface, p. i) explicitly rejected Marxism as a paradigm to diagnose and understand the laws of motion of capitalism and as an erroneous programme for improving the welfare of the worker and peasant classes. His rejection of Marxism was based on knowledge of Marx's analysis and not on *a priori* prejudice; actually honesty in this regard inflicted a cost in terms of Wicksell's popularity, since Scandinavia was no exception to the rule that Marxism generated much political appeal in the three decades before World War I, the epoch just after Karl Marx's own death.

Despite his admiration for Ricardo, Wicksell denounced the unrealism of that writer's labour theory of value. Even the great editor of Ricardo, in Sraffa (1951, p. xxiii), lets that writer get away with transparent murder in fallaciously claiming to be able to 'get rid of [the complication of land and] rent' by setting each good's price to its labour cost on extensive-margin zero-rent land. Wicksell (1934, p. 24) points out that where the extensive margin for land will fall is itself

909

an *endogenous* variable that is changed when the composition of demand alters away from land-intensive corn and toward labour-intensive cloth. Along with dozens of other self-contradictions in Ricardo's writings, there is clear recognition in his new chapter on machinery that a wartime shift of demand toward labour services of soldiers rather than toward rural produce would alter the distribution of income – a passage which is the root source for J.S. Mill's later overblown doctrine that 'demand for goods is not demand for labour'. If taste changes can alter distributive shares, then hopeless is Ricardo's attempt to separate distribution theory from value theory – and Wicksell was not loathe to call a spade a spade and a hopeless task hopeless.

One is left, most of all, with an impression of Wicksell's depth and breadth. Except for the Åkermans and Lindahl, Wicksell in his brief end-of-life professorship at Lund had almost no career-economist pupils. But it is no accident that Eli Heckscher and Bertil Ohlin should have originated the paradigm of factor–price equalization by free trade in goods. For, in his post-retirement years back at Stockholm, Knut Wicksell was a national treasure who inspired a generation of younger economists (and succeeded, partially, in keeping Gustav Cassel scientifically honest).

One of the many harvests of his versatility is the 'voluntary exchange' (or 'benefit') theory of public finance and taxation. Wicksell [1896] began this Wicksell–Lindahl–Musgrave–Samuelson–Vickrey theory of pure public goods and the work of his pupil, Erik Lindahl (1919), created its foundation. When private goods consumed by a single person only are supplemented by a public good that is simultaneously enjoyed by many people, Pareto optimality requires that production of the public good be carried to a point where its marginal (opportunity) cost just equals the sum of all citizen's marginal-rates-of substitution between the public good and any private good. Relying on a hoped-for Scandinavian consensus or 'unanimity', Wicksell perhaps worried too little about the 'free rider' problem (that results from the fact that every citizen in a Lindahl market is tempted to pretend not to much want the public good).

Finally, Wicksell's civility towards his great rival Gustav Cassel sets us all a noble example. Cassel had every gift except the gift of 'maybe'. Tutor to the King, Cassel pleased the Establishment and, prior to the post-1930 age of Keynes, was the economist most quoted by the international press. Although Schumpeter called Cassel '90% Walras and 10% water', I judge him to be a creative scientist, underrated today because of his egotistical failures to acknowledge doctrinal borrowings. (When his secretary wrote his biography, she alibied for this failing on the grounds that friction with his father blotted out from Cassel's memory all writers from whom he learned in early life!)

Wicksell (1934, pp. 219–52) gives his final reckoning with Cassel. His verdicts are unsparing, often harsh, but by no means malicious. Moreover, by modern standards, often it is Wicksell who must be judged to have the weaker case. Cassel (1918) brilliantly anticipated the Harrod–Domar mode of balanced exponential growth, and deserves praise not blame for soft-pedalling diminishing returns to land in modern Europe. Cassel, like Pareto, was right to downplay cardinal-measurable marginal utility even though he went too far in hypothesizing reduced-form, positivistic demand functions. Wicksell was not wrong in wishing for individual tastes to underlie welfare economics; but, as Abram Bergson (1938) was later to demonstrate, ordinal welfare economics does not necessarily require independently addable Benthamite utility functions for individuals. Wicksell, better than Marshall or Mises or Walras, realized from the beginning that competitive equilibrium of *laissez faire* does not necessarily achieve or approximate to a state of maximal social welfare or equity. He recognized, dimly, that the algorithm of perfect competition (not to be confused with *laissez faire*) does achieve the efficiency of production and exchange that we have since 1950 called 'Pareto optimality'; so, with the aid of feasible-best prior redistribution of people's endowments, the competitive market mechanism might be used to contrive a state of ethical optimality. Better to see obscurely in 1893 what we came to understand only after 1938. But, short of that, better for Wicksell to stubbornly insist that the emperor of market competition wore no ethical clothes than fall in with capitalistic apologias.

Wicksell's economics, because of its eclecticism and generality, adapts well to the present post-neoclassical age. As with Cournot, his writings speak eloquently to readers of a later century.

PAUL A. SAMUELSON

BIBLIOGRAPHY

Bergson, A. 1938. A reformulation of certain aspects of welfare economics. *Quarterly Journal of Economics* 52, February, 310–34.
Cassel, G. 1918. *Theory of Social Economy*. Trans., New York: Harcourt, Brace & Co., 1932.
Clark, J.B. 1899. *The Distribution of Wealth*. New York: Macmillan.
Gårdlund, T. 1956. *The Life of Knut Wicksell*. Trans. N. Adler, Stockholm: Almqvist & Wiksell, 1958.
Hicks, J.R. 1932. *The Theory of Wages*. London: Macmillan.
Patinkin, D. 1982. *Anticipations of the General Theory? and Other Essays on Keynes*. Chicago: University of Chicago Press.
Radcliffe, Lord (Chairman). 1959–60. *Committee on the Working of the Economy: Report, Minutes of Evidence, and Memoranda*. London: HMSO.
Robinson, J. 1956. *The Accumulation of Capital*. London: Macmillan.
Samuelson, P.A. 1983. Thünen at 200. *Journal of Economic Literature* 21, December, 1468–88.
Stigler, G.J. 1941. *Production and Distribution Theories: The Formative Period*. New York: Macmillan.
Sraffa, P. 1960. *Production of Commodities by Means of Commodities*. Cambridge: Cambridge University Press.
Sraffa, P. (With the collaboration of M.H. Dobb.) 1951. General Preface to D. Ricardo, *On the Principles of Political Economy and Taxation*, Cambridge: Cambridge University Press for the Royal Economic Society.
von Thünen, J.H. 1826, 1850. *Der Isolierte Staat*, Pts I and II.
Wicksell, K. 1893. *Über Wert, Kapital und Rente*. Jena: Gustav Fischer. Trans. as *Value, Capital and Rent*, London: George Allen & Unwin, 1954. This contains a fairly complete Wicksell bibliography, on pp. 169–75, completed by Arne Amundsen.
Wicksell, K. 1896. *Finanztheoretische Untersuchungen nebst Darstellung und Kritik des Steuerwesens Schwedens*. Jena: Gustav Fischer.
Wicksell, K. 1898. *Interest and Prices*. Trans., London: Macmillan, 1936.
Wicksell, K. 1934. *Lectures on Political Economy*. Vol. I: *General Theory*; Vol. II: *Money*. London: George Allen & Unwin.

552

HAROLD FREEMAN (1909-1997)
Paul A. Samuelson, MIT, 10 March 1998

The old *Reader's Digest* used to run a monthly contributed volume called, "The Most Unforgettable Person I Ever Met." Certainly Harold Freeman would be my choice as a character encountered on life's path. He was one of a kind: 99.44% Peer Gynt, and the residual had to be Baron Munchausen. No one friend of Harold's could be his Boswell; he was a diamond with a thousand faces, each one different.

Harold grew up in the mined-out hard coal region of Pennsylvania. He was the only child of parents who trace back, I believe, to Austria. That may explain why he was Harold Adolph Freeman. His folks ran a little general store, which he claimed was mostly a saloon. Disaster struck when America in 1919 passed the Prohibition Amendment against liquor. Harold's version is that his Uncle Looey, the only relative of affluence, bought them a 100-gallon barrel of straight kootch. That kept the family afloat until Franklin Roosevelt restored civil rights in 1933. When I questioned his tale on arithmetic grounds--after all Harold Hotelling proved in 1929 that a finite stock will be depleted in a finite time--Harold trumped my ace by claiming that each night they kept the barrel full by adding water. That way, he said, they could withstand any siege, however long.

I want to get Harold to MIT. But I must tell two alleged stories about Uncle Looey. Harold's mother is supposed to have said to him, "Cotton up to Uncle Looey. He might leave you his money." Alas, that caper came to nought. According to Harold, two fast-talking managers persuaded Looey to invest in their scheme for counterfeiting $20 bills. Apparently those items could not have fooled a six-year-old school girl! So, in the end, all of Uncle Looey's fortune went into bribing a federal judge in order to stay out of jail. Did all of that ever happen? Did any of it happen? With Harold, we will never know. He saw reality in a different light. Whenever he and I witnessed the same event, my excellent memory could rarely corroborate his version.

In 1927, seventy years ago last September, Harold somehow arrived as an MIT freshman. In those days, and still when I began teaching here, MIT's tuition was 50% higher than Harvard's. Our hero was then six feet tall, but his weight was less than his I.Q.: and I speak with measured exactitude. You may ask, What's the big deal? Isaac Newton was no heavyweight wrestler. Well, back in those pre-Karl Compton MIT days, Tech was indeed Hell. Every freshman, along with taking math, physics, chemistry and mechanical drawing, was required to take a class called "Forge." Handling a ladle full of molten steel nearly proved Harold's undoing at the beginning of his academic career. That is the same Harold who was a basketball starter well into his forties on the Econ Department's league-winning basketball team! I will have more to report later on Harold Freeman's caloric intake.

MIT's courses in statistics were in those days nothing to boast about. In later years Harold could speak well only of a course he took in mathematical probability from Dick Struick. But it did not matter. With exquisite timing Harold's MIT degree jumped him into the job market in the middle of 1931, when the Great Depression was moving into its final grim stage.

In those days there was neither federal, state nor local welfare relief for the unemployed. By great good luck Harold got a job at the Watertown Hood Rubber Plant, pounding cheap heels into cheap shoes at 19 cents an hour. Walking both ways between Central Square and Watertown Square gave him plenty of time to think about the Pareto Optimality of the capitalistic system.

When I came to Harvard in 1935 there was only one Peer Gynt to be seen in the graduate classroom. Always he took notes but never spoke. But occasionally, after the lecture, while I was sucking up to Professor Schumpeter or Edward Bidwell Wilson, Harold would ask a question. It was not that economics kidnapped Harold Freeman's imagination or ravished his soul. But by then, as an Assistant Professor of Statistics, he had to do his share of 14.01 teaching and he probably wanted to do the job right. He certainly didn't make the trip to Harvard to learn statistics. He had the good taste to avoid William Leonard Crum and Edwin Frickey, who taught something *they* called statistics. And in the math department the offering in the Harvard Yard was also pretty lean.

To concentrate on Harold the person, let me rush over his crucial role in bringing to MIT a world-class economics department. Early on he tried to interest me in a chair at MIT. It was Harold who talked me into my first teaching job, sixty-one years ago, at the MIT summer school. I was younger than the upperclassmen in the class. (Yes, they happened to be all men, and some of them could speak English.) Unbeknownst to me it was part of Harold's campaign to talk me up with Department Head Ralph Freeman (no relation). Allegedly, I was the hottest thing since chicken pot pie was invented and yet, shucks, I was just plain folk. Actually, he convinced the mercurial Rupert Maclaurin, who had a back door to President Compton's office, that Samuelson was the wave of the future for economics. As I have already hinted, Baron Munchausen Freeman could tell a good story. Later I learned from Ralph, who became a dear friend, how Harold operated. Rhodes Scholar Ralph said, "I know Paul is a good scholar. But is he a *cooperator*?" Never at a loss, Harold replied, "Is Samuelson a cooperator? Why the man writes joint articles." Now the sober truth was that only one of my papers had been written jointly. It was with Russ Nixon, Harvard's village radical. It was an empirical investigation on the measurement of U.S. unemployment and I understood it only because a local go-getter was elbowing Nixon unfairly to the side. The record shows that since that time only about 10,500 ft. of my publications have been with collaborators.

Harold deserves even more credit for bringing Bob Solow to MIT. At the time, in late 1948, veteran-soldier Solow had zero publications and Ph.D.'s. Like Oscar Wilde at the U.S. Customs, Solow had nothing to declare but his genius. But Bob is the one to tell you presently about Harold and his coming to MIT.

I could spend all day talking about Harold's individuality. Here are a few sample items to document that he was no run-of-the-mill Rotarian.

Item 1. Every day from 1931 to 1939, inclusive of Sundays and February 29th, Harold's lunch consisted of a chicken pot pie at Walton's Cafeteria outside of MIT's main entrance. Then, suddenly, Harold never ate another chicken pie. He could not explain why. When he was brainwashed to try Chinese food, he chanced on sub gum chow mein. From then on it was that item only.

Item 2. Harold was a gregarious person, full of gossip and ready to discuss your current troubles. I was as close to Harold as anyone, and scores of times with each of my six children, I would visit Harold and Margaret out in Belmont. But never once, in 40 years, did Marion and I succeed in getting Harold to accept a party invitation. It wasn't that he refused. Always he said, Yes. But then an out-of-town emergency prevented his coming. At least once he actually went to Providence so as not to have to tell a white lie.

Item 3. During World War II Harold traveled around the country, in Aberdeen testing grounds and elsewhere, providing consulting to the military on quality control. But he refused to accept any compensation for the voluntary service. As far as he would go was to take on his tax return a travel-expense deduction. Of course that led to an IRS audit. "Show me, Professor Freeman, the non-MIT income against which you claim these deductions," the auditor demanded. Harold explained his voluntary expert services for the beleaguered nation only to be told, "You can be as generous as you like, Professor, but not at our expense." Harold never appealed the decision.

Item 4. Once Harold received a small inheritance. Maybe it was when his mother died. He came to me for financial advice. No, it was not for the hottest stock tip or for an optimal program of diversification. He set an impossible problem: "Paul, how can I invest this so that no stock will benefit from cold-war armament expenditures?" Knowing the Leontief input-output table, I knew that even the Avon lady was part of the military-industrial complex. In the end I had to flim-flam Harold with a black lie: "Gillette," I said, "is squeaky clean."

Item 5. A Harvard graduate student came around to take some of our courses. His name was Nathan Belfer, who ended up in Wall

Street as a futures trader. Harold said to me in all seriousness, "And, I always liked that Belfer kid."

Final item. Harold was an excellent teacher, even for business executives innocent of mathematics. His seminar for Sloan Executives was held in the basement of the Sloan building. When the bell rang to end the hour, Harold bolted for the door. It was the wrong door--the door to the closet. The class didn't know what to do. They hung around for a while. Harold knew what to do. He stayed put until silence proved the coast was clear. Then he made the getaway. That really happened, in just that way.

* * *

Harold is missed. But he is not forgotten. The many hours I spent with him--swapping stories about Norbert Weiner or R.A. Fisher or Casey Stengel or Milton Friedman--are among the happiest in my life. He ended his career as he began it--the perpetual scholar with books but no Ph.D. thesis. Yet he advised more scientists and engineers on statistical matters than Fisher or Deming or Neyman put together.

We used to have a Happy Hour at the MIT Faculty Club. One Wednesday I said to Harold, "Let's go up and have a drink." He refused, saying, "I don't want to drink with those 25-cent drinkers." I shall always miss that drink with Harold--the one we never had.

553

CHAPTER - 1

MY JOHN HICKS

Paul A. Samuelson

ABSTRACT

In this paper, contributions of J.R. Hicks have been evaluated briefly. The landmarks in Hicks's working life are described. Among the major works of Hicks, *"Value and Capital"* written at the age of 35, is a scientific epic saga – full of new and beautiful things and a springboard towards future advances. Even before the *'General Theory'* if Keynes was considered as the greatest economist of the world, J.R. Hicks was the greatest young economist at that time. Hick's works are immortal.

I was lucky in my teachers at Chicago and Harvard. But being in love with the subject of economics and possessed of boundless youthful energy and a ferocious power to read and focus on everything that interested me, most of what I learned was not by word of mouth in lectures and conversations with economists at those two great universities in the 1932–1940 period. The wide world was my school. It was from books and journal articles that I learned what were the important scientific questions to ponder over; and many of the best answers that could be then given to those questions came from those away-from-home sources, from the great "invisible college" of economic and other sciences. With two great libraries at hand, I read essentially *all* the journals when they were, so to speak, still hot, and I was excessively eclectic in sampling almost all of their contents.

It was a wonder that I had time to do independent thinking! And if the brain has only so much room in it (as Sherlock Holmes insisted to Dr. Watson), then my excellent memory could have endangered my own

[1]

originality. But there was little danger of that, for as Chicago's Professor Paul Douglas wrote to Professor Jacob Viner in recommending that as an undergraduate I be admitted to Viner's celebrated Chicago graduate seminar in economic theory: "Young Samuelson is able if cantankerous and argumentative".

All this is by way of saying that John Hicks (born 1904), early and late, was a major intellectual stimulus for me. I went over his contributions with a powerful microscope, a much more intensive analysis than he ever gave either to my own work or to that of any other economist. That was the way Hicks was. Always he preferred to do things *his* way. And that was the source both of his creative originality and prolific scientific productivity. Of course such a scientific style can lead to blind spots even in the best of scholars, and to the rediscovery of a certain number of round wheels. But the completed record shows that, if this was a Faustian bargain with the Devil, it was one with high net payoff.

More than once I have recorded the autobiographical fact that, as a teenager at Chicago, I was told by an early tutor that John Maynard Keynes was then – 1932 or 1933, well before *The General Theory* (1936) – "the greatest economist in the world" and told also, that at Harvard around 1935 by an Assistant Professor friend J.R. Hicks was the greatest *young* economist at that time. Both evaluations squared with my own early impressions. I spent a lot of time dissecting Hicks's (1932) *Theory of Wages*; and, incidentally, I later disagreed with Hicks's own damning-with-faint-praise that early first book. By then I had learned to accept only with guarded reservations John's claims and disclaimers about his own contributions. Expressions of modesty can sometimes be veiled signs both of vanity and Napoleonic ambition.

I wish present readers to understand that I always regarded Hicks as having been somewhat undervalued, particularly in Britain, his own country. As he learned during his brief and not happy sojourn at Cambridge University – in between his nine golden years at the LSE and his decade of loner productivity at Manchester – Hicks was not "politically correct" and therefore not popular with the leftish elite at Oxbridge. Dennis Robertson engineered Hicks's Cambridge appointment to keep down Joan Robinson; but subsequently Robertson kept somewhat at a distance. Moreover, in England an early failure to earn a First leaves scars on the ego that will not fade. If I ran the world I would heap every honor early on whomever was later to shine in the scientific barnyard; that might get out of the way some of the pathology of unbridled ambition, which can never be satiated even by the greatest of accomplishments. (I think of Joseph Schumpeter and of the mathematician Norbert Wiener as examples in point.)

John Hicks had another fault. He wrote well. This is not a common crime among economists. And it meant that his was a wide audience among readers, some of whom were not very expert in mathematical jargon and techniques. The good fairies balance their gifts. Hicks was not a terribly good lecturer. He did not stammer but his flow of words was not smooth, and in a personal dialogue with a Nicholas Kaldor or Milton Friedman he did not excel in quick repartee.

At Oxford over the years Hicks had some very good students. To name just two, these included the American Lionel McKenzie and the Japanese Michio Morishima. On their travels all over the world, John and Ursula Hicks would be met by admiring former pupils. But the master was not a warm, outgoing personality. He wrote few joint papers and tended to concentrate most on his own research puzzles. It was not a rash decision for him to retire early from his Drummond Professorship: that kept him in step with his older wife; and it in no way inhibited twenty more years of prolific and provocative innovative contributions.

In *The New Palgrave A Dictionary of Economics* (1987, pp. 641–646), Christopher Bliss gives an admirable selective description of J.R. Hicks's many and fine contributions to varied fields of economic theory. I shall not duplicate that here. Let me merely sing the praises of *Value and Capital* (1939, 1946). Written when the author was 35, this is a scientific epic saga – full of new and beautiful things and a springboard toward future advances. No single misprint mars its mathematical text; and the one major omission in its first edition he was able to repair by altering a few pages only.

To summarize my superlative evaluation of John Hicks, I believe it would have been as well for the Royal Swedish Academy of Science to have named Hicks *alone* for the second Nobel Prize in 1970, following immediately after Ragner Frisch and Jan Tinbergen in 1969. That would have left Kenneth Arrow to receive later an unshared award: the Hicks and Arrow coupling was not particularly optimal; and it came about, I suspect, from the happenstance that some of the judging committee resented Hicks's cavalier citings of contemporary work by other scholars – a non-Scandinavian practise not uncommon in the British senior common rooms of that time. (I should add that Kenneth Arrow, in my book, deserves at least two Nobel Prizes).

I remember Sir John the last time I saw him in person, toward the end of his life, at the Saltzesbaden 1987 conference near Stockholm in honor of Erik Lundberg. He was in good form for an octogenarian. "Fortunately I am dying from my feet up rather than from my brain down", he quipped.[1] Years before John Hicks had confided to me, "When one of us – Ursula or I – dies, the other will be left lonely". And so it was for this childless couple; when Ursula (born in 1896!) died first, Sir John lived alone at his Blockley family property in the Cotswolds near Oxford. Fortunately younger economists on the Oxford scene helped him travel to conferences in Italy and elsewhere.

To the end Sir John Hicks was as he had been throughout his life: a loner scholar, for whom the sun rose in the morning when first he opened his eyes. His works constitute his immortality.

REFERENCES

Bliss, Christopher, 1987. "Hicks, John, R." in J. Eatwell, M. Milgate and P. Newman, eds., *The New Palgrave A Dictionary of Economics*, Vol. 2, London. Macmillan.

Hicks, John, R., 1932, 1963. *The Theory of Wages*. London. Macmillan.

Hicks, John, R. 1937. *La Théorie Mathématique de la valeur end régime de libre concurrence.*. Trans. G. Lutfalla. Paris: Hermann.

Hicks, John, R. 1939, 1946. *Value and Capital*. Oxford: Clarendon Press.

Keynes, John Maynard. 1936. *The General Theory of Employment, Interest and Money*. London. Macmillan.

---

[1] Wanting to square the books before it was too late, John Hicks in private at Saltzesbaden expressed worry that he had been remiss in properly citing my works parallel to his. Long earlier I had made the optimal adjustment to his manner of composition and I could see no point in worrying a doughty warrior at that stage of life. Therefore I assured him that always I had learned much from him (a literal truth); and that indeed I had early known the brief 1937 French version of his developed 1939 classic. Reassured, he confided: "Now that I am old and working alone, getting the big books off the library shelf is quite a chore and that inhibits my bibliographical accuracy". When I told Bob Solow this story I added: "Those books were always heavy on Sir John's shelves".

Foreword

Paul A. Samuelson

Murray Kemp a sexagenarian? That is hard to believe for those of us who remember the Australian Lochinvar come out of the West to liven up Johns Hopkins, McGill, MIT, and his own native stomping grounds. On the other hand, the scores of analytical contributions that have come from his quill and his workshop of colleagues have created the feeling that Kemp has always been there on the frontier of science, pushing it forward.

Kemp is one of the postwar generation who, along with Ronald Jones, Harry Johnson, John Chipman, and many others, have put trade theory on firm and wide foundations. The great Maxwell spoke of thermodynamics as "a science with secure foundations, clear definitions, and distinct boundaries". Willard Gibbs asserted that all this could be said to be true only after the 1850 synthesis by Clausius of the heuristics of Carnot, Thomson, and Joule. When I pick up the first edition of Kemp's *The Pure Theory of International Trade* and compare it with the fine prewar texts of Marshall, Haberler, and Ohlin, I can only use words like those of Gibbs. At last, coherence and closure was achieved. Originality is not the hallmark of us textbook writers, but *early* authors who set a standard for coverage and rigor do get seated by Saint Peter in the very front pews of the cathedral of science.

Let me elucidate that I am not engaged in the pleasant puffery appropriate to conventional birthday celebrations. I recently had occasion to do some research on the state of the pure theory of international trade six or seven decades ago—just before Ohlin, Haberler, and Viner moved it a quantum jump beyond Ricardian comparative (labor) costs. In the last century, J. S. Mill, Mangoldt, Marshall, and Edgeworth provided a beginning toward a science of international trade, and Taussig embalmed the received paradigms in an excellent exposition. But the quality of those contemporary debates has to be sampled to be believed. One point will illustrate. Two leading scholars, Luigi Einaudi and James Angell, accused Ricardo's initial discussion of trade between Portugal and England in wine and cloth as being logically self-contradictory. It took Viner and the young Straffa to rebut this charge, showing that Ricardo's only misdemeanor was that of incompleteness on the side of discussing where, between the autarky cost ratio limits, the actual free-trade price equilibrium would come. Even Pareto, whose polemics in favor of general equilibrium were mostly on the mark, engaged in quibbles when it came to his rejection of comparative cost methodology.

Ohlin, Haberler, and Viner opened the way for Lerner, Leontief, Meade, Stolper and Samuelson, and the many virtuosos of my generation. But just as economic theory needed its Debreus, Arrows, and Walds to whip its diversity into a rigorous synthesis, Murray Kemp's generation inherited the priceless opportunity to create a secure and coherent theory of international trade. As always, when an Arrow or a Kemp sets out to tidy up an inchoate domain, they perceive along the way wonderful new gems never dreamed of in the philosophy of their predecessors.

Trade in mobile goods—in books, articles, and manuscripts—serves as a partial substitute for the mobility of factors of production. All over the world, therefore, economists have been splashed with consumer's surplus from the stream of Kemp contributions exported out of New South Wales. Better still, Murray Kemp has himself been a moveable agent, serving as visiting professor in various places. Like Johnny Appleseed, everywhere that Murray goes he entices into originality a corps of new collaborators. The result is a multiplier chain that happily fails to converge finitely.

To be a recognized scholar it is neither necessary nor sufficient that a person be friendly, generous, humanitarian, or likeable. We who have encountered Murray Kemp in the great game of economic science, therefore, feel singularly blessed that he is so many standard deviations above the mean in these attributes that define character.

A scientist earns the only mortality worth having. Of the good scholar we say: *Rex numquam moritur.*

Foreword

Paul A. Samuelson

Nicholas Georgescu-Roegen was a great mind. Future history may reveal that he was one of those who is so far ahead of his time that he fails to get the recognition he deserves. I met him often in Schumpeter's 1935–6 Harvard Graduate Seminar, when he was a 30-year-old Romanian Rockefeller Fellow and I was a 20-year-old beginning graduate student.

Schumpeter ardently admired Nicholas and proposed to join him in writing a great theoretical treatise. One of history's might-have-beens would be a Georgescu–Schumpeter classic to sit on the bookshelf next to the grand von Neumann–Morgenstern opus. Alas, a Balkan patriot could not be lured away from the Motherland that was soon to implode. (Georgescu later regretted his own decision, but a Maxwell Demon who understood the intricacies of Byzantine Harvard politics in that golden dawn might have warned him that Schumpeter himself lacked the power base to procure for Georgescu-Roegen the tenure chair dangled before him as bait. Genius flourishes anyway where no Medici beams. Still, along that path not taken by history, Harvard would have provided for Georgescu-Roegen a bully pulpit to amplify and spread his influence.)

Looking at a puzzling modernist painting by Picasso, you are reassured to know that, when he did try to create in the classical mode, his canvases were masterpieces. So with Nicholas. After the age of 60 he moved ahead from his mainstream mathematical economics researches into a new phase. It is not easy to be both profound and at the same time clear. What is his new kind of economics that goes beyond the Newton–Bacon logic of observation and theoretical rationalization thereof, and which asserts that 'B can be *both* A and non-A?' What will be the fruits of a methodology that rejects the 'superstition as dangerous as the animism of old: that of the Almighty Arithmophonic Concept'?

When you read these puzzling words it is reassuring to know that Georgescu-Roegen, whenever he did set his pen to it, had been a topnotch innovator: on Paretian utility theory; on the integrability and transitivity problem in demand theory; on Non-Substitution Theorems in Leontief–Sraffa paradigms of input/output; on topological implications of addable independent cardinal utilities; and much more. I for one scrutinized intensely each new Georgescu *tour de force* and learned much from him. Therefore, when the Harvard University Press asked for my opinion about publishing in 1966 his collected papers, mine was an enthusiastic affirmation. I added that it would be a bonus to get from him a new Introduction. (They were somewhat taken aback when it turned out to exceed 100 printed pages. Rejoice, I said, you have induced from a deep scholar in effect a new book! And in the end, after the 1971 *Entropy* classic, they got from him two new classics.)

Modern concern for man's destroying of the environment gives poignancy to Georgescu-Roegen's second phase of entropy economics. From before 1776 Adam Smith, through 1911 Joseph Schumpeter and into the present day, economists contemplated scenarios that settled down (in the absence of new disturbances) into a stationary state that in season and out repeats its appointed rounds indefinitely. The logo for old economics, Georgescu-Roegen suggested, could therefore be the frictionless Newtonian pendulum which swings forever. (Maybe that pendulum, immersed in the syrup of resisting air, would be as apt an image: this captures the settling down of the economic system to an asymptotic sustainable steady state and it avoids the gratuitous razor's-edge between damping and anti-damping that characterizes rational mechanics of the Newton–Lagrange–Hamilton species.)

What Georgescu-Roegen proposes to replace the logo of the pendulum is the logo of an *hourglass* whose sands run downward as the arrow of time advances: an irreversible process that admits of no permanently renewable steady state for maintainable economic consumption. Absent from this scenario is any *deus ex machina* to immediately turn upside down the empty hourglass and thereby to preserve a permanently sustainable periodic clocklike motion.

Georgescu-Roegen proposes that the economic theorist should advance beyond the eighteenth-century kindergarten of the First (conserved-energy) Law of Thermodynamics to the next-higher grade of the nineteenth-century Second Law of Thermodynamics, whereby a definable measure of 'entropy' (or 'disorder') ever rises as time grows in one direction. Aside from today's fashionable chic of the 'green' movement, Georgescu-Roegen's methodological proposal evokes a resonant appeal to post-Marshallian economists who hanker for a shift in emphasis away from reductionist physics methodology and toward a 'biological' and 'organic' orientation for economic theory. This topic deserves explication in its own right. Bare description gains from *gestalts* of understanding.

First, there is actually nothing at all biological about the rise in the summed entropy of two flasks of a perfect gas (H_2O vapor at high temperatures) when they are joined by a non-insulating inner wall: the maximizing of Σ Entropy is as much 'reductionism' as the conserving of the gases' Σ Energy.

Second, the settling down of the newly-connected flasks to their envisaged equal-temperature steady state is covered by the old logo of the damped pendulum just as well as it is covered by the logo of the hourglass. The steady state of the glass when all its sand is in the lower hemisphere is indeed a maintainable (but non-productive!) equilibrium, quite like Schumpeter's 1911 scenario of circular-flow (zero interest rate) stationary state, which would persist until the damped-down violin string gets newly plucked by the good fairy of entrepreneurial innovation.

Third, I do not perceive that new eclectic dialectic of the NON-excluded Middle was ever involved in the prosaic domain of nineteenth-century thermodynamics. *Au contraire.*

Fourth, the last half of the twentieth century has seen the triumph of biology. In the DNA age of Crick–Watson, in the time of the Darwinian synthesis by Ernst Mayr, E.O. Wilson, W.D. Hamilton, R.H. MacArthur, J. Maynard Smith and predecessors, there has not been a retreat from or an advance beyond the physics methodology of Alfred Marshall's day. You will see this most clearly in the mathematics of dynamical genetic demography by the great triad of R.A. Fisher–J.B.S. Haldane–Sewall Wright, to say nothing of the ecological paradigms of Lotka, Volterra, Gauss, May, Joel Cohen and Karlin. No weed of vitalism ever surfaced in their gardens, and history has not been kind to the dialectics of Lynsenko or of Sunday-night Haldane, Bernal and Lewontin. Nicholas's methodological revolutions will presumptively have to earn their way autonomously on their own merits past and future.

But I come to praise Caesar, not to bury him (or undercut him). My point is not to deny that ecological dynamics has a need to face up to, and *resist*, irreversible degenerations. After all, the stationary state with all the sand in the lower globe is a different one from that in which you can turn a flour mill and earn a dollar by the thrust of falling sand. My point is that those of us with hardened arteries who resist the prophet of a new and revolutionary economics methodology can still accept and admire the insights about external diseconomies that Georgescu-Roegen contributed in his new phase.

Let me merely illustrate by his, so to speak, Fourth Law of Thermodynamics. Before the industrial revolution, rich seams of high concentration copper resided in Minnesota's Mesabi range. In World War I and the 1920s, they were dispersed to make durable goods and to end up in the waste dumps of society. Those no-longer-available configurations of concentrated matter could not help to fight World War II: they were already gone with the winds.

Modern PhDs cannot understand two-plus-two unless put in equation form. Let me therefore write down the simplest Georgescu-Roegen scenario (as I did at the Yale Centenary for Willard Gibbs in 1989). I first pilfer from Smith–Ricardo–Mill ancient texts two archetypes.

Archetype 1. Labor (or labor-cum-capital), L, works with fixed land (inexhaustible and unaugmentable in supply) to produce Corn. Choose units so that 1 of Corn in wage just suffices as subsistence to keep population neither growing nor declining.

More of L lowers the market-clearing wage rate:

$$w = f^{(1)}(L) = \text{say } 1/\sqrt{L}; f^{(2)} < 0: \text{ diminishing returns.} \tag{1}$$

More of L raises output, Q, when land is fixed:

$$Q = f(L) = \text{say } 2\sqrt{L}: \text{ concavity.} \tag{2}$$

Rent's share of competitive output, is residually,

$$R = Q - Lw = 2\sqrt{L} - L/\sqrt{L} = \sqrt{L} = \tfrac{1}{2}Q. \tag{3}$$

Population grows when $w > \bar{w} = 1$, the subsistence real wage:

$$dL/dt = \bar{a}(w - 1) = \bar{a}(L^{-\frac{1}{2}} - 1), \bar{a} > 0. \tag{4}$$

Permanent equilibrium comes when $L^* = 1$, the root of

$$0 = \bar{a}(L^{-\frac{1}{2}} - 1), L^* = 1 \tag{5a}$$

$$\lim_{t \to \infty} L(t) = 1 = L(\infty) = L^*, \tag{5b}$$

for any positive initial $L(0)$. QED.

All this is barebones classical economics, pre-Georgescu but post-Malthus. Now let us put the powerful microscope of logic on this specified economic organism. Where does the physics *energy* come from to grow corn century after century? Implicitly, there is the noonday sun whose rays by photosynthesis convert light into starch. However, as the pop song says, nothing is forever. This holds for the sun too. X million years from now it will be gone (or will be a dwarf star, or a blackhole, or ...). But, say, for the next 500 years the pre-Georgescu renewable equilibrium model does suffice.

Archetype 2. Now I turn to a second scenario that illuminates the simplest case of non-sustainable equilibrium. Let the Corn of subsistence, or some indispensable part of it, be a commodity that must be *mined* from finitely exhaustible mines. Now Q, aside from needing labor and land, is also adversely dependent on the past cumulative total of itself as mined over the years. For example.

$$Q = f[L, \textstyle\int_{-\infty}^{t} Q(\tau)d\tau] \tag{6a}$$

$$= \text{say } 2\sqrt{L}/\textstyle\int_{-\infty}^{t} Q(\tau)d\tau \tag{6b}$$

$$\equiv 2\sqrt{L}/Z \equiv Q \equiv dZ/dt. \tag{6c}$$

791

As before,

$$\text{real wage} = w = 1/Z\sqrt{L}, \qquad (7)$$

$$dL/dt = \bar{a}[Z^{-1}L^{\frac{1}{2}} - 1], \text{ as in (4)}, \qquad (8)$$

$$dZ/dt = 2\sqrt{L}/Z, \text{ as in (6c)}. \qquad (9)$$

The two differential equations, (8) and (9), plainly admit of *no stationary* positive (L^*, Z^*) solution. (The classical economists knew this about exhaustible mines.) From any positive initial $[L(0), Z(0)]$, the cumulative total of $Z(t)$ always will be growing, and that cumulation must eventually lower productivity and the wage rate below subsistence need: therefore, penultimately, population and output, $[L(t), Q(t)]$ must then both be shrinking *ad infinitum*.

What underlies this inevitability? It is Georgescu-Roegen's Law of Inevitable Dissipation of Useful Concentrated Matter. This is a good-sense certainty, not some esoteric probability of physicists Boltzmann and Clausius: only if all useful copper and gold and helium could be 100 per cent recycled would a *perpetuum mobile* be possible. If pigs could fly, if my Aunt Sally were a stagecoach, if . . . and if . . . .

A final word will speak of the man inside the scholar's armor. Nicholas was an intense, even a passionate, personality. He did not strive to be 'politically correct'. He suffered neither fools nor mediocrities gladly. Some of his best friends lost that precarious status. Others had to work hard to keep it, walking with him the second and third mile. Despite his proud, even haughty, demeanor, never in oral dialogue, correspondence or written commentary was Nicholas other than courteous and meticulously just. To those who know well the nature and practice of scholars and human beings, what I have just said is high praise – praise which does not go without saying.

The novelist Stendhal comforted himself that the fame he did not fully realize in life would be his from posterity. Many are called to have such a fate, but few are chosen. As a surviving friend of Nicholas, I will be delighted if Stendhal's happy fate turns out to be Georgescu-Roegen's too.

Hans-E. Loef and Hans G. Monissen (eds) *The Economics of Irving Fisher. Reviewing the Scientific Work of a Great Economist.* Cheltenham: Edward Elgar, 1999. Pp. xx + 343. £59.95. ISBN 1-84064-037-5.

Irving Fisher (1867–1947) was a great world economist, a theorist and empiricist (Newton and Bacon entwined), a pioneer in both micro- and macroeconomics, the first great master in intertemporal economics from whom modern finance theory (J.B. Williams to Black–Scholes–Merton) evolved. This fine book, written by 15 German-language and five American experts, objectively reviews Fisher's publications over more than five decades of productive scholarship.

After the editor of his collected works, Barber, devotes two chapters to personal biography, Fisher's pure theory (1892–1940) is audited by Chipman, Schwalbe and Schultz, Barta, Schefold and Caspari, and in their policy and statistical applications by Brolle-Milde and Gintschel, Entorf, Fuest and Scheer.

Undergraduates knew Fisher as the macroeconomist with thoughts and afterthoughts on MV=PQ Quantity Theory. Dimand, Humphrey, Loef-Monissen (the editors), V. Alexander and F. Steindl provide valuable commentary. What overlap exists between chapter authors I judge to have been useful rather than repetitious.

My review begins with Fisher's 1911 classic on *The Purchasing Power of Money*. He attributes his variant of MV=PQ to the American-Canadian astronomer Simon Newcomb (1835–1909); however, classical writers early in the nineteenth century, such as the pedantic James Mill, had arrived pretty close to the neoclassical Quantity Theory. Alfred Marshall, A.C. Pigou and J.M. Keynes had independently written down M=(1/V)PQ, an equivalent tautology to MV=PQ. Despite some initial provincial puffery by Keynes for his local team's superiority, we can agree that Fisher, Marshall, Wicksell and the preponderance of mainstream monetary economists were all of essentially the same paradigm – which manipulated the tautology to derive longest-run *neutrality* of the price level and impotence of the *nominal* M supply to affect systematically real (Q, P_i/P_j, P_i/W, interest rate) magnitudes in comparative stationary states. (From Copernicus to Locke to our own nursery-school days, we all knew the King Midas lesson that *ceteris paribus* mere doubling of the nominal M level, when at the same time all nominal p's of goods and services were doubled in stationary-state plateau levels, need not alter any real price ratios or q levels.) From the time of David Hume and Robert Thornton, these mainstream macroeconomists did recognize certain transient dynamics of non-neutrality – as did 1911 Fisher and, more importantly, post-1929 Fisher and Keynes.

Thomas Humphrey persuasively argues that Wicksell was a *Quantity Theorist*, one who regarded M in MV=PQ as an *endogenous* variable systematically shiftable by central bank *exogenous* alterations of the interest rate: too low an i thus produces an opposite rise in M and P. Irving Fisher and Alfred Marshall would not disagree. This Knut Wicksell slant, when adopted by Model T early Keynesians, obscured their understanding of the Pigou-Haberler effects' ability to raise real demand and employment after general price deflation elevates the *real* purchasing effectiveness of a maintained stock of external hard M. Contrariwise, the Wicksell slant may better serve understanding of how interest rate policy can maintain potency in a new era when technological economies in computerized clearings could make explicit M almost extinct.

The Ohlin-Myrdal generations misled themselves and us into thinking that Wicksell had a paradigm of output determination inconsistent with Say's Law. Actually he (1) minimized real effects of 'the great deflation' in the 1865–96 epoch and (2) miscalculated the depressive effects of a return to 1914 gold parity in the 1920s when that represented an over-valued currency. Very late in life Knut's view became shaken by the actual facts. The post-1930 Fisher also died a wiser and better monetarist, as Robert Dimand discusses. His debt-deflation theory, whereby bankruptcies and layoffs become self-fulfilling vicious syndromes, rejected any comfortable belief in the tolerable constancy of Q/V and P/M in the MV=PQ tautology. The anti-monetarist post-1930 John Maynard Keynes ended up as the best of that lot, restressing that the PQ/M ratio was strongly an increasing function of the *nominal* interest rate: $v(i)$, $v'(\mathbf{i}) > 0$ and $v_i'(\mathbf{i}) \gg 0$ when nominal i $\gg$ real i because $\dot{\mathbf{P}}/\mathbf{P} \gg 0$. At lowest i, as in the 'liquidity trap' times of 1935± and Japan 1992–9 (not dreamed of in my teachers' generation) a contrived rise in M induced a near-cancelling fall of V (as Henry Simons early sensed at Chicago in negation of Milton Friedman's later positivistic monetarism). See Friedman's 1968 quantity theory summing up in the 1968 *International Encyclopedia of the Social Sciences* where he hypothesized only weak $v'(\mathbf{i})$ effects, not a happy leaning. When money substitutes make almost all my assets (common stocks, mutual funds, money market funds, home equity loans, margin loans, ...) be *readily spendable* assets, my inventory of M becomes more and more negligible as a *cause* of spending and as a stable element in the equation(s) of my demand for money. Thus the golden age of the MV=PQ Quantity Theory proved to be its swansong age.

Fisher was much more than a Quantity Theorist. Modern finance theory evolved from Fisher: present discounted values; total returns; real interest rate plus inflation rate = nominal interest rate; and more. Not understanding Fisher, Sidney Homer's *A History of Interest Rates* in its early editions was a chronicle of surprises to the author.

Reality did make old-age Fisher a crypto-Keynesian. But mind set inhibited his understanding of how V and Q and i are affectable by deep depression fiscal policy. Price level reflation was, alas, his only hope for society's recovery and personal nest-egg recovery.

As a theorist I must say some words about Fisher's 1892 and later mathematical economics. If born in a decade earlier than 1867, he would have been even more original. Before him Stanley Jevons, Carl Menger and Léon Walras were the first wave. Then came Francis Edgeworth, Marshall and evolving Walras. Auspitz-Lieben, Wicksell, Vilfredo Pareto and Philip Wicksteed were Fisher's contemporaries in the third wave. His own system went beyond Jevons' simplest exchange model in the direction of partial equilibrium and Auspitz-Lieben. Schwalbe is correct that Fisher's theory of production *sans* use of labour, land and produced inputs was primitive in comparison to that of Walras. His general equilibrium equations involved for each person and each good: cardinal addable Utility − Disutility = $U(q) - V(\bar{q})$, with $U'(q) > 0 > U''(q)$, $V'(\bar{q}) > 0 < V'''(\bar{q})$; q depicts consumptions and $\bar{q}$ productions, with not even labour explicitly in V. If we impose strong modern 'Inada conditions', so that $U'(q)$ falls from ∞ to 0 as q rises from 0 to ∞ while $V'(\bar{q})$ rises with $\bar{q}$ from 0 to ∞, then Fisher's exchange-cum-production system does have a unique interior solution for *all* persons' $(q_i^*, \bar{q}_i^*, p_i^*/p_i^*)$ variables. No modern commentator need apologize then for Fisher's old-fashioned counting of equations and unknowns. Yale's Willard Gibbs of 1892 and Steven Smale of 1966 knew that *such non*-linear equations have as necessary-and-sufficient conditions exactly such counting rules. (The famous Gibbs Phase Rule is one such procedure, as the Gibbsian E.B. Wilson taught me at Harvard.) Fisher and Wicksell, already in the early 1890s and long before Abraham Wald, knew that when Inada conditions fail, equalities of price ratios and marginal utility ratios can fail as when zero use of a good leads to its price becoming indeterminate and excess of supply over demand entails duality vanishing of price.

Fisher went beyond additive-separability when he put away his toy hydraulic model, which could teach us nothing new about comparative statics. Gratuitously added to pad out a thesis already overflowing with novelties − sufficiency of using indifference contours of *ordinality*, possibility of cross-commodity complementarities, problem of integrability conditions when goods exceed two in number, etc. − the hydraulic plumbing probably did further harm to Fisher's already primitive disutility functions. In a first go, Jevons, Walras and Marshall might contemplate that utility of cloth and of tea be somehow 'independent'. But how can one's disutility of producing more cloth not be contaminated by how many hours of the finite day one also spends on producing tea? $V(\bar{q}_1, \bar{q}_2)$ or $V(\bar{q}_1 + \bar{q}_2)$, and not $V_1(\bar{q}_1) + V_2(\bar{q}_2)$ is almost mandatory − except that the cute plumbing would veto that.

No commentator mentions the complete irrelevance and mistaken identifications of Fisher's physics analogies to his independent new and valid economics. Physics envy did not guide his walks across the *pons assinorum* of economics. Primitive *hydraulics physics* does not remotely mirror the economics functions in the 1892 thesis. School children understood that by sweaty work to turn a crank they can recharge their electric batteries. Then when playing their portable phonograph and draining those batteries, they can enjoy the utility of hearing Beethoven's Fifth. Young Irving therefore can be forgiven the venial sin of trying to write out a little Physics Economics Glossary: Work and Disutility; Energy and Utility. Understandable? Yes. Harmless? Not quite. Looked at to find mathematical isomorphism between physics theory and economics theory, it is simply wrong. Adam Smith's Invisible Hand maximizes some kind of 'utility'. Mother Nature's laws of physics (1) keep total energy *Constant*; (2) it is Clausius *Entropy* that gets itself maximized. Fisher, like Homer, nodded; (3) when an apple drops dynamically in thinnest air toward Isaac Newton's head, its time arc has it losing potential energy while gaining equivalent kinetic energy; always P.E.+K.E. is conserved. Something is maximized – something different from entropy or energy or utility, namely the negative of 'Action'.

Fisher's economics or mine gain or lose not a whit from any apt or inept analogy to crystallography, Sanskrit or Pig Latin. The LeChatelier-Samuelson Principle in economics, about when long-run elasticity will exceed short-, stems from a mathematical theorem about sub-determinants, applicable if and only if the contemplated empirical relationships arise from maximizing scenarios. Gibbs, Yale legend authenticates, sponsored few theses and for those insisted that aspirants not require his motherings. Their triumphs were theirs alone, and so were their mistakes.

Bertram Schefold brings post-Sraffian insights to the relationships between Fisher's magnificent intertemporal capital theory and that of Eugen von Böhm-Bawerk. I used to understand Joan Robinson and sometimes agreed with her. Joan only rarely understood Paul. Irving pretty much understood Eugen; but their relationship was not symmetric. Already in 1907, Fisher criticized Böhm's effort to correlate Kapital's metric and productiveness by the approximation of labour's average period of investment in a roundabout technology that could begin with labour alone. Call this a circulating-capital model. In Fisher's 1907 counter-example, Technique A and Technique B cannot be ranked as to which is 'more roundabout, more mechanized, more productive or more capitalistic'. At low interest rates A is more viable than B; at intermediate i levels, B will competitively drive out A; but at still higher i levels, A will dominate so that lowest and highest interest rates are produced by the *same* technology. Properly understood, this qualifies Böhm's incautious claim – his third reason for positive interest – that the inevitable productivity of capital properly understood can both explain and justify interest rate as a cost and as a source of permanent income. QED.

Schefold's deep analysis seems to argue that neither of the two scholars dominates the other in proper understanding. All this is not old hat. Piero Sraffa's 1960 classic leaves his followers with an incipient but unfinished critique of marginalism; it also leaves them and us with an incomplete theory to determine real world interest rates, their levels, trends and oscillations. In my own MIT seminars I used to nominate alternative *supplements* to pluck out from Sraffa's infinity of menu one or more definite equilibrium plateaux of interest and modes of trend dynamics. All these seem compatible with 1930 Fisher.

It is not clear how precisely Fisher did understand the senses in which competitive arbitrage relations are or are not *intertemporally-Pareto-Optimal* and 'efficient'. Sraffa's sparse writings miss out on this issue. What Fisher's own double-switching does do is remind theorists of what they already knew from Marshall's 1879 *The Pure Theory of Foreign Trade. The Pure Theory of Domestic Values* – namely that where an existence theorem applies to guarantee at least one equilibrium, there is no guarantee at all against *multiplicity* of alternative equilibria, each with different ethical implications and different stability properties. In some of my own nominated augmented paradigms, without double reswitchings there can be multiple equilibria, some locally stable and some unstable. With double switching or without, there can be complete models that are locally and globally stable around a unique equilibrium. The observable facts of economic history (technology and institutions) must decide. I am uncertain as to whether Fisher explicitly understood how at his own reswitching points, one which lowered i from one plateau to another might bring with it a new *lower* (!) plateau of consumptions for all. Schefold's subtleties merit studying and restudying.

Space prevents me more than commending the excellent chapters on consumption taxing, separation theorems, rational stochastic investing and much else. Hail Fisher, a great ancestor who elevates us from beyond the grave. He was an odd duck who could have posed for Grant Woods' 'American Gothic'. He was a do-gooder lusting for personal fame. When pursuing a good cause, he was most prone to become sloppy, as three examples can illustrate. (1) Fisher tried to test *statistically* the *tautological* definition $V = PQ/M$! Better would it have been to regress PQ/M against various exploratory independent variables. (2) Don Patinkin could show lapses in connection with Fisher's exposition of his compensated gold dollar. Finally, (3) John Chipman correctly identifies expositional blunders in Fisher's 1927 measurement of [utility of cloth + utility of tea = $f(x) + g(y)$]. These are but venial sins. Fisher did understand that the observable marginal rate of substitution $g'(y)/f'(x) \equiv R(x,y) = P_y/P_x$, if separable additive utility were empirically satisfied, would have to satisfy the box relation: $R(a,b)R(A,B) \equiv R(a,B)R(A,b)$ for *any* positive (a b A B). Then, eschewing explanation for the mathematically illiterate, Fisher could have done what Robert Bishop did in the 1943 *QJE*, namely write out: $f(x) + g(y) = \int_a^X R(X,b) dX + \int_b^Y R(a,Y)^{-1} dY$. Then, like Ragnar Frisch in that same first third of the century, Fisher could have provided all the testable content of the singular and special tastes involved in Gossen-Jevons-Walras-Marshall partial equilibrium efforts.

268

But *cui bono* 1927 Fisher's effort and intention? He naively thought to make ethics *scientific*. Having measured Peter's and Paul's separately and now (for *each*!) addable $f+g$ functions, he hoped to use them to decide how rich Peter and poor Paul should each be taxed to buy a public fire engine. Frisch and Fisher were sleep-walking. If Peter did have 'independence (ordinal)' tastes, Fisher could help Peter to say: I lose the same Fisherine utility when I am taxed $2 out of a $10,000 income as I lose in Fisherine utility when taxed $1 out of a $4,567.89 income. So what? Paul's and Peter's Fisherine utilities are interpersonally incommensurable. Fisherine utility, like Fahrenheit temperature, can be stretched in an infinite number of different ways. As John Harsanyi (1955) showed, Peter's and Paul's *gambling von Neumann utility* might have some place in ethical discussions of distributive justice. When Fisher measures for both Peter and Paul $f(x)+g(y) = \log x + \log y$, John von Neumann might still measure $x^{\frac{1}{2}} y^{\frac{1}{2}}$ for risk-neutral Peter and $x^{\frac{1}{4}} y^{\frac{1}{4}}$ for risk-averse Paul, inferring these from their observed gambling choices – a procedure quite different from non-stochastic choices observed by Fisher. Irving, I fear, never thought through all his paths to fame and to improving mankind's welfare.

Newton was not invariably nice in every respect. We cherish scientific heroes by their permanent hits not by their personal biographies. Fisher's place in economists' Hall of Fame is made even more secure by this fine book that reviews and judges fairly his many works.

References

Auspitz R. and Lieben, R. (1889). *Untersuchungen über die Theorie des Preises*. Leipzig: Duncker & Humblot. French translation by Louis Suret, Paris: M. Giard & E. Brière, 1914.

Bishop, R. (1943). Consumer's surplus and cardinal utility. *Quarterly Journal of Economics*, 57: 421–49.

von Böhm-Bawerk, E. (1889). *Kapital und Kapitalzins. Zweite Abteilung: Positive Theorie des Kapitales.* Innsbruck: Wagner. Translated as *The Positive Theory of Capital*, London: Macmillan, 1891.

Fisher, I. (1892). Mathematical investigations in the theory of value and prices. In *Transactions of the Connecticut Academy*, 9: 1–124. Reprinted New Haven: Yale University Press, 1925.

—— (1907). *The Rate of Interest, Its Nature, Determination and Relation to Economic Phenomena*. New York: Macmillan.

—— (1911). *The Purchasing Power of Money: Its Determination and Relation to Credit, Interest and Crises*. New York: Macmillan.

—— (1927). A statistical method for measuring marginal utility and testing the justice of a progressive income tax. In J. H. Hollander (ed.) *Economic Essays Contributed in Honor of John Bates Clark*, New York: Macmillan, pp. 157–93.

—— (1930). *The Theory of Interest as Determined by Impatience to Spend Income and Opportunity to Invest It.* New York: Macmillan.

Friedman, M. (1968). Quantity Theory. In D. Sills (ed.) *International Encyclopedia of the Social Sciences*, Vol. 10, New York: Macmillan.

Frisch, R. (1932). *New Methods of Measuring Marginal Utility.* Tübingen: J. C. B. Mohr.

Harsanyi, J. (1955). Cardinal welfare, individualistic ethics, and interpersonal comparisons of utility. *Journal of Political Economy*, 63: 309–21.

Homer, S. (1963). *A History of Interest Rates.* New Brunswick, NJ: Rutgers University Press.

Hume, D. (1955) [1752]. *Writings on Economics.* Ed. E. Rotwein, Edinburgh, London, Melbourne, Cape Town: Thomas Nelson and Sons, Ltd.

Marshall, A. (1879). *The Pure Theory of Foreign Trade. The Pure Theory of Domestic Values,* privately published. Reprinted in London: London School of Economics, Scarce Works in Political Economy No. 1, 1930.

Smale, S. (1966). Structurally stable systems are not dense. *American Journal of Mathematics*, 88: 491–6.

Sraffa, P. (1960). *Production of Commodities by Means of Commodities, Prelude to a Critique of Economic Theory.* Cambridge: Cambridge University Press.

Thornton, H. (1802). *An Enquiry into the Nature and Effects of the Paper Credit of Great Britain.* Together with his evidence given before the Committees of Secrecy of the two Houses of Parliament in the Bank of England, March and April 1797, some manuscript notes, and his speeches on the Bullion Report, May 1811. Edited and with an introduction by F. A. von Hayek, London: George Allen & Unwin, 1939. Reprinted, London: Frank Cass & Co.; New York: Augustus Kelley, 1962.

Paul A. Samuelson
Massachusetts Institute of Technology

A Personal Tribute to John Harsanyi

Paul A. Samuelson

Department of Economics, Massachusetts Institute of Technology, Cambridge, Massachusetts 02142-1347

I first learned the name Harsanyi in a chance reading of a deep article from an unknown author in a distant corner of Australia. It is a reflection of my U.S. East Coast provincialism that this came as a surprise to me. However, and this betrays more about my naiveté, all mystery disappeared when I learned that John Harsanyi was in fact a Hungarian—one of the Wigner, von Neumann, and von Karman clan.

Each new Harsanyi published gem added to my silent admiration. Indeed, after Abram Bergson's important 1938 work, my own views on welfare economies hardened into pretty much their final form. (How unprogressive!) This attached no special or canonical significance to interpersonal ordinal ethical normings that were *additive across people* in the pre-1930 Benthamite hedonistic fashion. Therefore, my first reaction to Harsanyi's 1955 *Econometrica* paper was to be skeptical of his theorem, which can be expressed approximately as follows: (1) if each of N persons subscribes to the Laplacian dogma of acting as if to maximize $\text{Exp}\{U\{x_1^i, \ldots, x_S^i\}\}$, for Ramsey–Marschak–Savage reasons, and (2) if an ethical observer shares each person's rationality of reasoning, and (3) if the ethical observer must deem situation A ethically superior to situation B whenever every person personally deems A to be better than B, then this Laplacian individualistic ethical observer must agree that his or her Bergsonian social welfare is Bentham-hedonistic or in the form

$$W_{\text{BH}} = \sum_{i=1}^{N} \alpha_i U^i\{x_1^i, \ldots, x_S^i\}, \qquad \alpha_1 \geq 0. \tag{1}$$

In Eq. (1) the form of the $\alpha_1 + b_1 U^i\{\ \}$ function is determinable from ordinal stochastic experiments on person i. And the ethical observer is restrained to encapsulate *all* ethical decisions by specifying the $N - 1$ positive constants $(\alpha_2/\alpha_1, \ldots, \alpha_N/\alpha_1)$.

Although Eq. (1) may be congenial to much of the economist literature, most thoughtful ethicists will not want to go all the way with such individualism. Surviving Darwinian humans are usually deemed not to be omniscient about their own well-being. Importantly, most complete ethical systems violate to some degree Arrow's axiom of not being **IMPOSED**. This does not give privileged power to Hitler, the family father, the local mayor, or some historical philosopher king. Kenneth Arrow borrowed the word "social welfare function" when he arrived at his great impossibility theorem(s) about democratic voting functions—more power to him. But still I prefer nonconfusion to its opposite.

The proof of (1) that I came to accept will be found in the 1983 enlarged edition of *Foundations of Economic Analysis* and in *The Collected Scientific Papers of Paul A. Samuelson* (1966, 1966, 1972, 1977, 1986). I am not aware that the classic John Rawles' *A Theory of Justice* takes notice of this Harsanyi profundity.

One is left with an element of paradox. Here seems to be a case where behavior in a *nonstochastic* universe is made to obey a special restriction by consideration of how behavior ought to be restricted in a *stochastic* universe. Perhaps someone has somewhere resolved this paradox?

Ricardo, David (1772–1823)

Among the educated public only a few names of economists stand out: Adam Smith, the spokesman for capitalism; (T.) Robert Malthus, who earned for economics the title of 'the dismal science,' by virtue of his belief that any temporary gain in well-being would self-destruct by inducing population explosion that would entail diminishing returns and a retreat back to a subsistence ration of real wages; Karl Marx, the prophet of capitalism's doom and the exponent of allegedly scientific socialism; John Maynard Keynes, proponent of the Mixed Economy, who rescued capitalism from the post-1929 Great Depression by activistic governmental macroeconomic policies and public regulation.

Within the economics profession, it is a different story. David Ricardo was the archetypical classical economist, the economist's economist who supposedly improved upon Smith and spelled out with Euclidean logic the eternal behavior of the market system. In amiable epistolary debates with his friend Malthus, Ricardo used to be reckoned the hands-down winner: Malthusian fears of recurrent depression stemming from under-consumption spending were argued to be fallacies. Like poet Robert Frost, beloved by both highbrows and lowbrows, the self-made millionaire David Ricardo captured the respect of the Victorian devotees to *laissez faire* as well as socialistic critics of Marxian or romantic stripe.

Schooled only in the Darwinian jungle of speculative finance, the broker Ricardo wrote as an autodidact, often in an obscure style that impressed his limited number of readers as being profound. Since 1817 literally scores of articles have appeared in learned journals debating whether or not David Ricardo did believe in 'a labor theory of value.' This is the stuff of which PhD theses can be made.

Ricardo was also lucky in having the learned Piero Sraffa edit for the Royal Economic Society, over a period of 25 years, a magnificent and complete edition in 11 volumes of *The Works and Correspondence of David Ricardo* (1951–73). Although this brought Ricardo's name back into the limelight, oddly it seems to have contributed to a revisionist erosion of his analytic reputation. Whereas the late-Victorian Alfred Marshall, pillar of post-1870 neoclassicism, had idiosyncratically argued that the good modern stuff was *already* in Ricardo, and whereas Keynes had written in the 1920s that David Ricardo's was 'the finest mind that had come to economics'—neither Ricardo's late-twentieth-century admirers nor detractors could agree among themselves as to what his different virtues and vices actually were. A scholar who is much misunderstood cannot be acquitted of all responsibility for ambiguity.

Ricardo's parents were Sephardic Jews who migrated to England from Amsterdam in the mid-eighteenth century. His ancestors had gone from Spain to Italy and then on to Holland. They seem to have been for the most part successful dealers in finance, an occupation that young David took up at the age of 14. When he married a Quaker, he was cut off by his father with the proverbial shilling; but within a score of years, working as a broker in the City of London, he had by his early forties amassed a comfortable fortune—the period of the Napoleonic Wars offered windows of opportunity for an alert and nimble financier. During vacation, when he picked up by chance Smith's *The Wealth of Nations* (1776), Ricardo was hooked for political economy.

Reversing the usual order of study, Ricardo first made his mark in what has come to be called *macro*economics. His unqualified verdict typifies his non-eclectic style. To finance a very long war against Napoleon, Britain expanded its money supply of paper currency in order to procure goods at home and abroad for its armies. Price-level inflation, not surprisingly, was part of the economic history in that period. Eclectic Smithian theory would no doubt have predicted as well a worsening of Britain's terms of trade as she and other belligerents bid up the relative prices of needed imports. Had gold and silver been the sole money used then in England and elsewhere, the 1750 theories of David Hume would have predicted a drain of specie from London to pay for the war-induced trade deficit of exports compared to imports.

However, even in those distant times much of the money employed for purchase and sale transactions involved use of paper-money currency. And, as is customary in times of war, whatever the supply of domestic gold or silver, there ensued a considerable rotation of the printing press to finance government needs and accommodate the desire for the enhanced cash necessary to conduct the enlarged volume of goods transactions and their higher average prices. Under these circumstances, whenever a government chooses *not* to redeem paper currency notes into specie at their previous face value, those notes will depreciate in price relative to ounces of specie. The high price of gold is what the person in the street calls this phenomenon and passionate voices debated its cause(s). Young Ricardo attributed *all* of the rise in gold prices to over-issue of paper notes.

Today one can write counterfactual history. Somehow the British government might have taxed the populace more heavily to finance in a balanced-budget fashion the enhanced war effort and the irreducible rise in relative import prices; imposed tightness in bank lending, enforceable only at higher interest rates, conceivably could have kept the stock of paper currency unchanged, at the same time almost certainly imposing unemployment and extra loss of consumption on the civilian populace. With heroic tightness, trade balances might even have been forced to cancel out to zero. (It is hard to envisage how normal peacetime unemployment levels could have somehow been made to prevail from say 1795 to 1810 in this contrafactual scenario.) An inflation-free war can thus be painfully conjured up in contrafactual history; and with no wartime increment of paper-currency issue.

In actual history, paper notes did depreciate and price levels did soar. As happened a century later during the 1920–23 German hyperinflation, economists lined up in opposing camps. Young David argued: over-issue in currency M explained virtually *all* of the rise in the price of bullion. Henry Thornton, practical banker and Bank of England authority, (at first) argued that the microeconomic phenomena of adverse trade balances and war-induced buoyant business activity explained a significant fraction of the observed appreciation of bullion.

Ricardo's 1809–10 strong assertion of what was called the 'bullionist view' won him instant celebrity, particularly with the dogmatic James Mill. But this economic debate was not really a zero-sum game in which Ricardo's gain had to equal Thornton's loss. Both men agreed on the likely longest-run outlook. The price of gold in terms of paper would be the same in 1850 if, in the many preceding decades, the supply of paper currency was limited enough to permit free specie–currency convertibility at the old 1790 ratio. The so-called 'Ricardian vice' was his use of *long-run* true relations to characterize actual short-run patterns in economic history.

After the first decade of the nineteenth century, Ricardo concentrated mostly on *microeconomics*. In 1815 (and *not* prior to then), along with Malthus and Edward West he helped articulate the 'law of diminishing returns' and its consequences for land-rent determination. Society's product, call it corn, is produced by labor and by land, both working together. When you increase labor in two *equal* increments, working on fixed land, you acquire two successive increments of corn. But the second gain is presumptively *less* than the first—a technological law of nature. Thus the wage that the competitive market can pay to labor goes down when labor/land density increases; and the rent that the market will pay for land will go up. This is not a new idea—it is in Benjamin Franklin (1755) early in the eighteenth century and already in Smith (1776)—but it is an important insight that needed being made explicit.

Already Ricardo had perceived what he considers faults in Adam Smith. Posterity can be grateful that

13331

this perception tempted Ricardo into economics, even though it can be argued convincingly that Smith is mostly the more correct thinker in the cases where Ricardo criticizes him. For example, in the capital-and-land-and-produced-capital models that both writers worked with, Smith was right to jettison the 'labor theory of value' as soon as the interest rate and/or the land rent rate becomes significantly positive.

As between the two tasks of political economy—(a) understanding how relative scarcities of factors of production constrain the alternative availabilities of different goods and their valuation relations; and (b) how society's harvest gets *distributed* among and between the different social classes of workers and owners of property—Ricardo arbitrarily declared it to be distribution that was all important. Yet nowhere in the 11 volumes of his *Works and Correspondence* (1951–73) will the reader find a *complete* and satisfactory theory of distribution that goes beyond what is in Smith, Malthus, Mill or modern mainstream writers.

Perhaps Ricardo's lack of a university education contributed to his methodological style. Frequently he asserts general 'truths' that do admit of important exceptions; repeatedly he fails to distinguish between *necessary* and *sufficient* conditions for an argument. He is a superb miniaturist but with an absence of coherence, particularly in his post-1815 textbook phase. (Ricardo's theory of comparative advantage in international trade, similar to that of the contemporary Colonel Robert Torrens, is a brilliant example of his miniaturist virtuosity.)

If it be thought that, by use of hindsight, I am a bit harsh on 1810–23 David Ricardo, let it be understood that I am even harsher on Ricardo's twentieth-century commentators: the brightest and the best of them—Piero Sraffa, George Stigler, Samuel Hollander, Mark Blaug and scores of others—while understanding that the positive interest and time-phasing of production do generically invalidate Ricardo's championing of the *labor theory of value* (as, indeed, Ricardo himself intermittently admitted), at the same time seem blind to the parallel fact that positive rent(s) on scarce land(s) must similarly invalidate the labor theory of value. (Edwin Cannan, Knut Wicksell, Jacob Viner and Lionel Robbins are honorable exceptions to this indictment of blindness about how labor/land intensities do generically invalidate any labor theory of value in the same logical way that time-intensities are known to do so.)

Around 1815, between his macro works on gold and his *Principles of Political Economy and Taxation* (1817, 1819, 1821), Ricardo did puzzle over a simple scenario involving a farm good (corn) and one or more manufactured goods (cloth, ...), all produced by, say, homogeneous labor, homogeneous land and by one or more *produced* inputs (corn seed, raw materials from farming used for manufactures, durable tools). He may even have worked out, in an unpublished manuscript that has not survived, a one-sector farm-only model. In it, a determinate model of distribution could have cogently defined long-run stationary-state equilibrium for (real corn wage rate, interest rate, real corn rent rate) = $(W/P_{corn} = \bar{w}, \bar{r}, Rent/P_{corn} = R^*)$. How would it have gone?

Like Malthus and other predecessors, Ricardo would have specified *exogenously* a classical 'subsistence wage' rate, $\bar{w}$, needed to keep population just reproducing itself. Like classical successors he would have specified *exogenously* a minimal interest rate, $\bar{r}$, needed to keep capital(s) just reproducing themselves. Land being a classical constant, $\bar{A}$, its stationary equilibrium rent rate he would *residually* determine once variable labor-and-capital stocks, L_t and K_t, dynamically converged to their long-run, asymptotic stationary equilibrium levels: $L_t \to L^*$; $K_t \to K^*$, when K is a single scalar. Finally, short-run determination of w_t and r_t would be market-clearing rates dependent on the relative transitional abundances of L_t and K_t.

Here is how in the spirit of Prokofiev's 'Classical' Symphony, an ambitious neophyte in a 1932 Hicks–Wicksell *neo*classical workshop might synthesize these classical insights into a coherent simplistic dynamic equation system, using the notational convention $dY_t/dt \equiv \dot{Y}_t$:

factor supplies: $\dot{L}_t/L_t = |\bar{\alpha}|(w_t - \bar{w})$,

$$\dot{K}_t/K_t = |\bar{\beta}|(r_t - \bar{r}), A_t \equiv \bar{A} = 1 \quad (1)$$

factor demands: $w_t = \bar{\sigma} K_t^{1/3}/L^{2/3}$,

$$r_t = \bar{\sigma} L_t^{1/3}/K_t^{2/3} \quad (2)$$

where $\bar{\sigma}$ is an exogenous parameter denoting level of technical productivity.

When the modern crank of deduction gets turned, Ricardo's (1) and (2) do lead convergently to a determinate classical stationary state. From any *initial* $(L_0, K_0, \bar{A})$, as $t \to \infty$,

$$(w_t, r_t; L_t/\bar{A}, K_t/\bar{A}; R_t) \to (\bar{w}, \bar{r}; \tfrac{1}{3}\bar{\sigma}/[\bar{w}^2 \bar{r}],$$
$$\tfrac{1}{3}\bar{\sigma}/[\bar{r}^2 \bar{w}]; \tfrac{1}{3}\bar{\sigma}[\bar{r} w]). \quad (3)$$

One must commend the classical tradition for so subtle an accomplishment. (Note the version worked out here differs from the Samuelson (1978) 'canonical' model, which had more faithfully adhered to the conventional labor-capital 'dose' version.)

This above supply–demand equilibrium is definitely *not* independent of the problem of how consumers wish to allocate their earned incomes among the many goods, when there are many non-corn goods in the picture. Then in it there are no 'natural prices' definable independently of how consumers choose to spend their incomes.

Definitely goods' relative price ratios do not remain close to proportionality with their respective embodied-labor contents, $P_t^i/P_t^j \neq (L_t^i/q_t^i)/(L^j/q_t^j)$.

Likewise embodied land contents $(A_t^i/q_t^i)/(A_t^j/q_t^j)$ and embodied capital contents $(K_t^i/q_t^i)/(K_t^j/q_t^j)$ similarly fail as approximations to empirical actual P^i/P^j ratios.

Since Ricardo did not coherently understand the intricacies of his own classical scenario, he never realized how unattainable was his hankering to have all relative prices determinable purely *by objective technology and cost data*. *Subjective* variabilities (a) of consumers' utilities and demand choices and (b) of intertemporal saving-and-consuming choices—which became central preoccupations of post-1870 neoclassical successors to the classical school—were thus *already* unavoidable in the classicals' own capital, land and labor models and in the competitive scenarios that Marx grappled with all his working life. This inevitability will come with pain for the small sect of Sraffian neo-Ricardians who proliferated after 1925 and especially 1960.

Ricardo was low-keyed and civil in argumentation, albeit firm in holding to his strong positions. The letters between Ricardo and Malthus, notwithstanding these scholars' deep differences, are a model of courtesy and affection. Despite Ricardo's typical unqualified dicta, he did not hesitate to change his mind and admit to previous mistakes. Marx, who abhorred classical authorities and for whom 'Parson' Malthus was a particular *bête noir*, was uncharacteristically soft toward Ricardo. Here is an illustrative incident. After Ricardo's first edition of *Principles*, but prior to its third edition, David, Humpty-Dumpty like, had declared that technical invention *must always* help *all* factors of production, including the working man. He encouraged disciples, like J. R. McCulloch, to affirm this strong view. However, on reconsideration, Ricardo came to realize that some inventions can assuredly *replace labor and reduce the demand for labor in the short and the long run*. Therefore, despite friends' warnings that this would weaken the case for *laissez faire*, Ricardo added a new chapter on Machinery to the third (1821) edition of the *Principles*, presenting exposition and numerical examples designed to show how labor's share of national income could suffer from certain possible inventions and how long-run equilibrium populations and gross-income levels could be permanently lowered. With virtually no exceptions, ancient and twentieth century authorities agreed that for once Homer had nodded. For once David must have invoked rigidity of wage rates with its resulting unemployment, thus for once denying J.-B. Say's sacred dogma that over-production is impossible in a capitalist system. Karl Marx praised the scholar for his honesty.

It is a story that casts discredit on virtually all. The Ricardo–McCulloch original sweeping position was gratuitously wrong. A new wind that raises an economy's *potential* for production and consumption most certainly can do harm to *some* competitors while helping others. (Ricardo did not, as J. S. Mill and Vilfredo Pareto were later to do, argue that gainers could always bribe losers so that *with intervention all could gain*.) Nor did Ricardo's new understanding motivate him to abandon a dogmatic defense of *laissez faire*. His critics on Machinery, both then and in our time—including Knut Wicksell, Nicholas Kaldor, Joseph Schumpeter, George Stigler, ...—failed to see the absence in Ricardo's exposition of any denial of dogmatic Say's Law and its ruling out theoretical harm from under-consumption; instead his usual classical scenario of population decline dictated by the induced drop in the wage below an alleged equilibrium *subsistence* rate would, as the Machinery chapter alleged, call for an ultimate drop in population and gross product as a result of labor-saving invention(s). Just as the industrial revolution was beginning to raise wages by a genuine filter-down process, the philosophers of the Chair were getting first intimations of the complexity of how a market system metes out its distributive awards.

In that long ago age before antibiotics, David Ricardo in 1823, at the peak of his powers, died from an ear infection. Thus he never lived to see the 1836 Repeal of the Corn Laws, a vindication of his pamphleteering for free trade; and he did not live to witness Ireland's great famine of the 1840s, with its brutal confirmation of the laws of the free market.

In summary, David Ricardo, like the twentieth-century economists Friedrich Hayek and Milton Friedman, importantly pushed voters and public opinion toward libertarian *laissez faire*. Victorian England's Whig society and Manchester School owed much to him. In the modern debate about how a modern mixed economy can optimally compromise between market mechanisms and democratic rules of the road, Adam Smith and John Stuart Mill seem more subtle classical thinkers. From these two, rulers like Lenin, Stalin and Mao could have had the most to learn. But among the worldly philosophers, David Ricardo must be counted as an important shaper of the twenty-first-century mind.

See also: Asset Pricing: Emerging Markets; Economic Growth: Measurement; Economic Growth: Theory; Economics, History of; Economics: Overview; Income Distribution; Innovation and Technological Change, Economics of; Libertarianism; Malthus, Thomas Robert (1766–1834); Market Structure and Performance; Marx, Karl (1818–89); Marxian Economic Thought; Monetary Policy; Political Economy, History of; Regulation, Economic Theory of; Smith, Adam (1723–90); Stock Market Predictability

Bibliography

Franklin B 1755 *Observations Concerning the Increase of Mankind and the Peopling of Countries*

Keynes J M 1936 *The General Theory of Employment, Interest and Money.* [Reprinted in: 1977–81 *The Collected Writings of John Maynard Keynes.* Macmillan, London]

Malthus T R 1798 *An Essay on the Principle of Population as it Affects the Future Improvement of Society, with Remarks on the Speculations of Mr. Godwin, M. Condorcet and Other Writers.* J. Johnson, London [Reprinted by Macmillan, London, 1926]

Marshall A 1890–1920 *Principles of Economics.* Macmillan, London

Marx K 1867, 1885, 1894 *Capital,* Volumes I, II, and III. Verlag von Otto Meissner, Hamburg; [Penguin Books, Harmondsworth 1976, 1978, 1981]

Niehans J 1990 *A History of Economic Theory. Classic Contributions, 1720–1980.* The Johns Hopkins University Press, Baltimore

Ricardo D 1817 *Principles of Political Economy and Taxation.* John Murray, London

Ricardo D 1951–73 *The Works and Correspondence of David Ricardo* [ed. P. Sraffa with M. H. Dobb] 9 vols. Cambridge University Press, Cambridge, UK

Samuelson P A 1978 The canonical classical model of political economy. *Journal of Economic Literature* **16**: 1415–34

Samuelson P A 1989 Ricardo was right! *Scandinavian Journal of Economics* **91**: 47–62

Schumpeter J 1954 *History of Economic Analysis.* Oxford University Press, New York

Smith A 1776 *An Inquiry into the Nature and Causes of the Wealth of Nations* [ed. E. Cannan]. The Modern Library, New York, 1937

Sraffa P 1926 The laws of returns under competitive conditions. *The Economic Journal* **36**: 535–50

Sraffa P 1960 *Production of Commodities by Means of Commodities.* Cambridge University Press, Cambridge, UK

Thornton H 1802 *An Enquiry into the Nature and Effects of the Paper Credit of Great Britain.* Reprinted, Frank Cass, London; Augustus Kelley, New York, 1962

P. A. Samuelson

4 My Bertil Ohlin

Paul A. Samuelson

A Pearl of Analysis

Ask newly minted economics Ph.D.'s at century's end, "What do you associate with Ohlin's name?" Probably they would answer: "Ohlin explained geographical trade and specialization patterns as depending on *differences* in geographical *endowments* of factor inputs. Free trade causes a region to export goods intensive in its relatively abundant factor, in exchange for goods intensive in its scarce factor. That way trade raises in each place the return of each region's superabundant factor, tending to move real factor prices nearer to equality everywhere. Moving goods thus substitutes for moving factors themselves."

It is a beautiful insight, one only vaguely noticed in the classical Ricardian literature. Ohlin deserves praise for it, even after he acknowledged that in 1919 his teacher Eli Heckscher had glimpsed its essence, and acknowledged that he used his teacher Gustav Cassel's version of the Léon Walras general equilibrium to perfect and develop its analytics. When I, the pupil of Jacob Viner and Gottfried Haberler, arrived on the scene, we called this *the Ohlin* system.

Knowing no Swedish, Lloyd Metzler and I wisely urged the then-Danish couple Svend Laursen and Agnete Laursen (later Kalckar) to translate into English Heckscher's 1919 classic article. Inadvertently, and I would say somewhat unjustly, gradually Ohlin lost some kudos for his crucial role in "the Heckscher-Ohlin" breakthrough. Further, after 1948, Ohlin sometimes became the meat in a Heckscher-Ohlin-Samuelson sandwich. Robert K. Merton, the historian and sociologist of science, aptly calls this, "obliteration by incorporation." Eventually no one cites a precept of Isaac Newton or John Maynard Keynes because we are all inhaling and exhaling what those masters have breathed. On this occasion of remembering Ohlin—my Ohlin—

it is proper to emphasize that it was he who launched half a hundred dissertations and learned-journal articles. Lionel McKenzie could do the great crowning work on this topic before and after 1967 because 40 years earlier a precociously original young scholar performed the alchemy of turning two noble metals into an alloy of pure gold.

The Scholar as a Young Virtuoso

The history that perforce has to be lived forward cannot be adequately told any other way. Bertil Ohlin by fate was born precocious and by family opportunity and timing lived up to his potential. Sweden is a small country. Early in the century Scandinavia was a northern outpost of Europe with moderate GDP per capita. But for whatever reason where economists were concerned, Sweden was fat city—a veritable Vienna. In the first wave were (alphabetically) Gustav Cassel, David Davidson, Heckscher, and Knut Wicksell. From their loins sprung the crown princes: (chronologically) Bertil Ohlin, Gunnar Myrdal, Erik Lindahl, Erik Lundberg, and Ingvar Svennilson.

Ohlin's chief masters were Heckscher and Cassel. What best illustrates how precocious young Bertil really was is an attested story. The austere Heckscher was a learned economic historian as well as a subtle theorist. In politics he was "liberal"—which then meant, staunchly in favor of laissez faire. Four great contemporaries are not required to love each other equally, or at all.

In his seminar at the Stockholm Business School, Heckscher asserted the dictum: the rational age to chop down a tree is just when its *percentage* rate of growing wood has fallen to precise equality with the (instantaneous) rate of interest. Not a wild notion and one (I believe) also held by Fisher (yes, Irving) and Johann von Thünen. "'Tain't so," in effect said the teenage Ohlin. "When you chop down the tree, that makes room to plant a new tree. And where forest land is scarce enough to earn a market-clearing *positive* rent rate, you should chop the tree *before* Heckscher's specified age."

The Emperor of the Seminar stood his ground. Ohlin, sitting with four aces in his hand, would not give way. When asked by forestry experts to adjudicate the same issue some sixty years later, by use of dynamic Bellman nonlinear programming, Samuelson (1976) had to rule against the Heckscher view. (Harold Hotelling would have thought well of Ohlin had he been told this story; for, in Hotelling's [1925] classic maiden article on depreciation, he had not spoken about this subtlety—a subtlety long hidden in the 1849 writings of the German forestry expert Martin Faustmann.) What is remarkable is that despite little advanced training in mathematics, Ohlin could still exhibit his native mathematical talent.

Time of Crucial Change

Just after I began my Chicago undergraduate study in January 1932, Ohlin published his thick English tome on interregional and international trade. During the 1930 to 1933 years, Ohlin's was one of the many seminal works that went beyond the labor-only models of comparative advantage that had prevailed in the writings of David Ricardo, Robert Torrens, J. S. Mill, Hans von Mangoldt, Francis Edgeworth, and Frank Taussig. Notable contributors to this renaissance were Jacob Viner, Gottfried Haberler, Abba Lerner, Wassily Leontief, and James Meade. As we in the Anglo-Saxon world learned later, Ohlin's contributions had been largely independent of the others. Already in his 1924 Swedish dissertation, Ohlin had written out much of what was later in his 1933 English book.

When Ohlin and James Meade received their well-deserved, shared 1977 Nobel Prizes, I estimated that most of what Ohlin accomplished in the pure theory of international trade he had already accomplished by the age of twenty-five. Joseph Schumpeter sentimentalized—oversentimentalized—the importance for scientific originality of youth, the importance of one's sacred third decade of life. Certainly Ohlin's career fitted in with Schumpeter's conceit. (But what about the great Wicksell, who got a late start and died with his boots on, running fast?) My appendix will say more about the 1933 Ohlin classic book.

The Transfer Controversy

Actually Ohlin's first world notoriety, his hour of Andy Warhol celebrity, came around 1929 when as a little known chairholder in Copenhagen and Stockholm, he crossed swords with the great John Maynard Keynes on the transfer or reparations problem.

As part of his critique of the Versailles Treaty, Keynes uncharacteristically espoused the "orthodox view" on the transfer problem. This maintained that when Germany had to make unrequited reparation payments to England, two burdens would necessarily fall on her: (1) the *primary* burden of the excess goods she must export abroad and do without at home, plus (2) the *secondary* burden stemming from the induced drop in her terms of trade—her drop in real $\sum P_j \text{Exports}_j / \sum P_k \text{Imports}_k$—(allegedly) made necessary to effectuate transfer of the reparations. Twenty-nine-year-old Bertil said to 45-year-old Maynard (my paraphrase): "Not necessarily so. You have taken account of the loss-in-income effect on Germany, but left intact England's (Marshallian) reciprocal demand. *Both* nations will experience opposite directional income shifts, so there is no presumption that the payer's terms of trade need fall, rise, or stay the same."

There is a landscape in Provence that may not be the world's most beautiful—or even the best in France. But it is the best known one because so many painters have addressed it over the years. The transfer problem is like that. Viner's 1937 survey of its earlier literature shows that David Ricardo, J. S. Mill, Frank Taussig, Keynes, A. C. Pigou, Dennis Robertson, and a score of other luminaries, had failed to reach agreement on the transfer problem. For Haberler's Harvard seminar I devoted around 1937 a term paper to clearing up the analysis. My former teacher, Jacob Viner, turned it down for the *JPE*, forcing me years later, in 1952 to 1954, to devote two *Economic Journal* articles to the subject. Notable post-1935 authorities included James Meade, Ronald Jones, Martin Bronfenbrenner, and many others. (With several regions and many goods, ambiguities in outcomes multiply.)

If called on to adjudicate between Keynes and Ohlin, under oath as a friend of the court, I would have to find for Ohlin. The agnostic and eclectic verdict on indefinite algebraic signs of secondary burdens is the better conclusion. If Keynes had understood this, his bestselling *Economic Consequences of the Peace* (1919) would have been a less exciting book but not a less accurate one.

The "Stockholm School" as Independent Keynesians?

The Great Depression drew from the 53-year-old Keynes a new macro paradigm of effective demand. *The General Theory* (1936) was not without earlier anticipation: 1931 Richard Kahn, 1931 J. M. Clark, 1934 Michal Kalecki, 1935 Ragnar Frisch, and so on. Bertil Ohlin (1937) argued eloquently that what he called the Stockholm School had been Keynesian even before Keynes. Ohlin's generation early advocated and justified use by the Labor Party of fiscal stimulus to

811

reduce unemployment and increase demand. (Even the conservative Cassel and Heckscher had favored activistic lean-against-the-wind monetary policy, which was in marked contrast to Austrians like Friedrich von Hayek and Ludwig von Mises who subscribed to their version of neo-Wicksellianism.)

My considered judgment is that several anticipations of Keynes did arrive at the multiplier version of *The General Theory*— $Y = C(Y) + I + G$, $dY/d(I + G) > 1$, and all that. But the *full* Keynes system of the LM-IS type was not needed to rationalize *deficit* fiscal spending, and perhaps Ohlin overreached in his claims for mid-1930s Swedish macroeconomics. Myrdal's contemporary works, like earlier ones of Wicksell, presented no theory of output as a whole, instead concentrating on the ups and downs of the price level as such. Wicksell was and remains a favorite economic hero of mine. Still it was unwarranted for Ohlin and others to attribute their stimulation programs to Wicksell's leadings. Only after more extensive acquaintanceship with Wicksell's total bibliography did I come to realize how much that radical Bohemian believed in Say's law of markets clearing and in the macro Pareto-optimality of the capitalistic system.

Thus, after World War I, Wicksell advocated a return to 1914 currency parity, stressing that equity-justice required this and minimizing the deadweight losses that would be created by the process of deflation. Conservative Cassel was more realistic. Grudgingly Wicksell learned how overly optimistic he had been, but death overtook him before he could arrive at a final judgment in the matter. History runs a cruel casino: in a career you are called on to make only a few key judgments, and on the neutrality of deflation, Knut seems to have backed the wrong horse. When writing his *Treatise on Money* (1930), Keynes sinned in neglecting Wicksell; for the 1936 *General Theory*, there was no similar sin, and the famous Keynes circus, I suspect, had not much to learn from the Swedish learned journals of the early 1930s.

The Scholar as Politician

Economists in Sweden were accorded much respect and wielded considerable political power. Somehow the Marxian virus that flourished in Bismarck's Germany and elsewhere never took firm root in Scandinavia's northern soils. Politics' gain was economics' loss when

Bertil Ohlin after 1938 became a parliamentarian and leader of the Liberal Party. (Heckscher and Cassel were conservatives; Myrdal, Dag Hammarskjöld, and many of the university professionals began as Labor stalwarts; but as is the way with critical scholars, successers in the younger Swedish generations became somewhat disillusioned with the workings out of Sweden's middle way.) When I first visited Stockholm in the fall 1948, Bertil Ohlin came as close to being voted prime minister as he was ever to do. For the purpose of the present memoir, what needs reminding is that even before Bertil was forty he became virtually a part-time scholar.

What energy Ohlin must have had: to lead a party, to debate in parliament, to write often for the daily press and the quarterly bank journals. As a selfish theorist, I must regret Ohlin's preoccupations with politics; as a humanitarian and citizen of the world, I know there is rejoicing in heaven when a gifted mind helps to elevate democracy. Arthur Okun offers a similar case. From 1949 to 1980 we in America knew him as the wisest of our generation. By deliberate choice Okun left Yale and full-time academic life. That was no Faustian bargain with the devil. It was a rational choice in terms of comparative advantage, and it must have been envy of the gods that killed off an Okun at so early an age and just when the mixed economy needed so urgently the rare wisdoms that he could muster.

Quick of mind and energetic of spirit, part-time Ohlin kept up with the dynamic trends of mainstream economics. I remember when he visited Columbia University in 1947 to help celebrate its bicentennial. On his way home, at Harvard, I heard him give one of the earliest analyses of the over-full-employment economy. Masters with absolute pitch know when to change their focus. While a brilliant generation of Oxbridge economists stayed mired in Model T Keynesianism of the Great Depression—remember only the British Radcliffe Committee of 1959—Ohlin had moved on to late-twentieth-century issues and challenges.

To be a virtuoso of fixed-point theorems, I do not need the virtues of judgment and eclecticism. Our house of economics has many mansions, and we can certainly use the innovations of impractical ivory-towered shut-ins. Indeed, evolving excesses in unrealistic doctrines will not be cured by the prosaic wisdoms of full-time sages. Always it takes a better theory to kill off an imperfect theory: from *within* the camp of academic research will come, eventually, the cleaning of the Augean Stables, rather than from a Hans Christian Andersen child or a Homeric sage.

My Bertil Ohlin 57

The Bertil Ohlin I knew and admired added to the political economy of his teachers and contributed to the originality of his contemporaries and students. His was a fulfilled life.

Appendix: Gemstones in Ohlin's Great Book

Ohlin's 1933 classic was notable for several features. (1) In the spirit of Adam Smith, Frank Graham, and Allyn Young, Ohlin emphasized the importance for trade and location theory of *increasing returns to scale*. Such models deviate from the nice competitive models built on *constant* returns to scale. Such models become very difficult to analyze and to say new and elegant things about. At the end of this century Paul Krugman and other economists have had to return to Ohlin's courageous emphasis.[1]

(2) Ohlin tried to integrate *location* theory with economist's trade theory, a return toward von Thünen. Domestic (or untradable) goods interacted with easily tradable manufactures and raw materials. With technological improvements in transportation and communication, again paradoxically, trade may have now become more unified and production less balkanized.

(3) As I mentioned in my beginning, for reasons of theoretical elegance, increasingly Ohlin gained prominence for his theory (with Heckscher) to explain patterns of geographical specialization and trade in terms of differences in regions' proportionate factor endowments.

All this is simple general equilibrium filtered through Cassel's borrowings from Léon Walras. Ohlin applied Heckscher's 1919 factor-endowment insight to the Walras-Cassel constant-returns-to-scale model with *uniform* production functions everywhere in the world—a strategic oversimplification but not one that had been emphasized by earlier Ricardian trade theorists. Actually Ohlin generalized beyond Cassel's borrowing from 1889 second-edition Walras, with its *constant* (input/output) technical coefficients. These a_{ij} coefficients Ohlin makes be variable and endogenous cost-minimizing variables.

Ohlin writes the *prices* of n goods as $(p_1 \ldots p_n)$; their *quantities* he writes as $(D_1 \ldots D_n)$. For r primary factors of production, $r \lesseqgtr n$, he writes their total quantities as $(R_1 \ldots R_r)$, writes $(R_{11} \ldots R_{1n}; \ldots; R_{r1} \ldots R_{rn})$ for industries' factor inputs by industries, and writes $(q_1 \ldots q_r)$ for their factor prices. Clearly, he postulates a smooth neoclassical Clark-Solow technology connecting outputs to inputs; I write these for him as strongly concave and smooth, linear-homogeneous neoclassical production functions

$$D_1 = F^1(R_{11}, R_{12}, \ldots, R_{1r})$$

$$\vdots$$

$$D_n = F^n(R_{n1}, R_{n2}, \ldots, R_{nr}). \tag{1a}$$

For any $1 \leq i \leq n$, constant returns to scale implies that

$$1 = F^i\left(\frac{R_{i1}}{D_i}, \frac{R_{i2}}{D_i}, \ldots, \frac{R_{in}}{D_i}\right)$$

$$\equiv F^i(a_{i1}, a_{i2}, \ldots, a_{ir}), \tag{1b}$$

where the a's are Walras's technical coefficients of production, now *endogenous* unknowns. Unlike Cassel and early Walras who made the a's constant, Ohlin makes them infinitely substitutable in the J. B. Clark sense. Thus, for $r = 2$, instead of F^1 being $\text{Min}(R_{11}/\bar{a}_{11}, R_{12}/\bar{a}_{12})$, it could be Cobb-Douglas $R_{11}^{1/4} R_{12}^{3/4}$ or could be $(\rho_1 R_{11}^{-1} + R_{12}^{-1})^{-1} + (\gamma_1 R_{11}^{1/2} + R_{12}^{1/2})^2$: strong Inada conditions specify that as $\partial F^1/\partial a_{ij} \to \infty$ as $a_{ij} \to 0$, and $\partial F^1/\partial a_{ij} \to 0$ as $a_{ij} \to \infty$.

Under autarky Ohlin specifies personal factor endowments to be exogenously given at $(\bar{R}_1^s \bar{R}_2^s \ldots \bar{R}_r^s)$ in his abbreviated mathematical appendix. Each of S persons, $s = 1, \ldots, S$ has endowments given at $(\bar{R}_1^s \bar{R}_2^s \ldots \bar{R}_r^s)$. Each gets an income to spend on consumption goods of $\sum_1^r q_j R_j^s = I^s$, just as the logician Gödel suggested to Wald later that they should do.

What Ohlin intuitively senses (but does not write out) is correct:

THEOREM There exists always a positive equilibrium for $(p_2^*/p_1^* \ldots p_n^*/p_1; q_1^*/p_1^* \ldots q_r^*/p_1^*; [I^1/p_1]^* \ldots [I^S/p_1]^*)$ and for $(D_1 \ldots D_n)^*$ satisfying the full equations

$$p_i^* = \text{Min} \sum_{j=1}^r q_j R_{ij}, \quad i = 1, \ldots n, \tag{2}$$

$$\sum_{i=1}^n R_{ij} = \bar{R}_j = \sum_{s=1}^S \bar{R}_j^S, \quad j = 1, \ldots, r. \tag{3}$$

Also Ohlin adds Cassel-like consumer demands for goods in terms of income relations (which do *not* mention marginal utilities but which do behave like quasi-concave indifference contours):

815

$$D_i = f^i\left(p_1,\ldots,p_n; \sum_{j=1}^{r}\bar{R}_j^1 q_j,\ldots, \sum_{j=1}^{r}\bar{R}_j^S q_j\right), \qquad i=1,\ldots,n, \qquad (4)$$

$$\sum_{i=1}^{n} p_i D_i \equiv \sum_{s=1}^{S}\left(\sum_{j=1}^{r}\bar{R}_j^2 q_j\right) = \sum_{j=1}^{r}\bar{R}_j q_j, \qquad \text{Walras's law.} \qquad (5)$$

The upshot is this. If Abraham Wald in the mid-1930s, instead of dealing with Cassel's and Schlesinger's imperfect version of Walras had dealt with Ohlin's 1933 extension, then he could immediately have proved the existence of one or more positive equilibria and could have proved (as Marshall knew in 1879) that multiple equilibria could easily occur. In this sense (of providing *sufficiency* conditions for a general equilibrium solution) Bertil Ohlin the non-mathematician was ahead of his time and of such mathematical stars as Abraham Wald, F. Zeuthen, H. Neisser, J. R. Hicks, and others. As Ohlin explicitly warns, his appendix does not grapple with intertemporal complexities of "capital and interest" theory. Rome was not built at one sitting! The modern reader can put in for Ohlin the Sraffa-Leontief input/output coefficients to bring the 1933 appendix fully up to date.

Note

1. In his 1931 preface, Ohlin strangely omits from his outlined claims his important advance into increasing returns. Paradoxically, modern "globalization" has vastly expanded the range of markets. Therefore the old competitive model in many ways seems somewhat more realistic than it used to be during the vogue of Joan Robinson's and Edward Chamberlin's imperfect competition. The U.S. Fortune 500 corporations probably enjoyed more oligopoly rents then (which they had to share with labor union employees) than they do today. As size of market grows with globalization and domestic integration, the early stages of increasing returns to scale exhaust themselves, making governmental trust-busting and regulation perhaps less important.

References

Cassel, Gustav. 1918. *Theoretische Sozialökonomie*. Leipzig: C. F. Winter. Translated as *Theory of Social Economy*, London: T. F. Unwin, 1923.

Clark, John M. 1931. *The Costs of the World War to the American People*. New Haven: Yale University Press; New York: H. Milford, Oxford University Press for the Carnegie Endowment for International Peace.

Faustmann, Martin. 1849. On the determination of the value which forest land and immature stands possess for forestry. English translation in M. Gane, ed., *Oxford In-*

stitute Paper 42, 1968 (entitled "Martin Faustmann and the Evolution of Discounted Cash Flow").

Frisch, Ragnar. 1935. Circulation planning: Proposal for a national organization of a commodity and service exchange. Parts I–II. *Econometrica* 2:258–336, 422–35.

Heckscher, Eli. 1919. Effects of foreign trade on distribution of income. *Ekonomisk Tidskrift*: 497–512. Translated in H. S. Ellis and L. Metzler, eds., AEA, *Readings in the Theory of International Trade*. Philadelphia: Blakiston, 1949, ch. 13, pp. 272–300.

Hicks, John. 1932. Marginal productivity and the principle of variation. *Economica* 12:79–88.

Hotelling, Harold. 1925. A general mathematical theory of depreciation. *Journal of the American Statistical Association* 20:340–53.

Kahn, Richard. 1931. The relation of home investment to unemployment. *Economic Journal*, 41:173–98. Reprinted in R. Kahn, *Selected Essays on Employment and Growth*. Cambridge: Cambridge University Press, 1972.

Kalecki, Michal. 1934, 1971. *Selected Essays on the Dynamics of the Capitalist Economy 1933–1970*. Cambridge: Cambridge University Press.

Keynes, John Maynard. 1919. *The Economic Consequences of the Peace*. New York: Harcourt Brace. Reprinted in *The Collected Writings of John Maynard Keynes*, vol. 2. London: Macmillan for the Royal Economic Society, 1971.

Keynes, John Maynard. 1929. The reparation problem. A rejoinder. *Economic Journal* 39:179–82.

Keynes, John Maynard. 1929. Mr. Keynes' views on the transfer problem. Reply. *Economic Journal* 39:404–408.

Keynes, John Maynard. 1930. *Treatise on Money: The Pure Theory of Money*, vol. 1. Reprinted in *The Collected Writings of John Maynard Keynes*, vol. 5. London: Macmillan for the Royal Economic Society, 1971.

Keynes, John Maynard. 1936. *The General Theory of Employment, Interest and Money*. Reprinted in *The Collected Writings of John Maynard Keynes*, vol. 7. London: Macmillan for the Royal Economic Society, 1973.

Marshall, Alfred. 1879. *The Pure Theory of Foreign Trade. The Pure Theory of Domestic Values*. Privately printed. Reprinted in *Scarce Works in Political Economy*, no. 1. London: London School of Economics, 1930.

McKenzie, Lionel. 1967. The inversion of cost functions: a counter-example. *International Economic Review* 8:271–78.

McKenzie, Lionel. 1967. Theorem and counter-example. *International Economic Review* 8:279–85.

Myrdal, Gunnar. 1939. *Monetary Equilibrium*. London: Hodge.

Neisser, Hans. 1932. Lohnhöhe und Beschèftigungsgrad im Marketgleichgewicht. *Weltwirtschaftliches Archiv* 36:413–55.

Ohlin, Bertil. 1924. *Handelns Teori*. Stockholm: Nordiska. Ph.D. Thesis. Translated into English as "Theory of Trade," in H. Flam and M. J. Flanders, eds., *Heckscher-Ohlin Trade Theory*. Cambridge: MIT Press, 1991.

Ohlin, Bertil. 1929. The reparation problem: A discussion. *Economic Journal* 39:172–78.

Ohlin, Bertil. 1933. *Interregional and International Trade.* Cambridge: Harvard University Press.

Ohlin, Bertil. 1937. Some notes on the Stockholm theory of savings and investment. Parts I–II. *Economic Journal* 47:53–69; 221–40.

Samuelson, Paul A. 1966, 1972. *The Collected Scientific Papers of Paul A. Samuelson*, vols. 2 and 3. Cambridge: MIT Press. For reference to factor price equalization, see chapters 67, 68, 69, 70, 74 and 75 in volume 2; and chapter 161 in volume 3.

Samuelson, Paul A. 1976. Economics of forestry in an evolving society. *Economic Inquiry* 14:466–92. Reproduced as chapter 218 in *The Collected Scientific Papers of Paul A. Samuelson*, vol. 4. Cambridge: MIT Press.

Schlesinger, Karl. 1934. Über die Produktionsgleichungen der ökonomischen Wertlehre. *Ergebnisse eines mathematischen Kolloquiums* 6:10–11.

Viner, Jacob. 1937. *Studies in the Theory of International Trade.* New York: Harper.

von Mises, Ludwig. 1912. *The Theory of Money and Credit*, 3rd English ed. Indianapolis: Liberty Classics, 1981.

Wald, Abraham. 1934. Über die eindeutige positive Lösbarkeit der neuen Produktionsgleichungen I. In K. Menger, ed., *Ergebnisse eines mathematischen Kolloquiums, 1933–34*. Translated by W. Baumol as "On the unique non-negative solvability of the new production equations, Part I." In W. Baumol and S. M. Goldfeld, eds., *Precursors in Mathematical Economics*. London School of Economics Series of Reprints of Scarce Works on Political Economy No. 19. London: London School of Economics, 1968.

Wald, Abraham. 1935. Über die Produktionsgleichungen der ökonomischen Wertlehre II. In K. Menger, ed., *Ergebnisse eines mathematischen Kolloquiums, 1934–35*. Translated by W. Baumol as "On the production equations of economic value theory, Part II." In W. Baumol and S. M. Goldfeld, eds., *Precursors in Mathematical Economics*. London School of Economics Series of Reprints of Scarce Works on Political Economy No 19. London: London School of Economics, 1968.

Wald, Abraham. 1936. Über einige Gleichungssysteme der mathematischen Ökonomie, *Zeitschrift für Nationalökonomie*. Translated by O. Eckstein as "On some systems of equations in mathematical economics." *Econometrica* 19:368–403.

Walras, Léon. 1889. *Eléments d'économie politique pure.* 2nd ed. Lausanne: F. Rouge; Paris: Guillaumin; Leipzig: Duncker & Humblot.

Walras, Léon. 1900. *Eléments d'économie politique pure.* 4th ed. Lausanne: F. Rouge; Paris: F. Pichon. Translated by W. Jaffe, as *Elements of Pure Economics*, 1954. Homewood, IL: Irwin; London: Allen & Unwin.

Wicksell, Knut. 1898. *Geldzins und Güterpreise bestimmenden Ursachen.* Jena: G. Fischer. Translated by R. F. Kahn as *Interest and Prices. A Study of the Causes Regulating the Value of Money.* London: Macmillan.

Zeuthen, Frederik Ludvig. 1932–33. Das Prinzip der Knappheit, technische Kombination und ökonomische Qualität. *Zeitschrift für Nationalökonomie* 4:1–24.

560

Edmund Phelps, Insider-Economists' Insider

PAUL A. SAMUELSON

Of Arms and the Man we Virgilians gather here to sing. Lest the keynote speaker steal in his overture the best tunes of the seminars that will appraise and praise the Ned Phelps feats of arms, my function now is to talk of the scholar himself as a person in his times.

In politics you know you are getting old when you hear yourself saying repeatedly, "I gave him his first job." Let the record show that Ned Phelps's rise to scientific fame owed nothing to interventions by me. However, that was not because of lack of trying on my part. When Phelps was a bright senior at Amherst, I lectured there solely in order to recruit him for MIT. His case was a no-brainer lay-down hand. But Ned was one of the fish that got away. And it was Yale's good fortune that he went there. One cannot deny that his was a good choice, for out of the ashes of Old Eli's glory in the days of Fairchild, Furness, and Buck—an interlude between the Gibbs and Irving Fisher era—Jim Tobin gathered to New Haven the refugee Cowles clan and many more. Eclectically, Ned learned from them and from the Fellner-Wallich-Triffin crowd too, and what he borrowed from his elders, he paid back at golden compound interest.

In no time at all he became known for golden rule theorems, for the Phelps-Koopmans permanent inefficiencies, for optimal intertemporal stochastic programming, for models of *endogenous* technological change, and for the concept of a natural rate of unemployment defined at the point where the algebraic rate of inflation passes from being permanently minus to permanently plus.

You might say this was Picasso's classical period. I knew of his innovations well, and not only because Solow and I were pedaling in the same bicycle marathon. Often I was a free rider boosted ahead by Ned's windbreaking lead efforts. Truly Phelps has been external-economy. Thus, my much-cited 1969 paper on optimal intertemporal portfolio programming opportunistically used the Bellman-Beckman-Phelps recursive techniques to analyze what defines the best qualitative asset-portfolio mix of the Phelps 1962 aggregate saving. It was not plagiarism but it was horning in on a created public good there for the taking.

The biography of a Phelps illuminates the nature of scientific advance and of innovators' behavior. Physics or mathematics or botany or anthropology, all of them are group efforts—you might call them overlapping generations of clique efforts. On the Midway at the University of Chicago, there stands a statue depicting Time, the work of Sculptor Lorado Taft (Senator-Professor Paul Douglas's father-in-law). It portrays the stationary figure of Time, before whom draped figures of succeeding generations pass from left to right. Etched in the marble base is the legend that I paraphrase from imperfect memory. "Time passes, you say? Ah no. 'Tis we who go."

The inner history of economics is a bit like that. Into the main ring of the circus each of us enters from the left and departs from the right. But it is not a simply ordered sequence ABC . . . XYZ: The better image is that of each epoch's chorus of scholars: Smith, Malthus, Ricardo, and the two Mills in the prime classical age. Then, in Victorian times, Jevons, Menger, Walras, Marshall, Pareto, Slutsky, Wicksell, and Cassel. Contemporaries of my teachers were Pigou, the Clarks, von Bortkiewicz, Keynes, Knight, Young, Viner, Schumpeter, and Hotelling—followed by the 1900+ vintages of Hayek, Haberler, Leontief, Hicks, Lerner, Kaldor, Robinson(s), Robertson, Tinbergen, Frisch, Ohlin, and Meade. Never are the hall lights so dimmed that a previous chorus can be replaced in one fell swoop by a new set of singers. Rather, imperceptibly new voices come on stage while old ones quietly slip off, humming ever more softly as they first linger and then fade away.

This construct enables me to place today's birthday boy in his generation. For a surprisingly long time most of our productive economists had their roots in the pre-World War II epoch. This is true of Tobin, Modigliani, Alexander, McKenzie, Arrow, Kaysen, Baumol, and Solow—to say nothing of Methuselahs like Bergson and me—and all of us had a head start over graduate students of the post-1945 years—the hot breath of ingenious youth at first burned less scorchingly on our necks.

But of course that could not last. The 1950s began with the Beckers, Ecksteins, Jorgensons, Gricheses, von Weizackers, Diamonds, Fishers, and Phelpses, all of whom were still singing soprano when the Pearl Harbor attack took place, and soon to come were the invading hosts of the Halls, Gordons, Stiglitzes, Mertons, Dornbusches, Fischers, and . . . but now I must stop because a countable infinity is still an infinity and a lunchtime speech is of finite duration, however boring it may become.

Returning to our rags-to-riches Horatio Alger, Jr., hero, Phelps established his credentials in the easy micro and macro of Hicks-Dantzig-Debreu: Santa Claus domains of convex sets and the differentiable calculus of variations. Would he advance into the unpromising lands of increasing scale returns, asymmetric information, lumpinesses, and all those other imperfections undreamed of in the philosophies of the equilibrium mongers?

The answer is a resounding, Yes. To sum up my hagiographic panegyric, I shall steal a few lines from Philippe Aghion, who "sees Phelps's contribution [to economics] as basically *one* project: *to introduce imperfect information and knowledge, imperfect competition, and market frictions* into macroeconomics"—and, I would add, into microeconomics as well. To polish Max Planck's dictum: Science does progress funeral by funeral—as the chorus of Phelpses and Stiglitzes explicates those many ways that palsy can afflict the invisible hand of Smith, Say, and Lucas.

Reflections on the Schumpeter I knew well

Paul A. Samuelson

Department of Economics, Massachusetts Institute of Technology, 50 Memorial Drive, Cambridge, MA 02142, USA

> "Ah, did you once see Shelley plain,
> And did he stop and speak to you,
> And did you speak to him again?
> How strange it seems, and new!"
>
> Robert Browning, Memorabilia, 1855.

In December of 1934, when I was an acne aged senior at the University of Chicago cleaning off pictures of Adam Smith, Böhm-Bawerk, and Alfred Marshall for the Economics Department, George Stigler and Allen Wallis were gigantic graduate students exercising squatter sovereignty over a basement storage room in the new Social Science Research Building. They told me that the American Economic Association was holding its Christmas annual meeting downtown in the Palmer House and suggested that I might want to pay that zoo a visit.

That is how I first saw Shelley plain. In one statistics section a roly-poly Harold Hotelling introduced Bill Madow who put some of the biggest matrices known to man on the blackboard. (That left its mark on me.)

Then, down the hall, to an overflow audience a florid Arthur Marget sang the flowery praises of a Harvard speaker whose name I could not catch. From Harvard he may have come, but I could catch no meaning from his energetic gibberish about "kitchens" and "spaghettis". Only a year later did I come to realize his Germanic-English was preaching about short-term Crum-Kitchen business cycles, intermediate-length Juglar cycles and longest-run Kondratief waves. He spoke dynamically and dramatically, and since his own jokes made him laugh, I nervously joined in with the crowd's frequent applauses. It was not love at first sight but he did capture my interest.

Still, the following week when Walllis and Stigler asked what I had learned at the AEA, I replied "Harry Carver from Michigan math department suggested, 'to avoid the sample assumption of normality, permute the sample's measured properties with that universe's means properties'." Wallis then observed, "Samuelson, that's the silliest idea I've ever heard." This is really a story about Allen Wallis since the famous bootstrap technique did become important in statistics only some forty years later.

When I finally came to mention Schumpeter, George Stigler snorted, "Isn't he the nut who believes the interest rate to be zero in the stationary state?" I didn't then have the wit or the brashness to reply, "Yes, and Frank Knight is the nut who believes that the interest rate can *never* be zero in the stationary state." Knight was then our local Chicago Isaac Newton.

A year later I won a juicy SSRC fellowship that would pay all my graduate school expenses provided I went to a different university. So I was bribed to leave the midway Valhalla. In June 1935, without exception my Chicago teachers – Simons, Director, Knight, Douglas, Viner, Gideonse, Mints, Nef, and Yntema – recommended Columbia over Harvard. By lucky miscalculation I brashly ignored their wisdom. But it was not in order to sit at the Schumpeter knee. My hallucination was that the Harvard Yard would be, like the Dartmouth lawns at Hanover, New Hampshire: a pretty white church on the hill, and much green ivy. Ed Chamberlain's 1933 *Theory of Monopolistic Competition*, which had never been assigned in any of my numerous Chicago courses, I found on a Reserve shelf and much enjoyed. But it took scarcely a month in the busy Harvard Yard to realise that Chamberlin was indeed a one-book-only man.

By sheer luck – my good luck – Harvard was about to come out of a lean period, led by an infusion of European talent: Schumpeter, Leontief and Haberler; buttressed too by the powerful soon-to-be arrival of Alvin Hansen, and my discovery of Edwin Bidwell Wilson, mathematician, physicist, statistician and only protégé of Yale's Willard Gibbs. Had I stayed at my beloved Chicago I would have missed completely, or had to fabricate alone, three great revolutions: the Keynesian revolution, the mathematical revolution, and the imperfect-competition revolution; besides, the Chicago ideology was an infantile eczema okay for one's teens but much in need of outside sunshine.

Today's lecture began with meeting Schumpeter for the first time. Lest the fast-moving clock choke off an account of how exactly fifteen years later I was the last professional economist to talk at length with Joseph Schumpeter, let me postpone for another occasion those intervening years. In 1949, this time in New York City, the AEA again met just after Christmas. Joseph and Paul had no inkling then that within a dozen days Professor Schumpeter would die in his sleep at the Taconic, Connecticut country estate of his American third wife, Elizabeth Boody Schumpeter. It can be said that Schumpeter's death was the gift of the gods – it came unannounced; with his boots on, he died going full-tilt. Born February 8, 1883 (four months before Keynes), Schumpeter died January 7-8, 1950 at but age 67.

(Keynes, perhaps from a heart damaged at Eton by rheumatic fever, was granted only 63 crowded years.) Best of all for a scholar like Schumpeter, his huge *History of Economic Analysis* was near enough to completion that his economic historian widow could supervise its final editing with the help of a few friends (Wassily Leontief, Richard M. Goodwin, Gottfried Haberler,...).

822

Pascal and Felix Mendelssohn were prodigiously precocious. But when each died before reaching age forty, each was physiologically an old man. Not so with Mozart – from him could have been extrapolated as much again in the future as had generously erupted in the past.

Schumpeter used to joke that in his seventies he would write his treatise on logic. In his eighties would come his sociological novel, and in preparation for it, he would for a second time ride the Boston subway. That was not to be.

When Schumpeter received an honorary Columbia degree – at age 30! – old Frank Fetter took him to a Princeton football game. Once was enough for a quick learner like Joseph Alois. Less promising was the attempt by Bob Bishop and me to initiate Schumpeter into the intricacies of poker following a semiriotous cocktail party. The gallant scholar could not seem to realise that if he financed everbody's losings, the game might lose some of its zest.

I recollect that Schumpeter was an active participant at several of the 1949 AEA sessions. His *Capitalism, Socialism, and Democracy,* which he professed to despise as an off-the-cuff pot-boiler, had been a great success in the 1940s. By contrast the two volumes of *Business cycles,* which drained much of his energies in the 1930s, made no considerable splash. Perhaps Keynes' 1936 *General Theory* made it seem anti-climatic.

When we met in the hotel bar, Schumpeter told me of plans to prepare an important invited Chicago lecture during the coming January. Significant to me was a seeming recantation expressed by Schumpeter at an autumn 1949 NBER Business Cycles conference held just prior to the Christmas AEA meeting. Remember that Schumpeter, from the time of his first German book in his Edwardian-Age youth, had been the Viennese heretic who did not believe Walrasian general equilibrium; moreover, Schumpeter was the electic who shocked continental contemporaries by praising J.B. Clark and Knut Wicksell. As far as my own career was concerned, he egged me on to discover and utilize new mathematical tools in economics – even though, Moses-like, JAS himself was never to cross over into the Promised Land of Pareto, Hotelling, Tinbergen, and Frisch – to say nothing of Arrow, Debreu and Koopmans.

Imagine then the surprise that greeted his 1949 NBER statement, which I paraphrase as follows :

> Yes, econometric mathematics and statistics are fruitful tools for the future science of economics.
>
> But if the good fairies will allot you only one of *economic history* or *Mathematical econometrics,* then to become an outstanding economist, master the corpus of economic history.

Was this the ranting of a decaying arteriosclerotic mind, poised two months from extinction? My evidence is against that. The terminal Schumpeter was lucid and witty and often wise. Wicksell, late in life, lost some of his earlier unearned faith in Say's Law and Neutral Money. The realities of the 1930s Great Depression, which Irving Fisher personally suffered from especially, left Fisher before his death with a wiser and more qualified version of the *Quantity Theory of Money* than graced

823

the pre-1927 macro writings of Fisher, Marshall, Pigou and even pre-1925 John Maynard Keynes.

Let me return to, so to speak, our last supper. One topic the two of us discussed was if I could help Dick Goodwin get a good job, one that he would think good enough for him to accept.

> JAS: I wish Harvard would give Goodwin a tenured chair. But that limited crew will veto any such nomination. As an alternative, I have offered to fight for a lifetime fellowship for this worthy scholar of simple tastes and a desire to be a modern painter part time. But Dick is a proud man and says, "If I cannot be a first-class member of the club, it is not the club for me."

Amherst, or Williams, or the University of Michigan Schumpeter mentioned as possible destinations but Goodwin (this Rhodes Scholar from a small Indiana high school that had never previously sent a graduate to Harvard) was just not interested.

> PAS: I am at a loss. Perhaps going abroad to Oxbridge will be the most hopeful exploration.

I digress to report that Goodwin was welcomed to Peterhouse, Cambridge University, where he taught and did research until his middle sixties, when he retired to a second career as an Italian professor in Sienna. This was an Indian summer for Richard Goodwin. Senator Joseph McCarthy's early 1950s research witch hunts played some role in the Goodwin saga, although in late 1949 I had no inkling of that. I ought to add that although Schumpeter made plain after 1932 that he himself had not been a refugee from Adolph Hitler's Bonn University, many refugees were helped by Schumpeter to settle in an American university.

At this point the two of us were joined at the hotel bar by Gottfried Haberler, Schumpeter's younger Vienna colleague at Harvard and by the colourful Imre de Vegh, who became Schumpeter's financial executor and who was a Hungarian aristocrat trained at Cambridge University. De Vegh was one of the first of the post-World War II "performers" as a Wall Street money-manager investor, first at Scudders, Stevens and Clark, and then later for his own firm. De Vegh had a great penchant for academies and was prone to press his hospitality on visitors from out of town.

To put it plainly, de Vegh then proceeded to kidnap us three academics, pouring us into a taxicab on the way to his penthouse apartment where his (surprised) wife was to cook us dinner. When we arrived, Mrs. de Vegh was in her kimono, curling the hair of her cute young daughter. She assured us that it was no imposition and that she did have a frozen Bird's-Eye chicken (then an innovation) to cook up for our dinner. In the meantime, our kidnapper host lay down for a noisy nap, leaving us three to amuse ourselves in the living room.

Crafty Gottfried Haberler soon escaped quietly. Schumpeter and I were again a twosome. We talked of many things. One, I remember, was Estelle Leontief's novel that John Day was contemplating publishing. Schumpeter judged it to be promising, but he didn't know whether she could meet the publisher's request to add more sex to it.

824

Finally, my wise master said: "What are we doing here? Gottfried is smarter than us." So we sneaked into the bedroom where our coats were hung and where our host dreamed on. Tiptoeing, we made our way to a taxi. That was the last I saw of my master. And a dozen days later, on snowy roads from Boston to Connecticut, Gottfried and wife Friedl in the front seat drove me surrounded by Goodwin on the right and by Schumpeter's then current assistant Alf Conrad on the left, to Schumpeter's funeral.

Of course we gossiped of good old days in the Harvard Yard and Littauer Hall. Did we find many good things to say about the late departed? Indeed we did. Was he completely without faults? Of course not, and long ago I've commented on some of them. Remember this, though: In chess you are only as good as your worst move. In creative science you are as good as your best moves.

Let me again solemnly affirm, at this place and before this company, that Joseph Schumpeter greatly enriched my life and enriched that of my late wife Marion Crawford who was perhaps his earliest research assistant. His support for my scholarly career was intense and without limits.

When Schumpeter died, he may have been the most frequently cited living economist.

Now, at the turn of the millennia, when total-factor-productivity has remarkably soared in America and abroad, both fools and sages sing Schumpeter's praise. That would have amused and pleased this worldly scholar who in some dark hours of the night used to despair in his German-shorthand diaries of justly deserved praises passing him by. So Keynes was wrong: in the long run not all of us are dead.

1 A portrait of the master as a young man

Paul A. Samuelson

1. The Harvard background

Leontief had a long and picturesque life in three countries, on two continents. Over sixty years his was a first-rate lectureship at Harvard University and New York University (NYU).[1] At the editors' invitation, I speak here for an early generation of Leontief's boys: those in his special workshop within a golden pre-war Cambridge age. Listed in approximate chronological order, I bear witness for Abram Bergson, Sidney Alexander, Shigeto Tsuru, Lloyd Metzler, Dick Goodwin, Jim Duesenberry, Hollis Chenery, Bob Solow and myself. A baker's half dozen that, owing only to age-related inadvertence, omits to mention a few other celebrated names.[2]

For a long time I was as much younger than Leontief as Solow is younger than I am. However, late in the era of the Soviet Union, revisionist research into Czarist vital statistics pushed back from 1906 to 1905 the birth year of my beloved master. But what signifies age? When I first glimpsed Wassily, brown-suited, dark, scarred and handsome, at the 1934 Palmer House Chicago meeting of the American Economic Association (AEA), he looked much the same as when at 69 he left Harvard in a huff for NYU. Even in the months before he died, in 1999, his appearance had not changed much. I may also add that his foreign accent softened little over the years; but, after my first hour of hearing him lecture, his soft-spoken words came through loud and clear.

We graduate students spun legends in the junior common room about our mentor. At the age of puberty, as a Menshevik, his life was spared by the Bolsheviks in the hope that he would grow up to know better. The scar on his neck was not the wound from a student's duel; actually the

---

[1] It was a nineteenth-century Harvard graduate who said: "Good Americans, when they die, go to Paris." It is I who says: "Good economists, before they die, go to NYU." Fritz Machlup, Oskar Morgenstern, Will Baumol and Wassily Wassilyovitch Leontief will know I state the truth.

[2] Marion Crawford (Samuelson) was at least one gender exception; her 1937 summa senior honors thesis was written as Leontief's Radcliffe tutee.

3

German operation that produced it did provide him the exit visa to leave the Soviet Union.[3] Like an earlier immigrant, Simon Kuznets, the young Leontief at first seemed quite apolitical in America. Later he reversed the usual life cycle: with age, conservative cynicism peeled off – particularly after the Republicans cut back on input-output development.

In 1935 Harvard was just moving from torpor into an Elizabethan renaissance. Frank Taussig had aged. Allyn Young had died prior to returning from the London School of Economics to Harvard. Failing to achieve tenure, Laughlin Currie had recently been banished to Washington. Charles Jesse Bullock and Thomas Nixon Carver had at long last retired. Economic historian Edwin Gay, although he may not have known it, was in his last year at Harvard (thereby liberating Abbott Payson Usher to teach graduate students). John Williams led dynamic seminars that were respectable and, after Alvin Hansen arrived (in 1937, by a Harvard miscalculation!), the two made a great macroeconomic duo. Edward Chamberlin at 35 was, judged retrospectively, at the zenith of his scholarly career; Edward Mason was not yet the important elder statesman he was to become. Other local worthies can mostly be overlooked.

Thanks only in part to Adolf Hitler, the foreign rescuers were on their way: Schumpeter from Austria and Weimar Germany; Haberler from Vienna and the League of Nations. It must have been the newly-arrived-in-Cambridge Schumpeter who plucked Leontief from a brief National Bureau stint to Harvard. I suspect Schumpeter fastened on Leontief as a genius on the basis of the 24-year-old's German article (Leontief, 1929) on how to identify demand and supply elasticities from a time-series sample – a brilliant investment decision even if not 100 percent cogent.

2. Early teaching

It was only in the calendar year 1935 that Schumpeter and Leontief were permitted to lecture on their specialties. That was luck for me since it provided both a telescopic and a microscopic add-on to my training. It rescued me from my miscalculation, which had diverted me from Morningside Heights to the Harvard Yard.[4]

---

[3] Unlike Prokofiev he never went back, except to preach to his fatherland the virtues of input-output analysis.
[4] When the Social Science Research Council (SSRC), my Medicis, dictated that I leave Chicago, midway locals without exception advised choosing the Columbia of Wesley Mitchell, Harold Hotelling and J. M. Clark. Joseph Schumpeter, I was told, was the eccentric who believed in a zero interest rate for the stationary state. Leontief neither I nor they knew anything about. Before Seymour Harris was an "inflationist," Lloyd Mints warned me against him as one. Independently of any Chicago reading list, I had

That first registration day I gladly burned my bridges. Defying indescribable high authority, William Tell refused to take economic history from Gay. (I already knew it from John U. Nef.) That made room to take two advanced courses – one of which was from Chamberlin. Twenty-one years later, when I substituted for him to teach the basic elementary Harvard graduate course in theory, I encountered precisely the same unchanged reading list: J. S. Mill, A. Marshall, E. H. Chamberlin and J. V. Robinson! Eschewing Gay in the spring semester, I was able to learn genuine modern statistics from E. B. Wilson, bypassing Edwin Frickey (who, with Leonard Crum, taught at Harvard courses *against* modern statistics!). But all was not lost.

For the first time Wassily gave a one-semester mathematical economics seminar; it was camouflaged as "Price Analysis" but that didn't fool me. We were a small class. Abe Bergson, then a third-year graduate student, was one attendee. Another was Harvard honors senior Sidney Alexander. Maybe Shigeto Tsuru and Philip Bradley were auditors, as was Schumpeter occasionally.

Here is what we learned from late September to almost November Thanksgiving. (a) Specified two-good indifference contours, non-intersecting and "convex to the origin." (b) A negatively sloped budget line. (c) No indicator of *cardinal* utility at all. The commodity (numbered 2) on the vertical axis was specified to be numeraire good, so that P_1/P_2 determined the absolute slope of the budget line. (d) As this price ratio changed, the budget line pivoted around the intercept where it hit the vertical axis. (e) What could we *prove* about the signs of $\partial q_1/\partial(P_1/P_2)$ and $\partial q_2/\partial(P_1/P_2)$? But first, (f), what might be true of the signs of income elasticities or of $\partial q_i/\partial(I/P_1)$ when I/P_1 is defined as $(P_2/P_1)q_1 + q_2 = I/P_1$, the budget constraint?

We learned that, in so-called "normal" case(s), *both income* elasticities would be positive. But also there could be cases where one, but *not both*, of the income elasticities could be negative. Finally, somewhere between Columbus Day and Thanksgiving, we found the Holy Grail at the North Pole.

Theorem. In all "normal" cases, own-price elasticities were indeed negative. However, in a case where a good's income elasticity was negative and much was spent on it, Giffenosity could obtain to make $\partial q_i/\partial(P_i/P_j) > 0$!

discovered on my own the *Theory of Monopolistic Competition* (Chamberlin, 1933) on the SSRC reserve room shelf. That predisposed me toward Harvard. But, truth to tell, it was because I expected Harvard to be like Dartmouth – located around a New England green common, with a white chapel tower and much ivy on the walls – that I arrived by tram, unannounced, at the Harvard Yard.

We didn't learn this by writing down in our notebooks the professor's dictated statements of the theorem. We *proved* it by 2 × 2 determinants! Ah, bliss.

No other course I ever took so profoundly set me on the way of my life career. It was, so to speak, slow motion, and all the better for that. It prepared me to master Edwin Bidwell Wilson's exposition of Willard Gibbs' thermodynamic analysis. Leontief assigned no readings in Pareto or Allen-Hicks; or, for that matter, W. E. Johnson (1913) or Eugen Slutsky (1915) – only our own laboratory work. Then, after Thanksgiving, we replaced the linear budget equation by Haberler's (1933) concave "opportunity-cost" curve – thereby mastering Leontief's (1933) own vindication of Marshallian (1879) offer curves in international trade. Obviously we were prepared for James Meade's (1952) later graphics of international trade.

I have told more than once how Haberler's resistance to indifference curves provoked from one brash Leontief student the rebuke: "Well, without indifference curves, your 1925 Vienna Ph.D. thesis on index numbers evaporates into thin air" (see Haberler, 1927). The theory of revealed preference (see Samuelson, 1938a, and 1938b) was born one second later as I listened to what *I* was saying.

Although Wassily rarely lectured on *his* current researches, this was a golden decade in his own life. (Also, it was that for Abba Lerner far away in London. And for the Oskar Lange whose muse left him after his patriotic return to post-war Soviet-satellite Poland.) Notable and already mentioned was Leontief's (1933) paper on indifference curves in international trade. Less noticed was his (1934) paper – in German, but translated in Leontief (1966) – on cobweb dynamics of non-linear supply and demand curves. Here his topological explorations into multiple periodic motions came close to chancing on modern *chaos* theory. Already his Harvard lectures introduced testable partial differential equations for disaggregation separability. In my 1941 thesis (see Samuelson, 1947, p. 178), I referred to the *Leontief* condition for additive-utility independence of goods x and y, namely the vanishing of $\partial^2 \log M(x, y)/\partial x \partial y$, where M denotes the observable marginal rate of substitution between x and y.

3. Afterthoughts on input-output

Leontief's middle and final decades were increasingly preoccupied by input-output researches (see Leontief et al., 1953; Leontief, 1966). These were of tremendous value to society and to him. His Nobel Prize properly cited them. Well and good; a scholar should follow his own instincts and volitions. Still, I have to confess to a certain regret. Max

Born (the physics Nobel laureate who helped to found the better post-Planck and post-Bohr quantum mechanics theory) expressed my sentiments when he wrote to the Albert Einstein who, from the age of 45 on, concentrated all his energies on creating a new unified field theory combining gravity, relativity, quantum theory and cosmology. To do this, Einstein chose to cut himself off from most of the frontier developments in 1925–1955 physics. Born wrote to his admired master: "We are left to struggle on without our leader." I am much like Oliver Twist, who always asks for "More!" So original and lively an economist as Leontief, in my contra-factual history, could well have given us another volume of diverse and sparkling collected papers like those in his classic 1966 book. The whole world appreciated the genius of Wassily W. Leontief. But we his disciples knew the full measure of his inspiration and potential.

At Berlin Leontief was lucky in his teacher Ladislaus von Bortkiewicz, a keen contributor to statistics and to mathematical economics. Matching this depth came the width from Werner Sombat, the grandiose creator of theories for economic history. From von Bortkiewicz's improvements on Marx must have come an early interest in the Quesnay-like circular interdependence of input-output. But, from my later explicit quizzing of him, I can rebut the innuendo that he ever did know the work of Vladimir Dmitriev (1898). Just as Sraffa's (1960) book on input-output never cited Leontief, Leontief's 1925–1999 writings seem never to have cited the work of Sraffa.

I try not to make those venial mistakes. I am conscious of how much I have benefited from teachers like Leontief: at Chicago Jacob Viner, Henry Simons, Frank Knight and Paul Douglas; at Harvard Edwin Bidwell Wilson, Joseph Schumpeter, Leontief, Gottfried Haberler and Alvin Hansen. It is humbling when one weighs accomplishments against advantages. Old school ties are dummy variables that unfairly boost one's R^2. And, when your teachers pass off the stage, your students step in to add on their push. All the while the wind is broken for us by contemporaries such as Abram Bergson, Robert Solow, Kenneth Arrow, Gerard Debreu, Abraham Wald, Lionel McKenzie and the rest of the Invisible College.

Sixty-five years have not dimmed memories of that golden age in the Harvard Yard: so to speak, Wassily Leontief on one end of the log and I on the other.

REFERENCES

Chamberlin, E. H. (1933) *The Theory of Monopolistic Competition* (Cambridge, MA, Harvard University Press, 6th edn., 1948).

Dmitriev, V. K. (1898) The theory of value of David Ricardo: an attempt at a rigorous analysis, in *Economic Essays on Value, Competition and Utility* (London, Cambridge University Press, 1974), 37–95. [Translated by D. Fry from a 1904 Moscow Russian-language publication, and published with an introduction by D. M. Nuti.]

Haberler, G. (1927) *Der Sinn der Indexzahlen* (Tübingen, J. C. B. Mohr).

(1933) *Der internationale Handel. Theorie der weltwirtschaftlichen Zusammenhange sowie Darstellung und Analyse der Aussenhandelspolitik* (Berlin, Julius Springer). [Translated as: *The Theory of International Trade with its Applications to Commercial Policy* (London, William Hodge & Co., 1936).]

Johnson, W. E. (1913) The pure theory of utility curves, *Economic Journal*, 23, 483–515.

Leontief, W. W. (1929) Ein Versuch zur statistischen Analyse von Angebot und Nachfrage, *Weltwirtschaftlichs Archiv*, 30, 1–53.

(1933) The use of indifference curves in the analysis of foreign trade, *Quarterly Journal of Economics*, 47, 493–503.

(1966) *Essays in Economics: Theories and Theorizing* (New York, Oxford University Press).

Leontief, W. W., et al. (1953) *Studies in the Structure of the American Economy* (New York, Oxford University Press).

Marshall, A. (1879) *The Pure Theory of International Trade. The Pure Theory of Domestic Values*. [Privately printed 1879. First published (London, London School of Economics, 1930), reprinted (Clifton, New Jersey, Augustus M. Kelley, 1974).]

Meade, J. (1952) *A Geometry of International Trade* (London, Allen & Unwin).

Samuelson, P. A. (1938a) A note on the pure theory of consumer's behavior, *Economica*, 5, 61–71.

(1938b) An addendum, *Economica*, 5, 353–354.

(1947) *Foundations of Economic Analysis* (Cambridge, MA, Harvard University Press).

Slutsky, E. (1915) Sulla teoria del bilancio del consumatore, *Giornale degli Economisti e Rivista di Statistica*, 51, 1–26. [Translated as: On the theory of the budget of the consumer, in K. E. Boulding and G. Stigler (eds.) *Readings in Price Theory* (London, Allen & Unwin, 1953).]

Sraffa, P. (1960) *Production of Commodities by Means of Commodities. Prelude to a Critique of Economic Theory* (Cambridge, Cambridge University Press).

ABRAM BERGSON

April 21, 1914–April 23, 2003

BY PAUL A. SAMUELSON

OVER THE LAST TWO-THIRDS of the twentieth century Abram Bergson was a leading American and world economist. He was a creative theorist, both literary and mathematical. Bergson was also a careful statistical empiricist who, from a bully pulpit at Harvard, earned a reputation as the dean of Soviet studies and teacher of that subject's major scholars.

At a young age in 1933 Abram came to the Harvard Graduate School in economics after undergraduate training at Johns Hopkins (where he was a hometown commuter). Adolph Hitler was responsible for new foreign blood arriving in Cambridge to trigger a prewar Harvard renaissance in economics. When Bergson died at age 89, he was the last survivor of Harvard's age of Frank Taussig, and had been a young star in the new age of Joseph Schumpeter, youthful Wassily Leontief, eclectic Gottfried Haberler, and after 1937 Alvin Hansen, the "American Keynesian." As Leontief's second protégé I am proud to have been preceded by Abram Bergson, his first protégé. I would be honored to be known as Bergson's first protégé, for much of my own work in welfare economics owes virtually everything to his classic 1938 *Quarterly Journal of Economics* article that for the first time clarified this subject.

Two of Bergson's most cited papers actually appeared

under the authorship of Abram Burk. Burk was indeed the name he had been born with. How A. Burk became A. Bergson is a tale worth telling, both as a reflection of what American academic and ordinary life was like 70 years ago, and for what it tells about his own straight-arrow character.

Abram's older brother Gus (Gustav Burk) studied Harvard graduate physics at the same time that Abe was studying economics. (Reliable family legend tells that Gus's skill in Baltimore poker games won for his junior brother private tutoring in the economics that he would need at Harvard.) Gus Burk particularly felt uncomfortable in having a name that did not correctly identify him as being the son of Russian immigrant Jews. So the two decided legally to change their surname. Abram sought my advice on the tentative substitution of Bergson for Burk. That struck me as an excellent choice: "It makes the point, but does not rub it in." Still Abram dithered: "You don't suspect, Paul, that some will think I'm trying to travel on the prestige of the great French philosopher Henri Bergson?" I put that probability down to near zero. The rest is history. And the old Brahmin *Boston Transcript* wrote a laudatory editorial commending this reverse instance of an opposite common pattern. In the end no significant citation confusion resulted from this early career decision.

Having by 1937 already achieved wide respect as a mathematical economist, serious Abram decided he would add a second string to his bow. Accordingly he learned the Russian language, and made a lengthy research visit to Moscow. Nineteen thirty-seven was the precise year when Stalin was liquidating on a large scale dissidents and innocents as enemies of the revolution. In later reflection Bergson reported how astonishing it had been that none of the many scholars he talked to—most of whom must have known family members and neighbors who were imprisoned or killed—communicated complaints to a naive American visitor.

By 1940 Bergson had written for publication his Harvard Ph.D. thesis. Thereafter at the wartime Office of Strategic Services, at Columbia, at the RAND think tank in Santa Monica, and after 1956 as tenured Harvard professor, Abram Bergson divided his time and energies between pure economic theory and the Soviet economics specialty. After the 1940-42 years at the University of Texas, Austin, Bergson spent most of the World War II years as head of the Russian desk at the Office of Strategic Services. Then at war's end Columbia called him to an economics chair. A decade later at Harvard, after 1956, he taught scores of theorists and Kremlinologists.

Many of the *cognoscenti* at the frontier of modern welfare economics—I being one of them—expected Stockholm to wake up to Bergson's merits. Alone, along with Ian Little or John Harsanyi or John Rawls, a Bergson prize could have added luster to the new post-1968 Alfred Nobel awards in economics. My tentative guess as to why that never did happen goes as follows. Kenneth Arrow's monumental work on the impossibility of *any* constitutional method of voting that would satisfy half-a-dozen plausible desirable axioms, that great theorem somehow got confused in nonspecialists' minds as being a proof against *the possible existence* of the quite different animal of the Bergson Ethical Normative Function. The history of every science contains some history of confusions, and economics is no exception to this.

In connection with ethical value judgments Bergson clarified how they could be distinguishable from testable empirical relations, a problem inadequately grappled with by Lionel Robbins (1932). Bentham, J. S. Mill, Edgeworth, as well as Pareto, Myrdahl, Lerner, Hicks, Kaldor, Scitovsky,

Vickery, and Little could be given *coherent* interpretation in light of Burk-Bergson (1938).

Vilfredo Pareto in the years 1892-1913 brought important excellent insights into the post-Bentham utilitarian methodologies of Anglo-Saxon normative economics. But Pareto was an isolated pioneer, self-indulgent in his expositions as is not surprising in an autodidact. Serious Abram pondered important questions such as whether what we have come to call "Pareto optimality," which in even vaguer formulations is already in Mill (1848) if not indeed already in Adam Smith's "invisible hand" (1776), was a singular "*the* optimum" rather than (as in Francis Edgeworth [1881]) an infinity of incommensurable optima. My re-readings with him could not resolve the interpretations. Bergson's insightful happy thought was first to understand that *any* ethical code is, in the language of Arrow (1951), "imposed." The "just" person does not give his second coat to a naked beggar because that happens to tickle his fancy that Monday. It is his credo that requires him to do that.

However, using the useful device of an Individualistic Social Welfare Function—a special case that economists like to contemplate—Bergson could derive Pareto optimality conditions as *necessary* but not sufficient conditions for defining interpersonal normative equity. (Later Leontief and Franklin Fisher elaborated on "weak" mathematical separability and "strong" separability; earlier Irving Fisher had formulated testable conditions for Bentham-like additive hedonism; and as late as 1955 John Harsanyi restored some credence to pre-Bergson cardinality of individual utilities and of Social Cardinal Utility in the light of stochastic choosers sometimes feeling obliged to pay respect to the Independence Axiom in post-von Neumann argumentations about Laplacian Expected Utility. Few National Academy of Sciences readers need to understand this name dropping, inasmuch as out of any one hundred 2003 graduate economic students in the Ivy League and Big Ten, my Bayesian estimate is that almost none of these professionals do comprehend these nuances.)

What needs to be stressed is that Bergson's Social Welfare Function(s) left plenty of room for ethical credos that ordained *duties* and for which separate Pareto-optimality conditions could not even be defined. In the language of Richard Musgrave's magisterial *The Theory of Public Finance* (1958), "merit wants" that are so unpopular on the University of Chicago midway do exist. Some societies might even be unanimous in voting a fair military draft, even though every young voter is unwilling to be a volunteer. (God is in the ad libs. I knew a libertarian economist who was against the tyranny of coercive traffic lights. My spies reported that, nevertheless, commuting to daily work he revealed a preference for the longer route over the lights-free shorter router: His gut knew more about the algebraic pluses and minuses of the calculus of "liberty" than his conscious mind did.)

Abram Bergson was a realist par excellence. He applied generous reasoned discounts to the statistical growth claims of the Stalinist and post-Stalinist statisticians. And yet, after the dozen post-Gorbachev years of communist dissolution the emerging evidence suggests to me—and I think to "Honest Abe" as he was known at Harvard—that the Soviet system was even less productive in most sectors than the international almanacs had estimated. Why? Plain Machiavellian lying? No doubt there was some of that, as all our experts did recognize.

More important, I suggest after much reflection, is the fact that what are called "prices" in a controlled society have little true relationship to relative scarcities and technical trade-off costs. From copious nonmeaningful statistical inputs will have to come quite nonmeaningful statistical estimates. One wonders whether some future transformation of Mao's Chinese economic system will thereafter reveal how hard it is for scholars to gauge correctly how deep China's present-day discount factors ought to be.

Before Schumpeter died in 1950 that learned scholar had to feel some jealousy of John Maynard Keynes, who gained recognition as the twentieth century's greatest economist. Our master therefore missed what he would have certainly relished, namely, his burgeoning posthumous fame. Innovation and long-term trends today command some of the interest and energy that had previously belonged to equilibrium statics and macroeconomic business cycle fluctuations.

Moreover, the fact that widow Elizabeth Boody Schumpeter bequeathed to the Harvard Archives *all* his papers, personal and private, and even those that discuss in an obscure German shorthand the pros and cons of not marrying her, that understandably created a cottage industry in Schumpeter biographies. One of the best and most balanced of those biographies on Joseph Schumpeter, that by the Swedish economic sociologist Richard Swedberg (1991), raised an important question. In my paraphrase the biographer at one point writes, "Now I must ask the following question. Can we judge Joseph Alois Schumpeter to have been a fervent friend to mankind? On the basis of all the known evidence, perhaps no firm answer can be given to this question."

No biographer of Abram Bergson could be in doubt about his personal attitudes and modesty. I have made stronger claims on his behalf than he ever made in print. He was no shrinking violet. Thus when he found some faults in the mathematical writing of Ragnar Frisch (who later was deservedly to share the *first* Bank of Sweden-established Nobel Prize in Economics in 1969), Bergson did stand up to that great and self-confident man. (In Bergson [1936], written when the author was only 24, will be found an earliest formulation of the Constant Elasticity of Substitution Function, which outside of consumer utility analysis, became widely used in production theory; it is also a workhorse in modern finance theory as the one case where optimal portfolio ratios are independent to whether wealth is large or small. This is but one of Bergson's theoretical novelties.)

Those who knew Abram Bergson and knew his informed views on Smith, Marx, Franklin D. Roosevelt, Lenin, and Stalin will judge him to have been a man of the center with a personal preference toward less economic inequality. That majority view among his generation of economists (and mine), perusal of the published literature will confirm, has lost its preponderant majority as the Great Depression and World War II recede farther into history. Libertarianism à la Milton Friedman and Friedrich Hayek has gained in strength. Outside the academy, among voters in general there has been a similar erosion of "altruism." However, with the weakening of "altruism" and the gaining of "my wallet" motivations, I detect no logical or empirical tie-up with libertarianism as such. Also among academics in or outside economics there has taken place little popularity for fundamentalist religions.

Straight-arrow honest people can sometimes seem to many of us naïve—refreshingly naive. Bergson provides such an example. His lack of guile is illustrated by the following anecdote. Abram was a close friend of Harvard's learned Alexander Gerschenkron, who taught economic history and did so as a tough nonelective. Among students and young faculty almost a rebellion was brewing. Therefore a committee was appointed to review requirements. Bergson was asked to be its chairman. If he had asked advice from his Machiavellian MIT friend, Paul Anthony Samuelson, he would not have touched that third-rail topic with a 10-foot insulated pole. Honest Abe was never Machiavellian. He accepted the draft. And, inevitably, by strong majority the committee recommended new and much lighter economic history requirements. Gerschenkron, a strong believer in what he believed in, never quite forgave Honest Abe. A lifetime friendship was strained. Someone else could have been chairperson, as I think Abe came to realize belatedly.

Once in Bergson's rare reminiscing about his Baltimore youth, he mentioned that Gus and he would organize a number of new neighborhood clubs. Their main purpose seemed to be primarily to decide who would be *excluded* from them. Later I learned that being elected to honorific academies was somewhat similar. Energy on research gets you into the Academy; for example, Bergson was elected to the National Academy of Sciences in 1980. After that your time for research becomes compromised by duties to serve on research and nominating membership committees, whose main function is to decide just which worthies will be the ones *not* to be elected.

Back a long time before Bergson's death we had lunch together at the Harvard Faculty Club. A Harvard scholar came by whom I had known a long time, saying hello to me and passing on. At this point, as old friends will gossip to each other, big-mouth Samuelson said: "I wish that guy would not be so sharp with his wife." Abe's response was: "I'm glad to hear you say that." Surprised, I said, "Why should you want an acquaintance to be unkind?" "I don't," Bergson explained, "It's just that he's being so mean to me, and I thought it was something personal."

In the high-pressure atmosphere of modern university life, true character ultimately reveals itself—for better or worse. Abram Bergson over a long career earned from teachers, pupils, colleagues, and friends much affection and admiration. His wife, Rita Macht Bergson, herself from an academic Baltimore background, played an important role in their family and professional lives. I owe to their three achieving daughters—Judy, Mimi, and Lucy—much informal help in preparing this affectionate memoir.

REFERENCES

Arrow, K. 1951. *Social Choice and Individual Values.* New York: John Wiley.

Bentham, J. 1789. *An Introduction to the Principles of Morals and Legislation.* London: T. Payne. Reissued 1970, eds. J. H. Burns and H. L. A. Hart. London: Athlone Press.

Bergson (Burk), A. 1936. Real income, expenditure proportionality, and Frisch's "New methods of measuring marginal utility." *Rev. Econ. Stud.* 4:33-52.

Bergson (Burk), A. 1938. A reformulation of certain aspects of welfare economics. *Q. J. Econ.* 52:310-34.

Bergson, A. 1944. *The Structure of Soviet Wages: A Study in Socialist Economics.* Cambridge, Mass.: Harvard University Press.

Edgeworth, F. Y. 1881. *Mathematical Psychics.* London: C. Kegan Paul.

Harsanyi, J. 1955. Cardinal welfare, individualistic ethics, and interpersonal comparisons of utility. *J. Polit. Econ.* 63:309-21.

Mill, J. S. 1848. *Principles of Political Economy with Some of Their Applications to Social Philosophy.* Boston: Charles C. Little and James Brown; 1908, New York: Appleton.

Musgrave, R. 1958. *The Theory of Public Finance.* New York: McGraw-Hill.

Robbins, L. 1932. *An Essay on the Nature and Significance of Economic Science.* London: Macmillan.

Smith, A. 1776. *An Inquiry into the Nature and Causes of the Wealth of Nations.* Modern Library ed., 1937. New York: Random House.

Swedberg, R. 1991. *Schumpeter: A Biography.* Princeton, N.J.: Princeton University Press.

564

REMEMBRANCE AND APPRECIATION ROUNDTABLE

Harry G. Johnson (1923–1977):

Scholar, Mentor, Editor, and Relentless World Traveler

By MAX CORDEN, JAMES S. DUESENBERRY, CRAUFURD D. GOODWIN,
J. ALLAN HYNES, RICHARD G. LIPSEY, GIDEON ROSENBLUTH,
PAUL A. SAMUELSON, ELIZABETH JOHNSON SIMPSON

Edited and arranged by LAURENCE S. MOSS[*]

I

Samuelson on Harry, the Full Achiever

IN THE BRITISH ACADEMY OBITUARY OF Harry, James Tobin called ours the Age of Johnson. That was a bit of a stretch, but admissible in an eulogy where, as Dr. S. Johnson observed, one is not under strict oath. Undeniably our Johnson did penetrate into every nook and corner of post-1940 mainstream economics. He was certainly among the most prolific of our clan. Indeed, although he died at age 54, the intensity at which he lived added up to at least two normal lifetimes.

[*]On July 3, 2000, at the History of Economics Society meeting at the University of British Columbia in Vancouver, B. C., Canada, the current editor of this journal, in consultation with the incoming president of the Society, Professor John Davis, organized a special remembrance session in honor of Professor Harry G. Johnson. Contributors to this session were: Professor Max Corden, Johns Hopkins University, 1740 Mass Avenue, N.W., Washington, D.C. 20036; Professor Robert Dimand, Brock University, St. Catherines, Ontario L2S 3A1 Canada; Professor James S. Duesenberry, Harvard University, c/o 25 Fairmont Street, Belmont, MA 02178; Professor Craufurd D. Goodwin, Duke University, Box 90097, Durham, N.C. 27708-0097; Professor Allan J. Hynes, University of Toronto, 150 St. George Street, Toronto, Ontario M5S 1A1 Canada; Professor Richard G. Lipsey, Simon Fraser University, Harbour Centre, 515 W. Hastings St., Vancouver, B.C. V6B 5K3, Canada; Professor Donald Moggridge, University of Toronto, 150 St. George

American Journal of Economics and Sociology, Vol. 60, No. 3 (July, 2001).
© 2001 American Journal of Economics and Sociology, Inc.

841

Harry seemed a driven man—self-driven. Articles bubbled out of him like songs from Franz Schubert and varied melodies from Mozart. He would travel 3,000 miles to attend a meeting, whittle away while the program droned on, polish off a nightcap quart of scotch, and then on the plane trip back home compose a paper dealing with some aspect of the subjects discussed. Before the word processor amplified scholars' capacity for good or ill, Harry's little portable typed out print-ready copy.

Johnson surfaced in big-time science at Harvard following the war's end. He was born on a Toronto street where (I believe) Lorie Tarshis, Harold Somers, A. F. W. Plumptre, and a number of other eminent Canadian economists had lived. Like Jacob Viner in an earlier Montreal generation, Harry had a distinguished physician brother. During the war itself Harry did have a brief sojourn in the Other Cambridge. Unaccountably, he did not at Harvard stand out remarkably in comparison with the several hundred post-war graduate students in economics. At MIT, three miles away, I would hear tales about Bob Solow, Jim Tobin, Carl Kaysen, and Tom Schelling. However, when Harry called on me at my office (along with a forgotten second face), I was obtuse enough to regard him as just another competent student. However, Sidney Alexander alerted me to Harry's unusual versatility

---

Street, Toronto, Canada M5S 3G7; Professor Laurence S. Moss, Babson College, Mustard Hall, Babson Park, MA 02457; Professor Gideon Rosenbluth, c/o 4639 Simpson Avenue, Vancouver, B.C. V6R 1C2, Canada; Professor Paul A. Samuelson, Massachusetts Institute of Technology, E52-383, 50 Memorial Drive, Cambridge, MA 02142-1347; Mrs. Elizabeth Johnson Simpson, Chicago, IL. Professors Goodwin and Samuelson were not able to attend in person but prepared contributions. Mrs. Simpson made it all the way to Vancouver but the day before the sessions she took a fall, broke her ankle, and was hospitalized, and as a result Professor Anthony Scott of the University of British Columbia was kind enough to step in and read Simpson's contribution. The photographs of the session participants were taken by the talented economist and photographer Dr. Niels Korgard of Denmark. The cartoon of Professor Johnson was sketched by his then graduate student, Mr. Robert Vaughn. The actual photo of Professor Johnson and his various woodcuts were supplied by Mrs. Elizabeth Johnson Simpson. Professors Robert Dimand and Donald Moggridge's contributions appear separately in the journal as full-length articles, and they are not listed in this essay despite the fact that they participated in the session. I wish to acknowledge the help Donald Moggridge provided when planning this session.

and speed. Needing a grader to handle examination books, Alexander hired the first to volunteer, namely H. J. Later that day the books came back expertly graded and ranked. Since the normal expected time was three blue books per hour, Sidney was suspicious of a slovenly job. Checking, he reported to me, "They were optimally evaluated. Clearly we deal here with an extraordinary talent." Fellow editors were later to learn the same lesson.

John Chipman was surprised to find out how prolific Pareto had been: his words of publication exceeded those of Keynes and Ricardo put together. When I mentioned this to the late, erudite Alexander Gerschenkron, I was told that Eli Heckscher, Bertil Ohlin, and Luigi Einaudi put Pareto to shame. Like him they wrote often for newspapers and general magazines; a book merely listing Einaudi's bibliography made a volume thicker than Marshall's *Principles*. Johnson, by contrast, concentrated on learned journal publishing. Certainly he was aiming for a lifetime total of more than 1,000 scientific articles. Given a normal life span of the Bible's three score and ten, he would surely have reached that goal. It was said that at Johnson's death he had 18 articles in proof. I wager that there wasn't a dud in the whole lot. The classical scholar and poet A. E. Housman was asked by a colleague about an item he had not included in his collected papers: "Did you think it not good?" Housman answered, "I thought it good. But not good enough for me." I doubt that Harry let the wet rag of doubt kill off many of his plane-ride progeny. Friedrich Lutz said of a super-productive Harvard professional contemporary, "That man Seymour Harris can't hold his ink." A similar case was the mathematician Richard Bellman: he wrote important innovative analyses, but he may have written too much—so much that readers were not always sure whether they had or had not already read the Bellman result that arrived in the morning mail. (The same can never be said about the mathematician Paul Erdös, who died recently in his 80s, having authored or co-authored highly respected mathematical articles in excess of 4,000. Erdös was without wife or family and lived only to conjecture and prove mathematical theorems. On his own, in the forest or city, he could never have survived a full week or met a payroll at either end.)

Harry burned the candle at both ends. Alas, that does not give you

843

two candles. Felix Mendelssohn and Gustav Mahler, their contemporaries report, were both over-busy persons; while they talked to you they repeatedly checked their watches; both died young. Mendelssohn, like Pascal, died before 40, each already an old man. Harry chose to teach a full stint at Chicago, while teaching a full stint at the LSE; some periods he could tuck between them a teaching assignment Down Under, in Australia or Hong Kong or Singapore. At no place were students and colleagues cheated or stinted. Perhaps his arteries paid the price, although even had he eschewed tobacco and barley-corn and cholesterol, always his meter was running.

I recall an early encounter during my 1948 Guggenheim Fellowship year. At Will and Hilda Baumol's London lodgings, Frank Hahn introduced Harry, who had come from Cambridge to address an informal seminar of lively LSE prodigies. At no time was Harry without a cigarette; before one burned out he left it glued to his lip while lighting another; a third of the time he kept two going. Later when he swore off smoking, he took up whittling wood. He was good at everything he tried, whittling being no exception. I remember a masterpiece of three little monkeys, ducking their heads and covering their ears. The legend on the piece read: "Don't hurt me, Milton!"

What made Harry run? Who can provide cogent psycho-babble to explain these data? Of course, ambition was one explanatory factor. All the scholars I have known, without exception, have possessed ambition—even humanist saints like Jan Tinbergen or James Meade. Beethoven had no need for any self-doubt. Still, the early Beethoven went out of his way to try to top every mentor at his own game: Bach, Haydn, or whomever. When arrived at success, Beethoven deplored aristocratic patronage; while climbing the greasy pole he sought it out. Harry would go out of his way to drum up chair offers that he would certainly not accept. (The young Queen Victoria was counseled by Lord Melbourne on how a queen should act. Loving him, she observed her mentor closely. This led her to ask, "When the apples are passed around at dinner's end, I notice that you often take one or two even though you rarely eat even one. Why?" Melbourne replied gravely, "Mum, I like the feeling of command over them." Harry, I suppose, liked the feeling of first refusal.)

I spoke earlier of Johnson as driven. Also, his seemed to be a restless physiology. Stocky types are sometimes stereotyped as calm and ponderous. Well, when Pascal wrote that man can do everything but sit calmly alone in a room doing nothing, he might have been describing Johnson. (Newton, sitting with eyes closed in his Trinity room, working out mentally the elliptical differential equations of the two-body problem, cannot be classified as doing nothing!) Harry at rest could have beads of perspiration on his forehead. Enrico Caruso, the all-time great tenor, before every performance had butterflies in his stomach. Why then be surprised that so fertile an economist would show signs of insecurity? Victor Hugo, we learn, could demolish a dozen oranges and two haunches of beef at any meal. When late in life for no fathomable reason Harry opted to collect a Harvard Ph.D., on the eve of his final Orals he consumed an amazing run of freshly-picked sweet corn.

Some high achievers by nature require only a few hours of sleep. I think back to wonder whether Harry was one such. In today's pharmaceutical age, the elixirs that would have extended his life expectancy might have curbed his originality. Who can say?

On the evidences thus far provided, you would not expect Harry Johnson to be a namby-pamby, two-armed economist. And he was not. He formed decisive views and expressed them strongly. He was a formidable polemicist. Capable of random acts of gratuitous kindness, there was inside Harry also trace elements of acerbic reprobation: If we put George Stigler at 100 in this department, Harry earned a solid 50. It did not make things better that Harry first served time at Cambridge, England when the factionalism there was intense and bitter. This did not nurture the St. Francis latent in him. Then, later, fate carried him to the University of Chicago, never known as a particularly harmonious environment even back in the time of Frank Knight, Jacob Viner, and President Robert Hutchins—or in its later reincarnations.

At first, in Cambridge during the late 1940s, Harry was the only scholar maintaining good relations with both the Keynesian mob (Kahn, Joan Robinson, Kaldor, Sraffa) and the Robertsonian opposition. That could not last. Eventually Johnson lost patience with the politically correct British leftist Keynesians. At Chicago, Johnson resisted the monistic tides of Friedman, Stigler, and Gary Becker, but at the same time evolved away from 1936 Ur-Keynesianism. One supposes that Johnson was good for Chicago, but wonders whether Chicago was good for Johnson? We can never know the answer to such a question.

Literally hundreds of students and scores of colleagues benefited from Harry Johnson's many and varied economic researches and teachings. This is quite aside from the thousands who read his works. Canada, his native land, the UK where he trained and taught, and the United States all owe much to this sophisticated thinker. He had many warm friends. And, if I may say so, even his few enemies have mostly to be put to his credit.

Franco: a mind never at rest

PAUL A. SAMUELSON

Modigliani was never a 9-to-5 worker. The night he died in his sleep he attended a charitable fundraiser, then stayed up late to dot some 'i's' and cross some 't's'. Intensity was ever his forte and that is why his basic scientific contributions were so many, so diverse, and so *deep*.

Madame Currie received Nobel Prizes in physics and in chemistry. Linus Pauling capped his chemistry prize with a prize for peace. If they had given prizes for vitamin C, he might have received a third one for curing cancer and the common cold. Some great scholars are great for just one thing: Max Planck for stumbling onto quantum mechanics comes to mind and, in economics, Edward Chamberlin was clearly a one-book man. Franco's Nobel Prize stressed his theoretical finance but I can perceive other equally important contributions: intergenerational accounting, macroeconomics, microeconomics, and policy wisdoms.

And what he did, Modigliani always did *his* way. At 20, as a recent immigrant who sold books to finance advanced study, his was not a background from Exeter Academy or New Trier High, or from Harvard, Chicago or MIT. Indeed, at The New School in New York by great good luck he tied in with Jacob Marschak and Hans Neisser, themselves gifts from Hitler to American science. Later, after Franco joined up with Herb Simon at Carnegie Tech, the rest was history.

Gottfried Haberler, recognizing Franco's quantum improvements on Keynes's 1936 Model T *General Theory*, engineered an early call to Harvard. Scouting the mediocrities and bigots then cluttering corners of the Harvard Yard, Franco and Serena politely refused the offer. Strangely, when Harvard later began to get its act together, they let MIT capture the arrived and arriving Franco Modigliani.

☐ MIT, Department of Economics, Cambridge, Mass. (USA).

Meanwhile, Modigliani at Carnegie Tech (and during the short-lived renaissance at the University of Illinois) had been publishing profusely on a great variety of subjects – literary and mathematical. This earned him early reputation as a frontier world economist. And, because he was so gifted in finding and inspiring co-authors, his workshops were of the Titian and Rembrandt quality.

A Gilbert and Sullivan patter song could be composed about Modigliani and Grunberg, Modigliani and Brumberg, Modigliani and Miller, Modigliani and Ando, Modigliani and Drèze, Modigliani and Cohen, Modigliani and Sutch, Modigliani and Shiller, even M&M (grandfather and Wall Street's Leah Modigliani). That way a whole generation of leading scholars began as proteges of one Master.

Franco never did really leave Italy. At MIT a revolving circle of Italian graduate students spiced our common rooms. Moreover, Modigliani's advice concerning policy as Italy advanced within the surging European Common Market – when heeded – greatly helped his homeland. To know one country you must know more than one. Modigliani was a deeper adviser on American matters because of his Italian understandings.

Here is but one example. In the late 1970s Modigliani (with Cohen) made Wall Street headlines when he declared that the Dow Jones Index deserved a doubling of evaluation. More important than this prediction was the reason for it. Wall Street tipsters understood that, under anticipated inflation, bonds deserved (so to speak) a much lower price/earnings (P/E) ratio. What's sauce for the goose is sauce for the gander: investment bankers therefore believed that stocks should also be priced down to equally low P/E ratios.

Knowing European inflation experience, Modigliani and Cohen reminded us that accounting earnings for corporations never do include price-tag increments on the firms' steady state ownership of machinery, structures and inventories. Their needed correction mandated that marking down stocks' P/E ratio fully to match bonds' P/E would prove to be a mistake in the long run. Subsequent events proved how right they were, when what had been a 700 Dow Jones was soon on its way far beyond 1400.

Clever economists are not always wise economists. When I came to know Harvard's Schumpeter well, I was not surprised to learn that this sparkling mind had been president of a bankrupt Austrian bank during the post-World War I inflation. Even at age 20, I would never have chosen one so limited in gravitas to be custodian of my paltry nest egg.

By contrast at MIT and for other non-profit academies, Modigliani's advice proved useful, especially in the longer run. In China, before earthquakes, dogs are supposed to whine. The week before the 1987 Black October record Wall Street crash, Modigliani did not like the atmospheric noises. As portfolio insurance, he bought normally-priced puts. Doing so well with them, he went back for some more of that good stuff. But now they were twelve times more expensive. His smaller coup was to pass them up as over-priced.

The same shrewdness characterized Modigliani's advice against President Bush's program to "save social security" by letting participants take into self-managed private accounts part of their compulsory contributions. Knowing Chilean and Swedish experiments, Modigliani understood 1) that this was an inefficient way to get help from equities, and 2) that withdrawals by the more affluent would be for them to renege on the solemn covenants the historic system was premised upon. The week he died, Franco was working hard to explain the intergenerational accounting involved.

* * * *

The Modigliani brain children are too numerous and varied to be noticed in my limited space. A brief sample can be listed.

    1. At Carnegie, with Simon and others, Franco contributed to dynamic control theory. Although Franco never did accept as gospel the Lucas-Sargent rational expectationism, he did apply at the micro level the Richard Muth version of mean expectation.

    2. To the economics masses, perhaps the Modigliani-Miller theorem is best known. It reaches the counterintuitive conclusion that *any* degree of debt leverage can be optimal for a firm. Why? Because share buyers can *undo* algebraically whatever the firm has done. Two pitfalls must be warned against. 1) Readers forget that often firms can borrow cheaper and more safely than median investors can. 2) If people in Society A are more risk averse than people in Society B, do realize that in the ideal normative steady state, B will be choosing somewhat riskier methods of corn production than A will. For each person and polity, there will not be indifference over what degree of stochastic risk-taking will end up being chosen. Modigliani-Miller, properly understood, does comprehend that.

3. For me, Modigliani's life-cycle theory of saving and bequeathing is first among equals. It is rooted in intergenerational accounting and explains why rapidly growing societies tend to be higher-saving than are slowly-declining societies. I rank this paradigm far above Friedman's permanent income hypothesis and various post-Harrod exponential tautologies.

4. Particularly with Ando, Modigliani was a parent of the MIT-Penn-Fed macro model. This had for years an informal usefulness at both the Federal Reserve and the Bank of Italy. Nihilists opine that economists have zero edge to forecast future macroeconomic trajectories. Not only did the MIT-Penn-Fed prove useful, but inside the confidential bureaucracy of the Fed pieces of it live on. As Chairman Walter Wriston learned the hard way at Citibank, MV = PQ models of 1950 type generated excessive squared errors of estimates and did so even after Ptolemaic epicycles were glued on to St. Louis Federal Reserve Bank versions. Paradoxically, today's Taylor-like rules, which were generated out of actual past economic history, could also have been generated out of the MIT-Penn-Fed equations themselves. Street-smart Franco never believed in the rational expectations view that policy changes can in the end affect only nominal price levels, being impotent to perturb significantly such real variables as unemployment and real outputs.

5. With Sutch and others, Modigliani grappled with the term structure of interest rates. (Paradoxically, his recognition that different investor types had favorite domiciles of particular debt instruments partially qualifies the Modigliani-Miller theorem.) From 1950 to 1975, lower-income families put their savings in three percent saving accounts; proceeds from them were lent to leveraged purchasers of new and old homes. In a reverse Robin Hood operation, with the connivance of bureaucratic fiats, it was kind of a case where the richer 'rob' the 'poorer'. Only amateurs in the art of trading believe that there are easy pickings to be had if only one reads the term structure of the public debt cleverly. Most of what is obvious is *already* in the posted market prices. The superlative long-term trader somehow successfully second guesses what is obvious and moves ahead of next market moves. Nihilists misunderstand their self-contradiction between belief that economic events are unpredictable at the same time that no safe excess returns are earnable. Modigliani's multi-variable causal models

contrasted well with the Friedman monistic positivisms. Franco understood that economic history is neither a stationary time series nor is it meaningless chaos. During Friedman's own lifetime, the M in MV = PQ became, because of endogenous exogenous innovational institutional change, a vector of money substitutes, thereby vitiating that some one M_0 or M_{13} could invariably move price levels.

A final anecdote

I never expected to make the grade of being a co-author with Franco. Just as a revolution once began on a tennis court, it was on a Belmont, Massachusetts, doubles court that the Samuelson-Modigliani article(s) were born. Between serves partner Franco asked partner Paul: "What do you think of Luigi Pasinetti's new result?" "Don't know it. How does it go?" "Pasinetti deduces that a rise in the fraction of income that workers save cannot raise the ultimate equilibrium." "Can it be that simple? In a plain vanilla Harrod model, the saving fractions of workers and rentiers are equal. Why won't a further *ceteris paribus* rise in workers fraction alone raise Harrod's average saving ratio and thereby eventually create a higher K/L ratio?"

That's what I vaguely remember. There followed for me a tiring three months. Once a week we met to discuss our joint findings. Busy Franco had to catch up with where we had left off before we could advance one inch. My English assistant thought him to be maybe slow. I corrected her: No, he is *deep* and will not leave anything unresolved. In the end our dialogue with Pasinetti I hope did leave each side correct under the *different* technological and institutional structures brought to the problem.

In memoriam

These days more than once a month events occur that make me wish Franco were alive to give his take on them. That's the true immortality that only scholars can hope for.

851

BOURNEUF, Alice. October 2, 1912–December 7, 1980. Economist.

In an age when career opportunities for women were significantly limited in economics and other disciplines, Alice Bourneuf by merit and force of character earned entrance into the elite group of Harvard-Radcliffe scholars when the Age of Schumpeter was replacing the venerable age of Taussig. She was born in Haverhill, Massachusetts, the tenth of eleven children in a very religious family, and she remained a devoted Catholic all her life. Her ancestry stemmed from early Acadian settlers. Her Canadian-born father, Volusien Modeste Bourneuf, was a carpenter who ran a successful construction business. Her mother, Jessie Marie d'Entremont, had been trained as a teacher before she left her native Nova Scotia. After Alice's father died, when she was two, the family moved to the Boston area, where Alice graduated from Newton High School in 1929. During her Radcliffe College years she was a commuter; she graduated Phi Beta Kappa and magna cum laude in 1933.

With the encouragement of her professors, she decided to continue her graduate studies at Harvard. Bourneuf belonged to two minorities: she was a woman; and in the epoch when Boston Cardinal O'Connell and Harvard president A. Lawrence Lowell had guarded interrelations, Bourneuf, like Joseph Kennedy, was the rather rare Catholic who chose to go to Harvard. In Professor Frank Taussig's famous graduate course, the few women were relegated to the rear rows; deemed even worse than children, they were to be neither seen nor heard in Taussig's famous Socratic dialogues. Taussig had a reputation for automatically giving women students the grade of C, while in Joseph Schumpeter's succeeding graduate seminar the grade was transformed into the perfunctory "woman's A," but Bourneuf later confided to a fellow economist that Taussig had in fact given her an A. Among her Harvard classmates were John Kenneth Galbraith and Paul Samuelson.

Job prospects were bleak during the Great Depression, especially for women economists, and Bourneuf took a job teaching at Rosemont College in Pennsylvania from 1937 to 1939. After receiving her MA from Radcliffe in 1939, she went to Belgium to undertake research for her doctoral dissertation. Her stay ended abruptly in May 1940 when the Germans invaded Belgium, forcing her to leave her research notes behind as she fled Hitler's war. Then at Harvard she became Professor Seymour Harris's research assistant prior to joining federal government service in Washington. Her first position was with the Office of Price Administration, specializing in wartime administration of export-import prices. Her stature as an economist soared at the Federal Reserve Board, where she worked on international monetary plans for the postwar period. At the famous Bretton Woods conference in 1944 that set up the International Monetary Fund (IMF) and the World Bank, there were only two women economists: Bourneuf from the Federal Reserve and the State Department's ELEANOR LANSING DULLES.

After the war Bourneuf worked in the research department of the IMF in Washington from 1946 to 1948, and then moved to Oslo, Norway, to represent there the Marshall Plan's program of large-scale economic and military aid to European economies devastated by the war. Many colleagues believe she regarded her work in Oslo, where she served as local representative of executive director Richard Bissell, to have been the high point in her public policy career. Important too was her tour of duty from 1951 to 1953 in the Paris office of the Marshall Plan as guardian helper for Norway's amazing postwar recovery. Her 1958 book, *Norway: The Planned Revival*, won kudos as a definitive work on the Marshall Plan's Scandinavian efforts.

When Bourneuf left government service in 1953, she returned to academic life, which may have seemed something of an anticlimax—a common experience for many of her generation. A Littauer School of Public Administration Fellowship at Harvard in 1953–54 allowed her to write up her Norway research and receive the PhD from Radcliffe in 1955. She joined the economics department of Mount Holyoke College in 1954, and was appointed a visiting associate professor at the University of California at Berkeley from 1957 to 1959.

Bourneuf's finest moment, however, was perhaps still to come—when she chose to accept the challenge of an important role in bringing Boston College's adequate economics department up into the very frontier of modern mainstream economics. Before World War II, the leading Catholic colleges were largely staffed by ordained Jesuits; some of Joseph Schumpeter's best graduate students had been recruited from their ranks. With the postwar explosion in student numbers, both undergraduate and graduate, the center of gravity was to shift more toward lay careerists; and with the permanent slowdown in recruitment of ordained orders, the secular component had continued to increase in the various Catholic universities. In 1959 Alice Bourneuf became the first woman appointed a full professor in the College of Arts and Sciences at Boston College.

At Boston College, the team of department-head Father Robert McEwen and Professor Bourneuf must have seemed, if not like a hurricane, at least like a Grade 3 tropical storm. Aside from Bourneuf's expertise, energy, and creative public research in the field of macroeconomics, her major asset was guileless devotion to excellence. What she lost in the short run from adhering to stubborn meritocracy, she and her colleagues more than won in the long run. What you saw in her was what you got. Her fulfilled life disproved Leo Durocher's Darwinian maxim, "Good guys end up last."

Alice Bourneuf never married, but she always maintained an amazingly wide circle of friends. After her retirement from Boston College in 1977, she moved to Ogunquit, Maine, stoically battling terminal cancer while still maintaining her research and training activities. She died in Boston on December 7, 1980, at the age of sixty-eight. Her many scholarly co-workers and students kept alive the memory of an important player in what is remembered as a golden age in economics.

Bibliography: Biographical material about Alice Bourneuf is found in the Radcliffe College Archives at the Schlesinger Library, Radcliffe Institute for Advanced Study, Harvard University. The Boston College Archives also contains material about her career. In addition to *Norway: The Planned Revival* (1958), Bourneuf published extensively in journals such as the *American Economic Review,* the *Review of Economic Statistics,* and the *Review of Social Economy.* Bourneuf's own account of her wartime experience appeared as "Chestnut Hill Girl Tells Thrilling Story of Fleeing Belgium," *Boston Daily Globe,* June 1, 1940. David A. Belsley, Edward J. Kanes, Paul A. Samuelson, and Robert M. Solow, eds., *Inflation, Trade and Taxes: Essays in Honor of Alice Bourneuf* (1976), includes a tribute by Samuelson. An obituary appeared in the *Boston Globe* on December 12, 1980.

PAUL A. SAMUELSON

166 Atkinson, Cnossen, Ladd, Mieszkowski, Pestieau, and Samuelson

6. Affectionate Reminiscences of Richard Musgrave
Paul A. Samuelson[16]

When I arrived by (lucky) miscalculation at Harvard's Graduate Economics, I found already there such stars as Richard Musgrave, Abram Bergson, Wolfgang Stolper, Shigeto Tsuru, and Alice Bourneuf. I have forgotten why and how Richard's hegira to America began at Rochester University. Already at age 24, Musgrave had the gravitas that our master Schumpeter never did attain.

Thanks in part to the beastliness of Adolf Hitler, Harvard's economics was then reviving from a somewhat lean period. Allyn Young had died young in London. The venerable Frank Taussig was winding down his legendary EC11 graduate theory course, which was famous for his masterful use of something called "the Socratic method." (Taussig told me privately, around 1938, that after his Washington wartime service in World War I, he had never been able to catch up to current economic theory. For that reason, he had reverted to trade theory, and under his direction important Ph.D. theses were published by Jacob Viner, Harry White, James Angell, and other yesteryear worthies.)

After 1932 Schumpeter had stolen Wassily Leontief for Harvard from Wesley Mitchell's National Bureau in New York. By 1936 Gottfried Haberler had switched permanently from the League of Nations to Harvard. One year later when the new Littauer School of Public Administration was funded, Alvin Hansen came from Minnesota to Harvard. (Paradoxically, his early somewhat critical review of Keynes's general theory led to this lucky if uncharacteristic Harvard appointment. With Hansen's arrival, Harvard's primacy in Keynesian macroeconomics was assured.)

Like Dick's luck, all of this was my good luck, too. Had I remained at my Chicago alma mater, I'd have missed participating in any of the three great twentieth-century revolutions in economics: in (a) the Cournot–Chamberlin–Robinson imperfect-competition revolution; in (b) the Keynesian macro revolution; and finally (c) in the mathematization-of-economics revolution. (For me, aside from the luck to be in Leontief's first permitted Harvard seminar on mathematical economics, I was able to become a protegé [maybe the only protegé] of the mathematician Edwin Bidwell Wilson, who himself had been Willard Gibbs's only protegé at Yale.)

Richard, five years my senior, was more judicious than I in discerning some merit both in Hayek's 1931 *Prices and Production* and in Keynesianisms and Hansenisms.

---
[16] Professor emeritus, Massachusetts Institute of Technology, Department of Economics, 50 Memorial Drive, Cambridge MA 02142-1347, Fax: +1-617-253-0560

It is no great stretch to say that it was Musgrave's Harvard Ph.D. thesis that brought to America news and details about the Wicksell–Lindahl theory of public goods. I look back with considerable embarrassment on the fact that my 1954 *Review of Economics and Statistics* paper on public goods received so many citations. Certainly all that I knew of the historic public-goods literature came from oral communication with Musgrave and perusal of his 1939 dissertation.

It will help readers to know that my sole reason for writing up the 1954 paper came from the fact that an obscure Rand researcher, David Novick, submitted to Seymour Harris as editor of the *Review of Economics and Statistics* a screed denying that mathematics had anywhere previously been useful in economics. Harris deputized me to be judge and prosecuting attorney and defense counsel, as well as final jury (a not untypical Harris caper). For no other reason than to specify one example where math could manifestly be useful, my tossing of the dice led to the topic of Lindahl public goods.

Imagining counterfactual history, surely it would have been better if there had been a 1954 item by Musgrave and Samuelson that led to a post-1970 Nobel Prize in economics. Indeed, many discerning academics believe that Stockholm erred in not honoring the author of Musgrave's *Theory of Public Finance* – the acknowledged successor in the second half of the twentieth century to A. C. Pigou's *The Economics of Welfare* and *A Study in Public Finance*.

My generation knew Dick Musgrave as the Prince of Wales to Alvin Hansen's eclectic macroeconomics. Wherever he was – at Michigan, Hopkins, Princeton, or Harvard – Musgrave sat at the head of the table. On my own gravestone it ought to read: "Served on the Harvard *ad hoc* committee that rubber-stamped Musgrave's return to Harvard."

Sciences both progress and regress. Since about 1980, under the influence of libertarians like Milton Friedman, the quasi-paternalistic "merit wants" of Musgrave have too often become forgotten. When competitive markets accomplish mere Pareto optimality sans Rawls–Aquinas distributive justice, it can be preferable to sacrifice Pareto optimality in some degree for agreed-upon incremental ethical optimality. A good enough cause can be worth its cost in mere Pareto optimality – a subtle tautology. We'll need future Musgraves to remind us of the pragmatic limits to state-enforced equalization programs.

One trait of great scholars will be their versatility. Too little appreciated is the wartime *Quarterly Journal of Economics* gem by R. A. Musgrave and E. D. Domar, "Proportional Income Taxation and Risk Taking." Years before either Modigliani and Miller, Harry Markowitz, or behavioral economists, this item provides an early specification of the optimal-portfolio problem. Critics of New Deal progressive tax structures alleged that they inhibit invest-

855

ing in productive but risky ventures. Domar and Musgrave cogently argued that the reverse was true. Under full tax offsets for losses, high marginal tax rates *mandated* enhanced risk-taking.

In closing I permit myself one last anecdote. Years ago, when MIT was competing with Harvard for Kenneth Arrow, Dick phoned me. "Paul," he said. "Harvard needs Arrow more than MIT does. He should come here." My reply was, "Dick, you may be right. But by that logic maybe you should never have left Princeton."

2 An economist even greater than his high reputation

Paul A. Samuelson

In print I have told the story more than once how my University of Chicago tutor, Eugene Staley, answered my naive beginner's question, 'Who's the world's greatest economist?' Without hesitation he answered, 'John Maynard Keynes (rhymes with "brains").' That was a good call, especially since it was made before the classic 1936 *General Theory* and just after the disappointing two-volume *Treatise on Money*.

Once not bitten, twice non-shy. After arriving at the Harvard Graduate School I asked a lively assistant professor there, John Cassells, 'Who is the world's best young economist?' 'John Hicks,' he said. I came to verify this on my own, from reading Hicks's 1932 *Theory of Wages*. My reason for particularly mentioning this is because Hicks in his characteristic way disclaimed in middle life that his first book had been a good one. We authors cannot be trusted in evaluating our own brainchildren.

Neither can award committees be trusted in awarding honors. In the fourth year of the Bank of Sweden's new Alfred Nobel Prize in economics, the Stockholm Committee of the Royal Swedish Academy of Science made two qualitative misjudgments: they gave only one-half a Nobel to each of Sir John Hicks and Kenneth Arrow. In my considered judgment, Arrow deserved two Nobel Prizes in economics: one for his *Social Choice* classics and one more at least for his novel theory of complete stochastic markets. Hicks himself, meanwhile, certainly deserved an early full prize for his large corpus of important contributions. At the time I suspected that punctilious Swedish resentment against an English scholar who was cavalier in recognizing and documenting the related publications of contemporary researchers – as when Hicks learned a lot about non-linear business cycles from Richard Goodwin, a less appreciated economist – persuaded a committee majority to pair the names of Hicks and Arrow. Certainly, it was a stretch to justify the pairing by pointing out that both had contributed to general equilibrium theory. That they did do. But what each did was quite different. Arrow and Gerard Debreu, or Arrow and Lionel McKenzie, would have made better sense.

Within the United Kingdom itself, Hicks's home country, in my calibration he never did quite receive his full measure of recognition. For one

49

thing, he was not primarily in the tradition of 'pope' Alfred Marshall. No capital offense, since at the LSE Hicks drifted more into the better tradition of the Swedish Knut Wicksell. Second, Hicks was an Oxford undergraduate during lean seasons there. Third, without being a Mt. Pelerin conservative such as Friedrich Hayek or Milton Friedman, centrist John Hicks was not quite 'politically correct' by contemporary leftish Oxbridge standards. It may be no mortal sin in academia to be a bit Napoleonic, but sometimes it will be held against you.

The purist economist Tjalling Koopmans was against fine writing by scientists: it gave, he believed, undeserved weight to your views. If it is criminal to be a facile writer, few economists need fear indictment. Hicks was an exception. He wrote understandable prose and, being satisfied with his thoughts, he never suffered writer's block. R. G. D. Allen, Hicks's more mathematical comrade at the LSE, told me that, when Hicks asked about the theory of determinants and quadratic forms, Roy Allen lent him Eugen Netto's little book on the subject. 'And in a few months, John came back with his 1939 *Value and Capital*.' William Makepeace Thackeray declared that *Vanity Fair* was a novel without a heroine. I declare that the Oxford University Press first edition of *Value and Capital* was without improvements, without resetting a single page. Although Allen and Hicks's articles (1934a, 1934b) were written without knowledge of the wartime Italian classics of Eugen Slutsky, their papers did essentially complete Vilfredo Pareto's quest for the testable structure of consumer's demand theory. It says something for Hicks's good judgment that, while G. C. Evans (1930), Allen (1932), Nicholas Georgescu-Roegen (1936), and Samuelson (1947) allocated considerable space to non-integrable demand structures, Hicks fairly early on concentrated on the more relevant case of integrable demand structures. Along with H. Hotelling (1932, 1935) and M. Allais (1943), Hicks wrote sure-footedly about generalized consumers' surplus.

When Hicks was an early reviewer of Keynes's *General Theory* he seemed to think that he and Keynes were competing rivals to arrive at the North Pole, where the Holy Grail of a new paradigm was to be found. I never quite understood that belief. Later, Hicks's famous 1937 graphical model of intersecting IS and LM curves did become a classroom workhorse to exposit Keynes's paradigm. There was nothing that I remember in Hicks's 'A Suggestion for Simplifying the Theory of Money' (1935a) that implied *those* curves, however. In any case, very much of 1937 Hicks (1937a) was derived from Roy Harrod, who had himself earlier commuted from Oxford to Cambridge to join the famous Kahn–Robinson–Meade–Harrod 'circus' that helped generate, in 1932–5, Keynes's 1936 *General Theory*.

We must accept great scholars as they are, warts and all. In 1962, a decade after Harry Markowitz (1952, 1959) had published the much-used quadratic programming mean:variance approach to optimal portfolio construction, Hicks published that same approach. If Hicks had already worked it out for himself beforehand and independently, it would still have been inexcusable to submit this to *The Economic Journal*. Alas, more likely Hicks and the peer reviewers of this one-time world-beating learned journal were so out of touch with the frontier of modern finance theory that they were still unaware of Markowitz's Nobel-calibre contributions.

I need to admit explicitly that being Napoleonic can itself contribute to important scholarly progress. It led Hicks to nominate as an important organizing theme for economic history the origins and evolution of the market mechanism. Although his suggestion may not have caught on with history-trained experts in economic history, I believe that economics-trained experts would do well to explore Hicks's lead further. Interestingly, no large society has been known to achieve progressive growth and a high standard of living with prolonged life expectancies without considerable reliance on supply-and-demand market-clearing mechanisms. Utopian reformers, impressed by self-sufficient biological families and occasional kibbutz-like small groups, have favored socialist regimens. (Albert Einstein was one such. Perhaps Noam Chomsky, the famous linguistics innovator and formidable polemicist, is another. We are not preprogrammed from birth to answer such questions by *a priori* thought alone. Analytical sifting of relevant evidence can alone balance the imponderables concerning this conundrum.)

Indulge me to add one further example of Hicks's sage judgment. In 1958 the annual meeting of the International Economic Association (IEA) was held on the Greek island of Corfu. Sir Austin Robinson had scheduled it there to trap Piero Sraffa into attending. The mountain was brought to Mohammed, but that did not coax Sraffa into uttering any memorable words on capital theory. Still, nature abhors a vacuum, which Nicholas Kaldor helped fill with *two* late papers: along with the draft the Kaldor commentator was handed on the day of the Kaldor lecture, was the stenographer's different text of what came out of the Kaldor mouth. The published 1958 IEA volume was a vintage issue. All the same, the single remark that has stayed with me longest was an off-the-cuff intervention by Hicks, saying (in paraphrase): 'Do you realize that, in between two neighboring items listed in the order catalogue of a toolmaker, there are a plethora of intermediate items that the supplier will offer if only he is confronted with a critical demand for such an offering.' To the degree that this is correct, the gulf between (i) Clarkian neoclassical marginalism, with an uncountable infinity of alternative techniques, and (ii) a von Neumann technology, with only a finite number of alternative techniques, becomes importantly narrowed.

859

CHAPTER II

REMEMBERING MILTON FRIEDMAN

Paul A. Samuelson

ABSTRACT

Milton Friedman's Contributions from 1929 to 1939, during Depression and later, during the Second World War, 1939-45, are presented in this paper briefly. The pros and cons of his contributions to Monetary Economics are briefly discribed. There are some conceptual differences between Paul A. Samuelson and Milton Friedman, logically elucidated, which is natural at the highest level of intellect. Samuelson's affection to and contact with Milton Friedman are mentioned at every stage in the paper which shows how they were great friends and colleagues.

.....Editor

Milton Friedman's 2006 death in his nineties ended a remarkable epoch. Electorates in most places have moved rightward from the 1929-1939 years of the Great Depression and the 1939-1945 years of World War II.

With the general lay public, Ludwig von Mises, Friedrich Hayek and non-economists like William Buckley have been important writers promoting that change. But the remarkable move to the right inside the economists guild was by far most persuaded by Milton Friedman at Chicago and the Stanford Hoover Institute.

Friedman and I - Milton and Paul - rarely agreed on substantive issues. However, for 74 years since 1932, we have remained friends. That's a tribute to two people. And it contrasts with the historic polemical of debates between Cassel and Wicksell in Sweden and between Hayek and Keynes in Britain.

Here I begin by quoting verbatim my 1976 *Newsweek* column praising Milton Friedman's being awarded the Nobel Prize in economics.

I conclude with some needed second thoughts on different Friedman writings. Time and space preclude me from articulating much more about his pros and his cons. In particular I do not deal here with the fact that the modern computer destroys the notion of any reliable definition of an M in $MV=PQ$.

Milton Friedman, *Newsweek*, October 25, 1976

The economics profession has long expected that Milton Friedman would win the Nobel Prize in Economics. His 1976 award is fitting recognition of his scientific contributions and his scholarly leadership.

There is no need for me to describe in these columns his important views as a conservative economist. His own words speak eloquently for themselves.

What I have to emphasize is that Friedman is the *architect* of much that is best in our conservative tradition and not merely the *expositor* of that viewpoint. Furthermore, the adjective "conservative" does not do proper justice to a thinker who would refuse the steel industry its import quotas, strip Texas of its oil subsidies and deprive the railroads and the trucking interests of their protective regulations.

Why is Milton Friedman "an economist's economist"? Let me point out the ways.

Curriculam Vitae

He started as an undergraduate student of Arthur Burns at Rutgers. No bad beginning. He went on to become a graduate-student star at Columbia and Chicago.

The "Chicago School", with its emphasis on human freedoms and the efficiency of market pricing, can be said to have been founded by Frank Knight, his revered teacher. Under Friedman it has been led to new heights of influence and profundity.

MIT, Harvard, Oxford and every topnotch economics department would today feel deprived and one-sided if the fruitful Chicago viewpoint were not represented on its faculty. This new fact is tribute to one great leader. Scholars are known by their original scientific discoveries. Friedman early made his mark in statistics and mathematical economics. Without being a Keynesian, he pioneered early budgetary measurements of income-consumption patterns and taught our wartime Treasury how to reduce the inflationary gap. Abraham Wald's great breakthrough in the statistical technique called "sequential analysis" stemmed in part from Friedman's realization that it is not necessary to finish testing every egg to infer that a batch is bad. Does this seem simple? So now does Newton's falling apple.

If it pays to reduce risk by insuring, how at the same time can it pay to increase risk by backing long shots? Friedman (with L.J. Savage) provided an answer. Also, Friedman (with Simon Kuznets, Nobel laureate 1971) first analyzed and measured "human capital," the investment we make in our medical and other education and the interest return on this investment.

Do not the rich save more from each dollar than the poor? If so, redistributing income from rich to poor will raise consumption spending and stimulate business. Friedman's investigation of "*the permanent income hypothesis*" revealed that, once we get used to being permanently at a higher income, we in fact save *much the same fraction* of income! That this finding stood up so well to adversary attack demonstrated his Nobel caliber.

Of course it is monetarism that marks Friedman's lifework of the last twenty years. His monumental *A Monetary History of the United States, 1867-1960*, written with Anna Schwartz, clinched his international reputation.

Missions Accomplished

The story the facts tell Friedman is that the price level is determined in the long run by the quantity of money. Contrary to the view of 1939 Keynesians and the stubborn 1959 view of many English economists, the short-run changes in the money supply provide the one factor reliably to half the variance in nominal GNP changes. The rest being primarily noise, *M growth* is the only such significant factor. From this follows his basic prescription: *Keep aggregate M growth constant.*

The fact that he and I, despite our policy disagreements and scientific differences, have remained good friends over 40 years says something perhaps about us, but even more I dare to think about political economy as a science. (*Newsweek*, 25 October 1976).

At birthday parties or eulogies or congratulatory events, as Dr. Samuel Johnson observed, "Speakers are not under [strict] oath." It is appropriate therefore that, at this later date, I should elaborate further on my principal 1976 themes: Friedman's positive additions to modern evolving micro theory; his formulations of the "permanent income" hypothesis; his take on modern mathematical statistics; and finally, in too abbreviated space, Friedman's MV=PQ revivals of 1911 Irving Fisher-Alfred Marshall.

1. Like most frontier scholars, Friedman shared a high I.Q. with contemporaries such as A.P. Lerner, John R. Hicks, Nicky Kaldor or James Meade. His especial forte was quickness in polemical debate. An illuminating scenario is Milton telling Abraham Wald, the creator of sequential analysis, "What you mean, Abe, is this and not that". Only sometimes would it be the case that Abe agreed with Milton later on the staircase.

Because of limited youthful income, Milton was not an early precocious publisher. He was already 23 when his first *Quarterly Journal of Economics* paper appeared. His first substantial book on human capital (with Simon Kuznets) appeared when he was 33. Gary Becker, an important

1867–1960

admiring colleague, noted that when Chicago called Friedman to a tenured professorial chair in the 1940's, that was based on his personal reputation and promise and not on a substantial inventory of important publishing.

A prolific scholar like Hicks or Lerner had a bibliography measured in terms of items or words many times greater than Friedman's. Becker's summing up on Friedman in the 1991 Shils book on great Chicago Scholars speaks mostly of his persuasive ideological dominance on the Midway and on the post-1960 libertarian *Weltanschauung* of the economics profession.

2. Milton's publications on the "permanent income" hypothesis was of seminal importance. My generation of wartime Keynesians was crucially wrong in fearing that the 1939-1945 prodigious propensities to save rather than consume could be extrapolated into the after war years, and would mandate massive deficit fiscal spending to offset mass unemployment.

Evolving science is usually a group effort. Contemporaneously with Friedman, the names of Kuznets, Dension, Duesenberry, Modigliani, Tobin, Woytinsky and Fellner must be noted as other correctors of the 1945 paranoia. (Tom Kuhn documents that a dozen names discovered—in Darwin-Wallace or Newton-Leibniz fashion—the Law of Conservation of Energy. In this respect macroeconomic advance apes the harder natural science.)

It should be pointed out that among that mob, it is Friedman who goes all the way—beyond the assertion that temporary income tends to be saved more than permanent income—on to the view that numerical saving propensity of the millionaires is significantly the same as those for the lowest quartiles of income and wealth. What documented *that?*

3. The subject of human capital that Kuznets-Friedman pioneered won for Chicago's Theodore Schultz a Nobel Prize in 1979. The Kuznets Friedman NBER paper on that subject had been delayed because its manuscript was criticized for its claim that physicians' incomes were as high as they were because certification for competence was kept irrationally high in order to keep doctors scarce and prosperous.

All can agree that trade associations do always have selfish monopolistic motives to pump up their incomes. But only Milton Friedman could argue—argue seriously—*that therefore everyone should be able to practice surgery.* That is a bizarre stretch, bred out of Friedman's libertarian gut rather than his syllogistic brain. Proof is that Friedman seriously opposed legislation requiring drivers on the public highways to pass a competence test.

Once conservative Bill Buckley dialogued with conservative Milton Friedman. I paraphrase this discussion:

B.B. Yes, some public regulation can be necessary. Suppose the democratic legislature made prostitution legal. Surely then requiring prostitutes to pass a monthly test for venereal disease is a worthy idea.

M.F. Not at all. If a woman on the street, professing to be disease-free does infect a customer, that will hurt her reputation. If, nevertheless, she does infect you, then that is a *tort* that you can sue her for in court.

When Friedman's conservative Chicago colleagues chided him for such extremisms, he was unrepentant. Someone in each generation must go all the way with the truth, however much that dissipates his influence - that was his credo.

Darwin gave Friedman every good gift of I.Q. and originality. But withheld from him was the precious gift of "maybe".

4. Space does not permit needed criticism of Friedman's mono-monetarism, which seriously prescribed abolishing all central banks, replacing each by a machine that, in accordance with $MV = PQ$, always spits out $M(t)$ currency at the same exponential rate that full employment $Q(t)$ grows; then, because of his belief that $V(t)$ is a quasi-constant (the *only* macro constant!), the $P(t)$ level will be free of inflation and Say's Law will keep outputs and consumption optimal.

Once around 1970 *Time* magazine opined: Keynes is dead as Keynesianism failed to solve the stagflation of the 1970's. Friedman is the new King successor to king Keynes.

Time never did notice that OPEC and other supply shocks, including having to dismantle Nixon-Burns price and wage controls, would not have been cured by Friedman's M Machine.

Before and after the Friedman-Schwartz. *A Monetary History of the United States* (1963) macroeconomists understood that Money Matters. Jim Tobin was the Hans Christian Andersen child who pointed out that it does not follow from this that *only* Money matters. Great "quantity" theorists like Fisher and Wicksell, before they died, lost confidence about V's constancy. Before Friedman died, no scrap of writing known to me registered regrets for his mono-monetarism:

Positivists measure a theory's merits by its degree of agreement with empirical economic history. Walter Wriston—head of Citigroup, the world's largest bank—abolished overnight his monetarist economic staff when even by specifying epicycle after epicycle, $MV = PQ$ could not approximate to the imperfect accuracies of Greenspan, Eckstein, and Federal Reserve Bank forecasting. Friedman's monetary proved to be neither tasty nor nutritious. Rest in Peace.

REFERENCES

Fisher, I. 1991. *The Purchasing Power of Money.* New York, Macmillan.

Friedman, M.1935. Professor Pigou's methods for measuring elasticities of demand from budgetary data, *Quarterly Journal of Economics (*Nov): 151-63

Friedman, M. and S. Kuznets. 1945. *Income from Independent Professional Practice.* New York: National Bureau of Economic Research.

Friedman, M. and L.J. Savage. 1948. The Utility analysis of choices involving risk, *Journal of Political Economy,* 56: 279-304.

Friedman, M. and A. J. Schwartz. 1963. *A Monetary History of the United States. 1867-1960.* Princeton. Princeton University Press for the National Bureau of Economic Research.

Keynes, J.M. 1936. *The General Theory of Employment, Interest and Money.* Reprinted in **The Collected Writing of John Maynard Keynes**, Vol. VII. London, Macmillan for the Royal Economic Society.

Marshall, A. 1923. *Money, Credit and Commerce.* London, Macmillan.

Shils, E. 1991. *Remembering the University of Chicago: Teachers, Scientists and Scholars* Chicago, Centennial Publications.of the University of Chicago Press.

Personal report

A few remembrances of Friedrich von Hayek (1899–1992)

Paul A. Samuelson

Department of Economics, Massachusetts Institute of Technology, Cambridge, MA 02142, USA

Hayek was the seventh to receive the Bank of Sweden's new Nobel Prize in economics. In my judgment his was a worthy choice. And yet in the 1974 senior common rooms of Harvard and MIT, the majority of the inhabitants there seemed not to even know the name of this new laureate. (By contrast, the following year when I was in Stockholm to celebrate the 75th anniversary of the original five Nobel Prizes, it was my vague impression that the Royal Swedish Academy electors paid greater deference to Hayek than to their own native son Myrdal. Some majority fiends on the election committee must have known that they were making two opposite ideologues furious over their being ironically paired.)

Rise and Fall of 1931 *Prices and Production*

There were good historical reasons for fading memories of Hayek within the mainstream last half of the twentieth century economist fraternity. In 1931, Hayek's *Prices and Production* had enjoyed an ultra-short Byronic success. In retrospect hindsight tells us that its mumbo-jumbo about the period of production grossly misdiagnosed the macroeconomics of the 1927–1931 (and the 1931–2007) historical scene.

When a centrist like me says this about an extremist like Hayek, readers have a right to reserve judgment. More weighty was the later opinion to the same effect of the conservative Lionel Robbins. It was Robbins who had brought Hayek out of Austria to the LSE. It was Robbins who wrote a 1934 Hayekian book entitled *The Great Depression*. Not so very long after 1934, Robbins repudiated his own early take, saying in effect, I must have been a bit loony at the time.

Aside from the substance of Hayek's (1931) text, part of his short-lived popularity came from the fact that many in England, annoyed by Maynard Keynes's unorthodox testimonies before the 1930 Macmillan Committee, hoped that Hayek would be the White Knight to slay the Black Dragon.

Productivity and reputation of Keynes itself fluctuated in Kondratief waves. His 1930 two-volume *Treatise on Money* posterity judged to have been an anti-climatic flop. But the deeper the drop into the 1929–1935 Great Depression, the more rapidly came the recognition of Keynes as top dog in the twentieth century. (In 1932 as a 16-year-old freshman, I asked my Chicago tutor, Eugene Staley: "Who is the world's greatest economist?" He answered, "John Maynard Keynes." For once I never became tempted to question the authority of my many great teachers.)

Gentle Charles Darwin had Thomas Huxley to be his bulldog for evolution. Sraffa (1932) must have been editor Keynes's bulldog to annihilate *Prices and Production*, and its author. I never much admired Sraffa's methodological contentions in that debate but at least his item did have the merit of introducing for the first time Sraffa's novel concept of "the *own* rate of interest" in terms of corn or rye or caviar.

For my money more to the point was Richard Kahn's simple oral 1932 statement: If Hayek believes that the spending of newly printed currency on employment and consumption will *worsen* our current terrible depression, then Hayek is a nut. Alas, one fatal error eclipses a few elementary true truths á la Mises and Hayek: Easy money *now* often does entail tighter money *later* which will come as a surprise to uncompleted projects and new contingent contemplated investment projects.

Hayek himself, naively, diagnosed the fall of his 1931 opus as due to the fact that his period-of-production mutterings there did not do full justice to the not-yet-completed Austrian theory of capital (Menger, Böhm et al.).

Therefore, heroically but hopelessly, he wasted years on a task that he was grossly under-equipped to handle. Hayek's (1941) *The Pure Theory of Capital* was not stillborn. But it was a pebble thrown into the pool of economic science that seemingly left nary a ripple.

Hayek's grave defeats in the early 1930s predisposed him in the World War II years to write what he entitled, *The Road to Serfdom* (1944). I will postpone my take on that bestseller.

0167-2681/$ – see front matter
doi:10.1016/j.jebo.2008.07.001

So you might say Hayek as an economist fell into what physicists call a black hole. Wisely, libertarian Hayek turned away to weighty constitutional and philosophical interests. And from his pen came commendable items on history of economics doctrines. (One example is Hayek's biographical item on the love affair and marriage between John Stuart Mill and Harriet Taylor.)

The Jewel in Economist Hayek's Crown: Information Economics

Just prior to Hayek's departure from post World War II mainstream economics came what must be hailed as his greatest important contribution to economic science. It can be well understood if I make reference to the famous debate between Lerner–Lange and Ludwig von Mises (1935) over the role of the supply-and-demand mechanism in a socialist state. Lerner (1934), as well as Lange and Taylor (1938) quasi-independently, suggested that playing the game of parametric supply–demand auctioning could optimally organize a socialist society that had evolved beyond historic capitalism.

Arguably this general notion might be traced back to Adam Smith's legendary Invisible Hand, which led society unconsciously to achieve the maximal "general good." Individual avarice, under market checks and balances, achieved this happy state. A more sophisticated version of the same idea came in the 1890s from Pareto (1896–97) and Barone (1908), long before Arrow-Debreu breakthroughs. Pareto deduced the mathematical theorem that the determinative equations of Walrasian general equilibrium mimicked exactly the maximizing welfare conditions for utopias.

By contrast, Mises in his polemics prior to Lerner–Lange, had contended that only under *actual* capitalism could one *even define* a post-Bentham welfare economics. Autobiographically, I can testify that most economists born after 1910 at that time would have voted Lerner and Lange to be the debate winner, with Mises as the prime loser. (Even my Harvard mentor Schumpeter saw some merit in the Lerner–Lange conjectures.[1])

In the 1940s Friedrich Hayek in an invited Harvard lecture introduced a new dynamic element into the debate. Call it "information economics." The broad competitive markets, Hayek proclaimed, were the recipients of heterogeneous idiosyncratic bits of individuals' information. Playing for matches rather than for real money or blood was as different an economic dynamics as night is from day.

I was not at all the only one to be converted to the view that, as between Abba Lerner, Oskar Lange and Ludwig von mises, Friedrich Hayek was actually the debate's winner. (After the U.S. State Department persuaded Lange to go back to Stalinesque Poland, Lange reportedly lost his lust for auction markets.)

The jury of history judges innovators not by adding linearly their plus and minus contributions. Hayek's 1974 Stockholm Nobel Prize was importantly won for him by his notions about decentralized information economics discussed that day in Cambridge, Massachusetts.

Never mind that Hayek over-praised the optimality of individualistic *spontaneity*. Charles Darwin's genius long earlier had eclectically enumerated both the *pluses and minuses* of individualistic natural selection.

I do not know how much George Stigler had ever been influenced by Hayek when later Stigler's work on information economics helped bring him his Nobel medal. Senior Robert K. Merton, as sociologist, historian and philosopher of history of science, taught us again and again that great things come in pairs and triplets. Darwin had his Wallace. Newton had his Leibniz. Leibniz had his Newton. Thomas Kuhn documented the case that the fundamental Law of Conservation of Energy had a dozen different fathers. Although what each had discovered was not precisely the same thing, maybe at most one of the dozen did understand *all* the nuances.

The Road to "Exactly What?"

The history of economic science is distinguishable from the history of ideas. Adam Smith is little remembered by the lay public for how and whether he got right the pricing of corn and the rent of land. Smith's thumb-nail popular fame comes from his glorification of free enterprise and market capitalism.

So it is with Friedrich Hayek's celebrity as author of the bestseller *The Road to Serfdom*. It was written in London, so to speak on a bus driver's holiday, during the first years of World War II when its author was readjusting himself to the popular rejection of his 1931 *Prices and Production*. As he has written many times, the book was a political polemic against the evolution *away* from pre-1929 market capitalism *toward* the cruel totalitarian state, in which almost certainly the worst type leaders will forge up to the top. (Laboristic Fabian socialists in Britain and Franklin Roosevelt New Deal legislation in America, by innuendo and coherent argument, were believed to be the vulnerable stepping stones toward the serfdom(s) already realized in Lenin-Stalin Russia and Adolph Hitler Nazi Germany.)

Biography is important for the understanding of a scholar's writing. Hayek himself was the son of a Viennese professor of botany. For a century his ancestors, moving from Bohemia to Vienna, were supporters of Emperor Franz Josef's Austro-Hungary Hapsburg empire. (Hence, the respectable honorific "von" in Hayek's own name.)

On Hayek's return from Austria's military defeat by the Allied Italian army, Hayek reports a short infatuation with "socialism." Like a common cold its incidence must have been brief. He has acknowledged the influence of Ludwig von Mises to

---

[1] For the vast 1930s literature on the Lerner–Lange mechanism, see Lange references in Palgrave (1987, vol. 3, pp. 129–131). Aside from nineteenth century related notions by von Mises, it is of interest that ultra-conservative Fred Taylor at the University of Michigan, a textbook writer much admired by Frank Knight and Edward H. Chamberlin, had in his 1928 AEA Presidential Address already sketched the trial and error procedures of Lerner-Lange (Taylor, 1929).

convert him to his lifelong libertarian quasi-*laissez faire* market capitalism. Hayek, along with Mises and Milton Friedman and other libertarians, attended periodic meetings of the Mt. Pelerin Society. (Once it had been suggested to be named the Acton Society, in honor of Lord Acton who was thought to have coined the phrase: "Power corrupts; and absolute power corrupts absolutely." However, Acton's earlier role in Vatican debates disqualified him for the honor. Having spent a lifetime near libertarians, I can confirm that they are an individualistic idiosyncratic bunch. For example, my conservative mentor Gottfried Haberler was defined by Mises to be a "communist." The number of Mt. Pelerin resignations never quite reached the number of its new members.)

Anthropological experts in "content analysis," focusing their microscopes on the Hayek text (1944), might score its impact to be traceable to both (1) its version of history and (2) its projection of the future. Post Bismarck social legislation and Weimar unorthodoxies allegedly bred Hitler's horror state and horror camps (sic). When Frank Knight peer reviewed Hayek's book for an American edition, he blessed its message but demurred at its shallow handling of history (see Hayek, 2007).

Two-thirds of a century after the book got written, hindsight confirms how inaccurate its innuendo about the *future* turned out to be. Consider only Sweden's fig-leaf middle way. As I write in 2007, Sweden and other Scandinavian places have somewhat lowered the fraction of GDP they use to devote through government. But still they are the most "socialistic" by Hayek's crude definition. Where are their horror camps? Have the vilest elements risen there to absolute power? When reports are compiled on "measurable unhappiness," do places like Sweden, Denmark, Finland and Norway best epitomize serfdoms?

No. Of course not. American conservatives like my old friend the late David McCord Wright, confronted by such counter evidence would say to me up to his last years: "Paul, just you wait." I never tired of waiting.

Actually, let the contents-analyst anthropologist go on to put her microscope on the many forewords to *The Road to Serfdom* quoted in forewords by the late Milton Friedman (see Hayek, 1994). She will conclude that the "serfdoms" believed to have occurred in accordance with Hayek's 1940 crystal ball are not at all the Nazi-Burma-Mao-Castro totalitarian catastrophies. Instead *they are the mixed economies that have flourished almost everywhere in the post-1945 years*!

The Hayek I met on various occasions – at the LSE, at the University of Chicago, in Stockholm (1945), at Lake Constance-Lindau Nobel summer conferences – definitely bemoaned progressive income taxation, state-provided medical care and retirement pensions, fiat currencies remote from gold and subject to discretionary policy decisions by central bank and treasury agents. Not only is this what constitutes his predicted serfdoms, do notice that when the same anthropologist scans Milton Friedman's various admiring forewords, her verdict will be that Hayek and Friedman were in essential agreement on what their singular verbal definitions are connoting.[2]

I can bear witness that, for twentieth century professional economists. Milton Friedman was infinitely more important for turning economists toward conservatism than Hayek. For the lay public maybe Hayek may have been more important?

---

[2] In this journal's same issue, Professors Edward McPhail and Andrew Farrant of Dickinson College have published letters between Hayek and me, along with their comments. I desist from providing any peer-reviewer comments of my own.

But, since I happen to be still alive at so late a date, I jot down here certain *ad hominem* nuances that only I could be privy to.

Hayekian biography confirms a few commonplaces. His was a highly original mind. That meant he had to work out everything for himself rather than learning stuff from teachers. Also, his was a slightly depressive personality. Popularity, unpopularity and virtual anonymity added to this. Once he told me (and I quote from memory) that (in his seventies) he feared he had become stale and uncreative. But later his originality did come back. In hindsight he learned that his two periods of letdown had in fact turned out to have coincided with two incidents of heart infarction. In paraphrase: Right there is the brain-mind connection that had preoccupied Hayek when writing his psychology treatise *The Sensory Order* (Hayek, 1952).

Add to the above that as I myself aged beyond seventy and eighty and ninety, it came to my notice that one must learn to appreciate that elderly friends do need to be handled gently. Here is a germane example. After Harry Johnson's stroke in Venice he still produced many worthy research articles. But he became easily irritated. He argued with various long-time friends. When the publisher who had carried his stuff for decades was three weeks late in sending a book out for review, he broke off relations with that company. Often I heard myself saying to good mutual friends of Harry and me: "That's not our Harry arguing. It's his arteries. Let's just go with the flow and remember Johnson's fertility and admirable versatility."

So it was when I began to receive complaints from my long-time acquaintance Friedrich Hayek. Why at so late a date should I belabor the persisting differences between us on ideological issues?

No good deeds go unpunished! Never then, or before, or later did I have reason to think or to say: Yes, I have misunderstood you. Yes, I have incorrectly quoted from you. *Mea culpa.*

Exactly what I have written above evaluating *The Road to Serfdom* is precisely what I believed about it in the 1940s and continued to believe about it up to the present 2007.

Why agitate ourselves when we are each entitled to harbor different analyses? One learns that often it is better to *avoid* an argument than to *win* one. Amen. In this footnote on *ad hominem* matters, some few additional remarks may be useful. Most of my gifted mentors, born in the nineteenth century, lacked today's "political (and ethnic) correctness." There were of course some honorable exceptions among both my Yankee and European teachers. Reder (2000) has provided a useful exploration of such unpleasantries. Central to his expositions were appraisals of the triad John Maynard Keynes, Joseph A. Schumpeter and Friedrich Hayek on the subject of anti-semitism.

Unexpectedly, I was forced in the end to conclude that Keynes's lifetime profile was the worst of the three. In the record of his letters to wife and other Bloomsbury buddies, Keynes apparently remained in viewpoint much the same as in his Eton essay on that subject as a callow seventeen-year-old.

Hayek, I came to realize, seemed to be the one of the three who at least *tried* to grow beyond his early conditioning. The full record suggests that he did not succeed fully in cleansing those Augean Stables. Still, a B grade for effort does trump a C-grade.

Keynes's visceral social repugnance would interest future historians less if it never contaminated his intellectual judgments. However early on, like Bertrand Russell, Keynes did recognize barbaric evils in Lenin's utopia. Strange though that instead of discovering the key role of Georgian Josef Stalin, it was the beastliness of Leon (Lev) Trotsky that Keynes's pen picks up on.

References

Barone, E., 1908. Il Ministro della Produzione nello Stato Collettivista. Giornale degli Economisti, September/October. In: Hayek, F.A. (Ed.), Collectivist Economic Planning. Routledge, London, Reprinted 1935 as: The ministry of production in the collectivist state.
Hayek, F., 1931 (Rpt 1967). Prices and Production. Augustus M. Kelley, New York.
Hayek, F., 1941. The Pure Theory of Capital. University of Chicago Press, Chicago.
Hayek, F., 1944. The Road to Serfdom. University of Chicago Press, Chicago.
Hayek, F., 1994. The Road to Serfdom. Fiftieth Anniversary Edition with Introduction by Milton Friedman. University of Chicago Press, Chicago.
Hayek, F., 2007. In: Caldwell, B. (Ed.), The Road to Serfdom: Text and Documents. University of Chicago Press, Chicago. See especially the reader's reports written by Frank Knight and Jacob Marschak.
Hayek, F., 1952 (paperback edition 1976). The Sensory Order. University of Chicago Press, Chicago.
Keynes, J.M., 1930. Treatise on Money. Vol. I: The Pure Theory of Money; Vol II: The Applied Theory of Money. Reproduced in: The Collected Writings of John Maynard Keynes, Vols. V and VI. Macmillan for the Royal Economic Society, London.
Lange, O., Taylor, F., 1938. In: Lippincott, B. (Ed.), On the Economic Theory of Socialism. University of Minnesota Press, Minneapolis.
Lerner, A., 1934. Economic theory and socialist economy. Review of Economic Studies 2, 51–61.
Palgrave, New, 1987. A dictionary of economics. In: Eatwell, J., Milgate, M., Newman, P. (Eds.). Lange–Lerner Mechanism, vol. 3. The Macmillan Press Limited and New York: the Stockton Press, London, pp. 129–131.
Pareto, V., 1896-97. Cours d'économie politique, two volumes. Librairie de l'Université, Lausanne.
Reder, M., 2000. The anti-Semitism of some eminent economists. History of Political Economy 32, 833–856.
Robbins, L., 1934. The Great Depression. Macmillan, London.
Sraffa, P., 1932. Dr. Hayek on money and capital. Economic Journal 44, 539–544.
Taylor, F., 1929. The guidance of production in a socialist state. AEA Presidential address, 1928. American Economic Review 19, 1–8.
von Mises, L., 1935. Economic Calculation in the Socialist Commonwealth. In: von Hayek, F.A. (Ed.), Collectivist Economic Planning. Routledge, London.

571

Preface
Thünen: An Economist ahead of His Times

Both Alfred Marshall and Joseph Schumpeter paid homage to Johann Heinrich von Thünen as a prophet way ahead of his own times. Thünen was not only a theorist. He deduced the principles best suited to run his agricultural estate in the far east of Germany, hundreds of miles away from the epicentre of the Scottish Enlightenment where lived such as David Hume, Adam Smith, John Stuart and James Mill. Like France's Augustin Cournot (1838), Thünen anticipated the kind of mathematics later employed by Stanley Jevons, Léon Walras, Francis Edgeworth and Vilfredo Pareto.

While deserving notice and praise from his contemporaries, Thünen's work never really received the recognition it deserved. His was not the luck of Austrian German language writers (such as Böhm-Bawerk) whose works were promptly translated into English in the period when Anglo-Saxon economic literature dominated frontier discussions.

Admirers of Thünen have differed in what interested them most. Thünen's picturesque circular zones of specialization around a city eclipsed his later (1850s) anticipation of post-1890 marginal productivity theory. As late as 1983, coinciding with Thünen's 200th birthday, Samuelson (1983) for the first time puzzled out the general equilibrium system implicit in Thünen's natural wage as the geometric mean between workers' average productivity and their marginal productivity.

Only in the present millennium has Thünen's late work on forestry optimization been translated into English and become the object of renewed discussion. In World War II, when Allied physicists stumbled onto operation research, analyses like Thünen's came into fashion. By the mid-nineteenth century, when he was deep into middle age, in his solitary study Thünen deployed not only calculus but also Cardan's formula for finding the roots of a cubic equation. Applied maths work is never done. Whether to fell trees at 30 years or 90 years is sensitive to assumptions about numerical parameters and on the scope of included variables.

Not all great scholars are great human beings. At George Washington's death, he freed his slaves. Thomas Jefferson never did free his own slaves. This was not because he approved of that institution, but rather because of his own spendthrift ways. Thünen seems to have been one of those rare species of *homo economicus* who did indulge in random acts of altruism. And non-random ones, too.

The importance of German science was recognized in the nineteenth and early twentieth centuries: Gauss, Humboldt, Einstein and beyond. My generation of economists knew too little about the sophisticated analytical economist literature – Austrian and non-Austrian – independently generated on the continent. David Ricardo had his Robert Malthus and Mill. Thünen perforce remained a pre-Gossen loner.

It is fitting then that 225 years after his birth, Johann Heinrich von Thünen still speaks to us. It is appropriate to conclude this tribute with hot-off-the-press news about Thünen's capital theory, maybe the jewel in his crown.

Samuelson (1983) sketched Thünen's scenario in which, for example, final consumable corn gets produced by direct land and direct labour working with a produced capital input, K. That K, in Thünen's simplest mid-nineteenth century model, could be produced by labour alone. At my suggestion, a perceptive young Finn from the Massachusetts Institute of Technology and Harvard, Erkko Etula (2008), analysed definitely the more complicated Thünen case where K as well as corn gets produced by K and labour. Both in terms of post-1890 Clark–Wicksteed differentiable marginal productivities and (Samuelson and Etula, 2006) completion of the limited substitutability technology of Sraffa (1960) type, a cogent Thünen-inspired answer can finally be given to David Ricardo's fundamental query: how does a competitive regime answer the puzzle of how society's total harvest gets divided among (1) the rent to landowner (2) the wages of laborers and (3) the interest yield of (vectoral!) K's.

Yes. Science does advance funeral by funeral. And science does advance also birth by birth. Thünen's brainchildren live on and proliferate.

Paul A. Samuelson
Massachusetts Institute of Technology

References

Cournot, Antoine-Augustin (1838) *Recherches sur les Principles mathématiques de la Théorie des Richesses*. Paris: Hachette.

Etula, Erkko (2008) 'The Two Sector von Thünen Original Marginal Productivity Model of Capital; and beyond', *Metroeconomica* 59(1), pp. 85–104.

Samuelson, Paul A. (1983) 'Thünen at Two Hundred', *Journal of Economic Literature*, pp. 148–1488.

Samuelson, Paul A. and Erkko Etula (2006) 'Complete Work-Up of the One-Sector Scalar-Capital Theory of Interest Rate: Third Installment Auditing Sraffa's Never-Completed "Critique of Modern Economic Theory"', in *Japan and the World Economy*, pp. 331–56.

Sraffa, Piero (1960) *Production of Commodities by Means of Commodities: Prelude to a Critique of Economic Theory*. Cambridge: Cambridge University Press.

572

THE SCHUMPETER CIRCLE AT HARVARD: 1932-1950
Paul A. Samuelson

I write briefly and only from undocumented memory. My arrival in 1935 at the Harvard Economics Graduate School accidentally coincided with the first year that Joseph Schumpeter took over Frank Taussig's legendary Ec11, the first course in economic theory. (It was also the first year for Leontief to teach his course in mathematical economics, which was great good luck for me.) In 1936 the Harvard scene was improved by the permanent coming from Vienna and Geneva of Gottfried Haberler. And after 1937, when the new Littauer School of Public Administration was founded, the arrival of Alvin Hansen at Harvard from the University of Minnesota consolidated a new era for Harvard economics.

Up until the summer of 1937 when Schumpeter surprised us all by marrying his Yankee third wife, Elizabeth Boody, widower Schumpeter lived with widower Taussig in Taussig's big Scott Road house. Schumpeter, along with economists Edward Mason, Seymour Harris, and Wassily Leontief, was an official economics tutor at Harvard's Dunster House. That would have given him the option of living in a suite there--as Mason did before his 1935 marriage, and as Harris did in the long intervals when Ruth Harris's TB confined her to a sanitorium.

Taussig was then quite old so that Schumpeter's frequent party-giving took place primarily at the Harvard Faculty Club. Bachelor student Abram Bergson (nee Burk), who had been a star in Taussig's 1933-34 Ec11 class, was drafted to replace newly-wedded Schumpeter as Taussig's house companion. I think he found it no house of mirth and soon thereafter the venerable Taussig went to live with a neighboring daughter.

Wassily Leontief was the colleague Schumpeter admired most. Certainly it was Schumpeter who coaxed Harvard to steal Leontief from the New York National Bureau of Economic Research, back then in its Wesley Mitchell phase. What Schumpeter admired most about Leontief's early research was his alleged almost miraculous ability to identify both a dd demand curve and an ss supply curve from the *same* $[q(t),p(t)]$ time series sample. Ragnar Frisch in Norway was less admiring and that is why later I tried (unsuccessfully) to interest econometricians to do a post mortem on the polemics.

The Schumpeter couple's residence on Acacia Street bordered closely the Leontief residence on Ash Street. When Wassily and Estelle jumped ship from Cambridge, Massachusetts, in favor of New York University, the Leontief summer house shifted from Vermont to not far from Elizabeth Schumpeter's Connecticut country estate. And, later, when Leontief was Schumpeter's literary executor, there turned out to be more than enough room on the Schumpeter burial plot for the four of them to lie permanently together.

In the 1930's and 1940's the Harvard Economics Department was somewhat split between a sterile old-guard that lacked enthusiasm for foreign high-fallutin theorist newcomers not trained at Harvard. This helps explain why Schumpeter never achieved the departmental powers that later James Tobin did attain during Yale's economic renaissance.

Also, Schumpeter's influence in the wider Harvard community never reached the level to be expected for such a world famous scholar. I never heard that he spoke at a university-wide faculty meeting. Perhaps it was his temperamental lack of *gravitas* that helps explain this lack of university-wide prominence.

When a depressed Schumpeter was temporarily tempted to leave Harvard for a Sterling Professorship at Yale, I formed part of the young student group who helped persuade him to stay. (I digress to speculate that Yale of that day would have turned out to be significantly worse than Harvard for Schumpeter.)

Alan and Paul Sweezy were special friends of Schumpeter. Particularly Paul, the younger brother, who became Schumpeter's official assistant lecturer for Ec11. Paul gave up an assured career in neoclassical economics to become a Marxist and an authority on Marxian theoretical analysis. The Sweezy father had been a vice president of J.P. Morgan's New York Bank; the family had money and the boys went to the elite Exeter School. Paul was the American editor for the LSE group that founded *The Review of Economic Studies*. (Later I was his successor.) Alan was, I believe, one of the earliest Harvard graduates approved to live in John Harvard's rooms at Cambridge University.

If I were to drop names conscientiously, I ought to mention Redvers Opie, who did the 1934 English revised edition of the 1911-12 German *Theory of Economic Development*. Opie also was for a time son-in-law of Frank Taussig. Arthur Smithies, Australian scholar at Oxford's Magdalen College and Commonwealth Fellow visiting America, was a Schumpeter devotee. Surely Schumpeter was one who helped him become a tenured Harvard professor.

Another Schumpeter favorite was Richard Goodwin, who from Indiana farm country had landed in Harvard College and later became a Rhodes Scholar at Oxford. At the 1949 Christmas AEA convention, a few nights before Schumpeter's January death, I was the last economist to talk to him. The main subject of our bar room conversation was on how to find for Goodwin the good job that he deserved and would accept. (Prior to Stalin's 1939 pact with Hitler, Goodwin had been in a three-person Oxford communist party cell--not then an illegal U.S. act. One never knew whether a Paul Sweezy or a Piero Sraffa did ever officially become a CP member. Certainly Paul Sweezy and Paul Baran invariable did follow every Stalinist wiggle.)

Returning to a more chronological ordering, before my 1935 Cambridge arrival in the Schumpeter circle were Abe Bergson and Alice Bourneuf (maybe the only woman Taussig ever gave an A rather than a C, and the only female academic at the Bretton Woods conference that created the IMF and the World Bank), Wolfgang Stolper and Richard Musgrave. Shigeto Tsuru, I, Robert Triffin, Sidney Alexander, David Rockefeller and Marion Crawford (Samuelson) were followed by Joe Bain, John Lintner, Lloyd Metzler and Bob Bishop. And of course, after 1945, a slew of war veterans swamped the Harvard Yard: James Tobin, Jim Duesenberry, Carl Kaysen, Bob Solow, Richard Ruggles--the list is endless. From my perch three miles down the Charles River, I recognized that an Elizabethan Golden Age coincided with the late Age of Schumpeter.

However, factually it had been globally more the Age of Keynes then than the Age of Schumpeter. Graduate students imitated Alvin

Hansen's green eye shade rather than Schumpeter's imported tweeds and pigskin gloves. Was Schumpeter jealous of Keynes? How could it be otherwise?

Tom Kuhn's (1962) *The Structure of Scientific Revolutions* explains why a Schumpeter could not understand the defection of the young. A quite false explanation gave him some cold comfort. The young could be Keynesians only because they were leftist socialists--so he thought. What Schumpeter never quite understood was that there could be another paradigm than the classical Say's Law paradigm of Alfred Marshall--one that could *give a handle to understanding the Great Depression* and how to ameliorate it by spending newly created currency.

The young deserted Schumpeter mainly because *he was such a bad depression macroeconomist*. Indeed he was a very bad one, as bad as 1931 Hayek. At the prime age of 51, in the ludicrous book by several Harvard senior professors Schumpeter praised the great depression as a "healthy catharsis" of the economic system. This was a garish "*uncreative*" version of what 1942 Schumpeter later called "creative capitalistic destruction."

Actually, in the 1929-1934 epoch, AT&T's Bell Laboratory, along with General Electric, Westinghouse and Dupont Labs, decimated their research efforts. Schumpeter's beloved entrepreneurial innovators were in fact paralyzed and aborted during Schumpeter's epoch of health catharsis. Like all of us, Schumpeter contradicted in some writings what he had proclaimed in others. He should have remembered his own words that depressions and booms unnecessarily go too far under capitalism.

For every thing there is a season. That fame which came to Keynes from his 1936 *General Theory* eclipsed Schumpeter's hoped-for fame.

But lo and behold. Decades later, when unemployment moved to the back burner, Schumpeter's elucidation of how innovation is the wellspring of improved total factor productivity moved him front and center in the Valhalla of great economic thinkers.

Underneath Schumpeter's gay Viennese demeanor, one sensed a sad person. His posthumous biographers found in Harvard's Schumpeter archives how very depressed he had become after that month in the early 1920's when his mother died and soon after his beloved second wife died while trying to give birth to their stillborn son.

Creatively his fifties were wasted on producing *Business Cycles*, a disappointing treatise whose taxonomy of economic cycles--short Kitchen-Crum cycles, intermediate Juglar cycles, and long Kondratief waves--attracted few readers. Wisely during his isolated World War I years in Cambridge and Connecticut, he turned to the much-cited *Capitalism, Socialism and Democracy*--maybe his best work since 1912--and worked away on his magisterial *History of Economic Analysis*. I believe his ghost must be appreciating the twenty-first century fame that his personality lusted for and would have savored.

Who were the contemporary economists Schumpeter admired most? From his young days he singled out a surprising trio of greatest economists. They were Léon Walras (for his original general equilibrium); Cournot (the younger) for his 1838 mathematical masterpiece; and, surprisingly, Quesnay for his tableau of multi-sectoral dynamic equilibrium.

Schumpeter's popularity in Vienna probably suffered when he came to praise J.B. Clark and Irving Fisher. A discernible pattern was Schumpeter's admiration for technicians whose mathematical nuances he did not fully understand. I recollect in this regard Schumpeter's particular admiration for Norway's Ragnar Frisch, Holland's Jan Tinbergen and Romania's Nicholas Georgescu-Roegen.

His was a fulfilled life. He died, so to speak, with his boots on, after a productive day split between preparing an important University of Chicago invited lecture and planning penultimate drafts for his *History of Economic Analysis*.

Not afraid to formulate bold conjectures that might be wrong, he earned high grades as a creative economist. His wrong guesses--as for example his diagnosis that capitalism decayed *because of its very successes*--are easily forgotten. What will ever be remembered was his now century-old emphasis on entrepreneurial innovation as a cardinal catalyst for economic progress.

* * * * *

In this memoir I am purposely only touching on Schumpeter's ideology. Both in his night thoughts and occasional verbal utterances, his view of the world was definitely "politically incorrect" in modern parlance. No wonder. By the time he was 35 in 1938 his preferred outer world had been killed off by the unnecessary World War I. From early on Schumpeter had been an Austrian who was anti-German and pro-British. Quixotically, late in World War I he seriously proposed that Austria should make a separate peace with the allies--as if Kaiser's Germany would have permitted that.

By the time Schumpeter was 40, his inner world of wife, son and mother had also died. These were enough to explain his hidden inner melancholy. We can add to them the familiar trap that youthful brilliance or maidenly beauty can engender. This can leave one with a Napoleonic lust for fame, generally an insatiable ambition.

World War II did not add to his joy. He feared that Hitler would win that struggle. (In the dark days of 1940 that was not a rash guess.)

After 1941 Pearl Harbor when America joined the Allies, the Schumpeter couple were rather isolated in an emptied-out Cambridge. That helps explain why, until a very, very late date, Schumpeter expected that Hitler would end up the winner. Better informed analysts, after Germany's debacle at Stalingrad and Japan's fiasco at Midway, had earlier come to realize that both Germany and Japan were doomed.

For Joseph Schumpeter the Allies' victory may have seemed a mixed blessing. Throughout the conflict it was his conviction that the war was being fought against the wrong enemy--not a belief that could go down well in the Senior Common Rooms of U.S. universities.

Leaving psychoanalytical babble and ideology aside, I return to basic political economy. Earlier I wrote that Schumpeter was a poor depression economist. Longer lived was a related serious fault. The Schumpeter I knew lacked sophisticated deep understanding of the Mixed Economy. On the day before he died, if a omniscient spirit had told him that the mixed economy (which he disparagingly called "capitalism in an oxygen tent") was to accomplish in the 1950-2008 epoch what it did accomplish, he would have dismissed that as a fairy tale fashioned out of wishful thinking.

Do I exaggerate? Consider his flippant answer when asked in 1936 whom he would vote for in the U.S. presidential election. "Madam, if my choice were between Franklin Roosevelt and Genghis Khan, I would vote for Genghis Khan." Only a Viennese conceit? I wish it were so. *In vino veritas* does hold. But also there often holds too: One's *jokes* may betray one's visceral and mental beliefs.

The house of economics has many diverse occupants. In my own life and that of my contemporaries, Joseph Alois Schumpeter was one who played a leading role.

References

Cournot, A. 1838. *Researches into the Mathematical Principles of the Theory or Wealth.* Trans. N.T. Bacon. New York, Macmillan, 1929.

Hayek, F. 1931. *Prices and Production.* New York, August M. Kelley, 1967.

Keynes, J.M. 1936. *The General Theory of Employment, Interest and Money.* Reprinted in *The Collected Writings of John Maynard Keynes*, Vol. VII. London, Macmillan for the Royal Economic Society.

Kuhn, T. 1962. *The Structure of Scientific Revolutions.* Chicago, University of Chicago Press.

Quesney, F. 1758. *Tableau économique.*

Schumpeter, J. 1912. *The Theory of Economic Development.* Liepzig, Duncker & Humblot.

Schumpeter, J. 1939. *Business Cycles.* New York, McGraw-Hill.

Schumpeter, J. 1942, 1944. *Capitalism, Socialism and Democracy.* New York, Harper & Brothers; London, George Allen & Unwin, 1943.

Walras, L. 1874. *Eléments d'économique politique pure: ou théorie de la richesse sociale.* Two parts. Lausanne, L. Corbaz; Paris, Guillaumin; Basil, H. George.

573

3 The Richard Goodwin circle at Harvard (1938–1950)

Paul A. Samuelson

These will be selective affectionate remembrances of times long gone by. Any errors in memory may themselves be of interest. Surprisingly, the bare biographical facts about Dick cannot be found in the 1999 *Who's Who in Economics* (3rd edn), for the reason that its editors scandalously omitted to include Goodwin's name.

When I arrived at the Harvard Graduate School in 1935, already present were the two Sweezys (Alan and Paul); and also Abram Bergson, Alice Bourneuf, Wolfgang Stolper and Richard Musgrave. Memories still were fresh of earlier staff and students – Professors Lauchlin Currie and Allyn Young; students Emile Despres and Albert Hart, class of 1930; Moe Abramowitz and Walter Salant, class of 1934.

But never in the 1935–1937 period did I ever hear the name of Richard Goodwin (class of 1934).

I think it was early in 1938 that a lunchtime guest at Harvard's Society of Fellows mentioned that a bright friend of his, one Richard Murphy Goodwin, would be soon returning to Harvard economics after his three years at Oxford as a Rhodes Scholar.

New boy on the block

My 1938–1950 period of course followed an earlier 1930–1934 Harvard era, and was followed by the longer 1950–1996 third act. If copies of Dick's undergraduate articles for the *Harvard Advocate* still exist, they would be worth examining microscopically. How naive or sophisticated were his youthful Marxist views? He once described himself as both a lapsed Catholic and a lapsed Marxian. This resembles the sociologist Paul Lazarfeld who once claimed to be a 'Marxist on leave'. 'Who gave you leave?' Lazarfeld's friend Jacob Marschak enquired. In Goodwin's post-1938 Harvard Yard sojourn, I don't remember hearing that he had any connection with the senior Marxist *Science and Society* periodical.

That Goodwin from Indiana had ever been a Catholic would have surprised his Cambridge, Massachusetts friends. Such were not common in the Hoosier state of Indiana that he and I were born in. The middle name 'Murphy' should perhaps have lessened our surprise.

An important fact should be mentioned. When Dick and I were boys in Indiana, at the time he and I were in grade school, Indiana was a leading northern centre for the extremist Klu Klux Klan. When Dick was 12, the Indiana KKK numbered almost half a million members (a tenth of total US membership), and the Klan controlled virtually all elected officials from the governorship downward. With a private slogan, 'Join the Klan and lynch a [what shall I write?] "black"', there weren't all that many folk of colour around Greencastle, Indiana. So in the north, the KKK's anti-Catholicism had to trump its anti-Negroism. 'The only good Catholic is a dead Catholic', was a borrowed KKK locker-room phrase. Maybe it was non-Darwinian creative design that the Klan's northern head, in a drunken orgy, raped, mutilated and killed a woman – who lived long enough to provide the data that sent the Klan leader to prison for life, while the governor and other high officials' careers were terminated by criminal indictments. Richard and I, as two Hoosier natives, never happened to discuss these historic factoids.

An open question is this. How, within a year after the October 1929 stock market crash, did Dick get the money to attend Harvard? Unlike Jim Tobin, class of 1939, who was a first-time Conant Merit Scholar, Goodwin must have had to rely on private financing to attend the Harvard that was in his time still an eastern private school destination.

Settled in

After 1938 the attractive couple of Dick and his Dutch-born wife Jackie were popular ornaments to the Harvard social scene. Before the 1939 Second World War, America's Great Depression had not fully ended. Therefore, a backlog of untenured instructors and assistant professors marked time at Harvard until good jobs elsewhere could be attained.

Closest to Dick and Jackie were her sister Suzanne and Dick's Oxford buddy, Dick Schlatter (later Provost at Rutgers University). Unmarried Dan Bourstin completed a threesome of recent Rhodes Scholars. I must mention them specifically because later, when Joe McCarthy's witch hunting for subversive communists was burgeoning, the FBI publicly announced that Richard Goodwin, Richard Schlatter and Dan Bourstin had been part of a small cell of communist party members at Oxford.

This news seemed almost comical: three such unworldly academics, scarcely capable of catching a mosquito. Professor Wassily Leontief and his wife Estelle were stunned at the news; and even resentful that they had not been 'told'! My wife Marion and I were glad that we had been kept in the dark. In these matters dates can be important. 'When did you join the French resistance movement? And did you, two months before me, succumb to Vichy blandishments?'

In the US before post-1945 cold war days, it was no crime to be a 'card-carrying' member of the Communist Party. Apparently the members of the Oxford cell broke with the Communist Party when Stalin in 1939 formed a pact with the Nazi Adolph Hitler. A good time to jump ship. By hindsight, we know that each of these Rhodes troika later did achieve deserved scholarly and academic recognition.

No exact answer can be given to the following question: Was Goodwin deprived of a tenured Harvard professorship because of his radical associations? Before Cambridge folk had been able to know about the Oxford cell connection, my guess is that the prognosis of Goodwin's future at Harvard was a gloomy one. Why should a good teacher and fruitful researcher not be a shoo-in for retention and promotion? Here are some reasons.

1. The Economics Department at Harvard in the 1930–1950 period, records show, resented excellence in scholarship. In Goodwin's 1930–1934 undergraduate time, outmoded luminaries such as Professors Gay, Bullock and Carver still ruled the roost. Statistics at Harvard both in Goodwin's time and mine were a feeble jest. How come top student Jim Tobin was permitted to go to Yale around 1950? He was brilliant from age five on in Champagne, Illinois. Why no Lloyd Metzler permanently at Harvard? To the department chairman Metzler's name may have sounded Jewish, but actually Lloyd was a Kansan-born Protestant. Why did Chairman Burbank discourage Franco Modigliani from accepting the Harvard offer to come there? Why no Solow permanently at Harvard? The list of like cases is a long and unsavoury one.

2. Dick was regarded as a 'dilettante' – an eccentric who preferred half-time pay to full-time. He liked to do serious painting. His later aristocratic love for once-expensive Edwardian automobiles belied his frugal, ascetic living style. It wasn't easy to find in Cambridge the Revere Street living quarters that lacked central heating, but Dick and Jackie managed to do so. They bought whisky by the pints, not litres. When we students persuaded Schumpeter not to let his disgust for Harvard colleagues make him accept a Yale chair, we celebrated by holding in his honour a dinner at an expensive Boston restaurant. Though Dick had been a leader in the full-court press to keep Schumpeter at Harvard, he protested at the cash outlay. Probably the pro-rated restaurant bill equalled his monthly living-expenses budget.

Witch hunt days

Somewhere I have published that during the 1949 American Economics Association meetings, I was the last economist to talk to Schumpeter a few days before his death. What we talked about in the hotel bar was how to get a good job for Dick Goodwin.

Said Schumpeter, 'I told Dick I would try to gain for him a permanent non-professorial lectureship at Harvard even though such deals are being phased out. Goodwin replied, "I'm not willing to be a second-class member of any club." I understood that.'

My next suggestion was, 'What about a good big-ten university like Michigan or Wisconsin?' Schumpeter said that Dick had no interest in them. Even Amherst or Williams were not to his taste.

So, the only root to our equation had to be a British elite university. This carried the extra advantage that going abroad would free Goodwin from having to testify before the bullying McCarthy committees that would require naming of names of one's associates (which the Committee of course already knew). Also part of that ordeal was arm-twisting pressure to express remorse and regret over earlier quite legal decisions. Hindsight confirms that the Oxford three all achieved highest academic and scholarly achievements.

If Schumpeter believed that only he and Haberler would vote tenure for Goodwin, I believe he miscalculated. Surely Hansen and Leontief valued Goodwin's scholarly merits.

On the road to the wake

I ought not to ramble on and on. So let me conclude with an account connected with Schumpeter's Connecticut funeral only ten days into 1950. Schumpeter died, so to speak, with his boots on. He expired in his sleep after a day spent on composing an important University of Chicago lecture, and working on his almost finished *History of Economic Analysis*.[1]

On a snowy New England January day, in the back seat of Gottfried Haberler's car, I was sandwiched between instructor Alfred Conrad on the left and Dick on my right. Professor Haberler drove, while his wife Friedl sat in the front passenger seat. Naturally we back three talked during the long drive. Most of it was about Schumpeter. But some concerned the arch enemy, Harold Hitching Burbank. Burbank was a rogue scholar with zero scholarly credentials. From 1913 to 1930 he had wormed his way to the long-term chairmanship of the Harvard economics department. Burbank would have preferred an affable Goodwin to an able Abram Bergson, but Dick was not the type to suck up to his bullyings.

For the record I will reconstruct some of our random car conversations.

GOODWIN: Burbie urged me to accept every job offer I ever got except, strangely, one from Amherst. Go figure.
SAMUELSON: I can explain that. It had nothing to do with you. As a 1913 Dartmouth College ruffian, he had a life long distaste for Amherst.
CONRAD: Say what you will, in the cold Cambridge milieu, it was Burbank who knew that I once was tubercular. Often he would ask about my health. Once he invited me in to talk about a thesis topic. 'Alf', he said, 'you are a warm human being. You should not pick an arid subject in pure theory.' It was not easy to have to tell him then that I had just decided on a topic involving Leontief's input/output matrix algebra.
GOODWIN: You say Burbank was in a warm human relationship with some students. One day he did call me in to say, 'Dick, I'd like to tie you to a wagon much the way my father did with me, and whip you into sense.' That's warmth for you.[2]

My next vignette is a bit of a digression, but illuminates what gets lost below the radar screen of history writers. Alf Conrad was co-author with Harvard's John Meyer of the seminal paper (1958) that launched the *cliometrics* vogue among economic historians. (The seed that they sowed, denying that ante-bellum slavery was doomed to die of its own weight as a bankruptcy operation, was harvested more intensely by Robert Fogel later.) At the time of Schumpeter's death, Conrad was his paid assistant.

CONRAD: Recently I asked Professor Schumpeter what he thought of the economist Nicky Kaldor. His reply, which I will quote, mystified me.
SCHUMPETER: Oh, these Asiatic Magyars. They are only early bloomers as scholars, thereby usurping chairs away from deeper thinkers.
CONRAD: Magyars. Are you referring to Professor Kaldor's Hungarian birth?
SCHUMPETER: No, my dear Alf. To spare your sensibilities, that was my way of identifying Kaldor's Mosaic heritage.[3]

One anecdote begets another. One of Schumpeter's best subsequent biographers, the Swedish econ-sociologist Richard Swedberg, at one point writes (in my paraphrase): 'And now we must address the question, was Schumpeter anti-Semitic? Stolper and Galbraith say No. X and Samuelson say Yes.' Surprised by the last part of the previous sentence, I read its footnote, which read: 'From personal conversation with Samuelson' (at earlier specified date).

This persuaded me to write to my admired acquaintance Swedberg that I wished he had quoted exactly what I said to him, which was, 'One of the many forms of anti-Semitism is to say that Jews do not lack competence, but are only "early bloomers". Schumpeter's view was shared by America's great mathematician George Birkhoff at Harvard, who believed in just that.' Conrad's 1950 account was precisely that which I had reported to Swedberg. The nuances of Schumpeter's 'politically incorrect' (or correct) views are so complex that I have avoided reporting on them. I will only venture here the following vague summary. After reading Melvin Reder (2000) on anti-Semitism among eminent economists, I judged that Keynes was worse than Schumpeter or Hayek; and that Hayek, incompletely successful, at least tried hardest to overcome what he could not completely overcome. Long and late he believed his Indian students at the LSE were offspring of 'money lenders'.

Personal piffle, like all of the above, is admissible in a family portrait. But even more important, the following information may be new. As the five of us wended our 100+ snowy miles between eastern Massachusetts and western Connecticut, Dick Goodwin engaged in extensive conversations with Friedl Haberler about their respective painful and frequent migraine headaches. Never had any in our circle even known that Goodwin had a migraine problem at all. In my mind this puts a new light on his role as a 'dilettante painter'. Half-time leisure and recreation may at some point in one's life in fact be the optimal paradigm for maximizing one's inherited biblical pound.[4]

Limit-cycle stable periodic limit cycles

My frenetic pen has left me epsilon time to discuss the Goodwin–LeCorbeiller greatest claim to theoretical fame. Just as John Hicks gained much from talking to Harrod, Meade and whomever about Keynesian matters, in my recollection much of what ended up in Hick's 1950 *A Contribution to the Theory of the Trade Cycle* would not have been possible if he had not earlier talked over those issues with Dick Goodwin. That's the way the dynamics of scientific discovery works. Bees take elsewhere my honey; and much of what is 'mine' was brought to me by those same busy bees. Insiders know these things. But historians never can get things perfectly right.

Notes

1 Goodwin was one of the few who helped widow Elizabeth Boody (Firuski) Schumpeter edit uncompleted fragments of the great history-of-thought book.
2 A story has been told that Goodman faced up to command Burbank to destroy 'the little black book' containing the names of minority students he was opposed to. One must wonder whether memory got somehow garbled. Burbank needed no written list to identify non-favourites. Breakfast, lunch and supper he fretted over them.
3 Alfred Conrad, I believe, may have been born Alfred Cohen. I ought to add that in the 37 years between 1949 and his 1986 death at age 78, Kaldor was as prolific as he had been in his post-1932 youth – with about the same fraction of interesting speculations and a few doubtful ones.
4 Often later in life, migraine sufferers do enjoy some relief; maybe one of the few benefits from getting old. Certainly Goodwin did find in Siena, Italy, a new burst of scholarly productivity.

References

Blaug, M. (ed.) (1999) *Who's Who in Economics*, 3rd edn, Cheltenham: Edward Elgar Publishing Limited.

Conrad, A. and Meyer, J. (1958) 'The economics of slavery in the ante-bellum south', *Journal of Political Economy*, 66(April): 95–130.

Hicks, J. (1950) *A Contribution to the Theory of the Trade Cycle*, Oxford: Clarendon Press.

Reder, M. (2000) 'The anti-semitism of some eminent economists', *History of Political Economy*, 32(winter): 833–56.

Schumpeter, J. (1954) *History of Economic Analysis*, New York: Oxford University Press.

PART X.

Autobiographical Writings

574

PAUL A. SAMUELSON

My Life Philosophy: Policy Credos and Working Ways

ETHICS

Many economists – Alfred Marshall, Knut Wicksell, Léon Walras, ... – became economists, they tell us, to do good for the world. I became an economist quite by chance, primarily because the analysis was so interesting and easy – indeed so easy that at first I thought that there must be more to it than I was recognizing, else why were my older classmates making such heavy weather over supply and demand? (How could an increased demand for wool help but lower the price of pork and beef?)

Although positivistic analysis of what the actual world is like commands and constrains my every move as an economist, there is never far from my consciousness a concern for the ethics of the outcome. Mine is a simple ideology that favors the underdog and (other things equal) abhors inequality.

I take no credit for this moral stance. My parents were "liberals" (in the American sense of the word, not in the European "Manchester School" sense), and I was conditioned in that general *Weltanschauung*. It is an easy faith to adhere to. When my income came to rise above the median, no guilt attached to that. Nor was there a compulsion to give away all my extra coats to shirtsleeved strangers: my parents would have thought me daft to do so, and neurotic to toss at night for not having done so. Some personal obligation for distributive justice liberals do expect of themselves: but what is far more important than acts of private charity is to weight the counterclaims of efficiency and equity, whenever public policy is concerned, in the direction of equity. As my University of Chicago teacher and friend Henry Simons used to say, "Any *good* cause is worth incurring some *costs* for. Everything should be pushed beyond the point of diminishing returns (else, why desist from pushing it still further?)."

Persons who will not volunteer to serve in the army can with good logic vote to pass a fair conscription law that will entail their being drafted with the same positive probability as any other persons. I have generally voted against my own economic interests when questions of redistributive taxation have come up. The fact that I have favored closing tax loopholes has not precluded seeking some advantage from those left in the tax code. But too avid an effort in that direction would seem not only unaesthetic but also a source of some discomfort and self-reproach.

Without exception all the economists I know regard themselves as humanitarians. This includes communists who toe the Stalinist line and Chicago-school zealots for laissez-faire. Yet we all pretty much know what to expect of each other when it comes to policy recommendations and judgments. It is not unanimity. If political economy were an exact, hard science, then more agreement on probable outcomes would occur. If economics were no science at all, only a tissue of value judgments and prejudices, then soliciting an opinion from an economist would tell the Prince or Parliament nothing about the merits or demerits of the proposal under deliberation but only give a reconfirmation that Economist Jones is a bleeding-heart liberal and Economist Smith a selfish elitist.

Political economy as we know it falls in-between. Economists do agree on much in any situation. Where Milton Friedman and I disagree, we are quick to be able to identify the source and texture of our disagreements in a way that non-economists cannot perceive. The disparity of our recommendations is not an unbiased estimator of the dispersion of our inductive and deductive beliefs. With my *social welfare function* (or, in Waldian statisticians' terminology, my "loss function") concerning the relative importance of unemployment and business freedoms, I could disagree 180° with his policy conclusion and yet concur in diagnosis of the empirical observations and inferred probabilities. Yet such is the imperfection of the human scientist, an anthropologist studying us academic guinea pigs will record the sad fact that our hearts do often contaminate our minds and eyes. The conservative will forecast high inflation danger on the basis of the same data that lead the do-gooder to warn against recession. (Conscious of this unconscious source of bias, as the subsequent discussion will elaborate on, I make a special effort toward self-criticism and eclecticism – with what success, the record must testify to.)

An economist who has been preoccupied over the years solely with *Pareto optimality* wrote me long ago that I would be surprised to know how liberal he is. Indeed I would be. Reflecting on his writings, I wondered how he knew he had a heart: it had been so long since he had used it. Organs atrophy without exercise. "Use it or lose it" is nature's law.

It is not only the arteries that harden with age. Economists are said to appear to grow more conservative as they rise in seniority. This they often deny.

In my own case, I do not perceive that my value-judgment ideology has changed systematically since the age of 25. For a decade now mainstream economics has been moving a bit rightward. But I have not been tempted to chase it. What does tend to change with the accumulation of years and experience is one's degree of optimism about what is feasible and one's faith in good intentions alone. My enhanced skepticism about government ownership of the means of production or the efficacy of planning is not a reflection of ossifying sympathies and benevolence, but rather is a response to the testimony of proliferating real-world experiences.

I am conscious of one occasion in which my respect for the market mechanism took a quantum leap upward. This change had nothing to do with improved performing of the market system. Nor was it related to any new arguments brought forward by Hayek about generating and utilizing information, or to any old arguments about market efficiencies and freedoms by Adam Smith, Frederic Bastiat, or Frank Knight. Rather my changed viewpoint came from observing the communist witchhunting episode of the 1950s.

The McCarthy era, in my judgment, posed a serious threat of American fascism. I knew plenty of people in government and the universities whose civil liberties and careers came into jeopardy. I observed at close hand the fears and tremblings that the Harvard and MIT authorities experienced, and these were the boldest of the American academic institutions. As Wellington said of Waterloo, it was a close-run thing that Senator McCarthy was discredited: the Richard Nixon "enemy list" was a joke in comparison, and my being named on it only added to my fading credentials as a New Dealer. What I learned from the McCarthy incident was the perils of a one-employer society. When you are blackballed from government employment, there is great safety from the existence of thousands of anonymous employers out there in the market. I knew of people who got some kind of work in private industry, usually smaller industry since large firms tend to try to keep on the safe side of government. To me this became a newly perceived argument, not so much for laissez-faire capitalism as for the *mixed* economy.

How did free-market advocates among the economists score as defenders of personal freedoms and civil liberties? This was a subject of great interest to me and over several years I kept a quiet tally of the behavior and private utterances of scores of the leading American and Continental libertarians, almost all of whom I knew intimately. Like a visiting anthropologist I would ask innocent questions designed to elicit relaxed and spontaneous views. If it was churlish to keep a record of private conversations, then I was a churl. The results surprised and distressed me. Worshippers of laissez-faire à la Bastiat and Spencer were insensitive and on the whole unsympathetic toward the rights and personal freedoms of scholars. Alone among the members of the Mt. Pelerin Society the name of Fritz Machlup stood out as one willing to incur personal costs to speak up for John Stuart Mill values. It is not the failure of people to be heroes that I am speaking about. There is little of the heroic in my own makeup and I have learned not to expect much of human nature. What my research found was a sad lack of genuine concern for human values.

I was taught at the University of Chicago that business freedoms and personal freedoms have to be strongly linked, as a matter both of brute empirical fact and of cogent deductive syllogism. For a long time I believed what I was taught. Gradually I had to acknowledge that the paradigm could not fit the facts. By most Millian criteria, regimented Scandinavia was freer than my America – or certainly at least as free. When I used to bring up these inconvenient facts to my conservative friend David McCord Wright, he would warn: "Just you wait. British and Swedish citizens, it is true, have not yet lost their freedoms. But it cannot last that the market is interfered with and people remain politically free." We have all waited for more than thirty years now.

Friedrick Hayek wrote his bestseller, *The Road to Serfdom*, at the end of World War II, warning that partial reform was the sure path to total tyranny. Cross-sectional and time-series analysis of the relationship between politics and economics suggest to me important truths.

1. Controlled socialist societies are rarely efficient and virtually never freely democratic. (There is considerable validity then for the non-novel part of Hayek's warning.)
2. Societies which resisted partial reforms have often been those overtaken by revolutionary change. If it is the free market or nothing, often it has then had to be nothing. Indeed, after midcentury the finest archetypes of efficient free markets have often been quasi-fascist or outright fascist societies in which a dictatorial leader or single party *imposes* a political order – without which imposition the market could not politically survive. Chile with its military dictatorship cum-the-Chicago boys is only one dramatic case. Taiwan, South Korea, and Singapore are less dramatic but more representative cases.
3. I can nurture a dream. Like Martin Luther King, I have a dream of a humane economy that is at the same time efficient and respecting of personal (if not business) freedoms. Much of producing and consuming decisions involve use of the market mechanism. But the worst inequalities of condition that result from reliance on market forces – even in the presence of equality of ex ante opportunity – can be mitigated by the transfer powers of the democratic state. Does the enhancement of equity by the welfare state take no toll in terms of efficiency? Yes, there will be some trade-off of enhanced total output against enhanced equality, some trade-off between security and progress. I call the resultant optimizing compromise *economics with a heart*, and it is my dream to keep it also economics with a head.

MY METHODOLOGY

It is some relief to move from the exalted realm of philosophical ethics to the mundane realm of scientific methodology. However, I rather shy away from discussions of Methodology with a capital M. To paraphrase Shaw: Those who can, do science; those who can't prattle about its methodology.

Of course I can't deny that I have a methodology. It's just that there seems little appeal in making it explicit to an outsider. Or for that matter, in spelling it out to my own consciousness.

I am primarily a theorist. But my first and last allegiance is to the facts. When I began study at the University of Chicago, Frank Knight and Aaron Director planted in me the false notion that somehow deduction was more important than induction. This was a confused tenet of Austrian methodology at the time, and I certainly do not mean by the word "Austrian" the logical positivism of the Vienna Circle. Rather, such direct and indirect disciples of Carl Menger as Ludwig von Mises, Friedrich Hayek, and Lionel Robbins seemed to put on their own heads the dunce caps of the classical Ricardians who believed that by thinking in one's study one could arrive at the basic immutable laws of political economy. I remember believing Director when he pooh-poohed Wesley Mitchell's empirical work on business cycles, claiming instead that the greatest breakthroughs in the subject were coming from Hayek's a priorisms on the subject.

I grew out of this phase fast. Once Lionel Robbins explained lucidly in the first edition of his *An Essay on the Nature and Significance of Economic Science* his claims for Kantian a priorism in economics, his case was lost. Logical positivism is now judged to be an oversimplified doctrine, but it was enormously useful in deflating the pretensions of deductionists. If one had to choose between the methodologies of the warring brothers – Ludwig the economist and Richard von Mises the mathematical physicist – Richard would win hands down.

Let me not be misunderstood. I abhor the sins of scientism. I recognize that, as social scientists, we can have relationships with the data we study that the astronomers cannot have with the data they study. I am aware that my old friend Willard van Orman Quine, one of this age's greatest logicians, has cast doubt that anyone can in every case distinguish between "analytic" a priorisms and the "synthetic" propositions that positivists take to be empirical facts. Furthermore, Wesley Mitchell's empiricisms on the business cycle do seem to me to have been overrated – not because they are empirical, but rather because his was an eclecticism that never had much luck in discovering anything very interesting, as the lifecycle profile of his post-1913 career sadly reveals. Some of the skepticisms of Knight and Jacob Viner concerning the empirical statistical studies that their colleagues Paul Douglas and Henry Schultz were attempting, I readily admit, were well taken – just as some of Keynes's corrosive 1939 criticisms of Jan Tinbergen's econometric macromodels were. But it is on *empirical* grounds that these empirical attempts have to be rejected or accepted, and not because deductive syllogisms can claim a primacy to vulgar fact grabbing. What was wrong with the German Historical School was not that it was historical, but rather that its sampling of the facts was incomplete and incoherent. The facts don't tell their own story. You can't enunciate all the facts. And if you could, the job of the scientists would just begin – to organize those facts into useful and meaningful gestalts, into patterns that are less multifarious than the data themselves and which provide economical *descriptions* of the data that afford tolerably accurate extrapolations and interpolations.

Whatever logical positivism's faults and superficialities are in science at large, it gets an undeservedly bad name in economics from being confused with Milton Friedman's peculiar version of positive economics. Much of what is in Friedman's 1953 essay on this topic is unexceptional and a story so old as to seem almost platitudinous. But what is novel in his formulation and commands most attention is that which I have called "the F twist" – the dictum that a scientific theory is none the worse if its premises are unrealistic (in the usual meaning of "unrealistic" as stating hypotheses that are false and/or far-from-true assertions about what obtains in the actual world), so long as the theory's "predictions" are usefully true. Thought suggests, and experience confirms, that such a dogma will be self-indulging, permitting its practitioners to ignore or play down inconvenient departures of their theories from the observable real world. A hypothesis's full set of predictions includes its own descriptive contents: so, literally understood, an unrealistic hypothesis entails some unrealistic predictions and is all the worse for those false predictions – albeit it is all the better for its (other) empirically correct predictions. We are left then validly with only the prosaic reminder that few theories have all their consequences exactly correct; and it can be the case that a scientific theory is deemed valuable because we have reason to give great weight to those of its predictions that happen to be true and to give little weight to those that are found to be false. In no case is unrealistic falsity a virtue; and there is danger of self-serving Humpty-Dumptyism in letting the theorist judge for himself which of his errors he is going to extenuate or ignore.

Unpopular these days are the views of Ernst Mach and crude logical positivists, who deem good theories to be merely economical descriptions of the complex facts that tolerably well replicate those already-observed or still-to-be-observed facts. Not for philosophical reasons but purely out of long experience in doing economics that other people will like and that I myself will like, I find myself in the minority who take the Machian view. "Understanding" of classical thermodynamics (the archetype of a successful scientific theory) I find to be the capacity to "describe" how fluids and solids will actually behave under various specifiable conditions. When we are able to give a pleasingly satisfactory "HOW" for the way of the world, that gives the only approach to "WHY" that we shall ever attain.

Always when I read new literary and mathematical paradigms, I seek to learn what descriptions they imply for the observable data. The paradigm's full set of entailed descriptions is what is of interest and forms the basis for a complete judgment on it. My work in revealed preference, in *Foundations of Economic Analysis*, and in the several volumes of *Collected Scientific Papers*, consistently bears out this general methodological procedure.

I dislike being wrong. Long before knowing of Karl Popper's writings, I sought to be my own strictest critic. Why give that fun to the other chap? All this explains why I am an eclectic economist. It is not because of inability to make up my mind. I am eclectic only because experience has shown that Mother Nature is eclectic. If all the evidence points to a single-factor causation, I have no internal resistance to accepting that. But there is a big "if" involved in the previous sentence.

Being prepared to be eclectic does not have to inhibit bold theory building. One creates boldly knowing that this does not commit one to exaggerated belief in the sole potency of one's brain child.

We all have secret vanities. He prides himself on his good looks. She takes satisfaction in her sense of humor. I do delight in producing still another beautiful model that illuminates important terrains of economics. But in my heart of hearts I nurture the claim that I have good judgment. Be wise, sweet maid, and let them who will be clever. My theories must run the gauntlet of my judgment, an ordeal more fearsome than mere peer review. (Of course one can have one's cake and eat it too by presenting a theoretical gem as an unpretentious mirror of some aspects of some corner of the economic terrain under observation.) Why let sagacity degenerate into well-informed nihilism? The mindless naysayer is no better than the mindless yeasayer. Neither adds anything to the silent scientist's cipher.

Joseph Schumpeter, who all his life whored after beautiful theories, just before he died testified at the 1949 National Bureau conference on business cycles: If he had to choose between mastery of mathematics and statistics, or of economic history, he would have to choose mastery of economic history. I won't disagree. But I deny the need for dichotomous choice. Give apes in the Widener Library a data bank of all that's there and you don't get a master economic historian. What you get back is the data bank and a curator.

Let me make a confession. Back when I was 20 I could perceive the great progress that was being made in econometric *methods*. Even without foreseeing the onset of the computer age, with its cheapening of calculations, I expected that the new econometrics would enable us to narrow down the uncertainties of our economic theories. We would be able to test and reject false theories. We would be able to infer new good theories.

My confession is that this expectation has not worked out. From several thousands of monthly and quarterly time series, which cover the last few decades or even centuries, it has turned out not to be possible to arrive at a close approximation to indisputable truth. I never ignore econometric studies, but I have learned from sad experience to take them with large grains of salt. It takes one econometric study to calibrate another; a priori thought can't do the job. But it seems objectively to be the case that there does not accumulate a convergent body of econometric findings, convergent on a testable truth.

Does this mean that I belong to the camp which regards truth as in the eye of the beholder? Which denies the existence of an objective truth out there, in political economy as well as in astronomy and biochemistry? Which recognizes in the truth of mainstream economics only the class interests of the bourgeoisie, and in the truth of Marxian economics either the class interests of the nascent proletariat or the objective truth of the final classless and universal society?

No. Observing myself over fifty years and a vast number of scientists in various disciplines, I do recognize that truth has many facets. Precision in deterministic facts or in their probability laws can at best be only partial and approximate. Which of the objective facts out there are worthy of study and description or explanation depends admittedly on subjective properties of the scientists. Admittedly, a given field of data can be described in terms of alternative patterns of description, particularly by disputing authorities who differ in the error tolerances they display toward different aspects of the data. Admittedly, observations are not merely seen or sensed but rather often are perceived in gestalt patterns that impose themselves on the data and even distort those data.

But still, having admitted all of the above, as you observe scientists and study the developments of disciplines when schools evolve and paradigms are born and die, it is forced upon you that *what ultimately shapes the verdicts of the scientist juries is an empirical reality out there*. When a Marxist scores a triumph it is not by employing a useful alternative to 2 + 2 = 4 logic, or cultivating a different Hegelian dialectic. We esteem a Pavlov, Lysenko, Haldane or Bernal, Landau or Baran for what they can or cannot accomplish with respect to animal experiments, plant breeding, hydrogen-bomb explodings or phase transitions, or insights into the observable paths of economic development.

When Thomas Kuhn's book, *The Structure of Scientific Revolutions,* came out in 1962, I made two lucky predictions: one, that in the physical and life sciences its thesis would have to be modified to recognize that there is a cumulative property of knowledge that makes later paradigms ultimately dominate earlier ones, however differently the struggle may transiently look; two, that Kuhn's doctrine of incommensurability of alternative paradigms would cater to a strong desire on the part of polemical social scientists who will be delighted to be able to say, "That's all very well in your paradigm, but your white is black in my paradigm – and who's to say that we'uns have to agree with you'uns." Kuhn has correctly discerned the warts on the countenance of evolving science. His readers must not lose the face for the warts.

HOW I WORK

As a theorist I have great advantages. All I need is a pencil (now a ball pen) and an empty pad of paper. There are analysts who sit and look vacantly out the window, but after the age of 20 I was not one of them. I ought to envy the new generation who have grown up with the computer, but I don't. None of them known to me sit idly at the console, improvising and experimenting in the way that a composer does at the piano. That ought to become increasingly possible. But up to now, in my observation, the computer is largely a black box into which researchers feed raw input and out from which they draw various summarizing measures and simulations. Not having access to look around in the box, the investigator has less intuitive familiarity with the data than used to be the case in the bad old days.

I have been blessed with an abundance of interesting problems to puzzle out. Many artists and writers run into long fallow periods when new creative ideas just will not come. Luckily, that has not been my experience. Perhaps I am insufficiently self-critical to recognize when problems of lower quality are involved. In any case mine has never been the Carlylean view of Schumpeter that only the greatest ideas count, and only a few great men are important in history and in the development of science. One tackles the most important unsolved problem at hand. Then the next one. If that leads down the path of diminishing returns in the absence of dramatic new challenges and breakthroughs, so be it.

"What are you working on now?" This is a question I have been asked all my life. And never in my life have I known how to answer it. At any one time I have several balls in the air. And always there is an inventory of questions just below the threshold of my explicit attention. Some of these slumber in that limbo for two decades. There is no hurry; they will keep. Some morning (or at night in a dream) the evolving wheel of chance will turn their number up.

Poets testify that often their lines gush up from within. They merely write down what their muse is dictating. That sounds rather highfalutin, but there is something in it. When I was young I used to explore a topic; write down equations and syllogisms dealing with different aspects of it; then outline the final work. After that the final draft could be written out. Perhaps what I am describing is the optimal way to write a paper.

Increasingly after the age of 35 that is not how I have in fact operated. Instead I have often let the paper write itself. A problem is posed. One begins to solve it, writing out the steps in the solution. One development leads naturally to another, as one exposits in writing. Finally, what can be solved of the problem has been solved. The paper is finished. What has been finished is not something that has ever been envisaged, waiting only to be written down. All this is reminiscent of Franklin Roosevelt's dictum, "How do I know what I think until I hear myself saying it?"

This means that some articles might be composed in half a day. Of course the first draft need not be the final draft. There may follow many hours of revisings, involving additions, deletions, rearrangements, and corrections. Perhaps it would be better to follow the first draft with a completely new rewrite. But that is not my usual practice, as I trade some perfection against more time for new topics. This means I am a prisoner of my first drafts, and it is a source of exquisite pain if a manuscript is lost: my mind rebels at having to reconstruct a lost argument, and impatience is likely to make a recollected version abridge some essential matter.

Prolific scholars are addicted to writing. A day spent in committee meetings is for me a day lost. After an interval of fasting, you are hungry. After an interval of doing no analytical research, there is so to speak a fluid inside you that wants to get free. I used to think that the unconscious mind, which Henri Poincaré described so beautifully as working away at specific puzzles the mathematician is interested in, was accumulating findings on the particular problems that routine duties prevented me from dealing with. But I have come to think that not to be quite correct. For *any* new topic can capture one's enthusiastic and fruitful attention after a period of deprivation. One snowy day in New England I was told at the airport gate that Washington was snowed in. A friend hearing me inquire, "Can you go to New York?" asked, "Are you just bound to go somewhere this day?" That's exactly what it's like with the creative urge: It doesn't have to spend itself on the theory of capital that has been engaging the scholar's recent attention; it just wants to go about doing something creative, and its motors seem revved up to be effective in whatever direction it is pointed.

Reporters used to speak of a nose for news. What is important in scholarship is an aesthetic sense for what is an important problem. Otherwise the facile mind can spend itself on patterns that are merely pretty. For recreation I would rather play tennis than play chess, or read pedestrian detective stories than solve the mathematical conundrums that appear in the back pages of learned journals. My unconscious motivation, I suspect, is that chess and problem-solving involve the same energies as innovative scholarship does. They will usurp some of the limited supply of precious brainpower that might better go toward learning something new; and, involving use of the same workday muscles so to speak, those recreations do not provide as refreshing rest periods. I daresay that the powerful pure mathematician faces a different problem from the applied scientist. A great mathematician is only as great as his greatest deeds. The revolutionary idea that might lead to great deeds comes very rarely.

One marks time in between and one might as well mark time while keeping the brain tuned up in chess or bridge as in any other way. However, I do not have too much confidence in the distinction that I have just made. For it certainly does not cover the case of prolific mathematicians such as Poincaré or Euler. A mathematical snob like G. H. Hardy might judge that much of Euler and Poincaré could just as well have never been written. But even from the snobbish viewpoint, we must reckon with the fact that some of their best work would not have gotten done if it had not been an outgrowth of some of their less transcendental achievements.

I said that my working tools are only pen and paper, and that an airplane cabin provides as good an environment for research as a library study. That is true as far as analytical creativity is concerned. On the other hand to stay well informed on what it is that is important to be done, a scholar must have access to books and to learned journals. In this regard I have always been very lucky. Whatever works the MIT libraries have not had, the neighboring Harvard libraries can be counted on to provide. There are very few great scholars working off by themselves with paper and pen far from the centers of creative economic thought. Those who pride themselves on being most autonomous usually end up most idiosyncratic.

Long ago I set myself the grandiose challenge of not being merely subjectively original. More useful to science – and more truly fulfilling if you can bring it off – is to try to stay informed on what other scientists have done and to advance the frontier by your own quantum jumps. In terms of the old song: "Good work if you can get it. And you can get it if you try."

Paul Samuelson is Institute Professor, Emeritus, Massachusetts Institute of Technology, and 1970 winner of the Nobel Memorial Prize in economic science.

Statistical Flowers Caught in Amber

Paul A. Samuelson

Since I remember well the war-time MIT seminars in statistics now being reproduced in abstract form, I am happy to accept the editors' invitation to reminisce about those times.

Chance alone turned up these Abstracts in the University of Chicago libraries. Although it was my secretary (and Harold Freeman's), Eleanor Prescott Clemence, who typed up these mathematical abstracts, all of us had forgotten they were ever compiled. With probability not minute, Harold Freeman would have sent a copy of them to our friend W. Allen Wallis, who with certainty approaching unity throws away nothing. (The initials W. A. W. on the manuscript Stephen Stigler stumbled upon in the Chicago archives are in the unmistakable schoolboy hand of the Honorable W. Allen Wallis.)

Actually, with faculty blessings, this seminar series was conceived and executed by two graduate students: Lawrence Klein, who was to become MIT's first Ph.D. in Economics and our first home-grown Nobel Laureate; and Joseph Ullman, then studying economics but in the course of the war's windup in Europe later to be enticed into a career in mathematics by Gabor Szegö. Laurie and Joe both alternated as introducers of the speakers; Harold Freeman and I would both cringe and delight in the unpredictable algebraic felicities of their unrehearsed introductions. (Sample: when the illustrious Richard von Mises was to be presented, his many fames as a pioneer had not run ahead of him; so our student impresario left it at, "Although I don't know why, our speaker is supposed to be a very famous scholar.")

It is amazing that, in this epoch after Pearl Harbor, when faculty was dispersing to various war-time labs and graduate student bodies were shrinking to a small core of transients and women, two active students could still attract without stipends so brilliant a group of speakers. Most were

---

Paul A. Samuelson is Institute Professor Emeritus, Massachusetts Institute of Technology, E52-383C, Cambridge, Massachusetts 02139.

locals who came of course by foot or, in those days of rationing, by streetcar or at worst by rail from Rhode Island; two lecturers traveled from New York and one from Washington. It is a disappointment to find no women on the list: at the least Hilda Geiringer might have been invited, along with Richard von Mises.

The quality of the papers has high variance. Mine, for example, is a mere finger exercise in curve fitting, excusable only in someone young who volunteers to help keep the local pot boiling. On the other hand, the Haavelmo piece is a gem, which contains the essence of his contribution to the problem for which he quite properly got his 1989 Nobel Prize, and which was later to stimulate the important Cowles Commission works at Chicago by Koopmans, Marschak, Rubin, Hood, Hurwicz and many others.

In alphabetical order I shall recall some personal features of the baker's dozen of speakers.

ARNOLD

MIT never lived up to its promise in statistics but the mathematics and economics departments had a smattering of statisticians. George Wadsworth, an applied mathematician, consulted widely for the armed forces and for various private interests. Probably Kenneth J. Arnold was connected with the Wadsworth group, as Albert Bowker would have been.

One interesting feature of Arnold's analysis was its inversion of the maximum-likelihood procedure. Instead of seeking to show, as R. A. Fisher did in Gauss's wake, that the arithmetic mean of a Gaussian sample is the estimator that maximizes the sample's likelihood, one can ask in the Gauss and 1911 Keynes fashion: "For what family of distributions is the *median* the maximum-likelihood estimator? For what, the *harmonic mean*?" And so forth.

Gauss himself, in a demonstration he ceased to be proud of, had purported to prove that the Normal Curve was the "most-likely" probability law. Had he gone whole hog, and asked what probability distribution was truly most likely to have given rise to the observed sample ($x_1 \leq x_2 \leq \cdots \leq x_n$), he should have given as his answer the stepfunction that has jumps at those points of size proportional to the frequency of each such x_j value—a case of absurdly close curve fitting.

Arnold takes notice of a common procedure: to find characterizing properties of the Normal Law. Examples are:

a. Its max-likelihood central tendency is the sample mean (Gauss-Fisher).

b. Its joint (m, σ) sampling distribution involves independent probabilities (Kaplansky).

c. For its normalized density, $N'(x) = p(x)$, $p'(x) = xp(x)$ (K. Pearson).

d. For joint (x, y) samplings from it, if x and y are independently distributed, any orthogonal rotation of them leaves independence invariant (Herschel, Maxwell).

Actually, as Stephen Stigler (1980) might have more strongly emphasized, the de Moivre "reproductive" property of the Normal Law is by all odds its important singularity:

e. It is the only law with finite moments for which the mean of a sample obeys the same law as each item does after rescaling (by $1/\sqrt{\text{sample size}}$). This guarantees that *it* is the asymptote when a valid Central Limit Law applies.

f. As Arnold explicitly noted, it is defined by the Edgeworth-Bachelier-Einstein-Folker-Planck partial-differential (heat Fourier) equation of radiating probabilities.

Arnold himself, who served in later years a tour of duty as Secretary of the Institute of Mathematical Statistics, left MIT for the Wisconsin and Michigan State mathematics departments. Good Americans when they die go to Paris; lucky American professors retire to Cape Cod where Kenneth Arnold resides.

BOWKER

Harold Freeman had several statistics students who made their mark. The late Jack Kiefer is a case in point—at Columbia, Cornell and Berkeley. So is Albert Bowker who tied up with Wallis' wartime Statistical Research Group at Columbia. His subsequent career as Stanford Dean, Berkeley Chancellor, CUNY Head and University of Maryland executive extenuates some loss of concentration on Latin Squares.

FELLER

Willy Feller was then at Brown's strong war-time group in mathematics assembled by Dean Richardson. Later he was a mainstay at Cornell and Princeton. He had arrived in America from Yugoslavia by way of Harald Cramér's Stockholm seminar. Feller had not yet published his classic textbook, but already he was known to be a superb lecturer. Stochastic processes (the name traces to Bachelier c. 1900) were as old as Adam, but were just on the verge of a self-conscious renaissance.

Within economics, Markov processes were also about to take off. (Before 1938, I had to work out for myself that the transition-probability matrix for grandchildren of the elite was the square of the first-generation matrix—such was the state of economics education of the time.) The integral equation of renewal was a hot topic in business-cycle demographics and in Lotka population analysis. Feller had already shown the need for rigor when one claims to give infinite series of exponentials as exact solutions. Later, Ansley Coale and his pupil A. Lopez were able to defend demographer's heuristics since the inability of the very old and the very young to have children guaranteed the completeness of the infinite-series representation. And it was a refugee economist in New Zealand, Harro Bernardelli, who first pioneered the Leslie matrix version of Lotka's demographic integral equations. Much later, Nathan Keyfitz was able to show how the first term(s) in the Lotka infinite series enable calculating the penultimate transition timing to a population's maximum. When I wrote for the 1980 Merton *Festschrift* on R. A. Fisher's economic calculus of "reproductive value," I was delighted to see how his heuristics had touched against those of Keyfitz.

FREEMAN

Harold Freeman was the true leader of MIT's scientific activity in statistics. I always thought of him as Ibsen's Peer Gynt: Peer Gynt with touches of Thorstein Veblen. A perpetual student, Harold never took a Ph.D. degree. MIT didn't care; why should God?

A picture of him on his sickbed in 1936 showed what Jesus would have looked like. When Harold arrived here as a freshman a few years before the 1929 Crash, he topped six feet but weighed less than 100 pounds. He was too weak to carry the molten steel then required at the Forge Lab—even though 20 years later he led our pickup teams to league victory in basketball.

Although he once resembled Jesus, he told stories like Baron Munchhausen. I never heard him describe an event as it happened. Usually his accounts were better than the real thing. Harold was responsible for my coming to MIT. Harold was responsible for Bob Solow's coming here. When emeritus he wrote a bestseller on the evils of American capitalism. Joan Robinson wrote to him in the following vein: "How can a pearl like you coexist with swine like Paul Samuelson and Bob Solow?" He replied: "Easily. They are my best friends."

During the Korean decade, Harold asked me how he could invest a small inheritance so as not to benefit from any war activity. It was a tough question in Leontief input-output networking. In the end I had to cheat him by not mentioning that Gillette and International Harvester did have some Pentagon contracts. During World War II he refused fees for consulting on quartermaster and ordnance matters. He did claim his travel expenses as tax deductions. The local IRS agent said: "Nix. You can be a good guy. But not at our expense."

Every single day from September 10, 1927, to November 3, 1943, Harold ordered a chicken pie at the Walton Cafeteria outside MIT's main gate. By Laplace's Law of Succession, November 4, 1943, had an all but certain outcome. But never since has he eaten chicken.

Once I asked him: "If the Devil promised you a theorem in return for your immortal soul, would you accept the bargain?" Without hesitation he replied, "No. But I would for an inequality."

In his eighties I salute Harold Freeman. *Hail Apollo!*

HAAVELMO

Trygve Haavelmo began as Ragnar Frisch's favorite assistant at Oslo. World War II caught Haavelmo in America when Hitler's *Blitzkrieg* took over Norway. He was prepared to row back to Europe but that proved to be impractical. So there was naught for him to do but work on his own in Cambridge and Chicago, achieving a breakthrough in connection with identifying stochastic relationships in interdependent systems; he was to join up with the exiled Norwegian Shipping and Trade Mission. His MIT Lecture is not at all a routine review. Rather it is a first revelation of what was to be a major stimulus for the Chicago Cowles group already mentioned.

From time series data on price and quantity of, say, wheat, $[p_t, q_t]$, the economist wishes to estimate the best slope and intercept of wheat's linear *demand* curve. But every such point lies as much on wheat's supply curve. What meaning can we give to a least-squares fit of a line as a demand curve? Frisch, Haavelmo's master, had already struggled with this identification problem and had noticed that a fitted line would have its slope biased toward some mean of the two curves' respective dq/dp slopes.

Haavelmo chose to tackle in this lecture the Keynesian macro scenario called the multiplier-accelerator. I note in 1991 that he chose to use the 1939 version that had brought me an excess of youthful fame. Before Haavelmo, we would have regressed Consumption$_t$ on Income$_t$ or Income$_{t-1}$; and we'd have regressed Capital$_t$ − Capital$_{t-1}$ on Income$_t$ − Income$_{t-1}$ or have regressed Capital$_t$ on Income$_t$. Haavelmo shows how wrong this can be (and indicates when it might be a correct thing to do). Econometrics was never quite the same after his famous *Supplement*.

Being a scholar of no fuss, Trygve simply typed up his big manuscript and ran off copies on the purple ditto process of the day. He sent copies to the few interested experts and would probably not have published it in a special Supplement to *Econometrica* had it not been for insistence by Jacob Marschak and Ragnar Frisch.

It was a coup for Klein and Ullman to have persuaded Trygve Haavelmo to lecture on his new work red hot off the griddle.

HOTELLING

Today most people understand the term econometrics to cover the part of statistics useful in economics. But the original meaning of the term back in 1930 when the Econometric Society was founded (by Joseph Schumpeter, Irving Fisher and Ragnar Frisch) was the triple combination of mathematics, statistical theory and economic theory mobilized for the scientific measurement of economic reality.

In this extended sense of the term, Harold Hotelling qualified in the years 1925-1960 as America's leading econometrician. Trained in mathematics at the University of Washington and Princeton, he came to Columbia from Stanford. And, after 1946, he helped lead the statistical initiatives in North Carolina. At a time when R. A. Fisher's statistics was just beginning to affect American students, Hotelling at Columbia trained many of the nation's teachers. (Later, Wilks at Princeton and Neyman at Berkeley contributed much, and it was Hotelling who found for Abraham Wald a permanent home at Columbia.) Besides being a transmitter of statistical knowledge, Hotelling was also a creator, contributing to canonical correlation, principal components and much else, as well as forging computational algorithms for accelerated convergence of matrix inversion and matrix *eigenvectors*.

In economic theory Hotelling did not go up to bat often, but every article he wrote was a home run. Early on (1925, 1931) he worked out the variational conditions for optimum replacing of a machine and exploitation of exhaustible resources. Parallel to, and independently of, the contributions to demand theory of Slutsky (1915-1953) and Hicks-Allen (1934), Hotelling (1932, 1935) definitively established integrability and curvature conditions for budget unconstrained and budget constrained demand decisions, founding duality theory along the way. Parallel to, and independently of, the new welfare economics of Pareto, Lerner, Kaldor and Hicks, Hotelling (1938) demonstrated that equality of prices and marginal costs were a necessary condition for both Pareto-optimality and Bergson-optimality. Hotelling (1929) enriched permanently the literature of duopoly theory in its spatial aspects: sellers on a line move too close together; ciders are too homogeneous; Republicans and Democrats, sure of the stalwarts at their extremes, vie for the shiftable voters at the center.

Hotelling was an amiable leader with many admiring students. To have helped shape one Kenneth Arrow is fame enow. He was also something of a character. Thus, in the present MIT Lecture, delivered after Pearl Harbor when the Allied cause looked dark, Hotelling announced: "Have no fear. I have surveyed the statisticians possessed by Germany and Japan. They cannot compare with those in Britain, America and Russia. All will be well." He was serious.

Columbia's great physicist, I. I. Rabi, received the Nobel Prize while he was the assistant director of MIT's war-time Radiation Laboratory. Rabi asked me one day if I knew a Harold Hotelling; I replied that of course I knew so great an economist and statistician.

"Is he all there?" Rabi asked.

"Why would you ask that?"

"Well, at a Columbia faculty meeting Hotelling declared that the land the University was on was too valuable for that purpose and we should move elsewhere. 'What new location do you have in mind?' I asked.

"Hotelling replied, 'Seattle'."

I am sure Hotelling was serious.

It is a pity that Hotelling died in 1973 before being awarded the Nobel Prize he richly earned.

KLEIN

Lawrence Klein was too young to vote when he came to our graduate school, fresh from the Berkeley of Jerzy Neyman, Francis Dresch and William Fellner. After 15 months of course work he qualified for MIT's first Ph.D. in Economics, fast work even in war-time. His thesis became a classic, *The Keynesian Revolution*, and it gave the name to an epoch. His Nobel Prize traced primarily to his innovations in econometric macroeconomic forecasting, first at the University of Michigan and then later with the Penn Wharton model.

Klein has been a leader in modern econometrics. He was one of the important Cowles circle, in its Chicago existence. Along with Theodore Anderson he was a Post-Doc in Scandinavia: Klein at Ragnar Frisch's Oslo, and Anderson with Harald Cramér in Stockholm. Klein had a tour of duty at the Oxford Institute of Statistics. Many present-day chair holders call him Master and through him I have grandchildren aplenty.

SAMUELSON

At Chicago and Harvard I had the best economist training available in the 1930s. Therefore, the statistical education, or miseducation, of Paul A. Samuelson would tell something about the scene 50 years ago.

Often I ask couples exactly how they met. They rise to that fly. Where did I first meet the Normal Curve—often called the Gaussian or Laplace-Gaussian curve, but obviously best called de Moivre's Law? I was luckier than I deserved. The Chicago botanist Coulter, in an exposition during the Biology Survey I had to take in my sophomore autumn of 1932, explained simple Mendel laws of peas pink-and-white and smooth-or-curly. When he made tallness depend on the sum of independent genes that could be T_j or t_j, he hinted at a limiting bell-shaped "normal curve" for heights: not bad to get de Moivre's Central-Limit Theorem for the binomial as one's first introduction.

My second introduction came when I accompanied a girlfriend from the Social Service School to an afternoon lecture by the sociologist Ogburn. (He turned out to be the old boy who played tennis at the Quadrangle Club each mid-day. It was he who picked for the new Social Science Research Building its wall motto by Kelvin about scientific knowledge coming only when you could measure it.) Ogburn drew a symmetric unimodal curve on the board and asserted that, within what he called two standard deviations centered on its middle, 95% of any sample would have to fall. I saw that needn't be so: Alas, he didn't mention that, for something called the Normal Curve, it would be true.

I suppose it was soon thereafter that I happened to find on the Social Science Reserve shelf a little statistics primer by the psychologist Thurston. It defined mean, mode, median, geometric and harmonic means, standard deviation (not variance), mean-absolute-deviation and percentiles. It gave histograms for grouped data and may even have prattled about Sheppard's Corrections. A chapter dealt with the Normal Curve; and, I believe, an Appendix may have given Gauss' purported proof that the Normal Curve was the most probable (symmetric) one to have produced the specified sample (under the proviso that for some reason the sample mean had to be the estimator of the parameter a in the density function $p(x - a)\,dx$). What was not gratuitous was to recognize that only for $f(x - a) = (2\pi)^{-1/2} \exp[-\frac{1}{2}(x - a)^2]$ would the maximum likelihood estimator for a be the mean of a random sample $[x_1, \ldots, x_n]$.

I think Thurston described 2-variate linear correlation à la Karl Pearson. But in reading for a nature-versus-nurture term paper, I encountered Pearson's detailed description of Galton's regression-toward-the-mean analysis of parents and children. Later I learned from Ezekiel's treatise all about multiple regression.

Where were my classroom teachers in all this? Aaron Director—who was my first-quarter teacher in beginning economics and later in labor economics—taught me statistics. He relied on a pedestrian text and Mitchell's 1927 *Business Cycles*. I ended up knowing that people used the mean and standard deviation because they were "mathematically tractable." The median and mean-absolute-deviation, though intractable, had the saving grace of not being too much affected by "extreme deviations." Multiple regression I learned on my own, computing on automatic Monroe desk calculators Gauss-Doolittle least-squares equations. I learned about collinearity and ill-conditioned matrixes the hard way, grinding out approximations to 0/0 by ϵ_1/ϵ_2 expressions incident to roundoff errors in connection with a Paul Douglas production-function model based upon labor and capital inputs that grew in the *same* proportion. (Later from Ezekiel I learned the "free-hand curvilinear correlation" techniques of Louis Bean: knowing our data points lovingly, in those days we could almost feel the free play of collinear independent variables. My students in the post-computer age never got introduced to their time-series data points, except through the chaperonage of their summarizing product moments.)

A shocking undergraduate education in statistics at America's second-best university? Yes. But it was worse at the first-best university; at Harvard there were only hand calculators, and honors students learned virtually nothing. By the time I was a graduate student there, I was one out of 20 who discovered the small and exclusive E. B. Wilson seminar given every other year. Maybe at Iowa State things were better for undergraduates lucky enough to be majoring in agricultural economics. Maybe, but don't give 2-to-1 odds on it.

One advantage of a miseducation was much independent reading. Like a drunken sailor I staggered randomly through the many derivative works on least squares in astronomy and geodesy, all tracing back to Gauss. (A typical passage: "In triangulating the Lake Superior region, we solved 75 simultaneous equations between April, 1898 and September, helped by the sparse pattern of nonzeroes in our array of coefficients.") Not until Wilson steered me to Whittaker and Robinson did I learn about characteristic functions ("Fourier integrals") or that some linear sum of variates each normally distributed might *not* itself be normally distributed. I was bothered where I should have been bothered, as to read in R. A. Fisher that an over-small chi-square might be as significant as an over-large one—this from the genius who declared Neyman–Pearson to be totalitarian idiots.

One who did not live through the *ancien régime* would not believe how spotty it could be!

STRUIK

Dirk Struik in his tenth decade is certainly MIT's senior professor, and he must be one of the world's oldest mathematicians. Trained in Leiden, his specialty was differential geometry and he was coauthor with Schouten of a work on tensors. As a departmental volunteer he taught MIT's course on probability for many years. (I seem to remember that he had a cute axiomatic basis for the Poisson distribution.) As a writer on the history of mathematics, Struik attained world fame.

America has gained much from immigrants and Struik was a decade ahead of the avalanche to our shores propelled by Hitler. Struik took an active interest in a teacher's union for universities. In the witchhunt days of Senator Joseph McCarthy, Struik came under various attacks. Although Marxism can hardly infiltrate students' notes on quaternions, Dirk Struik had to sit out his pre-retirement years on a leave of absence with pay—a sad reflection of an ignoble epoch and a definite loss to the community of scholarship. Survival is one form of revenge and it lifts spirit to see the Struik couple striding vigorously as erect nonagenarians.

VON MISES

Richard von Mises indeed had many claims to scholarly fame. He was the kind of pure mathematician who worked in many applied areas of physics, engineering and statistics—a type like von Karman, not rare in Europe and almost nonexistent in America. During World War I he built Austria's first military airplane. With Einstein's friend and biographer Philip Frank, who was also brought to war-time Cambridge, Massachusetts by Hitler's fascism, von Mises edited a famous treatise on partial differential equations.

Von Mises was perhaps best known to mathematicians for his attempt to build the foundations of probability, not on Laplace–Kolmogorov definitions of measure and generalized notions of equally-likely sets, but rather on the concept of an infinite series whose successive terms lacked all order. The approach never much caught on. Some considered it circular; its consistency and rigor were questioned (even though Wald wrote a paper giving it some support). Hilda Geiringer, long von Mises' good friend and ultimately his wife, wrote and lectured in the von Mises vein.

I remember von Mises in a different statistical connection. R. A. Fisher had in those days made inverse and Bayesian probabilities dirty words, with only Harold Jeffreys and von Mises keeping that old faith alive among working mathematicians. A von Mises piece, I think in an early issue of the *Annals of Mathematical Statistics*, was my first source for the important theorem, that as one's sample of new data grows indefinitely, the sensitivity of one's inferences to one's *prior* probabilities goes to zero.

The occupancy problem von Mises treated in this lecture series arose from a famous argument among actuaries in a Vienna insurance firm, who had arrived at inconsistent answers. They called on von Mises, who resolved the quarrels by recourse to elementary combinatorics relevant to Boltzmann's probability-entropy. Cocktail parties still are entertained and surprised by von Mises' demonstration of how few must be the assemblage if no two are likely to have the same birthday in this year's calendar.

A few personal remarks about von Mises. The conservative economist Ludwig von Mises was Richard's older brother, but their views were opposed. Ludwig believed in *a priori* truths; Richard wrote a trenchant book on *positivism*. Ludwig hated mathematics and deplored any attempts by economists to use natural science methodology. Both were strong minds and personalities. (Out of disapproval of Hitler, Richard for a time dropped his "von" and wrote his signature as Richard de Mises. Like John von Neumann he could not, in America, quite give up his honorific—even though both had titles of fairly recent family origin that were unconnected with ancient feats of military glory and were tainted by either bureaucratic merit or financial lobbying!) I remember as an instance of von Mises' high quality a war-time discussion in one of the Harvard Houses on *turbulence*, in which he touched on notions now recognizable under the categories of chaos, bifurcation and computer Monte Carlo explorations.

WALD

Abraham Wald was simply our best. Fisher, Neyman and Wald were the top trio for statistics in the twentieth century. Abe was solid, deep and wide—completely without flash. Virtually self-taught in the boondocks of Hungarian Romania, he sought to study pure mathematics in Vienna. Karl Menger (the mathematician son of Carl Menger the economist) recognized his potential; but prospects for an outlander Jew in depression Austria were minimal. To survive, the racehorse harnessed himself to the cart of economic statistics. Oskar Morgenstern and the banker Karl Schlesinger scratched up bare financial support. Wald's proof of the existence and uniqueness of a Walrasian equilibrium owed its origins to Schlesinger; along the way Wald made a significant contribution to modern index number theory, and useful additions to seasonal adjusting and to Slutsky cycle analysis. Economics, he discovered, was fun and but for his accidental death in a 1950 Indian Air crash, he would have innovated much in theoretical economics along with continued work in statistics and pure mathematics.

Once Wald got to America, places like Harvard could have had him for a song but the mathematicians and administrators of my days in the Harvard Yard were tone deaf to his kinds of quality. It was Harold Hotelling who engineered his appointment at Columbia, where he lived happily ever afterward.

I seem to recall as the interesting feature of this Wald lecture at MIT the fact that Wilks' nice analysis of tolerance intervals, which was distribution-free in the 1-variable case, simply did not generalize to the case of 2-or-more-variables. With all Wald's ingenuity, he had to treat the variables asymmetrically to get anywhere with a generalization. At that time we may not have realized that soon Wald was to encounter and solve definitely the important problem of sequential analysis.[1]

More than 40 years ago a good friend of Wald told me the following charming story. It is second-hand hearsay but has some ring of truth.

Wald to Wolfowitz: Funny thing, I'm proving more theorems than ever but somehow I don't seem to be as happy as I used to be.

Wolfowitz to Wald: Maybe you ought to get Menger's advice at Notre Dame in South Bend.

Wald to Menger: Funny thing, ...

Menger to Wald: Maybe what you need is to get married?

Wald to Wolfowitz: Menger says maybe what I need is to get married.

Wolfowitz: Of course, what a fool I've been not to see it. And I have a cousin . . . .

The rest was history, happy history, but all too stochastically short.

WIENER

Much has been written about Norbert Wiener as prodigy and character. His own two autobiographies, *Ex-Prodigy* and *I Am a Mathematician*, give his version of reality. One biographer has grouped in a book Wiener as Mr. Clean and John von Neumann as the Lucifer who put his genius at the service of the bad guys. We shall not see Norbert's like again soon, but at the MIT of 1922-1964 he was ever-present. I always felt he might have accomplished twice as much if his restlessness and neuroses did not keep him so much in other people's offices. Those who were not themselves geniuses may even have lost a theorem or two because of time occupied with Norbert.

Dozens of stories were told about Wiener, many undoubtedly apocryphal since one had heard similar tales about local characters at colleges ranging from Ripon, Wisconsin, to Cambridge, England. An instance (that might even be true) can illustrate the genre. When the Wieners moved from one Belmont, Massachusetts house to another, Norbert drove near-sightedly back to the old home. It was empty and the door was locked. In perplexity he asked an urchin playing in the street where the Wieners lived. "Mama sent me to take you there, Father. Come along." Wiener's lack of skill at bridge and chess was awesome. A businessman studying at the MIT School of Management was amazed to be able to trounce him at a Faculty Club chess game. "How, Professor Wiener, can you be such a genius in mathematics and such an idiot at chess?" For once, Wiener's answer was on the mark: "In mathematics you're as good as your best move. In chess you're as bad as your worst." The wonder is that one who could play his chess would.

Along with Birkhoff, von Neumann, B. O. Koopman, Hopf and some of the great Russians, Wiener

---

[1] Remarkably, what Wald did was done in record time, reckoned in days and not months. To go much beyond this initial killing seems still to be frustrating. (It is well-known that preoccupation with priorities of discovery was virulent among the shipmates on the Wallis Statistical Research Group cruise: What did Milton say to Allen in the presence of Major Something-or-other at 10:03 a.m.? Was Jack Wolfowitz paranoid in his concerns for Wald's priorities? Before the last octogenarian is gone and history embalms myths, I ought to preserve in the record the fact that Walter Bartky of the University of Chicago Astronomy Department circulated widely for the Bell System around 1929 one well-specified formulation of the sequential-analysis problem that went beyond the Dodge-Romig procedures and included a complete solution for the binomial case. In July of 1940 at the Cowles Colorado Springs Conference, in the presence of Wald, Samuelson, Haavelmo, Flood and many others, Bartky lectured on this matter. Robert K. Merton as sociologist of science will not be surprised that straight-arrow Wald would have forgotten this event when Wallis threw at him the sequential-analysis challenge. Only one thing matters: It was Abraham Wald who did for the first time the general analysis that it is possible to do. And it is a matter of regret that subsequent generations have been so powerless to advance significantly beyond where he had arrived.)

was a major contributor to ergodic theory, then in the flush of its first decade. His lecture in this series was, as I remember it, purely expository but he began with the solemn warning: "Gentlemen, we are at war. And nothing you hear in this room must be repeated outside these walls lest it give aid and comfort to the Enemy."

Ralph Freeman—no kin to Harold Freeman and quite illiterate in mathematics—Head of MIT's Economics Department, attended Wiener's lecture by miscalculation and was trapped into being a captive audience. As the small group disbanded, Ralph whispered to me, "Hell, Hitler and Himmler couldn't get a word out of me even if the speaker had been a coherent lecturer."

WILSON

Edwin Bidwell Wilson was a polymath, Willard Gibbs' last protégé at Yale and my Harvard Master in mathematical economics and statistics. Since I wrote recently about him for the Yale Symposium celebrating the 150th Anniversary of Gibbs' birthday, I cannot do better than paraphrase extensively what I said there.

Wilson's merits are in danger of being lost in the mists of history. His forebears went to Yale until he went to Harvard, graduating in 1899 at the age of 20 with the alleged designation of *summa summorum cum laude*. By miscalculation he went to the Yale Graduate School. Gibbs turned out to compensate for Yale's inadequacies in pure mathematics; this pushed Wilson toward mathematical physics and, in the end, toward many novel fields. He wrote the first studies on stability of an airplane and contributed to the following areas: psychometrics (principal components and generalized Spearman–Thurston factor analysis), population analysis and actuarial statistics, Fisherine mathematical statistics and mathematical economics.

MIT called Wilson from Yale. At MIT he headed mathematical physics, wrote his serviceable and durable *Advanced Calculus* and was drafted to be the acting president in the early 1920s. Then President Lowell called him to be the dean of what is now the Harvard School of Public Health. Each spring he taught for the Economics Department in alternate years a seminar in mathematical economics and mathematical statistics, and I was one of the small contingent of economists who benefited from his broad knowledge and wry wit.

E. B. was the only intelligent man I ever knew who liked committee meetings. He was long Chairman of the Social Science Research Council, and much longer Editor of the *Proceedings of the National Academy of Sciences, U.S.A.* He headed the watchdog committee that Harvard set up to monitor its new venture into sociology à la Sorokin, Parsons and Merton.

Statistics at Harvard in the 1930s was a scandal. The course on probability in the Mathematics Department was often not offered; when offered it was usually by Mr. X, who could not escape impressment. In the Economics Department Leonard W. Crum and Edwin Frickey taught bizarre versions of Yule's statistics and a smattering of correlation analysis. (Something close to the Central-Limit Theorem appeared in my notes from Crum as the Law of Large Numbers.) What we all learned was, never trust statistics.

Wilson was a saving remnant. He gave intelligent exposition of Fisherine statistics. He knew R. A. Fisher, admired him but also knew him as unreliable in experimental matters. Both Wilson and Fisher goofed in appraising the evidence against cigarette smoking; both were enlisted by the tobacco industry; but Wilson's follies were misdemeanors of skepticism whereas Fisher's were felonies of stubborn idiocy. Retrospective audits have only worsened Fisher's report card in this matter.

FINALE

Reading these embalmed abstracts is a bit like experiencing the time warp of a visit to Pompeii. It brought the same déjà vu as I experienced in reading the resurrected report by Erik Lundberg of his 1931-1933 sojourn in America as a Stockholm Rockefeller Fellow. Names almost forgotten came back to instant life after one gazed upon the snapshots caught at that time.

Does nostalgia make it seem a time better than it was? Perhaps not. Was there ever a more uncivil pair than Karl Pearson and R. A. Fisher? Alfred North Whitehead told me that he was the only person in England who could stay on speaking terms with both Pearson the Galtonian and Bateson the Mendelian. Pearson in power abused Ronald Fisher as untenured scholar. Beaten children become child beaters, it is said. And that was the alibi admirers of Fisher offered to extenuate his hauteurs. (At the Galton Laboratory of the University of London, when Karl Pearson's kingship was divided into chairs for both Fisher and Egon Pearson, a separate staircase was built so that Fisher would not have to encounter the face of Neyman. Honest Injun? That's what we youngsters were told.)

The years 1935-1950 represent an inflection point in the growth of intensive science. The generation of scholars willed to America by Adolph Hitler were unusually dedicated people and they stoked the furnaces of native American research establishments. I believe this rediscovered MIT war-time seminar catches something of the flavor of those unusual times.

ON THE HISTORIOGRAPHY OF ECONOMICS: A CORRESPONDENCE

BY

PAUL A. SAMUELSON, DON PATINKIN, AND MARK BLAUG

SAMUELSON TO BLAUG, JULY 3, 1990

I read your "...Historiography..." (Blaug 1990) with interest and profit. You were kind to me — probably too kind. But let me explore a point. Let's accept for the sake of the argument that in some instances a "rational reconstruction" can deviate from a "historical reconstruction." Query: When I attributed to Smith the "canonical classical model" (Samuelson 1978), did I provide your readers with such an instance of deviation? No, I say. And your text does not adduce otherwise. Nor does Hollander's rhetoric (1980) in reaction to me. Actually, Hollander said: Yes, that model is in Smith but one has to work hard not to overlook it (particularly because its pieces are in scattered and unlikely places).

If you had reported that, your readers would have been in a position to take with a grain of salt the sentence you report (Blaug 1990, p. 31) about Hollander: "Thus, Hollander concludes, the canonical model is a Ricardian [sic][1] construction...in terms of analytic logic...and should not be attributed to Adam Smith." This reminds me of a lame admission by Hans Staehle, in a 1938 letter to Keynes (see p. 272 of Volume XIV of Keynes's *Collected Writings*), that indeed he had incorrectly described a 1936 Keynes argument but that was because he had so marked up his copy of the *General Theory* that he could not read the words written there. What Hollander might have claimed was that Smith's exposition was sufficiently obscure so that Ricardo might have had to rediscover Smith's argument for himself. But in that case

---

Massachusettes Institute of Technology; Hebrew University of Jerusalem; University of Exeter and University of Buckingham.

In order to save space, the editor has eliminated the salutations and the complimentary closes from the letters. The references in parentheses were inserted after the letters were written.

1. Square brackets in original.

Journal of the History of Economic Thought, 13, Fall 1991.
©1991 by the History of Economics Society.

your charge against me would still be vitiated and you would have to say: Ricardo's *historical* reconstruction of Smith was faulty in not recognizing the correct *analytical* reconstruction to be found in Smith.

Let me babble on a bit. Suppose I give an analytic reconstruction of an old writer and we imagine the thought experiment of showing it to that writer. If he says, "Clever, why didn't I notice that?", then my effort hardly qualifies as a historical reconstruction. But it is different when he reacts with, "Yes, that's a way of putting what I was trying to say." This leads me to the Fallacy of Pedantical literalness, which infests writers on history of doctrines. When you show them that Smith and Malthus (and Eve-Adam) perceived and wrote down that limitation of land constrains output even when labor and capital grow, they say: "That's not THE LAW OF DIMINISHING RETURNS. How could it be? since West-Malthus-Ricardo discovered this LAW only in 1815, which *follows* 1798, 1776 (and minus 4106)." I say, fingers were made before forks and before they were named forks.

God punishes all good deeds. Your reward for praising me was an Oliver Twist whine for more.

SAMUELSON TO PATINKIN, JULY 3, 1990[2]

For your interest in our long dialogue between liberal and strict interpretations. I could have added for Blaug that writers do not at all times perceive what is in their own words (and which they may sometimes perceive)....

PATINKIN TO SAMUELSON, JULY 25, 1990

Many thanks for sending me a copy of your letter to Mark Blaug. I have no expertise on the subject of classical economics, and so have nothing to say about the specific issues you discuss with respect to Smith and Ricardo. But, as you wrote in the note to me that you added to your letter, these issues are indeed related to "our long dialogue between liberal and strict interpretations," so let me say a few words from that viewpoint.

In your letter to Blaug, as on earlier occasions, you make use in your treatment of the history of doctrines of "thought-experiments" in which you hypothetically ask an author about his writings in order to determine what can properly be attributed to him. My reservations about these experiments is that you both pose the question and give the answer. And what if I should conduct the same thought-experiment and give a different answer? What do we do then? In brief, our respective thought-experiments are simply a way of presenting our respective interpretations of a text, carried out in each case by whatever method of interpretation we respectively use. The

2. *P.A.S.*: Note attached to a copy of my letter to Blaug.

909

thought-experiments in themselves provide no criterion for choosing between different interpretations.

I must nevertheless go on to say that, on two occasions that I am aware of, the answers you have given to thought-experiments you have conducted are contradicted by the evidence — in one case unequivocally, and in one case circumstantially. The first case was in an exchange we had many years ago in the pages of the *Canadian Journal of Economics* with respect to what I had in my 1949 *Econometrica* article called the invalid dichotomy, which I contrasted with the valid one, and in which I contended that "classical economics" (a misnomer that I then used to describe those economists of the end of the nineteenth century and first quarter of the twentieth whose writings inter alia I was discussing — e.g., Walras, Fisher, Cassel et al.) had in fact advocated the invalid one. In your 1968 paper in the *Canadian Journal* on "What Classical and Neoclassical Monetary Theory Really Was" (reprinted on pp. 529-43 of volume 3 of your *Collected Scientific Papers*) you rejected my contention on the basis of the following thought-experiment: "If one could subpoena Cassel, show him the two systems and the defects in one, and then ask him which fits in best with his over-all intuitions, I believe he would pick (A,B) [the valid dichotomy] and not his own (A',B') [the invalid one]" (ibid., p. 542). In my 1972 comment on your paper (reprinted on pp. 149-153 of my *Essays On and In the Chicago Tradition*), I pointed out that such an experiment (though of course not with Cassel!) had actually been carried out in your presence, only to yield results the opposite of those predicted by you: namely, at a session of the 1949 Econometrics Society meetings that you chaired, Leontief and Hickman had criticized my 1949 article, and had explicitly chosen (A',B') in preference to (A,B). And I also pointed out that Archibald and Lipsey had also done so in an article published almost a decade later.

The second case is the ongoing disagreement that we have had about your contention that there is a "logical equivalence" between Kahn's 1931 multiplier article and the "output determination model" of the *General Theory*, as you first contended in the 1975 conference that we both participated in on "Keynes, Cambridge and the General Theory" (see p. 83 of the proceedings volume of this conference (Patinkin and Leith, eds., 1977)), and as you repeated at the 1987 conference on the Stockholm School, where you described them as being "logically isomorphic." Instead of going over all that again, let me simply enclose a copy of my discussion of your paper at the 1987 Stockholm conference, which discussion is primarily devoted to that contention. And the circumstantial evidence that I have in mind is Kahn's 1974 letter to me in response to my query as to what he saw as the "primary purpose" of his 1931 article. In this letter there is not even a hint that Kahn saw any connection between it and the *General Theory* — and this despite Schumpeter's well-known comment that Kahn's "share in the historic achievement [viz., writing the *General Theory*] cannot have fallen very far short of co-authorship," a comment of which Kahn could not have been unaware. (Kahn's letter is reproduced on pp. 146-8 of the aforementioned proceedings volume; Schumpeter's comment is on p. 1172 of his *History of Economic Analysis*.)

A related problem that I have with your thought-experiments is that they don't provide for the possibility of our saying that we don't believe the hypothetical answer given by our hypothetical questionee – and here too I am thinking of a specific instance, one which to my mind is not unrepresentative of the temptations to which our hypothetical questionee might well be subject. It is the instance that I have discussed on pp. 196-97 of my chapter on "Keynes and the Multiplier" in my 1982 book on *Anticipations of the General Theory*. This chapter is an abridgment of a 1978 article of mine in which I cited an unpublished 1930 memorandum by Colin Clark in which he had written that "the 'repercussive' effects of any considerable increase in the export trade...would lead to assuming an infinite series of beneficial repercussions...the limiting factors [of which] are obscure and economic theory cannot state the possibilities with precision." In my original paper, I interpreted this statement as expressing the view that "while there was no doubt that the multiplier (which term was not yet in use) was greater than unity; but the theoretical question to which no satisfactory answer had yet been formulated was, why was it not infinity?"

I also reported that in his discussion of my paper, John Flemming had suggested that "as a graduate of the physical sciences...Clark must have surely known that the sum of an infinite series was not necessarily infinite," so that "Clark might have simply meant that he did not know how to provide a precise mathematical description of the 'infinite series of beneficial repercussions' – and hence obviously could not sum it up." I was visiting the University of Chicago in 1978, and at a later point in it Clark also paid a brief visit to Chicago, and I took advantage of it to ask him (and I'm quoting now from the additional material that I added to the footnote on p. 197 of the reprinted article) "which of the two interpretations of what he had in mind in the aforementioned passage from this memorandum, mine or Flemming's, was correct – and he unhesitatingly replied that Flemming's was. But as we continued with our conversation, Clark suddenly remarked that he actually had no recollection of ever having written the 1930 memorandum!"

In your letter to Mark Blaug, you refer to the "Fallacy of Pedantical Literalness." Is the counterpart to that the "Fallacy of Impressionistic Interpretation"? Or should we denote the distinction as one between "Documented and Undocumented Interpretations"? Nor do I think that the different interpretations you and I have of texts are properly described as the difference between "liberal and strict interpretations." For I feel that these differences between us stem primarily from two more basic differences.

First, our different notions of the creative process. You feel that if A implies B, then one can attribute B even to a writer who has only stated A. But the personal experiences I have on several occasions had of not seeing B—in some cases, not seeing it until later (see pp. 11 and 14 of my *Essays On and In the Chicago Tradition* and p. 1 of my new introduction to the 1989 reissue of *Money, Interest and Prices*), and in some cases not seeing it until someone else had pointed it out (see my discussion of Clower on pp. xvii-xviii of that introduction)—make it impossible for me to accept that approach. And I have said enough about this in the concluding paragraphs of my comment on your 1987 Stockholm paper.

Second, my emphasis on the central message of a writer, which is indeed the central message of the first half of my *Anticipations of the General Theory*. I summarized that discussion elsewhere (Patinkin 1983). In the note to me that you have added to your letter to Blaug, you say that "writers do not at all times perceive what is in their own words." In such a case it is not part of their respective central messages, and accordingly (for reasons explained on pp. 85-87 of *Anticipations*) I would say that there is no justification for attributing to these writers what they themselves did not perceive.

As relevant to all this as another example of my own approach to the writing of the history of doctrine, I am also enclosing a copy of an extended version of the Keynes Lecture that I gave last November "On Different Interpretations of the *General Theory*," which is forthcoming in the *Journal of Monetary Economics*. Would I be hitting below the belt if I were to say that Joan Robinson would contend that her interpretation of the *General Theory* is the result of a thought-experiment that she conducted with Keynes?

Since all this started with the copy you sent me of your letter to Mark Blaug, I am sending him a copy of this too. By coincidence, in some comments he sent me on the Keynes Lecture, he too has alluded to his article "On the Historiography of Economics," though on a different aspect of it.

I would be very interested in getting your reaction to all this.

BLAUG TO SAMUELSON, AUGUST 1, 1990

Thanks for your letter of July 3. I take your point but actually it is you who are committing the Fallacy of Pedantic Literalness: Because Adam Smith did say X, therefore he knew/understood/recognized the significance of X. The old Stigler point applies here as elsewhere: If contemporaries do not register X, the fact that someone did say X counts for naught. Is Gossen a true forerunner of the Marginal Revolution? No, because no one read him.

It is not enough to have great ideas, as Schumpeter always said; you have to get them across to your colleagues.

I enjoyed Patinkin's letter to you and your reply to him about the judo trick.[3]

SAMUELSON TO PATINKIN, AUGUST 14, 1990

I sent you a copy of some scrappy remarks to Blaug and you replied with 4 single-lined pages of thoughtful comments plus enclosures of old and new reprints. That is unbalanced trade and an exploding multiplier! I started to draft some reactions but found that on a hit-and-run basis they were incomplete and seemed to be argumentative — when it was not so much disagreement that I was trying to register but rather elucidating distinctions that are vital to my position.

I applaud those who study history of scholars — their writings, ideologies, influence, and changing reputations. My own special interest is in the history of economic theories, models, paradigms, measurements, hypotheses, etc. Abraham Pais's *scientific* biography of Einstein's contributions or his survey of the development of modern unified field theory in physics is something like what I have always had in mind. John Chipman's trade-theory survey (1965, 1966) is also relevant. In my earlier excursion into history (c. 1957?), I spoke of "Marx-like Models" and subsequently gallons of ink were spent by Meek, Dobb, Seton, Morishima, Steedman,... on similar issues.

When Quesnay and the Physiocrats are unclear on *why* they regard non-agricultural industries as "sterile," I find their discussion other than boring only when I can use the Hume-Smith-Ricardo perception of land rent as a residual to made good sense of the physiocatic distinction.

You speak of your 1974 letter from Richard Kahn in which he gave no hint that he saw a connection between his 1931 article and Keynes's 1936 *General Theory* model. Interesting. But it does not alter the verdict on the logical equivalence of Kahn's 1931

$$(1 + c + c^2 + ...) \Delta(\text{spending}) = 1/(1-c) \Delta(\text{spending}), \quad 0 < c < 1$$

and Keynes's system

$$y = C + \bar{I} = cy + \bar{I} = 1/(1-c)\bar{I} = \left(\sum_{0}^{\infty} c^k\right)\bar{I}$$

---

3. *M.B.*: Don Patinkin's "Comment" on Samuelson's paper at the 1987 conference on the Stockholm School concluded with a paragraph reminding the reader that he had disagreed once before with Samuelson on doctrinal questions because Samuelson was too fast on his feet to be a good historian of economic thought. Samuelson's reaction to this gibe was to accuse Patinkin of fighting judo: using an opponent's strength against himself. Hence my reference to "the judo trick."

or

$$\Delta y = \Delta C + \Delta \overline{I} = c \Delta y + \Delta \overline{I} = 1/(1-c) \Delta \overline{I} = (\sum_{0}^{\infty} c^k) \Delta \overline{I}$$

I agree that we humans are often imperfect logical machines—particularly in the early stages of discovery and exploration. Truly, I would not want to write: "If A implies B and Cohen asserts that A obtains, then he asserts (and understands) that B does obtain." When you present me with my sentences that are of this form, I will authorize you to say that "Samuelson admits and regrets error." But also, in pursuing my study of the history of (A, B, logical relationships, empirical relevances), I'd reproach myself for failing to recognize when the A's do imply the B's.

Enough for now. (By the way, before 1930 C. Clark, J. M. Clark for his Carnegie study of World War I articulated the *convergent* chain of 1914-1916:

Δ(National Income) = (ΔAllies' Imports from U.S.)$(1 + c + c^2 + ...)$, where $1 + c + c^2 + ... < 1 + 1 + 1 + ... = \infty$.

P.S. You claim no knowledge of classical economics. Nonetheless, I ought to clarify my remarks on pedantical literalness in connection with the presence in Petty, Locke, Cantillon, Smith, Turgot, and 1798 Malthus of a distinct perception of "diminishing returns to land" in the sense of recognizing that crowding much labor and produced-input-goods on limited land can be expected to reduce real wage rates, raise land rent, and (probably) lower the profit rate. With you, I insist on the need to "document" that these recognitions are indeed in their sentences. What I dubbed the fallacy was a belief that failure to find there "the law of diminishing returns" in the form of the 1815 West-Malthus-Ricardo assertion that Q(land, labor + 2[Δlabor]) - Q(land, labor + Δlabor) < Q(land, labor + Δlabor) - Q(land, labor) — that such a failure would cogently rebut those early writers' recognition of "diminishing returns." I can use your own mode (which is also mine) to elucidate. "When x and y are equivalent logically, each implying the other, failure of Aristotle to recognize that x obtains does not prove that Aristotle fails to recognize that y obtains."[4]

SAMUELSON TO PATINKIN, AUGUST 27, 1990

In another connection I consulted Cassel's 1925 lectures: *Fundamental Thoughts in Economics,* on his thoughts about any possible "dichotomy" between barter- and money-economy. Then I tried to write down a faithful

---

4. *P.A.S.*: See my 1990 article commemorating the bicentenary of Smith's death for further elucidation of why Hollander and Blaug ought to concede his mastery of substantive "diminishing returns." See also Samuelson (1992) summing up on Kahn and Keynes.

translation into math of Cassel's view, as applied to the following world: All are alike, owning equal acres of land, equal fixed supplies of labor (they live forever!), and of a produceable-depreciable machine. They consume corn and silk, each of which are produceable by Cobb-Douglas production functions involving labor, land, and machines. New machines are produced by a Cobb-Douglas function of the same three inputs. All people have a 5% time preference and machines depreciate exponentially independently of age. To humor Cassel's allergy to marginal utility, I'll let him assume that people spend half their net incomes on corn and half on silk. Remark: At interest rates above 5%, people will accumulate capital until the market interest rate is brought down to the 5% equilibrium. All use a fiat M to buy corn and silk; and firms use it to buy labor and land and machines.

To make a long story long, my Walrasian steady-state unknowns would be three outputs (q_1, q_2, q_3), nine allocated inputs $(L_1, L_2, L_3; T_1, T_2, T_3; K_1, K_2, K_3)$, three output prices (P_1, P_2, P_3), two factor prices (Wage, Rent), real interest rate r, and net rental of machines as deducible from rP_3. All prices are in fiat money, and if the total of M is fixed as $\overline{M}$, Cassel and everyone will deduce that $(P_1, P_2, P_3,$ Wage, Rent) is a vector proportional in equilibrium to $\overline{M}$.

To make the long story short, I could validly reduce it to the following equations:

I $\quad r =$ exogenous time preference rate

II $\quad f^j(P_1/M, P_2/M, P_3/M, \text{Wage}/M, \text{Rent}/M, r) = 0$

$$j = 1, 2, 3, 4, 5$$

III $\quad M = \overline{M}$

Now, I-II can indeed be solved for relative prices

$$([P_2/P_1]^*, [P_3/P_1]^*, [W/P_1]^*, [R/P_1]^*, r^*).$$

I-II-III determine absolute prices proportional to M. Query: Have I not been faithful to Cassel and to *Canadian Journal* PAS? What illegitimate dichotomy have Cassel or PAS done? Surely I am cycling in my old age?

P.S. The way *I* would spell out how M itself enters into equations II might well differ from Cassel's way. I might use the utility function he despises:

$$U(P_1, P_2, M; q_1, q_2)$$

$$= U(P_1/M, P_2/M, 1; q_1, q_2)$$

915

$$= (q_1 q_2)^{1/2} V(P_1/M, P_2/M).$$

Subject to $rM + P_1 q_1 + P_2 q_2 = W\overline{L}_1 + R\overline{T} + rP_3\overline{K} + r\overline{M}.$

$$\underset{q_1, q_2, M}{\text{Max}} \ U(P_1/M, P_2/M, 1; q_1, q_2)$$

Need I stress the point that in 1935, fresh at Harvard out of Chicago, this is in the spirit of how I would have tried to answer the Exam question: "How do Cassel and Fisher regard M as entering into the behavior equations of their two elementary textbooks?" No post-1936 new wisdoms are involved in I-II-III. At Harvard circa 1936 I did learn from Schumpeter:

Four independent equations in $[P_2/P_1, P_3/P_1, W/P_1, R/P_1]$

and

$$\sum_1^3 P_j q_j + W\overline{L} + R\overline{T} = v\overline{M}, \quad v \text{ a velocity parameter.}$$

Undoubtedly, I failed to note Schumpeter's step backward in capturing neoclassical reality.

P.P.S. People spend equal amounts on corn and silk, and spend one-tenth of those amounts on the convenience of a cash balance (foregoing that much of opportunity cost interest, earnable at 5% on their endowment of fiat cash $\overline{M}$): This might be Cassel's own simplified version of how M enters into his II.

PATINKIN TO SAMUELSON, AUGUST 28, 1990

Thanks for your fax of August 14. You say that your "special interest is in the history of economic theories, models, paradigms, measurements, hypotheses, etc." I would describe my interests in the same way, though I would add that I also have an interest in what this history reveals about the wonders of the workings of the human mind. I would also confess that for various reasons my interest is limited to the development in the twentieth century of those ideas in monetary and macroeconomic theory with which I have been concerned in my own theoretical work.

There is, however, a difference between us, and I still think it is nicely illustrated by our ongoing discussion of Kahn and the multiplier. I have never questioned your demonstration that *implicit* in his development is the theory of effective demand. What we differ about is the cerebral distance between the implicit and the explicit, the width of the synaptic gap between the two. And I continue to believe that this difference in the way we interpret a text is itself a reflection of the difference between the respective speeds with which our own minds work.

P.S. Incidentally, J. M. Clark's Carnegie study was published in 1931, and so did not precede Colin Clark's 1930 memorandum.

P.P.S. I have just received your fax of August 27. The dichotomy which you present in it is equivalent to the one that I present on p. 474, section (i) of the second edition of my *Money, Interest, and Prices* as the first valid dichotomy. It differs from the third and invalid dichotomy (ibid., pp. 475-6) in that the additional information that it provides in order to determine nominal prices is the specification of some nominal quantity (which in both your discussion and mine is the nominal quantity of money), as distinct from specifying the excess-demand equation for money (which is the critical feature of the dichotomy presented by Divisia, Modigliani and the other writers cited on pp. 624-29 of my book, and reaffirmed by Hickman and Leontief even after I had demonstrated its invalidity). Note too that the valid dichotomy violates Leontief's "homogeneity postulate," which is satisfied by the commodity equations of the invalid dichotomy: for in the valid dichotomy, an equi-proportionate change in the money prices of all commodities *will* affect the amounts demanded of them.

Might I also note that in Supplementary Note H of my book I have discussed Cassel's system, and in this context also cited from the same pages of his *Fundamental Thoughts in Economics* that you have faxed me (see p. 620, n. 24). I must, however, admit that I would now probably agree with you that these passages should be interpreted as a statement of the first valid dichotomy, and not (as in my discussion there) as one of the invalid dichotomy. At the same time, the passage that I quote from Cassel's *Theory of Social Economy* (see p. 619, text at n. 20) shows that Cassel confused these two dichotomies.

SAMUELSON TO PATINKIN, AUGUST 28, 1990

Thanks for your valuable 8/28 fax. An executive in an MIT advanced management program beat Norbert Wiener so easily in chess that he asked of him: "How can you be such a great mathematician and so lousy a chess player?" Wiener answered: "In chess you're only as good as your worst moves. In mathematics you're as good as your *best* moves." This suggests to me a small difference between our approaches to science history. When a Cassel tries to *formalize* his money theory in the 1918 *Theory of Social Economy*, that best effort falls below his best elementary expositions. A strict documentarian is right to nail him with his failure(s). A loose constructionist is right to recognize in his overall corpus the good perceptions that are really there. (The danger for the loose constructionist is that he has few guards against proclaiming falsely that those good perceptions are truly there and not solely in his own eyes.)

I was glad to be given the reminder that I needed, namely that you had indeed dealt with Cassel's 1925 text. I had a selfish and ignoble reason for feeling happy that you do recognize a "valid dichotomy." When I wrote the *Canadian Journal* piece on what I remembered neoclassical monetary theory to have been, I feared that you regarded me as having inadvertently introduced hindsight into the piece. I could not prove that to be less than justice but in my heart and mind I believed in my own innocence. The not very profound words of Cassel, if they can now pass muster, make me less fearful that mine could have been a case of self-delusion. My recent fax to you did not speak accidentally of the "elementary textbooks" of Fisher and Cassel.

Permit to write a small quibble. If my system's relations all involve $(P_1/M,...,P_n/M, W_1/M,...,W_m/M)$ as variables, then Leontief's "homogeneity" is substantively realized. More generally, when M is also a vector, homogeneity of degree 0 in the vector (P, W, M) is what the Quantity Theory is all about and what 1936 Keynes momentarily denied.

PATINKIN TO SAMUELSON, AUGUST 30, 1990

Thanks for your fax of the 28th. It bears nicely on my point that an additional interest of mine in the history of doctrines is what it reveals about the wondrous workings of the human mind. You seem to say that Cassel stated the dichotomy incorrectly in his 1918 *Theory of Social Economy* and then consciously corrected himself and stated it correctly in his 1925 *Fundamental Thoughts in Economics*. Whereas I would say that he was and remained confused about these two forms of the dichotomy and did not realize that they were quite different.[5] On pp. 600-602 of *Money, Interest, and Prices* I bring evidence to the effect that Fisher was involved in the same confusion. And the same was true of other writers.

Of course your model as well as mine assumes that the commodity demand functions are homogeneous of degree zero in the prices *and* in M. Leontief's "homogeneity postulate," however, states that the homogeneity exists *in the prices alone*. That is the distinction that I emphasize ad nauseam in my book. And if Leontief "really" meant what the two of us meant, why

---

5. *D.P.:* I forgot here to support this view with the fact that my evidence in *Money, Interest and Prices* (1965, pp. 618-19) for Cassel's involvement in the invalid dichotomy was based on the 1932 English translation of the 5th (1932) edition of Cassel's *Theoretische Sozialökonomie*; and that the corresponding discussion in the 1924 translation of the 2nd (1921) German edition was much the same. It is also noteworthy that Cassel wrote a preface to the 1932 translation in which he stated that he had "gone through the whole work several times, made many additions, and brought it up-to-date" (ibid., p. v).

did he criticize my 1949 article in his 1950 *Econometrica* note?

On p. 188 of my book I say that "I have no doubt that neoclassical economists would have readily accepted the criticisms involved [i.e., of the invalid dichotomy]; would have declared the explicit introduction of the real-balance effect into the commodity demand functions to be a more precise reflection of their thinking on this matter all along and, indeed, a modification that could only strengthen their quantity-theory conclusions." This sounds very much like what you said in our subsequent *Canadian Journal* exchange. The difference between us, however, is that while you seem to continue to feel that such economists would immediately recognize the incorrect aspect of their original statements and immediately embrace the corrected one, my experience with Leontief, Hickman, Archibald and Lipsey et al. has made me realize that such acceptance will frequently come only after an extended effort of explanation and persuasion, and sometimes not even then. In brief, I would today delete the word "readily" from the above passage.

Let me also say that the issue between us is not whether we should judge a writer by his best or his worst. When I point out that Cassel and Fisher were confused, I am not trying to downgrade them, and not trying to say that I am smarter than they were. I am simply pointing out that they too were fallible human beings. And I am also pointing out the fascinating way in which even great minds have confused two statements which are deceivingly similar, but actually quite different. This is the fascinating intellectual phenomenon that is lost sight of by the "loose constructionist."

SOME AFTERTHOUGHTS:

P.A.S., April 11, 1991: One fruit of this "Trialogue" means much to me: Don Patinkin's August 28 words "...I would now probably agree with you that these (1925 Cassel) passages should be interpreted as a statement of the first valid dichotomy, and not...as one of the invalid dichotomy." It means much because it fortifies my confidence that hindsight gleaned from the 1935-1968 years had not contaminated my recollection of what my neoclassical notions of monetary theory were in the 1933-1935 era. Convergence to agreement of Don and me represents genuine progress. And I must declare that the third sentence of Patinkin's August 30 letter — inferring that I ever believed that Cassel improved his understanding of the dichotomies between 1918 and 1925 — is quite unwarranted. Rather, and this is another highly valuable instance of convergence of viewpoint, Patinkin's stated views in the final two sentences of that paragraph are almost exactly those I had also arrived at — namely, long continued confusions persisted in the minds of Cassel and Fisher on how to give proper mathematical formulation of their common-sense perception about monetary reality. Amen to agreement.

D.P., April 29, 1991: And as further evidence of the confusion that existed with reference to the dichotomy issue, I am glad to have Paul's testimony in his postscript to his letter of August 27 that what Schumpeter presented in his lectures to Paul and his classmates at Harvard in 1936 was actually the invalid dichotomy. So amen again to agreement.

REFERENCES

Blaug, Mark. 1990. "On the Historiography of Economics," *Journal of the History of Economic Thought*, *12*, Spring, 27-37.

Cassel, G. 1918. *Theoretische Sozialökonomie*, 2d ed., 1921; 3d ed., 1923; 4th ed., 1927; 5th ed., 1932, C. F. Winter, Leipzig.

_____. 1924. *Theory of Social Economy*, translation by Joseph McCabe of the 2d edition of *Theoretische Sozialökonomie*, T. Fisher Unwin, London.

_____. 1925. *Fundamental Thoughts in Economics*, Harcourt, Brace, New York.

_____. 1932. *Theory of Social Economy*, translation by S. L. Barron of the 5th ed. of *Theoretische Sozialökonomie*, Harcourt, Brace, New York.

Chipman, John S. 1965, 1966. "A Survey of the Theory of International Trade," *Econometrica*, *33*, 477-519,685-760; *34*; 18-76.

_____. 1987. "International Trade," in *The New Palgrave: A Dictionary of Economics*, 2, 922-55, edited by John Eatwell, Murray Milgate, and Peter Newman, Macmillan, London.

Clark, J. M. 1931. *The Costs of the World War to the American People*, Yale University Press, for the Carnegie Endowment for International Peace, New Haven, Conn.

Fisher, Irving. 1912. *Elementary Principles of Economics*, Macmillan, New York.

Hollander, S. 1980. "On Professor Samuelson's Canonical Classical Model of Political Economy," *Journal of Economic Literature*, *18*, June, 559-74.

Jonung, Lars, ed. 1991. *The Stockholm School of Economics Revisited*, Cambridge University Press, New York.

Kahn, R. F. 1931. "The Relation of Home Investment to Unemployment," *Economic Journal*, *41*, June, 173-98.

Keynes, J. M. 1936. *The General Theory of Employment, Interest and Money*, Macmillan, London.

_____. 1973. *The General Theory and After: Part II: Defence and Development*, edited by Donald Moggridge, in *The Collected Writings of John Maynard Keynes, 14,* Macmillan, for the Royal Economics Society, London.

Leontief, W. W. 1950. "The Consistency of the Classical Theory of Money and Prices," *Econometrica*, *18*, January, 21-24.

Pais, Abraham. 1982. *Subtle is the Lord: The Science and the Life of Albert Einstein*, Oxford University Press, Oxford.

———. 1986. *Inward Bound: Of Matter and Forces in the Physical World*, Oxford University Press, Oxford.

Patinkin, Don. 1949. "The Indeterminacy of Absolute Prices in Classical Economic Theory," *Econometrica*, *17*, January, 1-27, as reprinted in Patinkin 1981, 125-48.

———. 1965. *Money, Interest, and Prices: An Integration of Monetary and Value Theory*, 2nd ed., Harper and Row, New York.

———. 1972. "Samuelson on the Neoclassical Dichotomy: A Comment," *Canadian Journal of Economics*, *5*, May, 279-83; as reprinted in Patinkin 1981, 149-53.

———. 1981. *Essays On and In the Chicago Tradition*, Duke University Press, Durham, NC.

———. 1982. *Anticipations of the General Theory? And Other Essays on Keynes*, University of Chicago Press, Chicago.

———. 1983. "Multiple Discoveries and the Central Message," *American Journal of Sociology*, 89, September, 306-23.

———. 1987. See Patinkin 1991.

———. 1989. *Money, Interest, and Prices: An Integration of Monetary and Value Theory*, 2d ed. abridged, with a new Introduction, MIT Press, Cambridge, MA.

———. 1990. "On Different Interpretations of the General Theory," *Journal of Monetary Economics*, 26, October, 205-43.

———. 1991. "Comment [on Samuelson 1991]" in Jonung 1991, 407-10.

———. and J. Clark Leith, eds. 1977. *Keynes, Cambridge and The General Theory: The Process of Criticism and Discussion Connected with the Development of The General Theory*, Macmillan, London.

Samuelson, Paul A. 1957. "Wages and Interest: A Modern Dissection of Marxian Economic Models," *American Economic Review*, *47*, December, 884-912.

———. 1968. "What Classical and Neoclassical Monetary Theory Really Was," *Canadian Journal of Economics*, *1*, February, 1-15.

———. 1978. "The Canonical Classical Model of Political Economy," *Journal of Economic Literature*, 16, December, 1415-34.

———. 1987a. "Out of the Closet: A Program for the Whig History of Economic Science," *History of Economics Society Bulletin*, 9, Fall, 51-60.

———. 1987b. See Samuelson 1991.

———. 1988. "Keeping Whig History Honest," *History of Economics Society Bulletin*, 10, Fall, 161-67.

———. 1990. "The Overdue Recovery of Adam Smith's Reputation as an Economic Theorist," to be published in a volume commemorating the bicentenary of Adam Smith's death.

———. 1991. "Thoughts on the Stockholm School and on Scandinavian Economics," in Jonung 1991, 391-407.

———. 1992. "Richard Kahn: His Welfare Economics and Lifetime Achievement," *Cambridge Journal of Economics*, forthcoming.

Schumpeter, Joseph A. 1954. *A History of Economic Analysis*, Oxford University Press, New York.

"The Passing of the Guard in Economics"

Paul A. Samuelson*

This is a lucky audience. When I accepted the invitation to give the present lecture, my first temptation was to choose for a topic *A Sweeping New Non-Substitution Theorem Valid for Technologies Lacking Primary Factors of Production*. How did you miss that dire fate? By chance I remembered what Raymond Goldsmith said three decades ago when the two of us walked out at the conclusion of Arthur F. Burns' AEA Presidential Address: "Let this be a lesson to you, Paul. When you come to give yours, don't impose on a captive audience at the end of a long day a complex scientific discourse."

Therefore, I have chosen to talk tonight about the great generation of economists who dominated our science in the 1930–1980 half century. You know their names: Ragnar Frisch and Jan Tinbergen; Joan Robinson and Nicky Kaldor; Abba Lerner and Oskar Lange; Harold Hotelling and John Hicks; Tjalling Koopmans and Jacob Marschak; Frank Knight and Jacob Viner; Piero Sraffa and Wassily Leontief, Simon Kuznets and Michal Kalecki; James Meade and Roy Harrod; Gottfried Haberler and Friedrich Hayek; Erik Lundberg and Bertil Ohlin; and many others just as colorful and original as the names I have happened to mention in this helter-skelter ordering.

Not all on my list are dead. A living scholar could make the cut by being over the age of 80. (That goes the *New Palgrave Dictionary* one better: to be embalmed in its pages, you had to be dead or merely 70. Even I was eligible.) Have I committed myself to the view that scholars over 80 have already run their race? That is not my intention: Hicks, Tinbergen, Leontief, Haberler, Hayek, and Meade—at this very hour that we are meeting—are busily engaged in the creative destruction that is called scientific productivity.

What do these various names have in common? All were born after 1885. Most are not American, even though the triumphant rise of American economics after 1940 was enormously accelerated by importation of scholars from Hitlerian Europe. In addition, as we say in Heckscher-Ohlin trade theory, free trade in ideas is a powerful substitute for free trade in the productive factor called professors. How very much we American economists have learned from studying the writings of Frisch, Robinson, and all the rest who resisted calls to cushy American chairs.

Some of these named economists have received the Nobel Prize. Most have not. In my judgment every one deserved that award or higher. Each time when a Kalecki died, or a Harrod or Robinson, or Blankety-Blank, it made my blood boil that the Committee in Stockholm had missed doing its duty. It was small consolation to realize that Einstein got his Nobel late, and that Tolstoy was passed over, so to speak in favor of Pearl Buck and John Galsworthy.

I included in a footnote of a 1981 obituary for Ohlin a fictional list of Nobel Winners in Economics for the years 1901 to 1930, prior to the 1969 funding of such a prize by the Bank of Sweden. As Casey Stengel would say, "You could look it up in the *Journal of International*

---

*Department of Economics, Massachusetts Institute of Technology. Invited Dinner Lecture, Eastern Economic Association, March 10, 1988, Boston Mass.

Economics." Many on tonight's list would have earned their laurel wreaths during the 1931–1968 hiatus that discretion made me leave blank.

Back when I was a graduate student, characters roamed the quadrangles. My wife and I agreed that all our teachers and friends were characters. As time passed, we used to speculate whether there really had come to be fewer characters; or whether, as we were prepared to believe, it was just the case that less colorful people now came our way or that our palates had lost the power to detect nuances of character because of overexposure to spicy sensations.

Besides being creative intellects and energetic researchers, my heroes are a colorful collection of human beings. One of them at most could pass in a crowd without being noticed, but I shall not give a hint as to who that one might be. However, the temptation to tell the following story is at this point irresistible:

> On a visit to Princeton I once attended the usual afternoon tea in Fine Hall where the mathematicians always gathered. As I looked around the room, my eye was struck by the oddball characteristics of everyone present. I shall skip names. But when I mentioned this to my host, inviting him to notice what a Polaroid picture would preserve from that room in that instant, he was in no way offended or surprised. "Yes," he said, "it was only the other day that a stranger appeared here looking for a mathematician whose name he had forgotten. When we asked him to describe the chap, he could only say that there was nothing unusual about him. With one voice everyone cried out, 'You must mean Al Tucker'! And we were right.

If someone like me does not describe what these great scholars were like in personal terms, that information will be lost forever. Their good scholarly works will live forever in the learned journals and book publications. Being called a character is not equivalent to a derogatory description. These were admirable and lovable people, who were much admired and loved—not least by me. So, when I record that Nicky Kaldor was sometimes deemed to be self-centered or unthin, I shall hasten to include mention of some incredible Kaldorian feats of theoretical intuition.

NICHOLAS KALDOR

Specifically, in Kaldor's case, it was a sight to see him and Joan Robinson argue at the Monday night Secret Seminar in Cambridge. Literally, each talked 90 percent of the time. Impossible, you say, for 100 to be divided into a pair of 90's? Well, who said anything about how much listening was getting done?

I have told elsewhere, but without full disclosure of all names, how in the early 1930s Thomas Balogh came upon his two London roommates arguing, the erudite Paul Rosenstein-Rodan and the exuberant Nicholas Kaldor. When he later left the apartment with Kaldor, Balogh said, "I didn't realize, Nicky, that you knew Pareto's work." "Actually, I don't," Kaldor replied, "but after Rosie described the problem, I saw how it had to go."

Of Kaldor's many intellectual feats, let me mention only two. His 1940 "Model of the Trade Cycle" involves Keynesian curvaceous saving and investing schedules that intersect 3 times, involving 1 unstable income level surrounded by 2 stable intersections. Adding a flexible accelerator element to this multiplier mechanism, Kaldor assumed that accumulation of positive investment would raise the stock of capital and depress the propensity to invest at each income level. Knowing nothing about differential equations, much less about van der Pol-Rayleigh second-order equations of autorelaxation type, Kaldor by mere intuition inferred the existence of a limit-cycle fluctuation of determinate amplitude and period, which would be stably approached by the system after any perturbation from the stable long-term equilibrium. Hats off to him!

Less well-known is Kaldor's independent 1937 discovery of the von Neumann model where outputs are produced by themselves as inputs, with no reliance on the *primary* factors of labor or land. In a polemic with Knight on capital theory, Kaldor (1938) pointed out that when slaves and machines are producible by slaves and machines, the absence of any non-augmentable primary factor rules out the good old law of diminishing returns! In steady-state equilibrium *sans* joint products, there is a unique interest rate (equal in own-rate terms for all goods). Alterations in tastes for the respective goods or in the propensity to save and invest various proportions of the goods, Kaldor somehow perceived, could not alter his unique interest rate. Therefore, he could validly infer that always his equilibrium interest rate equaled the maximum potential growth rate of the consumptionless von Neumann growth model. Just as Kaldor didn't know Pareto's works, he didn't know von Neumann's work. But once Kaldor was confronted with the problem, he did see how it had to go!

KNIGHT, VINER, AND HABERLER

Who could forget Frank Knight, a little dumpy figure in a workman's cap when he first gave a guest lecture to us University of Chicago sophomores? His squeaky voice emitted a mixture of Will Rogers' profundities and Ludwig Wittgenstein one-liners. Anyone so ununderstandable you knew had to be a deep thinker.

Or consider Jacob Viner, Knight's colleague, who towered above him by a full inch. Viner not only made female graduate-students cry, he reduced lieutenant-colonels and first sergeants to tears in his postwar seminars. When I wrote an official Viner obituary, I investigated the accusation that he had mellowed with the years. Notarized testimony about his final year at Chicago suggested that, if Viner ever did mellow, it was on the train from LaSalle Street station to Princeton Junction.

According to my doctrine of balancing reportage of personality traits by reportage of scientific breakthroughs, let me say a few words about the works of Knight and Viner. The Second Chicago School, that of Milton Friedman, George Stigler, and Aaron Director, is distinguishable from the First Chicago School of Knight and Henry Simons. Science does not stand still. But sometimes in the current Cook County preoccupation with Pareto optimality and libertarianism, something of the Knightian concern for interpersonal equity seems sadly lost.

Knight used to say that he became an economist because his feet hurt: so, rather than follow the plow, he signed on in our subject. The true reason is no less interesting. Either from the autobiography of Alvin Johnson or of Norbert Weiner, I learned that Knight began at the Cornell Graduate School in philosophy. But he talked too much. When the exasperated chairman gave Knight the choice of talking less or leaving the field of philosophy, legend has it that he levitated down into economics. Luckily he did not have to drop one notch further for it was Knight who used to say: Sociology is the science of talk; and there is only one law in sociology—Bad talk drives out good!

Knight's atheism was almost prurient in his disdain for religion, particularly Christianity. This was a violent reaction from his fundamentalist parental indoctrination. In *New Palgrave* [1987, volume 3, p. 55], Stigler retells brother Bruce's account of how under parental suasion the eleven Knight children "... signed pledges to attend church the rest of their lives. Returning home, Frank (then 14 or 15 [and the eldest]) gathered the children behind the barn, built a fire and said: 'Burn these things because pledges and promises made under duress are not binding'." Sadly though, Knight could not burn away the scars. Never could he leave religion alone. And I found it infinitely sad, to learn from Donald Dewey [1986], that even in old age

925

Knight was plagued by insomnia as he could not stop thinking about the follies of organized religion.

With respect to Jacob Viner, this favorite pupil of Frank Taussig fully anticipated in his non-mathematical way the Lerner-Leontief pure theory of international exchange—which is isomorphic with the competitive equilibrium of *Value and Capital*. Viner's boner in trying to get Wong, the mathematical draftsman, to make the envelope to the family of descending U-shaped cost curves pass through their bottoms amused his admirers and mortified him. As his graduate class was ending, he admitted to me he had been in error for some mysterious mathematical reason. "But," he proclaimed, "I can do it." Being all of 19 I quipped brashly, "Yes, with a good thick pencil you can." Make no mistake though, Viner's 1937 *Studies in the Theory of International Trade* is incredibly erudite and acute and the hundreds of hours I have spent with that book rank with the most delightful interludes in my professional life. Along with Viner, the Haberler who in 1930 broke out of the fetters of Ricardian one-factor-of-labor models by use of the *production-possibility frontier*, surely deserved a Nobel Prize; or together they deserved a joint one for their trade innovations.

Personally, I owe much to my teacher Gottfried Haberler. From Schumpeter I got encouragement and praise; it was Haberler who marked my early manuscripts with scores of needed emendations. With the impatience of youth, I sometimes rebelled at Haberler's eclecticism—until he one day pulled me up short by saying: "Paul, how do you know Mother Nature is not eclectic"? Thanks to him, I have felt little tempted by narrow positivism and Napoleonic reductionism. The model on my shield and sword is this: "Be as eclectic as the data require, seeking to avoid two kinds of error: over-simplicity and shapeless description."

Joseph Schumpeter, like Keynes, was born before 1885 and is ruled out of the present review of the troops. Alvin Hansen, my surrogate father in academic life, I have omitted in tonight's lecture for the reason that my 1986 Godkin Lectures, " How Keynes Came to America via Harvard and Hansen," were largely devoted to his genius. As I documented there, Hansen was more than a great policy advocate—the so-called American Keynes. His analytic writings, and those of his disciples in his workshop, pioneered developments of macroeconomic modelling. Here I shall only cite my recent write up of the third multiplier-accelerator model—that of Keynes-Hansen, which deserves to be remembered more vividly than it is.

You and I would be here all night if I were to do full justice to all the names mentioned in my original list. So I must be brief, indulging in hit-and-run comments.

FRISCH, TINBERGEN, AND MEADE

Just as our Lord's house has many mansions, the edifice of science needs varied personality types. Ragnar Frisch was the loner scholar, much like John Hicks. Frisch had able students—Trygve Haavelmo, Leif Johansen, and others—but Frisch also had the need to be alone and follow his own star. He believed in that star. After being appointed to a United Nations' economics commission around 1950, he became impatient with its literary deliberations. The cure, he decided, was for him to teach mathematics to his fellow commissioners. Since Frisch had just discovered Marshall's doctrine of external economies, he picked that for the text of his first sermon. Roy Harrod and the other distinguished international economists did not come back for the second lesson. Frisch found this inexplicable and went out of channels in pressing upon his countryman, Trygve Lie, the first Secretary General of the United Nations, the need for Lie to compel the commission members to attend the needed remedial sessions.

The economist world applauded when Jan Tinbergen and Frisch received the first Alfred Nobel Award in 1969. I called Tinbergen a "humanist saint" in a *Newsweek* column. Not many of us scholars are saints of any kind. But James Meade might be paired with Tinbergen in this beatification. When Meade received his Nobel in 1976 along with Bertil Ohlin, I described him in the *New York Times* as the last of the utilitarians ". . . who, meeting a coatless person on the street, would give him his coat." James corrected me by return post, saying in effect: "It is true that I would believe I ought to do just that, but can I be confident that I would live up to my ideals?"

Don't make the mistake of thinking that saints have to be fuzzy thinkers. Our encyclopedias are chock-full of important hard theorems discovered by Tinbergen and Meade. One instance that concerned my own work will illustrate. After my 1948 article deduced that goods mobility would often suffice to ensure complete (rather than partial) factor price equalization in international trade, half the economist world was engaged in proving this wrong and the other half in proving why it was indeed the case. Tinbergen was quickest off the mark in writing down the conclusive mathematical equations. And Meade led the crowd in showing why more goods than factors would, in a zero-transport-cost world, lead to an uncountable infinity of (inessentially) indeterminante geographical specialization patterns. Neither of these saints thrusts forward his claims for scientific innovation. But be assured that neither is unaware of his just merits.

MARSCHAK AND KOOPMANS

If Frisch was a loner, Jacob Marschak was a warm and tireless member of the working parties seeking scientific truth. At age 79, as at age 30, Marschak worshipped the pursuit of science. Jane Austen spoke of spinsters who lost the bloom of youth at 25 and of admirals who were old crocks at 39. In science it is not the legs that are the first to go. It is enthusiasm that oozes away as cynicism seeps in. Not so with Jacob Marschak. To the end he pursued the Holy Grail and knew it to be worth pursuing. For my money Marschak's axioms on expected utility are the definitive ones, preferable to those of von Neumann and of Ramsey—no mean accomplishment.

Tjalling Koopmans was a serious scholar, with many deep and versatile analytic discoveries to his credit. He did superlative empirical work on tanker shipping rates. Long before the dawn of modern finance theory, he worked out for Penn Mutual insurance company how it could hedge in the bond market its predictable future cash outlays—a pearl he cast before swine who ignored it. With Trygve Haavelmo he pioneered the technique of *identification* in time series. Before there was a subject of linear programming, at the War Shipping Board Koopmans discovered that subject while knowing nothing about the works of Kantorovitch, Hitchcock, or Dantzig. His researches in turnpike theory, like those of Radner, McKenzie, and Morishima, were deep. I could go on and on.

Tjalling was also a serious person. At a Nobel conference on Lake Constance some students took his picture. It was a charming likeness of a smiling and handsome scholar, but he and his wife didn't like it. When Risha and I pressed them as to why they didn't like it, they finally said it wasn't typical. At second glance I realized that it was the smiling that the camera caught which they regarded as non-representative. That was false advertising! Koopmans was seriously opposed to fine writing in economics, not a common crime in our field. According to his code of scientific honor, mere elegance must not give ideas an unfair boost.

LUNDBERG, HAYEK, HARROD AND HOTELLING

If Koopmans was content to be serious, Erik Lundberg was an ungloomy Swede, ever with a quip to puncture pretension or stuffiness. Last summer, fifteen days before he died at the age of 80, he reminisced from his sick bed with Assar Lindbeck and me. We talked about Alvin Hansen whom he liked. Lundberg remarked: "In 1937 I was waiting for Hansen in his Harvard office. Seeing my book on his shelf, I naturally took it down, rather expecting its pages not to be cut. But every spread was underlined with copious marginal notes." At this point, there was a twinkle in Lundberg's eye when he went on to say. "So naturally, when Hansen's next book came out on similar matters I was a little disappointed to see that no mention had been made of my *Studies in the Theory of Economic Expansion*." I am glad to add, that this Lundberg classic is still the most quoted treatise of the Stockholm School of macroeconomics. And it deserves to be.

You all know the works of Hayek. Perhaps not all have read his little memoir concerning his World War I encounter with his cousin Ludwig Wittgenstein; few may know that his University of Chicago Press book on psychology is held in awe by such Nobel physiologists as Gerald Edelman of Rockefeller University. (When those two corresponded about the mind-body problem, Hayek wrote to this effect: "When I was in my low seventies, I suddenly became depressed and scientifically sterile. Unaccountably, a year later the old zest returned. But once again a similar pattern came to pass a few years later. With the discovery of new instruments of anatomical observation, I learned for the first time of two scars of coronary infarcts dating from those periods. There's the mind-body problem for you." Who said Hayek disdained Baconian empiricism?)

It is a scandal that so original and prolific a scholar as Roy Harrod never held a chair at Oxford or any other British university. The quintessential don, Harrod looked a bit like a handsome American Indian. His microeconomic contributions were first class: the correct form of Viner's envelope is given in Harrod's 1934 paper on imperfect competition. Only 90 years after Cournot he independently discovered the marginal revenue (or dR/dq) concept, and he was robbed of acknowledged credit for naming the concept only by Frank Ramsey's high standards as the referee that editor Keynes relied on. His growth theories you all know.

Though Harrod was like Kaldor in lacking mathematical training, like Kaldor he was brilliantly intuitive. As of 1935 he may have understood Keynes' *General Theory* better than the Master did. His 1937 definitive account of that model antedates Hick's better known one, and is isomorphic with it. Harrod did not have to be a great reader: easier it was for him to invent the principle of acceleration than read about it in musty journals of the World War I period; that way, besides, he could more likely improve upon received theories.

Like Frisch and Hotelling, Roy believed completely in his star. If Keynes could revolutionize economics, so could Harrod. If Keynes could in addition clear up the theory of probability, so could Harrod. ("How long is an unknown road?" Harrod was the first to answer this basic question of induction: "As long again, on the average, as you have already come on it." The question, "How big is the square of the road's length?" is not one he addressed in print.)

Gilbert Ryle said that at Oxford Faculty meetings he always first determined which side of an issue Roy was on. That way he knew which motions to vote against. Rarely, Ryle observed, did Harrod prevail. But Ryle thought it a beautiful sight to see a battleship being attacked by a foil, and often hard pressed thereby. Freudian memory makes me remember lines like these from Harrod's 1959 biography of Lindemann (Lord Cherwell), Churchill's physicist braintruster. "Lindemann was not too popular in the pre-war common rooms. But the Prof was a genius.

Unfortunately you had to be a genius to recognize that fact. I was the first at Oxford to fully appreciate him."

When I was Harrod's guest at Christ Church High Table in 1948, he told me he was scheduled to give a public lecture on the atomic bomb.

Samuelson: But do you know anything about the atomic bomb?

Harrod: No. And at first I was inclined to turn down the invitation. But as I got to thinking about the subject, I realized my ideas on the subject were as good as anyone else's and so I accepted.

Harrod did me one good turn. He published in book form [1952] his fugitive financial journalism from newspapers and brokerage letters. When he looked at his handiwork, he found it good. When I looked ex post at his ex ante predictions, I was less sure of that. So I resolved never to republish my similar items and have been a happy man ever since.

Harold Hotelling had two great careers. He applied his mathematical arsenal to microeconomics: We still use his discount formulas for allocating machines and resources over time. His neat model of competition along a line illuminated both oligopoly and the tendency in politics for two rival parties to push platforms toward the center. The duality theorems that Shephard and I polished up are already present, *ab ovo,* in Hotelling's 1932 masterpiece of competitive pricing. His 1938 Presidential Address on welfare-pricing is a jewel, fit to be mounted next to Frank Ramsey's classic of the 1920's on second-best taxing and pricing. Besides all this, Hotelling revolutionized statistics teaching in America, leading us into the age of Fisher, Neyman, and Wald.

One story is enough to dramatize Hotelling's complete belief in the vital importance of the subjects he studied. In the black year after Pearl Harbor, Hotelling in a 1942 M.I.T. seminar on statistics declared in all seriousness: "Despair not. The Allies, in Britain, America, India and the USSR, have by far the better statisticians. Germany and Japan are doomed to ignominious defeat." And so it came to pass.

HICKS AND LERNER

I shall reserve for another occasion fuller remarks about John Hicks, whose work and my work have exhibited many parallels. Let me at the beginning pay him the highest compliment that one scholar can give to another. It was Mayor Gibson of the wasteland we call Newark, N.J. who said, "I don't know where America is going. But wherever it is, Newark will be found there waiting." Time and again when I arrived at some interesting discovery in value theory, there Hicks was already waiting for my arrival. Hicks being the kind of scholar who works from inside his own mind, I could often joke that I take unfair advantage of him: he depends on his own originality, whereas I had the advantage of what it is that both of us know. As I once said in a University of London Stamp Lecture, my own code is to recognize and acknowledge all that anyone has ever discovered in my science and then go after the bigger game of seeking to advance the subject under that constraint. Glory aside, it is an efficient procedure for science to follow.

When I was 21, John Cassels at Harvard told me that Hicks was the world leader among the younger economists. In 1936 Hicks was 32 and this was a prescient judgment since he was something of a late bloomer. I thought that later his countrymen insufficiently recognized Hicks' quality, in part because he was no part of the coteries that Balkanized British economics during the 1935–1950 epoch. As a grand old man, as *the* grand old man, Sir John Hicks today is seen to be the scientific innovator he has always been.

Abba Lerner was in a class of his own. Starting LSE night school at older than usual age, in two years he was turning out classic papers in economic theory. If Lagrange's mechanics is a Shakespeare poem, Lerner's 1944 *Economics of Control* is a Mozart concerto. His Model T Keynesian writings, looked at from today, are truly ferocious. His simple policy programs are chastely logical. If Kaldor reminds one of the physicist Pauli, Lerner reminds us of the brilliant Szillard (who patented nuclear fission before Fermi or Hahn invented it).

Abba was a dean's nightmare. When Oskar Lange, a Polish socialist, was being offered chairs at Chicago, Berkeley, Ann Arbor, and everywhere, Lerner was receiving only guest professorship invitations. He was a premature Bohemian, and I do not mean from Czechoslovakia. Under his sandals were no socks, and for a score of years it was a reflection on American academic life that a post worthy of Lerner's genius was not to be found.

Three Lerner stories I have told many times. When he developed his functional finance at the University of Kansas around 1940, his disciples suggested he call it Lernerism. But he told me in all seriousness that he refused lest it lessen the program's appeal. This is the Lerner who visited Trotsky in Mexico City to persuade him to use Lerner-Lange pricing under communism. The assassin dispatched from Moscow scotched that campaign in the bud. It was this same Lerner whose friends had to suppress his wartime publication of a scheme to run the war by giving Generals Eisenhower and MacArthur each abstract purchasing power to be used in bidding for resources in auction markets. At the 1946 Cleveland AEA meeting, Lerner commandeered an empty hall to propose that the Russians be given the choice of introducing democracy or being atom bombed. When I told Lionel Robbins and Hayek at LSE about these activities, Hayek said concerning the auction proposal, "What's the matter with that? I've proposed as much." And concerning the preemptive bomb strike, Robbins uttered the exact same words.

Dogmengeschichte would be incomplete if 1) I did not refer you to Tibor Scitovsky's wonderful appreciation of Lerner's contributions, and 2) remind you of Lerner's ingenious wire handicrafts. Once when I told him about just having seen in Paris a wonderful exhibit of Caldor mobiles, Abba replied, "Mine are better."

LANGE, KALECKI, AND KUZNETS

Oskar Lange was the organized teacher and disciplined researcher that his friend Lerner never tried to be. Lange offered to return from Chicago to Berkeley if Lerner could be part of the package deal, but the Associate Dean said no dice. The years 1934–1944 were a marvelously productive decade for Lange in microeconomics, macroeconomics, and Marxian analysis. An erstwhile Polish social democrat, Lange was persuaded by patriotism to go back as Polish U.N. Ambassador and subsequently as Vice President. Unlike Kalecki, Lange got caught in the bureaucracy and in power politics. His scientific muse suffered in consequence and he died too young.

Michal Kalecki was led to his independent discovery of Keynes *General Theory* from his study of Marx. That is Joan Robinson's considered view, and she used to tell the story of Kalecki's taking to his bed when he learned he had been forestalled by Keynes' *General Theory*. Like Tinbergen, Kalecki pioneered econometric measurement of business-cycle models. He was a brilliant simplifier: If capitalists saved less, that would add to their profits, raising real income just enough to keep labor's fractional share constant at the level determined by the system's degree of monopoly.

McCarthy harassments aside, I fear Kalecki was not a success in the late 1940s at the United Nations. He could not believe in the prosperity that came to pass in the Age after

Keynes, and he always was firmly a man of principle. Kalecki always stood by his guns and died out of favor in Poland, a victim of anti-semitism and totalitarian politics.

Simon Kuznets is the one scholar on my list linked least with economic theory. His skills with history and statistics more than compensate for this preference of his. When he wanted to, Kuznets could do theory—as Hicks and I learned when we studied his 1940 *Economica* paper on how to interpret in welfare terms the aggregative ΣPQ data that are known as national income. I first learned from Kuznets's early writings about the fabricating of Slutsky cycles by the differencing and the moving-averaging of random numbers. Like Marschack and Leontief, Kuznets had been a Menshevist rather than a Leninist Bolshevik: their backing the wrong horse was our gain in American economics. Simon was as soft-spoken as I am boisterous. When students would call out, "Speak louder," Kuznets would whisper, "Move closer"—a case of the fallacy of composition and of advice that would not be needed if it could be received.

LEONTIEF AND SRAFFA

Wassily Leontief was my beloved teacher. I am as much younger than him as I am older than Bob Solow, another foal from the Leontief stable. Wassily was 29 when we first met, and last time I saw him at NYU, in his ninth decade of life, he had not changed an epsilon. It now turns out that while Calvin Coolidge was napping in the White House, the young Sraffa and the young Leontief were forging the tools of input/output. As far as I can remember, neither of the two has ever referred to publications of the other and I suspect that this is an honest reflection of what each has felt to be the need to know about the other's work. Mine is a different philosophy. With the Germans I say of their two Works: "Herring is good. Chocolate is good. How good must be chocolate and herring."

Piero Sraffa's writings speak for themselves. In his seventh decade he unveiled his researches on producing commodities by means of commodities. In villages throughout Italy, India, and East Anglia seekers of truth burn the midnight oil studying the truths contained in the 99 pages of Sraffa's 1960 classic. All over the globe Sraffa's magnificent edition of Ricardo's *Works* graces the coffee tables of the educated elite.

If our profession has a Sir Galahad, Piero Sraffa is it. That explains Michal Kalecki's famous story: "When I first went to Britain, I hoped to meet an Englishman. Throughout the British Isles I could discover only two. One was a communist [presumably Maurice Dobb]; and the other turned out to be an Italian."

A sadder property of Sraffa as a producing scholar is encapsulated in the following sample of Maynard Keynes's wit. When told what was finally decided to be the diagnosis of a mysterious ailment of Kaldor in wartime Cambridge, Keynes replied: "What, Nicky with athletes' foot? I don't believe it. Next you'll be telling me that Piero has writer's cramp!" Soberly speaking, it was a tragedy that Sraffa had a psychological block against lecturing, and a blessing that his writer's block was less than absolute. I was proud to be his friend.

THE INCOMPARABLE JOAN

My time is almost up. Joan Robinson I've left to the end. In my measured judgment, she was a great economist. Since I have written recently on "Remembering Joan" Samuelson [1989], I shall briefly sample a few of my remarks.

In the years 1932 to 1982 Joan Robinson contributed to every field of economics. Her 1933 *Economics of Imperfect Competition* is a classic that nicely complements Chamberlin's classic of the same year. She was in the Kahn-et-al Circus that helped Keynes gestate the *General*

Theory. Her article on output as a whole, Robinson [1933], was the first leak to outsiders of the Keynesian revolution to come. Her books on Model T Keynesianism were invaluable. In Robinson [1938] she made quantum improvement on stability of trade theory: she corrected the error that a currency depreciation must, in a stable system, depreciate the terms of trade of the country depreciating. Her 1942 *Essay on Marxian Economics* is a masterpiece: she is pro his ideology but unsparingly she rejects his faulty labor theory of value. Robinson's 1956 *Accumulation of Capital* is a pre-Sraffa classic. On the inadmissibility of a *scalar* aggregate of capital to serve as a productive factor, she was dead right. She pioneered with Kahn, Kaldor, and Pasinetti the post-Keynesian macro tautologies of income distribution, but rejected their applicability to the real world because of its stubborn failure to display balanced growth.

The daughter of a Major General and descendent of Maurice the Christian socialist, Joan Robinson first admired Stalin's USSR, then Castro's Cuba, then Mao's China, and even North Korea. During the cultural revolution she told me that work in the countryside would be good for a sedentary professor of economics. (I must admit that I prefer tennis.) What Samuel Johnson applied to second marriages applied to Joan's passion for social reform; it was a triumph of hope over experience.

When Diogenes reached Joan, he could douse his lamp and end his search. Here are some words I wrote in the 1989 piece entitled "Remembering Joan":

> I once remarked to an old Cambridge hand that she [Joan] must think well of another leftist scholar there. He corrected me: 'Oh no, she is contemptuous of him as a lackey of the Party Line'.
> A Polish scholar once volunteered to me: 'I love that woman. When she visited Poland, all the brass turned out to give her the royal treatment. Replying to the toasts and fine words, she proceeded at once to the forbidden topic that all of us were thinking about, saying, "Why are we wasting our time on these matters when the workers in Posen are rebelling? What is the reason for that'? We young people revered her for that.'

I learned more from Joan than she learned from me. And that is not a snide comment—at least not solely. She despaired of Solow and me as perverse or worse. Here is the first paragraph of a late letter from her to my colleague Harold Freeman who had just written the first edition of his indictment of American capitalism under the title of *Towards Socialism:*

29 October 1979

Dear Professor Freeman

I was absolutely amazed that such a sensible book could be written in the Economics Department at MIT.

How did you hit it off with Samuelson and company?

Harold did not have the heart to inform her that we were dear friends and that it was he who had got MIT to hire me and also Bob Solow.

Robinson was not a great woman economist. She was a great economist.

FINALE

The drama of science is that of the Golden Bough, where ruling chiefs are slain by new contenders. "What have you done for me lately"? is the query of the Muse of Science. King

Isaac Newton is dead. Long live King Clerk Maxwell. King Maxwell is dead, long live King Albert Einstein. And so it goes.

My pinup-stars labored well in the vineyard. All of them, with no exception, enjoyed the game of science and it rewarded them mightily.

Yes, we do know more than our predecessors in science. We do so because it is they that we know.

REFERENCES

Dewey, D. 1986. "Frank Knight Before Cornell: Some Light on the Dark Years," in *Research in the History of Economic Thought and Methodology*, vol. 4, ed. W. J. Samuels. Greenwich, Conn.: JAI Press.

Eatwell, J., M. Milgate, P. Newman, eds. 1987. *The New Palgrave Dictionary of Economics*, vol. 3. London, New York and Tokyo: The Macmillan Press, Ltd.

Harrod, R. 1934. "Doctrines of imperfect competition," *Quarterly Journal of Economics* 48(May):442-70.

Harrod, R. 1937. "Mr. Keynes and the traditional theory," *Econometrica* 5(January): 74-86.

Harrod, R. 1959. *The Prof: A Personal Memoir of Lord Cherwell*. London: Macmillan.

Harrod, R. 1952. *Economic Essays*. London and New York: Macmillan.

Hicks, J. 1939. *Value and Capital*. Oxford: Clarendon Press.

Hicks, J. 1940. "The valuation of the social income," *Economica* 7(May):105-24.

Hotelling, H. 1932. "Edgeworth's Taxation Paradox and the Nature of Supply and Demand Functions," *Journal of Political Economy* 40(October):577-616.

Hotelling, H. 1938. "The general welfare in relation to problems of taxation and of railway and utility rates," *Econometrica* 6(July):242-69.

Kaldor, N. 1937. "Annual survey of economic theory: the recent controversy on the theory of capital," *Econometrica* 5(July):201-33.

Kaldor, N. 1938. "On the theory of capital: a rejoinder to Professor Knight," *Econometrica* 6(April):163-76.

Kaldor, N. 1940. "A model of the trade cycle," *Economic Journal* 50(March):78-92.

Lerner, A. 1944. *The Economics of Control*. New York: The Macmillan Co.

Lundberg, E. 1937. *Studies in the Theory of Economic Expansion*. London: P.S. King and Sons; Oxford: Blackwell, 1955.

Ramsey, F. 1927. "A contribution to the theory of taxation," *Economic Journal* 37(May):47-61.

Robinson, J. 1933a. *Economics of Imperfect Competition*. London: Macmillan.

Robinson, J. 1933b. "The Theory of Money and the Analysis of Output," *Review of Economic Studies* 1(October):22-26.

Robinson, J. 1938. "The concept of hoarding," *Economic Journal* 48(June): 231-36.

Robinson, J. 1942. *An Essay on Marxian Economics*. London: Macmillan.

Robinson, J. 1956. *The Accumulation of Capital*. London: Macmillan.

Samuelson, P.A. 1969. "Two Remarkable Men," *Newsweek*, 17 November 1969, p. 108.

Samuelson, P.A. 1986. "How Keynes Came to America via Harvard and Hansen," Godkin Lecture I, Harvard University, 19 November 1986.

Samuelson, P.A. 1988. "The Keynes-Hansen third multiplier-accelerator model of secular stagnation," *Japan and the World Economy* 1(October):3-19.

Samuelson, P.A. 1989. "Remembering Joan," in *Joan Robinson and Modern Economic Theory, G. Feiwel, ed.*. New York: New York University Press.

Sraffa, P. 1951-73. *The Works and Correspondence of David Ricardo*. 11 volumes. Cambridge: Cambridge University Press.

Sraffa, P. 1960. *Production of Commodities by Means of Commodities, Prelude to a Critique of Economic Theory*. Cambridge: Cambridge University Press.

Viner, J. 1937. *Studies in the Theory of International Trade*. New York: Harper.

578

Economics in Our Time
Stockholm, 6 December 1991

I could have named this lecture with the alternative title--Sixty Years in Paradise--to celebrate in prose the utter joy that came from a career in economics which began almost exactly six decades ago. My intention is not to drop names. Nay, rather I shall catapult into the sky names of the many great scholars who have made the last two-thirds of the twentieth century a Golden Age in the study of economics. To borrow and extend a borrowing from Noel Annan, we could dub this "Our Age" or "Our Crowd."

This is a birthday party. You don't have to come to it, but if you do you must say nice things. On such occasions, Dr. Samuel Johnson said: One is not under oath. If I err, I shall err on the up side. When Thackeray wrote *Vanity Fair*, he called it a novel without a heroine. Well, this affectionate lecture is a survey without a single villain. Here then will be the truth, and only the truth; but you are on notice that it will not be the *whole* truth.

I shall follow the practice of Diaghilev when he revived his ballet. He made the Bakst stage sets even more colorful than the originals "so that they would be as vivid as people remembered them." It is like the case of a newspaper venture that some time ago proposed only to publish good news. To others was to be given the task of telling about war, rape, and cosmic misadventure. The enterprise was not a commercial success and it did not last. Some say there was no viable demand for good news. More sophisticated students of the identification problem traced the publication's demise not to insufficient demand but to an insufficiency of supply of cheery items.

Insufficiency of supply of great economists and superlative scientific breakthroughs is not my problem. The period 1932-1991 has seen a veritable avalanche of progress in economics. One way to document this claim would be by describing the great classic articles of the not-so-distant past, and then showing how they contrast with what is standard treatment of those same topics in today's literature. That documentation I cannot do without violating my self-imposed rule of only good things to say. My listeners can read for themselves the great works of Marshall, Wicksell, and Pigou to confirm the fact of extraordinary progress in what Keynes once called "our most agreeable branch of the moral sciences." Yes, they were giants whose shoulders we stand upon. Our grandsires drew a good long bow at Hastings, but each generation stands at a higher altitude in a cumulative discipline, and Saddam Hussein has more firepower today than any Genghis Khan could muster in past history!

Just as business cycles have long waves, so do sciences. Isaac Newton was himself a veritable scientific revolution. Then, as Britain came on hard times, one had to go to the Continent with its post-Leibniz stars of the Bernoullis, Euler, Lagrange and Laplace, and finally the incomparable Gauss. So in our field we have the epoch of Hume, the Physiocrats, and Smith. Then the lull until the outburst of Malthus, Ricardo, and the Mills. A fire engine on its way back from the last fire is really on its way to the next fire. Jevons, Walras, Menger, Edgeworth, Marshall, Wicksell, and Pareto soared beyond five standard deviations.

All this is a polite way of saying that the third quarter of the nineteenth century was not a good time for an economist to be born. The first third of the twentieth century was not a vintage time for economic science. It was of course not a wasteland. How could any acres be so described that produced an Irving Fisher, an Allyn Young, and an A.C. Pigou? But that generation was not really a hard act to follow.

It was my good luck to begin economics study on January 2, 1932. The greatest depression ever was at its worst. Keynes was engaged in changing his snake skin and the young Hicks was just finding his métier. Why do I begin with those two names? Autobiography mandates it. My Chicago tutor Eugene Staley volunteered to his 16-year old charge: Keynes is the world's leading economist. Not a bad judgment considering that by this time the *Treatise on Money* was considered Keynes's masterpiece. Then later when I levitated up to Harvard, the young assistant professor John Cassels informed me: "Hicks is the coming man." By then I was prepared for the message.

Three years ago, by invitation from the Eastern Economic Association, I gave a lecture entitled, "The Passing of the Guard in Economics." In telling anecdotes about economists living and dead, I have already covered some of the present ground in print. Legal counsel, however, assures me that one cannot plagiarize one's self. Guests, like fish, stink after two days but good stories only improve in the retelling.

Schumpeter

But where to begin? I begin with Joseph Schumpeter. My Schumpeter. There is raging today a veritable Schumpeter epidemic. No less than four biographies have just appeared. All discuss whether Schumpeter's nose was out of joint because of jealousy towards Keynes's success with the *General Theory*. Yes, I believe it was. Abraham Lincoln's law partner reported that there was a little clock ticking inside of Abe lusting for fame. So with the brilliant only-child born on the margin of the Viennese aristocracy. Each night his diary recorded a self-awarded grade. Depreciating the currency shamelessly, he awarded people like me A+++. But aching for a theorist's fame that was not to be his, Schumpeter's self-judgments were severe. In death Schumpeter, like Stendahl, hit the jackpot. As

Hemingway's friend said, "Living well is the best revenge." So also is dying well. "Schumpeter Ascendent" is the fitting title of a recent article.

Schumpeter in the end stumbled into his comparative advantage, which did not involve zero-ness of the rate of interest in the steady state or the epicycles of Kondratiev, Juglar, and Kitchen-Crum periodicities. Schumpeter had an unparalleled quickness in mastering past literature. He had fresh and uninhibited viewpoints on politics, sociology, and economic history. His 1920 sociology of politicians seeking rents antedated modern cynical trends in the public choice literature. Richard Swedberg is right that as a literary stylist (and, I would add, speaker) Schumpeter is in the class with Keynes. Eastern Europeans now need Schumpeter's emphasis that ours is not a system of profit but rather a system of profit-and-loss; and they need Schumpeter's insight that competition is inescapably a cutting of losses and a process of *creative destruction*. When I notice failures of Schumpeterian prophecies, or Pareto-like warts of bigotry and reactionism, I think of what Justice Holmes more or less wrote to Pollock: Although Alfred Marshall does not sing to me, I read Spengler--not because Spengler is right, but because the rascal gives you a run for your money.

The Schumpeter story is an example that one can earn top fame and still not be part of what are the essential trends of one's own time. To see this let me contrast with the Schumpeter effort these main trends in the economics of the last sixty years.

The Zeitgeist

In 1932 economics was poised to become mathematical. Isolated pioneers like Cournot, Jevons, Walras, Edgeworth, Pareto, and Fisher had used symbolisms before, but now suddenly the dam burst in economic theory and statistics. Before econometrics came to be known as the statistics appropriate for economics, it began its dictionary life meaning the combination of mathematics, economic theory, and economic statistics. Harold Hotelling was quick off the mark. Arthur Bowley taught at the LSE in the Edgeworth tradition. Henry Schultz carried on at Chicago in the H.L. Moore tradition of Columbia. With Frisch and Tinbergen, the invaders had become triumphant. Pure mathematicians were only occasionally central: Volterra and Griffith Evans are examples; but later we were to come to know the seminal works of von Neumann (two-person zero-sum game theory and his time-phased production of outputs by means of inputs), and of Frank Ramsey (optimally-controlled saving, second-best feasible excise taxation, subjective probabilities and *deduced* maximization of a canonical cardinal utility of state outcomes). Mostly, though, economists were self-taught virtuosos. I thought to be paying a compliment to John Hicks when I wrote for the press about his 1972 Nobel Prize and described him as a brilliant quick study. Some people will not take yes for an answer: Hicks wrote reproachfully, to tell me how excellent had been his maths training at Clifford and Oxford. I spared him what had been my excuse--namely, Roy Allen's story that he had lent J.R.H. Netto's little book on determinants and soon after Hicks had returned with *Value and Capital*!

Alas, we are leaving behind the age when a few brilliant minds are able *sans* mathematics to keep up and even move ahead in economic science. It is rather marvelous to see a Kaldor, quite innocent of differential equations, deduce cogently a van der Pol-Rayleigh limit cycle for a curvilinear-multiplier-quasi-accelerator model; or to observe a Lerner glimpse necessary conditions for Pareto-optimality by sheer I.Q. alone. It is like clapping for a tumbler who operates with one hand tied. When one ticks off a hundred-odd valuable relationships of recent decades, one perceives the answer to the nineteenth century challenge: What did mathematics ever add to economic theory? Namely, 90 out of the last 100 findings. Still, nostalgia arises for times gone by.

If at the beginning it was a matter of catch-as-catch-can in mathematics, once the tidal wave hit economics, economists went all the way to Nickolaus Bourbaki and beyond. This is well indicated by Herbert Simon's thought experiment. "Perform content analysis," he suggested "on the leading journal *Physical Review* and on *Econometrica*, evaluating each for the degree of sophistication of the mathematical techniques employed. You will find that *Econometrica* goes farthest to stretch the resources of modern analysis." Lest this be thought to be a reflection of smugness on the part of the reporting economist, let me add for the record that Simon is more than an economist and that he regards our fanciness as a sign of degeneracy, not of creative strength. My own postscript points out that better logic never hurts, and few of my acquaintances are kept from finding pearls in the slime of reality because of their preoccupation with elegance. They also go whole hours playing tennis, bridge, put-and-call options, and inter-gender dalliance --waiting in between times for arrival of new paradigms and great empirical findings. We climb mountains because they're there. We travel down curves of diminishing returns because that is all you can do while waiting for curves to shift exogenously.

My lot in life has been to live intimately with some of the leading mathematicians, physicists, chemists, and molecular biologists of this age. Critics of current economic methodologies could not be more wrong if they believe that economists like me bend every effort to win praise from such as these. To a person, non-economics scientists lack interest in the axiomatics of economics.

The Harvard mathematician George Mackey would never want to discuss with me my *Foundations*. It is my elementary *Economics* (or John Rae's theory of interest) that captures his attention and not the Debreu niceties that fascinate the likes of me.

All my scientist friends believe in their heart of hearts that if they took time off from their laboratories they could clean up economics and the social sciences in half a sabbatical year and then live happily ever after. It reminds me of what the Cambridge topologist Whitehead said when a colleague asked: "What are we going to do about Bertrand Russell who claims all mathematics is mere tautology?" Whitehead replied: "Tautology maths may be, but how come Bertie can't do any of the bloody stuff?" Economics looks as easy as a Mondrian drawing. All you need to better it is a ruler and a few colored lines. With Somerset Maugham I say: "Try it."

The generation of my teachers found mathematics a sore cross to bear. In their presidential addresses they inveighed against it as pretentious and sterile, seeking comfort by quoting the view of Marshall, Pigou, and Keynes on the triviality of mathematical economics. But that wolf at their door just would not go away. Funeral by funeral they lost their battle.

Population Explosion

A second trend in the economics profession has been its sheer growth in size and numbers. Time was when the number of American economists just about equalled the number of our chiropractors. For better or worse we have left those quacks behind. Introductory economics has become the largest single class at most colleges. Tens of thousands of economists attend the Christmas meetings of the AEA. And about the same story unfolds in developed and developing societies. Since the propensity to write is a universal constant while the propensity to read is quite limited, this means the journals are more competitive than ever--even after there has grown up a splintering of specializations.

Life was sweet in the *ancien regime*. A few of us wrote for a moderate-size circle of readers. Now the jungle is crowded and nasty. All this applies as well to the physical and natural sciences: young scholars are oppressed by the difficulty of being the one who tops the pole when the number of climbers has doubled and redoubled. The law of conservation of number of Nobel Prizes leads to an increasing number of disappointments.

The Westward Tide

Related to the previous trends of mathematization and explosion in scale has been the massive move of our subjects' center of gravity from Europe to America. Part of this resulted as a gift of Hitler to the New World--as the Schumpeters, Haberlers, Machlups, Marschaks, Lerners, and Leontiefs gravitated to our shores and stayed here. Part of it reflects the sheer weight of American GNP in the total of world GNP. Money talks. I mean inflation-corrected money. Real money means more college students. More students means more professors and more research. Nowadays factors of production move in international trade, toward job opportunity and higher salaries.

When I was young we read British authors. We spent sabbaticals abroad. Now, alas, our brightest and best aspire to winter in Stanford and not at Oxbridge, Oslo, or Rotterdam. My young graduate students patronize the traditional centers of economic eminence. Don't shoot the messenger: I only report what's out there.

Location and concentration of location fortunately do not matter as much in the present age as they used to. Before the war it was my great good luck to be trained at the University of Chicago and at Harvard. Cambridge University, Columbia, the LSE, Oslo, Rotterdam, or Stockholm would have been quite passable alternatives. But when pressed to give career advice to pre-war economists, candor required me to counsel: "Beg, borrow, or steal but get to where the real action is." Today I could name three-score-and-ten strong centers for economic study. And better informed folk could double my list.

Revolutions: Monopolistic Competition and Keynes

Early on following 1932 were three great breakthroughs: the first, in microeconomics, was associated with Edward Chamberlin and Joan Robinson. It was overdue and brought the Marshallian tradition kicking and screaming into catch-up with Cournot's 1838 analysis of imperfect competition. Except in its incorporation into game theory and managerial economics, the Chamberlin-Robinson revolution has almost disappeared from contemporary notice. I believe that to be a mistake and a retrogression, explicable in part because of Chicago-School desire to favor *laissez faire* and in part because of mathematicians' hankering to be able to stay in the green acres of easy convex-set theory. However, this is not the place or the time to argue the point.

Postponing Keynes's *General Theory*, I date the third revolution to just about fifty years ago. The abrupt paradigm shift from the classroom microeconomics of *partial equilibrium* to the few-goods-few-factors diagrams of general equilibrium dates at around 1941. I was reminded of this a fortnight back when invited to a 50th birthday party at Ann Arbor. Wolfgang Stolper and Paul Samuelson were the honored scholars, but really people came from thousands of miles around to celebrate the jubilee of a lemma--the so-called Stolper-Samuelson theorem and its myriad generalizations. As I said on that occasion, what made the great impact was not the tariff's successful protection subsidy to real wages or to whichever factor of production is geographically scarce in the Heckscher-Ohlin framework. What mattered was bringing into the undergraduate classroom the manageable *box diagram of production* and its implied guns-vs.-butter *possibility frontier*. So long as Walras, Cassel, and Ohlin remained in the abstract realm of N+M equations in N+M unknowns, Marshall held on to the elementary classroom and primers. As if hit at the same time by the same colliding asteroid, Joan Robinson, Jacob Viner, Stolper-Samuelson, and others occupied the manageable ground of general equilibrium.

In between the beginning and the ending of the 1930s came the bombshell of Keynes's *General Theory*. Before its name had been coined in the literature or embalmed in the dictionary, substantive "macroeconomics" was born. The Einstein-Bohr debates concerning the ultimate foundation for quantum theory in physics were not more dramatic than the pre- and post-war debates on the micro-foundations of macroeconomics. Model T Ur-Keynesianism of the 1930's depression cut the Gordian Knot by largely ignoring micro-foundations. The only wheel in town to handle the depression decade was the best wheel in town. As the war came, and as both depression and war receded into the past, the behavior equations of central-bank and fiscal policy changed. Epicycle by epicycle the Keynesian paradigm evolved, as a stock variable was added here and a cumulative lag there. Once $MV = PQ$ had its V become a rising function of the interest rate, the neoclassical and Keynesian tracks began to converge.

"We are all Keynesians now" became a conscious echo of Harcourt's *fin de siecle* complaint that "We are all socialists now." Only now we had splintered into post-Keynesians, eclectic-Keynesians, new-Keynesians, and new-new-Keynesians. To one like me who bade adieu to Model T Keynesianism when the post-war depression self-aborted, I find Keynes's scientific greatness in the fact that my best shot at explicating "the new classical economics of rational expectations," or explicating the post-Patinkin Quantity Theory of Money and Prices, involves employment of the variables and functions that were absent in the pre-Keynes writings of J-B Say and Marshall and even at best implicit in the writings of Wicksell and Fisher. Greater fame hath no one! "Obliteration by incorporation" is the Mertonian tag for the process.

My purpose now is not to claim truth for post-1936 macroeconomics. Rather I have to call attention to the sheer fun, vitality, and progress that has characterized economics in our time. We never ran out of challenges. Or surprises. And, with all, there were triumphs aplenty along the way!

Around the Campfire

My seven children, and later the 15 grandchildren, always asked for good stories about the olden times when we were growing up. I must hasten to fulfill the promise of jolly anecdotes about various of our crowd.

Here are three for the price of one. At war's end at the LSE, Lionel Robbins and Friedrich Hayek asked me about their old student Abba Lerner. I reported that Abba was in top form, producing new theorems, lemmas, paradoxes, reform movements, and wire sculptures every hour on the hour. "However," I added, "his friends had to protect him against himself during the War and just afterward."

"What do you mean?" these fervent libertarians asked me.

"Well, Lerner wrote a little book proposing that General Eisenhower in Europe and General MacArthur in the Pacific each be given abstract purchasing power in proportion to the importance of their theatres. Then each would divvy this up among their colonels, for division among the lieutenants and privates so that the war could be fought in an efficient and decentralized way by use of auction markets. Abba never understood why his friends talked him out of publishing to protect his reputation."

Hayek interrupted me, saying: "What's the matter with that? I've proposed exactly the same thing."

To change the subject, I continued on. "At the last AEA Christmas meeting, Lerner commandeered an empty hotel ballroom to launch his new political platform. His program? The West is to give Joseph Stalin the ultimatum: Introduce immediately in the USSR free speech, free press, free religion, and free marginal-cost pricing or we shall drop on you the atomic bomb."

It was Robbins' turn. "What's the matter with that? I myself have sponsored just that proposal."

Last January I had the honor to give the Second Lionel Robbins Lecture in Claremont, California and I quote two items from it.

> Lionel was a tall and handsome and impressive presence. Once during a polished Robbins lecture at Harvard, young Bob Solow whispered in my ear: "People who don't lecture like that should be shot."
>
> Back in Marshall Plan days, Robbins was in Paris for an inflation commission. I encountered him at an economists' cocktail party, and encounter is the right word. In cutaway garb, he looked more distinguished than any person could possibly be. Stimulated by his polite and flattering interest, I became more and more

animated--until in a crescendo of hyper-ventilated brilliance, I spilled all of my dry martini over his beautiful tailoring. Guilt-stricken, I proffered wrinkled tissue to sop up the flood. Lionel turned not one hair. "Think nothing of it, my dear Paul. Have no concern."

What could I say? As an amateur anthropologist, I opined this to Robbins. "On my plane from Boston to Paris, a colonial from the fringe of the British Empire moved from passenger to passenger to convey his unease concerning missing his further connection in Paris. His nervousness quite annoyed more than 50 people. And here you, Lionel, have put me completely at ease despite my gaucherie. There really is something to the English Empire Builder and his phlegm."

Lionel gently punctured my pretentious balloon saying, "Yes, Paul, that good public school I never went to did wonders for me."

Here is another three-for-one anecdote.
Once Nicky Kaldor, Tommy Balogh, and Paul Rosenstein-Rodan were bachelor roommates. Balogh came in on the other two furiously arguing. As he left with Kaldor, Balogh said: "I didn't know you knew Pareto's economics."

Said Nicky, "I don't. But once Rosie explained the problem to me, I saw how it had to go."

Nicky was legendary on the Allied Bombing Survey. When they found Hermann Goering's private railroad car loaded with Scotch whiskey, the American privates touched not a drop, which was unheard of abstinence. Nicky drank and got down to work. At the end of exactly 60 minutes, the well-trained Yanks looked at their watches and proceeded to get roaring drunk. Nicky never understood the story.

To explain to me Maynard's reputed humor I was told of the time in Cambridge when Kaldor had foot trouble. When Keynes was told it turned out to be athlete's foot, he refused to believe it. "Next," he said, "you'll be telling me that Piero Sraffa suffers from writer's cramp."

In debate with Milton Friedman, Bob Solow used to quote Sydney Smith's words to Thomas Babington Macaulay, "I wish, Babington, I were as sure of anything as you are of everything."

In badinage with my dear friend and tennis mate Franco Modigliani, I would make the mock complaint that the same Sydney Smith made to Macaulay: "When I am dead, Franco, you'll be sorry you never heard the sound of my voice." Economists used to debate over who was the faster talker, Modigliani or Arrow. The verdict was: Kenneth for the short sprint; but for the long marathon put your money on Franco. Albert Gaylord Hart has also been a strong contender in those sweepstakes. He once explained to me that he and John Hicks spent an enjoyable evening in contented silence. I admitted to half believing the story.

Oskar Morgenstern, reputed to be the grandson of Kaiser Friedrich of Prussia, was a delightful mixture of boyishness and sophistication. When Abraham Wald was a starving mathematician in Vienna, Oskar found him work in economics. The rest is history. Oskar once told me that Hitler's censorship was not so bad as he had thought. He learned this by sending his Mother in Austria ever more provocative letters, to determine the point at which they ceased to pass through. There's scientific ardor for you.

Morgenstern's name makes one think of Johnny von Neumann. Von Neumann was a phenomenon. The medieval protocol at a doctor's examination involved propounding to the candidate an Impossible Problem. Legend has it that von Neumann found its solution! The great Hilbert never spoke at exam ceremonies. But he stunned the crowd at von Neumann's exam by begging to ask a question. "Never," he said, "have I seen such fine evening clothes at Göttingen examinations. Is it permitted to ask who is the candidate's tailor?" I like the following story about von Neumann, who was notoriously helpful if you could capture a few minutes of his time. To an ardent researcher, the great man said: "Perhaps if you do A, then B, then C, you'll make progress on your problem." Back at the lab, A got done. Then B. As the sun was rising, C got finished and miraculously all was solved. The grateful researcher immediately called up von Neumann on the telephone: "Just as you said, A, B, and C did the trick, completely and perfectly." "Next time," von Neumann said drowsily, "call me up only if things *don't* work out."

In the school yard anyone two years older or younger than you belongs to a different generation. Sixty years on readers will giggle when I speak of my elders at the University of Chicago and refer to George Stigler, Milton Friedman, and Allen Wallis. Ever since, despite our differences in value judgments we have stayed good friends. Indirectly I owe this success to the bad personal relations between the conservative Gustav Cassel and the bohemian Knut Wicksell. Before I had met Gunnar Myrdal or Bertil Ohlin, I heard that the bad example of their elders had persuaded them to keep personal animus out of ideological differing. And I remembered the saying that Albert Einstein and Max Planck were such fine characters that between them they elevated the tone of German physics in several generations.

Scholars, I have observed, can learn from their friends better than from enemies. A Hawtrey criticism of Keynes's early *General Theory* drafts was more acceptable if it came from Richard Kahn. This is human, but it is 180° wrong. Karl Popper advises: Be your own best critic. Why leave the fun to the enemy? I suggest in the same vein: Concentrate on the other fellow's data and syllogisms. Your friends' works largely reflect what you already think you know.

I have learned a lot from Milton Friedman. Stigler said Friedman's propositions are likely to be weightier than most people's because they are always subjected to a barrage of adverse testing. Stigler's truth is only half the story. We ought to chalk up to his credit the many false propositions that Friedman's critiques have caused to miscarry and abort. I count as a bonus some of Milton's quotable quips. Here are only two.

In one of our many public debates, I once said. "Diderot was given every gift by the Gods. Every gift but the gift of *dialogue*. Milton, the gods gave you every gift: a quick mind and a coherent set of values. They gave you every gift, Milton, every gift but the gift of `maybe.'" The crowd laughed but then Dr. Friedman put me in my place, with the telling phrase: "Paul, one man with the truth is a majority."

Also, I like to quote what I first heard from Milton's lips. "The future is longer than the present." Put that one back-to-back with "In the long run we are all dead," and you will have what Hegel, Thomas Mann and Niels Bohr called a deep truth:

> A deep truth is a truth whose negation is also a deep truth.

Of George Stigler what can I say that has already not been established in his many writings on information, policy, and history? My copy of Bartlett's quotation is interlaced with George's many witticisms. If St. Peter told George that to get into heaven he would have to tell no joke for a whole week, I am sure he could not last past Wednesday. When I told George that his son Stephen, the distinguished historian of statistics, was a chip off the old block, Stigler took his lines from the mathematician George Birkhoff: "I'm glad to hear you say it. I knew he was good, but I didn't realize he was that good." Actually, Stigler never had reason to be immodest.

Chicago in our times can boast such names as Knight, Viner, Paul Douglas, Henry Simons, Aaron Director, two Schultz's and a Shultz, Lange, Friedman, Metzler, Harberger, Koopmans, Marschak, Becker, Coase, Harry Johnson, Fama, Merton Miller--but I had better leave the list incomplete lest I lose two friends for each one I make. Why this brilliance? Chance? Yes, in part. What else? I think the Midway has for a century been a meritocracy, albeit a tough jungle. Although I am on record as being skeptical of the adversary procedure in the advancement of science, one must admit that sometimes it takes grit to make pearls. The Chicago I have known had plenty of that good irritating stuff.

The Cambridge of Pigou, Keynes, Kahn, Sraffa, Kaldor, Dennis Robertson and two Robinsons was not your peaceful backwater. Will I be departing from my pledge of sweetness and light if I remark that too much sand can spoil the pearls?

I am reminded of Viner's teacher at McGill, the humorist Stephen Leacock. He was a great wit. However, for reasons of family sorrow, he began to spend much time in the university bar. A faithful colleague kept him company. After Leacock's liver went West that colleague was left with his mentor's habit, but alas Leacock could take his genius with him and did. So it was that I used to wonder back in the 1940s, 1950s, and 1960s, what would happen to the Cambridge dominance when the brilliant personalities of that great epoch retired to Cornwall or Elysian fields. After regression toward the mean could the university afford its habit? I would take comfort in the fact that the elite places--with the secure material base of a Harvard or Yale or Princeton or Cambridge or Oxford--can come back after a dry season in a way that cannot be counted on by an Iowa State, Purdue, or University of Illinois after their Elizabethan Ages meet their James First.

A Little List

Your time is limited and the hour is late. For brevity let me sing praises by awarding hypothetical Nobel Prizes among our crowd. Before 1969 Economics was a Johnny-Not-Yet-Come in the Nobel barnyard. Never bothered by a brute fact, when writing up an obituary appreciation of Bertil Ohlin, I awarded the Economics Nobel Prize for the missing years of 1901-1930. Here is my 1981 list for 1902-1930.[1] It was a case of art improving on nature: I doubt that the

---

[1][For reference, here is my 1981 footnote]. One cannot forbear playing the game of might-have-been. Here is the most likely scenario of awards from 1901 on: Böhm-Bawerk, Marshall, J.B. Clark, Walras, and Wicksell; Carl Menger, Pareto, Wicksteed, Irving Fisher, and Edgeworth; Sombart, Mitchell, Pigou, Adolph Wagner, Allyn Young, and Cannan; Davenport, Taussig, Schumpeter, Veblen, and Bortkiewicz; Cassel, J.M. Keynes, Heckscher, J.R. Commons, and J.M. Clark; Hawtrey; von Mises, Robertson, H.L. Moore, and F.H. Knight. My list breaks off at 1930 and the dawn of the modern age. Of course there would have to be the usual grumblings and criticism. Why were Eugen Slutsky and Frank Ramsey missed? If Davenport, why not Carver and Fetter? Why Böhm before Menger?

Swedish Royal Academy of Science would have had in those years the wisdom imparted to me by hindsight.

Now the Statute of Limitations permits me to fill in for the years 1931-1968. This time, however, I shall cheat a little. To make up for what God and I consider imperfections in the 1959-1991 record, I shall award too-early time slots to some great overlooked economists. I beg the reader's indulgence.

Semicolons separate each year's winner(s), beginning with 1931:

> Viner ('31); the Webbs; Paul Douglas; A. Bowley and R.G.D. Allen; E. Chamberlin and J.V. Robinson; Henry Schultz; Alvin Hansen; Lundberg and Lindahl; A.P. Lerner; Boulding; Kaldor; Lange; Kalecki; Harrod; von Neumann; Colin Clark; Holbrook Working; Lösch and Palander; Frank D. Graham; Marschak; Slichter; Metzler; Bergson and Harsanyi; J. Meyer and A. Conrad; Vickrey and Musgrave; Scitovsky and Hurwicz; George Dantzig; Fleming and Mundell; Harry Johnson and Arthur Okun.

No apology is needed for including some names before their time. Someone as wise as Okun, in a crowd that is stronger on flash than on judgment, deserves a prize at any time; a Harry Johnson crowded two lifetimes in one fore-shortened one. A second try at such a list would be just about as excellent as this first stab.

We Happy Few

This is a symphony, not a concerto: Our Crowd not My Crowd. Personally I have been a pioneer on the mainstream, helping to form it and helping to define its established channels.

But for you to be able to calibrate and allow for my personal biases, the record should show who my special comrades at arms

---

If Mises, why not Foxwell, Nicholson, Aftalion, Seligman, Spiethoff, von Wieser, Bowley, Pierson, Birke, Einaudi, Pantaleoni, or Barone? If Veblen, what about Hobson, Luxemburg, the Webbs, Hilferding, or Lenin himself for the 1917 Prize? The listing I have given compliments the taste of the Swedish Royal Academy of Sciences, being a compromise between (1) what I with hindsight judge to be true scientific merit, and (2) what would likely have been recognized as merit by conscientious but fallible committees.

have been. Compared to me James Tobin is without guile and possesses sharper Bayesian priors than I do. But it would make me specially uneasy if, on some major topic, I continued to differ with him--or with Bob Solow, or Franco Modigliani, or Dick Musgrave, or Ken Arrow, or Art Okun. By contrast my admiration for the depth, breadth, and originality of Roy Harrod or Joan Robinson would not lead to unease when differing with their empirical and policy views. And over the years my consumer's surplus from the works of Lionel McKenzie, John Chipman, Nicholas Georgescu-Roegen, and Bob Merton tells you something about me and about them.

Requiem

In closing, we need to pay homage to those in our age cut off in midcourse by the envy of the gods. Pascal died at 39, but his body was that of an old man. Felix Mendelsohn, who "began as a genius but ended as a talent", died at a similar age. Again, if we think of him as having already run race after race, his last 10 years' work is all we should expect of a fulfilled life. Mozart's death at 35 is something else again: extrapolation of his productivity profile shows how great was our loss.

Readers will hardly recognize such names as Victor Edelberg (LSE) or Miguel Sidrauski (Chicago and MIT), bright talents cut off before they could run their race. All, however, will know Lloyd Metzler and Harry Johnson. Like Galois, Maxwell, and Hertz, catastrophe struck for them while still at their inflection point of promise and accomplishment. When a Jan van der Graaf leaves science of his own free choice we grieve, but we respect his right to choose. With these others, I am once again made to agree with that wise King Alphonse of Spain who said:

> If I had been in on the Creation, I could have done a better job of it.
> Amen.

Remembered Heroes

The Alfred Nobel Award in Economics is a parvenue, a Johnny-Come-Lately and not properly a Nobel Prize. Twenty-three times (before 1992) our own ranks have grown in number. Brief our time may be, but not so brief as to be spared deaths among our comrades. It is proper that I call the roll of our eight departed. Alas, poor Yorick. I knew each one well.

| 1959 | Ragnar Frisch, first among equals |

1971	Simon Kuznets, analyst of economic history
1972	John Hicks, versatile theorist
1974	Gunnar Myrdal, Viking navigator into distant disciplines
1975	Tjalling Koopmans and Leonid Kantorovich, mathematical programmer and pioneer
1977	Arthur Lewis, son of underdevelopment who modelled development theory
1978	Bertil Ohlin, innovator in trade and macro

I wrote down this little list prior to departing from Stockholm. Only here did I learn of George Stigler's recent death. That news strikes close to the bone--my bone. For Stigler was like an older brother to me back on the Chicago Midway. I remember when I complained to him about the boredom of learning 3x3 determinants. What use was that ballast to an economist? George showed me his notebook from Henry Schultz's seminar. 3x3? Why these were NxN, where N is an integer that can be indefinitely large. From now on out, to whom shall I submit my untested notions on Ricardo or von Thünen?

George Stigler will be long remembered by all economists. To me he had a special significance. He was my first mentor back in the Chicago Midway of 1932-1935.

In every lecture one finds a nodder who nods once through the lecture. Also, when one writes a lecture one needs a point of view. For what person is one shaping the discussion? It was George Stigler whom I had in mind when preparing this lecture on Economics in Our Time--his time and mine. I shall write many more future articles directed at the same target.

That is scientific immortality. *Earned* immortality.

Stigler left our subject permanently altered and that is the only immortality a scholar can have, or want to have.

Our Crowd salutes his memory.

ME AND KENNEDY
Examiner Club, January, 1994

My title is stolen from the shrewd bartender Mr. Dooley, who claimed that the name of the book Teddy Roosevelt was writing on the Spanish-American War read *Me and Cuba*. It began with the tribute

> The bravest man I ever knew was the black sergeant
> who followed me up San Juan Hill.

History records a more modest role for me as an economic guru to John F. Kennedy. But for about a year, from late 1959 to Inauguration Day in January 1961, I may well have been the principal economic adviser to Candidate Kennedy and President-Elect Kennedy. Moses-like, it was not given to me to enter into the promised land of Camelot. But Andy Warhol would have understood my brief season of celebrity.

How did a clean-cut mathematical economist fall into such strange company? For that matter how did a mathematical economist come to write an all-time best-selling textbook in more than 40 languages? Teddy Roosevelt would no doubt say, "Shucks, it was nothing any American go-getter could not have done." But let me tell my own story about an interesting time in American history, a time that is already fading away within memory of living people.

Franklin Roosevelt was, and remains, my hero. I began the study of economics when American capitalism was essentially undiluted. That means I remember vividly the Wall Street boom (to say nothing of the 1925-1926 Florida land bubble, which I enjoyed--if that is the right verb--on the spot). I witnessed the Great Crash, and in my corner of the Middle West virtually all the banks went bust.

Naturally then I was a Democratic economist. There was virtually no other kind. I recall how, during the 1952 Stevenson-Eisenhower election campaign, economists such as Max Millikan and Dick Bissell became so disillusioned by Eisenhower's refusal to defend General Marshall against the vicious attacks by Senator Joseph McCarthy that they resigned from Republican ranks. "Go back, Max," I pleaded. "We don't need you, and a Republican Administration will desperately require competent economists." All to no avail. When our six-year-olds would say, "Who is it we're for, Dad? All the kids are for Ike", I knew the jig was up. Anyone who pleased the likes of me the way Adlai did was obviously not going to win a majority of the American electorate. And so it did come to pass. Except for Arthur Burns, who was not a notoriously nice character, the Republican infield was not a very competent one. People remember the Eisenhower years as pleasant, just as they claimed to do for the Calvin Coolidge years. That shows how much non-economists know about economic history. Ike managed to have three recessions within his two terms of office. I read that in the Guiness Book of Records.

And Gladly Teach

But I must not digress from me. Unsuccessful candidates have time on their hands. Tom Finletter, the New York lawyer, arranged for Adlai and New York Governor Averell Harriman to be coached in post-Keynesian economics. That was around 1955. One of the usual suspects must have mentioned my name; it could have been Alvin Hansen, Seymour Harris, or Kenneth Galbraith. As an undergraduate I had tutored the Chicago football team to try to keep them eligible, so I was game for anything. It was an experience having to reassure Adlai Stevenson repeatedly that deficit spending was genuinely a good thing in recessionary times. Averell was not of higher I.Q. than Adlai, but his Index of Self-Confidence was distinctly higher.

As they say in court, I can now connect up with Jack Kennedy. From 1956 when Senator Kefauver stole from Senator Kennedy the privilege of running for Vice President on a losing Stevenson ticket, old Joe Kennedy was aiming for JFK to run for the top spot. Ted Sorenson and JFK may not have been convinced that every candidate needs an economist. Probably they felt the way Louis Howe felt about economists. When Leon Henderson reported for duty in 1932 as the first economist ever on a campaign staff, Howe as FDR's loyal lieutenant is supposed to have said to him: "Leon, see these buttons on the sleeves of my suitcoat. They're not worth a damn, but everyone says I have to have them. That's the way I feel about economists on a campaign staff." In a Pascal wager, Senator Kennedy wanted to have an economics brain trust just in case people expected that of him. Archibald Cox was to be his Tom Finletter. And I was only a 10-cent phone call away.

Seduction of the Innocent

But was Barkis willing? Ken Galbraith found a formula to sign on the Kennedy bandwagon. Pols, he read somewhere, should be for Favorite Sons from their own states. I recall that Jerry Wiesner was recruited to advise on science and cold-war military strategy.

I, however, was still for Adlai. Old Joe Kennedy I knew as an appeaser and a bigot. (I will tell a story out of school. When Harvard mounted its first big Funds Campaign in the 1950s, McGeorge Bundy pencilled in on the mailing to alumnus Joseph Kennedy, Sr.: "We're counting on you, Joe." He is said to have received by return mail, "You won't get one red cent from me, and if you come by I'll tell you why." Provost Bundy will do anything for Yale or Harvard and so he did drop by. What he is supposed to have learned is this: "I am the only Harvard graduate who has been Ambassador to England and not received an Honorary Degree. Which is because Harvard is anti-Catholic and I'll be damned if you'll get money from me." Bundy knew, but could not say, it was not Kennedy's theology that blackballed him, but rather the fact that internationalists on the Harvard Corporation like Grenville Clark were adamant against such an appeaser of Adolph Hitler.)

In my mind there seemed further guilt by association. I recalled Robert Kennedy as being somehow associated with such McCarthy henchmen as Cohn and Schine, perhaps not an unfair identification. John F. Kennedy's own role in the McCarthy witch-hunt days was not precisely what would form a chapter in a tome on *Profiles in Courage*. Although JFK had been my own Cambridge-Belmont Congressman when he displaced Jim Curley who had displaced egghead Tom Eliot, I only vaguely knew what he stood for. Many a time in the 1940s and 1950s I testified before the Joint Economic Committee. Imagine then my surprise to learn that Senator Kennedy was on it, for never could I recall his attending even a single session.

A third of a century later it seems incredible but a major query about supporting Kennedy enthusiastically--maybe the major block--was the question of a Catholic holding the U.S. Presidency. Usually bigotry is the privilege of the common folk not the academic intelligentsia. But on this issue we academics were as benighted as any class.

I don't know who said it, but there was truth in the taunt: anti-Catholicism is the anti-semitism of the Senior Common Room. Catholic universities were well represented in the schools of law and of theology. But in arts and sciences and engineering generally, Catholic institutions and students were distinctly underrepresented at that time. However, it was not this factor of numbers that mattered. After all, in economics scarcity is supposed to make for high value.

Rather it was the case that the church hierarchy was thought to have an asymmetric stance on politics. While in a definite minority, it insisted on the privileges of each and every sect. But when in a strong majority--as in Ireland, Spain and Quebec--God's law was to prevail over man-made constitutions. So its critics alleged.

Any middle-westerner who came to Boston in the mid-thirties, back in good old Cardinal O'Connell's time, was struck by the presence and power of the local hierarchy. Since Pope John and Vatican II, this all reads like the ancient history that it has truly become. John F. Kennedy's election enabled all to see that what was thought to be an issue was really no issue at all. One must read in the history books that the Unitarian William Howard Taft had to overcome resistance from those who said, "How can a person who does not believe in the Holy Trinity sleep in the White House?" One should add that President Eisenhower helped Kennedy's campaign by refusing to discuss the issue of birth control, saying that it belonged in the bedroom and not the political arena. As far as I can remember, JFK never pronounced on the legitimacy of birth control. And after his primary victory against Hubert Humphrey in the Protestant state of West Virginia, the Catholic issue evaporated away. Similarly, the dogma that a divorced man could not occupy the White House evaporated away under the sunshine of Ronald Reagan's attractive style on the stump.

I dwell on this inner struggle, not because I was anyone of primal important, then or now. Nor was my dithering especially interesting, or influential. Rather because my process of warming up toward JFK as a liberal was typical of what was about to take place in millions of Democratic minds.

But I am running ahead of the story. When asked to come to meetings in Boston with Kennedy and his people, I replied candidly: "I am not your supporter. I am for Adlai Stevenson." Stevenson was still in the running for a third time, and saints like Eleanor Roosevelt were squarely behind him. Kennedy and Sorenson disarmed me: "Hell, we don't need your vote. If you have expert counsel that you think can benefit the country, won't you want to make it available to someone who will have a shot at the Presidency?"

What could I say? That was precisely the reasoning I had used in attending academic seminars called at Brookings across the street from the White House by Ike's Chairman, Arthur Burns, of the Council of Economic Advisers. And that I was to use again in regimens of Nixon and Ford. I owed it to my fatherland and world society to share the wisdoms of my magnificent brain and expensive research education. Would I draw the line in counseling Adolph Hitler or Ghengis Khan? Those moments of truth never came my way. And later I was able to nag at the Reaganomics supply-sider nonsense from the bully pulpit of Congressional hearings. Always my advice was worth every penny paid for it.

So the issue of loyalty was left moot. I was an unpaid gun who volunteered for semi-anonymous duty. Later I imperceptibly evolved into a Kennedy believer. Yes, his father may have been a son-of-a-bitch. Still, I could detect no particular Joe Kennedy, Sr. influencing on policy decisions. I was never privy to John F. Kennedy's *inner* feelings and sentiments. But observing his black-box exterior, I was driven to the judgment that for better or worse, JFK's political future was tied up with Democratic liberalism.

(Digression. Subsequently, when Teddy Kennedy insisted on running for the 1962 Senatorial seat Jack had won in 1958, I was one of half-a-dozen Massachusetts academics who came out for him. True, he was only thirty and owed the shot to family influence. But Pitt the Younger had not become Prime Minister at 23 because of his beautiful blue eyes or superlative IQ. Yes, Teddy seemed less bright than Bobby, who seemed less bright than Jack. And he then did seem less humanely committed than either. But in 1962, the choices on the menu were Junior McCormick, Lawrence Curtis, and the academic pinup boy Stuart Hughes. I extrapolated that Edward Kennedy would make a better than median senator; and, by my lights, he has turned out in the last three decades to be both topnotch and effective. I have no informed opinion on how he spends his after-five hours. Indeed, in Kennedy's White House years, my contacts were always in the oval office. Chaps like Ken Galbraith visited the family wings and had personal chit-chat with Jacqueline Kennedy on the economics of arts. That was not my beat, and candidly, I preferred things that way.)

The Way Things Were
In the open discussion of this memoir I can elaborate on what the economic problems of the nation were as the 1960s loomed into view. Let me give a few of my own diagnoses at the time, pearls of wisdom that I was prepared to cast before any Presidential aspirants.

Compared to nations abroad, particularly measured against the miracle sprints of our erstwhile enemies--West Germany, Japan, and even Italy--U.S.A. real growth was relatively weak. Absolutely in this Age After Keynes we were doing well compared to our long-run and between-the-Wars history. But compared to remarkable world growth, America's 5 1/2 percent of world population was having its percentage share of global output fall from over 40 percent in 1945, to 35 percent, and showing a trend to 30 percent and below. (Today, U.S. GDP is perhaps 22 percent of the world total.)

Stagflation was a new disease beginning to rear its ugly head in the late 1950s. This is the phenomenon in which, at the same time, a modern mixed economy can be facing both peril of too much unemployment and of too much inflation. Economists know how to act against either one of these evils: we turn up the monetary and fiscal taps to stimulate employment and production; contrariwise, to reduce inflationary overheating, we turn down either or both of those macroeconomic taps. But the rub in stagflation is precisely this: whatever you do to ameliorate the "stag" of stagflation, that tends to worsen the "flation" aspect. And vice versa, when you act to control accelerating inflation, you worsen the unemployment problems.

General Eisenhower, discovering late in life that he was a Republican and not a Democrat, had by and large operated in the 1950s to combat inflation. And, with a little bad luck, he had contrived for America three recessions in the 1953-1960 time span. I could confirm for Kennedy-Sorenson that the economic weather was being favorable for a Democratic comeback after eight years of Republican austerity. It was not I who coined the Kennedy goal of "Getting the Country Moving Again." Even a lawyer could think of that. But it was a slogan with resonant appeal.

I did have a personal and private heresy. Ever since first visiting Japan in the late 1950s, I became convinced that the yen was a much undervalued currency. And, hush-hush, whisper it quietly, the U.S. dollar was becoming ever more overvalued within the Bretton Woods version of the good old gold standard. Here most mainstream economists disagreed with me. Memoirists tend to remember issues like these in which subsequent history confirmed the correctness of their minority view. So, as you listen to my words, I warn you to hold on to your wallets.

Bold social thinkers hoped to break out of the bind of stagflation by creating a new supplement to fiscal and monetary policies in the form of Wage-Price Guidelines. These had worked quite well in World War II, up until almost the last months of the conflict. Lord Beveridge in Britain and Alvin Hansen here had warned that Keynesian full employment might need controls on goods' prices and workers' wage rates.

Old friends of mine like Walt Rostow (and, I think, Ken Galbraith) were urging on the Democrats new forms of wage-price guidelines. We tried not to call them wage-price *controls*. The magnificent Camelot Council of Economic Advisers trio--Walter Heller of Minnesota, Jim Tobin of Yale, Kermit Gordon of Williams, not on the scene until Inauguration Day 1961--was later to innovate and monitor the best attempt to make such fat guidelines operate.

I have to confess to having been more skeptical. Indeed a reason, maybe the main reason, that this Cincinnatus was willing to leave his MIT plow was because of a private conviction:

> America is too great a nation to have its economic destiny determined by big-picture thinkers like Rostows and Galbraiths. A small-picture aficionado of cyclical macroeconomics like me must needs be in on the policy deliberations.

Such is vanity. Before we oversell the Prince, we first oversell ourselves. The second task is the easier one to pull off!

Every potential winner is surrounded by a bevy of would-be volunteers. I was only one of many who thought of themselves as Kennedy's economic adviser. In the Bible, many are called but few are chosen. In practical politics, many call themselves even though few really count. Never is the candid word spread to say, "We welcome your support but, in brute truth, you are only a spear-carrying extra in the Grand Opera presentation." Right now as I speak, there may be a dozen other New England worthies telling how *they* masterminded the Kennedy game plan. I was acquainted with a few score of folk who thought of themselves as king-makers in the

Kennedy camp, and there was no useful purpose to be served in puncturing this illusion.

An optimist might say that the King gets the advisers he deserves, while a pessimist fears that this may indeed be so. It was not that my persuasive words converted JFK to my viewpoints, as that his was a cool intellect that distrusted visionary gabble.

Here is an example: Chester Bowles began on short lists for a very high post in the State Department. It was his bad luck to take a two-hour plane trip with a candidate who disliked talkative optimists.

Here are some further examples of John F. Kennedy's intellectual temperament. The first story is one I heard around 1962 from Ben Lewis, beloved economist at Oberlin College. The Lewis daughter worked on JFK's senatorial staff before the bid for the presidency began. She was fired. Jack called her in and said: "You've been a great asset here. I'd dearly love to keep you. But you and Ted don't get along. And the simple truth is that I need Ted more than I need you." There is no graceful way of being fired. But this candid explanation -- which one cannot imagine unctuous Richard Nixon ever performing -- took the personal sting out of it. Sorenson was more important and the two did not hit it off.

In my own experience I was constantly urging on the Senator, the Candidate, the President-Elect and (from a distance) the President to do A and B. I was careful not to overstate the case too much because JFK was amazing at remembering who had misjudged the future and got him into trouble. He, with Sorenson's help, kept the score. More often than not, he would say: "No, we won't come out for A and B. We haven't got the votes." Or, "To get them we'd have to risk too much capital." When I would suggest the virtue in fighting the good fight even when you might lose, he often reminded me: "That's vanity, Professor. You feel justified but your total cause loses net."

There was another characteristic of his mental style. He was a quick reader. I daresay that Dick Nixon would have made a better professor at a third-rank law school. But Kennedy was his superior in the art of decision-making. In particular, it would be disconcerting when one repeated for emphasis a point that had not carried the day when first uttered. The wind went quite out of your sails when he would say: "You are only repeating what I understood you to say the first time. That doesn't add to the weight of your evidence." It certainly didn't and I learned to avoid the Bowles kind of mistake.

I reveal a secret of the trade when I tell you that every rational adviser to the Prince must learn to overstate his case. The sovereign, like the electorate, needs to be bamboozled a bit to develop the conviction to act as needs to be done. When you are asked, "If I don't get a tax cut by 1962, are you assuring me that unemployment will rise to 10 percent and blood will run in the ghetto streets?," then you must swallow and decide whether to make a good and dramatic story of it. But woe to you as a Kennedy adviser if you overdo it. Thus, Bob Roosa, who died this last month, was Undersecretary of Treasury for Foreign Economics in considerable degree on the basis of my recommendation. (I'll tell the full story later if time permits.) But in a sense that was my mistake. Roosa bucked the good cowboys at the Council for Economic Advisers -- my blood brothers -- and played footsy-footsy with Wall Street and Zurich aborigines. For reasons of personal chemistry that I would not have predicted and never did understand, the President didn't much care for Bob. Often he would say, "Isn't this Roosa who is telling us we can't lower interest rates for fear of alienating foreign investors the same guy who told me last year that our balance of payments would be cured before this time? Next time you're all in Paris take him to a bordello to loosen up." My memory is excellent for a 78-year-old, but I warn you to take with a grain of salt the poetic licenses involved in such a story. If not literally true, it is a well-told story truly indicative of what actually transpired.

A Day at the Hyannisport Compound

My title for this section comes from Turgenev. After the victory in the West Virginia primary, Kennedy's nomination was virtually certain. The week after the Democratic Convention the uranium pile at Hyannisport went active. Archie Cox called for an economic briefing of JFK. Present was to be Seymour Harris of Harvard, who had a nearby Cape home. Also Dick Lester, a Princeton labor economist prominent in New Jersey Democratic circles and also a nearby summer resident. Besides the nominee and Cox, there were Galbraith and me. The morning was lovely and sunny and Ken hitched a ride with me.

The press surrounded the Kennedy compound like Henry V's troops at Agincourt. When we got admitted, a three-ring circus was in view. Infant Kennedy cousins played in one corner. Celebrity after celebrity posed for the press with JFK. Walter Reuther of the UAW was the biggest card. During the interval of waiting Ken and I were introduced to Jackie Kennedy in a yellow bathing suit -- she in yellow, we in civvies. She had read Ken's essay on economics and leisure and they hit it off.

Finally, things quieted down and we formed a seminar in the Kennedy living room, deep in comfortable chairs. Archie Cox, to my mind an unsung hero in the campaign who never got his due of appreciation, was moderator of the seminar. Walter Reuther, who had not yet left for Detroit, sat in at the beginning. He was asked for his wisdoms before departing. His advice was not so cogent as to be memorable, but the following is a good enough indicator of its flavor.

What we need is more purchasing power. That means higher wages for workers, who won't hoard what they get. You can meet with our economists at the UAW and work out concrete programs for getting the job done.

The candidate nodded politely. We all nodded appreciatively. As soon as Reuther left the room, Kennedy said: "Forget what we heard. Work out what you think needs to be done. I'll decide among proposals."

I knew I was going to like it there. Father Kennedy could give advice and Son Kennedy would listen attentively. Afterwards the economics team could go about its job.

Or take Galbraith. He had a new idea every day just after the sun rose in the sky. Some of them were good ideas. Jack found Ken amusing. When the author of *The Affluent Society* would speak out against obscene private spending, JFK would listen closely and nod. Later he could tell his economics team to cook up their best program on tax rates and give justification for their recommendations. Issues were to be decided on their merits--merits for the economy, merits for re-election odds in 1964.

Cox turned to Seymour Harris as second lead speaker. Seymour, even a fond protegé would have to admit, was not a great teacher. He began talking a mile a minute, stating how each dollar of fiscal stimulus would get spent and respent in a multiplier chain infinite in its number of links but adding up eventually to a finite multiple of the original dollars.

"Slow down, Seymour," Archie advised. "Think of this as EcA."

"EcA? Why Jack has already taken EcA."

JFK intervened: "Yes, Seymour. But I got a C in it. And Russ Nixon [a radical friend of mine] was the teacher. So don't take anything for granted."

On the whole the tenor of the discussion was in favor of Keynesian fiscalism. Not much mention of monetary policy by the Federal Reserve under William McChesney Martin, Jr., ostensibly a Democrat but one who had not kept his union card renewed recently.

I seem to remember that Sorenson and Feldman, lawyers on the Kennedy team, as present but remaining cautiously quiet. We adjourned for lunch on the family yacht (I believe the *Marlin*). Personally, I was looking forward to a bang-up meal on sparkling Nantucket Bay. The black cook in a white chef's hat raised my hopes. The Bloody Marys whetted my appetite. Frankfurters and beans, fried in a skillet, came as an anti-climax. I felt I had never left home.

In the afternoon John F. Kennedy and I went off alone to talk about the problems looming up on the horizon. I told him about the drain of gold that was resulting from America's export-trade deficit. Ford Motors was threatening to increase that deficit appreciably by investing heavily in Ford Motors, Ltd.--as indeed they did subsequently do in the face of only sighs from the Eisenhower Treasury. After an hour with the dismal science of economics, I on one end of the log and he on the other, JFK concluded with the remark: "Well you haven't made me feel happier than I felt before."

When I got home and polished off a rare steak, I judged it had indeed been an exciting day.

Lawyers and Economists

Theodore Sorenson was John F. Kennedy's right hand. Also his left ear and an important part of both brain hemispheres. Later, during Richard Nixon's first term I used to wonder how much autonomous influence Henry Kissinger was able to exert on his own. Were Kissinger's doctrines those ordered by Nixon? Or did Kissinger, by persuasion and force of intellect, swing Nixon into the desired directions? Could Kissinger be Svengali to Nixon's Trilby, the Rasputin who controlled the Romanoff actions?

I lacked the data to resolve this question. Therefore I tried to answer it by using the analogy of Sorenson's relation to Kennedy. Often Sorenson settled policy dilemmas. Was he following the boss's orders? Or helping form by his actions the shape of Kennedy opinions? As I surveyed events that came into my camera sights, my best hypothesis was the following:

> Ted was completely loyal to Jack. When it came to him to make a decision in Jack's name, he acted in the way that long experience had taught him Jack would want to do, which was also the way that would best advance Jack's career in politics and history.

Once Galbraith was sharing experience gained as a speech writer for Stevenson and other Democratic aspirants. "Before the campaign is over, we'll all find ourselves at times hating the candidate." "I know one exception to that rule," Sorenson replied. And I believe he turned out to be a good prophet. Bobby Kennedy, it seemed was a similar resource. At meetings he always addressed his brother as "Mr. President," a formality not always followed in FDR's New Deal circles.

It is significant that I cannot remember the names of early staff members in the Kennedy camp. Certainly none professed to be trained economists. Larry O'Brien was important in politics but I don't recall his cutting ice in any decision making. Kenny O'Donnell became an important figure from the Irish Mafia once he had the role of doorkeeper who shaped people's chances of getting an appointment to see the President. Mostly in the power struggles that became chronic between the Heller Council and the Dillon Treasury--these two groups were on good terms but inevitably Treasury resisted the CEA pace of activism--O'Donnell seemed a bit more friendly toward the Council gang. It was an Administration of tall men, tall men who laughed a lot.

Quickest off the mark of the new team were Bundy in the White House and Arthur Goldberg at Labor. Someone like Abraham Ribicoff counted for nothing and there were no meaningful cabinet meetings. Kennedy with his staff was a hands-on president--180° different from Eisenhower and Reagan.

But prior to 1960 Election Day, most Kennedy staffers were lawyers. I remember how shocked they were, all of them, when we economists had to break the news that you can't get the economy moving again by rhetoric or prayers. You would have to *do* something. Since dollar weakness and gold drains constrained the monetary policy you could hope to get from the Fed, all this spelled DE---IT. As late as December, 1960, when the country was known to be officially in the 1959-1961 Recession, Feldman and Sorenson did not want to hear that dread D-word spoken.

Indeed, just before the Inauguration, Kennedy promised Speaker Rayburn and Majority Leader Senator Kerr that he would "balance the budget, in the sense of not deliberately unbalancing it except to the degree that the recession itself occasioned that." I was heart sick to learn that news. Tobin, Heller, and even lawyer Joe Fowler on my Task Force were more vocally upset. They threatened not to sign their names to any recommendations that excluded some cut in taxes. That is why, early in January, it was decided that there would be no task force report. Instead, under my name and responsibility, there was issued my Report on the State of the American Economy. I dodged mention of a tax cut. We Democrats were to go swimming without getting our clothes wet near the water.

It took another full year to persuade the President that a tax cut was prudent and mandatory. It stuck in his craw to be asked to say to the public:

> Ask not what your country can do for you. Ask what you can do for your country.
>
> And the first sacrifice I demand of you to make for your country is to accept a generous tax cut.

Before Dallas this cause was won with business and the people. Even then it took Lyndon Johnson to push the tax cut through congress, along with the poverty program already on the drawing board. Even Congressman Wilbur Mills and Undersecretary

Henry (Joe) Fowler could not slow down that tide. By hindsight, knowing that in the late 1960s Viet Nam war escalation would overheat the Johnson economy if it maintained Great Society programs full scale, we realize losing the 1961-1963 years was a costly error.

Campaign and Victory

You know as much about the great Kennedy-Nixon debate as I do. I was frightened that Tricky Dick would make our boy look bad. I hoped the public would develop sympathy for the beat-up underdog.

That shows what I know. When I saw the debate--seeing it on TV rather than hearing it on radio--my fear vanished. The next day when Republican friends called to say that it hadn't changed as much as one percent of the vote, I thought victory to be assured.

An economist like me reads in the newspapers about LBJ being put on the ticket. Was Joe Kennedy, Sr., involved in that decision? Probably. Phil Graham of *The Washington Post*? Probably. Eliot Janeway? Probably not. Was Bobby against? Probably. Since the outcome was so close, by hindsight it was a brilliant decision. I expected that so great a wheeler-dealer would be a great asset. In my observation Vice President Johnson was foolishly not used at all. He visited with camel drivers in Pakistan. He was figure-head chairman of a committee to recommend a supersonic airplane. That recommendation, wisely, was in the end turned down. Only after the assassination in Dallas did Arthur Schlesinger, Jr. and the likes of my friends begin to ask: "Who is the attractive young Bill Moyers on LBJ's staff and how do we get to know him better?"

Mover, Shaker, King-maker

My time tonight is short. I shall have to skip the Task Force on the State of the Economy that I chaired for JFK. And the Working Party on Tax Reform chaired by Stan Surrey, which came up with the idea of an investment tax credit in an MIT seminar room. And the Task Force on International Economics, the George Ball task force, that had economists Robert Triffin and Eddie Bernstein on it, along with Paul Nitze.

At JFK's request, I sat in on many of these different committees' deliberations. Later someone asked me what the Ball Committee had accomplished. I could say that it did help to make Ball Assistant Secretary of State and later Undersecretary of State. Certainly it did not solve the problem of America's overvalued dollar. That had to wait on John Connolly's cynical advice to Richard Nixon in August of 1971. God works his wonders in mysterious ways.

I witnessed what I never expected to see. Every cabinet officer was selected by the small Kennedy team. That's no surprise. But it was a surprise to observe that *every major officer in each cabinet department was handpicked for them by the same narrow White House team.*

My true claim to fame, my true gift to the nation, was having much to do with getting Walter Heller selected as Chairman of the CEA. He was the perfect choice and he wasn't from Massachusetts but rather from some strange place called Minnesota. Heller and I had a lot to do with getting Jim Tobin, the sage from Yale, as Number Two man. (When Jack Kennedy met Jim, he said: "Don't I know you?" "Yes, I was in the 1939 class, between you and your brother Joe." "Hell, and I thought I was getting away from the Harvard monopoly.")

Douglas Dillon, a Republican, doesn't know that he owes something to me for his appointment. He was regarded as a good actor in the Eisenhower State Department and I was afraid they'd make the mistake of picking Alfred Hayes of the New York Federal Reserve Bank. Concerning Robert V. Roosa from that bank I've already said enough, maybe too much.

I have to laugh in memory at the gatherings in the Galbraith home where Ken, Arthur Schlesinger, Seymour Harris, and I would recommend and blackball possibilities for about 50-to-100 top cabinet jobs. We could never know how much or little our counsel mattered. In retrospect I am amazed on how much influence our information and prejudices could have, not on how little.

When asked about my own role, I have always given the one true answer: "Had I wanted a top job for which I was qualified, I could have had it. I got precisely the role I best desired -- out-of-town sage, who in a few critical times reinforced the recommendations of his admired colleagues at the CEA: Heller-Tobin-Gordon, the all-time star infield of Tinker-to-Evans-to-Chance."

What did Ken Galbraith want? Certainly JKG would never have accepted the CEA top command. As Galbraith's pal, Young Arthur, revealed at a press conference trial balloon, he would have best loved being named to fill out JFK's unfinished senatorial team.

When I was dumb enough to suggest: "Ken, you'd keep the seat warm for Teddy?", I was set straight. "No, I'd later run on my own and be elected in my own right." Pat Moynihan proves that it was I who suffered from too little faith.

As I read over my prepared text, I see that I have given some indications of how much fun it was to march with Dorothy, Toto, and the rest on the road to Camelot. I have not, I fear, conveyed well how successful and rational the Kennedy Years 1961-1963 were in terms of economic policy and performance. By a Gresham's Law that bad talk drives out good, history will increasingly remember John F. Kennedy the philanderer and cynic. Predecessors such as Eisenhower and successors such as Nixon and Reagan conspired to make JFK look good in economics. But actually those in the know realize that

President Kennedy with Theodore Sorenson's faithful and intelligent loyalty, themselves brought about much of America's good luck.

580

AT EIGHTY: MIT AND I
April 30, 1995

As Abraham Lincoln left to take up the duty of the Presidency in Washington, he gave a farewell address to his neighbors in Springfield, Illinois. He said something like the following: "Here I lived, and worked, and became old. Here I've married and brought up a family. Here I've buried a child. I don't know when I'll be back but I know where I've been. Etc. Etc."

Well, I'm not going anywhere. But it is MIT where I've been and worked for more than 55 years. Since I first taught summer school at MIT, it's actually nearer to sixty years.

A legend has grown up that Harvard treated me badly, to its shame, and that therefore I had the misfortune of not getting tenure there. So to speak after this terrible setback I made good and, to paraphrase Ernest Hemingway's friends, Doing well is the best revenge. In this case, revenge on Harvard.

Such a melodrama may somewhat fit Norbert Wiener's career. Certainly all his life, Norbert lived in the shadow of the Harvard Yard and never did the trauma of his expulsion from Eden fade away from his conscious mind.

Legend and history never get things quite right. At no time had Marion and I expected much from Harvard. There were no fervent promises later reneged on. Of course I never for a moment thought that my dim prospects at Harvard were remotely connected with a lack of competence on my part. I knew precisely my worth and future potential. And I knew accurately the merits and demerits of all those already on the tenured faculty and those ultimately to be there. (I digress to mention that subsequent years completely confirmed my diagnoses: Lloyd Metzler, Jim Tobin, Bob Solow--the bars of Central Square are full of village Newtonians destined to shed their fragrance some distance from the Fogg Museum. The case of James Tobin was the most surprising in retrospect. He was in Cambridge, England when Yale made him an excellent offer. To his legitimate surprise, and *ex post* to that of everybody else's since, no one at Harvard said boo. And his worst stigma was that he came from the Middle West.)

But back to me and MIT. Late in October 1940, I simply transferred from teaching Harvard undergraduates to teaching MIT undergraduates. My research never missed a beat. But now I had my own telephone--as Schumpeter and Haberler still did not. With Harold Freeman I had my own secretary. All this accelerated the tattoo of published articles.

Why MIT and not, after a few years as a tutor and instructor, Michigan or Berkeley or Purdue? I can give you the logical reasons. But probably the real reason was that at the age of 17 months I was sent by my Mother, a premature feminist, to live with Aunt Frieda on the farm in Indiana near Valparaiso, the county seat. What should have been an analyst's disaster was not. Newton and I were both shipped off to foster homes for most of the time between birth and five years of age, but both of us made good. As I can quote from a recent premature 80th birthday party for family members only:

> One dollar a day for room, board, and *love*. That's a bargain hard to beat. Actually I remember the farm with great nostalgia, exaggerated nostalgia. It did deliver me from the legacy of bad cooking. And maybe it gave me a look into two cultures, my native one and also the Protestant culture of nineteenth century rural Indiana. Nineteenth century because the farm lacked electricity and indoor plumbing. We went to Valpo by horse and buggy. In winter the roads were never ploughed because that would have prevented sleighs from replacing wagons.

Why this present blubbering about infancy? As they say in court, I will connect up with my choosing MIT. All my life I have clung to home. Two weeks in Rome or Paradise leaves me hankering for my Belmont tennis courts. When it was the fashion to go on sabbaticals to Cambridge, London, or Stanford, the Samuelsons stayed near good old Hayes-Bickford. In 1940 I already lived between Harvard and MIT. All I now had to do was turn left in the morning rather than right. So I never left home.

There was a second, and maybe deceptive reason for my choice. Edwin Bidwell Wilson, Willard Gibbs's sole protegé, was a cherished mentor in mathematical economics and statistics. He wrote to me how, when he went from Yale to MIT in 1907, friends thought him crazy. But in *ex post* fact, it was the best move he ever made. That persuaded me to overlook the fact that MIT economics was then a service department for nerds in engineering. (Let me digress to mention what I learned only recently when a biographer of Schumpeter sent me an item from the Harvard archives. Wilson with the kindliest intentions was working to pass me on from Harvard: he might have said good things about my taking a job at CCNY.)

Indulge me to digress once more to read a relevant message from my recent speech to 15 grandchildren and 11 children of the next generation.

> To tell the truth I never expected to reach 80. My father died at 52 and that hit me hard. For a year I dreamt it really hadn't happened. And I was always supposed to be like him.
>
> With a bad history of male heredity I had a rational belief that whatever I was to do I would have to do early. Perhaps that added to my natural quantum of *wunderkind* brashness.
>
> Well, what happened? Science happened. By 1955 anti-hypertension treatment was perfected. And in part by my Boston doctor. So here I am 40 years later playing tennis most days, in the hours after being at McDonald's or Albioni's, where I still spit out monthly, ahem, learned papers.

Rupert Maclaurin was the final force in getting me here. I say final because Harold Freeman was the initial source in my getting MIT's call, just as he was later to be in the case of Bob Solow. When Harold told Ralph Freeman I was the hottest thing since cheesecake, Ralph said: "I know he's good. But is he a cooperator?" Harold Freeman replied: "Is he a cooperator? He writes joint articles."

Indeed I had written one such on measuring unemployment with Russ Nixon, our village radical, who was getting a bad deal from a contemporary go-getter. And that was the last one for a long, long time. What Rupert did was call up incessantly and dangle prospects of research funds, like that from Roger Babson to study Newton's Law of Action and Reaction for economics. Rupert was a loose cannon, but without him MIT's explosive development in economics could not have happened. He was a good friend and later a tragic figure.

The rest, as they say, is history. In 1941 we started our Ph.D. program. Money talks. That first year we had nearly as many applicants as Harvard. And within our first two years we had turned down no less than Ken Arrow. Charlie Myers explained that he interviewed him at the end of a long day.

Of course I'm proud of how our department exploded upward. It helped a lot that around 1950 Harvard never wanted the people we did. Usually Yale was our tough competition.

But what I am most proud of is that we accomplished our sociological revolution avoiding the usual pattern in which the old boys get pushed aside and humiliated. The new team of Bishop, Millikan, Kindleberger, Adelman, Brown, Modigliani, Solow, and the other suspects created a new island of smug amiability. We all ate lunch together, eschewing the non-economists. None of us knew each other's salaries. No one ever asked for a raise.

For twenty years it was a benevolent despotism. Ralph Freeman's will was law and I told him whether A or B needed a raise and whether C could simmer awhile after his recent big promotion.

When Ralph retired he said, with obvious exaggeration, that all he had to do for 25 years was keep me happy. I replied that it was a tribute to both of us that he had never refused any request I ever made of him. And never did MIT meet an outside offer, even though I got millions of them because in those good old days no one believed I was here because I wanted to be. Somehow my salary stayed competitive. That's why I later understood it when Ronnie Gierson, a partner at Warburg's in London, told me they never named a fee. "How do firms know what to pay you?" I asked naively. "Oh, somehow they do know," he replied smugly.

In 1947 I heard a call from Chicago. Thinking, wrongly thinking, that there I might encounter better students over my career, I accepted for 24 hours. As soon as I made the bad decision, I knew it was a mistake and immediately cut my losses. At that instant, and only then, might I have succumbed to a Harvard temptation. And when those came a couple of times soon after, I did a cost-benefit analysis and knew which was the better place for me to be.

I learned from Wiener's example to have no rancor against Harvard. My best friends were there. My rarest books came from there. I enjoyed the best of two worlds. I was like the Soprano Melba who named to Mrs. Vanderbilt a stiff 1900 fee of $5000 to sing for her guests. Mrs. Vanderbilt said stiffly, "Very well. I'll pay it, but you're not to mingle with the guests." "Oh, in that case $3,000 will be enough." I even spent a sabbatical hiding in Bob Dorfman's office. Like New York City it was a great place to spend a weekend, but not the best place to live in.

Once a Washington University Chairman told me how great MIT treated recruiting professors. "Doesn't everybody?" I asked. "Not up the river," he said and asked, "Why is that?" I heard myself giving that famous logo. "We're Avis, Number Two, and so we try harder." But actually the polls then showed that Hertz was no longer in first place for mainstream economics.

Just because I am 80, I must not babble endlessly. It can all be summed up this way.

> MIT and I were made for each other. And when you come back for my Ninetieth we can count the ways that prove the theorem.

581

8. Paul Anthony Samuelson (b. 1915)

Birthplace: Gary, Indiana

Education:
1935: A.B. University of Chicago
1941: Ph.D. Harvard

Significant publications:
'A Note on the Pure Theory of Consumers' Behavior', *Economica,* Feb. 1938.
'Interactions Between the Multiplier Analysis and the Principle of Acceleration', *Review of Economics and Statistics,* May 1939.
Foundations of Economic Analysis, Cambridge, Mass.: Harvard University Press, 1947; 2nd edn 1982.
'International Trade and the Equalisation of Factor Prices', *Economic Journal,* June 1948.
Economics, an Introductory Analysis, New York: McGraw-Hill, 1948; 12th edn 1985.
'The Pure Theory of Public Expenditure', *Review of Economics and Statistics,* November 1954.
Linear Programming and Economic Activity, New York: McGraw-Hill, 1958.
The Collected Scientific Papers of Paul A. Samuelson, vols I–V (various editors).

Significant honors:
1941: David A. Wells Award (best thesis, Harvard University)
1947: John Bates Clark Award

1953:   President, Econometric Society
1961:   President, American Economic Association
1965–8: President, International Economic Association
1970:   Albert Einstein Medal
1970:   Nobel Prize in Economics

Experience:

1940– : Massachusetts Institute of Technology

The interview was conducted in Samuelson's office at MIT in August 1986

I was born in Gary, Indiana. My father was a pharmacist. My family was lower middle class, made up of upwardly mobile immigrants who had prospered considerably in World War I because Gary was a brand new steel town when my family went there. By the 1920s, however, already my father was engaged in losing a good deal of his net worth, so I was a premature sufferer from the Great Depression. When I was eight-and-a-half we moved to the Chicago region; and later I spent a couple of years in grade school in Florida. Then I went to Hyde Park High School in Chicago. One thing I remember about high school is the stock market boom. I remember helping my freshman algebra teacher pick out her stocks: Hupp Motors and some other losers. My Aunt Sophie was caught in the last of the new issues of the boom, the Ford Limited issue of Canada.

Just before I graduated from high school – in the middle of the year – I went on to the University of Chicago. I started at the University January 2, 8 a.m., 1932, when I attended a lecture by the sociologist, Louis Wirth, on Malthus. Before that lecture I knew nothing of economics, even though we had the *Harvard Classics* in our home, that five-foot shelf has *The Wealth of Nations* in it, but it would never have occurred to me to pick up *The Wealth of Nations*. Except for a Virgil poem and one boring look into *Two Years Before the Mast*, that opportunity for culture was completely wasted on me. Because I became a Freshman in the middle of the year, I missed the new economics part of the compulsory Social Science Survey course, which Harry Gideonse, as colonel in charge of the staff, had lectured on and assigned readings in. As it turned out this was very fortunate, because I was put in an old-fashioned elementary economics course taught by Aaron Director that was being phased out and had all upperclassmen in it. My first textbook at Chicago, which was also Jim Tobin's first textbook at Harvard, was Sumner Slichter's *Modern Economic Society*. It was kind of an Institutionalist textbook, and was pretty good – very full of the data of the 1920s. (His publisher begged him to keep it up to date, but he wasn't hungry and he let it go. Because it had been in date, it went out of date – most textbooks were never in date and so don't get out of date.)

I had a very strong grounding at the University of Chicago, where I took a record number of economics courses and did well in pre-Keynesian economics. My second teacher, under the quarter system, was Lloyd Mints, who used Ely's *Outline of Economics* – I think maybe the 7th edition – the theoretical parts of which were written by Allyn Young. I also took Statistics and Labor Problems from Aaron Director, and labor again from Paul Douglas. Henry Simons was very influential at Chicago. I took Public Finance from him. I knew Simons quite well, and talked to him a lot, so I knew about his 100 per cent money proposal and about his positive program for laissez-faire.

During this time (and this is what is not sufficiently in the record), there was a lot of dissatisfaction, even among orthodox economists, with the simple notion, "Let prices fall enough and there will be equilibrium." Simons already had the notion: what good does it do to have open market operations when short-term interest rates are already infinitesimal? Short-term bonds, Treasury bills, are then very close substitutes for money. What's the advantage of issuing new money and retiring an equivalent amount of a close money substitute when the efficacy of monetary policy per unit is very low? You begin to see here liquidity trap notions of later date.

Although the term "macroeconomics" had not yet come into use, we had a kind of macroeconomics before 1936. It was mostly taught in Business Cycles and Money and Banking courses. There wasn't very much relationship between the Business Cycles courses and the Value Theory that Jacob Viner and Frank Knight taught at the University of Chicago. There was a kind of schizophrenia. In the Business Cycles courses, people were very sensible; they talked about unemployment, and increases and decreases in unemployment. But when you studied Walras or a rigorous course in Value Theory, markets cleared and there was no unemployment. It wasn't that Say's Law was invoked – it wasn't necessary, because by definition of a market clearing system there was no unemployment problem. (People didn't worry about the niceties of existence and uniqueness; in those days they were taken for granted.) This was being taught while in South Chicago, not all that far from the University of Chicago, everything was closed down most of the time. In the early years of the Depression, you could have bought *anything* merely by assuming the mortgage.

Frank Knight wrote some polemics against Slichter's textbook in *The Journal of Political Economy* in the early 1930s. He smelled some kind of heresy in Slichter. But Knight's discussion was methodological. He argued that old Slichter was a do-gooder who thought he could change human nature, and that governments can do some good. Hardened, experienced people, by contrast, know that people are cussed. I think there's a lot of merit in Knight, but a lot of demerit, too. Whether his total effect on me was more bad than good I'm not sure. But from 1932 to 1936 I was besotted on Frank Knight.

It's not true, I'll say categorically, what Milton Friedman at one time tried to sell: that there was a very subtle Chicago oral tradition on the demand for money and monetary theory. Read Robertson's handbook on *Money*, and you will have plumbed the depths of Chicago's monetary sophistication.

I left Chicago in 1935.

How did your teachers explain the Depression?

Well, I got the impression from Aaron Director and Henry Simons and maybe Lloyd Mints that it was the tariff. The Smoot–Hawley

Tariff had been a bad thing. We were also taught the ups and downs of the money supply and the banking system, the Phillips multiplier, expansion of bank credit. During my time at Chicago I was a believer. Just to give you an example of how brainwashed I was by my Jesuitical training, I found it incomprehensible that Jacob Viner, who'd been away when I first came to Chicago, refused to sign a petition in favor of 100 per cent money. By 1934 I thought that, if only we had 100 per cent money, then no leverage between bank reserves and total money would ever be variable because one is a constant number, and if you didn't have variability in the money supply you wouldn't have the ups and downs of the dollar.

I think Frank Knight himself, by the time the Great Depression had dragged on for a long time, remained with the conclusion that in all ordinary times it's only frictions that cause depressions, and sometimes you get a double whammy or a triple whammy. If you read *The Economics of the Recovery Program* (it's a terrible book) by what was called the Harvard second team (Schumpeter, Leontief, Mason, Chamberlin, Harris, Douglass V. Brown), you will see the argument that depressions are inevitable and are even a little bit healthy. They're catharsis for the system. But the Great Depression was a particularly bad one, Schumpeter thought, because you got the Kitchen–Crum 40-month cycle interfering with the eight-year Juglar cycle, which interfered with the long-wave Kondratieff cycle. The ham bone was attached to the shin bone, and so you got triple whammy, and once it got itself spread out the market system would be okay.

The exception to this schizophrenia at Chicago was given by Paul Douglas, who was a reflationist, and not on very good terms with Simons and Knight; they regarded him as a power-hungry do-gooder. Jacob Viner actually appeared as a moderate in that environment, although I would say that he was on the sagacious conservative side of the ideological spectrum in economic doctrine in general.

Books that I remember include D.H. Robertson's little Cambridge handbook, *Money*, which was used in my Money course with Mints. The other book used in that course was *The Banking*

Process, written by an undistinguished professor at the University of Michigan. In it I was taught $MV = PQ$. I think I also was assigned – but I can't think in what course it would have been, but maybe it was a supplementary reading – Currie on *The Supply of Money in the United States*. According to my best recollection it was not a precursor of the Keynesian analysis. In that book he's worried about the instability of money supply, but that was because the non-member banks and the small banks have a different reserve ratio from the member banks; therefore when you get a change in the ratio of relative reserves in different parts of the banking system, the resulting volatility in the money supply exceeds the volatility in M reserves.

Did the explanation of the Depression convince the students?

Yes, but remember: in all these courses we didn't much address the underemployment problem, and we didn't primarily address the Wesley Mitchell fat years/lean years problem of being above some norm and below some norm. It was just a way of talking about past inflations and panics.

Did the students talk among themselves and say, "What explains the unemployment in the economy?" Or did they just not deal with that issue?

I would say that there was some preoccupation with things such as were propounded in William T. Foster and Waddell Catchings who published, I think even before the mid-twenties, two or three different books in which they argued the underconsumptionist view. Now, it's obvious to me, since I knew Catchings in his old age around 1950, that Foster must have been the brains because, extrapolating backward age-specific qualities, Catchings was not. Waddell Catchings was head of Goldman-Sachs when they were bankrupt in the twenties. Earlier he was part angel in setting up the Pollack Foundation which helped support Irving Fisher's *The Making of Index Numbers*.[1]

Well, Foster and Catchings had a challenge or contest. You got $5000 or $10,000 if you could find a flaw in their theory. That was quite a lot of money then, and a lot of economists joined in. The guy who won was something of a nut, named Souter, a New Zealander or Australian. If you looked up the series of Columbia theses that were published in those days, there's one called *Prolegomena to Economic Science*, or something. It's a very mystical book, dedicated to those anti-Marshallians who think they have replaced the master but haven't. I don't know what the quality of his critique was or whether he patted them on the back, but Alvin Hansen entered the contest and did not win, although he might have been second or third and gotten some prize money.

Hansen was most famous in my year for Garver and Hansen, and he had done, from what I understood, the macro primarily, and Garver had done the micro part. It was an interesting textbook because, unlike most American economists, Hansen is in the Spiethoff, Wicksell, Cassel, Schumpeter tradition, arguing that it is technological change and things like that, the external shocks, that mainly cause the business cycle.

The Foster and Catchings theory, like that of Major Douglas and so many of the underconsumptionists, is really quite obscure: and therefore specifying just what's wrong – or right – with it is not easy. I want to emphasize that because I think that either Foster or Catchings might have been a student of my Harvard money teacher John Williams, or his contemporary, at Brown University many years ago. John Williams himself was a fairly conservative fellow, but enough of an iconoclast to devote class attention to the Foster and Catchings book. If a student said, "Say's Law is exactly right," he'd say, "Well, wait a minute! There may be something in Foster and Catchings. And if there is something wrong with it, I can't tell you exactly what that is." That's as near to a Keynesian influence in the early Harvard environment as you could find.

Did the students talk about Foster and Catchings and say it didn't make sense? Was that the general consensus?

No, probably some of us students and some of the graduate students flirted a little bit with [Gesell-type] stamped money, or scrip. You know, there was scrip being issued in the Great Depression, since a lot of towns couldn't pay their teachers and police in cash. And there were notions afoot that if you could only date the money it would lose value unless you spent it, and that would make the money be spent. There were even floating around – I can't date exactly when this was, but I'm inclined to think before my June 1935 commencement day – stories like the following. A counterfeiter comes to town, creates some fake bills, buys a suit of clothes; the tailor uses the money to go to the baker – and finally the money comes back to the counterfeiter, who tears it up. Who lost? Everybody gained because there was extra production. In other words, there was a very strong notion – which I probably heard Stuart Chase orally espouse, maybe in my last months of high school – that we lived in poverty in the midst of plenty.

Even somebody like Princeton's Frank Graham, who was a pretty orthodox economist, had a scheme. He argued, "Why can't we organize all the unemployed people and the unemployed plants and have a dual economy alongside the market economy which can pay for itself; have everybody take in each other's washings and enjoy its extra employment?" There was a strong feeling in most of American academia, probably stronger outside the economics departments than in, and probably stronger in most economics departments than in the University of Chicago economics department, that something should be done.

But the students didn't really force the professors to deal with those plans and say what's wrong or right with them – is that a fair statement?

Yes. It's a bit curious because I don't remember in economics classes the loud radical who interrupts things, asks the questions that shouldn't be asked or that are hard to answer. Also, by the time I finished my undergraduate work, and up to that time, I met almost no communists. If you read memoirs, honest memoirs, of the various New York colleges, Columbia or NYU or CCNY in the period from 1930 to 1940, you would find either a tremendous antipathy or attraction towards communism. Communism didn't seem to loom large at the University of Chicago in the

1931–1935 period. But maybe as a commuter I was oblivious to it.

Keynes wasn't discussed much either, except by an instructor named Eugene Staley, who was a student of Viner's. I remember asking him, probably at the end of my freshman year (about 1932), "Who's the greatest economist alive?" He replied, "John Maynard Keynes." This was on the basis of Keynes' *Treatise*, which I had sampled, and *Monetary Reform*, which I probably had read. I wasn't assigned these books by Mints, Director, Simons or other undergraduate teachers.

Who else was there at Chicago?

Well, Jacob Mosak was my undergraduate colleague, and we were in friendly competition for prizes and honors. He probably is now retired from the United Nations, where he's been for many years. He wrote a classic book on trade theory for his Chicago Ph.D. Mosak played a key role later, in World War II, when he was chief macro expert for Richard Gilbert at the OPA, the most Keynesian shop in that town in the war's last months.

At this time Mosak was very much in the camp of Henry Schultz's econometric researches. Schultz was an object of derision to Frank Knight and maybe Henry Simons, and this was picked up by George Stigler and Allen Wallis, who were graduate students. I was an undergraduate student, but I came to know them pretty well. And I knew Albert Hart and Milton Friedman, but not quite so well. About that time Milton Friedman married Rose Director, Aaron Director's sister. The Knight crowd didn't need much to get an attitude of derision towards people and theories. Schultz was a self-trained mathematician and econometrician and a little unsure of his ground. He was a student of H.L. Moore's, and I would say a somewhat limited man, but he did perform a valuable role at that time. Wallis and Stigler used to make him nervous by trading on his insecurity.

In "Succumbing to Keynesianism", I wrote of the frustration that I felt of not being able to rationalize what was going on in the world around me with what I was being taught. I remember arguing with my parents. My father thought that Father Coughlin, who spoke frequently on the radio, was great. He would declaim against the bankers and against "fountain pen money". Only as certain anti-Semitic undertones began to appear in his addresses broadcast from Detroit did my father begin to lose enthusiasm for him. I couldn't really explain why Coughlin was wrong. I remember my mother saying to me, what would have been regarded as great heresy in the classroom, "Don't you know that times are only good during war?" (She had World War I in mind and the Gary steel boom.) And I had to admit there was some empirical basis for that.

So you did have a certain amount of internal confusion?

Yes. But my friends who were not economists regarded me as very conservative, a person who would debunk schemes for reform and things, because the system would take care of itself, or you would only make things worse. On the other hand I became very enthusiastic for Franklin Roosevelt. It was a little hard to explain how I could rationalize that.

Despite any doubts, I thought Chicago was wonderful. The only reason I left was that I won a fellowship from the Social Science Research Council for my entire graduate study. This fellowship had a requirement that you could not stay where you were. Were it not for this fellowship I would not have left the University of Chicago; I thought it was perfect. But I had to leave. I'm not sure whether or not it was open to me to go to the London School or Cambridge, which might have tempted me; and I wouldn't for an instant have thought of going to Oxford. That left the realistic choice between Columbia and Harvard.

There was a strong connection between Columbia and Chicago in those days because people like Allen Wallis and Milton Friedman had studied under Hotelling. Because of this connection most of my advisers – and I was on quite good terms with the Chicago faculty – thought I should go to Columbia. Harry Gideonse said, "How could you go to Cambridge if you could go to Morningside Heights?" (He came from Columbia.) I was warned that Schumpeter was kind of a crank, who believed in a zero interest rate. I was warned by Lloyd Mints that Seymour

Harris in macroeconomics was an inflationist. This is interesting, because if you read *The Economics of the Recovery Program*, 1934, you'll see that Harris, not yet having tenure at Harvard and still under the influence of Harold Hitchings Burbank, is a stout reactionary. Lloyd Mints must have had some keen sense of smell, because after Harris did get tenure he became a flaming Keynesian.

Despite these urgings I chose Harvard, but for the wrong reason. I thought it was going to be like Middlebury or Dartmouth – a green common and a white church – nice quiet surroundings. My irrational expectations were frustrated when I saw Harvard Square. One reason I chose Harvard was because Edward Chamberlin was there. I had looked into *The Theory of Monopolistic Competition* and Joan Robinson's *Economics of Imperfect Competition* as an undergraduate. They weren't assigned but were discussed vaguely in the advanced undergraduate theory course given by Paul Douglas. At the very end of the class he said, "This is the best class I've ever had. Because you're such a wonderful class, I'm going to give you something extra." That something extra was the following. He put a U-shaped average cost curve on the blackboard, and he drew a marginal cost curve and said, "For reasons I can't quite explain, that marginal curve must go right through the bottom of the average curve." A graduate student from the business school who was in that class told me that Joan Robinson had proved that in equilibrium you've got to be to the left of the bottom of the curve. But I drew lots of equilibria which proved to me that this wasn't the case. What he hadn't hold me was that it had to be an equilibrium with a downward-sloping demand curve and *no profits*. As you can see, it was a pretty primitive state of affairs.

Thomas Nixon Carver had an article – I can't remember whether it was in the *Quarterly Journal* or where it was – that if you get the real wage down to the intersection with the supply curve of labor, there will be no unemployment problem. It was much the same argument that was in Pigou's *Theory of Unemployment*. Finally, old Edwin Cannan in *The Economic Journal* had an article in 1932 in which the market got cleared at the right low-enough real wage.

We spent a lot of inconclusive time, wasted time I would say, on stuff like this: if you cut the wage and the demand for labor is elastic, then you really will be dealing a benefit to the laboring class as a whole because it will get more income. On the other hand, if you cut the wage and the demand for labor is inelastic, then there will be a loss in total purchasing power. Just what this general demand for labor was that we were talking about, and what these sterile totalities were, never got clarified; all this wasn't any statement about the real world, it was just a statement about what is meant by the elasticity of demand being above or below unity.

There is quite a lot of this type of argument in a book authored by Douglas and Director: it seemed to be a book concerned to reduce the seasonal fluctuations of employment. Director appeared ashamed of his earlier collaboration with Douglas. He probably was making a living, just barely keeping on good terms with Douglas, for whom he had some contempt as a sentimental, empty-headed do-gooder.

There was some dissatisfaction with these Say's Law views. Earlier I mentioned that Simons had the beginnings of a notion of the liquidity trap. I also remember that John Williams, who gave the first graduate course in Money that every graduate student took, was by 1935–1936 not a Keynesian – the *General Theory* book was hardly out; it *hadn't* been out; and it took him time to get up to speed (I don't know whether he ever got up to speed) on the Keynesian system, but he certainly did a lot better than, say, Schumpeter did in learning what Keynes's system was all about. Williams would say things like, "You can pull on a string but you can't push on it." By my Harvard entry, we were ready for public spending and budget deficits, and not just monetary policy, even though monetary policy was the principal thing taught.

I should also remind you of the Harris Foundation Lectures, a subsidized series at the University of Chicago, which had John Maynard Keynes as a visiting professor around 1931, and published a volume. That was before my time and I never met him. If you read that volume carefully (as I did only after 1945), there is already a notion that the flow of income is the primary determinant of saving and, when income falls enough, then the saving falls to equality with the reduced investment. Keynes' *Means to Prosperity* came out in 1933, although I was never assigned that, I believe, in any University of Chicago course.

To give you the Chicago flavor, once around 1944 or 1945 I wrote in *The New Republic* an article in favor of the Bretton Woods system. In it I had as a final sentence something like this: "History will learn who's the better friend of the capitalistic system, Alvin Hansen or Henry Simons." After I'd written this, I sent Henry Simons, who was a friend, a postcard and I said, "You and I come from a part of the country where if you call a man a son-of-a-bitch you'd better be smiling. Well, I was smiling when I wrote that." Henry Simons wrote back and said, "I took no offense but I want to remind you that I had no wild oats of deflationism to live down, as Alvin Hansen did." And I say that because in Alvin Hansen's business cycle book, written in 1929, he argues that the business cycle may be a thing of the past, it may be just part of the growing pains of capitalism. He also argues that in the debate between Malthus and Ricardo on whether mass unemployment is possible, because of ineffective demand, no one who thinks it through could fail to realize that Malthus was wrong and Ricardo was right(!). Up until, I would say, as late as 1932 or maybe even later, Hansen is still espousing sweating it out. Henry Simons, on the other hand, was part of the University of Chicago group which was in favor of deficit spending when that was still unfashionable.

Once Arthur Burns, after he'd been at the Council of Economic Advisors, to boost himself in the history of thought, said to me that he was one of the deficit financiers, that he had written a letter to *The Herald Tribune* in 1931 or 1932. I said, "Yes, Arthur."

You went to Harvard in 1935? How did Harvard differ from Chicago?

A lot. In Chicago everybody knew the answer; economics was a completed science. Allen Wallis never got a Ph.D.; Homer Jones never got a Ph.D.; Al Hart had terrible problems in getting his

Ph.D. past Knight because he wrote about the period of production. George Stigler told me that everything good in economics was already in Frank Knight. His thesis was essentially on Menger; he argued that there's a lot of good stuff in Menger, but it's all better in Frank Knight.

Actually, this is a bit strong. There was this three-way split at Chicago. Henry Schultz was an empiricist and empiricism was looked down on very much by Knight and Viner, although Viner's position was more complicated: in principle he did not look down on it; in fact he did, because all the models that were being measured were more abstract than any sensible man could believe in. Then there was this little wing of Paul Douglas liberals, liberal in the American sense. Even Frank Knight was never your simple conservative in the sense that Milton Friedman was, or even in the sense of Henry Simons. He just was against any government action, but he really was also cynical about the market at that time. Williams, who was a very good teacher, was certainly very open-minded.

Mathematics, which I was beginning to get interested in, was laughed at by the Knight wing. Chicago was happy when the Cowles Commission left Chicago after the war, and they left because they felt that it was a hostile environment.

At Harvard there were lots of different viewpoints. There wasn't homogeneity. Schumpeter made economics seem a very developing subject. *You* would be doing great things, everything was left to be done. If you'd asked me five years after I went to Harvard, in 1940 when I left Harvard for MIT and after being a Junior Fellow for three years, I would have said, "Thank God I left Chicago. Because the three biggest things in economics have been the Keynesian revolution, the monopolistic competition revolution, and the mathematicization of economics", and Chicago was against all of these things during that period of time.

When did you first hear of The General Theory*?*

I first heard of *The General Theory* in the academic year 1935–1936 from the Canadian Bob Bryce. Bob Bryce, fresh from Cambridge University, was in John Williams's graduate class. Bob

Bryce arranged for *The General Theory* to be available to us as soon as it was published. I don't know whether I still have my copy. It cost five shillings. But before it came out he wrote up a summary of it. I still have a copy somewhere in my files, but I don't know where I can put my hands on it.

I heard Lorie Tarshis and Bob Bryce at London, Ontario, at the conference that Patinkin and others held, and I found it disappointing. That is, I could not learn from their accounts just what parts of *The General Theory* they were able to acquire from Keynes's lectures. I'm not sure that it all came from lectures. It may have come from what we would call research students, talking among themselves. I don't know, if I were to read Bob Bryce's memorandum today in the Patinkin fashion, exactly what it is I would find.

Even after I read *The General Theory* I resisted. In a sense I was sampling the whiskey and finding it unpalatable. Leontief was my teacher then and Leontief, in his way, which has not changed at all, was derisive. He argued that the ideas in *The General Theory* were nonsense, and that he and I know better.

I took my general exams in my first year, which was a little unusual, around May 15, 1936, so I was either twenty or twenty-one. On the whole, they were a breeze, but there was one question asked me by Seymour Harris which I thought was off limits and I felt uneasy about it. He asked me about the leakages in the multiplier. Of course, that was too soon for me. *He* knew about the leakages in the multiplier, but I didn't.

What I resisted in Keynes the most was the notion that there could be equilibrium unemployment. I'd argue with Bob Bryce, and discuss with Leontief, that first chapter where workers react differently to an increase in money wages from the way they react to a change in real wages that comes from inflation. The way I finally convinced myself was to just stop worrying about it. I asked myself: why do I want to refuse a paradigm that enables me to understand the Roosevelt upturn from 1933 till 1937? It's not sufficiently realized – I don't know why people don't discuss this – that money supply did not grow according to Friedman formulas, it had much more rapid rate of growth during this period; and it's completely untrue that the New Deal didn't work until World War II came and bailed it out. Some of the highest rates of real increase in and highest levels of plant and equipment capital formation are in the period 1934 to 1937. I was content to assume that there was enough rigidity in relative prices and wages to make the Keynesian alternative to Walras operative.

Another thing, of course, that confirmed me much more, and this is where Hansen had an influence on me: it was so patent in the last part of the thirties that monetary policy had little potency. When I came to Harvard I could not get a bank account. Neither Cambridge Trust nor Harvard Trust would take my account. They didn't want students' accounts, and they didn't want them because they only got a fraction of a per cent on Treasury bills. By 1938, Treasury bills would pay less than three-eights of a per cent. There were times in the year when they'd go negative. I once asked someone at the Treasury, "I understand a lot of million dollar Treasury bills are not turned in. How come?" And he said, "Do you know a better way to hold a million dollars?" I had to use the Postal Savings system. It's gone now. It also had the advantage that you could go there later in the day.

What happened with the Keynesian revolution and the monopolistic competition revolution? Did the Keynesian revolution just wipe out the monopolistic competition revolution?

I don't think there was any direct competition between them. When I wrote to Jim Tobin – he asked me for any comments [on his interview] – I said, "I want privately to correct you on one matter. You said that for the most part we early Keynesians were satisfied to assume perfect competition as an understructure." And I said that that was not my feeling about myself, and I've checked it with Bob Bishop. We always assumed that the Keynesian underemployment equilibrium floated on a substructure of administered prices and imperfect competition. I stopped thinking about what was meant by rigid wages and whether you could get the real wage down; I knew it was a good working principle, a good hypothesis to explain that the real wage does not move down indefinitely so long as there is still some unemployment. Thus I assumed a disequilibrium system, in which people could not get on the supply-of-labor curve.

I worried most of all in my Chicago years and the first part of the time I was at Harvard. You know, I was like a tuna: the Keynesian system had to land me, and I was fighting every inch of the line. I was worried about the micro foundations. I had worked out in my mind naively that one of the reasons that you could have unemployed people who wanted a job alongside people who were employed was the people who were employed would be damned unhappy if they lost that job. My answer to the question: "Why don't firms cut the wages of the people who are at work?" – was that if employees developed rents of special knowledge then it wouldn't be good economics for the employer to cut the wage rate on the differentiated specific factors.

I guess I should emphasize this: I spent four summers of my college career on the beach at Lake Michigan. I did not have a wealthy family and they could have used the income that I would have produced if I had worked, but it was pointless to look for work. I didn't even have to test the market because I had friends who would go to 350 potential employers and not be able to get any job at all. I was very conscious that the unemployed had no way of going to General Motors and offering to work for less than those who were already working there, no way of displacing already employed workers. Moreover, the question would be: why didn't little firms take over the automobile industry, or the steel industry, by starting up in Tennessee with low wages? And the answer to that was we thought of the Fortune 500 companies as requiring a tremendous amount of capital. Free entry was not a feasible thing and there was overcapacity in all lines. This goes back to the system being floated on imperfect competition and increasing returns technologies.

But that was never really formalized?
There was no need to.

What do you mean, "no need to"?

I think that I took a positivistic attitude that we know that there are ups and downs in the degree of utilization, and the Keynesian model has given us an apparatus that moves up and down to explain this. Just because I don't understand the process of digestion, should I refuse my beefsteak? Actually, the opposition of somebody like Schumpeter to the Keynesian system was rationally based. He couldn't see – in fact he found it very disappointing – that Larry Klein could write (under my direction) the thesis *The Keynesian Revolution* in which there existed in the market system a mismatch of supply and demand for labor. How can that be in an equilibrium system? The underemployment equilibrium system lacked the properties of full equilibrium, but the real world behaved in that way.

It's a modern desire to have impeccable micro foundations for macro. You see, the original people, like Leontief, Taussig and Viner, who criticized 1936 Keynes in the *Quarterly Journal* – his homogeneity axiom, for instance – were worried about this sort of thing. I decided that life was more fruitful not worrying about it. You weren't making any progress on it. Moreover, the search today for micro foundations for macro does not have a rich set of results. It's a methodological principle with me that in the longer run people will find more ways of getting around the disequilibrium. For instance, if union wages are too high in the steel industry, somebody will be working on electric furnaces, which don't require that you replicate the size of Bethlehem Steel, and you can begin to chisel away on the market. It's because I get a better positivistic macroeconomics to do some worrying about the micro foundations that I do that worrying, and not because I have a conscience that everybody's micro foundations must be tidy.

But your work in mathematical economics and foundations is tidying up enormous amounts of confusion at the same time. Is there schizophrenia there?

Remember that I was able (in *Foundations*) through the correspondence principle and other things, to take systems like the simple multiplier system and work out what its comparative static properties were, and how you were able to predict them in advance – even though the full Walrasian equilibrium was not realized. I also probably had in mind, if you want to know why my conscience wasn't worse, the lectures I had in mathematical economics from Old Edwin Bidwell Wilson. He started life as a mathematician and mathematical physicist and was Willard Gibbs's last protégé. He would describe equilibrium like this: You leave your car in the MIT parking lot overnight. The rubber tire is a membrane which separates the inside of the tire from the atmosphere, and because of this stiff wall there's an equilibrium difference in pressure. Wilson would say, "Come back a thousand years later, and that tire will be flat." That was not strict equilibrium. It's just a very slowly adjusting disequilibrium. The time period was involved.

It was a model that worked. I should also say that I was very much influenced – moving to the 1935–1937 period – by Schumpeter's off-the-cuff general methodological remarks. Schumpeter was Kuhnian in Tom Kuhn's sense long before Tom Kuhn was in high school. He always said, "You never in economics kill a theory by fact; you kill a theory by a better theory." L.J. Henderson, who was the chairman of the Society of Fellows, head Senior Fellow, was very anti-economist. (I was a Junior Fellow from 1937 to 1940 and was really the first proper economist: I got elected because I was a mathematical economist. Henderson was in favor of Pareto, but he thought all the rest of economics was no good.) He always emphasized, probably derivatively from Pareto but also from his own methodological work, that you can't be a pure empiricist; you've got to have a systematic way of thinking about things. So the Keynesian system gave one a systematic way of thinking about things.

I don't think it's systematic if your great uncle was a heretical underconsumptionist and then said, "Look, Keynes stole my stuff. I already had it way back then." There was a German banker named Albert Hahn who was a refugee in this country and who turned very conservative. In the 1920s he'd been an underconsumptionist. He'd always say, "Keynesian notions are all wrong but I had them first." That's why I think that Leijonhufvud's interpretations are a complete distortion of how it happened and what happened. Keynes versus the Keynesians gets it all wrong. Keynes the master was supposed to have very subtle, deep insights which he can hardly articulate – those are the good things. Then you have this terrible Keynesian cross – we can draw it all with the Hicks–Hansen diagram. And that's a perversion. Well, about eight different people *independently* discerned in Keynes' book that Keynesian system. Six, at least, of those eight were close friends of John Maynard Keynes. Keynes read them in his lifetime, had plenty of opportunity to disclaim them if that was not what he had in mind. But more than that, I go to the positivistic fact that what counts in science is not your vague inarticulations. It's what you can write down, what you can use, what people do use; it's really even what people *mis*-use, the things that don't fit.

Who else was there besides Bryce, among the students?

Well, I would say that people who became early Keynesians would be Paul and Alan Sweezy. Jay Raymond Walsh of the Walsh–Sweezy case was also there. J. Raymond Walsh and Alan Sweezy were popular undergraduate teachers, but they did not have great claims to tenure at Harvard. And they were radical.

How about Lauchlin Currie?

He was gone before 1935. If you had asked me in 1937 or 1936, "Is Lauchlin Currie a leading Keynesian?" I would have said, "I'm not aware he's a Keynesian at all." If you'd asked me in 1938, I would have realized he was because he was at the Federal Reserve and influencing fiscal policy. I should also tell you that I didn't myself quite realize that the Roosevelt New Deal Administration was not Keynesian until about 1937. The early, first-term Tugwell, Moley, Kirkland, Kahn group were really Veblenian. They were in favor of restructuring American life, and they ended up being enemies of Keynesianism. For them, Keynesianism was a palliative.

Most economists – you could have said this up to 1962 or 1963 – thought that it was a crime that Franklin Roosevelt jettisoned the World Economic Conference in 1933 by devaluing the dollar. (Fritz Machlup, as late as 1962 or 1963, spoke of that as a crime.) In 1935 I probably thought it was a crime – in 1933 John Williams was on the boat to Europe and the rug was pulled out from under him. But later I became convinced, as Seymour Harris became convinced, that, although America didn't have to devalue, it gave us extra leeway, and that Belgium was very smart to devalue in 1936 – it should have done it earlier; and France was very stupid never to have done it. The way that Britain and Scandinavia came out of the Great Depression earlier – by 1932 they were on their way up – was not by beggaring-my-neighbor devaluation, but it gave them the room to expand so they made an impact on their neighbor in a neutral way at worst. That was somewhat in Seymour Harris's book of 1936 on currency depreciation.[2]

What about the Hansen seminars?

Hansen came to the Littauer School in 1937 before the school had any students. That's when I met him; he was never a teacher of mine. In 1937 I became a Junior Fellow, so I had a generous fellowship and no classes. I wasn't allowed to work for a degree, but I was able to drop in on Alvin Hansen's seminar. By then I had finished my graduate course work. But I often attended his and Williams's seminar the next year, 1938. Hansen would try out his new books. The seminar had a lot of important visitors.

When would you date your conversion to Keynesianism?

I was already a Keynesian at the time of the Hansen–Williams seminar. If you think of Michael Farraday as the fellow who measured electromagnetism, and Maxwell as the theoretician who took the insights of Farraday and made models of them, in some ways that was my relationship to Alvin Hansen. I remember being proud that I got him to put the income on the horizontal axis and not on the vertical axis. If you put it on the vertical axis, when you have an increase in the propensity to consume, there's a rightward shift, just like your demand curve, Hansen protested. And I said, "Just like the demand curve; and the demand curve's been wrong because of Alfred Marshall these fifty years. Why should we get off on the wrong foot again?" I formalized the Keynesian cross, where you add the investment to the consumption function and look for the forty-five degree line and I worked out the mathematics of the accelerator/multiplier model. I simply took a numerical model of Hansen's, from which he was drawing over-strong conclusions, and showed that if you actually carried it further it would come back and you'd have self-generated cycles.

Then there is the story about how the original theorem of the balanced budget multiplier originated independently in four or five places. The first I knew about were I, Bill Salant and Alvin Hansen – this at a time when Perloff and Hansen were writing their book. Also the B-B-Multiplier Theorem is to be discerned in the speech which Keynes wrote for the Chancellor of the Exchequer on financing the British war, and possibly – although this was a little later – in Nicholas Kaldor's exercises in alternative means to full employment.

I waited a long time to publish the theorem because Bill Salant and I were going to publish it together and he was engaged in public service. Also Hansen had found a different way of looking at it. He was quite intrigued when I was able to show that the Keynesian cross measure of the stimulus would not be a correct stimulus. The miracle to me was not that several discovered this balanced budget multiplier with the remarkable feature of the multiplier being exactly one; it was surprising that everybody didn't see it earlier. And the reasons we didn't see it earlier were completely accidental. It was primarily taxonomic. When Kuznets first measured national income, he did not include in national income government expenditure financed by a deficit – something strange like that. His definition would have been absolutely impossible once the war made the government fully half of the GNP and half of that financed by fiscal deficit. People realized they couldn't live with that definition and it was rightly dropped.

So I realized that I'd actually had the balanced budget multiplier back in 1937/1938 in earlier papers, but it was not counted as kosher income. [A rise in government spending with taxes unchanged gave no first-round increase in old-Kuznets income. With no rise in income, no secondary multiplier effects would follow.]

I should also say that the majority of the able students by 1937/1938 were Keynesians. I may be off a year, but I don't think I am. Emile Despres came to Harvard in 1937 as a senior civil servant, and Walter Salant stayed a second year. I thought of Richard Gilbert as a Keynesian, but I don't remember why. James Tobin thought that maybe Richard Gilbert was influenced a lot by Hansen, but I don't remember much interaction between Dick Gilbert and the rest. At Harvard he was having to teach and lecture outside to support his family. He had no tenure. Phil Wernette at the business school was a heretical underconsumptionist. He, in my time, didn't teach on our side of the river. I was impressed by Sumner Slichter, whom I didn't particularly like at that time – I thought of him as a conservative. He had some University of Utah lectures in which he said that consumption is passive and investment is active; and, years later, I said to Alvin Hansen that I thought there were some good notions in Slichter. He said, "Well, to tell the truth, I always thought of Sumner as a closet Keynesian, who wouldn't admit it." I suspect that Sumner Slichter was kidding himself; that he didn't really face himself in the mirror and perceive that a lot of his notions were Keynesian.

The two books which show the change in viewpoint in the Harvard community are *The Economics of the Recovery Program* – the stupid book I already mentioned by Schumpeter, *et al.* – and *An Economic Program for American Democracy*. I once said to Alvin Hansen years later that I thought that *An Economic Program for American Democracy* in program and analysis was most like what went on in the next twenty years. I had the opportunity to be one of the members of that group but I wasn't much of a joiner. Hansen replied, "I never thought it was very original. I thought it was just about what was in my lectures." Hansen was not a terribly vain man, as scholars go. He surprised me a few times. Practically everyone speaks well of Allyn Young. Allyn Young was the great theorist at Harvard in the twenties. When Edwin Cannan retired from the London School, Young answered a call to a chair there. He was only there a year or two when he died of pneumonia, at about the age of 50. He never wrote much, but was one of America's leading economists. He was a great teacher who supposedly didn't publish because he knew so much. Supposedly Young was just ready to publish when he died. But Alvin Hansen said to me, uncharacteristically, "You know, I always thought he was a stuffed shirt."

You asked me about other people in the seminar. Always things looked different to people on the scene. For example, at that time we had Richard Musgrave (the quintessential Hansenian) down as an anti-Keynesian. The same with Benjamin Higgins, if you know that name. Soon Musgrave left Harvard – went to Swarthmore, I think, then to the Federal Reserve, then to Michigan, Hopkins and Princeton, and finally to Harvard. I would judge Richard Musgrave became number one of his generation in the field of public finance and in the top few in the field of money and Keynesianism. But that seemed not yet the case in the Hansen seminar days. The same thing about Higgins. But Higgins was in Washington only about three months when he told me at the Christmas AEA convention, "We're going to spend three billion here and 17 billion there." I concluded, "Boy! Marx was right. The job makes the man."

To a degree what I'm saying is also true about Henry Wallich, who was of a slightly later period. I always thought of Henry Wallich as trying to be conservative. He was an intelligent critic of Keynes's system, but also a good practitioner of that system. There was a little bit of a Williams camp at Harvard, and a Hansen camp. It was kind of embarrassing because the Williams camp was so skimpy compared to the Hansen camp. Gabriel Hauge of Eisenhower White House prominence was in the Williams camp.

Ken Galbraith has written of his role as an early American Keynesian. In the Hansen seminar group Ken was not thought of as primarily a macroeconomist at all. We were bigots.

In 1940 I became an instructor and tutor, but got a better offer at MIT and I decided to take it. When I came here our department was a service department and there was just beginning to be a labor economics group and an industrial relations section. A year after I came here we started a graduate program and we started to acquire people like Bob Bishop and Dan Vandermeulen. And then, after the war, we began to acquire people like Cary Brown, Charlie Kindleberger, Max Millikan and Bob Solow.

During the war, how would you characterize most people's beliefs about Keynesian economics?

I would say that within university life, if you tried to get a job for somebody in 1938, you had to suppress that he was a Keynesian. Roland Robinson, a name you would not know, was at the Federal Reserve for some years. He was a pretty good money economist and he went from the Federal Reserve to be the chief economist for the main trade association of the banks, or saving banks. He had some interesting ideas. Somebody once said to him, "Whose idea is that?" and he said, "Well, it's Keynesian." And he said the temperature went to zero in the room, and he finally decided he couldn't live in that environment and went to Michigan State University.

However, I would say that Keynesianism at the beginning of the war was a majority view among the active young people at the elite universities, with some exceptions like maybe Chicago. By the end of the war the entire academic profession was Keynesian.

Did you ever meet Keynes?

No. Keynes knew about me because he told somebody – I can't remember who – that I was a comer. He never lectured at Harvard in my time; I think because he was not invited. I have to be careful, because in an earlier period, before my time, he was invited and didn't come. He definitely was blackballed shamefully when Harvard passed him by for their 1936 Tercentenary gathering of great world scholars.

You can see that the profession was Keynesian by the success of Lorie Tarshis's 1947 textbook and my post-1948 textbook. One of the reasons for the triumph was that during the war the Keynesian wing of the U.S. civil service had been vindicated. This was actually supply-side economics, not aggregate demand-side economics. Most of the business civil servants, called to the War Production Board and so forth, believed that the expandability of production was very limited. People like Richard Gilbert at OPA argued that there was big room for further expansion. I remember being told that Keynes came over and was asked his opinion. He said, "Well, how much was 1929 real output over 1913?" He was given the numbers. He said, "Well, that was a 15-year period and it's been 12 years since 1929. So let's take 12/15 of that increment, and I think that that would be a reasonable goal for potential GNP." That crystallized the problem. And that was about the number that Gilbert and others of that Keynesian wing had chosen. It turned out that they were right. Of course there was no problem of explicit inflation because of price controls.

"Keynesianism" was a naughty word politically outside economics long after the war. Inside the profession it was another matter. Fiscal policy dominated monetary policy. One interesting exception was Clark Warburton, who antedated Milton Friedman as a monetarist. But he got little attention.

Why did Keynesianism sweep everything?

Because it seemed to work on war finance. Nobody cared a rap about money. The head of the Federal Reserve, Mariner Eccles, felt guilty that while boys were dying in the field he was fiddling at the Fed. A rumor went around Washington in the early forties that the Federal Reserve was going to lose its air-conditioning system. It was going to be transferred to WPB, OPA, or some other important wartime agency. You can't transfer such units. What's interesting is two things: one, that someone would contemplate doing this; and the other that everybody would believe such a rumor.

De facto, government spending became half the GNP by the late war years. Rationing and shortages kept people from consuming much of their incomes; perforce they saved, at banks and buying government bonds issued to mop up excessive income and finance the deficits that matched the tax share of the public spending. The need for high interest rates to confine private spending was thus minimal. Such a disequilibrium system might not have lasted for a long war; but it did set the stage for a postwar reconversion and boom fed by cumulative private liquidity and cumulative longings for consumption.

There's another reason, I think, why Keynesianism swept the field. It's the same reason rational expectations attracts people today. It provided a lot of Ph.D. fodder, a lot of clever models to work on. An example is an issue of *Econometrica* on the balanced budget multiplier, the first time it surfaced belatedly in print, in which Musgrave, Haberler, Hagen, Haavelmo, Goodwin and Arthur Smithies could spin their elegant theories. Theory is the lifeblood of science: if that's decadent, well that's the way it is.

Tarshis's textbook lasted for one year. He said that the reason for that was that the publishers got scared, everybody started calling it Commie, and an enormous amount of hate mail.

It's true. Two things: he had a very good first year, and then – do you know Hope Ingal's and Rose Wilder Lane's children stories, *The Little House in the Forest* and *The Little House on the Prairie*? They are novels, semi-true family stories. The daughter is Rose Wilder, and she wrote a well-received novel, *Let the Hurricane Roar*, about some Swedish immigrants in the northwest fighting snow blizzards and so forth. She later turned semi-Fascist and jumped on Tarshis and his books as being Marxist–Keynesian poison. There were many others, too. Young William Buckley, just grinding his baby teeth, wrote a hatchet job called *God and Man at Yale* on my book. (Part of the indictment is there's a Protestant minister at Yale and the other is Yale's bad economics.) The criticisms my book got pale against those leveled against Tarshis. I don't quite know why Tarshis got those undeserved calumnies. In fact, the Tarshis book was stopped right in its tracks. But I think what's important is not its being stopped in its tracks, but the resonant response that the Keynesian approach met with in the universities. My *Economics* generated a lot of imitative clones.

What kind of attacks did your book get and how did you deal with it?

For some reason that I have no understanding of, the virulence of the attack on Tarshis was of a higher order of magnitude than on my book, but there were plenty of attacks on my book, and there was a lot of work done by people. Also I wrote carefully and lawyer-like so that there were a lot of complaints that Samuelson was playing peek-a-boo with the Commies. The whole thing was a sad scene that did not reflect well on conservative business pressuring of colleges.

Why did you decide to do the textbook?

I started the textbook because the head of my department, Ralph Freeman, came to me and said, "I'll give you half time off: write a textbook so that our juniors, who have economics only as a compulsory subject, will like it, and believe in economics." He said, "It doesn't have to be long; there are no topics you *have* to cover. Just make it interesting." So I undertook to do it. I was very conscious of the lack of a text. I didn't know the Tarshis textbook then; I knew Lorie, but I didn't know he was writing a textbook. I was very sanguine that the field was waiting for a modern book, and that this would be a good seller. I didn't know it would be a good seller over forty-five years! I didn't know it would be as good a seller as it was, but I thought it would do very well. Writing the book took a lot longer than I thought it would. Instead of taking a semester, it took about two or three years. In the interim I had mimeographed preliminary chapters to try out on MIT classes.

Was your book the first to use the term "macroeconomics"?

No. In the 1960s Edwin Nourse, who was the first Chairman of the Council of Economic Advisors and a distinguished agricultural economist at Brookings, wrote to Alvin Hansen and said, "Who invented the word 'macroeconomics'?" Hansen sent me a card with his answer. He said, "I don't know – probably Samuelson." But I was pretty sure I hadn't. When I did some research for Hansen, I found that the terms "microeconomics" and "macroeconomics" do not surface early in the literature. Even at the time of my first edition they're not in my index. I looked in the index of *Econometrica* because I thought it was Frisch and Tinbergen who'd first used "macroeconomics", but what they had used in the early thirties was "macro dynamic systems". "Macroeconomics" appears in the *Econometrica* cumulative index, but that was some editor's afterthought.

The earliest case of the word "macroeconomics" that I could find was by Larry Klein, but his usage is somewhat different than normal. You and I think of macroeconomics primarily as involving effective demand, total amount of unemployment, the rate of inflation, and such. But the other sense in which "macroeconomics" has been used is a J.B. Clark aggregative model, which is a black box, with one output and two or three inputs. And that's the sense in Larry Klein's 1946 *Econometrica* discussion. (Hendrik Houthakker later found for me this 1941 *Econometrica* reference by Pieter de Wolff: "Income elasticity of demand, a micro-economic and a macro-economic interpretation.")

How about full employment after the war? Was there a big concern?

The general profession, I would say, and particularly some leading members of the profession, laid a big egg for which they paid in acclaim, dis-esteem, recrimination. That is the famous prediction that there would be mass unemployment after the war unless the government slowed down the return of soldiers and did a lot of deficit spending. This culminated in an official governmental estimate of all the agencies. The titular author of it was Everett

Hagen, my late MIT colleague who I believe was on the War Production Board; but Dick Gilbert's stalwarts David Lusher and Jacob Mosak and Arthur Smithers of Budget were also very important. They went public, around the spring of 1945.

I can remember being told by Roy Blough, the head of economics at the Treasury, about a famous meeting. I wasn't in on this because I was at the Radiation Laboratory doing mathematical wartime work. This was a meeting at the Treasury where William Fellner, an eminent anti-Keynesian, gave a talk arguing that there would be a big boom after the war. His argument was the same as W.W. Woytinski's and Sumner Slichter's. He said, "There's a tremendous post-war nest egg that's been accumulated by the American people because of deficit financing and swollen liquid holdings. The counterpart of that is a tremendous built-up hunger for durables and other consumption items and vacations that people couldn't have; and the juxtaposition of these two things will mean a tremendous period of buoyant demand." Probably he added in the accelerator, that the wartime step-up in the real income which would remain would require new equipment. You couldn't work the factories three shifts and expect that to last forever. Roy Blough told me that the seminar was a slaughter, with Jacob Mosak leading the assault: "Do you think that housing can go up three years in a row by such-and-such?" Fellner said, "They tore me to pieces every way." Yet as we look back now, that's much what happened. Fellner was very near the mark. I would say that the Keynesian branch of the profession was tarred very much with this gizmo prediction, which was quite wrong. I do not absolve myself from this error; I did allow for secular shifts in the saving function but I failed to anticipate the Friedman–Modigliani–Duesenberry–Kuznets–Dennison analyses of how much long-run saving patterns could fall below short-run extrapolations.

But it didn't seem to hurt them.

Oh, it did. It slowed down the spread of Keynesianism. By the end of the war Keynes was a very respectable figure in Britain, an establishment figure, but that still was not the case here. Now, there were some exceptions. In the Department of Commerce there were rosier post-war forecasts. Paul McCracken and Dick Bissell were working on viewpoints that would later be espoused by the Committee for Economic Development. Dick Bissell was the effective person running the Marshall Plan. And he was head of the CIA at the time of the Bay of Pigs fiasco. His career was ended by that. They and the C.E.D. believed that, if all businesses knew what the post-war GNP would be and made their investment plans conditional upon that, then all of them doing that would create a boom. (This does resemble De Gaulle's *Le Plan*.)

I might mention that Alvin Hansen was not a believer in postwar unemployment. He said, "There'll be a big restocking boom." Alvin Hansen also – because I've heard Alvin Hansen rationalize – said that one of the reasons there wasn't a problem of effective demand stagnation after the war was that economists had warned so against it. For example, he said that his wartime projections of what the budget should be post-war were the highest by far of anybody's and, he said, "I was a piker; the reality was way ahead of what I had, and that's what made the difference." By and large, the error was something to be expected occasionally in any inexact science. There was an extrapolation of short-run saving habits that was both unwarranted in terms of long-term history and implausible when you really think about it, and which, by hindsight, was very wrong. My contribution in Seymour Harris's book, *Postwar Economics*, argued that there would be no secular increase in the savings rate at full employment. So there was nothing in my toolbox that required me to help lay a big egg, but I did. My brother Bob Summers asked me, oh, maybe five years after the war, "Paul, were you right or wrong about the post-war thing?" and I said, "I was wrong." But I didn't, until I looked it up, realize *how* wrong in the stuff I'd written, some of it unsigned in *The New Republic*.

How did that hurt the Keynesian revolution?

Principally because it seemed to suggest that macroeconomic models are all wrong. However, it was Keynesian macro modelers like Lawrence Klein who made their reputations correcting those models that had wrongly predicted unemployment. Not until after Camelot, when stagflation persisted and monetarists offered their alternative *theory* to Model T Keynesianism, did Keynesianism lose its glamour.

Still, in terms of the development of the field, Keynesian economics ruled.

Well, yes. It's like rational expectations. I get maybe fifty yellow-jacketed National Bureau papers a year that have a bearing on the rational expectations model. Of that fifty, maybe fifteen are actually tests of the model, one form or another of it. Of those fifteen, about fourteen out of fifteen are rejections of the model, using ordinary statistical technology. Still I don't see much of an effect on what they'll be discussing at the Kansas City Federal Reserve meeting at the Tetons today. All the young bloods will be there. But it does have an effect in the long run; and actually, rational expectations is not doing as well in the mid-eighties as it was in the late seventies because it hasn't worked very well.

In science there is always cultural lag. A lot of people were just catching on to Keynesianism in the first post-war years. Remember, a whole new generation was being born who had just learned it, who didn't know what pre-Keynesian life was like. If you look at my textbook you can see that it starts out – because all textbooks simplify – mostly with flow models. There is a little chatter about the money stock having an influence, but it's never really in the early editions given very much emphasis. You have to realize that it was about 1950 before American Keynesians, to say nothing of the anti-Keynesians, began to realize that the quasi-liquidity trap behavior of 1938 and the artificial wartime situation were things of the past. Model T Keynesianism, in America, but alas less so in Britain, was evolving into its Post-Keynesian emphases on wealth stocks and money stocks. The Hicks–Keynes diagrams could have served a Fellner as well as a Hagen or Mosak!

I think Howard Ellis used the expression "the rediscovery of money". Money was rediscovered by Keynesians, American

Keynesians, as well as by anti-Keynesians. The money was already in the Keynesian system. You also have to emphasize, if you want to be fair, the Pigou Effect began to be perceived in the literature, after about 1940. So Keynesianism was already becoming eclectic, and moving beyond what I call Model T Keynesianism – which is just the one-variable system with $Y = C + I = f(Y) + g(Y)$. When you remember to include the interest rate and money supply, i and M, as variables and remember to write liquidity preference as $PQ = Y = MV = Mv(i)$, then you realize that Friedman's monetarism of 1955 and beyond is agreeing with rather than debunking the Keynes–Hicks diagrams. I consider it a great advance when monetarist anti-Keynesians can share with Keynesians the post-1936 paradigms. It's a bit like bipartisan foreign policy in politics! The New Classicists are something else again.

There are some stories I've been told about the Lerner/Keynes exchanges. Can you shed any light on them?

Keynes gave two famous Federal Reserve seminars, which I was not able to attend. However, from accounts at the time – probably from Hansen – I know what happened. At the first one he was utterly charming but was kind of reactionary and, in particular, he jumped on Abba Lerner, who had written about functional finance. One of the things he said – and I can never remember whether it was Aristotle or Plato – was, "Plato said, 'The art of politics is the art of telling plausible lies.' But you know, Abba, those lies have got to be *plausible*", implying that Lerner's weren't. He must have felt, maybe at the time, that Lerner had overdone it; or maybe he came to feel that. But anyway, in the meantime, Lerner's *The Economics of Control* came out. He must have paged through it – he was a very quick reader – and in the second seminar he made redress and went out of his way to say nice things. How Lerner happened to be in Washington on these two occasions I don't know. Lerner was a brilliant mind, and only his lack of *gravitas* limited his influence on actual policy.

Notes

1. Samuelson elaborated: "By this time Fisher was a wealthy man twice. He'd married the chemical heiress and he invented a visual filing system which became Remington Rand, or something like that, and that went way up in the stock market. It kind of pleased him that he could do it on his own. And so he undoubtedly subsidized a lot of his own research. There are a lot of formulas in that book, and you didn't have giant computers in those days – they were probably computed by his assistants in his New Haven basement.
2. Jeff Sachs has gone back to review the period in National Bureau papers. Before I read his paper, I wrote down what my bunch thought in 1936, to see how we came out. I think we came out pretty good, first rate.

Credo of a Lucky Textbook Author

Paul A. Samuelson

When a scholarly discipline is in a fruitful phase of innovative advance, it spares little time in studying its own history. Few know the revolutions that hit economic introductory textbooks half a century ago. This is a good occasion to sketch that story and, as Schumpeter would say, to review the troops. Also, I conclude with notes for historians on ideological pressures brought against postwar economics teachers.

The 1920s and 1930s were a fallow period in textbook writing. Frank Taussig's (1911) classic was nearing its end: in 1940 at Harvard, we taught Economics I from it. The bestseller out of Yale was still Fairchild, Furniss and Buck (1936), a watered-down version of Irving Fisher's (1911) text with coverage of Marshall's dd and ss intersections. At Chicago in the 1931–32 years, Aaron Director assigned me Sumner Slichter's (1931) new text, poor-mouthing it from the beginning. Actually, it gave a pretty fair institutional picture of the 1920s: when I recently reread Frank Knight's (1932a,b) polemics in the *Journal of Political Economy* against it, what all the shooting was about was hard to discern. The next quarter, Lloyd Mints shifted to Richard Ely's *Outlines of Economics*, which dated from church materials in the 1890s. Ely's later editions were written by a committee, presided over by the gifted Allyn Young.

The list of competing texts was not short. Among the competent was the Garver and Hansen (1938) text (Alvin did the macro). Among the pedestrian were perennials like Wisconsin's Kiekhoffer (1936) text: it was "institutional," but primarily in the sense of being "NON-theoretical." Digression: just 60 years ago, Kiekhoffer never began his lectures before a thousand Madison undergraduates until delegated cheerleaders led the crowd in a Wisconsin locomotive. No kidding!

■ *Paul A. Samuelson is Institute Professor Emeritus of Economics, Massachusetts Institute of Technology, Cambridge, Massachusetts.*

Book content is what matters. So much less was taught then in economics as compared to today. When 5,000 banks failed and mortgage delinquencies were in the millions, the bestselling texts limned the certainties of Say's Law! Taussig was little better on that when Harvard gentlemen learned it from my knee. No wonder economics enrollments eroded just when real-world problems and actions were most dramatic.

An Offer I Couldn't Refuse

How did all this relate to brash Paul Samuelson, whippersnapper go-getter in esoteric theory? I returned from the wartime Radiation Lab to rejoin the MIT economics department. My department head and pal, Ralph Freeman, entered my office and closed the door. This is what he said.

Eight hundred MIT juniors must take a full year of compulsory economics. They hate it. We've tried everything. They still hate it. We even did a departmental joint product. It was the worst editorial experience of my life. After our senior colleague turned in his chapter, I had to say, "Floyd, this is not a chapter on public finance. It's a chapter *against* public finance." Paul, will you go on half time for a semester or two? Write a text the students will like. If they like it, yours will be good economics. Leave out whatever you like. Be as short as you wish. Whatever you come up with, that will be a vast improvement on where we are.

Little did I know of the devil's blandishments. Why not give it a whirl? Here's a window of opportunity when all the books are 15 years out of date at least. Then, next summer I can put the finishing touches on *Foundations*, which has been awaiting publication since before Pearl Harbor. Truth defies fiction. Three years later, after night and summer slaving and following up on uncountable mimeograph handouts, the deed was done. The rest, as they say, is history.

Skousen's Critique

When you read the novels of Jane Austen, never do you learn that the Napoleonic wars were going on while her characters were angling for life-cycle security with amiable spouses. When I read Mark Skousen's account of how macroeconomics and public policy discussions evolved in the successive editions of Samuelson's *Economics*, I was left with something of the same feeling as Jane Austen's readers: missed in his Whiggish retrospective is all of the drama that went into the decisions to revise; and, what matters to an audience of economist teachers and researchers, scarce hints are given about the scientific developments and innovations impinging on me as the textbook writer and teacher. (Since Bill Nordhaus cannot be held liable for my imperfections, the present pages concentrate mostly on those 11 Samuelson-only editions before the last decade. No distortion of the debate is thereby entailed.)

The bare facts are simple. My 1948 first edition's macro concentrated on the early *General Theory* paradigm in which the level of money and real aggregate income, Y, got determined by the interplay of saving and investing propensities: Y^* is the (diagrammatic) root where an ascending Saving schedule rises to intersect an Investment schedule. Fed interest rates were at that time frozen by President Truman's fiat; in consequence, there was no great need to go into Keynesian liquidity preference schedules, à la Hicks and Hansen; and postwar price levels had not yet the impetus (nor the freedom!) to soar. By the second edition, these things were changing outside the scholar's window, and his quill was busy sketching those changes. Already I lost some Keynesian partisans, a process that turned out to be "perseverant."

I am pleading no alibi nor extenuation. My present-day eyes do discern regrettable lags in sloughing off earlier skins. My kind of Keynesianism was never a religion. "What have you done for me lately?" was always the battle cry. Besides, the American Keynesians—Alvin Hansen, James Tobin in his 1939 Harvard undergraduate thesis that had already added *wealth* to income as a determinant of spending, Franco Modigliani during the war itself—all these were evolving beyond Model T Neanderthal Keynesianism. I raced along with the avant garde.

The recent biography of Abraham Lincoln by David Herbert Donald (1995) is such great history because its author endeavors at every stage to describe Abe's actions and decisions *using only that knowledge which at each moment was available to his protagonist*. When Milton Friedman wrote for the Treasury in 1943 about war finance or proposed a 1948 macro stabilization program, no latter-day commentator can validly indict him for not employing his own *later* Model T Monetarism model.

When you use paleontological fossils to outline the history of species, use them all. Was the Samuelson elementary text lagging behind the plethora of emerging intermediate macroeconomic textbooks in the 1948–1985 era or a pioneering engine in evolutionary progress? I know the answer to that, but will Professor Skousen's readers?

Objectivity is in the eye of the beholder. By my third edition, the "neoclassical synthesis" got set forth. To Joan Robinson, this was surrender to the enemy: one more Keynesian friend lost. To Mark Skousen, this, incredibly, boils down to "demand management." What actually was it? And why in later editions did those words get revised out? The "neoclassical synthesis" was no more and no less than a matter-of-fact statement that there are alternative mixes of central bank money/credit configurations and fiscal expenditure/tax configurations that are compatible with full employment and price-level stability. By logical implication, *arbitrary* configurations of these—demand mismanagement?—can and will induce hyperinflations and recessionary unemployments.

For two reasons I later dropped the "neoclassical synthesis" verbiage. First, it smacked too much of complacency: perfection is at hand, economics is an exact science, blah, blah. Second, and more important, from early on I (along with Lord Beveridge and Alvin Hansen) was fearful of a *stagflation* problem in a mixed-economy welfare state that strove hard for full employment while at the same time helping the unemployed in a humane way. In Camelot counsels, I was at first too pessimistic about stagflation ahead. Alas, by 1965 and for 15 years, my fears proved only too prescient. The post-1965 decline in Keynesianism's esteem was *not* a Kuhnian consequence of a better paradigm replacing it. Monetarism à la Friedman for a bare two years around 1970, at the St. Louis Fed and Citibank, positivistically then did only *almost* as well; after that, Cinderella's hour had struck. Rather, what lowered even the self-esteem of the Keynesians and macroeconomists generally was the onset of stagflation (supply-side shocks and all that), a scourge difficult to prescribe for by any of the competing macro paradigms and quite uncalled for in the logic of either monetarism or later-time's rational expectationism. The Skousen paragraphs should be reread in light of this.

Here, I do not enumerate the several places at which Skousen's critiques appear to me to be inexact and nonoptimal. Space is scarce. I do strongly protest, though, when I am called an *antisaving* Keynesian. (At Harvard's 350th birthday symposium before an overflow crowd of 2,000, Tobin, Benjamin Friedman, Martin Feldstein and I debated this topic. Holding up his end, Feldstein similarly complained that Harvard had mistaught him about the virtue of thrift.) I baldly proclaim my nonguilt. From 1950 on, in congressional testimony and writings, both Tobin and I were nagging Democratic leaders and urchins in the street toward a high-employment mix, *weighted toward capital formation and away from current consumption*: see Samuelson (1965; see the congressional testimony in chapter 100; see also chapters 98, 99 and 105) and Tobin (1955, 1959, 1960 and 1983, especially pp. 197–200). To this day, we still nag. In my case it was precisely the tools of the "neoclassical synthesis" (used in the 1955 edition assigned to Ec10 Harvard students) that were employed to deduce how austere budget surpluses cum expansionary Fed mode could augment a low-saving nation's productivity growth rate without occasioning structural unemployment. We were heroes before our time and long before the infelicities of Laffer-Kemp-Reagan!

Competent scholars in macroeconomics will understand the neoclassical deductive reasonings and the economic-historical facts that can bring back into relevance the paradox of thrift that my critic scorns. Yes, when the Bank of Japan's 1996 short-term interest rate is half of 1 percent, there is less new punch from open-market purchases than when nominal interest rates average 10 percent. Yes, Virginia, there can be in such times shades of liquidity traps and a genuine paradox of thrift. Maybe future college sophomores will learn this the hard way—perhaps after a populist majority has temporarily put a balanced-budget amendment into the Constitution and when real-and-nominal exogenous forces cause securities markets to clear at low interest rates like those prevailing back in the late 1930s. The Bible tells us: there is a time to remember and a time to forget. Alas, the Good Book does not reveal when those times occur in connection with delicate syndromes like the heretical paradox of thrift. Slogans and excommunications do not a good economics make.

Mark Skousen is more of a libertarian than I am. That is obvious. He was born with a more devout belief in Say's Law than I was. That is obvious. Much could be usefully added on our many differences, but it will be a better use of my page ration to conclude with some account about past ideological pressures on teachers and textbooks, from the right and left. It is a story not well known, but fraught with historical significance.

Tale of Two Texts

As indicated, in the mid-1940s I suspected that it was a time of singular opportunity. The colleges were crowded with returning veterans. For those who had lived through the 1929–1935 Great Depression, the best of the existing texts were almost comical in their *macroeconomics*. That word had not yet been invented. When Edwin Nourse, the first chairman of the Council of Economic Advisers, asked Alvin Hansen who invented the newfangled word *macroeconomics*, Hansen wrote back: "I don't know. Probably Samuelson." I have much to declare before St. Peter, but I was pretty sure that Frisch or Tinbergen was the culprit. *Macroeconomics* was not in the index of my *Economics* first edition. Subsequent research suggests, however, that Erik Lindahl (1939) first used the word in Swedish and English print.

I did cash in on bringing simple Keynes to the elementary classroom. But in doing that, I was packaging some of my own hooch, since it was I who had invented (at Harvard and MIT) the 45° $I + C + G$ diagrams that became a staple on postwar blackboards. But of course they were already lurking there in the mathematics and the words of the Keynes-Kahn multiplier paradigm. What I did not anticipate was how strong this new virus would be and how durable would be the market prominence of my evolving brainchild.

One guy's luck may be augmented by another's bad luck. The tale I shall tell has its primary interest as an important chapter in the attempts by noneconomists to censor what is taught in the university. Censors seek suppression both from the right and from the left.

The 1948 Samuelson text was not the first to add a Keynesian analysis to the received versions of $MV = PQ$. The late Lorie Tarshis was a Canadian who taught at Tufts University in the latter 1930s. Tarshis had been a Cambridge student from Toronto in John Maynard Keynes' lectures during the formative years of the 1936 *General Theory*. He began before World War II to write an elementary text; on returning from the war, he finished *The Elements of Economics* at Stanford, and Houghton-Mifflin published it a full year before 1948. Lorie was a neighbor and good personal friend, but I first heard of his book when as a 1947 MIT teacher I was given a promotional copy. It was a good book; a very good book. Maybe in 1945 I would have stuck to my mathematical-economics knitting if the Tarshis text had then been available.

For one year the Tarshis opus had a good sale. Under normal circumstances, my book would have inevitably become a competitor. But of course, the beginners' market is gigantic in scope, big enough for several worthy competitors: once good textbooks became available, the economics courses at most universities shot toward or to the very top in enrollment. What almost killed the Tarshis book in its tracks were vicious political and personal attacks on him as a "Keynesian-Marxist." (Earlier, Herbert Hoover popularized that one-word combination.) I knew well the diversities of ideologies in 1930–1950 America, but never could I understand the variety and virulence of the attackers on Tarshis from the right. Tarshis was not notorious as a leftist; before then and until his death in 1994 at a ripe, ripe age, Lorie Tarshis was a low-keyed teacher and researcher. Independently of John Dunlop, Tarshis did important empirical work criticizing (!) Keynes' treatment in the *General Theory* of a necessarily declining wage rate when the total of employment rose. His later textbook on international trade was also an excellent middle-of-the-road contribution to that subject.

The attackers, I recall, included names then considered extremely on the right: a Colonel Namm, who owned a Brooklyn department store; also someone named Zoll, from a small fascist-leaning group on the right. There was, too, a Philip Cortney, who headed the Cody cosmetic company and lectured at Harvard that Sumner Slichter (who was actually the academic most beloved by business-group audiences) was "the most dangerous man in America. Worse than an avowed Keynesian is this closet-Keynesian poisoning America's policy formation." Running with that pack was Rose Wilder Lane. All of us have had read to us Laura Ingalls Wilder's *The Little House in the Prairie* (. . .*in the Forest*, . . .*in the*. . .) or we have read them to our own children. Rose Wilder Lane, little Rose grown up, became the author of *Let the Hurricane Roar* (1933), an epic about Norwegian immigrants freezing in the Dakotas. Somewhere along the line the no-longer-young Rose became possessed of economic truth and proclaimed that it was not to be found in the dangerous Tarshis canon.

I know of these details only because, later, having tasted blood in trying to root the Tarshis text out of colleges everywhere, some of the same people turned toward my effort. *God and Man at Yale* by the young Bill Buckley (1951) quoted from some of them; and others of his critiques I could recognize (from the coincidental inexactitudes of the quoted words) were taken from the writings of these earlier critics. The joke is that Buckley's Yale was notorious in those days for its conservative old guard economists (Fred Fairchild, Hudson Hastings, Ray Westerfield, O. Glenn Saxon). I cannot judge Yale's religious orthodoxies and heresies, but its economics at that time was devoutly orthodox.

All this may now seem bizarre and comical, but it was not a joke to earnest professors at scores of colleges who came under attack by regents and alumni visiting committees who had been alerted to the heresies being imposed on innocent college youth. Person-years were imposed on earnest professors who had to defend the objectivity of their assigned curricula. Fortunately for me, I had considered it good business to articulate carefully just when and why an unorthodox paradigm might make sense under certain conditions, whereas at other times orthodox paradigms would commend themselves. Interested in maximizing not *PQ* book revenues but rather Q influence, I could only gain from being eclectic and centrist. Critics from both right and left began to complain that I wrote carefully (as if a lawyer were at my elbow). Actually, such critics did me a favor. Where one person stays unconvinced, so will another. Eclectically qualifying principles makes for better principles, rather than for wishy-washy banalities, and it makes for better scholarship.

Prior to publication, my preliminary classroom versions came under intense attack from several MIT businessmen alumni and board members. One spotted a list of 100 heresies. When I took pains to explicate their expositions, he reacted with frustration: "The whole tone is wrong. You do not inculcate sound economics. That is your trouble. To protect your own reputation, a good man like Professor Fairchild of Yale must vet your text to cleanse out its heresies." That command exceeded my tolerance and amiability. President Karl Compton of MIT intervened with a letter in which he proclaimed that any time one of his professors became censorable by some outsider, he would hand in his own resignation from office. (Later, when my book was accorded bestseller status, this particular businessman critic even developed some grudging admiration for it. Money talks. Lorie Tarshis was never so lucky with any of his opponents.)

All this, mind you, was just *prior* to the Joseph McCarthy era of witch-hunting in government, academia and the clergy. During that period and still afterwards, there was often a full-court press by various conservative groups to emphasize sound principles in high school and corporate in-house courses in economics. When the AEA cosponsored with numerous foundations a TV Continental Classroom course in economics, much time and energy was expended to ensure a balanced curriculum. (This "ethical cleansing" did not speed up creative innovations in the direction of "monetarism" or later "rational expectationism.")

By the time of the 1960s and 1970s, the shoe began to pinch on the other foot. Student unrest at the time of the Vietnam War led to bitter attacks on mainstream economics. To the New Left, Samuelson became the personification of what was bad about the running jackals of capitalism. Out of Denmark, in German and English, came a two-volume *Anti-Samuelson* (Linder and Sensat, 1977). Like the miniskirt, the radical faction gradually subsided; but when I lectured in 1973 at Australian universities, I discovered that students were disappointed that I wore neither a top silk hat nor spats. It is hard to please everyone. See Assar Lindbeck's (1971) *The Political Economy of the New Left: An Outsider's View* for a valuable account of what turned out to be a nondurable movement.

I believe it is healthy for a discipline like economics to evolve in response to new developments and better understandings of historical reality. That is quite another thing from Stalinist or Chamber of Commerce coercion on the educational system. Funeral by funeral, economics does make progress. Darwinian impact of reality melts away even the prettiest of fanciful theories and the hottest of ideological frenzies. But there are fits and starts along the way.

References

Buckley, William F., Jr., *God and Man at Yale.* Chicago: Regnery, 1951.

Donald, David Herbert, *Lincoln.* New York: Simon and Schuster, 1995.

Ely, Richard T., *Outlines of Economics.* New York: Macmillan, 1893, 1908, 1918, 1926, 1931, 1938; after 1908 the revisions are by Thomas S. Adams, Max O. Lorenz and Allyn Young, and later by Ralph Hess.

Fairchild, Fred R., Edgar S. Furniss, and Norman S. Buck, *Elementary Economics.* Vols. 1 and 2, 3rd edition, New York: Macmillan, 1936.

Fisher, Irving, *Elementary Principles of Economics.* New York: Macmillan, 1911.

Friedman, Milton, "The Spendings Tax as a Wartime Fiscal Measure," *American Economic Review,* March 1943, *33,* 50–62.

Friedman, Milton, "A Monetary and Fiscal Framework for Economic Stability," *American Economic Review,* June 1948, *38,* 245–64.

Garver, F. B., and Alvin Hansen, *Principles of Economics.* Boston: Ginn, 1938.

Keynes, John Maynard, *The General Theory of Employment, Interest and Money.* London: Macmillan, 1936.

Kiekhoffer, William H., *Economic Principles, Problems and Policies.* New York and London: Appleton-Century, 1936, the successor to a 1921 version.

Knight, Frank, "The Newer Economics and the Control of Economic Activity," *Journal of Political Economy,* August 1932a, *40,* 433–76.

Knight, Frank, "Comment on Mr. Slichter's Comment on the Issues," *Journal of Political Economy,* December 1932b, *40,* 820–25.

Lane, Rose Wilder, *Let the Hurricane Roar.* London: Longmans Green & Co., 1933.

Lindahl, Erik R., *Studies in the Theory of Money and Capital.* London: Allen & Unwin, 1939.

Lindbeck, Assar, *The Political Economy of the New Left: An Outsider's View.* New York: Harper & Row, 1971.

Linder, Marc, with Julius Sensat, *Anti-Samuelson.* Vols. 1 and 2, New York: Urizen Books, 1977.

Samuelson Paul A., *Foundations of Economic Analysis.* 1947. Enlarged edition, Cambridge: Harvard University Press, 1983.

Samuelson, Paul A., *Economics.* New York: McGraw-Hill, 1948, 1952, 1955, 1958, 1961, 1964, 1967, 1970, 1973, 1980; with William D. Nordhaus, 12th, 13th, 14th, and 15th editions, 1985, 1989, 1992, 1995.

Samuelson, Paul A., *The Collected Scientific Papers of Paul A. Samuelson.* Vol. 2, Cambridge, Mass.: Massachusetts Institute of Technology Press, 1965 (see especially chapter 100, "The New Look in Tax and Fiscal Policy"); see also chapter 98, "Principles and Rules in Modern Fiscal Policy: A Neo-Classical Reformulation," chapter 99, "Full Employment Versus Progress and Other Economic Goals," and chapter 105, "Fiscal and Financial Policies for Growth").

Slichter, Sumner H., *Modern Economic Society.* New York: Henry Holt, 1931.

Slichter, Sumner H., "Modern Economic Society Further Considered: Comments on Mr. Knight's Review," *Journal of Political Economy,* December 1932, *40,* 814–20.

Slichter, Sumner H., "Pseudo-Scientific Method in Economics: A Reply," *Econometrica,* October 1933, *1,* 428–29.

Tarshis, Lorie, *The Elements of Economics.* Boston: Houghton-Mifflin, 1947.

Tarshis, Lorie, *Introduction to International Trade and Finance.* New York: Wiley, and London: Chapman & Hall, 1955.

Taussig, Frank W., *Principles of Economics.* New York: Macmillan, 1911.

Tobin, James, "A Dynamic Aggregative Model," *Journal of Political Economy,* April 1955, *31,* 103–15.

Tobin, James, "Reply to Professor Eisner," *Economic Journal,* September 1959, *69,* 599–608.

Tobin, James, "Growth Through Taxation," *The New Republic,* July 25, 1960, 15–18; reproduced in Tobin, J., ed., *National Economic Policy, Essays.* New Haven: Yale University Press, 1966, pp. 78–88.

Tobin, James. "Macroeconomics and Fiscal Policy." In Brown, E. C., and R. M. Solow, eds., *Paul Samuelson and Modern Economic Theory.* Cambridge, Mass.: Massachusetts Institute of Technology Press, 1983, pp. 189–202; particularly 197–200.

Wilder, Laura Ingalls, *The Little House on the Prairie.* New York: Harper & Bros., 1935.

ON COLLABORATION

by Paul A. Samuelson*

Asking me to write about joint authorship is rather like going to a vegetarian for a treatise on the proper cooking of steak. Mostly I have been a loner: out of half a thousand papers in my collected volumes, perhaps five percent have been jointly authored. Still that leaves more than a score of collaborations. Towards the end of his life Maynard Keynes was asked: If you had to do it over what would you do differently? He is supposed to have answered: "I'd have drunk more champagne." Well, in a second Monte Carlo run of history, I'd write more joint papers. More with Bob Solow. And if the gods were kind a second classic with Wolfgang Stolper.

Many say they find scholarship a lonely business. It's you and your pencil in a closed room. (I know one busy professor who was beset by teaching and administrative duties. Finally after years of this he carved out a sabbatical year at the Stanford Behavioral Science Center: nice stipend, serene office, great secretarial backup. The anticlimax was writer's block!) Collaboration with a congenial mind may well then be a prescription for enjoyable research achievement.

I am against the Carlyle-Schumpeter Great Person theory of history. Science is knowledge—*public* knowledge. We each add our bit: the result is the sum, and the product, of its parts.

R.A. Fisher was a great statistician, even though he was a cantankerous individualist and a capricious genius. Neyman & Pearson—one word, like Gilbert & Sullivan or Rodgers & Hart—were also great statisticians. Their cooperation was carried on by slow mail between prewar Poland and England with turnaround time measured in months and not in today's e-mail nanoseconds.

It is nonsense to say that nothing wonderful was ever created by a committee. The maligned camel is a magnificent adaptation of form and function. The King James Version of the Bible is a Beethoven symphony. Never ask about *Principia Mathematica:* How much was Bertie (Russell)? how much Alfred (Whitehead)?

G. H. Hardy, dean of British mathematicians in the World War I era, said: "Mine has been a good life; I have collaborated with Littlewood (and Ramanajuan!) on not too uneven terms." Stealing Hardy's line, I can boast that Solow and I have made good music together.

As they say, cut out the cackle and get down to the facts. By chance, it was writing a 1940 joint article with Russ Nixon, a fellow graduate student in the prewar Harvard graduate barnyard, that got me my lifetime job at MIT. Let me explain. Harold Freeman, a non-Rotarian statistician (more Peer Gynt than Baron Munchhausen), started a one-man crusade to move me from Harvard to MIT. Harvard, it developed, was no great obstacle. But the MIT Department Head (Ralph Freeman, later a dear friend and no relation to Harold) resisted. "Yes," he said, "I know Samuelson is a promising economist, but is he a cooperator?" "A cooperator?" Harold replied, "Why, he even writes joint articles." Clio the Muse of History has a sense of humor. It was my *first* joint article; and in a decade it was the only one. Besides, as a theorist I was not destined to be a prolific writer on empirical statistical matters like the pre-1939 measurement of total U.S. unemployment. I came to write on that subject only because I learned that a third-party go-getter was elbowing Nixon out of a joint venture: it was none of my business but I have had some weakness for the underdog. (No good deed goes entirely unpunished. The late Russell Nixon, who had been John F. Kennedy's instructor in EcA, pursued an active career in CIO and leftist labor unionism. I am sure J. Edgar Hoover has my name in his FBI files as a collaborator with Nixon, but I have not had the curiosity to use the Freedom of Information Act to learn the details. There were no untoward consequences in the McCarthy Witchhunt days, but it is not a laughing matter

---

*Institute Professor Emeritus, MIT 1970 Nobel laureate in economic science.

that careers of useful folk were destroyed for less.)

I move on to less accidental collaboration. One of the most cited articles in trade theory is the 1941 Stolper-Samuelson paper on "Protectionism and Real Wages." Fifty years after its publication, the University of Michigan called a two-day conference to commemorate its content and extend its scope. Note that Samuelson beats out Stolper in alphabetical order, but the name of Stolper comes first on the paper. This is only as it should be. Wolfgang Stolper had been a pupil of Schumpeter at Bonn and followed him to Harvard. The newly-married Samuelsons and Stolpers lived on the same Ware Street two blocks from the Harvard Yard. (In those days I needed no watch: every quarter hour the Memorial Hall bells told me the time; being absent-minded I was not equally sure of the date but mostly I did have a good guess as to the month.) One day Wolfi mentioned to me: Ohlin's factor-price equalization theorem must imply that an American tariff ought legitimately to raise U.S. wage rates. Obvious. Yes, *today* obvious. But then in the shadow of Frank Taussig, Gottfried Haberler, and Jacob Viner this was heresy. I replied: "By George, you're right. Work it out." And that he began to do. But there were snags and surprises, which he would discuss with Midwife Paul A. Samuelson. Kibitzers do not deserve to have their names on a paper; a footnote acknowledgement is adequate. But Stolper is a person of excessive conscience. He declared that he could not publish the paper without my name as joint author. Not wishing to be an aborter, I gave in.

The rest is history. We were turned down by the best editors of the best journals. (This is written up somewhere.) Also, we have here a prime example of Robert K. Merton's Matthew Effect in the history of science. TO HIM WHO HATH SHALL BE GIVEN.

Broadly I have been given too much credit and Stolper too little—except by experts who know better. If A and B make the same discovery at the same time, and B is the more prolific name, then A will fail to get the deserved 50% of the credit. (Whitehead and Russell display the same effect: Bertrand Russell's fame as a logician exceeds Whitehead's, so that the *Principia* began to be called Russell's *Principia*; Russell had to scold Keynes in print for this provocation.)

I am not digressing when I mention here "Samuelson's" classic 1939 article on the "Interactions Between the Multiplier Analysis and the Principle of Acceleration." It is published as the work of one author only. Written in an afternoon it brought that young economist instant international fame. Yet, as I later explained in print, Samuelson was only correcting a subtle mathematical mistake in the writings of his beloved mentor Alvin Hansen ("the American Keynes"). It was all Hansen's exact model, prettied up, generalized, and mathematically explicated. In a world where it is so often the case that an older scholar gets his name on a manuscript largely done by an assistant, and gets his name first on it, this counter-example of generosity deserves special notice. (In organic chemistry, a star publishes as many as half a hundred papers a year, probably with a score of junior authors. I asked MIT's late chemist John Sheehan—the synthesizer of penicillin—how his authors' names were listed. He replied: "I used to put my name last, but that didn't fool anybody and it did make bibliographical referencing more confused. So now it reads Sheehan and Smith, Sheehan and Jones, Sheehan and Tom, Dick, and Harry." "Do you think that's fair?" I asked. Prior to Jack Kennedy, he replied: "Is life fair? Besides I have an unrealistic hope that it all evens up in the end. When you're young you get too little credit, when you're old too much." But what about premature dying and also the inevitable narrowing down that leaves fewer on top than began at the bottom?)

Unlike R. G. D. Allen and J. R. Hicks who teamed up from the beginning to write their classic 1934 "Reconsideration of the Theory of Value," it is apparent that often my few joint efforts came when my midwife role grew too large for the conscience of some friend. Thus, in my first 1953 collaboration with Solow, uncharacteristically I contributed to the proof of his original conjectured theorem. (I happened to remember a similar case in A. J. Lotka's mathematical demography.) A footnote would have sufficed but he insisted on joint authorship. The shoes were on the other feet in our second 1956 collaboration: he saved me from a wrong conjecture. My name did not appear on a different article denying the possibility of double reswitching in a Sraffa input/output model; but since its author wrote as an MIT student of mine, it was proper that I be given much blame for what was an inexplicable stupidity.

I could go on spinning anecdotes about Merton and Me, Hansen and Me, Modigliani and Me, ... But space is short and more representative matters need mention.

Let me therefore report only on working with Franco, a unique and grueling experience. We all envied the legendary cooperations of Modigliani and Gruenberg, Modigliani and Brumberg, Modigliani and Ando, Modigliani and Drèze, Modigliani and Miller, Modigliani and .... I used to say facetiously, "Franco, when I am dead you will regret never having heard the sound of my voice." So even in my Walter Mitty dreams of Napoleonic glory, I never dared hope for Franco and Paul. But fate destined me to be the man who had everything.

Like a French revolution, it all began on the tennis court. (*The New Yorker* carried under the heading "Things We Doubt Ever Happened" a news bite describing this; but it was the literal truth.) Franco, not wishing to waste time between his first and second serve, had said to me: "Do you believe Luigi Pasinetti's new theory?" "Tell me what it is and I'll let you know." "Pasinetti claims that a rise in workers' saving rate can't affect long-run capital stock or interest rate." "Impossible," I said after Franco had double faulted. "Only begin with Harrod's model and now increase workers' saving propensity above *rentiers*'. That does raise K/L and does lower longrun profit rate." Thus, the dual anti-Pasinetti equilibrium regimen was conceived; but the child was not delivered into print without painful travail. Every line had to be argued out at length. It was like going over Niagara Falls in a barrel. I wouldn't have missed the experience for a million dollars but I wouldn't give two cents for a second helping. (I jest. My sky high opinion of Modigliani went up. I knew it was a deep well but had not realized its unbounded dimension.)

Just as scholars divide up into soloists and duet singers, diverse patterns of collaboration abound. Even the same composer Richard Rodgers worked differently with the undisciplined Lorenz Hart and the on-schedule Oscar Hammerstein III. With Hart, Rodgers wrote the music first and then tried to trap Hart into an afternoon of inspiration. Oscar's autonomous lyrics, by Granger causality (an inside econometrician's joke), evoked Rodgers' beautiful music.

Dale Jorgenson and Franco Modigliani are similar and different. Dale's is the chemists' pattern (recall John Sheehan) in which workshop participants join with the Master and themselves later become Masters. Complex data call for such group efforts. Von Neumann and Morgenstern represent the pairing of one who knows mathematics with one who knows economics: it was a fertile marriage even though each brought out some of the foibles of the other. (When asked what was Morgenstern's role in the game theory book, von Neumann gave the waggish answer: "Without Oskar I could never have written the book." Humor, as George Stigler has instructed us, can often be cruel. Truth should never be told so as to be interesting. It is enough that it be true.) In the development of linear programming, the economist W. W. Cooper and the mathematician A. Charnes, formed a synergestic team. Dick Zeckhauser's restless mind has identified many new problems for him and one or another statistician to put to rest. Milton Friedman's innovative boldness and Jimmie Savage's mathematical power conspired to forge the classic 1948 "The Utility Analysis of the Choices Involving Risk." Savage told me Friedman's virtuosity educated him on how research should be formulated: the wood Milton chopped warmed science twice.

Some authors almost always work with others. In modern physics it seems ludicrous when 100 names are on a paper. But that kind of research may involve giant machines that need numerous attenders. When Segré and Chamberlain got the Nobel Prize in Physics, Owen Chamberlain was a visiting professor at Harvard from Berkeley. He told the press: "A committee at Berkeley gave me that prize, by happening to pick me for early use of the new cyclotron." A surgeon friend of mine was one of many co-authors of a paper relating cancer and coffee consumption. He told me laughingly, "I provided some of their patients, that's all I did." When the paper's initial result didn't pan out under replication, my friend was very little put out. As Mark Twain said, "Most men will defend their home but few will go to the stake to save a boarding house."

One young Harvard M.D. in a hurry wrote 50 papers a year with names on their masthead of all his mentors. When his jealous peer group caught him creating on the computer before their eyes 24 hours of data, the fat was in the fire. Under microscopic examination, the skein of wool completely unraveled. Like Typhoid Mary this crook had contaminated dozens of teachers, who revealed how little was their knowledge of what bore their names. I hasten to point out that my casual investigations over the years into outright plagiarism among economists reveals that our field is better refereed and audited than seems to be the case in the harder sciences where there is much dependence on "soft money" for research, and where pressure for publication fabricates most papers that go widely unread. In economics, plagiarism is a rare phenomenon in which fourth rate people with high time preference steal from third rate people and where what is pilfered has not much value in the market place. On a cost/benefit basis crime does not pay: even with a 99% chance of not getting caught the penalty to permanent reputation is too great to make it a rational gamble. (Mining data and selective stopping rules are more serious blemishes in scholarly Machiavellism, and are harder to spot early. Still, facts are remorseless and over time it all tends to come out in the wash.)

Ours is not a field of Saints and Sir Galahads only. Just as some brokers "front run" and "back run" to capture rents on their knowledge of others' intentions, certain scholars earn repute for joining band wagons early; give them a paper to referee and they are off to the races; it is even worse when an editor is too quick off the mark just after the post brings a new batch of manuscripts. These are not felonies nor even indictable misdemeanors, but they are lapses of taste that do not escape notice. (In the eyes of paranoids everyone is a predatory enemy.)

A more difficult normative problem arises for fast-thinking scholars. Mention to them your lemma and they know your theorem before you do. It is fair that the race should go to the swift—if it is a footrace against time. But what is golden about an Invisible Hand that makes a speculator rich just because she digests new news a minute before her slower brother-in-law?

Would science be much hurt if West, Malthus, and Ricardo had stumbled over the Law of Diminishing Returns in 1816 rather than 1815? Yet the coin we poor scholars work for is priority in discovery. The perversity of Prisoners' Dilemma applies widely in real life. Alas.

One pattern that recurs occasionally is the monogamous Damon & Pythias syndrome: two scholars, Brothers Grimm so to speak, who *always* write together. When asked to evaluate one of them for a university chair, that can become problematic. Also, there have been cases where longtime partners came to a parting of the ways. After all, marriage itself is a cause for divorce. Sir Arthur Sullivan thought himself too good for the vulgar W. S. Gilbert.

When a team publishes always under, say, the names Aaron and Zeiss, that alphabetical ordering does less injustice to Zeiss. But the repeated trademark of Zeiss-Aaron, if it is a truly symmetric cooperation, would be an unfair syndrome. Better surely to use A–Z on Monday-Wednesday-Fridays and Z–A on Tuesday-Thursday-Saturdays. The injustice seems even worse when by historic chance, a long series of researchers got first published under say the heading Thompson-Dickson-Harrison—maybe for no better reason than that Thompson was a full professor first and carried most initial weight in fundraising. Twenty years later, and n publications on, it is hard cheese if citation indexes concentrate on Thompson *et al.* only. I would not like to have to explain to St. Peter that I was legitimately in the Et al category. A sensitive Harrison would insist, in early times, on the doctrine "Each of equals is more equal than the others" and drive home this point by a scrupulous permutation of names.

Does all this seem like making heavy weather about a tempest in a teapot? It is not. Dorfman, Samuelson, Solow was the meticulous alphabetical ordering on the spine of a 1958 treatise. Merton's *Sociology of Science* demonstrates that proper credit is all important to scholars. Who steals my legitimate claim for innovation steals all. Indeed it is only natural that junior assistants should if anything exaggerate their unique contribution to a research enterprise, while those who wear medals all over their chests can be expected often to be insensitive to the legitimate inputs of their rotating coworkers. It is tempting to hope that *in advance* all these imputations and

Vol. 40, No. 2 (Fall 1996)

acknowledgments be agreed upon and codified by contract. But experience teaches that in real dynamic life imputation and property rights cannot be unambiguously quantified. (Gossips said that one professor got a Nobel Prize historically for making an observation that his female assistant had to call repeatedly to his notice! Another got the Prize for curing a disease today not believed ever to have existed: maybe his lab slave let him down? — an unlikely alibi.)

Success has a thousand fathers. Failure is an orphan. John F. Kennedy — or Theodore Sorenson — said that: but before them, this was noted in the wartime diary of Count Cianno, Mussolini's son-in-law. Quarrels can arise when time comes to cash in on the wages of fame. James Watson's *Double Helix* is the greatest account ever written about a scientific breakthrough told by a breakerthrough. It is not a pretty story; but if a chap will write it, it should get published (as written). The Harvard Press and the lawyers of the Harvard Corporation decided otherwise. It was feared that Sir Lawrence Bragg, head of the Cambridge Cavendish Lab, might sue. Defenders of women's rights regarded Rosalind Franklin (whose crystallography data pointed Crick-Watson toward the helix hypothesis) as the one most cruelly libeled. When I read the manuscript, it was Crick who seemed most harmed: if he was a full 50–50 partner and one less ruthlessly ambitious, to my mind he would have a grievance. In any case it took some years for a complete reconciliation between the young comrades at arms.

Hard cases make bad law. In my overall experience scholars and scientists have been no better or worse as persons than judges or ditchdiggers. Maybe I've been lucky, but in another run of the game I'd settle for the same crew that have been my teachers, colleagues, and students.

Conclusion

Collaboration is wrongly measured — for anyone and especially for me — by relative number of researches jointly authored. I can genuinely say "Adam and I" about the Smith who wrote in 1776. And can say "Black-Scholes and I" about the pair who discovered the options-price formula that I never quite arrived at. I revealed a preference to learn more (of what there was to learn) from Sir John Hicks than he cared to learn from me: who said life is symmetric? I advanced Keynes' football beyond the yardline where he left it. Why should I expect any record of mine to stand throughout time eternal?

I cannot help but feel sorry for libertarians. It is a personal failing for which I should reproach myself. Whenever I feel myself feeling too egotistical, I try to reread the following 1922 words of L. T. Hobhouse:

> The organizer of industry [the achieving scholar] who thinks that he has "made" himself . . . has found a whole social system ready to his hand in skilled workers, machinery, a market, peace and order [a corpus of past knowledge and contemporary researchers] — a vast apparatus and a pervasive atmosphere, the joint creation of millions of humans and scores of generations. Take away the whole social factor and we have not Robinson Crusoe, with his salvage from the wreck and his acquired knowledge, but the naked savage living on roots, berries, and vermin.

References

Allen, R. G. D. and Hicks, J. R. 1934. A Reconsideration of the Theory of Value, Parts I–II. *Economica N.S.* 1 (February–May):52–67; 196–219.

Dorfman, R., Samuelson, P. A., and Solow, R. M. 1958. *Linear Programming and Economic Analysis*. New York: McGraw-Hill.

Friedman, M. and Savage, L. J. 1948. The Utility Analysis of Choices Involving Risk. *Journal of Political Economy* 56 (August):279–304.

Hobhouse, L. T. 1922. *The Elements of Social Justice*. New York: Holt, pp. 162–63.

Merton, R. K. 1973. *The Sociology of Science*. Chicago: The University of Chicago Press.

Nixon, R. A. and Samuelson, P. A. 1940. Estimates of Unemployment in the United States. *Review of Economic Statistics* 22 (August):101–11.

Samuelson, P. A. 1939. Interactions Between the Multiplier Analysis and the Principle of Acceleration. *Review of Economic Statistics* 21 (May):75–78. Reproduced as Chapter 82 in *The Collected Scientific Papers of Paul A. Samuelson*, Vol. 2. Cambridge, Mass.: The MIT Press, 1966.

Samuelson, P. A. and Modigliani, F. 1966. The Pasinetti Paradox in Neoclassical and More General Models. *Review of Economic Studies* 32

(October):269–301. Reproduced as Chapter 146 in *The Collected Papers of Paul A. Samuelson*, Vol. 3. Cambridge, Mass.: The MIT Press, 1972.

Samuelson, P. A. and Solow, R. M. 1956. A Complete Capital Model Involving Heterogeneous Capital Goods. *Quarterly Journal of Economics* 70 (November):537–62. Reproduced as Chapter 25 in *The Collected Scientific Papers of Paul A. Samuelson*, Vol. 1. Cambridge, Mass.: The MIT Press, 1966.

Samuelson, P. A. and Solow, R. M. 1960. Analytical Aspects of Anti-Inflation Policy. *American Economic Review* 2 (May):177–94. Reproduced as Chapter 102 in *The Collected Scientific Papers of Paul A. Samuelson*, Vol. 2. Cambridge, Mass.: The MIT Press, 1966.

Solow, R. M. and Samuelson, P. A. 1953. Balanced Growth Under Constant Returns to Scale. *Econometrica* 21 (July):412–24. Reproduced as Chapter 24 in *The Collected Scientific Papers of Paul A. Samuelson*, Vol. 1. Cambridge, Mass.: The MIT Press, 1966.

Stolper, W. F. and Samuelson, P. A. 1941. Protectionism and Real Wages. *Review of Economic Studies* 9 (November):58–73. Reproduced as Chapter 66 in *The Collected Scientific Papers of Paul A. Samuelson*, Vol. 2. Cambridge, Mass.: The MIT Press, 1966.

Watson, J. D. 1968. *The Double Helix; a personal account of the discovery of the structure of DNA.* New York: Atheneum.

Joint Authorship in Science: Serendipity with Wolfgang Stolper*

by

Paul A. Samuelson**

It is almost five decades since the Stolper-Samuelson paper on *Protection and Real Wages* started trade and value theory on the fruitful path of connecting relative prices with relative factor scarcities. Aside from the incremental reputation the joint work brought, the whole operation was to me an undiluted pleasure from beginning to end.

I propose here, while in a mood of nostalgic tribute to Wolfgang Stolper, to reflect on the role of joint authorship in the house of science.

Romantic Individualism

"A camel is a beast perpetrated by a committee." This canard epitomizes a popular view glorifying the scientist and artist as a creative loner. Alfred Marshall tried to construct a defense of the free market against socialism by asking in effect: "What collectivity ever composed a great symphony, painted a masterpiece, or wrote a great book?"

The question is rhetorical but I cannot agree that its answer is self-evident. The camel is actually an organism of incredible efficiency for the functions evolution has designed it for. The Cambridge sage perhaps momentarily forgot that the magnificent King James version of the Bible was literally written by a committee. The *Encyclopédie* of the French enlightenment was greater than the sum of its parts. If Isaac Newton's *Principia* was written by a solitary don, the *Principia Mathematica* was the product of both Bertrand Russell and Alfred North Whitehead. If William James was the sole author of his classic text on psychology, the magisterial treatise on nineteenth century natural philosophy (physics) was written by Thomas and Tait – "tee" and "tee prime" they used to be called.

---

* Written on the occasion of Wolfgang Stolper's 75th birthday May 13, 1987 (ed).
** I owe thanks to the MIT Sloan School of Management for partial support from my Gordon Y. Billard post-doctoral fellowship; and to Aase Huggins for appreciated editorial assistance.

Within modern economics the 1934 gem of Hicks and Allen brought consumption theory back to the high road that was begun by Pareto and Slutsky. Many of Franco Modigliani's finest constribusions have been jointly authored, as we know from the familiar trademarks: Modigliani-Brumberg, Modigliani-Miller, Miller-Modigliani, Modigliani-Ando, Grunberg-Modigliani, and so forth. Neyman and [Egon] Pearson revolutionized orthodox Fisher paradigms of statistical inference by their distinguishing Type B as well as Type A errors. Mirrlees-Diamond breathed new life into the 1927 Frank Ramsey theory of second-best taxation. So it goes.

Gilbert and Sullivan – the phrase rings in our ears like one word (backeast or damnyankee). Gershwin and Gershwin, Rogers and Hart, Hammerstein and Rogers, these are just as natural. Indeed the cases of Cole Porter or Richard Wagner, who provided both their words and their music, are the exception rather than the rule.

Strained Relations

Partnership, like marriage, can be a stormy affair. Sullivan the musician came to believe that his genius was being dirtied by having to deal with the vulgar satirist Gilbert. In the end jealousy and irritation brought their lucrative collaboration to an end.

Disinterested scientists are no exception: where money leaves off and fame begins, their disinterest dissipates. Lee and Yang, who discovered together that nature does not maintain left-right parity, had a friendship that was a casualty of their Nobel fame. (The divorced wife of a Chemistry laureate told me bitterly that she should have coaxed a different scholar into transcendental creativity.) When Watson wrote *Double Helix*, it was Crick his codiscoverer of how DNA reproduced, and not Rosalyn Franklin, who had reason to be most resentful. It took years for some *rapprochement* to take place between the two conquerors.

Even the Russell-Whitehead intimacy disintegrated. Bertie's pacifism in World War I grated on the patriotism of the bereaved Whitehead parental couple. Alfred's ambiguities in philosophy grated on Russell's intolerance for fuzziness. These factors must be acknowledged. But the rift may have been exacerbated by the fact, be it a correct or wrong one, that Russell came to be credited with much of the *Principia's* novelty and profundity.

As a digression, let me mention that Keynes played a role in this. The ancient Whitehead claimed to me at Harvard in 1939 that he had twice recognized genius before others did: once in the case of Eddington, and once for Keynes. Memory can betray. The sober record suggests another story. It appears that Whitehead as a reader of Keynes' fellowship dissertation on probability played the role of his critic, delaying (to Maynard's resentment) his appointment to a King's College fellowship. Pigou's intervention was needed to save the day. I may add that Evelyn Whitehead exercised a disproportionate influence on her husband's opinions, being in this respect his Harriet Taylor. She regarded Maynard as too "teutonic," lacking her own gallic charm. Aside from being too serious and being associated with Bloomsbury homosexuality, Keynes suffered in her eyes from the crime of being pro-German in his criticisms of the Versailles Treaty as being punitive and unfeasible. Perhaps it is therefore understandable that Keynes tended to denigrate Whitehead, persistently referring to *Russell's Principia*. So flagrant was such practise, that Russell was impelled to scold its perpetrators in print, insisting that the work had been joint in every sense. (So to speak, whom God joined together let no man cast asunder.)

What the historian and sociologist of science, Robert K. Merton, calls the *Matthew Effect* works here as elsewhere. *To him who hath shall be given.* As one of two authors who has done, or will subsequently come to do, the most outstanding work in the same field as the jointly-authored work, he will tend to be given disproportionate credit for what both published.

I can attest that, in the case of the 1941 *Protection* paper with Stolper, mine was definitely the role of the junior author and the reverse-alphabetical listing of our names was advisedly the proper one. More on this later.

Modes of Collaborating

My Gilbert and Sullivan anology is an imperfect one for the sociologist of science. A string quartet would not be one if it did not include violins, viola, and cello. Lorenz Hart, aside from being of different temperament from Richard Rodgers, was there to do something different; and it would not have mattered if he were tone-deaf, so long as he could turn out such perfect words-of-one-syllable lines: "I took one look at you/that's all I had to do/and then my heart stood still." The team never had to meet in the same room. Rodgers wrote the music first. Then, after much delaying, Hart produced the lyrics. By contrast, it was Oscar Hammerstein III, who wrote the words first, which Rodgers then set to music. None of the fun of sitting in the same room and engaging in exploratory dialogue is basic to composer-lyricist collaboration.

These days, especially in physics but increasingly in biology, there is another and different kind of authorship. I refer to articles that appear with a listing of 100 authors. I do not exaggerate. Crucial experiments require ever larger equipment[1]. It is almost as if the janitor in the laboratory gets included for part of the fame. But where every one gets fame, no one gains much in reputation. Fortunately, in economics the senior mentor who helped to get a research grant does not automatically add his name to the paper's authorship list. In modern

---

[1] One Nobel physicist felt obliged to say, on the occasion of the award's announcement, that in effect a committee at Berkeley had given him the prize by its decision to give him first access to some new equipment.

medicine it is otherwise. One young postdoc put it to me this way: "If we don't put Professor Senex's name on the title page, how will he be able to get us money for our next grant? Besides it helps librarians to file a sequence of related papers under the heading, Senex & Aaron, Senex & Brown, ..., Senex and Zabel." It has been seriously proposed that a scholar ought not have her name on more than 100 papers in each year. No wonder that each headline of scientific fraud in the biological literature implicates some academic bigwig: surely the Lord will forgive them, for they assuredly do not know what is in all the papers they author. (A friend of mine was one of a dozen authors of a celebrated paper on coffee and cancer. I asked him about it, but he disengaged on the ground that all he had done was provide the patients for the investigation.) A Japanese scientist, refused tenure in an American institution, sued because the cancerous tissues cultured there had come from his own mother, in consequence of which he claimed to deserve a credit share in all subsequent research findings.

Joint authorship is tangentially related to plagiarism. There is no harm when all the scholarly world recognizes that a Dean's name on a paper is there only by courtesy. But at least one Nobel Prize – that for the important discovery of insulin as a remedy for diabetes – was clouded by the protest of one of the recipients that the head of his department deserved no such award, underlining his point by publicly sharing his half of the prize with his young co-worker. (A careful historical investigation of the matter has suggested that all three persons, and a fourth, deserved recognition for significantly contributing to the final result. Paradoxically, of the four, the one who did least in important scientific work subsequently, was the protester.)

Years ago I made a casual study of plagiarism and reached the conclusion that, in economics, it played no significant role. So I desist from further discussion of it, except to point to the universal propensity to exaggerate one's own worth: each of a Crick and a Watson, in his heart of hearts, might believe that the respective contributions were 55% – 45%; especially are young persons, tapped by a successful scholar for cooperating, likely to forget how many other young people could have been found to accomplish much the same thing. Economists, cognizant that the joint fruits of labor and land *cannot* be partitioned into the independently-additive contributions of each, realize that there is no objective par against which to rectify the claims of the respective partisans. (Marginal-product imputation *prices* the inputs; it does not cut the Gordian Knot of *causality* imputation.)

Some collaborations in science are based upon complementarity between the collaborators. The economist Morgenstern brought his social knowledge to the analytical skills of the mathematician von Neumann. It was a synergistic combination. I suppose the combinations of Cooper and Charnes, or of Shubick and Shapley, displayed some of the same happy meshings of talents.

Still another complementarity pattern is the case of the brilliant scholar with a writer's block or a creator's inhibition. Such a person is brilliant in the coffee house. He – usually this type is a *he* – talks away his potential scholarly performance. Since ideas, like mother's milk, must be drawn upon if the fountain from which they flow is to refill and gush forth fruitfully, much is permanently and irreversibly lost. Sometimes to the rescue of this Don Quixote comes a collegial Sancho Panza, a partner who takes down the pearls of wisdom as they emerge; who organizes the flow of thought and captures it in ink; who arranges the time of the next day get-together and, on the necessary occasions, provides the needed naggings. The respected Stonier and Hague book, I understand, had just this kind of origin. I believe that Paul Sweezy was able to perform for Paul Baran some of that which Friedrich Engels was able to do for (and with) Karl Marx. James Mill bullied and praised David Ricardo into writing his *Principles* in much this fashion.

Joys of Working Together

G. H. Hardy, a great mathematician of the early twentieth century, praised his collaborator and himself when he was able to write proudly, I collaborated with Littlewood. (His discovery of genius in a poor Madras clerk, Ramanujan, and his working with him until Ramanujan's early death from tuberculosis, Hardy declared to be the one romance of his life.) There are few pleasures like that of working successfully with one's equal on a hard but tractable problem.

Research is said to be a lonely business. (I must confess not to have found it so. A *solitary* business, yes. But time stands still when one grapples with an interesting challenge. Perhaps mine is a minority view.) How refreshing then to meet with a kindred spirit, upon whom one can bounce off conjectures and proofs and whose suggestions can be savored and digested.

Most of my work has been one-authored. I cannot say it has been independently conceived, for in a real sense all economists have been my coauthors. Take Sir John Hicks for example. Both of our names appear on no book or article. Rarely do my papers include his name among the list of my creditors. But through the years, poring over his many works has been of enormous aid (and interest) to me. Indeed, I have often said that we Americans take unfair advantage of the English: we look at each other through polarized glass, that asymmetrically favors passage of light in one direction; we can read and benefit from both of our languages!

But in my time I have written a fair number of jointly-authored papers. The one with Stolper was, I believe, the second. Several papers have been with Solow. Among my co-authors have been Dorfman, Dornbusch, Fischer, Hagen, Hansen, Modigliani, Nordhaus, R. Sato, Swamy, and still others.

No two love affairs, it is said, are alike. The same holds for joint researching. A glance across a crowded room can begin love. My paper with Franco Modigliani, like a revolution, began on the tennis court. Between serves he said, "An odd result, that of Pasinetti, where increased worker's savings leaves ultimate capital/labor ratios and interest rates unchanged?" Rising to the bait, I said: "That can hardly be true, since the substantive difference between Harrod's equilibrium and Kalecki's can be thought of as due to a rise in the workers' saving rates from zero to that fraction which profit-receivers save." The rest is history.

Bliss in That Youthful Dawn

This is not the place for autobiographical memoirs but is rather a tribute to Wolfgang Stolper. When I came as a minor to the Harvard graduate school, Stolper was already there in the Schumpeter stable. Indeed he was the only link between Schumpeter's time in Bonn and in Cambridge, Massachusetts. (Herbert Zassenhaus, Hans Staehle, Erich Schneider were some others whom I later came to meet.) Gustav Stolper, Wolfgang's remarkable father, had transmitted to his next new generation an appreciation of Schumpeter's brilliance.

Those were great days in the Harvard Yard. Richard Musgrave, Lloyd Metzler, Richard Goodwin, Paul Sweezy, William and Walter Salant, Emile Despres, Kenneth Galbraith, and a host of rising stars elevated the seminars of Leontief, Schumpeter, Hansen, Williams, Chamberlin, and Mason.

Wolfgang and I were neighbors on Ware Street near the Harvard Yard. Married in the same year, he and I were tutors together in Leverett House. Given my middlewestern past, Stolper was my first contact with the Continent: Viennese waltzes and *Lederhosen*. I admired his indignation when, after complaining to a waiter that the chablis was warm, that functionary returned with an ice cube plopped into the glass. Wolfgang did not admire – he found it incredible! – that I would listen to a Beethoven Symphony in the order of its movements 1, 4, 2, 3 – because I was too lazy to get up and turn the 78 RPM records over in their old-fashioned automatic mechanisms. (Since then I have readily understood the scientific finding that Mozart listened to music with the half of the brain different from the one I use.)

One day in the late 1930s, Stolper mentioned to me a curiosity: "Old Taussig [still very much alive] asserts that free trade raises American wages by drawing workers into the sectors of maximum comparative advantage. How do we square this with Ohlin's notion that the input America is most niggardly endowed with can have its return *lowered* by free trade in comparison with autarky?"

The point was a new one to me. I said, "You've got something there. Work it out."

He did. And in the course of his explorations we talked endlessly about the many ramifications of the problem. The analysis soon went beyond the point about free trade, which fell naturally into place after one had sorted out the issues. The discussion led naturally into the new tool of the factors-of-production box diagram, which has a generalization into production theory of the construction used by Edgeworth and Bowley for competitive *goods'* exchange. The time was ripe for this breakthrough. And in the end it led to the post-Heckscher-Ohlin analysis of factor-price equalization and geographical specialization.

When the job was through, Wolfgang Stolper insisted that his conscience would not be at rest unless I agreed to have the article appear under joint authorship. Although I realized that my function had been that of midwife to Stolper's baby, I acquiesced – under the agreement that our names would not appear in misleading alphabetical order.

What Travail Had Wrought

After the fact, most deductive theorems seem natural, even obvious. But as some sage has written, *ex ante* ain't *ex post*. I remember with what excited surprise we discovered that a rise in the price ratio between land-intensive wheat and labor-intensive watches could be proved to raise the real wage expressed in *every* good, and without requiring recourse to an ambiguous index-number problem.

We made a conscientious search of the earlier literature for an anticipation of our results. After evaluating Taussig, Haberler, Viner, Ohlin and Heckscher, Wicksell, Carver, Nicholson, Bastable, and Manoilescu, the only cogent reference we could come up with was to a little known 1935 analysis of taxation by Fredric Bentham.[2]

Our brainchild reads well in retrospect. It has been much cited and appears in many an anthology. Perhaps aspiring scholars will take comfort from the knowledge that, after we sent our fine baby to the *American Economic Review* for publication there, it was rejected. (Howard Ellis as referee found its argument convoluted; and besides it might bestow comfort on the forces of protectionism. I may add as an aside that the universe of my papers that have been

---

[2] The previous literature was strong on the mathematical equilibrium of exchange, thanks to works by Torrens, Ricardo, J. S. Mill, Mangoldt, Marshall, Edgeworth, and Graham. After 1930, the increasing-cost scenario yielded to analytic treatment at the hands of Haberler, Viner, Lerner, and Leontief (and, subsequently, Meade). I have told elsewhere the romantic story concerning Lionel Robbins' memory being triggered by my 1948 paper on factor-price equalization, and his discovering in the files a copy of the 1933 seminar paper on that subject that Abba Lerner himself had forgotten and which nicely anticipated my results and methods. The lamented Victor Edelberg, whose scientific career at the LSE was prematurely aborted by mental illness, had also some anticipations of the production-box diagram. Neither Heckscher nor Ohlin had tried to put their intuitions on a firm analytical basis. Needless to say, I at least had very much in mind at the time of the Stolper-Samuelson investigations the definitive 1939 findings by Marion Samuelson that verified the correctness of the "Australian case for a tariff," which alleged that a tariff on labor-intensive manufactures could increase real wage rates there and increase the population. See P. A. SAMUELSON [1981] for a post mortem on this last matter.

rejected for publication have been of average merit certainly no less than that of those in the universe of papers accepted for publication.)

Two imperfections I notice in my 1987 rereading. We failed to question Ohlin's dictum that goods' trade could equalize factor prices *only partially* [sic]. Not until later in the decade did recognition of that error belatedly come to me. Also, it was left for Lloyd Metzler in 1945 to show that we were too glib in our (implicit) assumption that a rise in tariff on an import good results in an enhanced domestic price ratio of it relative to the other export good. Beginning with free trade, Metzler showed that under quite admissible inelasticity of reciprocal demand(s), imposing a small tariff could *lower* the dollar p_{wa} of labor-intensive watches (imports) relative to the dollar p_{wh} of land-intensive wheat (exports). Then our line of argument would apply precisely – *but in reverse*, as such a tariff harms the real wage of labor *relatively* to the real return of land and in absolute terms.

Happy Recall

As I have said, this collaboration was an undiluted pleasure. So imagine my reaction a few years back when I received a telephone call from a subeditor of the *Quarterly Journal of Economics*. "Can you help me with a reference," she asked, "One of our submissions speaks of your polemic with Stolper. Where did that appear?"

I was amazed. "Read me the context." I said. When she read the words, "According to the Stolper-Samuelson argument ...," I burst out laughing and explained that this was an argument on which we belonged to the same side.

At Swarthmore, in Michigan, in Switzerland and elsewhere on the Continent, Wolfgang Stolper has developed admiring students and colleagues. His works have spanned international trade, colonial development and growth, comparative study of East and West Germany and much else.

While his moral strength matures, his boyish wistfulness endures. Joseph Schumpeter has much to be proud of. His pupil and friend Wolfgang Stolper carries on the grand tradition. I appreciate that he has touched my own life, personally and professionally.

Hail Alexander!

References

METZLER, L. [1949], "Tariffs, the Terms of Trade, and the Distribution of National Income", *Journal of Political Economy*, 57, 1–29; reproduced in Lloyd Metzler *Collected Papers*, Cambridge, Mass., 1973, Chapter 6. Chapter 7, published later in 1949 in the same journal, also has relevance.

ROBINSON, J. [1937], *Essays in the Theory of Employment*, London.

SAMUELSON, M. C. [1939], "The Case for Australian Protection Re-examined", *Quarterly Journal of Economics*, 54, 143–149.
SAMUELSON, P. A. [1948], "International Trade and Equalisation of Factor Prices", *Economic Journal*, 58, 163–184, reproduced as Chapter 67 in J. E. Stiglitz (ed.), *Collected Scientific Papers of Paul A. Samuelson,* Vol. II, Cambridge, Mass., 1965. Relevant also are Chapters 68–71, and in later Volumes Chapters 161, 251–255, 320.
– –, [1981] "Summing Up on the Australian Case for Protection", *Quarterly Journal of Economics*, 96, 147–160; also reproduced as Chapter 318 in K. Crowley (ed.), *Collected Scientific Papers of Paul A. Samuelson,* Vol. V, Cambridge, Mass., 1986.
STOLPER, W. F. and SAMUELSON, P. A. [1941], "Protection and Real Wages", *Review of Economic Studies*, 9, 58–73.

Professor Paul A. Samuelson
Mass. Institute of Technology
Cambridge, MA 02139
U.S.A.

585

The Fallibility of Economic Science*

Paul A. Samuelson, MIT

When I showed the title of my lecture to a sharp-tongued colleague, he observed, "Well, fallibility is a subject you are well qualified to speak upon." That same title may have drawn some members of this audience in the hope to learn how pretentiously phoney modern economics is. Everyone unconsciously resents complacent winners in the struggle for existence. And that's why it is easy to make the crowd laugh when a corpulent tycoon is brought down by a slippery banana peel.

The oldest of the social sciences, political economy always prided itself as their peer leader. And for a long time economics was riding high. It is one thing if some opinionated editor or legislator blasts this economics as a pseudo-science. But it is quite another matter if a longtime worker in the vineyard of political economy goes public with a blast of self-criticism. In a court of law, admissions against (self)interest are accorded special weight—and rightly so.

However, it is only fair for me to give warning, at the beginning, that my sermon tonight is not to be a diatribe on the inadequacies of this scholarly discipline. So, for those who have come here on a miscalculation, now is the time to cut your losses and beat a hasty retreat.

My proposal to examine some of the fallibilities of modern economics could equally well have been given the title: *Some of the Things Economists Know*. It is like the case of Middle East oil explorings that took place before the OPEC era. Under the constant pressure of local potentates eager for more immediate oil revenues, a friend in the oil industry told me that his company often responded not by drilling to find out where oil *is* but by drilling to mark off *where it is*

---

*I owe thanks to the MIT Sloan School of Management for my Gordon Y. Billard Fellowship, and to Kate Crowley and Aase Huggins for editorial assistance.

not. In economics learning what is not true is an indispensable aspect of establishing where the truth does lie.

There is another point, too deep for exhaustive analysis here tonight, but important for any science. As the philosopher of science Karl Popper reminded us fifty years ago, any body of thought that cannot possibly be falsified by any conceivable factual observations must *ipso facto* not be a science at all. Newton and Galileo did not prove that cannon balls and moons do obey the inverse square law of gravity. What they empirically observed might well be accounted for by still other theories (for example, Einstein's). What Newton and Galileo did do was to *refute* factually Aristotle's theory, according to which a body in motion needs a new push at every instant to keep it whirling through empty space at the observed constant speed. Scientists test meaningful theories, trying to falsify them if they can. Their understanding grows as they determine more and more of the possible theories to be false.

The present point is not an academic irrelevancy. One weakness of classical economics, the Act I phase of our subject which lasted for a century after 1776, lay in the delusion harbored by many followers of Adam Smith, David Ricardo, and John Stuart Mill, the delusion that political economy could be deduced as a science by *a priori* thought, and without dirtying one's fingers with grubby digging into economic history. Even when I began my studies at the University of Chicago, only yesterday so to speak, I was encouraged by many of my great professors not to waste my time on the empirical researches of Wesley Mitchell and Simon Kuznets. If I really desired to understand the business cycle, I should instead concentrate on the deductive syllogisms of someone like Friedrich Hayek with his period-of-production paradigms.

Whatever are the weaknesses of modern economics, neglect of econometric measurement is not one of them. As we fiddle here in this room, thousands of computers throughout the land are burning up the midnight voltage estimating 3-stage least-squares regression equations to explain overvaluation of the dollar and to refute the Laffer-Curve hypothesis that less is more when it comes to taxes.

2

Pride Before the Fall

Winston Churchill once said about his Labor Party rival: "Clement Atlee is a modest man. And he has much to be modest about." Economists can never be convicted of being modest, but an index of self-complacency for the profession would probably have peaked out around 1965. That index reached 100 just after Kennedy's Camelot got the country moving again and just before the Indo Chinese entanglement ignited inflation. By 1980 the index of economists' self-esteem had dropped from 100 to 37. Now in 1985 it has revived a bit, but still hovers in the low 40s.

Why has mainstream post-Keynesian macroeconomics moved into a crisis of self-doubt? Is it a case where, in the terminology of Thomas Kuhn's *The Structure of Scientific Revolutions,* a ruling paradigm began to run into conflict with newly observed facts? And, according to the Kuhnian scenario, finally a new paradigm emerged that better fits the facts and as a result captured most of the emerging younger scientists? Was it then the success of the competing macroeconomic methodology of *monetarism,* in the version of Clark Warburton, Milton Friedman, Alan Meltzer, or Karl Brunner, that succeeded in giving better forecasts and descriptions of business cycle developments, and thereby outsurvived post-Keynesianism in the Darwinian struggle for existence among economic theories? As I shall explain, the realities of doctrinal development in the last twenty years will not accord with any such simple interpretation.

More serious than monetarism as a long-term challenger to the eclectic post-Keynesianism has been the "New Classical School" or the "Rational Expectationism" of Robert Lucas and Tom Sargent. But even here Kuhnian dogma will have to be modified to take recognition of the fact that whatever else rational expectationists can do they have been damnably unlucky in forecasting how the economic system will be developing. If you want to become an instant millionaire by creating a new DRI, Chase Econometrics, Townsend-Greenspan, or Wharton model, you can't do it with black box monetarism or neutral-money Ricardianism: to keep squared errors of estimates down, you still need oldfangled C+I+G models—

3

albeit, for forecasting several quarters ahead, Robert Litterman's vectoral autoregressive techniques do provide a respectable control.

What lowered the public reputation of economic science was something out there in the real world rather than new findings of the graduate school seminar room. I refer of course to the scourge of stagflation. This was a new disease that modern mixed economies became afflicted with—namely, a tendency for the general price level to accelerate even before desirable levels of full employment were reached.

It is not true that economists are unable to tell how to curb inflation. It is not true that economists are powerless to recommend policies that will lower unemployment. We know what the Federal Reserve Central Bank must do in combination with the fiscal authorities to expand the nominal GNP or to contract it.

It is a fallibility of economic science—or to speak more accurately it is a regrettable property of today's mixed capitalism—that whatever is done to help in the short run the inflation part of stagnation will simultaneously worsen the stagnation part of stagflation; and, similarly, whatever we contrive that ameliorates the stag part of the problem will, in the short run, aggravate the 'flation part.

The first duty of a scientist is to tell the truth. If physicians cannot cure certain cancers, that is too bad, but it is an admission that must be made.

I once knew of a refugee from Hitler's Germany who was called to operate on the Turkish dictator Kemal Atatürk. It did not help his hand's skill to be told just as he entered the operating room, "Of course your life is forfeited, if your knife slips." So, nobody is proposing economists be flogged or exiled just because their theories don't work perfectly. It is natural, however, to admire and extoll physicians when they can prevent polio and provide miracle cures for hypertension and other life-threatening ailments. He who takes credit for the sun must expect to be blamed for the rain. If the stock of political economy rose when Kennedy's marvelous council of economic advisors of Heller, Tobin and Gordon did get the country moving again, we must be prepared to see economics

4

in a bear market when Ackley, McCracken, and Charles Schultze are economic advisors at a time when prices get out of hand while slum jobs are scarce.

It is no secret that the consensus forecasters at banks, in government, and inside university computers have had their batting averages deteriorate in recent years. Dr. Stephen McNees of the Boston Federal Reserve can salve our vanity by pointing out that the movements in real GNP are truly more choppy than they used to be and hence are intrinsically more difficult to anticipate accurately. As far as the general public is concerned though, this explanation does not provide an adequate alibi for economic science. And in terms of my chosen title for this evening, I must acknowledge for the record that one of the fallibilities of economic science is its limited accuracy in forecasting the future.

More than once I have told the story of the late Nobel Laureate Tjalling Koopmans of Yale. A great scholar of serious purpose, Koopmans long ago took a year's sabbatical to formulate essays on the nature of economic science. He came to my office to ask whether our improving data bases, our computer hardware, and our sophistication in statistical methodology would enable economic science to converge toward ultimate accuracy in prediction. I could only answer with a hunch that a fundamental indeterminacy principle, only superficially reminiscent of Heisenberg's principle in physics, would prevent us from going above a certain barrier of accuracy. I wish my view had proved wrong. And I hope that young economists are making it obsolete. But so far our powers have remained limited.

Lest you think I am succumbing to uncharacteristic modesty, let me emphasize this: though economics cannot forecast perfectly, there is no other discipline, science, or occupation that can do as well. Businessmen, brokers, astrologers, and the entrails of geese, experience shows, are significantly worse forecasters than economists.

The Post-War Booboo

The post-Camelot deflating of economists' pretensions reminds me of the single greatest error of economic science in my time as an economist. I don't know whether the failure of our profession to foresee the stockmarket crash of 1929 and the Great Depression that ensued represents any culpability of economic science or of the generation of economists who occupied the stage before I began the study of economics. That was before my time. I do know that most leading American economists participated in the general 1945 forecast that at the end of World War II there would follow a serious depression.

Everett Hagen had the responsibility to coordinate the diverse forecasts from economists in all the governmental agencies: the Treasury, Federal Reserve, OPA, and the rest. Their general consensus was that rapid curtailment of military spending and of the colossal government deficit would leave the nation with such a surplus of full-employment saving over motivated private investment as to lead to massive unemployment.

My brother Robert Summers once asked me how I had stood on that issue. Sigmund Freud would not be surprised to learn that one's mind tends to forget its own gross errors in judgment. However, when I looked up the exact words my quill had written for *The New Republic* and the *National Resources Planning Board's* studies on post-war planning, I had to admit that I shared in the guilt of my generation.

Always, I tell my students to ignore the advice of Satchel Paige, who said, "Never look back; someone may be gaining on you." I say, "Always look back. Study your residuals. You might even learn something".

This end-of-war example of the fallibility of economic science is an instructive one. Our science can even take some comfort in it. First, it was not a simple case of erroneous Keynesianism versus sound shirt-sleeve economics. America's arch-Keynesian, my old friend and mentor Alvin Hansen, always predicted that there would be a restocking boom immediately after war's end. The actual postwar fiscal stimulus, Hansen told me at the time, was even more than he

6

had predicted and his had been the highest of the predictions. Sumner Slichter, a Keynesian writer although of the closet variety, was also one who predicted the vigor of the postwar recovery. So did W.W. Woytinski and William Fellner: moreover, theirs were not the usual know-nothing boiler plate; rather, they came out with the right answers for the right reasons.

What is instructive is not the count of the good guys and the bad guys. It is learning, after the fact, the hard way, that it is a misidentification to extrapolate for the intermediate and long run, short run saving patterns of the business cycle and of wartime scatter. Here was a case where science learned from its losses. The later *permanent-income* hypothesis of Milton Friedman, the *lifecycle saving* model of Franco Modigliani, and James Dusenberry's Veblenesque model of saving were useful antidotes to the simple short-term saving-income regressions of the 1920-45 years. Better of course to be right *before* the fact; but nonetheless important not to stay wrong right after the fact.

Speaking at this university, I should call attention to the fact that one of your greatest professors of yesteryear, Simon Kuznets, whose recent death we currently mourn, gave a historical survey of long-term American saving trends at a famous University of Pennsylvania convocation: in this magisterial recapitulation, Kuznets showed that the ratio of saving to income with full employment tended to be constant over the decades rather than rising; and this same invariance is what economists refer to when they speak of Denison's Law. I should also mention the name of two young Keynesians, or more accurately two young post-Keynesians: Lawrence Klein and Franco Modigliani. Economists may make errors but, unlike demographers, we are quick on our feet and a shifty lot. We cut our losses and don't stay wrong. Both Klein and Modigliani independently in the last half of the 1940s warned against the vulgar error of exaggerating the saving that will characterize higher-income regimes.

7

'Twixt Art and Science

Economics is not an exact science. That is obvious. Actually most of the so-called exact sciences are not exact: experts still differ on Saturn's rings; the areas where experts unequivocally agree are peculiar and special subsets of the data—as for example weights falling slowly in a vacuum, and not the afternoon perambulations of an autumn leaf. Still, there are some aspects in physics and engineering where a rigor obtains that our subject will never attain.

Here is a story to illustrate, a true story. Some decades ago the head of mechanical engineering at one of our technical schools developed a new theory. It was so sweeping in its novel conclusions that my publisher signed him up to edit a series of forty volumes working out its implications and expositions in a great variety of practical applications. I asked an MIT friend who was an eminent thermodynamicist about the new theory. "It's novel all right," Joseph Keenen said, "the only trouble is it violates the second law of thermodynamics." To make a long story short, McGraw-Hill had no legal problem in voiding its contract to publish what competent scientists rejected as incompetent.

Can you imagine this happening in economics? I often say that there is no theory in economics so bizarre as not to have a proponent, usually some friend of mine. Weekly I get crank letters to set the economic system aright. The German mathematician Landau used to have postcards printed up so that he could write to cranks: "Your proof of Fermat's Last Theorem—or, as the case might be, your proof on how to trisect the angle or square the circle—first goes wrong on page blank." And then he would dispose of the matter by filling in the blank with the appropriate page number.

That kind of deductive certainty is not relevant for economics. I don't believe there is anything in the sunspot theory of the business cycle, even though Stanley Jevons and at least one other great economist did. But I can't prove to a believer that he's crazy. I can't even prove that Walt Rostow, Jay Forrester, Miyohei Shinohara, Christopher Freedman, and other revivers of the Kondratieff theory of long waves are barking up the wrong tree. That is why, back in

8

1934, my teacher Joseph Schumpeter insisted that Harvard's *Quarterly Journal of Economics* publish a long manuscript on sunspots. "Its statistical methodology," he argued, "is little worse than in articles we do publish and our scientific duty is clear." Schumpeter's conscience is nicer than mine, but one has to face up to an important difference in degree between the certitude that a non-experimental subject can aspire to, relative to a luckier science.

Lest you think sunspots a wayout case, consider the issue of whether higher interest rates will coax out more saving and investment. Theorists know that, when our assets earn more, we may decide we can achieve our old-age needs with lower saving today—even though the prospect of more future chocolates growing from each chocolate abstained from today may, other things equal, tempt us to eat fewer chocolates now. I suppose that in fifty years I've seen fifty inconclusive empirical articles on this vital topic. Doubling the number of inconclusive studies, alas, does not double our knowledge or halve our ignorance. The topic is not hopeless; it deserves further researching; but I can't advise you to hold your breath until we get a good answer to this microeconomic question posed. (Remark: this example is taken from microeconomics, which unlike macroeconomics, is still riding high.)

Here is a hot second topic. Reaganomics has given us an unprecedented budget deficit—perhaps 5 or 6 percent of GNP, of which more than a half is a *structural* not *cyclical* deficit. Neoclassical economics, as well as post-Keynesian economics, suggests to me that this huge Reagan-O'Neill deficit is one important cause of the unusually high real interest rates of the 1980s, and thus one important cause of the dollar's being overvalued on current account with the entailed huge trade deficit.

"Good common sense," you say?—as if common sense and good sense are the same thing. I must remind you that the Regan Treasury produced a study purporting to demonstrate that there is *no* relation between budget deficits and interest rates or exchange rates. On three continents I used to tell audiences that this Treasury memo would not pass peer review and be accepted by any of our economic journals.

9

I was an optimist. Recently the *American Economic Review* published a paper that was worse than the Treasury memo by far; and I have to report to you that the *AER* has the greatest circulation of any of our learned journals. I rest my case that economics still has a way to go on the road to becoming an accurate science—a distillation of agreed-upon public knowledge.

Scientist Inside the Black Box

Actually, an economist like me has some advantages over a physicist or molecular biologist. A physicist cannot say to herself, "What if I were an autumn leaf? How would I blow?" No more can a biologist apply introspection to understand DNA better.

Here is a third case to show that introspection, subjective and treacherous as it can sometimes be, may be an aid to an economic scientist. When Reaganomics began in 1981 to give us those large budget deficits, Robert Barro of the Universities of Chicago and Rochester used modern rational expectationism to argue against the dogma that such deficits will "crowd out" investment and capital formation. In effect he said the following:

> First, the deficit is not really as big as newspapers let on. With the price level rising, the real value of the old public debt is falling to offset in part the new debt being incurred; and the domestic interest burden, swollen by the inflation component, is income to Americans as well as being costs to them.
> But even if there is a net rise in deficit, that will not crowd out investment because we people, realizing that in the future they and their heirs will face extra taxes by virtue of the enhanced public debt, we will increase our savings by as much as the government is perpetrating dissaving—just as David Ricardo argued back around 1820.

How would you appraise this argument in 1981? In 1985, after four years of Kemp-Laffer-Reaganomics?

Hindsight is easier than foresight. The crude facts of economic history are that saving rates did *not* rise after 1981. They now seem low, as low as they

10

have been in history. So to speak, we have had almost a controlled experiment like one in a chemist's laboratory, and the result has not seemed favorable to Ricardo-Barro rational expectations.

Before the fact, here is how I reacted in 1981 to the Barro argument. I offered myself up as a guinea pig. I am more reflective than most pigs, and go whole hours thinking about my heirs. The Reagan tax programs that I voted against, it seemed to me in 1981, were signals that I, my heirs, and others at the affluent end of the wealth pyramid would probably be paying *less* of the total tax burden than in the past when marginal tax rates were 70 percent, 77 percent, and even 91 percent. Rather than thinking about belt tightening, I was induced by Reaganomics to turn the pages of the Sears catalog looking for more luxurious jackknives and baubles.

The first moral then is that we did not really have a controlled experiment in which only the deficit was made to change.

More important than this, though, was the following chain of reasoning that went on in my mind: "My purpose in making bequests is to help my numerous children live a little better than their peers. I can't turn them into Rockefellers or Rothschilds. If tax rates have to be higher in 1999 and 2019 because Ronald Reagan, in order to keep downward pressure on welfare spending programs, refuses to raise tax rates now, then my children will only be in the same boat as those who inherit nothing. No need for me to save now in anticipation of next century's tax load."

Finally, I have learned not to put undue weight on my own idiosyncratic introspections. As I listened to the Barro arguments, I recalled little talk of extra bequests down at the club next to the swimming pool. Nor did lawyer and accountant friends report new queues of activist clients. So, prior to knowing the facts of 1982-5, my judgment prepared me for what turns out to have transpired.

Introspection can nominate hypotheses. In the last analysis it is the facts that judge them. Franco Modigliani's statistical rejections of the Barro supposition are of course more important than any personal ruminations.

11

The Dream That Failed

There is an old Chinese proverb that extolls the merit of econometric measurement over *a priori* speculating. "One peek is worth a thousand finesses"—or as Robert Bishop reminds me, "is worth *two* finesses." Economics has made great strides in statistical methodology during my time. On the honor roll in this regard are such names as Henry Schultz, Harold Hotelling, Jan Tinbergen, Simon Kuznets, Ragnar Frisch, Trygve Haavelmo, Tjalling Koopmans, Herman Wold, R. A. Fisher, Jerzi Neyman, Abraham Wald, L. J. Savage, Jacob Marschak, James Tobin, Lawrence Klein, Henri Theil and many others. The statistical tools appropriate for agricultural experimentation had to be augmented to handle the time series of uncontrolled observations and cross-sectional surveys.

Boy and man I have watched this progress with measured hope and have deplored criticism of the effort by Keynes and less educated practical people. I did not expect perfection. But back in 1940 if you had told me of the goodies that were to come in high-speed computers, data bases and sample surveys, I would have been optimistic that many of our basic controversies could by now be brought to an end by means of empirical testing.

That of course has not happened. Nor does it look likely to happen in the foreseeable future. Quarterly time series covering several decades and involving scores of variables, it turns out, just do not have the power to settle the questions that arise in connection with economists' behavior functions.

The Lack-of-Consensus Libel

In order to preserve time for a valuable period of questioning from the floor, I shall bring to a close what could be an endless series of methodological observations. My final topic will deal with the alleged propensity of economists never to agree on anything.

You know the tired jokes. "Five economists, six opinions: two from Mr. Keynes." "If you laid all the economists end to end, they'd still not reach a conclusion." So forth, and so forth *ad nauseam*.

Actually, as I have many times observed, the truth is the reverse of this. Economists, if anything,

12

are *too much alike* in their expectations. The standard deviation between their views is miniscule compared to the standard deviation of their departures from the true facts.

It was President Harry Truman who is supposed to have said in exasperation: "What I want is a one-handed economist." For him, none of this pussy-footing "On the one hand this, on the other hand that." Princes think that it is sure-thing advice that they need. I have to say: "Sire, with respect, it is not one-handed economists you need. For in our subject, one-handed economists come in two varieties: those with only a right hand; and those with a left hand only. And then, Sire, you need a two-handed economist like me to adjudicate between them and calibrate the quantitative odds concerning possible outcomes."

Once in a *Newsweek* column I wrote an unkind thing about a prominent contemporary economist: "The good fairies," I said, "gave him the gifts of cleverness, erudition, and originality—every good endowment save, alas, the most important gift of all, the gift of 'maybe.'" In an economist this is no small lack. For the whole corpus of economic science, it can, however, be fruitful to have one overzealous scientist. The wolf pack can cut the lone tiger down to size.

My teacher at Harvard, Gottfried Haberler, who is still going strong in his eighty-sixth year, once defended himself against the charge of being an eclectic, saying, "How do you know Mother Nature isn't ecletic?" Paradoxically, it is an art to be properly scientific.

There is much still to know in economics. I say this in humility and arrogance. The humility part needs no amplification. The great scholars I have most admired—the Knut Wicksells and not the Gustav Cassels—have had an informed if not arrogant knowledge about our true scientific ignorances. And theirs has been the greater fun of neither claiming too much nor too little. The pleasure of testing critically their own theories they have not given away to others but have selfishly reserved for themselves—advice I press on new students.

In the long run we are all dead, yes. But in science good work lasts longest.

586

HOW *FOUNDATIONS* CAME TO BE

If there are people born under a lucky star, there must be books that are lucky too. *Foundations of Economic Analysis* (Samuelson, 1947) was one such. Unlike a biological embryo, this work had no definite moment of conception. Gradually, over the period 1936 to 1941, it got itself evolved. As I was mastering the existent corpus of economic theory, I recognized that a limited number of qualitative truths obtained, along with a greater number of indefinite relationships. Puzzled to understand this, I ransacked the mathematical libraries of Chicago and Harvard to explain to myself what made the difference. Reading widely I was a child of my time, but it was the *internal* logic of the economic puzzles that guided *Foundations*' growth.

When you read biographies and obituaries of scholars, they fall into a few familiar patterns. The most interesting--like Albert Einstein's or Knut Wicksell's--are cases of early adversity and then final irresistible triumphs. My autobiography is of the duller kind. I began as a precocious infant, with unusually early conscious memories. Parents and two brothers were congenially supportive. Though it was fashionable to hate school, I loved it. Early bloomers develop ridiculous heights of self-confidence, not realizing that even the duller academic scholars have above-average I.Q.'s.

By accident the public schools I attended--in Gary, Indiana and Chicago--were unusually good ones that turned out many future scholars and scientists. By chance of geography, I went to the University of Chicago at a young age and under its experimental New Hutchins Plan I got a deep and wide undergraduate education. By chance my freshman courses included economics under Aaron Director (1901- !), who was later to be founder of the *second* Chicago School of Milton Friedman, George Stigler and Gary Becker. In that academic year of 1931-1932, although I didn't know it at the time, Chicago was the leading world center *for neoclassical economics*: next in the hierarchy would probably have come the London School of Economics, Cambridge University, and Columbia University. Harvard, then as now, was the greatest university in the world; but with the 1929 death of Allyn Young and the aging of Frank Taussig, its theory was then in a lean period.

The stars at Chicago's First School in economics were Frank Knight, Jacob Viner, Henry Schultz, Paul Douglas and Henry Simons. As an undergraduate I came to know them all well. A legend grew about an un-selfconscious teenager who used to correct the omniscient Jacob Viner on the topography of his graduate seminar blackboard diagrams.

Given my way I would have stayed at Chicago forever. Why leave Nirvana? However, by chance, that happened to be the year when the Social Science Research Council began an educational experiment: they would scour America for the eight best economics undergraduates and generously underwrite their several years of graduate study. (Later I learned from the late Frank Fetter--Fetter the younger--that he had been the examiner who discovered me: success, President Kennedy observed, has a thousand fathers; failure is an orphan.) There was just one catch to the awards: you could not stay where you had done your undergraduate study. So my choice reduced effectively to Columbia or Harvard. My Chicago mentors recommended the Columbia of Wesley Mitchell, John Maurice Clark and Harold Hotelling. Never one to follow slavishly the advice of mentors, I opted for Harvard. (Joseph Schumpeter and Wassily Leontief were not my magnets: at Chicago Schumpeter was known as the eccentric who believed the rate of interest would be zero in the stationary state. Edward H. Chamberlin of monopolistic competition fame, by my miscalculation, attracted me to Harvard; but more important was my naive notion that Cambridge, Massachusetts would be a peaceful green village where book learning could explode.)

As mentioned, again by good chance, Harvard economics was just then awakening from a fallow period of sleepiness. New European blood--Schumpeter, Leontief, Gottfried Haberler--plus soon-to-come Alvin Hansen, the "American Keynes," was beginning to make Harvard the mecca for advanced economic research. Perhaps most relevant of all for the genesis of *Foundations*, Edwin Bidwell Wilson (1879-1964) was at Harvard. Wilson was the great Willard Gibbs's last (and, essentially, only) protégé at Yale. He was a mathematician, a mathematical physicist, a mathematical statistician, a mathematical economist, a polymath who had done first-class work in many fields of the natural and social sciences. I was perhaps his only disciple: in 1935-1936, Abram Bergson, Sidney Alexander, Joseph Schumpeter, and I were the only students in his mathematical economics seminar. (Our ages were 21, 19, 52, and 20.) Aside from the fact that E.B. knew everything and everybody, his great virtue was his contempt for social scientists who aped the more exact sciences in a parrot-like way. He detested pseudo-learning and debunked many a pretentious theory (such as the Pearl-Verhulst infatuation with the *logistic curve* in demography). I was vaccinated early to understand that economics and physics could share the same formal mathematical theorems (Euler's theorem on homogeneous functions, Weierstrass's theorems on constrained maxima, Jacobi determinant identities underlying LeChatelier reactions, etc.), while still not resting on the same empirical foundations and certainties.

Publications flowed merrily from my pen. It was my good luck to be appointed as the first proper economist to Harvard's prestigious Society of Fellows--24 youthful princes in all fields, free to work on whatever they liked, but forbidden for three years to work toward any degree or Ph.D. dissertation. For me those 1937-1940 years were veritable heaven, and had I been offered the Faustian bargain of staying a Junior Fellow forever, I would have joyfully embraced it.

This explains how citations of my journal articles had won me in my early twenties an international reputation as a comer. Their topics were diverse: capital theory, lifecycle saving, utility theory, international trade, Keynesian multiplier-accelerator dynamics, revealed preference, and much else. Miraculously it dawned on me that there was some unity of method and logic underlying much of these researches as well as much of current and historical economic theory.

In mid-1940 my Society of Fellows prohibition against writing a Ph.D. dissertation expired. Harvard's original Senior Fellows--President A. Lawrence Lowell, Alfred North Whitehead, John Livingston Lowes, and Lawrence J. Henderson--had launched the Society as a vendetta to reform the mediocre American Ph.D. system. My colleagues as Junior Fellows--Willard van Quine, the mathematical logician; George Birkhoff, the founder of lattice theory mathematics; Harry Levin, the youthful doyen of comparative literature--each deigned not to become Doctors of Philosophy. Their Harvard careers never suffered from this. My Protestant wife, Marion Crawford, and I decided to follow the prudent course of taking a Ph.D. degree. Lucky that we did, or perhaps *Foundations* might have been pushed off my agenda by the outflow of new publishable ideas.

From mid-1940 to January 1941, I composed and rearranged at fever pace; some got dictated to Marion, all got typed in first draft by her even though she was a graduate-school economist in her own right. Although I have always insisted that *Foundations* was formulated on Harvard grounds, before degree time I was an Assistant Professor at MIT. With or without a Ph.D., I was not to get an early tenure offer from Harvard and, without malice, I revealed a preference for MIT. To everyone's surprise, including my own, that turned out to be the happiest decision of my life.

A learned treatise, like a poem, stands on its own bottom or text. *Ad hominem* gabble about its author is at best secondary. The times were ripe for *Foundations*. Nature abhors a vacuum, and *Foundations* helped fill the vacuum. I have written elsewhere about how much there was back in the 1930s waiting to be discovered, and aching to be codified. I was like a fisher for trout in a virginal Canadian brook. You had only to cast your line and the fish jumped to meet your hook.

Let me give a few examples. Jacob Viner (1931) made a famous error, when his draftsman Y.K. Wong refused to draw a family of *descending* U-shaped cost curves with a lower envelope that went through their bottoms. Viner was ever after sensitive, but he conceded his error. That same Viner (1929), in a discussion of his hero David Ricardo, had discovered that the domestic price ratio of cloth to wheat, P_C/P_W, was as much equal to their respective (Marginal Cost in *Land*)$_C$/(Marginal Cost in *Land*)$_W$ as it was to (Marginal Cost in *Labour*)$_C$/(Marginal Cost in *Labour*)$_W$. Viner sensed that this in the deepest sense invalidated the hoary Labour Theory of Value, a truth not understood by David Ricardo, Piero Sraffa, or George Stigler. But Viner never connected this insight with what I waggishly called in *Foundations* the Wong-Viner *Envelope* Theorem. Actually, that theorem is a kaleidoscope which yields multiple insights: the direction of change of a maximum system when an external parameter gets perturbed; the LeChatelier theorem on constrained variables; the duality property that makes Lagrange-multipliers measure optimizing prices (and marginal costs or utilities).

In postwar years I used to receive letters from all over the world reporting groups of students who met in teams to puzzle out the contents of *Foundations*. Memorable is the London-Cambridge cell that included Jan de Van Graaff, Harry Johnson, Will Baumol, and Frank Hahn: soldiers of destiny on their way to destiny.

Even the book's mistakes generated a history. When I was apprised of a double error of sign in a LeChatelier-Jacobi determinant, I would write back: "Congratulations! You are the seventeenth non-Japanese to notice this."

The book won Harvard's David A. Wells Prize in 1941 for best publishable thesis. Because an earlier winner had pocketed the money but never revised his manuscript, I was required to submit my revised draft. Alas, World War II came to U.S. shores via Pearl Harbor. Nights and Sundays, while working on radar and mathematical fire control at the Radiation Laboratory, I toiled over revisions and expansions. By 1944 I handed in the finished draft. Harvard's long-time Economics Department Chairman was no admirer of me; long before, he had counseled me against working in economic theory before I had reached (his) ripe old age of 50+. Once a month I checked that the manuscript still gathered dust in the anteroom of Economics headquarters. That was an unintentional boon to me: a wartime publication would have been an anti-climax before any climax.

Less lucky was the department Chairman's decision to have a first printing of only 500 copies. I objected. We compromised on 750 copies. But he had the last word. His orders were to destroy all that beautiful mathematical type after the first run. When the first printing sold out immediately, all subsequent printings had to be done by photo offset. This turned out to be just as well for a busy author who had no relish for proofreading complicated mathematics.

Young authors expect a respectable demand for their brainchild. I was no exception. But I never dreamed of the repeated printings that were to come, the paperback editions, or the many translations into foreign languages. I decided not to revise the text, instead merely correcting any errors brought to my attention. (They were relatively few and trivial: reversed algebraic signs; an occasional treacherous double limit. However, early in 1997, one new one got reported to me: it was an inexplicable error alleging that when one of many independent utilities involved a permissible *rising* marginal utility, then that good could have negative income elasticity. The gentle Leontief would have horsewhipped me in my first Harvard year for so crude a slip!)

When *Foundations* was 35 years old, I finally agreed to an enlarged edition. Rather than tamper with the original text, I added a second part that almost doubled the book's length. I wrote compactly to cover three decades of exploding new results. It was good stuff. A good deal of it was deeper than much of the original. But the result was dramatic confirmation of my suspicion that *Foundations*' success came from its being the needed exposition for its time. The new stone caused no great ripples in the pond of modern mainstream economics. By 1983 we were all, so to speak, mathematical economists; and several hundred specialized books were available to cover each corner of up-to-date economics.

This is as it should be. Soft and hard sciences are cumulative disciplines. We each bring our contributions of "value added" to the pot of progress. In Max Planck's much-quoted words: Science progresses funeral by funeral. Inside tomorrow's physics treatise will be the lasting truths of Isaac Newton and also of the professor who works down the hall from you. Something of the same goes for economics, where often the dance must proceed Two Steps Forward and One Step Back.

Some fool (it was Henry Ford) has said, History is bunk. Actually good history does debunk, by means of detailed reporting, the mystiques of scientific biography. "The lone genius toiling in a garret, and producing the Mona Lisa," that kind of gush. What was the background knowledge that led to *Foundations*? John Livingston Lowes, in his classic *The Road to Xanadu*, perused the books Samuel Taylor Coleridge was known to have read. The library withdrawal records at Chicago's Harper Library and Harvard's Widener and Baker libraries would be an unreliable source for my 1932-1941 readings. I lived and breathed economics much of those days' 24 hours. What this autodidact learned (belatedly) came from auditing math lectures and reading while standing up deep in the stacks of Widener Library. Edward Gibbon had the seat of an historian; I had the feet of a zealot.

By the time I came to Harvard, though I was still too young to vote, I had taken more varied courses in economics than my fellow students would attend in all their graduate study: labor economics, economic history (both European and American), public finance, money and banking (there was no macro then), business cycles, statistics, everything but agricultural economics. Fellow students--our true teachers--included at Chicago, George Stigler, Albert Hart, Allen Wallis, Milton Friedman, Jacob Mosak; at Harvard Abram Bergson, Shigeto Tsuru, Robert Triffin, Wolfgang Stolper, Richard Musgrave, Sidney Alexander, Joe Bain, Alice Bourneuf, Lloyd Metzler, John Lintner, Robert Bishop, Paul and Alan Sweezy, Richard Goodwin, Henry Wallich, James Tobin, Evsey Domar, Walter and William Salant, Emile Despres, Robert Solow, ...; the list is endless. As I later wrote: "Yes, Harvard made us. But it is we who made Harvard." The Cambridge, Massachusetts which had begun as Keynes-hostile, ended up as the chosen place to spend your postwar sabbatical year. It came to supplant Oslo and Rotterdam, the London School of Economics and Cambridge, England. Had I remained on the Chicago Midway, I might well have missed out on the three revolutions that remade mainstream economics: the Keynesian revolution, the imperfect-competition revolution, and the mathematical-economics revolution. Instead I had a front-row seat. In races, once you get a lead you have only to run as fast as the rest to stay up front. (In my own sober self-audit, my 500-odd collected scientific papers outweigh for me all textbook bestsellers or *Newsweek* columns or governmental testimonies.)

I. The Revealed Preference Story

In 1938 I had proposed a novel paradigm of "revealed preference." For the 2-good case this could provide a *complete* description of *all* the observable (and testable, and refutable) empirical (price, quantity) data of a coherent demand system. As an example, it could prove, for as many as n-1 out of n goods, there could be *negative* income elasticity at any specified income and prices; and that an own price elasticity, $(\Delta \log q_i/\Delta \log p_i)_{I,p_j}$, could be Giffen *positive* for any such "inferior" good and *only* for such. Also, *necessarily* $\partial q_i/\partial p_i \leq q_i(\partial q_i/\partial I) \gtreqless 0$ for *all* goods. It could also deduce cogently that q_j demands remain invariant when all prices double (or halve) at the same time that nominal expendable income doubles (or halves). These stated results are essentially the *only* and the *exhaustive* empirical content of received preference-maximization formulations. As I have reported, my revealed-preference innovation came from a marriage between Haberler-Könus index number theory and Gibbs finite-difference formulations of classical phenomenological thermodynamics of the 1870s.

My approach looked backward in summarizing "economically" (in the Mach-Vienna Circle sense) the "meaningful" (testable and, in principle, refutable) core of constrained-budget demand theory. It could do so without mention of "mind" or "brain" or "introspection." It had no explicit need for a utility metric by which beans could be judged to yield twice the utils of peas; or for statements like "My love for Mary exceeds that for Jane in exactly the degree that my love for Jane exceeds that for Fifi." In non-stochastic conditions, I cared not whether the observed demander was risk-neutral or risk-averting or risk-relishing.

My good day's work was well rewarded. My Master, Professor Schumpeter, oh-ed and ah-ed. But in *Foundations* I chose to downplay this paradigm. One reason was substantive. For more than two goods, n ≥ 3, my so-called Weak Axiom was recognized to be *necessary* but *not* to be alone *sufficient* to deduce *transitivity* of preferences. It could not rule out "Jones chooses (3 rye, 2 corn, 2 peas) over (2 rye, 2 corn, 3 peas) and chooses (2 rye, 2 corn, 3 peas) over (2 rye, 3 corn, 2 peas); but also (!) chooses (2 rye, 3 corn, 2 peas) over the initial (3 rye, 2 corn, 2 peas)!" For n > 2 goods, *always* satisfying the Weak Axiom as *applied pair by pair* could, in the most general case, decidedly lead to a *transitivity contradiction* -- if not after three comparisons then after 3,333 comparisons. (This could not occur if Jones really did adhere to a transitive partial preference ordering.) What was needed to be added to the Weak Axiom so that (p_j, q_j) observable-data tests could be strengthened to their maximal extent? Young Hendrik Houthakker (1950) on his own in Holland later supplied the needed Strong Axiom. Already in 1938, before I could know of Houthakker, I had conjectured that it might be enough to specify that "no chain of weak-axiom rulings can ever lead to a contradiction like (A weak-revealed better than B, B weak-revealed better than C, ..., Y revealed better than Z--but Z weak-revealed better than A!)." I propounded this conjecture to two of the best young mathematicians anywhere: Stan Ulam and Lynn Loomis, Harvard Junior Fellows of my time. (Ulam later invented for Teller the American hydrogen bomb at Los Alamos; Loomis, knowing nothing of game theory, after hearing John von Neumann issue a challenge for an algebraic, non-topological proof of his [1928] two-person, zero-sum game theorem, went home and found the needed proof that night.) But, as I have discovered in life, the great pure mathematicians I have known, except for John Nash, sensibly resist concentrating on puzzles arising from esoteric fields like economics. At the time *Foundations* went to press, the revealed preference paradigm still lacked completion.

The second reason I soft-pedaled claims for it went deeper and remained after Houthakker's *tour de force*. The Samuelson-Houthakker paradigm, α, properly exposited, became equal in empirical meaning to the indifference field approach of Pareto-Allen-Hicks-Hotelling, β; and equal to the ordinal-utility formulation of Eugen Slutsky (1915) or John Hicks (1939), γ; and equal to a Kenneth Arrow (1959) lattice-theory partial ordering, δ. When members of a class are equal, each is *first* among equals. Also, each is *last* among equals. Why debate the different merits of essential equals? Since the δ version is the most "intuitive" one, be satisfied when you demonstrate that α does exhaust *all* the valid empirical content of $(\alpha, \beta, \gamma, \delta)$.

Professor E. Roy Weintraub (1983) has astutely recognized that Samuelson's (1938) Weak Axiom was already in Abraham Wald's (1934-35) second paper on determinateness of Walras-Cassel-Schlesinger general equilibrium. But I did not in 1938 "refine" that: as often mentioned, my approach arose from considering Haberlerian restrictions that apply to Laspeyres and Paasche quantity index numbers for a "rational consumer." Wald's arose from a search for a set of sufficient conditions to guarantee uniqueness of equilibrium; if I had known Wald's paper and had had the wit to see in it the Weak Axiom, I would certainly have invoked the prestige of Wald's name to help sell the Weak Axiom to readers.

It has been said that no good deed goes unpunished. As a result of my (uncharacteristic) modesty in playing down revealed preference in *Foundations*, some writers have suspected some failure in the paradigm. On reflection, thanks to Houthakker, all I hoped for (or could rationally have hoped for) was attained by it.

Revealed preference, aside from looking backward to consolidate and elucidate received doctrines, inadvertently looked ahead into the finite-mathematics of inequality-duality relationships that formed the modern Age of Debreu in economics. Gibbs led me to the promised land before there was a promised land. Indeed, among my alternative 1938 formulations (with respect to ">" or "≥"), can be found valid relations applicable to admissible specifications of *non-convex* sets. (Example: If a good *never* displays *negative* income elasticity, it can never display a *positive* [Giffen] own-price elasticity--even if indifference contours cease to be convex and demand functions are neither single-valued nor uniquely invertible.)[1]

II. Admired Influences

Who were the major writers influencing *Foundations*? They were many and various. E. Roy Weintraub (1989, 1991) suggests that there is some mystery here, even maybe some cover up. Interested readers will want to compare the following paragraphs with his account and with earlier memoirs by me.

First, my heroes in economics were scholars such as Léon Walras, Antoine Augustin Cournot, Francis Edgeworth, Vilfredo Pareto, Irving Fisher, and Knut Wicksell. (This was after my infantile infatuation with Frank Knight simmered down to measured respect for a brilliant but erratic economist and theologian.) Among working economists during the 1930s, John Hicks and Ragnar Frisch (two very different egoists) got most attention from me. (In my 1932 Chicago freshman year, my tutor Eugene Staley told me that John Maynard Keynes was then the world's greatest economist. This was after the *Treatise on Money* (1930) but before *The General Theory* (1936). I had no reason to disagree. In 1936 at Harvard, Assistant Professor John M. Cassels told me that John Hicks was the world's leading *younger* economist. I could believe that based on the *Theory of Wages* (1932) and the Hicks-Allen (1934) collaboration. Allen, who visited Harvard,

---

[1] Prior to Houthakker, for $n > 2$, I tended to side with Roy G.D. Allen rather than with Hicks's insistence upon integrability. Why not be general and be happy to posit non-integrability and global non-transitivity? In those cases, only the Weak Axiom could be validly posited as a constraint on empirical demand observations. My reading of Griffith Evans (1930), Allen (1932), and Nicholas Georgescu-Roegen (1936) softened me up for such a half-way house compromise. But, Freudianly, that was perhaps making a virtue of necessity. Once Houthakker delivered me from such necessity, in a 1950 exchange with Herman Wold I lost my tolerance for *global* intransitivity, which came to smack of uninteresting formalism for its own sake. See Stanley Wong (1978) for related discussions. A reader of Philip Mirowski (1989) may find some difficulty in reconciling remarks there and remarks here.

Remark: The deep points raised by Dr. Wong can, I believe, be argued out in the 2-good case without prejudice to their evaluations. Presence or lack of presence of Giovanni Antonelli's (1886) observable integrability conditions introduce interesting technical points but Wong's preoccupations will remain to be addressed even when integrability is assured (as in the 2-good case).

became a good friend and I always thought he received too little credit. Jan Tinbergen was an admired role model and I approved when Frisch and Tinbergen shared the first Nobel Prize in 1969.)

In 1935 Alfred Marshall still ruled the roost in fame. What goes up too far comes down too low. Like Gustav Cassel's, his textbook filled a real need; but, like Isaac Newton, he had an inhibiting influence on two generations of followers. Marshall never lived up to his potential, for reasons of health and temperament. Before 1890 he knew the defects in his own constructs (consumers surplus, partial equilibrium, ...) but never did he follow up with the needed improvements. As Whitehead said to me, "Marshall was more Popish than saintly. We liked Mary Paley Marshall better."

When I came to know John and Ursula Hicks well, I said to him: "I have the best of both worlds. I know your work and know my own, too." In this relative neglect of other scholars Hicks was even-handed. For him the sun rose when he opened his eyes. He wrote well and lectured badly. In Britain, Hicks's originality and breadth never received its full due, perhaps in part for reasons of personality and of "political incorrectness." Hicks's *Value and Capital* (1939) was an expository *tour de force* of great originality, which built up a readership for the problems *Foundations* grappled with and for the explosion of mathematical economics that soon came.

III. Mysteries Deciphered

In this English version of my published German essay (Jurg Niehans, *et al.*, 1997), I can be brief on certain queries that over the years have arisen about *Foundations*. (1) Why does it seem to say nought about use of a Lyapunov Function that ever decreases towards a zero rendezvous at the equilibrium asymptote of a dynamic system, and thereby deprive itself of a classic method of proving damped stability of an economic system? (2) Herbert Simon (1959) and Joel Cohen (1987) have noted that Paul Samuelson was an admirer of Alfred Lotka the mathematical biologist; but did he covertly owe more to Lotka than is explicitly acknowledged in footnotes and bibliographic references? (3) How important an influence on Samuelson was the Gibbsian biochemist L.J. Henderson at the Society of Fellows and in connection with his Pareto cell at Harvard? E. Roy Weintraub (1989, 1991) has nominated questions like these and assayed in a lengthy article on *Foundations*' dynamics to provide them with critical answers. Interested readers may be referred to my German text's detailed attempts to provide dialogue on these topics. Here I can be brief.

1. I did not use the *name* "Lyapunov Function" in stability analysis for a simple reason: not until World War II did I know that *name* for this 1892-and-earlier technique. But repeatedly *Foundations* did use such Lyapunov Functions, roses by whatever name. Thus, from J.W.S. Rayleigh's monumental *Theory of Sound* (1870), I had early learned to prove stability in the following fashion:

(1) $\quad x + a\dot{x} + x = 0 \to \frac{1}{2}\dot{x}x + \frac{1}{2}a\dot{x}^2 + \frac{1}{2}\dot{x}x = 0$

$$\to (d/dt)[\dot{x}^2 + x^2] = -\frac{1}{2}a\dot{x}^2 < 0 \text{ for } a > 0.$$

The above bracketed expression is a Lyapunov Function that ever declines toward zero, thereby entailing $[(x(t) \ \dot{x}(t)] \to [0 \ 0]$ as $t \to \infty$.

Similarly, *Foundations* repeatedly studied gradient motions:

(2) $\quad \dot{x}_i = a\partial F(x_1,...x_n)/\partial x_i, \ 0, \ i = 1,2,...,n; \ a > 0.$

For F, a *strictly* concave function with a maximum at $(\bar{x}_j) = (0)$,

(3) $\quad \lim_{t \to \infty} [x_1(t) \ ... \ x_n(t)] = [0 \ ... \ 0]$

by virtue of strict concavity's entailing the following Lyapunov Function relations:

(4) $\quad \dot{F}(x_1,...,x_n) - \dot{F}(\bar{x}_1,...,\bar{x}_n) = \sum_1^n x_j \partial F/\partial x_j < 0.$

Again, *Foundations* innovated the then new concept of *quasi-definiteness* for an n^2 matrix $[a_{ij}]$, and demonstrated by Lyapunov Function reasoning that

(5) $\quad \dot{x}_i = -\sum_1^n a_{ij}x_j, \ [a_{ij} + a_{ji}] = a^S, \text{ pos.def.}$

is locally and globally stable. My German text gives page references that dispel mystery about a failure in *Foundations* to employ the rudimentary Lyapunov technique. My actual 1947 explicit references to Alexander Lyapunov, Emile Picard and Birkhoff had mostly to do with the more delicate cases of borderline stability related to measure-preserving conservative Hamiltonian and more general systems; prior to the 1960s breakthroughs in *chaos* theory, I in the late 1930s was too unsophisticated to grapple with Henri Poincaré, George Birkhoff, Edward Lorenz and Stephen Smale subtleties.

2. My major benefit from Lotka came in connection with *dynamics* (as for example his autonomous one-sex population growth model, and his Lotka-Volterra predator-prey model). My three Lotka references came *appropriately* late in the book because dynamics came late. See the German text for more detail on my admiration for Lotka. Here I need only stress that it was his *physical*-reductionist biology that interested me, and this is far removed from Marshall's palaver about a biological paradigm in economics. A century on, it is Darwin-Lotka-Fisher-Haldane-Wright-Hamilton mechanisms that have made some progress in economics.

3. My relation to the Pareto-Henderson-Homans-Curtis coterie at the Society of Fellows can be simply put. These turned out to be purely social. I went but once to the famous Henderson sociology seminar. That was either once too many or many too few. When I would want to talk about Gibbs to Henderson, he would prefer to enumerate

the shortcomings of Franklin Delano Roosevelt. In 1937 it was a case of Henderson's being too old or Samuelson's being too young; or both. My guarded admiration for Pareto the economist has been great; but during the vogue for his sociology, I stayed out to lunch. (For the complete section published in the German version, see "The Weintraub Effort" appended here.)

IV. The Road Not Taken

Foundations, for the most part, had a unifying theme: how and why one could predict with qualitative certainty the direction of change for an optimizing *maximal* variable when its exogenous price in the bilinear product ...--$p_j q_j$--... is perturbed upward. Chapter 3 outlined the general deductive logic; Chapter 4 applied it to cost minimization and supply response; Chapters 5-7 handled the implications for constrained-budget demand optimization. Had I been a strict constitutionalist, I might well have stopped there. The result would have been a shorter 200-page book with one fully-integrated theme.

Young men in a hurry are prone to want to tell all they know (and sometimes we overshoot!). It seemed a pity not to add an eighth chapter which would explicate, à la Bergson, for the great pioneers in "modern" welfare economics--Arthur C. Pigou, Lionel Robbins, Hotelling, Hicks, Nicholas Kaldor, Pareto, Tibor Scitovsky, John Stuart Mill, Ian Little, John Harsanyi, ... (note the admixture of nineteenth century savants, 1930s pioneers, and writers not yet born in the *ante bellum status quo*)--their *own* meanings. Having, in King Alphonso's words, "been present at the creation," I understood precisely the clarification achieved for welfare economics by Bergson's (1938) magisterial synthesis. Using the words the poet Alexander Pope addressed to Newton, I later wrote,

> Ethics and Ethics' laws lay hid in night:
> God said, "Let Bergson be!"
> And all was light.

Bergson's Welfare Function of Individualistic Type made clear for Hicks and Kaldor--had they deigned to pay heed--exactly how their Mill-Pareto Optimality calculus (in which winners can overcompensate losers) fits in with exogenously prescribed interpersonal value norms. Responsive to Geoffrey Chaucer's, "And gladly teach," I composed Chapter 8's exposition of Bergsonian welfare economics even though that strayed from early chapters' central theme. Ralph Waldo Emerson and Albert Einstein would have approved: consistency can be a hobgoblin; and elegance is indeed for tailors rather than serious scholars.

One liberty begets another. I could not resist the temptation to add Part Two on *dynamics*, even though much of my focus there was on "macroeconomics" (a word not yet coined by Erik Lindahl, Peter de

Wolff, or Lawrence Klein). No one associates a Keynesian system with a maximizing single mind or even to an as-if-pretend maximizing system. Yet from consideration of *The General Theory*'s (1936) "stable" dynamics, one could predict that a rise in the propensity to invest would increase, not lower, underemployment equilibrium output and GNP. Why that might be possible needed to be researched in the late 1930s. Catastrophe theory and chaos theory were not yet born or reborn in the math literature, but I caught a look at heuristic "correspondence" between dampening in dynamics and qualitative direction of (comparative-statics) equilibrium responses to exogenous perturbations. "If one's reach cannot exceed one's grasp," what is innovating for?[2]

In retrospect, I have never regretted not taking the road not taken. *Foundations* came a bit too late to be responsible for the first J.B. Clark Medal of the AEA in 1947. But it is a safe guess that it did accelerate a 1970 Nobel Prize that came, if anything, a little too early for Platonic justice.

V. Finale

The above memoir was written *before* I could read the many kind words of Schefold, Niehans and von Weizsäcker. As Dr. Samuel Johnson observed, those who communicate at a birthday party are not strictly under oath. Nonetheless among the compliments were just qualifications: thus, Niehans and Schefold are right to hint that the heuristic "correspondence principle" failed to develop the scope of the "maximizing principles." And von Weizsäcker, himself a deep analyst of Marxian and non-Marxian capital theories, is all too correct in the observation that my demonstrations on the confusions and sterilities of the Marxian novelties--equalized rates of surplus values, the transformation problem as simply an initial return by Marx back from his *Mehrwert cul de sac* to the bourgeois square one--has had few converts on the Left. Still, like Galileo, I mutter under my breath the symbolic, "But it does move."

---

[2] In reading this essay, Robert Solow remarks on the surprising absence of general equilibrium as an explicit topic in *Foundations*. Why? I reconstruct memory of my then state of mind as follows. When many folks are alike with (quasi-concave, smooth) tastes, and like initial endowments of goods, it is easily provable that a general equilibrium would exist and be unique. From 1879 on, Marshall and I knew that the exchange equilibrium need not be unique when tastes and/or endowments differed; but I sensed topologically that at least one equilibrium existed. (Only later, from Gerard Debreu, did I realize that "almost always" the number of possible equilibria would be finite.) From Irving Fisher (1892) and Wicksell (1893), Franz Zeuthen (1933), Hans Neisser (1932), Heinrich v. Stackleberg (1933) and Hicks (1931), I understood the Schlesinger-Wald duality relation, according to which a good's non-negative price would be zero when its supply was redundant. And from early Pareto I had learned that a competitive equilibrium could support any defined feasible normative optimum à la Adam Smith. So with the naive optimism of youth I didn't know enough to miss the fixed-point theorems of Debreu-Arrow (1954) and Lionel McKenzie (1959).

* * *

Worse than an ungrateful child is an ungrateful parent. And I have many times been a grateful parent. At its Fiftieth Birthday, I hail *Foundations of Economic Analysis*: PARENS GRATVS FILIO PERGRATO GRATIAS AGIT.

Appendix

The Weintraub Effort

One of the most detailed discussions of *Foundations*, most specifically of its dynamics, is given in E. Roy Weintraub (1989, 1991). It makes some valid points but I will comment briefly on some questionable issues it raises. For brevity I will paraphrase in numbered statements what any fair-minded reader will construe to be what Professor Weintraub's text is contending. (His circulated 1989 draft is even more accusatory.)

1. Samuelson's early autobiographical accounts, particularly Samuelson (1972), give a rhetorical account involving both brash posturing and pretended Olympian detachments--a typical creating of a mythic past by elderly scholars whose accounts are the Caesarian, "I came, I saw, I conquered."

2. Insufficiently noticed is the biological stimulus to *Foundations*, and particularly Samuelson's deep dependencies on A.J. Lotka, which is insufficiently acknowledged (only "three" cited references, and all of them "late" in *Foundations*).

3. *Foundations* defectively handles Lyapunov's (1892) stellar techniques for analyzing dynamic "stability" of a system of differential equations, despite Samuelson's (imperfect) citings of Emile Picard's classic treatise.

4. Besides the self-evident influences on Samuelson of Edwin Bidwell Wilson, a mathematician mentor at Harvard, Dr. Weintraub wishes to nominate emphasis on influences from Harvard's mathematician George Birkhoff, Harvard's biochemist L.J. Henderson and Henderson's circle of 1930s enthusiasts for Pareto (including the Brahmin sociologist George Homans).

I could list further less important points, some of which are given stronger form in Weintraub's circulated 1989 draft of his 1991 paper. Here are my comments on the above-numbered paraphrases.

1. A close reader of the Samuelson (1972) and Weintraub (1991) texts will, I believe, detect nothing substantive in the latter that evidentially justifies any of the stated innuendos. At best it is a case of "I do not like your style, Dr. Fell/The reason why I cannot tell/... ." I boasted of no kissings that never took place. Among economics authors I have been known, comically known, for my fulsome attributions to numerous earlier scholars--"freight train" citations, in the kindly quip of

1051

sociologist of science Robert K. Merton--of the type Frobenius-Perron-Hertz-Fréchet-Keynes-Kahn-Minkowski-Marx-Chipman-Goodwin-Markov non-negative matrixes. *Foundations* wrote up half a decade of grappling with economic problems by one who was learning mathematics to further that task.

2. As Herbert Simon and Joel Cohen have noted, I was an acknowledged admirer of A.J. Lotka. His *Elements of Physical Biology* (1924) was only the peak of an iceberg of some hundred papers he wrote on mathematical demography. I corresponded with him, listened to him at AEA and ASA annual meetings, scored his heated debates with the creative accountant-mathematician Gabriel Preinreich, and by invitation wrote for the Smith-Keyfitz *Contributions to Mathematical Demography* (1976) the definitive chapter clarifying the Lotka-Sharpe (1911) masterpiece of one-gender, linear, self-propelling population models in its relationship to Ladislaus von Bortkiewicz, R.R. Kuczynski and other contemporaries. It was I who in 1980 censured R.A. Fisher for his Cassel-like borrowing of Lotka's growth model with no shred of attribution. (I did point out that Fisher, being a genius, did add value to what he borrowed--in the form of his proposed concept of "biological reproductive values.")

But all that said, I have to state for Weintraub's readers that Lotka was *not* a major influence on *Foundations*' genesis. Dynamics came *late* in my book, and therefore the three appropriate references came appropriately late and they appropriately record my indebtedness.

Defensive argument can be Freudianly self-deceiving. So let me therefore walk the extra mile to ask in 1997: "Why no reference to Lotka in the earlier statics dealing with the LeChatelier Principle? When grappling with that topic, did I not read Lotka's pages?" Yes, I did--along with fifty other less-than-optimal thermodynamic authorities such as Max Planck, Edward Guggenheim, Constantin Carathéodory, Joseph Keenan, Paul Epstein, Percy Bridgman, E.B. Wilson, A.H. Wilson, R.H. Fowler, Subramanian Chandrasekhar, ... Many such authors did recognize in their LeChatelier expositions inequalities like $(\partial p/\partial V)_T < (\partial p/\partial V)_S$, but I could not locate in them exactly what general *mathematical* principle was involved.

In a sense *Foundations* might with a stretch be said to have begun when, as a 17-year-old social science major in the captive audience of the University of Chicago's required Survey Course on the Physical Sciences, I heard Professor Harvey Lemon (Birkhoff's physicist brother-in-law) say: "As LeChatelier has shown, when you put a stress on a system it reacts so as to relieve that stress." I bridled at the presumed anthromorphism and teleology: a system has no mind; it has no will; how can it act so as to accomplish something like that?

Half a dozen years later, around 1940, I still had to puzzle out *my* version of LeChatelier: it was a theorem about the value of a positive-definite-matrix's ratios of principal minors, as you lop off successive rows and columns. Experience repeatedly teaches, "If you find a pearl in a well-trodden scholarly field, you can be sure someone else found it earlier." Only later (well after 1947!), in a German science encyclopedia of 1911 vintage, did I run across this identical exposition and reproached myself for not finding it earlier in many places. On retrospective reflection, I judge it proper not to have cited Lotka on this topic even though his is far from the worst of many standard expositions.

Alfred Marshall predicted, wrongly predicted, that the biological method would displace the mechanical method in economic theory. Where *Foundations* did benefit from *The Elements of Physical Biology* (Lotka, 1924) was in its cited pages that were "least biological" and most reductionist mathematical. (I should add that any reader of Philip Mirowski [1989] who guessed that Lotka's "energetics" ever interested me much would have been an unlucky gambler.)

3. Mysteries can arise in the darkness of limited information, which evaporate under the light of explanation. Did *Foundations* somehow miss out on the valuable Lyapunov technique, whereby stability of a dynamic flow or iteration can be established by showing that at each point of time along any trajectory there is definable for the system a positive scalar that always erodes towards its lowest value at the stationary and stable equilibrium point? Neither in the book's index nor its printed pages is the nomenclature of such a Lyapunov Function mentioned. But at dozens of places precisely that technique was used to provide sufficiency conditions for local or global stability of an economic dynamic scenario. An unnamed rose is still a flower that smells as sweet.

The self-taught author first encountered the technique in connection with J.W.S. Rayleigh's *Theory of Sound* (1870), which he did not realize antedated the turn-of-the-century treatment by Lyapunov. (Only during World War II, from the works of Solomon Lefschetz and of N. Minorsky, did he learn of the Lyapunov label.) Thus, Rayleigh contemplated first a harmonic oscillator obeying the differential equation $y'' + y = 0$; along any motion defined by a non-equilibrium initial condition $[y(0), y'(0)] = [a,b] \neq [0,0]$ there will be satisfied for all $t > 0$:

$$2y'(y'' + y) = [d/dt][(y')^2 + (y)^2] \equiv 0.$$

Therefore, without calculating the explicit sinusoidal solution $y(t) = a \cos t + b \sin t$ as being periodic (neither damped nor anti-damped), we infer that no motion which begins out of equilibrium can ever asymptotically move into stationary equilibrium. With this "conservation insight," Rayleigh proceeds to prove the damped and dissipative property for the frictional pendulum: now for $c > 0$, and $y'' + cy' + y \equiv 0$, we deduce that

$$2y'[y'' + y] \equiv -2c(y')^2 \equiv [d/dt][y']^2 < 0.$$

If you call $[(y')^2 + (y)^2]$ the system's positive Lyapunov Function, you can thus deduce that this always declines out of equilibrium and has a rendezvous with the equilibrium asymptote of $[y(\infty), y'(\infty)] = [0,0]$, where the L.F. vanishes.

This example is child's play. But it motivated me to "invent" numerous more sophisticated "Lyapunov" Functions. Thus, when a firm seeks to maximize its profit as a function of factor inputs, Max $[f(x_1,...,x_n) - \Sigma_1^n w_j x_j]$ = Max $\pi(x_1,...,x_n)$, it can employ for successive approximations the gradient dynamics, $\dot{x}_j = \partial \pi(x_1,...,x_n)/\partial x_j$, and always its calculable profit will be (if anything) rising, by virtue of the identity

$$d/dt \text{ Profit} = \Sigma_1^n [\partial \pi / \partial x_j] \dot{x}_j \equiv \Sigma_1^n [\partial \pi / \partial x_j]^2 \geq 0.$$

The profit function $[\pi - \text{Max } \pi]$ thus serves as a L.F. More subtle was the proved stability of $[dx_i/dt] = [a_{ij}]x_j]$ but where $[a_{ij} + a_{ji}]$ is known to be a negative definite matrix. Molière would understand how one can speak good prose without knowing that. Under any name Uranus pursues its same elliptical milk run.[3]

Actually, Lyapunov made at least two distinct contributions to the subject of "stability of dynamic motions." I have mentioned the one which was important for *Foundations*' concentration on dissipative systems that damped down their divergences from equilibrium. The second contribution had to do with the more delicate problem of motions that are neither damped nor anti-damped, but in which "near by" initial points generate respectively future points that "stay near by." George D. Birkhoff and Henri Poincaré pioneered in this more advanced terrain of pure mathematics. Their subtleties were beyond my full youthful understanding, and through subsequent works by Edward Lorenz, Stephen Smale, and other writers on "chaos theory" all this remains a lively field of mathematical research bordering on the ergodic theorems of the 1930s. I did pick up from Birkhoff and Lotka references to both Lyapunov and Emile Picard, and that explains why my only references to Lyapunov did not relate to his techniques applicable to dissipative systems. Thus, no mystery remains to be explained.

4. It would be an understandable speculation that a mathematical economist in Harvard's Society of Fellows would be part of the Pareto Circle associated with its Chairman L.J. Henderson. But speculation, however reasonable, can be wrong; and in this case is wrong. Henderson disliked economists but swallowed me because his hero Pareto was (like me) a mathematical economist. I expected great help from Henderson,

---

[3] A reader who knows the name and nature of a "Lyapunov Function" will find its anonymous spoor in *Foundations* on (backward listed) pages 438, 431, 373, 334, 307-30, 262, 140, 108-15 and perhaps elsewhere.

a biochemist who had applied Gibbs's techniques to the study of blood. It turned out that with me he discussed the radical iniquities of President Franklin Roosevelt's New Deal rather than stability of equilibrium. I attended his famous sociology seminar only once: every time, or no time at all, would have been more diplomatic; but hoping for nothing from him and fearing nothing, I went my independent way. George Homans, also in the Pareto Circle, was a lively Junior Fellow colleague. For fifty years until his death our paths crossed occasionally and amiably in Cambridge. A sociologist and an Adams, Homans was not much impressed by economists' judgment. He thought me a cut better than the rest--until he found me in the company of those who expected high U.S. unemployment after World War II. That lowered his esteem for my predictive powers--as it did my own esteem for any economist's forecasting precision.

References

Allen, Roy G.D. "The Foundations of a Mathematical Theory of
　　Exchange," *Economica*, June 1932, 42, 323-26.
Antonelli, Giovanni B. *Sulla teoria matematica dell'economia politica*.
　　Pisa, 1886. Reprinted, with an introduction by G. Demaria, Milan: Malfasi, 1952.
Arrow, Kenneth. "Rational Choice Functions and Orderings,"
　　Economica, N.S., May 1995, 73, 292-308.
Arrow, Kenneth and Debreu, Gerard. "Existence of an Equilibrium for
　　a Competitive Economy," *Econometrica*, July 1954, 22, 265-90.
Bergson, Abram. "A Reformulation of Certain Aspects of Welfare
　　Economics," *Quarterly Journal of Economics*, February 1938, 52, 310-34.
Birkhoff, George D. *Dynamical Systems*. New York: The American
　　Mathematical Society, 1927.
Cassel, Gustav. *The Theory of Social Economy*. New York: Harcourt,
　　Brace and Company, 1932. English translation of 1918 German version.
Cohen, Joel E. "Lotka, Alfred James," in John Eatwell, Murray
　　Milgate, and Peter Newman, eds., *The New Palgrave a Dictionary of Economics*. London: Macmillan, 1987, 245-47.
Evans, Griffith C. *Mathematical Introduction to Economics*. New
　　York: McGraw-Hill Book Company, Inc., 1930.
Fisher, Irving. *Mathematical Investigations in the Theory of Value and
　　Prices*. New Haven: Connecticut Academy of Arts and Sciences. Reprinted 1961, New York: Augustus M. Kelley.
Georgescu-Roegen, Nicholas. "The Theory of Consumers' Behavior,"
　　Quarterly Journal of Economics, August, 1936, 50, 545-93.
Hicks, John R. "The Theory of Uncertainty and Profit," *Economica*,
　　May 1931, 11, 170-89.
Hicks, John R. *The Theory of Wages*. London: Macmillan and Co.,
　　1932.
Hicks, John R. *Value and Capital, an Inquiry into Some Fundamental
　　Principles of Economic Theory*. Oxford: The Clarendon Press, 1939.
Hicks, John R., and Allen, Roy G.D. "A Reconsideration of the
　　Theory of Value," Pt. I-II, *Economica* N.S., February, 1934, 1, 52-76; May, 1932, 1, 196-219.

Houthakker, Hendrik. "Revealed Preference and the Utility Function," *Economica*, N.S., May, 1950, 17, 159-74.
Keynes, John Maynard. *A Treatise on Money*. Reprinted in *The Collected Writings of John Maynard Keynes*, Vol. V. London: Macmillan for the Royal Economic Society, 1930.
Keynes, John Maynard. *The General Theory of Employment, Interest and Money*. Reprinted in *The Collected Writings of John Maynard Keynes*, Vol. VII. London: Macmillan for the Royal Economic Society, 1936.
Lefschetz, Solomon. *Differential Equations: Geometric Theory*, 2nd edn. New York: Interscience Publishers, 1946.
Lorenz, Edward. *The Essence of Chaos*. Seattle: University of Washington Press, 1993.
Lotka, Alfred J. *Elements of Physical Biology*. Baltimore: Williams & Wilkins Co., Inc., 1934. Reprinted with a Lotka bibliography as *Elements of Mathematical Biology*. New York: Dover Publications, 1924.
Lowes, John Livingston. *The Road to Xanadu, a Study in the Ways of the Imagination*. Princeton: Princeton University Press, 1927.
Lyapunov, Alexander. "Obshčaya zadača ob ustoičivosti dviženiya," *Soc. Math. Kharkov*, 1892. English translation, *The General Problem of the Stability of Motion*. London: Taylor & Francis, 1992.
Marshall, Alfred. *Principles of Economics*. London: Macmillan and Co., 1890, 1891, 1895, 1898, 1907, 1910, 1916, 1920, 1961.
McKenzie, Lionel. "On the Existence of General Equilibrium for a Competitive Market," *Econometrica*, January 1959, 27, 54-77.
Minorsky, Nicolai. *Introduction to Non-linear Mechanics: Topological Methods, Analytical Methods, Non-linear Resonances, Relaxation Oscillations*. Ann Arbor, Mich.: J.W. Edwards, 1947.
Mirowski, Philip. *More Heat than Light*. New York: Cambridge University Press, 1989.
Neisser, Hans. "Lohnhöhe und Beschäftigungsgrad im Marktgleichgewicht," *Weltwirtschaftliches Archiv*, 1932, 36, 413-55.
Niehans, Jürg, Samuelson, Paul A. and von Weizsäcker, Carl Christian. *Paul Samuelson's "Foundations of Economic Analysis", Vademecum zu einem Klassiker der Gegenwart*. Dusseldorf: Verlag Wirtschaft und Finanzen, 1997.
Picard, Emile. *Traité d'analyse*. Volumes I-III. Paris: Gauthier-Billars, 1891, 1893, 1896.
Poincaré, Henri. *The méthodes nouvelles de la mécanique céleste*. Paris: Gauthiers-Villar, 1893.
Rayleigh, John William Strut. *The Theory of Sound, by John William Strutt, Baron Raleigh, with a Historical Introduction by Robert Bruce Lindsay*, 1870. Second revised and enlarged edition published 1894. Reprint of 2nd edition, New York: Dover Publications, 1945.
Samuelson, Paul A. "A Note on the Pure Theory of Consumer's Behavior," *Economica*, N.S., February 1938, 5, 61-71. Reproduced as Chapter 1 in *The Collected Scientific Papers of Paul A. Samuelson*, Vol. 1. Cambridge, Mass.: The MIT Press, 1966.
Samuelson, Paul A. *Foundations of Economic Analysis*. Cambridge, Mass.: Harvard University Press, 1947. Enlarged edition, 1983.
Samuelson, Paul A. "The Problem of Integrability in Utility Theory," *Economica*, November 1950, 17, 355-85. Reproduced as Chapter 10 in *The Collected Scientific Papers of Paul A. Samuelson*, Vol. 1. Cambridge, Mass.: The MIT Press, 1966.

Samuelson, Paul A. "Economics in a Golden Age: A Personal Memoir," in Holton, George, ed., *The Twentieth Eentury Sciences: Studies in the Biography of Ideas*. New York: W.W. Norton & Co., Inc., 1972. Reproduced as Chapter 278 in *The Collected Scientific Papers of Paul A. Samuelson*, Vol. 4. Cambridge, Mass.: The MIT Press, 1977. Reprinted also in Brown, E. Cary and Solow, Robert M., eds., *Paul Samuelson and Modern Economic Theory*. New York: McGraw-Hill, 1983.

Samuelson, Paul A. "Resolving a Historical Confusion in Population Analysis," *Human Biology*, September 1976, 48, 559-80. Detroit, Mich.: Wayne State University Press. Reproduced as Chapter 236 in *The Collected Scientific Papers of Paul A. Samuelson*, Vol. 4. Cambridge, Mass.: The MIT Press, 1977. This appears in the Smith-Keyfitz anthology referenced below.

Samuelson, Paul A. "Fisher's 'Reproductive Value' as an Economic Specimen in Merton's Zoo," *Transactions of the New York Academy of Sciences*, Serial 2, April 1980, 39, 126-42. Reproduced as Chapter 350 in *The Collected Scientific Papers of Paul A. Samuelson*, Vol. 5. Cambridge, Mass.: The MIT Press, 1986.

Sharpe, F.R. and Lotka, Alfred J. "A problem in age-distribution," *Philosophical Magazine*, 1911, 21, 435-38.

Simon, Herbert. "Review of *Elements of Mathematical [physical] biology*," *Econometrica*, July 1959, 27, 493-95.

Slutsky, Eugen. "Sulla teoria del bilancio de consumatore," *Giornale degli Economisti e Rivista di Statistica*, July 1915, 51, 1-26. Translated as "On the Theory of the Budget of the Consumer," in Boulding, Kenneth E. and Stigler, George J., eds., *Readings in Price Theory*. London: Allen & Unwin, 1953, 26-56.

Smale, Stephen. *The mathematics of time*. New York: Springer-Verlag, 1980.

Smith, David and Keyfitz, Nathan, eds. *Contributions to Mathematical Demography*. Berlin, Heidelberg, New York: Springer-Verlag, 1976. Also Chapter 236 in the Samuelson (1976) reference above.

Stackleberg, Heinrich v. "Zwei kritische Bemerkungen zur Preistheorie Gustav Cassels," *Zeitschrift für Nationalökonomie*, 1933, 4, 456-72.

Viner, Jacob. *The Long View and the Short: Studies in Economic Theory and Policy*. Glencoe, Ill.: The Free Press, 1958. See particularly Viner's (1929) review of Edwin Cannan.

Viner, Jacob. "Cost Curves and Supply Curves," *Zeitschrift für Nationalökonomie*, September 1931, 3, 23-46.

von Neumann, John. "Zur Theorie der Gesellschafts-spiele," *Mathematische Annalan*, 1928, 100, 295-320.

Wald, Abraham. "Über die Produktionsgleichungen der ökonomischen Wertlehre II. In *Ergebnisse eines mathematischen Kolloquiums*. Ed. K. Menger, 1934-35. Translated by W. Baumol as "On the Production Equations of Economic Value Theory, Part II," in Baumol, William J. and Goldfeld, Stephen M., eds., *Precursors in Mathematical Economics*. London School of Economics Series of Reprints of Scarce Works on Political Economy No. 19. London: London School of Economics, 1968.

Weintraub, E. Roy. "On the Existence of a Competitive Equilibrium: 1930-1954," *Journal of Economic Literature*, March 1989, 21, 1-39.

Weintraub, E. Roy. "The Foundations of Samuelson's Dynamics," September 8, 1989 draft of paper published in 1991 (see below).

Weintraub, E.Roy. *Stabilizing Dynamics, Constructing Economic Knowledge*. Cambridge, UK and New York: Cambridge University Press, 1991. See Chapter 3, 39-67.

Wicksell, J.G. Knut. *Über Wert, Kapital, und Rente*. Jena: G. Fischer, 1893. Translated by Frowein, S.H. as *Value, Capital and Rent*. London: Allen & Unwin, 1954. Reprinted 1970, New York: Augustus M. Kelley.

Wong, Stanley. *The Foundations of Paul Samuelson's Revealed Preference Theory*. Boston: Routledge & Kegan Paul, 1978.

Zeuthen, Franz. "Das Prinzip der Knappheit, technische Kombination und ökonomische Qualität," *Zeitschrift für Nationalökonomie*, 1933, 7, 1-24.

A GOLDEN BIRTHDAY

At its fiftieth birthday, this *Economics* has witnessed an exciting half-century of progress in economics. Our subject has come a long way. But there is so much farther to go before this, or any social science, can make pretense to be anywhere near an exact science. Economics will always be as much an art as a science, but still there's a world of difference between informed economics and just plain bad economics.

Today the number of jobs for economists has exploded. Statistical databases—inside government, in private industry, and within academia—are many times more comprehensive than they were in the late 1940s. Now information gets reported sooner, and computers give us access to statistical facts and knowledge with the speed of light. No branch of production has benefited more from the advance of computer hardware and technology than research in political economy itself. And that includes economic theory and applied economics.

And yet the fundamentals remain broadly intact. History—at least economic history—has taught the world certain basic economic principles that have been learned and tested the hard way. Repeated recessions and inflationary booms have been the economists' substitute for the chemists' controlled laboratory experiments. The tragic comedies of Russian and Chinese communistic organization of production and distribution have robbed three generations of the potential fruits of rising standards of material life. At the same time, the completely free market mechanism has not been able to bring all of humankind measurable near-equality of opportunity and outcome.

Because of "the poor we have always with us," the modern democratic state has evolved everywhere into a "mixed economy"—neither pure laissez-faire market mechanism nor Robin Hood utopia. Alas, only by their study of the rudiments of economics can the citizenry understand and decide about where should lie the *golden mean* between the selfishness of individual initiative and the regulatory, stabilizing, and redistributive functions of government. The mixed economy must, perforce, be the "limited mixed economy."

A Time to Look Back

A fiftieth birthday is a good time to look back. What is the story that emerges from this history of a trend-setting bestseller? How did this textbook come to be? Gaze back to 1945. Germany and Japan were defeated and American colleges were nearly overflowing with people returning from World War II. At the same time, the science of economics was entering a golden age. The Great Depression of 1929–1935 had finally been licked by forceful programs that threw out the window the old orthodoxies of do-nothing monetary and fiscal policies. Britain and America had later mobilized their economies for war in a way that Hitler, Mussolini, and Hirohito had never dreamed of. And, though we could not know it in 1945, the Marshall Plan and American occupation of Japan were about to set the stage for miraculous decades of postwar economic growth.

College students deserved to understand all this. But, as teachers of my generation knew to our sorrow, the best-selling economics textbooks were seriously out-of-date. No wonder beginners were bored. My students at Harvard and MIT often had that glassy-eyed look.

In 1948, when *Economics* was first published, the word "macroeconomics"—the study of what determines a society's unemployment, its price level and inflation rate, and its rate of overall real GNP growth—was not even in the dictionary! But had *Economics* not brought guns-and-butter choices into elementary microeconomics, someone, somewhere, would soon have done so. The time was ripe for a revolutionary approach to introductory economics. The real question is: Why me?

I was back from the MIT Radiation Laboratory, where I had worked at the mathematical job of designing automatic servomechanisms to ward off enemy bombers, and I "thirsted" for a return to economic research and teaching. And I was 30 years old, a good age to write a text or innovate a treatise. By chance, my advanced work, *Foundations of Economic Analysis,* which was to win me a Nobel Prize in economics 25 years later, was already in press.

However, in those days, a promising scholar was not supposed to write textbooks—certainly not basic texts for freshmen and sophomores. Only hacks were supposed to do that. But because I had already published so many research articles, it seemed that my reputation and prospects for lifetime tenure could allow me the elbowroom to respond positively to the request for a new textbook by my department head at MIT. Being cocky, even brash, in those good old days, I had only myself to please. And I agreed it was high time that we got some of the leaders in economic research back in the trenches of general education.

The Long Grind of Creation

Starting a project is easy. Bringing it to full term involves enormous labor and great travail. As soon as each chapter was written, the mimeograph machine ground it out for testing on our MIT students. I found it demanding but pleasant work. But what I naively thought might be a year's job turned into three years of writing and rewriting. And my tennis suffered, as weekends and summer vacation had to be devoted to the task of reducing to plain and understandable prose the fundamental complexities of economic science. Even the traditional diagrams of economics, I discovered, needed redesigning if the "dismal science of economics" was to become the exciting subject it really is.

The Moment of Truth

In the autumn of 1948 the first edition of *Economics* rolled off the presses. No matter how hard the advance work or how optimistic the dreams, one can of course never be sure how the future will turn out. Fortunately, from the word go, this novel approach to economics seemed to have hit a responsive chord. Colleges big and small opted for the new book, and as each fresh printing was sold out, *Economics* was back again for new press runs.

When a Guggenheim fellowship took me to Europe, I checked each main bookstore in major cities for the availability of translations into French, German, Italian, Spanish, and Swedish. And in addition to experiencing the natural vanity of an author, I was pleased as an educator to see that the citizenry, who would be deciding global policies, was being exposed to the pros and cons of up-to-date mainstream economics.

Reviews of the book speeded up the bandwagon. The first came from the pen of John Kenneth Galbraith, then an editor of the conservative business magazine *Fortune.* He predicted that the next generation would learn its economics from Samuelson's *Economics.* And although praise is sweet to an author's ears, I confess that the durability of the book's dominance did surprise me. Galbraith turned out to be more prescient than I, and *Economics* did set a new and lasting pattern. Most of its successful rivals have been written in its general evolving mode, and it is heartwarming that much of the competition has come from the pens of personal friends.

Rough Pebbles along the Way

Not always has it been fun and games. In the reactionary days of Senator Joseph McCarthy, when accusations of radicalism were being launched from the pulpit and in the classroom, my book got its share of condemnation. A conservative alumnus of MIT warned university president Karl Compton that Paul Samuelson would jeopardize his scholarly reputation if he were allowed to publish his apologetics for the "mixed economy." Dr. Compton replied that the day his faculty was subjected to censorship would be the day of his resignation from office. It all seems slightly comical four decades later, but it was no joke to be a teacher at a public university when many of the fashionable textbooks of the time were being denounced as subversive. (One excellent text, which came out a year before mine, was killed in its infancy by vicious charges of Marxism that were false from the beginning.) Actually, when your cheek is smacked from the Right, the pain may be assuaged in part by a slap from the Left. *Anti-Samuelson,* a two-volume critique authored in the 1960s when student activism was boiling over on campuses here and abroad, portrayed me as an apologist for the laissez-faire world of markets where dog eats dog, a veritable running jackal of capitalism.

Each cold wind imparts a useful lesson, and I learned to write with special care wherever controversial matters were concerned. It was certainly not that I was perfect in all things. Rather, it was that I could only gain by leaning over backward to state fairly the arguments against the positions popular in mainstream economics.

And by dealing carefully and fully with the contending schools within the mainstream, the work kept its representative status as a reference source book. Even Soviet Russia had felt a translation was mandatory, and within a month the entire supply of translated copies had been exhausted. (Experts tell me that in Stalin's day my book was kept on the special reserve shelf in the library, along with books on sex, forbidden to all but the specially licensed readers.) In the post–Cold War era, new translations have been authorized in Hungary, the Czech Republic, Croatia, Bosnia, Serbia, Romania, and other Eastern European countries as well as in China, Japan, Vietnam, and two-score other countries.

The Ever-Young Child

Just as a child takes on an individual identity distinct from a parent's, so it was with the *Economics.* At first I was in command of it; later it took over in its own right and came to be in charge of me. As the years passed, my hair turned from blond to brown and then to gray. But like the portrait of Dorian Gray, which never grew old, *Economics* remained forever 21. Its cover turned from green to blue and from brown to black; and now it turns to gold. Aided by hundreds of letters and suggestions to the author from students and teachers, the economics inside the covers evolved and developed. A historian of mainstream economic doctrines, like a paleontologist who studies the bones and fossils in different layers of the earth, could date the ebb and flow of ideas by analyzing how Edition 1 was revised to Edition 2 and, eventually, to Edition 16.

And so it went. Hard, hard work—but ever so rewarding. Finally came the day when the call of tennis was too strong to be denied. To McGraw-Hill I said: "I've paid my dues. Let others carry on as I enjoy the good life of an emeritus professor, cultivating the researches that interest me most." McGraw-Hill had a ready answer: "Let us find you a coauthor. We'll make a list of congenial economists whose competence and views you admire." And so the search for the perfect William Nordhaus began.

Yale is only 150 miles from MIT, and it was there that the real Nordhaus was to be found. It only helped that Bill had earned his Ph.D. at MIT. And in the days since then he has won his spurs serving on the President's Council of Economic Advisers and doing tours of duty in Cambridge (England), Delhi, and Vienna. Like Gilbert and Sullivan or Rogers and Hart, we turned out to be a most congenial team.

And so, as in the classic tales, we have lived happily ever after. What matters is that the book stays young, pointing to where the mainstream of economics will be flowing.

Science or Art?

Why has economics become in most colleges one of the largest elective courses? The reasons are many. Economics deals with the real life around us. On the job. At the store. When inflation comes, it hits us all. When recession strikes, the tide goes out for all the boats. And the early bird that seeks the worm needs to know about supply and demand. The same goes for the senior citizen constrained to live on a limited pension and for the young idealist determined to improve and reform society.

Good sense economics is not all obvious. The common sense you bring with you from home to college will not let you understand why a rich country and a poor country can both gain great benefit from free international trade at the same time. (And your senator won't understand the point either without taking a good course in *comparative advantage*.) On the other hand, *after* you have mastered instruction in so-called microeconomics and macroeconomics, there will remain no mysteries. If it doesn't make good sense, it isn't good economics.

A first course in economics will not make you a master of all its intricate and esoteric topics. But this I can tell you, based upon students' experience everywhere: your best course in economics will be your introductory course. After you have stepped into this new strange garden of ideas, the world will never be quite the same. And when, years from now, you look back on the experience, even what you didn't quite understand at the time will have perceptibly ripened.

Enjoy!

Paul A. Samuelson
Massachusetts Institute of Technology
Cambridge, Massachusetts
1998

FOREWORD

Chaucer, seeing three men at work in the Middle Ages, asked them what they were doing. The first replied: "I'm earning pay, pretty good pay." The second said: "I'm shaping together intricate patterns of stone and glass." The third proclaimed: "I am building a cathedral." When I wrote this first edition of *Economics*, I was doing all three of these things without knowing it. But it was not the case that I started out with any such grandiloquent goals in mind.

Just as the story has already been told, this 1948 introductory textbook to economics was first conceived when my department head came to me with an offer I could not refuse—and could not have refused even if he had not been a valued friend. "Paul," he said, "800 MIT engineers are made to take a full year of economics. And they hate it. We've tried every one of the prominent texts. We've even written an in-house text. And still they don't like economics.

"Please lighten teaching duties for a semester or two and write a book that will be both interesting and accurate. Take as much or as little time as you want. Leave out whatever you want to. With your background in research and teaching, I know it will be a landmark text."

Well, flattery always wins over the young and brash. I was just back from the war and overflowing with ideas and energy. Even the available good contemporary introductory textbooks—such as that of Frank Taussig which I had taught from at Harvard—were woefully out of date. I knew in my bones that a window of opportunity was at hand: beginners in economics would be excited to study the macroeconomics of great depressions and hyperinflations. (The word "macroeconomics" had not yet come into the dictionary; it was not in this first edition's index!) Even the *micro*economics of supply and demand—how competition determines the relative prices of tea, coffee, lemons, cream, and salt—was still mired at the 1890 level of the art and science of economics.

So the die was cast. And my life was never the same afterward. What I thought would take three months took most of the 1945–1948 years. Yes, as I had suspected, I woke up to a Byronic success as a bestselling author. But what I had never expected was the durability of the book's dominance. Authorized and pirated translations appeared in scores of languages, so that sales abroad dominated the field even more than sales at home did. The coin I lusted for was not so much gold as it was scientific influence. When asked to testify before Congress on copyright protection, I abdicated in favor of more specialized and disinterested authorities.

I truly felt that imitation was the sincerest form of flattery; so that when in the course of four of five passing decades some other texts began to rival or outsell mine, I was pleased to find in them good things that had first entered the public domain in the present commemorative volume. Once, when Author X sued Author Y for plagiarism and copyright infringement, the exasperated judge threw the suit out of court with the curt remark: "They all seem to be Samuelson clones anyway." I hasten to stress the many innovations in contemporary textbooks that trace to the invisible college of economic researchers.

If it is anything, science is *public* knowledge, contributed to by all and rebuttable by anyone. As I had dared hope from the beginning, the authors most successful in competing with this work have frequently been friends of mine and not a few have been cherished pupils.

It will be clear by now that I think economics is an interesting and exciting and useful subject. Nor it its usefulness primarily to students in the West where competitive market mechanisms are predominantly relied upon. Just last month, when asked to prepare a foreword for the new Russian translation of Samuelson and Nordhaus's sixteenth edition, I wrote, "An introduction to modern mainstream economics will be even more valuable to a Russia or an emerging-market country than to college students in a Switzerland, America, or other quasi-capitalistic mixed economies. What our children absorb, so to speak with their mother's milk, you out there must learn from university studies—not in order to be converted to our way of life, but so that you can choose and pick rationally to best achieve your own cultural goals and desired standard of living."

An old classic, by definition, captures the state of the art in its time of conception. No living science stands still. But, as I have turned these pages at random, it has been a pleasant surprise to discover how much of the original verve and relevance is still there, preserved forever in amber on the library shelf.

That is the only kind of immortality that an author could have or want. And the same goes for this author's brainchild.

Paul A. Samuelson
Cambridge, MA
October, 1997

Samuelson's *Economics* at Fifty: Remarks on the Occasion of the Anniversary of Publication

Paul A. Samuelson

Dr. Samuel Johnson went to see the revival of his earlier play, *Irene,* which had been a failure. When Boswell asked him what he thought of the performance, Johnson replied sadly, "I had thought it better."

My experience was a happier one in reviewing today's commemorative reissue of the first 1948 edition of Samuelson's *Economics*. With the objectivity that 50 years of perspective brings, I examined it minutely. To my surprise, it read much better than I could ever have suspected. No wonder it was an instant bestseller, which set a new pattern for all the late 20th-century economic textbooks. For, as I had almost forgotten, it was not merely the first text to bring effectively to beginners macroeconomic modeling along Keynesian and post-Keynesian lines. It was that. But in addition, this book brought into the basic economics course numerous innovations in microeconomics that are today taken for granted. Even a fond author forgets the merits of a favorite brainchild.

Before Stockholm gave Nobel Prizes for researches into *human capital*, the 1948 text introduced students to the theoretical and factual payoffs from additional years of schooling. I do not recall any previous texts that discussed the economics of *social security* and that included long ago a warning that the dynamics of demography would mandate an inevitable increase in the funding needed to provide for the foreseeable growth in the ratio of aged dependents to working-age numbers.

What sex is to the biology classroom, stocks and investment riskiness is to the sophomore economics lecture hall. That chapter on *personal finance,* put there to keep hard-boiled MIT electrical engineers awake, helped make introductory economics the largest elective course at hundreds of colleges. My great predecessors—John Stuart Mill, Alfred Marshall, Frank Taussig and Irving Fisher—were writing for their times. I was writing for the last half of the 20th century—an epoch that surpassed even my youthful optimism. Those classic authors had dealt with essentially pure capitalism. I had to grapple with the tradeoffs and opportunities inherent in the mixed economy, a social pattern that by now spreads across the continents of the Americas, Europe, Asia, and Africa.

1948 was then. 1998 is now. Because mine was a text shaped to be in date at mid-century, the reviewing author has to wince at various nonoptimalities that are obvious from hindsight. Fiscal policy was given too much emphasis at the expense of monetary policy. Yes. Can this be excused by the fact that not until the 1951 Accord did the Federal Reserve get back its freedom to exercise an autonomous monetary policy? Admittedly, that is an excuse in part. But is it not a duty for the economics writer to pound on the table and nag against bad institutional policies?

Enough of self-congratulations and excuses. Let me try to describe how being a successful textbook author changed my career. Already at 30, I had been a recognized researcher at the frontier of mathematical economics and statistics. That trajectory went on little affected by my success as a textbook author.

Financially hitting the best-seller jackpot is of course luck like no other. Students do not buy books; they are captive slaves of their instructors. Fiction and nonfiction works usually have their single year of glory. A lucky textbook, however, can go on for a long, long time. And royalties that arrived in the form of 1940's dollars came at a time when stocks typically sold at 8-to-1 price/earnings ratios and not infrequently carried 6 percent or higher dividend yields.

I am not here to talk about personal finance. A McGraw-Hill vice president once said to me: "You can't buy happiness with money. You can't buy love with it, or buy good health. Of course, I mean *Confederate* money." He was not wrong. But I have found you are rich if you have a little more money than those around you. In consequence, for 50 years money has meant nothing in my life. I have always refused to testify in court for money. I do not criticize colleagues who do. I have not taught night school or summer school. I cheerfully paid 92 cents out of each marginal dollar to the IRS back in those days when U.S. GDP (gross domestic product) grew at a real rate of more than 4 percent per annum.

I never received one penny in the form of a publisher's book advance. Out of two dozen clamoring publishers—big and small—I selected McGraw-Hill solely for two reasons. Reason 1: Macmillan and Prentice-Hall, the other giants back then, already had best-selling textbooks; McGraw-Hill did not. Reason 2: What clinched the deal was that McGraw-Hill had published the scholarly 2-volume treatise on *Business Cycles* by my Harvard teacher Joseph Schumpeter and had also published the 15-volume compendium on what had been learned at the MIT Radiation Laboratory where I had spent the War. Besides, as a bonus, McGraw-Hill's representative, Basil Dandison, was a gentleman, and when the other publishers saw that he left his raincoat and galoshes in my office whenever he visited MIT, they gave up all hope.

I was able recently to reach Basil Dandison at his home in Lexington, Massachusetts. He is 97 years old but completely with it mentally. I explained McGraw-Hill's reissue of the 1948 edition. I asked him what message I could repeat on this occasion. Basil's modesty has not changed. Here is what he said: "It was a great thing for McGraw-Hill when Paul Samuelson decided to sign up with us." I say, "What a gentleman!"

At this point I must digress. At McGraw-Hill scores of names float in memory—Curtis Benjamin, Harold McGraw, the tax lawyer Bill Cady. It was Cady who asked me how often I was audited by the IRS. When I replied, "Never," he said, "You are definitely not living right." I knew better: Justice Oliver Wendell Holmes taught me that "Taxes are the price we pay for civilization." When I passed this wisdom on to my colleague Franco Modigliani, he said "That is a very non-Italian attitude."

Bob Locke, Jack Taylor, Betty Binns, Mary Griffin—the list of McGraw-Hill co-workers is endless. Between us, we pioneered the use of multiple colors in the textbook field. I advanced the cause of education by being the first McGraw-Hill author to accept lower royalty rates on special international English-language editions. My interest was not so much in dollars as in influencing minds.

A new layer of fame that I never dreamed of evolved. At annual American Economic Association meetings I was besieged by groupies reminiscent of Talmudic students crowding around famous rabbis. I never knew what to say when people would tell me: "We use your book." One day, I heard myself saying, "Mrs. Samuelson will be pleased," and that has solved my problem ever since.

The policeman at the door of the White House whispers, "I am using your book at Georgetown night school." The chap who sells me a newspaper at Harvard Square confides that at Northeastern he studied my book. No folks, alas, ever remember the name of their economic analysis instructor; at best they may recall that he was fat. But I can always tell a woman her age from the color of the edition she claims to have used.

Wherever I go in Europe, Asia, or Latin America, strangers greet me as an old friend or old tormenter. I have never been to India, Russia, or China, but in my MIT office, I am asked to autograph copies of translations. In one lifetime, while adhering to the same eclectic liberalism, I have been at first denounced as *avant garde* and later castigated as a running jackal of capitalism.

All this is pleasant enough, but in honest truth, the few hundred of scientific articles that have never earned back their editorial costs mean more to me than all the financial journalisms and congressional testimonies that overflow my MIT file drawers.

I tell no secret when I repeat that fame and reputation are much a matter of luck and chance. Yes, one capitalizes on one's luck, but without something to capitalize on, how far can mere talent and effort take you? I came into economics at a fortunate time—when the world was misbehaving in depression and inflation and just when academic opportunity was exploding at more than exponential rates. At Chicago, Harvard, and MIT, precisely when and where the action was heating up, I was there. The tide raises all ships, and once among the leaders, I had only to sail as fast as the fleet to retain lead position. Best of all have been the hundreds of companions at arms acquired along the way. Always it is better to travel than to arrive. Remember where you heard that last.

Paul A. Samuelson is Institute Professor Emeritus at MIT.

590

ECONOMICS AND THE KENNEDY PRESIDENCY
Brookings Institution, Washington, D.C.
12 November 1999

Preamble
When old Nazis meet in convention, they glory in war stories. "We're just as great now as we were in those good old days," I could tell a lot of insider stuff from the pre-Camelot and Camelot days. How we economists had to educate the lawyers in the old Kennedy Mafia. Typical was this conversation.

  Ted Sorenson: Paul, if he misbehaves, how can we make William McChesney Martin Jr., do what we want? Can we turn off the heat in the Fed building? Cut their budget?

  Paul Samuelson: The Fed prints money rather than getting M from the Executive. In fourteen years you can contrive a change in personnel. For better or worse we'll have to get along with the independent Federal Reserve.

  Actually, the triplets Heller-Tobin-Gordon in the end converted the lawyers, contained Bob Roosa at the Dillon-Fowler Treasury and Professor Galbraith in New Delhi, while pretending to work under the constraint that dampened my spirits when a week before Inauguration Day President-elect Kennedy announced that he had just promised Majority Leader Senator Kerr and Speaker Sam Rayburn that we would balance the federal budget. I pitied Heller as I passed on to him *that* baton.

  Before I make a few substantive remarks, I must mention Jim Tobin who can't be here. That's like Hamlet without the flawless Dane. When Walter and I introduced Jim to the about-to-be President, Kennedy said: "Don't I know you?" "Yes, I was in the '39 class between your brother Joe's and your class at Harvard." "Darn it. I thought I was at last getting a non-Harvard economist and a true blue Yalie. Are you at least related to Tobin the black baseball player?" Jim had to decline that honor.

  Jim was the man of principle come to Washington. What he lost in Machiavellianism he gained when all learned that he was completely without guile. What you saw was what you got. And what the doctor knew you ought to have.

  Now for brief substance because I learned at age 16 that history never gets things quite right.

"Substance"
I believe a key fact of economic history is that, by the end of the 1950s, the U.S. dollar had become an overvalued currency. This followed after the 1945-55 epoch of the opposite "dollar shortage," which enabled America to contribute so much to post-war reconstruction: Truman Doctrine, MacArthur Occupation of Japan, Marshall Plan, launching of the Bretton Woods regime.

Our kind of economists was slow to recognize the change. Machlup on the right and Despres on the left both believed that a credible lowering of the price of gold would work. (Herman Goring said, "When I hear the word culture, I reach for my gun." In view of the rot and whimsy that goes on in modern economics in connection with the word "credibility," when I hear it I reach for my razor.) Bob Triffin and Eddie Bernstein each had their alleged cures. As a good soldier I shut up and backed the Administration's grappling with the problem. I was amused to receive last week a paper with a title suggesting that a malignant preoccupation with a malignant cancer was deplorable. I am using retrospective Kalman filtering in patting myself on the back for prescience.

In the two-term Eisenhower presidency, the U.S. underwent *three* National Bureau business cycles.[1] The last of these was probably the main reason that the close 1960 election went against Candidate Nixon. The Kennedy slogan "Get the country moving again" was perhaps the winning theme of the 1960 campaign.

Under Bretton Woods, the U.S. dollar was the anchor. Persuading many foreign nations to appreciate *their* currencies was a no-win strategy. (Germany did make a small move. France was obdurate.) Machiavelli would have told the Young Prince: "Depreciate the dollar your first day in offer (maybe along with the U.K.)." The political chemistry for that was all wrong. Result: America for a decade was hamstrung by the overvalued dollar. (Fed policy had to aim for an interest rate *no lower than 3%*; fiscal policy was the only remaining general macro card--and before Dallas the Heller-Tobin-Gordon CEA had converted JFK and the Dillon Treasury [and the Congress and the country] to a sizeable tax cut. The inside story of the 1931 depreciation of the Sterling Bloc was not that it was a beggar-my-neighbor tactic; its true virtue was that it let the U.K. and Scandinavia get over the depression factor by engineering harm to more sluggish neighbors.)

After 1965, as we now know from the Johnson memoirs, Gardner Ackley (Heller's successor at the CEA) did tell LBJ: If you keep your Great Society (*cum* poverty battle) programs and escalate the Vietnam involvement, you will overheat the economy, risk inflation and impel the Fed to put on the brakes and end the recovery. Johnson judged it bad politics to raise tax rates and/or triage spending just to accommodate Vietnam actions.

---

[1] It was my view in mid-1960 that "Eisenhower's investment in austerity-sadism" would give Kennedy times some respite from stagflationary pressures, an eroding asset. Before the inauguration I bet Tobin they would be back soon. In the end I was right but until 1965 I was glad to have Jim win the wager.

No sage believes that presidents are irrelevant to economic history, or that they are omnipotent. The Fed was, and is, quasi-independent. Congress has its unilateral legislative powers, subject to White House vetoes and to override.

To understand Nixon's August 1971 (1) suspension of gold redemptions and effective burying of Bretton Woods, (2) 10% temporary emergency tariff on imports, *and* (3) price-wage controls, you must understand the previous Truman-Eisenhower-Kennedy-Johnson history. Arthur Burns at the 1972 Fed, Nixon's volunteer "boy," privately advised Nixon to put in Wage-Price controls. After the controls' predictable pre-election benefits and post-election burdens, the 1973-75 recession and the stagflation of the 1970s (*cum* OPEC and harvest supply shocks) were the consequences. That serious recession cooked Ford's goose and elected Carter. Carter's appointee Paul Volcker, by engineering two back-to-back recessions and use of skilled hypocrisy (I am a "monetarist" now: 1979) and by good luck, did break the back of stagflation. And *despite* the early Reagan supply-side crazies (Art Laffer, David Stockman, Jack Kemp, Judy Somebody, Bob Mundell), Volcker's subsequent adroit 1982 disregard of monetarism set the U.S. GDP on a growth trend (prior and subsequent) to the October '87 Stock Market Crash. That Crash the new Fed chief, Alan Greenspan, handled in the proper Victorian (and lucky) way.

All this needs amplifying, documenting and guardedly qualifying. But not on your eating time.

591

The First Fifteen Nobel Laureates in Economics, and Fifteen More Might-Have-Beens
Paul A. Samuelson
Lindau Economics Nobel Laureates Conference
September, 2004

Back I think in 1958 I received a letter from the Bank of Sweden, asking for my view on the feasibility and desirability of there being established an Alfred Nobel Award in economics, running in parallel with the official Nobel Prizes in Physics, Chemistry, Physiology and Medicine, Literature and Peace. After reflection I gave my opinions pro and con: fields like mathematics and economics, experience suggests, do lend themselves to approximate ranking by peers. However, providing rewards to one elite would exclude from tribute a larger group of worthies whose body of research achievements is, if anything, only slightly different in quality and quantity.

To explicate the above contentions, I dared to provide in 1958 a list of names of living economists who might be considered for such awards in the coming decade(s). According to my hazy recollections, some on my list died before they could have received the new award. A number on my list did turn out eventually to receive the call from Stockholm. And, of course, quite a number of names were neither included in the actual first fifteen nor, up to this date, been selected by the relevant Committee of the Royal Swedish Academy of Science.

All of the first fifteen winners listed here in Table 1 were my friends, some of course on a more or less intimate basis. However-- and this is what really counts--I did happen to know essentially all of each person's published writings in economics.

Table 1: First Fifteen Nobelists

1969	Ragnar Frisch (1895-1973), Norway; Jan Tinbergen (1903-1994), The Netherlands
1970	Paul A. Samuelson (1915-), USA
1971	Simon Kuznets (1901-1985), Russia
1972	John Hicks (1904-1989), U.K.; Kenneth Arrow (1921-), USA
1973	Wassily Leontief (1905-1999), Russia
1974	Friedrich Hayek (1899-1992), Austria; Gunnar Myrdal (1898-1987), Sweden

1975	Tjalling Koopmans (1910-1985), The Netherlands; Leonid Kantorovich (1912-1986), Russia
1976	Milton Friedman (1912-), USA
1977	Bertil Ohlin (1899-1979), Sweden; James Meade (1907-1994), U.K.
1978	Herbert Simon (1916-2001), USA

In these ten years that were under consideration by the Stockholm choosers, I meticulously refrained from nominating any of them or commenting for the record on any scholars' respective merits. That was because it was my determined personal resolve *not* to take advantage of my open annual opportunity to offer a name for nomination. Having so to speak shot my bolt in the 1958 letter to the Bank of Sweden, and in view of my dislike for creation of a self-perpetuating elite, only once and far later did I break this resolve: when many of us feared that a clearly great scholar was in danger of dying before Stockholm got around to anointing him, I did join in a successful full-court press to speed up his choice.

As I write, twelve of the fifteen have died. This frees me to record (what is not important) that in my personal judgment the 1969-to-1978 awards were all commendable and in no case surprising. This does not deny pronouncements by some informed scholars that a subset of the winners ought in those years to have been replaced by later winners or by worthies who died and never did receive the Stockholm nod.

The oldest of the fifteen, Frisch, was born in 1895. The youngest, Arrow, was born in 1921. Surprisingly only four of the fifteen were born in America. (None of them came from the typical small-town origins of Frank Knight, Wesley Mitchell or others of my teachers' generation.)

No less than three were born in Russia. Three also hailed from Scandinavia. Only two were born in the British Isles, the birthplace of mainstream economics. Holland also bred two. Finally, the Austrian Hayek was the only laureate whose native language was German. Early on, neither France, nor Italy nor Germany contributed to the first fifteen. Perhaps it is not accidental that continental places where economics was located in the law schools lost ground to places where economics flourished in the engineering and commerce faculties.

In all fairness, we should add to the native-born four Americans Kuznets and Leontief and Koopmans as immigrants to America where they did their primary research. Similar reasoning could reallocate Hayek to England where his main publications were authored.

Notably absent from the list are the great economists from my teachers' generation. Reference books tell me that Jacob Viner, Frank Knight, Alvin Hansen, and Paul Douglas could have been picked in the first years of the new award. Evidently Erik Lundberg and his committee made a conscious resolve to start out with the present and the future, rather than pack the first several years with great but retiring scholars.

Evident too was a bias that inclined the first laureates toward economists fairly adept at mathematics. Only Hayek, Myrdal, and Kuznets could be regarded as exceptions. And even the latter showed himself to be mathematically competent by his publicizing Eugen Slutsky's seminal statistical work demonstrating that cyclical artifacts could be the result of applying repeated differencings and moving averagings to uncorrelated random time series; also Kuznets published important articles on the post-Könus definitions of economic index numbers. (One guesses that because economics is necessarily a soft social science, the Nobel group hoped that a stress on mathematics might minimize the subjectivities and ideologies that had always simmered in connection with the original Nobel Prizes in Literature and Peace.)

Can one discern distinct ideological biases present in the first sub-sample? One's own ideology contaminates what one subjectively discerns in addressing such a question. Without doubt Hayek and Friedman would be counted as "conservative" economists. Frisch, Tinbergen, amd Myrdal would certainly be classified as social democrats and "do-gooders." Adopting that filtering designation, from what I knew of them, in those days both Kuznets and Leontief tended to be apolitical--as one might expect from burnt-out Menshevists migrating out of Lenin's Soviet Union. On the grounds that a Soviet academician would not be free in 1975 to express publicly a personal ideological credo, I make no attempt to score Kantorovich's social attitudes. By Swedish standards, Ohlin would be judged to be more conservative than the majority of his fellow voters and I would be inclined to bracket him in the middle along with Hicks. That leaves half a dozen left to be graded. At even-money odds, I'd bet that all (or most) of them, when choosing between a slightly right-of-center and a slightly left-of-center head of state, would vote left of center. Since most Swedish economists I have known have been somewhat to the right of their ruling party's ideology, it might not be too far off the mark to opine that the majority of the Stockholm committee end up choosing most laureates who were similar to themselves. I must make clear that one will find it hard to document that any one of the scholar group was there *only* because of his congenial ideology. Instead, having the reputation of being a strong ideologist of any kind would probably have worked against your winning an early Alfred Nobel award in economics.

Nominating a Second Fifteen
Historians and sociologists of science have learned that great discoveries are rarely the sole work of a single scholar. A Darwin and a Wallace are almost more the rule than the exception. Same goes for Newton and Leibniz. Thomas Kuhn has documented that a dozen quasi-independent researchers had claims to have discovered the Law of Conservation of Energy; exactly what each discovered was not known to all.

This brute truth works against Carlylean myths about single great giants as all important actors on the stage of history. Also this truth makes harder the task of Stockholm Nobel committees. For myself this leads toward the pragmatic suggestion that each year, *ceteris paribus*, there should be three awards rather than only one. (Yes, yes, Einstein deserved to shake the King of Sweden's hand alone on the platform.)

Simple arithmetic confirms that in the first ten years, 1969 through 1978, instead of recognizing only our fifteen economists the Royal Academy could have filled twice fifteen slots. Out of curiosity and in the interest of both fairness and justice, I am pursuing the antifactual thought experiment of nominating fifteen more available might-have-beens. Each of my readers, like me, could have picked randomly among fifty acknowledged worthies to replace my slate of 15 hundreds of other slates of 15.

Here is my hypothetical list for 1969-1978. The chronological order is inessential and is here somewhat scrambled.

Table 2. Reality Augmented by Fifteen Nominated Might-Have-Beens
(new names in bold face type)

1969	Frisch; Tinbergen; Hicks
1970	Kuznets; Friedman; **Irving Kravis** (1916-1992), USA
1971	Arrow; **Harold Hotelling** (1895-1973), USA; **Holbrook Working** (1895-1985), USA
1972	Hayek; Myrdal; **Joan Robinson** (1903-1983), U.K.
1973	Ohlin; Meade; **Gottfried Haberler** (1901-1995), Austria

1974	Leontief; **Piero Sraffa** (1898-1993), Italy; **Nicholas Georgescu-Roegen** (1906-1994), Romania
1975	Koopmans; Kantorovich; Simon
1976	**Abba Lerner** (1903-1982), Russia; **Lionel McKenzie** (1919-), USA; **Roy Harrod** (1900-1978), U.K.
1977	**John Rawls** (1921-1982), US; **Kenneth Boulding** (1910-1993), U.K.; **Thomas Schelling** (1921-), USA
1978	Samuelson; **Abram Bergson** (1914-2003), USA; **Richard Musgrave** (1910-), Germany

It is evident that my selection leans toward the mathematical side. A Hayek list would be very different. Also, my rankings are idiosyncratic. A name like Holbrook Working is not even in the official *Who's Who in Economics*, but it is that book's editors' fault that they have omitted the scholar who first and most extensively documented the random walk properties of futures and spot prices in the 1925-1960 period.

When I picked out John Rawls, it was not because I believed the philosopher to be deeper than such economists as Arrow, Little or Harsanyi. However, Rawls' general acceptance merited recognition. Why name Kravis and not Summers and Heston? The first leader of an orchestra creating purchasing-power-corrected comparative per capita real incomes must stand for all when award slots must be severely rationed. Behind every Berkeley physicist, numerous teams of co-workers perforce go prizeless. Who said life will be fair?

Table 2 makes it more fair than Table 1. At least that is its purpose. Debate about the above choices will be more interesting than they themselves are.

Conclusion

I hope that this new set of fifteen will not tend to rob the originals their deserved due. Scientific scholarship is not--or ought not to be --a zero-sum game, where elevating A perforce demotes B.

The original award winners, taken as a group, score almost as workaholics. But this blunts Aristotle's point that people enjoy working at what they are good at--and my point, that such work is not algebraically work at all. Most of the group seem to have achieved all that could have been expected of them. Possible exceptions are the few whom an outsider might judge did not choose to realize their likely scholarly potential. The reason for this was generally not laziness or a desire to earn lots of money. In individuals of this high caliber, it can be ideological zeal that tempts effort away from scholarly creativity. In a free universe what right has an outsider to second guess the aspirations of another?

The notion has floated around that Nobel physicists, chemists, and biologists become more sterile *after* their Stockholm beatification. Eyeballing the time profile of these first guinea pigs, I do not discern any discontinuous descent into sterility. Yes, vanity may swell after Stockholm, but the normal age-corrected time profile of creativity seems generally preserved.

I want to develop a last point. The 1901-1968 prizes in the exact sciences tended to award Nobels to scholars for *specific* accomplishments: a physics prize for Robert Millikan for measuring the electron's charge; a prize for the "Compton effect" or the "Mossbauer effect." If a lucky apple didn't drop on your head, you went prizeless. A fruitful career in many eclectic domains went unrewarded. I feared that the economic committees would be unduly influenced to ape this questionable practice. Actually the first fifteen choices, in retrospect, somewhat avoided this temptation. The last fifteen appointed up until now, maybe, if anything have seemed more prone to break ties between worthy nominees by the dubious method of selecting the ones whose names are attached to particular techniques to the neglect of all-around many excellences. I realize many will disagree with me on this viewpoint.

CHAPTER 11

Paul A. Samuelson

Professor (Emeritus) of Economics, Massachusetts Institute of Economics

This interview was conducted by mail in May 2003. Paul read the introduction and earlier interviews and was kind enough to answer the following questions.

You are probably the person who is most responsible for shaping modern economics. Are you happy with the way it has turned out? How do you view new fruitful trends and view others as likely dead ends?

I hesitate to speak off the cuff about your last question. I am reminded that the great physicist Lord Rayleigh was asked early in the last century, "What do you think of quantum mechanics?" He replied, "You must not ask a scholar over sixty that question." Actually, this was excessive modesty since Max Planck's first breakthrough owed much to Rayleigh's investigations of black-body radiation's observable frequency distributions. I am well over sixty and feisty with pro and con judgments about new century trends in economics. However, research deadlines usurp my time for leisurely reflection. I go with A. E. Housman, the poet who wrote *A Shropshire Lad* in his spare time between his admired publications as a classic scholar. "Why did you not include item A in your collection of papers? Do you not think it good?" he was asked by a colleague. He replied, "I do think it good, but not good enough for me." Rather than compose evaluations that lack coherence and *detailed* understandings, I'll take a pass.

Where the influence of 1947 *Foundations* is concerned, one must understand that this 1937–1945 composition was exceedingly lucky in its timing. At that time it was still the case that so much of literary economics could still benefit from straightforward intermediate applied mathematics. That is why, in many diverse places around the globe, a baker's dozen of graduate students would meet to discuss and learn from this book, which was written largely in the latter 1930s, when I myself was a privileged Harvard Junior Fellow leisurely learning the tools that it contained.

For almost forty years the book went through successive printings that corrected its various typos but left its original text untouched. In 1983 I finally decided to enlarge it, strictly by adding compact analyses of the very many subsequent postwar theoretical developments: linear and nonlinear programming; Arrow-Debreu-McKenzie general equilibrium; post Heckscher-Ohlin and Jones trade theories, stochastic and intertemporal maximizing; modern finance theory à la Markowitz, Modigliani, Mandelbrot, Merton, Bachelier, Tobin, Sharpe, Fama; also many Ramsey and von Neumann goodies. In this effort completeness and not pedagogical verve was my goal.

The result: moderate sales and impact from what, objectively speaking, was a better book. Why? Presumptively because the end-of-century generation had by then been converted to the newer, more technical economics, and for whom learned journals and books had proliferated mightily to teach those willing to learn.

Foundations, *your long-time best-selling pattern-setting elementary* Economics, *and five (soon to be seven) volumes of* Collected Scientific Papers *have given you perhaps the reputation of Mr. Neoclassical Economics. Is that take right? And how do you feel about it?*

Mine is a more nuanced view. If the label *neoclassical* excludes the Keynesian abandonment of Marshallian-Wicksellian-Walrasian belief in Say's Law as a guarantor of quasi-full-employment equilibrium, then I am a heretic. Decades ago I initiated the popular notion of a *neoclassical synthesis.* Its two-word essence was that by use of non–Say's Law macro tools, a modern mixed economy could restore to relevance the microeconomic verities absent from Great

Depression or hyperinflation scenarios in economic history. My prescriptions and policy nostrums were not at all identical to Milton Friedman's monistic monetarism. But to "new classicist, rational expectationists" Robert Lucas or Tom Sargent, we might be lumped together as odd-couple bedfellows. (That would annoy *two* people!)

Bona fide neoclassicists—such as Sweden's Eli Heckscher or Gustav Cassel—were admirers of laissez-faire. In *Foundations,* I tirelessly stressed how empirical realities of technology and divided knowledge could vitiate Adam Smith's comfortable views on good-thing Invisible Hands. What I learned from Abram Bergson was how to distinguish between the efficiencies of (the infinite) Pareto Optima and the spread of distributive inequalities that they entailed. (My personal credo mandates: Never think about Pareto Optimality without at the same time contemplating differential effects on different peoples' well-being. Henry Simon tattooed my mind on the old Chicago Midway with the dictum: Any good cause can justify moves into realms of diminishing returns—which is why those moves need rational limiting.) When a Rawls or Bentham is persuasive, a good democracy can be justified in trading off some efficiency against the goal of some social harmony or equality. This is not a license for romantic utopianism that might in brute fact create horrendous and *gratuitous deadweight loss* as it misses the nice-sounding target of utopia.

Surely you have experienced some disappointments with real world trends and historical evolutions of economist tools and accomplishments?

Yes, and the day is not long enough to dig out all of them. Thus, I was more hopeful at age thirty that future statistical tools and techniques would pinpoint better understandings and forecasting. I knew that "Nature" (i.e., the economic history record) would not perform for us useful scatters of data like those achieved in the chemistry or physiology laboratory. However, early advances in multivariable regression techniques and identification were already in a degree useful. Still the best objective economists can be in disagreement, at the same time that both admit to limitations on their self-confidence about their best guesses.

On the macro front, we've done perhaps better than I had reason to guess half a century ago. *Quasi-micro* efficiency of securities markets exceeded my original guessings. However, macro *inefficiency* of

𝒫ᴀᴜʟ ᴀ. sᴀᴍᴜᴇʟsᴏɴ

aggregate stock market oscillations has also (slightly) exceeded my expectations for the new century. Net, though, my overall impression rebuts Tom Kuhn's relativisms in the history of science. In economics "later" generally is "better." Such a whig inference we are not free to believe in or to deny for personal subjective reasons.

When I sample novel proposals of today's brightest and best, my pulses rise but not yet wildly. Experience has taught: Give each new idea a friendly hearing. Expect most to fail. But better to be a bit gullible for the reason that overblown novelties will likely get cut down to size by future critical researchers. Overambitious claims are unlikely permanently to be taken seriously.

Experience early converted me to eclecticism. Try to be as eclectic as complex reality requires. But try not to be more eclectic than reality needs: an open mind can be an empty mind. Psychologically, I am averse to being wrong. Before Karl Popper recommended being your own best critic, I tried to capture for myself the fun of rebutting my own nominations. Nevertheless in the interest of being explorative, I've been willing to be occasionally wrong. ("That's big of you," Bob Solow says.) But what I hate most in life is to *stay wrong*.

It is not a paradox that I scrutinize most carefully the writings of contemporaries whose views differ systematically from mine. I can learn least from rereading expositions of buddies who concur with me. Most of us can learn least from "enemies." (When Keynes was resisting criticisms of his 1936 *General Theory* by Ralph Hawtrey in the years when the book was being written, those same exact arguments, if expressed by Keynes's protégé Richard Kahn, might well have seemed acceptable! That is why when I hope to convert an opponent out of what I believe to be a nonoptimal view, my devious mind seeks to plant the rebuttal into a mutual friend who will not raise the hackles that I might do.)

I might add in connection with this present book's efforts that in my experience *biography* of contemporaries does *usefully* help in understanding and testing their nominated novelties.

Paul A. Samuelson

Professor (Emeritus) of Economics, Massachusetts Institute of Economics

INFORMATION ON THE WEB ABOUT PAUL A. SAMUELSON
http://ideas.repec.org/e/psa57.html

EDUCATION
A.B. Economics, University of Chicago, 1935
Ph.D. Economics, Harvard University, 1941

SELECTED PUBLICATIONS
"A Note on the Pure Theory of Consumers' Behavior." *Economica,* February 1938.
"Interactions between the Multiplier Analysis and the Principle of Acceleration." *Review of Economics and Statistics,* May 1939.
Economics. 1st ed. New York: McGraw-Hill, 1948.
"The Pure Theory of Public Expenditure." *Review of Economics and Statistics,* November 1954.
Foundations of Economic Analysis. Cambridge: Harvard University Press, 1947; enlarged ed., 1983.
"An Exact Consumption-Loan Model of Interest with or without the Social Contrivance of Money." *Journal of Political Economy* 66 (1958).

SPECIAL HONORS AND EXPERIENCE
David A. Wells Award (best thesis, Harvard University), 1941
John Bates Clark Award, 1947
President, Econometric Society, 1953
President, American Economic Association, 1961
Albert Einstein Medal, 1970
Nobel Prize in Economics, 1970
Gold Scanno Prize in Economy, 1990
National Medal of Science, 1996
34 Honorary Degrees

593

3 Pastiches from an earlier politically incorrect academic age

Paul A. Samuelson

Father and son teams are famous in economics: James and John Stuart Mill; John Neville and John Maynard Keynes; John Bates and John Maurice Clark. Therefore, to contribute for a Mark Perlman *Festschrift*, I select a topic that would have interested Selig Perlman, Mark's father and an acclaimed historian of the American Labor Movement in his own right.

Selig Perlman made his academic way at Wisconsin in the pre-World War I period when Jews were few in U.S. academic life. If scarcity makes for high price, those few ought to have enjoyed astronomical salaries. (Alvin Hansen told me that it was Perlman who first discovered him. While on sabbatical leave, Selig looked over the term papers in John R. Commons' Wisconsin graduate class. 'The one by Hansen is the only paper with real scholarly promise,' Perlman reported. The rest is history.)

Some careerists, after they have elbowed their way into Valhalla, wish to pull up the ladder behind them. Not Selig Perlman. By reputation, he was singularly zealous in speaking up for promising scholars who encountered theological bigotries: as we have seen, he even spoke up for a Danish-American farmboy, whose parents had independently migrated to America to escape the repressions against Baptists by the mid-nineteenth century established Danish Lutheran Church.

I am not an expert on anti-semitism and various racial prejudices. Nor can I claim personally to have particularly suffered the pains of bias. If anything the marketplace has imputed to me perhaps even more than my intrinsic worth. All the better then may be my qualifications to report on what the world was really like in the years from 1920 to 1945. Before then, we can be sure that Selig Perlman could have painted an infinitely worse portrait.

What my anecdotes lack in quantitative validation may be a bit atoned for by their authenticity. I was present at world centers of importance and confine myself largely to incidents and events of which my knowledge has been first hand. Although the present purpose pardons an unbalanced preoccupation with anti-semitism, strongly correlated with it factually will be found to be anti-Black, anti-female, anti-Catholic, anti-homosexual, anti-radical and even anti-class attitudes. No discrimination is intended here against the valid complaints of Hispanics, gypsies or Native Americans – it is just that their sample was very small in the academia of my early times, which is itself a testimony to something significant.

The good old days

Put bluntly, there were no tenured Jews in the Ivy League. None at all? Well, virtually none at all. And it was not all that different at the large state universities, particularly in the engineering faculties. Since almost no chemical companies would hire a Jew with a diploma in chemistry, graduates of the City College of New York (CCNY) sensibly opted to apply to law schools or schools of dentistry. Was the DNA of the Chosen People exceptionally biased in favor of tooth care and against care of the heart and kidney? Or was it more likely that Junior Phi Beta Kappa's from CCNY were largely unable to gain admission to medical schools?

In my older times, if you went to college at all, it was generally (a) to your father's college, or (b) to the university near to where you lived. That explains why, as a visiting lecturer, I would encounter a richer mixture of brilliant students at the University of Buffalo in 1940 than at State University of New York (Buffalo) in 1965: by 1965, the best and brightest in upstate New York often got drained off to Cornell or Harvard. That explains why in 1941 our crack MIT graduate school recruited much of the entering class from the University of Kansas and DePauw rather than as today so much more frequently from Princeton, Stanford and Harvard. This seems a case of *class* stratification giving way to meritocracy stratification.

I was lucky that the University of Chicago was near my home. It was a great age for the (Hutchins) Midway. The Rosenwald Foundation rightly ranked Chicago second only to Harvard *c.* 1935, with Columbia and Berkeley hot on their heels. What was Chicago's transient advantage? John D. Rockefeller's largesse as a Baptist? Yes, of course. But, also, I give importance to Chicago's monopoly advantage as a place that would hire some extraordinarily able Jews. That made their money go farther. Not that there was no anti-semitism at Chicago. There was some of that anywhere (and even in the CCNY faculty!). In the 1920s when Frank Knight, Jacob Viner and other Chicago economists decided to recruit Henry Schultz, protegé of H.L. Moore and an early econometrician, they were told: 'But President Max Mason does not like Jews.' 'Well, let him veto the appointment then. We think he's the best man for the post.' (I have this story from my Chicago classmate Jacob Mosak, who became Schultz's protegé and assistant. I may add that by general 1920–35 opinion, Jacob Viner had been Frank Taussig's prize student at Harvard and, as the world authority on both international trade and history of economics, he arguably deserved a Harvard chair more than most then sitting in those chairs.)

My next anecdote is exceptional because it represented something so rare. In my undergraduate time, a Chicago coach was reported to have said aloud (there is no other way to say something): 'There are getting to be too many Jews around here.' When this was reported to the venerable head-coach Amos Alonzo Stagg, Stagg called in the accused. 'Did you say that?' 'Yes, in a thoughtless moment I did say those words.' 'Well then, as of this hour, you are fired. Collect your pay and sweat garb and go.' Now what's unusual about that story? It is its rarity. In simple truth *most* non-Jews were not virulently anti-semitic at that time. Or even anti-semitic in any *significant sense.* (I exclude the racial slurs that peppered within-family conversations of your typical American family folk. 'You can't jew me down to a lower price.' etc., etc.)

Everywhere and at all times most humans are social cowards. We will not make waves just for an abstract principle. Even if you would not mind having proportionate Jewish representation in social or athletic clubs, you are not willing to go clubless on that account or join up with a largely Jewish group to make a point. Similar stratifications were observable within ethnic groups: successful Eastern European Jews becoming token members in exclusive clubs formed by wealthy German immigrants from an earlier age.

The Harvard of 1920–45 was not worse than other Ivy League schools. Since President Eliot's effort to make Harvard a great *university*, it had become distinctly better than Yale or Princeton. That is not saying much. Harvard presidents alternate between university and college leaders. A. Lawrence Lowell, as Eliot's successor, was a college person. I came to know him later – at Harvard's Society of Fellows, which he personally endowed with the last of his family fortune. Lowell denounced Sacco and Vanzetti because he believed them to be murderers, and therefore he said so publicly. He believed that the pushy 'new races' were pressing against the fine Yankee talent. And therefore he injudiciously announced that Harvard would apply a numerical quota on admissions. Better candid truth than under-the-table hypocrisy? This led to an unexpected public uproar. When he gave a speech to alumni in New York, apparently he explained the problem of uncouth immigrants with pushy manners. Besides, he is supposed to have validly pointed out that race-blind admissions at Harvard would vastly increase the number of New York Jews in the freshman class. One old-timer reported to me the following (so all this is hearsay and should be checked with the new history of Harvard that is in the making), that a number of wealthy listeners deemed this personally insulting and began to reconsider their charitable giving.

It is a matter of record that, for whatever reason, in 1923 Harvard introduced a new policy according to which *any* boy who finished in the highest *seven* of his high school class would be admitted to Harvard. In consequence, 1927 was a brilliant class that included Judge Charles Wyzanski, Professor Milton Katz of Marshall Plan and Ford Foundation fame and many others. A surviving member of 1927 believes that as many as twenty percent of his fellow freshmen were Jews. And pins on the map for subsequent Harvard students did become dispersed to include entrants from outside the Philadelphia–Portland axis. Not until 1935 did President Conant introduce Harvard's regional scholarships, which brought James Tobin all the way from Champaign-Urbana, Illinois, to Cambridge, Massachusetts.

Where were Yale and Princeton then? At Yale President Angell tried to be a university rather than college president. A call was sent out to Morris Cohen, CCNY's famous philosopher. In weighing it, Dr Cohen made a point of asking whether the philosophy department really wanted him. Since he asked, he is said to have been told: 'President Angell wants you. But we do not.' Yale's loss was CCNY's gain, and later Chicago's gain. Princeton's eating clubs, which operated much like private fraternities, effectively kept its undergraduate composition mainstream Protestant. Its graduate school stayed limited to the couple of hundred who could be housed in one gothic structure, where Oxbridge robes were *de rigueur* at meal times. So strong was Princeton's mathematics and physics that a Maxwell Demon passed a Richard

Feynman through the system's filter. Stars like Ansley Coale and Lionel McKenzie were relatively rare until Morgenstern-von Neumann mathematics attracted Shapleys, Nashes and Shubiks.

It used to be quipped: Anti-Catholicism is the anti-semitism of the academics. Less than the demographic quotas of brilliant Catholics were to be found in pre-World War II elite universities. Bias begets backlash. Cardinal O'Connell, the powerful archbishop of the Boston diocese, frowned on members of the flock who selected Harvard over Boston College. It was a wonder that Ambassador Joseph Kennedy, father of the Kennedy clan, went to Harvard back in the Teens. Alice Bourneuf, who was the one woman who got an A from the femmophobe Frank Taussig, was considered exceptional when she and her sister came to Radcliffe. After her time the two-sided barriers largely broke down.

In the 1930s Radcliffe and Harvard were not integrated at the undergraduate level. Edward Mason would lecture on Industrial Organization to 200 Harvard men at 9 am. Then from 11 am to 12 noon he would repeat that same lecture before eight Radcliffe women. When my fiancée would want to use Widener Library, she was supposed to wear hat and gloves and speak in hushed tones in the special ghetto space for females. In economics, graduate study was by then integrated. But not in delicate subjects like English. When I expressed surprise at this to Mr. Lowell, he expressed surprise at my surprise. 'Would you want your sister to be in the same Shakespeare class with men?' That, as the French say, gave one to think. (I by chance was at Cambridge University in 1948 the first day a woman received a Cambridge degree. It was the Queen Mother. I heard an old don mutter, 'Next they'll be riding their bikes in caps and gowns.') Joan Robinson, at Girton in the early 1920s, got a certificate, not a degree – even though Florence Brown Keynes and Mary Paley Marshall had received a Cambridge education back in the late 1870s. The great Alfred Marshall was a notorious femmophobe.

A proposal, around 1937, to admit a black undergraduate into Lowell House at Harvard gave rise to hot debate. (This was decades after Paul Robeson had starred in Ivy League football!) Finally, non-resident tutor Professor William Yandell Elliott, southern gentleman and lecturer in huge Freshman Government 1 caved in and said, 'All right, but don't expect me to sit next to him.' I tell this discreditable story only to make a point about the timing of the Great Change. Just ten years later, this same Elliott, as Chairman of the Government Department, went on hands and knees to Ralph Bunche hoping to fill a distinguished Harvard chair. Bunche by that time had bigger fish to fry elsewhere at the United Nations.

Repeating the same kind of anecdote N times does not proportionally multiply its importance or accuracy. However, to illustrate the positive correlation between one kind of bigotry and other kinds of bigotry here is a true account *within* economics itself. When I arrived at Harvard in 1935, Harold Hitchings Burbank had been department chairman since time immemorial. Burbank's incompetence as a scholar could not be exaggerated. I once thought to have caught him out with a publication: on the spine of a volume at old Phillips Bookstore across from Widener was written Burbank. But after incredulous auditing, it turned out to be an edited symposium where it was the other editors who had done the work. The easiest A I ever got was in Burbank's graduate Public Finance course. (Irreverent students called it a course, not *on* public finance but *against* public finance.) Class contents were a crib from the Princeton textbook of conservative Harley Lutz, which itself was a crib from Charles Bullock's reactionary Harvard lectures of 1901–33.

Burbank suffered fools gladly, but not Jews. On major departmental appointments, he could count on a near-majority of cronies. Where patronage appointments in the lower ranks were concerned, he was absolute king. Being myself royally supported by Social Science Research and Harvard Society of Fellows stipends, like William Tell I felt no need to cozy up to him. That did not stop Burbank from advising me: 'Samuelson, you are narrow. Keynes and Hawtrey are narrow. Don't take up economic theory until *after* you are fifty. This is what our great Allyn Young used to say.' Alas, I had already lost my heart, and aspired to become even more narrow; and furthermore Young died young, just before his rendezvous with greatness. Believing my male heredity to be (I write this in my ninth decade of life!) problematic, I was always a young man in a hurry.

Faced with a plethora of unsavory talent, H.H.B. solved his dilemma by confining the best of them to a ghetto of assistants in statistics and accounting under W. L. Crum and his satellite Edwin Frickey. Because Burbank had almost absolute pitch in his distaste for talent, such names as R. A. Gordon, Abram Bergson, Joe Bain and Lloyd Metzler made this a legion of honor. Metzler, a boy from Kansas with a German-sounding name, used to sing hymn duets with Marion Crawford – such as, 'Jesus Wants Me For a Sunbeam.' But as has been said, an anti-semite can smell out the last nine out of six Jews who have entered the room.

Burbank was catholic in his distastes. *Ceteris paribus*, he did not like foreigners. (As he discovered, they didn't speak accentless English.) He did not like radicals. Richard Murphy Goodwin, fresh from the farm country of Newcastle, Indiana, and Rhodes House, Oxford, drove him up the wall by asking: 'How little must I teach if I want a salary of only $1800 a year? I do like to paint.' When Senator Sinclair Weeks leaked an FBI report to Harvard concerning Goodwin's leftisms, that confirmed Burbank's distrust of dilettantes. (Neither Burbank nor Dick's friends knew that Goodwin did suffer from debilitating migraines. Painting may have been optimal decision making – at least up to Goodwin's post-Cambridge Indian Summer of scientific creativity late in life at Siena.) Under the Freedom of Information Act, Ken Galbraith learned that Burbie had reported to the FBI that Galbraith was as dangerous as President Franklin Delano Roosevelt. (I paraphrase from memory.)

I believe I have laid the background for the promised anecdote to come. (But before proceeding, one must face up to the complexity of real life. Yes, Burbie did have in him a sadistic streak which he took out on bullied graduate students: he did once call in Goodwin to say, 'Dick, I'd like to do to you what my father once did to me – tie you up to a wagon wheel and give you the whipping you deserve.' I learned this when sitting in the back of Gottfried Haberler's car on our way to Taconic, Connecticut, for Schumpeter's funeral in January 1950. On my right was Goodwin. On my left was Alfred Conrad, co-generator of Cliometrics with John Meyer. Alf chipped in: 'Say what you will about Burbie, he was the only one in the cold Harvard environment who asked me how my post-T.B. health was developing. One day he called me in to say: "I've got you figured, Alf, as a warm human being, and that's the kind of PhD thesis you ought to decide on." How could I then say that just yesterday I'd settled on a topic about matrices of Leontief input/output type!')

There is a different beast from every angle you view an elephant. My first run in with Burbie came on Registration Day 1935 when I refused to take the standard economic history course from the boring Edwin Gay. Yet, just yesterday, as I write, I read a charming memoir from Theodore Morgan of the University of Wisconsin. In 1938 when Ted was dithering between English (with two years of old English and one of Middle German as a graduate requirement) and economics, he reports, '... nice old Burbie... overweight and pleasant... talked to me with interest and kindness.... [and] let me sign up for the courses I fancied.' Also, as I have written elsewhere, our dear friend Jeanette Arnold (Whitmer) became Burbank's last departmental secretary. She worshipped the man we held in contempt. It was no strain on our friendship: by tacit agreement we never talked about H.H.B.

One summer day in 1937 or 1938, Russ Nixon our class radical and Radcliffe students' pin-up boy, told me about his tennis morning playing doubles with full professors Edward Chamberlin and Edward Mason and Instructor Paul Sweezy. Between sets, Nixon reported that Paul S. remarked, 'Wasn't that terrible what Burbie said as yesterday's departmental meeting was ending?' 'What was that?' Chamberlin asked. Paul filled him in: 'You'll remember that attendance was light and that encouraged me to move that we make Shigeto Tsuru a Teaching Fellow – a post he richly deserved. *Mirabile dictu*, we got a majority and the motion was carried. As we were breaking up, Burbie grumbled, "Next thing you know they'll be making Dean an instructor."' (Voice from the Greek chorus, me, PAS: Dean was one of two black graduate students, whose research under Abbott Payson Usher on location theory applied to economic history was deemed to be path-breaking.)

Ed Chamberlin, always logical, Russ reports as saying: 'Burbank wasn't wrong. If you appoint a Japanese, you can't refuse to appoint a colored man. Actually, the French do it right: if you're not trained in France, no chair for you.' Paul then replied: 'But if national residence is your test, then a Dean whose people have been in America for 300 years must surely qualify.' Chamberlin, always logical, replied: 'Yes to Dean. No to a foreigner.' (Greek chorus: Shigeto Tsuru was the only Harvard College graduate in the 1935 entering economics graduate class. His senior thesis, written in Adams House, won high honors. Later he was a bulwark for the MacArthur Occupation team, a primary bridge between Japanese and Western economics, Professor and President of Hitotsubashi University and a scholar whose collected papers filled more than thirteen volumes! He was also an authority on Marxian and on environmental economics.) To wind up this two-bigotry anecdote, at the next departmental meeting with a full complement attending, the provisional Tsuru appointment was rescinded and he had to settle for being Schumpeter's prize research assistant. As an honorable postscript to this tennis-court conversation, I can report that during World War II when Emile Despres was recruiting the famous team of pre-CIA Office of Strategic Services (OSS) economists, he felt duty bound to go to head honcho Mason and say, 'Ed, I've been recruiting many crack economists and a number of them turn out to be Jews. Is this a problem?' Mason replied: 'Pick the best you can. If ever it becomes a problem, let me worry about that.' The story ended there.

1088

Summing up

There was once a time when many scholars honestly dismissed Jews as being incompetent – especially in Humanities departments. The early Binet I.Q. tests, culture bound, when applied to pre-World War I immigrants allegedly confirmed this thesis of racial inability. But by the time of my early days, attitudes were best understood as stemming from a contrary fear that ethnic-blind promotions might unleash an undesired avalanche. Few thought Einstein to be a dunce or a shallow master of physics. When Nazis in Hitler's Germany called Werner Heisenberg a 'White Jew' that was taken by him to be something of an honor.

Frisky Merriman, Master of Harvard's fashionable Eliot House, was a candid anti-semite. He never justified his position in terms of competence or incompetence. I am sure that, as a historian of the Spanish and Turkish Empires, he had never heard of Eli Heckscher's histories of Sweden or of Mercantilism. In 1940 I was an Instructor and Tutor in Harvard's Leverett House – known then as 'Moscow on the Charles.' Our Boston blue-blood Master, Kenneth Murdock, mischievously read to us members of the Senior Common Room the letter Merriman had written to all his 'cousins' serving as House Masters: 'What, oh what, are we going to do about this Jew problem? We are supposed to have a quota of twenty per cent [was he right in this?] but you have only to use your eyes to realize that they are more than forty per cent and growing.' It was *a* last gasp – but not *the* last gasp – of a decaying order.

Today Harvard, Princeton and Yale have presidents who, by Nazi calculus, are two-and-a-half Jewish and one-half Italian. This is not an equilibrium of maximal entropy, but one envisages well-born corpses rotating in their graves at the fact of it.

I have concentrated on MIT and the few Ivy League places I knew best. But one could write much about the great state universities and the smaller crack colleges. Wisconsin itself, Selig Perlman's academic base, once went through an intense bout of anti-semitism. Chancellor Dykstra, who left the University of Wisconsin to go to UCLA, confided in me that he had gone literally out of the frying pan only to end up in the fire. (On another bigotry front, a University of Virginia president for some odd reason came to me to ask my advice: 'What can I do about my overly conservative economics department?' I, always a realist and pacifist, replied: 'Probably nothing. Why don't you work the other side of the street and try to develop the best conservative department outside of Cook County and indeed anywhere in the world?')

I have named names. This is all right. But I have failed to name names that I might have named. George Birkhoff of Harvard was America's first great mathematician. I saw a good deal of him in the years 1937–40. He was considered to be a strong anti-semite. That was not what he believed about himself. Being of a Napoleonic temperament, he genuinely believed that no one was quite as good as himself and he would have taken grave offense if anyone thought his Dutch-German name was Jewish. He ludicrously rationalized the peculiar composition of Harvard's math department in the 1920–45 period as being merely the consequence of their wanting to belong to a 'congenial' group. (In mathematics intrinsic ability is self-revealing. *Ergo* race bigotry becomes self-revealing.)

At a deeper level, G.B. believed that Jews were 'early bloomers' who tended to worm their way into prestigious posts while their deeper competitors were still maturing into genius. (Incidentally, George Birkhoff was an early bloomer – and also a late one. MIT's Norbert Wiener, who was Birkhoff's *bête noir*, was actually something of a *late* bloomer in his great researches even though he went to college as a boy in knickerbockers.)

By coincidence my teacher Joseph Schumpeter shared this view with Birkhoff. Alfred Conrad was Schumpeter's assistant when he died, and he relayed to Goodwin and me on our drive to the 1950 funeral a recent dialogue with Schumpeter.

> Alf: Professor Schumpeter, what do you think of Nicky Kaldor?
> Joe: Oh, these Asiatics. They are only early bloomers.
> Alf: I am puzzled. Are you perhaps referring to Kaldor's Hungarian Magyar ancestry?
> Joe: My dear Alfred. My figure of speech was to spare *your* sensibilities. It was my delicate way of referring to Kaldor's Mosaic ancestry.

The Greek chorus can report that in Kaldor's 78 years of life he was more prolific toward its end than early on; in my book, he deserved to split a Nobel Prize with Roy Harrod and Joan Robinson; any detectable foolishnesses in his work smacked of youth-like enthusiasms rather than senile dementias.

Final reflections

Maynard Keynes and Joseph Schumpeter were creatures of an earlier time. Can one be surprised that their diaries and letters to pals reflect the folkways and mores of Eton-Bloomsbury and Emperor Franz Joseph's Austria? Keynes's brilliant early discernment of a rottenness in Lenin-Stalin Russia becomes blemished by a Keynesian denunciation of Trotsky's Jewishness. This is from the pen of Richard Kahn's mentor, and from the pen that exaggerates the Old Testament virtues of Weimar's Melchior as elder statesman.

Elizabeth Schumpeter, widow, chucked into the Harvard archives *all* her husband's literary remains (including arguments with himself pro and con on marrying Elizabeth). Naturally a cottage industry of biographers sprang up. How should we weigh in the balance vulgar night thoughts against the fact that more refugees from Hitler were landed in U.S. professorial chairs by Schumpeter than probably by any other single person? When Schumpeter singled me out as a favorite protégé, did this betoken a belief that my candle would burn out quickly by virtue of defective DNA?

Things are often not quite what they seem. Mathematical polymath Edwin Bidwell Wilson, Willard Gibbs' sole protégé at Yale and my revered mentor, encouraged me to go to MIT, telling how he himself had never regretted leaving Yale for MIT early in the century. That carried weight with me: I was touched by his admiring solicitude. Years later Richard Swedberg, Schumpeter's best biographer, sent me an item he found in the Harvard archives of E. B. Wilson and Talcott Parsons.

It threw a new and different light on that Wilson-Samuelson 1940 correspondence. I paraphrase for brevity.

> Wilson to Parsons: I write to avoid misunderstanding. You left our Sociology Division meeting just after I had said: You must never appoint an able Jew to a temporary assignment. I fear you may have got the wrong impression that I am anti-semitic. That is not at all the case. I was merely warning that, since one will not be able to make him a tenured academic, his very ability will be the cause of embarrassment and heartburn later.

Pass-on-the-good-penny is a genuine problem in an imperfect, bigoted society.

Later ages will find it hard to identify the sheep and the goats of an earlier time but, with unearned self-confidence, they will not be deterred from making the effort.

52

Memoirs of an Early Finance Theorist

Paul A. Samuelson

Massachusetts Institute of Technology

When once asked to describe my specialisations in economics, I replied that perhaps I was the "last generalist" in economics – because pure theory, literary and mathematical economics, macro and micro, statistics and probability, foreign trade and managerial economics, were all principal research objects for me. This would imply, on a random basis, some preoccupation with finance and risk theory. But actually that would understate my degree of interest in and dedication to that area. Finance in general – personal and economy-wide – has been one of the most successful areas evolved in this last century, my century, and I've loved being a player.

Not everyone agrees. The record shows that Milton Friedman was cool toward Harry Markowitz's seminal 1952 Chicago PhD thesis, which to paraphrase, he thought *was hardly at all economics and not even interesting applied mathematics*. That this was not a temporary aberration was revealed when the press quoted his surprise years later that Stockholm would beatify the threesome of Markowitz, Sharpe and Miller, putting them ahead of a hundred other worthies. By contrast, I have found my extensive forays into finance rewarding. No other economic paradigms of elegance have equal intellectual and practical interest. Before I could vote, as a Chicago undergraduate, I began to follow the research efforts of Alfred Cowles III in testing forecasting methods and their batting averages. Before 1953 when Maurice Kendall documented the whiteness of noise in the speculative markets for shares, commodity spot and futures, and mutual fund markets, I pored over Holbrook Working's overlooked analyses of quasi-random grain prices. In 1935–37, newly at the Harvard Graduate School, I wrote my first paper on optimal life cycle consumption and saving. What led me to it was a notion, already in the air, that people's utility-of-wealth functions, subjective and introspective, could be measured non-introspectively from observing their stochastic choices. I even discovered then that knowledge of a Laplacian's smallest bets would pin down exactly how all his bets would behave. But I was so green as not to realise how extraordinary this finding was.

My family background, as interpreted to me by my risk-averse mother, involved World War prosperity and mid-1920s Florida real estate ventures that culminated in 1926 burst-bubble losses. My teacher of freshman high school math, with my juvenile help, became a victim of the 1929 Wall Street crash. I was not affluent in my early academic years, but being off to an early start, I was surrounded by good friends who could make do with less. So in the beginning, and later with my wife, I began to explore actual security selection. Avarice was not my guiding motive. Instead, it was an economist's curiosity. What was it like to sell short? What was it like to bet on a Packard–Studebaker merger? What was it like to dabble in puts and calls? My first interest in calls and warrants arose from a mistaken notion that their price patterns could tell me whether the public's expectational sentiments were "bullish" or "bearish". Only later, when I had perfected the arbitrage vector equivalences of puts and calls, did I come to realise that options were related to market volatility and not to expected levels or trends.

In the first half of the last century, practically nothing had been rigorously demonstrated in finance theory. "Don't put all your eggs in one basket" and anecdotes about "selling coal in winter and ice in summer" encoded the bare wisdom about the efficiency of diversification. That motivated my early publications to *prove* that the best meld of two independent but otherwise probabilistically identical stocks had to be a portfolio with *equal* weighting.

False aphorisms proliferated. At TIAA-CREF, a trustee destined for future ennoblement insisted that the Law of Large Numbers implied that an investor with an investment horizon ahead of 2N-periods must rationally be more equity-risk tolerant than a similar investor with only an N-period horizon. Evidently, he had not read my 1969 "Review of Economics and Statistics" paper, or those of a rash of others at the same time, which proved that constant-relative-risk aversion utility functions

$$\log(W) \quad \text{or} \quad W^{1-\gamma}/(1-\gamma), 0 < \gamma \neq 1$$

must myopically choose at all times in the future to aim for exactly the *same* optimised equity fraction.

Cleaning out Augean stables is not pleasant work, but someone has to do it. Again and again I have had to slay a new dragon who is tripping himself up on the notion that the geometric mean maximiser will achieve meaningful maximisation of a portfolio's "growth rate". If your one-period maximum is always the harmonic mean, because you are truly more risk-averse than Daniel Bernoulli's 1,738 U (W) = logW person, then following the GM maximising criterion will do you harm for all N however great, and the harm measured in your own risk-corrected dollars will soar with N!

When Savage asked economists: "who's this Bachelier guy?", I was able to locate that scholar's great 1900 Paris thesis. Converting its Gaussian–Brownian motion cum unlimited liability to Log-Gaussian motion, the astronomer Osborne and I independently were to provide Ito, Merton and Black–Scholes with a jumping-off place for instantaneous probabilities and rebalancings – a wonderland for elegant and virtually risk-free perfect hedgings. Separately, Eugene Fama and I could axiomatise efficient Martingale pricings, much like, but not identical to, Wiener random-walk noise.

Two-thirds of a century after my acne-age beginnings, I am still engaged in publishing basic critiques of Markowitz–Tobin–Sharpe quadratic-programming approximations involving means and variances. And side by side with Mark Machina, I have been developing the exact differential geometry that separates Laplacian expected {utility of outcomes} from more general functionals that do rank order any two or more probability distributions confronting the decision maker.

As the advertisements say, "we've come a long way, baby. And there's much more to come." As an adviser to non-profit agencies and as a theorist, I've certainly enjoyed the ride.

Reflections

Three Moles

Paul A. Samuelson

Paul A. Samuelson

Paul A. Samuelson, a Fellow of the American Academy since 1942, is Institute Professor of Economics Emeritus at the Massachusetts Institute of Technology. He was awarded a Noble Prize in Economics in 1970.

After Easter 1945, within the World War II research labs, conviction grew that Hitler's defeat was just around the corner. Understandably, hopes for a return to peacetime academic life began to emerge. Canny guys within the Office of Strategic Services and intelligence units knew that Germany, after its Stalingrad defeat, could not hope to win the war. In the Pacific, after the Battle of Midway, Allied code breakers had made certain that Japan, too, could not win its war. But Main-Street Yanks and Brits, almost up to the last gunshots, could still fear the worst. (As a dramatic example, Joseph Schumpeter, my Austrian Harvard mentor, isolated in Cambridge, Massachusetts, from December 7, 1941 to August 1945, when the nuclear bombs fell on Japan, could still believe until very late that Hitler was winning the war.)

In that 1945 springtime, as one of the few mathematical social scientists in the Radiation Laboratory at the Massachusetts Institute of Technology (MIT), I was sounded out for the job of writing the history of the Los Alamos nuclear bomb project – a paradoxical offer since officially I couldn't know that there was such a project. But no matter: wild horses could not have drawn me to that, or any, history job. Postwar macroeconomic challenges were already keeping me awake at night.

However, a second challenge arose that I felt I could not, in good conscience, refuse. Vannevar Bush, former Vice President of my own MIT, had become Roosevelt's virtual czar for science. To map out the government's peacetime organizations for science, based on lessons learned during World War II itself, Bush was formulating the basic document that became *Science: The Endless Frontier*. Advising Bush was a stellar committee of representative eminent scientists, including I. I. Rabi from Columbia and elsewhere; Oliver Buckley, head of the prestigious Bell Labs; and *wunderkind* Edwin Land, a Harvard dropout who pioneered Polaroid, where organic chemist Bob Woodward had just synthesized quinine.

A member of and secretary to Bush's committee was my MIT colleague, Rupert Maclaurin, son of Richard Maclaurin, the former President of MIT who in 1916 converted what had been Boston Tech into the modern Massachusetts Institute of Technology. Rupert, a dynamic go-getter who earned the first Harvard Business School PhD in economics (and who was the first to ski over the Andes), knew that as a non-scientist he would need to recruit a knowledgeable staff of helpers. Three of us were picked as scriveners to the secretariat and, thus, indirectly to Bush's scientific advisors and potentially to Bush himself.

John (Jack) Edsall, a biochemist at Harvard, was the oldest of us three. Next came Robert (Rob) Morison, physiologist, M.D., and head of biology for the powerful Rockefeller Foundation. (Rob and his brother, my MIT colleague Elting Morison, were cousins of Harvard historian Samuel Eliot Morison.) I, not yet thirty, was the most junior, but I was the one most conversant with the mathematical branches of the social sciences.

Throughout it was made clear to one and all that we three were to be solely helpers in drafting and in arranging and recording interviews of myriad viewpoints. We finished our part of the job within a couple of months, I think, but the three of us learned a lot that went beyond what we knew about the Ivy League or the Big Ten. There was much to learn about labs at AT&T, IBM, Mayo, Westinghouse, Brookings, or United Shoe Machines. We learned that at President Robert Hutchins's University of Chicago, my undergraduate alma mater, never were equal percentage pay raises ever given. In terms of 1945 dollars, a tenured woman full professor in classics might have a $3,900 salary, while a physicist-chemist might have a $70,000 salary, a vast difference traced, partially, to how much of a chemist's consulting earnings accrued to the university itself.

On Bush's advisory committee there was a diversity of opinions: cautious, conservative, activistic. (Bush himself never met personally with his committee's deliberators.) For brevity's sake, I'll focus on the main split in scientists' views and in academic administrators' views.

Many persons, maybe most, were impressed with how much had been accomplished during the war in governmental scientific agencies: early radar at the National Bureau of Standards; operations research at MIT and the Air Force; underwater sound research at

Reflections

Harvard; research in the Radiation Laboratory at MIT; physics research in labs at Chicago, Columbia, and UC Berkeley; and the Los Alamos project. There was cryptology research, too, but this was hush-hush.

By contrast, a minority on the committee with strong libertarian views feared these accomplishments, lest the camel of government take over the whole tent. Two reputable presidents of great universities (who can be nameless) favored dividing whatever billions the federal government would allocate to science in strict proportion to state and county populations. Equal-sized geographical counties in, say, Massachusetts and rural South Dakota should have the same dollars to "spend on science." Otherwise, they alleged, certain pushy New York City scholars with sharp elbows would end up with the lion's share of federal grants. (Remember that notions of political correctness change a lot every half century, and I have softened their language.)

At another extreme, a committee member like Edwin Land favored U.S. merit grants to support university dropouts, like Land himself had been and what Bill Gates was later to be.

As the only living survivor of our trio, how should I describe the rather eclectic middle-of-the-road policies we three came to hope for? The best policies of what the Edsall-Morison-Samuelson trio actually hoped for did come to be realized – fortunately realized – by what *Science: The Endless Frontier* recommended, including, prominently, Pentagon support for technical innovations; National Institutes of Health (NIH) for broad medical research; National Science Foundation for soft-money grants to applicants in physics, biology, and in the more metric branches of such social sciences as psychology, mathematical statistics, and econometrics; and NASA. It should be stressed, however, that the three of us were in no sense movers and shakers: Yankee Vannevar Bush was not one to be swayed by ribbon clerks' syllogisms or dreams. Causation went the other way; we scriveners adjusted toward what might become feasible.

Our own views, in retrospect, were less than perfect. We were a bit fearsome that non-university laboratories might grow stale and non-innovative in the absence of university teachers and students; NIH and RAND think tanks proved us to have been overly skeptical.

A reader may say the nation got much that was needed because it was all an obvious "lay-down hand." Yes, maybe. But let me mention that my longtime Harvard friend, Willard Van Orman Quine, arguably one of the three greatest logicians of the twentieth century, wrote in *Dædalus* in 1974 that, to paraphrase, all those dollars of federal aid to science and scholarship had (net!) a *negative* effect on the advancement of science! Go figure. Though both Maclaurin and I were whelped in Schumpeter's entrepreneurial innovation workshop at Harvard, we underestimated the burgeoning of Silicon Valley and venture-capital innovational productivity centers.

Deductive logic cannot prove or disprove policy propositions. Speaking for myself, I am glad that I was drafted for a couple of months for duties on this new frontier, where my specialized training and aptitudes could be useful. As I sum up in memory those months devoted to postwar scientific institutions, I must suspect that my per-hour contribution to the good society was accidentally near to my lifetime maximal do-gooding.

Maybe through my many writings and advising to Congress, the Federal Reserve, presidents, and voters over the years I have been a useful citizen. Those end-of-war weeks with Jack and Rob delayed only a little my writing *Foundations of Economic Analysis* (1947), a seminal treatise that changed economics and won a Nobel Prize for me. Nor, fortunately, did they abort my planned career program to alter postwar introductory textbooks. After half-a-century and a score of revisions, Samuelson's ECONOMICS still survives as one of the best sellers (now especially to a million Chinese readers).

Summing up, ideologies do play a role in evolving scientific development. I dare to hope that a science with both a libertarian Milton Friedman and an eclectic centrist Paul Samuelson is all the better for its diversity. ∎

© 2009 by Paul A. Samuelson

596

Paul A. Samuelson

Massachusetts Institute of Technology (MIT), Cambridge, MA, USA

© *Peter Badge/Typos1 in cooperation with the Foundation Lindau Nobelprizewinners Meetings at Lake Constance, all rights reserved.*

The Sveriges Riksbank Prize in Economic Sciences in Memory of Alfred Nobel 1970 'for the scientific work through which he has developed static and dynamic economic theory and actively contributed to raising the level of analysis in economic sciences'.

INTRODUCTION

MIT spreads out squarely along the northern shore of the Charles River, just opposite Boston. That's however about the only flattering thing one can say about the place. Most buildings have seen better days. The Sloan School of Business is no exception, even though many stars of economic science have their offices here, amongst them Paul A. Samuelson, sitting right next door to Robert M. Solow, his all-time sparring partner in macroeconomic theory. His cubicle is somewhat larger than the others, but the windows badly need cleaning, and the worn-out furniture seems to have remained unchanged ever since the 1970s, including the bulky grey telephone with its anachronistic bell tone. In the antechamber, where Janice Murray, the secretary, has her empire, a series of relatively recent sports photographs up on the wall signal what kind of personalities are assembled here: Janice Murray, boxing; Robert

M. Solow, sailing; and Paul A. Samuelson, playing tennis. Right now, however, the small, frail figure of 92-year-old Samuelson almost disappears behind his desk. He warmly welcomes the interviewer and starts talking right away.[1]

Paul Anthony Samuelson is certainly one of the most awe-inspiring Nobel Laureates, extremely sharp, witty, playfully humble, but always with a harsh judgment on others coming rapidly and easily. Born in Gary, Indiana, on 15 May 1915, as the son of a Jewish pharmacist, he studied at Hyde Park High School in Chicago and then, starting at age 16, at the University of Chicago before switching to Harvard in Cambridge, Massachusetts. At Harvard, he got his MA together with the rank of a 'junior fellow' and, in 1941, his Ph.D. He was strongly influenced by Wassily Leontief, Joseph Schumpeter, and especially Alvin Hansen, who popularized the works of John Maynard Keynes in the United States. In 1940, at age 25, he was offered an assistant professorship at MIT – which he accepted, given that Harvard didn't step up the bid, perhaps for anti-Semitic reasons as some suspect. During the war, Samuelson worked on the National Resources Planning Board, the War Production Board, and the Office of War Mobilization and Reconstruction. In 1947, he received tenure at MIT and started to create the department as we know it today. He also worked for the RAND Corporation, for the American Treasury, for NATO and for American Presidents Dwight D. Eisenhower, John F. Kennedy and Lyndon B. Johnson. He was an advisor to the Federal Reserve Board. A prolific writer in almost every field of economics, he has published some books, most importantly *Foundations of Economic Analysis*[2] and *Economics*,[3] which is now in its eighteenth edition, as well as hundreds of papers, averaging almost one per month in his fully active years. He received the David A. Wells Award at Harvard in 1941, the John Bates Clark Award from the American Economic Association in 1947, and the Albert Einstein Medal in 1971.

With his never idly resting mind, he has covered almost every imaginable field of economics to which he contributed fundamental concepts and theories. In trade theory, for example, he left his mark, amongst other things, by explaining the conditions for beneficial trade and by showing that protectionism tends to raise the real wages of a country's relatively scarce production factor, while opening up the borders benefits the relatively abundant production factor ('Stolper–Samuelson theorem'). In consumption theory, he derived demand curves from the 'revealed preferences' that people display as they buy things, instead of messing around with marginal utilities which are impossible to observe otherwise. In capital theory, he showed how to deal with heterogeneous capital goods. In growth theory, he worked out the 'turnpike theorem' describing conditions for maximum growth. For dynamic theory and stability analysis, he invented the 'correspondence principle' that provides the missing link between static and dynamic theory and which thereby helps to understand situations outside equilibrium. In business cycle theory, he created accelerator-multiplier models that permit the phenomenon of business cycles to be understood in a rather simple way. And in public finance, he showed what optimal taxation for public goods should look like. One may want to call Samuelson's approach eclectic, but that misses the point. It would be more appropriate to say – and he does it himself – that he is one of the last generalists. The breadth of his research agenda is due to his genius, for one, but also very much to the fact that when he started out, economic theory was not yet as diversified. He has been active in an era when economics only started to unfold and flourish – and he himself made that happen.

Interestingly, outside and inside observers are divided when it comes to the question of whether Samuelson has created a school of thought of his own. Given the generality of his approach and his non-dogmatic way of using every tool available, some people deny this. It is our view, however, that his impact has been tremendous, and this because in all the fields that he has covered, Samuelson has brought his one major general innovation to bear: formalization, mathematization, or, as the Nobel Committee has it, he 'actively contributed to raising the level of analysis in economic sciences'. In this, Samuelson has turned out to be not only one of the most brilliant, but also one of the most influential economists ever. By demonstrating that all economic behavior can be studied in the form of some maximization problem, he fundamentally changed economics. In a sense, it is fair to say that all modern economics is economics of the Samuelson school. What had once been a more verbal, or literary field with close ties to classical philosophy now became a relatively rigorous, mathematical discipline, and this development seems to be irreversible. While this may be deplorable for what has been lost, it must be acknowledged that formalized theory simply has won out in the market for ideas. The profession wasn't satisfied with the more withdrawn philosophical approach any more; something more concrete and precise allowing for state action was desired.

The desire to have such an almost 'natural' hard science that would lend itself more easily to political action has really come up in economics ever since the late 1920s. The existing tools of (then) orthodox economics didn't seem to provide satisfactory explanations and answers to the Great Depression.[4] As Samuelson himself points out, the Great Depression made a deep impact on him; he still views it as the 'most important economic catastrophe so far'.[5] What was needed in this serious situation was a theoretical body that would allow the understanding of disequilibrium, on the one hand, or, even better, equilibrium with persistent unemployment, on the other hand. For this reason, the profession not only gracefully picked up the new trend that originated in England, with John Maynard Keynes's *General Theory of Employment, Interest, and Money*,[6] but also started looking out for tools that would make analysis more precise. Given this desire, mathematization was a natural, straightforward choice. Paul A. Samuelson indeed quotes John Maynard Keynes as one of his major role models – even though, when the *General Theory* came out, he 'didn't take to it at once',[7] as he says elsewhere, precisely because it didn't square with neoclassical equilibrium theory. He instantly set out to do what seemed impossible – to incorporate Keynes's insights into equilibrium theory. This is what became known as the 'neoclassical synthesis'. In doing so, he created a new orthodoxy, a new mainstream in economics.

Paul A. Samuelson looks at the world in what one might want to call an American liberal way. His personal experience in life and work have triggered and confirmed the feeling that the optimal economic system is something like a 'third way', that is a mixture between free markets and active collective choice, avoiding both libertarian and socialist extremes. The Great Depression forever disenchanted him with 'unfettered' capitalism. He therefore admires President Franklin Delano Roosevelt, whose 'New Deal' supposedly helped to end the disastrous effects of the Great Depression and established a social safety net in the United States. In Samuelson's view, 'Laissez-faire' just means that the state doesn't live up to its responsibilities. Libertarianism, for him, is a misleading philosophy. Samuelson likes to warn that the market is never and can never be perfect – and so, in one of his more recent papers, he has managed to stir up the whole profession once more by showing mathematically that there are situations in which free trade is not welfare-enhancing for everybody.[8] His paper encountered a lot of criticism for not taking technical progress into account, but his warning nevertheless met with particular interest as some Americans were growing more and more suspicious of the strong competition coming from China. Samuelson showed that even though customers on average benefit from this competition, some groups inside the United States, especially those with low professional qualifications, may lose out. Unlike some lobbies, however, Samuelson doesn't imply that the pace of globalization should be slowed down through protectionism. Instead, he advocates some compensation: the winners should share their gains with the losers.

Paul A. Samuelson's path is a perfect example of how the economic challenges of changing times, the evolution of economics as a field of science, and personal biographies all act together in the progress of economic theory. All these three lines of development were relevant and interacted. Samuelson's approach grew out of the puzzling times of the Great Depression, which he lived through as a child and was eager to understand, even though his family background was not a genuinely intellectual one. At any rate, Paul Samuelson discovered that economics wasn't quite apt to give satisfactory answers. In leaving his own mark in economics, in showing the way towards mathematization, Samuelson then triggered new debates that kept the process of theoretical refinement going. This developed some dynamism of its own. As he acknowledges, much of what he has been working on just came up as a topic because somebody else had written something that he felt the urge to straighten out. One might say therefore that Samuelson provided the mathematical tools that set the profession on its modern track and then browsed through the upcoming ramifications in a more or less leisurely way. In the interview, we can see that in many and recurring instances, he simply reacted to Milton Friedman, a figure that constantly gave him both annoyance and inspiration, as it seems. The dialectics of intellectual progress obviously requires one to have somebody resisting and somebody to resist.

INTERVIEW

Professor Samuelson, please tell me what made you turn to economics in the first place. What role did your upbringing play, if any? Let's go back to your first years.
I started out as a bright kid, I skipped grades. As I look back, I realize that I had an enormous amount of self-confidence as a child, most of it unearned. Just because I counted the numbers faster than anybody in the classroom, I thought I could be a great radio announcer, for example. I thought I would succeed in anything that I'd put my hand to. That was of course absurd. Well, I had a supportive family, I had a bright older brother, and as an afterthought, I must say that I also had a bright younger brother. My cousins were not quite as smart. Actually, I have one unusual part in my autobiography in that from the age of 17 months until 5½ years old, I spent half of my time at what I now have to think of as a foster family, on a farm in Porter County next to Lake County, near Gary, Indiana, where I was born.

How did that come about?
That's something I have never understood. It could have been a disaster, but it wasn't at all. This whole adventure cost one dollar a day for food, lodging and love from someone who was not my DNA. I learnt this from my mother, when she was in her late eighties – I never had any curiosity

about this before, but at that time, we needed something to talk about. The setting was just like a late nineteenth century protestant American rural environment. No inside-the-house plumbing, chamber pots in the alcoves, no electricity. That means you have to use oil lamps when it's dark. But those oil lamps are no good to read by, and therefore you end up going to bed early. I can't think there was a great deal of mental stimulation from that environment. By contrast, my younger brother Robert, who is the father of the former president of Harvard University, Lawrence Summers,[9] he and his son spent a lot of time every day talking about economic and other problems. I think the same was true for David and Milton Friedman.[10] If you talk to David Friedman, he says he's never been influenced by Milton, but in reality, David Friedman is like Milton squared, and not less. In my case, that wasn't so at all.

What about your supportive parents?
My parents both came from the same little part of Poland between Lithuania and East Prussia. As I learnt later, my mother pursued my father, her first cousin, to America. My father came over, and after a brief stop in the New York area, he went to the Midwest, became a registered pharmacist, druggist, and had his own drugstore. This was a common pattern for relatively poor immigrants who might otherwise have gone to medical school. In 1912, my parents eloped from Chicago to Kenosha, Wisconsin.

Why would they do that?
They had to do that because they were first cousins, as I mentioned earlier. In those days, they were illegal in Illinois, but not in Wisconsin. That's why I have six fingers, you see (*chuckles at his joke*). My father was quite good at a couple of things, at algebra for example, which he did discuss with me. We didn't discuss the state of the world, though.

So some mathematical affinities were in your blood, so to speak?
Yes. And I did actually learn something about solving simultaneous equations while I was still down at grade school.

What about your mother?
Well, my mother's case must have been somewhat unusual because in her kind of environment, a female would not be expected to get much education. But she had some proficiency in French and Latin. I don't know exactly where that came from. I think that her family was a bit more prosperous than the others around her because her grandfather had come to the US around the time of the Civil War in the middle of the century. He probably started out as a peddler, left his family in the old country, sent and brought

money back. That, too, was a very common pattern. He became a wheat merchant. My mother was a person whose metric of what was important was very much conditioned by how well off they were. I also think she was a premature feminine activist. She didn't like home duties. That's perhaps one reason why I went to the farm as a child. Maybe I was a difficult eater, too. At any rate, she was a wretched cook. It's all understandable.

What did the economic environment look like, and how did that influence you?
I was born into the boom of World War I. Actually, I was born in a frontier town, a new town, Gary, with the biggest steel mill in the world, where ten years before my birth, it had been all sand dunes. Being a big company town, it had a really excellent school system. The same is true for Milton Friedman, by the way, by coincidence. He was born in Brooklyn but they lived in Raleigh, New Jersey, which is nothing of a town. They had a good school system there, too. When we moved to Chicago later, after an interlude in Florida, I went to good schools, too. The city was also very important for my macroeconomic background. Anyway, my point is that I could feel around me the boom that the breakout of the war in 1914 had created. We weren't into the war, but all the allied countries bought steel, and the steel mills operated every hour of the week, you could see the fire. Men worked a twelve-hour day seven days a week. They probably got a dollar an hour. The population was mainly from Eastern and Central Europe. We called them 'Slawish'. They really were Slovenes, Serbs, Croats, Czechs and Poles. And on the other hand, also as a kid, I had already experienced the prosperity of a hundred-acre farm. The war sent up the price of grain, and the Keynesian multiplier was operating. Of course, I later also experienced the opposite of that at the end of the war, when there was the rather sharp, short-run recession, prior to the next boom period. Another key was when my family, in 1925, moved to Miami Beach, Florida, because there was a great land bubble that we wanted to take advantage of. We didn't see it coming to the burst. You know how to make a small fortune in Florida real estate? You start out with a bigger one *(laughter)*. So the relative degree of affluence that had been accumulated in the family from the World War I prosperity gradually was dissipated. That was something which I experienced. And it left a mark.

How did your schooling go?
After returning from Florida, I went to a good Chicago public school, Hyde Park high school. I had very good mathematics courses there. I had a great mathematics teacher, Ms Smith. She was a spinster, and she more or less wore the same dress every day. She later left 10 million dollars to the

University of Chicago, her Alma Mater. I was surprised to hear that, and when I inquired, I was told she probably just had a good broker. Anyway, even before I graduated from Hyde Park high school under a familiar arrangement, I could go already to Chicago University, which was only two miles away. It never occurred to me to go to Harvard, as would today be the pattern, or Princeton, or Yale, or Cornell, or whatever. I landed at the University of Chicago on 2 January 1932 and I walked into my first lecture class. I was still in my teens then. I can truly say that I was reborn that instant. The lecture that I heard which was actually given by a professor of sociology was on Malthus's theory of population.[11] It was very interesting. It seemed so simple, I thought I wasn't really understanding this, it must be more complicated. But it wasn't more complicated. Actually, I had come in one quarter late. The economics of the famous Chicago core curriculum had taken place during that first quarter. So to make up for my deficiency, I was put in an old-fashioned introductory course in economics. That worked out very well because the teacher was Aaron Director.[12] He was a person who has never published anything important, but he was very influential. He really was the one who converted the first Chicago School of Frank Knight, Jacob Viner and Paul Douglas, which was pretty eclectic, into the second one, with Milton Friedman and so forth. I guess with Gary Becker[13] et al. we're at the third right now. So there I was, completely by chance, and I discovered the subject that interested me and that I would be good at. Economics is a subject which is quite attractive to somebody who is both interested in statistics, analysis, metrics, but also in people and policies. And so I became a very good student there.

But with those interests, you could also have turned to political science or sociology. So economics was actually a coincidence?
To be sure, I came to Chicago only because of location. It was an accident that I liked the subject. I had not even thought about economics in my high school years. In my father's library, there was a copy of Adam Smith's *Wealth of Nations*[14] in the – abridged – Harvard Classics Series. I didn't even notice it was there. I only looked at two books of that famous series; one was a translation of Virgil that helped me cheat in Latin and the other one was some novel. It wasn't that with my mother's milk I was getting economics. But it was important – and it shows the importance of coincidence and chance – that Aaron Director assigned me a chapter in a famous advanced book by Gustav Cassel, the Swedish economist, on the arithmetic of the price system.[15] This was his plagiarism of Leon Walras's general equilibrium. It was exciting to see that the math that I knew could be used. And then I realized I didn't have enough math, so I spent the time at Chicago catching up on it.

So Chicago played an important role in giving you the necessary tools.
Oh yes, and it was also valuable that the Chicago I went to was the best place in the world at that time in neoclassical economics. But that does not mean it was the best place in the world to understand the Great Depression.[16] The Great Depression was not Euclidian geometry. I was very sensitive to this mismatch, that is to the fact that what I was learning in class could not rationalize for me that almost every bank in my neighborhoods in Northern Indiana and Illinois went broke and that almost all the money that my older brother had earned to go to college was lost. In a nutshell, about one third of the population had no jobs. And the two thirds who had jobs would not trade with them. The one third without jobs would gladly trade with them or gladly work for even less. But of course they couldn't do that. To try and handle this kind of disequilibrium system with the historic tools of economics that were in the textbooks I was being assigned was impossible. So you can understand why, then, by complete good luck, I happily got out of Chicago.

How did that happen?
The reason was that I had won an extraordinary new scholarship to pay all my graduate training but I couldn't stay where I had started out. All my mentors, all famous people like Frank Knight, Jacob Viner, Paul Douglas, Henry Simons, all of them said I should go to Columbia, not Harvard. At Columbia, there was better statistics, with Harold Hotelling, and there was also Wesley C. Mitchell, the institutionalist. But I didn't listen to my elders much. I picked Harvard mostly because I thought it would be like a nice small New England village with a white church and a good library and a lot of green there. I was pretty shocked then when I came on the streetcar across the river here and got to noisy Harvard Square. Every decision I have made in my life that has been at first the wrong one, I changed. But this one, by luck, was the right one. I didn't realize it then, but Harvard was in kind of a boom period because Adolf Hitler was so beastly and many refugees started out there. One effect of that was that I was by far the best prepared member of that entering class. I was kind of a brash youngster; I would correct my professors when they made mistakes. I was already publishing articles during my doctorate at Harvard.

When you started economics, was it clear to you from the very beginning that you were heading towards an academic career?
No, it wasn't clear to me. You see, I came from a family with a Jewish heritage, but not an observant family. One knew, for example, that you could be as bright as anything and do well in chemistry, but you

wouldn't get a job with DuPont or something. Different fields were different. There was anti-Semitism in some degree everywhere, but less in Chicago than at Harvard or Princeton. As a result, this gave Chicago a certain monopoly advantage; they could get talent that the others didn't think they wanted. So it would be wrong for me to think that in my freshman year at Chicago I had an academic life in mind. At that time, I would probably, like my older brother, have tried to become a lawyer. That was a more common path. However, once I got to be proficient with publications, I knew that I would get a good job, even though I didn't know where.

And when you were at Harvard?
I spent five wonderful years at Harvard, especially with the status of a fellow, which meant that I didn't have any duties. Most of what I got the Nobel Prize for, I did it at that time. I wasn't allowed to work for a degree, but I also didn't need to. And then, when I finished that stint, I was an instructor at Harvard, and I got a good offer here at MIT. In the meantime I was married. My wife was a small town banker's daughter, a WASP, that is, a white Anglo-Saxon protestant. We said, well, this will be a test, we will see whether Harvard can match this offer or do better. They didn't, and so we came three miles down the river. I have always been within three miles of Harvard yard, and I still live three miles off Harvard yard. At the time, the economics department at MIT, an engineering school, was a mediocre department. But I didn't need the stimulus of bright colleagues; I knew that I was a self-starter. Also, I still had all my Harvard friends and the great Harvard library which was important. I was very lucky in my marriage; she was bright and sensible.[17] Actually, she was Schumpeter's assistant at one time, and a protégée of Wassily Leontief.[18] So, summing up, I've always been overpaid and underworked. The reason why I'm underworked is because what I do is not work. And as you can see, at age 92, I'm still doing it.

How did you become a Keynesian?
I was dissatisfied with the analysis of economic fluctuations. By the way, the word macroeconomics was not yet coined then. But the alleged 'macroeconomics' of the orthodox neoclassical economists would have been that overall permanent unemployment is impossible, Say's law[19] prevails, and in the Walrasian general equilibrium system, there can be proved to always be a root.[20] But a disequilibrium system was no subject for them. In my very first year at Harvard, John Maynard Keynes' *General Theory*[21] came out, and we received books in advance of the publication. When I read it, I was not converted.

It is a difficult read
Yes, and actually, if you just have the words of the text, it's not completely coherent. But pragmatically, I said this is the best bicycle in town, you can't wait for that better bicycle. Maybe we don't know what its micro-foundations are, but it does explain why, in my sophomore year at the University of Chicago, Franklin D. Roosevelt came in to office and began to spend billions of dollars in his New Deal,[22] just as Hitler was beginning to do, too, and the same effects came. I understood this because I had experienced it in Gary, Indiana, in the World War I period. I had a certain amount of interest in the stock market. I had helped my freshman math teacher pick stocks, most of which ended up badly after the 1929 crash. I made a leap of faith. I really thank Darwin or whoever runs the universe that I wasn't stuck at Chicago. I would have missed out on the monopolistic competition revolution, which they didn't believe in. I would have missed out on the Keynesian revolution that they also didn't believe in. I would have missed out on mathematization of economics, although some of that did even take place at the University of Chicago. I was lucky. When I came here, to this mediocre department, with World War II just around the corner, some government money needed to be spent on computers, on radar, secretly on the atomic bomb, etc., so that MIT was 85 percent engineering. Now it is probably 15 percent engineering. Wherever the tide was rising, I was by good luck there.

What about your colleagues? Wasn't Milton Friedman one of your most important sparring partners?
Oh yes. Milton Friedman and I became known as two poles, early on, but we managed to stay on civil and fairly friendly terms. Milton Friedman never made a mistake in his whole life. That's remarkable, isn't it? He is as bright a guy as you would ever meet. But I don't think he realizes the tremendous number of mistakes he made in his life. I don't think anybody has read every item of Milton Friedman's work in the world except me. I always feel that I learn more from my enemy than I can learn from my friend, because my friend and I already are at the same point. Most of my jokes about Milton Friedman are actually deep truths. Sometimes I say he's got such a high IQ that he has no protection against himself. He looks at his work and is satisfied with it. However, I think that it is a tragedy when somebody really takes the wrong train in his life.

I'd rather talk a little bit more about you
This *is* about me. See, unlike Milton, I look at my work, I realize that my opinions are fallible opinions; they are always changing over time. That's not something I regard as a fault but rather as a virtue. I'm always self-conscious,[23] and I like to get not two viewpoints on every matter, but three!

After all, the great gift to be a skilled economist is to be eclectic. As I would tell my macro seminar: if you must forecast, forecast often. It sounds like a joke, but it's true. Also, I have changed my opinions in many ways, and in each case, that's no rejection of my earlier opinions. The earlier opinions were geared to a particular system.

Right. That sounds a bit like the Popperian position – the historical context matters. But let's turn to some of your own major contributions. First of all, and most importantly, what drew you so much towards mathematization, culminating in your dissertation, better known as your landmark 1947 book Foundations of Economic Analysis?[24] *It revolutionized economic theory.*
Mathematics has an evolution built into it, and that's what I like about it. You start out and it teaches you. You don't know what it teaches you until you've done it and you suddenly realize what it is. Fundamentally, all the different parts of the *Foundations of Economic Analysis* just grew out of actual lively topics that my teachers – a great generation – weren't able to handle adequately.

And what caused you to write your world-famous bestselling textbook?[25]
All that I just said had no bearing on my textbook. The textbook was actually written upon invitation by the head of the department here at MIT. Every MIT student in the third year had to take two full semesters of introductory economics, and they hated it. And so he said to me: 'Paul, would you take a few months off and write a text which they will like?' And I agreed: 'Sure, I'll do it.' What I didn't realize was that it would take me three years and more of beastly hard work. I had the choice: I could have made it a simple mathematical introduction, simple mathematics, but I decided not to do that, because MIT students like to do analytical problems. In the book, it's only diagrams and so forth. I spent a lot of time on expository virtues. I didn't do it for the money, although there was a lot of money to it, after the fact. But there was a different layer of fame that opened up for me this way: the book set a pattern for all textbooks ever after. Just this morning I was over at the medical department for some appointment, and a Chinese came up saying 'oh, Doctor Samuelson, you're still alive!? You're so well-named out there...' And I asked: 'Did you study my book in Mandarin or English?' In his case, he studied it in English, but you could do it in both. My book no longer has a monopoly on the field in America, but around the world, it still has an important role to play.

Did politics ever directly trigger the questions that you worked on?
Very uncharacteristic was the fact that for some time, I became the principal economic adviser to President John F. Kennedy. It is true that

this involved an internal dilemma, for a number of reasons, even though it was extremely interesting and pretty important for me. At the time, I was an Adlai Stevenson follower, so I had to warn Kennedy: 'I'm not even for you!' He said: 'I don't want your vote, see, that would be only one vote anyway. But I'm going to make a shot at the presidency and I may get it. And I think that your ideas are important for the country. Think about it.' And so I did think about it. And Kennedy ended up persuading me that this country is too important to have John Kenneth Galbraith and Walt Rostow act as the principal economic advisers. I could have gone to Washington in a high position, but I really preferred the academic life. I even had my doctor prepared to say that this wouldn't be good for my health. Fortunately, I never had to use that excuse. Anyway, it was a wonderful team that I helped to select: Walter Heller as the chairman of the Council of Economic Advisers, James Tobin,[26] etc. As a matter of fact, before the 1960 election, the American dollar had become an overvalued dollar. And so we proposed quietly that the first act of the President should be to depreciate the dollar, with the British. But Kennedy said: 'The last thing I want is to be known as a currency tinkerer.' What you learn when you are advising the prince is that the prince gets the kind of adviser that he wants. As a result, for a whole decade, we did everything possible to hide the fact that we were cheapening the dollar.

You've covered a vast area of topics throughout your career. What guided you there? For example, in Public Finance, the theory of taxation for public goods[27] – how did that very particular idea come about? Was it some kind of request from politics?
No. There is this much-cited article which, in a way, I regret because I should have gone to my friend Richard Musgrave[28] and said 'Let's make this a joint article'. Because everything I knew about the theory of voluntary taxation, I knew from Dick. I wrote the article because some fool out of the RAND Corporation[29] had written an article saying that mathematics was useless in social sciences, that nothing had ever been done by mathematics that was of any use. Seymour Harris who was the editor of the journal, made me lead a symposium on the topic. And so I thought I'd give this as an example that mathematics can be useful, since nobody had ever exactly clarified the Lindahl problem.[30] I wrote it probably in an afternoon or two. That's the genesis. This probably kept Musgrave from getting the Nobel Prize. Which is a shame. But that's the trouble with honors for one person. The people at the top tier who don't receive the prize are just as good. Science is a group activity.

As I can see, much of what you do seems to be a reaction to foolish papers of other people that needed correction. And also, a lot of your ideas seem to have come out of discussions with colleagues, e.g. Richard Musgrave and Wolfgang Stolper,[31] the latter in trade theory.

Yes, that's true. Talking of trade theory, there was a big fuss about an article a couple of years ago, a paper in the *Journal of Economic Perspectives*[32] in which I told a simple truth: if Toyota has innovations and takes away business from Ford and General Motors, then it is true that you get cheaper and better quality Toyotas for consumers, and therefore, a simple-minded answer would then be that all globalization and innovation anywhere is good for everywhere. But that's simply not true. But I had a new metric, a new way of measuring, just what the benefit of the cheapness of the import was against the drop in real wages produced in that country. And there was a clear case where it would be harmful. By and large, globalization has helped both China and the US. But the point is that the winners in the US are a very unbalanced group. In the old New Deal days, with Presidents Franklin D. Roosevelt, Harry Truman, John F. Kennedy, Lyndon Johnson, the government would have made the winners – with the use of the tax system and the expenditure system – share some of their winnings, so that potentially, everybody could be better off. However, there is a big change in my understanding: only to a limited degree can you take a market system and improve on it by government buy-out.

And why isn't state intervention a good remedy?

Mine is not the Hayekian argument that it would turn totalitarian.[33] To me, all of current history just shows that if you do that, as in Sweden, you kill the goose that lays the golden eggs. You can rectify distribution only to a very limited degree. The real trouble with the modern world from an ethical viewpoint is not an idiot like President George W. Bush or a mean guy like President Richard Nixon, it's the electorate. The more we get away from the Great Depression, when everybody felt we had the same problems and need of mutual reinsurance, and from the 'necessary war', World War II, the more the electorate no longer has altruism. But you can't just dispel the electorate, as the German playwright Bertolt Brecht noted sarcastically.[34] Yet, this emphasis upon the limited improvements that you can make within a modern democracy is a fundamental change in my thinking. The other thing that has changed is that because of Japan and Singapore and Hong Kong and Taiwan, the US economy in the ancient tradition of my textbook is a different one from the one of the current edition. In those old days, the Fortune 500 companies had a measure of oligopoly power which they were forced to share with the trade unions. Well, in the meantime, the trade unions are gone in America, except in a few localizations and in government. We have a cowed labor force. The result is that we are much more like in a Say's law situation. All that conversion to the disequilibrium system, into Keynesianism, seems no longer useful to me.

Why is Keynesianism losing ground?
What dethroned plain vanilla Keynesianism was stagflation. If you have a supply shock like in the seventies, you knew what to do: cure either the 'stag' or the 'flation'. But one would hurt the other. However, even nowadays, you still have to worry about liquidity traps[35] and stuff like that. So my attempt is to stay eclectic. That's a major gift, I think, a gift that major scholars should buy into. It allows you to focus on what's relevant. But of course, one explanation for anything is always short of the other things.

How would you define progress in economic theory?
Oh well, I would say that something like the Taylor rule[36] is progress. What I was espousing at the Federal Reserve academic classes is that you don't look at one thing, but you look at many things, and you have two goals. One is, if you are tolerant towards inflation, it will stop being tolerable inflation, and so you have to have a penalty on too much stimulus. And the other thing is that you have to look whether the economy is creating enough jobs and purchasing power etc. From this viewpoint, the problem is not that jobs disappear because they go to China. The problem is that the jobs that reappear in America are 20 percent below in wage as compared to what your last job was. That's good sound neoclassical economics. But politics doesn't deal with that. By the way, it's a very hard message for the public to understand.

Well, that's the problem with economics generally, I guess, it's often times just counterintuitive. . . Are you happy with economics the way it is being taught right now?
There is one thing that I'm not very happy about, even though I understand it. It's that the profession has gone very much to the right ideologically. And guess who was the most important person responsible for that. . . it was Milton Friedman, not Friedrich Hayek. The libertarianism which puts all the emphasis on Pareto optimality[37] efficiency doesn't realize that even if you get 100 percent of the market return, and therefore you have a Pareto optimum, this outcome would still not satisfy any distributive justice criteria. I hope that my colleagues under 45 years of age in this wonderful department here at MIT understand that.

And otherwise? In terms of topics?
The deeper truth is that people go where the money is, even in research. I know lots of economists who are drawn to financial engineering, but also to judicial testifying. You tell me which side I'm to testify on... and then... It's an honorable thing to do for a lawyer, and I won't say it is dishonorable for economists. But there is a famous story about this that tells it all: when Willie Sutton, the bank-robber, went to jail, a reporter asked him: 'Why do you rob banks?!' And the answer was, sure enough: 'That's where the money is'.[38] If you had a son who would go into economics and you advise him on his career, you say: 'Try to find a justification for non-regulation.' That will pay off best. And also, your self-esteem depends on public esteem, that is, on the public's esteem. Well, summing up: the old gang of people was nicer people than the new gang. That's not to say that there are not nice people in both. At any interdisciplinary meeting, economists always stick out, and they are being viewed as being crazy and mean, but often they're just realistic, which the others aren't.

That certainly has to do with the underlying idea of the self-centered, super-rational homo oeconomicus. People from other fields often tend to think that we really believe in it.
Well, Gary Becker has indeed explained that a smoker who shortens his life is maximizing his hedonistic pleasure from smoking. That's not very acute psychology. Anyway, what I have always known is that a lot of people who don't come to the same conclusions as I do are smart and hard-working people. What they find will always be interesting. Even though their findings may shift a lot along the way.

What do you think are the most important challenges for economic theory in the future?
The biggest challenge is probably globalization. As a big country, you can bear a lot of inefficiency. But with globalization, that leeway vanishes. The increase of globalization is inevitably associated with an increase in inequality, and also with an increase in anxiety. It used to be that if you were a graduate of Harvard business school, you would get a job, you get promoted with age, and then you retire in honor. It's not like that any more. The length of time in one job has been seriously shortened. This is a source of a lot of corporate misgovernance. You can make a big killing and laugh all the way to the bank, even though you've left havoc behind you. Well, economists will never run out of work. And good analytical economics is always a good cure for incoherent economic policy.

Thank you, Professor.

NOTES

1. The interview was held on 4 June 2007.
2. Paul A. Samuelson (1947). This book was also his dissertation, under the title 'The operational significance of economic theory'.
3. Paul A. Samuelson (1948a). The book has in recent years (after 1985) been co-authored by William Nordhaus. The book has been translated into 41 languages and has in total sold over 4 million copies.
4. 1929–1937. For a precise account of the Great Depression as such and how some major economists, including Paul A. Samuelson, experienced it, see Randall E. Parker (2002).
5. See questionnaire.
6. John Maynard Keynes (1936).
7. See Randall E. Parker (2002, p. 29).
8. Paul A. Samuelson (2004).
9. The Summers brothers changed their name in order to avoid anti-Semitic discrimination.
10. Milton Friedman (1912–2006) was awarded the Nobel Prize in 1976 'for his achievements in the fields of consumption analysis, monetary history and theory and for his demonstration of the complexity of stabilization policy'.
11. 'That day's lecture was on Malthus's theory that human populations would reproduce like rabbits until their density per acre of land reduced their wage to a bare subsistence level where an increased death rate came to equal the birth rate', explains Paul Samuelson in his 2003 paper 'How I became a economist', available at www.nobel.se. Thomas Malthus (1826).
12. Aaron Director (1901–2004), professor at the University of Chicago Law School and Rose Friedman's elder brother, played a central role in the development of the Chicago School of economics. He founded the *Journal of Law & Economics* in 1958, which he co-edited with Ronald Coase. Indeed, he didn't publish much, but as his colleague George Stigler once said, 'most of Aaron's articles have been published under the names of his colleagues'.
13. Gary S. Becker was awarded the Nobel Prize in 1992 'for having extended the domain of microeconomic analysis to a wide range of human behavior and interaction, including non-market behavior'.
14. Adam Smith (1776).
15. The book was Gustav Cassel's *Theory of Social Economy* (1923).
16. The Great Depression was a worldwide economic downturn starting in most places in 1929, following the stock market crash on 29 October 1929, and ending at different times in the 1930s or early 1940s. It was the largest and most important economic depression in modern history. It originated in the United States. The Great Depression had devastating effects in the whole world.
17. His first wife was Marion Crawford (1916–78), herself an economist, whom he had met in Cambridge. Since 1981, Samuelson has been married to Risha S. Eckaus.
18. Wassily Leontief (1906–1999) was awarded the Nobel Prize in 1973 'for the development of the input–output method and for its application to important economic problems'.
19. Say's law, named after the French economist Jean-Baptiste Say (1767–1832), states that supply always creates its own demand. The approach behind this 'law' focuses more on the conditions for supply, rather than concentrating on demand, as the Keynesians do (Jean-Baptiste Say, 1803).
20. This means simply that the system of equations mathematically depicting the economy can be solved, so that such an equilibrium does actually really exist.
21. John Maynard Keynes (1936).
22. Franklin D. Roosevelt became President of the US in 1933. The New Deal was a program of government interventions aiming at relaunching the economy, simultaneously

23. See, for a differing interpretation, the interview with Kenneth J. Arrow in this book.
24. Paul A. Samuelson (1947).
25. Paul A. Samuelson (1948a). Now in its eighteenth edition, the book has in recent years (after 1985) been co-authored by William Nordhaus. The book been translated into 41 languages and has in total sold over 4 million copies.
26. James Tobin was awarded the Nobel Prize in 1981, 'for his analysis of financial markets and their relations to expenditure decisions, employment, production and prices'.
27. In this paper, Samuelson establishes what later became dubbed the 'Samuelson Rule'. It says that the sum of the marginal rates of substitution between the public good and the private good for all members of the community should equal the marginal rate of transformation between the two goods (Paul A. Samuelson, 1954).
28. German-born Richard A. Musgrave (1910–2007) was an eminent scholar in public finance. He systematized his field by splitting it up into the three classical subdivisions of allocation, distribution and stabilization policy. He also invented the somewhat controversial idea of 'merit wants' that should be provided for by the state.
29. The RAND Corporation is a research institution created originally in 1946 by the United States Army Air Forces as Project RAND, under contract to the Douglas Aircraft Company. In 1946, they released the Preliminary Design of an Experimental World-Circling Spaceship. In 1948, Project RAND was separated from Douglas and became an independent non-profit organization, sponsored initially by the Ford Foundation, to 'further promote scientific, educational, and charitable purposes, all for the public welfare and security of the United States of America'. The ranged of topics has since expanded greatly. The acronym RAND actually stands for 'Research and Development'.
30. In the Lindahl problem, named after the Swedish economist Erik Robert Lindahl (1891–1960), it is asked how parties can contribute to the cost of a public good in proportion to the incremental benefit they derive from it.
31. In 1941, Paul Samuelson and Wolfgang Stolper postulated the Stolper–Samuelson theorem according to which under some assumptions such as constant returns and perfect competition, a rise in the relative price of a good will lead to a rise in the return to that factor which is used most intensively in the production of the good, and conversely, to a fall in the return to the other factor. Wolfgang F. Stolper and Paul A. Samuelson (1941).
32. Paul A. Samuelson (2004).
33. This is an allusion to Friedrich August von Hayek (1944). Hayek was awarded the Nobel Prize in 1974, together with Gunnar Myrdal – both received it 'for their pioneering work in the theory of money and economic fluctuations and for their penetrating analysis of the interdependence of economic, social and institutional phenomena'. With regard to Hayek, this is somewhat ironical, given that his major contributions are much rather to be found in his works in the field of social philosophy.
34. After the events of 17 June 1953, the suppressed widespread uprising against the East German government, Bertolt Brecht wrote in the famous poem 'Die Lösung' (the solution), one of his 'Buckower Elegien': 'Wäre es da nicht doch einfacher, die Regierung löste das Volk auf und wählte ein anderes?' – wouldn't it be simpler if government dissolved the people and elected a different one?
35. A liquidity trap is when people prefer to hold all their assets in cash, given that the nominal interest rate is too low, that is close or equal to zero. The classical tools of monetary policy, especially a further lowering of the interest rate, then don't work – but rather make things worse.
36. According to the Taylor rule, named after the American economist John B. Taylor, the central bank should change the nominal interest rate in response to divergences of actual GDP from potential GDP and divergences of actual rates of inflation from a target rate of inflation (John B. Taylor, 1993).

37. Pareto optimality, named after the Italian economist and sociologist Vilfredo Pareto (1848–1923), is a concept that refers to a situation in which none of the concerned parties can improve his or her welfare any further without impairing the other one's. In exchange relations, this demonstrates the optimal scope of mutually beneficial interaction.
38. William 'Willie' Sutton (1901–1980) was a prolific US bank robber. For his talent at executing robberies in disguises, he gained two nicknames, 'Willie the Actor' and 'Slick Willie'. He actually denied having uttered the famous quote and attributed it to the reporter.

In Search of George Stigler and the Chicago School— A Conversation with Paul Samuelson
Craig Freedman, Macquarie University

I held this interview with Paul Samuelson in his office in October 1997. He was gracious enough to spend approximately one hour and twenty minutes talking to me about George Stigler, who he had known throughout his adult life.

The reason for the interview was simple. As part of a long-term research project on George Stigler and his response to critics of neoclassical theory, I spent two months travelling throughout the US, interviewing many of George Stigler's colleagues and close friends. I included within my round of conversations both Paul Samuelson and Robert Solow as two people who enjoyed a long acquaintance and/or friendship with George Stigler, though perhaps not his economic or political standpoint.

This interview with Paul Samuelson differs markedly from many of the other ones I conducted. Those tend to be more directed. In other words, it is not difficult to discern the direction and purpose of the interview by the questions I pose. Interviewing Paul Samuelson, however, proved to be far easier than any other task I set for myself. Literally, close to an hour went by between my first innocent background question and my next fully articulated one.

I readily admit to coming across as a pale imitation of Socrates' slave boy in the Platonic dialogue, 'Meno.' My lines are reduced to the equivalent of 'Yes, O Socrates.' I leave these innocuous interjections in not intentionally to self-characterise myself as clueless, but to provide natural breaks which make reading such an interview a more comprehensible task.

Critical readers might wonder why I didn't do more to take control of the interview. I can only respond that it was a rapid and almost unconscious choice on my part. Given Paul Samuelson's flow of thought and its usefulness for my own purposes, to interrupt would not only display needlessly bad manners but be deliberately counter-productive as well.

Let's start with some background information. I know you met in the 30s in Chicago.

I probably met George Stigler some time in the calendar year 1932. But I'm not certain. It would have been at the same time that I met Milton Friedman and Allen Wallis. Those three I group together. But I also knew Albert Hart there. He just died, maybe you saw that?[1]

No, I haven't seen that.

Albert Gaylord Hart recently died. I knew Homer Jones as well. They were the elite guard in the Chicago Graduate School in the 30s. I came to the University of Chicago on January 2nd, 1932, and Aaron Director was my first teacher in economics. Aaron later played an important role in George's life. Aaron was the brother of Rose Director who later became Rose Friedman.

I probably saw George the most in my final senior year, which was the academic year 1934–35. George and Allen Wallis had taken squatters' rights possession of a storeroom in the basement of the social science research building where the economics department was. They had their little office there. And they were then, I suppose, second- or third-year graduate students. Was George born in 1911?

1911.

And did he come from The University of Washington?

Yeah, he had done an MBA at Northwestern and then did a year out in Washington before he came to Chicago.[2]

But he lived in the State of Washington?

Seattle.

And where did he do his undergraduate?

The University of Washington.

At the University of Washington, in Seattle?

Yeah.

And then he had an MBA at Northwestern. That was a strange interlude in his career. The reason that I saw them, and a good deal of them, was that to make some money during the Great Depression I had what was called an NYA (National Youth Administration), scholarship supplement. I suppose the department secured that for me. I don't know how much an hour I received, maybe twenty-five cents an hour, but they had to find some perfunctory work for me to do. And just as in *Pinafore*, I polished up the brass on the door. I was given the job of dusting off in that department records room the pictures of the great economists, Böhm-Bawerk, John Stuart Mill, David Ricardo, Adam Smith, and maybe Knut Wicksell. So I would be in that storage room doing my little 'make-work job' and talking to George and Allen who were, of course, exalted graduate students. Well, you must have an impression of what George was like. I thought of the two of them then as being closer together to one another than either was to Milton Friedman.

At that time.

At that time. But it was a mutual admiration society. And George was very amusing. Allen was very self-confident in any view that he had. One of the notable characteristics

1117

of George Stigler was his humour. There was an element of cruelty in that humour, and maybe that grew over the years. There are people who are still alive who carry the scars, and will to their grave. George had lunch, day after day, being very witty at their expense. I presume if you've spent some time examining his career you've encountered this.

Yes.

That was his reputation. George was a pretty self-confident person, also. At that stage he was, as many people were at the University of Chicago, quite besotted with Frank Knight.

Yes.

George's thesis topic was Carl Menger,[3] the father of the mathematician Karl Menger with a 'K.' I remember a sentence he said. He said, 'Carl Menger is very good, but everything good that is in him is already (I can't say already) in Frank Knight.'

Yeah.

Frank Knight's influence on the student body was profound and not, I say in retrospect, a hundred per cent positively constructive. Does Knight figure in your studies to any great degree? Knight is a most interesting character. You've seen, I'm sure, George's Palgrave article on Knight, his biographical piece.

Yes.

Knight had a very strong influence on George Stigler and all the graduate students. But Knight was in a kind of manic mood then about capital theory. He must have written some eight or ten articles in the 1930s. They were a mixture. Part was a proper correction of a view that some simple Böhm-Bawerkian period of production could serve as a surrogate for capital. But they were also full of Humpty Dumptyisms, such as the period of production is either zero or infinite by some particular Knightian definition of how it would be measured. I don't know that this aspect of Knight profoundly affected Stigler, yet it did have an effect on Albert Hart, who had trouble getting his thesis passed. In fact, Knight's major influence at that time resulted in the local view that Knight had done everything and there was nothing left to do. So, he was the cause that led to a pretty important generation of Chicago economists never getting their PhD degrees.

I've heard that Allen Wallis never got his degree. Allen Wallis was of course, a bit more mathematical than George. So there is no reason why, whatever it was that Knight did in economics, that this should have precluded Wallis from taking a degree. Aaron Director never got a doctorate as well. But George must have acquired a decent knowledge of German to be able to write his thesis. I never read his PhD dissertation. I, of course, read his book on the history of production[4] and there is a chapter devoted to Menger. I don't recall any particular profundity in his interpretation of Menger that I ever heard from George's lips or remember reading in any of his writings. But then I didn't read the dissertation. Now, George was a tall guy. Have you got that wonderful picture of Milton and George from the rear.[5] It's something those in the economics profession would instantly recognise. I think he had some kind of a minor limp.

Really?

I don't know what the nature of it was. His son might know.

He didn't mention it.

George though played tennis and he became a pretty avid golfer especially, I think, when he was a widower. So it wasn't a debilitating limp. Milton Friedman played tennis, and George and he must have been a sight on the tennis court, if they were doubles partners. Milton played to some degree up to a late stage. You know he has had a heart bypass. Two, at intervals of more than a decade I think. And I think that tennis and golf became a fairly important part of George's life maybe from the age of 50 onwards. Can you remind me what George's age was when his wife died?

Well, she died about '71, '72. He would have been ...

As late as that?

Yes.

Oh, I thought it was earlier.

She died just as that book he did with Kindahl came out on 'Prices.[6] *That was about '71. He would have been about sixty.*

Yes, he would have been. Well, that's interesting. I was always surprised, no reason why I should have been, that George never remarried. He was close to his sons. Were there three?

Three.

Now, I know Steve.

Yes.

Are you talking to Solow?

After you.

Good. Good. Bob Solow and George Stigler were an odd couple. They became very close friends, fine friends after they both spent a year at the Stanford Behavioural Centre. I'm a little shaky on that but I think it was about 1958. That same year Milton Friedman was there. And Karl Popper actually was there that year but only came in at midnight, when no smokers were allowed. It was a pretty stellar year and that's when they met. And, of course, they both were very witty. They had that in common. But the reason why it was such a surprising friendship was that George was known to be a very conservative fellow and many of the things about Bob Solow were not at all.

Well now. I think there were some changes in George's thought over the years. Did George go first to the University of Minnesota? Was he ever at Iowa State?[7]

That was his first job, for about a year.

He went to Iowa State?

Under Theodore Schultz who was there.

Yes, Theodore Schultz was building up a powerful department at Ames.

Yes, that's right.

I had never heard of Theodore Schultz at that time when he was beginning to build up his department. And there were some other very good people who went to Iowa State like Gerhart Tintner. He was not George's type particularly. He stayed there a long time. Oz Brownlee, I don't remember whether he had been at Chicago or not as a graduate in any sense.[8] But he was the one who broke up the Iowa department because he wrote a pamphlet in the early war years entitled something like, *Margarine Not Butter*[9]...

Oh, the margarine.

The margarine or butter pamphlet. He argued that in a time of scarcity, such as the war, the fat from the ox was a better social bargain than the fat from the cow. And then the fat was in the fire. The farmers really were hopping mad. They said, 'We don't want to pay to have a Harvard down here in Iowa.' And, what may have been momentarily the fourth or fifth best economics department in the country simply disintegrated. I don't know whether George went to Minnesota before that happened.

I think that he might have. He was only at Iowa for maybe about a year.

About that. There were damn few jobs in those years. And certainly damn few jobs at the University of Chicago. The Great Depression did hit Hutchins' Chicago pretty hard in the investments it had made.[10] And the number of full professors suffered attrition. So there were very few appointments. Lloyd Mints, he was my teacher in 1932, was probably already 45 in 1932. I haven't checked the date. He lived to be over 100.[11]

Yes.

But he was only an assistant professor. Henry Simons might have been an Associate Professor, but I don't think there were very many promotions. So, there is no need to explain why none of the people I am talking about were asked to stay on at the university. I'll give you an example of the characters of these people. I may say that Allen Wallis and George were very good to me. They formed an opinion that I was a person of some ability and they spent a lot of time talking to me. I'll tell you a Stigler story. This concerns Allen Wallis too. Neither one of them liked nor thought very well of Henry Schultz. They thought that he was not a bright mind, not a profound scholar and something of a bluffer in mathematical economics. I think they were too hard on Henry Schultz. Henry Schultz was a very serious, very hard-working guy who had been a student of H. L. Moore at Columbia, really his prize student. H. L. Moore was a strange man, who had some psychiatric problems later in his life. Henry Schultz got a call to the University of Chicago in late 1920s. Chicago was not free of anti-Semitism, but it was relatively free in those days. And as a result, I think that explains in part its greater pre-eminence in those years, the early Hutchins years—the years just before Hutchins and up until, say, the end of the 1930s. It kind of had a monopoly on talent because Harvard, Yale and Princeton and a lot of the prevailing academic life was discriminatory against the Jews. In any case this story about George and Allen I probably had from Allen, but it might be confirmed by Jacob Mosak. Does that name mean anything to you?

Yes.

Jacob Mosak didn't have a lot to do I think with George, or Allen, because he became an assistant to and a disciple of Henry Schultz.[12]

Right. I see.

Milton Friedman, actually, must have worked a brief time for Henry Schultz, because if you look in Schultz's *Theory of the Measurement of Demand* in 1938—published just scarcely a year before he died with all his family in an auto accident—there is an acknowledgment to Milton and a reproduced Friedman section.

But anyway, Wallis and Stigler took Schultz's course, which was a very serious assignment because he assigned a lot of work and you had to sign up for a double quarterly credit if you took the course at all. Under the quarter system each subject had a lot of hours attached. You spent a lot of hours on a subject for a third of the year, instead of the way things are divided under the more common two-semester system. Well, because they were contemptuous of Schultz, and kind of mean, they played mean games with him. In one case they went to Henry Schultz and said, 'Professor, we have an argument between us which we can't settle. We know the formula for the area of a unit square, and we know the formula for the area of a unit cube. But we can't agree on what the general formula is for a four-dimensional regular solid. Would you please decide between us?' They knew that Henry Schultz thought that Allen Wallis was a better mathematician than George Stigler, so they gave George Stigler the correct answer and they gave Allen Wallis the incorrect answer. And, as it was basically described to me, Henry Schultz was proven to be a four-flusher. I don't know if that word means anything to you. It means a bluffer. As they saw it, the insecure professor fell into their trap and came out in favour of the Wallis formula. Well, that's a story on three people. And not on Schultz alone.[13]

George obviously had an original mind, although he wasn't very deeply trained in mathematics. For example, I can think of two things that he did that a person who was illiterate in mathematics would not have been expected to do. His Least-Cost Diet article, I should think came out about 1939, or some date like that, it came out in the *Journal of Agricultural Economics*, done when he was at Minnesota.[14]

Yes.

It is a clear formulation of a particular version of a linear programming problem. George did not know there was a prior history of this kind of problem and he did not work out the Dantzig simplex method for solving it. But he was able to get lower bounds and upper bounds. He understood that the cost could be brought down to this level and that it would involve only a certain selection of the foods on the menu. He correctly understood that the data of the problem would be what the nutrient requirements are. This would include calories, vitamin A, vitamin B, all of which were prescribed by the National Research Council for Good Health. The prices of a large number of goods, and the nutrient loadings for each one of these goods, were based on what their calorie content was; what their vitamin A, vitamin B, vitamin C, vitamin D and so forth were. It's an early example of linear programming and got a good deal of attention. I think he specified that one should eat just beans and I can't remember what else ...

Cabbages, I think.

Something like that, anyway, I think his article ended with something like 'but don't invite me to dinner.' Now that was one of the things he did. The other thing...

He never developed the work he did on that particular article?

No, but very soon that ball got picked up, not from Stigler but from the operations research in the war, and got carried very far and very fast in that period. The work on it began in the war agencies around 1945. By the time of the 1949 Cowles Commission Conference at the University of Chicago, the volume that came out in 1951 edited by

Koopmans, the whole theory was developed and very little except details were left to do afterwards. His work was a footnote.

I'm not particularly aware that he had an interest in the theoretical problem. The other mathematical piece is of purely intellectual interest. Suppose you could go into any geographic almanac and you made an array of all the rivers shown by length. Out of the first ten digits: zero, one, two, three, four, five, six, seven, eight, nine, you will find a preponderance of zero, one, two, three, four digits over the five, six, seven, eight, nine digits in the lengths. That's a brute fact. The same is true in a table of logarithms. Let's say it's a seven-place table of logarithms that has these same digits. You can work out how often zeros occur, one and so forth. This is exemplified by the fact that the earliest pages in a book of logarithm tables are the dirtiest. And I think that this brute fact has been commented on in the literature. But George got interested in this when he was at the Applied Math Panel of which Allen Wallis was the head.

Yes.

It had been established under Mina Rees who in the war effort was the Chief of mathematical projects.

Now George must have a published or unpublished memorandum on this subject. There are many different publications on it. This is just the kind of thing his son would know. I think he would know it backwards and forwards.

Yes.

Not because, so much, that his father was involved, but it's the kind of thing that would much interest him. I know Wendell Furry, the physicist, and later one of the victims in the McCarthy era, from Harvard has written on the subject. I don't remember if I ever knew the degree to which its result is a purely logical one. It has nothing to do with anything factual about a river, but has something to do with a way of describing numbers in a decimal system, or in a system of zero and ones, a dyadic system. I suspect that, whatever it is, whether it has something to do with an empirical fact, or whether it is a pure artefact of logic, it would re-occur in all number systems. If the Mayans used twelves, or sixes, that wouldn't matter. Now, that's the kind of thing you would do in wartime, when you are working very hard and you just want a diversion. Of course that was a somewhat strange place for George to be, I would think, but I think it was purely that he had no interest in carrying a gun and exposing his chest to random bullets. It isn't always what you know, but whom you know. And he certainly had literary skills.

Yes.

And they were producing a lot of publications. If you needed to know more about that, I would think that if Milton Friedman's memory is good, he would know exactly what George was doing there. Milton was a more creative mathematical type in sequential analysis. I knew a lot about that Applied Math Panel because my colleague, Harold Freeman, who just died days ago at the age of eighty-eight, was there. He was quite a character in his own right. He would regale me with stories about that very group. His stories involved, on the one hand, Allen Wallis, George and Milton Friedman. The order in which I put them means nothing. Actually George would have been the least important. And on the other hand, the great statistician Abraham Wald and his pal and friend, I think it was Jacob Wolfowitz.[15] Wolfowitz in particular was incensed against the Friedman/Wallis group because he thought they were stealing Wald's stuff. And Allen

Wallis, because this is the kind of a guy he is, got everybody very conscious about priorities. So people were keeping notes, 'I was sitting on the toilet and it was ten-o-three when I happened to look at my watch, which is when I got this idea. This was earlier than somebody else who was sitting in a bathtub and said 'Eureka!' That kind of thing is like AIDS or herpes. It spreads. You just need one rotten apple and then everybody is doing it to a characteristic degree. Now I was saying that George was globally very witty and that there was an element of cruelty in it.

Hmm.

Allen Wallis wasn't that witty although he could be whimsical. But there was an element in him of ruthlessness. I remember a story—I don't remember the particular character, it may have been a guy named Schwartz—who was involved with one of the books which the Applied Math Panel put out. On it was a list of names—it's not important I get this right—let's say Wallis, Friedman, my colleague Harold Freeman and maybe a fourth. But Schwartz's name wasn't on it. So he went to Wallis and complained. He said 'I want you to know that I think I did the work and I deserve it. And it's important for my career that I receive proper credit for this.' Historians of the sociology of science, like Robert K. Merton, would understand this. It isn't just dollars that people work for directly. And Allen Wallis wrote this sort of letter back to him. He said, 'I take your point. I understand your point of view. But I've decided that your name will not be on the book. And I have to tell you the reason for it. Because your name doesn't deserve to be on the book.' End of letter. That would be quite difficult to deal with. I recall Al Bowker—has his name figured at all in what you're doing? If you were writing a biography of Allen Wallis, it would. Bowker was an undergraduate student here at MIT. He had a lot to do in his life with scientific and academic administration and also with Allen Wallis. I once said to him, 'Will Allen Wallis ever get to be President of Stanford University?' And he said 'I don't think so. But it's not because he wouldn't like to be. And it's not because he necessarily makes the wrong decisions. But he insists upon giving you the reasons for his decisions and they chill your blood.'

Well, this was just what that congenial group was like. But let's step forward. George's early work was primarily in the field of history of thought, of course, and in industrial organisation. I think in the course of his life he had a change in his viewpoint. And I believe this is evident in that short breezy autobiography that he was persuaded to write by the Sloan Foundation Committee on Scientific Autobiography.[16] He was reluctant to do it, but he then did it in a remarkably short time once he made up his mind. The key character in this change was probably Aaron Director.

Yes.

Which is surprising as Aaron Director was a scratch tenure appointment at the University of Chicago. He published almost nothing and never took his PhD degree, but he was—and I guess I should say 'is' because is still alive and in his nineties.[17]

Ninety-three.

But he's not in very robust health.

No.

I don't know what his mental state, his memory is. Are you seeing him?

I actually already have had an interview with him, and with Milton Friedman and Rose Friedman as well.

Right, well those are the most important interviews you could have, especially if you can add Allen Wallis.[18]

Aaron Director was extremely conservative. Why, I don't know. By the time I knew him he was already like that. And he was an iconoclast. But he didn't develop new data with respect to industrial organisation. He didn't develop and articulate new theories. He just said that the conventional belief wasn't so.

Now, the typical thing would be that George, I think in his early stage, believed it was all important to study the technology in the steel industry. And if it were the case that the market was large enough, you could replicate, in each market three, four, five, six, seven or eight equally shaped, u-shaped cost curves at about the same time. You get lumpiness, but that lumpiness when you have eight firms diminishes the monopoly power of any in such a way that you could have effective competition. Not perfect competition. Effective competition. And the government wouldn't have to necessarily do anything about it. But in the beginning he was of the belief that in some of these industries there were unexhausted economies of scale. I think he must have written an article at one time, maybe in the *JPE* saying that, almost in the title.[19] Smith was right that unexhausted economies of scale will render competition imperfect.

By the last part of his life, whether in the last half or the last third, it was my impression that George was of the opinion that *laissez-faire* itself pretty much approximated to tolerably effective competition. And I think Aaron Director was the prime source of this view. George also gave signs—I don't know whether it's in his biography of Frank Knight in *Palgrave*[20]—of real disaffection with Frank Knight. The besottedness faded away. And I think that may have also been [so with] Aaron Director, although Aaron Director and Frank Knight were close and intimate. It was only Frank Knight who got Aaron Director his professorship. Of course, Aaron Director became prominent as a university teacher, and really had an influence, a profound influence, upon American IO policy when he became a lecturer at the University of Chicago Law School. I think he was just replacing Henry Simons.[21]

Yes.

Who had been doing that and who committed suicide in one of the early post-World War II years. Frank Knight was conservative. His prime characteristic was that he was a flaming atheist and he just couldn't leave the subject alone. He was an iconoclast, but he was also very critical of simple conservatism. His views were complicated. I always think of the first Chicago school as Knight and Viner, and to a degree Schultz. You'd also have to include Douglas—although they all ganged up on Douglas, they were all very critical of him—and of course Henry Simons. There was also Harry Gideonse, probably a guy whose name you don't know, who was brought in to organise and teach a big undergraduate survey course in the social sciences. And that first Chicago group was conservative by standards of the time and less so by standards of today's time. But still, as a group, they were on the conservative side. It was no way as conservative as the second Chicago School of Director, Friedman. If you had to skip all names but one, I think Friedman's name should be the one you should keep, and Gary Becker's.

Mmm.

I'm sure I'm leaving out some people. But Stigler and Friedman jumped on to Ronald Coase and felt that the Coase doctrines about transaction costs and property rights—just get the property rights right then *laissez-faire* could be relied upon—was the lifeline that they sought. Now, all that I know about this part of the story is what's called the Coase Theorem.

Yes.

And that's a coinage of Stigler's.

Yes.

I don't think Coase knew what his theorem was. There's great argumentation as to whether there is a theorem. And in George's writings on that, but also in his little autobiography he discusses in detail the evening dinner at which Coase started out with everyone as his opponent, but then all of them got converted.[22]

Now, George was a very learned, he was hard-working. ... I'm now going into his history of thought work. He was perhaps not as learned as Jacob Viner or Edwin Cannan or Piero Sraffa, as far as the documents, but he had a lot of depth and breadth. George wrote short and dogmatic articles. I heard it said that that little book of the four lectures at the LSE—

Yes. Five.

Five?

Yeah.

That he went there and I don't know whether his first lecture was half an hour or something like that and then he left. He also never answered criticism. I never understood that. That's just alien to my nature. If George made a mistake, and I believe he did when he specified what Wicksell thought and what Nicky Kaldor thought. He thought that Ricardo—in his last edition chapter on machinery, where Ricardo recanted his earlier view and came to believe that machinery could hurt the demand for labour—that Ricardo simply made a mistake. Ricardo must have had a hardening of the arteries because he seemed to these people to be saying that what happens under competition is not Pareto optimal. (Pareto optimality is not an expression that would have meant anything to Ricardo.) I think that's a misreading of Ricardo. And, if Ricardo had been saying that, under the conditions of the problem, that would have been a mistake. But all Ricardo was saying was that there could be a change in technology. Technology could shift the incidence of distribution between labour and other produced inputs and that could destroy the total amount of national income. Because Ricardo believed that when the wage fell, in the short run, population would decline.

Yes.

Now it doesn't mean that the output with that population—whatever it is, before, after and during, isn't being produced at a Pareto optimal level of efficiency. There's just fewer inputs available. This describes labour as an endogenous variable in the classical Ricardian system.

Well, I wrote a couple of articles pointing it out and reiterating that there really wasn't anything, in my opinion, in Ricardo's language which relied upon sticky wage rates or on involuntary unemployment. What he was describing was perfectly consistent with what would happen in a classical scenario of his kind. And Pareto optimality would be maintained at all times. I published this in two places. I don't remember what the order was. There was some difference in the time frame. But one was the *Journal of Scandinavian Economics* that Wicksell had once edited, and the other was the *JPE*.[23] Now the *JPE* might even have been the first publication. George Stigler *de facto* was an editor of the *JPE* at that time. I don't know whether in that year he was a *de jure* editor because that was a shifting thing. And he accepted the article.

The article was accepted and he would surely have been asked since I directly referred it to him as an editor. I never got a note from George saying 'Well, this time around I've got to admit I was wrong. And your reading was right.' Not at any time. And a lot of people would tell me that if they wrote to him complaining about something, he would answer something like 'Well, if you're the kind of person who believes that, then you're just the kind of person who believes that.'

Yes.

Or to take a different case, and probably a case for which Stigler will remain well known, to the degree that anybody remains well known over time.

When he reviewed, I think it was Sraffa's edition of Ricardo, about the time that it came out—it may not have been in this same issue as the review—he also had an article with the title, 'The Ninety Three Percent Labour Theory of Value of Ricardo.'[24] And his argument was very simple. Certainly an argument like that can be found in Ricardo. I don't strictly believe that every industry has the same relative mix of interest cost, time cost, and labour cost. But, suppose you take a realistic example, and that's what Ricardo's typical examples—numerical examples—are. And you let the profit rate go through a great variation. Now calculate how much that affects the relative prices of costs for corn, let's say it's corn. It'll be only a five percent change, a three percent change or, to be liberal, a seven per cent change. So, it's ninety-three percent accurate.

Well, first, it depends on which numerical example you use. And particularly if you use those which Ricardo didn't much use. It is really more congenial to the Marxian literature and von Bortkiewicz to go into Sraffa-like input/output. Let the profit rate become very near the maximum it can become in such a market. You can have there extreme sensitivity. It can change the price ratio by—and indeed a good example to use—as much as ninety-nine per cent. That's a far cry from George's 3%.

I wrote about this and some Australians wrote about this, but I never saw any commentary from Stigler. It was almost a Schumpeter-like attitude. Schumpeter in 1911 wrote that the interest rate will become zero in a stationary state.[25] After there had been no exogenous development and no technological change, the violin strings plucked by innovation will dampen down. And when it dampens down, until the next perturbation, the interest rate will dampen down to zero.

Right.

Well this particular view is based on a number of what I believe to be intuitions in Schumpeter's mind, but he never really thought through the problem. Frank Knight made similar mistakes, but on the opposite side. For him, the interest rate can't ever go to zero. Schumpeter never lectured on this subject voluntarily, in all the Harvard days I knew him. But Paul Sweezy once persuaded him, and got him to do so.[26] I think that he believed you go down in history books for what your ideas are. You don't admit a mistake: 'Let's go down with all flags flying.' And there was something of that, I think, in George.

Mmm.

People in our profession have always been kind of scared of Milton Friedman as a polemicist. So, he gets away with a certain amount of murder. And when he's safely dead and when they've salted his grave against any revival, the daggers will come out. I'm flogging the point. That doesn't change his overall status.

No.

The same is true in some degree of George as a witty polemicist. People tended to be scared of him including those who deal with history of economics doctrine. George had lots of dicta that can be quoted.

I don't know that I'm getting any of these things just right, but one is that you should judge a person by his central message. What his impact was at the time and not what you can go back and read into it, but which nobody in those times would have done.

Yes.

Well, the answer is yes you should. And yes, you shouldn't. You should be pointing out this—I'm telling you what some of the other dicta are that usually sweep the field—but really the jury has to be permanently out on that. It's the kind of sweeping assertion whose negation also has something to it. I'm not talking about the truth content, because you can't have a proposition which is both true and untrue, but I'm talking about what is a truthful approach. Now let's see. Another strong characteristic is the unity of this group who properly felt that they were lone voices crying in the wilderness. And that most of the profession was against them.

Yes.

They defended each other. Now, Aaron Director, for example, would never have written a good letter of recommendation for somebody who wasn't a staunch conservative but neither would Milton. And I remember for years after I left the University of Chicago, when they were contemplating influential appointments they would ask me about the person, 'Is he really sound?' In fact, Milton once showed his naïveté to me, but it wasn't about appointments. He said, 'Tell me the truth, is Galbraith a Commie?' You know the amount of naïveté that's in that. I've done a lot of thinking about my old ... I can't say my old religion, although I was trained by the Jesuits, so I know it. But I once did a little informal investigation of whether people who were economic libertarians and tended to favour low taxation and low regulation and *laissez-faire,* were also people interested in civil liberties and freedom of expression, and that sort of thing. So I would ask innocent questions. 'Now what do you think of this group?' Of course, I had a placebo question control group. 'What do you think of the fact that this professor at the University of New Hampshire, the one who invited Paul Sweezy in the McCarthy era to give a lecture, is losing his job because neither he nor Paul Sweezy will testify as to what was the content of the lecture?' And Milton said, 'Gee, it's a simple case. It's a free speech society. If a man will not do what he should, this professor should be fired. Society has a right to know.' I said, 'You don't understand. They've got the notes on the lecture, verbatim. It's not a question of information.'

I mentioned the name of Wendell Furry earlier on, when we spoke about this problem of digits. Wendell Furry, who was a son of a minister, had been a member of the Communist Party. That was not a crime at that time. I don't know whether it ever became a crime to be a member of the Communist Party. Under legislation, it became a reason not to be admitted to the country, things like that. And many people like him in universities and in this community were called before the House Un-American Activities Committee and required to confess that they had been a member of a communist cell. Required to name names of those who were in the cell with them. And Wendell Furry was no exception. But he said, 'I freely admit I was a member of the Communist Party. I was a member from this date to that date, but I will not name any names.' Well his job at Harvard was in peril, he was in contempt of Congress, and all the rest. The Harvard lawyers said to him 'But don't you understand, they know those names already?' And he said, 'Of course I know that, but this is something that a person of character doesn't do.' And Wendell Furry was actually worthless at anything but teaching advanced physics and writing about it. He couldn't even run a shoe store or anything. But with him it was just never a question. And as it happened, the virus ran its course so he actually died a member of the Harvard faculty. The case against him, the Federal case, was dropped after a mistrial. It was never re-started.[27]

Well, the point of my story was, now, what would Milton Friedman think about such a case. I didn't actually ask Aaron Director this or receive an answer. I don't remember doing that. We can't simply use this story as evidence, but this group, they really had no interest in such things. I was only able to develop one case, and that was Fritz Machlup who came to this country as an immigrant from Austria. He was part of the very conservative Austrian tradition, but he became prominent in the American Association of Professors for Academic Freedom, and so forth. And when I said that to one of his students he said, 'You don't understand, it's just because Fritz liked professors.' I said, 'I don't care. You've got to put him down for where he stood on this issue. He actually had a thing for market freedoms and also had a thing for freedom of expression.' But I was sorry I wasn't able to get more, to ask more people and to arrive at a happier finding.

Now let's see. I think I've pretty much shot my bolt. I don't know a lot about George and the work he did on the importance of information in economics. I think this would be one of the things that his supporters would write down. And I don't know but whether there's a direct and strong link, in that later position of his, with his early study on Carl Menger.

But there is in fact an element of that in the earlier Austrian writing, all the time, all the way through actually up to Hayek. Now, I don't remember any particular adulation by George of Hayek. George, I think, was a member of the Mt. Pelerin Society, wasn't he?

Yeah, he was ...

And Milton, and so was Hayek who also went to the meetings, and von Mises. I never heard George make jokes about Ludwig von Mises' extremism, although there were a lot of jokes made at the time, but George was generally on the rightish side of most issues.

Now, I'll tell you two other unrelated facts. When I was at Harvard and left the University of Chicago, and when I thought of George as already an up-and-coming economist of reputation, my professor, Gottfried Haberler, who had just read the production book, said, 'Ah, mark my words Paul, I predict George Stigler as one of the coming leaders in our profession.' And I thought, 'Well, I'm already there in thinking that.'

Now George wasn't especially lucky in his academic career. He went from Minnesota to the war effort I guess.

Yes.

Then, did he go to Brown for a very short period?

One year.

And then he went to Columbia?

Yeah, because he had that problem with the Chicago job.

What was the problem?

He was offered the job but when he was interviewed by the president ...

Yeah. Who was a very opinionated person …

Yes. He claimed that Stigler was far too empirical. And they gave the job to Milton Friedman instead.

Yes. I see. I didn't know that. That would have been around 1947.[28]

Yes, '47, '48.

But what is a little bit surprising in the first place, Milton only got an offer of an associate professorship. And he accepted it. Which I think was too little and rather late. Now Milton had certain troubles, because of two things: anti-Semitism, but also people were afraid of him. His corrosiveness and so forth. Gottfried Haberler wanted Milton Friedman to be appointed to Harvard and somebody like Ed Chamberlin, who was a very conservative person was the department member most violently opposed, because the Chicago School hated both the theories of imperfect and of monopolistic competition.

Did you ever figure out exactly what was behind that?

It started with Knight. Knight was actually a teacher of Ed Chamberlin at the State University of Iowa. That's not at Ames.

No.

That's at Iowa City. And that isn't what its name is today. Its name today is the University of Iowa.

Yeah.

Knight always said, all that's good in Chamberlin he got from me and there isn't anything good in him. You know, something like that. And, there's no reason why this should have been of any importance, but it really riled Knight that Chamberlin was a Catholic convert.

I know.

'The man believes in the Immaculate Conception. What can you do with him?' Knight would say. So from the start, of course, they didn't like the notion that if you were analysing imperfect competition, you were analysing cases of market failure. They always played this down. Now, the early Stigler wasn't as strong on this as he was later on. But Friedman was from early on. And I think that part of the reason for it was this development of his—was it 1953—version of positivism?[29]

1129

Yes.

It's partly a licence for self-indulgence. You don't have to have a correspondence between a theory and the facts, or a close correspondence. In fact, the theory is all the better if it doesn't fit the facts closely. And I think that there are some profound errors in that form of positivism, but it is there for a purpose. It serves a purpose. Do you think the cigarette industry with only four big producers in it is not competitive?

Well, if one raises its price, another one will and so forth. That's the same paradigm of comparative statics that would happen under competition. So under the doctrine of 'as if,' we can use the competitive theory?

Yes.

And as I said, the early Stigler didn't quite believe that, but the late, greater Stigler sort of believed that the facts had changed or had only now been properly interpreted. You could see this in the role that information played for Stigler. It also extenuates what had seemed like market failure because it is all very well to have one price, but that's under the naive assumption that you could have ideal information.

Yes.

And, actually they're working out their own version of a theory of imperfect competition. It just isn't the Joan Robinson or the Ed Chamberlin version. But, go back to this 'civil liberties' versus 'economic freedom' discussion and this is tangential. When I first came to Harvard in 1935, the university got a grant from Thomas Lamont of the First National Bank, now the Morgan Guarantee Bank, to establish an Institute Professor. I don't know whether it was the first University Professorship at Harvard. I think it wasn't. I think the Dean of the Harvard Law School, Roscoe Pound, might have gotten the first one. But it was at least the second one. And they had a wide choice of applicants. It was a very cushy job, no teaching duties, a lot of surplus hours, and a salary for life essentially. Well, they scoured the world. They didn't give it to Schumpeter. They gave it to Sumner Slichter. You ever heard of him?

Yes. Labour.

Labour. Yeah. And a leader in labour economics. Also, a pretty good rough and ready macro forecaster. He was probably the most popular and the highest paid lecturer to the business community. But a complete loner. He never showed any manuscript of his to a colleague. He split his time between the business school and the economics department. And he had a little bit of the institutionalist colouring of the University of Wisconsin because he came from the University of Wisconsin where his father had been a famous dean of mathematics and engineering. Now, Aaron Director came to visit me for a weekend at Harvard and he said, 'Why didn't you give it to Frank Knight? He would have liked to have had the job.' And I said, 'Well, would he have accepted it?' Because I had heard the story that when Allyn Young went to England and they had to replace him, Harvard extended a call to Frank Knight who had earlier been Allyn Young's thesis student at Cornell University. And in fact, it was always rumoured that what was good in *Risk Under Uncertainty and Profit* came from Allyn Young, who never published much. The rumour about Chamberlin's economics was the same, the *Theory of Monopolistic Competition*. I think this is not true in either case, in my observation. And he said, 'Well, in 1927 Frank Knight refused the call and the reason was that he didn't approve of

President A. L. Lowell's treatment of the Sacco and Vanzetti case, because in that case ... I don't know if you know that case. Lowell, the head honcho in the review committee, said that there had been no miscarriage of justice and it was a *cause cèlébre* all over the world. That's the good part of the story. But then, according to Aaron Director, who shared a cabin in the sand dunes outside of Chicago with Knight, Knight now (1935) said, 'What a fool I was.' I found that sad.

Uh, huh.

Knight gave a famous lecture in 1932, I think it was, that the world was coming to an end, and that there was only a choice between fascism and communism.[30] He said that, 'As for me, I would choose communism.' He later tried to get all the copies back.

So, Knight who had been divorced about the time of the Great Depression had money worries. I don't know whether they were out of proportion to his actual alimony but he had worrying problems. Like Irving Fisher, who also had financial reverses, they not only affected in Fisher's case his personality, but these matters actually affected his policy formulations and recommendations.

I think I've shot my bolt. But sure, ask me any questions.

Oh, sure. George Stigler seems to have had, all through his life, a certain concentration on income distribution issues. Starting from his dissertation and ...

How did income distribution ...?

Well, even in his dissertation ...

You mean imputation.

Marginal productivity ...

Yeah, yeah, but that is different ...

Yes, he was keen ...

That's different from Gini coefficients ...

Not that, not that.

Right.

And at least in the later years, say in the '80s Tanner Lectures he gave, later published as "The Economist as a Preacher", he seemed to want to push that not only was it efficient, but it was also somehow ethical as well.

You mean, what is, is right.

What is, is right.

Okay, I imagine that he got this from Milton Friedman. This happened around 1952, at the Paris Colloquium or Conference on Risk, put on by The Econometric Society. Milton Friedman gave a paper which said in effect, life is a constant procession of events that impinge on us with a considerable amount of uncertainty out there. (This is my broad gloss on what he said.) At every stage on the road there are forks in the road, and we are making choices. And, in effect, we end up in the beds that we have made for ourselves. This would have grown, in Milton's mind, out of the Friedman/Savage article of 1948 on gambling.[31] You postulate an epicycle in the form of a convex stretch, a non-concave stretch of the utility function so that the people falling in that become inveterate gamblers. And so the inequality is the result of their own *ex ante* decisions. Now, it's undoubtedly true that if everybody started out exactly alike in genetic composition and environment— for this they would have to be clones, identical clones—and if for some reason, even though they are clones, they differ in their risk aversion, then, what you will find is that those with the greatest risk tolerance will end up bi-polarly at the extremes more than the people with less risk tolerance. And so what is, is right. Now, that's in a *JPE* article. Probably in 1953, I don't know.[32] I would speculate that this would have been an important source. Because George Stigler, who was very critical of people, was almost worshipful of Milton Friedman. I remember that one of his dicta was that a Milton Friedman theorem was more credible than any other theorem, because everybody picks on Milton. It's an unfair world and so forth, which means that he gets a more rigorous testing than anyone else.[33] Doesn't he have genuinely adulatory remarks in his autobiography about Milton?

Yes.

Now, what you have to understand with somebody like Allen Wallis, and so to a degree those people who were in his circle, is that Allen Wallis had the sharpest priors—I'm using the language of Bayesian probability—of anybody I ever knew. Almost no new data could change his view for this reason. On the other hand, if he thought of somebody as a dangerous, or an incompetent thinker, but Jimmy Savage assured him that the man was very smart and had good judgement, that carried more weight with Allen Wallis than a two-year study of the person's vitae and an audit of his writings. There's an in-group of the good guys and the much larger out-group. This showed itself in things that aren't even political. Just as an amusement I used to do a little Diogenes-like anthropological study of statistician friends of mine on what their attitude was on cigarette smoking. This was in the years when it had been nominated as an important cause of mortality, excess mortality. Let's say for my money that already the evidence was overwhelming. But this was denied. And when I went to Allen Wallis he said, 'There's nothing to it. Next thing you know they'll be saying coffee causes cancer.' Or something like that. And this was right on my prediction. Before I went to talk to him, I predicted what his response would be. I remember saying to him, 'Now, what about Milton?' And he said 'Well, Milton agrees with me. However, he has quit smoking.' But you know what my skeleton key, my variable was, in making these judgements? I went to Howard Raiffa[34] and he said, 'Oh, I wouldn't touch them on the basis of what we have.' Now, how much of an admirer of R.A. Fisher are you? R.A. Fisher was a genius. He was the genius of first half of the 20th century in statistical theory. But he was an extremely opinionated man, a man of strong opinions, including strong eugenic and race kinds of things, and a very disagreeable man in many regards. There is a very good biography of him by his daughter, who of course is not a critic, but you just have to read the facts. Well, R.A. Fisher refused to believe there was a link between smoking and cancer. That was all poppycock. In fact in one of his articles, he purports to have a sample in which the inhalers have less lung cancer than the others. One of my younger colleagues here, who is both an MD and an economist, once went through the Fisher literature to see whether there was any saving grace, and there really isn't. But, Fisher was the enemy of Neyman-Pearson[35] because Karl Pearson had been very mean to Fisher and Fisher in turn ... well, abused children become abusers.

Yes.

Now John Tukey, who was a very great American statistician, was also wrong. My maths teacher, Edwin Bidwell Wilson from Harvard, went on the payroll of the tobacco industry. In his case, he was Dean of the School of Vital Statistics and he was just so jaundiced by false understandings of probability. If six people in the same street get cancer, there would be a state legislative investigation. But it was interesting that in this particular group, this also was the case with Allen Wallis for example, they liked the complicated explanation better than the simple one.

The clever one.

Yeah, it was kind of like syncopation, always the after beat. So there was an awful lot of nonsense going on. I don't know if any important doctrinal differences ever developed among George Stigler and Allen Wallis and Milton Friedman. I'd say the only thing I can see at the very end is that Milton Friedman remained very much a policy person, pushing policy views.

Yes. George Stigler pushed his idea of 'what is, is best' to the degree where he would say, 'Suppose there is for instance, a sugar subsidy that's remained in place. Suppose we can actually calculate the social cost of maintaining it. However, if it has remained for 50 years and passed the test of time, it must be, as far as the public is concerned, an optimal way to redistribute income, and therefore economists can't really attack it, because it is all motivated by self-interest.

This is a little bit like Frank Knight's position against Henry George and the single tax. Land is inelastically supplied. There is no dead weight loss from imposing taxes on it, but why would you do it at this stage, when people in good faith have bought land over the years. Besides, how can you separate the investment that has been made in the land from the Ricardian original inexhaustible value of it?

Yes.

You know this argument that you're making is Gary Becker-like. I at times think some of the Chicago people are hopeless. Well, I wouldn't include Milton as among the hopeless because he was smart enough to punch his way out of a paper bag sometimes. But in the end he didn't want to do so. I think that's the case with 100% money, which was just a crotchety part of the first Chicago school. Irving Fisher also embraced it.

The only thing it fits into is Milton's later monistic monetarism where, if you have a 100% reserve ratio by law, then you can't have a variable *de facto* reserve ratio and therefore you won't get an additional component in the variance of the money supply. And of course getting a variance in the ups and downs of the money supply is the worst thing possible.

Yes.

Gary Becker, I think, cured him of that. Probably he said, 'Look. You have barriers to money in the banking system and private banking under one disguise or another will inevitably arise. You will simply make the banking system ineffective with a kind of Gresham's Law arising.' And I think Milton quietly changed; he just quietly dropped that. He doesn't particularly announce changes in positions, but instead, lets them just decay away. That idea actually became a prominent principle, that there's always a way out of bad regulations.

1133

The market rushes in.

If you do it by surprise ... This gets into the Lucas critique.

Yes.

If you do it by surprise people can be cheated the first time. But give them time and they'll work the market around. So don't worry. In fact, Lucas's rational expectations really stole the show from Friedman's monetarism. There's almost nobody left, including I think Milton quite quietly, who believes that there's a tight relationship between one of the M's and effective demand.

You can't even measure money supply anymore.

Yes. Now when George Stigler got the Nobel Prize and he actually went to Washington—he was given the Science Medal of Honor by Reagan—he was asked about what fiscal policy should be, or something like that. What was very uncharacteristic for an economist is that he said what Gerald Debreu said when he got the prize. 'I don't do that sort of thing. And so I don't have any interesting opinion on that.' I think George said, in effect, I'm a micro-economist and not a macro-economist. But I think like Armen Alchian[36], who is more Catholic than the Pope, and who never went to the University of Chicago but is a real Chicagoan, does end up doing some simple macro theory.

I imagine when all's said and done—I don't remember George writing particularly on the real bills doctrine or the quantity theory—George would say 'inflation is everywhere a monetary phenomenon.'[37] This is like taking a personality loan from people whom he admires, who believe that kind of thing. More than most, I think, George kept out of things that he felt he wasn't entitled to an opinion on.

Most economists would say 'How do you spell 'gold'? And then they'll tell you what we should be doing about gold or anything else that you can imagine.

One last question.

Yes.

This is related in a way to your last statement. In his writing, Stigler is very clear that he doesn't believe ideology has much to do with economics.

Well, this is a popular Friedman view too. And it's wrong. I say that flatly. But it's interesting that just recently—I have somewhere a National Bureau yellow jacket manuscript of a research study by Victor Fuchs from Stanford University, Jim Poterba from this university and Allan Krueger of the Woodrow Wilson School at Princeton.[38] They did an extensive sampling of economists in two areas of economics. One was labour economics and there was another, approximately equal size sample. I can't remember how large these samples were. Whether we're talking 50, 150 or 200 in each discipline, I'm not sure my memory's precise.[39] I don't remember what the other field was, whether it was IO or not, but I don't think so. It was an important field, but it wasn't fiscal policy versus monetary policy. And what they did was they gave a whole set of questions on what each person's factual opinion was on that question. What do you think is the elasticity of supply of labour under this condition? He had all these factual differences in the group. But they also asked questions about their value judgements.

Yes.

They asked these in whole different areas. The third less important area was their political affiliations, which I presume these days would be Republican or Democratic, but they might have gone further. Then they tried to see how you explained the differences in policy recommendations. Their finding is the opposite of Milton Friedman's. There was very considerable degree of consensus on factual matters. There were some differences in the degree of confidence they had in their answers. The confidence intervals varied quite considerably. And in particular, the people who in this sample had aberrant factual beliefs—if most people thought the elasticity of supply was a small plus, but you got somebody who had it a very large plus, or somebody who had it a very large minus—those people would have much wider confidence intervals as well because the authors got data on what they regarded as their confidence intervals. Now what they found was the difference in their policy recommendations were—I'm using your language, not their language—ideologically premised values. They were not fact driven. Now there are a few cases like the minimum wage or Ricardian comparative advantage where you can almost get certain unanimity, free of ideology. But these are exceptions in my opinion.

Notes

[1] Albert Hart (1909-1997) died on September 19, 1997, a month prior to this conversation with Paul Samuelson. He received his Ph.D. from the University of Chicago in 1936. He came to Columbia University in 1946 and stayed until his retirement in 1977. Thus Hart and Stigler were contemporaries not only as graduate students but also as colleagues at Columbia.

[2] George Stigler's career prior to coming to Chicago in 1933 consisted of an undergraduate degree in business administration from the University of Washington in 1931. He then received a master's degree from Northwestern after a year of study. Stigler returned to the University of Washington for a year before heading to Chicago.

[3] Carl Menger formed a chapter in his dissertation published in 1941. However, his first publication, prior to submitting his dissertation, appeared in 1937, "The Economics of Carl Menger," *Journal of Political Economy*. 45 (2): 229-50.

[4] George Stigler's dissertation became the basis for his first published book in 1941, *Production and Distribution Theories*. New York: Macmillan.

[5] This picture is reproduced in George Stigler's autobiography, *Memoirs of an Unregulated Economist*. New York: Basic Books, 1988. The picture is well worth a look being reminiscent of Don Quixote and Sancho Panza.

[6] The correct date is 1970. The precise title (written with James Kindahl) is *The Behavior of Industrial Prices*. National Bureau of Economic Research, New York: Columbia University Press.

[7] George Stigler started his professional career at Iowa State College in 1936. According to his own recollections (1988:38), 'It was one of only two available academic posts (the other was Ohio State) known to my professors at Chicago in that year, and it would not have been available if Homer Jones had not turned it down.' Stigler then moved on to the University of Minnesota in 1938 and remained there until 1946. However during the war years he was on leave, first at the National Bureau of Economic Research and then at the Statistical Research Group at Columbia University.

[8] Brownlee worked as a research associate at Iowa State, coming there in 1939 after completing a Master's Degree from the University of Wisconsin. He received a Ph.D. from Iowa State in 1945. Most of his career was spent at the University of Minnesota

(1950-1985). Before Minnesota he had taught at Carnegie Institute of Technology and the University of Chicago.

[9] Oswald H. Brownlee (1943) 'Putting Dairying on a War Footing," original (retracted) version of Pamphlet No. 5, *Wartime Farm and Food Policy Series* . Ames, Iowa: Iowa State College Press.

[10] Robert Hutchins was Chancellor of the University of Chicago 1946-1951. Prior to that he served as President of the University of Chicago from 1929-1946.

[11] Lloyd W. Mints (1888-1989) was a key figure of the University of Chicago economics department in the 1930s and 1940s. He was known for his contribution to monetary theory, particularly his reformulation of the quantity theory of money. He came to Chicago in 1928 and remained there until his retirement in 1953. At that time he turned his back on economics, starting a second career as a cabinet maker while living with his sister outside of Ft. Collins, Colorado.

[12] Jacob Mosak also was on the Cowles Commission research staff in the early forties and was associated with the Walrasians then at Chicago rather than the self-proclaimed Marshallians.

[13] Compare George Stigler's own recollection of this incident in his autobiography, *Memoirs of an Unregulated Economist*. New York: Basic Books. 1988:25-26.

[14] The article came out in the May edition of the *Journal of Farm Economics*. The title of the article is 'The Cost of Subsistence.' Stigler, George J. (1945) "The Cost of Subsistence," *Journal of Farm Economics*. 27(1): 303-314.

[15] His son, Paul Wolfowitz would become one of the more influential neo-conservative voices in the George W. Bush administration.

[16] George Stigler's autobiography appeared in 1988, *Memoirs of an Unregulated Economist*. New York: Basic Books. The book is a well written, enjoyable read of an academic life. The author reveals very little of his private life.

[17] Aaron Director born 1901, died on September 13, 2004 at the age of 102. At the time of the interview he would have been 95. His sister Rose married Milton Friedman, both having been graduate students at Chicago in the thirties with Aaron then part of the staff as an instructor.

[18] I unfortunately failed to do so. Wallis died in 1998, the year following this interview.

[19] This reference would seem to be to his 'The Economies of Scale' article published October 1958 in *The Journal of Law and Economics*. Stigler, George J. (1958) "The Economies of Scale," *The Journal of Law and Economics*. 1(1): 54-71.

[20] The reference is to *The New Palgrave: A Dictionary of Economics*. Edited by John Eatwell, Murray Milgate and Peter Newman in four volumes, London: Macmillan Press in 1987.

[21] This occurred in 1946.

[22] Aaron Director hosted that dinner at his house.

[23] The two articles are:
>Samuelson, Paul A. (1988) "Mathematical Vindication of Ricardo on Machinery," *Journal of Political Economy*. 96(2): 274-282.
>Samuelson, Paul A. (1989) "Ricardo was Right," *Scandinavian Journal of Economics*. 91(1): 47-63.

[24] The exact reference is:
>Stigler, George J. (1958) "Ricardo and the 93% Labor Theory of Value," *The American Economic Review*. 48(3): 357-367.

[25] The reference is to Schumpeter's (1911) *Theorie der wirtschaftlichen Entwicklung*. Leipzig: Duncker & Humblot. (transl. 1934, *The Theory of Economic Development: An inquiry into profits, capital, credit, interest and the business cycle*. London: Oxford University Press.)

[26] Surprisingly enough, Paul Sweezy was Schumpeter's graduate assistant at this time.
> I was there [Harvard] for eight years, I think from '34 until I went into the army in 1942. That was the period when Schumpeter was at his peak. He was a magnet for people from all over the world. They wanted to study with, or have an opportunity to study with, him at a higher level. For a year, or maybe for two years, I forget now, I was working with Schumpeter. I was his graduate assistant (Conversation with Paul Sweezy, November 1997).

[27] Wendell H. Furry (1907-1984) was defended by newly appointed Harvard president Nathan Pusey who in 1954 refused to cave in to McCarthy's demands to fire him.

[28] I am also not quite accurate here. The actual year was 1946. George Stigler took up a position at Brown instead. As Stigler relates the incident in his *Memoirs of an Unregulated Economist*:
> In the spring of 1946 I received the offer of a professorship from the University of Chicago, and of course was delighted at the prospect. The offer was contingent upon approval by the central administration after a personal interview. I went to Chicago, met with the President Ernest Colwell, because Chancellor Robert Hutchins was ill that day, and I was vetoed! I was too empirical, Colwell said, and no doubt that day I was. So the professorship was offered to Milton Friedman, and President Colwell and I had launched the new Chicago School. We both deserve credit for that appointment, although for a long time I was not inclined to share it with Colwell (Stigler 1988:40).

[29] Friedman, Milton (1953) *Essays in Positive Economics*. Chicago: University of Chicago Press.

[30] The lecture has been published as Frank Knight, "The Case for Communism: From the Standpoint of an Ex-liberal," in Warren J. Samuels, ed., *Research in the History of Economic Thought and Methodology*, archival supplement 2 (Greenwich, CT, 1991), 57–8. The lecture was privately published by Knight in 1933, along with two other speeches, in an edited volume: Frank Knight, *The Dilemma of Liberalism* (Ann Arbor, MI, 1933). The 1932 lecture in which Knight urged his audience to vote communist in the coming election was given under the auspices of the Communist Club and the National Student League at the University of Chicago.

[31] The article is: Friedman, Milton and Leonard Savage (1948) "Utility Analysis of Choices Involving Risk," *Journal of Political Economy*. 56(4): 279-304.

[32] The reference seems to be to Friedman, Milton (1953) "Choice, Chance and the Personal Distribution of Income," *Journal of Political Economy*. 61(4): 277-290.

[33] This particular dictum found its way into print at least once. Talking about the need to generate quite deliberately controversy, Stigler contrasts early Walrasian economics with the theories of his close friend Milton Friedman. In his (1982) evaluation of studying the history of economic thought ("Does Economics Have a Useful Past?" in *The Economist as Preacher*. Chicago: University of Chicago Press, pp. 107-118) he claims:
> The sterility of the early Walrasian system arose because it was ignored

by most economists and adopted by a few but criticized by almost none. Milton Friedman's work is bound to be spread rapidly in the science and to achieve a wide scope and high rigor because of his wondrous gift of eliciting the probing attention of eminent contemporaries (p.111).

[34] Howard Raiffa (1924-) is a pioneer in the field of decision science and game theory. He is currently the Frank P. Ramsey Professor (Emeritus) of Managerial Economics, a joint chair held by the Business School and the Kennedy School of Government at Harvard University.

[35] Egon Pearson (1895-1980) was the son of Karl Pearson (1857 – 1936). The Neyman-Pearson lemma was the joint work of Jerzy Neyman and Egon Pearson.

[36] Armen Alchian (1914 -) spend his academic career at U.C.L.A., starting there in 1946. The economics department became closely identified with the Chicago School. Alchian himself is best known for his pioneering work in the economics of property rights. A seminal work, "Uncertainty, Evolution and Economic Theory," appeared (1950) in the *Journal of Political Economy 58*: 211-21.

[37] In an interview conducted by *The* Region (May 1989) the official publication of the Federal Bank of Minneapolis, http://www.minneapolisfed.org/pubs/region/89-05/int895.cfm, George Stigler clearly confirms Paul Samuelson's claim.

Well, I'm a monetarist in the sense of believing that the control over some money supply is important (which measure of money and over what periods, for example, are decisive questions in the control over the rate of growth of the price level). I think that the rate of growth of money is a critical variable in controlling inflation and that, for example, the massive troubles we are having with the savings and loan industry are, in part, the product of the fanatical inflation we had at the end of the '70s and the beginning of the '80s. Those alone are indications of the kind of costs that are imposed upon a society. It wouldn't be too bad maybe if you went completely crazy, like the South American countries, and let inflation go on and everybody indexes on some more stable currency, and so forth and so on. But we aren't going to do that. We're going to put all kinds of strange regulations in: we won't let this go up, and we'll let this price go up. They cause immense distortions in an age of inflation. That's one of the great problems plaguing the Israeli economy.

[38] Fuchs, Victor R., Alan B. Krueger and James M. Poterba (1997) "Why Do Economists Disagree About Policy," *NBER Working Papers W6151* August: 1-49. This was later printed in the *Journal of Economic Literature*. Fuchs, Victor R., Alan B. Krueger and James M. Poterba (1998) "Economists' views about Parameters, Values and Policies: Survey Results in Labor and Public Economics," *Journal of Economic Literature*. 1387-1425. Curiously enough, Paul Samuelson has a published article in the same volume.

[39] The three authors base their work on surveys sent out to "specialists in labor economics and public economics at the 40 leading research Universities in the United States." (Fuchs, Krueger, and Poterba 1997:1).

CONTENTS

Volume I

Book One

Problems in Pure Theory: The Theory of Consumer's Behavior and Capital Theory

Part I. The Theory of Revealed Preference and Other Topics in Non-stochastic Consumption Theory

    1. "A Note on the Pure Theory of Consumer's Behavior" and "An Addendum" (*Economica*, February 1938 and August 1938)
    2. "The Numerical Representation of Ordered Classifications and the Concept of Utility" (*The Review of Economic Studies*, October 1938)
    3. "The Empirical Implications of Utility Analysis" (*Econometrica*, October 1938)
    4. "The End of Marginal Utility: A Note on Dr. Bernadelli's Article" (*Economica*, February 1939)
    5. "Constancy of the Marginal Utility of Income" (O. Lange *et al.*, eds., *Studies in Mathematical Economics and Econometrics, in Memory of Henry Schultz*, University of Chicago Press, 1942)
    6. "Comparative Statics and the Logic of Economic Maximizing" (*The Review of Economic Studies*, 1946–1947)
    7. With C. C. Holt, "The Graphic Depiction of Elasticity of Demand" (*The Journal of Political Economy*, August 1946)
    8. "Some Implications of 'Linearity'" (*The Review of Economic Studies*, 1947–1948)
    9. "Consumption Theory in Terms of Revealed Preference" (*Economica*, November 1948)

Contents

    10. "The Problem of Integrability in Utility Theory" (*Economica*, November 1950)
    11. "Consumption Theorems in Terms of Overcompensation rather than Indifference Comparisons" (*Economica*, February 1953)

Part II. Stochastic Models of Consumer's Behavior

    12. "Probability and the Attempts to Measure Utility" (*The Economic Review* (*Keizai Kenkyu*), Tokyo, Hitotsubashi University, July 1950)
    13. "Utility, Preference, and Probability" (brief abstract of paper given before the conference on "Les Fondements et Applications de la Théorie du Risque en Econométrie," May 1952)
    14. "Probability, Utility, and the Independence Axiom" (*Econometrica*, October 1952)
    15. "The St. Petersburg Paradox as a Divergent Double Limit" (*International Economic Review*, January 1960)
    16. "Risk and Uncertainty: A Fallacy of Large Numbers" (*Scientia*, April–May 1963)

Part III. The Pure Theory of Capital and Growth

    17. "Some Aspects of the Pure Theory of Capital" (*The Quarterly Journal of Economics*, May 1937)
    18. "The Rate of Interest under Ideal Conditions" (*The Quarterly Journal of Economics*, February 1939)
    19. "Dynamics, Statics, and the Stationary State" (*The Review of Economics and Statistics*, February 1943)
    20. "A Note on Measurement of Utility" (*The Review of Economic Studies*, February 1937)
    21. "An Exact Consumption-Loan Model of Interest with or without the Social Contrivance of Money" (*The Journal of Political Economy*, December 1958)
    22. A "Reply" to A. P. Lerner, "Consumption-Loan Interest and Money" (*The Journal of Political Economy*, October 1959)
    23. "Infinity, Unanimity, and Singularity: A Reply" (*The Journal of Political Economy*, February 1960)
    24. With R. M. Solow, "Balanced Growth under Constant Returns to Scale" (*Econometrica*, July 1953)
    25. With R. M. Solow, "A Complete Capital Model Involving Heterogeneous Capital Goods" (*The Quarterly Journal of Economics*, November 1956)
    26. "Efficient Paths of Capital Accumulation in Terms of the Calculus of Variations" (K. J. Arrow, S. Karlin, and P. Suppes, eds., *Mathematical Methods in the Social Sciences, 1959*, Stanford University Press, 1960)
    27. "The Evaluation of 'Social Income': Capital Formation and Wealth" (F. A. Lutz and D. C. Hague, eds., *The Theory of Capital*, London, Macmillian, 1961)
    28. "Parable and Realism in Capital Theory: The Surrogate Production Function" (*The Review of Economic Studies*, June 1962)

Part IV. On Ricardo and Marx

29. "Wages and Interest: A Modern Dissection of Marxian Economic Models" (*The American Economic Review*, December 1957)
30. "Wages and Interest — A Modern Dissection of Marxian Economic Models: Reply" (*The American Economic Review*, September 1960)
31. "A Modern Treatment of the Ricardian Economy: The Pricing of Goods and of Labor and Land Services" (*The Quarterly Journal of Economics*, February 1959)
32. "A Modern Treatment of the Ricardian Economy: Capital and Interest Aspects of the Pricing Process" (*The Quarterly Journal of Economics*, May 1959)

Book Two
Topics in Mathematical Economics

Part V. Essays on Linear Programming and Economic Analysis

33. *Market Mechanisms and Maximization* (RAND Corporation, Parts I and II, March 28, 1949; Part III, June 29, 1949)
34. "Linear Programming and Economic Theory" (*Proceedings of the Second Symposium in Linear Programming*, Washington, D.C., National Bureau of Standards and U.S. Air Force, January 27–29, 1955)
35. "Frank Knight's Theorem in Linear Programming" (*Zeitschrift Für National-ökonomie*, 1958)

Part VI. Nonsubstitution Theorems

36. "Abstract of a Theorem Concerning Substitutability in Open Leontief Models" (T. C. Koopmans, ed., *Activity Analysis of Production and Allocation*, Wiley, 1951)
37. "A New Theorem on Nonsubstitution" (Hugo Hegeland, ed., *Money, Growth and Methodology and Other Essays in Economics*, in honor of Johan Akerman, Lund, Sweden, CWK Gleerup, March 1961)

Part VII. Some Metaeconomic Propositions: Comparative Statics, Dynamics, and the Structure of Minimum Equilibrium Systems

38. "The Stability of Equilibrium: Comparative Statics and Dynamics" (*Econometrica*, April 1941)
39. "The Relation between Hicksian Stability and True Dynamic Stability" (*Econometrica*, July–October 1944)
40. "The Stability of Equilibrium: Linear and Nonlinear Systems" (*Econometrica*, January 1942)
41. "Dynamic Process Analysis" (Howard Ellis, ed., *A Survey of Contemporary Economics*, Richard D. Irwin, 1952)
42. "An Extension of the Le Chatelier Principle" (*Econometrica*, April 1960)
43. "The Le Chatelier Principle in Linear Programming" (RAND Corporation, August 4, 1949)

Contents

44. "Structure of a Minimum Equilibrium System" (Ralph W. Pfouts, ed., *Essays in Economics and Econometrics: A Volume in Honor of Harold Hotelling*, University of North Carolina Press, 1960)

Part VIII. Mathematical Investigations

45. "Conditions that the Roots of a Polynomial Be Less than Unity in Absolute Value" (*The Annals of Mathematical Statistics*, September 1941)
46. "A Note on Alternative Regressions" (*Econometrica*, January 1942)
47. "A Method of Determining Explicitly the Coefficients of the Characteristic Equation" (*The Annals of Mathematical Statistics*, December 1942)
48. "Fitting General Gram-Charlier Series" (*The Annals of Mathematical Statistics*, June 1943)
49. "A Simple Method of Interpolation" (*Proceedings of the National Academy of Sciences*, December 1943)
50. "Efficient Computation of the Latent Vectors of a Matrix" (*Proceedings of the National Academy of Sciences*, December 1943)
51. "A Convergent Iterative Process" (*Journal of Mathematics and Physics*, November 1945)
52. "Generalization of the Laplace Transform for Difference Equations" (*Bulletin of the American Mathematical Society*, March 1946)
53. "Computation of Characteristic Vectors" (*Bulletin of the American Mathematical Society*, March 1946)
54. "A Connection between the Bernoulli and Newton Iterative Processes" (*Bulletin of the American Mathematical Society*, March 1946)
55. "Generalization of the Laplace Transform for Any Operator" (*Bulletin of the American Mathematical Society*, March 1947)
56. "A Generalized Newton Iteration" (*Bulletin of the American Mathematical Society*, March 1947)
57. "Exact Distribution of Continuous Variables in Sequential Analysis" (*Econometrica*, April 1948)
58. "Iterative Computation of Complex Roots" (*Journal of Mathematics and Physics*, January 1950)
59. "Rapidly Converging Solutions to Integral Equations" (*Journal of Mathematics and Physics*, January 1953)

Contents of Volume II

Acknowledgments

CONTENTS

Volume II

Book Three

Trade, Welfare, and Fiscal Policy

Part IX. Trade

60. "Welfare Economics and International Trade" (*The American Economic Review*, June 1938)
61. "The Gains from International Trade" (*Canadian Journal of Economics and Political Science*, May 1939)
62. "The Gains from International Trade Once Again" (*The Economic Journal*, December 1962)
63. Review of Jacob L. Mosak, *General Equilibrium Theory in International Trade* (*The American Economic Review*, December 1945)
64. "Disparity in Postwar Exchange Rates" (Seymour Harris, ed., *Foreign Economic Policy for the United States*, Harvard University Press, 1948)
65. "Theoretical Notes on Trade Problems" (*The Review of Economics and Statistics*, May 1964)
66. With W. F. Stolper, "Protection and Real Wages" (*The Review of Economic Studies*, November 1941)
67. "International Trade and Equalisation of Factor Prices" (*Economic Journal*, June 1948)
68. "International Factor-Price Equalisation Once Again" (*Economic Journal*, June 1949)
69. "A Comment on Factor Price Equalisation" (*The Review of Economic Studies*, February 1952)
70. "Prices of Factors and Goods in General Equilibrium" (*The Review of Economic Studies*, 1953–1954)
71. "Equalization by Trade of the Interest Rate Along with the Real Wage" (*Trade, Growth and the Balance of Payments*, in honor of Gottfried Haberler, Rand McNally, 1965)
72. "Spatial Price Equilibrium and Linear Programming" (*The American Economic Review*, June 1952)
73. "Intertemporal Price Equilibrium: A Prologue to the Theory of Speculation" (*Weltwirtschaftliches Archiv*, December 1957)

Contents

74. "The Transfer Problem and Transport Costs: The Terms of Trade When Impediments Are Absent" (*Economic Journal,* June 1952)
75. "The Transfer Problem and Transport Costs: Analysis of Effects of Trade Impediments" (*Economic Journal,* June 1954)

Part X. Welfare Economics

76. "Commentary on Welfare Economics" (*The American Economic Review,* September 1943)
77. "Evaluation of Real National Income" (*Oxford Economic Papers,* January 1950)
78. "Social Indifference Curves" (*The Quarterly Journal of Economics,* February 1956)
79. Review of H. Myint, *Theories of Welfare Economics* (*Economica,* November 1949)
80. Review of J. de V. Graaff, *Theoretical Welfare Economics* (*The Economic Journal,* September 1958)
81. "Comment on Welfare Economics" (B. F. Haley, ed., *A Survey of Contemporary Economics,* Vol. II, Richard D. Irwin, 1952)

Part XI. Dynamics and Statics of Income Determination

82. "Interactions between the Multiplier Analysis and the Principle of Acceleration" (*The Review of Economics and Statistics,* May 1939)
83. "A Synthesis of the Principle of Acceleration and the Multiplier" (*The Journal of Political Economy,* December 1939)
84. "Alvin Hansen and the Interactions between the Multiplier Analysis and the Principle of Acceleration" (*The Review of Economics and Statistics,* May 1959)
85. "The Theory of Pump-Priming Reëxamined" (*The American Economic Review,* September 1940)
86. "Fiscal Policy and Income Determination" (*The Quarterly Journal of Economics,* August 1942)
87. "A Statistical Analysis of the Consumption Function" (Appendix in A. H. Hansen, *Fiscal Policy and Business Cycles,* Norton, 1941)
88. "Concerning Say's Law" (*Econometrica,* April 1941)
89. "Professor Pigou's *Employment and Equilibrium*" (*The American Economic Review,* September 1941)
90. "A Fundamental Multiplier Identity" (*Econometrica,* July-October 1943)
91. "The Simple Mathematics of Income Determination" (L. A. Metzler *et al., Income, Employment and Public Policy: Essays in Honor of Alvin Hansen,* Norton, 1948)

Book Four

Economics and Public Policy

Part XII. Pure Theory of Public Expenditure

92. "The Pure Theory of Public Expenditure" (*The Review of Economics and Statistics,* November 1964)
93. "Diagrammatic Exposition of a Theory of Public Expenditure" (*The Review of Economics and Statistics,* November 1955)
94. "Aspects of Public Expenditure Theories" (*The Review of Economics and Statistics,* November 1958)

Part XIII. Principles of Fiscal and Monetary Policy

95. "The Effect of Interest Rate Increases on the Banking System" (*The American Economic Review*, March 1945)
96. "The Turn of the Screw" (*The American Economic Review*, September, 1945)
97. "The Business Cycle and Urban Development" (Guy Greer, ed., *The Problem of the Cities and Towns*, Conference on Urbanism, Harvard University, March 5–6, 1942)
98. "Principles and Rules in Modern Fiscal Policy: A Neo-Classical Reformulation" (*Money, Trade and Economic Growth: Essays in Honor of John Henry Williams*, Macmillan, 1951)
99. "Full Employment versus Progress and Other Economic Goals" (Max Millikan, ed., *Income Stabilization for a Developing Economy*, Yale University Press, 1953)
100. "The New Look in Tax and Fiscal Policy" (*Federal Tax Policy for Economic Growth and Stability*, U.S. Government Printing Office, 1956)
101. "Economic Forecasting and National Policy" (Gerhard Colm, ed., *The Employment Act Past and Future: A Tenth Anniversary Symposium*, Washington, National Planning Association, Special Report No. 41, February 1956)
102. With R. M. Solow, "Analytical Aspects of Anti-Inflation Policy" (*The American Economic Review*, May 1960)
103. "Reflections on Monetary Policy" (*The Review of Economics and Statistics*, August 1960)
104. "Reflections on Central Banking" (Memorandum for the Royal Commission of Banking and Finance, Ottawa, Canada, October 19, 1962)
105. "Fiscal and Financial Policies for Growth" (*Proceedings — A Symposium on Economic Growth*, The American Bankers Association, February 25, 1963, Washington, D.C.)

Part XIV. The Individual and the State

106. "Modern Economic Realities and Individualism" (*The Texas Quarterly*, Summer 1963)
107. "The Economic Role of Private Activity" (*A Dialogue on the Proper Economic Role of the State*, Selected Papers No. 7, University of Chicago Graduate School of Business, 1963)

Part XV. Comments on Economic Programs

108. "Full Employment after the War" (S. E. Harris, ed., *Postwar Economic Problems*, McGraw-Hill, 1943)
109. "Recent American Monetary Controversy" (*Three Banks Review*, March 1956)
110. "The Economics of Eisenhower" (*The Review of Economics and Statistics*, November 1956)
111. "Economic Frontiers" (first published as "Prospects and Policies for the 1961 American Economy," Report to President-Elect Kennedy, January 6, 1961. Reprinted as "Economic Frontiers" in M. B. Schnapper, ed., *New Frontiers of the Kennedy Administration*, Public Affairs Press, 1961)
112. "Economic Policy for 1962" (*The Review of Economics and Statistics*, February 1962)

Contents

Book Five
Economics — Past and Present

Part XVI.   Essays in the History of Economics

113. "Economists and the History of Ideas" (Presidential Address, *The American Economic Review*, March 1962)
114. "The General Theory" (Robert Lekachman, ed., *Keynes' General Theory: Reports of Three Decades*, St. Martin's Press, 1964)
115. "A Brief Survey of Post-Keynesian Developments" (Robert Lekachman, ed., *Keynes' General Theory: Reports of Three Decades*, St. Martin's Press, 1964)
116. "Schumpeter as a Teacher and Economic Theorist" (*The Review of Economics and Statistics*, May 1951)
117. "Economic Theory and Wages" (David McCord Wright, ed., *The Impact of the Union: Eight Economic Theorists Evaluate the Labor Union Movement*, Harcourt, Brace, 1951)
118. "Harold Hotelling as Mathematical Economist" (*American Statistician*, June 1960)
119. "D. A. Robertson (1890–1963)" (*The Quarterly Journal of Economics*, November 1963)
120. Review of Torsten Gårdlund, *The Life of Knut Wicksell* (*The Review of Economics and Statistics*, February 1959)

Part XVII.   Lectures and Essays on Modern Economics

121. "What Economists Know" (Daniel Lerner, ed., *The Human Meaning of the Social Sciences*, Meridian Books, 1959)
122. "American Economics" (Ralph E. Freeman, ed., *Postwar Economic Trends in the U.S.*, Harpers, 1960)
123. "Problems of the American Economy: An Economist's View" (Stamp Memorial Lecture, University of London, The Athlone Press, 1962)
124. "Stability and Growth in the American Economy" (Wicksell Lectures, 1962, Stockholm, Alqvist and Wiksell, December 1962)
125. "Economic Thought and the New Industrialism" (A. M. Schlesinger and M. White, eds., *Paths of American Thought*, Houghton Mifflin, 1963)

Part XVIII.   Comments on Methodology

126. "Economic Theory and Mathematics: An Appraisal" (*The American Economic Review*, May 1952)
127. "Some Psychological Aspects of Mathematics and Economics" (*The Review of Economics and Statistics*, November 1954)
128. Comment on "'Professor Samuelson on Operationalism in Economic Theory' by Donald F. Gordon" (*The Quarterly Journal of Economics*, May 1955)
129. Comment on Ernest Nagel's "Assumptions in Economic Theory" (*Papers and Proceedings of the American Economic Association*, December 1962)

Contents of Volume I

Acknowledgments

Index

CONTENTS

Volume III

Book One

Problems in Pure Theory: The Theory of Consumer's Behavior and Capital Theory

Part I.   The Theory of Revealed Preference and Other Topics in Non-Stochastic Consumption Theory

    130. "Maximum Principles in Analytical Economics" (*Les Prix Nobel en 1970*, Stockholm, The Nobel Foundation, 1970).

    131. "The Monopolistic Competition Revolution" (R. E. Kuenne, ed., *Monopolistic Competition Theory: Studies in Impact. Essays in Honor of Edward H. Chamberlin*, New York, John Wiley, 1967).

    132. "Reply" (*Quarterly Journal of Economics*, May 1970).

    133. "Two Generalizations of the Elasticity of Substitution" (J. N. Wolfe, ed., *Value, Capital, and Growth: Papers in Honour of Sir John Hicks*, Edinburgh University Press, 1968).

    134. "Using Full Duality to Show that Simultaneously Additive Direct and Indirect Utilities Implies Unitary Price Elasticity of Demand" (*Econometrica*, October 1965).

    135. "Corrected Formulation of Direct and Indirect Additivity" (*Econometrica*, April 1969).

Part III.   The Pure Theory of Capital and Growth

    136. "A Catenary Turnpike Theorem Involving Consumption and the Golden Rule" (*American Economic Review*, June 1965).

Contents

137. "A Turnpike Refutation of the Golden Rule in a Welfare-Maximizing Many-Year Plan" (K. Shell, ed., *Essays on the Theory of Optimal Economic Growth*, M.I.T. Press, 1967).
138. "The Two-Part Golden Rule Deduced as the Asymptotic Turnpike of Catenary Motions" (*Western Economic Journal*, March 1968).
139. "Local Proof of the Turnpike Theorem" (*Western Economic Journal*, March 1969).
140. "Turnpike Theorems Even Though Tastes are Intertemporally Dependent" (*Western Economic Journal*, March 1971).
141. With N. Liviatan, "Notes on Turnpikes: Stable and Unstable" (*Journal of Economic Theory*, December 1969).
142. "Law of Conservation of the Capital-Output Ratio" (*Proceedings of the National Academy of Sciences*, November 1970).
143. "A Theory of Induced Innovation Along Kennedy-Weizsäcker Lines" (*Review of Economics and Statistics*, November 1965).
144. "Rejoinder: Agreements, Disagreements, Doubts, and the Case of Induced Harrod-Neutral Technical Change" (*Review of Economics and Statistics*, November 1966).
145. "The Fundamental Singularity Theorem for Non-Joint Production" (*International Economic Review*, January 1966).
146. With F. Modigliani, "The Pasinetti Paradox in Neoclassical and More General Models" (*Review of Economic Studies*, October 1966).
147. With F. Modigliani, "Reply to Pasinetti and Robinson" (*Review of Economic Studies*, October 1966).
148. "A Summing Up" (*Quarterly Journal of Economics*, November 1966).
149. With David Levhari, "The Nonswitching Theorem is False" (*Quarterly Journal of Economics*, November 1966).
150. "Indeterminacy of Development in a Heterogeneous-Capital Model with Constant Saving Propensity" (K. Shell, ed., *Essays on the Theory of Optimal Economic Growth*, M.I.T. Press, 1967).
151. "What Makes for a Beautiful Problem in Science?" (*Journal of Political Economy*, December 1970).

Part IV. On Ricardo and Marx

152. "Marxian Economics as Economics" (*American Economic Review*, May 1967).
153. "Understanding the Marxian Notion of Exploitation: A Summary of the So-Called Transformation Problem Between Marxian Values and Competitive Prices" (*Journal of Economic Literature*, June 1971).
154. "The 'Transformation' from Marxian 'Values' to Competitive 'Prices': A Process of Rejection and Replacement" (*Proceedings of the National Academy of Sciences*, September 1970).
155. With C. C. von Weizsäcker, "A New Labor Theory of Value for Rational Planning Through Use of the Bourgeois Profit Rate" (*Proceedings of the National Academy of Sciences*, June 1971).

Book Two
Topics in Mathematical Economics

Part VIII. Mathematical Investigations

156. "A Negative Report on Hertz's Program for Reformulating Mechanics" (*Scientia*, January-February 1966).
157. "Reciprocal Characteristic Root Property of Discrete-Time Maxima" (*Western Economic Journal*, March 1968).
158. "Classical Orbital Stability Deduced for Discrete-Time Maximum Systems" (*Western Economic Journal*, June 1970).
159. "Constructing an Unbiased Random Sequence" (*Journal of the American Statistical Association*, December 1968).
160. "How Deviant Can You Be?" (*Journal of the American Statistical Association*, December 1968).

Book Three
Trade, Welfare and Fiscal Policy

Part IX. Trade

161. "Summary on Factor-Price Equalization" (*International Economic Review*, October 1967).
162. "An Exact Hume-Ricardo-Marshall Model of International Trade" (*Journal of International Economics*, February 1971).
163. "On the Trail of Conventional Beliefs about the Transfer Problem," (J. Bhagwati et al., eds., *Trade, Balance of Payments, and Growth: Papers in International Economics in Honor of Charles P. Kindleberger*, Amsterdam, North-Holland Publishing Co., 1971).

Part X. Welfare Economics

164. "Principles of Efficiency—Discussion" (*American Economic Review*, May 1964).
165. "A Fallacy in the Interpretation of Pareto's Law of Alleged Constancy of Income Distribution" (*Rivista Internazionale di Scienze Economiche e Commerciali*, April 1965).
166. "Foreword" (J. de V. Graaff, *Theoretical Welfare Economics*, Cambridge University Press, 1967).
167. "Arrow's Mathematical Politics" (S. Hook, ed., *Human Values and Economic Policy: A Symposium*, New York University Press, 1967).
168. "Contrast Between Welfare Conditions for Joint Supply and for Public Goods" (*Review of Economics and Statistics*, February 1969).

Part XI. Dynamics and Statics of Income Determination

169. "Some Notions on Causality and Teleology in Economics" (D. Lerner, ed., *Cause and Effect*, New York, The Free Press, 1965).

Contents

170. "A Universal Cycle?" (R. Henn, ed., *Methods of Operations Research III*, Muhlgasse, Verlag Anton Hain, 1967).
171. "Generalized Predator-Prey Oscillations in Ecological and Economic Equalibrium" (*Proceedings of the National Academy of Sciences*, May 1971).

Book Four

Economics and Public Policy

Part XII.   Pure Theory of Public Expenditure

172. "Pure Theory of Public Expenditure and Taxation" (J. Margolis and H. Guitton, eds., *Public Economics: An Analysis of Public Production and Consumption and their Relations to the Private Sectors: Proceedings of a Conference held by the International Economic Association*, London: Macmillan, 1969).
173. "Public Goods and Subscription TV: Correction of the Record" (*Journal of Law and Economics*, October 1964).
174. "Indeterminacy of Governmental Role in Public-Good Theory" (*Papers on Non-Market Decision Making*, Vol. III, 1967).
175. "Pitfalls in the Analysis of Public Goods" (*Journal of Law and Economics*, January 1968).

Part XIII.   Principles of Fiscal and Monetary Policy

176. "What Classical and Neoclassical Monetary Theory Really Was" (*Canadian Journal of Economics*, February 1968).
177. "Nonoptimality of Money Holding Under *Laissez Faire*" (*Canadian Journal of Economics*, May 1969).
178. "Money, Interest Rates, and Economic Activity: Their Interrelationship in a Market Economy" (*Proceedings of a Symposium on Money, Interest Rates, and Economic Activity*, New York, American Bankers Association, 1967).
179. "Tax Deductibility of Economic Depreciation to Insure Invariant Valuations" (*Journal of Political Economy*, December 1964).
180. With the assistance of Felicity Skidmore, "An Analytic Evaluation of Interest Rate Ceilings for Savings and Loan Associations and Competitive Institutions" (*Study of the Savings and Loan Industry*, Washington, D.C., Federal Home Loan Bank Board, July 1969).

Part XIV.   The Individual and the State

181. "Personal Freedoms and Economic Freedoms in the Mixed Economy" (E. F. Cheit, ed., *The Business Establishment*, New York, John Wiley, 1964).

Book Five

Economics—Past and Present

Part XVI. Essays in the History of Economics

182. "Reply" to "D. H. Robertson: Comment" (*Quarterly Journal of Economics,* May 1964).
183. "A. P. Lerner at Sixty," (*Review of Economic Studies,* June 1964).
184. "Irving Fisher and the Theory of Capital" (W. Fellner et al., *Ten Economic Studies in the Tradition of Irving Fisher,* New York, John Wiley, 1967).
185. "Joseph Schumpeter" (*Newsweek,* April 13, 1970).
186. "The Way of an Economist" (P. A. Samuelson, ed., *International Economic Relations: Proceedings of the Third Congress of the International Economic Association,* London, Macmillan, 1969).
187. "Foreword" (P. A. Samuelson, *Foundations of Economic Analysis,* Japanese Edition, 1967).
188. "Foreword" (P. A. Samuelson, *Foundations of Economic Analysis,* Chinese Edition, 1971).
189. "Money and History" (H. E. Krooss, ed., *Documentary History of Banking and Currency in the United States,* New York, Chelsea House, 1969).
190. "Economic Growth" (*Gendaisekai Hyakka Daijiten,* Volume I., Tokyo, Kodansha Ltd., 1971).
191. "Memories" (*Newsweek,* June 2, 1969).

Part XVII. Lectures and Essays on Modern Economics

192. "Problems of the American Economy — Hard and Easy" (L. H. Seltzer, ed., *New Horizons of Economic Progress,* Wayne State University Press, 1964).
193. "Stabilization Policies in the Contemporary U.S. Economy" (G. Horwich, ed., *Monetary Process and Policy,* Homewood, Illinois, Richard D. Irwin, 1967).
194. "Reflections on Recent Federal Reserve Policy" (*Journal of Money, Credit, and Banking,* February 1970).

Part XVIII. Comments on Methodology

195. "Theory and Realism: A Reply" (*American Economic Review,* September 1964).
196. "Professor Samuelson on Theory and Realism: Reply" (*American Economic Review,* December 1965).
197. "Economic Forecasting and Science" (*Michigan Quarterly Review,* October 1965).

Contents

Part XIX. Portfolio Selection, Warrant Pricing, and the Theory of Speculative Markets

198. "Proof that Properly Anticipated Prices Fluctuate Randomly" (*Industrial Management Review*, Spring 1965).
199. "Rational Theory of Warrant Pricing" and "Appendix: A Free Boundary Problem for the Heat Equation Arising from a Problem in Mathematical Economics" by H. P. McKean, Jr. (*Industrial Management Review*, Spring 1965).
200. With R. C. Merton, "A Complete Model of Warrant Pricing that Maximizes Utility" (*Industrial Management Review*, Winter 1969).
201. "General Proof that Diversification Pays" (*Journal of Financial and Quantitative Analysis*, March 1967).
202. "Efficient Portfolio Selection for Pareto-Levy Investments" (*Journal of Financial and Quantitative Analysis*, June 1967).
203. "The Fundamental Approximation Theorem of Portfolio Analysis in Terms of Means, Variances, and Higher Moments" (*Review of Economic Studies*, October 1970).
204. "Lifetime Portfolio Selection by Dynamic Stochastic Programming" (*Review of Economics and Statistics*, August 1969).
205. "Foreword" (R. Roll, *The Behavior of Interest Rates: Application of the Efficient Market Model to U.S. Treasury Bills*, New York, Basic Books, 1970).
206. "Stochastic Speculative Price" (*Proceedings of the National Academy of Sciences*, February 1971).
207. "The 'Fallacy' of Maximizing the Geometric Mean in Long Sequences of Investing or Gambling (*Proceedings of the National Academy of Sciences*, October 1971).

Contents of Volumes I and II

Acknowledgments

Index

CONTENTS

Volume IV

Part I. Theory of Consumption and Production

208. Complementarity: An Essay on the 40th Anniversary of the Hicks-Allen Revolution in Demand Theory (*Journal of Economic Literature*, Vol. 12, No. 4, December 1974, 1255–1289).
209. Invariant Economic Index Numbers and Canonical Duality: Survey and Synthesis (with S. Swamy), (*American Economic Review*, Vol. 64, No. 4, August 1973, 566–593).
210. Analytical Notes on International Real-Income Measures (*Economic Journal*, Vol. 84, No. 33, September 1974, 595–608).
211. Remembrances of Frisch (*European Economic Review*, Vol. 5, 1974, 7–23).
212. Unification Theorem for the Two Basic Dualities of Homothetic Demand Theory (*Proceedings of the National Academy of Sciences, U.S.A.*, Vol. 69. No. 9, September 1972, 2673–2674).
213. Relative Shares and Elasticities Simplified: Comment (American Economic Review, Vol. 63, No. 4, September 1973, 770–771).
214. A Quantum-Theory Model of Economics: Is the Co-ordinating Entrepreneur Just Worth His Profit? (*Development and Planning, Essays in Honour of Paul Rosenstein-Rodan*, J. Bhagwati and R. S. Eckaus (eds.), London, John Allen and Unwin, Ltd., 329–335, 1973).

Part II. Theory of Capital and Growth

215. Interest Rate Determinations and Oversimplifying Parables: A Summing Up (*Essays in Modern Capital Theory*, M. Brown, K. Sato, and P. Zarembka (eds.), Amsterdam, North Holland Publishing Company, 1976).

216. Steady-State and Transient Relations: A Reply on Reswitching (*Quarterly Journal of Economics*, Vol. 89, February 1975, 40–47).
217. Paradoxes of Schumpeter's Zero Interest Rate (*Review of Economics and Statistics*, Vol. 3, No. 4, November 1971, 391–392).
218. Economics of Forestry in an Evolving Society (*Economic Inquiry*, Vol. 14, No. 4, December 1976, 466–492).
219. Capital Shortage, or Glut? (*Newsweek*, August 26, 1974, p. 73).
220. Optimum Social Security in a Life-Cycle Growth Model (*International Economic Review*, Vol. 16, No. 3, October 1975, 539–544).
221. The Optimum Growth Rate for Population (*International Economic Review*, Vol. 16, No. 3, October 1975, 531–538).
222. The Optimum Growth Rate for Population: Agreement and Evaluations (*International Economic Review*, Vol. 17, No. 2, June 1976, 516–525).
223. The General Saddlepoint Property of Optimum-Control Motions (*Journal of Economic Theory*, Vol. 5, No. 1, August 1972, 102–120).
224. The Periodic Turnpike Theorem (*Nonlinear Analysis, Theory, Methods and Applications*, Vol. 1, No. 1, 1976, 3–13).

Part III. On Marxian Economics

225. Marx as Mathematical Economist: Steady-State and Exponential Growth Equilibrium (*Trade, Stability and Macroeconomic Essays in Honor of Lloyd A. Metzler*, George Horwich, and Paul A. Samuelson (eds.), New York, Academic Press, 269–307, 1974).
226. Optimality of Profit-Including Prices Under Ideal Planning: Marx's Model (*Proceedings of the National Academy of Sciences, U.S.A.*, Vol. 70, No. 7, July 1973, 2109–2111).
227. The Economics of Marx: An Ecumenical Reply (*Journal of Economic Literature*, Vol. 10, No. 1, March 1972, 51–57).
228. Samuelson's "Reply on Marxian Matters" (*Journal of Economic Literature*, Vol. 11, No. 1, March 1973, 64–68).
229. Insight and Detour in the Theory of Exploitation: A Reply to Baumol (*Journal of Economic Literature, Colloquium on Marx, The Transformation Problem*, Vol. 12, March 1974, 62–70).
230. Rejoinder: Merlin Unclothed, A Final Word (*Journal of Economic Literature*, Vol. 12, No. 1, March 1974, 75–77).
231. Review of *Economic Essays on Values, Competition, and Utility* by V. K. Dmitriev (*Journal of Economic Literature*, June 1975, 491–495).

Part IV. Mathematical Biology and Economics of Population

232. A Biological Least-Action Principle for the Ecological Model of Volterra-Lotka (*Proceedings of the National Academy of Sciences, U.S.A.*, Vol. 71, No. 8, August 1974, 3041–3044).
233. Speeding Up of Time with Age in Recognition of Life as Fleeting (*Evolution, Welfare and Time in Economics: Essays in Honor of Nicholas Georgescu-Roegen*, Anthony M. Tang, Fred M. Westfield, James S. Worley (eds.), Lexington, Mass., Lexington Books, 1976).

234. A Dynamical Model for Human Population (with Joel Yellin), (*Proceedings of the National Academy of Sciences, U.S.A.*, Vol. 71, No. 7, July 1974, 2813–2817).

235. Time Symmetry and Asymmetry in Population and Deterministic Dynamic Systems (*Theoretical Population Biology*, Vol. 9, No. 1, February 1976, 81–122).

236. Resolving a Historical Confusion in Population Analysis (*Human Biology*, Vol. 48, No. 3, September 1976, 559–580).

237. An Economist's Non-Linear Model of Self-Generated Fertility Waves (*Population Studies*, Vol. 30, No. 2, July 1976, 243–247).

238. Scale Economies and Non-labor Returns at the Optimum Population (*Eastern Economic Journal*, April/June 1974, 125–127).

239. Social Darwinism (*Newsweek*, July 7. 1975, 55).

Part V. Stochastic Theory of Economics

240. Mathematics of Speculative Price (*SIAM Review*, Vol. 15, No. 1, January 1973, 1–42; first appeared in *Mathematical Topics in Economic Theory and Computation*, Richard H. Day and Stephen M. Robinson (eds.), Society for Industrial and Applied Mathematics, Philadelphia, 1972). Appendix by Robert C. Merton.

241. Proof that Properly Discounted Present Values of Assets Vibrate Randomly (*Bell Journal of Economics and Management Science*, Vol. 4, No. 2, Autumn 1973, 369–374).

242. Is Real-World Price a Tale Told by the Idiot of Chance? (*Review of Economics and Statistics*, Vol. 58, No. 1. February 1976, 120–123).

243. Challenge to Judgment (*Journal of Portfolio Management*, Vol. 1, No. 1, Fall 1974, 17–19).

244. Foreword to *Investment Portfolio Decision-Making* (James L. Bicksler and Paul A. Samuelson (eds.), Lexington, Mass., D. C. Heath and Company, 1974).

245. Fallacy of the Log-Normal Approximation to Optimal Portfolio Decision-Making Over Many Periods (with Robert C. Merton), (*Journal of Financial Economics*, Vol. 1, 1974, 67–94).

246. Generalized Mean-Variance Tradeoffs for Best Perturbation Corrections to Approximate Portfolio Decisions (with Robert C. Merton), (*Journal of Finance*, Vol. 29, No. 1, March 1974, 27–30).

247. Limited Liability, Short Selling, Bounded Utility, and Infinite-Variance Stable Distributions (*Journal of Financial and Quantitative Analysis*, September 1976, 485–503).

248. Comments on the Favorable-Bet Theorem (*Economic Inquiry*, Vol. 12, No. 3, September 1974, 345–355).

249. Optimality of Sluggish Predictors Under Ergodic Probability (*International Economic Review*, Vol. 17, No. 1, February 1976, 1–7).

Part VI. International Economics

250. International Trade for a Rich Country (Lectures before the Swedish-American Chamber of Commerce, New York City, May 10, 1972).

251. Trade Pattern Reversals in Time-Phased Ricardian Systems and Intertemporal Efficiency (*Journal of International Economics*, Vol. 5, 1974, 309–363).

252. Illogic of Neo-Marxian Doctrine of Unequal Exchange (*Inflation, Trade and Taxes: Essays in Honor of Alice Bourneuf*, P. A. Belsley, E. J. Kane, Paul A. Samuelson, Robert M. Solow (eds.), Columbus, Ohio State University Press, 1976).

253. Deadweight Loss in International Trade from the Profit Motive? (*Leading Issues in International Economic Policy: Essays in Honor of George N. Halm*, C. Fred Bersten and William G. Tyler (eds.), Lexington, Mass., D. C. Heath and Co., 1973).

254. Ohlin Was Right (*Swedish Journal of Economics*, Vol. 73, No. 4, 1971, 365–384).

255. Equalisation of Factor Prices by Sufficiently Diversified Production Under Conditions of Balanced Demand (*International Trade and Finance: Essays in Honor of Jan Tinbergen*, Willy Sellekaerts (ed.), London, Macmillan, 1974).

256. Heretical Doubts About the International Mechanisms (*Journal of International Economics*, Vol. 2, No. 4, 1972, 443–454).

Part VII. Welfare Economics

257. Optimal Compacts for Redistribution (*Public and Urban Economics*, Ronald E. Grieson (ed.), Lexington, Mass., D. C. Heath and Co., 1976).

258. A Curious Case Where Reallocation Cannot Achieve Optimum Welfare (*Public Finance and Stabilization Policy* (Musgrave Festschrift), Warren L. Smith and John C. Culbertson (eds.), New York, North-Holland, American Elsevier, 1974).

259. From GNP to NEW (*Newsweek*, April 9, 1973, 102).

260. Proof That Unsuccessful Speculators Confer Less Benefit to Society Than Their Losses (*Proceedings of the National Academy of Sciences, U.S.A.*, Vol. 69, May 1972, 1230–1233).

261. The Consumer Does Benefit From Feasible Price Stability (*Quarterly Journal of Economics*, Vol. 86, August 1972, 476–493).

262. Rejoinder (*Quarterly Journal of Economics*, Vol. 86, August 1972, 500–503).

263. Is the Rent-Collector Worthy of His Full Hire? (*Eastern Economic Journal*, Vol. 1, No. 1, January 1974, 7–10).

Part VIII. Theory of Money and Inflation

264. Reflections on the Merits and Demerits of Monetarism (*Issues in Fiscal and Monetary Policy: The Eclectic Economist Views the Controversy*, James J. Diamond (ed.), DePaul University, 1971).

265. Samuelson on the Neoclassical Dichotomy: A Reply (*Canadian Journal of Economics*, Vol. 5, No. 2, May 1972, 284–292).

266. Foreword to *The Geographical Aspects of Inflationary Processes* (Peter B. Corbin and Murray Sabin (eds.), Pleasantville, New York, Redgrave Publishing Company, 1976).

267. Economic Policy—Where Is It Leading? (*Boston University Journal*, No. 1, 1975, 30–36).

Part IX. Lectures and Essays on Current Economic Problems

268. Worldwide Stagflation (*The Morgan Guaranty Survey*, June 1974, 3–9).
269. Economics of Sex: A Discussion (Economic Problems of Women, Hearings Before the Joint Economic Council, Congress of the United States, 93rd Congress, July 10, 1973, 58–64).
270. The Convergence of the Law School and the University (*The American Scholar*, Vol. 44. No. 2, Spring 1971, 256–271).
271. Lessons From the Current Economic Expansion (*American Economic Review*, Vol. 64, No. 2, May 1974, 75–77).
272. Foreword to *The Retreat From Riches: Affluence and Its Enemies* (Peter Passell and Leonard Ross (eds.), New York, Viking Press, 1971).
273. Christmas Economics (*Newsweek*, December 25, 1976, 54).

Part X. Essays on the Evolution of Economics

274. The Balanced-Budget Multiplier: A Case Study in the Sociology and Psychology of Scientific Discovery (*History of Political Economy*, Vol. 7. No. 1, Spring 1975, 43–49).
275. The Art and Science of Macromodels Over 50 Years (*The Brookings Model: Perspective and Recent Developments*, Gary Fromm and L. R. Klein (eds.), North-Holland Publishing Co., 1975, 3–10).
276. Adam the Immortal (*Pennsylvania Gazette*, University of Pennsylvania, November 1976, 26–27).
277. Liberalism at Bay (Second Gerhard Colm Memorial Lecture, New School for Social Research, March 5, 1971. 16–31).
278. Economics in a Golden Age: A Personal Memoir (*The Twentieth Century Sciences: Studies in the Biography of Ideas*, Gerald Holton (ed.), New York, W. W. Norton, 1972, 155–170).
279. Reminiscences of Shigeto Tsuru (*Ad Multos Annos! Looking Back and Ahead on Shiget Tsuru*, Shigeto Tsuru (ed.), Tokyo, Dai Nippon Printing Company, 1976, 52–57).
280. Foreword to *Essays on Industrial Organization: Essays in Honor of Joe S. Bain* (Robert T. Masson and P. David Qualls (eds.), Cambridge, Massachusetts, Ballinger, 1976, xvii–xviii).
281. Preface to *Inflation, Trade and Taxes: Essays in Honor of Alice Bourneuf* (David A. Belsley, Edward J. Kane, Paul A. Samuelson, Robert M. Solow (eds.), Columbus, Ohio State University Press, 1976).
282. Jacob Viner, 1892–1970 (*Journal of Political Economy*, Vol. 80, No. 1, January/February 1972, 5–11).
283. Frank Knight, 1885–1972 (*Newsweek*, July 31, 1972, 55).
284. Seymour Harris as Political Economist (*Review of Economics and Statistics*, Vol. 57, No. 1, February 1975, i–v).
285. Alvin Hansen as a Creative Economic Theorist (*Quarterly Journal of Economics*, Vol. 90. February 1976, 24–31).
286. In Search of the Elusive Elite (*New York Times*, June 26, 1976, 39).
287. Alvin H. Hansen, 1889–1975 (*Newsweek*, June 16, 1975, 72).
288. The 1972 Nobel Prize for Economic Science (*Science*, Vol. 178, November 3, 1972, 487–489).

Contents

289. Pioneers of Economic Theory (*New York Times*, October 26, 1972, 71).
290. Nobel Laureate Leontief (*Newsweek*, November 5, 1973, 94).
291. Nobel Choice: Economists in Contrast (*New York Times*, October 10, 1975).
292. Milton Friedman (*Newsweek*, October 25, 1976, 89).

Contents of Volumes I, II, and III

Acknowledgments

Index

CONTENTS

Volume V

Author's Preface xi

Editor's Preface xii

Part I. Economic Theory

293. "Bergsonian Welfare Economics," in *Economic Welfare and the Economics of Soviet Socialism: Essays in Honor of Abram Bergson*, Steven Rosefielde (ed.). Cambridge: Cambridge University Press, 1981, 223–266. ... 3

294. "Reaffirming the Existence of 'Reasonable' Bergson-Samuelson Social Welfare Functions," *Economica*, vol. 44, February 1977, 81–88. ... 47

295. "When It Is Ethically Optimal to Allocate Money Income in Stipulated Fractional Shares," in *Natural Resources, Uncertainty, and General Equilibrium Systems: Essays in Memory of Rafael Lusky*, Alan S. Blinder and Philip Friedman (eds.). New York: Academic Press, 1977, 175–195. ... 55

296. "A Chapter in the History of Ramsey's Optimal Feasible Taxation and Optimal Public Utility Prices," in *Economic Essays in Honour of Jørgen H. Gelting*, Svend Andersen, Karsten Larsen, P. Norregaard Rusmussen, and J. Vibe-Pedersen (eds.). Copenhagen: Danish Economic Association, 1982, 157–181. ... 76

297. "Pseudo-Maximization to the Rescue of Derived Factor Demand of a Competitive Industry," in *Breadth and Depth in Economics: Fritz Machlup—The Man and His Ideas*, Jacob S. Dreyer (ed.). Lexington, Mass.: D. C. Heath, A Lexington Book, 1978, 87–118. ... 101

298. "St. Petersburg Paradoxes: Defanged, Dissected and Historically Described," *Journal of Economic Literature*, vol. 15, no. 1, March 1977, 24–55. ... 133

Contents

    299. "Second Thoughts on Analytical Income Comparisons," *Economic Journal*, vol. 94, June 1984, 267–278.   165

    300. "Unattainability of Integrability and Definiteness Conditions in the General Case of Demand for Money and Goods," with Ryuzo Sato, *American Economic Review*, vol. 74, no. 4, September 1984, 588–604.   177

    301. "Balanced Growth Equilibrium in the General Multi-Class Saving Model," *Quantitative Wirtschaftsforschung: Wilhelm Krelle zum 60. Geburstag*, Horst Albach, Ernst Helmstädter, and Rudolf Henn (eds.). Tübingen: J. C. B. Mohr, 1977, 569–577.   194

    302. "Paul Douglas's Measurement of Production Functions and Marginal Productivities," *The Journal of Political Economy*, vol. 87, no. 5, part 1, October 1979, 923–939.   203

    303. "Rigorous Observational Positivism: Klein's Envelope Aggregation; Thermodynamics and Economic Isomorphisms," in *Global Econometrics: Essays in Honor of Lawrence R. Klein*, F. Gerard Adams and Bert G. Hickman (eds.). Cambridge, Mass.: The MIT Press, 1983, 1–38.   220

Part II. Marx, Keynes, and Schumpeter

    304. "1983: Marx, Keynes and Schumpeter," *Eastern Economic Journal*, vol. 9, no. 3, July–September 1983, 166–180.   261

    305. "The Keynes Centenary," *The Economist*, 25 June 1983, 19–21.   275

    306. "The House That Keynes Built," *The New York Times*, 29 May 1983.   279

    307. "Succumbing to Keynesianism," *Challenge*, January–February 1985, 4–11.   283

    308. "Comment [on Axel Leijonhufvud's 'What Would Keynes Have Thought of Rational Expectation?']," in *Keynes and the Modern World*, David Worswick and James Trevithick (eds.). Cambridge: Cambridge University Press, 1983, 212–221.   291

    309. "Schumpeter as an Economic Theorist," in *Schumpeterian Economics*, Helmut Frisch (ed.). London: Praeger, 1982, 1–27.   301

    310. "Schumpeter's Capitalism, Socialism and Democracy," in *Schumpeter's Vision: Capitalism, Socialism and Democracy After 40 Years*, Arnold Heertje (ed.). London: Praeger, 1981, 1–21.   328

    311. Foreword to *Marx's Economics: Origin and Development*, by Alexander Balinky, Lexington, Mass.: D. C. Heath, 1970, xi–xii.   349

    312. "The Normative and Positivistic Inferiority of Marx's *Values* Paradigm," *Southern Economic Journal*, vol. 49, no. 1, July 1982, 11–18.   351

    313. "Marx Without Matrices: Understanding the Rate of Profit," in *Marxism, Central Planning, and the Soviet Economy: Economic Essays in Honor of Alexander Erlich*, Padma Desai (ed.). Cambridge, Mass.: The MIT Press, 1983, 3–18.   359

    314. "Durable Capital Inputs: Conditions for Price Ratios to be Invariant to Profit-Rate Changes," *Zeitschrift für Nationalökonomie*, vol. 43, no. 1, 1983, 1–20.   375

Part III. International Economics

    315. "A Corrected Version of Hume's Equilibrating Mechanism for International Trade," in *Flexible Exchange Rates and the Balance of Payments: Essays in Memory of Egon Sohmen*, John S. Chipman and Charles P. Kindleberger (eds.). Amsterdam: North-Holland, 1980, 141–158.   397

316. "Comparative Advantage, Trade, and Payments in a Ricardian Model with a Continuum of Goods," with Rudiger Dornbusch and Stanley Fischer, *American Economic Review*, vol. 67, no. 5, December 1977, 823–839. ... 415
317. "Heckscher-Ohlin Trade Theory with a Continuum of Goods," with Rudiger Dornbusch and Stanley Fischer, *The Quarterly Journal of Economics*, vol. 95, no. 2, September 1980, 203–224. ... 432
318. "Summing Up on the Australian Case for Protection," *The Quarterly Journal of Economics*, vol. 96, no. 1, February 1981, 147–160. ... 454
319. "Justice to the Australians," *The Quarterly Journal of Economics*, vol. 96, no. 1, February 1981, 169–170. ... 468
320. "Interest Rate Equalization and Nonequalization by Trade in Leontief-Sraffa Models," *Journal of International Economics*, vol. 8, 1978, 21–27. ... 470
321. "Free Trade's Intertemporal Pareto-Optimality," *Journal of International Economics*, vol. 8, 1978, 147–149. ... 477
322. "Analytics of Free-Trade or Protectionist Response by America to Japan's Growth Spurt," in *Economic Policy and Development: New Perspectives*, Toshio Shishido and Ryuzo Sato (eds.). Dover, Mass.: Auburn House, 1985, 3–18. ... 480
323. "Japan and the World at the Century's End," *NEXT Magazine*, August 1984, 4–15. (Original English version provided for translation into Japanese.) ... 496
324. "To Protect Manufacturing?" *Zeitschrift für die gesamte Staatswissenschaft (Journal of Institutional and Theoretical Economics)*, Band 137, Heft 3, September 1981, 407–414. ... 510
325. "America's Interest in International Trade," in *New England Merchants Company, Inc., 1979 Annual*, 4–5. ... 518
326. "The Future of American Industry in a Changing Economy," *The Journalist*, Fall 1984, 3–5, 19. ... 520

Part IV. Stochastic Theory

327. "Stochastic Land Valuation: Total Return as Martingale Implying Price Changes—A Negatively Correlated Walk," speech given 19 January 1984, University of California, San Diego. ... 527
328. "Paul Cootner's Reconciliation of Economic Law with Chance," in *Financial Economics: Essays in Honor of Paul Cootner*, William F. Sharpe and Cathryn M. Cootner (eds.). Englewood Cliffs, N.J.: Prentice-Hall, 1982, 101–117. ... 537
329. "Why We Should Not Make Mean Log of Wealth Big though Years to Act Are Long," *Journal of Banking and Finance*, vol. 3, 1979, 305–307. ... 554
330. "Economics of Futures Contracts in Basic Macroeconomic Indexes: An Economist's Appraisal," *Futures: Policy and Prospects for a Dynamic Market*. Washington, D.C.: National Journal, 1983, 43–44. ... 557
331. "Hanging in There," *Newsweek*, 13 February 1978, 80. ... 559
332. "Coping Sensibly," *Newsweek*, 6 March 1978, 88. ... 560
333. "Gold and Common Stocks," *Newsweek*, 21 August 1978, 65. ... 561
334. "Time to Sell," *Newsweek*, 11 December 1978, 90. ... 562
335. "No-Fuss Canny Investing," *Newsweek*, 4 February 1980, 68. ... 563
336. "Crackpot Investing," *Newsweek*, 26 January 1981, 67. ... 564
337. "Canny Investing," *McGraw-Hill Economics Newsletter*, Spring 1981. ... 565

Contents

338. Foreword to *On the Factorial Approach to Index Number Problems, Consumption Analysis and Orthogonal Decomposition of National Income: A Summary*, by K. S. Banerjee. College Park, Md.: World Academy of Development and Cooperation, Special Studies Publication, no. 2, 1985, ii–iv.   570

Part V. Classical Economics

339. "Thünen at Two Hundred," *Journal of Economic Literature*, vol. 21, December 1983, 1468–1488.   575
340. "The Canonical Classical Model of Political Economy," *Journal of Economic Literature*, vol. 16, December 1978, 1415–1434.   598
341. "Noise and Signal in Debates Among Classical Economists: A Reply," *Journal of International Literature*, vol. 18, June 1980, 575–578.   618
342. "A Modern Theorist's Vindication of Adam Smith," *The American Economic Review*, vol. 67, no. 1, February 1977, 42–49.   622
343. "Quesnay's 'Tableau Economique' as a Theorist would Formulate it Today," in *Classical and Marxian Political Economy: Essays in Honor of Ronald L. Meek*, Ian Bradley and Michael Howard (eds.). New York: St. Martin's Press, 1982, 45–78.   630
344. "Land and the Rate of Interest," in *Theory for Economic Efficiency: Essays in Honor of Abba P. Lerner*, Harry I. Greenfield, Albert M. Levenson, Wiliam Hamovitch, and Eugene Rotwein (eds.). Cambridge, Mass.: The MIT Press, 1979, 167–185.   664
345. "Correcting the Ricardo Error Spotted in Harry Johnson's Maiden Paper," *The Quarterly Journal of Economics*, vol. 91, no. 4, November 1977, 519–530.   683

Part VI. Mathematical Biology

346. "Maximizing and Biology," *Economic Inquiry*, vol. 16, April 1978, 171–183.   697
347. "Complete Genetic Models for Altruism, Kin Selection and Like-Gene Selection," *Journal of Social and Biological Structures*, vol. 6, 1983, 3–15.   710
348. "Modes of Thought in Economics and Biology," *The American Economic Review*, vol. 75, no. 2, May 1985, 166–172.   723
349. "Comparison of Linear and Nonlinear Models for Human Population Dynamics," with Joel Yellin, *Theoretical Population Biology*, vol. 11, no. 1, February 1977, 105–126.   730
350. "Fischer's 'Reproductive Value' as an Economic Specimen in Merton's Zoo," *Transactions of the New York Academy of Sciences*, series 2, vol. 39, April 1980, 126–142.   752
351. "Generalizing Fischer's 'Reproductive Value': Linear Differential and Difference Equations of 'Dilute' Biological Systems," *Proceedings of the National Academy of Sciences USA*, vol. 74, no. 11, November 1977, 5189–5192.   769
352. "Generalizing Fischer's 'Reproductive Value': Nonlinear, Homogeneous, Biparental Systems," *Proceedings of the National Academy of Sciences USA*, vol. 74, no. 12, December 1977, 5772–5775.   773
353. "Generalizing Fischer's 'Reproductive Value': Overlapping and Nonoverlapping Generations with Competing Genotypes," *Proceedings of the National Academy of Sciences USA*, vol. 75, no. 8, August 1978, 4062–4066.   777
354. "Generalizing Fischer's 'Reproductive Value': 'Incipient' and 'Penultimate' Reproductive-Value Functions When Environment Limits Growth; Linear Approximants for Nonlinear Mendelian Mating Mod-

els," *Proceedings of the National Academy of Sciences USA*, vol. 75, no. 12, December 1978, 6327–6331. ... 782

Part VII. Biographical and Autobiographical Writings

355. "My Life Philosophy," *The American Economist*, vol. 27, no. 2, Fall 1983, 5–12. ... 789
356. "Economics in My Time," in *Lives of the Laureates*, William Breit and Roger W. Spencer (eds.). Cambridge, Mass.: The MIT Press, 1986, 59–76. ... 797
357. "Bertil Ohlin, 1899–1979," *The Scandinavian Journal of Economics*, vol. 83, no. 3, 1981, 355–371. Also appeared in *Journal of International Economics*, vol. 11, 1981, 147–163. ... 809
358. "Arthur Okun, 1928–1980," *Newsweek*, 7 April 1980, 67. ... 826
359. "Lloyd Metzler (April 3, 1913–October 26, 1980)," Memorial Service, Memorial Church, Harvard University, 12 December 1980. ... 827
360. "Two Nobel Laureates' Theories on Trade," *The New York Times*, 15 October 1977. ... 831
361. "A Nobel for Forecasting," *Newsweek*, 3 November 1980, 72. ... 833
362. "1981 Nobel Prize in Economics," *Science*, vol. 214, 30 October 1981, 520–522. ... 834
363. "The 1983 Nobel Prize in Economics," *Science*, vol. 222, 2 December 1983, 987–989. ... 838
364. "The 1984 Nobel Prize in Economics," *Science*, vol. 227, January 1985, 20–22. ... 841
365. Seventieth Birthday Remarks, given 18 May 1985, at Wellesley College Club. ... 844
366. Introduction to the Enlarged Edition of *Foundations of Economic Analysis*. Cambridge, Mass.: Harvard University Press, 1983, xv–xxvi. ... 846
367. Forewords to the Japanese edition of *The Collected Scientific Papers of Paul A. Samuelson*, vols. 1, 2, 4, 5, 6, 8, 9, M. Shinohara and R. Sato (eds.). Tokyo: Keiso Shobo, 1982. ... 858
368. Foreword to *Theory of Technical Change and Economic Invariance: Application to Lie Groups*, by Ryuzo Sato. New York: Academic Press, 1981, xi–xii. ... 876

Part VIII. Current Economics and Policy

369. "The World Economy at Century's End," in *Human Resources, Employment and Development, Volume, 1. The Issues*, Shigeto Tsuru (ed.). London,: Macmillan, 1983, 58–77. ... 881
370. "Evaluating Reaganomics" (Horowitz Lecture), *Challenge*, November–December 1984, 4–12. ... 901
371. "The U.S. Fiscal Crisis of the 1980s," in *Reconstructing the Federal Budget: A Trillion Dollar Quandary*, Albert T. Sommers (ed.). New York: Praeger, 1984, 75–86. ... 909
372. "Myths and Realities about the Crash and Depression," *The Journal of Portfolio Managment*, vol. 6, no. 1, Fall 1979, 7–10. ... 921
373. "The Crash of '29: Lessons for '79," *Newsday*, 28 October 1979. ... 925
374. "The Role of Profits in a Mixed Economy: Changes in the Perceived Reality" (John Diebold Lecture), in *New Challenges to the Role of Profit*, Benjamin M. Friedman (ed.). Lexington, Mass.: D. C. Heath, 1978, 13–29. ... 929
375. "The Public Role in the Modern American Economy," in *The American Economy in Transition*, Martin Feldstein (ed.). Cambridge, Mass.: National Bureau of Economic Research, 1980, 665–671. ... 946

Contents

376. "Thoughts on Profit-Sharing," *Zeitschrift für die gesamte Staatswissenschaft*, Special Issue on Profit-Sharing, A Symposium, Heinz Sauermann and Rudolf Richter (eds.). Tübingen: J. C. B. Mohr, 1977, 9–18. ... 953
377. "The Roots of Inflation," in *Encyclopaedia Britannica, 1979 Book of the Year*. Chicago, Ill.: Encyclopaedia Britannica, 1979, 60–64. ... 963
378. "Recession: Causes and Consequences," with William F. Samuelson, in *The Americana Annual 1980, Yearbook of the Encyclopedia Americana*. Danbury, Conn.: Grolier, 1980, 25–28. ... 968
379. "Living with Stagflation," in *Collier's Year Book 1980*. London: Macmillan, 1980, 89. ... 972
380. "Government and Business," in *Emerging Issues Affecting U.S. Corporations*. Washington, D.C.: The Public Affairs Council, 1977, 99–105. ... 973
381. "Policy Advising in Economics," *Challenge*, March-April 1978, 37–38. ... 980
382. Foreword to *Health Controls Out of Control*, by David M. Kinzer. Chicago, Ill.: teach'em, 1977, ix–xi. ... 982
383. "An Economist's View," *Environmental Protection Agency Journal*, vol. 5, no. 1, January 1979, 4–5, 36. ... 985
384. "Lofty Aims Alone Cannot Create Efficiency, Growth and Equity," *The Japan Economic Journal*, 17 June 1980, 20. ... 992
385. "Inequality of Incomes and Wealth Can Lessen amid Competition," *The Japan Economic Journal*, 24 June 1980, 24. ... 995
386. "Afternoon of the Mixed Economy?" *Ökonomisk Rapport*, March 1981. ... 998
387. "World Economy of the Eighties," speech broadcast over *Westdeutscher Rundfunk*, December 1979. ... 1002
388. "That Constitutional Budget Amendment—'Tremendous Potential for Harm,'" *AEI Economist, The Conference Board Magazine*, April 1979, 4–6. ... 1005

Contents of Volumes I–IV ... 1009

Acknowledgments ... 1029

Index ... 1037

CONTENTS

Volume VI

Editor's Preface

Part I. Classical Economics

389. Out of the Closet: A Program for the Whig History of Economic Science
    History of Economics Society Bulletin, 9(1), 51–60, 1987. 3
390. Keeping Whig History Honest
    History of Economics Society Bulletin, 10(2), 161–167, 1988. 13
391. The Overdue Recovery of Adam Smith's Reputation as an Economic Theorist
    Adam Smith's Legacy, His Place in the Development of Modern Economics, M. Fry (ed.). New York: Routledge, Chapman and Hall, Inc., 1–14, 1992. 20
392. The Classical Classical Fallacy
    Journal of Economic Literature, 32(2), 620–639, 1994. 34
393. Mathematical Vindication of Ricardo on Machinery
    Journal of Political Economy, 96(2), 274–282, 1988. 54
394. Ricardo was Right!
    Scandinavian Journal of Economics, 91(1), 47–62, 1989. 63
395. Yes, to Robert Dorfman's Vindication of Thünen's Natural-Wage Derivation
    Journal of Economic Literature, 24(4), 1777–1785, 1986. 79
396. Conversations with my History-of-Economics Critics
    Economics, Culture and Education, Essays in Honour of Mark Blaug, G.K. Shaw (ed.). Aldershot: Edward Elgar Publishing Co., 3–13, 1991. 88

Contents

397. A Classical Theorem for John Chipman: Maximal and Minimal Malthusian Population; A Sweeping Non-Substitution Theorem at the Core of the Canonical Classical Model
Trade, Theory and Econometrics, Essays in Honor of John S. Chipman, J. C. Monroe, R. Riezman and J.R. Melvin (eds). London and New York: Routledge, 338–352, 1999. 99

398. Land
The Elgar Companion to Classical Economics, Volume L-Z, H. Kurz and N. Salvadori (eds). Cheltenham, UK: Edward Elgar, 27–37, 1998. 114

399. Non-Substitution Theorems
The Elgar Companion to Classical Economics, Volume L-Z, H. Kurz and N. Salvadori (eds.). Cheltenham, UK: Edward Elgar, 183–188, 1998. 125

400. Samuelson, Paul Anthony, as an Interpreter of the Classical Economists
The Elgar Companion to Classical Economics, Volume L-Z, H. Kurz and N. Salvadori (eds.). Cheltenham, UK: Edward Elgar, 329–333, 1998. 131

401. A Quintessential (ahistorical) Tableau Economique: To Sum up Pre- and Post-Smith Classical Paradigms
Economics Broadly Considered, Essays in Honour of Warren Samuels, J. Biddle, J. Davis and S. Medema (eds.). London: Taylor & Francis Books Ltd., 49–63, 2001. 136

402. A Modern Post-Mortem on Böhm's Capital Theory: Its Vital Normative Flaw Shared by Pre-Sraffian Mainstream Capital Theory
Journal of the History of Economic Thought, 23(3), 301–317, 2001. 151

403. What Ricardo et al. Didn't Quite Understand About Their Own System
Faith, Reason, and Economics, Essays in Honour of Anthony Waterman, D. Hum (ed.). Winnipeg: St. John's College Press, 203–211, 2003. 168

404. An Elizabethan Age for Pure Trade Theory: 1925–55
Review of International Economics, 13(5), 1001–1003, 2005. 177

405. Two Alternative Hypothetical "Lost" 1814 Ricardo Manuscripts: New-Century Bearings (with Erkko Etula)
History of Political Economy, 38(1), 1–14, 2006. 180

Part II. Neoclassical, Marxian and Sraffian Economics

406. A Revisionist View of von Neumann's Growth Model
John von Neumann and Modern Economics, M. Dore, S. Chakravarty and R. Goodwin (eds.). Oxford: Oxford University Press, 100–122, 1989. 197

407. A Sweeping New Non-Substitution Theorem: Kaldor's Discovery of the von Neumann Input-Output Model
Nicholas Kaldor and Mainstream Economics, Confrontation or Convergence? E.J. Nell and W. Semmler (eds.). Basingstoke: The Macmillan Press Limited, 72–87, 1991. 220

408. Logic of the Historical Transformation Problem: Exchange Ratios Under Simple Commodity Production
Marx and Modern Economic Analysis, Volume I: Values, Prices and Exploitation, G.A. Caravale (ed.). Aldershot: Edward Elgar, 145–168, 1991. 236

409. Marx on Rent: A Failure to Transform Correctly
Journal of the History of Economic Thought, 14, 143–167, 1992. 260

410. Revisionist Findings on Sraffa
Essays on Piero Sraffa, K. Bharadwaj and B. Schefold (eds.). London: Unwin Hyman, 263–279, 1990. 285

411. Sraffian Economics
The New Palgrave: A Dictionary of Economics, Vol. IV, J. Eatwell, M. Milgate and P. Newman (eds.). London and Basingstoke: The Macmillan Press, 452–461, 1987. 302

412. Sraffa's Other Leg
    Economic Journal, 101(406), 570–574, May, 1991. ... 312
413. Two Classics: Böhm-Bawerk's *Positive Theory* and Fisher's *Rate of Interest* Through Modern Prisms
    Journal of the History of Economic Thought, 16(2), 202–228, 1994. ... 317
414. Isolating Sources of Sterility In Marx's Theoretical Paradigms
    Capital Controversy, Post-Keynesian Economics and the History of Economics, Essays in Honour of Geoff Harcourt, Vol. 1, P. Arestis, G. Palma and M. Sawyer (eds.). London and New York: Routledge, 187–198, 1996. ... 344
415. Book Review of *Socialism and Marginalism in Economics, 1870–1930*, I. Steedman (ed.)
    The European Journal of the History of Economic Thought, 4(1), 179–187, 1997. ... 356
416. Report Card on Sraffa at 100
    The European Journal of the History of Economic Thought, 5(3), 458–67, 1998. ... 365
417. The Special Thing I Learned from Sraffa
    Value, Distribution and Capital, Essays in Honour of Pierangelo Garegnani, G. Mongiovi and F. Petri (eds.). London and New York: Routledge, 230–237, 1999. ... 375
418. Sherlock Holmes and the Swarthy German: the Case of Inanely 'Transforming' *Mehrwert* to Prices
    Economics, Welfare Policy and the History of Economic Thought, Essays in Honour of Arnold Heertje, M. Fase, W. Kanning and D. Walker (eds.). Cheltenham, UK and Northampton, Mass.: Edward Elgar, 345–363, 1999. ... 383
419. Sraffa's Hits and Misses
    Critical Essays on Piero Sraffa's Legacy in Economics, H. Kurz (ed.). Cambridge: Cambridge University Press, 111–152, 2000. ... 402
420. Comment (on Sraffa's "Hits and Misses") by H. Kurz and N. Salvadori. Reactions to Kurz-Salvadori's Comment on "Sraffa's Hits and Misses"
    Critical Essays on Piero Sraffa's Legacy in Economics, H. Kurz (ed.). Cambridge: Cambridge University Press, 163–180, 2000. ... 444
421. Sparks and Grit from the Anvil of Growth
    Frontiers of Development Economics, G. Meier and J. Stiglitz (eds.). A co-publication of the World Bank and Oxford University Press, 492–505, 2001. ... 473
422. A Ricardo-Sraffa Paradigm Comparing Gains from Trade in Inputs and Finished Goods
    Journal of Economic Literature, 39(4), 1204–1214, 2001. ... 487
423. Brief First Critique of Sraffa's Unfinished Critique of Marginalism
    Regulation, Competition and the Market Economy, Festschrift für Carl Christian von Weizsäcker, H.G. Nutzinger (ed.). Göttingen: Vandenhoeck & Ruprecht, 3–21, 2003. ... 498
424. The Hawkins and Simon Story Revisited
    Models of a Man, Essays in Memory of Herbert A. Simon, M. Augier and J.G. March (eds.). Cambridge, Mass.: The MIT Press, 153–162, 2004. ... 517
425. Testing to Confirm that Leontief-Sraffa Matrix Equations for Input/Output Must Obey Constancy of Returns to Scale (with Erkko Etula)
    Journal of Economics Letters, 90, 183–188, 2006. ... 527
426. Complete Work-up of the One-sector Scalar-Capital Theory of Interest Rate: Third Installment Auditing Sraffa's Never-completed "Critique of Modern Economic Theory" (with Erkko Etula)
    Japan and the World Economy, 18(3), 331–356, 2006. ... 533

427. Classical and Neoclassical Harmonies and Dissonances
The European Journal of the History of Economic Thought, 14(2), 243–271, 2007.   559

Part III. Modern Macroeconomics

428. The Keynes-Hansen-Samuelson Multiplier-Accelerator Model of Secular Stagnation
Japan and the World Economy, 1, 13–19, 1988.   591
429. Extirpating Error Contamination Concerning the Post-Keynesian Anti-Pasinetti Equilibrium
Oxford Economic Papers, 43, 177–186, 1991.   608
430. In the Beginning (Keynesian Economics and Harvard)
Challenge, 31(4), 32–34, 1988.   618
431. Who Innovated the Keynesian Revolution?
Economics, Econometrics and the LINK, Essays in Honor of Lawrence R. Klein, M. J. Dutta, D.W. Jorgenson, J-J. Laffont, T. Persson, and H.K. Van Dijk (eds.). Amsterdam: Elsevier Science, B.V., 3–19, 1995.   621
432. How Keynes Came to America via Harvard
Godkin Lecture I, Harvard University, Cambridge, Massachusetts, November, 1986.   638
433. Structure of a Scientific Revolution
Godkin Lecture II, Harvard University, Cambridge, Massachusetts, November, 1986.   661
434. Requiem for the Classic Tarshis Textbook that First Brought Keynes to Introductory Economics
Keynesianism and the Keynesian Revolution in America: A Memorial Volume in Honour of Lorie Tarshis, O.F. Hamouda and B. Price (eds.). Cheltenham, UK and Northampton, Mass.: Edward Elgar, 53–58, 1998.   676
435. Reply: Complementary Innovations by Roy Harrod and Alvin Hansen
History of Political Economy, 34(1), 219–223, 2002.   682
436. Multiple Priorities in Evolving Scholarly Disciplines
History of Political Economy, 35(2), 333–334, 2003.   687
437. Paul Samuelson, interview
Reflections on the Great Depression, R.E. Parker. Cheltenham, UK and Northampton, Mass.: Edward Elgar, 25–40, 2002.   689

Part IV. Welfare and Efficiency Economics

438. Theory of Optimal Taxation
Journal of Public Economics, 30(2), 137–143, 1986.   707
439. How a Certain Internal Consistency Entails the Expected Utility Dogma
Journal of Risk and Uncertainty, 1, 389–393, 1988.   714
440. Sparks from Arrow's Anvil
Arrow and the Foundations of the Theory of Economic Policy, G.R. Feiwel (ed.). Basingstoke: The Macmillan Press, 154–178, 1987.   719
441. Tragedy of the Commons: Efficiency Rents to the Rescue of Free-Road Inefficiencies and Paradoxes
Does Economic Space Matter? Essays in Honour of Melvin L. Greenhut. H. Ohta and J-F. Thisse (eds.). New York: St. Martin's Press, 71–80, 1993.   744
442. When Deregulation Makes Things Worse Before They Get Better
Competition and Markets, Essays in Honour of Margaret Hall, C. Moir and J. Dawson (eds.). Basingstoke: The Macmillan Press, 11–20, 1990.   754

443. Tragedy of the Open Road: Avoiding Paradox by Use of Regulated Public Utilities that Charge Corrected Knightian Tolls
Journal of International and Comparative Economics, 1(1), 3–12, 1992. ... 764
444. Richard Kahn: His Welfare Economics and Lifetime Achievement
Cambridge Journal of Economics, 18(1), 55–72, 1994. ... 774
445. Some Uneasiness with the Coase Theorem
Japan and the World Economy, 7(1), 1–7, 1995. ... 792
446. Graduated Income Taxation, Which Reduces Inequality, Leaves Pareto's Coefficient Invariant: A Pseudo-paradox That Debunks Pareto's Coefficient
Correspondence, *Journal of Economic Perspectives*, 6(4), 205–206, 1992. ... 799
447. John Bates Clark: America's First Great Theorist
John Bates Clark's "The Distribution of Wealth, Vademecum Zu Einem Amerikanischen Neoklassiker, Klassiker der Nationalökonomie" (published in German). Dusseldorf: Verlag Wirtschaft und Finanzen, 55–72, 1999. ... 801
448. Where Ricardo and Mill Rebut and Confirm Arguments of Mainstream Economists Supporting Globalization
Journal of Economic Perspectives, 18(3), 135–146, 2004. ... 816
449. As Bad As Ricardo
Comments, *Journal of Economic Perspectives*, 19(3), 242–244, 2005. ... 839
450. An Interview with Paul Samuelson: Welfare Economics, 'Old' and 'New,' and Social Choice Theory
Social Choice and Welfare, K. Suzumura, vol. 25, 327–356, 2005. ... 843

Part V. Economic and Scientific Theories

451. Deterministic Chaos in Economics: An Occurrence in Axiomatic Utility Theory
Nonlinear and Multisectoral Macrodynamics: Essays in Honour of Richard Goodwin, K. Velupillai (ed.). Basingstoke: The Macmillan Press, 42–63, 1990. ... 875
452. A Long-Open Question on Utility and Conserved Energy Functions
Equilibrium and Dynamics, Essays in Honour of David Gale, M. Majumdar (ed.). Basingstoke: The Macmillan Press, 287–306, 1992. ... 897
453. Two Conservation Laws in Theoretical Economics
Conservation Laws and Symmetry: Applications to Economics and Finance, R. Ramachandran and R. Sato (eds.). Norwell, Mass.: Kluwer Academic Publishers, 57–70, 1990. ... 917
454. Trimming Consumers' Surplus Down to Size
A Century of Economics, 100 Years of the Royal Economic Society and the Economic Journal, J.D. Hey and D. Winch (eds.). Oxford: Blackwell Limited, 265–297, 1990. ... 931
455. Characterizing an Area Condition Associated with Minimizing Systems (with James Cooper and Thomas Russell)
Economic Theory, Dynamics and Markets, Essays in Honor of Ryuzo Sato, T. Negishi, R. Ramachandran and K. Mino (eds.). Norwell, Mass.: Kluwer Academic Publishers, 391–403, 2001. ... 968
456. Economic History and Mainstream Economic Analysis
Rivista di Storia Economica, Nuova serie, anno XVII, 17(2), 271–277, 2001. ... 981
457. Conservation Laws in Economics
Japan and the World Economy, 16, 243–246, 2004. ... 988

Contents

458. Testing the Expected Utility Maximization Hypothesis with Limited Experimental Data (with James Cooper and Thomas Russell)
Japan and the World Economy, 16, 391–407, 2004.   992

459. Testing Whether the "Capital Reversal" Syndrome Mandates Deadweight Loss in Competitive Intertemporal Equilibrium
Economic Theory and Economic Thought, Essays in Honour of Ian Steedman, J. Vint, J. Metcalfe, H. Kurz, N. Salvadori and P.A. Samuelson (eds.). London and New York: Routledge, 167–173, 2010.   1009

Contents of Volumes I–V   1017

Acknowledgments   1043

Index   1065

ACKNOWLEDGMENTS

The editor and The MIT Press wish to thank the publishers of the following essays for permission to reprint them here. The selections are arranged chronologically, with cross references to the chapter numbers in volumes six and seven in brackets.

"The Economic Brownian Motion," speech delivered to the American Philosophical Society, Philadelphia, 11 November 1960. **[490]**

Foreword to *The Political Economy of the New Left—An Outsider's View*, Assar Lindbeck. New York: Harper & Row Publishers, 1971, ix–xxi. Copyright © 1971 by Harper Collins Publishers, New York. Reprinted with permission of Addison-Wesley Educational Publishers, Inc. All rights reserved. **[525]**

Book Review of *Beat the Market: A Scientific Stock Market System*, Edward O. Thorp and Sheen T. Kassouf, New York: Random House, 1967, *Journal of the American Statistical Association*, vol. 63, September, 1968, 1049–1051. Reprinted with permission of the *Journal of the American Statistical Association*. © American Statistical Association. See the 2009 preamble. **[493]**

"Schumpeter, Joseph Alois," in *Dictionary of American Biography, Supplement 4, 1946–1950*, John A. Garrity and Edward T. James (eds.). New York: Charles Scribner's Sons, 1974, 720–723. Copyright © 1974 by American Council of Learned Societies, New York, New York. Reprinted with permission. All rights reserved. Included here is "1991 Afterthoughts on Schumpeter," unpublished. **[537]**

Acknowledgments

"Piero Sraffa (1898–1983)" published as "Un genio con poche opere," *Corriere della Sera*, 6 March 1983. Reprinted with permission of R.C.S. Editoriale Quotidiani, S.p.A., Milano, Italy. [547]

"How Not to Cure the Imbalance of Trade," published as "Where Iacocca and Common Sense Err," *The New York Times*, 15 September 1985. Copyright © 1985 by The New York Times Company, New York. Reprinted with permission. [501]

"The Fallibility of Economic Science." The Third Julius Steinberg Memorial Lecture, The Wharton School of the University of Pennsylvania, Philadelphia, 2 October 1985. [585]

"The 1985 Nobel Prize in Economics," *Science*, vol. 231, March 1986, 1399–1401. Copyright © 1986 by American Association for the Advancement of Science, Washington, D.C. Reprinted with permission. [530]

"Theory of Optimal Taxation," *Journal of Public Economics*, vol. 30, no. 2, July 1986, 137–143. Reprinted with permission of Elsevier Science Publishers, B.V., Amsterdam. [438]

"Has Economic Science Improved the System?", in *American Society, Public and Private Responsibilities*, William Knowlton and Richard Zeckhauser (eds.). New York: Harper Collins Publishers, 1986, 299–315. Copyright © 1986 by Harper Collins Publishers. All rights reserved. [498]

"The Present State of Economic Science and Its Probable Future Development," in *Zeugen des Wissens*, H. Maier-Leibnitz (ed.). Mainz: v. Hase & Koehler Verlag, 1986. Reprinted in *Journal of Business Administration*, vol. 18, nos. 1 and 2, 1988/89, 21–32. Reprinted with permission of v. Hase & Koehler Verlag. [494]

"How Keynes Came to America Via Harvard." Godkin Lecture I, Harvard University, Cambridge, Massachusetts, November 1986. [432]

"Structure of a Scientific Revolution." Godkin Lecture II, Harvard University, Cambridge, Massachusetts, November 1986. [433]

"Yes to Robert Dorfman's Vindication of Thünen's Natural-Wage Derivation," *Journal of Economic Literature*, vol. 24, no. 4, December 1986, 1777–1785. Copyright © 1986 by American Economics Association, Nashville, Tennessee. All rights reserved. [395]

"Paradise Lost and Refound: The Harvard ABC Barometers," *The Journal of Portfolio Management*, vol. 13, no. 3, Spring 1987, 4–9. This copyrighted material is reprinted with permission of *The Journal of Portfolio Management*, 488 Madison Ave., New York, NY 10022. All rights reserved. [461]

Acknowledgments

"Joint Authorship in Sciences: Serendipity with Wolfgang Stolper," *Journal of Institutional and Theoretical Economics*, vol. 143, no. 2, June 1987, 235–243. Reprinted with permission. **[584]**

"How Economics Has Changed," *Journal of Economic Education*, vol. 18, no. 2, Spring, 1987, 107–110. Reprinted with permission of the Helen Dwight Reid Educational Foundation. Published by Heldref Publications, 1319 18th Street, N.W., Washington, D.C. 20036-1802. Copyright © 1987. **[505]**

"An Economist's Economist," obituary of Walter Heller, *The New York Times*, 23 June 1987. Copyright © 1985/1987 by The New York Times Company, New York. Reprinted with permission. **[533]**

"Out of the Closet: A Program for the Whig History of Economic Science," *History of Economics Society Bulletin*, vol. 9, no. 1, 1987, 51–60. Reprinted with permission. **[389]**

"Sparks from Arrow's Anvil," in *Arrow and the Foundations of the Theory of Economic Policy*, George R. Feiwel (ed.). Basingstoke: The Macmillan Press, Limited, 1987, 154–178. Copyright © 1987 by The Macmillan Press, Limited. All rights reserved. **[440]**

"Sraffian Economics," in *The New Palgrave: A Dictionary of Economics*, Volume IV, John Eatwell, Murray Milgate and Peter Newman (eds.). London and Basingstoke: The Macmillan Press Limited, 1987, 452–461. Copyright © 1987 by The Macmillan Press, Limited. All rights reserved. **[411]**

"Wicksell and Neoclassical Economics," in *The New Palgrave: A Dictionary of Economics*, Vol. IV, John Eatwell, Murray Milgate and Peter Newman (eds.). London and Basingstoke: The Macmillan Press Limited, 1987, 908–910. Copyright © 1987 by The Macmillan Press, Limited. All rights reserved. **[551]**

"Mathematical Vindication of Ricardo on Machinery," *Journal of Political Economy*, vol. 96, no. 2, April 1988, 274–282. Copyright © 1988 by The University of Chicago Press. All rights reserved. **[393]**

"Recurring Quandaries in International Trade." Keynote Address at Conference on International Finance Markets, New York University, New York, 5 May 1988. **[508]**

"Keeping Whig History Honest," *History of Economics Society Bulletin*, vol. 10, no. 2, Fall 1988, 161–167. Reprinted with permission. **[390]**

"In the Beginning" (Keynesian Economics and Harvard), *Challenge*, vol. 31, no. 4, July/August 1988, 32–34. Reprinted with permission of M.E. Sharpe, Inc., Armonk, New York. All rights reserved. **[430]**

Acknowledgments

"Knut Wicksell," published in German as "Wicksells Werk und Persönlichkeit - Eine kritische Analyse in moderner Sicht," in *Klassiker der Nationalökonomie*. Foreword to Faksimile-Edition of Wicksell's "Finanztheoretische Untersuchungen." Düsseldorf: Verlag Wirtschaft und Finanzen GmbH, 1988, 25–36. **[548]**

"The Science of Economics at Century's End," *Mainichi Shimbun*, no. 65, 7 November 1988, 17–23. Reprinted with permission. **[495]**

"The Number One Economic Problem is the Structural Budget Deficit," in "Business, Economics and the Oval Office: Advice to the New President and Other CEOs," *Harvard Business Review*, no. 6, November/December 1988, 67–69. Copyright © 1988 by the President and Fellows of Harvard College. All rights reserved. **[496]**

"The Keynes-Hansen-Samuelson Multiplier-Accelerator Model of Secular Stagnation," *Japan and the World Economy*, vol. 1, 1988, 13–19. Reprinted with permission of Elsevier Science Publishers, B.V., Amsterdam. All rights reserved. **[428]**

"The Passing of the Guard in Economics," *Eastern Economic Journal*, vol. 14, no. 4, October-December 1988, 312–329. Copyright © 1988 by the Eastern Economic Association, Smithfield, Rhode island. All rights reserved. **[577]**

"How a Certain Internal Consistency Entails the Expected Utility Dogma," *Journal of Risk and Uncertainty*, vol. 1, 1988, 389–393. Copyright © 1988 by Kluwer Academic Publishers, Dordrecht, The Netherlands. Reprinted with permission. All rights reserved. **[439]**

"U.S. Economic Prospects and Policy Options: Impact on Japan-U.S. Relations," in *Unkept Promises, Unclear Consequences: U.S. Economic Policy and the Japanese Response*, John A. Rizzo and Ryuzo Sato (eds.). Cambridge: Cambridge University Press, 1988, 109–136. **[502]**

"Robert Solow: An Affectionate Portrait," *Journal of Economic Perspectives*, vol. 3, no. 3, Summer 1989, 91–97. Copyright © 1989 by American Economic Association, Nashville, Tennessee. All rights reserved. **[534]**

"Ricardo Was Right!", *The Scandinavian Journal of Economics*, vol. 91, no. 1, 1989, 47–62. Reprinted with permission. **[394]**

"The $\sqrt{N}$ Law and Repeated Risktaking," in *Probability, Statistics and Mathematics, Papers in Honor of Samuel Karlin*, T.W. Anderson, Krishna B. Athreya, and Donald L. Iglehart (eds.). San Diego, California, and Orlando, Florida: The Academic Press, Inc., 1989, 291–306. Copyright © 1989 by The Academic Press, Inc., Orlando, Florida. All rights reserved. **[462]**

"Remembering Joan," in *Joan Robinson and Modern Economic Theory*, George R. Feiwel (ed.). New York: The New York University Press,

Acknowledgments

1989, 121–143. Basingstoke: The Macmillan Press Limited. Reprinted with permission. **[540]**

"The Judgment of Economic Science on Rational Portfolio Management: Indexing, Timing, and Long-Horizon Effects," *The Journal of Portfolio Management*, Fall 1989, 4–12. This copyrighted material is reprinted with permission of *The Journal of Portfolio Management*, 488 Madison Avenue, New York, NY 10022. All rights reserved. **[468]**

"A Case at Last for Age-Phased Reduction in Equity," *Proceedings of the National Academy of Sciences, USA*, vol. 86, November 1989, 9048–9051. **[470]**

"Galbraith as Artist and Scientist," in *Unconventional Wisdom, Essays in Economics in Honor of John Kenneth Galbraith*, Samuel Bowles, Richard Edwards, and William G. Shepherd (eds.). Boston: The Houghton Mifflin Co., 1989, 123–128. Copyright © 1989 by The Institute for Economic Studies, Inc. Reprinted with permission of Houghton Mifflin Co., Boston, Massachusetts. All rights reserved. **[535]**

"A Revisionist View of von Neumann's Growth Model," in *John von Neumann and Modern Economics*, Mohammed Dore, Sukhamoy Chakravarty, and Richard Goodwin (eds.). Oxford: Oxford University Press, 1989, 100–122. Reprinted with permission. **[406]**

"Gibbs in Economics," *Proceedings of the Gibbs Symposium Yale University May 15–17, 1989*, Daniel G. Caldi and George D. Mostow (eds.). Providence, Rhode Island: American Mathematical Society, 1989, 255–267. Reprinted with permission. **[539]**

"Deterministic Chaos in Economics: An Occurrence in Axiomatic Utility Theory," in *Nonlinear and Multisectoral Macrodynamics: Essays in Honour of Richard Goodwin*, Kumaraswamy Velupillai (ed.). Basingstoke: The Macmillan Press Limited, 1990, 42–63. Copyright © 1990 by The Macmillan Press Limited. All rights reserved. **[451]**

"Asset Allocation Could Be Dangerous to Your Health," *The Journal of Portfolio Management*, vol. 16, no. 3, Spring 1990, 5–8. Reprinted with permission of *The Journal of Portfolio Management*, 488 Madison Ave., New York, New York 10022. All rights reserved. **[463]**

"Gottfried Haberler as Economic Sage and Trade Theory Innovator," in *Wirtschafts Politische Blätter*, vol. 37, 1990, 310–317. Reprinted with permission. **[550]**

Foreword to *Continuous-Time Finance*, Robert C. Merton. Cambridge, Mass.: Basil Blackwell, Inc., 1990, xi–xii. Copyright © 1990 by Robert C. Merton. Reprinted with permission of Basil Blackwell Publishers, Oxford. **[475]**

Acknowledgments

"The Law Beats Maxwell's Demon," Scientific Correspondence in *Nature*, vol. 347, no .6 September 1990, 24–25. Reprinted with permission of *Nature*. Copyright © 1990 by Macmillan Magazines Limited, London. All rights reserved. [519]

"When Deregulation Makes Things Worse Before They Get Better," in *Competition and Markets, Essays in Honour of Margaret Hall*, Christopher Moir and John Dawson (eds.). Basingstoke: The Macmillan Press Limited, 1990, 11–20. Copyright © 1990 by The Macmillan Press Limited. All rights reserved. [442]

"Two Conservation Laws in Theoretical Economics," in *Conservation Laws and Symmetry: Applications to Economics and Finance*, Rama Ramachandran and Ryuzo Sato (eds.). Norwell, Mass.: Kluwer Academic Publishers, 1990, 57–70. Reprinted with the kind permission of Elsevier Academic Publishers. [453]

"Trimming Consumers' Surplus Down to Size," in *A Century of Economics, 100 Years of the Royal Economic Society and the Economic Journal*, John D. Hey and Donald Winch (eds.). Oxford: Blackwell Limited, 1990, 265–297. Reprinted with permission. [454]

"Revisionist Findings on Sraffa," in *Essays on Piero Sraffa*, Krishna Bharadwaj and Bertram Schefold (eds.). London: Unwin Hyman, 1990, 263–279. Reprinted with permission. [410]

"Tribute to Nicholas Georgescu-Roegen on His 85th Birthday," *Libertas Mathematica*, vol. 10, 1990, 1–4. Reprinted with permission. [536]

"Logic of the Historical Transformation Problem: Exchange Ratios Under Simple Commodity Production," in *Marx and Modern Economic Analysis, Volume I: Values, Prices and Exploitation*, Giovanni A. Caravale (ed.). Aldershot: Edward Elgar Publishing Co., 1991, 145–168. Reprinted with permission. [408]

"Conversations with my History-of-Economics Critics," in *Economics, Culture and Education, Essays in Honour of Mark Blaug*, G.K. Shaw (ed). Aldershot: Edward Elgar Publishing Co., 1991, 3–13. Reprinted with permission. [396]

"Economic Science Grapples with Dilemmas of International Finance." Lionel Robbins Memorial Lecture, Claremont College, California, 28 January 1991. [507]

"Thoughts on the Stockholm School and on Scandinavian Economics," in *The Stockholm School of Economics Revisited*, Lars Jonung (ed.). New York: Cambridge University Press, 1991, 391–407. Reprinted with permission. [499]

Acknowledgments

"Sraffa's Other Leg," *The Economic Journal*, vol. 101, no. 406, May 1991, 570–574. Reprinted with permission of Blackwell Publishers, Oxford. **[412]**

"A Personal View on Crises and Economic Cycles," in *The Risk of Economic Crisis*, Martin Feldstein (ed.). Chicago: The University of Chicago Press, 1991, 167–170. Copyright © 1991 by The University of Chicago Press. All rights reserved. **[497]**

"Extirpating Error Contamination Concerning the Post-Keynesian Anti-Pasinetti Equilibrium," *Oxford Economic Papers*, vol. 43, 1991, 177–186. Reprinted with permission of Oxford University Press, Oxford. **[429]**

"Leontief's 'The Economy as a Circular Flow': An Introduction," *Structural Change and Economic Dynamics* vol. 2, no. 1, 1991, 177–179. Reprinted with permission of Oxford University Press, Oxford. **[542]**

"Jacob Viner 1892–1970," in *Remembering the University of Chicago Teachers, Scientists, and Scholars*, Edward Shils (ed.). Chicago: The University of Chicago Press, 1991, 533–547. Copyright © 1991 by The University of Chicago Press. All rights reserved. **[531]**

"Long-Run Risk Tolerance When Equity Returns Are Mean Progressing: Pseudoparadoxes and Vindication of 'Businessman's Risk'," in *Money, Macroeconomics, and Economic Policy*, William C. Brainard, William D. Nordhaus, and Harold W. Watts (eds.). Cambridge, Mass.: The MIT Press, 1991, 181–204. Reprinted with permission. **[460]**

"My Life Philosophy: Policy Credos and Working Ways," in *Eminent Economists, Their Life Philosophies*, Michael Szenberg (ed.). New York: Cambridge University Press, 1991, 236–247. Reprinted with permission. **[574]**

"On the Historiography of Economics: A Correspondence," with Mark Blaug and Don Patinkin, *Journal of the History of Economic Thought*, vol. 13, no. 2, Fall 1991, 144–158. Reprinted with permission. **[576]**

"A Sweeping New Non-Substitution Theorem: Kaldor's Discovery of the von Neumann Input-Output Model," in *Nicholas Kaldor and Mainstream Economics, Confrontation or Convergence?*, Edward J. Nell and Will Semmler (eds.). Basingstoke: The Macmillan Press Limited, 1991, 72–87. Copyright © 1991 by The Macmillan Press Limited. All rights reserved. **[407]**

"Statistical Flowers Caught in Amber," *Statistical Science*, vol. 6, no. 4, 1991, 330–338. Reprinted with permission of Institute of Mathematical Statistics, Hayward, California. **[575]**

"Irving Fisher 1867–1947", published in German in *Irving Fisher's 'The Nature of Capital and Income'—Vademecum zu einem Klassiker*

Acknowledgments

der amerkanischen Nationalökonomie, Klassiker der Nationalökonomie, Paul A. Samuelson, Bertram Schefold, and James Tobin, Michael Tochtermann (ed.). Düsseldorf: Verlag Wirtschaft und Finanzen, GmbH, 1991, 47–55. [532]

"Economics in Our Time." Speech delivered on the occasion of the 90th anniversary of the Nobel Prize, Stockholm, Sweden, 6 December 1991. [578]

"Conserved Energy Without Heat or Light," *Proceedings of the National Academy of Sciences, USA*, vol. 89, February 1992, 1090–1094. [520]

"Economics and Thermodynamics: von Neumann's Problematic Conjecture," in *Rational Interaction, Essays in Honor of John C. Harsanyi*, Richard Selten, (ed.). New York: Springer Verlag, 1992, 377–389. Reprinted with permission. [521]

Foreword to "The Theory of Security Pricing and Market Structure," by Marshall E. Blume and Jeremy J. Siegel, *Journal of Financial Markets, Institutions & Instruments*, vol. 1, no. 3, July 1992, 1–2. Reprinted with permission of Blackwell Publishers. [479]

"Risk Tolerances, Distributive Inequality, and Track Bettors' Equilibrium," in *Economic Analysis of Markets and Games, Essays in Honor of Frank Hahn*, Partha Dasgupta, David Gale, Oliver Hart, and Eric Maskin (eds.). Cambridge, Mass.: The MIT Press, 1992, 602–620. Reprinted with permission. [471]

"The Overdue Recovery of Adam Smith's Reputation as an Economic Theorist," in *Adam Smith's Legacy, His Place in the Development of Modern Economics*, Michael Fry (ed.). New York: Routledge, Chapman and Hall, Inc., 1992, 1–14. Reprinted with permission. [391]

"Tragedy of the Open Road: Avoiding Paradox by Use of Regulated Public Utilities that Charge Corrected Knightian Tolls," *Journal of International and Comparative Economics*, vol. 1, issue 1, 1992, 3–12. Reprinted with permission of Springer Verlag, New York. [443]

"At Last, a Rational Case for Long-Horizon Risk Tolerance and for Asset-Allocation Timing?", in *Active Asset Allocation, State of the Art Portfolio Policies, Strategies and Tactics*, Robert Arnold and Frank Fabozzi (eds.). Chicago: Probus Publishing Co., 1992, 411–416. Reprinted with permission. [469]

"A Long-Open Question on Utility and Conserved Energy Functions," in *Equilibrium and Dynamics, Essays in Honour of David Gale*, Mukul Majumdar (ed.). Basingstoke: The Macmillan Press Limited, 1992, 287–306. Copyright © 1992 by The Macmillan Press Limited. All rights reserved. [452]

"Correspondence" (regarding "Graduated Income Taxation, Which Reduces Inequality, Leaves Pareto's Coefficient Invariant: A Pseudo-Paradox That Debunks Pareto's Coefficient"), *Journal of Economic Perspectives*, vol. 6, no. 4, Fall 1992, 205–206. Copyright © by American Economic Association, Nashville, Tennessee. All rights reserved. **[446]**

"Marx on Rent: A Failure to Transform Correctly," *Journal of the History of Economic Thought*, vol. 14, Fall 1992, 143–167. Reprinted with permission. **[409]**

"Factor Price Equalization by Trade in Joint and Non-Joint Production," *Review of International Economics*, vol. 1, issue 1, November 1992, 1–9. Reprinted with permission of Blackwell Publishers, Oxford. **[522]**

"The Fitness Maximized by the Classical Canonical Economy: A Theme from Houthakker and R.A. Fisher," in *Aggregation, Consumption and Trade, Essays in Honor of H.S. Houthakker*, Louis Phlips and Lester D. Taylor (eds.). Dordrecht: Kluwer Academic Publishers, 1992, 9–19. Copyright © 1992 by Kluwer Academic Publishers. Reprinted with permission. All rights reserved. **[541]**

"Altruism as a Problem Involving Group versus Individual Selection in Economics and Biology," *American Economic Review*, vol. 83, no. 2, May 1992, 143–148. Copyright © 1993 by American Economic Association, Nashville, Tennessee. All rights reserved. **[523]**

"Gustav Cassel's Scientific Innovations: Claims and Realities," *History of Political Economy*, vol. 25, no. 3, Fall 1993, 515–527. Reprinted with permission of Duke University Press, Durham, North Carolina. **[546]**

"Tragedy of the Commons: Efficiency Rents to the Rescue of Free-Road Inefficiencies and Paradoxes," in *Does Economic Space Matter? Essays in Honour of Melvin L. Greenhut*, Hiroshi Ohta and Jacques-François Thisse (eds.). New York: St. Martin's Press, 1993, 71–80. Basingstoke: The Macmillan Press Limited. Copyright © 1993 in the U.S. by St. Martin's Press. Copyright © 1993 for the rest of the world by The Macmillan Press Limited. All rights reserved. **[441]**

"Homage to Chakravarty: Thoughts on His Lumping Schumpeter with Marx to Define a Paradigm Alternative to Mainstream Growth Theories," in *Capital, Investment and Development, Essays in Memory of Sukhamoy Chakravarty*, Kaushik Basu, Mukul Majumdar, and Tapan Mitra (eds.). Oxford: Blackwell Publishers, 1993, 244–258. Reprinted with permission. **[543]**

"Realities for a Fine June Day." Speech at Harvard Business School Class of 1948 Reunion, Cambridge, Massachusetts, 5 June 1993. **[509]**

"Leaning Against What Inflationary Wind?", *Challenge*, vol. 36, no. 5, September/October 1993, 20–26. Reprinted with permission of the

Acknowledgments

publisher, M.E. Sharpe, Inc., 80 Business Park Drive, Armonk, NY 10504, USA, from the September/October 1993 issue of *Challenge*. All rights reserved. [506]

"Reflections on Investing for Foundations and Colleges." Speech delivered to U.S. Trust/Rutgers University Conference, New York, 17 November 1993. [476]

Foreword to *Bogle on Mutual Funds, New Perspectives for the Intelligent Investor*, John C. Bogle. New York: Irwin Professional Publishing, 1993, iii–iv. Reprinted with permission. [478]

Foreword to *Trade, Welfare, and Economic Policies, Essays in Honor of Murray C. Kemp*, Horst Herberg and Ngo Van Long (eds.). Ann Arbor: The University of Michigan Press, 1993, vii–viii. Copyright © 1993 by The University of Michigan Press. All rights reserved. [554]

"Me and Kennedy." Speech delivered to the Examiner Club, Boston, Massachusetts, 3 January 1994. [578]

"Richard Kahn: His Welfare Economics and Lifetime Achievement," *Cambridge Journal of Economics*, vol. 18, no. 1, 1994, 55–72. Copyright © 1994 by Cambridge Political Economy Society. Reprinted with the permission of Academic Press Limited, Orlando, Florida. All rights reserved. [444]

"The Classical Classical Fallacy," *Journal of Economic Literature*, vol. 32, no. 2, June 1994, 620–639. Copyright © 1994 by the American Economic Association, Nashville, Tennessee. All rights reserved. [392]

"The To-Be-Expected Angst Created for Economists by Mathematics," *Eastern Economic Journal*, vol. 20, no. 3, Summer 1994, 267–273. Copyright © 1994 by The Eastern Economic Association, Smithfield, Rhode Island. All rights reserved. [500]

"Tribute to Wolfgang Stolper on the Fiftieth Anniversary of the Stolper-Samuelson Theorem," in *The Stolper-Samuelson Theorem, A Golden Jubilee*, Alan V. Deardorff and Robert M. Stern (eds.). Ann Arbor: The University of Michigan Press, 1994, 343–349. Copyright © 1994 by The University of Michigan Press. All rights reserved. [544]

"Two Classics: Böhm-Bawerk's *Positive Theory* and Fisher's *Rate of Interest* Through Modern Prisms," *Journal of the History of Economic Thought*, vol. 16, no. 2, Fall 1994, 202–228. Reprinted with permission. [413]

"The Long-Term Case For Equities and How It Can Be Oversold," *The Journal of Portfolio Management*, vol. 21, no. 1, Fall 1994, 15–24. Copyright © 1994 by Institutional Investor, New York. This copyrighted material is reprinted with permission of *The Journal of Portfo-*

lio Management, 488 Madison Ave., New York, NY 10022. All rights reserved. **[464]**

"Facets of Balassa-Samuelson Thirty Years Later," *Review of International Economics*, vol. 2, no. 3, October 1994, 201–226. Reprinted with permission of Blackwell Publishers, Oxford, U.K. **[524]**

"Who Innovated the Keynesian Revolution?", in *Economics, Econometrics and the LINK, Essays in Honor of Lawrence R. Klein*, M. Jan Dutta (ed.). Amsterdam: Elsevier Science, B.V., 1995, 3–19. Reprinted with the kind permission of Elsevier Science, B.V., Amsterdam, The Netherlands. **[431]**

"Some Uneasiness with the Coase Theorem," *Japan and the World Economy*, vol. 7, no. 1, 1995, 1–7. Reprinted with permission of Elsevier Science, B.V., Amsterdam, The Netherlands. **[445]**

"At Eighty: MIT and I." Speech delivered at Paul A. Samuelson's 80th birthday party given by MIT, Boston, Massachusetts, 30 April 1995. **[580]**

"The Past and Future of International Trade Theory," in *New Directions in Trade Theory*, Jim Levinsohn, Alan Deardorff, and Robert M. Stern (eds.). Ann Arbor, Michigan: The University of Michigan Press, 1995, 17–22. Copyright © 1995 by The University of Michigan Press. All rights reserved. **[503]**

"Paul Anthony Samuelson (b. 1915)," in *The Coming of Keynesianism to America, Conversations with the Founders of Keynesian Economics*, David Colander and Harry Landreth (eds.). Cheltenham, U.K.: Edward Elgar Publishing Limited, 1995, 145–178. Copyright © 1995 by Edward Elgar Publishing Limited. All rights reserved. **[581]**

"Grappling with the Rational Case for Long-Horizon Risky-Equities Tolerance." Speech at the University of Rome, Rome, Italy, 5 April 1995. **[472]**

"American and European Economic Divergences at Century's End." Lecture at Institut d'Economic Industrielle, University of Toulouse, Toulouse, France, 9 May 1996. **[504]**

"Tribute to Jan Tinbergen: One Exact Match for Economics and Physics," *Indian Journal of Applied Economics*, vol. 5, no. 3, April-June 1996, 1–16. Reprinted with permission. **[545]**

"The Irreducible Role of Derived Marginal Utility in Dynamic Stochastic Programming," *Pacific Economic Review*, vol. 1, no. 1, June 1996, 3–11. Reprinted with permission of Blackwell Publishers, Ltd., Oxford, U.K. **[465]**

"Gottfried Haberler (1900–1995)," *Economic Journal*, vol. 106, no. 439, November 1996, 1679–1687. Reprinted with permission. **[536]**

Acknowledgments

"On Collaboration," *The American Economist*, vol. 40, no. 2, Fall 1996, 16–21. Reprinted with permission. [583]

"Isolating Sources of Sterility in Marx's Theoretical Paradigms," in *Capital Controversy, Post-Keynesian Economics and the History of Economics, Essays in Honour of Geoff Harcourt,* Vol 1., Philip Arestis, Gabriel Palma, and Malcolm Sawyer, (eds.). London and New York: Routledge, 1996, 187–198. Reprinted with permission of Routledge Publishers, London, U.K. [414]

"Dogma of the Decade: Sure-Thing Risk Erosion for Long-Horizon Investors," uncut version of edited article, "Dogma of the Day," *Bloomberg Personal*, January-February 1997, 33–34. Reprinted with permission. [467]

"Credo of a Lucky Textbook Author," *Journal of Economic Perspectives*, vol. 11, no. 2, Spring 1997, 153–160. Copyright © 1997 by American Economic Association, Nashville, Tennessee. All rights reserved. [582]

"Some Memories of Norbert Wiener," in *Proceedings of Symposia in Pure Mathematics, Vol. 60, The Legacy of Norbert Wiener: A Centennial Symposium*, David Jerison, Isadore M. Singer and David W. Stroock (eds.). Providence, Rhode Island: American Mathematical Society, 1997, 37–42. Reprinted with permission. [549]

"Proof by Certainty Equivalents that Diversification-Across-Time Does Worse, Risk Corrected, than Diversification-Throughout-Time," *Journal of Risk and Uncertainty*, vol. 14, no. 2, March 1997, 129–142. Reprinted with the kind permission of Kluwer Academic Publishers, Dordrecht, The Netherlands. [466]

Book Review of *Socialism and Marginalism in Economics, 1870–1930*, Ian Steedman (ed.), London and New York: Routledge, 1995, *The European Journal of the History of Economic Thought*, vol. 4, no. 1, Spring 1997, 179–187. Reprinted with the permission of Routledge. [415]

"How *Foundations* Came To Be," published in German in *Paul A. Samuelson's "Foundations of Economic Analysis," Vademecum zu einem Klassiker der Gegenwart*, with Jürg Niehans, Paul A. Samuelson and C. Christian von Weizsäcker, 1997, 27–52. Dusseldorf: Verlag Wirtschaft und Finanzen. Extracts reprinted (English, unabridged version) with permission of the publisher. Published in English (abridged) in *Journal of Economic Literature*, vol. 36, no. 3, September 1998, 1375–1386. Reprinted with permission of the American Economic Association. [586]

"Informal Thoughts about Macroeconomics." Roundtable discussion at Banca d'Italia, Rome, Italy, 3 October 1997. [510]

"How Best to Flip-Flop if You Must: Integer Dynamic Stochastic Programming for Either-Or," *Journal of Risk and Uncertainty*, vol. 15, no. 3, December 1997, 183–190. Reprinted with the kind permission of Kluwer Academic Publishers, Dordrecht, The Netherlands. [473]

"Estimating Probabilities Relevant to Calculating Relative Risk-Corrected Returns of Alternative Portfolios," *Journal of Risk and Uncertainty*, vol. 15, no. 3, December 1997, 191–200. Reprinted with the kind permission of Kluwer Academic Publishers, Dordrecht, The Netherlands. [474]

Foreword to *Economics, An Introductory Analysis,* Paul A. Samuelson. Reissued first edition (1948). New York: McGraw-Hill, 1998, iii–iv. Reprinted with permission. [588]

"A Golden Birthday," in *Economics*, 16th edition, Paul A. Samuelson and William D. Nordhaus. New York: Irwin McGraw-Hill, 1998, xxiv–xxvii. Reprinted with permission. [587]

"Harold Freeman (1909–1997)." Memorial Service Tribute, MIT, Cambridge, Massachusetts, 10 March 1998. [552]

"'Tis Folly to be Wise." Interview in *Dow Jones Asset Management*, March/April 1998, 20–28. Uncut version of edited article. Reprinted with permission. [477]

"Report Card on Sraffa at 100," *The European Journal of the History of Economic Thought*, vol. 5, no. 3, Autumn 1998, 458–467. Reprinted with the kind permission of Routledge Limited, UK. [416]

"My John Hicks," *Indian Journal of Applied Economics*, vol. 7, no. 4, October-December, 1998, 1–4. Reprinted with permission. Reproduced in *John Hicks, His Contribution to Economic Theory and Application*, K. Puttaswamaiah (ed.). New Brunswick and London: Transaction Publishers, 2001, 1–4. Reprinted with permission of Transaction Publishers. Copyright © 2001 by Transaction Publishers. [553]

Foreword to *Passion and Craft, Economists at Work*, Michael Szenberg (ed.). Ann Arbor, Michigan: The University of Michigan Press, 1998, xi–xiv. Copyright © 1998 by the University of Michigan Press. All rights reserved. [512]

"Requiem for the Classic Tarshis Textbook that First Brought Keynes to Introductory Economics," in *Keynesianism and the Keynesian Revolution in America: A Memorial Volume in Honour of Lorie Tarshis*, Omar F. Hamouda and Betsey Price (eds.). Cheltenham, UK and Northampton, Mass.: Edward Elgar, 1998, 53–58. Reprinted with permission. [434]

"Land," in *The Elgar Companion to Classical Economics, Volume L-Z*, Heinz Kurz and Neri Salvadori (eds.). Cheltenham, UK: Edward Elgar, 1998, 27–37. Reprinted with permission. [398]

Acknowledgments

"Non-substitution Theorems," in *The Elgar Companion to Classical Economics, Volume L-Z*, Heinz Kurz and Neri Salvadori, (eds.). Cheltenham, UK: Edward Elgar, 1998, 183-188. [399] Reprinted with permission. [399]

"Samuelson, Paul Anthony, as an Interpreter of the Classical Economists," in *The Elgar Companion to Classical Economics, Volume L-Z*, H. Kurz and N. Salvadori (eds.). Cheltenham, UK: Edward Elgar, 1998, 329-333. Reprinted with permission. [400]

"John Bates Clark: America's First Great Theorist," published in German in *John Bates Clark, the Distribution of Wealth, Klassiker der Nationalökonomie*. Dusseldorf: Verlag Wirtschaft und Finanzen, Verlagsgruppe Handelsblatt, GmbH, 1999, 55-72. Reprinted with permission. [447]

"The Special Thing I Learned from Sraffa," in *Value, Distribution and Capital, Essays in Honour of Pierangelo Garegnani*, Gary Mongiovi and Fabio Petri (eds.). London and New York: Routledge, 1999, 230-237. Reprinted with permission. [417]

"A Classical Theorem for John Chipman: Maximal and Minimal Malthusian Population; A Sweeping Non-Substitution Theorem at the Core of the Canonical Classical Model," in *Trade, Theory and Econometrics, Essays in Honor of John S. Chipman*, James C. Moore, Raymond Riezman and James R. Melvin (eds.). London and New York: Routledge, 1999, 338-352. Reprinted with permission. [397]

"Two Gods That Fail," *Challenge*, vol. 42, no. 5, September-October 1999, 29-33. Reprinted with permission. [511]

Foreword to *Bioeconomics and Sustainablity, Essays in Honor of Nicholas Georgescu-Roegen*, Kozo Mayumi and John M. Gowdy (eds.). Cheltenham, UK and Northampton, Mass.: Edward Elgar Publishing, 1999, xiii-xvii. Reprinted with permission. [555]

"Samuelson's *Economics* at Fifty: Remarks on the Occasion of the Anniversary of Publication," *Journal of Economic Education*, vol. 30, no. 4, Fall, 1999, 352-355. Reprinted with permission of the Helen Dwight Reid Education Foundation. Published by Heldref Publications, 1319 18th St., NW, Washington, DC 20036-1802. Copyright © 1999. [589]

"The Classical Theory of Commodity Money Under a Microscope," in *From Classical Economics to the Theory of the Firm, Essays in Honour of D. P. O'Brien*, Roger Backhouse and John Creedy (eds.). Cheltenham, UK: Edward Elgar, 1999, 47-64. Reprinted with permission. [482]

"Economics and the Kennedy Presidency." Speech delivered at the Brookings Institution, Washington, D.C., 12 November 1999. [590]

Acknowledgments

"Sherlock Holmes and the Swarthy German: the Case of Inanely 'Transforming' *Mehrwert* to Prices," in *Economics, Welfare Policy and the History of Economic Thought, Essays in Honour of Arnold Heertje*, Martin M.G. Fase, Walter Kanning and Donald Walker (eds.). Cheltenham, UK and Northampton, Mass.: Edward Elgar Publishing, 1999, 345–363. Reprinted with permission. [418]

Foreword to *Finance*, Zvi Bodie and Robert C. Merton. Upper Saddle River, New Jersey: Prentice-Hall, 2000, v. Reprinted with permission. [481]

"Comment: Clarifying Getting Older and Getting Richer Effects," *Journal of Private Portfolio Management*, vol. 2, no. 1, Spring 2000, 25–26. Reprinted with permission. [480]

"Sraffa's Hits and Misses," in *Critical Essays on Piero Sraffa's Legacy in Economics*, Heinz Kurz (ed.). Cambridge: Cambridge University Press, 2000, 111–152. Reprinted with permission of Cambridge University Press. [419]

"Comment" (on "Sraffa's Hits and Misses") by Heinz Kurz and Neri Salvadori, 152–163, reprinted with permission of the authors. "Reactions" (to Kurz-Salvadori "Comment"), in *Critical Essays on Piero Sraffa's Legacy in Economics*, Heinz Kurz (ed.). Cambridge: Cambridge University Press, 2000, 163–180. Reprinted with permission of Cambridge University Press. [420]

"Sparks and Grit from the Anvil of Growth," in *Frontiers of Development Economics*, Gerald Meier and Joseph Stiglitz (eds.). A co-publication of the World Bank and Oxford University Press, 2001, 492–505. Used with permission of Oxford University Press, Inc. [421]

"A Quintessential (ahistorical) Tableau Economique: To Sum Up Pre- and Post-Smith Classical Paradigms," in *Economics Broadly Considered, Essays in Honour of Warren Samuels*, Jeff Biddle, John B. Davis and Steven G. Medema (eds.). London: Taylor & Francis Books Ltd., 2001, 49–63. Reprinted with permission. [401]

Book Review of *The Economics of Irving Fisher. Reviewing the Scientific Work of a Great Economist*, Hans-E. Loef and Hans G. Monissen (eds.). Cheltenham: Edward Elgar, 1999. *The European Journal of the History of Economic Thought*, vol. 8, no. 2, Summer 2001, 263–270. Reprinted with permission of Taylor & Francis. [556]

"A Modern Post-Mortem on Böhm's Capital Theory: Its Vital Normative Flaw Shared by Pre-Sraffian Mainstream Capital Theory," *Journal of the History of Economic Thought*, vol. 23, no. 3, September 2001, 301–317. Reprinted with the permission of Taylor and Francis Ltd., Basingstoke, UK, whose website is www.tandf.co.uk. [402]

Acknowledgments

"A Personal Tribute to John Harsanyi," *Games and Economic Behavior*, no. 36, 2001, 28–29. Reprinted with the permission of Academic Press, San Diego, California. **[557]**

"One Way to Measure How Much Second Best 'Second Best' Is," in *Economic Theory, Dynamics, and Markets, Essays in Honor of Ryuzo Sato*, Takashi Negishi, Rama Ramachandran and Kazuo Mino (eds.). Norwell, Mass.: Kluwer Academic Publishers, 2001, 1–17. Reprinted with permission. **[484]**

With James Cooper and Thomas Russell. "Characterizing an Area Condition Associated with Minimizing Systems," in *Economic Theory, Dynamics and Markets, Essays in Honor of Ryuzo Sato*, Takashi Negishi, Rama Ramachandran and Kazuo Mino (eds.). Norwell Mass.: Kluwer Academic Publishers, 2001, 391–403. Reprinted with permission. **[455]**

"Economic History and Mainstream Economic Analysis," *Rivista di Storia Economica*, Nuova serie, anno XVII, vol. 17, no. 2, 2001, 271–277. Reprinted with permission. **[456]**

"On Just How Great 'Great Books' Are," *The European Journal of the History of Economic Thought*, vol. 8, no. 3, Autumn 2001, 301–308. Reprinted with permission of Taylor & Francis Ltd., Oxfordshire, UK, whose website is www.tandf.co.uk. **[526]**

"David Ricardo (1772–1823)," *International Encyclopedia of the Social and Behavioral Sciences*, Neil J. Smelser and Paul B. Baltes (eds.). Oxford: Pergamon, 2001, 13330–13334. Copyright © 2001 by Elsevier Science. Reprinted with permission. All rights reserved. **[558]**

"A Ricardo-Sraffa Paradigm Comparing Gains from Trade in Inputs and Finished Goods," *Journal of Economic Literature*, vol. 39, no. 4, December 2001, 1204–1214. Copyright © 2001 by American Economic Association, Nashville, Tennessee. All rights reserved. **[422]**

"Modern Finance Theory Within One Lifetime," in *Mathematical Finance-Bachelier Congress 2000*, Hélyette Geman, Dilip Madan, Stanley R. Pliska, and Ton Vorst (eds). Berlin, Heidelberg and New York: Springer Verlag, 2001, 41–45. Reprinted with permission. **[483]**

Book Review of *Globalization and the Theory of Input Trade*, Ronald W. Jones, Cambridge, Mass.: The MIT Press, *Review of International Economics*, vol. 9, no. 3, 2001, 547–549. Reprinted with permission of Blackwell Publishers Limited. **[513]**

"Samuelson on Harry [Gordon Johnson], The Full Achiever," *The American Journal of Economics and Sociology*, vol. 60, no. 3, July, 2001, 601–606. Reprinted with permission of Blackwell Publishers, Inc. All rights reserved. **[564]**

"Paul Samuelson," interview in *Reflections on the Great Depression*, Randall E. Parker. Cheltenham, U.K. and Northampton, Mass.: Edward Elgar, 2002, 25–40. Reprinted with permission. **[437]**

"Pastiches From an Earlier Politically Incorrect Academic Age," in *Editing Economics: Essays in Honour of Mark Perlman*, Hank Lim, Ungsuh K. Park and Geoffrey C. Harcourt (eds.). London and New York: Routledge, 2002, 47–55. Reprinted with permission. All rights reserved. **[593]**

"Reply: Complementary Innovations by Roy Harrod and Alvin Hansen," *History of Political Economy*, vol. 34, no. 1, Spring 2002, 219–223. Reprinted with permission of Duke University Press. Copyright © 2002 Duke University Press. **[435]**

"My Bertil Ohlin," in *Bertil Ohlin, A Centennial Celebration (1899–1999)*, Ronald Findlay, Lars Jonung and Mats Lundahl (eds.). Cambridge, Mass.: The MIT Press, 2002, 51–61. Reprinted with permission. **[559]**

"Innovational Progress Sans Thrifts," *Japan and the World Economy*, vol. 14, no. 3, 2002, 281–84. Copyright © 2002, with permission of Elsevier Science, B.V., Amsterdam. All rights reserved. **[514]**

"The State of the World Economy," in *Monetary Stability and Economic Growth, A Dialog Between Leading Economists*, Robert A. Mundell and Paul J. Zak (eds.). Cheltenham: Edward Elgar Publishing Limited, 2002, 24–37. Reprinted with permission. **[515]**

"Edmund Phelps, Insider-Economists' Insider," in *Knowledge, Information and Expectations in Modern Macroeconomics, in Honor of Edmund S. Phelps*, Philippe Aghion, Roman Frydman, Joseph Stiglitz and Michael Woodward (eds.). Princeton: Princeton University Press, 2003, 1–2. Copyright © 2003 by Princeton University Press. Reprinted with permission of Princeton University Press. **[560]**

"Brief First Critique of Sraffa's Unfinished Critique of Marginalism," in *Regulation, Competition and the Market Economy, Festschrift für Carl Christian von Weizsäcker*, Hans G. Nutzinger (ed.). Göttingen: Vandenhoeck & Ruprecht, 2003, 3–21. Reprinted with permission. **[423]**

"What Ricardo et al. Didn't Quite Understand about Their Own System," in *Faith, Reason, and Economics, Essays in Honour of Anthony Waterman*, Derek Hum (ed.). Winnipeg: St. John's College Press, 2003, 203–211. Reprinted with permission. **[403]**

"A Few Theoretical Aspects of Deregulation," *Japan and the World Economy*, vol. 15, no. 1, 2003, 131–133. **[517]**

"Pure Theory Aspects of Industrial Organization and Globalization," *Japan and the World Economy*, vol. 15, no. 1, 2003, 89–90. **[516]**

Acknowledgments

"Multiple Priorities in Evolving Scholarly Disciplines," *History of Political Economy*, vol. 35, no. 2, 2003, 333–334. Reprinted with permission of Duke University Press, Durham, North Carolina. **[436]**

"A Small Pearl for Doctor Stiglitz's Sixtieth Birthday: When Risk Averters Positively Relish 'Excess Volatility,'" in *Economics for an Imperfect World, Essays in Honor of Joseph E. Stiglitz*, Richard Arnott, Bruce Greenwald, Ravi Kanbur and Barry Nalebuff (eds.). Cambridge, Mass.: The MIT Press, 2003, 11–16. Reprinted with permission. **[485]**

"Reflections on the Schumpeter I Knew Well," *Journal of Evolutionary Economics*, vol. 13, no. 5, December, 2003, 463–467. Reproduced in *Entrepreneurship, the New Economy and Public Policy, Schumpeterian Perspectives*, Uwe Cantner, Elias Dinopoulos and Robert Lanzillotti (eds.). Berlin, Heidelberg and New York: Springer Verlag. Copyright © 2005 by Springer Verlag. Reprinted with permission. **[561]**

"Memoirs of an Early Finance Theorist," in *Modern Risk Management: A History*, introduced by Peter Field. London: Risk Books, 2003, 587–589. Reprinted with permission. **[594]**

"The Hawkins and Simon Story Revisited," in *Models of a Man, Essays in Memory of Herbert A. Simon*, Mie Augier and James G. March (eds.). Cambridge, Mass.: The MIT Press, 2004, 153–162. Reprinted with permission. **[424]**

"A Portrait of the Master as a Young Man," in *Wassily Leontief and Input-Output Economics*, Erik Dietzenbacher and Michael L. Lahr (eds.). Cambridge: Cambridge University Press, 2004, 3–8. Reprinted with permission of Cambridge University Press. All rights reserved. **[562]**

"Abram Bergson, 1914–2003, A Biographical Memoir by Paul A. Samuelson," in *Biographical Memoirs*, vol. 84. Washington, DC: The National Academies Press, 2004, 3–14. Reprinted with permission of **Biographical Memoirs V. 84** © 2004 by the National Academy of Sciences, courtesy of the National Academies Press, Washington, DC. **[563]**

"Paul A. Samuelson," in *The Changing Face of Economics, Conversations with Cutting Edge Economists*, David Colander, Richard P.F. Holt and J. Barkley Rosser, Jr. (eds.). Ann Arbor, Michigan: The University of Michigan Press, 2004, 309–313. Reprinted with permission. All rights reserved. **[592]**

"Alice Bourneuf," in *Notable American Women, A Biographical Dictionary Completing the 20th Century*, Susan Ware (ed.). Cambridge, Massachusetts and London: The Belknap Press of Harvard University Press, 2004, 72–73. Reprinted with permission. **[566]**

Acknowledgments

"The First Fifteen Nobel Laureates in Economics, and Fifteen More Might-Have-Beens." Speech delivered at the Lindau Economics Nobel Laureates Conference, Lindau, Germany, September, 2004. **[591]**

"Where Ricardo and Mill Rebut and Confirm Arguments of Mainstream Economists Supporting Globalization," *Journal of Economic Perspectives*, vol. 18, no. 3, Summer 2004, 135–146. Reprinted with permission of the American Economic Association. Copyright © 2004, American Economic Association, Nashville, Tennessee. All rights reserved. With Erkko Etula, revised, unpublished Appendices I and II. **[448]**

"Conservation Laws in Economics," *Japan and the World Economy*, 16, 2004, 243–246. **[457]**

With James B. Cooper and Thomas Russell. "Testing the Expected Utility Maximization Hypothesis with Limited Experimental Data," *Japan and the World Economy* 16, 2004, 391–407. **[458]**

"The Backward Art of Investing Money," *The Journal of Portfolio Management*, 30th Anniversary Issue, September, 2004, 30–33. Reprinted with permission of *The Journal of Portfolio Management*, 488 Madison Avenue, New York, New York 10022. All rights reserved. **[486]**

"As Bad As Ricardo," in Comments, *Journal of Economic Perspectives*, vol. 19, no. 3, Summer, 2005, 242–244. Reprinted with permission of American Economic Association. **[449]**

"An Elizabethan Age for Pure Trade Theory: 1925–55," *Review of International Economics*, vol. 13, no. 5, 2005, 1001–1003. Reprinted with permission of Blackwell Publishing, Ltd. All rights reserved. **[404]**

"Franco: A Mind Never at Rest," *Banco Nazionale del Lavoro Quarterly Review*, vol. 58, nos. 233–234, June-September, 2005, 5–6. Reprinted with permission. **[565]**

"An Interview with Paul Samuelson: Welfare Economics, 'Old' and 'New', and Social Choice Theory," Kotaro Suzumura, *Social Choice and Welfare*, vol. 25, 2005, 327–356. Reprinted with the kind permission of Springer Science and Business Media, and Kotaro Suzumura. **[450]**

With Erkko Etula. "Testing to Confirm that Leontief-Sraffa Matrix Equations for Input/Output Must Obey Constancy of Returns to Scale," *Journal of Economics Letters*, vol. 90, 2006, 183–188. Reprinted with permission of Elsevier Science, B.V., Amsterdam. **[425]**

With Erkko Etula. "Two Alternative Hypothetical 'Lost' 1814 Ricardo Manuscripts: New-Century Bearings," *History of Political Economy*, vol. 38, no. 1, Spring, 2006, 1–14. Reprinted with permission of Duke University Press, Durham, North Carolina. **[405]**

Acknowledgments

With Erkko Etula. "Complete Work-up of the One-sector Scalar-Capital Theory of Interest Rate: Third Installment Auditing Sraffa's Never-completed 'Critique of Modern Economic Theory,'" *Japan and the World Economy*, vol. 18, no. 3, August 2006, 331–356. Reprinted with permission of Elsevier Science, B.V., Amsterdam. **[426]**

"The Pros and Cons of Globalization," *Japan and the World Economy*, vol. 18, no. 4, December 2006, 593–594. Reprinted with permission of Elsevier Science, Ireland. **[518]**

Foreword to *Louis Bachelier's Theory of Speculation, the Origins of Modern Finance*. Translated and commentary by Mark Davis and Alison Etheridge. Princeton: Princeton University Press, 2006, vii–xi. Reprinted with permission. **[487]**

"Reflections on How Biographies of Individual Scholars Can Relate to a Science's Biography," Foreword to *Inside the Economists's Mind, Conversations with Eminent Economists*, Paul A. Samuelson and William A. Barnett (eds.). Oxford: Blackwell Publishing Ltd., 2007, viii–x. Reprinted with permission. All rights reserved. **[527]**

By William Barnett, "An Interview with Paul A. Samuelson," in *Inside the Economist's Mind, Conversations with Eminent Economists*, Paul A. Samuelson and William A. Barnett (eds.). Oxford: Blackwell Publishing Ltd., 2007, 143–164. Reprinted with permission. All rights reserved. **[528]**

"Classical and Neoclassical Harmonies and Dissonances," *The European Journal of the History of Economic Thought*, vol. 14, no. 2, June 2007, 243–271. Reprinted with permission. All rights reserved. **[427]**

"Is Personal Finance a Science?", in *The Future of Life-Cycle Saving and Investing*, Zvi Bodie, Dennis McLeavey and Laurence B. Siegel, (eds.). Charlottesville, VA: The Research Foundation of CFA Institute, 2007, 1–4. Reproduced and republished from the Research Foundation of CFA Institute publication *The Future of Life-Cycle Saving and Investing* (October 2007). **[488]**

"Affectionate Reminiscences of Richard Musgrave," *FinanzArchiv*, vol. 64, no. 2, June 2008, 166–168. Reprinted with permission. All rights reserved. **[567]**

"Asymmetric or Symmetric Time Preference and Discounting in Many Facets of Economic Theory: A Miscellany," *Journal of Risk and Uncertainty*, vol. 37, nos. 2/3, December 2008, 107–114. Reprinted with permission of Springer Science and Business Media. **[489]**

"An Economist Even Greater Than His High Reputation," in *Markets, Money and Capital: Hicksian Economics for the Twenty First Century*, Roberto Scazzeri, Amartya Sen and Stefano Zamagni (eds.). Cambridge: Cambridge University Press, 2009, 49–51. Reprinted with permission. All rights reserved. **[568]**

"Three Moles," *Bulletin*, vol. 62, no. 2, Winter 2009, 83–84. Cambridge, Mass.: American Academy of Arts and Sciences. © Paul A. Samuelson. **[595]**

"Remembering Milton Friedman," in *Milton Friedman, Nobel Monetary Economist, a review of his theories and policies*, K. Puttaswamaiah (ed.). Enfield, New Hampshire: Isle Publishing Company, 2009, 31–36. Reprinted with permission. **[569]**

"Advance of Total Factor Productivity from Entrepreneurial Innovations," in *Entrepreneurship, Growth, and Public Policy*, Zoltan J. Acs, David B. Audrestch and Robert J. Strom (eds.). Cambridge and New York: Cambridge University Press, 2009, 71–78. **[529]**

"Paul A. Samuelson," interview in *Roads to Wisdom, Conversations with Ten Nobel Laureates in Economics*, Karen Ilse Horn. Cheltenham: Edward Elgar Publishing Limited, 2009, 39–57. Reprinted with permission. **[596]**

"Thünen: An Economist Ahead of His Times," Preface to *The Isolated State in Relation to Agriculture and Political Economy, Part III: Principles for the Determination of Rent, the Most Advantageous Rotation Period and the Value of Stands of Varying Age in Pinewoods, Johann Heinrich von Thünen*, Ulrich van Suntum (ed.). New York: Palgrave Macmillan, St. Martin's Press, 2009, xii–xiv. Preface © Paul A. Samuelson. **[571]**

"A Few Remembrances of Friedrich von Hayek (1899–1992)," *Journal of Economic Behavior and Organization*, 69, January 2009, 1–4. Reprinted with permission. All rights reserved. **[570]**

"An Enjoyable Life Puzzling over Modern Finance Theory," *Annual Review of Financial Economics*, vol. 1, December 2009, 19–35. Palo Alto: Annual Reviews. Reprinted with permission from the *Annual Review of Financial Economics*, Volume 1. © Annual Reviews www.annualreviews.org. **[491]**

"Testing Whether the 'Capital Reversal' Syndrome Mandates Deadweight Loss in Competitive Intertemporal Equilibrium," in *Economic Theory and Economic Thought, Essays in Honour of Ian Steedman*, John Vint, J. Stanley Metcalfe, Heinz D. Kurz, Neri Salvadori and Paul A. Samuelson (eds.). Abingdon: Routledge, 2010, 167–173. Reprinted with permission of Taylor & Francis Group. All rights reserved. **[459]**

"The Richard Goodwin Circle at Harvard (1938–1950)" in *Computable, Constructive and Behavioural Economic Dynamics, Essays in Honour of Kumaraswamy (Vela) Velupillai*, Stefano Zambelli (ed.). Abingdon:

Routledge, 2010, 49–54. Reprinted with permission of Taylor & Francis Group. All rights reserved. [573]

"On the Himalayan Shoulders of Harry Markowitz," in *Handbook of Portfolio Construction: Contemporary Applications of Markowitz Techniques*, John B. Guerard (ed.). New York: Springer U.S., 2010, 125–132. Reprinted with permission. [492]

"In Search of George Stigler and the Chicago School—A Conversation with Paul Samuelson," *Southside Blues: Conversations in Search of George Stigler*, Craig Friedman. Cheltenham: Edward Elgar Publishing. Forthcoming. Printed with permission of Craig Friedman. [597]

"The Schumpeter Circle at Harvard: 1932–1950," *Journal of Evolutionary Economics*. Forthcoming in a special issue on Joseph Schumpeter. Printed with permission of the editor. [572]

INDEX

Abernathy, William J., 314
Accumulation of Capital (Robinson), 932
Addison-Wesley publishers, 255–256
Additive separability, 626–627
Additive-utility independence of goods, Leontief condition, 829
Adiabatic contour, 655
Aging, risk tolerance and, 159
Allen, Robert Loring, 634
Altruism, 505, 871
　inclusive fitness doctrine and, 501–502
　trend away from, 428, 572
　weakness of, 838
Alzati, Fausto, 453
An American Dilemma (Myrdal), 533–534
American Economic Association, 306, 632, 880
American Economic Review, 590
American economists, 278, 287
American Keynes, 302–303
Annuity, variable lifetime, 226
Anti-Catholicism, 952, 1086
Anticipations of the General Theory (Patinkin), 911, 912
Anti-Keynesianism, 291, 423, 998, 1000–1001
Anti-Samuelson (Linder & Sensat), 1009, 1061

Anti-Semitism
　among eminent economists, 566, 882, 978
　against Friedman, 1129
　at Ivy League colleges, 1083–1084, 1088–1090
　at MIT, 764
　at University of Chicago, 1120
Argentina, 454
Arnold, Kenneth J., 900
Arrow, Kenneth J., 32, 105, 834, 1072, 1073, 1075
Asia, 453
Asset allocation timing, 45–48, 95–100
Austrian opportunity-cost doctrines, 772$n.$3
Austrian School, 287, 637
Autarky, 343, 435–436
　Haberler's view on, 640
　per capita incomes, 524
　personal factor endowments, 815

Bachelier, Louis, 187–188, 218–218, 235–236, 249
Bachelier-Kruizenga theory of price formulation, 236
Balanced budget multiplier theorem, 330, 990–991
Balance-of-payment deficit, U.S., 294
Bank failures, 297
Banking Process, The (Rodkey), 973–974

Index

Baran, Paul, 642
Barnett, William, 553–574
Barone, Enrico, 639
Barro, Robert, 1035
Beat the Market: A Scientific Stock Market System (Thorp & Kassof), 248, 270–272
Becker, Gary, 592, 862–863, 1112, 1133
Belgium, 451–452
Bellman-Beckman-Phelps recursive techniques, 819
Bellman type algorithm, *vs.* Lagrange multiplier technique, 59, 61, 137–138
Bergson, Abram (Burk, Abram), 832–840, 1076
Bergson-Samuelson social welfare functions, 554
Bernoulli utility maximizer (Bernoulli logarithmic utility), 6–10, 13–16, 46, 47
Bhagwati, Jagdish, 514–516, 527–528
Bicksler, Jim, 151
Bigotry, 1086–1087
Birkhoff, George, 765, 1089–1090
Bishop, Robert, 105
Bismarck, Otto von, 347–348
Bissell, Dick, 999
Blacks, racial discrimination and, 312, 1086, 1088
Black-Scholes-Merton formula for equilibrium, 190–191, 248
Black-Scholes option pricing formula, 165, 221
Blaug, Mark, 908, 909, 912–913
Bliss, Christopher, 784
Blough, Roger, 296
Bodie, Zvi, 101, 168
Bodie-other Samuelson effect, 93
Böhm-Bawerk, Eugen von, 637
Böhm-Bawerk period of production, 1118
Bohr, Jarald, 618
Bohr, Neils, 638
Bond market, 159
Books. (*See also specific books*)
  Schumpeter's recommendations on, 546–549
  textbook sales, 287
  writing economic textbooks, 1003
Bortkiewicz, Ladislaus, 830
Boulding, Kenneth, 1076
Bourneuf, Alice, 852–853, 874, 1086
Bowker, Albert, 900, 1123
Bragg, Sir William, 712
Bretton Woods system, 509, 981, 1070

Brody, Andrew, 474
Brownian motion, economic, 235–244
Buckley, William, 863–864, 995, 1008
Budget deficits, U.S.
  Federal Reserve policy and, 392–394
  Reaganomics and, 343–344, 1034–1036
  structural, 293–295, 392
Buffalo, University of, 1084
Buffett, Warren, 88, 152–153, 249
Bullock, C.W., 25–26
Bundesbank, 363, 392–393, 395
Bundy, McGeorge, 27
Burbank, Harold Hitchings, 1086–1088
Burk, Abram (Bergson, Abram), 832–840, 1076
Burns, Arthur, 981
Bush, George W., 225
Bush, Vannevar, 761, 1095
Business cycles
  between-wars period, 20*n*.1
  persistence, 301–304
  phases, 641
  prediction, 283
Business Cycles (Schumpeter), 547, 633, 823, 875
Business cycle theory, 321, 1099

Cabot, Paul, 27
Call or put options, 235–236
Cambridge capital controversy, 555
Cambridge Handbook on Money (Robertson), 561
Cambridge University, 696, 747, 845, 1086
Canada, military personnel, 348
Cannan, Edwin, 979, 992
Canonical classical growth model, 685–690, 908
Capital and interest theory, 816
Capital-budgeting techniques, 314
Capital disposal concept, 741
Capital formation, failed, 440
Capital input, 871–872
Capitalism
  criticisms of, 625
  laissez-faire (*See Laissez-faire*)
  realization problem, 699
Capitalism, Socialism, and Democracy (Schumpeter), 308, 631, 632, 702, 823, 875
Capital theory, 871–872, 1098
Carlyle, Thomas, 428
Carter administration, 309
Carver, Thomas Nixon, 979

Index

Cassel, Gustav
  dichotomy between barter-and-money economy, 914–919
  general equilibrium (*See* General equilibrium theory)
  influences on, 741
  personality of, 739–740, 743–744
  posthumous fame, 742–743
  purchasing power parity and, 507–508
  revealed demand approach, 734, 736
  revealed preference theory and, 736–739
  standard utility equilibrium, 735–736
  theory of output, 320
  Walras-Cassel constant-returns-to-scale model, 814–815
  Wicksell, Knut and, 757
  writings of, 705, 740
Cassels, John, 936
Catchings, Waddell, 974–976
Central banks
  Deutsche Bundesbank, 363, 392–393, 395
  expansion, 310
  money supply and, 751–752
  poor performance of, 392–393
  in U.S. (*See* Federal Reserve)
Central limit law, 31
Chakravarty, Sukhamoy, 696–701, 703, 707
Chamberlain, Owen, 1013
Chamberlin, Edward
  monopolistic competition revolution, 747
  on racial discrimination, 1088
  Robinson, Joan and, 240, 940
  writings of, 306, 665, 822, 979, 1130
Chapman, John Jay, 620
Chicago, University of, 1084, 1107, 1120
  anti-Semitism, 1120
  Columbia University and, 978
  Cowles Commission Conference of 1949, 1121–1122
  explanation of Great Depression, 972–973
  faculty (*See* Chicago School)
  Harris Foundation Lectures, 980–981
  oral tradition, 362, 560–561
  Samuelson, Paul A. and, 562–566, 569–570, 891–892, 971–972, 977–978 1105, 1039–1040
  vs. Harvard University, 981–982
Chicago Federal Reserve Bank, 562
Chicago School
  Becker, Gary and, 592
  first (1920–1950), 592, 1039 (*See also* Knight, Frank; Simons, Henry; Viner, Jacob)
  laissez faire and, 940
  macro paradigms, 560
  Markowitz, Harry and, 220, 262–263, 548, 1092
  optimality of market mechanisms, 283
  second (1960), 592, 1039 (*See also* Friedman, Milton; Stigler, George)
Chile, 451
China, 279, 347, 457, 463, 577
City College of New York, 1085, 1086
Clapham, J.H., 664
Clark, Colin, 519, 911, 917
Clark, J.M., 324, 917
Clark, John Bates, 632, 876
Classical economics
  canonical growth model, 685–690, 908
  economists of 1750–1870, 578
  Malthus, Robert and, 330, 576–577, 981
  math, thermodynamics and, 478–479
  Mill, John Stuart and (*See* Mill, John Stuart)
  in other countries, 276–277
  Patinken's view on, 910
  Ricardo, David and (*See* Ricardo, David)
  Say's Law (*See* Say's Law)
  Smith, Adam and, 578, 835, 867, 908 (*See also* Invisible Hand doctrine)
  weaknesses of, 1027
Classical theory of commodity money, 169–186
  generalizations, 181–185
  gold mined at risking supply cost and, 176–181
  labor-theory-of-value scenario, 170–176
  qualifications, 181–185
Clausius-Boltzmann-Georgescu second law. (*See* Thermodynamics, second law)
Cliometrics, 882
Club-of-Rome model of exhaustible resources, 657
Coase Theorem, 1125
Cobb-Douglas production functions, 915
Cohen, Morris, 1085
Collaboration, in science, 1017–1025
  advantages of, 1021–1022
  joint authorship, 1011–1016
  modes of, 1019–1021
  strained relationships and, 1018–1019
  vs. individualism, 1017–1018

1195

Index

Colleges and foundations, investing for, 151–157
Common Fund, 27
Communism
    party members at universities, 879–880, 976–977, 1128 (*See also* McCarthy committee)
    perfect competition and, 623–624
    vs. mixed-market economy, 427
Communist Manifesto (1848), 578
Comparative advantage, 462
Comparative advantage theory, 405–407
Competitive arbitrage, 728
Compound interest, 228
Compton, Karl, 1009
Conrad, Alfred, 882, 1087
Constant absolute risk aversion, 36–41
Constant elasticity of substitution function, 838
Constant relative risk aversion, 33, 35–37, 166–167
Consumer demand theory, 626
Consumption, 606
Contact structures, 647
A Contribution to the Theory of the Trade Cycle (Hicks), 883
Copper, 489, 657
Cornell University, 1084
Correspondence principle, 554, 1050, 1099
Cost-of-living index, 298
Cowles Commission, 189, 1121–1122
Cox, Archie, 957–958
Cramer, Gabriel, 10
Cramer utility, 9, 10
CREF (S&P 500 Index), 27
Culbertson, John M., 342
Currency systems
    dollar (*See* Dollar)
    exchange rate (*See* Exchange rate)
    single, 454–455
Currie, Lauchlin, 988–989

Danzig linear programming, 476
Darwin, Charles, 330, 501, 502, 503, 547, 578*n*.1
Debreu, Gerald, 1134
Debt-deflation theory, 428, 795
Defense expenditures, 295
Denison, Edward, 306, 313
Depression of 1929–1935. (*See* Great Depression of 1929–1935)
Deregulation, 458–460
Derived marginal utility, in dynamic stochastic programming, 59–67

Deutsche Bundesbank, 363, 392–393, 395
De Vegh, Imre, 824
Dewing, Arthur, 25
Differential equations, second-order, 328
Dillon, Douglas, 962
Director, Aaron
    Chicago School and, 590, 592
    Samuelson, Paul A. and, 1117, 1124, 1127, 1131
Discounted dividends model, 607
Discounting, intertemporal, 230
Displaced constant relative risk aversion, 166–167
Distributive inequality, 105–122
Diversification
    across-time *vs.* within-time, 45–48, 56, 68–81, 124, 125, 131–138, 160
    after 1950, 420
    broad, 86–87
    canny principle, 54–56
    many-period, 77–78
    optimal, 75, 263–267
    risk corrected returns and, 154, 156–157, 162, 165
Dollar
    averaging, 50, 155
    depreciation, 294–295, 1070
    foreign exchange value, 360, 361, 364, 365
    overevaluation, 508–509, 1069
    shortage, 346
Double Helix (Watson & Crick), 547, 712, 1015
Douglas, Paul, 228, 579, 590, 591, 980
Dow Jones Index, 446, 848

East Germany, 427
Eccles, Mariner, 994
Eclectism, 291
Econometrica, 938, 997
Econometric measurement, 1027
Econometrics, 288, 605, 894–895, 937
Econometric Society, 605, 652
Economic Consequences of the Peace (Keynes), 811
Economic crises, 296–299
Economic cycles, 296–299
Economic growth, post-war, 308
Economic history, 414–419, 851, 1069
The Economic Journal (Cannan), 979
An Economic Program for American Democracy (Hansen), 991
Economics, 287–292
    classical (*See* Classical economics)
    education, 388–391, 1111–1112

1196

Index

evolution of, 388–391, 1100–1101
fallibility of, 1026–1038
future development, 284–285
geographic convergence, 276–277
growth of, 939
historiography of, 908–922
inexactness of, 420–421
institutionalist, 278
internal advances, 427–428
interrelationship with physics, 720–723
Islamic, 278–279
Kennedy administration and, 1069–1071
Keynesian (*See* Keynesianism)
language barriers and, 317–318
Marxism and, 278–279
migration-of-factor scenarios, 723–731
neoclassical (*See* Neoclassical economics)
Nobel Prize in, 585–587, 863, 948–949, 1072–1077
patterns, differentiation of, 317–318
physics and, 720–723, 727–731
politics and (*See* Political economy)
postwar, 280, 580–581
present state, 275–285
progress from 1932–1991, 935–949
public reputation, 1029
thermodynamics and, 474–491, 647, 654–685
twentieth century trends, 288–289
Economics: An Introductory Analysis (Samuelson)
criticisms of, 996
decision to write, 996, 1060
enlargement in 1983, 1079
evolution of, 1061
fiftieth anniversary of, 224, 1065–1068
first edition (1948), 1060, 1063–1064, 1079
graph of historical real wage growth, 577
reviews, 1060
Economic science. (*See* Economics)
Economics of Control, The (Lerner), 930, 1001
Economics of Imperfect Competition, The (Robinson), 931, 979
Economics of Irving Fisher, The (Loef & Monissen), 793–800
Economics of Planning Public Works (Clark), 324
Economics of the Recovery Program, The (Schumpeter, Leontief & Chamberlin), 556, 973, 979, 991
Economic theory
  discounting in, 227–234
  of finance (*See* Finance theory)
  in future, 1112
  of index numbers, 637
  progress, 1111
Economists. (*See also specific economists*)
  of 1930–1980, 923–934
  classical of 1750–1870, 578
  conservative, 861, 889
  English, 862
  generalist, 568
  Keynesian, 641, 863
  liberal, 982
  mathematical, 569–570
  neoclassical, 728
  Nobel laureate, 1072–1077
  personal motive/experiences of, 550–552
  self-complacency and, 1028
  Swedish (*See* Heckscher, Eli; Ohlin, Bertil)
  technical change and, 576–577
  uneasiness with altruism, 501
Economy as a Circular Flow, The (Leontief), 693–695
Economy as hourglass rather than pendulum, 488, 627–628, 647n.1, 657, 789
Efficient market hypotheses, 249–250
Einstein, Albert, 218, 638, 765, 830
Eisenhower, Ike, 950–951, 953, 954, 1070
E-K-S system, 518–519
Elements of Economics, The (Tarshis), 1007–1008
Elkana, Yehuda, 329–330
Ellis, Howard, 1000–1001
Eminent Economists: Their Life Philosophies (Szenberg), 433–434
Employment. (*See also* Unemployment)
  full, 311–312, 558–559, 997–998
  government, 890
Energy functions, 469–473, 729–731
  conserved, 469–470, 656
  of Gibbs, 476–477, 482
  of Joule, 654–655
Engels, Friedrich, 578
Enthalpy, Gibbsian, 479
Entrepreneurial innovation, total factor productivity and, 575–582
Entropy, 729, 789, 797
  fixed, 482–483
  max-entropy formulation, 730
  maximization, 481–485, 488
Equilibrium discount rates, 231
Equilibrium of Heterogeneous Substances (Fisher), 653–654

1197

Index

Equity/equities
  age-phase reduction, 101–103
  long-horizon risk tolerance, 124–130
  long-term case, 49–58, 158–159
  market exposure shifts, 160
  premium, excessive, 233
  return rates, 92, 98–99
Erdös, Paul, 843
Escrow, 102
Essay on Marxian Economics (Robinson), 660–663, 932
Essay on the Nature and Significance of Economic Science (Robbins), 892
Essays on Employment (Robinson), 312
Euler's principle, 328
Euro, 454
European economics, divergence with American economics, 379–387
European Union, 385
Exchange rate
  collapse, with currency meltdowns, 452–453
  dollar-euro, 443–445
  flexible, 283
  instability, 405
  Penn effect and, 507, 509–512
  purchasing power parity and, 507–509
Export trade, 643, 911

Factor-price equalization, 576, 728
  factor intensity reversals and, 494–496
  incomplete, 493–494
  joint products and, 496–498
  no-joint products and, 492–493
  perfect, 493
  Robinson, Joan and, 666–668
  theory, 555, 1012
  Tinbergen, Jan and, 719–720
Factor price returns, regional, 580–581
Fallacy of composition, 501
False weight coin puzzle, 750
Fama, Eugene, 250
Farm production, total value, 303
Farnam, Henry W., 649
Fascism, American, 889–890
Fascist societies, 891
Federal Reserve
  from 1989–1993, 392–398
  in 1931, 306
  budget deficits and, 392–394
  Eccles, Mariner and, 994
  efficacy of, 310–311
  inflation targeting, 395–398
  overstimulus in 1972–73, 395
  policy, 392–394, 450
  production index fluctuations and, 301–302
  rates, 559–560
  rational-expectationist forecast, 309
  success, 308
  understimulus in 1929–33, 395
  Volcker, Paul and, 293, 294, 343, 392, 393, 396, 398, 425, 429
Feller, Willy, 900–901
Fellner, William, 998
Finance (Bodie & Merton), 168
Finance theory, modern, 164, 188–190, 245–261
First law of thermodynamics, 627
Fischer, Stan, 296
Fisher, A.G.B., 519
Fisher, Irving, 771n.2, 794–800, 876
  contributions to economics, 604–605, 651–652
  free trade and, 435
  Gibbs, Willard and, 652–653
  Haberler, Gottfried and, 637, 639
  neoclassical capital theory, 651–652
  personal biography, 603, 652, 1131
  quantity theory of money and, 259
  scientific standing, 603–604
  theory of capital and interest, 605–609
  writings of, 602–603, 605–607, 609, 651–654, 794, 823–824, 1003
Fisher, R.A., 503, 764, 1011, 1132
Fisher-Marshall-Pigou MV=PQ paradigm, 561
Fitness functions, for classical economics, 684–690
Flemming, John, 911
Ford Foundation, 27
Ford Motors, 959
Forecasting
  post-Camelot models, 422–423
  short-term, 447–448
Foreign competition, 381–383
Forestry optimization, 871
Fortune-500 companies, 381
Foster, William T., 974–976
Foundations and colleges, investing for, 151–157
Foundations of Economic Analysis (Samuelson)
  awards/prizes for, 1042, 1050
  background knowledge, 1043–1044
  criticisms, 1005–1006
  decision to write, 1108
  enlarged edition, 1042–1043

1198

Index

first edition (1948), 1004–1005, 1007
influences on, 1046–1047
mathematical economics and, 554, 986–987
mistakes in, 1042
neoclassical economics and, 554
organization of, 1049–1050
readers queries, answers for, 1047–1049
revealed preference paradigm and, 1044–1046
success, 1043
third edition, 1005
timing of, 565, 1039–1041
topics, 555, 1049, 1050*n*.2
Weintraub effect, 1051–1055
Fractals, 764
Franklin, Rosalind, 712
Free energy
Gibbsian, 479
Helmholz, 479
Freeman, Harold, 778–781, 901, 966, 967
Freeman, Ralph, 779
Free markets, 312, 891
Free trade
factor-price equalization and (*See* Factor-price equalization)
with foreign innovation, 353–356
Haberler, Gottfried and, 639, 642, 773
harm, reactions to, 356–357
merits, 353
Samuelson's view on, 1100
United States and, 351
U.S. standard of living and, 342–343
vs. fair trade, 341, 357–368
Friedman, Milton, 220, 259, 560, 860–865
Buckley, Bill and, 863–864
Chicago School and, 592
curriculum vitae, 861–862
Hayek, Friedrich von and, 868
I.Q., 862
marriage, 977
monetarism and, 281, 556, 560–561, 573, 795
Nobel Prize, 1073
permanent-income hypothesis, 1032
as polemicist, 1127
positive economics, 892–893
Stigler, George and, 1133
stock risk and, 225
writings of, 389, 391, 562, 626, 862–863, 1005
Friedman-Chicago School. (*See* Chicago School, second)
Friedman-Savage effect, 106, 119–120

Frisch, Ragnar, 322, 837, 926, 1072, 1073, 1075
Fundamental Thoughts in Economics (Cassel), 917, 918
Furry, Wendell, 1128
Future prices, 160

Galbraith, John Kenneth, 620–625, 992
Kennedy administration and, 958, 959, 962
new consciousness and, 538–540
reviews of *Economics: An Introductory Analysis* (Samuelson), 1060
Gale-Kuhn-Tucker concave programming, 476
Galileo, 327, 329
Gambling
horse racing (*See* Track bettor's equilibrium model)
risk tolerance and, 106–108
von Neumann utility, 799
GDP (gross domestic product), 454
General Electric, 621
General equilibrium theory, 713, 736, 773, 940
multi-period price clearing, 607–608
time-phased, 608
Walras's law, 816
General Motors, 621
General Theory of Employment, Interest and Money, The (Keynes)
anticipation of, 323–324, 811–812, 911, 912
connection with Kahn's multiplier, 910, 913–914, 916
criticisms/reviews of, 325–326, 547, 556, 561, 945
Haberler's critique of, 641
Harrod and, 928
Hicks' views on, 858
importance of, 1100
interpretations, 912
Kalecki, Michal and, 930
Model T, 422
multiplier version, 812
paradigms of, 558, 561
Samuelson's views on, 565, 982–984, 1106–1107
Wicksell, Knut and, 752–753
Georgescu-Roegen, Nicholas, 788–793, 1076
economy as hourglass rather than pendulum concept, 488, 627–628, 647*n*.1, 657, 789
entropy economics, 789
writings of, 788–789

1199

Index

German Historical School, 278, 892
Germany
  Bismarck era, 577
  Bundesbank, 363, 392–393, 395
  East, 427
  GNP, 347–348
  West, 347, 363
Gerschenkron, Alexander, 838–839
Gibbs, Willard
  as colleague, 650
  death, 646
  disciples of (*See* Fisher, Irving; Wilson, Edwin Bidwell)
  personal biography, 648–650, 657
  as teacher, 650
  thermodynamics impact on economics, 654–685
  writings of, 648, 649
  at Yale, 646–647, 650
Gibbs growth model, *vs.* von Neumann's growth model, 480–481
Gibbs-Maxwell rule, 486–487
Gibbs thermodynamics
  energy function, 476–477, 482
  enthalpy, 479
  entropy, 482
  free energy, 479
  Min-Min property, 477
  phase transitions, 486
Gibbs-Tisza thermodynamic potentials, 488
Gideonse, Harry, 1124
Gilbert, Richard, 991, 994
Globalization
  industrial organization and, 456–457
  input trade theory and, 435–436
  pros and cons, 461–463
Global production, maximization, 724, 728
GNP. (*See* Gross national product)
God and Man at Yale (Buckley), 1008
God That Failed, The (Koestler), 427
Gold
  mined at risking supply cost, 176–181
  prices, 804
Goods, tradeable, 523–524
Goodwin, Richard
  at Harvard, 879–883
  personal biography, 874, 878–880
Gordon, Robert J., 308, 424–425
Government employment, 890
Graham, Frank, 976
Granger causality tests, 573
Great Britain, 577
Great Challenge symposia of 1961, 557
Great Depression, The (Robbins), 866

Great Depression of 1929–1935
  ending of, 989, 1059–1060
  explanations of, 972–974
  failure to predict, 1021–1032
  forestalling, 310
  impact on Samuelson, 1099–1100
  Roosevelt, Franklin D. and, 305
  University of Chicago and, 1120
Greenough, William C., 27, 92
Greenspan, Alan, 259, 392, 395, 396–398, 423, 429, 438–439, 448–449
Grinnell College, 152–153
Gross domestic product (GDP), 454
Gross national product (GNP)
  budget deficit and, 295
  business cycles and, 304
  cyclical variability, 303
  German, 347–348
  global, 348
  nominal changes, 862
  real, movements in, 1030
  response to panic, 298–299
Growth models
  canonical classical, 685–690, 908
  Gibbs *vs.* von Neumann's, 480–481
  von Neumann's, 474–478
Growth theory, 700, 1098–1099

Haavelmo, Trygve, 901–902, 927
Haberler, Gottfried
  Austrian opportunity-cost doctrines, 772$n.$3
  critique of *The General Theory,* 641
  eclectisim and, 1038
  free trade and, 639, 642, 773
  at Harvard, 767–768, 769, 824, 1129
  influences on, 641
  lectures, 642
  macroeconomics and, 640–642, 769–770
  personal biography, 637, 643–644, 768–769
  as political analyst, 642–643
  positivistic equilibrium, 772–774
  trade theory and, 637, 639–640, 770–772
  writings of, 638, 639, 640, 643, 767
Haberler-Jones-Samuelson 1974 model of labor, 715
Haberler-Pigou effect, 770
Hadley, Arthur T., 649
Haldane, J.B.S., 501–502
Hamilton, W.D., 502
Hansen, Alvin
  on post-war economy, 999
  public *vs.* private expenditure, 302–303

Index

Samuelson, Paul A. and, 438, 991–992
seminars, 989
Williams, John and, 306–307
writings of, 981
Harberger, Al, 447
Hardy, G.H.
collaborations of, 218, 562, 613, 711, 1011, 1021
Wiener, Norbert and, 764
Harriman, Averell, 951
Harris, Seymour, 27, 306, 958
Harrod, Roy, 513–514, 928–929, 1076
Harsanyi, John, 801–802
Hart, Albert Gaylord, 117, 977, 1118
Harvard Economic Society, ABC barometers of business activity, 23–28
Harvard University, 1084, 1086, 1089, 1120
admissions policy of 1923, 1085
anti-Semitism, 566, 1085
departmental appointments, 1087
depression and, 25, 26
economics department, 854–855, 880, 1040
Goodwin circle, 879–883
Jewish students, 1085
Keynes, John Maynard and, 993
portfolio, 27, 151
Samuelson at, 979–980
Schumpeter circle, 873–877 (*See also specific members of Schumpeter circle*)
vs. University of Chicago, 981–982
Harvard University Press, 712, 789
Hawtrey, Ralph, 26
Hayek, Friedrich von
influence on Samuelson, 891–892
information economics and, 867
Nobel Prize of 1974, 866, 867, 1072, 1073, 1074
Pareto efficiency and, 624
view on poverty, 280
writings of, 546, 866, 867–868, 928
Hayes, Robert H., 314
Heckscher, Eli, 580
Heckscher-Ohlin model, 435–436, 808
Heckscher-Ohlin-Samuelson research, 571, 808
Heisenberg, Werner, 1089
Heisenberg indeterminancy principle, 764
Heller, Walter W., 611–612, 962
Henderson, Ernest, 296
Hicks, John, 782–785, 857–859
economic cycles and, 297
influences on, 783
Lerner, Abba and, 929–930

Nobel Prize, 784, 857, 938, 1072
students of, 784
view on *The General Theory*, 858
writings of, 783, 784, 857, 883, 1021
Hicks-Hansen IS-LM diagram, 558
Higgins, Benjamin, 992
Historiography, of economics, 908–922
History of Economic Analysis (Schumpeter), 631, 633, 875, 876
Holland, 451–452
Horizons, 99, 159. (*See also* Long-horizon portfolio)
different, portfolio investing for, 60–61
general t-period decision, 134–135
law of large numbers and, 1093–1094
length of, 3, 19, 166–167, 215–217
long-run, 86–94, 804
multiperiod, 9–11, 16–19, 63–64
one-period, 6–9, 61–62, 128–129, 132–134
portfolio proportions and, 51–52
risk tolerance and, 215–217
two-period, 62–63, 129, 134
Horse racing. (*See* Track bettor's equilibrium model)
Hotelling, Harold, 809–810, 902, 928, 937, 1075
Hotelling function, 478
Houthakker, Hendrik
personal biography, 682–683
purchasing power parity and, 508–509
real-life process movements and, 249
strong axiom of revealed preference, 682, 739, 1045
Human capital, 101, 103, 440*n*.2, 861, 862, 863
Hume, David, 728
Hydraulic physics, 796–797
Hyperinflation, 804

Iacocca, Lee, 341
Identification in time series, 927
Imperfect competition, 288, 593, 1130
Import competition, 342
Import quotas, 341
Import substitution, 643
Inclusive fitness doctrine, 501–504
Income-consumption patterns, 861
Income elasticities, 828
Income inequality, 312–313
Income taxation, 652
Index investing, 86–94, 156, 161–163, 165
Index number theory, 605, 736
India, 347, 696–697

1201

Index

Indifference curves, 637, 773, 815, 829
Industrial organization, globalization and, 456–457
Inflation
  containment, 398
  mid-1960's, 312
  Reagan administration and, 282, 294
  stagnation and, 1029
Information economics, 867
Input-output research of Leontief, 829–830
Input trade theory, 435–436
Instability, macroeconomic, 625
Institutionalist economics, 278
Insurance, 34, 84
Integer dynamic stochastic programming, 131–138
Interest
  as excessive usury, opposition to, 231–232
  Fisher diagram, 606
  simple *vs.* compound, 230
  sources, 228–230
Interest rates
  futures on, 448
  migration scenario and, 724
  natural, 751
  nominal, 751
  real, 293–294
  reductions, 395–396
  targeting, 397–398
  term structure, 850
  to zero in stationary state, 822
Interest theory, 603
International Economic Association, 632
International Encyclopedia of Social Sciences (Baumol; Seiler), 595
International finance, 399–413
International trade, 435–436
International Trade of 1927 (Taussig), 770
International trade theory, 373–378, 593
Intertemporal capital theory, 797
Invariance law of nature, 469–473
Investing, for foundations/colleges, 151–157
Investment horizons. (*See* Horizons)
Investors
  long-run, 3, 15, 96, 152
  with long-run positive alphas, 250–252
  risk-averse, 3, 8–9, 99
  short-run, 15, 152
Invisible Hand doctrine, 276–277, 726, 727, 754, 835, 867
Islamic economics, 278–279
Isotherms, 486
Ivy League colleges, 1089

Japan, 349, 453, 454, 457, 795
  factor price returns, 580–581
  free trade and, 341–342
  innovation and, 353–354
  interest rates, 394
  in late 1950's, 955
  1987 market crash and, 155
  Marxism and, 279, 288–289
  output stagnation, 428
  per capital real income, 346–347
  postwar prosperity, 345–348
  relationship with U.S. (*See* United States-Japan relations)
Jews
  discrimination against (*See* Anti-Semitism)
  early Binet I.Q. tests and, 1089
Johnson, Christopher, 449
Johnson, Harry G.
  at Cambridge, 845
  death, 841, 843
  personal biography, 842–846
  at University of Chicago, 845–846
  writings of, 843
Johnson, Samuel, 862
Joint authorship, 1011–1016. (*See also* Collaboration)
Jones, Paul Tudor, 89
Jorgenson, Dale, 1013
Journal of Political Economy, 590, 972, 1126
Juglar, Clement, 297

Kahn, Richard
  factor-price equalization and, 666, 667
  Keynes *General Theory* and, 910–911, 913–914, 916
Kaldor, Nicholas, 924–925, 943
  theory of distribution, 668–669
  U.K. protectionism and, 353
  writings of, 859
Kalecki, Michal (Michael), 930–931
Kantorovich, Leonid, 1073, 1075
Katz, Milton, 1085
Kellogg, Oliver, 765
Kelvin absolute temperature, 655, 727
Kemp, Murray, 786–787
Kennedy, John F.
  anti-Catholicism and, 952
  Blough, Roger and, 296
  debate with Nixon, 961
  economic advisors, 569, 951–963
  intellectual temperament, 956
  during McCarthy era, 952
  Presidential election, 393, 952–953

Index

Kennedy, Joseph, 1086
Kennedy, Ted, 953–954
Kennedy administration, economic programs of, 289–292, 1069–1071
Keynes, Florence Brown, 1086
Keynes, John Maynard
   bull markets of 1920's, 25–26
   at Cambridge University, 696
   equilibrium theory and, 1100
   Federal Reserve seminars, 1001
   Harvard University and, 993
   King's College and, 603
   Lerner, Abba and, 1001
   market system and, 427
   monopolistic competition and, 940–941
   multiplier, 641
   personal biography, 153–154, 980–981, 988, 993–994
   personality of, 250, 304–305
   PQ/M ratio, 795
   Schumpeter's jealousy of, 575, 631, 823, 837, 875, 936
   writings of, 977
Keynes' General Theory: A Retrospective View (Pigou), 556
Keynesian economists
   American, 1005 (*See also* Hansen, Alvin; Tobin, James)
   early, 988
   Model T, 290
   Samuelson, Paul A., 1106
   students in 1937/1938, 991
Keynesianism, 328–329, 980, 987–988
   decline, 864, 1111
   evolution of, 558–559
   Model T, 813, 932, 941, 1000, 1001
   money and, 1000–1001
   opposition to, 986
   popularity of, 994–995
   post-1965 decline, 1006
   post-war spread of, 998–999
   Samuelson, Paul A. and, 565, 989–993
   during World War II, 993
Keynesian revolution, 279–280, 420
   after Kennedy administration, 999–1000
   monopolistic competition revolution and, 984–985
   theory of output as whole, 324
Keynesian Revolution, The (Klein), 986
Keynes-Walras-Lucas economic relations, 15
K-H-S effect (Penn effect), 507, 509–528
Kissinger, Henry A., 557
Klein, Lawrence, 902–903, 1000

Knight, Frank, 972, 977, 982
   atheism, 925
   Chicago School and, 592, 1118, 1124
   lectures, 1131
   personality of, 591, 1124
   real-cost determinants of price, 595
   students of, 1118, 1129
Knightian Chicago School. (*See* Chicago School, first (1920–1950))
Koopmans, Tjalling, 420–421, 647
   identification in time series, 927
   Nobel Prize, 721, 1073
   writings of, 858
Korea, 347, 349
Kravis, Irving, 1075
Kuhn, Thomas, 189, 282, 875, 1028
Kuznets, Simon
   Friedman, Milton and, 861, 862
   long-term savings trends, 1032
   Nobel Prize, 1072–1075
   writings of, 306, 931
Kuznets-Denison productivity growth rates, 313

Labor economics, 1130, 1134
   land and, 657, 790–792
   migrations scenario, 723–727
   supplies, 731
Labor theory of value, 512–513, 805, 1041
LaChatelier principle of convexity, 487
Lagrange multiplier technique, *vs.* Bellman type algorithm, 59, 61, 137–138
Laissez-faire, 698, 1127
   Carlyle, Thomas and, 428–429
   Chicago School and, 940
   competition, 462
   earning capacity and, 754
   efficiency of, 623
   inequality, 625
   libertarian, 429, 430
   Marx, Karl and, 699
   money markets, 395
   pure, 427
   Samuelson's view of, 1100
   stagnation and, 303
   Stigler, George and, 1124, 1125
   Wicksell, Knut and, 756
Lane, Rose Wilder, 1008
Lange, Oskar, 623, 930
Law of conservation of energy, 483–384, 731
Law of diminishing returns, 231, 576, 578, 724, 914, 1014

1203

Index

Law of large numbers
  fallacies/misunderstandings, 52, 53, 97, 126, 152, 1093–1094
  length of investment horizon and, 50, 82–85, 125, 166
  repeated risk taking and, 29–43
Leading indicators methodology, ABC barometers and, 25
LeChatelier-Samuelson principle, 797
LeChatelier theorem, 654, 1041–1042
Legendre transformations, 655
Lending, 228–230
Lenin, Vladimir, 624
Leontief, Wassily, 693–695, 983
  at Harvard, 826–829, 873
  homogeneity postulate, 917, 918–919
  input-output research, 829–830
  Nobel Prize, 1072, 1073, 1074
  Sraffa, Piero and, 693–694
  writings of, 306, 693, 931
Leontief paradox, 516–518
Lerner, Abba, 317, 930, 942
  economic planning in socialist state, 623
  Keynes, John Maynard and, 1001
  writings of, 714, 930
Lerner-Lange system, 623, 624
Lerner-Leontief pure theory of international exchange, 925
Leveraging
  indifference of, 585–586
  optimal, 263–267
Levinson, Norman, 764
Liberal and Illiberal Development Policy (Haberler), 643
Libertarianism, 1100
Life-cycle theory of saving, 585, 850, 1032
Lindahl, Erik, 754–755, 1007
Lindbeck, Assar, 534–541, 545, 1009
Lindner, Kurt, 89
Linear programming, 721
Liquidity traps, 259, 561–562
List, Friedrich, 277
Littauer School, 306–307
Living standards, 295
Location theory, 814
Logarithmic utility, one-period, 6–7
Logical positivism, 892–893
Long-horizon portfolio, 86–94
  buy and hold equities, 50–53
  risk and, 225
  sure-think risk erosion, 82–85
Long-run risk tolerance, 3–21
  canonical test case, 4–6

dynamic programming solutions for multistage timing, 16–19
  multiperiod horizons, 9–11
  one-period logarithmic, 6–7
  one-period nonlogarithmic, 7–9
Long Term Capital Management, 447
Lord Acton, 868
Loss-win innovations, 463
Lotka-Volterra predator-prey model, 1048
Lowell, A. Laurence, 24, 26, 1131
Lucas, Robert, 282, 308. (*See also* Rational expectationism)
Lundberg, Erik, 317, 322, 928
Lyapunov function, 1047–1048, 1053, 1054
Lynch, Peter, 89

Mach, Ernst, 893
Maclaurin, Rupert, 966, 1095
Macroeconomic Dynamics (Tobin & Shiller), 572
Macroeconomics, 420–425
  before 1936, 971–972
  diversity in (*See* Diversification)
  first use of term, 1007
  Haberler, Gottfried and, 640–642, 769–770
  inexactness of, 420–421
  internal stimulation, 319
  new American, 383–384
  political economy and, 300
  positivistic, 986
  Samuelson's view on, 555–556, 573–574
  textbooks, 1007
  use of word, 997
  Wicksell's theory of, 751–752
Macroefficiency, 160
Making of Index Numbers, The (Fisher), 605, 974–975
Malaysia, 451–452
Malthus, Robert, 330. 576–577, 981
Margarine Not Butter pamphlet (Stigler), 1120
Marginal-cost pricing, for railroads/public utilities, 754
Marginalism, 722, 750
Marginal productivities, positive, 724
Market-clearing real interest rate level, 569
Markets
  absence of, 623
  efficient, 87, 220–221
  macro-efficient, 90–91, 165, 445–447
  macro-inefficient, 57, 429
  micro-efficient, 87, 90–91, 165, 252, 429–430, 445–447
  structure, 164

1204

A Market Theory of Money (Hicks), 297
Market timer, 99
Markov matrixes, 4–6, 11–13
Markov processes, 47, 98
Markowitz, Harry, 220, 262–263, 548, 1092
Markowitz-Sharpe-Tobin quadratic programming, 216
Marschak, Jacob, 927
Marshall, Alfred, 663–664, 1017, 1047, 1086
Marx, Karl, 578, 632, 699–706
Marxism, 426–430, 541–542, 708
 disillusionment with, 427
 Japan and, 279, 288–289
 mainstream economics and, 278–279
 militarism and, 350–351
 Robinson, Joan and, 660–663, 932
 surplus value, 699
 upsurges in 1960's, 291
Mason, Edward, 306, 1088
Massachusetts Institute of Technology. (*See* MIT)
Mathematical economics, 795–796, 986–987. (*See also* Econometrics)
Mathematics
 Bachelier's, 218–219
 economist's views on, 334–340, 982
 isomorphisms, 647
Maximizing principles, 1050
Maxwell's demon, 221, 467–468
McCarthy committee
 American fascism and, 889–890
 Eisenhower, Ike and, 950
 ethnic cleansing and, 1009
 Goodwin, Richard and, 881
 Kennedy, John F. and, 952
 Samuelson, Paul A. and, 1060–1061
McDougall, Sir Donald, 719
McKenzie, Lionel, 1076
Meade, James, 927, 1073, 1075
Mean regression, 97–100
Means to Prosperity (Keynes), 324, 981
Memoirs of an Unregulated Economist (Stigler), 621
Menger, Carl, 637, 1118
Merriman, Frisky, 1089
Merton, Robert C.
 Brownian motion and, 101
 collaboration with Zvi Bodie, 168
 Matthew effect, 712, 1019
Merton, Robert K., 149–150, 808, 1019
Merton paradox, 103
Meyer, John, 882

Microeconomics
 nonstationary time series, 560
 Samuelson, Paul A. and, 554
Migration-of-factor scenarios of economics, 723–731
Militarism, 348, 350–351
Mill, John Stuart, 578, 771
 canonical model of growth, 700–701
 progressive steady state, 438
 thriftless case, 440n.2
 writings of, 277
Mills-Ricardo comparative advantage, 462
Min-energy, for thermostatics, 484–485
Mints, Lloyd, 978–979, 1120
Mirowski, Philip, 722–723
Mises, Ludwig von, 637, 768, 867–868
 economic planning in socialist state, 623
 influence on Samuelson, 891–892
Mises, Richard von, 904
MIT, 1089
 anti-Semitism, 764
 economics department, 779, 1004
 graduate school recruiting, 1084
 mathematics department, 761
 postwar, 566
 Radiation Laboratory, 1095
 Wiener, Norbert and, 761
Mitchell, Wesley, 892
MIT-Penn-Federal Reserve Bank macro model, 296, 309–310, 850
Mixed-market economy, 302, 308–314
 argument for, 890
 post-Keynesian, 280, 427
 Samuelson's view on, 1061
 vs. communism, 427
Model of the trade cycle, 924
"Modern consciousness," 540
Modigliani, Franco, 641, 847–851, 1013
 at Carnegie Tech, 848, 849
 contributions to economics, 585–586, 849–851
 lifecycle model, 224, 643, 1032
 MIT-Penn-Fed model, 296, 309–310, 850
 Nobel Prize, 847
 personal biography, 560, 585–586, 943–944
 rational expectationism and, 586–587
 view on Harvard University, 566
 writings of, 559, 848, 1018
Modigliani-Miller theorem, 253–254, 263–267, 849, 850
Modigliani-Tobin partial derivatives, 298
Momentum model of positive autocorrelation, 3–6

1205

Index

Monetarism, 305–306, 390, 396, 1028
  Friedman, Milton and, 281, 556, 560–561, 573, 795
  monistic, 422–423, 429, 448, 864
  renouncement, 396
  scientific development of, 311
A Monetary History of the United States, 1867–1960 (Friedman & Schwartz), 397, 862, 864
Money
  bank creation of, 705
  growth, 862
  lending, 228–230
  and money substitutes, 556
  monoistic monetarism and, 864
  supply (*See* Money supply)
  theories, 917–918 (*See also* Classical theory of commodity money; Quantity theory of money)
  velocity *vs.* interest rates, 290
Money (Robertson), 973
Money, Interest, and Prices (Patinkin), 917, 918
Money managers, 86–87, 156
Money market funds, 556
Money-metric-utility, 462
Money supply, 556–558, 751, 775. (*See also* Quantity theory of money)
  acceleration, 298–299
  central banks and, 751–752
  growth rate, 751
  short-run changes, 862
Monopolistic competition, 747, 940–941, 984–985
Moore, Geoffrey, 303–304
Morgan, Theodore, 1088
Mosak, Jacob, 977, 998, 1084
Mt. Pelerin Society, 868, 890
Multiplier-accelerator macrodynamic model, 555
Multiplier doctrine, 324
Mundell, Robert, 455
Musgrave, Richard, 854–856, 992, 1076
Mutual funds, 90, 125, 224
Myrdal (Myrdahl), Gunnar, 323, 533–534, 1072–1075

Napoleonic fundamental theorem of natural selection, 503
Natural selection, 501–505
Nature of Capital and Income, The (Fisher), 602–603
Neff, John, 89

Neoclassical economics, 422–423, 1039
  Chicago school of (*See* Chicago School)
  Clarkian, 750
  Clark-Solow technology, 814–815
  equilibrium theory, 280
  Foundations of Economic Analysis (Samuelson) and, 554
  Friedman, Milton and, 290
  Samuelson, Paul A. and, 1079–1080
  vs. classical economics, 277
  Wicksell, Knut and, 775–777
Neoclassical synthesis, 422, 1005–1006, 1100
Neo-Keynesians, 283
Neumann, John von
  game theory, 722
  growth model, 474–478
  personality of, 944
  time-phased general equilibrium model, 608
  two-person zero-sum game theory, 475, 721
New classical economics, 282, 290, 429, 572, 752, 1028. (*See also* Rational expectationism)
New Deal of Franklin Roosevelt, 305, 591, 1100, 1107
New left movement, 533, 535, 537–538, 539, 540
New Palgrave: A Dictionary of Economics, The, 602, 752–753, 771, 784, 925, 1124
Newton, Sir Isaac, 327, 329
Nixon, Russ, 1011, 1088
Nixon-Kennedy debate, 961
Nobel Prize, in economics, 585–587, 863, 948–949, 1072–1077
Non-Marxist countries, militarism and, 350–351
Non-profit finance committees, Samuelson, Paul A. and, 258
Non-substitution theorems, 555
Nontradables, labor-intensive, 514–516, 524–528
Normal law, 900, 903

O'Donnell, Ken, 959–960
OECD economies, 304
Ohlin, Bertil, 580, 595, 713, 773
  education, 809
  factor-price-equalization by trade, 719
  geographical trade, 808
  at Harvard, 323
  influences on, 808, 809

Index

Nobel Prize, 810, 1073, 1074
personal biography, 809–810
as politician, 812–814
price-level occupation, 321–322
Stockholm School and, 811–812
theory of output as a whole, 320, 327
trade theory and, 770
transfer controversy, 810–811
writings of, 317, 810, 814–816
Ohlin system, 808
Okun, Arthur, 813
One-employer society, 890
Online trading, 448–449
OPEC crisis of 1973, 294
Opie, Redvers, 874
Opportunity-cost transformation locus. (*See* Production-possibility frontiers)
Optimal equity ratio rule, 75–77
Outlines of Economics (Ely), 1003
Overlapping generations model, 555
Own-price elasticities, 828–829
Own rate of interest concept, 866
Oxford University, 879–880

Pareto, Vilfredo, 639, 713, 806, 835
Pareto-Champernowne distribution, 108
Pareto optimality, 429, 771–772, 835, 889, 1125–1126
Pasinetti, Luigi, 1013
Passion and Craft, 431–432
Patinkin, Don, 317, 324–326, 329, 909–912, 913–920
Pedantical literalness, 911–914
Penn effect, 507–532
P/E ratio, 158–159 (*See also* Price/Earnings ratio)
Per capita incomes, under autarky, 524
Perfect competition, 663
Periodic limit cycles, limit-cycle stable, 883
Perlman, Selig, 1083, 1089
Permanent-income hypothesis, 862, 863, 1032
Personal finance, 223–226, 247–249
Persons, Warren M., ABC barometer and, 23–28
Phelps, Edmund (Ned), 819–820
Phelps-Koopmans permanent inefficiencies, 819
Phillips curve, 311–312, 555
Physics, interrelationship with economics, 720–723, 727–731
Pigou, A.C., 556, 626, 719, 979
Pigou effect, 641, 1001

Plagiarism, 1020
Planck, Max, 431
Poincaré, Henri, 221, 235
Political economy, 576, 625, 699, 805, 890–891
Political Economy of the New Left: An Outsider's View, The (Lindbeck), 1009
Population theory of Malthus, 330
Portfolio
alternative, probability estimations, 139–147
certainty equivalent wealth of actual stochastic wealth, 71
discretionary selection, 86
diversification (*See* Diversification)
indexing (*See* Index investing)
investing for different time horizons, 60–61
life-cycle investing, 233
long-horizon (*See* Long-horizon portfolio)
long-run growth rate, 216
one-period choice, 70
optimization by mean-variance quadratic progamming, 220
proportions, investment horizon and, 51–52
pyramiding, 161
rational management, 86–94
rebalancing, 161
short-horizon, risk and, 225
total return, 156
Portfolio insurance, 56, 247–248
Portfolio managers, 161
Portfolio theory, modern, 608–609
Positivistic equilibrium, 772–774
Post-Keynesians, 312
Postwar Economics (Harris), 999
Poverty, 280
PPP. (*See* Purchasing power parity)
Pre-Houthakker theory, 2-good case, 736–737
Pressure, 470–471, 655–656, 729
Price, Michael, 89
Price/earnings (P/E) ratio, 157, 158–159, 296, 848
Price-level occupation, 320–322
Price levels
microshocks, 395
stability, 298, 328, 395, 752, 775
stationary, 312
Prices and Production (Hayek), 546, 562, 641, 866, 867

1207

Index

Princeton, 1085–1086, 1089
Principia (Newton), 547, 1012
Principles of Political Economy (1848) (Mill), 277, 580*n*.2
Principles of Political Economy and Taxation (Ricardo), 805, 806
Prisoner's dilemma, 501
Probability estimation, relative risk-corrected returns of alternative portfolios, 139–147
Production index, fluctuations, 301–302
Production of Commodities by Means of Commodities, The (Sraffa), 694, 747, 749–750
Production-possibility frontiers, 639, 773, 926
Production theory, modern, 555
Productivity growth, 314
Proper utility, 32
Prosperity and Depression (Haberler), 640, 767
Protective tariff surcharges, 341
Public expenditure, 302
Purchasing Power of Money, The (Fisher), 604, 794
Purchasing power parity (PPP)
  Penn effect and, 507, 509–512
  theoretical development, 402, 406, 522–523
Pure Theory of Capital, The (Hayek), 866
Pure theory of trade, 349, 351–357
Put and call prices, 247

q factor, 27
Q(t) likelihoods, 429
Quadratic utility, 267–268
Quantity theory of money
  Cassel, Gustav and, 741–742
  price level growth rate and, 751, 752
  price levels in short-run, 169
  Wicksell, Knut and, 321, 794–795
Quantity Theory of Money, The (Fisher), 823–824
Quarterly Journal of Economics, 590
Quesnay, François, 632, 875
Quine, Willard van Orman, 892
Quotas, 343, 353, 642

R.A. Fisher paradox, 684
Racial discrimination, 312, 1086, 1088
Radcliffe, 1086
Radcliffe Committee Report of 1959, 559
Radical economics, 540
Ramanujan-Hardy collaboration, 218

Ramsey-Solow one-sector model, 607–608
Random-walk model, 3–16, 92, 96–102, 216, 237
Rate of Interest, The (Fisher), 603, 606
Rational age, effects on risk-taking, 91
Rational expectationism, 282, 429, 430, 995, 1028
  budget deficits and, 1035
  forecasts, 309
  model, 309
  Modigliani, Franco and, 586–587
  money and, 290
  post-Keynesian eclecticism and, 290, 390–391
  Samuelson's view on, 572–573
  Say's Law and, 423–424
  stabilization programs, 309–310
Rational life-cycle investing, 96
Rawls, John, 1076
Reagan, Ronald, 294, 306, 309, 313
Reaganomics
  budget deficits, 343–344, 1034–1036
  supply-side economics, 293–295, 384–386
Real-business-cycle theory, 572
Real wage rate, 298
Rebound model, 3–7, 11–16, 99
Red-noise process, of random walk, 52, 91, 98
Relative risk aversion, constant, 17–18
Relative risk-corrected returns, of alternative portfolios, 139–147
Resource allocation, 283
Retirement, 314
Returns to scale, increasing, 814
Revealed demand paradigms, 734, 736
Revealed preference theory, 734, 737–739, 1044–1046
Review of Economics and Statistics, 23, 855
Review of Economic Studies, The, 874
Ricardian comparative advantage, 342
Ricardo, David, 374, 627, 803–807
  death, 806
  education, 805
  historical reconstruction of Smith, 908–909
  influences on, 804
  on investment, 251
  labor-only model, 435–436, 771
  labor theory of value, 512–513, 805
  macroeconomics and, 804
  on mass unemployment, 981
  microeconomics and, 804–805
  personal biography, 804
  Sraffa's work on writings of, 747, 749

Index

views in later years, 1125
writings of, 776, 803–804
Ricardo-Barro rational expectations, 1035–1036
Ricardo-Mill comparative advantage theory, 721
Ricardo-Mill exact 2-good models, 526–527
Ricardo-Viner equality, 640$n.2$
Riegle, Donald W., Jr., 394–396
Risk
  across-time diversification and, 45–48
  aversion (*See* Risk aversion)
  in long-horizon portfolio, 225
  long-term stocks and, 158
  optimal returns, 269
  reduction, diversification and, 162
  in short-horizon portfolio, 225
  time factors and, 91–92, 97, 159–160
  tolerance (*See* Risk tolerance)
  total absolute, 97
Risk aversion, 92, 135–137, 229
  with concave utility function, 70
  constant, 33
  constant absolute, 36–41
  constant relative, 69, 71–73, 77
  diminishing absolute, 32–33
  excess volatility and, 209–214
  portfolio investing for different horizons, 60–61
  relative, elasticity of, 14
  variance and, 11
Risk-taking
  rational age effects on, 91
  repeated, law of large numbers and, 29–43
Risk tolerance
  aging and, 159
  degree of, 209
  family wealth and, 217
  gambling and, 106–108
  individual differences, 263–267
  investment horizon length and, 215–217
  law of large numbers, 1093–1094
  long-horizon, 95–100, 124–130
  as personal feature, 159
  relative, 52–53
Risk Under Uncertainty and Profit (Young), 1130
Road to Serfdom, The (Hayek), 546, 866, 867, 868, 890
Robbins, Lionel
  Hayek, Friedrich von and, 866
  influence on Samuelson, 891–892
  personal biography, 275, 400–401, 942–943

real-cost determinants of price, 595
trade policy, 401–403
writings of, 399–400, 714, 719, 892
Robinson, Joan, 663–665
  Chamberlin, Edward and, 290, 940
  contributions to economics, 659
  debates with Solow, 617, 675–677
  education, 659
  factor-price equalization, 666–668, 719
  influences on, 663
  leftist viewpoint, 673–675
  Marxian studies, 660–663
  monopolistic competition revolution, 747
  Nobel Prize, 1075
  opposition to U.K. entry into European Market, 551
  personal biography, 665–666, 932
  Samuelson, Paul A. and, 555
  ultra-surrogate capital, 670–673
  writings of, 312, 659–660, 665, 714, 931–932, 979
Romer, Christina, 302
Roofs or Ceilings (Friedman & Stigler), 389
Roosevelt, Franklin D., 989, 1100
Rosovsky, Henry, 352
Royal Statistical Society, 189
Ryle, Gilbert, 928

Sacco and Vanzetti case, 1131
Samuelson, Marion Crawford, 248, 714–715
Samuelson, Paul A., 887, 903–904, 1078–1082, 1092–1094, 1097
  academic career, 1105–1106
  Addison-Wesley publishers and, 255–256
  age 80, 964–968
  autobiographical writings, 887–898, 964–968
  birthplace, 969, 970
  childhood, 970
  on collaboration, 1011–1016
  colleagues, professional, 1107
  contemporary economists and, 1081
  contributions to economics, 553–555, 1098–1099, 1108 (*See also specific contributions*)
  eclecticism, 894, 1108
  education, 563–564, 969, 970, 1082, 1103–1105
  evolution of economist tools and, 1080–1081
  Friedman, Milton and, 1107
  at Harvard, 248, 554, 564, 565–567, 570–572, 715–716, 1106
  honors/awards, 969–970, 1082

1209

Index

Samuelson, Paul A. (*cont.*)
  impact of Great Depression on, 1099–1100, 1101
  influences on, 564, 891–892, 1098, 1100, 1103, 1105
  "International Trade for a Rich Country" lecture, 571–572
  international trade theory, 555
  interviews with, 158–161, 553–574, 970–1002, 1101–1112
  Kennedy, John F. and, 569, 951–963, 1108–1109
  Keynesianism and, 565, 1106
  on macroeconomics, 555–556, 573–574
  on microeconomics, 554
  at MIT, 964–968, 970, 1098
  move from Harvard to MIT, 1011
  neoclassical synthesis and, 1079–1080
  Nobel Prize, 1072
  non-profit finance committees and, 258
  personal biography, 557, 560, 1092, 1095–1096, 1098, 1101–1103
  physical sciences and, 567–568
  political economy and, 888–889
  politics and, 1108–1109
  Robinson, Joan and, 555
  scientific methodology of, 891–895
  Social Science Research Council fellowship, 978
  state intervention and, 1110–1111
  on state of world economy, 442–455
  theory of taxation for public goods, 1109
  as TIAA-CREF trustee, 257
  trade theory, 1110
  at University of Chicago, 562–566, 569–570, 891–892, 971–972, 977–978 1105, 1039–1040
  value-judgment ideology, 888–889
  Viner, Jacob and, 596–599
  web resources, 1082
  work ethic, 896–898
  world view, 1100
  writings of, 553–554, 893, 969, 981, 1012, 1040–1041, 1047, 1082, 1098, 1108
Samuelson, William, 101
Samuelson-Houthakker paradigm, 1045
Sargent, Thomas, 282. (*See also* Rational expectationism)
Savage, Jimmie, 106, 218
Say's Law, 561, 564, 565, 980
  new classical school and, 423–424
  underutilization of resources, 308–309
  U.S. economy and, 572
  Wicksell, Knut and, 795

Scandinavia
  second golden age of economics, 323
  Stockholm School (*See* Stockholm School)
Schelling, Thomas, 1076
Schultz, Henry, 590, 982, 1084, 1120
Schultz, Theodore, 863, 1119
Schumpeter, Elizabeth Brody, 630, 634–635, 837, 1090
Schumpeter, Joseph Alois, 982, 987
  anti-Semitism and, 882
  awards/honorary degrees, 630–631, 823
  on capitalism, 289, 426, 624–625, 632, 703, 704–705, 877
  circular-flow equilibrium, 632
  comparative advantage, 937
  creative capitalist destruction, 426, 440, 581
  death, 822, 825, 881, 936–937
  depression macroeconomics and, 875
  education, 629
  entrepreneurial innovation and, 352, 439–440, 457, 578–579, 875, 876
  failures of, 937
  fame, posthumous, 575
  general equilibrium concept, 632
  Goodwin, Richard and, 880
  Haberler, Gottfried and, 768
  at Harvard, 631–632, 822, 824–825, 873–877
  influences on, 632, 875
  jealousy of Keynes's success, 575, 631, 823, 837, 875, 936
  in later years, 575, 823
  marriages of, 630, 631, 634–635, 825, 875
  Marx, Karl and, 701–706, 708
  methodological character and, 632
  personal biography, 434, 629, 630, 634–635, 765, 837, 873, 875, 876, 894, 926
  personal finance, view on, 223
  political economy, 876–877
  post-WWI, 629–630
  potentials in economics, 722
  theory of money, 637
  view on General Motors, 621
  world view, 876
  writings of, 306, 308, 547, 575, 629, 631, 633, 823, 875
  zero interest rate, 1126
Science
  American postwar, 567
  economic (*See* Economics)
  inexactness of, 420–421
  joint authorship in, 1017–1025
  modern, evolution of, 217–221

1210

Index

Scientific discovery, age of, 577–579
Scientific tariffs, 352–353
Scott, Bruce, 353
Self-insuring, 34
Sequential analysis, 861
Sex ratio, unbalanced, 503
Sexual selection, *vs.* natural selection, 502
Sheehan, John, 1012
Shelton, Judy, 452
Shiller, Robert, 572
Shinohara, Miyohei, 353
Shoesmith, Beulah, 569–570
Simon, Herbert, 1073, 1075
Simons, Henry, 888, 981
   "liquidity trap" phenomenon, 561–562
   at University of Chicago, 590–592, 982
Sims, Christopher, 556
Skousen, Mark, 1005–1007
Slichter, Sumner, 324, 991
Smale, Stephen, 721
Smith, Adam, 578, 835, 867, 908. (*See also* Invisible hand doctrine)
Smith, Howard K., 557
Smoot-Hawley tariff, 972–973
Social Darwinism, 430, 503
Social Democrats, 535
Socialism, 867
   Marxian (*See* Marxism)
   supply-and-demand mechanism, 867
Socialist societies, controlled, 891
Social science, 533–534
Social Security, 225–226
Social welfare function, 835–836, 888–889
Sociology of Science (Merton), 1014–1015
Solomon, Robert, 450–451
Solow, Robert, 613–619
   debates with Robinson, Joan, 617, 675–677
   Harvard thesis, 616
   at MIT, 615–616, 780
   Nobel Prize, 579–580
   writings of, 614
Solow-Ramsey models, 439
Sorenson, Theodore, 959, 963, 1069
Soros, George, 154–155
South Korea, 347
Soviet Union
   per capital real income, 346, 347
   restructuring or *perestroika,* 623, 624
S&P 500 Index (CREF), 27
Sraffa, Piero, 436, 663, 859, 866, 1076
   at Cambridge, 747
   contributions to economics, 747, 749–750
   Leontief, Wassily and, 693–694

   personal biography, 748–749
   political economy, 750
   as Ricardo's biographer, 251
   unfinished critique of marginalism, 722, 797
   writings of, 593, 664, 747, 748, 749–750, 803, 931, 1126
Sraffa-Robinson-Chamberlin paradigm of imperfect competition, 592–593
Stackelberg-Edgeworth one-sided duopolist, 357
Stagflation, 282, 290, 954, 1006, 1029
Stagg, Amos Alonzo, 1084
State intervention, 1110–1111
Stationary probability process, 51
Statistical methodology, 1037. (*See also* Econometrics)
Steel industry, 381–382
Stevenson, Adlai E., 557
Stigler, George, 867, 945, 977, 1116–1138
   academic career, 1119–1120, 1129
   Chicago School and, 592, 621
   education, 1117–1118
   influences on, 1118
   Nobel Prize, 1134
   personal biography, 1117–1119
   as polemicist, 1127
   political affiliations, 1135
   writings of, 389, 621, 1120, 1123, 1125, 1134
Stochastic programming, dynamic, 59–67, 131–138
Stockholm School, 317–333, 753, 910
   economists of, 319 (*See also specific Stockholm School economists*)
   history-of-science precedent, 327
   as independent Keynesians, 811–812
   macrotheorists, 322–323
   origins, 323–326
   theory of output, 320
Stock index fund, 163
Stocks
   discount-for-risk, 73–75
   linear optimal equity ratio rule, 75–77
   long run, market risk and, 158
   prices, $20n.1$, $21n.4$, 158
   regression to the mean, 161
   risk and, 225–226
Stolper, Wolfgang, 711–717, 1022–1023
Stopler-Samuelson theorem, 555, 571, 941, 1098
Strauss, Louis L., 557
Strong axiom of revealed preference, 682, 739, 1045

Index

Structure of Scientific Revolutions, The (Kuhn), 282, 557–558, 875, 895, 1028
Struik, Dirk, 904
Studies in the Theory of Economic Expansion (Lundberg), 317
Studies in the Theory of International Trade (Viner), 593, 926
Subsistence-consumption level, 101
Substitution frontier, 637
Supply-demand equilibrium, 805
Supply of Money in the United States, The (Currie), 974
Supply-side economics, 315
Swedberg, Richard, 837, 882
Swedish economists, 322–323, 752. (*See also* specific Swedish economists)
Sweezy, Alan, 874, 988
Sweezy, Paul, 622, 642, 874, 1088, 1127
Switzerland, 348, 451
Syll, Pålsson, 738$n.2$, 743–744
Szenberg, Michael, 433–434

Taiwan, 347
Tariffs, 343, 352–353, 457, 642
Tarshis, Lorie, 995–996, 1007–1008
Taussig, Frank, 589, 771
  at Harvard, 873
  Socratic method, 600
  students of (*See* Viner, Jacob)
  writings of, 770, 1003
Taxes, 313–314
  cuts, 960
  income, 652
  low rate, 295
  progressive, 439
  on short-term capital flows, 451
Taylor, O.H., 306
Technical economic paradigms, 579–580
Technological change rate, 439–440
Temperature, 655–656, 727, 729
Temperature equalization, 469–473
Templeton, John, 88, 154
Thailand, 453
Thatcher, Margaret, 428
Theorists, monetary, 641
Theory/theories. *See also* specific theories
  exogenous, 641
  psychological, 641
  testing, 1027
  unrealistic premises and, 893
Theory of capital and interest, 605–609
Theory of distribution, 668–669
Theory of Economic Development (1911–12), The (Opie), 874

Theory of Economic Development, The (Schumpeter), 575, 631
Theory of Interest, The (Fisher), 603, 606
Theory of International Trade with its Applications to Commercial Policy, The (Haberler), 639
Theory of Investment Value, The (Williams), 607
Theory of Monopolistic Competition, The (Chamberlin), 665, 822, 979, 1130
Theory of output as a whole, 320, 327
Theory of Public Finance, The (Musgrave), 836
Theory of revealed preference, 734
Theory of scientific revolutions, 189
Theory of Social Economy, The (Cassel), 705, 917–918
Theory of taxation for public goods, 1109
Theory of the Measurement of Demand, The (Schultz), 1120
Theory of Unemployment, The (Pigou), 979
Theory of Wages, The (Hicks), 783, 857, 1046
Thermodynamics
  classical, 654
  classical math economics and, 478–479
  connection with economics, 474–491, 647, 654–685
  entropy (*See* Entropy)
  first law, 627, 728, 789
  fourth law, 790
  functions, 479–481
  Gibbs (*See* Gibbs thermodynamics)
  impact on economics, 654–685
  maximum-minimum systems, 647
  Maxwell's demon, 467–468
  mixed functions, 479–481
  physics and, 727–731
  post-1840, 727–728
  second law of, 481–482, 627, 683, 728, 789, 1033
Thermostatics, min-energy, 484–485
Thought experiments, 670–673, 909–911, 938
Thünen, Johann Heinrich von, 870–872
TIAA, 27
TIAA-CREF, 96, 257
Time
  discounting, 228
  horizons (*See* Horizons)
  risk and, 91–92, 97
Time diversification theory, 159–160
Tinbergen, Jan
  econometric macromodels, 892

factor price equalization and, 719–720
macromodeling paradigm, 718
migration-of-factor scenarios of economics, 723–731
Nobel Prize, 647, 718, 927, 1072
physics-economics interrelationship, 720–723
Tobin, James, 559, 560, 572, 864
Tobin's q, 27, 157
Topology, separable independence and, 626–627
Total factor productivity, from entrepreneurial innovations, 575–582
Toynbee, Arnold J., 557
Track bettors' equilibrium model, 105–122
  bet sizes, 114–116
  bettor laws, 112–114, 119–120
  final market-clearing conditions, 117–118
  pitfalls, 118–119
  premises, 110–111
  properties, 112–113
  risk tolerance and, 106–108
Trade imbalance, 341–344
Trade theory, 637, 639–640, 770–772, 1110
Trade unions, 381, 622
Transactions of the Connecticut Academy (Gibbs), 648
Transfer or reparations problem, 810–811
Treasury bills, 310, 562, 984
Treatise on Money (Keynes), 547, 812, 866
Trends in American Economic Growth, 1920–1982 (Kuznets & Denison), 306
Truman, President Harry S., 428, 1028
Tukey, John, 1133
Turnpike growth theory, 1098–1099
Two-factor model, 354
Two-person zero-sum game theory, 475, 721

Ultra-surrogate capital, 670–673
Uncertainties, decision-making under, 252–253
Unemployment. (*See also* Stagflation)
  black male, 312
  measures, 302
  natural rates, 312
  rates, 385
United Kingdom, 347, 353
United States
  balance of payments, 294, 346, 366, 368, 449–450
  budget deficits (*See* Budget deficits, U.S.)
  consumer price index, 361, 364
  economic divergence with European economics, 379–387
  free trade and, 351
  government expenditures, 384
  interest rates exchange value, 360, 362
  job creation after OPEC crisis of 1973, 294
  labor market, 386–387
  long-range projections, 366, 367, 368
  merchandise trade balance, 359–360
  per capital real income, 346–347
  production index, 579
  real GNP, 360–363
  real growth in 1960's, 954
  real income per capita, 294
  real wage rates, 355
  standard of living, 342–343, 349, 351
  stock market, assessment of, 160
  trade deficit, 341
United States corporations, 161, 296, 352
United States-Japan relations, 345–372, 379
  free trade, *vs.* fair trade, 357–368
  free trade with foreign innovation, 353–356
  n-good equilibrium, 368–371
  reactions to free trade harm, 356–357
  scientific protectionism, 356–357
United States Steel, 296
Utilitarian theories of demand, 734
Utility equilibrium, standard, 735–736

Value and Capital (Hicks), 784, 858, 1047
Value theory, 972
Vassar system, 155
Veblen, Thorstein, 538
Versailles Treaty transfer or reparations problem, 810–811
Vienna, University of, 637
Viner, Jacob
  Austrian opportunity-cost doctrines, 772*n*.3
  Chicago School and, 592, 601
  childhood, 588–589
  as conservative economist, 591
  contributions to economics, 592–595
  education, 589
  at Harvard Graduate School, 589–590
  influences on, 593–594, 597, 600
  in later years, 594–595
  lectures, 594–595
  liquidity trap times, 562
  personality of, 591, 594, 596, 597, 925
  at Princeton, 594, 601
  pure theory of trade, 770, 771
  at University of Chicago, 588, 589, 590–592, 596–600
  Wong, Y.K. and, 926, 1041
  writings of, 589–590, 593, 594, 926

1213

Index

Violet-noise process, of random walk, 98
Virginia, University of, 1089
Virtual rent, 688–690
Volatility
  excess, risk aversion and, 209–214
  online trading and, 448–449
Volcker, Paul, 293, 294, 343, 392, 393, 396, 398, 425, 429
Voluntary-exchange taxation, 754
Von Neumann, John. (*See* Neumann, John von)
Von Neumann's growth model, 474–478, 925
  saddlepoint property, 480
  vs. Gibbs model, 480–481

Wage-price controls, 955
Wald, Abraham, 736–737, 773, 816, 861, 904–905
Wallich, Henry, 992
Wallis, Allen, 977, 1118, 1120–1123, 1132–1133
Wall Street
  bubble of 1995–2000, 438–439
  as random walk, 219
Walras, Léon, 632, 713, 875
Walras-Cassel constant-returns-to-scale model, 814–815
Walras-Cassel-Schlesinger general equilibrium. (*See* General equilibrium theory)
Walras-Debreu economics
  cost-profit-utility systems, 647
  equilibrium systems, 655
Walrasian market-clearing equilibrium, 324
Walrasian theory, pure, 603
Walras-Mill economics, 704
Walras's law, 816
Walsh, Jay Raymond, 988
Warburton, Clark, 994
War financing, 804
Warren, G.F., 305
Washington, University of, 1117
Watson, James, 712
Weak axiom, 736, 773, 1044–1045
Weintraub effect, 1051–1055
Welfare economics, post-Bentham, 867
Welfare state, 311–315, 428
West Germany, 347, 363
Whitehead, Evelyn, 1018–1019
White-noise process, of random walk, 91, 98, 1092–1093
Wicksell, Knut
  age and, 433
  business cycle theory, 321
  Cassel, Gustav and, 757
  death, 751, 812
  Lindahl, Erik and, 754–755
  macroeconomic theory, 751–753
  neoclassical economics and, 775–777
  output determination, 795
  personality of, 756–758
  post WWI return to 1914 currency parity, 812
  price-level occupation, 320–322
  quantity theory of money and, 259, 321
  theory of output, 320
  Victorian era and, 755–756
  writings of, 751, 753–754, 755, 775
Wiener, Norbert, 761–765, 905–906
  autobiography, 762–763
  personality of, 762–764
Wiener Probability Process, 762
Wieser, Friedrich von, 637
Williams, John Burr, 607
Williams, John H., 306–307, 975, 980
Wilson, Edwin Bidwell, 650–651
  personal biography, 761–762, 906, 965–966, 1040
  Samuelson, Paul A. and, 1090–1091
  view on equilibrium, 987
Win-loss innovations, 463
Win-win innovations, 463
Wisconsin, University of, 1089
Wolfowitz, Jacob, 1122–1123
Wong, Y.K., 593, 1041
Wong-Viner envelope theorem, 1041
Working, Holbrook, 155, 1075, 1076
Works and Correspondence of David Ricardo, The (Sraffa), 803–804, 805
World economy
  foreign competition and, 381–383
  post-1945, 304
  pre-1920, 304
  stability, 300
  state of, 442–455
Worldly Philosophers, The (Heilbroner), 426
World War I, 454
World War II
  economic consequences of, 568–569
  economy after, 301–302
Wright, David McCord, 890
Wriston, Walter, 423, 624, 864
Wyzanski, Charles, 1085

Yale, 649, 1085, 1089
Young, Allyn, 992, 1087, 1130

Zeiss-Aaron, 1014
Zinsser, Hans, 433

1214